THE ROYAL HORTICULTURAL SOCIETY

ENCYCLOPEDIA OF GARDENING

THE ROYAL HORTICULTURAL SOCIETY

ENCYCLOPEDIA OF GARDENING

Editor-in-chief

CHRISTOPHER BRICKELL

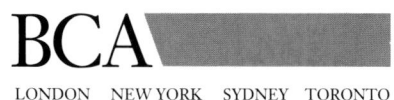

LONDON   NEW YORK   SYDNEY   TORONTO

A Dorling Kindersley Book

Managing Editor Jane Aspden
Managing Art Editor Ina Stradins

Senior Editor Kate Swainson
Senior Art Editor Lynne Brown

Editors Claire Calman, Alison Copland,
Annelise Evans, Helen Partington, Jane Simmonds

Editorial assistants Judith Chambers, Katie John, Teresa Pritlove

Additional editorial assistance from Jackie Bennett, Carolyn Burch, Joanna Chisholm,
Allen Coombes, Heather Dewhurst, Angela Gair, Lin Hawthorne, Jonathan Hilton,
Jane Mason, Ferdie McDonald, Andrew Mikolajski, Christine Murdock, Lesley Riley

Editorial Director Jackie Douglas

Art Editor Gillian Shaw
Designers Gillian Andrews, Johnny Pau, Vicky Short, Chris Walker

Additional design assistance from Rhonda Fisher, Bob Gordon, Sally Powell, Steve Wooster

Photography Peter Anderson (with Steve Gorton and Matthew Ward)

Demonstrators Anne-Marie Dorenbos (with Peter Bainbridge, Mark Lamey,
Dorling Kindersley staff, and RHS Wisley staff)

Location assistants Diana Mitchell, Reg Perryman

Illustrations Karen Cochrane, Simone End, Will Giles, Vanessa Luff, Sandra Pond,
John Woodcock (with Andrew Farmer, Aziz Khan, Liz Peperall, Barbara Walker, Ann Winterbotham)

Picture research Sue Mennell, assisted by Ginny Fitzgerald

Page make-up and typesetting Cooling Brown Partnership, Icon Associates,
Johnny Pau, Debbie Rhodes, assisted by Melanie Tham

Production Hilary Stephens

Index Dorothy Frame

Special thanks to the staff of the Royal Horticultural Society
at Wisley Garden, Surrey, and Vincent Square, London

This edition published 1992 by BCA
by arrangement with Dorling Kindersley

CN 9270

Reproduced by Colourscan, Singapore
Printed and bound in England by Jarrold Printing

PREFACE

THE UPSURGE OF GARDENING as a leisure activity during the last two or three decades has been very marked and, as interest has increased and garden centres have burgeoned, a demand for information on practical gardening and plants to be grown in gardens has developed very rapidly.

The Royal Horticultural Society has, as part of its remit under its Charter, a duty to "encourage interest in the practice and theory of horticulture in all its branches". Much of this dissemination of knowledge takes place through displaying plants, demonstrating plant practices and providing advice to gardeners at the RHS Gardens at Wisley in Surrey and Rosemoor in Devon; additionally, and very importantly, the society has a long tradition of producing publications of excellence to help achieve its aim of increasing interest in and knowledge of gardens and gardening.

The *Royal Horticultural Society Gardeners' Encyclopedia of Plants & Flowers*, published by Dorling Kindersley in 1989 in close co-operation with the RHS, has already provided a major reference source of information on over 8,000 plants that gardeners (world-wide) can grow. The success of *Plants & Flowers* has created not only a tremendous interest in plants to grow in our gardens but a thirst for knowledge on how to grow them.

This complementary volume, the *Royal Horticultural Society Encyclopedia of Gardening*, caters for that demand and has been designed to provide, in a clear, practical and authoritative manner, advice on how to cultivate, maintain and increase virtually any group of flowers, fruits or vegetables that gardeners may wish to grow. Gardening involves both art and practice and, in addition to the practical step-by-step instructions provided, there is guidance on how to use and place plants in the most appropriate garden situation.

The major focus is, however, on the practical techniques involved in cultivating plants of all types. The concise and accurate information on the techniques and cultivation practices has been provided by a range of authors with specialist knowledge and is greatly enhanced and clarified by the inclusion of over 3,400 photographs as well as over 360 finely drawn artworks. The *Encyclopedia* has been carefully planned to cover, in a logical sequence, all the major plant groups of ornamentals, fruits and vegetables, providing, in addition, detailed coverage of soil and climate, pests and diseases, weed control and the tools and equipment required to carry out tasks. Each plant chapter is structured in a similar manner to cover soil preparation, planting, routine care, pruning (if appropriate) and propagation, as well as how to site the plants in a garden to obtain the best effects and results.

A work of this nature involves many individuals with diverse skills – contributors, editors, designers, photographers and many others – and inevitably demands an extraordinary degree of co-operation if it is to succeed. Ensuring that each piece fits into place in the complex jigsaw that eventually emerges as the completed book is a daunting task and I am most grateful to all those whose immense patience and meticulous attention to detail has made this publication possible, in particular the Managing Editor, Jane Aspden, who has been untiring in her efforts to bring this project to fruition.

The *Encyclopedia*, like its predecessor, is intended to provide gardeners, however great or limited their experience and knowledge may be, with a continuing source of reference on how best to plan their gardens and grow plants to obtain the maximum pleasure from this most stimulating and satisfying of leisure activities.

Christopher Brickell
Director General, Royal Horticultural Society
London, 1992

CONTENTS

Part II: Maintaining the garden

— CONTRIBUTORS —

Tom Wright *Garden Planning and Design*
Jim Gardiner *Ornamental Trees, Dwarf Conifers, Topiary, Hedges and Screens, Ornamental Shrubs*
John Wright *Fuchsias*
Caroline Boisset *Climbing Plants*
Raymond Evison *Clematis*
Michael Gibson *The Rose Garden*
Roy Cheek *Perennials* **(with Graham Rice)**, *Ground Cover*
Mervyn Feesey *Grasses, Bamboos, Sedges, and Rushes*
Jack Elliott *Irises, Bulbous Plants, Tulips and Daffodils*
Larry Barlow *Chrysanthemums*
Hazel Key *Ferns, Pelargoniums*
John Galbally *Carnations and Pinks*
Arthur Hellyer *Annuals and Biennials*
Bill Maishman *Sweet Peas*
Kath Dryden and Christopher Grey-Wilson
The Rock Garden **(with John Warwick)**, *Alpine Houses*
Roger Aylett *Dahlias*
Bill Baker *Lilies*
Peter Robinson *The Water Garden, Water Lilies, Aquariums*
Clive Innes *Cacti and other Succulents, Bromeliads*
John Hacker *The Lawn*
Deni Bown *The Herb Garden*
Joy Larkcom *The Vegetable Garden*
George Gilbert *The Fruit Garden*
Don Tindall *Tender vegetables and fruits*
Deenagh Goold-Adams *The Indoor Garden*
(with Arthur Hayward-Costa *Hydroculture)*
Alec Bristow *Orchids*
Peter McHoy *Tools and Equipment, Greenhouses and Frames, Structures and Surfaces*
Michael Pollock *Climate and the Garden*
Trevor Cole *Frost and Wind Protection*
Tony Kendle *Soils and Fertilizers*
Keith Loach *Principles of Propagation, Basic Botany*
Pippa Greenwood and Andrew Halstead *Plant Problems*
(with David Pycraft *Weeds)*

How to Use this Book

Clear, concise, and easy-to-use, *The Royal Horticultural Society Encyclopedia of Gardening* is the perfect horticultural reference library. It gives detailed information on how to create and design an attractive garden, and demonstrates a vast range of horticultural techniques that apply to both ornamental and productive plants.

Written to appeal to the novice and the experienced gardener alike, the text is lavishly illustrated with full-colour photographs and artworks showing design ideas, planting plans, and practical techniques. Illustrated lists of plants help the reader to choose the right plants and act as a quick-reference source on how to care for them.

Part I: Creating the Garden is a complete guide to garden design and all aspects of plant cultivation and care, including pruning and propagation. **Part II: Maintaining the Garden** helps you to choose garden equipment and materials, provides a practical guide to building a framework for the plants, and sets the plants in the context of their physical environment.

A glossary and a comprehensive index make this book easy to use and understand.

Plant names

In general, plants are referred to by their botanical name. Some plants, however, including vegetables, fruits, and herbs are referred to by their common name in preference to their botanical name. To find out the botanical names of these plants, consult the index.

The index includes common and botanical names for all plants mentioned in the book.

Part I: Creating the Garden

The chapters in Part I cover everything you need to know to choose and grow plants successfully. Each chapter is dedicated to either a different plant group – for example ORNAMENTAL TREES and CLIMBING PLANTS – or an area of the garden, such as THE HERB GARDEN and THE WATER GARDEN.

The chapters are all structured in a similar way, so readers can become familiar with where to find the information they need quickly and easily. Each chapter has sections on design (using the particular plant group), as well as soil preparation and planting, routine care, propagation, and, where appropriate, pruning and training. Some chapters have other sections that are appropriate to the subject matter: for example THE HERB GARDEN has a directory of common herbs while THE LAWN has a section on establishing a lawn.

The chapters on vegetables and fruits have a general section at the beginning describing techniques that are common to all vegetables or fruits; this has the same structure as the other chapters. Entries on individual vegetables and fruits follow, grouped according to their type (for example, podded vegetables, leafy and salad vegetables, tree fruits, or soft fruits). Within these groupings entries are ordered by botanical name.

CHAPTER STRUCTURE

SECTION HEADINGS
All chapters are split into sections covering "Design", "Soil preparation and planting", "Routine care", "Pruning and training", and "Propagation". The headings are clearly displayed at the beginning of each section and in the running head.

RUNNING HEADS
Clear running heads help you find the section of the book that you want. The running head on the left-hand page has the name of the chapter; the running head on the right has the title of the section.

CHAPTER HEADING
This indicates which plant group or area of the garden is discussed in this chapter. It has a short introduction giving general information about the plant group.

Feature boxes

Part I of the encyclopedia includes a number of short features that focus on a specific plant group or area of interest, for example PELARGONIUMS, TOPIARY, and ALPINE HOUSES AND FRAMES. Because of their importance to the gardener, each of these subjects is given separate coverage in a feature box containing more detailed information than would be possible within a chapter. The boxes include explanations of techniques that are specific to that group of plants; for example the FERNS feature shows you how to raise new plants from spores while the ORCHIDS feature tells you how to cultivate and propagate this specialist group of plants.

The feature boxes accompany the most closely related chapter: the feature on CLEMATIS appears in the chapter on CLIMBING PLANTS while that on SWEET PEAS is found in the ANNUALS AND BIENNIALS chapter. All the feature boxes are listed on the Contents pages.

BOX RULE
A rule round a feature box sets it apart from the chapter and makes it easy to find.

PLANT PORTRAITS
These indicate the range and types of plant covered in the feature box.

PLANTING SUGGESTION
Text and photographs suggest ways of creating a display.

TECHNIQUES
Techniques that are specific to the subject of the feature box are explained fully both in the text and in the step-by-step picture sequences.

THE ELEMENTS ON A PAGE

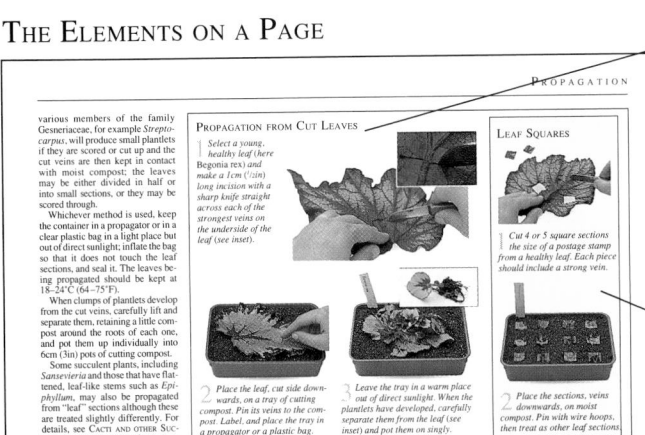

PROPAGATION

PROPAGATION FROM CUT LEAVES

1 Select a young, healthy leaf (here Begonia rex) and make a 1cm (½in) long incision with a sharp knife straight across each of the strongest veins on the underside of the leaf (see inset).

LEAF SQUARES

1 Cut 4 or 5 square sections the size of a postage stamp from a healthy leaf. Each piece should include a strong vein.

2 Place the leaf, cut side downwards, on a tray of cutting compost. Pin its veins to the compost. Label, and place the tray in a propagator or a plastic bag.

3 Leave the tray in a warm place out of direct sunlight. When the plantlets have developed, carefully separate them from the leaf (see inset) and pot them on singly.

2 Place the sections, veins downwards, on moist compost. Pin with wire hoops, then treat as other leaf sections.

ALTERNATIVE METHOD
One or more photographs in a tinted box within a sequence explain an alternative method to the main one shown.

Propagation of tuberous begonias

When begonia tubers die back naturally in autumn, store them in their pots at 5–10°C (41–50°F) in a dry place over winter. Alternatively, lift and clean the tubers, dust their crowns with fungicide, and store them in boxes of dry sand, peat substitute, or peat.

At the beginning of the growing season, place the tubers in a tray of moist, sandy compost (1 part sharp sand, 1 part peat-substitute- or peat-based compost). Store them at a minimum temperature of 13–16°C (55–61°F). When new buds are clearly visible, cut the tubers into sections, making sure that each has at least one bud and some roots. Dust the sections with fungicide and leave them to dry for a few hours in a warm place. When the cut surfaces have formed calluses, pot up the sections in loam-based compost. Do not firm the compost heavily or water it, since this encourages fungal attack.

Alternatively, allow new shoots to develop on the tubers, and use these as basal cuttings. Take the cuttings so that each retains an eye. Dip the base of each cutting in hormone rooting powder and insert them, 2cm (¾in) deep, around the edge of a pot or pan of loam-based potting compost.

1 In autumn, lift the dormant tubers and clean them. Dust the crowns with fungicide and overwinter them in a dry place.

2 In spring, place the tubers, concave side upwards, 5cm (2in) apart and 2.5cm (1in) deep, in a tray of moist, sandy compost.

3 When shoots appear, cut the tubers into sections, each with a bud and some roots. Dust cut surfaces with fungicide and allow to dry.

BASAL CUTTINGS

4 Pot up the sections singly in 13cm (5in) pots, with the top of each level with the compost surface. Water a little, and label.

5 Keep the pots in a propagator in a warm, frost-free place until the sections are established, then pot them on singly.

Remove 5cm (2in) shoots from the tuber, each with an eye of tuber at the base. Pot them up and treat as divided tubers.

455

TEXT BOX
A text box comprises text and pictures that relate to a specific plant or to a technique that is not explained in the running text.

INSETS
Inset photographs provide a close-up view for more detail or to show a "before" or "after" step.

PRUNING AND TRAINING ARTWORKS

CAPTION
The caption gives general information on what to do.

ARTWORK
The artwork shows the extent of pruning in relation to the whole plant. The grey tone indicates the parts of the plant that should be cut out. The green and brown areas delineate the appearance of the plant after pruning and training.

CUT MARKS AND ARROWS
The red marks show where to cut. The light green areas show the shoots before they have been trained in and the red arrows show where to tie them.

INSETS
The insets are photographic representations of parts of the artwork, showing a symptom or a pruning cut. Leader lines point to the appropriate place on the artwork. The captions explain in detail what to do.

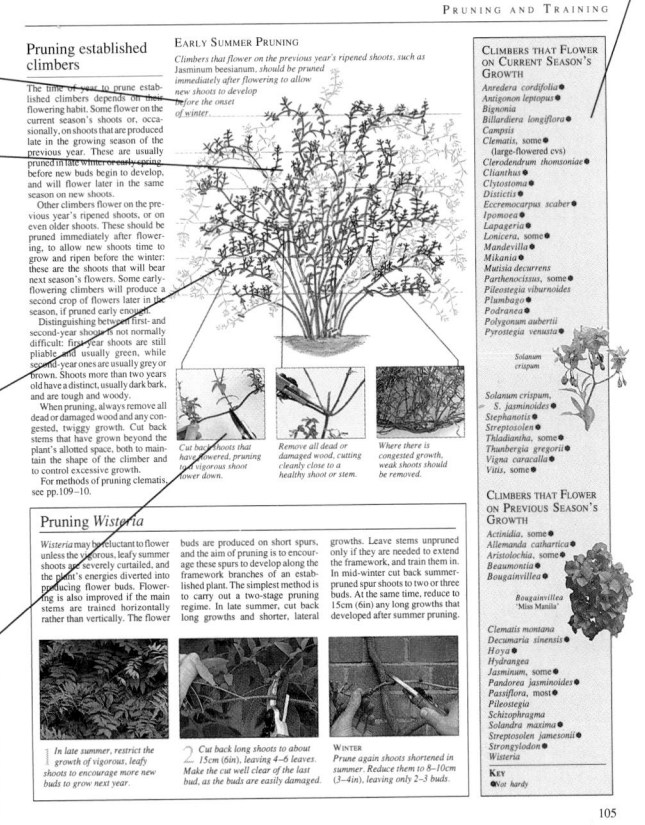

PRUNING AND TRAINING

Pruning established climbers

EARLY SUMMER PRUNING
Climbers that flower on the previous year's ripened shoots, such as Jasminum beesianum, should be pruned immediately after flowering to allow new shoots to develop before the onset of winter.

The time of year to prune established climbers depends on their flowering habit. Some flower on the current season's shoots or, occasionally, on shoots that are produced late in the growing season of the previous year. These are usually pruned in late winter or early spring before new buds begin to develop, and will flower later in the same season on new shoots.

Other climbers flower on the previous year's ripened shoots, or on even older shoots. These should be pruned immediately after flowering, to allow new shoots time to grow and ripen before the winter: these are the shoots that will bear next season's flowers. Some early-flowering climbers will produce a second crop of flowers later in the season, if pruned early enough.

Distinguishing between first- and second-year shoots is not normally difficult: first-year shoots are still pliable and usually green, while second-year ones are usually grey or brown. Shoots more than two years old have a distinct, usually dark bark, and are tough and woody.

When pruning, always remove all dead or damaged wood and any congested, twiggy growth. Cut back stems that have grown beyond the plant's allotted space, both to maintain the shape of the climber and to control excessive growth.

For methods of pruning clematis, see pp.109–10.

Cut back shoots that have flowered, pruning the vigorous shoot farthest down.

Remove all dead or damaged wood, cutting cleanly close to a healthy shoot or stem.

Where there is congested growth, weak shoots should be removed.

Pruning Wisteria

Wisteria may be reluctant to flower unless the vigorous, leafy summer shoots are severely curtailed, and the plant's energies diverted into producing flower buds. Flowering is also improved if the main stems are trained horizontally rather than vertically. The flower buds are produced on short spurs, and the aim of pruning is to encourage these spurs to develop along the framework branches of an established plant. The simplest method is to carry out a two-stage pruning regime. In late summer, cut back long growths and shorter, lateral growths. Leave stems unpruned only if they are needed to extend the framework, and train them in. In mid-winter cut back summer-pruned spur shoots to two or three buds. At the same time, reduce to 15cm (6in) any long growths that developed after summer pruning.

1 In late summer, restrict the growth of vigorous, leafy shoots to encourage more new buds to grow next year.

2 Cut back long shoots to about 15cm (6in), leaving 4–6 leaves. Make the cut well clear of the last bud, as the buds are easily damaged.

WINTER Prune again shoots shortened in summer. Reduce them to 8–10cm (3–4in), leaving only 2–3 buds.

105

CLIMBERS THAT FLOWER ON CURRENT SEASON'S GROWTH
Anredera cordifolia ●
Antigonon leptopus ●
Bignonia
Billardiera longiflora ●
Campsis
Clematis, some ●
    (large-flowered cvs)
Clerodendrum thomsoniae ●
Clianthus ●
Clytostoma ●
Distictis ●
Eccremocarpus scaber ●
Ipomoea ●
Lapageria ●
Lonicera, some ●
Mandevilla ●
Mikania ●
Mutisia decurrens
Parthenocissus, some ●
Pileostegia viburnoides
Plumbago ●
Podranea ●
Polygonum aubertii
Pyrostegia venusta ●

Solanum crispum

Solanum crispum,
    S. jasminoides ●
Stephanotis ●
Streptosolen ●
Thladiantha, some ●
Thunbergia gregorii ●
Vigna caracalla ●
Vitis, some ●

CLIMBERS THAT FLOWER ON PREVIOUS SEASON'S GROWTH
Actinidia, some ●
Allamanda cathartica ●
Aristolochia, some ●
Beaumontia ●
Bougainvillea ●

Bougainvillea
'Miss Manila'

Clematis montana
Decumaria sinensis
Hoya ●
Hydrangea
Jasminum, some ●
Pandorea jasminoides ●
Passiflora, most ●
Pileostegia
Schizophragma
Solandra maxima ●
Streptosolen jamesonii ●
Strongylodon ●
Wisteria

KEY
● Not hardy

Part II: Maintaining the Garden

The second part of the encyclopedia comprises chapters on equipping the garden and on the garden environment – all the background information you need to supplement Part 1.

Equipping the garden

Guidelines on choosing and using garden equipment are given in the chapter on tools. The chapter on greenhouses and frames gives information on how to choose and erect a greenhouse and how to maximize the available space. There is also advice on how to ensure that the greenhouse will provide the environment you need. The chapter on structures and surfaces shows you how to build walls, pergolas, and raised beds, for example, to create a framework for the garden, and explores the variety of materials that are available.

The garden environment

The environment of the garden has a direct impact on the health and vigour of the plants that grow there. The chapter on soils and fertilizers explains how to cultivate and improve your soil, and that on Climate and the Garden explains what effect the climate has upon plants and how to make the most of the microclimate in your garden.

Principles of propagation

This chapter sets out the basics of propagation and explains why certain plants are best propagated by a particular method so that the gardener can better understand the processes involved.

Plant problems

The chapter on plant problems helps you to identify the causes of problems in the garden such as pests, diseases, disorders, and weeds, and tells you how to control or prevent them. It takes a symptomatic approach and is divided into sections, each on a part of the plant that may be affected.

Quick reference

The chapter on basic botany provides a brief explanation of a plant's make-up to help the gardener understand the principles behind the practical techniques demonstrated elsewhere in the book.

The glossary provides concise definitions of horticultural terms used in the encyclopedia. A chart of seasonal reminders tells you at a glance what needs to be done in the garden and when. It follows the same structure as the chapters in Part 1 so that you can turn to the appropriate chapter and section for full details.

The comprehensive index will help the reader to find plants or techniques in the book. It includes both the botanical and the common name of plants. Page numbers in italic denote that a picture of the subject appears on that page.

GARDEN EQUIPMENT AND STRUCTURES

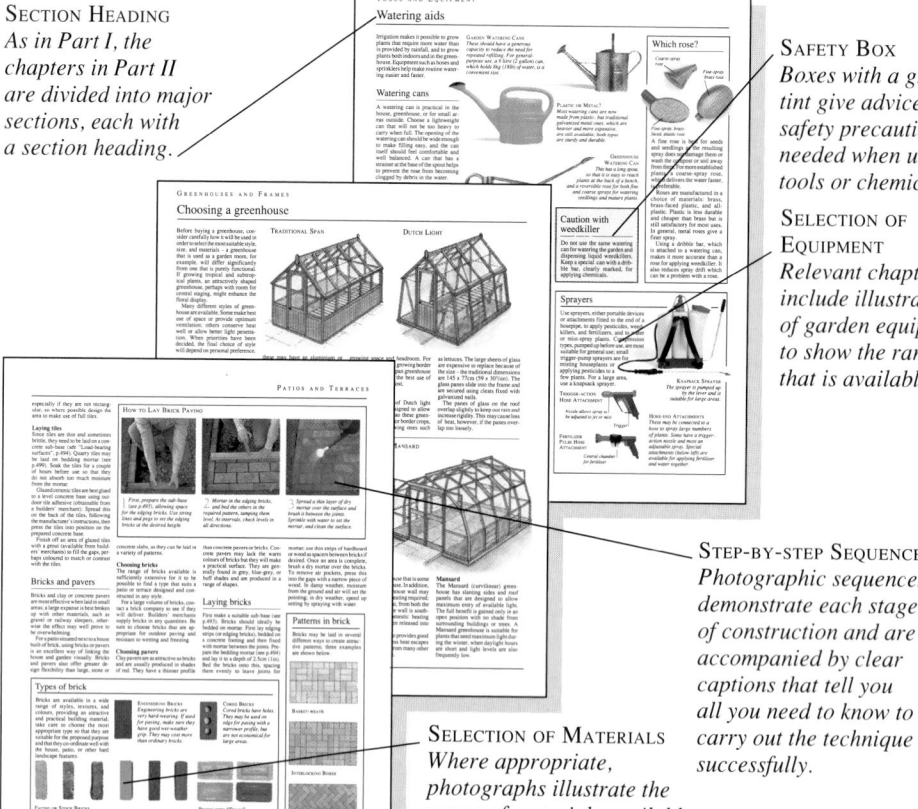

SECTION HEADING
As in Part I, the chapters in Part II are divided into major sections, each with a section heading.

SAFETY BOX
Boxes with a grey tint give advice on safety precautions needed when using tools or chemicals.

SELECTION OF EQUIPMENT
Relevant chapters include illustrations of garden equipment to show the range that is available.

STEP-BY-STEP SEQUENCES
Photographic sequences demonstrate each stage of construction and are accompanied by clear captions that tell you all you need to know to carry out the technique successfully.

SELECTION OF MATERIALS
Where appropriate, photographs illustrate the range of materials available for a particular project.

PLANT PROBLEMS

MAIN HEADING
This indicates the area of the plant on which symptoms are most visible. A problem that affects a plant's roots may have an entry in the "Leaf problems" section if the symptoms are most commonly seen in the leaves.

SUB-HEADING
This gives the main visible symptom. Problems with similar symptoms under this are grouped together.

ENTRY HEADING
This gives the name of the pest, disease, or physiological disorder.

TEXT
The text for each entry lists the plants that are most commonly affected, the most visible symptoms, the cause of the problem, and information on how to control it. Controls include organic and chemical treatments as well as preventive measures. At the end of the chapter is a list of chemicals that are mentioned in the chapter with names of products currently available.

Earwigs

Plants affected Shrubs, perennials, and annuals, commonly dahlias, chrysanthemums, and clematis. Also apricots and peaches.
Symptoms Young leaves are eaten in summer. See p.561 for other symptoms.
Cause The earwig (*Forficula auricularia*), which is a yellowish-brown insect 15mm (³/₄in) long with a pair of curved pincers. Earwigs hide during the day and feed at night.
Control Place inverted pots, that have been loosely stuffed with hay or straw, on canes among susceptible plants; earwigs use these as daytime shelters from which they can be removed and destroyed. Alternatively, spray at dusk with permethrin, pirimiphos-methyl, or HCH.

Adult earwigs

Leaves eaten away

SYMPTOM
Photographs show the pest and the damage it causes to the plant.

CROSS-REFERENCES
If you cannot find the apparent cause of the symptoms of your plant, see the entries listed in the grey tint box at the end of a page.

PART ONE

CREATING THE GARDEN

*How to design your garden, select,
cultivate, and propagate plants, and display
them to their best advantage*

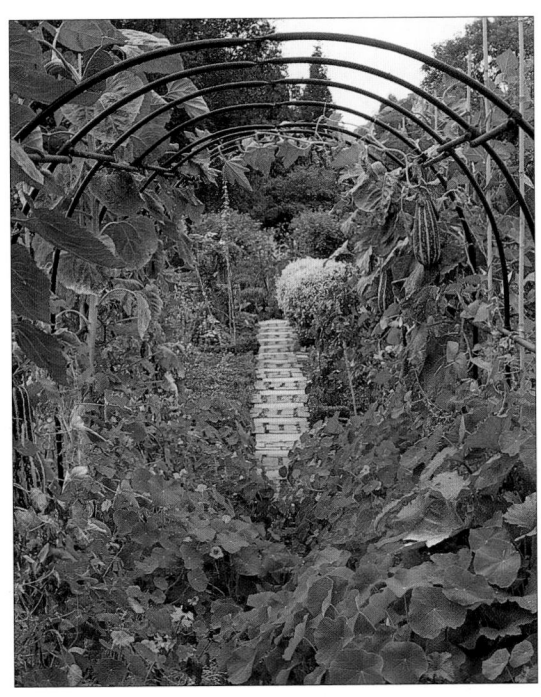

1

GARDEN PLANNING
AND DESIGN

SOME OF THE *finest gardens may look as though they have not been designed at all, but have simply sprung up – rich tapestries of colours, textures, and shapes in apparently artless concord. This may be an illusion, however, for the casual cascade of a rambling rose or the lazy sprawl of a lavender bush onto a path often owes almost as much to the gardener's forethought as to nature. Whether informal and cheerfully chaotic or elegant and formal, a successful design is usually the result of careful planning. There is a great difference between a garden where the plants and features are haphazardly arranged and one that, although seemingly naturalistic, is actually well controlled so that all the elements work together to form a cohesive and attractive scheme. Planning is the key to creating a beautiful garden – one with a sense of unity and style, balance and proportion, in harmony with its surroundings, and, perhaps most important, a relaxing place, a joy to the senses, and a panacea to the mind.*

Planning the garden

WHEN creating or redesigning a garden, the main aim is to provide a personal place that satisfies the needs and tastes of those who are going to use it. In many ways, it is like designing the interior decor of a house: the three major governing factors are the practical considerations of the site, its proposed functions, and personal taste – in other words, what you have, what you need, and what you like. Both garden and interior design are also influenced by a number of variables such as the size, character, and period of the garden or house.

Unlike a house, however, a garden does not remain static, even from one week to the next; indeed, this element of change and surprise is the essence of gardening. Certain plants may be spectacular in one season yet quite unobtrusive in the next. Even after the garden has been created, a continuous design process will be required to accommodate and enhance it as it develops.

The importance of planning
Although much of the pleasure in gardening derives from unforeseen effects, thorough planning is essential to ensure a cohesive design. Determining at least the basic framework of the garden on paper before making any actual changes helps prevent costly mistakes. Minor alterations may be made later, of

INFORMAL ABUNDANCE
The charm of this informal garden owes more to sound design than serendipity. A simple path leads the eye to the fields beyond, which act as a foil for the jewel-like planting. The predominantly pink and mauve colour scheme is enlivened by the inclusion of boldly placed splashes of red, yellow, and white.

BALANCING FORMAL DESIGN ELEMENTS
*The upright, geometric shapes of the clipped hedge and the classic elegance
of the statue complement the large, circular pool with its restrained
planting of irises and water lilies.*

the functional and desirable with the realistic. The budget as well as the design may determine how much, if any, of the work you want to undertake yourself. If it is simply a matter of cultivation, seeding or turfing grass, and planting, then you may well feel able to tackle it. However, levelling and construction work, such as building retaining walls, terraces, ponds, and patios, involve expensive materials and require experience and skill. As these elements are permanent and mistakes expensive to rectify, it is better to hire professional help if you do not possess building skills (see also STRUCTURES AND SURFACES, pp.492–513). Decide also whether help will be needed for routine maintenance once the garden is established. It is possible to plan a garden so that relatively little upkeep is required.

Changing an existing garden

In most cases, planning involves modifying an existing garden rather than creating a completely new one, and there are various reasons for wishing to redesign.

After moving house, you may wish to change part or all of the existing garden design to suit personal preferences. The layout or character of a garden may need to be adapted to accommodate a different use, such as providing play areas, space for fruit and vegetables, or greater privacy.

If the garden requires a high level of maintenance, it may be necessary to adapt its style in order to reduce the amount of work needed. More rarely, an overgrown or neglected garden may require restoration or, for some elements, renewal, to re-establish its original design (see also "Restoring old and historic gardens", p.31).

Initial assessment
Resist the temptation to be hasty: if faced with a jungle-like tangle of overhanging trees, neglected shrubs, and weeds, it may seem simplest to dig up the entire garden and start again, but it is better to proceed with caution. The disarray may conceal some interesting or useful plants that should be retained. The inclusion of one or two more mature specimens in a new garden provides a framework around which to design the planting scheme and also helps to counteract a raw appearance.

Let ideas for redesigning the garden develop gradually so that they incorporate the best of the inherited features rather than impose a preconceived image on the site. If possible, live with the garden as it is for a calendar year, keeping notes on any features that may be worth saving, such as an overgrown hedge that provides valuable shelter from prevailing winds, or a shrub that brightens a dull corner with a display of attractive berries in winter.

During this initial period, additional colour and interest may be provided by containers, bedding plants, and fast-growing annual

course, but the position of long-term features such as patios, walls, and trees should be worked out in advance. Plan the garden as a whole rather than tackling different parts piecemeal; this makes it easier to

create a sense of continuity, so that the separate elements are not merely interesting in their own right but effective when viewed as a whole.

Planning should be a logical process to create a design that combines

DESIGNING A GARDEN TO SUIT YOUR NEEDS

LOW-MAINTENANCE DESIGN
*Hard paving facilitates care of the lawn and borders,
which are closely planted with low-maintenance
shrubs, small trees, and ground-cover plants.*

HIGH-MAINTENANCE GARDEN
*Here, there is a more varied range of plants, including fruit, vegetables,
container-grown plants, and climbers trained on trellis, all requiring
detailed attention and regular maintenance throughout the year.*

climbers trained on trellis. Routine maintenance work such as pruning dead and damaged wood from trees and shrubs, cutting grass, removing perennial weeds, and clipping hedges should be carried out as usual to keep the garden in good condition.

Creating a new garden

Making a garden on a new "green-field" site (one that has not previously been cultivated as a garden) may be daunting, but it should also prove to be an exciting challenge. As there are fewer constraints imposed by existing garden features, there is more freedom to follow the dictates of the imagination. It is important, however, to design the garden in relation to its setting and to take account of such factors as soil type and climate.

Types of garden
There is a style of garden to suit every personality; for some, a productive kitchen garden is a priority, for others an area for entertaining or a secluded place to relax is more important. The following are examples of some common garden types, but it is, of course, possible to combine elements of two or three different types or, indeed, to create something entirely different.
Family garden Usually fairly formal in design, this type of garden provides a safe space where children may play, as well as areas for flower borders, fruit and vegetables, and a patio or terrace.
Cottage garden This is probably informal in layout and contains many

FORMAL, OPEN-PLAN GARDEN

FORMAL, OPEN-PLAN GARDEN
A framework of tall hedges surrounds this garden, making it a peaceful and secluded place. An ornamental bench provides a strong focal point as well as somewhere to enjoy the pink and white borders densely planted with heavily scented Nicotiana, *white* Buddleja, *and stately* Cleome.

unusual and interesting plants; it may also include some wild or conservation areas and a water feature. The maintenance of this type of garden may require a high degree of horticultural expertise.
Formal, outdoor living room With such constructions as a patio, low walls, steps, and perhaps a raised pool, this style of garden may have plenty of plants in containers but little other planting and probably no lawn. It usually requires only minimal maintenance. This formal style is often especially suitable for small, urban gardens.
Open-plan garden Possibly on ground sloping away from the house, this type of garden is generally low-maintenance, ideal for passive recreation, and with good views of the surrounding landscape. It may be terraced and have space for growing some fruit and vegetables.

Screened, secluded sanctuary Where privacy is a priority or where the garden is overlooked or has ugly views, this type of enclosed design usually incorporates a pergola or arbour and plenty of climbing plants.

Making a rough plan
At the preliminary design stage, it is useful to sketch a rough outline of the garden site simply to note down the main elements that are to be included. Mark in the position of the house and any other fixed features, such as the boundaries, then allocate approximate areas for beds, borders, a lawn, pool, patio, or whatever else is required. Allow space, where necessary, for purely functional fixtures too, such as a compost heap or a tool shed; these are best sited away from the house, or hidden from view.

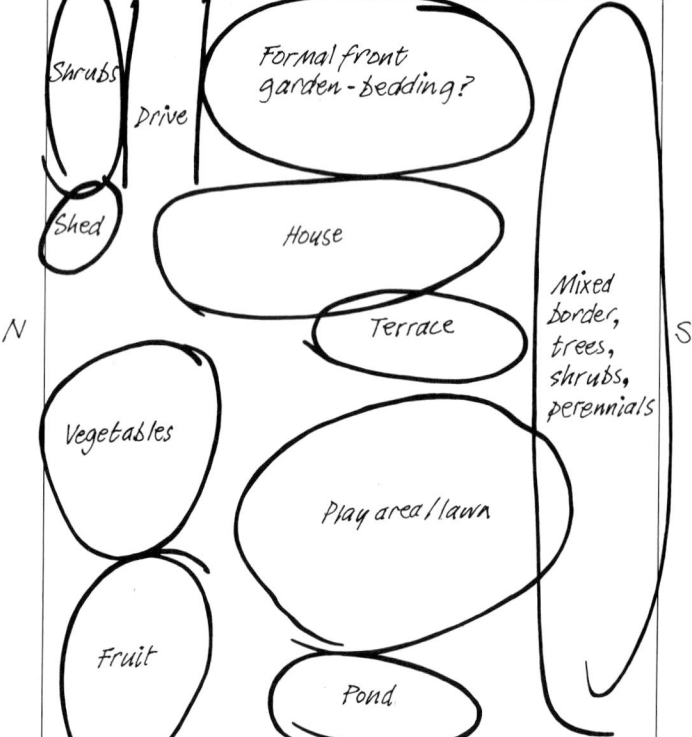

PLANNING THE GARDEN'S COMPONENTS
Make a simple, graphic note of all the features you intend to have in the garden, roughly sketching their position in relation to the house and any other fixed features as well as external boundaries.

URBAN, PATIO GARDEN
Wide, timber decking forms an unusual, stepped patio with a dynamic, diagonal pattern. Plants have been chosen for their low-maintenance requirements and attractive, architectural foliage.

Appraising the site

Before drawing up the next stage of the plan, assess the site thoroughly: good preparation now pays rich dividends later. The survey should detail factors such as climate and soil type, as this sort of information is invaluable when making decisions about drainage, shelter, which plants to grow, and where to site them.

Climate considerations

It is helpful to find out the local figures for annual rainfall, temperatures, and sunshine hours, as well as details of any special climatic influences, such as frost pockets. The geographical setting may also make a difference: for example, hilltop sites over 150–200m (480–640ft) above sea-level may be several degrees colder than nearby low-lying places, so the growing season could be later. Town gardens are usually warmer and more sheltered all year round than those in rural areas. Coastal gardens are vulnerable to salt-laden winds but, due to the moderating effect of the sea, temperatures are less extreme than inland.

In addition, the microclimate should be assessed: note which way the garden faces and which parts receive most sun and shade from

PLANNING TO SUIT LOCAL CONDITIONS
In this waterfront garden, tall trees help to reduce the force of the wind without spoiling outward views. Low-growing plants such as Eupatorium *species and* Tagetes *are untroubled by the wind and the flexible stems of* Miscanthus *grasses sway in the breeze without being damaged.*

one season to the next and at different times of day. For example, the shade cast by a deciduous tree is more dense in late spring and summer than during the rest of the year.

Some corners of the garden may be sheltered, while others may be exposed and need screening if they are to be used fully, depending on the direction and force of the wind. There may also be damp and dry patches and hot and cold spots; none of these is necessarily bad, but they all affect which plants will thrive. Try to exploit the different microclimates that occur within the garden itself, growing plants that enjoy the given conditions rather than trying to nurture species that are inappropriate. For further details, see "Microclimate", p.519.

Soil

Unless planning to create a "hard" garden with mostly paving or gravel, it is essential to find out the type, texture, and acidity level (pH) of the soil; it may be heavy clay, light and sandy, chalky or limey, or peaty and acidic. The soil type affects drainage, the type of plants that may be grown, and the ease of cultivation tasks such as digging and planting.

Proprietary soil-testing kits are widely available from nurseries for determining the pH level of a soil, although the presence of certain plants may also give a rough indication: for example, rhododendrons, blue hydrangeas, heathers, and bracken usually thrive on acid soil. For further details, see "Acidity and alkalinity", p.523.

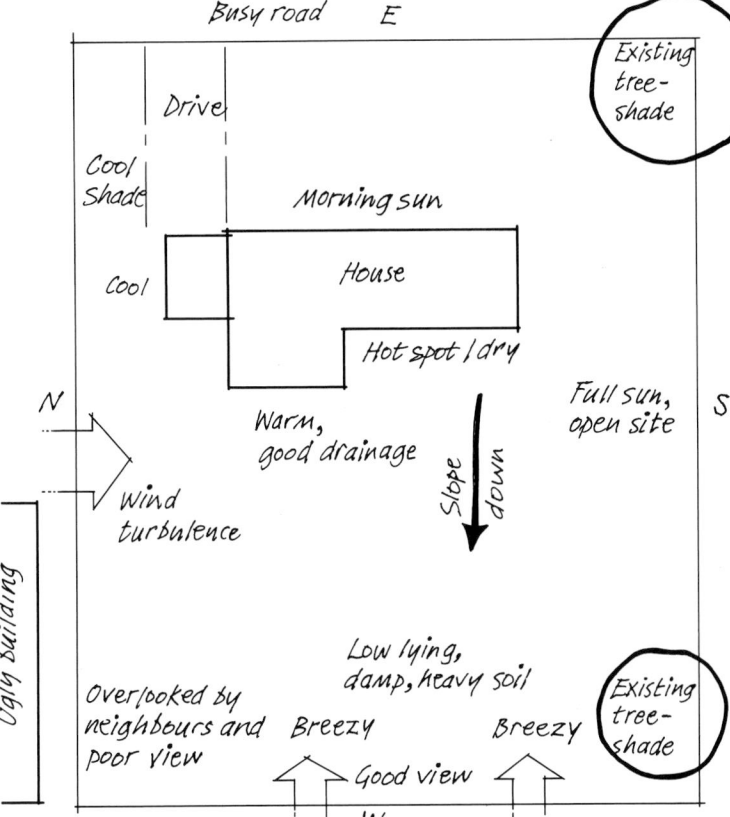

GARDEN MICROCLIMATE PLAN
Assess the conditions and site features and plants appropriately – a pond in the dampest spot, for instance, and sun-loving species in the warmest place.

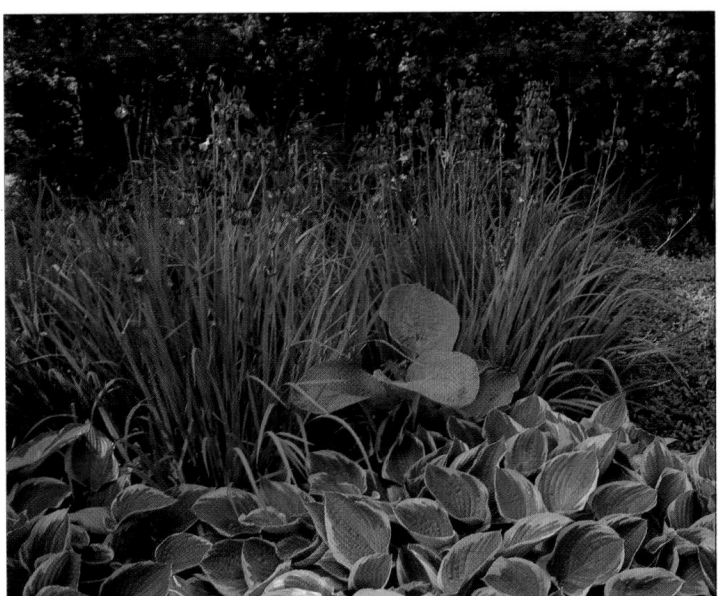

PLANTING FOR MOIST SHADE
Check the garden's soil type before selecting plants. Here, a damp, shady site provides a perfect environment for plants such as these blue-green and variegated hostas and beautiful, intense blue Iris sibirica.

The garden setting

When designing a garden, consider it in the context of its immediate surroundings rather than in isolation. It may be in a terrace or suburban setting with both good and bad outlooks, for example, or in an elevated position that has fine prospects but needs shelter from strong winds.

A more detailed plan may now be drawn, showing good and bad views, the direction of prevailing winds, and an indication of where additional shelter or screening may be required. Another factor that may be a concern is noise; if it is minor, dense, evergreen planting or solid banks of soil may help. A simpler and sometimes equally effective approach is to create a competing distraction with, for example, a tinkling fountain or splashing waterfall.

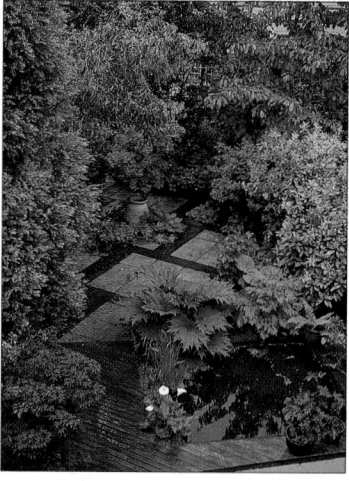

LOW-MAINTENANCE GARDEN
A balanced framework of hard materials and trees and shrubs forms an effective, low-maintenance design.

Maintenance considerations

All gardens, even if informal or wild, need some care and attention to keep them in good condition. Before deciding on a design, be realistic about the amount of work and energy that you are prepared to expend – if you want upkeep to be minimal, opt for a garden style that does not demand a constant round of mowing, clipping, staking, weeding, and tidying to be attractive. Assess how much time and help will be available or affordable to keep it looking good and match this to the maintenance regimes most gardens need. Some periods are particularly busy – spring and early summer, for example – so extra assistance may be necessary at these times of the year.

BORROWED LANDSCAPE
This slightly raised garden takes advantage of uninterrupted views over open countryside. A low fence allows a clear outlook, while the winding path and upright conifer echo the twisting river and tall tree beyond.

Long- and short-term expectations

Plants grow, mature, and decline at different rates so certain parts of a garden look well established while others are still some way from their prime. Trees are usually the largest and most long-lived plants, but some species may live many times longer than others; oaks (*Quercus*) may last for more than 200 years whereas some flowering cherries (*Prunus*) and birches (*Betula*) may decline after only 50 or 60. This also applies to shrubs. In general, the faster the growth of a tree or shrub, the shorter may be its effective life.

Although the life expectancy of herbaceous perennials is less variable, certain plants, for example peonies (*Paeonia*) and *Acanthus*, live for many years; others, such as delphiniums and phlox, are short-lived.

When planning a garden, take into account the rates at which the components will look well established. Structures such as paving, pergolas, or walls, have an immediate effect; a lawn soon looks presentable if turfed but will take longer if sown from seed; some herbaceous plants, shrubs, and hedges mature within five years. More patient gardeners may plan to a ten-year timescale, including some slow-growing plants interspersed with those that are faster maturing but more ephemeral.

SHORT- AND LONG-TERM PLANTING EFFECTS
An abundant, full effect can be created quickly using fast-growing perennials interspersed with annuals to fill gaps and provide plenty of colour, but such a scheme may require more maintenance in the long term (right). A more structured design with a sculptural framework of trees, shrubs, and clipped hedges will take much longer to reach maturity (far right).

Creating a design

Once the soil type and climatic conditions have been checked, a more detailed site study should be carried out. Assess the condition of any existing constructions and plants in the garden to decide whether they should be included in the new garden design and measure the site to provide a base plan.

Exploiting natural characteristics

Always work with the given conditions initially, using natural site features as part of the design where possible. Slopes, banks, and changes in level may offer scope for constructing terraces, retaining walls, stepped beds, a watercourse, or a rock garden, as well as providing good views out over the garden. Woodland ground-cover plants and bulbs can be used to colonize shaded banks and provide colour.

Poorly drained and damp problem areas make a good home for many bog and moisture-loving plants. These areas are often difficult (and expensive) to drain so use plants that have adapted naturally to the conditions. If there is a large piece of damp ground, there may be space for ornamental willows (*Salix*) and alders (*Alnus*), with candelabra primulas (*Primula*), some *Caltha*, and other small, moisture-loving plants around them (see also THE WATER GARDEN, "Bog gardens", p.245).

If large areas of rubble or subsoil have been left from building and construction works, they may be used successfully to form the base of a scree or gravel garden, rather than spending time and effort on digging them out and replacing them with good soil. This type of site provides ideal conditions for plants that prefer sharply drained soil. An advantage with gravel and scree gardens is that they often require minimal maintenance once they are established (see also THE ROCK GARDEN, "The scree bed", p.192).

Assessing existing features

Make a list of the long-lived plants in the garden, identifying them where possible. Note the condition of the trees, shrubs, hedges, and perennial plants, as well as the lawn, and work out how much pruning or renovation is required. Then make an estimate of the current and eventual sizes of the trees and shrubs.

Make a separate list of all the "hard" elements of the garden, such as patios, walls, paths, greenhouse, pools, and pergolas. Indicate the materials these structures are made from, their condition, and their aspect. When preparing your garden plan, this information will help you to decide which plants to reposition or remove, and which "hard" elements to retain or modify.

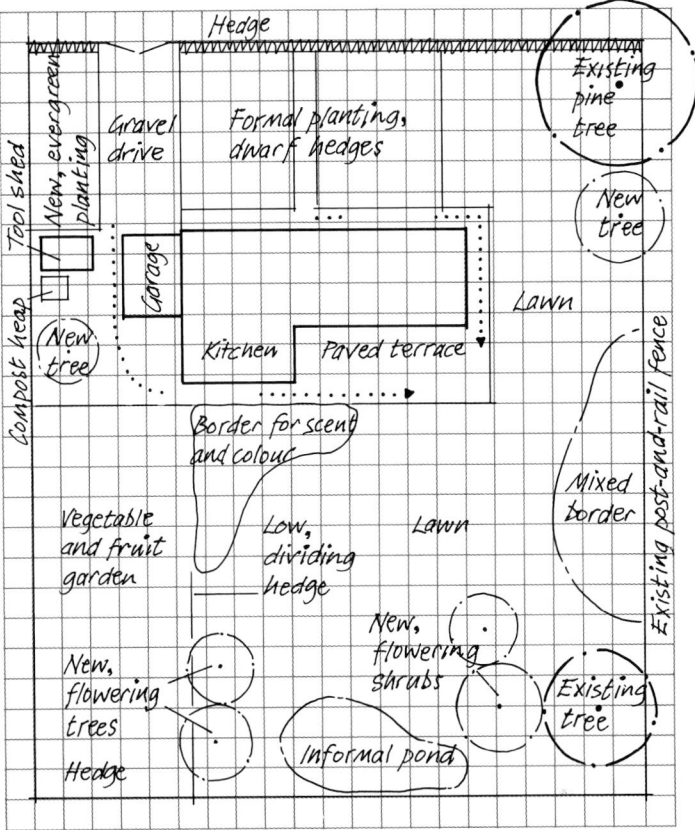

DRAWING THE DESIGN TO SCALE
Make a scale plan of the garden, marking in boundaries, existing structures, and other features you plan to keep, then add the proposed new elements.

Making a scale plan

Unless the proposed alterations are very minor, draw a scale diagram of the site as a basic plan on which various designs may be drawn. These may differ greatly in the style, the space allocated for each feature, and the sense of proportion, but make each one on a scale plan so that it has a realistic basis.

Measuring the site
First measure the boundaries of the plot, using an extra-long measuring tape. If the site is irregularly shaped, divide it into small sections with clear, fixed points and measure each section individually. Alternatively, a surveyor may be employed to prepare a scale plan.

It may be possible to use an existing plan – perhaps one that is part of the house deeds – although these are often inaccurate and may only include the boundaries of the garden and the position of the house.

Changes of level
If there are marked changes of level on the site, indicate this at the survey stage as the new design may have to

incorporate certain features to accommodate the gradient. A steeply sloping garden may necessitate the building of terraces or retaining walls. A gentle, downwards slope away from the house is usually worth keeping as it facilitates drainage for a lawn or patio next to the house.

Preparing the first plan
Transfer the site measurements onto paper to create a scale base plan of the garden; it should include all the boundaries together with any elements that you want to retain from the existing garden, such as trees, shrubs, paths, and walls. If making several different designs for comparison purposes, draw each one on tracing paper stuck over this scale plan so that the details can be altered easily without redrawing the original outline.

Sketch in the design elements that you consider essential but be realistic about what you can fit in the garden, otherwise the design may lack cohesion and appear muddled. Refrain from including too many garden structures or potentially large trees in a relatively small plot since they will overpower the design.

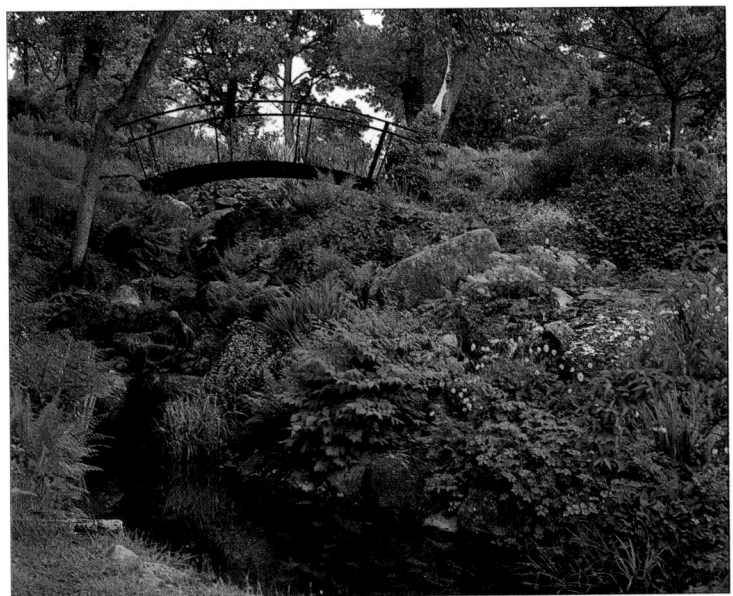

MAKING THE MOST OF NATURAL SITE FEATURES
The informal planting on these steep, rocky banks effectively integrates the natural features of the site to create a richly planted, woodland garden.

Choosing the design style

There are many variations of style that provide potential for creating a unique design; personal taste may be the main deciding factor. Some people prefer plenty of open space, others a more divided and secret garden; there may be symmetrical, formal areas or irregular and flowing shapes. It is possible to create strikingly different effects depending on whether straight-sided shapes or curves are used while maintaining a well-proportioned design.

There are a few basic principles of design that should be observed whatever the style. Balance and harmony are very important: try to include features that complement each other and the overall setting to create a cohesive whole. Scale and proportion should also be considered; this can be quite difficult with a living composition like a garden as plants change in size and shape over a number of seasons. Always take into account the eventual height, spread, habit, and growth rate of plants before including them in the design. Relate the plants to each other and to adjacent features such as walls and paths (see also "Height and scale relationships", p.22).

Vistas or focal points may also help to give more substance and definition; they are best worked out on site to begin with before incorporating them into the design. As with all features, some adjustment may be needed when finally marking out the scheme on the ground.

DETERMINING SHAPE AND STYLE
Within the same framework, gardens of radically different tone and style have been created. The first garden (right) is based on rectilinear design principles of straight lines and blocks that give it regularity and formality, and draw attention to each distinct element within the framework. In contrast, the garden on the far right uses a softly sweeping, curvilinear design for a much more flowing, informal style.

Perspective and proportion

It is possible to make a garden appear shorter and wider or longer and narrower by manipulating the apparent perspective and proportion.

Make a garden seem longer by establishing a long axis and then accentuating it. Site tall plants in the foreground, grading down to shorter ones along the axis, perhaps with a focal point such as a specimen tree at the end. This must not be too tall or the perspective will be altered. Alternatively, consider exaggerating the perspective (see below).

In a long, narrow garden, breaking up the length may often improve the apparent proportions as well as making it more mysterious, inviting exploration. The choice of divisions should depend on the garden: a trellis with an off-centre archway provides a pronounced division, whereas a border that intrudes across the long axis creates a gentler break.

Colours can also affect the sense of distance: strong, hot colours have a shortening effect since they seem to come forward in a scheme; cooler, misty colours appear to recede.

Deceiving the eye

A garden may be designed so that its shape is altered visually and its apparent proportions made more appealing. In the first design on the right, the urn at the back is the same size as the one in the foreground, whereas in the garden in the centre a smaller urn of the same shape is placed at the far end, suggesting that the garden is longer than is really the case. This imitation of natural perspective creates an impression of length, which is reinforced by the rest of the design: the path narrows at the rear of the garden, successively smaller trees recede into the distance, and even the hedge has been cut lower at the back to strengthen the illusion. The garden on the far right is made to seem shorter and wider by partitions placed at intervals along its length.

ORDINARY PERSPECTIVE
This design does not alter the garden's apparent size or perspective.

EXAGGERATED PERSPECTIVE
A tapering path and trees decreasing in size visually lengthen a garden.

BREAKING UP THE LENGTH
Partial divisions foreshorten the perspective in a long, narrow garden.

Drawing up the final design plan

All the elements may now be brought together in the completed jigsaw puzzle that will provide the final design. Draw this working plan accurately to scale on squared paper, using numbers or symbols for the various features. Indicate the spread of trees and shrubs precisely to make sure that sufficient space is allowed for them in relation to other plants and elements.

Plans on paper may sometimes appear unsatisfactory when they are transferred to the ground so, before preparing the final design on site, mark out the different areas using string and pegs to indicate the proportions and size of the features. It will almost certainly be necessary to make adjustments on site at this stage, so try out some variations, Once you are satisfied that the sizes and proportions of the features and areas work well together, incorporate them into the design.

When designing beds and borders, mark their outlines on the main plan but work out the detailed planting plan separately, preferably to a larger scale (see p.20). It is only necessary to draw in framework and specimen plants accurately.

THE FINISHED GARDEN

The final design plan (right) is drawn to scale, with each element clearly indicated; the mature garden (below) makes good use of the natural features of the site and incorporates practical considerations too.

1 Existing pine tree

2 Raised urns on pedestals planted up with pelargoniums and *Helichrysum*

3 Low edging of cotton lavender (*Santolina chamaecyparissus*)

4 Warm-coloured gravel for drive and path to garden

5 Low-maintenance shrubs

6 Pre-fabricated wooden shed for tools

7 Compost heap in wooden bin

8 Ornamental cherry (*Prunus* 'Shirofugen')

9 Restricted colour scheme for bed with herbs, pinks (*Dianthus*), and other scented plants

10 Vegetable garden including salad vegetables

11 Archway to kitchen garden, covered with clematis and climbing roses

12 Fruit garden including currants, raspberries, and other soft fruit

13 Low box (*Buxus sempervirens*) hedge to border kitchen garden

14 Crab apple (*Malus* 'Profusion')

15 *Pyrus calleryana* 'Chanticleer'

16 Informal pond with water lilies and bordered with irises and other moisture-loving plants

17 *Deutzia longifolia*

18 *Magnolia stellata*

19 Existing crab apple tree (*Malus*)

20 Evergreen *Fatsia japonica*

21 Mixed border of shrubs and perennials chosen to provide interest throughout the year

22 Patio constructed from pre-cast paving slabs with containers for specimen plants and annuals

23 Silver birch (*Betula papyrifera*)

Planting plans

Once the basic design of the garden has been determined, more detailed planning can follow, including deciding exactly which plants to grow and where to site them. The site survey will have noted any existing plants that may be worth incorporating in the new design. If there are useful trees, shrubs, and hedges that are to be retained but are in poor condition, they should be pruned and fed to renovate them.

Planting plans are best drawn separately to a larger scale. They do not need to be works of art – aim to sketch a planting plan that is simple and realistic and include other features immediately adjacent or that relate to the planting, for example a shed that will have climbing plants trained against the sides.

When siting plants, allow sufficient space for each to develop fully to the ultimate height and spread that it is likely to achieve. This is particularly important for trees and shrubs because they usually form the major, permanent "skeleton" in the design (see also "Principles of planting", pp.21–6).

MIXED BORDER

A detail of the mixed border from the main planting plan shows how a limited colour scheme creates a harmonious effect. Shrubs give height and structure, while perennials flesh out the design, forming a balanced display.

Planning the work

Before embarking on construction and cultivation, prepare a schedule to minimize disruption on the site: tackle the work in a logical order, so that the messiest and most elaborate operations, such as constructing a patio or wall, are carried out first.

Operations such as sowing, planting, transplanting, or turfing should be undertaken at an appropriate time otherwise the plants may not survive – autumn, winter, or early spring may be best; construction work may be better in summer or autumn when bad weather conditions are less likely to affect operations. Plan these stages first, then structure the rest of the timetable around them.

Schedule of operations
Existing hard features Repair or renovate existing garden structures. This may be done at any time of year, weather conditions permitting.
Existing planting If necessary, protect any plants to be retained in their present positions, to avoid damage from construction work. Remove unwanted plants. In the dormant season, lift any plants that are required elsewhere, transplant them, or heel them in temporarily.
Existing turf If turf is in reasonable condition and the lawn's shape or position is to be changed, lift the turf and relay it as soon as possible (see "Moving turf", p.283). Turf should also be lifted if it is likely to be damaged by construction work, then relaid afterwards. It is best to move turf in early spring or early autumn but if moved in winter it may be kept stacked for three or four weeks before relaying (see "Storing turf", p.282). Do not lift turf in summer unless essential.
New construction work If possible, complete this before beginning any cultivation or planting. Before major site works are started, check the location of all service pipes and cables (gas, water, etc.) to ensure that they are not damaged.
Soil cultivation Get rid of all debris, rubble, or scrub. If the soil has been compacted by machinery or trampling, cultivate it deeply (see "Simple digging", p.525, and "Double digging", p.526). Spring or early summer are the best times as the ground may be left fallow for a while and any weeds removed (see "Weeds", pp.572–7). Also remove any stumps and roots as they can be the source of honey fungus (p.565). Preparing the soil before planting may involve incorporating well-rotted organic matter, removing stones, fertilizing, and raking the soil to a fine tilth. Do this just before planting or a few weeks beforehand.
New planting and lawns This is best carried out in autumn, although it is also satisfactory in spring. Plant up beds, borders, and containers in accordance with the detailed plans. Lay turf or sow grass seed as required. Plants that have been kept in temporary positions should be transplanted now into their final, allotted places.

Principles of planting

PLANTS are the most important features of a garden, determining the style, character, scents, and the changing effects from season to season and year to year. They are the living essence of gardening and give tremendous potential for creating a pleasurable, individual design.

Some modern garden designers often favour the "outdoor living-room" concept, using a large number of hard elements such as walls, paths, paving, patios, and gravel. In these gardens there is still plenty of opportunity to use plants in interesting ways and they are essential to balance and soften the hard features. They should be included as an integral part of the design rather than added as a final cosmetic touch.

Most gardens are designed either so that there is a balance between planting and hard landscape, or using plants as the dominant features with limited hard structures included, carefully blended into the garden to provide focal points or fulfil practical functions.

Planting design

There is an infinite number of ways of growing and combining ornamental plants, and there are many thousands of readily available plants with which to plan a scheme. In a small-sized garden, it is particularly difficult to decide which plants to include. The fewer plants that can be used, the more value each should provide for maximum interest – whether from flowers, foliage, shape, or attractive fruit or bark. Plants with a showy but very brief display may be tempting to grow but are unlikely to merit inclusion.

Deciding on a theme or planting design concept is helpful as a basis for selecting and siting plants. The following broad categories of planting styles provide a few examples.

Formal planting

This type of planting is suitable to provide a simple, symmetrical, and architectural theme, with precisely clipped boundary or dividing hedges. Formal beds, knots, or parterres may be included, with well-balanced and controlled planting within the beds using limited colours, shapes, and textures (see also "Formal gardens", p.29; "Knot gardens" and "Parterres", p.31). Considerable discipline is necessary in both the design and maintenance of this style. If dividing up a large garden, it may be appropriate to treat only one section in this way.

Framed planting

Sometimes used in large gardens, this style is also quite easily modified to suit smaller sites. The principle is to create a clearly defined framework using hedges, fences, or walls; the area between them is usually divided by a simple, often formal network of paths that form a frame for planting. The design is structured and ordered but has plenty of scope for very different planting designs within the frame.

Usually a theme is used to link the planting: perhaps aromatic plants and herbs, or old roses underplanted with pinks or violas. It may also be effective to have a restricted colour scheme or to create a seasonal garden that contains plants chiefly for spring or winter interest.

The term "framed planting" also describes the use of a background or living frame to enhance a special feature, plant group, specimen tree or shrub, or a distant view. For example, a flight of steps or the start of a pathway could be framed by formal, clipped shrubs or upright conifers to form living gateposts. A charming, tantalizing view into another part of the garden or the world outside may be highlighted by creating "window" effects in a hedge or screen to offer a surprise in an otherwise enclosed space.

Free and mingled planting

This style allows planting to be free-flowing and more natural than formal or framed schemes. Charming and unstructured, sometimes even a little chaotic, free planting may combine a wide range of plants in an attractive, informal way. While considerations of balance and uniformity are incidental, there should be a feeling of rich profusion, and the overall effect should be harmonious in both colour and form. These gardens are rarely easy to manage and are usually the creations of keen gardeners who have the time and the inclination to cultivate comprehensive collections of plants.

FREE PLANTING
A joyous array of plants thrives in this informal garden, creating a feeling of spontaneity and abundance. The cool blues of Eryngium *and* Campanula *contrast effectively with the orange and yellow* Helenium *and* Hemerocallis.

FRAMED PLANTING
A geometric design delineated by paths and low, evergreen box (Buxus sempervirens) *hedges forms a permanent framework for a mixed and quite unstructured planting of low shrubs and perennials. The use of limited colour gives a sense of continuity, while the bright touches of white and yellow stand out well against a predominantly green backcloth, adding highlights to the planting, yet preserving the tranquillity of the garden.*

Garden backgrounds

The boundaries of a garden and any internal divisions are often not fully exploited in the design, but their materials, size, and character affect the overall tone; whether hedges, screens, walls, or fences, they may be used as backgrounds, perhaps to act as a foil for planting or ornamental seats or statuary. Try to use complementary textures, colours, and styles: for example, while a clipped yew hedge may set off a classical stone figure to perfection, a larchlap fence would be inappropriate.

Hedges and screens

As well as having a practical value for bordering or dividing the garden, hedges and plant screens form ornamental living barriers and provide attractive backgrounds. White or pale flowers or foliage, for example, are offset particularly well against the dark green of a dense cypress (*Cupressus*) or yew (*Taxus baccata*) hedge. Seats, urns, and statues also look effective set in an alcove in a well-clipped hedge.

Evergreen hedges make excellent backgrounds for shrub and herbaceous borders, and for showing off specimen plants, but some hedging plants have very fibrous, spreading roots and may compete for moisture and nutrients with nearby plants. Density of growth is particularly important if the hedge is intended primarily as a background foil for an ornamental feature.

Flowering or berrying shrubs, for example roses or pyracanthas, may also be used, especially in informal gardens, to provide a visual boundary or division. Growth is usually less dense than in a traditional hedge.

Hedges may take several years to become established and need more maintenance than walls or fences, but the interest they provide in terms of texture, colour, and shape is invaluable. Most are also long-lived and so are often more permanent features than fences (see also HEDGES AND SCREENS, pp.60–62).

Walls

Although expensive to build, walls of stone or brick provide excellent boundaries for gardens and offer considerable scope for "vertical" gardening. The height and aspect of a wall usually determines what may be grown on or against it. Plants that grow well on a south-facing wall, for example, are usually unsuitable for one facing north.

When choosing climbers, make sure that the colour of the flowers or foliage harmonizes well with that of

BACKGROUND PLANTING
Here, a high brick wall supports the magnificent, purple swathe of a clematis, which forms a living canopy above the ornamental garden seat.

the walls. Red or yellow brick walls show off greens, dark reds, blues, purples, and whites well, while pale or grey walls accentuate pinks, yellows, reds, and blues.

Golden- or silver-variegated forms of ivy (*Hedera*) can lighten up dark or gloomy walls, and are ideal for such sites. Although they should not damage walls in good condition, they are not recommended for walls in poor repair as their aerial roots frequently loosen the mortar. For more information, see CLIMBING PLANTS, pp.94–115.

Even when unadorned with plants, some walls, especially old, mellow ones, make attractive backgrounds and it may be desirable to leave a quarter or a half uncovered.

Fences

Where an instant physical boundary is required, fencing may be the best solution. Usually relatively inexpensive and easy to install, fences are available in a wide range of heights and styles and may be used to set or emphasize the tone of the garden. Woven, wattle hurdles are attractive in an informal, rural setting, while white picket fencing is pretty around a cottage garden, and wrought iron railings are in keeping with the formality of an elegant town garden. Fences that are purely utilitarian are often better covered with climbing or scrambling plants.

Trellis

Trellis, both square- and diamond-patterned designs, may be used against a fence or wall to provide support for plants; if sufficiently sturdy, it may be used on its own provided that it is attached to strong supports. This is a good option where

a screen or division is required that does not block out light or an attractive view. Trellis may be stained or painted for decorative effect.

Height and scale relationships

When deciding on a planting scheme, take the height and shape of a plant into account, both in relation to other plants and to the scale and size of the area. For example, a small garden would look overcrowded if it contained a large tree such as a horse chestnut (*Aesculus*), while a smaller-growing species, such as rowan (*Sorbus aucuparia*), would be more in proportion.

Successful plant associations often depend on harmony of scale; a grouping that combines many different plants, all of greatly differing heights, may simply look unplanned and unco-ordinated. Equally, there should be some variation so that the scheme does not look regimented. Even on a small scale, such as in a rock garden, consider how dwarf shrubs and conifers may be combined with cushion- and carpet-forming rock plants to create variety and interest through height and scale relationships while appearing in well-balanced proportion with each other. If grouped with larger species, these plants often appear insignificant and are easily overlooked.

Perennial and shrub borders are often arranged by height, with the tallest plants at the back and the lowest in the front, so that they may all be clearly seen. Such a scheme seems less formal, however, if the regularity is broken in one or two places, perhaps by including a tall plant mid-way. In this case, plants that allow a view beyond them should be chosen, for example a narrow, columnar tree such as a columnar yew (*Taxus baccata* 'Fastigiata') or a plant with airy, filigree foliage such as fennel (*Foeniculum vulgare*).

Structural planting

A number of plants have a striking architectural or sculptural impact – some from their natural growth habit, others from their foliage, stems, or flowers. There is a great variety of forms and effects, ranging from the low, spreading mass of a prostrate

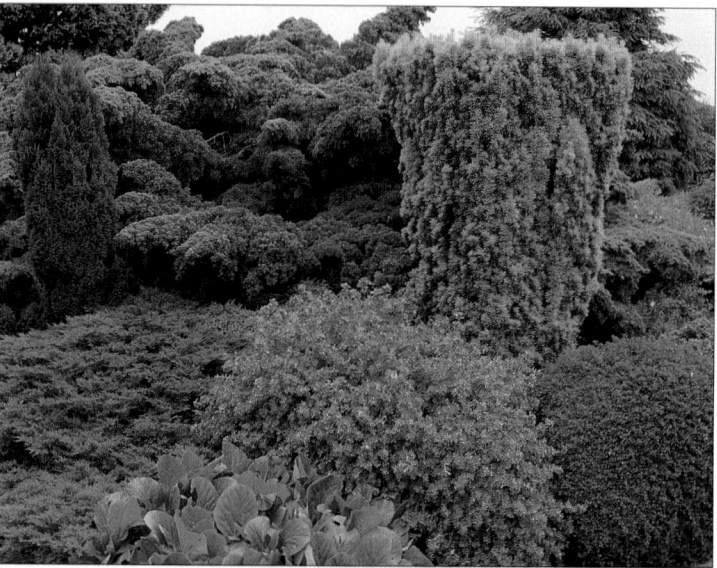

STRUCTURE AND MASS
This planting design adopts a sculptural approach to make a tableau of abstract shapes and textured masses with a variety of shrubs and conifers.

juniper (*Juniperus communis* 'Prostrata') to the stately, upright flower spikes and arching, thistle-like leaves of *Acanthus spinosus*.

Structural plants are often used singly as a focal point, but they are also effective as part of the design framework. Placing a structural plant at the end of a border provides a distinctive full stop, while a pair, one on either side of a path or doorway, acts as an enhancing frame. Architectural plants are excellent for visually linking the house (or other hard feature) with the garden – the sculptural, but living, forms span the transition from hard materials to soft planting. Including a few strongly shaped plants in an otherwise unstructured and informal plan helps to give the design a focus and contrasts well with the soft lines of the free planting.

With deciduous or herbaceous plants, plan the scheme so that other features or plants provide a similar function during winter months. For example, a group of red-barked dogwoods (*Cornus alba*) could be planted next to a clump of *Gunnera magellanica* so that the dogwoods become a spectacular feature once the *Gunnera* dies back.

Specimen plants

Plants that have a particularly fine shape or those with very attractive flowers, foliage, fruit, or stems are best grown with enough space around them for them to be seen and appreciated individually. Site them so that they form focal points from the house, terrace, or lawn. In large gardens, such plants may be

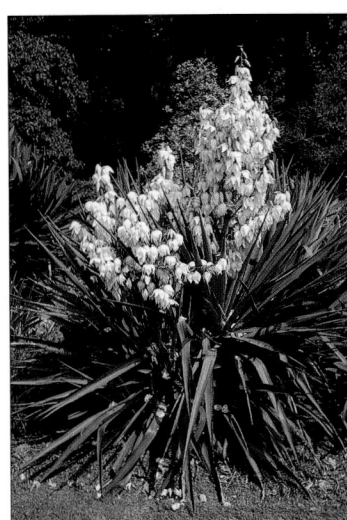

SINGLE SPECIMEN
The sculptural form, foliage, and flower panicles of Yucca gloriosa *make it an ideal specimen plant.*

IMITATING NATURE
Moisture-loving plants such as candelabra primulas and the white-flowered Anthericum liliago *form a natural-looking scheme on this waterside bank.*

grouped in threes or fours for bolder impact. Some plants may also be enhanced if grown in ornamental containers.

Planting in groups

Although single specimens may be used on their own or as part of a scheme, a much bolder and more harmonious effect is achieved by planting in groups or drifts, particularly with small plants. This avoids the cluttered effect that may result from "dot" planting of many different single plants. Growing a group of the same plants together provides a stronger impact, especially when viewed from a distance, and makes any planned colour scheme more emphatic. Usually groups look best if planted in odd numbers of three, five, or seven plants as this avoids a regimented look.

Groups of plants with bold foliage or other striking characteristics may also be used, informally, to divide or screen areas effectively in a less formal manner than hedges.

Naturalistic plant associations

The way in which plants are combined is an important part of garden design. There are many familiar groupings that are successful but, as there are so many plants available, many more combinations of colour, texture, and form remain to be tried.

When deciding which plants to place together, bear in mind how they would grow naturally so that the grouping as well as the selection of plants is appropriate. Imitating

plant associations from nature has two important advantages. In every natural or semi-natural habitat, associations of plants have developed that blend well together in different layers and groupings. These plant communities are adapted to the local soil and climate or microclimate and they thrive in the same growing conditions. In addition, the range of plants that thrive may be affected by other factors. For example, chalk downland, if left ungrazed, will be invaded by shrubs and trees and the grassland plants quickly decline.

Monocultures of one species seldom occur in nature and with some soils and habitats the variety is very rich indeed. Any bare soil is rapidly colonized by local flora. Different

CONTRASTING FORMS
Foliage plants of different shapes and forms have been combined to create an interesting but balanced design. The upright spears of Iris laevigata 'Variegata' *are effectively offset by the rounded, giant leaves of a* Hosta 'Buckshaw Blue' *and the open form and horizontal, divided foliage of* Heracleum mantegazzianum.

layers of vegetation may all be found on the same piece of ground. The highest layer is the tree canopy; below this there are shrubs and sometimes climbers, while the herbaceous plants and bulbs form the ground layer (see also "Layer planting", p.26). Such layered planting is easily copied, using both native and exotic species.

Wildlife gardens contain mostly indigenous plants to encourage birds, insects, and other wildlife, but the use of some appropriate exotics and selected cultivars of suitable species will often add to the interest and quality of the planting, particularly in autumn and winter.

Shape and form

The thoughtful planting and grouping of plants to exploit their shape and form is fundamental in creating a lively, satisfying design. Each plant has a natural growth form and silhouette that may change as it grows and matures. Some may also be pruned to develop a different growth form to be effective in a particular design, for example by coppicing to provide young, coloured shoots on willows (*Salix*) for winter display. The shapes and sizes of young plants in a nursery or garden centre may not give a reliable indication of their adult form, so it is a good idea to see more mature specimens in gardens or parks where possible.

Combining plants with different shapes and forms provides endless possibilities for inventing interesting, well-balanced schemes. When

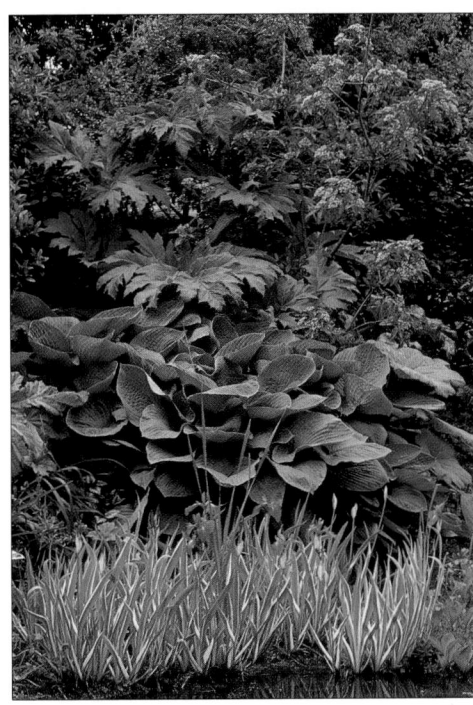

designing, always look at the habit of a plant in addition to its foliage, flowers, and other features. Elegant shapes and forms are especially important for specimen planting.

Many shrubs and perennials have a rounded, hummocky shape, which may be contrasted with different forms – such as a columnar tree or prostrate ground-cover plants – for extra interest. Shrubs with bare, basal stems may be used with low, bushy plants in front to hide the base. Those with rounded contours and dense habits are better suited to undulating ground-cover schemes.

Many herbaceous and bulbous plants provide striking shapes and forms with bold foliage and flower spikes when in growth, but in winter when they have died down are of little interest. The problem may be solved by placing an evergreen plant or suitable feature nearby to provide continuing interest (see also "Successional interest", p.25).

Colour

The most striking but sometimes rather transient colour in plants generally comes from the flowers, with

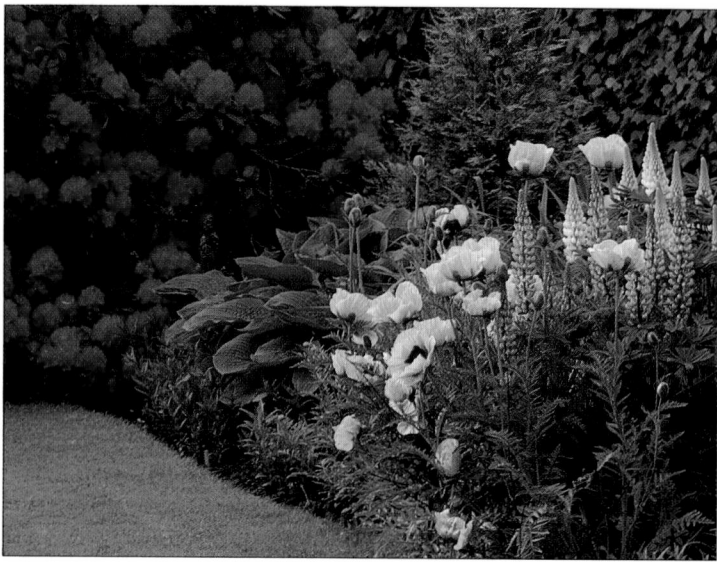

BREAKING THE COLOUR RULES
This clashing scheme of red rhododendrons and pink lupins (Lupinus) *and giant poppies* (Papaver) *shows how the rules may be broken successfully.*

a dazzling range of shades and tints. Flowers are not the only source of colour, however, as foliage is often ornamental, while many plants have attractive stems, bark, berries, or seedheads that provide interest during autumn and winter.

Colour preferences are often a question of personal taste, but there are general guidelines that may be followed. The colour spectrum may be divided into two ranges – the blues and the yellows. The blue range includes the bluish-whites, bluish-pinks, magenta, fuchsia, crimson-reds, blues, and purples. The yellow range includes the creamy-whites, ivories, salmon-pinks, scarlet-reds, oranges, and yellows.

Associations between the two ranges generally harmonize well, but mixing colours within a range may be less successful. In the blue range, for example, pinks and reds may not always be restful together, whereas taking a colour from each

range and mixing them, such as blue and yellow, can be effective. There are exceptions, however; blues and mauves usually combine well, for example. Restricting the colours included often helps to create a harmonious and attractive scheme; if a wide range of colours is used, the effect may be disjointed and fussy.

With all colour planting, light is a major factor: in countries where the light is soft and on the blue side, prominence given to pastel colours such as pale pinks, lilacs, and blue-greys is often effective; with stronger light and the more brilliant sunshine of Mediterranean or Californian landscapes, hotter colours may have more impact than pale colours, which often appear bleached in strong sun. On the other hand, a shaded, rather sunless court or terrace may be enlivened with salmon-pinks, oranges, reds, and yellows, while a hot, sun-baked courtyard may seem cooler if greys, blues, and whites are used.

Strong colour may also be used to lead the eye to a particular feature, while soft blues and greys are less distinct and therefore seem to recede. This effect may sometimes be used to create an illusion of distance – for example planting red roses in the foreground with blue-green grasses at the rear of the garden could make it seem longer (see also "Perspective and proportion", p.18).

Texture

This is largely provided by foliage, but other features, such as fruit and bark, and the effect of a plant's silhouette, may also have interesting

RESTRICTED COLOUR
Here, the colours have been limited to create a calm, co-ordinated effect, while the relaxed plant groupings underline the informality of the scheme.

THE EFFECT OF LIGHT
In strong sun, plants with intense colours, here lavender (Lavandula) *and* Nerium oleander, *make a dazzling impact; subtle shades may look bleached.*

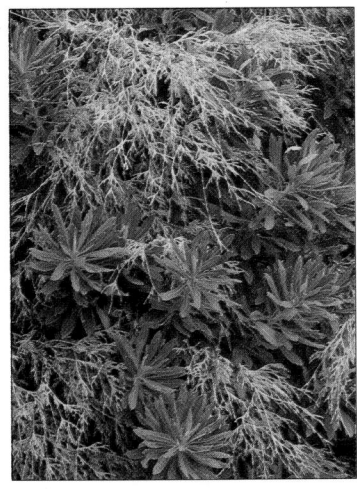

TEXTURAL CONTRASTS
The feathery branchlets of Chamaecyparis pisifera 'Filifera Aurea' *and the succulent foliage of* Euphorbia characias *subsp.* wulfenii *form a striking contrast.*

textures. When grouping different plants, consider how their varying textures will work together, and aim to set up contrasting effects so that they complement each other. For example, the lacy fronds of a clump of ferns would be attractively offset by the ridged leaves of a hosta.

Successional interest

Many gardens are at their peak in summer, with colourful schemes that rely largely on herbaceous plants. These usually provide little interest for the rest of the year, however, and a planting plan that creates a succession of interest is likely to give more pleasure. Shrubs, trees, and hedges are invaluable for establishing a lasting framework, while including

a variety of bulbs and herbaceous plants provides changing colour and texture in successive seasons.

Spring
Bulbs are excellent for bringing colour to the garden early in the year, from the white snowdrops (*Galanthus*) of late winter to the bright crocuses and daffodils of spring; many, such as tulips, flower almost into summer. Bulbs may be grown with ground-cover plants to provide interest once the bulbs' foliage dies down. Spring-flowering climbers, such as *Clematis armandii*, may be grown up a light-foliaged, deciduous tree to add colour while the tree is coming into leaf.

Summer
In summer, most herbaceous plants are at their best, with an enormous range of species from which to create a rich tapestry of colour. These include perennials, contributing interest year after year, and annuals and biennials, for example poppies (*Papaver*) and sweet peas (*Lathyrus odoratus*), to add variety and to fill in between established plants. The foliage of some bulbous plants such as *Eremurus* and ornamental onions (*Allium*) begins to die down before the plants come into flower. These bulbs should be planted behind late-flowering herbaceous plants so that their leaves will be hidden.

Autumn
Autumn-flowering bulbs, berrying shrubs, and dwarf conifers all provide interest in autumn. Many trees and shrubs that have attractive foliage, such as the fiery hues of many Japanese maples (*Acer palmatum* and *A. japonicum*), are particularly spectacular at this time.

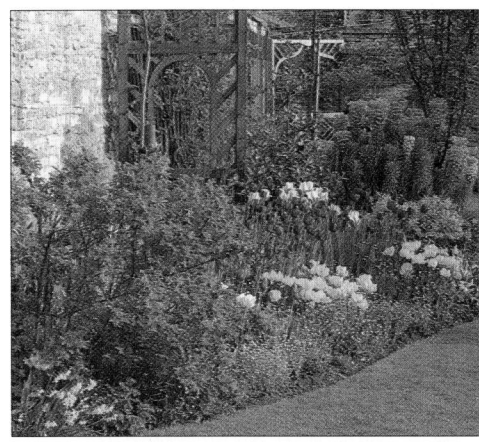

SPRING
The proud heads of colourful and striped tulips bring a wealth of colour to the border in spring, while the airy, blue flowers of forget-me-nots (Myosotis) add extra interest at ground level.

SUMMER
An old garden rose is at its prime in summer, its deep magenta blooms complementing the pink, mauve, and blue colour scheme. Perennials such as ornamental onions (Allium), hardy Geranium, and irises fill out the design of the shrub framework.

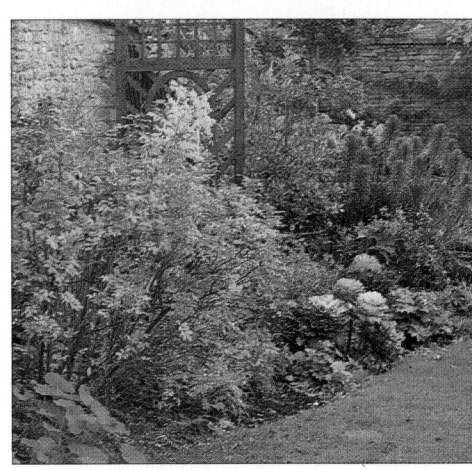

AUTUMN
Ornamental cabbages with attractive, pink and green leaves add soft colour while the golden yellow foliage of the rose brightens up the border. The structural elements of the painted trellis and the Euphorbia now start to become more prominent.

WINTER
As the perennials die down, the skeleton of the design comes to the fore – the bare stems of the rose, the bold cone shape of the gold-variegated holly (Ilex), the frost-tinged heads of the Euphorbia, and the distinctive arch of the trellis.

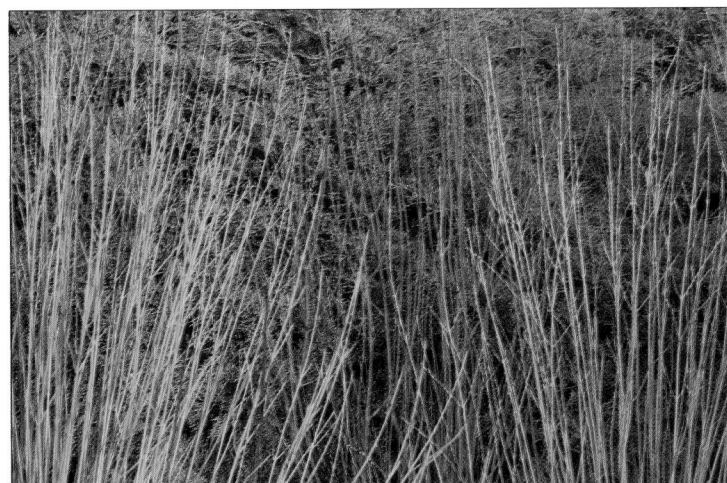

WINTER EFFECTS
The bright colours of red- and yellow-stemmed dogwoods (Cornus alba 'Sibirica' and C. stolonifera 'Flaviramea') are seen at their best in winter.

Winter

Although often regarded as a dull period in the garden, winter is a time when many plants have attractive foliage, flowers, fruits, bark, or stems. If there is the space, an area of the garden may be devoted to plants of winter interest, perhaps where they can be seen from the house. Trees and shrubs with ornamental bark provide structural features as well as colour and texture, for example the glossy, mahogany trunk of *Prunus serrula*. Evergreen ground-cover plants or winter-flowering heathers can be grown at the front of a border for extra winter colour.

Layer planting

The principle of layer planting is to achieve continuity and balance of colour, form, and texture in the same area. This mirrors natural habitats where plants grow in close proximity but often have distinct lifecycles which minimizes competition for moisture, food, and light. A good natural example is a bluebell wood where the bluebells bloom in late spring and die down before bracken, brambles, and foxgloves have developed fully. This interplanting or tiered planting may be copied, using associations of cultivated plants; for example, white-stemmed birches (*Betula*) could form the tree layer, in whose light shade could be planted Japanese maples (*Acer*) or dogwoods (*Cornus*) as the shrub layer. These could be underplanted with hostas or ferns and, as these do not come into leaf until late spring, they might be interplanted with spring bulbs.

On a smaller scale, the same principles may be followed using specimen shrubs surrounded by carpets of ground-cover plants and bulbs. Trees that have dense canopies, such as beech (*Fagus*), or evergreen trees such as hollies (*Ilex*), often cast deep shade or have branches right to the ground, making it difficult for plants beneath to grow well.

Plant spacing

When designing a planting scheme, leave enough space between plants so that they have room to develop to

GROUPING CONTAINERS
Siting containers together creates bold effects; here, a group ranged by height – from a striking Nerium oleander *at the rear to white candytuft* (Iberis) *at the front – forms a transition between house and garden.*

their full size; if planted too closely, they may soon need to be thinned to avoid becoming overcrowded. There may be occasions, however, when close planting may be employed to provide a particular design feature, such as a knot garden.

Planting distances and spacings also depend upon the soil, climatic conditions, and the maturity period for the species or cultivar while the scheme is developing. Young plants are less costly than more mature specimens of the same species or cultivar that provide an immediate impact, but there may be a delay of several years before the planting begins to look mature. The decision on which to plant will depend on the budget available.

As a general rule, close planting and the use of fast-maturing plants creates a good short-term impact, but more thinning, maintenance, and renewal is required in the longer term. A balance between fast- and slow-growing plants yields the most satisfactory results; using temporary "fillers" such as colourful annuals and bulbs in the gaps is a way of providing plenty of interest initially while the other plants are becoming well established.

Gardening in containers

There is plenty of scope for including planted containers in a garden, especially on terraces, patios, and steps, where they create attractive changes of level and soften the rigid appearance. Containers form structural points of interest and may be used in various ways – singly to enhance specimen plants, in pairs to frame a view or flight of steps, or in small groups to link the house with the terrace and garden, for example.

It is possible to grow most plants in containers: bedding plants or bulbs are often grown this way, while more permanent planting of small shrubs, trees, and conifers provides long-term interest. Even climbers may be planted in containers next to a wall.

Containers are available in a wide range of shapes and sizes, and may often be very stylish. Select those that complement the materials and character of the house, as well as the planting. For example, a clipped box (*Buxus*) would be perfectly enhanced by an elegant, stone trough, but would be less appropriate in a wooden half-barrel.

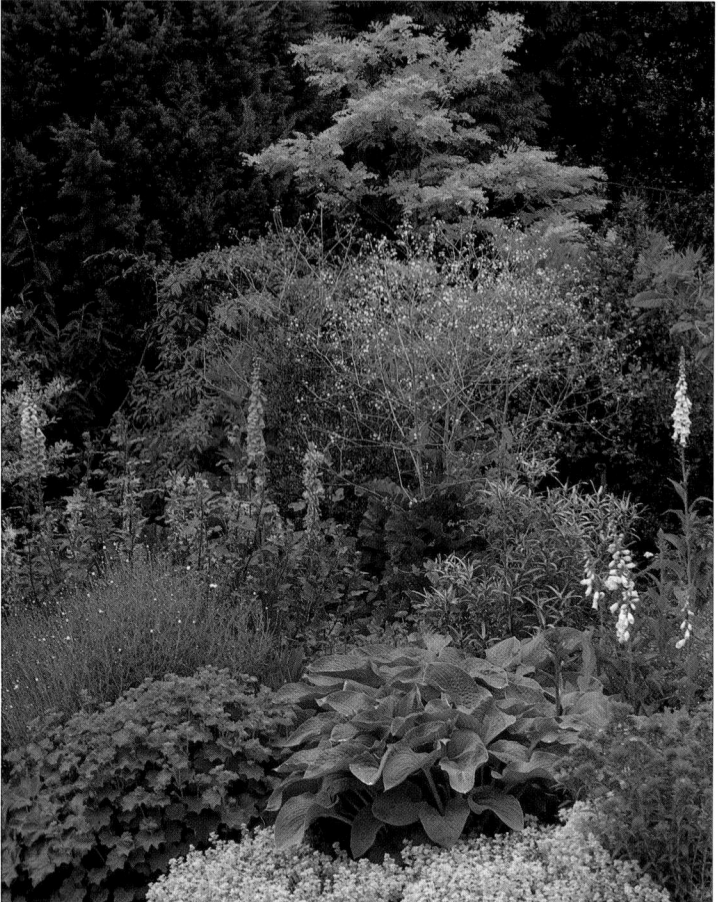

TIERED PLANTING
The small canopy and light foliage of a Robinia pseudoacacia 'Frisia' *allow many plants to grow underneath it; similarly, the foxgloves* (Digitalis) *and* Crambe cordifolia *do not restrict the growth of low perennials beneath.*

Garden styles

W HILE there are almost no limits to the potential range of garden designs, several classical and natural styles have provided inspiration for gardeners for centuries. These may assist you in planning and combining all the various elements to create a well-focused and consistent design.

Combining two or more styles may also be effective, perhaps by dividing the garden into smaller "rooms" with ornamental hedges or trellis. Even in quite a small area, stylistic contrasts may provide an interesting change of key: the strong, clean lines of a contemporary, formal pond may be effectively offset by a background border overflowing with old-fashioned rambling roses and attractive annuals. Plan the linking of areas or the juxtaposition of different styles with great care, however, to avoid a discordant effect. Mixing formal and informal styles is best achieved by framed planting (see p.21).

Informal and naturalistic gardens

These garden styles, as their names imply, tend generally to have no strong, symmetrical, rigid, or ordered lines; more flowing shapes, less regulated and controlled planting, and soft, curved patterns are typical. Informal groups of plants in overflowing beds and borders, such as are found in cottage gardens, are often included, while if a more naturalistic effect is required, the planting design may be even simpler.

The concept of a wild garden is to grow native species in natural associations and groups, imitating the best of nature while exerting some selection and control. Simply letting a garden run wild does not achieve the same result: it tends to be messy rather than pleasantly relaxed and flowing. A degree of maintenance is necessary in a naturalistic garden but the effect of this should be unobtrusive. Use the natural characteristics of the site as much as possible, whether developing a woodland garden, a wild-flower meadow, or a sanctuary to attract forms of wildlife.

Cottage gardens

In the past, cottage gardens were primarily utilitarian, with fruit, vegetables, herbs, flowers, and shrubs crowded into a very small area.

COTTAGE GARDEN
A productive screen of scarlet runner beans effectively combines the functional with the ornamental, while wigwams support scented sweet peas (Lathyrus odoratus) *which may be cut for indoor decoration.*

Lawns were rare, since any spare ground was thought better used for growing more plants. The garden was typically divided by paths of trodden earth edged with stones, tiles, shells, or clumps of flowers such as pansies (*Viola* x *wittrockiana*). A great variety of plants, often highly fragrant, was grown – old roses billowing over cabbages, Madonna lilies (*Lilium candidum*) next to marigolds (*Calendula*), while towering hollyhocks (*Alcea rosea*) and sunflowers (*Helianthus annuus*) might frame the doorway.

While it is possible to re-create a traditional cottage garden effectively, the maintenance demands are high and the characteristic plants do not usually provide much interest in autumn and winter. Many of the principles are valuable ideas for modern gardens, however, and may be borrowed or adapted to suit individual sites, while certain typical plants and features are often used today to create a relaxed and rural effect in a scheme.

Paths made from bricks, cobbles, or gravel are practical as well as appropriate in style, while an edging of lavender (*Lavandula*) provides scented flowers outdoors and for drying as well as attractive evergreen foliage. A rustic, wooden arch is an ideal feature for supporting scented climbing plants such as roses or honeysuckle (*Lonicera*), and borders overflowing with peonies (*Paeonia*), lupins (*Lupinus*), wallflowers (*Cheiranthus*), and pinks (*Dianthus*) re-create the feeling of unchecked abundance.

Woodland gardens

A woodland garden should be a peaceful, sheltered place based on a natural grouping of trees, and perhaps with appropriate underplanting of shrubs, herbaceous plants, and bulbs. Trees such as oak (*Quercus*),

silver birch (*Betula pendula*), and wild cherry (*Prunus avium*) that cast light or dappled shade allow a greater range of plants to grow beneath them, so are usually preferred to conifers and other trees that have a dense canopy (see also "Layer planting", p.26).

Growing other plants as well as trees makes it easier to create a succession of interest and provides a display at different levels of height. Hardy cyclamen and bluebells (*Hyacinthoides non-scriptus*) may be planted in drifts to form swathes of colour, while ornamental members of the nettle family (e.g. *Lamium maculatum*) are attractive as ground cover. In moist sites, for example

near a woodland stream, primroses (*Primula vulgaris*) and many ferns thrive, while foxgloves (*Digitalis*) tolerate the dry, shady conditions found beneath tree canopies. There are a number of shrubs such as rhododendrons and Japanese maples (*Acer*) that grow well in shady woodland sites and, as they also form a transition between low bulbs and perennials and tall trees, they help to create an interesting, well-balanced planting scheme.

Fast-growing species such as alders (*Alnus*) and willows (*Salix*) will provide a tree canopy fairly quickly, but may then soon form shade that is too heavy for many woodland plants

WILD GARDEN
Wild species such as tall, pink willow herb (Epilobium) *and yellow loosestrife* (Lysimachia punctata) *thrive in this naturalistic corner. The pond and dense cover of the reeds and other plants make it an alluring haven for wildlife.*

to thrive. Slower-growing species such as Scots pine (*Pinus sylvestris*), red oak (*Quercus rubra*), and wild cherry (*Prunus avium*) will provide more satisfactory top cover.

If the site is partially wooded already, it may be necessary to clear areas for glades and underplanting by removing unwanted scrub and saplings or thinning the tree canopy. Dense planting at the edges of the site is best left as it provides valuable shelter from the wind, although it may be cut back.

Given plenty of space, it is possible to create a new woodland garden but patience is essential; even if large sites are planted, a true woodland takes some years to establish. A minimum area of about 1,000sq m (¹/₄ acre) is needed, although on a smaller scale a few groups of birches (*Betula*), maples (*Acer*), or other trees with light foliage will provide sufficient shade in which to grow a succession of woodlanders, such as *Anemone nemorosa*, *Trillium*, and snowdrops (*Galanthus*).

When establishing a woodland on an open site, it is best to keep the area around the trees clear so that for the first year or two they develop with little or no competition from other plants.

Access to the garden is best provided by informal paths which can be made from loose materials such as bark chippings, pine needles, or, if the site tends to be wet, local gravel. For an informal garden environment, naturally meandering paths that are neither very wide (except for maintenance purposes) nor conspicuous are most suitable. Straight, formal paths look inappropriate in a woodland garden.

Wildlife and conservation gardens

In many areas, the natural habitat of much of the flora and fauna is being eroded, and therefore the idea of providing a refuge for wildlife in the garden is appealing. Any garden with a wide range of plants will attract some animals and birds but growing a greater variety of plant communities will provide better conditions for a diversity of wildlife.

The main aim of this style of garden should be to provide both habitats and food; if preferred, these can be selected to attract particular creatures. For example, hawthorn (*Crataegus*) hedges are suitable nesting sites for birds, while berrying trees and shrubs are a source of food in winter. Including a pond should attract a great many different forms of wildlife such as birds, frogs, newts, dragonflies, and other insects.

SHADY WOODLAND
The canopy created by deciduous trees provides the right conditions for many shade-loving plants and a cool refuge in which to sit in summer.

Meadows

Pastures and meadows with a rich abundance of wild flowers were once common in the countryside, but are now becoming increasingly rare, and the interest in meadow gardens has risen accordingly. It is important to select plants that are suitable for the site and conditions and to establish and maintain them properly if they are to look effective. A meadow garden may be developed easily and satisfactorily on even relatively poor soil because some of the most attractive grassland species prefer these conditions rather than richer, well-fertilized garden soils.

Many meadow wild flowers are perennials that persist well once they are established in an appropriate, correctly managed habitat. Seed mixtures of "cornfield annuals" are sometimes recommended for meadow gardening but are not always suitable, as they require regularly cultivated soil to thrive, and would soon die out in grassland. For more information, see WILD-FLOWER AND MEADOW GARDENING, p.169.

Water gardens

The allure of water brings a special fascination to any garden: a pool has an inherent tranquillity, while a stream offers the extra pleasures of sound and movement. If incorporating a water feature into the garden scheme, ensure that its design is congruous with the rest of the garden and the house.

In a formal garden, a symmetrical pool with a distinct edge is usually appropriate. A waterspout, fountain, or evenly stepped waterfall could also be included to add an interesting change of level as well as movement. A more naturalistic pond with a curving, irregular shape would be desirable in an informal setting; the edge is best partially softened or disguised by moisture-loving plants and attractive stones.

If there is sufficient space, a stream or watercourse leading into the pond and channelled over stones or cobbles creates an appealing sight and sound. It is best to use local stone or slate if constructing a water feature that is to blend in well with the

WATER IN THE GARDEN
This delightful pool forms the centrepiece of an informal area set apart from the formality glimpsed beyond and framed by a clipped hedge. The water's calm, reflective surface is attractive in its own right, while the pond margin also provides an ideal spot to grow moisture-loving plants, such as hostas and Rodgersia.

natural landscape. For more information on design, construction, and planting, see THE WATER GARDEN, pp.244–57.

Patios and courtyards

These hard-surfaced and usually enclosed gardens are often ideal in towns and cities where garden space is typically very restricted and lawns are difficult to establish and maintain well. Even in a small area, an enchanting garden can be created. To create the best effect, the design should be simple and the temptation to pack in many different features or plants should be resisted.

In addition to providing an area for sitting out and an informal eating place in fine weather, a patio may be used as a setting for displaying a wide range of plants in containers, including bulbs, alpines, herbs, small trees, shrubs, roses, and fruit. Raised beds around a patio or courtyard area may also be planted with climbers and trailing plants to spill over the edge and soften the rigid effect of the hard materials. Ensure that the materials selected for use are appropriate to the style and character of the house.

When designing a patio, bear in mind which parts of the site are sunny or shaded at different times of day, and plan areas for sitting out in the morning or evening accordingly. Shade cast by trees and adjacent buildings will vary during the year, depending on the density of foliage present and the differences in the angle of the sun.

An enclosing screen or trellis clothed in decorative climbers, vines, or even runner beans in summer,

BALCONY GARDEN·
Raised wooden beds and large terracotta pots are planted with standard shrubs, ground-cover plants, and bright annuals such as copper-leaved begonias to enliven this roof-top terrace. The square-patterned trellis picks up the design of the windows, linking the inside with the outside.

provides some protection from wind as well as seclusion. Trees in pots may be used as movable shelters for the same purpose. Privacy and shade can be increased by including a pergola or arbour, which also provides an ornamental framework to support fragrant and colourful honeysuckles (*Lonicera*), roses, and clematis.

Changes of level are often useful in developing a compact space effectively; steps may be enhanced by pots or by growing climbers up a handrail or railings. If the patio can be seen from an upstairs window, make sure that the overall design will also be pleasing from above, since small gardens often have a mosaic-like quality that is particularly attractive from this viewpoint.

Artificial lighting is often both practical and attractive in a courtyard or patio garden. It may be used in various ways, for example to cast

the shadow of a tree or statue against a brick wall, or to backlight a striking, architectural plant; in a pool, illuminate the fine spray of a fountain from underneath or shed light across the water surface to enjoy its reflections after dark.

Roof gardens and balconies

Many of the same considerations apply to roof gardens and balconies as to patios, although they are more exposed to both sun and wind. Low-maintenance design and planting are usually priorities, while the weight of containers is also important; if there are weight restrictions, plastic or fibreglass containers are preferable to those made from terracotta or stone. Similarly, if additional flooring is required, choose light-weight materials rather than heavy paving slabs.

If the garden is subject to strong winds, sturdy trellis screens or other windbreak filters provide shelter for both plants and people, although they may also obstruct views. Any screens used must be very securely fixed to permanent roof structures for safety reasons.

Balconies are usually more sheltered than roof gardens and may also be shaded from above. Exploit all the available space, adding sturdy brackets and shelves to the house wall to support pots and troughs of trailing plants, or grow climbers up ornamental trellis (see "Gardening in containers", p.26).

Formal gardens

From the simplicity of a lawn punctuated by a single island bed to the complexity of an intricate parterre, many types of formal garden may be

designed. However simple they may be, formal designs are characteristically elegant and ordered, balanced and well proportioned, and often strongly patterned or symmetrical. Features typically include closely mown lawns, straight paths, neatly clipped hedges or topiary, borders defined by low hedges or edging plants, framed vistas and focal points, formal bedding in blocks of strong colour, and, on occasion, parterres and knot gardens.

Formal gardens require very precise and regular maintenance and are usually labour-intensive. The more regular the design, the more any minor flaws will stand out.

Classical and Italianate gardens

The formal gardens that existed in ancient Greece and Rome were the inspiration for the splendid palatial and villa gardens of Italy and France in the 17th and 18th centuries. The essential characteristics of these gardens are their strong architectural and symmetrical designs which follow closely the proportion and scale of the building that they surround or enhance.

Italianate gardens are often set on elevated or dominating sites, with terraced gardens and flights of steps leading to long, shaded walks, fountains, cascades, and canals. In a hot, Mediterranean climate, the cooling effects of water and avenues or canopies of – usually evergreen – trees are all part of the pleasures of these gardens. On the terraces there might be parterre designs with box-lined scrolls of flower beds and symmetrically sited topiary obelisks or pyramids. Colour is generally limited, however, to the dark green of the plants, the pale colours of the

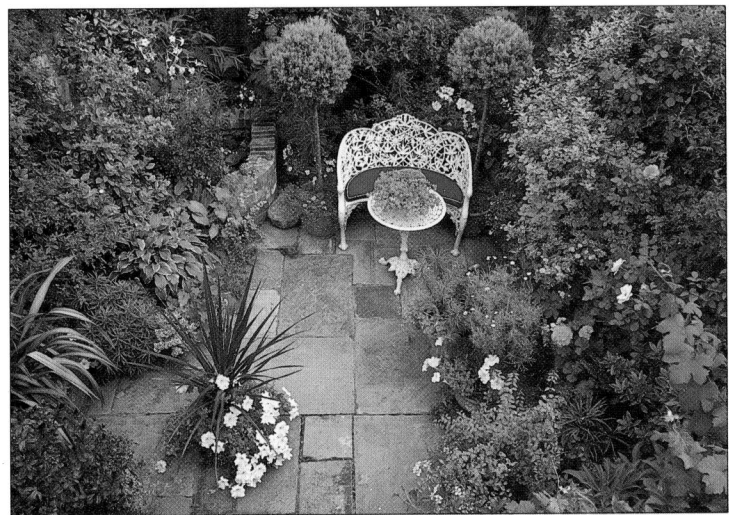

ENCLOSED PATIO
A table and seat, framed by clipped willow standards (Salix repens var. argentea) *and foliage plants, form an elegant focal point in this patio garden.*

stone and gravel, and the "white" waters. Other typical features include statuary, balustrades, and well-proportioned urns or vases for citrus and ornamental plants.

Many of these features may be incorporated into contemporary garden designs to create a sense of elegance, formality, and ordered calm. Even in a small area, the careful attention to scale, proportion, balance, and harmony noticeable in classical gardens may be copied to create a simple, effective design.

Oriental influences

Garden design in China is an ancient art, going back over 3,000 years. Gardens were created by scholars and philosophers as essentially quiet, sublimely peaceful places for contemplation and meditation. Traditionally, the elements are simple and symbolic, mirroring China's vast and superb landscape of mountains, rocks, falling water, green valleys, and lakes. The inclusion of a few small, scaled-down features, especially rocks, in a walled enclosure are sufficient to suggest these distant scenes. Paths wind or zig-zag, to reveal different views and prospects gradually, while steeply arched bridges over water offer views of fish or reflections. Glimpses out from these secret gardens were often through "key-hole" shapes in the walls, allowing the imagination to fly out of the garden into these borrowed landscapes.

Planting is restrained and limited, each tree or shrub in the garden having a meaning or symbolic place in the overall composition. Although

FORMAL DESIGN
Striking for both its simplicity and symmetry, this formal garden has a pleasing restfulness and is a splendid example of nature tamed by art.

China has one of the richest, natural floras in the world, only a relatively small range of plants is to be found in traditional Chinese gardens; this is primarily because these gardens were conceived by artists, poets, and scholars rather than botanists or plantsmen.

Japanese gardens were borrowed from the Chinese some 1,200 years ago and have their sources of inspiration in the hills, lakes, and islands of Japan. They differ from the Chinese in that they have richer, denser plantings of carefully shaped and dwarfed trees and shrubs, symbolic groups of shaped stones, raked gravels or sands around mounded "islands", and stone lanterns. Over the centuries three types of oriental garden have evolved. The first is the

flat garden containing the simplest elements of raked sand or gravel, a vertical or flat stone, and a bamboo. The second is the dry garden, which consists of hills and stones in dry watercourses and channels, and is more like a Chinese composition. The third oriental garden is the hill and water, or tea, garden, which comprises a complete landscape of hills, a watercourse, and pines and other trees among rocks and a lake.

Simple buildings are an essential feature of Chinese and Japanese gardens, with tea houses, pavilions, or temples all intended for resting, viewing, and contemplation.

While it is difficult to reproduce these oriental gardens accurately in a modern garden, some of the design principles may be copied: balance,

simplicity, symbolism, and calm are the elements that may be effective in various garden designs. The imaginative use of hard materials and water should provide inspiration for designing even the smallest garden, while on a larger scale the idea of sculpting the landscape may be helpful in planning garden outlooks.

Formal bedding

With their ordered groups of colourful plants, formal beds have declined in popularity in favour of informal styles, but their bold blocks of colour make an immediate and vivid impact. Flowers with strong, even clashing, colours are often included side by side, but the colour combinations should be carefully selected so that the use of too many different shades does not detract from the overall design. Try limiting the range of plants used, perhaps with only two or three cultivars or colours, using a formal frame to create a striking display that is also relatively easy to plant and maintain (see also ANNUALS AND BIENNIALS "Formal bedding schemes", p.174).

Many of the plants used traditionally are annuals or half-hardy plants; It may be expensive to buy a large number of these, but most may easily be raised from seed or cuttings. Perennials, bulbs, and some shrubs, provide a background structure in planting schemes and also help to extend the period of interest.

Topiary

For over 2,000 years, the art and craft of topiary has been practised in gardens: with time, patience, and

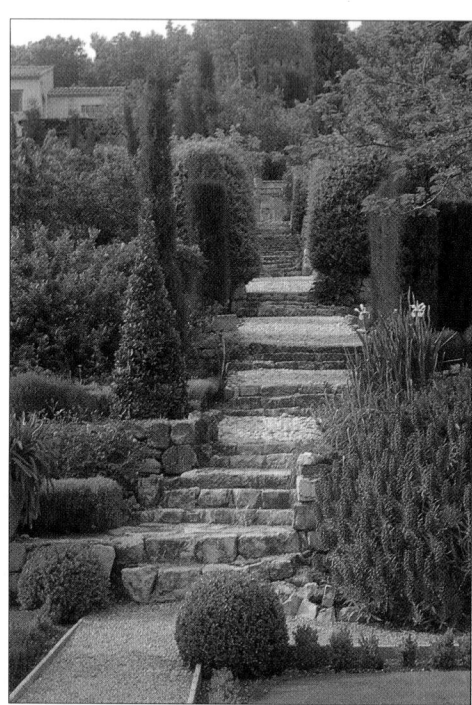

CLASSICAL ELEGANCE
The framed steps, controlled use of colour, and carefully sited, clipped evergreen topiary and hedges show how a classical approach can be adapted to suit a modern garden. Offsetting the steps to one side of the path and mixing different hard materials has helped to soften the formality of the design.

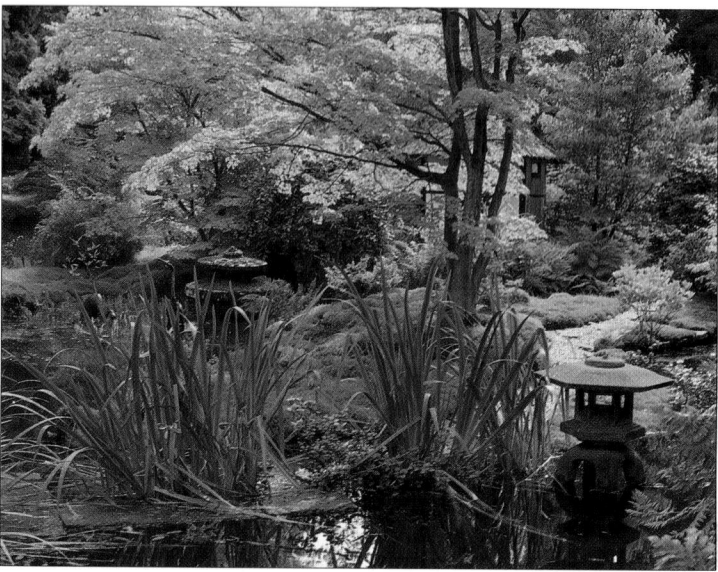

JAPANESE STYLE
The calming water, winding paths, strictly limited colour, and half-hidden views and features in this garden are characteristic of the mood and style of many oriental gardens.

suitable plants, "living sculptures" may be produced without too much skill being required.

Topiary is often used in formal gardens to add height, shape, and sculptural interest; well-clipped columns, pyramids, or spirals are used to provide vertical punctuation points and accentuate the symmetry and proportion of a design. A single piece of topiary forms a strong focal point while several clipped shrubs or trees may provide cornerstones to the garden or a well-defined framework as a foil for more informal and unstructured planting.

Simple, geometric shapes such as spheres or cones are best used if topiary is required for a classical or formal garden. More fanciful forms such as birds and animals, objects or even chess pieces, that add a lively and amusing touch, may be suitable in both formal and informal gardens, depending on the style, but would be inappropriate in a naturalistic or wild garden setting.

The best plants to use are generally those that are evergreen, dense, and slow-growing: yew (*Taxus baccata*) and box (*Buxus*) are ideal and provide interest all year round. Ivies (*Hedera*) may also be clipped and trained over frames into appropriate shapes. For further details, see TOPIARY, pp.52–3.

Knot gardens

These were particularly popular in the 16th century, and took the form of interlacing bands and abstract patterns, containing coloured sands, gravels, or plants, marked out and framed by low hedges. They often reflected the knots and strapwork patterns of English Elizabethan and Tudor needlework and plaster ceiling decorations. To appreciate the detail, knot gardens are best viewed

A TOPIARY GARDEN
Shrubs shaped into tall spirals, rectangles, and globes add sculptural interest to this formal garden and emphasize the symmetry of its design.

from above and should be designed so that they can be seen easily from a raised terrace or house window.

Given an appropriate setting and a level, well-drained site, knot gardens are not difficult to create and are fairly easy to maintain. The patterns should be kept simple or the design may be ineffective as well as making maintenance more difficult. Some suitable plants include dwarf box, *Teucrium chamaedrys*, and cotton lavender (*Santolina chamaecyparissus*). If using plants rather than coloured gravels to fill in the areas between the hedges, select those that are are in keeping with the scale and character of the knot; low-growing plants are usually suitable, although more unusual plantings, perhaps using succulents such as houseleeks (*Sempervivum*), may also be considered. Weeds that appear on the gravel surfaces should be removed by hand as weedkillers could damage the shallow-rooting hedges.

Parterres

Often confused with knot gardens, parterres are larger in scale, and consist of more or less flat, regular flower beds which form decorative patterns within a particular design. These designs are often very ambitious and complicated, with flowering, scroll-like patterns or symbolic themes. The outlines are usually formed from low hedges of box, and the area in between the hedges is then filled with gravels of different hues, compact and colourful bedding plants, or plants that have subdued pastel shades. Evergreen shrubs trimmed into neat pyramids or globes, and

other clipped, formal shapes in yew or box may also be included. Parterres became very popular in the Victorian and Edwardian periods, especially in municipal parks and gardens, where they were transformed into elaborate floral displays and extravagant bedding schemes.

If designing a parterre in a modern garden, make sure that it is in scale with the size of the house or adjacent terrace.

Sunken gardens

Changes of level, even comparatively small ones, provide interesting features in a garden, and a sunken garden that is well devised can add a feeling of space and adventure, as well as bringing another dimension to the design.

Traditional sunken gardens were usually square or rectangular, enclosed by walls, and surrounded by raised grass or paved paths so that they could be viewed from above. The layout was typically simple and geometrical, with flower beds divided by a symmetrical framework of paths and walkways, perhaps with a central sculptural feature such as a fountain or sundial.

As they are lower than the rest of the garden, sunken gardens are often sheltered and very secluded, with a secret, sanctuary-like quality that is particularly restful and appealing. Herbs, roses, and formal bedding lend themselves particularly well for use in sunken gardens.

PARTERRE
The intricate and decorative design of low, interlacing box hedges enclosing blocks of pink and red dahlias recreates the deliberately neat and tailored effect of a classical parterre.

Restoring old and historic gardens

If recreating or restoring an old garden, the degree and nature of the work will vary widely, depending on its size, condition, and character. As well as surveying the site and assessing the condition of the main existing features (see "Appraising the site", p.15), try to research the history and development of the garden.

A cautious approach is advisable: seeing the garden through a year helps to establish an idea of the original planting scheme, as well as making it easier to determine which plants may be pruned or renovated and which should be replaced. Clearing paths, steps, and other hard elements that are overgrown may also be helpful in revealing the original framework of the design. Work on the site should respect any elements of the original garden that remain. Unusual plants may also have survived, such as rare old rose or rhododendron cultivars. There

may be old trees that could be preserved with prudent surgery but, if they are diseased or dangerous, they should be removed (see "Cutting down a tree", p.45) and, if appropriate, replaced.

Overgrown hedges may sometimes be cut back hard to renovate them (see HEDGES AND SCREENS, pp.60–62). If neglected box hedges remain from an old knot garden or parterre, they may also be renovated if not too old or overgrown, but they do not respond well to severe pruning; if there is any doubt concerning their survival, it is better to replant.

Lawns and other turfed areas, if part of the original design, may not be beyond restoration. Often high-quality turf was used in lawnmaking a century or more ago and, if this is still in place, it may respond well to the necessary levelling, feeding, and proper mowing regimes (see "Renovating a neglected lawn", p.289).

2

ORNAMENTAL TREES

ORE THAN ANY *other plants, trees give a sense of permanence and maturity to a garden and link it with the broader, external landscape. They add height, structure, and sculptural focal points to a design, while their large-scale and distinctive silhouettes form an attractive contrast with the softer lines of other planting. There is an enormous variety of trees, differing in shape and form as well as in the colour and texture of foliage, flowers, and bark. Each has a particular appeal, from the dark,* pointing column of a cypress to the blazing autumn colour of a Japanese maple or the patterned cinnamon trunk of Eucalyptus. Trees may be grown in many ways: in an informal setting, a woodland grouping of hazels and silver birches, surrounded by bulbs, is highly effective, while, in a formal garden, an avenue of copper beeches or pleached limes is suitably elegant. Some trees – such as magnolias with their exquisite, goblet-like blooms – are best sited on their own as a garden feature.

Designing with trees

ORNAMENTAL trees are grown for the beauty of their flowers, bark, or decorative fruits, rather than for edible or timber crops. Many fruit trees, however, are graced by beautiful flowers and a few ornamental trees, such as crab apples (*Malus*), bear rich crops of fruits for preserving. The distinction between trees and shrubs is similarly blurred, the former usually, but not always,

with a single trunk and the latter, for example lilacs (*Syringa*), multi-stemmed although sometimes reaching tree-like proportions.

Choosing trees

Trees are generally the largest, most expensive, and longest-lived garden plants, and selecting and siting them

are major design decisions. The fewer trees a garden can accommodate, the more important careful choice and siting become; in a "one-tree garden" these points are crucial to the success of the design. A tree's general appearance and special features obviously matter, but its suitability for a garden's soil, climate, and aspect, and its ultimate height, spread, and growth rate are

equally important. Once a tree is chosen, the design process continues, in deciding where to plant it (see "Choosing a planting site", p.39). Garden centres carry a limited range of the most popular ornamental trees; specialist nurseries, some with a mail-order service, offer a wider choice.

Heights range from around just 1m (3ft) for some dwarf conifers to the massive 90m (300ft) of a redwood (*Sequoia*). Growth rates vary from 2.5cm (1in) or less a year for dwarf conifers to 1m (3ft) or more for some poplars (*Populus*). A young tree in a garden centre gives little or no indication of its potential size and some species, particularly conifers, include both miniature and giant cultivars. Select cultivars with care and, if offered substitutes, make sure that they will be equally appropriate for your needs.

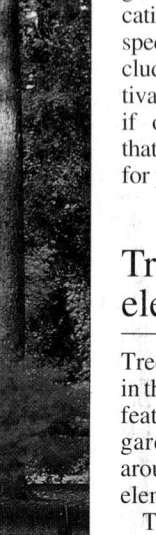

Trees as design elements

Trees create a strong visual impact in the same way as hard landscaping features. They also help to form a garden's permanent framework, around which the more temporary elements come and go.

Trees may be used as living sculptures (see "Specimen trees as focal points", p.33): a simple, contrasting setting is most likely to enhance a tree used in this way. A tree with pale foliage looks striking against a

TREES IN THE GARDEN
The architectural outlines of trees add structure to a garden and form a long-term part of the design framework. In a large garden, several trees may be *grouped together to create a strong impact of colour and form, as with this informal arrangement of maples* (Acer) *and other deciduous trees.*

ENCLOSING SPACE
The arching fronds of palms are used as structural features to enclose and delineate a seating area. They create a lush, cool screen that forms a less rigid division than a wall or fence.

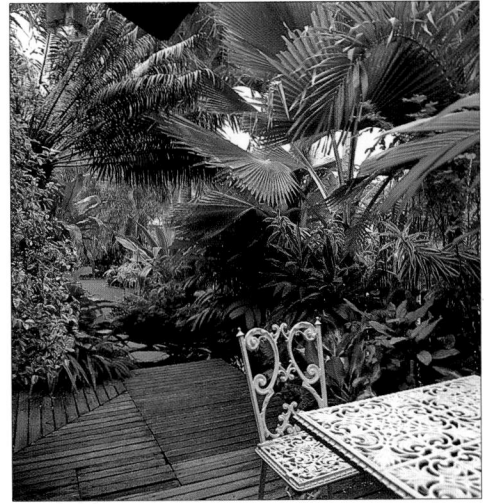

SPECIMEN TREE
Trees that are particularly attractive or well shaped look good sited on their own so that they stand out in the scheme. This double pink hawthorn (Crataegus laevigata) *has a fine show of blossom that may be enjoyed from all viewpoints as well as forming a cornerstone in the design.*

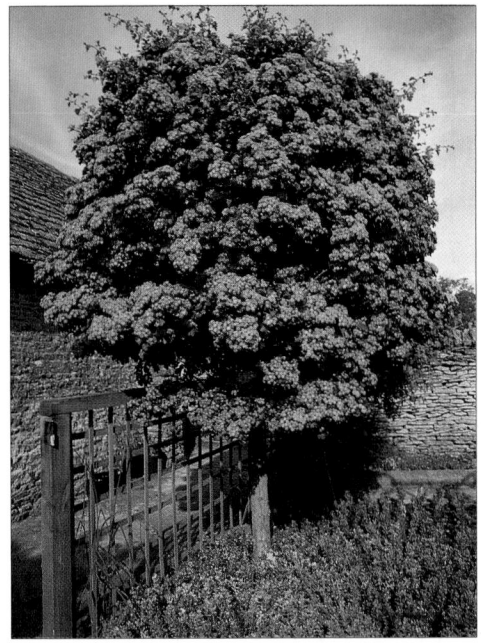

hedge of dark-green yew (*Taxus baccata*), for example, while the bold winter tracery of bare branches stands out well in front of a white-painted wall.

Used structurally, trees can also define or enclose space. A row or informal clump of trees can mark the boundary of a property, separate one part of the garden from another, or emphasize a path. A pair of trees might act as a verdant frame for a distant view or form a living arch through which the garden is entered.

Shape and form

A tree's shape and form are as important as its size – in setting the mood and style as well as in practical considerations of space. Some trees, such as many ornamental cherries (*Prunus*), are small and charming, while others, such as cedars (*Cedrus*), are grand and monumental. Most can be formal or informal, according to the setting and treatment. *Rhus typhina* has a striking architectural form, ideal for a modern, paved garden, while the arching fronds of many palms bring lushness to a courtyard or conservatory. Rowans (*Sorbus aucuparia*) and hollies (*Ilex*) are typical English cottage garden trees; Japanese maples (*Acer palmatum*) and the large *Salix matsudana* 'Tortuosa' are suitable for Oriental gardens; native species are ideal for wild gardens.

Narrow, upright trees, such as *Malus tschonoskii*, are suitable for small gardens but have a formal, almost artificial appearance. Round-headed or wide-spreading trees seem more informal but cast much more shade and rain shadow, making underplanting difficult, while those with an irregular, open-branch framework have a naturalistic appeal. Cone- or pyramid-shaped trees have a sculptural effect, while weeping trees have a softer silhouette.

Consider how long the tree takes to develop its characteristic shape – in some cases, it can be decades. *Prunus* 'Kanzan', for example, has a stiff growth habit when young, with awkwardly angled branches; yet after ten years the branches begin to arch and by 30 years the tree has a graceful, rounded crown.

Where space allows, combining contrasting tree shapes can create a dynamic effect, but planting many differently shaped trees may simply appear fussy and unco-ordinated.

Specimen trees as focal points

A specimen tree is grown on its own and so can develop and display its full natural beauty without competition from other trees. Depending on the climate, weeping willow (*Salix* x *sepulcralis* 'Chrysocoma'), flowering dogwood (*Cornus florida*), various ornamental cherries (*Prunus*), and palms such as *Howea* and *Phoenix* are popular specimen trees. Select a tree that is the right size for its setting – tiny specimen trees look lost in vast gardens and outsized ones overbearing in confined spaces.

TREE SHAPES

SPREADING
Prunus americana

PYRAMIDAL
Carpinus betulus 'Fastigiata' (Common hornbeam)

CONICAL
Pseudotsuga menziesii var. *glauca* (Blue Douglas fir)

WEEPING
Salix caprea 'Kilmarnock' (Kilmarnock willow)

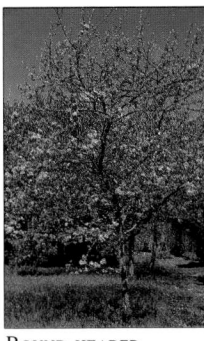

ROUND-HEADED
Malus 'Magdeburgensis' (Crab apple)

ARCHING
Archontophoenix alexandrae (King palm)

COLUMNAR
Acer rubrum 'Columnare' (Red maple)

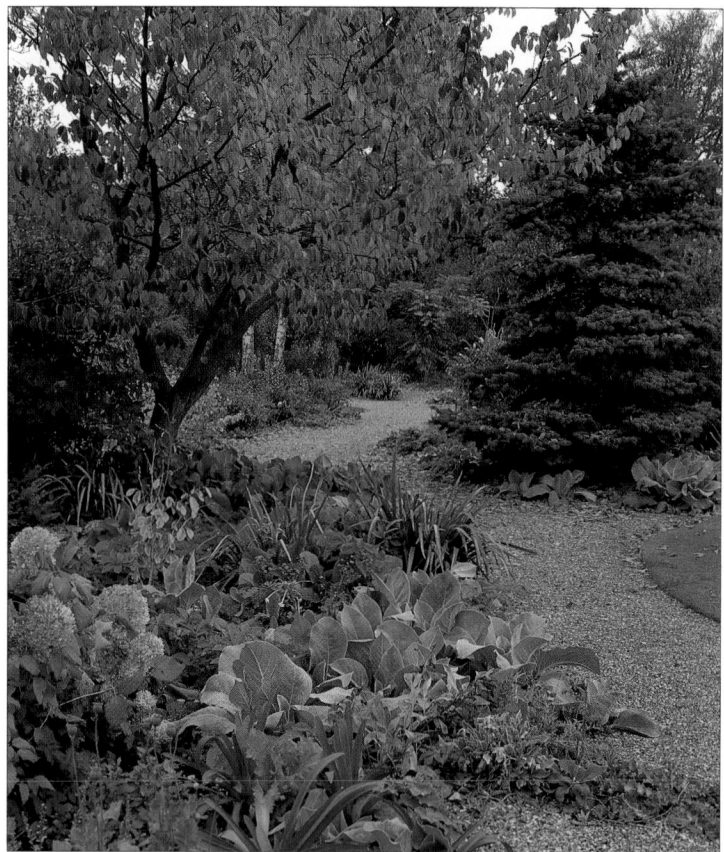

FOLIAGE COLOUR AND TEXTURE
Here, the autumn foliage of a deciduous tree is offset by the blue-green mass of a conifer, creating a contrasting tableau of colour, texture, and shape.

Specimen trees, particularly in formal gardens, are traditionally placed in the centre of a lawn. Siting a specimen tree to one side, however, can add a sense of liveliness and informality to a scheme as well as allowing a view down the garden. Other options include planting a specimen tree next to a gate or garden entrance, or at the bottom or top of a flight of steps, to mark the transition from one space in the garden to another.

Planting in a swathe of gravel or ground-cover plants such as ivy (*Hedera*) or periwinkle (*Vinca*) provides a complementary foil for a specimen tree. In a mixed border, use a tree as the keystone around which to build the colour and form of the surrounding groups of plants. A specimen tree may be reflected in a garden pond or offset by a statue or white-painted bench beneath it, so that each element enhances the other.

Grouping trees

If space allows, consider planting three or more trees together in informal clumps of the same or different species. A group of trees also creates a more substantial, curtain-like frame than a single tree for one or both sides of a view. Clumps of large trees such as oaks (*Quercus*) or beeches (*Fagus*) make focal points on a grand scale, as exemplified in the landscapes of the great 18th-century English landscape gardener, Capability Brown. In warmer climates, stands of tall, bare-trunked palms can be equally impressive on their own in grass or interplanted with lower-growing or multi-stemmed species.

On a smaller scale, a modest group of deciduous trees with light foliage, such as aspens (*Populus tremula*) or maples (*Acer*), can form the backbone of a miniature woodland. The dappled shade and leafy soil are perfect for bluebells (*Hyacinthoides non-scriptus*), daffodils, and primroses (*Primula vulgaris*).

Trees in informal groups can be planted closer than the combined potential spread of their crowns. Relatively tall, narrow, or asymmetrical growth may result but the effect can be pleasantly informal, with intermingled branches forming attractive tracery against the sky.

Features of interest

Although trees are most often valued for their architectural qualities, they also provide interest through particular features such as flowers, foliage, berries, and bark. Site a tree so that its attractive characteristics are shown off to advantage (see also "Successional interest", p.35).

Leaves

For sheer mass and duration of display, leaves are by far the most important feature. Their shape, size, and colour offer infinite variation, from the delicate, golden, ferny foliage of *Gleditsia triacanthos* 'Sunburst' to the huge, architectural leaves of palms such as *Phoenix*. Surface texture affects how light is reflected, with glossy leaves adding a bright touch. The density of the canopy ranges from opaque to airy, an important factor if considering underplanting around a tree.

Trees with coloured or variegated foliage, such as the reddish-purple of *Cercis canadensis* 'Forest Pansy' or the white-edged leaves of *Acer negundo* 'Variegatum', provide a mass of colour that contrasts especially well with green-leaved trees.

Some leaves, such as those of *Eucalyptus*, are pleasantly aromatic, while others, such as those of an aspen, quiver in the slightest breeze, adding the extra pleasure of sound.

Flowers

Flowers have a fleeting but memorable presence and range from modest to opulent. Autumn, winter, and early spring flowers are especially valuable to provide a display when there may be less interest from the other plants.

Flower colour should complement the larger scheme. Pale flowers stand out against dark leaves, while dark flowers show up best in a pale setting. By training climbers such as clematis or roses up mature trees, you can extend the floral display.

Fragrance is a bonus, ranging from the subtle, winter perfume of *Acacia dealbata* to the heady, summer scent of frangipani (*Plumeria rubra* var. *acutifolia*). For flowers and fragrance a sheltered spot is best, while growing a tree next to a path or patio makes it easy to enjoy its scent.

Fruits, berries, and pods

These can rival or exceed flowers in beauty, ranging from the bright red, strawberry-like fruits of *Arbutus*, and the yellow crab apples of *Malus*

COLOUR FROM FLOWERS
The large blooms of Magnolia campbellii *var.* mollicomata *stand out against the bare branches.*

INTEREST FROM BARK AND STEMS
The striking, white skeleton of a silver birch (Betula utilis *var.* jacquemontii) *brings bright relief to the garden in the gloom of winter, while its bold silhouette forms a strong focal point in the planting design all year round.*

'Golden Hornet', to the sculptural seed pods of magnolias. In warm climates, trees such as lemons and figs may be laden with eye-catching fruits.

Certain trees, such as hollies (*Ilex*), need cross-pollination to fruit; others fruit only when mature or when particular climatic conditions are met. Birds find some ornamental berries such as those of rowan (*Sorbus aucuparia*) tempting and may strip them when barely ripe, but you can choose trees with less appealing berries. Ask garden centre staff for advice.

Bark and branches
Bark can provide colour and textural interest, especially in winter. Options include the mahogany-red, silky sheen of *Prunus serrula*, the ghostly white bark of *Betula utilis* var. *jacquemontii*, and the exotic-looking *Eucalyptus niphophila* with its python-like, green, grey, and creamy-white bark.

The scarlet willow (*Salix alba* 'Britzensis') has scarlet-orange young branches, brilliant when lit from behind, and the golden willow (*S.a.* var. *vitellina*) has rich yellow shoots. These fast-growing trees are best pruned regularly to produce new shoots as these have the strongest colour. Some trees produce showy bark only when mature, others colour well when young.

Successional interest

Plants that change character with the seasons give a garden a lively tempo. With careful choice and planning, orchestrate their display as foliage, flowers, fruits, berries, and pods come and go against a permanent framework of branches and bark. By planting trees that flower successively, such as a Judas tree (*Cercis siliquastrum*) for spring, *Catalpa bignonioides* for summer, *Eucryphia* x *nymansensis* for early autumn, and *Prunus subhirtella* 'Autumnalis' for winter, ongoing interest is maintained, with the focal point altering as the seasons change. Some trees provide interest all year round, either from their evergreen foliage, or from their fine shape.

Deciduous trees offer the greatest scope to exploit seasonal changes, especially in spring, when many ornamental cherries (*Prunus*) are covered with beautiful blossom, and in autumn, when many maples (*Acer*) have brilliantly coloured foliage. Evergreen trees, on the other hand, provide a sense of continuity rather than change. Selecting and planting a mixture of deciduous and evergreen

TREES WITH ORNAMENTAL BARK

Acer capillipes

Eucalyptus dalrympleana

Betula utilis var. *jacquemontii*

Acer griseum

Acer pensylvanicum

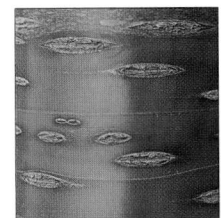
Prunus serrula

trees provides lasting interest in the garden that changes with the seasons to create a dynamic rather than a static effect.

Spring and summer
In spring, emerging leaves and flower buds bring fresh life to the bare branches of deciduous trees. Some – such as the silver-leaved *Sorbus aria* 'Lutescens' – have particularly fine young foliage. As the trees come fully into leaf, they take on their characteristic outlines while the canopies provide striking blocks of colour and texture as well as shade.

In late spring and summer, flowers, ranging in colour and form from the trailing, yellow chains of *Laburnum* to the upright cream or reddish-pink candles of horse chestnuts (*Aesculus*), add extra colour and interest to lighten the dense effect of the massed leaves.

Autumn and winter
When most herbaceous plants die down in autumn, the colour provided by trees is particularly welcome, whether from leaves turning from green through shades of yellow, orange, and red to brown, or from the bright flecks of colour from fruits or berries. Ornamental members of the Rosaceae, especially those from the genera *Cotoneaster*, *Crataegus*, *Malus*, and *Sorbus*, include many species, cultivars, and hybrids that have a handsome display in autumn; in some cases, the fruits will remain on the tree right through the winter months.

Winter is often regarded as a bleak time, but this is when many trees stand out most effectively with little

else in the garden to compete with them. It is in winter that a tree's skeleton or silhouette becomes most noticeable and creates the greatest sculptural impact. The colour and texture provided by coniferous and broad-leaved evergreens may be used to complement and soften the architectural, "hard" look of nearby deciduous trees, while patterned, textured, or peeling bark adds an extra point of interest. A few conifers such as forms of Japanese cedar

(*Cryptomeria japonica*) have foliage that takes on attractive russet overtones in winter.

Trees for small gardens

For small gardens, trees that do not reach more than about 6m (20ft) in height are the most suitable. There may only be space for one tree (see "Specimen trees as focal points", p.33), so those that provide more than one season of interest are especially valuable. A Japanese crab apple (*Malus floribunda*), for example, produces masses of crimson buds, then pale pink or white flowers, and finally small red or yellow fruits, on arching branches.

A deciduous tree's appearance when leafless is very important in a small garden, since the tree may be bare for six months each year and visible from every window facing the garden. Good choices include *Rhus typhina*, fig (*Ficus carica*), and *Pyrus salicifolia* 'Pendula'. None has showy flowers but all have handsome foliage and winter silhouettes with character.

Heavily thorned or prickly trees such as hawthorns (*Crataegus*) or hollies (*Ilex*) may be unsuitable in a very small garden as they may restrict access on either side, while those such as limes (*Tilia*) that drip

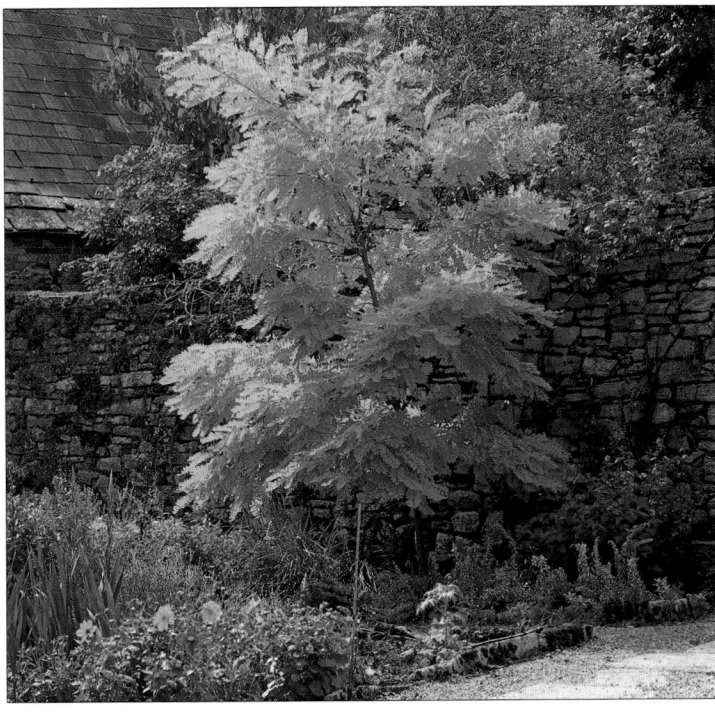

SMALL-GARDEN TREE
The modest stature of this Robinia pseudoacacia 'Frisia' *makes it a suitable choice for a small garden. Its airy foliage brightens up the grey stone wall behind and casts only light shade, allowing other plants to grow beneath it.*

sticky honeydew should not be sited where they will overhang an area for sitting out. If planning to underplant, choose a light-foliaged, deep-rooted tree, as it is hard for small plants to compete with the shallow, greedy roots of ornamental cherries (*Prunus*), for example.

Trees for avenues

Primarily used in formal settings, avenues rely on the uniformity of trees and spacing for their grand effect. The longer and straighter the avenue, the more impact the rhythm of the trees and their shadows has on the landscape. Trees should be sited so that they lead the eye to an impressive feature or focal point; large trees are often used on either side of a drive to line the route to the house. Long-term, forest trees such as beeches (*Fagus*) and horse chestnuts (*Aesculus*) are traditionally used for avenues, while the strong shapes of conifers may be more striking in a contemporary design.

Informal avenues may also be created, perhaps with the trees trained to form an arch over a walkway. The spacing may be less rigid than for a formal avenue to avoid a regimented appearance. Trees such as whitebeam (*Sorbus aria*) or the evergreen Chinese privet (*Ligustrum lucidum*) are particularly suitable for smaller gardens.

Training for effect
Trees may be pleached to create an elegant formality. The side branches are trained to meet in horizontal, parallel lines and other growth is

INFORMAL WALKWAY
Flowering cherries, arching over a path, bring height and structure to a garden with free, informal planting while complementing the character of the setting. The spring display of the arch draws attention up and away from the borders which will in turn fill out and become the centre of interest as the blossom fades.

FORMAL, PLEACHED AVENUE
In this large, formal garden, rows of pleached limes lead the eye to the two arches framing the view beyond, linking the garden with the landscape.

cut back or interwoven to form a vertical screen. Beeches, limes (*Tilia*), hornbeams (*Carpinus*), and planes (*Platanus*) are traditional trees for pleaching and, in the fruit garden, espaliered apples and pears are a variation of this technique.

Pollarding involves regularly lopping back the entire crown to short stumps that produce dense, thin branches and a single, tight ball of foliage. It achieves a formal, if artificial, effect and is useful in urban areas where a natural crown would cast too much shade or impede traffic. Some willows (*Salix*) are often pollarded or coppiced (cut back to ground level) for their colourful young shoots. Coppiced trees look appropriate in a naturalistic or informal setting such as a woodland garden or on the banks of a pond.

Trees for screens and shelter belts

Large-scale tree planting can screen buildings and roads, deaden noise, and provide shelter from wind and frost. A single, straight row of fast-growing Lombardy poplars (*Populus nigra* 'Italica') is often planted to screen eyesores, but their great

height and finger-like shape tend to highlight what they are intended to conceal. Looser, wider stands of mixed deciduous and evergreen trees are usually more natural-looking and effective. Hedges are the most compact and densest form of screening and their size can be controlled (see HEDGES AND SCREENS, pp.60–62).

Trees *en masse* can filter wind, reducing potential damage more effectively than solid barriers, which often create wind swirl on the leeward side. A shelter belt or group of trees can protect vulnerable plants from frost, especially in spring.

Trees in containers

Growing trees in large pots or tubs greatly extends their design potential. In roof, patio, or courtyard gardens, a collection of containerized trees is the quickest way to create a well-established appearance, adding height and structure to the design.

Use trees in large pots or tubs to frame a doorway that is surrounded by hard paving or to flank wide steps; these positions are particularly appropriate for topiary (see TOPIARY, pp.52–3). Trees too tender to overwinter outside may be grown in containers, displayed outdoors in summer, and moved to a frost-free place as cold weather approaches. Annuals and tender plants such as petunias, fuchsias, or trailing nasturtiums (*Tropaeolum*) may be included in the container for seasonal colour and interest, or ivy (*Hedera*) for permanent ground cover.

Containerized trees are long-term features, so use containers that are durable and attractive. A wide range of styles and materials is available, such as plain or decorated terracotta, stone or reconstituted stone pots, wooden half-barrels, or wooden Versailles planters. Make sure that the containers are frost-proof, if they are to be permanent features in an area subject to frost.

CONTAINER-PLANTED
TREES
Small trees grown in containers are valuable for bringing colour, vitality, and sculptural interest to a patio, terrace, or balcony. Here, a plain paving acts as a stage on which to display a striking Japanese maple (Acer palmatum 'Dissectum Atropurpureum') *in an ornamental trough.*

Planter's guide to trees

EXPOSED SITES

Trees that tolerate exposed or windy sites; those marked ✹ are not suitable for coastal sites

Acer pseudoplatanus
Betula pendula ✹, B. pubescens ✹
Crataegus x lavallei, C. monogyna
Fraxinus excelsior
Laburnum (spp. and cvs)
Picea abies ✹, P. sitchensis ✹
Pinus contorta, P. nigra,
  P. sylvestris
Quercus robur
Salix alba
Sorbus aria, S. aucuparia (and cvs)

AIR POLLUTION

Trees that tolerate polluted air

Acer platanoides (and cvs),
  A. pseudoplatanus (and cvs),
  A. saccharinum (and cvs)
Aesculus hippocastanum
Alnus cordata, A. glutinosa
Betula pendula
Carpinus betulus (and cvs)
Catalpa bignonioides
Corylus colurna
Crataegus
Fraxinus
Ginkgo biloba
Ilex x altaclerensis
Magnolia grandiflora
Malus
Populus
Pyrus
Robinia

Pyrus calleryana 'Chanticleer'

Salix
Sophora japonica
Sorbus aria,
  S. aucuparia, S. intermedia
Taxus baccata, T. x media

WINTER INTEREST

Decorative flowers
Acacia dealbata ✽
Magnolia campbellii (and forms)
Prunus mume, P. subhirtella
  'Autumnalis', P. s. 'Autumnalis
  Rosea'

Golden foliage
Chamaecyparis lawsoniana
  'Lanei', C. l. 'Stewartii',
  C. l. 'Winston Churchill'
x Cupressocyparis leylandii
  'Castlewellan Gold'
Cupressus macrocarpa 'Goldcrest'
Juniperus chinensis 'Aurea'
Pinus sylvestris 'Aurea'
Thuja plicata 'Zebrina'

Grey foliage
Cedrus atlantica f. glauca
Chamaecyparis lawsoniana
  'Pembury Blue'
Cupressus glabra 'Pyramidalis'
Eucalyptus coccifera ✽,
  E. pauciflora
Tsuga mertensiana f. argentea

Decorative bark
Acer capillipes, A. davidii,
  A. griseum, A. grosseri var. hersii,
  A. palmatum 'Senkaki',
  A. pensylvanicum (and forms),
  A. 'Silver Vein'
Arbutus x andrachnoides,
  A. menziesii
Betula albo-sinensis var.
  septentrionalis,
  B. 'Jermyns', B. pendula,
  B. utilis var. jacquemontii
Eucalyptus dalrympleana,
  E. niphophila, E. pauciflora
Myrtus luma
Pinus bungeana
Prunus maackii 'Amber Beauty',
  P. serrula
Salix acutifolia 'Blue Streak',
  S. alba 'Britzensis',
  S. daphnoides, S. x sepulcralis
  'Erythroflexuosa'
Stewartia pseudocamellia

TWO OR MORE SEASONS OF INTEREST

All year round
Acacia dealbata ✽
Arbutus x andrachnoides, A. menziesii
Betula albo-sinensis var.
  septentrionalis, B. ermanii,
  B. 'Jermyns', B. utilis var.
  jacquemontii
Eucalyptus ficifolia ✽
Ilex x altaclerensis 'Golden King'
Magnolia grandiflora

Winter/Spring
Acer negundo

Spring/Autumn
Amelanchier lamarckii
Crataegus x lavallei 'Carrierei'
Malus 'Crittenden', M. 'Golden
  Hornet'
Prunus 'Okame', P. sargentii
Sorbus scalaris

Summer/Autumn
Catalpa bignonioides
Cladrastis lutea
Cornus kousa, C. k. var. chinensis
Eucryphia glutinosa
Fagus sylvatica 'Dawyck Gold'
Liriodendron tulipifera
Stewartia pseudocamellia
Tilia tomentosa 'Petiolaris'

Autumn/Winter
Acer capillipes, A. davidii,
  A. griseum, A. palmatum
  'Senkaki', A. pensylvanicum
  'Erythrocladum'
Stewartia pseudocamellia

TREES FOR CONTAINERS
Acacia dealbata ✽
Chamaedorea ✽
Chamaerops humilis ✽
Citrus medica ✽
Cordyline australis ✽
Cupressus macrocarpa
  'Goldcrest', C. sempervirens
Ficus benjamina ✽

Ficus benjamina 'Variegata'

Howea ✽
Jacaranda mimosifolia ✽
Juniperus scopulorum 'Skyrocket'
Lagerstroemia indica ✽
Laurus nobilis
Olea europaea
Phoenix ✽
Prunus 'Amanogawa',
  P. 'Kiku-shidare'
Rhapis ✽
Sabal ✽
Taxus baccata 'Standishii'
Washingtonia ✽

TREES FOR SMALL GARDENS

Those marked ♠ may grow to 6m (20ft) or more

Acer capillipes, A. griseum ♠,
  A. palmatum, A. p. 'Senkaki',
  A. 'Silver Vein'
Amelanchier lamarckii
Arbutus x andrachnoides
Betula albo-sinensis var.
  septentrionalis ♠, B. ermanii ♠,
  B. pendula ♠,
  B. p. 'Dalecarlica' ♠, B. utilis
  var. jacquemontii ♠
Catalpa bignonioides 'Aurea'
Cercidiphyllum japonicum ♠
Cercis siliquastrum
Cinnamomum
Cornus kousa
Crataegus laevigata 'Paul's
  Scarlet', C. x lavallei 'Carrierei'
Eucalyptus niphophila ♠
Eucryphia x nymansensis
  'Nymansay' ♠
Fagus sylvatica 'Dawyck Gold' ♠
Gleditsia triacanthos 'Sunburst' ♠
Grevillea robusta ✽ ♠

Laburnum x watereri 'Vossii'
Magnolia 'Elizabeth',
  M. x loebneri 'Merrill',
  M. salicifolia
Malus 'Dartmouth', M. floribunda,
  M. 'Golden Hornet',
  M. tschonoskii ♠
Melia azedarach
Phoenix dactylifera ✽ ♠
Pinus halepensis ♠
Prunus – many including
  P. 'Okame', P. 'Pandora',
  P. 'Spire', P. subhirtella,
  P. x yedoensis
Pyrus calleryana 'Chanticleer',
  P. salicifolia 'Pendula'
Robinia pseudoacacia 'Frisia' ♠
Sorbus aria (some forms),
  S. aucuparia (some forms),
  S. cashmiriana,
  S. commixta 'Embley',
  S. vilmorinii
Stewartia pseudocamellia
Vitex agnus-castus

SPECIMEN TREES

Abies magnifica, A. procera
Acer pensylvanicum,
  A. pseudoplatanus, A. rubrum
Aesculus hippocastanum
Alnus cordata
Betula 'Jermyns',
  B. pendula 'Dalecarlica'
Cedrus
Eucalyptus coccifera ✽,
  E. dalrympleana
Fraxinus oxycarpa 'Raywood'
Liquidambar styraciflua

Liriodendron tulipifera

Liriodendron
  tulipifera
Livistona ✽
Magnolia campbellii,
  M. c. 'Charles Raffill'
Metasequoia glyptostroboides
Nothofagus procera
Nyssa sylvatica
Phoenix ✽
Picea breweriana, P. omorika
Pinus nigra, P. radiata,
  P. sylvestris, P. wallichiana
Platanus x hispanica
Roystonea ✽
Salix x sepulcralis 'Chrysocoma'
Sequoiadendron giganteum
Tilia 'Petiolaris', T. platyphyllos
Tsuga heterophylla
Zelkova carpinifolia

KEY
✽ Not hardy

Dwarf conifers

DWARF conifers, greatly valued for their ease of maintenance, are particularly suited to the small, modern garden, whether grown in compact beds or containers. Colours range from rich gold, through brilliant greens to pale blues and silvers, and shapes include globose, pyramidal, and slender, spire-shaped forms. Habits are diverse, with prostrate or mound-forming, erect or weeping types, and the variation in their foliage texture ranges from soft and feathery to dense and spiky. With careful planning, this rich variety of colour, form, and texture can provide interest throughout the year. For details on cultivation, routine care, and propagation, see ORNAMENTAL TREES, pp.39–43.

Selecting the plants

When selecting conifers for a small space, it is important to recognize the true dwarf and slow-growing species and cultivars; sometimes so-called "dwarf" conifers are simply slower-growing variants of large trees. Conifers can be very difficult to identify when young, since their juvenile foliage often differs widely from that when adult. Check that the plants are correctly named when buying, to avoid introducing plants that will rapidly outgrow their allotted space; if in any doubt seek advice from the retailer.

Designing with dwarf conifers

Dwarf conifers are suitable for a range of situations in the garden. They may be planted individually to form a feature or collectively to create a band of colours, and they may be used either to complement other plants or to provide ground cover. Rock gardens, heather gardens, and ornamental containers are also excellent locations for growing all types of dwarf conifer.

ENHANCING CONIFERS
To display dwarf conifers to their best advantage, add heathers to the planting scheme for bright splashes of year-round colour in the garden.

Specimen plants
Some of the slow-growing conifers are suitable for use as specimen plants. Spreading forms, for example, may be used to soften the edges of hard landscaping, while columnar specimens create a focal point.

Group planting
If space allows, a collection of dwarf conifers can make a very attractive feature. The colour spectrum in conifers may also be used to highlight areas at different times of year; blues and silvers, for example, are at their most beautiful in the cool light of winter, while golds and greens appear at their most fresh in spring.

Steep slopes and banks, which often prove difficult to plant effectively, can make striking landscape features when planted with bold drifts of prostrate conifers. Once plants are established, these often problematic areas are easy to maintain and are more or less weed-free.

Associating with other plants
Dwarf conifers associate well with other groups of plants that are similar in character. They are often used as components of heather gardens to extend the season of interest and provide contrast in colour and form with the main foliage and colour variants of *Calluna*, *Daboecia*, and *Erica* cultivars. Other complementary plants include *Cytisus*, *Genista*, *Cistus*, and the smaller cotoneaster species and cultivars.

Rock gardens
In the rock garden, dwarf conifers provide an air of permanence and create the framework for other plants.

The complete repertoire of colours, textures, and shapes can be used, but take care to select plants that will not become too large or dominant. The smaller species and cultivars, such as *Juniperus communis* 'Compressa', are ideal for the miniature landscapes of compact, raised beds as well as troughs, sink gardens, and other ornamental containers.

Ground cover
Many dwarf conifers make excellent weed-smothering ground cover, either by forming dense mats, as with *Juniperus horizontalis* and its cultivars, or by growing taller and spreading to exclude light beneath their canopy. Some Pfitzer junipers are particularly useful for covering manhole covers or concrete paving (see GROUND COVER, pp.150–51).

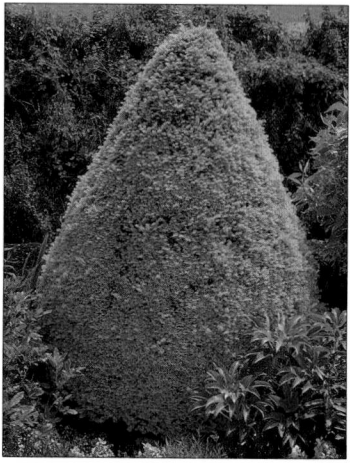

SPECIMEN PLANTING
Ideal for a focal point, the golden yew, Taxus baccata 'Aurea', has golden foliage all year round.

A RANGE OF DWARF CONIFERS

Thuja orientalis 'Aurea Nana'

Pinus sylvestris 'Gold Coin'

Juniperus squamata 'Blue Star'

Thuja occidentalis 'Caespitosa'

Juniperus scopulorum 'Skyrocket'

Picea pungens 'Montgomery'

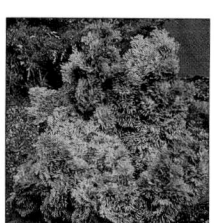

Chamaecyparis obtusa 'Nana Aurea'

Soil preparation and planting

ONCE planted, a tree may remain in place for decades or even centuries, so it is essential to provide it with the best possible growing conditions. Climate, soil type, and the amount of light and shelter available all affect a tree's growth, so take these factors into account when deciding on a planting position. Careful preparation and planting as well as aftercare are vital in helping a tree to establish quickly and grow well.

Climate considerations

Before selecting a tree, check that it will flourish in the temperature range, rainfall, and humidity levels of the site. Special local factors, such as strong winds on exposed hilltop sites, should also influence your choice. Even within a species, different cultivars may be more suited to certain conditions, so one plant may thrive while another may not: various cultivars of *Magnolia grandiflora*, for example, tolerate minimum temperatures ranging from -12°C to 6°C (10°–43°F).

In areas subject to spring frosts, choose trees that come into leaf late as frost frequently damages young growth. In cold areas, trees that are not fully hardy may be grown outdoors, but they may need protection from frost during winter (see FROST AND WIND PROTECTION, pp.520–21) and should be planted in a sheltered site. If growing tender or tropical species in temperate areas, keep them under cover or grow them in containers so that they may be brought indoors for the winter.

Trees rarely grow well in regions where the annual rainfall is less than 250mm (10in) and most prefer at least four times this amount. Most trees do not require irrigation, however, except when newly planted, as they obtain enough water from rain and, in some areas, from heavy mists condensing on their foliage.

Choosing a planting site

When planting a tree, try to choose the best position for it within the garden because the microclimate may vary considerably from one part to another. Make sure that the selected site will provide an appropriate amount of light and shelter: many

large-leaved trees, for example, will thrive in a sheltered, partially shaded position but may not grow well in an exposed site where the foliage would be subjected to strong winds and high light levels.

In coastal areas, choose a planting site that is sheltered because sea spray and salt-laden winds (even a few miles inland) may scorch foliage and cause damage to the growth buds. Some trees, however, tolerate coastal conditions (see "Planter's guide to trees", p.37), and may be planted as windbreaks to help screen other, more vulnerable, plants from strong winds.

Similarly, if trees are being planted on a slope, bear in mind that tender trees are more likely to succeed in a position half-way down where it is usually warmer and more sheltered than at either the top or the bottom (see also "Frost pockets and frost damage", p.515).

It is best not to plant trees very close to walls or buildings, otherwise, when young, the trees may suffer from reduced light and moisture

CHOOSING TREES
CONTAINER-GROWN TREE

GOOD EXAMPLE
Well-balanced branch framework

GOOD EXAMPLE
Well-established root system

POOR EXAMPLE
Tightly wound, congested roots

BARE-ROOT TREE

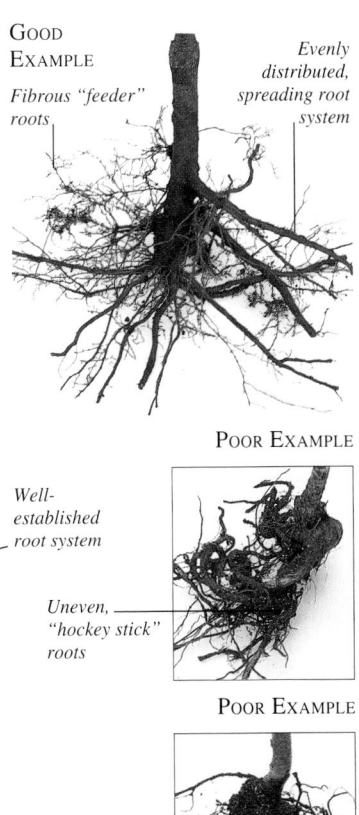

GOOD EXAMPLE
Fibrous "feeder" roots
Evenly distributed, spreading root system

POOR EXAMPLE
Uneven, "hockey stick" roots

POOR EXAMPLE
Tightly coiled roots

ROOT-BALLED TREE

GOOD EXAMPLE

x CUPRESSOCYPARIS LEYLANDII
Firm root ball with the covering intact

as a result of the "rain shadow" effect. In addition, the strong, fibrous roots of some trees, for example poplars (*Populus*) and willows (*Salix*), may damage drains and the foundations of buildings as they develop. Tender species may be planted near a warm wall, however; there they will benefit from the wall's retained heat and so may be grown in a region where they would fail to survive in more open conditions.

When choosing a site ensure that the trees will not interfere with overhead and underground cables and pipes, which may obstruct trees or be damaged by them.

Selecting a tree

Trees may be bought container-grown, bare-root, or root-balled, although conifers and palms are not usually available bare-root. They may be purchased in a variety of sizes and stages of maturity, from seedlings through to semi-mature trees. Young trees tend to become

established more quickly than older trees, while the latter create a strong and immediate impact in the garden but are more expensive. Whichever type you choose, check that the tree has healthy, vigorous top-growth and roots with no sign of pests, disease, or damage. Both the branch and root systems should be well developed and evenly balanced around the stem.

Container-grown trees
These are widely available and may be bought and planted at any time of year; container-grown trees are usually more expensive than bare-root or root-balled specimens of a comparable size. This is the best method of buying trees that do not establish easily when transplanted, such as magnolias and *Eucalyptus*, because there is less disturbance to the roots. Exotic and less common trees are usually sold this way.

Before buying a tree, remove it from its container, if possible, so that you can see the roots clearly: do not buy a pot-bound tree with a mass of congested roots or one with thick roots protruding through the drainage holes. Such trees may not establish well and, as the resulting root system is unstable and not well anchored, the mature tree will be liable to wind rock. Equally, if the compost does not cling to the root ball when the tree is removed from its container, do not buy it as its root system is not sufficiently established. Make sure that the container is large enough in relation to the tree: as a guide, the container's diameter should be at least one sixth of the tree's height. A tall tree growing in a small container will almost certainly be pot-bound.

The potting medium is also important: trees that are containerized in soil-based composts establish more quickly in open ground than those grown in other composts, as they have less of an adjustment to make to the surrounding soil.

Bare-root trees

Trees sold bare-root, which are almost always deciduous, are grown in open ground, then lifted with virtually no soil around the roots. It is essential to buy them when they are dormant, preferably in autumn or early spring; they are unlikely to survive transplanting if bought and planted when in leaf. Ash (*Fraxinus*), poplars (*Populus*), and many rosaceous trees, such as crab apples (*Malus*), are often sold bare-root.

Make sure that the tree you choose has well-developed roots spreading evenly in all directions. A number of small roots about 2–5mm ($^1/_{16}$–$^1/_4$in) in diameter is a good sign as it indicates that they have been undercut every year or so, a technique that encourages sturdy growth and vigorous root systems. Examine the roots to check that they are free from damage and disease and that there is no sign of dryness that may have been caused by exposure to wind. Do not buy trees with "hockey stick" roots, where all the growth is on one side; these will not establish well.

Root-balled trees

These trees are also grown in open ground but when the trees are lifted the roots and surrounding soil are wrapped in hessian or netting to hold the root ball together and stop the roots from drying out. Deciduous trees of more than 4m (12ft), and many evergreens, especially conifers and palms of more than 1.5m (5ft), are often sold in this way.

Buy and plant root-balled trees when dormant, in autumn or early spring, following the same criteria as for bare-root and container-grown

Staking

As the root system of a newly planted tree will need one or more growing seasons to anchor it firmly in the soil, staking against strong winds may be necessary initially. The stake must be driven in about 60cm (24in) below soil level so that it is completely stable. After two or three years, the tree should be sufficiently established for the stake to be removed. The method of support chosen depends on the tree, the proposed planting site, and personal preference.

Traditionally, a high, vertical stake has been used, placed on the side of the prevailing wind and long enough to reach to just below the crown. A low stake is now often preferred, as it allows the tree to move naturally in the wind.

With flexible-stemmed trees, such as crab apples, use a high stake in the first year after planting, cut it down to the lower level in the second year, and remove the stake in the third year.

For container-grown and root-balled trees, a low stake angled into the prevailing wind may be preferable as it can be driven in clear of the root ball even after the tree has been planted. Alternatively, space two or three vertical, low stakes evenly around the tree outside the area of the root ball.

In windy sites or for trees more than 4m (12ft) tall, insert two vertical stakes when planting, one on either side of the root ball, to provide support. Large trees are often secured by guy-ropes attached to low stakes. Covering the guys with hosepipe or white tape makes them more visible and so helps prevent the risk of people tripping over them.

HIGH STAKE
Drive in a single, high stake before planting. Secure the tree to the stake using two padded or buckle-and-spacer ties.

LOW STAKE
A low stake allows the tree's stem some movement; insert it so that only about 50cm (20in) protrudes above ground level.

ANGLED STAKE
A low, angled stake may be added after planting. Drive it into the ground at a 45° angle, leaning into the prevailing wind.

TWO STAKES
Insert two stakes so that they are on opposite sides of the tree, and secure them to the tree with heavy-duty rubber ties.

GUY-ROPES
For strong support, use guy-ropes attached to low stakes angled at 45° away from the tree. Space the guys evenly around the tree and secure them to the stakes with long eye bolts or "U" bolts which you can adjust when necessary (see inset, far right). Cushion the guys with hosepipe where they touch the tree to prevent damage (see inset, right).

Tree ties

Tree ties should be secure, long-lasting, and able to accommodate the tree's girth as it grows without cutting into the bark. Various proprietary ties are available, or you can make them from nylon webbing or rubber tubing. To prevent the stake from chafing the bark, use a spacer or form a padded tie into a figure of eight and nail it to the stake. When using two or three stakes, secure the tree to the stakes with heavy-duty rubber or plastic strips. If supporting a large tree with guys, use multistrand wire or nylon rope.

BUCKLE-AND-SPACER TIE
Thread the tie through the spacer, around the tree, and back through the spacer; buckle it so that it is taut but will not damage the bark.

RUBBER TIE
If using a rubber or plastic tie without a buckle, nail it to the stake to prevent bark damage caused by friction.

trees. Check that the root ball is firm and its wrapping is intact before purchase: if there is any sign of drying out or root damage, the tree is less likely to establish well.

Seedlings, transplants, and whips
Seedlings up to one year old are usually available only from specialist nurseries. Transplants are seedlings or cuttings that have been transplanted in the nursery and are up to four years old. They make sturdy, bushy plants and are usually 60cm–1.2m (2–4ft) tall. The age and treatment may be given by the nursery in shorthand: "1 + 1" denotes a seedling left for one year in the seedbed and then transplanted for a further season; "1 u 1" means that it was undercut (see "Bare-root trees", p.40) after the first year and remained *in situ* for a further year.

Whips are single, whip-like shoots sold by height; they are generally 1–2m (3–6ft) tall and will have been transplanted at least once.

Feathered trees
These trees have a single main leader with a spread of lateral branches, or "feathers", down to ground level. They will have been transplanted at least once and are usually 2–2.5m (6–8ft) tall.

Standards and large trees
Standard trees are approximately 3m (10ft) high and have been pruned to create one single main stem with no lateral branches for about 2m (6ft) above ground level. Central-leader standards are similar to feathered trees but have a clear length of stem at the base, while branched-head standards have been pruned so that they have an open centre.

HEELING IN

If planting is delayed, heel in the tree: first prepare a trench, then set the tree in it. Angle the tree so that the trunk is supported. Cover the roots and base of the trunk with moist, friable soil and do not allow the roots to dry out.

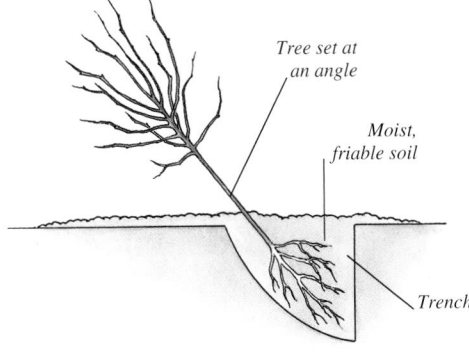

Tree set at an angle

Moist, friable soil

Trench

Trees of 2.1m (6½ft) in height, with a clear stem of 1.2–1.5m (4–5ft) are half-standards, while trees 3.5m (11ft) tall are selected standards. Larger trees, available from specialist nurseries, include extra-heavy standards which are 5m (15ft) tall and semi-mature trees which are 5–12m (15–40ft).

When to plant

Container-grown trees may be planted out at any time of year, except during drought or frost, while deciduous, bare-root trees should be planted between mid-autumn and mid-spring (avoiding periods of frost). Plant hardy evergreens and hardy, deciduous trees with fleshy roots in mid-autumn or mid- to late spring, and half-hardy trees in mid-spring. Root-balled trees are best planted in early to mid-autumn or mid- to late spring; if deciduous, they may be planted out in winter in mild conditions.

Autumn planting allows a tree's roots to become established before the onset of winter. This helps the tree to withstand any hot, dry spells the following summer. In cold regions, however, planting in spring may allow trees to establish more successfully. If planting in winter, the ground may be lifted by subsequent spells of frost and if so should be refirmed once it has thawed.

Heeling in
It is best to plant trees as soon as possible after purchase, although container-grown and root-balled trees may be stored in frost-free conditions for a few weeks if kept moist. If a further delay is unavoidable, heel in the trees in a sheltered place, and keep the soil moist.

Soil preparation

Preparing the site in advance allows the soil to settle and minimizes delay between buying and planting a tree. Choose a well-drained site; one that is poorly drained may need to be improved before planting (see "Improving drainage", p.529). Remove all plant growth in the immediate area to eliminate competition for nutrients and water in the soil, then double dig the soil, incorporating organic matter in the lower trench (see "Double digging", p.526).

Most trees require a soil depth of 50cm–1m (20in–3ft) to grow well. Some may grow on soils only 15cm (6in) deep, although they are then less stable and less drought-tolerant.

Planting trees

Once the site has been prepared, dig the planting hole, between two and four times the width of the tree's root ball, depending on whether the tree is container-grown, bare-root, or root-balled. If doing this in advance, backfill it loosely until ready to plant the tree so that the soil remains warm. Mix the removed soil with well-rotted organic matter and, if planting in spring, about 110g (4oz) of slow-release fertilizer. Fork over the sides and base of the hole to break up the surrounding soil and allow the tree roots to spread into it more easily; this is particularly important in heavy, sticky soils. If you are using a single stake, drive it into the hole just off-centre before planting the tree to ensure that the root ball is not damaged later (see also "Staking", p.40).

Container-grown trees

First thoroughly moisten the compost in the container – if it is very dry, stand the container in water for half an hour or until the compost is moist throughout. Then remove the container, cutting it away if necessary, taking care not to damage the roots. Gently tease out the roots with your fingers or a hand fork to encourage them to grow into the surrounding soil; this is essential with a pot-bound plant. If there are any broken or damaged roots, trim them back at this stage with secateurs. It is important to check that the planting depth is correct: if a tree is planted too deeply, its roots may not receive enough oxygen and may slow down in growth or even die; if planted too shallowly, the roots may dry out. Place the tree in the hole and locate the soil mark – a dark mark near the base of the stem indicating the soil

Tabebuia chrysotricha

Malus 'Cowichan'

KEY
❋ *Not hardy*

PLANTING A CONTAINER-GROWN TREE

1 *Mark out the area of the hole to be dug – about 3 or 4 times the diameter of the tree's root ball. Lift any turf or weeds, then dig out the hole to about 1 1/2 times the depth of the root ball.*

2 *Scarify the sides of the hole with a fork. Mix the removed soil with rotted organic matter.*

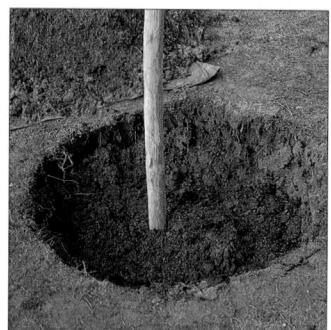

3 *If using one stake, hammer it into the hole, just off-centre and on the windward side. Add up to 20% of the organic matter and soil mixture to the pit.*

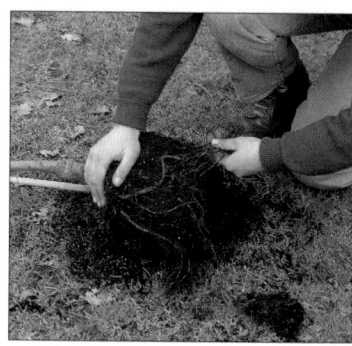

4 *Lay the tree on its side and slide it out of the pot. Gently tease out the roots without breaking up the root ball and remove any weeds from the compost.*

5 *Hold the tree next to the stake and spread out the roots. Lay a cane across the hole to check the planting depth. Adjust this by adding or removing some soil.*

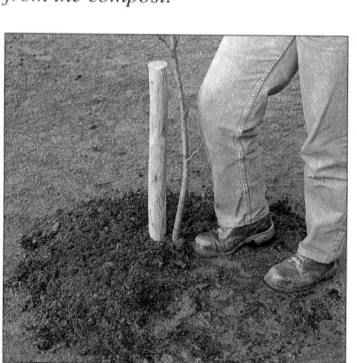

6 *Backfill around the tree with more of the topsoil and organic matter. Firm around the tree in stages by treading, then fork over lightly and water well.*

7 *Cut back damaged stems, long sideshoots, and lower feathers. Mulch 5–7cm (2–3in) deep around the tree.*

level when the tree was growing in the nursery. Place a cane across the hole alongside the stem and add or remove soil from beneath the root ball, if necessary, so that the soil mark is level with the cane.

Backfill the hole, firming the soil in stages to remove any air pockets; take care not to firm too heavily on clay soils as this may compact the ground and impede drainage. On sandy soils, a shallow moat around the tree helps to channel water to the roots. Conversely, on clay soils, a slight mound around the stem drains water away from the root ball.

Lightly prune the top-growth to balance it with the root system (see "Formative pruning", p.48), then secure the tree to the stake with one or more ties (see "Tree ties", p.41). Water thoroughly and apply a thick mulch to conserve moisture in the area where the roots will be developing.

Bare-root trees
Prepare the site in the same way as for container-grown trees, ensuring that the planting hole is wide enough for the tree's roots to be spread out fully; trim back any damaged roots to healthy growth. If using a single

stake, drive it in just off-centre of the planting hole, and spread out the tree's roots around it in the hole. Adjust the planting depth if necessary, then partly backfill the hole and gently shake the stem up and down to settle the soil around the roots. Firm the backfilled soil in stages, taking care not to damage the roots. Finally, water the tree well and mulch the area around it.

Root-balled trees
The method of planting root-balled trees is very similar to that used for container-grown trees. The planting hole should be twice the width of the root ball, however, or, in heavy, clay soils, three times the width. Place the tree in the hole at the correct depth, then remove the hessian or netting surrounding the root ball. If using an angled stake or two stakes, one on either side of the root ball, drive them in at this stage; they should rest firmly against the root ball without piercing it.

In heavy, clay soils, it is possible to improve drainage by planting so that the top of the root ball is slightly above soil level, and covering the exposed part with 5–7cm (2–3in)

of friable soil, leaving a gap of 2.5–5cm (1–2in) around the stem. Water thoroughly and mulch.

Aftercare
For the first two or three years after planting, it is important to provide trees with plenty of water, particularly in dry spells. Failure to do this may impede establishment, or the

tree may even die. Keep the surrounding area clear of grass and weeds, and feed and mulch regularly (see "Routine care", pp.44–6).

Some trees need extra protection from frost and wind; evergreens in an exposed site should be protected initially from drying winds with windbreaks, for example (see FROST AND WIND PROTECTION, pp.520–21).

PLANTING A ROOT-BALLED TREE

1 *Dig a planting hole 2–3 times the diameter of the tree's root ball. Mix the removed soil with well-rotted organic matter, then place the tree in the hole and untie the wrapping.*

2 *Tilt the tree to one side and roll the material up under the root ball, then tilt the tree the other way and carefully pull out the material. Backfill the hole, firm, and water well.*

Protecting the stem

In many regions, it is necessary to protect young trees from damage caused by rabbits or other animals that strip bark. Either surround the tree with a barrier of chicken wire or wire netting secured in place with several canes or stakes, or place a proprietary tree guard around the tree trunk. There are many types of guard available from garden centres and nurseries, including spiral, wrap-around guards made of flexible plastic,

as well as those made from heavy-duty plastic or wire mesh. Degradable, plastic-net tree guards are also available in a range of heights from 60cm (2ft) up to 2m (6ft).

In exposed sites, such as on hillsides, tree shelters may be used to assist young transplants and whips to become well established; these degradable plastic structures are up to 1.2m (4ft) long, and between 8cm (3in) and 15cm (6in) across.

A   B   C   D

Protect the bark of newly planted trees from animal damage with a barrier of wire mesh or netting secured to the ground with canes (A), a rigid, plastic tree shelter (B), a heavy-duty rubber or plastic stem guard (C), or a spiral, wrap-around, plastic guard (D).

Planting trees in containers

Containers are excellent for displaying trees on a patio, for tender trees that need to be brought under cover in winter, and for species that prefer a different soil type from that in the open garden.

Use a container that has a diameter of between one sixth and one quarter of the tree's height and a depth of at least one and a half times the tree's root ball. This provides a fairly even soil temperature and a good reserve of moisture, and also allows space for the roots to develop. Make sure that there are drainage holes to prevent waterlogging.

Preparing the container
If re-using an old container, scrub the inside with water to remove any disease-causing organisms. Cover all holes with broken crocks and add a layer at least 2.5cm (1in) deep of broken crocks or coarse gravel. Then add loam-based potting compost enriched with a slow-release fertilizer. If planting a standard, insert a stake into the compost before planting.

Planting
Prepare the tree and check the planting depth as for container-grown trees (see p.42). After

Insert the stake into the compost and then plant the tree so that the soil mark is about 4–5cm (1 1/2–2in) below the rim.

planting, firm the tree in well and top-dress with an organic or grit mulch 2.5–4cm (1–1 1/2in) deep to help retain moisture and prevent compaction of the compost. Then water well, using soft water or rainwater for lime-hating species. Stand the container on bricks or blocks to aid free drainage.

Routine care

THE amount of maintenance that a tree needs largely depends on the species, microclimate, soil type, and site. Most trees require watering, feeding, and a clear, weed-free area during the first few years if they are to establish well; container-planted trees should also be regularly top-dressed and occasionally repotted. In addition, other procedures such as removing suckers or controlling pests or diseases are sometimes necessary, while in certain circumstances – for example, if a tree is not thriving – the best solution may be either to fell the tree or to transplant it.

Watering

Most trees need plenty of water to grow well, especially on light, sandy soil or if trees have been planted within the previous two or three years. As a general guide, apply approximately 50–75 litres/sq m (10–15 gallons/sq yd) of water per tree each week in dry weather during the growing season. Once they have become well established, most trees only need to be artificially irrigated during spells of drought.

Fertilizing

All trees benefit from feeding, particularly on soils low in nutrients and during the first few years after planting. Older trees usually require feeding only occasionally. Trees grown for their flowers and fruit require more potash and phosphate than do trees grown for their foliage, which need more nitrogen.

Organic fertilizers such as well-rotted manure or compost are usually applied as a mulch: in autumn, or during any frost-free period in the dormant season, spread the material in a layer 5–8cm (2–3in) deep around the tree, keeping a clear area immediately around the trunk. When feeding a young tree, extend the mulch to the "drip line" – the ground beneath the outer edge of the canopy; an area 3–4m (10–12ft) in diameter is appropriate for a larger tree.

Artificial fertilizers are usually applied in spring. Broadcast the fertilizer around the base of the tree, at a rate of 50g/sq m (2oz/sq yd), or mix it with compost and insert it into small holes dug 2m (6ft) apart around the drip line. Alternatively, apply a proprietary liquid fertilizer around the tree.

Trees planted in grassed areas may need to be fed every year if they are not thriving. The grass between the trunk and the drip line may be removed by hand or with chemicals and a nutrient-rich mulch applied.

Mulching

Mulching around a tree keeps down weeds, reduces the effect of temperature extremes around the roots, and cuts down moisture loss from the soil surface. In general, organic materials such as pulverized bark are used as they are also attractive. Black plastic is also effective, but do not use clear plastic sheeting as heat is rapidly transferred to the soil and may damage surface roots. Mulches that are rich in nutrients are usually used only if a tree needs feeding.

Mulches are best applied in spring but, provided that the soil is moist, they may be spread at any time except during frost or drought. Apply mulch over an area about 30–45cm (12–18in) larger than the tree's root system. Top up the mulch every year or two under young trees.

Weeding

The area beneath a tree's canopy should be kept clear of weeds and grass as this ensures that the fibrous, feeding roots of the tree do not have to compete for water and nutrients.

Maintaining trees planted in containers

Container-planted trees generally require watering and feeding more frequently than those planted in open ground as the small amount of compost in which they are growing can store only limited reserves of water and nutrients. During hot, dry weather, they may need to be watered at least twice a day. Apply an annual mulch of bark chippings or similar material on top of the compost to help retain moisture. In addition, top-dress the tree each spring before it starts into growth. This involves replacing some of the old compost with fresh compost enriched with fertilizer. At the same time, prune back any dead, damaged, weak, or straggly stems to rejuvenate the tree and ensure that it produces healthy, vigorous growth.

Every three to five years, repot the tree completely either into the same container or, preferably, into a larger one. To do this, first remove the tree carefully from the container, then tease out the roots, cutting back by up to one third any that are large and coarse. Soak the root system well, if dry, then repot the tree into fresh compost (see "Planting trees in containers", p.43). If using the same container, wash it out before adding fresh compost and repotting.

TOP-DRESSING

1 Using a trowel or your hands, remove any mulch and the top 5cm (2in) of compost.

2 Replenish the container with fresh compost mixed with a slow-release fertilizer. Water the compost well, and mulch.

REPOTTING

1 Carefully lay the tree on its side and, with one hand supporting the stem and root ball, knock it out of its pot by sharply tapping the base. Remove any top-dressing or mulch material.

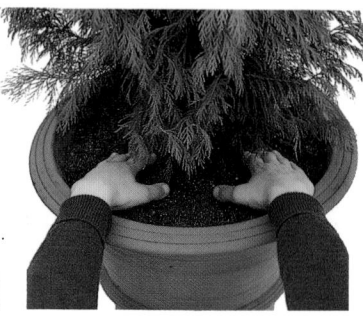

2 Using a hand fork, gently tease out the roots, removing some of the old compost from the root ball. Trim any long roots.

3 Repot the tree so that the fresh compost reaches the soil mark. Firm with your fingers, water well, and mulch.

REMOVING SUCKERS

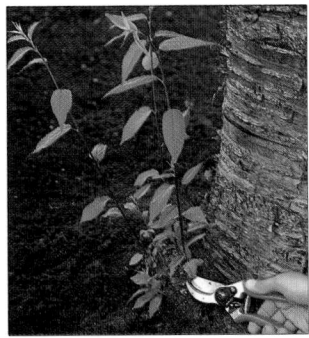

Using secateurs, cut off the suckers as close to the trunk as possible, then pare over the cut surface with a knife; rub out any regrowth as soon as it appears.

REMOVING WATER SHOOTS

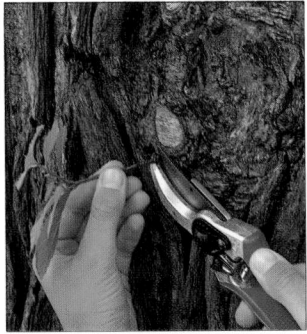

Cut back to the base with secateurs any water shoots that may grow through the bark or sprout at the edges of a wound where a branch has been removed.

If a tree's growth is too rapid, retaining, or establishing grass around it will help to reduce its vigour by competing for food and water.

Some weedkillers may be used around trees because they do not affect tree roots. Mulching, however, should make weeding largely unnecessary. For treatment of weeds, see "Weeds", pp.573–7.

Suckers and water shoots

Suckers and water shoots will divert nutrients from the main shoots of the tree if they are left to develop unchecked. Remove them as soon as they appear.

Stem and root suckers

A tree may produce both stem and root suckers: a stem sucker is a shoot that appears just beneath the graft union on the rootstock of a grafted tree, a root sucker is one that develops directly from the roots. Suckers of a grafted plant may quickly grow larger than the top-growth or even replace it within a few years so that the rootstock species predominates rather than the grafted cultivar.

Trees that are particularly vigorous or that have roots near the soil surface, such as poplars (*Populus*) and ornamental cherries (*Prunus*), may form root suckers if the root system is damaged. They may be used for propagation, but are a nuisance if they come up in lawns and paths.

Cut or pull off the suckers as close to the base as possible, digging down to where the sucker joins the root, if necessary. For some genera such as *Prunus*, painting the cuts on the roots with ammonium sulphamate usually prevents regrowth and, in small amounts, does not harm the tree.

Water shoots

Epicormic or water shoots may grow directly out of the trunk, often around pruning wounds. Rub them out with your fingers or thumb as soon as they appear, or cut them back to the base and rub them out as they regrow.

Frost and wind

Trees may be damaged by strong winds, and severe frosts may affect young growth, so provide protection such as windbreaks, particularly in exposed sites. Windbreaks may be artificial, such as fencing, or natural, such as hedges (see also "How a windbreak works", p.519).

The soil around newly planted trees may be lifted by frost; if this occurs, refirm it after thawing so that the roots do not dry out. For further information, see FROST AND WIND PROTECTION, pp.520–21.

Tree problems

Lack of vigour is a reliable indicator that there is a problem with a tree. As well as checking for pests and diseases, make sure that the tree has not been too deeply planted or that the roots and stems have not been damaged, as these are possible causes of poor growth and dieback.

The commonest pests are aphids (p.550) and red spider mites (p.550), while honey fungus (p.569) is the most damaging disease, affecting, and often killing, a wide range of trees. To minimize the risk of problems, keep trees properly fed and maintained, and the surrounding area clear of weeds and debris.

Cutting down a tree

Tree felling, which may be undertaken at any time of year, is a skilled and potentially dangerous operation; if the tree is taller than 5m (15ft), it should be tackled by a tree surgeon. Ensure that the tree is not subject to a Tree Preservation Order and, if on a boundary, that it legally belongs to you.

Make sure that there is space for the tree to fall safely and that there is an escape route at right angles to the proposed fall line, so that you can move out of the way.

A tree is usually taken down in stages. First remove any large branches in sections (see "Removing a branch", p.47), then cut down the rest of the trunk by taking out a wedge of wood on the side where you want the tree to fall and making another cut on the opposite side of the trunk. The tree can then be pushed over in the required direction. If felling a large tree, tie ropes around the trunk to guide its fall.

It is best to remove the stump but if this is impractical it may be treated with chemicals; if left to rot it could attract honey fungus (p.569), which may then spread. Dig out the stump, and any large roots with a spade. Tough roots should be severed with an axe. If the stump is large, you may need to employ a contractor to grind it or winch it out with special tools.

Alternatively, cut the stump flush with the ground and treat the cut surface with a proprietary solution of ammonium sulphamate. Allow at least 12 weeks before planting in the vicinity.

1 *On the side where you want the tree to fall, make an angled cut. It should be just over one third of the trunk diameter and about 1m (3ft) from the ground.*

2 *Cut out a wedge by sawing horizontally to meet the base of the angled cut. Remove the wedge; this ensures that the tree will fall in the right direction.*

3 *On the opposite side of the trunk, make the final cut just above the base of the wedge cut. As the tree starts to fall, push it in the right direction if necessary.*

4 *Remove the remaining stump by digging a wide trench around it, loosening the roots with a fork or spade, and then winching or digging it out.*

Transplanting a tree

It is best to prepare the tree a year in advance before transplanting as this will greatly increase its chances of re-establishing. Unless the tree is quite young, it may be difficult to transplant and may not adjust well; if taller than 2.5m (8ft), the tree may be difficult to establish in its new position. Large trees may need to be transplanted by specialist arborists.

Preparation

In early autumn the year before the planned move, while the soil is still warm and the tree roots are in active growth, mark out the optimum root-ball diameter for the tree – about one third of the tree's height. Dig a trench about 30cm (12in) wide and 60cm (24in) deep just outside the marked area and mix the removed soil with large quantities of well-rotted organic matter.

Using a sharp spade, undercut the root ball as far as possible to sever any large, coarse roots. This has the effect of stimulating the growth of fibrous "feeder" roots, which will help the tree to develop and grow successfully after transplanting. Then replace the mixture of soil and organic matter in the trench.

Lifting the tree

Transplant the tree the following autumn (see "When to plant", p.41), first carefully tying in the branches to the central stem to protect them and to increase the working space around the tree.

Dig a trench just outside the one made the previous year and of similar dimensions, and gradually fork away the excess soil until the root ball is of a manageable size and weight; take care not to damage the fibrous roots. Then cut through any roots underneath the root ball to separate it completely from the surrounding soil. Wrap the root ball securely in some hessian or plastic sheeting; this will hold it together and stop the roots drying out while the tree is removed from the hole and transported to its new position.

Replanting

The tree may then be replanted in its new site (see *Planting a Root-balled Tree*, p.43). Until it is well established, support the tree with guy-ropes (see "Staking", p.40), and keep it well watered and mulched. If it is impossible to replant the tree immediately, give it the same care as you would a newly purchased tree (see *Heeling in*, p.41).

HOW TO TRANSPLANT A YOUNG TREE

1 *Prepare the tree for transplanting a year ahead. To transplant, start by tying the branches in to the main stem to protect them from damage while working around the tree. Then, keeping outside the area of the root ball, dig a trench about 30cm (12in) wide and 60cm (24in) deep around the tree.*

2 *Carefully fork away the soil from around the root ball, removing a small amount at a time to avoid damaging the roots.*

3 *Undercut the root ball with a spade and cut back with secateurs any awkward roots protruding from the root ball.*

4 *Roll up a length of hessian (or plastic sheeting) and, tilting the tree to raise one side of the root ball, slide the hessian underneath.*

5 *Carefully tilt the tree back the other way and pull the hessian through underneath; the root ball should now be resting on the centre of the hessian.*

6 *Pull the hessian up around the root ball so that it is completely covered. Tie it securely in place with rope to keep the root ball intact while the tree is being moved.*

7 *Tilt the tree to one side and slide 2 planks underneath it to act as a ramp. Grasping the ropes around the root ball, ease the tree up the ramp.*

8 *Transport the tree to the new site. Holding the ropes, lower the tree into the prepared hole, then unwrap the root ball by reversing the procedure in steps 4–5. Remove any weeds from the root ball, then replant the tree to the soil mark on the stem.*

9 *Attach guy-ropes to the newly transplanted tree and secure them to angled stakes in the ground to provide support. Water the tree well, then spread a thick mulch about 10cm (4in) deep on the surrounding soil to retain moisture and suppress weeds.*

Pruning and training

CORRECT pruning and training helps to maintain a tree's health and vigour, regulate its shape and size, and, in some instances, improve ornamental qualities. It is important to prune young trees correctly to develop a strong framework of evenly spaced branches; thereafter most trees need minimal pruning.

The degree of pruning and training depends on the type of tree and the desired effect: relatively little is required to produce a well-balanced tree whereas creating a pleached avenue with interwoven branches demands considerably more work and expertise.

When to prune

Most deciduous trees are best pruned when dormant in late autumn or winter; they may also be pruned at other times, except in late winter or early spring when many trees "bleed" (exude sap) if cut. Maples (*Acer*), horse chestnuts (*Aesculus*), birches (*Betula*), walnuts (*Juglans*), and cherries (*Prunus*) all bleed extensively, even towards the end of their dormant season; prune these in midsummer after new growth has matured. Evergreens require little or no pruning except the removal of dead or diseased branches in late summer.

The principles of pruning

The first stage of pruning a tree is to remove any dead, diseased, or damaged wood, and to cut out weak or straggly shoots. Then assess the remaining framework and decide which branches should be pruned back or removed for well-balanced growth. Take care not to impair the natural growth habit of a tree by pruning unless aiming to produce a certain shape or form, such as an espalier. Hard pruning stimulates vigorous growth, whereas light pruning produces only limited growth.

It is important to make pruning cuts accurately to minimize damage to the tree. If cutting back a stem, cut just above a healthy bud, pair of buds, or sideshoot pointing in the required direction of growth. For example, if thinning out congested stems, cut back to a bud or shoot that is growing outwards so it will not rub against another stem as it grows. Cut neither too far from the bud, which leaves a stub that provides an entry point for disease, nor too close, which could damage the bud itself.

When pruning trees with opposite buds, make a straight cut with sharp secateurs directly above a pair of buds; for trees with alternate buds,

WHERE TO CUT

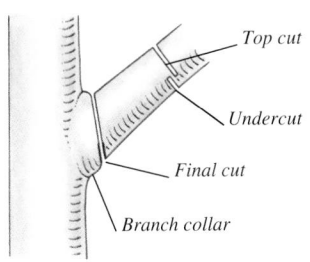

When removing a branch, take care not to damage the branch collar: first remove the bulk of the branch with 2 cuts, then cut off the stub just outside the collar.

CUTTING BACK A STEM

ALTERNATE BUDS
For trees with alternate buds, make a clean, angled cut just above a healthy, outward-facing bud.

OPPOSITE BUDS
For trees with opposite buds, make a clean, straight cut directly above a strong pair of buds.

make a sloping cut 3–5mm ($^1/_8$–$^1/_4$in) above a bud so that the base of the cut is just level with the top of the bud, on the opposite side of the stem.

If pruning back a branch completely, cut just outside the branch collar – the slight swelling on the branch where it joins the trunk. This is where the callus is formed that will eventually cover the wound. Never cut flush with the main stem as this damages the tree's natural protective zone, making it more vulnerable to disease. The branch collar on dead branches may extend some way along the branch, but it is still important to make any cut outside it.

Removing a branch

If removing whole branches of less than 2.5cm (1in) diameter, make a single cut with a pruning saw or secateurs. For branches thicker than this, first remove the bulk of the weight: partially undercut the branch at least 30cm (12in) from the trunk, then a little further out saw through from above. If no undercut is made, the branch may break off in mid-cut, ripping the bark back to the trunk so making it vulnerable to infection.

To remove the remaining stub, undercut it just outside the branch collar, then cut through from above. If you find it difficult to locate the branch collar, cut through the stub at a short distance from the trunk, making the cut so that it slopes outwards away from the tree.

If the angle between the branch and the trunk is very acute, it may be easier to cut through the stub from beneath. Do not apply a wound paint or dressing: there is no clear evidence that they speed up the healing process or prevent disease.

CUTTING OFF A BRANCH

1 *Using a pruning saw, undercut the branch 30cm (12in) away from the trunk by one quarter of its diameter. This stops the bark tearing back if the branch breaks.*

2 *Make the second cut about 2.5cm (1in) further away from the trunk, sawing through the branch from above. The undercut will close up, making sawing easier.*

3 *Remove the remaining stub by making a further 2 cuts. First make a small undercut just outside the branch collar.*

4 *Make the final cut just outside the branch collar, angling the saw slightly away from the trunk. Saw through cleanly until the top cut meets the undercut.*

Formative pruning

Young trees benefit from formative pruning to ensure that they develop a strong, well-balanced framework of evenly spaced branches. At its simplest, this involves the removal of dead, damaged, and diseased wood, as well as any weak or crossing branches.

Formative pruning may also be used to determine the tree's shape as it grows: for example, a young feathered tree may be pruned over several years to form a standard, or trained against a wall as an espalier. The extent of the pruning depends on both the type of tree selected and the required shape when mature. As with all types of pruning, care should be taken not to spoil the tree's natural growth characteristics.

It is particularly important to prune young tropical trees as the growth rate is very rapid and the girth of both main stems and branches develops very quickly; provided that they have been pruned correctly during the first few years after planting, they may then be left to grow naturally. Most other evergreens, on the other hand, will develop naturally into well-shaped specimens with little or no attention; pruning is usually restricted to the removal of dead, damaged, or crossing stems, and badly placed laterals.

The formative pruning of ornamental garden trees depends on the type of tree bought or required. Feathered trees have a single, central leader and laterals along the whole length of the stem. Central-leader standards have a clear length of stem at the base, while branched-head standards also have a clear stem but have their central leader removed to encourage the formation of vigorous lateral branches – as commonly seen in many Japanese cherries (*Prunus*).

Feathered trees

Feathered trees may either be simply pruned to enhance their natural shape or more extensively pruned to train them into standards. This process also occurs naturally sometimes. Although many feathered trees retain their lower branches, these die back in some species and the tree becomes a central-leader standard; other trees also lose their central-leader dominance and so become branched-head standards.

Early training is straightforward, however, regardless of the eventual habit of the tree. First remove any competing shoots to leave a single main leader. Then take out any small, weak, and poorly placed laterals,

PRUNING AND TRAINING YOUNG TREES

FEATHERED TREE

CENTRAL-LEADER STANDARD

Cut back laterals by half

Cut back laterals flush with stem

Remove congested and crossing shoots, then cut out any laterals that are small, spindly, or badly positioned, to achieve a well-balanced framework of branches.

YEAR 1
On the lowest third of the tree, cut back laterals to the main stem; on the middle third, cut back laterals by half. Remove any weak or competing leaders.

YEARS 2 AND 3
Continue the pruning process, removing the lowest laterals completely and cutting back by about half those laterals that are on the middle third of the tree.

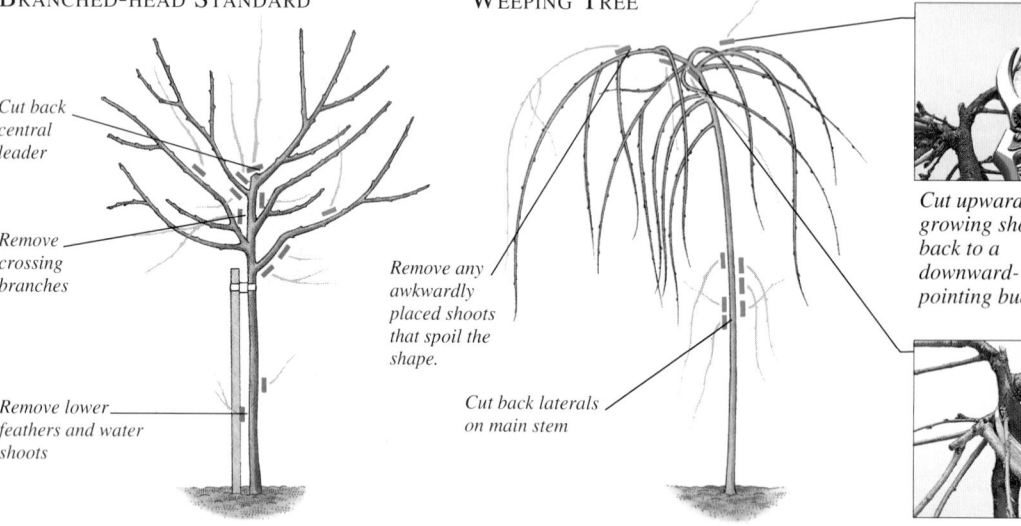

BRANCHED-HEAD STANDARD

Cut back central leader

Remove crossing branches

Remove lower feathers and water shoots

WEEPING TREE

Remove any awkwardly placed shoots that spoil the shape.

Cut back laterals on main stem

Cut upward-growing shoots back to a downward-pointing bud.

Cut out crossing, rubbing, or congested growth.

Remove crossing laterals and any growths on the lower third of the tree. Cut back the leader to a healthy bud or shoot.

Cut back crossing or vertical branches that spoil the symmetry of the tree. Remove any growths on the main stem.

so that the framework of branches around the main stem is evenly spaced and well balanced.

Central-leader standard trees

Feathered whips may be pruned over two to three years to form a standard; a technique called "feathering" is often used as it also channels food to the main stem which thickens and becomes sturdier. Initially, prune a feathered whip to remove any competing leaders or weak laterals. Then, on the lowest third of the tree, cut back all the feathers to the main stem; on the middle third, reduce the feathers by about half; leave the top

third unpruned, but remove any vigorous, upright shoots that might form a competing leader.

In late autumn or early winter, cut back the pruned laterals flush with the main stem. Repeat the procedure over the next two or three years to form a tree with approximately 1.8m (6ft) of clear stem.

Branched-head standard trees

To form a branched-head standard, train the tree initially as a central-leader standard to achieve the desired length of clear stem. Then, in mid- to late autumn, cut back the leader to a strong, healthy bud or

shoot to leave a framework of four or five strong, well-placed lateral branches. At this stage, also remove any crossing or congested laterals and any that spoil the balance of the branch framework.

In subsequent years, prune the tree as much as necessary to keep the crown well balanced and with an open centre; remove any vigorous, vertical shoots that may grow into a new leader and cut back any feathers to the main stem as soon as possible. Some branched-head standards can be formed by top-working (or top-grafting) as for weeping standards (see p.49).

Weeping standards

A weeping standard is formed by grafting one or two scions of a weeping cultivar onto a stock plant with a clear stem of about 1.8m (6ft). This is known as top-working or top-grafting, a technique that is most commonly used for fruit trees (see "Top-working", p.383) but also for weeping ash (*Fraxinus excelsior* 'Pendula'), the Kilmarnock willow (*Salix caprea* 'Kilmarnock'), and a large number of other weeping ornamentals. Young, pendulous branches start to develop once the grafts have taken.

Pruning is best restricted to the removal of crossing and vertical branches as well as any that spoil the overall symmetry of the framework. Although upward-growing branches are usually removed, leave some semi-upright stems to develop naturally as they often grow downwards later and produce tiers of weeping branches. If growths appear on the main stem, rub or pinch them out as soon as they appear.

Espalier- and fan-trained trees

The aim of both espalier- and fan-training is to form a symmetrical, attractive network of branches in a single plane by pruning and training a young tree over several years. These techniques are occasionally used for growing ornamental trees against fences or walls, but they are more commonly associated with growing fruit trees.

Pruning times vary according to the selected species: for example, *Magnolia grandiflora*, which flowers from mid- to late summer, should be pruned at the start of growth in spring, while the spring-flowering *Acacia dealbata* should be pruned directly after flowering. For full instructions on the pruning techniques, see THE FRUIT GARDEN, "Espalier", p.382, and "Fan", p.393.

Pruning established deciduous trees

Once a deciduous tree is well established, there is little need for further pruning. Major pruning of a mature tree is best carried out by a tree surgeon or arborist, as the work is both skilled and dangerous, and, if poorly executed, may ruin the tree.

Many branched-head trees become overcrowded in the centre as they mature, restricting the amounts of air and light that reach the central branches. Cut out inward-growing shoots and any branches that spoil the balance of the framework.

REMOVING A COMPETING LEADER

Prune out a competing leader by making a clean cut at the base with secateurs or loppers, taking care not to damage the remaining leader.

If a tree is too large for its situation, do not attempt to restrict its size by heading back all new growth each year; this "haircut" pruning produces an unsightly, congested cluster of shoots each season which spoils the tree's natural appearance and reduces flower and fruit production. The correct treatment is as for the renovation of old trees (see p.50).

As a result of hard pruning or the removal of large branches, a tree may produce a mass of epicormic or water shoots; rub or cut these out immediately (see p.45).

If the central leader is damaged, select a strong shoot close to the top of the main stem and train it vertically as a replacement leader. Tie the selected shoot to a cane or stake secured high on the main stem, and prune out any potential competing shoots. Once the shoot has developed into a strong, dominant growth, the cane may be removed.

If a tree develops two or more competing leaders, remove all but the strongest shoot. The very narrow crotch angle between rival leaders is a source of structural weakness and the tree could split open at this point in a high wind.

Vigorous, upright shoots may develop on young, branched-head trees. If left, these will quickly grow into competing leaders and so it is important to remove them entirely as soon as possible.

Pruning established evergreen trees

Broad-leaved evergreens need minimal pruning. Provided that the trees have an established leader and that any badly placed laterals have been cut out when young, it is only necessary to remove any dead, damaged, or diseased wood.

Conifers require only basic pruning once established, except when

they are grown as a hedge (see HEDGES AND SCREENS, pp.60–62). On some pines (*Pinus*), silver firs (*Abies*), and spruces (*Picea*), the terminal bud on the leader may die; if this occurs, train in the best placed lateral as a replacement leader (see above) and cut out any competing, upright shoots. Established palms require no pruning apart from the removal of dead leaves which should be cut back to the main stem.

Root pruning

If an established tree is growing vigorously, but producing very few flowers or fruit, pruning the roots will help slow down growth and stimulate better flowering or fruiting performance.

In early spring, dig a trench just outside the extent of the tree canopy. Then prune back any thick roots to the inner edge of the trench, using a pruning saw, secateurs, or loppers. Retain any fibrous roots at the inner edge of the trench, backfill the soil, and firm. For further details, see THE FRUIT GARDEN, "Root pruning", p.370. In some instances, it may be necessary to support the tree with stakes or guy-ropes if it seems unstable afterwards (see "Staking",

TRAINING A NEW LEADER

Replace a damaged leader by training in a strong shoot vertically. Attach a cane to the top of the main stem and tie the shoot to the cane. Prune out the old, damaged leader. Remove the cane once the new leader is dominant and growing strongly.

p.40). For root pruning of trees in containers, see "Maintaining trees planted in containers", p.44.

Pruning container-planted trees

Container-planted trees should be pruned annually, following the same principles as for other trees, to regulate their shape and size and maintain a strong, balanced framework of evenly spaced branches.

Coppicing and pollarding

Coppicing is the regular pruning of a tree close to the ground to encourage strong, basal shoots to grow. Pollarding is the pruning of a tree back to its main stem or branch framework, stimulating new shoots at this level. Traditionally, both techniques were practised to give a regular supply of firewood or pliable stems for basketwork and fencing. Now they are used in gardens to enhance leaf colour and size or the colour of ornamental stems, or to restrict tree size.

HOW TO COPPICE A TREE

Coppicing may be used to restrict a tree's size, enlarge leaves, or enhance stem colour.

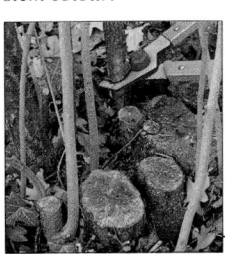

Use pruning loppers to cut back all stems to 7cm (3in); do not cut into the swollen, woody base of the tree.

Coppicing

Trees should be coppiced in late winter or early spring; some willows, when grown for their coloured or glaucous stems, may be left until mid-spring, however, and pruned just before or very shortly after the buds break into new growth. Cut back all stems to the base, leaving the swollen basal wood unpruned as all new growth forms from here.

Pollarding

To form a pollard, plant a young, branched-head standard (see p.48). When its trunk has reached 2m (6ft), or the desired height, prune back the branches to 2.5–5cm (1–2in) from the main stem in late winter or early spring. This results in a mass of shoots developing from the top of the cut stem. Prune back these shoots annually (or every second year) to stimulate further young shoots to grow from the enlarged head of the stem. Thin them if they become congested. Remove shoots that grow on the trunk as soon as they appear.

To produce a pollard with a main branch framework, allow the tree to develop a well-balanced branch system at the desired height. In late winter or early spring, prune back the branches to about 2m (6ft). Cut back the resulting, secondary shoots every two to five years, depending on the species, until the pollard is established. Thereafter, prune

TREES FOR COPPICING AND POLLARDING

Acer pensylvanicum
  'Erythrocladum'
Corylus avellana
  'Contorta' ∨
Eucalyptus dalrympleana,
  E. globulus ❁ ∨,
  E. gunnii ∨,
  E. pauciflora

Populus candicans
  'Aurora'

Populus x *canadensis*
  'Serotina Aurea',
  P. candicans 'Aurora'
Salix acutifolia 'Blue
  Streak', *S. alba*
  'Britzensis',
  S. a. var. *sericea*,
  S. a. var. *vitellina*,
  S. daphnoides 'Aglaia',
  S. irrorata ∨,
  S. x *sepulcralis*
  'Erythroflexuosa'
Tilia platyphyllos (cvs)
Toona sinensis 'Flamingo'

KEY
❁ *Not hardy*
∨ *Coppice only*

PRUNING AN ESTABLISHED, POLLARDED TREE

Prune back the shoots every 1–2 years in late winter or early spring to 1–2cm (¹/₂–³/₄in) from the pollarded head of the main stem. This will stimulate new shoot production the following spring. The new wood of trees such as this Salix alba *var.* vitellina, *grown for its ornamental stems, is particularly highly coloured.*

Using secateurs or pruning loppers, cut back the old stems to the base, taking care not to damage the enlarged head.

every year or two, and thin the shoots as required. If too many enlarged heads develop close together, cut out some of them entirely.

Renovating old trees

Trees that have outgrown their situation, or that have been neglected, should be either removed and replaced, or renovated to return them to full health and vigour. Renovation requires considerable care and expertise, and it is advisable to consult an experienced tree surgeon. In some cases, a tree may be too old and potentially dangerous to renovate, so it may be better to replace it.

Renovation may be undertaken at any time of year except at the start of growth in spring; for most trees, however, and particularly those that

produce a lot of sap, such as horse chestnuts (*Aesculus*) and birches (*Betula*), late autumn or early winter is the best time. Prune flowering cherries (and other *Prunus*) in early summer to reduce the risk of silver leaf (see p.551).

The first stage is to remove all dead, diseased, and damaged wood. Then prune out any crossing or congested branches and those that spoil the balance of the framework. It is best to carry out extensive renovation over two or three years to allow gradual recovery because drastic pruning may severely weaken or even kill a tree in poor health. If you need to remove any large branches, cut them off in sections (see "Removing a branch", p.47).

After renovating the tree, feed it by mulching with well-rotted manure and apply fertilizer to the ground

beneath the tree canopy in spring for two to three years. Hard pruning may stimulate the growth of a mass of sideshoots; if congested, thin some of them out to leave a well-balanced framework. Any suckers and water shoots should be removed as soon as they are noticed (see p.45).

Renovating "haircut" pruned trees

Trees that have had all their new growth trimmed back annually produce a congested cluster of shoots every season on knobbly branches, but without the balanced framework of a true pollard. Such "haircut" pruning is unsightly and reduces flowers and fruit. To correct it, first thin out the knobbly stumps at the ends of the main branches. Cut out most of the young shoots on the remaining stumps to leave just one or two and cut these back by about one third; repeat this procedure in the following three or four seasons to develop a more natural growth habit.

Tree surgeons

For pruning, renovation, or removal of large trees, it is advisable to consult a qualified tree surgeon. The nearest horticultural college or arboricultural association, may be able to supply a list of approved consultants and contractors, who comply with required standards of safe working practices and technical competence.

Before inviting contractors to tender, decide exactly what work is required, including the disposal of any debris which may be the most expensive part of tree surgery operations. Quotations are normally provided free, but a fee may be charged if advisory work is involved.

RENOVATING A TREE

YEAR 1
Cut out any dead, diseased, and damaged wood, and remove any branches that cross or rub against others and that spoil the balance of the framework.

YEARS 2 AND 3
The following year, thin out the new growth that results from the initial pruning and remove any water shoots. Repeat the next year if necessary.

Pleached trees

Pleached, or plashed, trees are clear-stemmed trees planted in one or more rows with their branches trained horizontally to intertwine, creating a formal, raised "wall" of foliage when in leaf (see "Trees for avenues", p.36). Hornbeams (*Carpinus*) and limes such as *Tilia platyphyllos* and *T.* 'Euchlora' make excellent pleached avenues, as they can be clipped precisely and, within four or five years, develop an effective, boxed appearance. It is best to use young trees with pliable stems; attempts to pleach mature trees are generally unsatisfactory.

Constructing the framework

Until the trees are established, they should be trained in to a framework. First, using one stake for each tree to be planted, set up a row of 2.5–3m (8–10ft) high, stout stakes an equal distance apart. Once driven into the ground to a depth of approximately 60cm–1m (2–3ft), they should be at the required height of the lowest branches – about 2m (6ft) or more if they are to allow people to walk underneath. Attach a secondary framework of wooden battens and stout canes to these stakes to create the desired, overall height.

Initial training

Plant a young tree next to each stake in late autumn or early winter. Choose trees that are sufficiently tall so that their laterals may be trained in to the framework. Cut back any lower feathers below the lowest horizontal batten, and prune out any sub-laterals that cannot be tied in easily. The leader may either be bent horizontally and tied in, if tall enough, or left to grow for another season before being trained.

Further training

Late the next summer, intertwine any untrained branches in to the framework and cut back any long laterals to stimulate new growth. Sub-laterals growing at right-angles to the branches may be tied in along the canes. Continue to develop a boxed effect in subsequent seasons by tying in branches and cutting back the laterals to stimulate new shoots and dense growth.

Once the pleached trees are fully established and the branches have intertwined, the framework may be dismantled. Maintain healthy, dense growth by removing any dead, damaged, or diseased wood, and strongly outward-growing laterals; rub out young shoots on main stems as soon as they are noticed.

ESTABLISHING THE FRAMEWORK

YEAR 1

Drive a row of stakes into the ground about 2.2–2.7m (7–9ft) apart. Secure strong, vertical battens to the stakes, then fix horizontal battens, about 60cm (24in) apart to these to form the framework. Plant a young standard or feathered tree next to each stake.

Bend over any laterals adjacent to the horizontal battens and tie them in without straining them excessively.

Prune laterals that cannot be tied in easily. Cut back to the main stem any feathers that are growing below the bottom horizontal batten.

YEAR 2

Late in the following summer, tie in any untrained branches to the framework to fill in spaces, and prune back long laterals to two or three buds to encourage the growth of new sideshoots.

Once the leader is tall enough, bend it over onto the top horizontal of the framework, and tie it in.

Prune back laterals to a strong side-shoot to encourage further branches to grow.

ANNUAL MAINTENANCE

Tie in all untidy and awkward branches to maintain the pleached effect, and prune back laterals to encourage new growth and a dense branch framework.

Cut back awkward stems growing away from the framework to maintain a neat, well-trained shape.

Continue to tie in new stems to the framework; check old ties and replace them where necessary.

Prune any long, awkward-pointing laterals to encourage further sideshoots to grow along the framework.

SUMMER PRUNING

Tie in untrained stems and cut back long laterals to 2 or 3 buds. Prune stems growing strongly from the framework to a well-placed bud or shoot.

Topiary

A FORM of training and pruning trees and shrubs to create attractive, boldly artificial shapes, topiary is a garden art that has been popular since Roman times. Traditionally used to produce strongly architectural and geometric shapes in formal gardens, it has been developed to include birds, animals, and unusual, even whimsical features such as giant chess-pieces and full-size trains.

Designing with topiary

Different styles of topiary may be used to create a variety of effects. Imaginative, living sculptures express personal style and add a humorous or bizarre touch. Using topiary for geometric shapes such as cones, obelisks, and columns provides a strong, structural element in a design. This type of topiary may be valuable both in formal gardens, perhaps to frame a vista or form an avenue, and in informal gardens, as a contrasting foil for less structured planting.

In some gardens, it may be appropriate to treat part of the hedge top as topiary, clipping it into one or more birds, spheres, or cubes, for example. Topiary may also be effective in containers; use a single container plant as a centrepiece, a pair to flank a doorway, or several to line a path.

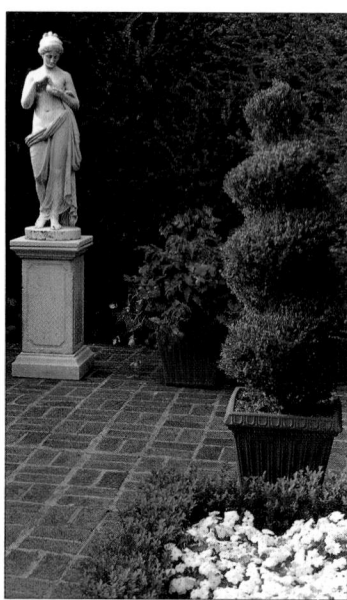

ELEGANT SIMPLICITY
This formal, spiral topiary perfectly complements the classical statue nearby and its square pot mirrors the statue's pedestal.

SUITABLE PLANTS FOR TOPIARY

Taxus baccata (yew)

Buxus sempervirens (box)

Ilex aquifolium 'Crispa -Aurea Picta' (holly)

Laurus nobilis (bay)

Ligustrum ovalifolium (privet)

Hedera helix 'Ivalace' (ivy)

Plants for topiary

Plants to be used for topiary need dense, pliable growth, small leaves, and the ability to recover quickly from clipping. Evergreens such as yew (*Taxus baccata*), box (*Buxus*), and *Lonicera nitida* are ideal in a temperate climate. *Cupressus sempervirens* can be trained to suit geometric designs, but only thrives in warmer climates. Bay (*Laurus nobilis*), holly (*Ilex*), and many other evergreens may be used, but are more difficult to train.

Ivies (*Hedera*) are very adaptable and may easily be trained to grow up a frame; alternatively, several cuttings can be taken from an existing plant to grow up a moss-padded structure.

Creating a shape

Most topiary designs are best formed with the aid of a guiding framework, although some simple shapes may also be cut freehand.

Simple designs

Using young plants, select the stem or stems that will form the core of the design; this can be either a single shoot or several shoots that are then spread out. The simplest shape to produce is a cone and for this only guiding canes are needed. For other shapes, attach a framework made from chicken wire or single wires attached to stakes placed in the ground next to the main group of shoots. Tie in the stems to the wire framework and then pinch back the shoots to encourage them to branch and cover the form.

Train new shoots into the framework to fill in any gaps, until they meet around its perimeter. Growth will vary around the plant, depending on the aspect. Shoots trained downwards always grow slowly.

Sandwich a 1cm (¹/₂in) layer of moss between 2 pieces of chicken wire, secure it, and form it into the desired shape. Place it in position and train ivies up around the frame.

Complex designs

To form complex topiary designs, make a basic framework from sturdy materials such as heavy-duty fencing wire. Chicken wire or thin-gauge wire may then be intertwined to form a more precise shape. Garden canes are also useful as a temporary aid in developing and shaping a framework. Tarred twine is good for tying shoots onto a framework, since it eventually decays.

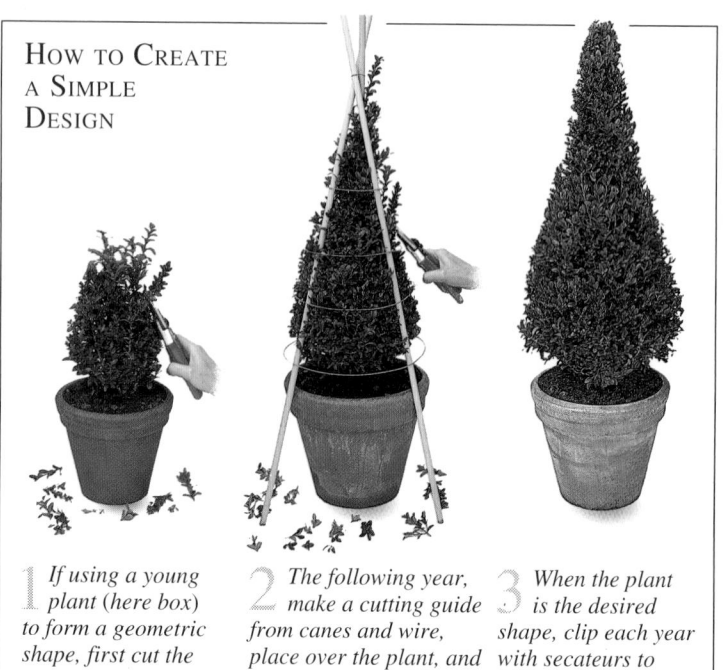

HOW TO CREATE A SIMPLE DESIGN

1 *If using a young plant (here box) to form a geometric shape, first cut the plant to shape by eye.*

2 *The following year, make a cutting guide from canes and wire, place over the plant, and cut the plant to shape.*

3 *When the plant is the desired shape, clip each year with secateurs to retain a crisp outline.*

CLIPPED BIRD
Traditional shapes are still the most popular for topiary. This delightful bird sits on top of its nest surveying the surrounding gardens.

Training stems

Young stems being trained onto a frame grow quickly and considerable work is thus required to tie in new shoots throughout the growing season. Tie in the shoots while they are young and pliable and check previous ties to make sure that they are not broken, rubbing, or in any way restricting the shoots.

If stakes have been used in the framework, make sure that they are still firm and have not cracked, snapped, or bent. If they are defective, replace them with new ones.

Clipping

Topiary involves much more precise clipping than is required for normal hedge cutting. Take time, particularly when initially forming topiary pieces, to cut the branchlets carefully to the required shape. Do not cut too much in one place as it may spoil the symmetry of a topiary design for a whole season until new replacement growth appears.

Even if you have a good eye for shaping plants, it is sensible to use levels, plumb lines, and any other aids available to check the accuracy of a cut. Always work from the top of the plant downwards and from the centre outwards, cutting both sides together in order to retain a balanced symmetry.

Rounded topiary pieces are easier to produce and maintain than angular, geometric shapes and may often be cut freehand. To produce a spherical shape, first trim the top of the plant and then cut a channel downwards around the circumference to leave a ring. A further ring at 90° should then be cut, leaving four distinct quarters to be trimmed.

Geometric topiary that has precise, flat surfaces and angled or squared edges is difficult to form and maintain successfully and needs to be tackled with confident, accurate clipping for a well-defined shape. Such geometric designs are best cut using guidelines attached to canes to maintain symmetry.

When to clip

Once a topiary feature is established, it will need frequent routine clipping during the growing season. The time between cuts will depend on the rate of growth. An intricate, geometric design in box may need to be cut at four- to six-week intervals. Trim as soon as any new growth begins to appear uneven.

ARCHITECTURAL DESIGNS
These complex, abstract shapes need frequent clipping but they form an impressive centrepiece, their forms echoing the cascade of the fountain.

If a perfect finish is not required throughout the growing season, two cuts during the growing season are usually sufficient for a reasonable effect, depending on the plant used. Yew, for example, need be cut only once a year, box (depending on the cultivar) usually needs to be cut twice, and *Lonicera nitida* three times.

Clip plants at the appropriate time of year. Do not clip bushes after early autumn as the young shoots produced after the first clip need to ripen sufficiently to withstand low winter temperatures. In warm climates where growth may be almost continuous, regular trimming will be required throughout the year.

Routine care

Weeding, watering, and mulching is essential in the same way as for free-growing shrubs (see p.72). It is important, however, to apply two or three feeds of a balanced fertilizer at a rate of 60g/sq m (2oz/sq yd) during the growing season.

Winter care

In regions where regular snowfalls occur, netting topiary pieces will help prevent the branches from breaking under the weight of snow. Knock snow off any flat surfaces as it may damage the framework.

Repairs and renovation

If a leader, a section, or a branch of topiary has been damaged or broken, cut it back cleanly with secateurs. Manipulate nearby shoots by tying them in to fill the gap.

If topiary plants have been left unclipped for one or two years, regular clipping should restore the original form within the season. If the topiary has been neglected for years, and the shape has been lost, severe pruning to restore the outline should be carried out the first spring, followed by two or three seasons of more precise clipping.

Scorch and dieback

The foliage of some evergreens may be scorched in fierce winters and can die. The damaged foliage will soon be covered by new growth in spring, but cut it back where it is unsightly, taking care to follow the shape of the topiary piece. If shoots do not fill the gap, there may be a root problem, which will need to be treated.

HOW TO CREATE A COMPLEX DESIGN

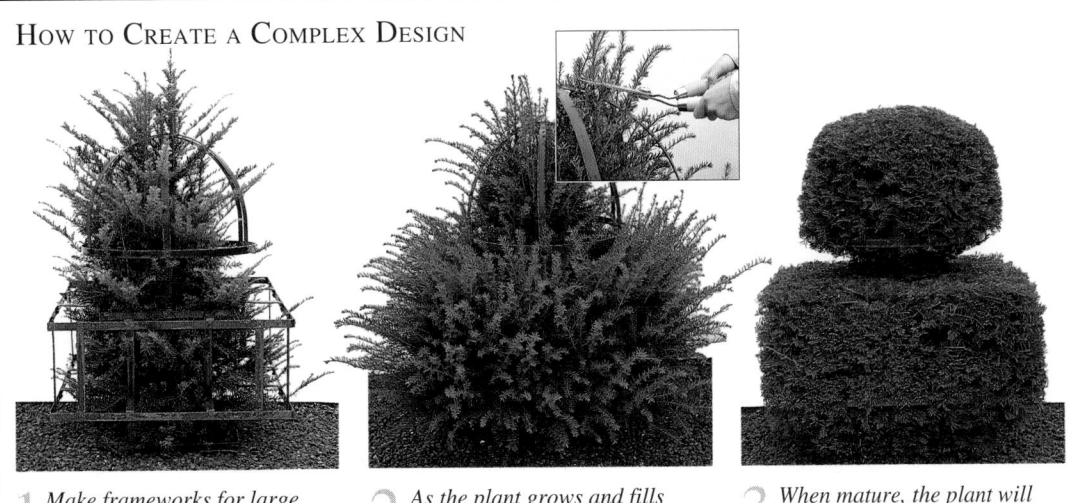

1 *Make frameworks for large topiary pieces from strong materials as they will be in place for several years. Clip a young plant (here yew) as necessary to keep it within the framework.*

2 *As the plant grows and fills the frame, clip it over once a year, following the outline of the framework and pinching out shoots to encourage bushy growth.*

3 *When mature, the plant will form a dense bush and cover the framework. It needs regular clipping to maintain the precise outline of the design.*

Propagation

TREES may be propagated from cuttings, seed, layering, or grafting. Taking cuttings is probably the most common method of propagation as it is fairly simple and provides new plants relatively quickly, while raising trees from seed or layering is easy but very slow. Grafting is rarely used by amateur gardeners because it requires considerable expertise to grow new plants successfully this way.

Tree species may be propagated from seed but hybrids and cultivars rarely come true to type. Vegetative methods of propagation, such as taking cuttings, layering, and grafting, may be used for hybrids and cultivars as well as species; however, some care in the selection of plant material is required in order to be successful.

Hardwood cuttings

Many deciduous trees may be propagated from hardwood, or dormant, cuttings. In early autumn, prepare the ground for the cuttings while it is still warm. Cuttings can be inserted either outdoors in open ground or, for trees that do not root very easily, in the more stable environment of a cold frame.

Cuttings of trees that root easily, such as willows (*Salix*), may be inserted directly into a trench, while those that are more difficult to root, such as *Metasequoia*, should be inserted in a sand bed, and then transplanted into a trench early the next spring. In either case, make the trench narrow and with one side vertical so that the cuttings are held upright while they root. The depth of the trench will depend on the type of plant required: for multi-stemmed trees, it should be 2.5cm (1in) shallower than the length of the cuttings; for single-stemmed trees, it should be the same depth as the cuttings so that the top bud is barely covered and the lack of light inhibits the growth of all other buds.

For best results, dig the trench in friable, well-drained soil; in heavy, clay soil, add some coarse sand to the base. If preparing a few trenches, space them 30–38cm (12–15in) apart in open ground, or about 10cm (4in) apart in a cold frame.

SLOW-ROOTING HARDWOOD CUTTINGS

1 *For species that do not root easily (here* Metasequoia*), tie cuttings into bundles. Dip the ends in hormone rooting powder.*

2 *Insert the bundles of cuttings in a sand bed and leave in a cold frame over winter. In spring, insert them individually in a trench in a prepared site outside.*

Preparing and inserting the cuttings

Select the cuttings just after leaf fall: choose strong, vigorous shoots of the current season's growth and remove them by cutting just above a bud or pair of buds at the junction between the current and the previous season's growth. Trim down the cuttings as shown and dip the basal cuts in hormone rooting powder to encourage them to root. Place the cuttings against the vertical side of the trench at the correct depth, and backfill with soil. Then firm in gently and water well.

For species that do not root easily, tie the cuttings with twine into small bundles and then plunge them into a sand bed (see p.544) in a cold frame for the winter, where they should root before being transplanted.

FAST-ROOTING HARDWOOD CUTTINGS

1 *To prepare the trench, push the spade vertically into the soil, then press it forwards slightly to form a flat-backed trench about 19cm (7in) deep.*

2 *Select strong, straight stems with healthy buds (right); avoid soft, spindly, old, or damaged stems (left). Remove about 30cm (12in) of the stem, cutting just above a bud.*

3 *Remove any leaves. Trim the cuttings to about 20cm (8in): make an angled cut just above the proposed top bud and a horizontal cut below the bottom one.*

4 *Insert the cuttings in the trench 10–15cm (4–6in) apart, and at the correct depth depending on whether a single- or a multi-stemmed tree is required.*

PLANTING DEPTHS

MULTI-STEMMED TREES
For multi-stemmed trees, insert cuttings with the top 2.5–3cm (1–1¹/₂in) above the soil surface.

SINGLE-STEMMED TREES
The top bud of each cutting should be just below the soil surface.

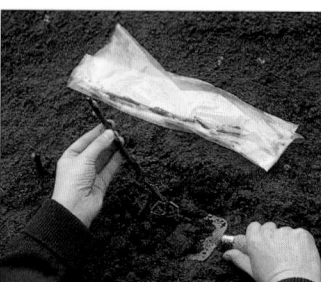

5 *Firm the soil around the cuttings, rake the surface, and label. Space any further rows 30–38cm (12–15in) apart.*

6 *Lift the rooted cuttings the following autumn. Then pot them up individually or transplant them into open ground in their final positions.*

Aftercare

Label the cuttings and leave them until the following autumn. During the winter, the ground may be lifted by frost; refirm the soil around the cuttings if this occurs. By autumn, the cuttings should be well rooted and may then be transplanted individually into open ground or into containers, as required. If they have been kept in a cold frame, harden them off in spring, then transplant outside; the following spring, pot them up or move them to their final positions in open ground.

Semi-ripe cuttings

Many conifers, as well as certain broad-leaved evergreens such as *Magnolia grandiflora* and *Prunus lusitanica*, may be propagated readily from semi-ripe cuttings. These cuttings are taken in late summer or autumn from stems that have virtually ripened, that is, when they have thickened and become harder (see also ORNAMENTAL SHRUBS, "Semi-ripe cuttings", p.84).

Selecting the cuttings

In a closed case, at 21°C (70°F), or in a cold frame, prepare a suitable rooting medium for the cuttings. This should consist of equal parts of grit and peat substitute or peat (see also "Standard cutting compost", p.534). Using a sharp knife, take heel cuttings from healthy sideshoots, including a sliver of hardened wood from the main stem. Alternatively, take 10–15cm (4–6in) long cuttings from leaders or sideshoots and trim immediately below a node with secateurs or a sharp knife.

For cuttings from conifers, choose leaders or sideshoots that are characteristic of the parent plant, as conifer shoots vary considerably in their growth patterns. It is particularly important to select cutting material carefully from slow-growing (dwarf) conifers; some plants may produce reverted or uncharacteristic shoots, but only use shoots that typify what you want to propagate.

Preparing and inserting the cuttings

With both types of cutting, cut off the lower pair of leaves with a sharp knife and reduce the remaining leaves by one third or a half to minimize the loss of moisture; if the cutting tips are soft, pinch them out. To encourage the cuttings to root, use the tip of the knife to make two shallow, vertical wounds, about 2.5cm (1in) long, on opposite sides of each cutting down to the base. Alternatively, make a longer wound along the side of each cutting with a knife, and remove a sliver of bark as well. In either case, dip the basal cut, including the wound, in hormone rooting powder.

Using a dibber, insert the bottom third of each cutting in the rooting medium, taking care to leave enough space between the cuttings so that they do not overlap; this allows air to circulate freely around them. Then firm the compost, water in thoroughly with a solution containing fungicide, and label.

Aftercare

Check the cuttings periodically, watering them only to keep them from drying out. Remove any fallen leaves as soon as they appear since these may rot and spread disease to the cuttings. In frosty conditions, cold frames should be insulated with hessian or a similar covering.

If the cuttings are being kept in a closed case with basal heating they should root by early spring. Cuttings in a cold frame are usually left until the following autumn, although it is preferable to leave them in the frame for a second winter and pot them up the following spring.

During the summer, mist-spray the cuttings frequently to stop them drying out and control any pest or disease infestations that might develop.

PREPARING A SEMI-RIPE CUTTING

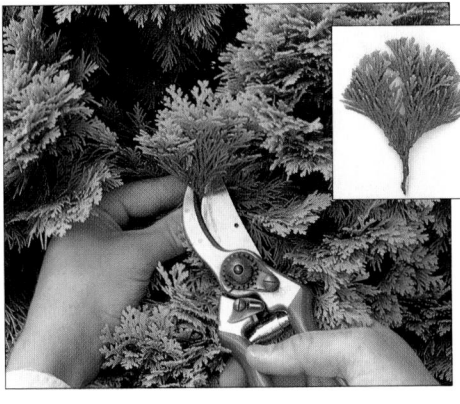

Cut a shoot 10–15cm (4–6in) long from a leader or sideshoot and trim immediately below a node. Strip off the lower leaves (here of Chamaecyparis obtusa *'Nana Aurea') and pinch out the tip if it is soft. Make a shallow wound, about 2.5cm (1in) long, down the side of the cutting and dip it in rooting hormone.*

If the cuttings are in strong, direct sunlight they risk being scorched and it may be necessary to shade them; apply a greenhouse shading paint or place shading material over the frame (see p.484). Once the cuttings root, lift them out carefully with a hand fork and transplant them into individual pots, then harden them off (see p.543) before potting them on further or planting them out in open ground. Rooted cuttings in a cold frame may be hardened off while still in the frame by raising the frame cover for short then longer periods. Give the cuttings a liquid feed and pot them up or transplant them outside.

Softwood cuttings

This method of propagation is suitable for some ornamental cherries (*Prunus*) and a few other tree species, although it is more commonly used for shrubs. Softwood cuttings are taken in spring from the fast-growing tips of new shoots and usually root very easily. They wilt rapidly, however, so it is vital to prepare and insert them as quickly as possible after removing them from the parent plant.

Preparing and inserting the cuttings

In spring, before taking the cuttings, prepare containers by filling them with an appropriate compost and then firming to just below the rim. Take the cuttings by removing the new growth from stem tips, cutting just above a bud or leaf joint with secateurs or a sharp knife. To reduce any moisture loss, immerse the cuttings in water straight away or place them in an opaque, plastic bag and seal it. Even a small loss of water will hinder the development of new roots.

Prepare the cuttings by trimming them with a sharp knife to about 6cm (2¹/₂in), cutting just below a leaf joint. Remove the lower leaves and dip the base of each cutting in hormone rooting powder to encourage rooting. Insert the cuttings into the prepared pots of compost, label them, and water them with a dilute solution of fungicide.

To encourage rapid rooting, place the containers in a mist unit or closed case at 21–4°C (70–75°F), preferably with basal heating, and water with a fungicide once a week to protect against rotting and disease. Once they are rooted, the cuttings may be hardened off gradually before they are transplanted carefully into individual pots.

TREES THAT MAY BE PROPAGATED BY CUTTINGS

Hardwood
Cordyline ❀
Ficus ❀
Metasequoia glyptostroboides
Morus
Platanus
Populus
Salix

Morus alba 'Laciniata'

Semi-ripe
Austrocedrus ▽
Calocedrus ▽
Chamaecyparis ▽
Cinnamomum ❀ ▽
x *Cupressocyparis* ▽
Cupressus ▽
Distylium racemosum ▽
Drimys winteri
Eucryphia x *nymansensis* 'Nymansay'

Eucryphia x nymansensis 'Nymansay'

Grevillea ❀
Ilex
Juniperus ▽
Ligustrum lucidum
Magnolia grandiflora ▽
Metrosideros excelsa ❀,
   M. robusta ❀,
   M. umbellata ❀
Michelia ❀ ▽
Nothofagus dombeyi
Podocarpus, some ❀, ▽
Prunus lusitanica
Quercus ilex ▽,
   Q. myrsinifolia ▽,
   Q. semecarpifolia ▽
Thuja ▽
Thujopsis ▽
Trochodendron aralioides ▽
Tsuga ▽
Weinmannia ❀

Softwood
Acer cappadocicum
Betula
Catalpa
Celtis occidentalis
Cotinus coggygria
Eucryphia lucida
Ginkgo biloba
Halesia
Koelreuteria paniculata
Lagerstroemia, some ❀
Liquidambar styraciflua
Metasequoia glyptostroboides
Prunus
Ulmus

KEY
❀ *Not hardy*
▽ *Take cuttings with a heel*

Raising trees from seed

Tree species may be propagated from seed as their seedlings usually retain the distinctive characteristics of the parent plant; hybrids and cultivars rarely come true to type. Raising a tree from seed is a relatively simple process; it is, however, a slow method if a tree is being grown mainly for its flowers, as the tree will take a number of years to reach flowering size.

Extracting seed

The protective covering of some seeds should be removed first. The method for this varies, depending on the type of seed coat. The coating on winged seed may be removed simply by rubbing it between finger and thumb. Some cones disintegrate naturally and the scales may then be separated. Place pine and spruce cones in a paper bag and keep them in a warm, dry place until the cone scales open and shed the seed into the bag; immerse cedar cones in hot water and leave them to soak until the scales open.

The method of extracting seed from fruits or berries depends on the seed size and type of flesh. Large fruits, such as those of crab apples (*Malus*), may be cut open and the seeds extracted. Soak smaller fruits, such as those of *Sorbus*, in warm water for several days; viable seed will sink. Discard the pulp and soak again until the seed can be removed and any remaining flesh picked off.

Storing

Once the seed has been extracted, dry it if necessary and place it in a sealed and labelled plastic bag. If planning to sow the seed within a few days, store it at room temperature; for longer-term storage, keep it on the top shelf of a refrigerator so that it is cool but not frozen.

CLEANING FLESHY SEED

1 Remove the fleshy seed with your fingers. Immerse it in warm water, and soak for 1–2 days. Once the fleshy coating has softened and split, drain off the water.

2 Pick off the remaining coating and dry the seed with tissue. Sow the seed fresh or store it in a plastic bag in a refrigerator for no more than a few weeks.

Breaking seed dormancy

Some seeds have a natural period of dormancy to prevent germination in adverse climatic conditions which would threaten the survival of the seedlings; this has to be overcome before the seed will germinate. Several kinds of dormancy occur, sometimes combined, which vary according to the species: most commonly, dormancy is achieved either by a hard, thick seed coat, which prevents water being taken up, or by a chemical inhibitor, which delays germination until there is a significant temperature change. In most cases, dormancy can be broken artificially by wearing away the seed coat or by chilling the seed.

Scarification

Before sowing seeds with an impermeable coating, scarify them to allow germination to occur: large seeds with a particularly hard covering, such as oaks (*Quercus*), may be nicked with a sharp knife, or a section of the seed coat filed away to let in moisture; smaller seeds that are

not easily nicked, such as those of pines, may be shaken in a jar that has been lined with sandpaper or partly filled with sharp grit, or they may be filed individually with an emery board. Seed from legumes (for example *Acacia* and *Robinia*) should simply be left to soak in a container of hot water for approximately 24 hours in a ratio of 3 parts hot water to 1 part seed.

Stratification

Dormancy in seed of trees from temperate climates is commonly overcome by chilling or "stratification". Seed may either be sown outside so that it is chilled naturally during winter or, more reliably, stratified artificially by being stored in a refrigerator.

If refrigerating seed, first mix it with moistened vermiculite, peat substitute, or peat. Place it in a clear plastic bag, then seal the bag and put it in a refrigerator. Check the seed regularly through the unopened bag – it should be sown as soon as there are signs of germination.

The length of chilling time required varies considerably: as a guideline, many deciduous species require about six to eight weeks of chilling at 0.5–1°C (33–4°F), while conifers need only about three weeks. Some seeds only germinate after they have been sown and once chilling has ceased. In such cases, sow batches of seed at intervals – for example after four, eight, and twelve weeks of chilling – as this should ensure that at least some seeds germinate.

Sowing seed in containers

This is a simple way of raising a small number of seedlings. Thoroughly clean any work surfaces and containers to be used before sowing the seed to avoid contamination from soil-borne pests and diseases. First fill the pots, pans, or seed trays with seed compost up to the rim.

Large seeds or those that produce seedlings with long tap roots, such as oaks (*Quercus*), should be sown about 8cm (3in) apart in deep seed trays or packs, or in individual pots that are about 10cm (4in) deep. Using a presser board, press the seeds into unfirmed compost, then cover them to their own depth with compost and firm to about 5mm (¼in) below the rim (see p.57).

Sow very large seeds, for example those of horse chestnut (*Aesculus*), singly in 10–15cm (4–6in) pots. Insert the seed in firmed compost, so that just the top of the seed is exposed above the surface.

Small seeds, for example those of *Sorbus*, may be either scattered evenly or, if sufficiently large, individually pressed into prepared pots or trays of firmed compost. They should then be barely covered with sieved compost followed by a layer of fine grit 5mm (¼in) deep.

After sowing, thoroughly water all seeds from above and label. Place the containers in a cold frame or,

SOWING IN CONTAINERS

1 Sow fine seed (here *Sorbus*) in containers of firmed seed compost, making sure they are scattered evenly; keep your hand low to stop the seeds bouncing.

2 Hold a sieve containing seed compost over the tray, then tap the side of the sieve until the seeds are just covered to their own depth with sieved compost.

3 Cover the sown seeds with a 5mm (¼in) deep layer of horticultural grit. Label and water the seeds, using a watering can fitted with a fine rose.

4 Once the seedlings are large enough to handle, gently prick them out into individual pots, taking care not to crush the delicate stems or roots.

SOWING LARGE SEED

1 Press large seeds and those of trees with long tap roots into unfirmed compost in individual pots. Cover with compost.

2 Sowing in long toms – deep pots – allows the tap root (see inset) of each seedling (here Quercus) to develop without any restriction.

within a greenhouse, in a closed propagation case or under a pane of glass. Temperate species are best kept at 12–15°C (54–9°F), and warm-temperate and tropical species at 21°C (70°F) to stimulate germination. Once the seeds have successfully germinated, spray them periodically with a fungicide to discourage damping off (see p.564).

Pricking out

When the seedlings are large enough to be handled by their seed leaves, prick them out so that they have more space to grow. This may be done by knocking the container sides to loosen the compost, and then lifting and transplanting the seedlings into individual pots. Alternatively, remove all the seedlings and compost together from the container so that the seedlings may be separated with minimal root disturbance. After transplanting, firm the compost gently around the seedlings, then level it by gently tapping the pot on the work surface.

Aftercare

Water and label the seedlings, and keep them out of direct sunlight in a temperature similar to that needed for germination until established. Gradually harden them off over a few weeks, feeding them regularly, and spraying them with fungicide. Do not overwater, but make sure that the compost does not dry out. Once hardened off, they may be planted out if there is no danger of frost.

Sowing seed outdoors

If raising a large number of seedlings, seed may be sown in an outdoor seedbed; with this method, the seedlings require less regular attention and their growth is less restricted than if sown in containers, but a special bed must be prepared. If possible, do this a few months before sowing by thoroughly digging the area to a spit deep (see "Single digging", p.525), incorporating organic matter and some coarse grit. Keep the ground clear of weeds.

When ready to sow, rake the soil down to a fine tilth, then broadcast small seeds or station sow larger ones individually. (For depth of sowing, see "Sowing seed in containers", p.56.) Lightly rake over the seeds, cover the bed evenly with a 0.5–1cm (1/4–1/2in) layer of grit, and firm with a presser. If the soil is at all dry, water thoroughly; then label with the plant name and sowing date.

In exposed sites, young seedlings may need to be protected with windbreak netting (see p.521) or with a floating cloche (see p.490). If the seeds are well spaced, disease should not be a problem and the seedlings may be grown on *in situ* for 12 months before being pricked out. Water the seedlings as necessary and check them regularly in case treatment is needed for pests such as greenfly (see "Aphids", p.550) and red spider mites (p.550).

Layering

Layering may be used to propagate hybrids and cultivars as well as species. This method of propagation occurs naturally in some plants, when a low-growing stem roots itself in the ground; once this happens, the stem may be removed from the parent plant and grown on. Air layering, where the shoot remains above ground, may be used for trees without low-growing stems.

The advantage of layering is that the layered stem needs very little attention while the roots become established. It is a slow method, however, because in order to obtain

SIMPLE LAYERING

Cut a 5cm (2in) tongue 30–45cm (12–18in) behind the tip of a vigorous shoot, or remove a narrow ring of bark at this point. Brush the wound with hormone rooting powder and peg the shoot into a shallow hole. Tie the shoot to a supporting cane and backfill the hole.

Vigorous shoot

Friable soil

Peg

Tongue

suitable material the plant must be prepared a year in advance and the layered stem may take a year or more to root.

Simple layering

In this method, a shoot is pegged down into the ground until it has rooted and is then cut off from the parent plant (see also *Propagating a Shrub by Simple Layering*, p.88).

Prepare the parent plant a year before layering is to take place: in late winter or early spring, prune a low branch to stimulate new, young shoots that will root easily. In early spring the following year, select a vigorous shoot and make a small wound 30–45cm (12–18in) from the tip. Brush this with hormone rooting powder to encourage rooting. Add plenty of leaf mould or similar organic matter and sharp grit to the soil where the shoot touches the ground and peg it down into a shallow hole, tying it to a vertical cane.

Backfill the hole and firm the soil well, leaving the shoot tip exposed, then water thoroughly and, if necessary, protect the shoot from rabbits and other animals with wire netting. About 12 months later, check to see whether the shoot has rooted; if it has, sever it from the parent and either plant it in open ground or pot it up; if it has not rooted, leave it in place and check a month later.

Air layering

The principle of air layering is the same as simple layering, except that the layered shoot roots above the ground rather than in it (see also *Air Layering a Shrub*, p.89). In spring, select a strong stem that has ripened in the previous year, and remove any leaves 30–45cm (12–18in) behind the growing tip. Prepare the stem either by cutting a tongue 5cm (2in) long in the bark, 22–30cm (9–12in) behind its tip, or by removing a 6–8mm (1/4–3/8in) wide ring of bark from the stem at this point; in either case, brush the wound with hormone rooting powder.

Surround the cut stem with a moist rooting medium and seal it in. To do this, first make a plastic sleeve by cutting off the sealed end of a plastic bag, then slide it along the stem until it surrounds the cut, and secure the lower end with string or tape. Moisten some well-aerated rooting medium (such as sphagnum moss or a mix of equal parts of peat substitute or peat and perlite), then use it to wedge open the tongue; add more medium around the stem inside the sleeve and seal the top.

If the layer has rooted by the next spring, sever the stem from the parent plant, remove the sleeve, and pot on; if not rooted, it should be left in place for another year.

TREE SEED REQUIRING STRATIFICATION

Acer
Betula
Carya
Fagus
Sorbus

TREES THAT MAY BE LAYERED

Simple layering
Cercidiphyllum
Chionanthus retusus
Corylus
Davidia
Dipteronia
Eucryphia
Halesia
Hoheria lyallii
Laurus
Magnolia campbellii,
   M. grandiflora,
   M. hypoleuca

Magnolia hypoleuca

Air layering
Ficus ✽
Magnolia campbellii,
   M. grandiflora

KEY
✽ *Not hardy*

Grafting

Grafted plants, unlike cuttings, have the benefit of a developed root system so they establish relatively quickly. Part of a stem (the scion), taken from the plant to be propagated, is joined to a compatible rootstock of another plant, usually of the same genus. In some cases, the rootstock may confer a desirable characteristic, such as a particular growth habit or high resistance to disease, on the resulting plant.

Grafting methods include side-veneer, chip-budding, apical-wedge, basal-whip (or splice), and whip-and-tongue. For details of basal-whip and whip-and-tongue grafting, see PRINCIPLES OF PROPAGATION, p.542. Check that the rootstocks and scions are compatible; if necessary, seek advice from a specialist nursery.

Side-veneer grafting

This is the most common grafting technique used for ornamental trees; a one-year-old stem is used for the scion and grafted onto the side of the prepared rootstock. It is usually carried out just before leaf break, in mid- to late winter, although for maples (*Acer*) summer-grafting is sometimes more successful.

Prepare the rootstocks a year in advance by potting up one- or two-year-old seedlings in autumn and establishing them in an open frame. About three weeks before grafting, bring them into a cool greenhouse to force them gently into growth. Keep the stocks dry, particularly those from trees that "bleed" sap, such as birches (*Betula*) and conifers, as excessive sap may prevent successful union with the scions.

For the scions, collect strong, one-year-old stems from the tree to be propagated; they should have a similar diameter to the rootstock stems if possible. Trim them down to 15–25cm (6–10in), cutting just above a bud or pair of buds, and place them in a plastic bag in a refrigerator until ready to graft. Either cut back the top-growth of the stocks to about 5–7cm (2–3in) or leave some top-growth above the graft and cut this back in stages later (see "Aftercare", p.59).

Prepare the stocks and scions, one pair at a time, with compatible cuts. It is important to unite the rootstock and scion as soon as they have been cut; if they are allowed to dry out even slightly, this is likely to impede successful union. If the scion is narrower than the stock, align one edge

---

TREES THAT MAY BE GRAFTED

Chip-budding
Crataegus
Laburnum
Magnolia
Malus
Prunus
Pyrus
Sorbus

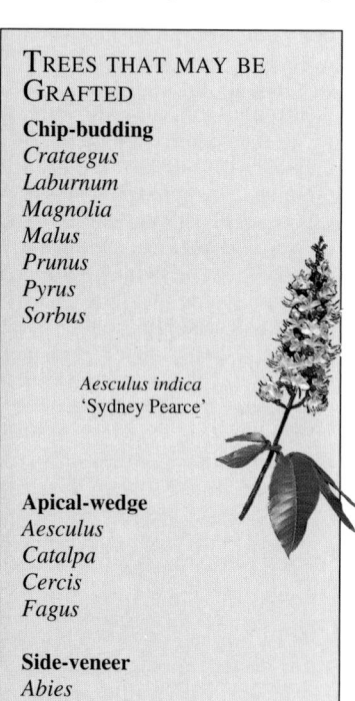

Aesculus indica
'Sydney Pearce'

Apical-wedge
Aesculus
Catalpa
Cercis
Fagus

Side-veneer
Abies
Acer
Betula
Carpinus
Cedrus
Cupressus
Fagus
Fraxinus
Ginkgo
Gleditsia
Larix
Magnolia
Picea
Pinus
Prunus
Robinia
Sorbus

Robinia pseudoacacia 'Frisia'

Whip-and-tongue
Fraxinus
Gleditsia
Robinia

PROPAGATING TREES BY SIDE-VENEER GRAFTING

1 *Trim the scion to a length of 15–25cm (6–10in), cutting just above a bud or pair of buds. Place it in a plastic bag and refrigerate until ready to graft.*

2 *Using a sharp knife, make a short, downward, inward nick about 2.5cm (1in) from the top of the rootstock.*

3 *Starting near the top of the stock, make a sloping, slightly inward cut down to meet the inner point of the first cut. Remove the resulting sliver of wood.*

4 *Make the final cut on the stock by slicing straight up with the knife from the first cut below. This leaves a flat cut on one side of the stock (see inset).*

5 *Now prepare the scion: make a shallow, sloping cut about 2.5cm (1in) long down to the base; then make a short, angled cut at the base, on the opposite side (see inset).*

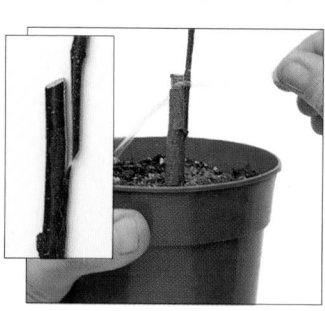

6 *Fit the base of the scion into the cut in the rootstock (see inset). Starting at the top, wrap a length of grafting tape around the union to secure it.*

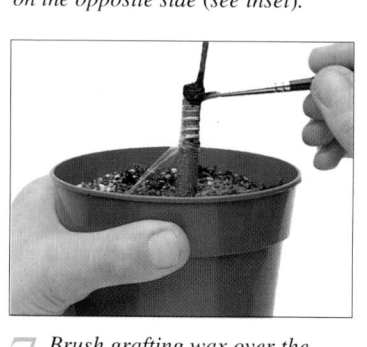

7 *Brush grafting wax over the external cut surfaces on both the stock and the scion. In addition, wax the top of the scion if it has been trimmed back.*

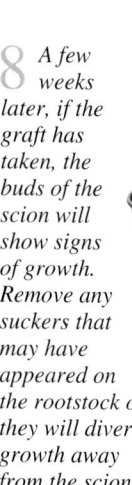

Growth visible from buds

8 *A few weeks later, if the graft has taken, the buds of the scion will show signs of growth. Remove any suckers that may have appeared on the rootstock or they will divert growth away from the scion.*

to ensure that at least one side of the cambium layer unites. Tie the scion in position with clear plastic, grafting tape, raffia, or a rubberized strip, then wax over all external cut surfaces to reduce moisture loss. For advice on aftercare, see right.

Chip-budding

Mainly used for fruit trees, this is also a good way to propagate plants of the Rosaceae family, for example crab apples (*Malus*). In this method, the scion includes a single bud from which the new growth develops, and the grafted plant remains outdoors rather than being potted up.

During winter, establish one- or two-year-old seedlings or hardwood cuttings in open ground for the rootstocks. In mid-summer, remove any lateral branches from the bottom 45cm (18in) of the stem. For the scions (or budsticks), select vegetative (non-flowering) shoots that are of a similar diameter to the rootstocks from well-ripened, current season's growth.

The rootstocks and budsticks are then prepared and united (see below). If successful, the graft should take within a few weeks; the tape or tie may then be removed and the bud should start to swell. For aftercare, see right.

Apical-wedge grafting

This grafting method is similar to side-veneer grafting, except that the scion is placed directly on top of the rootstock. In mid-winter, collect some stems of the previous season's growth from the plant to be propagated, and heel them into the ground.

In late winter or early spring, lift and wash one-year-old seedlings or vigorous plants for the rootstocks, then cut them back to 5cm (2in) above the roots. Make a vertical cut 2.5–3cm (1–1¼in) down the centre of each rootstock. Cut the base of each scion into a wedge, and insert them into the tops of the stocks; leave the top of the cut on the scion exposed. Bind and pot up the grafted plants, then follow the aftercare guidance given below (see also ORNAMENTAL SHRUBS, "Apical-wedge grafting", p.91).

Aftercare

Deciduous trees should be kept in the greenhouse at 10°C (50°F), while conifers, broad-leaved evergreens, and summer-grafted trees should be kept in a closed case in a humid environment at 15°C (59°F). The graft should take in a few weeks and new growth will be seen on the scion. Pinch off any suckers appearing below the union as these are growing from the rootstock. After six to ten weeks, harden off the grafted plants. If not cut back at grafting, reduce top-growth of the rootstock to within 10cm (4in) of the union.

Tie the growing bud to the remaining top of the rootstock to ensure that the new shoot grows straight. In mid-summer, cut back the rootstock to just above the union and tie in the new shoot to a supporting cane. Alternatively, the stock may be cut back to just above the union in late spring. Once they are beginning to grow vigorously, pot on the grafted trees or transplant them into open ground.

PROPAGATING TREES BY CHIP-BUDDING

1 *Select and cut the budstick (here* Malus), *choosing a long, vigorous shoot of the current season's ripened wood. It should have well-developed buds and be roughly the thickness of a pencil.*

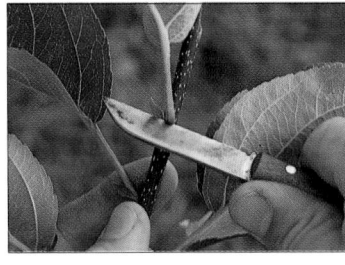

2 *Cut off the soft wood and strip away any leaves at the tip of the shoot.*

3 *Using a sharp knife, make the first cut 2cm (³/4in) below a healthy bud, inserting the blade about 5mm (¹/4in) deep at an angle of approximately 45°.*

4 *Start making a second cut about 4cm (1¹/2in) above the first. Cut down through the wood to meet the first cut, taking care not to damage the bud.*

5 *Remove the bud chip, holding it by the bud between finger and thumb to keep the cambium layer clean. Place it in a clean plastic bag to prevent it from drying out.*

6 *To prepare the rootstock, cut off all the shoots and leaves from the bottom 30cm (12in) of the stem; it is easiest to do this while standing astride the stock.*

7 *Make two cuts in the rootstock to correspond with those on the bud chip so that the stock can be united with the chip. Remove the resulting sliver of wood, taking care not to touch the stem's cut surface (see inset).*

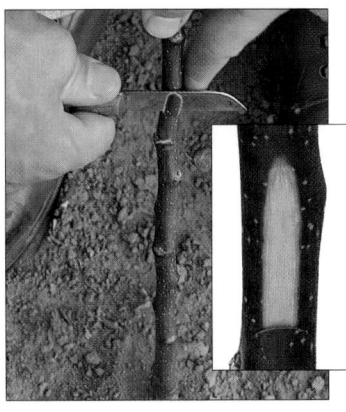

8 *Place the bud chip into the "lip" of the cut rootstock, so that the cambium layers of the chip and stock match as closely as possible (see inset). Bind the join tightly with grafting tape. If the graft takes, the bud will start to swell and develop; the tape can then be removed.*

9 *Next spring, cut back the stock just above the union; the bud will develop as the leader.*

Hedges and screens

HEDGES and screens, both formal and informal, can play an important role in the structure and character of a garden as well as having a variety of practical uses.

Practical uses

Most hedges, whether informal, open hedges or formal, solid, clipped ones, are planted for utilitarian purposes, to delineate boundaries, to provide shelter and shade, and to screen the garden. It is possible, however, to combine use with beauty.

Living barriers
As living barriers, hedges may take some years to establish, but, if properly maintained, they are often preferable to fences because they provide texture, colour, and shape. Most plants used for hedging are long-lived and if correctly maintained will provide effective and sometimes virtually impenetrable barriers for many years.

Shelter
Hedges make excellent windbreaks, filtering fast-moving air and reducing the impact caused by turbulence when wind hits a solid object such as a wall or fence. The porosity of a hedge varies between species and times of year; thus a close-clipped, evergreen yew hedge (*Taxus baccata*) will be considerably less porous than a deciduous beech hedge (*Fagus sylvatica*) during winter. At the ideal of 50 per cent porosity it has been calculated that with a 1.5m (5ft) hedge, windspeed is reduced

by 50 per cent at a distance of 7.5m (24ft) from the hedge; by 25 per cent at a distance of 15m (50ft); and by 10 per cent at a distance of 30m (100ft). The shelter provided by hedges is invaluable, particularly in windswept gardens where even hardy plants may suffer damage from gales and strong winds.

Noise barriers
Hedges may contribute to noise reduction by screening out unwelcome sounds. One of the most effective types in this respect is a green "environmental barrier", with a solid core of soil. A horizontal weave of osier (*Salix viminalis*) is threaded through vertical stakes and the core is packed with soil to form a wall. The osier roots into the soil core and the top and side growth is pruned back to the woven wall at intervals.

Ornamental hedges

A wealth of plants of diverse shape, size, texture, and colour can be used for hedges, deciduous or evergreen, formal or informal, or with flowers and fruit. Mixing evergreen and deciduous species selected for flower and foliage creates a living mosaic.

Formal
Yew (*Taxus baccata*) makes an excellent hedge, provided that six to ten years are allowed for establishment. A hedge of x *Cupressocyparis leylandii* grows extremely rapidly and has to be clipped at least twice a

year to keep it neat and within bounds. Low formal hedges are frequently seen in parterres as well as knot gardens. Various forms of box (*Buxus sempervirens*), especially 'Suffruticosa', are used widely, as are *Santolina* and *Lonicera nitida*.

YEAR-ROUND COLOUR
x Cupressocyparis leylandii *cultivars produce contrasting shades of foliage in a mixed conifer hedge.*

PLANTS FOR INFORMAL HEDGES

Pyracantha 'Golden Charmer'

Fuchsia magellanica

Escallonia 'Langleyensis'

Ilex aquifolium 'Madame Briot'

Rosa 'Roseraie de l'Haÿ'

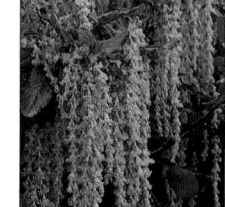
Garrya elliptica 'James Roof'

FORMAL, CLIPPED HEDGES

HEDGING PLANTS	PLANTING DISTANCE	APPROPRIATE HEIGHT	CLIPPING TIMES	RESPONDS TO RENOVATION
EVERGREEN				
Buxus sempervirens (box)	30cm (12in)	30–60cm (1–2ft)	Twice/3 times, in growing season	Yes
Chamaecyparis lawsoniana (Lawson cypress) – most cultivars except dwarf types	60cm (24in)	1.2–2.5m (4–8ft), but may be larger	Twice, in spring and early autumn	No
x *Cupressocyparis leylandii* (Leyland cypress)	75cm (30in)	2–4m (6–12ft), but up to 6m (20ft)	Twice/3 times, in growing season	No
Escallonia	45cm (18in)	1.2–2.5m (4–8ft)	Immediately after flowering	Yes
Ilex aquifolium (holly) and cultivars	45cm (18in)	2–4m (6–12ft)	In late summer	Yes
Lavandula (lavender)	30cm (12in)	45–90cm (18–36in)	In spring and after flowering	No
Ligustrum (privet)	30cm (12in)	1.5–3m (5–10ft)	Twice/3 times, in growing season	Yes
Lonicera nitida	30cm (12in)	1–1.2m (3–4ft)	Twice/3 times, in growing season	Yes
Taxus baccata (yew)	60cm (24in)	1.2–4m (4–12ft), but up to 6m (20ft)	Twice, in summer and autumn	Yes
Thuja plicata 'Fastigiata'	60cm (24in)	1.5–3m (5–10ft)	In spring and early autumn	No
DECIDUOUS				
Berberis thunbergii	45cm (18in)	60cm–1.2m (2–4ft)	Once, in summer	Yes
Carpinus betulus (hornbeam)	45–60cm (18–24in)	1.5–6m (5–20ft)	Once, in mid- to late summer	Yes
Crataegus monogyna (hawthorn)	30–45cm (12–18in)	1.5–3m (5–10ft)	Twice, in summer and autumn	Yes
Fagus sylvatica (beech)	30–60cm (12–24in)	1.2–6m (4–20ft)	Once, in late summer	Yes

Tapestry or mosaic hedges combine a number of compatible plants within the same hedge line, to provide changing visual effects throughout the year. Species used include *Taxus baccata*, *Ilex aquifolium*, *Carpinus betulus*, and *Fagus sylvatica*.

Mixing evergreen and deciduous species provides an interesting and colourful background throughout the year. Species used must have similar rates of growth if over-vigorous species are not to dominate.

Informal

Informal hedges combine practical and ornamental qualities. Although they are not suitable for creating strictly formal designs, they can be very decorative and still provide effective screening and shelter. Many of the plants used in these informal boundaries produce attractive flowers and fruit, or both, contributing form and colour to the garden.

Integrate the different colour backgrounds carefully into the overall design. *Cotoneaster lacteus*, *Berberis darwinii*, or *Forsythia* are often used; hybrid shrub roses and species also make fine informal hedges. Most strong-growing bamboos are suitable for areas where soil moisture is high and a wind filter is needed.

FORMAL ELEGANCE
The symmetrical pattern of dwarf hedges, in various shades of green, frames the brick path and draws attention to the ornamental sculpture.

Choosing plants

Before selecting species for hedging consider their eventual height, spread, and speed of development, and ensure that species chosen are hardy within the climatic zone, and suited to the soil type of the garden. Plants for formal hedges must have a dense habit of growth, and be tolerant of close clipping. For informal hedges grown for their flowers or berries, choose plants that need pruning only once a year. The timing of pruning is critical, otherwise the next season's display of flowers or fruit may be spoiled.

The choice of evergreens or deciduous species is partly a matter of taste, but bear in mind that evergreens and conifers provide a dense, wind-proof screen throughout the year, offering protection which may be critical in severe winters.

Soil preparation and planting

Hedges are a permanent feature of the garden. It is therefore important to prepare the site thoroughly before planting, and to top-dress each spring with a well-balanced fertilizer and mulch. Soil preparation and planting techniques are the same as for trees and shrubs (see pp.39–43 and pp.69–71). The width of ground preparation required will be between 60–90cm (24–36in).

Spacing for most hedging plants is 30–60cm (12–24in) – see the charts below. If a hedge 90cm (36in) thick or more is required, plant a double, staggered row with spacing of 90cm (36in) within the row, and 45cm (18in) between rows. Plants for all dwarf hedges, parterres, and knot gardens should be spaced about 10–15cm (4–6in) apart.

Pruning and training

The initial training of a formal hedge is crucial to promote even growth from the base of the hedge to the top. Careful attention to pruning in the first two to three years is essential.

Early pruning and shaping

Most deciduous plants, especially those with a naturally bushy, low-branching habit, need to be cut back by one third on planting, with strong laterals also cut back by one third of their length. In the second winter, cut back again by about one third.

INFORMAL AND FLOWERING HEDGES

HEDGING PLANT	ORNAMENTAL QUALITIES	PLANTING DISTANCE	APPROPRIATE HEIGHT	WHEN TO PRUNE
EVERGREEN				
Berberis darwinii	Yellow flowers, purple berries	45cm (18in)	1.5–2.5m (5–8ft)	Immediately after flowering
Cotoneaster lacteus	White flowers, red fruits	45–60cm (18–24in)	1.5–2.2m (5–7ft)	After fruiting
Escallonia	White, red, or pink flowers	45cm (18in)	1.2–2.5m (4–8ft)	Immediately after flowering
Garrya elliptica	Grey, green, red, or yellow catkins	45cm (18in)	1.5–2.2m (5–7ft)	Immediately after flowering
Ilex aquifolium	White flowers, berries	45–60cm (18–24in)	2–4m (6–12ft)	In late summer
Lavandula	Purple flowers, grey foliage	30cm (12in)	0.6–1m (2–3ft)	After flowering
Pyracantha	White flowers, red berries	60cm (24in)	2–3m (6–10ft)	For pruning, see p.81
DECIDUOUS				
Berberis thunbergii	Pale yellow flowers, red fruits, red autumn foliage	30–38cm (12–15in)	1–1.2m (3–4ft)	After flowering, if required to keep in check
Crataegus monogyna	Fragrant white flowers, red berries	45–60cm (18–24in)	3m+ (10ft+)	In winter, remove selected vigorous shoots
Corylus avellana	Yellow catkins	45–60cm (18–24in)	2–5m (6–15ft)	After flowering
Forsythia x intermedia 'Spectabilis'	Yellow flowers	45cm (18in)	1.5–2.2m (5–7ft)	After flowering, remove old stems
Fuchsia magellanica	Blue/red flowers, black berries	30–45cm (12–18in)	0.6–1.5m (2–5ft)	In spring, remove old stems
Potentilla fruticosa	Bright yellow flowers	30–45cm (12–18in)	0.6–1.2m (2–4ft)	In spring
Prunus spinosa cultivars	Pale pink or white flowers, red and purple foliage	45–60cm (18–24in)	2.5–4m (8–12ft)	In winter, remove selected vigorous shoots
Rosa 'Nevada'	Fragrant cream flowers	60cm (24in)	1.5–2m (5–6ft)	In spring, remove thin twigs
Rosa 'Roseraie de l'Haÿ'	Fragrant crimson flowers	45cm (18in)	1.5m (5ft)	In spring, remove thin twigs
Ribes sanguineum 'King Edward VII'	Deep pink flowers	30–45cm (12–18in)	1.5–2m (5–6ft)	After flowering, remove selected shoots

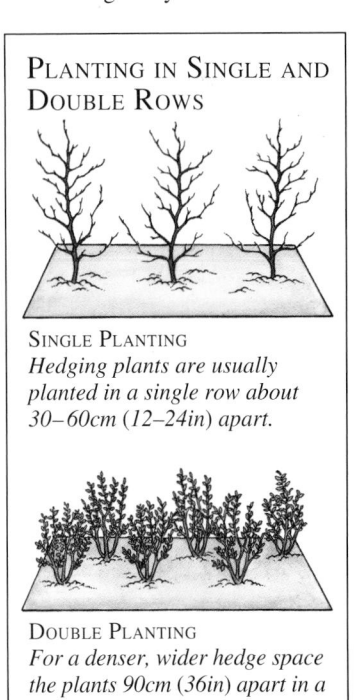

PLANTING IN SINGLE AND DOUBLE ROWS

SINGLE PLANTING
Hedging plants are usually planted in a single row about 30–60cm (12–24in) apart.

DOUBLE PLANTING
For a denser, wider hedge space the plants 90cm (36in) apart in a double, staggered row.

FORMATIVE PRUNING

BEFORE PRUNING
Leaders and laterals have grown unrestricted; the hedge (Lonicera nitida) needs formative pruning.

AFTER PRUNING
Cut back the laterals by half and prune the leaders to the required height to encourage bushy growth. Water, feed, and mulch if needed.

HOW TO SHAPE A HEDGE

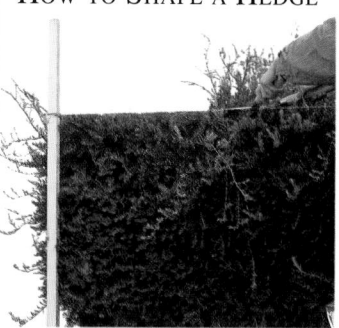

1 Stretch a taut, level string between two upright posts to act as a guideline for the highest point of the hedge, then cut the top of the hedge along this line.

2 Cut a template of the shape required. Place the template on the hedge and cut following the line of the template, moving it along as you proceed, then cut the sides.

3 Once you reach the end of the hedge, remove the template, posts, and lines of string. Clip the end of the hedge neatly.

To shape strong-growing plants and those with an upright habit of growth, such as privet (*Ligustrum*) and hawthorn (*Crataegus*) cut them back to within 15–30cm (6–12in) above ground level in late spring, followed by a further clipping back of laterals in late summer. During the second winter or early spring, cut hard back, removing at least half of the previous season's growth.

Even from this early stage the hedge sides should be cut at a more or less oblique angle (referred to as the batter), with the base as the widest point. A hedge with a flat-topped "A" shape or a gently curved,

pointed top is less vulnerable to snow and strong winds. Snow will quickly fall away down the sides of a tapered hedge; high winds or gales will be deflected by its sloping sides, causing minimal damage to the plants.

A level top is achieved by cutting to a straight edge or garden line stretched between canes. It is important to use a guide when clipping low hedges too, since discrepancies are just as likely to occur when looking down as when viewing from eye level. Once the size and batter have been achieved, clipping to keep the hedge in shape is all that is required in subsequent seasons.

Conifers and many evergreens are used extensively as hedges. In most cases, laterals only are pruned during the early years, particularly in the formative second year, allowing the apical shoot to grow to the desired height before trimming back.

Maintaining a hedge

A formal hedge needs to be clipped regularly to maintain its shape: in most cases the hedge should be

SHAPING HEDGES

Make hedges narrower at the top to deflect strong winds and snow. In heavy snowfall areas, hedges should have pointed tops to prevent snow settling and causing damage.

HORNBEAM

YEW

trimmed twice annually, in spring and late summer (see *Formal, Clipped Hedges*, p.60). Most formal hedges are cut with shears or an electric trimmer. Use a straight edge or a garden line as a guide when trimming the hedge to shape.

Informal hedges also need regular pruning to shape. Remove misplaced growths, and cut back within the required bounds. Flowering or fruiting hedges must be pruned only at the appropriate season (see *Informal and Flowering Hedges*, p.61). Informal hedges and those with large evergreen leaves should, where practical, be pruned with secateurs to avoid unsightly damage to the leaves.

Renovation

A number of hedging species, notably hornbeam (*Carpinus*), honeysuckle (*Lonicera*), and yew (*Taxus baccata*), respond well to renovation even where hedges have been neglected and have become overgrown. For best results, deciduous hedges should be renovated in winter, and evergreen ones in mid-spring.

If drastic pruning is required, alternate sides should be cut back in subsequent seasons. If the renovation is to be successful, it is most important to feed and mulch the plants in the season before pruning, and then again after cutting back to encourage healthy new growth.

TRIMMING HEDGES

TRIMMING WITH SHEARS
To ensure that the top of the hedge is cut level and flat keep the blades of the shears parallel to the line of the hedge at all times.

CUTTING WITH HEDGETRIMMERS
When using an electrical trimmer, keep the blade parallel to the hedge and use a wide, sweeping action.

HOW TO RENOVATE AN OVERGROWN HEDGE

Cut back growth to the main stems on one side only of a neglected, deciduous hedge, trimming the other side as usual (right). A year later, if growth has been vigorous, cut back growth on the other side to the main stems (far right).

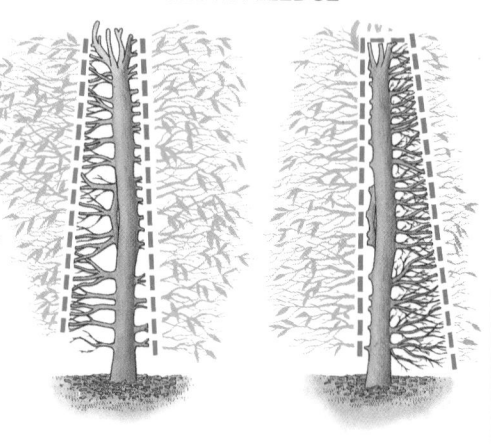

3

ORNAMENTAL SHRUBS

V ALUED BY GARDENERS *for their architectural quality and long-term interest, shrubs are excellent for forming the skeleton of a planting design. In a mixed border, they provide welcome solidity and substance, balancing the softer, more transitory pleasures provided by herbaceous plants. Grouping evergreen and deciduous shrubs together allows you to create an effective display all* *year round, which is also relatively low in maintenance. As well as a diversity of shapes and forms, shrubs possess a magnificent variety of features: from the shiny, palmate leaves of* Fatsia japonica *or the heavily perfumed plumes of lilac to the bead-like berries of pyracanthas or the spectral, white stems of* Rubus biflorus, *there is a shrub to suit every size of garden, wherever situated, and to satisfy every taste.*

Designing with shrubs

S HRUBS are woody-stemmed plants that typically produce a framework of branches from the base, unlike the single trunk characteristic of most trees. The division between shrubs and trees is not a rigid one, however, as some shrubs (such as fuchsias) may be trained as standards with a single trunk and a number of trees are multi-stemmed. Similarly, the difference in scale is not a clear demarcation, as some shrubs grow larger than some trees.

Whether the term "shrub" is used very strictly or rather more loosely, it covers an enormous choice of plants suitable for gardens of any size and style. Species have been collected from many parts of the world and these have given rise to numerous cultivars and hybrids of ornamental value.

Choosing shrubs

Shrubs are invaluable in the garden for many reasons; perhaps most important of all, they impart shape, structure, and substance to a design, and provide a framework. They are far from being purely functional keystones, however, for they are also endowed with a variety of ornamental qualities, including fragrant and colourful flowers, evergreen or variegated foliage, attractive fruits, and coloured or shapely stems.

These decorative attributes exert great influence on your choice of plants. There are, however, important practical considerations to take into account when deciding which shrubs to grow.

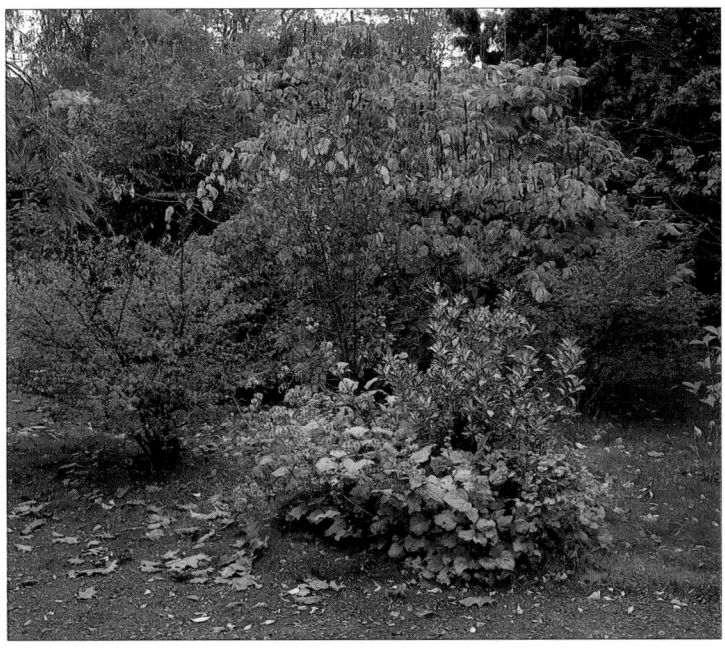

INFORMAL PLANTING
In this garden, an informal grouping of shrubs, including a variegated holly (Ilex aquifolium), *the fiery* Euonymus alatus, *and a tall* Aesculus parviflora, *provide an effective display of contrasting colours and shapes.*

Compatibility with the given or adapted growing conditions is essential (see "Suiting plants to site conditions", p.64), while a shrub's growth rate, habit, and eventual height and spread also determine whether it is suitable for a garden or not and where it is best sited.

Form and size
In size, shrubs range from dwarfs, such as the mat-forming *Penstemon newberryi* at only 15–20cm (6–8in) high, that are suitable for the rock garden, to much more substantial plants that are 5–6m (15–20ft) in height, such as some of the handsome, evergreen rhododendrons.

Shrubs have many different forms and habits, including rounded, arching, and vertical. Some – for example *Yucca gloriosa*, with its explosive spray of sword-like leaves and erect panicles of flowers – are worth growing for their form alone. Others, such as *Chaenomeles japonica*, have a sprawling habit that often looks better if wall-trained.

Shrubs as design features

When selecting shrubs, consider how they will associate with the other planting as well as any structural elements nearby, such as the house or patio. If they are to form part of the design framework, shrubs with distinctive, sculptural silhouettes are usually most suitable – for example the spreading, wave-like form of *Juniperus squamata* 'Blue Carpet' or the bold, upright mass of *Mahonia x media*. Think of them as abstract shapes that may be used singly or in combination to create a balanced scheme of contrasting and complementary forms.

Foundation planting
Shrubs are often used as foundation planting to link the house with the garden, forming a transition between the rigid lines of the building and the softer shapes and textures of border plants and lawn.

This type of planting is effective when used to mark the entrance to the house; symmetrical groups or rows of shrubs could flank the drive or the doorway, for example, or an informal curved bed might border a winding path to the door.

Design the planting so that it complements the style, colour, and scale of the building. Evergreen shrubs are often chosen because of their continuous display but, in an informal setting especially, including deciduous plants as well creates a greater variety of interest while still providing mass and structure.

Suiting plants to site conditions

To ensure that shrubs flourish and give pleasure for a long time, it is essential to invest in plants that will thrive in the particular conditions of your garden. Even within a small garden, these growing conditions often vary considerably. Since there are so many shrubs from which to make a selection, there is no need to grow plants that are unsuited to the chosen site.

Soil types

The character of the soil should be the first consideration; in many cases, it may be improved to widen the range of plants that can be grown satisfactorily. It is particularly important to make heavy soils more open and free-draining and light soils more moisture-retentive, as well as to moderate any excessive acidity or alkalinity that may be a problem.

Successful planting must take into account the soil's underlying character, however. Even for relatively extreme conditions, there are a number of plants from which to choose: dogwoods (*Cornus*) and willows (*Salix*) like moist soils, for example, while broom (*Cytisus/ Genista*), lavender (*Lavandula*), and *Phlomis* thrive on well-drained soils. Rhododendrons and other ericaceous plants generally require acidic conditions; but many shrubs do well on alkaline soils, including *Deutzia*, *Hypericum*, and *Philadelphus*.

Aspect and microclimate

A plant's preference for sun or shade should also be borne in mind. Sun-lovers such as *Cistus* will become drawn and straggly if not planted in full sun, but many shrubs tolerate or even prefer some shade. The latter are often ideal for town gardens, where instead of dappled light filtering through the tree canopy there tend to be sharp contrasts between full sun and deep shade cast by surrounding buildings.

The hardiness of shrubs is another factor to consider. The temperature range, altitude, degree of shelter, aspect, and distance from the sea all affect the range that may be grown. The sea has a moderating influence on temperature, but salt-laden winds can damage many plants in gardens near the coast. There are, however, shrubs (such as most *Escallonia* and

GROWING PLANTS IN THE RIGHT CONDITIONS
Light shade from the overhead tree canopy and acid soil are ideal for these impressive banks of rhododendrons lining an informal grass path. Clashing shades have been boldly mixed to create a spectacular avenue of colour.

Genista) that benefit from the mild conditions and tolerate salt spray. Plants of borderline hardiness for the area that might well succumb if grown in the open garden are more likely to thrive as wall-trained specimens in a sheltered position.

Successional interest

When selecting shrubs, take account of the seasonal interest that they provide and whether it is continuous, as from evergreen foliage, or transitory, as from a burst of summer blooms. A shrub with a brief period of splendour is often best sited near one that reaches its peak shortly afterwards to create a changing but unbroken display.

Spring

As well as new, emerging leaves, shrubs bearing spring flowers are valued for the colour and vitality that they bring early in the year. Combine them to provide interest throughout the season – from the early *Salix hastata* 'Wehrhahnii', with its bud-like, silver-grey catkins borne on deep purple stems, to the fragrant, white and pink flower clusters of *Daphne* x *burkwoodii* 'Somerset' in late spring.

Summer

The choice of summer-flowering shrubs is immense and, again, they are best combined to form a continuous display. Invaluable shrubs such as *Potentilla* 'Elizabeth' and *Syringa microphylla* 'Superba' deserve to be widely grown, since their flowering period extends from late spring until early autumn.

Autumn

This is the season when many deciduous shrubs really come to the fore, with colourful foliage providing an eye-catching spectacle. Shrubs for autumn interest include *Euonymus alatus*, with its intense red leaves, and the various cultivars of *Cotinus coggygria*, with yellow, red, or purple foliage. Colour from berries, such as the yellow clusters of *Pyracantha* 'Golden Dome' or the shiny red fruits of *Cotoneaster* 'Cornubia', is also valuable.

Winter

Shrubs are vital elements in the winter garden, with a rich variety of features. Evergreen foliage probably makes the greatest contribution, providing bold masses of colour and texture. Flowers also play their part, however, with a choice ranging from the sculptural *Mahonia japonica*, with its spreading, yellow sprays, to the spidery, red flowers borne by *Hamamelis* x *intermedia* 'Diane', while other fragrant shrubs such as *Viburnum* x *bodnantense* may be welcome. Less common are shrubs with ornamental stems, such as *Cornus stolonifera* 'Flaviramea', which has vivid, lime-green shoots.

Shrub borders

One of the most satisfactory ways of using shrubs in the garden is to grow them in a border on their own. From the large range available that will suit the soil, climate, and site, a selection may be made that will give a succession of colour and interest throughout the year. The aim is to create a balanced design, taking into

RECOMMENDED SHRUBS FOR ACID SOIL

Rhododendron 'Homebush'

Camellia x williamsii 'Donation'

Erica x williamsii 'P.D. Williams'

Eucryphia milliganii

Gaultheria shallon

Vaccinium parvifolium

Rhododendron wardii

Pernettya mucronata 'Wintertime'

Zenobia pulverulenta

DESIGN FOR A SHRUB BORDER
This plan includes a number of plants that provide interest in autumn and winter from foliage, form, flowers, and berries. Plants of different growth habit are combined to create a balanced design enlivened by contrasts.

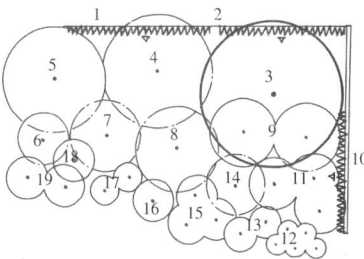

1 *Pyracantha coccinea*
2 *Pyracantha* 'Mohave'
3 *Hamamelis mollis*
4 *Garrya elliptica* 'James Roof'
5 *Viburnum* x *bodnantense*
6 *Perovskia atriplicifolia* 'Blue Spire'
7 *Daphne bholua*
8 *Viburnum tinus* 'Eve Price'
9 *Euonymus fortunei* 'Silver Queen'
10 *Jasminum nudiflorum*
11 *Daphne mezereum*
12 *Erica carnea* 'Vivellii'
13 *Ceratostigma willmottianum*
14 *Lonicera fragrantissima*
15 *Sarcococca confusa*
16 *Cotoneaster* 'Autumn Fire'
17 *Caryopteris* x *clandonensis*
   'Arthur Simmonds'
18 *Skimmia japonica* 'Fragrans'
19 *Skimmia japonica* subsp. *reevesiana*

account the shape, form, height, and spread of each shrub, as well as its ornamental qualities and any seasonal changes in its appearance.

The planting may rely almost entirely on a blend of foliage textures and colours, but other features may also play their part. Include shrubs with interesting shapes, for example, and others with colourful berries or stems to maintain interest throughout the year. Resist the temptation to rely on flowers, since their display may be impressive but transitory.

By careful selection, however, it is possible to sustain a long succession of flowers in the shrub border.

Some shrubs may be regarded as long-term plants while others tend to mature and fade quickly. When planning a border, space out the long-term shrubs so that they will not need thinning or drastic pruning to keep them in check once mature. Fast-growing shrubs may also be included but they should be thinned as soon as they threaten to crowd out the core planting of shrubs.

Herbaceous perennials, annuals, and other plants may be interplanted initially, so that in the short term the shrub border might have the same components as a mixed border. Dense planting, including ground cover, may help to keep down weeds although mulching is advisable to reduce weeds and water loss while the plants are becoming established.

Mixed borders

The idea of a mixed border is to combine a framework planting of shrubs with a variety of herbaceous plants to reap the benefits of both. Its main advantage is that the shrubs provide long-term, sometimes year-round, interest and a background to a succession of other plants. As the shrubs provide height and structure, there is less need to grow tall perennials that require staking than in a traditional herbaceous border.

The mixed border may be designed to suit various settings. If it is situated next to a wall, the planting may include a combination of wall-trained and other shrubs at the back as well as climbers, other plants being introduced in loosely shaped niches between shrubs in the foreground. In an island bed, shrubs are normally used to form an irregular core at the centre, surrounded by other plants in clumps or drifts.

Managing a mixed border is sometimes more complex than managing a shrub border, because the various

plants have different requirements. It is, however, one of the most effective ways of bringing together the wide-ranging qualities of many different groups of plants.

Specimen shrubs

Shrubs that are particularly attractive – perhaps because of their fine shape or a characteristic such as exquisite flowers or striking foliage – may be best planted as individual specimens, sited so that they can be seen from a number of viewpoints.

Suitable shrubs
Since a shrub grown in this way clearly stands out in the garden, it is important that its appearance warrants its prominent position. Shrubs with very shapely silhouettes are especially suitable, such as the dense, symmetrical cone of *Picea glauca* var. *albertiana* 'Conica', although a flowering shrub such as *Camellia japonica* 'Mathotiana' would also be an impressive focal point.

The long-term interest of the shrub must also stand up to the value placed on it. In a large garden, this may not be a problem, for a relatively short but magnificent display may be sufficient. A shrub occupying a prime spot in a small garden, on the other hand, needs to justify itself by contributing colour and form throughout the year or by having more than one interesting phase – flowers and good autumn foliage, for example.

RESTRICTED COLOUR BORDER
Here, a restricted colour scheme with a predominance of yellow, gold, and bright green creates a sunny, cheerful effect, with evergreen and deciduous shrubs including elders (Sambucus), *golden conifers, and* Euphorbia.

Siting a specimen shrub

When deciding where to site a specimen shrub, ensure its size will be in keeping with its position in the garden and that it relates well to the overall design. Often the best location is as the focal point of a view from a main window of the house or at the meeting point of two vistas. The background is as important as the shrub itself; usually, a uniform texture and colour, as provided by a dense, evergreen hedge or the green swathe of a lawn, forms the most complementary foil. There is, however, scope for experimenting with the positioning of specimen shrubs, particularly in combination with other garden features, such as a pool that creates appealing reflections. Before planting, roughly assess the effect of the shrub's scale and position in the design by substituting canes of the same height and width.

SPECIMEN SHRUB
In late spring and early summer, the spreading tiers of Viburnum plicatum 'Mariesii' *are richly clothed with* blooms but its unusual shape ensures its value as a strong feature throughout the year.

Wall shrubs

A border at the foot of a warm, sheltered wall is a prime site; although it often tends to be rather dry, if the plants are adequately watered, the conditions suit many shrubs that might otherwise be too tender.

Training shrubs against a wall is often the best option for lax shrubs such as *Forsythia suspensa* that make tangled growth unless supported. For a number of shrubs, it is the best way of displaying their ornamental features, such as the orange or red berries of pyracanthas. Some hardy shrubs, such as *Chaenomeles*, that may also be grown free-standing, look attractive wall-trained, and complement the unfussy background.

Sometimes no training is needed: shrubs such as myrtle (*Myrtus*) may simply be planted close to the foot of a wall for them to benefit from the warmth and shelter. Other shrubs such as *Buddleja crispa* do need training to flower well.

Dwarf and ground-cover shrubs

Planting low shrubs, such as many *Hebe* or *Daphne blagayana*, in raised beds or containers makes it easy to enjoy them at close quarters, as well as providing structure and long-term interest in the planting scheme. On a large scale, use low-growing shrubs to balance against contrasting, rounded, or upright forms in beds and borders.

These shrubs are also excellent where interest is needed at ground level; *Helianthemum* cultivars and a vast array of colourful heathers (*Calluna*, *Daboecia*, and *Erica*) brighten up the front of a mixed border or soften the hard edges of a path.

Some spread into an attractive carpet that forms a fine foil for other planting. Those that are relatively fast-growing may be used as ground cover (see pp.150–51). Ground-cover shrubs present one of the best solutions for sites such as steep banks that are difficult to cultivate; even in the unpromising, shady areas directly beneath trees, shrubs such as *Mahonia repens* and cultivars of *Euonymus fortunei* grow well.

Foliage

The substance and seasonal continuity of a garden depend to a large extent on foliage. Evergreen shrubs, in particular, hold the garden together all through the year. The leaves of deciduous shrubs – from spring growth to autumn leaf – also give a longer period of interest than most flowers.

Colour

Much may be made of foliage colour, which includes not only every shade of green but also silvers and greys, reds, and purples, as well as yellow, gold, and variegated forms.

The boldest leaf colour effects, such as the yellow of *Choisya ternata* 'Sundance', the red of the young growth of some *Pieris*, or the white-splashed green of *Euonymus fortunei* 'Silver Queen', may be used in much the same way as flower colour.

Shape and texture

There are many other attributes of shrub foliage that are worth exploiting in an ornamental display. Large or distinctively shaped leaves such as those of *Fatsia japonica* are particularly striking, and changes of texture, from smooth and glossy to matt and felted, also provide satisfying contrasts.

WALL-TRAINED SHRUBS
Growing a shrub such as this pyracantha against a wall enhances its display of ornamental, red berries.

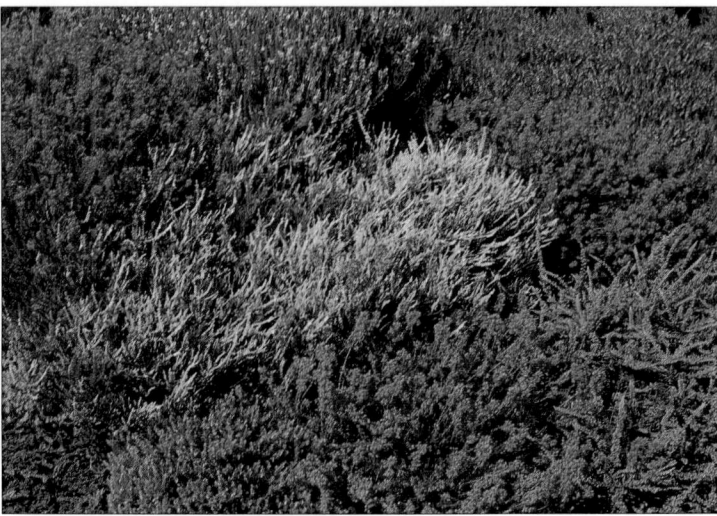

COLOURFUL GROUND COVER
To create a colourful patchwork effect use harmonizing and contrasting low-growing shrubs. Here, massed heathers make a fine display.

Flowers

Ranging from the tiny, pea-like flowers of many brooms (*Cytisus/ Genista*) to the large, heavy panicles of lilacs (*Syringa*), there is an impressive diversity of shrub flowers.

Colour and form

Shrubs have flowers in every colour, with endless variations of each; for example, shades of pink range from the pale pinkish-white of *Syringa yunnanensis* to the crimson of *Rhododendron* 'Hinodegiri'.

Sometimes it is the sheer mass of flowers that appeals, as with the dense blue clusters of *Ceanothus* or the sprays of star-like, yellow flowers of forsythias, while other shrubs – such as the exquisite but short-lived flowers of *Paeonia suffruticosa* – seduce by the sumptuous beauty of their individual blooms.

In a large garden it does not much matter that a plant's star turn is only brief; in a small garden, this may be a serious drawback, so consider a plant's form and foliage, too, if its floral display is very short.

Scent

While the appeal of some flowers lies largely in their colour and form, those that are scented give the garden another dimension. The flowers may be showy and also deliciously fragrant, as are many *Philadelphus,* or, like the minute flowers of *Sarcococca*, more muted in appearance but casting their fragrance through the garden in mid-winter.

Berries

Berrying shrubs are valuable for sustaining colour from late summer into winter, and also for attracting birds into the garden. On evergreens such as pyracanthas, bright berries framed by green foliage make an attractive contrast, while those on

ORNAMENTAL STEMS
An informal group of red-barked dogwoods (Cornus alba) forms a striking blaze of colour rising from a spreading mass of variegated Euonymus fortunei.

FLOWERS FOR SCENT
Fragrant shrubs are often best grown next to a path or patio so that their scent may be easily enjoyed. This sweetly perfumed Carpenteria californica *also benefits from the warmth and shelter of the wall behind it.*

deciduous shrubs such as *Viburnum opulus* are seen against a changing backdrop of autumn foliage followed by bare winter stems.

Orange and red berries are common, but there are other colours – from the yellow of *Cotoneaster* 'Rothschildianus' to the pretty pink of *Pernettya mucronata* 'Seashell'.

Bear in mind that with some species of shrubs male and female flowers are borne on separate plants. Thus satisfactory fruiting is only achieved when male and female plants are grown in proximity.

Bark and stems

In winter, the silhouettes of bare stems may be very striking. As well as their sculptural simplicity, some, such as dogwoods (*Cornus*), are strongly coloured while others, for example *Salix irrorata*, are overlaid with an attractive, glaucous bloom.

Group a few shrubs of the same type together to reap the benefit of their massed stems, or site a single

fine specimen against a simple background. Imagine the brilliant red stems of *Cornus alba* 'Sibirica' offset by a plain, white wall, or the chalk-white skeleton of *Rubus biflorus* by a dark one.

The delicate tracery of fine stems is often overlooked unless it is highlighted by vivid colouring, but unusual shapes and heavily thorned or contorted shoots provide added interest. The bizarrely twisted stems of *Corylus avellana* 'Contorta' and *Salix x erythroflexuosa* make them interesting curiosities to set against a plain wall or plants of more familiar growth pattern.

Many shrubs grown for their stems require regular pruning, because it is the new wood that is most effective (see "Coppicing and pollarding shrubs", p.79).

Shrubs in containers

Provided that they are watered regularly, many shrubs adapt happily to life in containers. Grown in this way, they make versatile as well as ornamental features. Use them as living sculptures to provide strong shapes and a framework to offset other planting. An evergreen shrub or dwarf conifer forms a fine centrepiece in a tub or planter all year round, which may be complemented by bulbs in spring and colourful and trailing annuals in summer.

A container-grown shrub is particularly valuable in a small, paved garden. It may be used alone as an isolated specimen or combined with a changing display of other plants in containers. In a larger garden, a single, handsomely potted shrub may make a more striking focal point

than a piece of garden statuary, for example. Container-grown shrubs may introduce a formal note simply, as a pair flanking a flight of steps or an archway, or, more elaborately, making a symmetrical framework or an avenue in grander schemes.

Selecting plants

The most suitable shrubs are those with a long season of interest. Good examples for containers include evergreen camellias and rhododendrons, which remain attractive even after their flowers have faded. For valuable foliage effects, consider the tender *Chamaerops humilis*, which has huge, palm-like, glossy fans, and conifers with their wide range of colours and textures.

Deciduous foliage can change from spring to autumn and, in the case of Japanese maples (*Acer palmatum*), an intricate pattern of delicate stems remains when all the leaves have fallen. Shrubs such as *Spiraea japonica* 'Goldflame', with its strikingly coloured leaves and heads of rose-pink flowers, often look particularly fine grown in an ornamental container.

Practical advantages

An advantage of growing shrubs in containers is that tender plants, such as *Nerium oleander* and palms, may be used to give the garden a Mediterranean or subtropical look in the summer, and then be moved to a protected site for winter. It is also an excellent way of including shrubs that would not otherwise tolerate the soil of the open garden: for example, given lime-free water and ericaceous compost, camellias and rhododendrons may be grown in pots or other containers even in chalky areas.

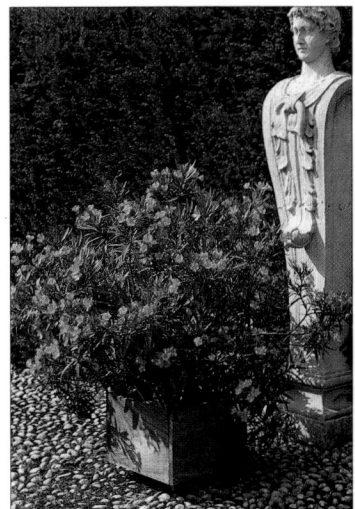

GROWING IN CONTAINERS
A bright Nerium oleander *brings colour to a cobbled area.*

Planter's guide to shrubs

EXPOSED SITES

Shrubs that tolerate exposed or windy sites; those marked ✿ are not suitable for coastal sites

Arctostaphylos uva-ursi ✿
Bupleurum fruticosum
Calluna vulgaris (and cvs)
Cassinia fulvida
Cistus, some ✿
Cordyline ✿
Cotoneaster (dwarf spp.),
    C. horizontalis
Elaeagnus commutata
Erica carnea (and cvs) ✿
Escallonia
Euonymus fortunei
    (and cvs)
Fuchsia magellanica
    (and cvs)

Fuchsia magellanica

Gaultheria shallon ✿
Genista, some ✿
Griselinia, some ✿
Halimodendron halodendron
Hebe, some ✿
Hippophäe rhamnoides
Ilex aquifolium
Lavatera
Olearia, some ✿
Ozothamnus, some ✿
Phormium
Prunus spinosa ✿
Pyracantha
Rhamnus alaternus
Rhododendron ponticum ✿
Salix
Senecio, some ✿
Spartium
Spiraea
Tamarix
Ulex
Yucca, some ✿

SHELTERED SITES

Shrubs that prefer sheltered sites

Abelia floribunda ✿
Abutilon, some ✿
Acer palmatum (cvs)
Ardisia ✿
Banksia ✿
Beschorneria ✿
Bouvardia ✿
Brachyglottis ✿
Citrus ✿
Coprosma ✿
Datura ✿
Dendromecon rigida ✿
Euryops pectinatus ✿
Musa basjoo ✿
Nerium ✿
Rhododendron maddenii (and
    subsection), *R. vireya* (sections) ✿

WALL SHRUBS

Abelia, some ✿
Abutilon, some ✿
Acacia dealbata ✿
Azara, some ✿
Buddleja crispa
Callistemon, some ✿
Camellia, some ✿
Ceanothus, some ✿
Cestrum, some ✿
Chaenomeles
Colquhounia
Daphne bholua
Fremontodendron
Itea ilicifolia
Pyracantha
Solanum crispum 'Glasnevin',
    S. jasminoides ✿

AIR POLLUTION

Shrubs that tolerate polluted air

Aucuba
Berberis
Buddleja davidii
Camellia japonica (and cvs)
Cornus stolonifera
Cotoneaster
Elaeagnus
Euonymus japonicus
Fatsia japonica
Fuchsia magellanica (and cvs)
Garrya
Ilex x *altaclerensis*, *I. aquifolium*
Leycesteria, some ✿
Ligustrum
Lonicera pileata
Magnolia grandiflora
Mahonia aquifolium
Philadelphus
Phillyrea
Salix
Spiraea
Viburnum

DRY SHADE

Shrubs that tolerate dry shade

Aucuba
Cornus canadensis
Daphne laureola
Euonymus fortunei, *E. japonicus*
Fatsia japonica
Hedera, some ✿
Ilex aquifolium
Pachysandra

MOIST SHADE

Shrubs that prefer moist shade

Aucuba
Buxus sempervirens
Camellia japonica
Cornus canadensis
Daphne laureola
Euonymus fortunei, *E. japonicus*
Fatsia japonica

*Sarcococca
hookeriana
var. digyna*

Ilex aquifolium
Lonicera pileata
Mahonia aquifolium
Osmanthus, some ✿
Rubus tricolor
Sarcococca
Skimmia
Vinca

TWO OR MORE SEASONS OF INTEREST

All year round
Acacia baileyana ✿
Ardisia japonica ✿
Convolvulus cneorum
Elaeagnus x *ebbingei* 'Gilt Edge'
Euryops acraeus
Lavandula stoechas
Ozothamnus ledifolius

Winter/Spring
Berberis temolaica
Corylus avellana 'Contorta'
Salix irrorata

Spring/Summer
Calycanthus occidentalis
Pieris 'Forest Flame'

Spring/Autumn
Cornus 'Eddie's White Wonder'

Summer/Autumn
Citrus 'Meyer's Lemon' ✿
Cornus mas 'Variegata'
Cotinus coggygria 'Flame'
Cotoneaster conspicuus
Dipelta yunnanensis
Hydrangea quercifolia
    'Snowflake'
Lonicera korolkowii
Myrtus communis var.
    tarentina

*Myrtus
communis*

Neillia thibetica
Phlomis chrysophylla
Pyracantha
Rosa 'Frau Dagmar Hastrup',
    R. moyesii 'Geranium'

Autumn/Winter
Arbutus unedo
Berberis temolaica
Cornus mas 'Variegata'

FRAGRANT FLOWERS

Abeliophyllum distichum
Buddleja alternifolia
Camellia sasanqua
Choisya 'Aztec Pearl', *C. ternata*
Clethra alnifolia 'Paniculata'
Colletia armata 'Rosea'
Cytisus battandieri
Daphne bholua, *D. blagayana*,
    D. cneorum, *D. odora*
Elaeagnus
Erica lusitanica
Hamamelis mollis 'Pallida'
Lonicera x *purpusii* 'Winter
    Beauty', *L. standishii*
Luculia gratissima
Magnolia sieboldii,
    M. x *thompsoniana*
Mahonia japonica
Osmanthus delavayi
Philadelphus (many)
Pittosporum tobira
Rhododendron auriculatum,
    R. 'Countess of Haddington' ✿,
    R. edgeworthii ✿,
    R. 'Fragrantissima' ✿, *R.*, Ghent
    hybrids, *R.*, Loderi group,
    R. luteum, *R. occidentale* (and
    hybrids), *R.* 'Polar Bear',
    R., Rustica hybrids, *R. viscosum*
Sarcococca
Viburnum (many)

*Rhododendron
luteum*

AROMATIC FOLIAGE

Caryopteris
Prostanthera ✿
Ruta graveolens
Santolina
Skimmia x *confusa*

ARCHITECTURAL SHRUBS

Agave ✿
Aralia elata 'Aureo-variegata'
Chamaerops ✿
Cocos ✿
Cordyline ✿
Cycas revoluta ✿
Dracaena ✿
Eriobotrya japonica
Howea ✿
Jubaea ✿
Pandanus ✿
Phoenix ✿
Phormium
Sabal ✿
Yucca, some ✿

KEY
✿ Not hardy

Soil preparation and planting

A wide range of shrubs can be grown in most gardens even if the soil falls short of ideal. The ideal soil is a fertile, well-drained but moisture-retentive loam. Improving the drainage of wet soils and, by the addition of humus, the structure and moisture-holding properties of dry soils greatly increases the range of shrubs that may be grown. The soil acidity or alkalinity, another factor limiting the range of plants that can be grown, may also be modified.

Important though these improvements may be, garden soil will still naturally tend towards being moist or dry, heavy or light, and acidic or alkaline. The best shrubs for your garden are those suited to the growing conditions available.

Selecting shrubs

Shrubs may be bought direct from garden centres, nurseries, and non-specialist outlets such as supermarkets. Some nurseries also sell shrubs by mail order; plants are normally dispatched during their dormant period. They are sold in containers, root-balled, or bare-root.

Shrubs on sale should be accurately labelled, healthy, undamaged, and free of pests and diseases. When buying direct, inspect the plants thoroughly and select a specimen with evenly distributed branches close to ground level or, with standard shrubs, at the head of a clear stem of the desired height. Shrubs sold in the warm, dry atmosphere of a supermarket have a short shelf life. Reliable suppliers may give a year's guarantee to replace the shrub if it is not true to name or if it dies within the first year, provided that it has been given reasonable care.

Shrubs in containers

Shrubs are most commonly sold as container-grown specimens, the containers ranging from rigid pots to plastic bags. Most shrubs sold in this way have been container-grown throughout their lives. Some are field-grown and potted up (containerized) in the season before sale to prolong their sale life. The two are difficult to distinguish, although container-grown shrubs normally have better-established root systems (often visible through the drainage holes of the pot).

If possible, slide the shrub out of its container; the roots should show healthy, white tips and the root system, if well established, will retain all or most of the compost from the pot. Reject plants with poorly developed root systems and those that are pot-bound (with roots protruding from the container), since these rarely grow well.

A major advantage of container-grown shrubs is that they may be bought and planted out at any time, except when there are extremes of temperature or drought. Containerized shrubs can be safely planted out in winter, but at other times may be slow to establish unless they have a well-developed root system.

Bare-root shrubs

Deciduous shrubs that are easily propagated are sometimes lifted from the open ground during their dormant season and sold with their roots bare of soil. The buying season for these bare-root shrubs is from autumn to spring. To prevent desiccation, they are normally heeled into the ground until they are sold. Before purchasing, check that bare-root shrubs have an evenly developed, fibrous root system.

Root-balled shrubs

These shrubs, usually available in autumn or early spring, have been grown in open ground, then lifted with soil around their root balls; the root balls are wrapped in hessian or netting. Conifers are often sold in this way. Always check that the wrapping is intact, as otherwise the roots may have been exposed to drying wind, and that the root ball is firm.

SELECTING A SHRUB

CONTAINER-GROWN SHRUBS

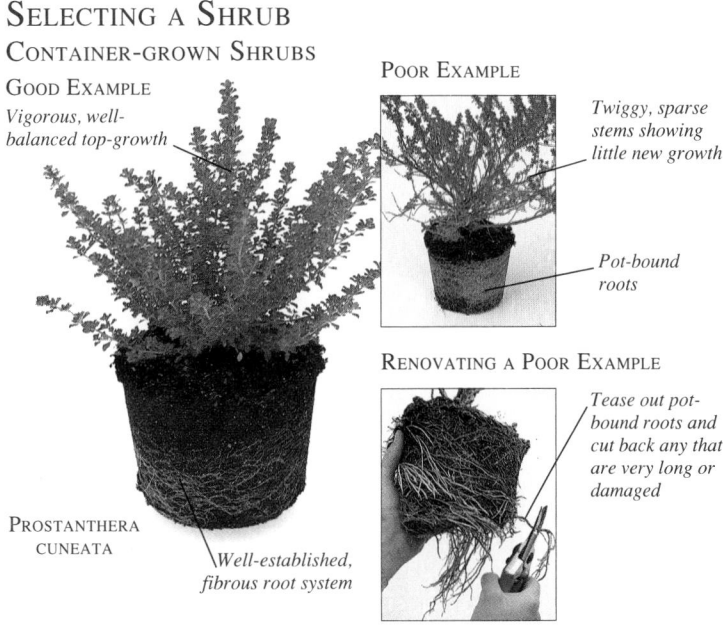

GOOD EXAMPLE

Vigorous, well-balanced top-growth

POOR EXAMPLE

Twiggy, sparse stems showing little new growth

Pot-bound roots

PROSTANTHERA CUNEATA

Well-established, fibrous root system

RENOVATING A POOR EXAMPLE

Tease out pot-bound roots and cut back any that are very long or damaged

GOOD EXAMPLE

Well-developed, even branch framework

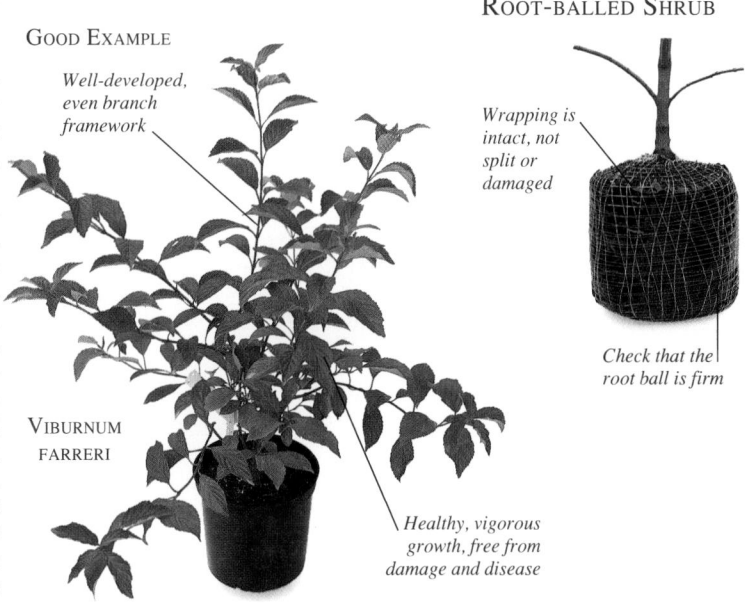

VIBURNUM FARRERI

Healthy, vigorous growth, free from damage and disease

ROOT-BALLED SHRUB

Wrapping is intact, not split or damaged

Check that the root ball is firm

SHRUBS THAT PREFER SANDY SOIL

Berberis empetrifolia
Calluna vulgaris (and cvs)
Ceanothus thyrsiflorus (and forms)
Cistus x cyprius

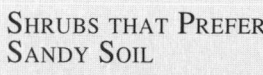

Cistus x cyprius

Cytisus scoparius (and forms)
Erica arborea var. alpina, E. cinerea (and cvs)
Fuchsia magellanica (and cvs)
Genista tinctoria
Hakea lissosperma
Halimodendron halodendron
Helianthemum
Helichrysum, some ✿
Lavandula, some ✿
Olearia, some ✿
Ozothamnus, some ✿
Phlomis
Phormium
Spartium junceum
Tamarix
Ulex europaeus
Yucca gloriosa

SHRUBS THAT TOLERATE CLAY SOIL

Amelanchier
Aralia ♦
Aronia arbutifolia ♦
Aucuba
Berberis ♦

Chaenomeles x superba 'Nicoline'

Chaenomeles x superba ♦
Citrus ✿
Clethra alnifolia ♦
Cornus alba 'Sibirica' ♦
Cotoneaster ♦
Forsythia
Garrya
Hippophäe
Kalmia latifolia
Lonicera, some ✿
Mahonia x media group ♦
Philadelphus
Pyracantha
Salix caprea ♦
Sambucus racemosa ♦
Taxus
Tetrapanax papyriferus ✿
Viburnum opulus ♦

KEY
✿ Not hardy
♦ Tolerates waterlogged soil

When to plant

Autumn to spring is the planting season for bare-root and root-balled shrubs, and the optimum time for container-grown and containerized shrubs. Planting in autumn allows the root system to establish while the ground is still warm, so the shrub should be growing vigorously before dry weather the next summer.

Planting may be carried out during mild weather in winter, but not when the ground is frozen. Roots will not grow away in very cold soil, and there is a risk that they may freeze and be killed.

The major disadvantage of spring planting is that top-growth is likely to develop before the roots establish and, if there is an early spell of dry weather, watering may be required to help the plants to survive.

Soil preparation

Many shrubs are potentially long-lived, so the ground needs to be thoroughly prepared before planting. The aim should be to cultivate an area well beyond the planting site for an individual shrub and, preferably, the entire bed.

The best seasons for cultivation are late summer and autumn. Remove or kill all weeds first, taking particular care to eradicate perennials (see "Weeds", pp.573–7). Double dig (see p.526), incorporating an 8–10cm (3–4in) layer of well-rotted organic matter in the lower trench. If this is impracticable, work large quantities of organic matter into the top 30–45cm (12–18in) of the soil. Add fertilizer if appropriate (see "Soil nutrients and fertilizers", pp.530–31).

How to plant

The planting hole for a shrub must be wide enough to accommodate the shrub's root ball. For container-grown or root-balled plants, make the hole twice the width of the contained root mass, or as much as three times the width if planting in clay soils. For bare-root shrubs, the hole must be large enough to allow the plant's roots to be spread out fully. The hole must also be sufficiently deep to allow the shrub to be planted at the same level as it was in its container or in the open ground. This is indicated by the soil mark – a dark mark near the base of the stem. A cane laid across the top of the planting hole provides a useful guide to the depth of planting. Treatment of a containerized shrub depends on how developed the root system is when removed from the pot. If the compost falls away, plant as for a bare-root shrub; if it does not, treat as if container-grown. Remove the hessian or netting surrounding a root-balled shrub after it is in the hole. When backfilling the hole, shake a bare-root plant gently to settle the soil. Firm the soil in stages but do not compact clay soils.

To improve drainage around shrubs planted in clay soils, plant

---

PLANTING A WALL SHRUB

 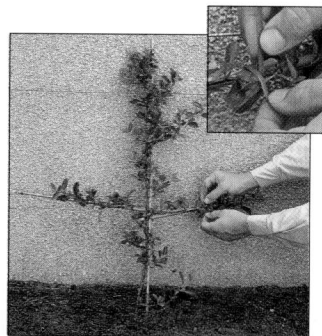

1 Dig a hole at least 22cm (9in) away from the wall. Plant the shrub (here a pyracantha) and tie in the supporting cane to a wire.

2 Firm back the soil. Secure lateral bamboo canes to the central cane and to the wires, so that the sideshoots can be supported and tied in (see inset).

PLANTING A CONTAINER-GROWN SHRUB

    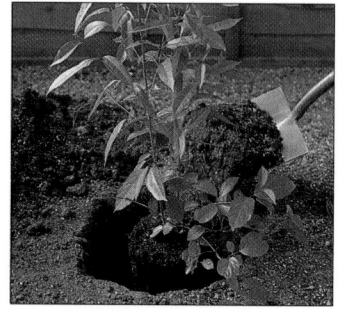

1 Dig a hole about twice the width of the shrub's root ball (here a Viburnum). Mix the removed soil with organic matter. Fork over the base and sides of the hole.

2 Placing one hand on top of the compost and around the shrub to support it, carefully ease the plant out of its container. Place the shrub in the prepared hole.

3 Lay a cane alongside to check that the soil level is the same as before. Adjust the planting depth, if necessary, by adding or removing topsoil beneath the shrub.

4 Backfill around the shrub with the removed soil and organic matter mixture, firming the soil in stages to prevent air pockets from forming.

5 Once the hole has been filled with the planting mixture, carefully firm the soil around the shrub with your heel or hands.

6 Prune any diseased or damaged wood back to healthy growth and cut back any inward-growing or crossing stems to an outward-growing shoot or bud. You should also remove any very long, weak, or straggly stems, or those that mar the overall balance of the shrub's framework.

7 Water the shrub thoroughly; apply a mulch of well-rotted compost or pulverized bark about 5–7cm (2–3in) deep and 30–45cm (12–18in) wide around the shrub.

the shrub slightly proud of the soil level and mound soil around the exposed section of the root ball up to the level of the soil mark. On sandy soils, plant the shrub in a slight dip to channel water around the plant's roots. Water the shrub and mulch.

Planting wall shrubs

Some shrubs may be trained on wires fixed to a wall or fence. Plant these as for free-standing shrubs, at least 22cm (9in) from the wall so that the roots are not in its rain shadow, and lean the plant in towards the wall. Support the main stem and laterals of the shrub with canes, which are then tied into the wires (see also "Wall shrubs", p.80).

Staking

Shrubs do not normally need staking, except for large, root-bound specimens and standards. The former, which ideally should not be selected, will almost certainly need some support in their first year or two at least, until their roots begin to spread out and they become stable.

The best method for any shrub that branches from near ground level is to brace the shrub with guys fixed to three stakes spaced evenly around a circle with a radius of about 1m (3ft) centred on the shrub. To prevent bark damage, cover the guys where they touch the branches with rubber or similar material (see also ORNAMENTAL TREES, "Staking", p.40).

For standards, insert the stake in the planting hole before planting to avoid damaging the root system. The top of the stake should be just below the first branches. Secure the stem to the stake, using a proprietary tie with a spacer or a homemade figure-of-eight tie to prevent chafing.

STAKING A STANDARD SHRUB

 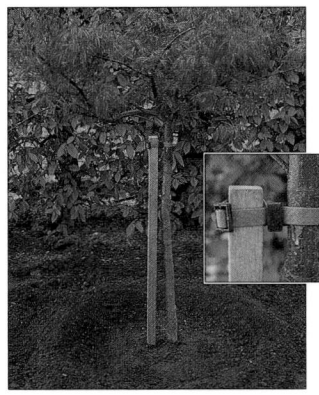

1 *Drive a stake into the hole just off-centre; the stake should reach to just below the head of the shrub after planting. Plant the shrub next to the stake.*

2 *If the depth is correct, backfill and firm in. On free-draining soil, form a dip around the shrub to retain moisture. Secure the stem with a suitable tie (see inset).*

Protecting newly planted shrubs

Newly planted shrubs may suffer from desiccation or cold if not protected. Broad-leaved evergreens and conifers in exposed positions are particularly vulnerable.

A screen of hessian or mesh significantly reduces the drying force of cold winds. Erect a strong, wooden framework 30cm (12in) away from the windward side of the shrub needing protection. Tack the hessian or the mesh to the frame, which should extend at least 30cm (12in) above and either side of the shrub. More complete protection is given by surrounding individual plants with a four-sided framework to which hessian or mesh is tacked.

Another measure, which may be used either alone or in addition to screening, is to spray the plants with an anti-transpirant to reduce drying out. Apply a thin film of spray to both sides of the leaves.

A mulch spread around the base of the shrub will help to protect the roots from ground frost. It is best to spread the mulch during periods of mild weather, preferably when the ground is reasonably warm and damp.

In areas of heavy snow, particularly vulnerable, evergreen shrubs may need additional protection. This is best provided by a timber and chicken-wire cage. Dislodge any heavy accumulations of snow promptly. More extreme measures may be needed to protect half-hardy and tender shrubs (see FROST AND WIND PROTECTION, pp. 520–21).

When removing the insulation in spring, check for pests and diseases that may have benefited from the winter protection.

Planting shrubs in containers

Late summer to autumn is the main period for planting shrubs in containers, although container-grown shrubs may be planted in an ornamental pot at most times.

Select a container that is the right size for the shrub. When transplanting a shrub, the new container should be about 5cm (2in) larger in depth and diameter than the previous one. If the container has already been used, scrub its inside surface thoroughly.

Heavy containers should be placed in position before planting. Stand the container on bricks or blocks to allow free drainage. Place broken crocks over the drainage holes and then add a 2.5cm (1in) layer of drainage material, such as coarse gravel.

A loam-based compost, which is nutrient-rich, is preferable to a peat-based compost, which contains only limited, added nutrients. Shrubs are likely to remain in their containers for years and any grown in peat-based composts will require frequent feeding. Additionally, peat-based composts dry out more rapidly than loam-based ones. Use an ericaceous compost for rhododendrons and other lime-haters, or to obtain blue flowers on hydrangeas. Ensure that the soil mark is level with the compost surface.

With container planting, ensure that the compost is at least 4cm (1¹/₂in) below the rim to allow room for mulching and watering.

Routine care

THE following guidelines for maintenance are generally applicable, although not all shrubs have the same requirements. Newly planted shrubs usually need watering and fertilizing, while those planted in containers should also be periodically top-dressed or repotted. In addition, dead-heading, removing suckers, weeding, and controlling pests and diseases may all be necessary.

Watering

Established shrubs need watering only in periods of prolonged drought, but young specimens may need regular watering. Apply the water to the ground around the shrub, soaking the soil. Do not water often and lightly, since this encourages root growth close to the surface. Shallow roots make shrubs vulnerable in drought conditions. The best time to water is in the evening, when evaporation is minimal.

Fertilizing and mulching

Most shrubs benefit from regular applications of organic or inorganic fertilizers. These are available in a variety of forms.

Mulching with well-rotted, bulky manures helps soil conserve moisture and, if nutrient-rich, improves soil fertility. It also moderates extremes of temperature around the roots and inhibits weeds.

Fertilizers

Shrubs, especially if pruned regularly, are usually fed with slow-release fertilizers, which are best applied in early spring. Some of these fertilizers release their nutrients only when temperatures are high enough for plants to use them. A standard rate of application is 60g/sq m (2oz/sq yd).

Quick-release powder fertilizers are useful to boost growth as it commences in spring. Liquid fertilizers work even faster than powders, and these should be applied once the shrub is in growth.

Fertilizers in granular or powder form should be worked into the soil over an area slightly wider than the spread of the top-growth of the shrub. With surface-rooting shrubs, allow the fertilizer to leach in naturally or water it in to avoid the risk of the roots being injured by forking. The application of fertilizers may affect the soil's pH level; most artificial fertilizers, for example, make the soil more acidic (see also "Soil nutrients and fertilizers", pp.530–31).

Mulches

Apply the mulch around newly planted shrubs over an area about 45cm (18in) wider in diameter than the plant's root system. The mulch around established shrubs should extend beyond the area of top-growth by 15–30cm (6–12in). A mulch of bark chippings, wood chips, or manure should be 5–10cm (2–4in) deep but kept clear of the stems of the shrub. Do not apply any mulch in cold weather or when the soil is dry.

Weeding

Weeds compete for nutrients and moisture, so it is essential to clear the ground of all weeds before planting. The area around newly planted ground-cover shrubs needs weeding until the plants form dense growth that suppresses competition. For treatment, see "Weeds", pp.573–7.

Removing suckers

Some grafted shrubs, including rhododendrons, are prone to producing growths, or suckers, beneath the graft union, from either stems or roots. Rub out suckers between finger and thumb as soon as they are noticed: if too large to treat in this way, cut them off as close as possible to the stems or roots from which they are growing. Pulling them off helps to remove any dormant growth buds, but take care not to damage the stem or root. Watch for further growth.

Reversion and mutation

Many variegated shrubs are propagated from green-leaved plants that have produced mutated branches, known as sports. From time to time, branches of variegated shrubs revert to the original foliage of the parent plant or mutate to plain cream or yellow leaves. Since these branches are usually more vigorous, they eventually crowd out those showing variegation, and should be cut out.

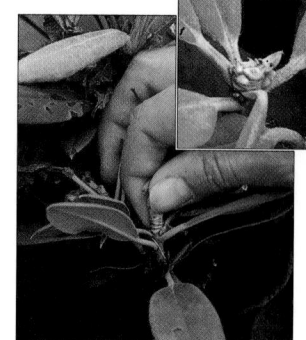
Dead-heading

Some shrubs, including rhododendrons, lilacs (*Syringa*), and *Kalmia*, benefit if their faded flowerheads are promptly removed, where practicable, before seed sets. Removing old flowers diverts energy into growth, improving the flowering potential for the following season, but it is not essential to the health of a shrub.

To avoid damage to new growth buds, dead-head as soon as the flowers fade, using fingers and thumb to pick off each one where it joins the stem. Most flowerheads come away cleanly but any snags should be trimmed with secateurs.

HOW TO REMOVE SUCKERS

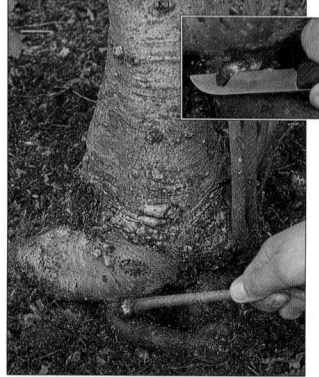

SUCKER REMOVAL
Pull or cut off the sucker (here on a Hamamelis*) at the base; if it is pulled off, pare over the wound to leave a clean cut (see inset).*

RECOGNIZING SUCKERS
A sucker may usually be distinguished by its leaves: a normal stem from the top-growth, left; a sucker from the root, right.

REMOVING NON-VARIEGATED AND REVERTED SHOOTS

NON-VARIEGATED SHOOT
With variegated shrubs (here Euonymus fortunei 'Emerald 'n' Gold')*, cut any plain shoots back to the variegated growth.*

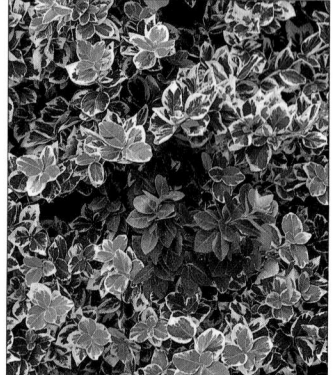

REVERTED SHOOT
Cut back reverted shoots (here on E. f. 'Emerald Gaiety') to the main stem. If necessary, remove the entire stem.

Maintaining shrubs in containers

Container-grown shrubs need more care and attention than those grown in open ground, since they have less access to any available moisture and nutrients.

Watering

Even in rainy weather conditions, check the compost at least once or twice a week, since the canopy formed by the leaves often prevents rain from reaching the compost beneath. In windy weather, plants are likely to need additional watering, since wind can cause rapid moisture loss.

The container itself also affects the rate at which the compost dries out – more quickly in terracotta pots than in wooden or plastic ones. When watering, soak the compost thoroughly until water starts to drain through the holes in the base of the container.

Feeding

Use a quick-release, balanced liquid fertilizer two or three times between the start of growth in early spring and mid-summer, at the rate recommended by the manufacturer.

Repotting and top-dressing

Until shrubs reach maturity, repot them every year or two in spring. When mature, instead of repotting just remove the top 5–10cm (2–4in) of compost in spring and replace it with a top-dressing of fresh compost and a slow-release fertilizer. Surface-rooting shrubs might be damaged by this, so ease the plant out of its container, take compost from the bottom, and replace it with a smaller quantity of enriched compost. The shrub will sit lower than before, leaving room for a top-dressing. Root pruning may be necessary when repotting a shrub if the roots are congested.

TOP-DRESSING

1 *If not repotting, top-dress shrubs in pots (here a rhododendron) annually. First, remove the top 5–10cm (2–4in) of the old compost, taking care not to damage the roots.*

2 *Replace with fresh compost to the same level as before. Water well and apply a mulch of bark chippings or grit if required.*

REPOTTING A CONTAINER-PLANTED SHRUB

1 *If a shrub (here Cestrum elegans) is lacking in vigour and appears either unbalanced or too large for its present container, it will almost certainly benefit from being repotted.*

2 *Carefully lay the shrub on its side; then, supporting the main stems with one hand, ease it out of its container. If necessary, slide a long-bladed knife between compost and pot to loosen the root ball.*

3 *If the roots have become very congested, gently tease them out. Remove the surface compost and any moss or weeds. Prune back about a quarter of the non-fibrous roots by up to two-thirds.*

6 *Leave 2.5–5cm (1–2in) of space below the rim of the container to allow for watering and top-dressing. Prune out any dead, twiggy, or damaged growth and remove any snags that may have been left by broken stems (see inset). Carry out additional pruning as necessary to create a well-balanced framework of stems.*

4 *Place crocks over the drainage holes of the pot and cover these with compost. Position the plant in the pot, spreading its roots out evenly.*

5 *Add more compost around the roots, gently firming it in stages, until the compost is at the same level on the plant as it was in its previous pot.*

Moving an established shrub

Careful selection and siting of a shrub should make transplanting unnecessary, although sometimes it may be desirable or unavoidable. In general, the younger the shrub, the more likely it is to re-establish after being moved.

When to transplant

Most young shrubs may be lifted bare-root when dormant. Established shrubs that have large root systems should be lifted with a ball of soil around the roots before being moved. Autumn is the best time to do this.

Root-balling a shrub

Most often, it is best to root-ball a shrub so that root damage is kept to a minimum. Prepare the new planting position before lifting the shrub.

Dig a trench around the shrub just beyond the spread of its branches. Cut through woody roots but leave fibrous ones intact. Use a fork to loosen the soil around the root ball and reduce its size. Then undercut it with a spade and use secateurs to sever any woody tap roots.

Once the root ball is free, work a sheet of hessian or similar material underneath it, tipping the shrub from side to side carefully so that the soil is not disturbed. Tie the hessian firmly around the ball, lift the shrub from the hole, and transplant it. Remove the hessian before replanting.

The shrub needs the same treatment as one that has been planted for the first time, but it may take longer to re-establish (see p.71).

Shrub problems

Plants are less likely to succumb to pest attack or disease if they are given good growing conditions and care. Many problems originate from poor drainage, lack of moisture, planting too deeply, compaction of the soil, or exposure to temperature extremes in an unsuitable site.

Physical damage

Wounds caused by a jagged pruning cut, a badly placed cut, or pruning at the wrong time may allow disease fungi to establish. This may also cause dieback. Mechanical wounding of bark, stems, or roots, for example by lawnmowers, also provides an entry point for disease.

Pests and diseases

As shrubs age, they lose vigour and become more prone to pests and diseases. Old or diseased shrubs that have lost their vigour are rarely worth saving and should be replaced.

Pests and diseases most likely to affect shrubs are aphids (p.550), red spider mites (p.550), fireblight (p.553), honey fungus (p.569), *Phytophthora* stem rots (see "*Phytophthora* root rots", p.558), and powdery mildew (p.550). Be alert to the signs of a problem, which include streaking and changes of foliage colour, drooping leaves, loss of leaves, distorted growth, and the development of fungi.

Maintaining good garden hygiene minimizes the chance of pests and diseases establishing a foothold. Remove dead and diseased wood, burning whatever is diseased, and keep the ground around a shrub free of debris such as old fruit.

Frost and wind

When selecting and siting shrubs it is vital to take account of the general weather pattern of the area as well as the garden's own individual microclimate; it is almost impossible, however, to take precautions against freak extremes of temperature or exceptional winds.

There is a wide range of hardy shrubs available and many gardeners choose to rely on these rather than risk the loss of more tender specimens. If growing shrubs that are of borderline hardiness for the area, then it is worth using the appropriate frost and wind protection methods (see pp.520–21).

Container-grown shrubs are more vulnerable to extremes of weather than those grown in the open garden. In areas where temperatures fall only occasionally below freezing, most container-grown hardy shrubs may be overwintered outdoors (except those, such as camellias, that are root-tender). In colder areas, however, move shrubs indoors where the ambient daytime temperature is about 7–13°C (45–55°F) or higher, according to species.

TRANSPLANTING A SHRUB

1 *Using a spade, mark out a circle around the extent of the shrub's branches (here* Ilex aquifolium *'Golden Milkboy'). If necessary, tie in any trailing stems or wrap the shrub in hessian to prevent the stems from being damaged.*

2 *Dig a trench around the circle, then use a fork to loosen the soil around the root ball. Take care not to damage any fibrous roots.*

3 *Continue carefully to fork away soil from around the shrub's root ball to reduce its size and weight.*

4 *Undercut the root ball with a spade, cutting through woody roots if necessary to separate them from the surrounding soil.*

5 *Roll up a length of hessian. Tilt the shrub to one side and unroll the hessian beneath the root ball. Tilt the root ball the other way, and unroll the rest of the hessian.*

6 *Pull the hessian up around the root ball and tie it securely. Remove the shrub from its hole and transport it to its new position.*

7 *Remove the hessian and replant the shrub in the new, prepared hole with the soil mark at the same level as before. Firm, water well, and mulch.*

Pruning and training

SOME shrubs, particularly evergreens of naturally compact habit such as *Sarcococca*, make attractive plants with little or no pruning or training. They may require no more than the removal of dead, damaged, and diseased wood. If left untreated, this will be unsightly and, more seriously, may put the health of the whole shrub in jeopardy. Many shrubs, however, need pruning or a combination of pruning and training in order to realize their full ornamental potential.

Aims and effects of pruning and training

The most common requirement is for formative pruning that creates a vigorous and well-shaped shrub. Many shrubs also require a regular regime of pruning to maintain or enhance the ornamental quality of their flowers, fruit, foliage, or stems. The timing of this pruning, which may often be critical, varies depending on the growth pattern of the shrub and the effect desired.

Pruning can also be a way of bringing neglected and overgrown plants back to healthy, manageable growth. It is a matter of judgment whether a shrub warrants being rescued. Replacement is often the best course when a shrub requires regular cutting back because it is too large for the space available.

Shrubs grown as topiary or hedges require specialized pruning from their formative stage. For further information see TOPIARY, pp.52–3, and HEDGES AND SCREENS, pp.60–62.

In training, the gardener plays an active role in directing the growth of plants. Most shrubs grown in the open require no training at all. Shrubs grown against supports, however, normally need a combination of pruning and training to form a well-spaced framework of branches.

Principles of pruning and training

Pruning normally stimulates growth. The terminal shoot or growth bud of a stem is often dominant, inhibiting by chemical means the growth of buds or shoots below it. Pruning that removes the ends of stems affects the control mechanism, resulting in more vigorous development of lower shoots or growth buds.

WHERE TO CUT

OPPOSITE SHOOTS
Prune stems with opposite buds to just above a strong pair of buds or shoots, using a clean, straight cut.

ALTERNATE SHOOTS
For shrubs with alternate buds, prune to just above a bud or shoot, using a clean, angled cut.

MAKING AN ANGLED CUT
Angle the cut so that its lowest point is opposite the base of the bud and the top just clears the bud.

Hard or light pruning
Hard pruning promotes more vigorous growth than light pruning; this needs to be borne in mind when correcting the shape of an unbalanced shrub. Hard cutting back of vigorous growth often encourages even stronger growth. Prune weak growth hard but strong growth only lightly.

How to prune
Pruning wounds, like other injuries that a shrub might suffer, are possible entry points for disease. The risk is reduced by making well-placed, clean cuts with sharp tools.

Stems with alternate or whorled arrangements of growth buds should be cut just above a bud pointing in the desired direction of growth – for example, an outward-facing bud that will not cross another shoot as its growth develops. Use an angled cut, starting opposite a healthy growth bud, and slant the cut so that it finishes slightly above the bud. If the cut is too close, the bud may die; if too far, the stem itself may die back.

With shrubs that have buds in opposite pairs, cut straight across the shoot just above a pair of healthy buds. Both buds will develop, resulting in a forked branch system.

In the past, gardeners have often been advised to use a wound paint on pruning cuts, but research now suggests that wound paints are not generally an effective way of controlling diseases and in some cases may even encourage them.

Pruning alone will not promote vigorous new growth. Shrubs that are renovated or regularly cut back benefit from feeding and mulching. Apply a general-purpose fertilizer at the beginning of the growing season at a rate of 120g/sq m (4oz/sq yd) and mulch to a depth of 5–10cm (2–4in) with well-rotted organic material in spring, when the ground has warmed up a little.

Training
The growth of lower buds or shoots on a stem may also be modified by training. When a stem is allowed to grow upright, the lower shoots on the stem usually grow weakly. With stems that are trained more horizontally, however, the lower shoots and buds grow more vigorously. Training branches near the horizontal can substantially increase the amount of flower and fruit that a shrub is able to carry. Wall-trained shrubs should be tied in to supports as growth develops. As stems ripen and turn woody they become far less flexible and are therefore more difficult to train successfully.

Formative pruning

The aim of formative pruning is to ensure that a shrub has a framework of well-spaced branches so that it will develop according to its natural habit. The amount of formative pruning required depends very much on the type of shrub and on the quality of the plants available. When

FORMATIVE PRUNING

After planting a young shrub (here a Philadelphus*), cut out any dead, damaged, and weak stems, and remove crossing and congested stems to form a well-balanced framework with an open centre.*

Prune back crossing or congested shoots to an outward-facing bud or, if necessary, right back to the base.

Prune out any very weak and spindly, or long and straggly stems, cutting them right back to the base.

Also remove any very awkward stems that spoil the shape of the shrub to leave an evenly branching framework.

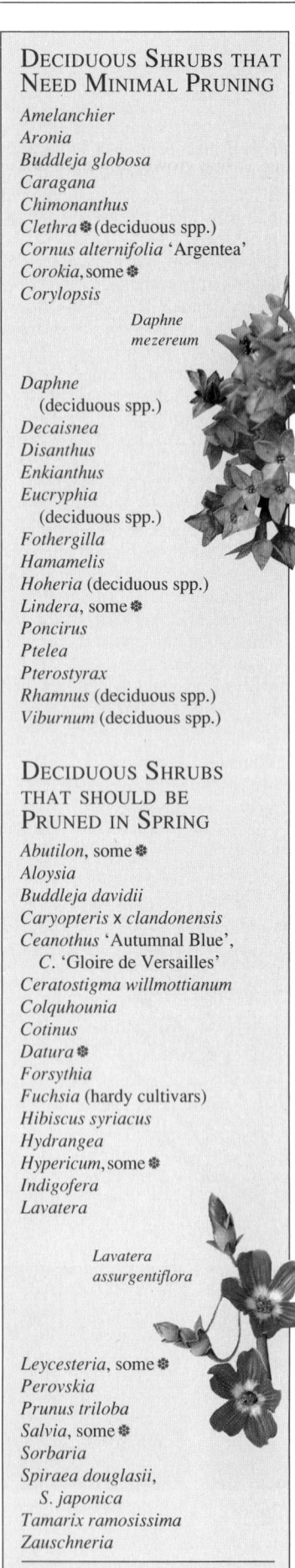

buying shrubs, look for sturdy specimens with a well-balanced branch formation.

Evergreen shrubs generally need little formative pruning. Excessive growth resulting in a lop-sided, unbalanced shape should be lightly pruned in mid-spring, after the shrub has been planted.

Deciduous shrubs are much more likely to require formative pruning than evergreen shrubs. This should be carried out in the dormant season, between mid-autumn and mid-spring, at or after planting.

The following guidelines apply to most deciduous shrubs. If a particularly vigorous shoot distorts the framework, cut it back lightly rather than severely. If the shrub does not have a well-spaced, branch framework, cut it back hard to promote strong growth.

In the case of most shrubs, remove completely any spindly and crossing branches that clutter the framework. An exception is made for a handful of slow-growing deciduous shrubs, in particular Japanese maples (*Acer japonicum* and *A. palmatum*). The numerous maple cultivars have a complex growth pattern that can be easily spoilt by this type of pruning.

Sometimes an apparently good specimen will make too much top-growth in relation to the size of its roots. Reducing the number of stems by up to one third, and then shortening those stems that remain, also by one third, will help to create a more stable plant.

MINIMAL PRUNING OF DECIDUOUS SHRUBS

Immediately after flowering, prune out any dead wood, weak stems, and congested growth to maintain a balanced, open-centred framework on shrubs such as Hamamelis.

Using secateurs, cut back any crossing or rubbing shoots to clear congested growth, especially from the centre of the shrub.

Cut back any weak, straggly, wayward, or misshapen shoots to the main stems.

Deciduous shrubs

These may be divided into four groups: those that require minimal pruning; those that are pruned in spring and usually flower on the current season's growth; those that are pruned after flowering in summer, and usually flower on the previous season's wood; and those of suckering habit. Two important factors are the degree to which shrubs produce replacement growths and the age of the flower-bearing wood.

SHRUBS THAT ARE PRUNED IN SPRING

Shrubs (here Spiraea) that flower on wood produced during the current growing season should be pruned in spring in order to encourage the growth of new, flowering stems.

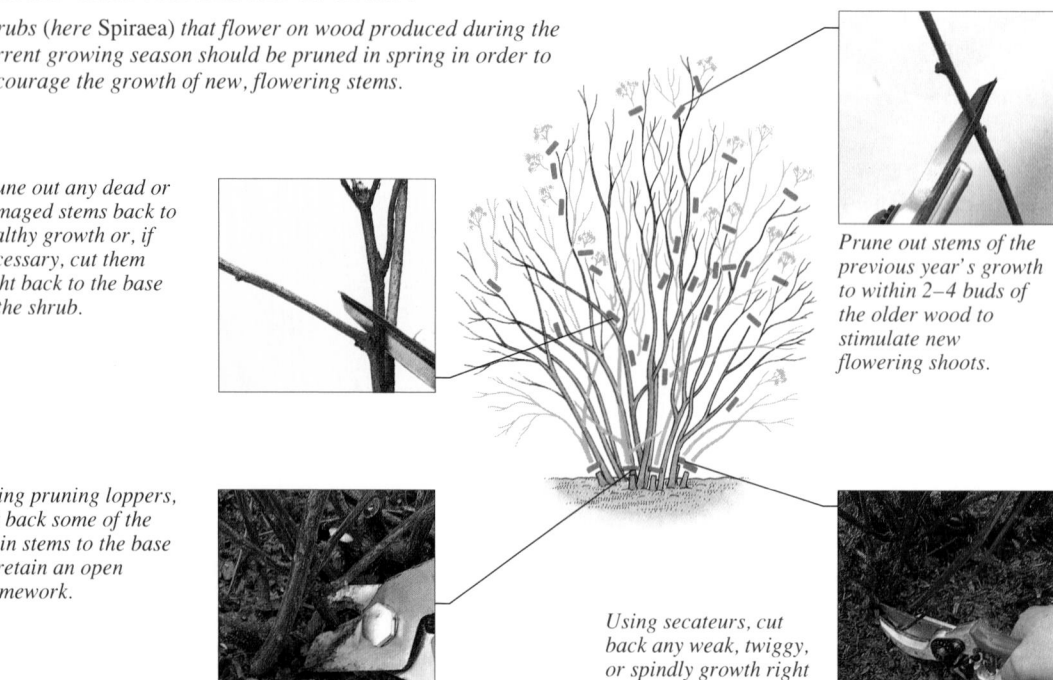

Prune out any dead or damaged stems back to healthy growth or, if necessary, cut them right back to the base of the shrub.

Using pruning loppers, cut back some of the main stems to the base to retain an open framework.

Prune out stems of the previous year's growth to within 2–4 buds of the older wood to stimulate new flowering shoots.

Using secateurs, cut back any weak, twiggy, or spindly growth right to the shrub's base.

Minimal pruning

Shrubs that do not regularly produce vigorous growths from the base or lower branches need little pruning; the chief need is to remove dead, diseased, and damaged wood and to cut out crossing or weak growth just after flowering. Many may require formative pruning. Feed and mulch in spring. Japanese maples and other shrubs prone to heavy bleeding if pruned in spring should be pruned in mid- to late summer, when their sap is least active.

Pruning in spring

Left unpruned, deciduous shrubs that bear flowers on the current season's growth tend to become congested and flower quality deteriorates. When pruned in spring, these shrubs generally produce vigorous shoots that carry flowers in summer or early autumn. Shorten flowered stems in autumn, as well, to minimize the risk of wind rock.

Some large shrubs, such as deciduous *Ceanothus*, develop a woody framework. In their first spring, lightly prune the main stems of less vigorous shrubs and, in the second spring, reduce the previous season's growth by half. In late winter or early spring of subsequent years, prune hard to leave only one to three pairs of buds of the previous season's growth. Prune framework branches to slightly different heights to encourage flower production at all levels. On mature specimens, cut out some of the oldest wood as part of the annual pruning operation to prevent congestion. For pruning *Buddleja davidii*, see above.

Some sub-shrubs, for example *Perovskia*, may form a woody base that allows them to be pruned hard back to a 15–30cm (6–12in) high framework. Cut back the previous season's growth annually in spring, leaving one or two buds.

A few shrubs, such as *Prunus triloba*, that flower in late winter or early spring on wood produced in the previous season are best pruned hard in spring after flowering, and so may be treated as other shrubs in this group. In the first spring after planting, shorten the main stems by about half to form a basal framework. After flowering in subsequent years, cut back all growth to two to three buds of the framework stems. In areas where annual growth is limited by cool summers, cut back only one third of shoots near to ground level, and the others to 15–30cm (6–12in).

For all shrubs in this group, apply fertilizer just after pruning. In mid-spring, mulch the area matching the spread of the shrub before pruning.

Pruning *Buddleja davidii*

As it is very vigorous, *Buddleja davidii* needs more drastic formative pruning than most other shrubs that flower on new wood. At the back of a border, where a tall plant is required, prune to leave a woody framework 90–120cm (3–4ft) high. In another position, however, this may be no more than 60cm (2ft) high.

In the first spring after planting, shorten main stems by a half to three-quarters, pruning to pairs of shoots or buds. Cut out growths other than main stems. In early to mid-spring of subsequent years, cut back the previous season's growth and shorten new growth from the base. To stop congestion, cut out one or two of the oldest branches as part of the annual pruning.

Using loppers, cut back some of the woody spurs to clear congested growth and produce an open, balanced framework.

Using secateurs, cut back all the main shoots that flowered the previous year to within 1–3 buds of the old wood.

Hydrangeas

For pruning purposes, hydrangeas (excluding climbing species such as *Hydrangea anomala* subsp. *petiolaris*) fall into three groups.

The first group (for example *H. paniculata*) flowers from mid-summer onwards on the current season's growth, and these plants should be treated in the same way as other shrubs that require hard pruning in spring (see opposite).

In early spring of the first year after planting, cut out all but two or three strong stems, pruning these back to a healthy pair of buds about 45cm (18in) from ground level. If the shrub is planted in an exposed position, and where summer temperatures will not ripen the stems sufficiently to withstand very cold winters, prune to just above ground level. Apply a quick-release fertilizer at a rate of about 120g/sq m (4oz/sq yd) and a 10cm (4in) deep mulch in a 60cm (24in) circle around the shrub. In early spring of subsequent years, cut back the previous year's growth to leave one or two strong pairs of growth buds. Then feed and mulch.

The second group, comprising mophead and lacecap hydrangeas (*H. macrophylla*), also flowers from mid-summer but on shoots made during the previous growing season. Lightly prune young plants in early spring, cutting out thin, twiggy growth and any old flowerheads. Once the plant is established and about three or four years old, remove some of the oldest wood annually in early spring. Cut out stems that are more than three years old and shorten the other stems that flowered in the previous season, cutting back to a strong pair of buds 15–30cm (6–12in) from the base. Then feed and mulch.

Other species, such as *H. aspera*, and related forms constitute a third group and need only minimal pruning in spring.

In spring, prune back all flowered stems, also damaged and weak growth, and cut back some older wood to the base.

H. MACROPHYLLA

Cut back any dead wood to healthy growth or right back to the base, if necessary.

Prune out all flowered stems, making a straight cut above a strong pair of growth buds.

Shrubs pruned in summer after flowering

Many deciduous shrubs that flower in spring or early summer carry their flowers on wood produced in the previous growing season. Sometimes, the flowers are formed on last year's wood, as with *Chaenomeles* and forsythias, for example. Other shrubs bear their flowers on short lateral growths produced from last year's wood – for example *Deutzia, Philadelphus,* and *Weigela.*

Without regular pruning to encourage development of vigorous, young growths from close to ground level, many shrubs in this group tend to become densely twiggy, often top-heavy, and the quantity and quality of flower deteriorate. The removal of spent flowerheads also prevents shrubs from expending energy in seed production.

When planting any shrub in this group, cut out all weak or damaged growth and trim back the main shoots to a healthy bud or pair of buds, to encourage the development of a strong framework. If any flowers are produced in the first year, prune again immediately after flowering. Cut back flowered shoots to a strong bud or pair of buds and remove any

spindly growth. After pruning, lightly work in fertilizer and apply a mulch around the shrub.

Carry out the same procedure immediately after flowering in subsequent years. Although it is desirable to cut back flowered wood to the strongest buds, do not adhere to this rigidly since it is also important to maintain a well-balanced shape. Feed and mulch as a matter of course after pruning.

As plants mature, more drastic pruning may be required to encourage growth. After the third year, up to one fifth of the oldest stems may be cut back annually to within 5–8cm (2–3in) of the ground.

Use your discretion when following these guidelines, since harsh pruning of young specimens of some shrubs in this group, for example forsythias, may result in an awkward and unnatural shape.

Other shrubs in this group, especially when grown as free-standing rather than as wall shrubs, require very little pruning. *Chaenomeles,* for example, has a naturally twiggy habit, with numerous crossing branches, and mature specimens need little pruning. Spur pruning will, however, encourage heavier flowering (see THE FRUIT GARDEN, "Spur pruning", p.378); shorten spurs and sideshoots to three to five leaves in mid-summer.

Particular care must be taken in pruning shrubs such as lilacs (*Syringa*) that come into growth during flowering. The new shoots that form below the flowers may be easily damaged when the old flowerheads are cut, and this reduces flowering in the next year.

Flowering shrubs of suckering habit

A few shrubs that are grown for their flowers produce flowers on wood of the previous year but make most of their new growth from ground level. These shrubs spread by suckers and are pruned in a different way from shrubs that form a permanent woody framework.

After planting, prune suckering shrubs by cutting out weak growth but retain vigorous stems and their sideshoots. The following year, immediately after flowering, remove any weak, dead, or damaged stems, then cut back flowered stems hard to a strong bud or pair of buds.

From the third year, annually cut back a quarter to a half of all flowered stems to 5–8cm (2–3in) above ground level and prune others by about half to vigorous, replacement shoots. After pruning, feed and mulch.

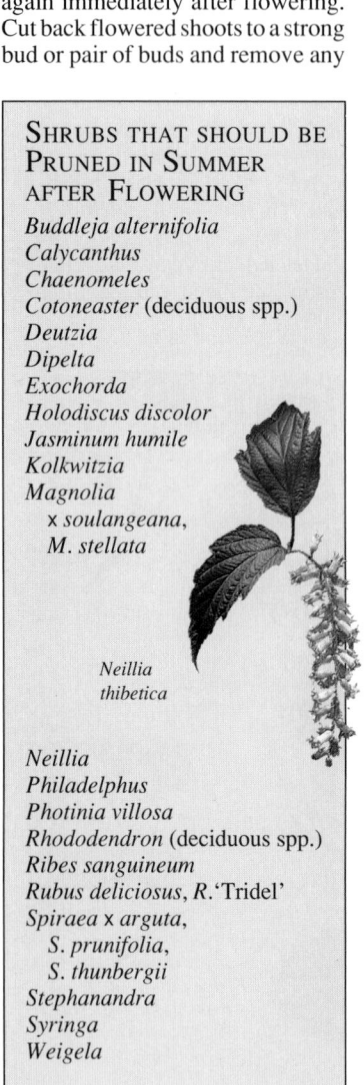

Neillia thibetica

PRUNING SHRUBS IN SUMMER

After shrubs such as Weigela *have flowered, cut back flowered shoots and remove dead and spindly stems. Also prune out some old, main stems.*

Using secateurs, cut any dead wood back to healthy growth.

BEFORE

AFTER

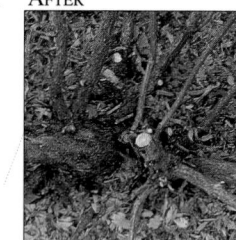

Cut out up to one fifth of the oldest wood to within 5–8 cm (2–3in) of the ground.

Cut out any very weak, twiggy, or straggly stems back to the base just above soil level.

Continue cutting out weak or crossing stems to form an open-centred, well-balanced shrub.

PRUNING A DECIDUOUS SUCKERING SHRUB

After flowering, prune back all flowered stems on deciduous suckering shrubs (here Kerria), *most by about half, the remainder almost to the ground. Cut out any weak, dead, or damaged growth.*

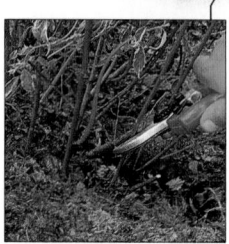

Prune the flowered stems by about half their length, cutting back to strongly growing, new shoots.

Cut back up to half of the flowered stems to within 5–8cm (2–3in) of the ground. Also cut to the ground any dead or damaged shoots.

Coppicing and pollarding shrubs

A number of deciduous shrubs grown for the ornamental value of their stems or leaves require severe pruning in spring. Most of these shrubs flower on shoots formed the previous season but, when grown for their stems or leaves, their flowers are sacrificed. The method of hard pruning used on these shrubs is essentially an adaptation of traditional methods of managing trees and shrubs to give a constant and renewable supply of wood for canework, firewood, and fencing materials. In coppicing, shrubs and trees are cut back regularly to near ground level. In pollarding, growth is cut back each year to a permanent framework of a single stem or several stems.

Coppicing shrubs such as *Cornus alba* ensures a regular supply of young growths, which are more strikingly coloured than older wood and effective in winter. On shrubs such as *Sambucus racemosa* 'Plumosa Aurea' that are grown for their foliage, hard pruning generally results in larger leaves. Just before growth commences in early to mid-spring, coppice vigorous shrubs such as *Salix alba* 'Britzensis' (syn. *S.a.* 'Chermesina') by pruning all shoots to within about 5–8cm (2–3in) of ground level. It may be preferable to vary the height to which stems are cut back to avoid a rigid, uniform effect. Weaker shrubs such as *Cornus alba* 'Sibirica' may be cut back less severely by coppicing only about one third to one half of the stems. Then apply a quick-release fertilizer and mulch liberally, covering a circle of 60cm (24in) radius around the shrub.

Shrubs that have been trained so that they have one or more clean, main stems are pruned back – or

POLLARDING A EUCALYPTUS

Establish a framework by cutting back a young shrub to one or more main stems (below). Each subsequent spring, cut the previous year's growth hard back either to within 5–8cm (2–3in) of the framework or to the base, as Eucalyptus can regenerate from ground level (right).

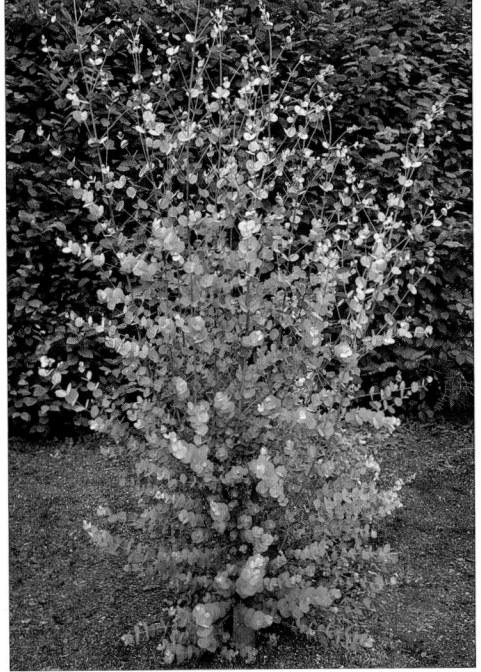

pollarded – to this stem framework each season. The aim of pruning in the first year is to establish the framework; after planting, before growth commences in spring, cut back a young plant to form a standard with a single stem of 30–90cm (1–3ft). Alternatively, leave three, five, or seven stems, depending on the size of plant required and the space available in the garden. Apply a quick-release fertilizer and mulch around the stem (or stems), as for shrubs that are coppiced.

During the plant's first growing season, restrict the number of shoots growing from below the cut to only four or five, rubbing out all others that are superfluous and any that develop low down on the main stem. Continue this process for the next year or two; this will allow the main stem to thicken so that it will be able to support heavier top-growth. In spring of the second and subsequent years, reduce the previous season's growths to above a bud within 5–8cm (2–3in) of the framework (see also *Pollarding a Eucalyptus, above*). If a larger specimen is needed, prune only a half or one third of the stems. Feed and mulch.

Evergreen shrubs

The appropriate method for pruning and training most evergreen shrubs depends on the size they are expected to reach when mature. All evergreens that show signs of dieback after a particularly hard winter, however, should be treated in the same way, regardless of size.

In mid-spring, prune out all dead wood to where the shrub has started to regenerate and thin out the new shoots if they are overcrowded or crossing. If a shrub shows no sign of life by mid-spring, nick the bark to see if there is any live, green wood beneath. Some shrubs may remain dormant for a whole growing season.

Small shrubs up to 90cm (3ft)
Low-growing, evergreen shrubs may be divided into two main groups, each requiring a different pruning technique. The first group includes a number of relatively short-lived shrubs that flower profusely, provided that they are trimmed each year and are not over-mature. Examples of these shrubs include lavender (*Lavandula*), cotton lavender

SHRUBS FOR COPPICING AND POLLARDING

Coppicing
Cornus alba 'Aurea',
    C.a. 'Elegantissima',
    C.a. 'Flaviramea',
    C.a. 'Kesselringii',
    C.a. 'Sibirica',
    C.a. 'Spaethii',
    C.a. 'Variegata'

Corylus maxima 'Purpurea'

Corylus maxima 'Purpurea'
Cotinus coggygria,
    C. 'Grace'
Hydrangea paniculata 'Floribunda',
    H.p. 'Grandiflora',
    H.p. 'Unique'
Rubus biflorus,
    R. cockburnianus,
    R. thibetanus
Salix alba 'Britzensis',
    S. daphnoides,
    S. irrorata
Sambucus racemosa 'Plumosa Aurea'

Pollarding
Cornus stolonifera
Eucalyptus, some ✿
Salix acutifolia

KEY
✿ *Not hardy*

(*Santolina chamaecyparissus*), and most heathers (*Calluna, Daboecia,* and *Erica*, but not tree heaths). These shrubs are generally best replaced about every ten years or so. Also replace plants that have been left unpruned for several years since they become weak and leggy and seldom flower or regenerate successfully.

In mid-spring, use secateurs or garden shears to cut out any weak growth or flowering shoots on newly planted shrubs. This ensures that new growth is generated from basal shoots in the centre of the plant. Each subsequent year in mid-spring, remove the old flowerheads, as well as any dead, diseased, or damaged shoots. Some heathers have attractive winter foliage and these, as well as other evergreens, are sometimes dead-headed in autumn. In very cold areas there is, however, a risk of dieback after autumn dead-heading and for this reason pruning is normally delayed until mid-spring. After pruning, apply slow-release fertilizer at a rate of 60g/sq m (2oz/sq yd) and apply a mulch to a depth of 5cm (2in).

COPPICING A SHRUB FOR WINTER STEM EFFECT

With shrubs that have coloured stems (here a Cornus stolonifera *cultivar) cut back hard all the shrub's stems to about 5–8cm (2–3in) from the base before growth begins in spring (see inset). Apply fertilizer around the shrub to promote new growth, and then mulch. Coppicing stimulates the growth of new, vigorous stems whose colour is especially strong.*

The second group comprises slow-growing shrubs, such as dwarf cotoneasters and hebes. These require less pruning than those in the first group, the main purpose in pruning them being to remove dead, diseased, or damaged shoots in mid-spring. Dead-heading, however, is not necessary.

Medium-sized, evergreen shrubs up to 3m (10ft) tall

Most medium-sized evergreen shrubs require little pruning once a well-balanced framework has been established. This principle applies to *Berberis darwinii*, camellias, *Escallonia*, *Hibiscus rosa-sinensis*, and many rhododendrons.

In mid-spring, just before growth is about to commence, remove any weak or crossing shoots as well as any that may affect the overall symmetry and balance of the shrub. Feed and mulch. Subsequent pruning is normally limited to cutting out straggly growth, restricting size, and shaping the plant to suit its position in the garden. Use secateurs or long-handled loppers to remove all or part of selected branches.

Winter- or spring-flowering shrubs, such as *Berberis darwinii* and *Viburnum tinus*, should be pruned immediately after flowering. Prune others that flower from mid-summer onwards, such as *Escallonia*, by removing older wood at the start of growth in mid-spring or by cutting

out flowered stems in late summer. *Hibiscus rosa-sinensis*, with a flowering season from spring to autumn, is best pruned in mid-spring. Feed and mulch spring-pruned shrubs after pruning, but shrubs pruned in late summer should not be fed or mulched until the following spring, since any new, soft growth produced would be vulnerable to damage from winter frosts.

Large, evergreen shrubs more than 3m (10ft) tall

Large rhododendrons and other tall evergreens require little pruning but may need shaping as young plants to create a well-balanced framework. Prune young plants in mid-spring or wait until the flowers have faded.

The aim of pruning here is to encourage an open-centred bush with well-spaced branches. Cut out all weak and crossing branches, and feed and mulch after pruning. Regular pruning is generally limited to the removal of dead, damaged, and diseased wood. Some large evergreens such as laurels (*Prunus laurocerasus*) may also be used for hedging (see pp.60–62).

Palms

These require little or no pruning apart from the removal of dead leaves. Certain rhizomatous palms, for example *Chamaedorea*, can be invasive, however, in which case unwanted stems should be removed at ground level in spring.

The palm-like *Cordyline* needs pruning only if it has suffered frost-damage or if a bushy, multi-stemmed specimen is required. Once new growth has started to appear, cut damaged branches back to just above newly formed shoots. Feed and apply a mulch. To create a multi-branched specimen, remove the growing point before growth commences in spring then feed and mulch.

Wall shrubs

There are three reasons for growing shrubs against walls. First, some are too tender for the open garden in frost-prone areas, but will thrive if sheltered against a warm wall. Second, training shrubs, including hardy shrubs such as pyracanthas, against a wall makes it possible to accommodate plants for which there might not otherwise be space. Third, some shrubs are natural scramblers (for example *Cestrum elegans*) and will therefore need support of some kind.

It is important to train and prune all wall shrubs from an early stage so that they present a compact and

"well-tailored" appearance and produce plenty of flowering shoots regularly. When training wall shrubs, provide a framework to which growth can be tied. Trellis, netting, or regularly spaced, horizontal wires as used for wall-trained fruit trees (see p.364) may be used. Plant hardy shrubs in autumn, half-hardy or tender shrubs in spring.

Recommendations for pruning free-standing shrubs also apply to wall-trained specimens, but more care is needed for formative training and pruning. It is vital to tie in shoots as they grow and cut back sub-laterals growing strongly away from the wall.

Formative training and pruning

During the first growing season, train in the leader and main laterals to form a framework; prune back any outward-growing laterals to encourage short sideshoots to develop close to the framework. Remove completely any laterals growing towards the wall or fence, and any shoots that are growing outwards in the wrong

direction. The aim should be to create a neat, vertical "carpet" of foliage to cover the allotted space.

Routine pruning

In the second and subsequent seasons, flowering laterals should be formed. After flowering, cut back the flowered shoots to within 7–10cm (3–4in) of the main framework. This encourages new flowering laterals to develop that will provide next season's display. Continue tying in framework shoots; trim outward-pointing laterals and remove inward-growing and other wrongly aligned shoots. Do not trim wall shrubs after mid-summer as this may reduce the following year's flowering shoots; this is particularly important with *Ceanothus* and many half-hardy evergreen shrubs which might otherwise produce soft growth liable to frost damage. Feed and mulch wall-trained shrubs annually in spring to maintain strong, healthy growth.

Shrubs such as pyracantha that are grown both for flowers and fruits or berries need slightly modified pruning. The shoots that have flowered

PRUNING EVERGREEN SHRUBS

After flowering, prune evergreen shrubs (here Prunus lusitanica*) by removing damaged or dead wood and cutting back flowered stems and any awkward or straggly stems that mar the shape.*

Cut back flowered stems to a main stem. Cut out thickly congested and crossing stems.

Cut back awkwardly growing stems to well-placed, healthy, outward-growing shoots.

Cut out any dead or damaged wood back to healthy growth or, if necessary, to the base.

PRUNING AND TRAINING A YOUNG WALL SHRUB

In the first year, prune the shrub (here a pyracantha) to build up a balanced framework, tying in main stems. In subsequent years, tie in new growth in spring; in mid-summer, cut back inward- and outward-growing shoots to form a vertical "carpet"; remove entirely dead, damaged, or spindly growth.

Using secateurs, cut back any weak, spindly stems as well as any dead or damaged wood.

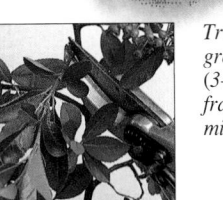

Trim back any outward-growing stems to 7–10cm (3–4in) from the framework in mid-summer.

Check and replace any broken ties, using garden twine tied in a figure of eight to resecure the stem to the wire.

PRUNING AN ESTABLISHED WALL SHRUB

Prune mature plants to maintain a well-balanced framework of stems and, on berrying shrubs, to expose the berries. In late summer, remove outward-growing shoots and, with the exception of shrubs grown for their fruits or berries, cut back flowered shoots to promote dense growth. The shrub shown here is a pyracantha.

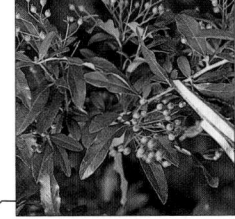

Cut back young shoots to 2–3 leaves from their base to expose the ripening berries.

In late summer, check and replace ties where necessary; in spring, tie in new shoots.

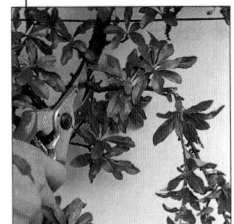

Using secateurs, cut back any damaged or dead wood to healthy growth.

---

are not cut back but are left to develop fruits. Trim back any laterals that develop to two to three leaves from their base as the fruits swell, so that they are exposed to more light and ripen well. Old fruit trusses may be cut out in spring as young growths develop.

Summer- and autumn-flowering wall shrubs, including some *Ceanothus*, should be trained as described earlier but pruned according to whether they flower on the previous season's wood (see "Shrubs pruned in summer after flowering", p.78) or that of the current season (see "Pruning in spring", p.77). Some half-hardy or tender shrubs, particularly *Ceanothus*, do not break readily from old wood and are difficult to renovate once neglected.

Scrambling shrubs

These also require careful training to contain their flexuous shoots. On some, such as the half-hardy *Cestrum elegans*, that produce flowers in late summer on terminal shoots or short laterals, the flowered shoots may be cut out entirely or cut back to strong, low, lateral growths in spring. Others flower in summer mainly on lateral growths, which should be cut back after flowering to 7–10cm (3–4in) and will often produce further sublaterals that flower the same season. In spring, these laterals are pruned back again to 7–10cm (3–4in) and will flower in summer.

Fan-training ornamental shrubs

A few shrubs, such as ornamental peaches (for example *Prunus persica* 'Klara Meyer'), are suitable for fan-training like fruit trees. In the first spring after planting, cut back the plant 38–45cm (15–18in) above the graft union, retaining three or four strong shoots. Train the shoots on canes tied to horizontal wires. Towards the end of the growing season, remove the central shoot if three strong shoots were retained; if four shoots were kept, space these out to form a fan. In winter, reduce all shoots by half their length.

The following growing season, select two or four new shoots on each stem; attach each of these to a cane tied to the wires. Then, in mid-summer, remove all other shoots. In the third year, immediately after flowering, cut back all framework shoots by a quarter to one third. Tie in two or three new shoots on each framework stem. Remove unwanted shoots in mid-summer. If there are gaps in the fan, prune back adjacent shoots by one third after flowering has finished to encourage new growth. Cut back all other extension growths to 5–8cm (2–3in) to encourage flowering on one-year-old spurs. For full details, see THE FRUIT GARDEN, "Fan", p.393.

PRUNING CEANOTHUS

Immediately after flowering, cut back new shoots of spring-flowering Ceanothus *to 2–3 leaves. Tie in new shoots and trim back outward-growing shoots to keep growth trained close to the wall or fence.*

FAN-TRAINING A SHRUB

This fan (Prunus mume 'Beni-shi-dare') has been trained to develop an evenly-spaced branch framework, in the same way as pruning fan-trained fruit trees.

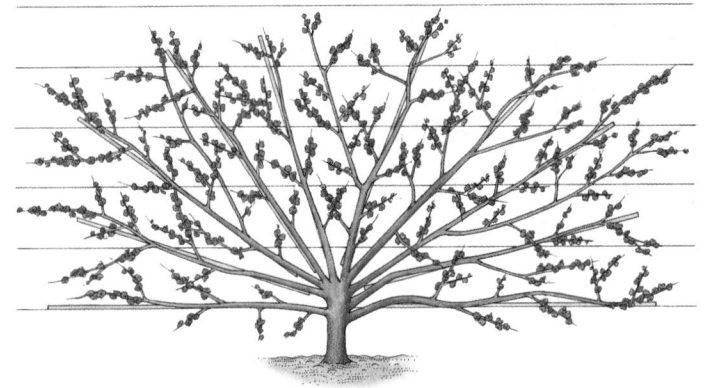

Training and pruning standard shrubs

Some shrubs, for example, fuchsias and *Buddleja alternifolia*, may be grown as standards. The height of the stem varies according to the vigour of the plant and the effect wanted. For details on training a standard fuchsia, see p.93; for pruning a standard rose, see p.128.

To train a shrub such as *Buddleja alternifolia* as a standard, tie a strong stem to a cane in the first growing season. Pinch all sideshoots back to two or three leaves, leaving a few growing near the stem tip. As the stem grows, continue to pinch out. When the clear stem is at the desired height, stop the terminal shoot to encourage shoots to form the head. In early spring of the following year, shorten the branches of the head to about 15cm (6in). Retain two or three of the shoots that each produces. Feed and mulch. Prune subsequently as for other shrubs pruned in summer after flowering (see p.78).

Some pendulous cultivars are grafted onto the clear stem of a rootstock. Remove any suckers (see p.72) from the stock and treat as for roses (see "Suckers and how to deal with them", p.125).

Root pruning

Root pruning is sometimes used to control the top-growth of vigorous shrubs and to make them flower more freely; grafted specimens that are making prolific leaf growth but producing few flowers or fruits usually benefit from root pruning.

In early spring, dig a trench around the shrub to a depth of 30–60cm (12–24in) with a circumference just beyond the spread of the top-growth. Use pruning loppers or a saw to cut back the thick, woody roots; as a guideline, shorten them to about half the radius of the trench. Leave fibrous roots unpruned. Control further spreading of the roots by inserting a barrier of slates or polycarbonate sheets around the circumference of the trench (see *Restricting the Spread of Bamboo*, p.145). After backfilling, mulch the area within the trench.

Root pruning is often used to control container-grown shrubs. This is best carried out when repotting the shrub. Shorten up to one fifth of woody roots by a quarter and cut back others so that they fit comfortably in the container. Repot, using fresh compost with a slow-release fertilizer added, and water thoroughly.

Renovation

Old, tangled, or overgrown shrubs may sometimes be renovated by extensive pruning. Shrubs that respond well usually produce young growth from the base. It is not worth trying to salvage a shrub that is badly diseased. Some shrubs do not tolerate drastic pruning; if in any doubt about a particular shrub, stagger a programme of heavy pruning over a period of two or three years.

Renovate deciduous shrubs, such as lilacs, after flowering or when dormant; for evergreens, such as *Viburnum tinus*, delay renovation until mid-spring.

Renovating old or overgrown shrubs

Cut out all weak and crossing stems and shorten main stems to 30–45cm (12–18in) above ground level, ensuring that a balanced framework is left. Apply a slow-release fertilizer at 120g/sq m (4oz/sq yd), and mulch the area around the shrub to a depth of 5–10cm (2–4in). Keep the shrub well watered throughout summer.

During the following growing season, a mass of shoots should grow from below the cuts on the main stems. Retain only two to four of the strongest on each stem to provide the new branch framework.

GRADUAL RENOVATION

On deciduous shrubs, cut out superfluous shoots during the dormant season. On evergreen shrubs, do this in mid-spring.

In the following growing season, some secondary growth may occur where shoots have been cut. Rub out these growths.

Staggered renovation

An alternative, less drastic method is to spread the pruning over two or three years. Prune deciduous shrubs after flowering, evergreens in mid-spring. Prune half of the oldest stems to 5–8cm (2–3in) from the ground. Where possible cut back the remaining stems by about half to new, vigorous, replacement shoots. Apply a slow-release fertilizer, water well, and mulch. At the same time the following year, repeat the process on the remaining old stems. Thereafter, prune the shrub according to its growth and flowering characteristics.

Renovate deciduous shrubs after flowering and evergreens in mid-spring. Cut back a third to a half of the oldest main stems (here on a Philadelphus) *almost to the ground and remove dead, twiggy stems. Over the next year or two cut back remaining old, main stems.*

DRASTIC RENOVATION

A shrub that produces new growth from the base (here lilac) can be renovated when dormant if it is deciduous or in mid-spring if evergreen. Cut back all main stems to within 30–45cm (12–18in) of the ground. Remove suckers by cutting them off at the base.

Cut back about half of the stems to within 5–8cm (2–3in) of the base. Remove the oldest stems and any that spoil the shrub's shape.

Cut back older stems by half to new, vigorous shoots, and remove any weak, twiggy growth or dead wood.

Prune back any crossing, rubbing, or congested stems to a bud or stem that will not cause another crossing shoot to develop.

Propagation

THERE are many ways to propagate shrubs to raise new plants, including taking cuttings, sowing seed, layering, division, and grafting.

Taking cuttings is a simple way of propagating many shrubs and, unlike seed, which may produce variable offspring, it may be used for cultivars, hybrids, and sports.

Sowing seed is simple and inexpensive but it is relatively slow to produce plants of flowering size. Some shrubs may be divided, while others may be layered – a method of stimulating stems to root while still attached to the parent plant.

Grafting involves uniting a stem from the plant to be propagated with the rootstock of a compatible plant. It is not commonly used since it requires more expertise and skill than other methods, but it is the most suitable method for some shrubs.

Softwood cuttings

This technique is suitable for raising several, mainly deciduous, shrubs, for example *Fuchsia* and *Perovskia*.

Softwood cuttings are taken in spring from fast-growing stem tips when these are about 6–8cm (2½–3in) long. The cuttings have a soft base and a higher capacity to root than cuttings of more mature wood.

Preparing the cuttings
Take the cuttings early in the morning. Select healthy, pliable, single-stemmed shoots and seal them in an opaque, plastic bag. Prepare the cuttings as soon as possible after collection: trim the cuttings just below a node and remove the lower leaves. Use a cutting compost of equal parts peat substitute (or peat) and either perlite or sharp sand. With a dibber, insert them into the compost. Water them in, applying a fungicide to minimize rot, label, and place in a mist unit or propagator.

Aftercare
Softwood cuttings wilt quickly if not kept in a humid atmosphere and aftercare is very important; remove dropped leaves daily, if possible, and apply a fungicidal spray every week. Once rooted, harden off the

cuttings and transplant them into individual pots or retain them in the container. If kept in the cutting medium, give a supplementary feed every two weeks during the growing season and pot up the rooted cuttings individually the following spring.

Greenwood cuttings

Almost all the shrubs that may be propagated by softwood cuttings may also be propagated by greenwood cuttings. Take greenwood cuttings, either nodal or heel cuttings (see p.85), from vigorous shoots in late spring when these are firm and slightly woody at the base. Follow the method for softwood cuttings, using the same potting mixture.

Remove the soft tips if the cuttings are more than 8–10cm (3–4in) long and trim off the bottom leaves. On a nodal cutting, make a straight cut with a sharp blade directly below the node. Trim off the tail on a heel cutting. Dip the cuttings in a rooting hormone and insert them into the compost. Water the cuttings with a

TAKING GREENWOOD CUTTINGS

Select and prepare greenwood cuttings (here of Philadelphus*) in late spring when growth has slowed and the new stems are firmer.*

fungicidal solution before placing them in a mist unit or propagator. Remove any fallen leaves daily and apply a fungicide once a week.

Once rooted, harden off the cuttings and transplant them or grow them on in the original container. If the latter, feed them regularly during the growing season and transplant them the following spring.

PROPAGATING SHRUBS BY SOFTWOOD CUTTINGS

1 *In spring, cut off young, non-flowering shoots (here from* Hydrangea macrophylla*) with 3–5 pairs of leaves. Seal them in an opaque plastic bag and keep shaded until they can be prepared.*

2 *Reduce each cutting to 8–10cm (3–4in) in length, making a straight cut just below a node (see inset). Trim off the lower leaves.*

3 *Insert the cuttings into prepared pots of cutting compost, ensuring that the leaves do not touch each other.*

4 *Water the cuttings with a fungicidal solution, then label and place them in a propagator. Maintain a temperature of 18–21°C (64–70°F).*

5 *Once the cuttings have rooted, harden them off, then remove them from the pot and carefully tease them apart.*

6 *Transplant the separated cuttings into individual pots and firm in. Water, label, and keep the cuttings in a shaded position until well established.*

SHRUBS THAT MAY BE PROPAGATED BY SOFT/ GREENWOOD CUTTINGS

Abelia, some ✻
Abutilon, some ✻
Aloysia, some ✻, ↡
Boronia ✻
Calluna
Caryopteris
Ceanothus, some ✻ (deciduous spp.)
Ceratostigma, some ✻, ↡
Cestrum ✻ ↡
Cotoneaster (deciduous spp.)
Cytisus, some ✻
Daboecia
Daphne x *burkwoodii*
Enkianthus
Erica
Forsythia
Fuchsia, some ✻
Genista, some ✻
Halesia
Hydrangea ↡
Kolkwitzia
Lagerstroemia ✻ ↡
Lantana ✻ ↡
Lavatera ↡
Nandina
Perovskia
Philadelphus
Potentilla
Viburnum (deciduous spp.)

KEY
✻ *Not hardy*
↡ *Softwood cuttings only*

PROPAGATING BY SEMI-RIPE CUTTINGS

1 *In mid- to late summer, select healthy shoots of the current season's growth for the cuttings. Sever them from the parent plant (here Ilex x altaclerensis 'Golden King') just above a node. They should be semi-ripe: still soft at the top but firm at the base.*

2 *Remove the sideshoots from the main stem. Trim each sideshoot to 10–15cm (4–6in) long, cutting just below a node.*

3 *Trim off the soft tip of each cutting and then remove the lowest pair of leaves, cutting flush with the stem.*

4 *Stimulate rooting by wounding the cutting: carefully cut away a piece of bark about 2.5–4cm (1–1¹/₂in) long from one side of the base.*

5 *Dip the base of each cutting in hormone rooting powder, then insert it into cutting compost in a propagator or in pots in a cold frame.*

6 *Once they are well rooted, carefully lift the cuttings and plant them individually. Gradually harden them off before growing them on in their pots or transplanting them outside.*

Semi-ripe cuttings

Many evergreen as well as some deciduous shrubs may be propagated from semi-ripe cuttings, including some, such as *Aucuba* and *Choisya*, that are difficult to propagate from hardwood cuttings.

Suitable cuttings

The cuttings are normally taken from mid- to late summer and sometimes into the early autumn. Select shoots from the current season's growth that are firm and woody near the base but still soft at the tip. Unlike softwood cuttings, they should offer some resistance when bent. Some shrubs are propagated by variations of this semi-ripe cuttings technique, such as mallet cuttings (see p.85) or leaf-bud cuttings (see p.85).

Preparing the rooting medium

Before collecting the cutting material from the parent shrub, fill sufficient containers of appropriate size, or a propagator (equipped with basal heating) with a suitable rooting medium: use fine-grade pine bark or a mixture of equal parts of peat substitute (or peat) and either grit or perlite.

Preparing the cuttings

Cuttings may be taken with a heel (see p.85) or as nodal cuttings. Heel cuttings should be 5–7cm (2–3in) long, trimmed to a short heel at the base; nodal cuttings should be 10–15cm (4–6in) long, taken from leaders or sideshoots, and cut with a sharp knife just below a node.

Remove the soft tips of nodal and heel cuttings. In both cases, remove the lowest pair of leaves and with large-leaved plants reduce the size of the remaining leaves by about a half to minimize moisture loss.

An optional step is to prepare the base of the cuttings by making a shallow wound at one side; on plants that are difficult to root, such as *Daphne sericea*, this cut should be made deeper so that a sliver of bark is also removed.

Potting up

Dip the bases of the cuttings, including the entire wound on wounded cuttings, in a rooting hormone before using a dibber to insert them in the prepared compost, either directly in a propagator, or in containers.

Space the cuttings approximately 8–10cm (3–4in) apart, and make certain that their leaves do not overlap, since this may create stagnant conditions in which rot fungi thrive. Firm the compost mixture around the cuttings. Label each container

and water the cuttings thoroughly with a fungicidal solution to protect them against damping off diseases (see p.568).

Correct temperature

Overwinter cuttings in containers in a cold frame or greenhouse. Those that have been inserted directly in a propagator should have basal heat maintained at 21°C (70°F).

Aftercare

Inspect the cuttings periodically during the winter period, removing any fallen leaves promptly. Water the containers if the compost mixture shows any signs of drying out, such as slight shrinking towards the edges of the container. If the cuttings are being overwintered in a cold frame, this may need some form of insulation, such as a hessian cover or a piece of old carpet, to protect the cuttings from damage by frost.

Cuttings kept in a cold frame or unheated greenhouse will almost certainly need a further growing season in their containers before rooting satisfactorily. Keep the frame closed, except on very mild days. The glass should be kept clean and free of any condensation, since the high moisture content of the air inside the frame provides ideal conditions for fungal infection to occur. In late spring and early summer, gradually open the cover for longer and longer periods to harden off the rooted cuttings. If necessary, protect the cuttings from strong, direct sunlight by covering the glass with suitable shading material.

Throughout the growing season, apply a liquid feed every two weeks to all semi-ripe cuttings. Check them regularly, and remove any that are weak or showing signs of disease.

Transplanting

Cuttings overwintered in a propagator should have rooted by early spring, since the basal heat helps to speed up root development. Check that there is strong root growth before transplanting the cuttings. Ease them from their containers, separate each cutting carefully, and either pot up individually or plant, clearly labelled, in the open ground. If some cuttings have not rooted but have formed a callus, scrape off some of the callus to stimulate rooting and re-insert the cuttings in the compost mixture.

Cuttings grown in a cold frame may be planted out in autumn, if well developed, or kept in a sheltered position outside or in the cold frame until spring. They are then potted up individually or planted out.

Heel cuttings

Heel cuttings, which may be taken from greenwood, semi-ripe, or hardwood stems, are vigorous sideshoots of the current season's growth. Each cutting is taken with a "heel" of old wood at its base, in which the growth hormones that assist the rooting process are concentrated.

Heel cuttings are particularly suitable for a number of evergreen shrubs such as *Pieris* and some azaleas (*Rhododendron*), deciduous shrubs that have pithy or hollow stems such as *Berberis* and *Sambucus*, and those shrubs that have greenwood stems such as broom (*Cytisus*/*Genista*).

Select as cuttings healthy sideshoots that are characteristic of the parent plant. Carefully pull the shoot away from the main stem so that a small strip of bark from the parent shoot comes away with it. Avoid tearing the bark of the main shoot as this may expose it to infection. Trim the heel with a sharp blade and then follow the technique for greenwood (see p.83), semi-ripe (p.84), or hardwood cuttings (see right), according to the particular stem's maturity.

1 *Pull away healthy sideshoots of the current season's growth (here on* Prunus laurocerasus *'Schipkaensis') with a heel of bark.*

2 *Using a sharp knife, trim off the "tail" at the base of the cutting before inserting it in cutting compost.*

Mallet cuttings

A mallet cutting, which is taken from semi-ripe stems, is a ripened shoot of the current season's growth attached to a piece of wood from the previous season, forming a mallet-shaped plug at its base. Mallet cuttings are often used to propagate shrubs with pithy or hollow stems, because rot fungi are less likely to affect older wood. It is particularly suitable for many *Spiraea* and deciduous *Berberis*, which produce short sideshoots on main branches.

In late summer, remove a stem of the last season's growth from the parent and cut it into sections, each containing a vigorous sideshoot of new growth. If the mallet is more than 5mm (¼in) in diameter, slit it lengthwise. Then treat as for semi-ripe cuttings (p.84).

Leaf-bud cuttings

A leaf-bud cutting is taken from semi-ripe stems and comprises a short piece of stem bearing a leaf and a leaf bud. In comparison with stem cuttings, leaf-bud cuttings make much more economical use of the material from the parent plant. This method of propagation is most commonly used for camellias.

In late summer or early autumn, select a vigorous shoot of the current season's growth, bearing healthy leaves and well-developed buds. Using a sharp knife or secateurs, cut the stem just above each leaf, then make a cut about 2cm (¾in) below the petiole so that the shoot is divided into several sections.

Leaf-bud cuttings do not need to be treated with hormone rooting powder before potting up, but may be wounded at the base to hasten rooting. Insert them in containers of cutting compost and treat as for semi-ripe cuttings (see p.84).

To save space in the cold frame or propagator, roll up any large leaves and secure them with rubber bands; a cane inserted down the middle of a rolled-up leaf will give extra support by helping to anchor it firmly in the compost. Trim compound leaves on shrubs such as *Mahonia* by a half.

Hardwood cuttings

An easy way to raise many deciduous and evergreen shrubs is from hardwood cuttings. Use fully ripe, vigorous growths of the current season, taken from mid-autumn to early winter. Take cuttings of deciduous shrubs just after leaf fall.

Preparing the ground

Cuttings are best rooted in a prepared bed or containers kept in a

Cotoneaster
'Firebird'

Olearia phlogopappa

KEY
✿ *Not hardy*
▽ *With a heel*

MALLET CUTTINGS

Remove a stem produced the previous year and cut it above each sideshoot and about 2.5cm (1in) below. Reduce it to 10–13cm (4–5in) and trim off lower leaves.

PROPAGATING BY LEAF-BUD CUTTINGS

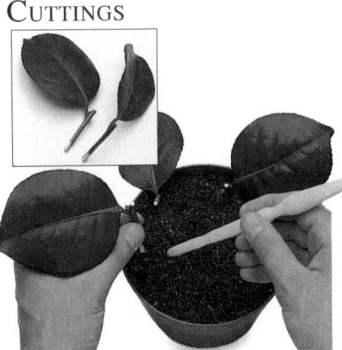

1 *Select semi-ripe shoots (here of* Camellia japonica*). Make a straight cut 2cm (¾in) below each leaf and a further cut just above.*

2 *Remove a 5mm (¼in) sliver of bark at the base of each cutting (see inset). Insert the cuttings in the compost so that the leaf axils are just visible above the surface.*

cold frame but they may also be inserted in a bed in open ground.

Prepare the bed in late summer or early autumn, first working the soil until it is friable, and then digging out a flat-backed trench 12–15cm (5–6in) deep. To encourage rooting, put a 2.5–5cm (1–2in) layer of coarse sand in the base of the trench; this is essential on heavy soils. Space the trenches 38cm (15in) apart.

Preparing the cuttings
Take cuttings that are about pencil thickness, cutting at the junction of the current and the previous season's growth.

Trim the cuttings into 15cm (6in) lengths, cutting at the top just above a bud or pair of buds and, at the bottom, below a bud or pair of buds; on evergreens, make the cuts above and below leaves. Take heel cuttings of pithy stems (see p.85). Remove all leaves on the bottom two-thirds of evergreen cuttings and cut large leaves in half. Treat the basal cut with a rooting hormone. Removing a sliver of bark near the base may encourage difficult cuttings to root.

Insert the cuttings in containers of cutting compost. Alternatively, place them against the vertical side of the prepared trench, 15cm (6in) apart in open ground or, in a cold frame, 10cm (4in) apart. Leave 2.5–5cm (1–2in) of the cuttings above ground. Backfill the trench and firm in the cuttings.

Aftercare
If the ground is lifted by frost, firm it down around the cuttings. Keep the bed weed-free and well watered during the growing season. Cuttings in a cold frame will normally root by the following spring. Harden them off before potting up or planting out. Those in the open ground should be left in place until the following autumn and then transplanted to their permanent position.

Root cuttings

Shrubs that may be propagated from root cuttings include *Aesculus parviflora*, *Aralia*, *Clerodendrum*, *Myrica*, *Rhus*, and *Xanthorhiza simplicissima*. Lift a young plant when dormant and tease the soil from its roots. If this is not practical, expose part of the shrub's root system. Cut off young roots – 5mm (¹/₄in) in diameter or more – close to the main stem. Keep them in moist sacking or a plastic bag until they can be prepared.

Preparing the cuttings
First remove and discard fibrous, lateral roots. Then make a straight cut on an undamaged root at the end where it was severed from the plant. At the opposite end of the root, make a slanting cut. Cuttings should be 5–15cm (2–6in) long, so several cuttings may be prepared from the same root. The colder the rooting environment and the thinner the root, the longer the cutting needs to be; cuttings to be rooted outdoors need to be at least 10cm (4in) long. Dust each cutting with fungicide but do not treat with a rooting powder, since this will tend to discourage the production of shoots.

Inserting the cuttings
Aralia and other shrubs that reproduce readily from root cuttings may be inserted in open ground. For shrubs that root less readily, a controlled environment is preferable. Prepare containers of cutting compost large enough for several cuttings. Firm the compost lightly and insert each cutting vertically 5cm (2in) apart with the slanted end down. Firm the compost so that the flat end of each cutting is just visible. Cover with 3mm (¹/₈in) of grit, and water. This watering may be sufficient to last until the shoots develop; excessive moisture may lead to rotting.

Aftercare
Cuttings will root in ten weeks outdoors, eight weeks in a cold frame or cool greenhouse. Under glass, cuttings will produce shoots in four to six weeks if they are kept at 18–24°C (64–75°F). Cuttings from shrubs that make rapid growth should be repotted as soon as they have rooted. Other root cuttings may be left in their containers for a further 12 months; apply a liquid feed once or twice a month. Then pot up singly or plant out in nursery beds.

Raising shrubs from seed

Growing shrubs from seed is simple and economical. In genera whose species hybridize readily, only use seed produced by controlled pollination.

Collecting and cleaning seed
Gather the seed capsules or fruits when ripe. Extract the seed, then clean and dry it before sowing or storing. Soak fleshy fruits in warm water or squash them so that the

PROPAGATING SHRUBS BY HARDWOOD CUTTINGS

1 *Select strong, healthy, ripened shoots from this year's growth for the cuttings (see inset, left); avoid weak, thin stems (centre) and older wood (right).*

Healthy Weak Old wood

2 *Remove any deciduous leaves and trim off the soft wood at the tip. Cut the stem into 15cm (6in) lengths, dipping the bases into hormone rooting powder.*

3 *Insert the cuttings into prepared pots of cutting compost so that approximately 2.5–5cm (1–2in) of each is visible. Label the pots and place in a cold frame.*

EXTRACTING SEED FROM BERRIES

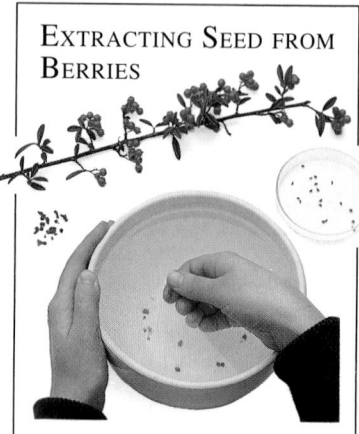

1 *Squash berries (here pyracantha) between finger and thumb, removing most of the outer flesh. Wash seeds by rubbing them in warm water.*

2 *Dry the seeds with tissue and place them in a clear plastic bag with a little coarse sand, then refrigerate them until ready to sow.*

seed may be picked out more easily. Collect fine seed by gathering whole capsules, preferably when they have already turned brown. Place the capsules in a paper bag and keep at room temperature until they split open.

Storing seed

The length of time seed is viable depends on the species and storage conditions. Oily seeds do not store well and should be sown soon after collection. The viability of seed may be prolonged if it is stored at a temperature of 3–5°C (37–41°F).

Breaking seed dormancy

The seeds of some shrubs have a form of dormancy to stop them germinating in adverse conditions. This dormancy may be broken artificially by scarification or stratification (see also PRINCIPLES OF PROPAGATION, "How to overcome dormancy", p.535).

To allow air and moisture to penetrate large seeds with hard coats, such as peonies (*Paeonia*), scarify them by nicking the seed coat with a knife or filing away a small section before sowing. Hard-coated seeds that are too small to be nicked may be rubbed with glasspaper. Germination of some seeds may be aided by soaking the seed in either cold water (for example *Camellia* and *Pittosporum*) or hot but not boiling water (for example *Caragana* and *Coronilla*) for a few hours. This softens the hard seed coat allowing water to enter and the germination process to begin.

Seeds that need a period of chilling are stratified. As soon as the seed is gathered, place a layer of crocks in the base of a container that has drainage holes, and scatter the seed between two layers of a sand and peat substitute (or peat) mix. Plunge the container in the open garden or place in a cold frame.

The next spring, by when some of the seed may have germinated, it may be separated out and space sown. Seed of certain hardy shrubs, such as some *Viburnum* species, may need further chilling in a refrigerator.

Refrigerating hardy seed may produce more reliable results. Mix the seed with moist vermiculite, peat substitute, or peat, then seal it in a clear plastic bag and refrigerate. The chilling period varies from species to species, but when the seeds have germinated, remove and sow them.

Sowing seed in containers

Most seed should be sown in autumn; however, seeds of tender shrubs that in temperate regions are germinated under glass should be sown in spring. Clean all containers, implements, and surfaces. Use a standard seed compost, but for lime-haters use an ericaceous compost.

Station sow large seeds. Overfill a pot or tray with compost and gently firm before scraping off the surplus. Firm again with a presser board so that the level is 1cm (½in) below the rim of the pot or tray. Sow the seeds 5cm (2in) apart, then firm them evenly into the compost. Cover with a 5mm (¼in) layer of sieved compost and a 5mm (¼in) layer of clean grit. Label and date each container and water the seeds. Many medium-sized seeds may also be sown in this way, but the gap between the rim and compost should be 5–8mm (¼–³⁄₈in). Cover seeds with sieved compost and then 5mm (¼in) of clean grit. Place wire netting over the container to protect the seedlings from small animals. When sowing fine seed, firm the compost to within 5mm (¼in) of the container rim. Water and allow the compost to drain before sowing, carefully shaking the seed out over the surface. Do not cover the seed or water it from above.

Aftercare for seedlings in containers

After sowing, place the containers in a propagator, greenhouse, or cold frame. Temperate species need a temperature of 12–15°C (54–9°F); warm-temperate and tropical species prefer 21°C (70°F). For seed sown in spring under glass, a temperature of 12–15°C (54–9°F) should be maintained. Inspect containers of seed regularly and water as necessary. Never water fine seed from above; place the container in a shallow water tank for a short time so that water is taken up by capillary action. When the seeds have germinated, spray occasionally with fungicide.

Pricking out

Once large enough to handle, prick out the seedlings. Knock the sides of the container to loosen the compost or remove the seedlings and compost together and separate the seedlings, disturbing their roots as little as possible.

Transfer the seedlings into clean pots or seed trays of cutting compost, levelled but not firmed. Make a hole in the compost using a widger and insert the seedling. Level the compost by tapping the top of the container and firm in, then label and water. Until the seedlings are established, place the pots out of direct sunlight in a temperature similar to that needed for germination.

Sowing seed outdoors

Open-ground seedbeds are useful for sowing large batches of seed that do not require daily attention. Prepare the bed between six months and a year before sowing.

In autumn, rake the soil to a fine tilth. Sow the seed in rows 45cm (18in) apart, station sowing medium or large seeds 10–15cm (4–6in) apart and sowing fine seed thinly.

Cover large and medium seeds to a depth of 0.5–1cm (¼–½in) but leave fine seed uncovered. Then place a 0.5–1cm (¼–½in) layer of grit over the seedbed. Firm the grit with a presser board, and label the rows.

Aftercare for seedlings outdoors

Protect seedlings from wind with 50 per cent permeable netting and from frosts with opaque sheeting. If the seeds are well spaced, they should not be troubled by disease, but greenfly (see "Aphids", p.550), red spider mites (p.550), and mice (p.566) may be a problem.

If the spacing is adequate, the seedlings may be left in the seedbed until the following autumn; they should then be either potted up or transplanted into a separate nursery bed.

SOWING SEED IN CONTAINERS

1 Sow seeds evenly onto a prepared tray of sieved seed compost by tapping them from a folded piece of paper.

2 Cover the seeds with a fine layer of compost, then add a 5mm (¼in) layer of grit. Label and place in a cold frame until the seeds have germinated.

3 When the seedlings are large enough to handle, prick them out, lifting them carefully with a widger and holding them gently by their leaves.

4 Transfer the seedlings into individual pots or insert 3 in a 13cm (5in) pot. After the second pair of leaves has formed, pot them up individually.

SHRUB SEED THAT REQUIRES SPECIAL TREATMENT

Stratification
Amelanchier
Cotoneaster
Euonymus
Hippophäe
Viburnum (some spp.)

Scarification
Camellia, some ❀
Paeonia

Soaking
Arbutus
Camellia, some ❀
Caragana
Coronilla, some ❀
Cytisus, some ❀
Pittosporum, some ❀

Sown when fresh
Acer palmatum
Daphne
Kalmia
Rhododendron, some ❀

KEY
❀ *Not hardy*

Andromeda
Aucuba
Carpenteria
Cassiope
Chaenomeles
Chionanthus
Corylopsis
Daphne blagayana
Disanthus
Elaeagnus commutata
Epigaea
Erica
Fothergilla
Gaultheria forrestii ❀
Illicium, some ❀
Kalmia
Laurus
Magnolia
Osmanthus,
   some ❀
Rhododendron,
   some ❀
Skimmia
Stachyurus, some ❀
Syringa
Vaccinium corymbosum

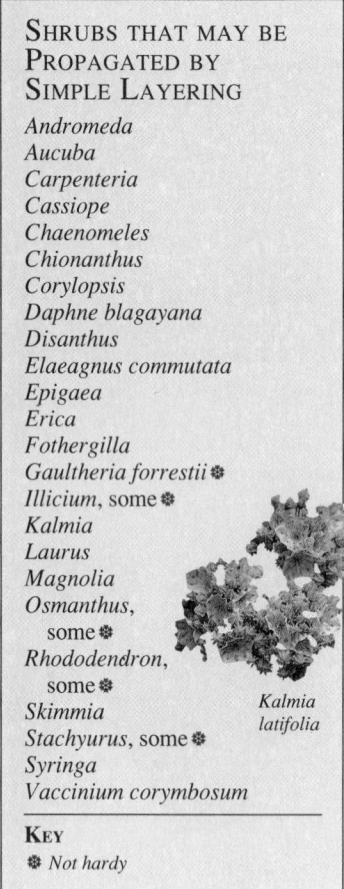

Kalmia latifolia

KEY
❀ Not hardy

Propagation by layering

Layering is a method of propagating shrubs whereby a stem is encouraged to develop roots before being removed from the parent plant. Dropping and stooling, techniques often used commercially, are variations of layering.

Simple layering
Many deciduous and evergreen shrubs may be propagated by this method. In autumn or spring, about 12 months before layering is to take place, prune a low branch on the parent plant to encourage vigorous shoots, which have a greater capacity to root. Between the following late autumn and early spring, prepare the soil around the stem to be layered so that it is friable. Add grit and humus if the ground is heavy.

Retain any leaves at the tip of the selected shoot but strip off others and any sideshoots. Bring the stem down to ground level and mark the ground about 22–30cm (9–12in) behind its tip. Dig a shallow hole or trench at this point for the stem. Wound the stem at the point where it will be pegged into the hole, that is about 30cm (12in) behind its tip, either with an angled cut or by removing a ring of bark. Dust the cut with rooting hormone, then peg the stem in the hole with bent wire, turning up the tip and securing it to a cane. Infill the trench and firm the soil, leaving the tip exposed.

Throughout the growing season keep the area around the layer moist. The layer should have rooted by autumn. In the following spring, check that there is a good root system before severing the layer from the parent plant and potting it up or planting it out in the open garden. If it has not rooted or there are only a few roots, keep it attached and in place for another growing season.

Air layering
This technique is particularly suitable for shrubs with branches that are difficult to lower to ground level.

In spring, choose a strong, healthy, one-year-old stem that has ripened. Trim the sideshoots or leaves to leave a clear length of stem behind the tip. Wound the stem with an angled cut and dust the cut surface with a rooting hormone.

Cut off the sealed end of a black or opaque plastic bag, about 22 x 18cm (9 x 7in). Slip it over the stem like a sleeve and secure the end farthest from the growing tip by tying the bag tightly around the stem using insulating tape, raffia, or string.

Moisten a well-aerated rooting medium of sphagnum moss or equal parts of perlite and peat substitute or peat so that it is wet but not sodden. Pack the moist medium into the bag around the stem's cut surface and seal the top end. Keep the bag in position for a complete season.

The following spring, check that the layer has rooted. If so, sever it immediately below the point of layering. Remove the bag and tease out the roots. Prune back any new growth on the layered stem to a leaf or bud close to the old wood. Pot up using a standard or ericaceous potting compost, as appropriate. Label and place the layer in a cool greenhouse or cold frame until the young plant is well established. If only a few (or no) roots have developed when the bag is removed, reseal it and leave it in place for several months more. Then carry out the process described above.

Tip layering
A few shrubs, mainly species and hybrids of the genus *Rubus*, root readily from the tips of stems and may be propagated in this way. In spring, select a vigorous, one-year-old shoot and pinch out the growing point to promote sideshoots. In late spring, cultivate the soil around the shoot. Work in organic matter and grit, if the soil is heavy.

In mid-summer, when the tip growth has firmed slightly, bring the stem down to ground level and mark the position of the tip. At that point, dig a trench about 7–10cm (3–4in) deep, with one side vertical and the other sloping towards the parent plant. Using inverted, "U"-shaped, wire staples, peg the growing tip at the bottom of the trench close to the vertical side. Infill the trench, firm lightly, and water.

By late autumn, well-rooted plants should have developed. Sever these at the point where the arched stem enters the trench. Lift the rooted layers and pot on or replant outdoors. (See also *Tip Layering*, p.411.)

Dropping
With this technique a plant is almost buried. It is used to raise dwarf shrubs, such as low-growing rhododendrons and heathers (*Erica, Daboecia, Calluna*), from parent plants that have become straggly.

In the dormant season, thin out branches of plants that have a mass of congested stems, to allow the remaining stems sufficient contact

PROPAGATING A SHRUB BY SIMPLE LAYERING

1 *Select a young, pliable, low-growing stem. Bring it down to the soil and mark its position with a cane about 22–30cm (9–12in) behind the tip.*

2 *At the marked point, dig a hole in the prepared soil about 8cm (3in) deep, with a shallow slope on the side where the stem joins the parent plant.*

3 *Trim off sideshoots and leaves on the selected stem. On the underside of the stem, at a point where it touches the ground, cut a tongue of bark.*

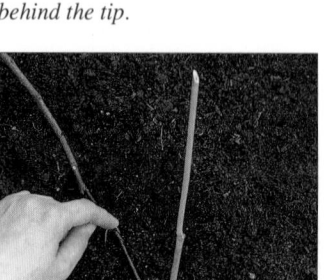

4 *Apply a rooting hormone to the wound on the stem. Peg down the stem with bent wire so that the stem's cut surface is held in contact with the soil.*

5 *Gently bend up the stem's tip vertically and secure it to the cane with a tie. Fill in the hole with more soil. Lightly firm with your fingers and water in.*

6 *Once rooted (see inset), lift the layered stem and cut it off the parent plant, severing it close to the new, young roots. Pot up the layer or plant it out.*

AIR LAYERING A SHRUB

1 Select a healthy, horizontal stem from the previous year's growth. Trim off any leaves and sideshoots to provide a 22–30cm (9–12in) section of clear stem.

2 Slide a plastic sleeve over and along the stem; seal and secure the lower end of the sleeve to the stem with adhesive tape.

3 Fold back the plastic. Make a 4cm (1¹/₂in) diagonal cut 5mm (¹/₄in) into the stem in the direction of growth, away from the shrub. Apply rooting hormone.

4 Soak about 2 handfuls of sphagnum moss in water, then gently squeeze it out. With the back of the knife, pack the cut with moss, wedging it open.

5 Pull back the plastic sleeve over the cut. Carefully pack the sleeve with more moistened moss so that the moss is all around the stem.

6 Continue to pack the sleeve until the moss is about 5cm (2in) from the open end. Close the end and secure it firmly in place with adhesive tape.

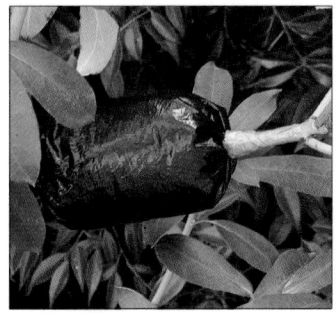

7 The sealed sleeve encourages rooting by retaining moisture. Leave it in place for at least a growing season to allow new roots to develop.

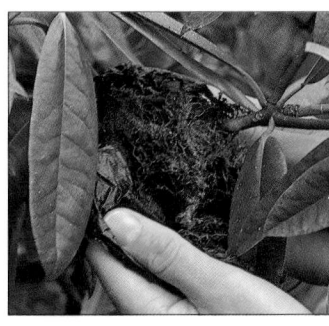

8 Once the layer has rooted, remove the sleeve and cut off the layer below the roots. Pot up or plant out the new shrub (here a rhododendron) in the open ground.

STOOLING

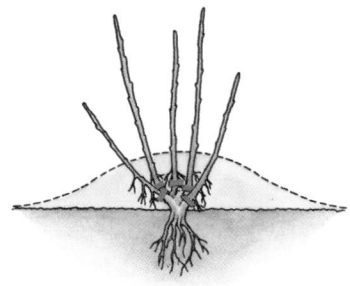

Cover shoots with free-draining soil, adding more as they grow. The shoots will root down and can be separated in autumn and potted on.

with the soil to develop roots once buried. Before growth starts, but after the risk of penetrating frosts has passed, dig a pit large enough to bury the plant with only the branch tips visible. If the soil is heavy, add grit and organic material.

Lift the parent plant with the root ball as complete as possible and "drop" it into the prepared hole. Work the soil around each stem, leaving 2.5–5cm (1–2in) of each tip exposed. Firm the soil and label the plant. In summer, keep the soil moist and, in autumn, carefully tease away the soil around the plant to check for rooting. Sever any rooted shoots from the parent plant, and pot up or plant out, clearly labelled. If rooting has not occurred, replace the soil and leave for a further 12 months.

Stooling

Although primarily used to raise fruit tree rootstocks, stooling may also be used to propagate deciduous ornamental shrubs such as dogwoods (*Cornus*) and lilacs (*Syringa*) from ungrafted plants.

Plant a rooted layer or other young plant in spring, label, and grow on for a season. The next spring, cut back the stem to within 8cm (3in) of the ground and apply a balanced fertilizer at 120g/sq m (4oz/sq yd). When the resulting shoots from this stem (or stool) are 15cm (6in) long, work friable soil enriched with organic matter between the shoots and bury them. Add grit if the ground is heavy. As the shoots grow, continue mounding up soil until about 22cm (9in) of each shoot is buried. Keep the soil moist in dry weather.

In autumn, gently fork away the soil to ground level straight after leaf fall, leaving the rooted shoots exposed. Cut them off and pot them up or plant them out. Provided that the stools are kept fertilized, the process may be repeated annually and the same stool used for propagation in subsequent years.

French layering

This method of propagating shrubs is a form of stooling and is suitable for increasing the stock of deciduous shrubs such as dogwoods (*Cornus alba*, *C. stolonifera*) and *Cotinus coggygria*.

In spring, plant a rooted layer or young plant, label it, and grow it on for a season. Then, in the dormant season, cut back the stool to within 8cm (3in) of the ground. In the following spring, apply a balanced fertilizer at the rate of 60–120g/sq m (2–4oz/sq yd).

The following autumn, cut out all but about the ten best stems; shorten the tips of these so that they are all about the same length. With "U"-shaped, wire staples, pin each stem to the ground, spreading the stems evenly around the parent stool. Each bud along the length of the stem should break evenly in spring.

When the new shoots on the pegged-down stems are approximately 5–8cm (2–3in) long, take out the pegs and cultivate the ground around the parent stool, incorporating a balanced fertilizer at a rate of 60–120g/sq m (2–4oz/sq yd). Space the stems evenly again, dropping each into a 5cm (2in) deep trench. Peg down each stem and cover with soil, leaving the shoot tips exposed. Earth up all but 5–8cm (2–3in) of the new shoots as they develop, until the mound is 15cm (6in) high. Water in dry weather.

After leaf fall, carefully fork away the soil from around the new shoots until the stems that were laid horizontally are exposed. Cut these flush with the central stool. Then cut the stems to separate the rooted sections. Pot these up or plant them out in the open garden, and label them. The same stool may be used to produce further layers.

Division

Division is a simple way of increasing shrubs that produce suckers. Suitable shrubs include *Ruscus*, *Kerria*, *Gaultheria*, and *Sarcococca*. Shrubs must be growing on their own roots not grafted onto another rootstock.

Before growth starts in spring, lift the plant. Break the clump into sections, retaining those with vigorous shoots and well-developed roots. Prune any damaged roots, and cut back the top-growth by one third to a half to reduce water loss. Replant the divisions in the open and water in dry weather. Alternatively, simply lift a suckering root, severing it from the parent plant, and then replant it in the open.

With a few shrubs, including *Rhus*, suckering may be encouraged

by digging deeply around the parent plant in summer or autumn. This damages the roots and stimulates adventitious buds to develop suckers in spring. These rooted suckers may then be lifted and potted up or planted out.

Grafting

This technique is used to unite two plants so that they grow together as one. One part, known as the scion, is taken from the plant to be propagated and provides the top-growth of the new plant, while the other part, known as the rootstock or stock, provides the root system. The rootstock and scion must be compatible and they are normally of the same or closely related species.

Grafting is an important way of propagating shrubs that are difficult to root or that are unlikely to come true from seed. By using selected rootstocks, it is possible to improve a plant's vigour, disease resistance, or tolerance to specific growing conditions, or sometimes to control its basic growth pattern.

Among the many variations of this particular technique, three that are widely used are saddle, side-

veneer, and apical-wedge grafting. In all cases, the stocks and scions should be joined immediately after they have been cut and the cut surfaces of each should be kept clean.

Saddle grafting

This grafting technique is predominantly used to propagate evergreen rhododendron species and hybrids, with *Rhododendron ponticum* generally serving as the rootstock. About one month before grafting is to commence, in late winter or early spring, bring the rootstock into a greenhouse maintained at a temperature of 10–12°C (50–59°F).

In late winter or very early spring, select the scion material so that it is ready for grafting. The scions selected should be about 5–13cm (2–5in) long, and taken from vigorous, non-flowering, one-year-old shoots on the plant to be propagated. If only shoots with flower buds are available, pinch these out. The scions should be labelled and stored in a plastic bag in a refrigerator.

Select a straight-stemmed rootstock of about pencil thickness and cut it back to within 5cm (2in) of the base, making a straight cut across the stem with secateurs. Then, using a knife, make two slanting cuts to

make an upside-down "V" wound on the top of the stock. Prepare the scion by making two corresponding angled cuts so that its base – the saddle – will fit snugly onto the apex of the rootstock.

Ensure that the two sections of the graft fit well together, and then bind the stock and scion together with a length of clear grafting tape. Cut back any very large leaves by half to reduce moisture loss. Label clearly, and then place the grafted plant in a propagator and shade it from direct sunlight. Check the plant daily for watering and hygiene, and spray it once a week with a fungicide solution. Union normally takes place within four to five weeks.

Once the scion starts to grow, remove the tape and gradually harden off the grafted plant – opening the propagator for longer periods each day. If the grafted plant is kept in the original pot for a season, give it a liquid feed once a month.

Side-veneer grafting

This grafting technique is used to propagate a variety of both evergreen and deciduous shrubs. Most side-veneer grafting is carried out in mid-winter, but deciduous shrubs, such as *Hamamelis*, may also be grafted during the summer.

For the appropriate rootstocks, choose one- to three-year-old seedlings that are compatible with the plant to be propagated. The stems should be of pencil thickness. About three weeks before grafting, bring the rootstock into the greenhouse. Water it sparingly so that the rootstock does not break dormancy too quickly, since vigorous sap movement may prevent successful grafting. If grafting in summer, use two-year-old seedlings for the rootstocks and keep them fairly dry for a month in advance.

For both summer and winter grafting, prepare and unite the stocks and scions in the same way.

Just before grafting takes place, collect vigorous, one-year-old shoots that have some mature wood to be used as scions. They should be of a similar thickness to the rootstocks onto which they will be grafted. If there is any delay, label the scions and place them in a plastic bag in a refrigerator.

When grafting, first trim the scion to a length of 15–20cm (5–8in), or 10–12cm (4–5in) for magnolias. Make a sloping cut at the base of the scion, 2.5–4cm (1–1½in) long then turn it over and make a small wedge-shaped cut on the other side.

Reduce the rootstock stem to about 30cm (12in). Make two cuts in the

---

SUCKERING SHRUBS THAT MAY BE DIVIDED

Amelanchier canadensis
Andromeda
Aronia
Aster albescens
Berberis buxifolia
Buxus sempervirens
Cassiope hypnoides
Ceratostigma plumbaginoides
Clerodendrum bungei
Cornus alba,
   C. canadensis,
   C. stolonifera

Cornus canadensis

Danäe racemosa
Diervilla lonicera
Erica
Euonymus fortunei
Gaultheria, some ✿
Itea virginica
Kerria
Mahonia repens
Menziesia ciliicalyx
Paxistima
Pernettya
Polygala, some ✿
Rhus, some ✿
Ruscus aculeatus
Sarcococca
Spiraea japonica (cvs)

KEY
✿ *Not hardy*

PROPAGATING SUCKERING SHRUBS BY DIVISION

1 *Lift a root with suckers on it, without disturbing the parent plant. Check that there are fibrous roots at the base of the suckers.*

2 *Remove the long, suckering root by cutting it off close to the parent plant. Firm back the soil around the parent plant.*

3 *Cut the main root back to the fibrous roots, then divide the suckers so that each has its own roots. Cut back the top growth by about half.*

4 *Replant the suckers in open ground in prepared planting holes. Firm the soil around the suckers and water in. (The plant used here is* Gaultheria shallon.)

SADDLE GRAFTING

1 Select vigorous, non-flowering shoots of the previous year's growth from the plant to be propagated (here a rhododendron) as scions.

2 Prepare a selected rootstock of about the same diameter as the scion by cutting it back to within about 5cm (2in) of the base.

3 Using a sharp knife, cut the stock with two upward angled cuts so that its apex is shaped like a slightly rounded, upside-down "V".

4 Make compatible, angled cuts on the scion (see inset), trimming its length to about 5–13cm (2–5in).

5 Place the cut scion (see inset) on top of the stock so that they fit together. If the scion is too narrow, place it so that one side of the cambium layer meets that of the stock.

6 Bind the scion in place with plastic grafting tape or raffia. Cut back very large leaves by half. Leave the grafted plant in a propagator until union occurs.

SHRUBS THAT MAY BE GRAFTED

Saddle
Rhododendron, some ❀ (many hybrids and species)

Side-veneer
Acer palmatum (cvs)
Aralia elata 'Aureovariegata'
Arbutus unedo (cvs)
Camellia reticulata,
  C. sasanqua
Caragana arborescens
Cotoneaster x 'Hybridus
  Pendulus'
Daphne bholua, D. petraea
Hamamelis
Magnolia
Pittosporum eugenioides
  'Variegatum' ❀
Prunus glandulosa
Rhaphiolepis

*Hibiscus
sinosyriacus
'Lilac Queen'*

Apical-wedge
Caragana arborescens
  'Walker'
Daphne arbuscula
Hibiscus, some ❀
Syringa

KEY
❀ *Not hardy*

---

stock, starting 8cm (3in) above soil level, to take out a sliver of wood, leaving a cut that roughly matches that on the scion.

Place the rootstock and scion together so that the cambium layers match as closely as possible, and if necessary on one side only for stocks and scions of differing widths; tie them securely in position with grafting tape. Label the grafted plant and place it in a propagator at an even temperature of 10–15°C (50–59°F). Water the plant regularly and, once a week, spray with a fungicide.

Union should occur in four to five weeks. Harden off the grafted plant over the next four weeks, then remove it from the propagator and grow it on in a cool greenhouse.

As the scion starts to grow, gradually cut back the stem of the stock; by the end of the first growing season, all the stock above the graft union should have been cut back. During the first season, remove the initial tie and, if growth is rapid, replace it with a single, raffia tie.

On plants that have been grafted in the summer, head back the stock just above the union before growth starts in spring. Replace the original tie with a small one around the union, since there is a tendency for the scion to be pushed off the stock. Support the leader with a cane after repotting. For further details, see *Propagating Trees by Side-veneer Grafting*, p.58.

Apical-wedge grafting

Apical-wedge grafting, or cleft grafting, is a comparatively straightforward technique and is suitable for the propagation of a number of shrubs, including *Caragana*, *Hibiscus*, and lilac (*Syringa*).

During mid-winter, collect vigorous, one-year-old stems for use as scions. Place these in a clearly labelled plastic bag and store them in a refrigerator in order to retard their development.

Also in mid-winter, select one-year-old seedlings of compatible shrubs as rootstocks. Stock and scion should both be about the thickness of a pencil. Immediately prior to grafting, lift the rootstock and wash it. Cut its stem horizontally, about 2.5cm (1in) above the roots. With a sharp knife, make a 2.5cm (1in), vertical cut down the centre of the rootstock stem.

Remove the scions from the refrigerator and select one with healthy buds that is of similar diameter to the rootstock. Trim it down by making a horizontal cut just above a healthy bud or buds and a similar cut 15cm (6in) below. To form the wedge, make a 2.5–4cm (1–1½in) long, sloping cut down towards the middle of the scion base, and a similar cut on the other side.

Push the scion into the prepared cut on the stock. If the scion is narrower than the stock, align one edge of the scion so that it is flush with one edge of the stock. Bind them with grafting tape or moist raffia. If raffia is used, coat the union edges with grafting wax to stop moisture loss and to seal the top of the scion.

Either pot up the grafted plants or insert them in potting compost in a seed tray. Label and then place them in a propagator at 10–15°C (50–59°F), the higher temperature inducing a faster union.

The union of the stock and scion should take place within about five to six weeks. Remove the tape or raffia when there is a firm union. Pot up the plants that are in seed trays and harden them off gradually. Grow the plants on for a further year in a cold frame before planting them out.

APICAL-WEDGE GRAFTING

Make a simple, vertical cut down into the stock. Cut the base of the scion with 2 downward cuts into a "V" and push the base into the stock. Bind them together, pot up, and place in a propagator.

Fuchsias

FUCHSIAS are extremely adaptable plants, cultivated for their very attractive, pendent flowers, which range from modest, slender tubes to fully double, bicoloured blooms with distinctive, swept-back sepals. All the species and cultivars may be used in summer bedding schemes or grown in containers, and many are hardy enough to be used in permanent plantings. Those of upright habit may be trained as standards or as other formal shapes, while lax or trailing cultivars look very attractive when planted in hanging baskets and windowboxes. Breeders have produced a vast range of hardy and slightly tender hybrids.

Most fuchsias cannot tolerate intense sun or warm greenhouse conditions; in cold areas, many may need frost protection in winter.

Propagation

Fuchsias grow easily from cuttings, and plants propagated in this way are almost always superior to those raised from seed. Cuttings may be taken at any time of year when plants have suitable, non-flowering shoots. If taken in early spring, they can make exhibition plants by late summer; if taken in late summer, cuttings may be overwintered in a greenhouse for late spring flowering. The tips removed when pinching out, or stopping, will also root.

Growing new plants from root cuttings is a slow process, only of use when the crown of a plant has been killed by frost (for further details, see "Root cuttings", p.86).

CUTTINGS

TIP CUTTING

STEM SECTION

Stem trimmed just above and below one set of leaves

SINGLE-LEAF CUTTING

Stem split vertically to retain only one leaf

Cuttings may be taken at any time of the year from growing tips, when stopping the plant, or from leaves.

Softwood cuttings

Cut the stem below a node, with the tip and three sets of leaves. Remove the lowest two sets and proceed as for other shrubs (see p.83).

To produce several cuttings, cut a young shoot into sections, each with a group of leaves and about 1cm (1/2 in) of stem above and below the leaves. These may be split to form single-leaf cuttings, provided that the bud in the leaf axil is undamaged. Provide bottom heat to accelerate rooting, especially early in the year.

Maintain a moist atmosphere, but allow air to circulate freely so that the cuttings do not damp off.

Once rooted, transplant them into 6cm (3in) pots of potting compost, and feed them weekly with a high-nitrogen liquid fertilizer. In the early stages, do not use feeds that are high in phosphate and potash.

Pot on into 13cm (5in) pots when the roots reach the outside of the soil ball. Use peat-substitute- or peat-based compost with good drainage. Plant out after the last frost.

HARDY AND TENDER FUCHSIAS

F. 'Celia Smedley' *Upright habit. Suitable for training as a standard. Half hardy.*

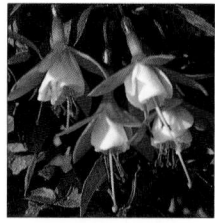
F. 'Lady Thumb' *Lax habit. Suitable for training as a miniature standard. Frost hardy.*

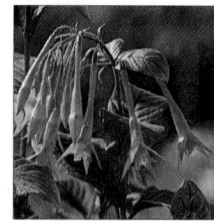
F. 'Thalia' *Upright habit. Suitable for summer bedding schemes. Frost tender.*

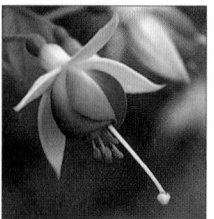
F. 'Estelle Marie' *Upright habit. Suitable for summer bedding. Half hardy.*

F. 'White Ann' *Upright habit. Suitable for training as a standard. Half hardy.*

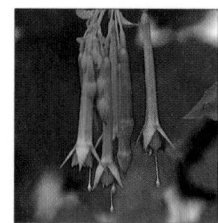
F. fulgens *Upright habit. Edible but acid fruits. Frost tender.*

Training

Fuchsias are most commonly trained into bushes or standards. Fans and espaliers may be created in the same way as fruit trees (see p.382, and "Peaches", p393).

Bush fuchsias

Begin training bushes as soon as the young plants have developed three sets of leaves. To form a bush, pinch out (stop) the growing tip to stimulate two to four sideshoots to grow.

HOW TO TRAIN A BUSH FUCHSIA

1 *When the fuchsia cutting has developed 3 sets of leaves, pinch out the growing point. This will stimulate the production of sideshoots lower down the stem.*

2 *A few weeks later, when several sideshoots have developed, pinch out the top set of leaves from each sideshoot to encourage further branching.*

3 *Continue to pinch out the growing points of new sideshoots as they develop.*

4 *Stop pinching out sideshoots when the plant has a symmetrical shape with evenly spaced shoots. Lax plants may need staking.*

HOW TO TRAIN A STANDARD FUCHSIA

1 When the cutting is about 15cm (6in) high, pinch out any sideshoots as they appear in the leaf axils.

2 Continue to do this to produce a long, straight stem. Tie the plant to a cane.

3 When the standard reaches the required height, leave it to produce 3 more sets of leaves, then pinch out the growing tip.

4 Pinch out the tips of the sideshoots that form at the top of the stem so that they will branch further.

5 Once the head has filled out, the leaves on the stem will usually drop off naturally, or they may be carefully removed.

When these have each developed two sets of leaves, stop the shoots until the plant is as bushy as needed.

Each pinching out increases the potential number of flowers but delays flowering. To time flowering for exhibition purposes, stop for the last time 60 days before the show for single cultivars, 70 days for semi-doubles, and 80 days for doubles.

Standard fuchsias
To train a standard, leave the tip of the young plant to grow and wait until sideshoots appear. Then pinch out all the sideshoots, but do not remove the leaves on the main stem. Tie the stem at intervals to a cane to provide support for the plant.

Continue until the required length of bare stem has been reached. The recognized stem lengths for a standard are: "miniature standard" less than 25cm (10in); "quarter standard" 25–45cm (10–18in); "half-standard" 45–75cm (18–30in); and "full standard" reaching 75–107cm (30–42in). Now allow a further three sets of leaves to develop, then pinch out the tip. After this, training involves the same stopping procedures as for a bush.

It will take 18 months to achieve a full standard and about six months for a quarter or miniature standard.

Growing fuchsias in containers

Fuchsias grow well in pots and hanging baskets and if well cared for will remain in flower from soon after planting until the first frosts. Position them where they will get some shade for part of the day. Choose just one cultivar per container, since different cultivars grow at different rates. Mixtures of fuchsias and other plants also make a successful display.

Planting
Use three good plants for a 24cm (9in) diameter basket or half basket, and a minimum of four for a 30cm (12in) basket, and more for a larger one. For a trailing effect, select young, bushy plants that have been stopped several times.

Use either a standard or a proprietary potting compost, both of which incorporate slow-release fertilizers to reduce the need for regular additional feeding.

HANGING BASKET

Line a basket with sphagnum moss and fill it with potting compost. Place a small pot of gravel, half the depth of the basket, in the centre with its rim at soil level; this will distribute water evenly around the roots. Plant small fuchsias around the edge, facing outwards at 45°.

Routine care

Water sufficiently to keep the soil moist but not waterlogged – at least once a day for hanging baskets, every few days for plastic pots. Never leave pots standing in saucers of water.

Fuchsias in hanging baskets benefit from a balanced liquid feed in late summer. Hardy garden fuchsias need a dressing of general fertilizer or bone meal after pruning in spring and again during summer. Mature plants do not need regular feeding, but give a high-potash liquid feed when flowering begins.

Vine weevil (p.549), greenfly (see "Aphids", p.550), whiteflies (p.550), red spider mites (p.550), and grey mould/*Botrytis* (p.550) can be troublesome. At the first signs of rusts (p.552) remove infected leaves and spray with a systemic fungicide.

Overwintering

Fuchsias are hardier than is thought and often bedded-out plants can be left *in situ*, although it is a good idea to take cuttings in early autumn as an insurance against frost damage. Standards should always be brought under cover in winter.

Hardy fuchsias
In areas that are cold in autumn, mulch fuchsias with straw, bracken, or bark over the crowns. Even if the plants are cut back by frost, they will shoot from the crown like a herbaceous plant. Do not prune until regrowth starts in spring, then cut back to ground level.

Non-hardy fuchsias
In late autumn, move frost-tender fuchsias into frost-free conditions. If a minimum temperature of 8°C (46°F) is maintained, they may continue flowering through the winter.

If there is no greenhouse available, place tender bedding fuchsias, standards, and other trained fuchsias in frost-free conditions. Lift and pot up plants that have been bedded out. Remove the green tips and leaves and keep all the plants dormant through the winter – not quite dry and as cool as possible.

In spring, shake the roots clear of soil, repot the plants into slightly smaller pots, and prune hard back. Water them and encourage fresh growth by lightly spraying the wood.

OVERWINTERING A HARDY FUCHSIA

Hardy fuchsias should be left in situ over the winter. In very cold areas, cover the base with bracken; the bare branches will also provide some frost protection. In the spring, prune them to strong new buds near ground level.

4

CLIMBING PLANTS

WOODY AND HERBACEOUS *climbers make up one of the most versatile of plant groups, providing enormous scope for imaginative design in the garden. Grown with support, whether against the house wall or on free-standing pillars and pergolas, climbing plants bring a strong vertical element to planting schemes. If unsupported, their branches sprawl luxuriantly, adding colour, texture, and horizontal line to plantings, while some function effectively as weed-smothering ground cover. When* allowed to scramble upwards through other tall plants, *climbers can extend the season of interest, and may be used to weave together other colour and textural elements of the garden design. Perhaps one of their greatest assets is their potential for clothing otherwise unsightly garden features, be they fences or walls, tree stumps, outhouses, or other garden buildings. Many of the most popular are also fragrant, their high and far-reaching stems bearing heavily scented flowers to perfume the garden.*

Designing with climbers

GARDENS of every size and aspect may be enhanced by climbing plants. Some, such as *Lapageria* and *Passiflora* species, are grown primarily for the exquisite beauty of their flowers; others – *Lonicera periclymenum*, for example – are equally valued for their fragrance. Many are appreciated for their handsome foliage, which can give year-round interest in the case of evergreens, or provide rich and spectacular autumn colour, as with *Parthenocissus* species and *Vitis coignetiae*. Even when leafless, their elegant habit and often strong architectural form enhance the stark, winter outlines of hard landscape features. A significant number of climbers carry fruits or berries that are attractive both to the gardener and to wildlife.

In their natural habitats, climbers use various techniques to climb through host plants to gain access to the light. In gardens, natural and purpose-built supports may be exploited to suit the particular mode of growth used by the plant selected.

A FLORAL ENTRANCE
Bougainvillea *artlessly links a series of archways in this elegant courtyard setting. The brilliant spectacle of its showy, pink bracts harmonizes well with the sun-baked supporting wall. In frost-free gardens, it is one of the most vigorous and luxuriant of all climbers.*

Climbing methods and supports

Some climbers are self-clinging, attaching themselves to their supports either by aerial roots (adventitious rootlets), as do ivies (*Hedera* spp.), or by adhesive tendril tips, as does Virginia creeper (*Parthenocissus quinquefolia*). These cling to any surface offering sufficient purchase, including walls and tree trunks, and need no additional support except during the early stages, when they require the guidance of a cane, string, or wire until they are able to establish secure contact. Climbers with aerial roots are also particularly well-suited for use as ground cover.

Twining species coil their stems in a spiralling motion around their support – clockwise or anticlockwise depending on their anatomical and morphological characteristics. Both *Lonicera periclymenum* and *Manettia inflata*, for instance, twine clockwise, whereas *Ceropegia sandersonii* and *Wisteria sinensis* twine anticlockwise. All twining species need permanent support, usually provided by trellis or wire. They may also be grown up the stems and branches of a sturdy host plant (see also "Growing climbers through other plants", p.96).

A few climbers like clematis and some nasturtiums (*Tropaeolum*) attach themselves to supports by means of curling leaf stalks. Many others are tendril climbers that twine around their supports by means of contact-sensitive tendrils, which are often modified leaves or leaflets as

GARDEN DESIGN
Framing a formal piece of statuary, Humulus lupulus 'Aureus' *helps to reinforce a striking focal point in this garden. Its fresh, lime-green leaves have a distinctive charm of their own.*

in *Bignonia capreolata* and sweet peas (*Lathyrus odoratus*); axillary shoots as in *Passiflora*; or terminal shoots as in vines. In *Parthenocissus*, the tendrils develop adhesive discs at the tips once they come into contact with a support.

Scandent, scrambling, and trailing climbers, such as *Bougainvillea* species, *Quisqualis indica*, and winter jasmine (*Jasminum nudiflorum*) produce long, arching stems that attach themselves only loosely, if at all, to their supports. These plants need to be tied in to a wire framework or trellis. Alternatively, they may be left to sprawl over walls and banks for a less formal effect. Plants in this group are also sometimes used as ground cover.

Some species, including climbing roses and certain *Rubus* species, are equipped with hooked thorns that help them to scramble naturally through host plants. If not grown through other plants, these need to be tied in to sturdy supports.

Site and aspect

To achieve their full potential, a number of climbers prefer a sunny position with their roots in shade, although some need a cooler spot. Others are less demanding and, while preferring a sunny aspect, may still tolerate shade – *Parthenocissus* and *Schizophragma* species are just two examples of many.

Tender climbers may require the protection of a south-facing wall in cool climates. There are numerous hardy climbers, however, that will perform perfectly well without any protection at all.

Sunny or sheltered sites

In temperate areas, a sheltered wall provides a suitable microclimate for growing tender or exotic-flowering climbers. *Lapageria rosea* and the common passion flower (*Passiflora caerulea*) both thrive with winter protection in such a position; the heat reflected by the wall helps to ripen the wood so that the plants are better able to withstand cold winter temperatures.

The wall itself also gives protection against several degrees of frost. If frost is likely to occur at flowering time, avoid planting such climbers in positions where the flower buds are exposed to early-morning sun, since the buds will often be damaged as a result of rapid thawing. Sun-loving herbaceous plants and bulbs may be planted at the base of the climbers to help keep their roots cool.

Cool or exposed sites

For shady, north-facing walls and those exposed to cold winds, vigorous, hardy climbers – some honeysuckles and many ivies, in particular – are the most suitable plants. In a heavily shaded site, use green-leaved ivies; those with variegated or yellow leaves prefer more light and are prone to frost damage.

Climbers on walls, buildings, and fences

Whether complementing or camouflaging their support, climbing plants make an immediate visual impact when trained against walls and buildings. Many provide strong colour, while others give a more diffuse and subtle backdrop to the whole garden design. Most buildings may be enhanced by the softening effect of a climber grown against them. In the same way, garden walls and fences become decorative features when clothed with plants bearing blossom and foliage.

Enhancing a building

Before planting, assess the architectural merits of a building and use the plants to emphasize its good points. A well-designed building may be complemented by climbers that have a strong visual impact, with, for example, distinctively shaped or coloured foliage or outstanding flowers. *Actinidia kolomikta*, with its pink- or white-tipped leaves and cup-shaped white flowers in summer, is one of the most spectacular climbers for this purpose.

A less visually pleasing building may also be made more attractive by using climbers. Regular panels of plants may be used to break up long stretches of blank wall, and may also serve to exaggerate or mitigate strong vertical or horizontal lines. Narrow panels of foliage that extend upwards can make a building seem taller than it is. On the other hand, wider panels of plants allowed to grow only as high as the first floor will make a tall, narrow building appear broader. The most suitable plants for this purpose include most species of ivy and other self-clinging root climbers, such as *Hydrangea anomala* subsp. *petiolaris* and *Schizophragma integrifolium*; these form rich panels of foliage that may be pruned into the desired shape.

In a more relaxed, informal setting, vigorous climbing plants may be combined for a profusion of flowers and fragrance: the dark green foliage and white flowers of *Clematis armandii*, together with the strongly fragrant red and yellow flowers of *Lonicera* x *americana*, combine well with many species of climbing rose, perhaps with annual sweet peas (*Lathyrus odoratus*) grown through them. This combination is particularly effective around a window or doorway, where the flowers and scents may be best appreciated.

Screening with climbers

The more vigorous climbing plants may be used to camouflage an unattractive outhouse, wall, or fence

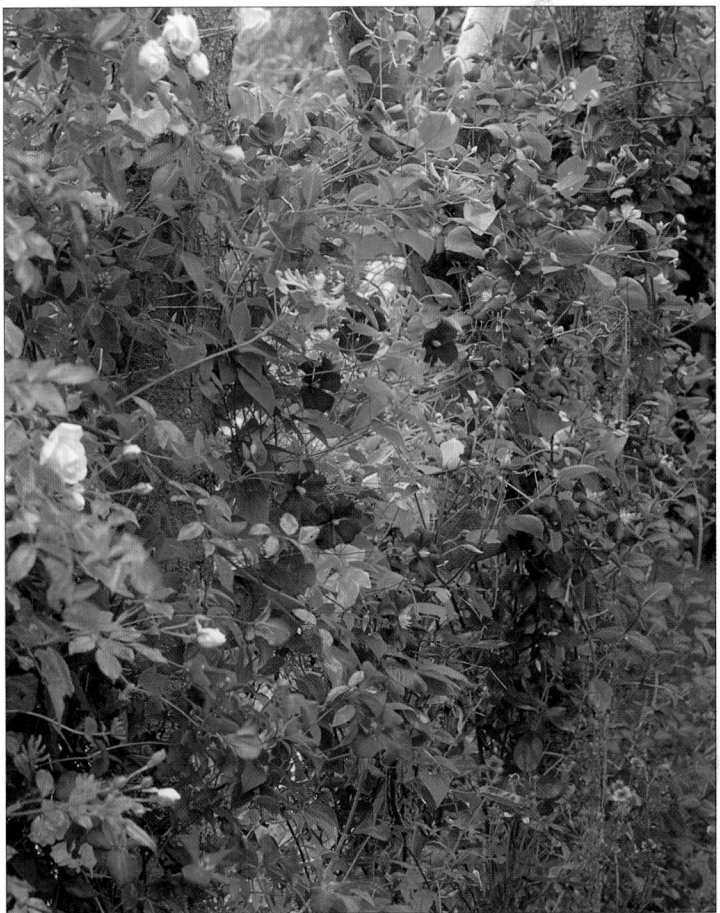

AN INFORMAL SCREEN
These clematis and yellow climbing roses weave through wires to provide an attractive mix of colour and a long season of interest.

remarkably quickly. Use plants such as *Clematis montana*, for its mass of creamy-white flowers in late spring, or Russian vine (*Fallopia aubertii*, syn. *Polygonum aubertii*), which soon produces dense cover combined with panicles of tiny flowers in late summer. Both *F. aubertii* and *F. baldschuanica* are known as mile-a-minute vine for a good reason – they are extremely rampant and must therefore be sited with great care, since they will swamp even reasonably vigorous neighbours. They also need regular and severe pruning to keep them within bounds.

Where all-year cover is required, ivies may be more appropriate. Alternatively, use a combination of evergreen and deciduous plants; the finely cut, evergreen leaves of *Clematis cirrhosa*, for instance, provide the perfect foil in summer for the soft-pink blooms of the climbing rose 'New Dawn'.

Climbers on pergolas and pillars

Pergolas, pillars, and other purpose-made structures enable climbers to be viewed from all sides and, in addition, contribute strong stylistic elements to the garden design. They may be used to add height to an otherwise flat garden. Depending on materials used, they may be formal and elegant, or informal and rustic. If well designed, they can be at their most attractive when only partially covered with plants. They must, however, be strong enough to carry the often considerable weight

of stems and foliage and should also be durable, as the plants will need their support for many years.

Pergolas

Pergolas or arbours festooned with climbers not only provide a cool, shady sitting area in the garden but also bring a sense of seclusion and privacy to an otherwise open site. The most suitable plants to choose are those that put on their best display at the time of day or during the particular season when the structure is most often used.

If an arbour is to be used often on summer evenings, suitable plants might include common jasmine (*Jasminum officinale*), *Lonicera periclymenum* 'Graham Thomas', or the climbing rose 'Mme Alfred Carrière', all with beautifully fragrant blooms in pale colours that show up well in the fading light. For summer shade, use large-leaved climbers such as *Vitis coignetiae* (which also gives splendid autumn colour) or *V. vinifera* 'Purpurea', whose claret-coloured young leaves turn dusky purple as they mature. Alternatively, use the massed floral display of *Wisteria sinensis* 'Alba' as a summer canopy. The flowers of this plant look very effective if grown up pergolas flanking walkways. Ensure that the crossbeams are high enough, however, so there is no need to stoop to avoid the flowers.

For winter interest, plant evergreens, such as ivy or, in mild areas, tender *Lardizabala biternata*. Alternatively, use deciduous plants such as *Celastrus* or *Wisteria* species, whose bare stems take on beautiful sculptural qualities in winter.

GROWING ON PERGOLAS
Wisteria sinensis 'Alba' is the ideal choice for a pergola over a walkway. It produces a mass of fragrant white blooms in early summer that hang down in garlands, releasing their welcome scent at just the right height to be appreciated.

Pillars

To add a strong vertical element to a mixed or herbaceous border, climbers such as clematis or *Passiflora* species may be grown up and around pillars. Also consider using pillars to mark an axis or focal point, perhaps at the corner of a border or at a point where the garden level changes. A series of pillars at the back of a flower bed or along a path may also be linked by rope or chain swags, and climbers trained along them.

For an evergreen climber, or as a temporary feature, a stout post with mesh panels wrapped around it will

provide adequate support. If growing a deciduous plant, which means that the pillar will be visible in winter, buy a ready-made trellis obelisk or column, which will be attractive when it is bare.

Growing climbers through other plants

In the wild, many climbers grow naturally through other plants, which is a habit that may be copied to great advantage in the garden – although

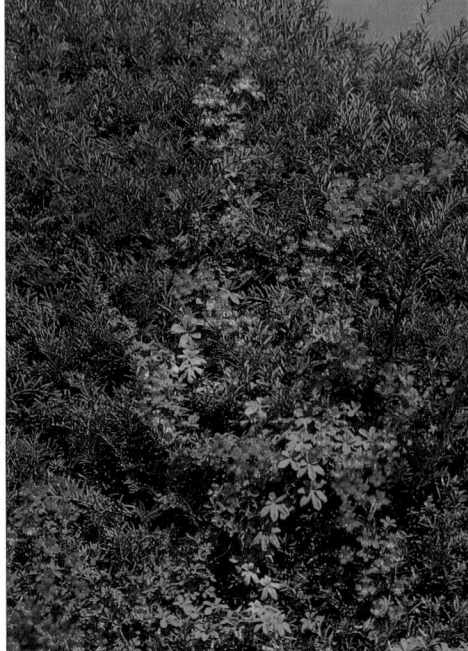

NATURAL SUPPORT
The scarlet flowers of Tropaeolum speciosum *are made yet more intense by the rich, deep-green backcloth provided by a hedge of yew (Taxus baccata).*

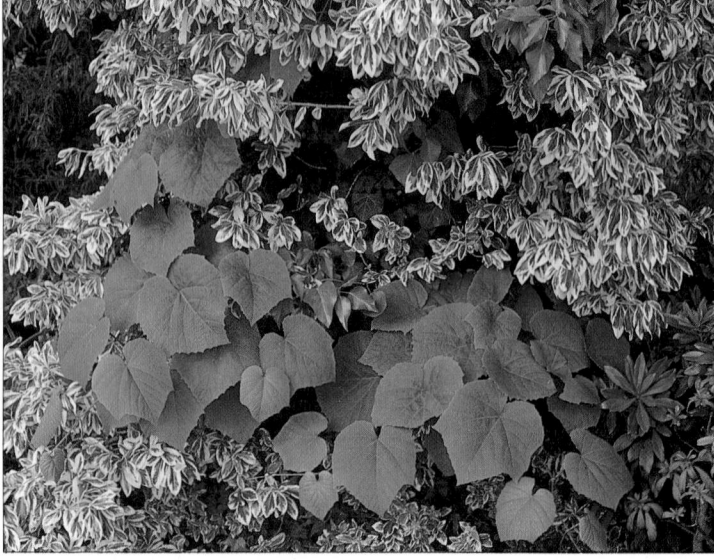

PLANT ASSOCIATION
The heart-shaped leaves of Vitis coignetiae *make a striking contrast of shape and texture with those of* Euonymus fortunei *'Silver Queen'.*

the climbers should not be too vigorous for the hosts. Always plan colour combinations carefully before planting, taking flowers, foliage, and fruit into consideration; the climber may either complement or contrast with its host when the latter is putting on its best display, or extend the season of interest.

Climbers that are suitable for growing through shrubs include *Clematis viticella* hybrids and those large-flowered clematis that are cut back each year. It is also a useful method of growing most annual climbing plants and *Tropaeolum speciosum*, whose stems and fiery red flowers are best supported by another plant.

For growing through trees, vigorous species, such as *Ampelopsis brevipedunculata* var. *maximowiczii* or *Schizophragma hydrangeoides*, produce beautiful combinations of foliage, fruit, and flower. Alternatively, try mingling the cascading blooms of *Rosa filipes* 'Kiftsgate' with the white or pink sprays of *Clematis montana*. Both produce strong, twining stems that quickly scramble into the branches of a tree.

Climbers as ground cover

Some climbers, particularly those with aerial roots or those with a scandent, trailing, or scrambling habit, may be grown without support to produce swathes of ground cover. They are particularly effective when allowed to sprawl over a sloping bank or when trailing over a wall, where they will often root in the soil beneath.

Climbers that attach themselves by means of adhesive tendrils, such as *Parthenocissus* species, and root climbers, are extremely effective at suppressing weeds when grown as ground cover. Take care when siting these plants, however, because if there is any other plant nearby that could serve as a support, it may be swamped. To reduce the risk of this, choose less vigorous climbing species or relocate other plants so that the climber has a free run.

Twining climbers may also be used as ground cover, provided that the shoots are spread evenly across the ground; if needed, wire hooks may be used to keep the shoots in place. The large, deeply coloured flowers of *Clematis* 'Ernest Markham' and *C.* 'Jackmanii' are very effective at ground level, as are the blue-green leaves and scarlet flowers of *Tropaeolum speciosum*.

GROUND COVER
Clematis viticella *cultivars* 'Abundance' *and* 'Etoile Violette' *make a carpet of colour, using winter-flowering heathers* (Erica) *as host plants.*

Colourful climbers

Colour effects vary according to light levels in different parts of the garden. In a sunny spot, bright or deep colours, which absorb light, show up more strongly than paler colours. The latter, on the other hand, may look washed out in bright light but successfully illuminate a dull space; they may be used to great effect in parts of the garden that are most often viewed in the evening.

Before planting climbing plants, consider the colour of the garden's permanent features. If the wall or support is already bright, use plants with more subtle colouring – unless you wish to create a particularly vibrant effect.

Colour combinations
Growing different climbers together or in combination with other plants adds another dimension to colour schemes. Climbers can be particularly useful for interweaving the different colour components of a planting scheme, creating brilliant effects with complementary colours or more subtle harmonies with closely related tones.

Flowers for colour
The flowers of climbers occur in colours across the spectrum, from the deep violet of *Clematis viticella* 'Etoile Violette' through the brilliant scarlet of *Campsis radicans* to the soft, creamy-white of *Araujia sericofera*. Many of the most vividly coloured climbers are tropical

in origin and may not always be hardy in temperate zones, however.

Climbers with strongly coloured flowers have a bold and exuberant appearance, but these usually need thoughtful placement if they are not to be overwhelming. Those that have softer colours, such as the pink *Clematis montana* 'Elizabeth'

or the pale violet-blue *Codonopsis convolvulacea*, are more suitable for subtle-hued planting schemes.

Foliage and fruits for colour
Use the leaves of climbers as well as their flowers: the skilful use of foliage can produce beautiful effects, the leaf tone providing soothing contrasts and balancing vivid flower colour. *Humulus lupulus* 'Aureus' has yellow leaves that appear almost gold if placed against a dark background. Even more striking is *Actinidia kolomikta*, which has leaves splashed with creamy-white and pink. The variegated ivies are almost as showy and, because evergreen, give a year-long display.

Other climbers bear fruits that are at least as colourful as their flowers: outstanding among these are the fruits of *Akebia quinata* (purplish), the slightly frost-tender *Billardiera longiflora* (purple-blue or white), and *Celastrus orbiculatus* (green, then black, splitting to show yellow insides with red seeds).

Interest through the seasons

For continuity of interest throughout the year, devise a planting scheme in which different climbers succeed each other as the seasons progress.

COMPLEMENTARY COLOURS
An old stone wall provides a natural setting for climbing plants. This one has an unobtrusive wire framework attached, with clematis and the golden-leaved Humulus lupulus 'Aureus' *twining around it.*

FOLIAGE EFFECTS
Actinidia kolomikta is a deciduous climber with highly unusual and decorative foliage; many of the leaves are tipped with bold splashes of pink or white. Small, cup-shaped, scented white flowers also appear in the summer.

CLIMBING ANNUALS
Lablab purpureus is often grown as an annual for quick cover in summer. This huge and gnarled old tree trunk lends its support to the twining stems and pea-like, pink and purple flowers.

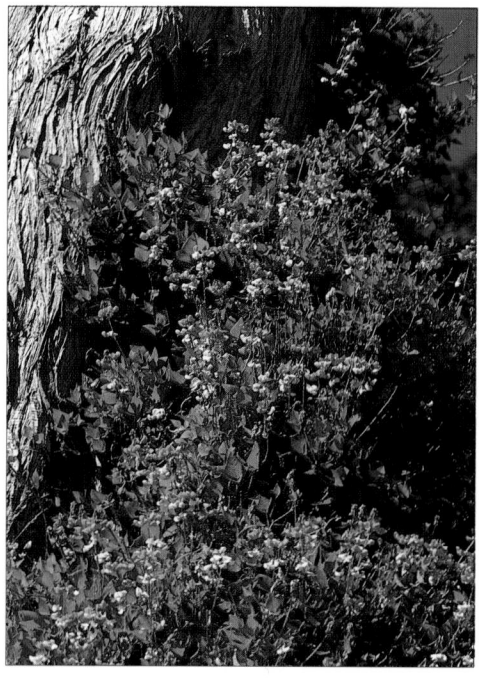

This technique may be applied to climbers that are being grown together or in separate parts of the garden, so that there is always something to catch the eye.

Spring and summer

Numerous climbers put on their best show in spring and summer. Early-flowering *Clematis macropetala* with *Lonicera periclymenum* 'Serotina', which reaches its peak in mid-summer, make an extremely effective combination. The flowers of the clematis also leave behind fluffy seedheads to augment the beauty of the honeysuckle's scented

tubular blooms, and often continue the display throughout autumn and sometimes even into winter.

Autumn colour

Some climbers provide glorious autumn leaf colour: the deeply cut, sometimes crinkled, leaves of *Parthenocissus tricuspidata* are perhaps the most spectacular of all, turning scarlet, crimson, and deepest burgundy before they fall.

Winter interest

Climbers that flower in winter are few and are not generally hardy; one rare exception is winter jasmine

(*Jasminum nudiflorum*), which produces delicate yellow blooms even on a north-facing wall. The slightly tender *J. polyanthum* produces a profusion of flowers in a sheltered situation, and *Clematis cirrhosa* flowers in all areas in frost-free weather.

Evergreens with unusual foliage provide interest in winter, too. Ivies are the most versatile, since most are hardy. Some are boldly variegated too: the colourful *Hedera helix* 'Buttercup' and 'Goldheart' are good examples. Others are grown for their leaf shape – the Bird's-foot ivy (*H. h.* 'Pedata'), with leaves shaped like a bird's foot, and 'Parsley Crested', with crinkly edged leaves, are two foliage plants of merit.

Scented climbers

Perfumed climbers, such as the tropical *Beaumontia grandiflora* and the sweet pea (*Lathyrus odoratus*), have special appeal. To appreciate the fragrance to the full, plant sweet peas near doorways or windows. If planted in a border, place them close to the outer edge.

Some release their fragrance at a particular time of day; jasmine species (*Jasminum*) are more heavily scented at night, so are well placed over an arbour or near a terrace or patio that is used in the evening.

Annual climbers

Annual climbers and those that are treated as annuals in cool-temperate climates, such as *Eccremocarpus scaber* and *Pueraria lobata*, are

particularly useful for short-term effects. Annuals provide an excellent way of introducing variety into planting schemes, since they can be changed every year, if desired. They may also be used to fill gaps in the border until more permanent plants become well established.

Climbers in containers

Climbers in containers may be trained over walls and pillars in the same way as those grown in the open ground; if the support is fixed to the container, the plant may be moved around as desired. Some lower-growing climbers, such as *Clematis macropetala*, may also be grown without support – plant these in tall containers, so that their stems trail gracefully to the ground. Ivies are well suited to being grown in this way but need regular pruning once established.

In gardens where space is limited, it is still possible to grow more rampant climbers, such as *Bougainvillea* and *Wisteria* species, in containers. Their growth will be checked but severe pruning will be required. Regular repotting will also be needed to keep them healthy.

Containers are especially suitable for less hardy climbing species that may need winter protection, such as *Hardenbergia comptoniana* and *Senecio macroglossus* 'Variegatus'. Simply take the containers indoors or into a heated greenhouse at the onset of autumn frosts, putting them outside again the following spring.

AUTUMN FOLIAGE
This striking display of autumn colour is produced by the crimson leaves of Parthenocissus tricuspidata *with the reddening foliage of* Vitis coignetiae.

Planter's guide to climbers

NORTH-FACING WALLS

Climbers that may be grown against north-facing walls

Agapetes ❀ (some spp.)
Akebia quinata
Allemanda cathartica ❀
Aristolochia elegans ❀
Berberidopsis corallina
Cissus ❀
Clematis, some ❀
Clerodendrum thomsoniae ❀
Clytostoma callistegioides ❀
Codonopsis convolvulacea
Dioscorea discolor ❀
Epipremnum ❀
Hardenbergia ❀
Hedera, some ❀
Hoya ❀
Humulus lupulus
Hydrangea anomala subsp.
   petiolaris
Kadsura japonica
Lapageria rosea ❀
Lathyrus latifolius
Lonicera x *americana*,
   L. x *brownii, L.* x *heckrottii*,
   L. sempervirens,
   L. x *tellmanniana*
Mitraria coccinea ❀
Monstera deliciosa ❀
Parthenocissus, some ❀
Philodendron ❀
Pileostegia viburnoides
Stigmaphyllon ciliatum ❀
Syngonium podophyllum ❀
Tetrastigma voinierianum ❀
Tropaeolum speciosum
Vitis coignetiae

AIR POLLUTION

Climbers that tolerate polluted air

Campsis radicans
Clematis, some ❀
Fallopia, syn. *Polygonum*

Clematis
'Elsa Spath'

Hedera, some ❀
Hydrangea anomala
   subsp. *petiolaris*
Parthenocissus, some ❀
Vitis, some ❀

SHADE

Climbers that tolerate shade

Asteranthera ovata
Euonymus fortunei and variants
Fallopia, syn. *Polygonum*
Humulus lupulus
Parthenocissus tricuspidata
Strongylodon macrobotrys ❀

FRAGRANT FLOWERS

Anredera cordifolia ❀
Beaumontia grandiflora ❀
Clematis armandii, C. montana
Hoya australis ❀, *H. carnosa* ❀
Jasminum officinale,
   J. polyanthum ❀
Lathyrus odoratus
Lonicera spp. (not *L. sempervirens*
   or *L.* x *tellmanniana*), some ❀
Quisqualis indica ❀
Solandra maxima ❀

*Stephanotis
floribunda*

Stephanotis floribunda ❀
Trachelospermum
Wisteria

CLIMBERS FOR CONTAINERS

Asarina erubescens ❀
Bougainvillea ❀ (prune very hard)
Cissus ❀ (some spp.)
Clematis alpina, C. macropetala
Dioscorea discolor ❀
Epipremnum ❀
Gynura aurantiaca ❀
Hardenbergia ❀
Hedera helix
Jasminum officinale,
   J. polyanthum ❀
Lapageria rosea ❀
Monstera deliciosa ❀
Philodendron ❀ (some spp.)
Senecio macroglossus
   'Variegatus' ❀
Stephanotis floribunda ❀
Streptosolen jamesonii ❀
Syngonium ❀ (some spp.)
Tetrastigma voinierianum ❀
Thunbergia alata ❀
Wisteria (prune very hard)

EVERGREEN CLIMBERS

Allemanda ❀
Anemopaegma ❀
Anredera ❀
Araujia ❀
Argyreia ❀
Asteranthera
Beaumontia ❀
Berberidopsis
Calceolaria pavonii ❀
Calochone ❀
Cissus ❀
Clerodendrum splendens ❀,
   C. thomsoniae ❀
Clytostoma ❀
Combretum grandiflorum ❀
Decumaria sinensis ❀
Dioscorea discolor ❀
Distictis ❀

Epipremnum ❀
Gynura ❀
Hardenbergia ❀
Hedera, some ❀
Hibbertia scandens ❀
Holboellia ❀
Hoya ❀
Jacquemontia ❀
Kennedia ❀
Lapageria ❀
Lardizabala
Macfadyena ❀
Mandevilla ❀
Merremia ❀
Monstera ❀
Mussaenda ❀
Mutisia, some ❀
Pandorea ❀
Pileostegia
Podranea ❀
Pyrostegia ❀
Rhoicissus ❀
Semele ❀
Senecio confusus ❀,
   S. macroglossus ❀,
   S. mikanioides ❀, *S. tamoides* ❀
Solandra ❀
Stauntonia
Stephanotis ❀
Stigmaphyllon ❀
Strongylodon ❀
Syngonium ❀
Tecomanthe ❀
Tecomaria ❀
Tetrastigma ❀
Trachelospermum
Wattakaka

CLIMBERS THAT MAY BE GROWN THROUGH OR OVER OTHER PLANTS

Bomarea caldasii ❀
Bougainvillea ❀

*Bomarea
caldasii*

Celastrus
Clematis, some ❀
Codonopsis convolvulacea
Humulus lupulus
Lonicera, some ❀
Mutisia, some ❀
Tropaeolum peregrinum ❀,
   T. speciosum
Vitis coignetiae
Wisteria sinensis

FAST-GROWING CLIMBERS

Allemanda cathartica ❀
Ampelopsis
Anredera cordifolia ❀

Antigonon leptopus ❀
Aristolochia elegans ❀
Clematis, some ❀
Clytostoma callistegioides ❀
Cobaea scandens ❀

*Cobaea
scandens
f. alba*

Epipremnum aureum ❀
Fallopia, syn. *Polygonum*
Humulus lupulus
Kennedia rubicunda ❀
Macfadyena unguis-cati ❀
Passiflora caerulea ❀,
   P. manicata ❀
Periploca
Philodendron scandens ❀
Plumbago auriculata ❀
Pyrostegia venusta ❀
Quisqualis indica ❀
Stigmaphyllon ciliatum ❀
Strongylodon macrobotrys ❀
Thladiantha dubia
Vitis vinifera

ANNUAL CLIMBERS

Asarina erubescens ❀
Convolvulus tricolor
Eccremocarpus scaber ❀
Ipomoea ❀ (some spp.)
Lablab purpureus
Lathyrus odoratus
Mikania scandens ❀
Quisqualis indica ❀
Thunbergia alata ❀
Tropaeolum peregrinum ❀

HERBACEOUS CLIMBERS

Bomarea caldasii ❀
Canarina canariensis ❀
Codonopsis convolvulacea
Humulus lupulus
Lathyrus grandiflorus, L. latifolius
Thladiantha dubia
Tropaeolum speciosum,
   T. tricolorum ❀, *T. tuberosum* ❀

CLIMBERS FOR GROUND COVER

Asteranthera
Hedera, some ❀
Kennedia ❀
Mitraria ❀
Pileostegia
Plumbago auriculata ❀
Senecio, some ❀
Tecomaria ❀
Trachelospermum

KEY
❀ Not hardy

Soil preparation and planting

G IVEN ideal growing conditions, climbing plants bring enduring rewards, so always ensure that they are well suited to the type of soil in which they are planted. Climbers seldom thrive in excessively damp or dry conditions. A few, such as *Agapetes* and *Mitraria*, do not tolerate alkaline conditions; others, such as clematis, thrive on alkaline soils but also grow well on all but the most acid soils. Many climbers are vigorous and require ample nutrients so dig and fertilize the soil well before planting (see also "Soil nutrients and fertilizers", pp.530–31).

When planting climbers, it is important to use the correct support. Choose one that will easily accommodate the eventual height, spread, and vigour of the plant.

Types of support

The three main types of support used are wooden or plastic trellis panels, wire or plastic mesh, and wires (usually plastic-covered) stretched between vine eyes or rust-proof nails. Horticultural string or reinforcing wire may be adequate for annuals or for herbaceous climbers if the supports are replaced each

year. Make sure that all supports are fixed securely in the correct position before planting. Do not use "U"-shaped metal staples to attach the stems of any plant to its support: plants rapidly outgrow these staples and the stems may become constricted and die back.

Choose a support that will match the size and strength of the climber. One that is not sufficiently sturdy for a vigorous climber may quickly become engulfed and will eventually collapse. Trellis is the most reliable support for all twining climbers, and may also be used for scramblers if they are tied in. Wires or mesh are appropriate supports for tendril climbers.

If the support is not to be a permanent structure, use climbers that are either herbaceous (*Lathyrus grandiflorus* and *L. latifolius*, for example) or cut to ground level each year (late-flowering *Clematis viticella* hybrids and cultivars), or annual climbers such as *Ipomoea hederacea*. When growing plants against a flat, free-standing trellis or over a pillar, bear in mind that climbers grow towards the light, and produce their flowers on one side of the support only, so position plants to provide their display where it will be most prominent.

Trellis and mesh

To allow air to circulate freely, fix a trellis panel or mesh so that it is held slightly away from the wall or fence and make sure that the base of the framework is approximately 30cm (12in) above soil level.

Walls are likely to need maintenance (repointing, painting, or rendering) at some time: wherever possible attach trellis and mesh with hooks at the top and hinges at the base, or hooks top and bottom. The whole plant may then be lowered from the wall or, if hooks only are used, taken down and laid flat on the ground while the wall is repaired.

Wires

Wires may be stretched horizontally or vertically between vine eyes or rust-proof nails. As with trellis panels, the wires should be held 5cm (2in) from the surface of the wall or fence, and must be kept taut to prevent sagging; either tighten the vine eyes with pliers or attach tensioners at approximately 2m (6ft) intervals. Space the wires 30–45cm (12–18in) apart, with the lowest horizontal wire (or the base of vertical wires) 30cm (12in) above soil level.

Climbing methods

Climbers attach themselves to supports by various means. Many climbers have aerial roots that readily attach to vertical surfaces without support. Other methods, all of which require some support, include twining stems and leaf stalks, and coiling tendrils. Scandent and scrambling climbers, such as *Bougainvillea*, produce long stems that need to be tied in at regular intervals.

AERIAL ROOTS
Ivy (Hedera) *is a self-clinging plant.*

LEAF STALKS
Clematis climbs using its leaf stalks.

COILING TENDRILS
Passiflora *attaches itself with tendrils.*

TWINING STEMS
Akebia *weaves its stems in a spiral around the support.*

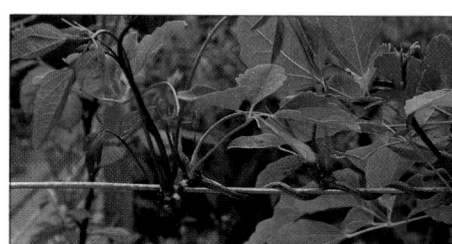

Fixing a trellis panel to a wall

To mount a trellis support, first securely attach vertical wooden battens at least 5cm (2in) thick to the wall and trellis. This allows the trellis to be suspended away from the wall and enables air to circulate freely. The trellis may then be permanently fixed to the battens with screws (right); this restricts access to the wall, however. Using hooks and hinges (below) allows the plant and support to be lowered, if required. Hooking the trellis to the battens at both top and bottom allows it to be removed from the wall altogether.

USING BATTENS
Screw the trellis to thick wooden battens.

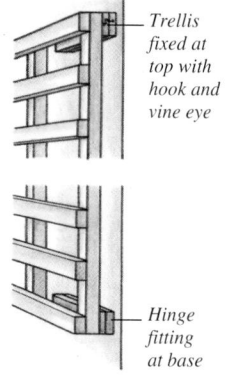

Trellis fixed at top with hook and vine eye

Hinge fitting at base

USING HOOKS AND HINGES
To allow access to the wall for maintenance, attach battens to both the wall and the trellis. Fix hinges along the bottom of the panel with hooks at the top to hold it in place.

CLIMBERS THAT HAVE A VIGOROUS HABIT

Actinidia chinensis
Akebia quinata
Beaumontia grandiflora ❀
Bougainvillea ❀
Cissus ❀
Clematis montana
Distictis buccinatoria ❀

Distictis buccinatoria

Fallopia aubertii
Ipomoea horsfalliae ❀
Mandevilla ❀
Parthenocissus quinquefolia,
   P. tricuspidata
Passiflora, most ❀
Petrea volubilis ❀
Solandra maxima ❀
Solanum wendlandii ❀
Tetrastigma voinierianum ❀
Vitis coignetiae
Wisteria sinensis

KEY
❀ *Not hardy*

How to Select Climbers

GOOD EXAMPLE

Label

Vigorous, sturdy stems

Healthy buds

HONEYSUCKLE (LONICERA)

POOR EXAMPLE

Spindly, weak growth with damaged buds

GOOD EXAMPLE

Roots are visible and healthy but not coiled

POOR EXAMPLE

Roots coiled tightly around the root ball

Buying climbers

Climbing plants are usually sold container-grown, although a few (including climbing roses) may be sold with bare roots. Choose a healthy plant with a well-balanced framework of strong shoots, and reject any that show signs of pest infestation or disease. Bare-root plants should have plenty of healthy, well-developed, fibrous roots that are in proportion to the amount of top-growth. For pot-grown plants, turn the pot over and check that the tips of the young roots are just showing; if so, the plant is well-rooted. Reject pot-bound plants – those that have tightly coiled roots around the root ball or a mass of roots protruding through the drainage holes in the pot – as they seldom grow on satisfactorily.

Planting outdoors

Climbers that are not fully hardy (such as *Solanum crispum* and *S. jasminoides*) should be planted in spring, so that they are well established before their first winter. Evergreen and herbaceous climbers are more quickly established if planted in spring when the soil is warming up, but they may also be planted in autumn in a protected situation or if the weather is mild. All other container-grown climbers may be planted in spring, autumn, or any other time of year as long as the ground is not frozen or water-logged. Planting during dry spells in summer is not recommended, but if this is unavoidable, make sure that the plant is watered daily while dry conditions persist.

Positioning the plant

Walls and solid fences create their own rain shadow, so plants that are to be trained against them should

Planting a climber in a container

Select a container large enough to accommodate the climber for at least two seasons. Concrete, stone, or terracotta pots are more stable than plastic ones. Shallow pots are not suitable. Choose a frost-proof pot if the climber is to remain outdoors in winter.

The potting medium should be moisture-retentive but also free-draining; use loam-based potting compost or a mixture of 2 parts peat substitute (or peat) to 1 part sharp sand. Supplement this with a slow-release fertilizer – mix it into the compost according to the manufacturer's instructions.

Trellis panels specially made for containers are available, with two "legs" at the base. Bed these into the compost before planting rather than after, to avoid damaging the plant's roots. Tie the top of the trellis to a wall or fence to keep it steady.

1 Put crocks at the base of the pot to assist drainage and bed the support into the base of the container with compost.

2 Plant the climber at the same level as in the original pot. Fill in with compost, leaving 5cm (2in) below the rim to allow for watering.

3 Tie the main shoots to the support, and water the plant thoroughly to settle the roots.

CLIMBERS THAT TOLERATE SANDY SOIL

Adlumia fungosa
Anredera cordifolia❀
Asarina❀
Bomarea andimarcana❀
Ceropegia❀ (spp. only)
Clianthus puniceus❀
Ercilla volubilis❀
Gloriosa superba❀
Ipomoea❀

Kennedia rubicunda

Kennedia rubicunda❀
Merremia tuberosa❀
Mutisia oligodon
Parthenocissus, some❀
Passiflora, most❀(some spp.)
Periploca graeca
Petrea volubilis❀
Solanum wendlandii❀
Streptosolen jamesonii❀

CLIMBERS THAT TOLERATE CLAY SOIL

Aristolochia durior
Campsis
Celastrus scandens
Clematis, some❀(most)
Distictis❀
Euonymus fortunei 'Silver Queen'
Hedera, some❀
Humulus lupulus 'Aureus'
Hydrangea anomala subsp. *petiolaris*
Lathyrus latifolius
Lonicera, some❀ (some spp.)

Parthenocissus tricuspidata 'Loweï'

Parthenocissus, some❀
Passiflora, most❀
Vitis coignetiae
Wisteria

CLIMBERS THAT REQUIRE ACID SOIL

Agapetes❀ (several spp.)
Asteranthera ovata❀
Beaumontia grandiflora❀
Berberidopsis corallina
Billardiera❀ (spp. only)
Kennedia❀
Lapageria rosea❀
Lardizabala biternata❀
Mitraria coccinea❀
Mutisia, some❀(some spp.)

KEY
❀ Not hardy

be planted at least 45cm (18in) from the foot of the support. In this way, they normally receive sufficient rain to be grown without additional water once established. A pillar or free-standing trellis does not produce the same density of rain shadow and so the planting distance need be only 20–30cm (8–12in).

When grown through another plant the climber will compete with the host plant for food and moisture; to minimize this, plant the climber so that its roots stay as far away as possible from those of its host. If the host plant has deep roots, and a sufficient depth of soil is available, plant the climber fairly close to the host's main stem. If the host plant has a mass of rhizomatous or shallow roots, however, plant the climber about 45cm (18in) from the main root spread. A cane tied to the host plant, inserted just behind the climber's main stems, may be used to train the climber towards it at an angle.

Preparing the soil
Remove all weeds from the planting area, using a systemic weedkiller to kill perennial weeds, if necessary,

---

CLIMBERS THAT TOLERATE VERY ALKALINE SOIL
Actinidia kolomikta
Akebia quinata
Ampelopsis brevipedunculata
Asarina antirrhiniflora
Campsis x *tagliabuana* 'Mme Galen'
Celastrus scandens
Clematis, some ✱ (cvs)
Eccremocarpus scaber✱
Fallopia aubertii,
    F. baldschuanica
Hedera, some ✱
Hydrangea anomala
    subsp. *petiolaris*

Lathyrus grandiflorus

Jasminum officinale,
    J. polyanthum ✱
Lathyrus grandiflorus,
    L. latifolius
Lonicera, some ✱ (some spp.)
Parthenocissus tricuspidata
Passiflora caerulea✱
Schizophragma integrifolium
Solanum crispum
Trachelospermum jasminoides
Vitis, some ✱
Wisteria sinensis

KEY
✱ *Not hardy*

---

then dig in bulky organic matter. This will improve the water retentiveness and fertility of sandy soils, and lighten the texture of heavy clay soils. Carefully fork in a dressing of slow-release fertilizer, at a rate of 50–85 g/sq m (2–3oz/sq yd).

The planting hole should be at least twice the diameter of the container in which the climber was grown in order to allow the roots ample room to spread in the prepared soil. This may not be possible, however, if the climber is to be encouraged to grow through a tree or shrub, in which case dig a hole large enough to accommodate the root ball and leave plenty of room for the roots to spread.

How to plant
Before removing the plant from its pot, make sure that the compost is moist – water the plant well so that the root ball is thoroughly wet and then leave it to drain for at least an hour. Remove the surface layer of compost to eliminate weed seeds, and then invert the pot, taking care to support the plant as it slides out. If the roots have begun to curl around inside the pot, gently tease them out. Any dead, damaged, or protruding roots should be cut back to the perimeter of the root ball.

Position the plant so that the top of the root ball is just level with the surrounding soil. It is advisable to plant clematis more deeply, however (see *Planting a Clematis*, p.109). Climbers that have been grafted (as is the case with most wisterias) should be planted with the graft union 6cm (2½in) below soil level. This encourages the scion itself to root, and reduces the incidence of sucker growths from the stock. For information on planting bare-root climbers, see "Planting a bush rose", p.123.

Fill the planting hole with soil, then firm the plant in and water well. Insert canes at the base of the plant and secure them to the support. Fan out the main shoots and tie them individually to the canes and to the support itself (if they will reach) to train them in. Do not damage the stems by attaching them too tightly. Remove dead or damaged growth and cut back wayward shoots.

Tendril climbers readily attach themselves to a support, but the shoots may require gentle guidance and some tying in until they become firmly established. Twining climbers soon fasten their shoots to a support in their natural direction of growth (clockwise or anticlockwise) but may also need initial tying in. Scramblers that do not support

themselves should have their shoots fastened to the support at regular intervals with appropriate ties. For further information, see "Training established climbers", p.106.

Watering and mulching
Water the newly planted climber thoroughly, then cover the surface of the soil surrounding the plant with a 5–7cm (2–3in) layer of mulch to a radius of about 60cm (2ft). This is beneficial to the roots because it retains moisture throughout the area, giving the roots a chance to establish themselves. In addition, the mulch discourages the germination of weeds that would otherwise compete with the newly planted climber for nutrients and moisture.

PLANTING A CLIMBER AGAINST A WALL

1 *Fix a support 30cm (12in) above the soil and 5cm (2in) from the wall. Dig a hole 45cm (18in) from the wall. Loosen the soil at the base and add compost.*

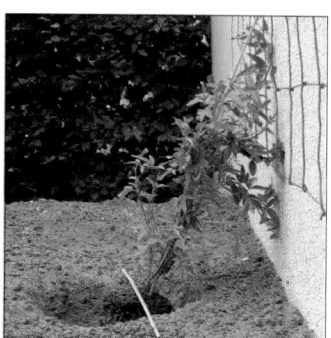

2 *Soak the climber's root ball well. Position it in the hole at a 45° angle, placing a cane across to check the planting level. Spread the roots away from the wall.*

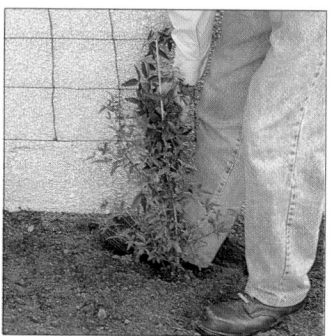

3 *Fill in around the plant and firm and level the soil, ensuring that no air pockets remain between the roots and that the plant is fully supported.*

4 *Untie the stems from the central stake and select 4 or 5 strong shoots. Insert a stake for each shoot and attach it to the lowest wire. Tie in the shoots.*

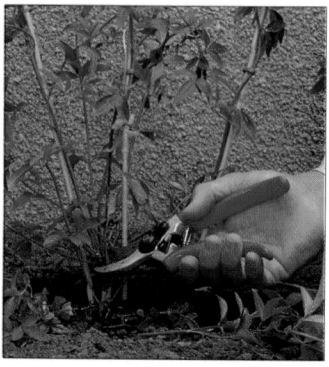

5 *Trim back any weak, damaged, or wayward shoots to the central stem using secateurs. This establishes the initial framework for the climber.*

6 *Water the plant thoroughly (here* Jasminum mesnyi). *Cover the surrounding soil with a deep mulch to retain moisture and discourage weeds.*

Routine care

CLIMBERS need feeding annually to maintain healthy growth, and the soil around their base should be kept moist. Climbers grown in containers need top-dressing or re-potting regularly, and adequate watering is essential. Regular dead-heading helps to prolong flowering. Plants also need protection from pests, diseases, and, if tender, frost.

Feeding
Feed climbers in spring during their first two seasons with a dressing of 50–85g (2–3oz) of a balanced fertilizer. Thereafter, apply a slow-release fertilizer annually at the manufacturer's recommended rate.

Watering
During dry periods, water climbers weekly. Soak thoroughly around the base of the plant; apply a 5–7cm (2–3in) mulch over the whole root area to prevent the soil drying out.

Dead-heading and tying in
Where practical, dead-head climbers as the flowers fade. This enables the plant to concentrate its energies on producing further flowers, rather than fruits or seedheads. If fruits or seedheads are needed for ornamental purposes, dead-head only a quarter to one third of the flowered shoots. This will be enough to encourage a continuing display of flowers.

Tie in new shoots as they develop, while still flexible, and cut back overgrown plants as needed (see "Pruning and training", pp.104–107).

Pests and diseases
Check carefully for signs of pests and diseases and treat any affected plants as recommended in PLANT PROBLEMS, pp.545–77.

Protecting tender climbers
In winter, and particularly in cold periods or when frost is likely, wrap up the top-growth and base of tender climbers grown outside in protective covering (see FROST AND WIND PROTECTION, pp.520–21).

CUTTING BACK CLIMBERS

Where a climber (here Hedera colchica 'Sulphur Heart') *has outgrown its allotted space, cut it back with secateurs. Trim the stems irregularly for a natural effect.*

Maintaining container-grown climbers

Container-grown climbers may need to be watered once or twice a day in dry weather. When frost is likely, they may be moved indoors or plunged in the ground in a sheltered part of the garden. During the year, a climber grown in a container uses up most of the nutrients in the potting medium. The top-dressing (i.e. the top layer of the compost and any mulch) should therefore be renewed annually. When the plant is watered, the fresh nutrients will gradually permeate and replenish the compost below. All but the most slow-growing climbers need to be moved into a larger container, using fresh compost, every three to four years. Spring-flowering plants should be repotted in autumn, others in autumn or spring.

RENEWING THE TOP-DRESSING OF A CONTAINER-GROWN CLIMBER

1 *In spring or early summer, scrape away and discard the top 2.5–5cm (1–2in) of compost in the container. Take care not to disturb any surface roots of the climber and the companion planting.*

2 *Replace the discarded compost with a layer of fresh compost mixed with a little slow-release fertilizer. Firm gently to eliminate air pockets. Make sure that the compost level is the same as before. Water well.*

3 *To aid moisture retention during the summer months, cover the compost in the container with a light, decorative mulch such as cocoa shells or bark chippings.*

REPOTTING A CONTAINER-GROWN CLIMBER

1 *Every 3 or 4 years repot container-grown climbers (such as this variegated ivy) to prevent them from becoming pot-bound (see inset). Soak the compost well, then carefully slide the root ball out of the container.*

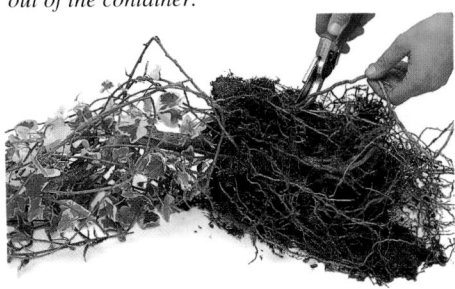

2 *Tease out the roots and trim back the thicker roots by about one third. Leave fibrous roots intact and retain as much compost as possible around them.*

3 *Prune the top-growth by a third and remove dead or damaged stems. Repot the plant in fresh, moist compost, adding slow-release fertilizer to the top 2.5–5cm (1–2in).*

4 *Ensure that the final planting level is the same as before. Insert a triangle of canes, and tie in the main shoots securely but not too tightly.*

Pruning and training

During the early years, pruning is carried out to build a strong framework for a plant, to promote vigorous growth of healthy, productive wood, and to facilitate training over the support. Training should be aimed at guiding a selected number of strong, major stems over and across a support while they are flexible to create a pleasing shape.

Some climbers, for example Russian vines (*Fallopia aubertii* and *F. baldschuanica*), send out a mass of small shoots in addition to main stems, and these need to be regularly tied in during initial training to retain the required shape. Frequently, however, vigorous climbers are difficult to train after the first year and are best left to grow freely; restrict them only when they grow beyond their allotted space.

Basic principles

Routine pruning is essential to the successful cultivation of almost all established climbers. Without this control the plants may fail to flower well, and, equally importantly, some of the more vigorous climbers may swamp nearby plants or damage roofs, gutters, and masonry. Training may be combined with pruning to achieve the most desirable structure and appearance for the plant.

Where to cut

The stems should be cut 2–3mm ($^1/_{16}$–$^1/_8$in) above a plump bud. Select an appropriately placed bud that faces the direction in which a new shoot is required. Then, as the shoot develops, it can be tied in to fill the framework or to replace an old shoot.

Make each pruning cut cleanly with sharp secateurs, at an angle slanting slightly away from the bud. This ensures that rainwater does not gather around the bud and encourage possible disease infection. The position of the cut is important: a cut that is made too close to the bud may damage it, while one made too far away from the bud will leave a stub that dies back and may provide an entry point for disease.

Using the correct tools

A pair of sharp secateurs is the best tool for most types of pruning. Long-handled loppers may also be useful, especially for thicker stems, and shears may be used where a great deal of dead or weak growth needs to be removed (see "How to prune honeysuckle", p.107).

Formative pruning and training

At planting time, and as the plant starts to grow, training consists of tying in the strongest shoots to the support to achieve a balanced framework. During the growing season, a little guidance will be needed to ensure that the soft, twining stems or tendrils attach themselves to their support while they are still pliable and before the wood becomes too mature, because hardened stems cannot be bent into the required position without damaging them.

In late winter or early spring following initial planting, once all danger of severe frost has passed, cut back each sideshoot to an appropriately placed bud that is near the central or main stem, tying the pruned shoots to the support. Several strong stems will grow from these during the following season, from which the framework of the plant develops. These should be trained in as they develop, as before.

The following year, cut back each stem and, possibly, the leader, to a bud that is pointing in the direction in which the stem is to be trained. This results in the growth of vigorous shoots with which to extend the main framework. Carefully tie in all the stems, and cut back any other shoots to within two buds of the nearest stem.

SPRING PRUNING

Climbers that flower on the current season's shoots, such as Solanum crispum *shown here, should be pruned in late winter or early spring.*

FORMATIVE PRUNING AND TRAINING

In order to establish a healthy, strong framework for a climbing plant, begin pruning and training as soon as possible after planting, in late winter or early spring. The plant here is Jasminum nudiflorum.

Remove any crossing shoots. Use sharp secateurs and cut just above a healthy bud.

To encourage new, strong growth, prune back sideshoots to an appropriately placed bud.

Cut out any congested growth from the centre of the plant.

Tie in all sideshoots securely to the support with horticultural string.

Cut out all congested growth, removing crossing shoots and the weaker of any shoots that are competing.

Remove dead or frost-damaged shoots and stems, cutting back to live, healthy wood.

To encourage flowering, cut back sideshoots to 5 or 6 strong, healthy buds, making an angled cut just above a bud.

Pruning established climbers

The time of year to prune established climbers depends on their flowering habit. Some flower on the current season's shoots or, occasionally, on shoots that are produced late in the growing season of the previous year. These are usually pruned in late winter or early spring, before new buds begin to develop, and will flower later in the same season on new shoots.

Other climbers flower on the previous year's ripened shoots, or on even older shoots. These should be pruned immediately after flowering, to allow new shoots time to grow and ripen before the winter: these are the shoots that will bear next season's flowers. Some early-flowering climbers will produce a second crop of flowers later in the season, if pruned early enough.

Distinguishing between first- and second-year shoots is not normally difficult: first-year shoots are still pliable and usually green, while second-year ones are usually grey or brown. Shoots more than two years old have a distinct, usually dark bark, and are tough and woody.

When pruning, always remove all dead or damaged wood and any congested, twiggy growth. Cut back stems that have grown beyond the plant's allotted space, both to maintain the shape of the climber and to control excessive growth.

For methods of pruning clematis, see pp.109–10.

EARLY SUMMER PRUNING

Climbers that flower on the previous year's ripened shoots, such as Jasminum beesianum, should be pruned immediately after flowering to allow new shoots to develop before the onset of winter.

Cut back shoots that have flowered, pruning to a vigorous shoot lower down.

Remove all dead or damaged wood, cutting cleanly close to a healthy shoot or stem.

Where there is congested growth, weak shoots should be removed.

Pruning *Wisteria*

Wisteria may be reluctant to flower unless the vigorous, leafy summer shoots are severely curtailed, and the plant's energies diverted into producing flower buds. Flowering is also improved if the main stems are trained horizontally rather than vertically. The flower buds are produced on short spurs, and the aim of pruning is to encourage these spurs to develop along the framework branches of an established plant. The simplest method is to carry out a two-stage pruning regime. In late summer, cut back long growths and shorter, lateral growths. Leave stems unpruned only if they are needed to extend the framework, and train them in. In mid-winter cut back summer-pruned spur shoots to two or three buds. At the same time, reduce to 15cm (6in) any long growths that developed after summer pruning.

1 *In late summer, restrict the growth of vigorous, leafy shoots to encourage more new buds to grow next year.*

2 *Cut back long shoots to about 15cm (6in), leaving 4–6 leaves. Make the cut well clear of the last bud, as the buds are easily damaged.*

WINTER
Prune again shoots shortened in summer. Reduce them to 8–10cm (3–4in), leaving only 2–3 buds.

CLIMBERS THAT FLOWER ON CURRENT SEASON'S GROWTH

Anredera cordifolia ✿
Antigonon leptopus ✿
Bignonia
Billardiera longiflora ✿
Campsis
Clematis, some ✿
  (large-flowered cvs)
Clerodendrum thomsoniae ✿
Clianthus ✿
Clytostoma ✿
Distictis ✿
Eccremocarpus scaber ✿
Ipomoea ✿
Lapageria ✿
Lonicera, some ✿
Mandevilla ✿
Mikania ✿
Mutisia decurrens
Parthenocissus, some ✿
Pileostegia viburnoides
Plumbago ✿
Podranea ✿
Polygonum aubertii
Pyrostegia venusta ✿

Solanum crispum

Solanum crispum,
  S. jasminoides ✿
Stephanotis ✿
Streptosolen ✿
Thladiantha, some ✿
Thunbergia gregorii ✿
Vigna caracalla ✿
Vitis, some ✿

CLIMBERS THAT FLOWER ON PREVIOUS SEASON'S GROWTH

Actinidia, some ✿
Allemanda cathartica ✿
Aristolochia, some ✿
Beaumontia ✿
Bougainvillea ✿

Bougainvillea 'Miss Manila'

Clematis montana
Decumaria sinensis ✿
Hoya ✿
Hydrangea
Jasminum, some ✿
Pandorea jasminoides ✿
Passiflora, most ✿
Pileostegia
Schizophragma
Solandra maxima ✿
Streptosolen jamesonii ✿
Strongylodon ✿
Wisteria

KEY
✿ Not hardy

EARLY WINTER PRUNING

When pruning climbers in early winter it is easy to assess the framework of the plant and train in any new growth. The climber shown here is Schisandra glaucescens.

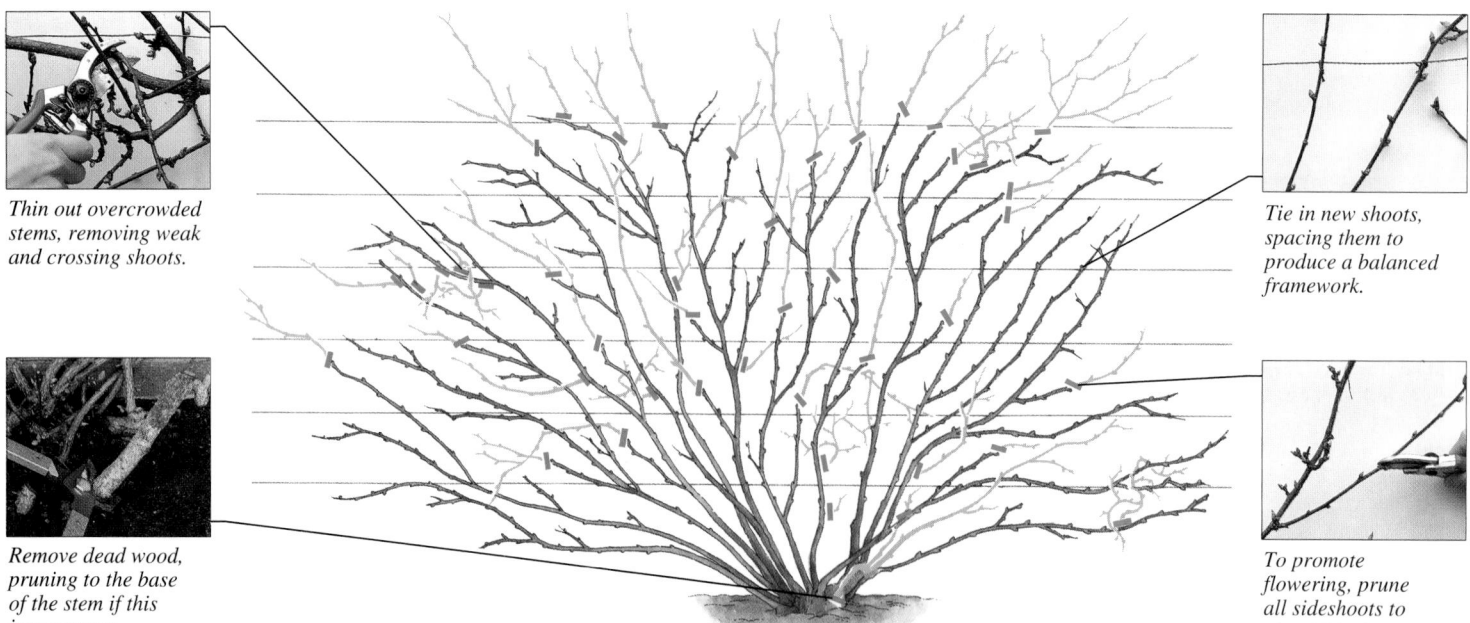

Thin out overcrowded stems, removing weak and crossing shoots.

Remove dead wood, pruning to the base of the stem if this is necessary.

Tie in new shoots, spacing them to produce a balanced framework.

To promote flowering, prune all sideshoots to about 5 buds.

Evergreen climbers

Prune evergreen climbers in early spring, after all danger of frost has passed and as the plants are about to begin fresh growth. Evergreen climbers that are grown for their flowers, as well as their foliage, produce flowers on the previous season's wood, so delay pruning these until after flowering. In both cases, simply remove dead or damaged wood and trim stray shoots to shape.

Early winter pruning

Climbers that have already had at least one pruning during the previous growing season may be pruned again in winter to tidy up their appearance (see illustrations above). This is particularly useful for deciduous plants, whose frameworks may be assessed more easily when the branches are bare. Do not remove ripened wood, which will carry the next season's flowers. If in mild spells winter-pruned plants are stimulated into new growth, the new young shoots may later be damaged by frost. Prune these back in spring.

Ornamental vines (*Vitis*) should be pruned in early winter, when the plants are dormant and pruning cuts may be made without the risk of "bleeding", or loss of sap, occurring. If the stems are cut in spring when the sap is rising, they "bleed" profusely; this is difficult to stop and weakens the plants. (For pruning of grape vines, see pp.402–406.)

Training established climbers

Climbers that attach themselves by means of aerial roots need very little training, except in the first few years until enough aerial roots have formed to support the plant. All other climbing plants need their new shoots trained in each year to establish the desired shape.

Each year during the growing season, select the strongest new stems, before they become hard and woody, and train them in to continue the basic framework. Follow the shape of the allocated space and allow the leading stem to extend in a straight line until it has reached the required height. Tie all stems securely to the

---

Pruning *Bougainvillea*

Bougainvillea is rampant and flowers reliably whether pruned or not. Prune between mid-winter and early spring to keep the plant in check. Shorten sideshoots to within a few centimetres of the main stems, but leave any needed to extend the main framework.

1 *Trim wayward sideshoots to within 2.5–5cm (1–2in) of the main framework stems.*

2 *Cut cleanly, close to a healthy bud. The buds will soon produce new growth.*

Training climbers on pergolas and pillars

To produce an even distribution of growth over a pergola or pillar, tie in the main stems throughout the growing season, spreading them out as required to fill any gaps. To promote flowering lower down a plant's stem, regularly train sideshoots of twining species around their support, making sure that the shoots are following their natural direction of growth: clockwise or anticlockwise.

After the flowering season, remove any dead or diseased shoots and prune the main stem and any leaders. This will encourage strong lateral growth to be produced in the following year.

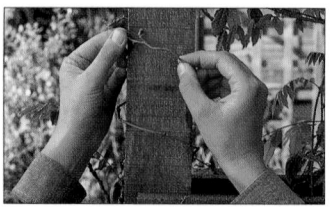

1 *Guide stray sideshoots onto the support in their natural direction of growth and tie in.*

2 *In late summer, cut back all the leading stems by one third to promote lateral growth.*

support at regular intervals using plastic twist-ties or vine ties. Make sure that the ties are tight enough to prevent the stems from being blown about in strong winds and rubbing against the support; they should not restrict development of the plant's stems, however. The ties will need to be loosened periodically as the stems thicken with age.

Renovating an old or neglected climber

Unpruned climbers – or those that have not been trained – often become a mass of tangled, woody stems, and produce a poor display of flowers. Such plants may be pruned hard to rejuvenate them. Most climbers withstand pruning close to the base or to main framework stems, but a plant in poor health may not survive this treatment. In this case, it is preferable to reduce the size of the plant gradually over a period of two or three years, in conjunction with annual feeding.

For a plant that is to be pruned to the base, cut down all existing growth in early spring to within 30–60cm (1–2ft) of the ground. To promote rapid new growth, apply a dressing

How to prune honeysuckle

Climbing honeysuckles (*Lonicera*) require little pruning to flower profusely but tend, if neglected, to develop into a mass of thin, tangled stems that bear foliage and flowers only at the top of the shoots. To renovate a honeysuckle in this condition, prune it severely in early to mid-spring, at the beginning of the growing season. New shoots will soon begin to develop and these should be trained in to provide an evenly balanced framework.

If such severe pruning is not required, it is still possible to renovate the plant by removing dead or damaged shoots and stems from beneath new, young growth. Use a pair of shears, rather than secateurs, for speed.

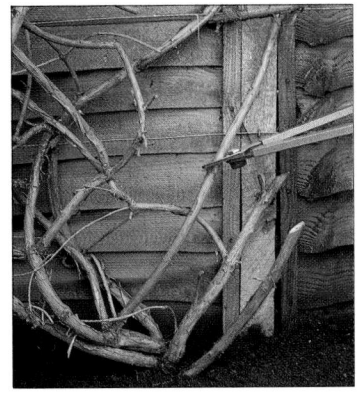

RENOVATION PRUNING
If the plant is badly overgrown, cut back all the stems with long-handled loppers to within 30–60cm (1–2ft) of ground level.

ALTERNATIVE METHOD
If it is undesirable or unnecessary to prune so severely, cut away all dead material from underneath the new, fresh growth.

of quick-acting, balanced fertilizer at a rate of 50–85g/sq m (2–3oz/sq yd). Soak the root area with water, and mulch. Train in all new growth as for newly planted climbers.

Renovation over a two- to three-year period (see below) is more difficult, as the stems frequently become entangled. In spring, remove

as much congested growth as possible, then cut to the base one in every two (or three) main stems. Gently unravel the top-growth of the severed stems. If any shoots are damaged, cut them out once the pruned main stems and their top-growth have been removed. Cut out any weak, spindly shoots, since these

will not flower satisfactorily, and any dead wood. Feed, water, and mulch, as when pruning to the base, to encourage healthy new growth. Train in fresh basal shoots to fill gaps, making sure they do not become entangled with old shoots. The following spring, repeat the process and feed, water, and mulch the plant.

RENOVATING A NEGLECTED CLIMBER

A neglected climber (here Celastrus orbiculatus) *may be renovated gradually over two or three seasons by pruning hard each spring.*

Remove as much congested growth as possible.

Remove weak, twiggy, or damaged shoots so that only strong shoots remain.

Using long-handled loppers, cut back to the base one third to one half of the old stems, retaining the more vigorous ones.

All dead or diseased wood should also be removed. Prune to a healthy bud, using sharp secateurs.

CLIMBERS THAT MAY BE CUT TO THE GROUND

Allemanda cathartica ❀
Anredera cordifolia ❀
Antigonon leptopus ❀
Aristolochia, some ❀
Campsis x *tagliabuana*
Clematis, some ❀ (most spp.)
Clerodendrum thomsoniae ❀
Clytostoma callistegioides ❀
Distictis buccinatoria ❀
Lonicera, some ❀ (most spp.)
Macfadyena unguis-cati ❀
Manettia cordifolia ❀,
    M. inflata ❀

Passiflora x *caponii*
'John Innes'

Passiflora, most ❀
Petrea volubilis ❀
Polygonum aubertii
Pyrostegia venusta ❀
Quisqualis indica ❀
Solandra maxima ❀
Solanum, some ❀
Stigmaphyllon ciliatum ❀
Strongylodon macrobotrys ❀
Thunbergia ❀

KEY
❀ *Not hardy*

Clematis

CLEMATIS are suited to almost any aspect and climate. Of all the climbers, they offer the longest flowering period with species or hybrids that bloom in almost every month of the year, many with the additional interest of silvery clustered seedheads appearing after flowering. They are diverse in habit, varying from herbaceous plants, such as *C. integrifolia* and the clump-forming *C. recta,* to sprawling sub-shrubs such as *C. x jouiniana,* as well as the better-known climbers.

Clematis also present a huge range of flower colour and flower forms, ranging from the attractive sprays of delicate, ivory-coloured bells in *C. rehderiana,* and exotic-looking, fleshy, golden lanterns in *C. tangutica,* to the simple but richly coloured blooms of *C. viticella* and its many hybrids, or the more complex forms of large-flowered double clematis such as *C.* 'Proteus' and *C.* 'Vyvyan Pennell'.

Where to grow clematis

Clematis can be chosen to suit almost any garden situation. The vigorous, spring-flowering species and cultivars are ideal for clothing and camouflaging unsightly buildings, fences and walls, or for scrambling over old trees, tree stumps, and arbours, adding colour and interest to otherwise dull features.

Less rampant types may be wall-trained on trellis and pergolas or allowed to cascade over terraces; at ground level more delicate species will sprawl where their blooms can be best appreciated.

Some clematis are suitable for container cultivation, on patios, or, for tender species, under glass. Others have great potential for being grown through host plants – trees, climbers, and sturdy shrubs, for example – to provide an extended season of interest, a splash of colour, or to create unusual and enchanting plant associations.

Clematis groups

Clematis may be divided into three main groups, based on their flowering time and habit.

Group 1 is made up of the early-flowering species and their cultivars, and the Alpina, Macropetala, and Montana groups, which flower directly from the previous season's ripened stems. In Group 2 are the early, large-flowered cultivars, blooming on short, current season's stems, which arise from the previous season's ripe wood. Groups 1 and 2 are sometimes known as "old wood"-flowering clematis. Group 3 includes the late-flowering species, late, large-flowered cultivars, and herbaceous types, which flower on the current season's growth.

Early-flowering species and cultivars

The slightly tender, early-flowering evergreen species and their forms originate from regions with warm climates and are best grown, therefore, with protection in areas with hard frosts. Among the hardiest ever-greens are the vigorous *C. armandii* and smaller *C. cirrhosa.* Both grow best in a south- or south-west-facing site and are effective when growing through other wall-trained plants.

The Alpina and Macropetala groups withstand very low winter temperatures and are ideal for growing through wall-trained trees and shrubs on any aspect. Do not grow them through climbing roses or other shrubs that need annual pruning, since these clematis need little or no cutting back. They are suitable in exposed sites such as north-east corners of buildings but also make superb container plants for the patio and can be trained to any support.

The members of the Montana group are fully hardy and vigorous, climbing 7–12m (22–40ft). These plants will cover walls and arbours and are effective growing through conifers or old fruit trees that are past their productive best, but may damage the foliage of evergreens with their rampant, dense growth.

Early, large-flowered cultivars

These are fully frost hardy, growing to 2.5–4m (8–12ft). The more compact cultivars such as *C.* 'Edith', which are normally the first to flower, are ideal for containers. The double and semi-double cultivars and the mid-summer flowering types with very large flowers are best grown through the branches of other wall-trained trees or shrubs, where their flowers are protected from severe wind or heavy rain. Paler-flowered cultivars with pink or mauve-striped flowers are best planted out of full sun, where their flowers may be used to lighten a dark wall and they will not be bleached. The deep reds and purples are more suited to sunny situations because they develop better colour in warmth.

Late-flowering species and cultivars

This group of clematis includes the late, large-flowered cultivars such as *C.* 'Jackmanii', small-flowered *C. viticella* and its hybrids, and a whole range of species and their forms, including the herbaceous clematis. The Jackmanii types are superb when grown through climbing roses, shrub roses, or through most medium-sized shrubs, both evergreen and deciduous, whether free-standing or wall-trained. The *C. viticella* hybrids in particular are excellent for growing through ground-cover plants, especially the summer- or winter-flowering heathers (*Calluna, Daboecia,* and *Erica*).

Of the other members in this group, *C.* x *jouiniana* makes ideal ground cover and the miniature, tulip-like flowers of *C. texensis* and its hybrids look well on a background of low-growing evergreens. The vigorous *C. orientalis* and *C. tangutica* need a large wall or tree where they can grow unconfined and display their many flowers and their fluffy seedheads. *C. heracleifolia* var. *davidiana* and other herbaceous species do not climb and should be grown in mixed or herbaceous borders; *C. integrifolia,* for example, associates very well with cluster-flowered bush roses.

Soil preparation and planting

When using vigorous clematis to clothe trellis or pergolas, ensure that the support structure is strong and sound before planting. Similarly, when growing clematis through old trees, the branches must be robust enough to bear the often

---

CLEMATIS

GROUP 1

C. montana var. *rubens*

C. alpina 'Frances Rivis'

C. macropetala 'Markham's Pink'

GROUP 2

C. 'The President'

C. 'Henryi'

C. 'Nelly Moser'

GROUP 3

C. 'Ernest Markham'

C. 'Jackmanii'

C. viticella 'Mme Julia Correvon'

considerable weight. For clematis grown through other host plants, it is essential to match the vigour of the clematis with that of its host, if the host is not to be swamped. Also ensure that the pruning requirements of host and clematis are compatible.

Most climbing species can be sited in part shade or in sun, provided that the roots are cool and shaded. Either underplant them with low shrubs or plant on the shaded side of the host tree or wall. The herbaceous species thrive in a sunny situation. To grow clematis on a patio, use a container with dimensions of 45cm diameter x 45cm deep (18 x 18in).

Most clematis will thrive in any rich, fertile, and well-drained soil, especially if it is neutral or slightly alkaline. The evergreens and species such as *C. tangutica* and *C. orientalis* should not be grown in soil that lies wet during the winter months as they have fine, fibrous root systems, which quickly rot. Planting details are the same as for other climbers (see "Soil preparation and planting", pp.100–102), except that clematis should be planted about 5cm (2in) deeper than normal to encourage basal buds to develop below soil level. If the stems are damaged the plant may then grow again from below soil level.

Routine care

Keep newly planted specimens well watered until established and mulch climbing and herbaceous species annually in spring with garden compost or well-rotted manure.

Fresh young growth is very susceptible to slug damage (p.548) in early spring. Clematis are prone to attack from aphids (p.550), and the later-flowering, large-flowered

Planting a Clematis

Plant clematis 5cm (2in) deeper than the nursery planting level. This helps buds to develop below soil level and overcome clematis wilt.

cultivars may be affected by powdery mildew (p.550). Clematis wilt, a condition caused by a fungus, can attack newly planted, large-flowered clematis (see p.569).

Pruning and training

Pruning requirements vary for each group so always check before cutting back. If pruned incorrectly, the flowering wood may be cut out.

Initial pruning and training for all groups

Clematis climb by means of leaf-stalk tendrils that attach themselves to their support. They need to be trained to reach their support and new growth will need tying in during spring and summer. Tie just below a node (or leaf axil buds), and space stems evenly on the support, leaving enough room for further growth to develop.

Clematis require special care in initial training and pruning. If they are left untrained, plants frequently

produce one or two stems that are 15–18m (50–60ft) long, and then a top-heavy tangle of growth leaving a bare base. To avoid this, all newly planted clematis should be pruned hard the first spring after planting.

Unless the plant already has three or four stems growing from the base, cut back all the stems just above a strong, healthy pair of leaf buds about 30cm (12in) above soil level. If this hard pruning does not produce three or four extra stems in early spring, any new stems should be pruned again to about 15cm (6in), just above a strong pair of leaf buds.

Group 1

Many of these vigorous clematis require little, if any, regular pruning, especially if cut back hard when first planted. If restricting the size or tidying tangled growth is necessary, pruning should be done after flowering. Any dead, weak, or damaged stems can also be removed at this time. New growth will ripen during late summer and autumn and provide flowers the following spring. Any excess growth may be reduced during the autumn, and tied into its support, but bear in mind that this will reduce the flowering display. *C. armandii*, which produces a mass of flowers on trailing stems, may be thinned annually to avoid congestion; cut back to well-placed, young shoots immediately after flowering.

Pruning Group 1 Clematis

Ripened stems of Group 1 clematis produce flower stems for the next season, so prune after flowering only if the plant has become overgrown.

Group 1 – Early-flowering Species

C. alpina and cvs
C. armandii and cvs
C. cirrhosa

Clematis armandii

C. macropetala and cvs
C. montana and cvs
C. montana
 var. *grandiflora*
C. montana
 var. *rubens*

Flower stem growing directly from last season's ripened stem

Cut back to a healthy pair of buds or to the main stem any shoots that are damaged.

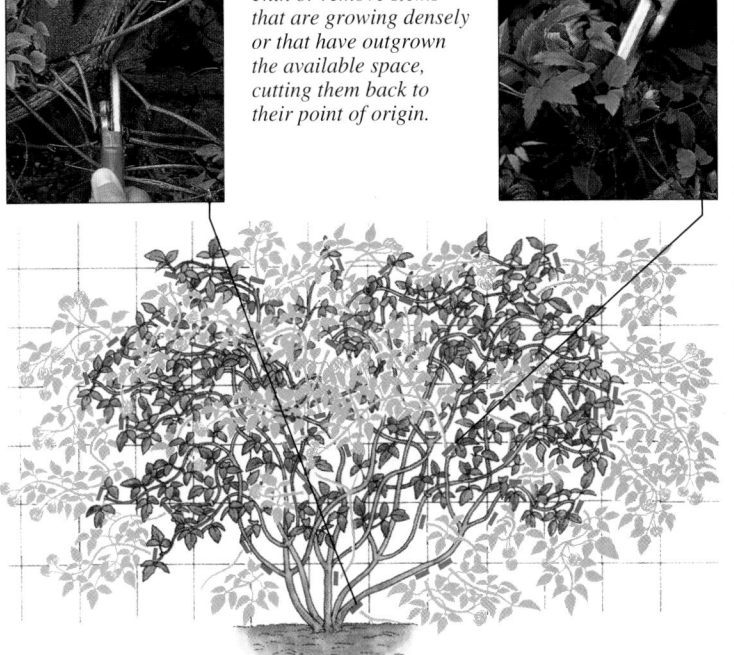

Thin or remove stems that are growing densely or that have outgrown the available space, cutting them back to their point of origin.

Colour Contrast
Clematis are excellent as companion plants and can be grown through a variety of host plants to create an unusual display. Here, the bright petals of C. viticella *'Venosa Violacea'* present an attractive contrast to the green of Juniperus sabina *var.* tamariscifolia *over which it is scrambling.*

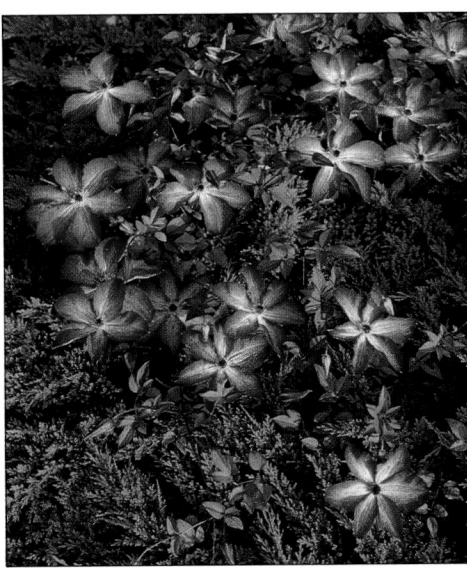

Group 2

The solitary, large flowers are produced on stems of lengths varying from 15cm to 60cm (6–24in) which arise from the previous season's ripened stems. Prune these plants in early spring before the new growth commences.

Remove any dead, weak, or damaged stems and cut back healthy stems to just above a strong pair of leaf buds. These buds will produce the first crop of flowers. This group may also produce a second, but smaller, flush of blooms on new shoots in late summer.

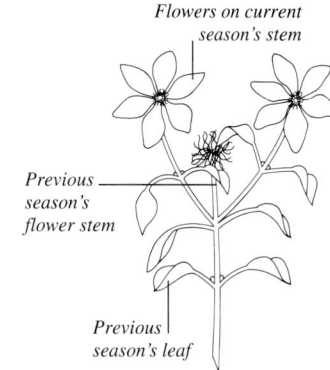

Flowers on current season's stem

Previous season's flower stem

Previous season's leaf

PRUNING GROUP 2 CLEMATIS

Group 2 clematis flower on current season's stems, so prune in early spring before growth starts.

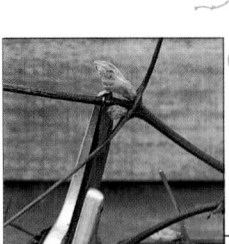

Cut back old stems to a strong pair of buds. Growth from these will produce this season's flowers.

Before new growth starts, cut out any damaged stems to their point of origin or to ground level.

Group 3

Flowers produced by this group are on stems of the current season's growth. Prune in early spring before new growth commences. Remove all the previous season's stems down to a strong pair of leaf buds just above the base of the previous season's growth, i.e. 15–30cm (6–12in) above soil level. As new growth appears, tie it to its support or host. Take care with the soft and often

brittle, new stems. Space them evenly and tie in at regular intervals.

Clematis growing over host or ground-cover plants, such as heathers, should also be pruned. In late autumn remove excessive growth to keep the plant and host tidy and less prone to wind damage. When clematis are grown over winter-flowering heathers, all clematis top-growth should be removed down to 30cm (12in) in late autumn, before the heathers come into flower.

Propagation

Clematis species can be propagated by seed sown in autumn and over-wintered in a cold glasshouse or frame (cultivars do not come true from seed). Cultivars are usually increased by softwood or semi-ripe cuttings (see pp.538–9) or layering (see p.537); division (see p.451) or basal cuttings (see p.166) are used for herbaceous types.

Internodal cuttings of softwood and semi-ripe wood are preferred to nodal cuttings. Take them in spring just above a node and trim the stem to 2.5–5cm (1–2in) below the node. Remove one of the pair of leaves 1cm (¼in) away from the node. Reduce the remaining leaf area by half and cut the stem above the node back to approximately 1cm (¼in). Treat the base with hormone rooting powder. Root in a closed propagating case with bottom heat. Harden off the new plants gradually (see p.543) before planting out the young clematis in spring.

PRUNING GROUP 3 CLEMATIS

Group 3 clematis produce flowers on the current season's growth, so prune in early spring before new growth begins.

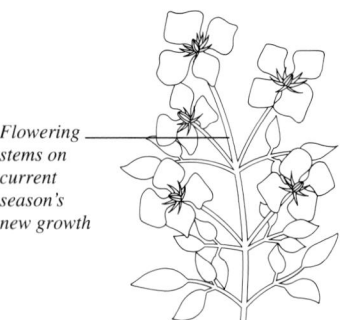

Flowering stems on current season's new growth

Cut just above the lowest pair of strong buds on each stem – this will be 15–30cm (6–12in) above soil level. Make a straight cut with sharp secateurs, ensuring that the buds are not damaged.

INTERNODAL CUTTINGS

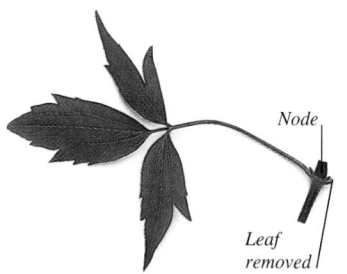

Node

Leaf removed

Make cuttings 5cm (2in) long by trimming just above a node and 3.5cm (1½in) below the node. Remove one leaf from each cutting.

GROUP 2 – EARLY, LARGE-FLOWERED CULTIVARS

C. 'Barbara Jackman'
C. 'Carnaby'
C. 'Daniel Deronda'

Clematis 'Vyvyan Pennell'

C. 'Duchess of Edinburgh'
C. 'Elsa Spath'
C. 'General Sikorski'
C. 'Henryi'
C. 'Lasurstern'
C. 'Marie Boisselot', syn. C. 'Mme Le Coultre'
C. 'Mrs N. Thompson'
C. 'Nelly Moser'
C. 'Niobe'
C. 'The President'
C. 'Vyvyan Pennell'

GROUP 3 – LATE-FLOWERING SPECIES AND CULTIVARS

C. 'Comtesse de Bouchaud'
C. 'Duchess of Albany'
C. 'Ernest Markham'

Clematis 'Perle d'Azure'

C. *florida* and cvs
C. 'Gipsy Queen'
C. 'Hagley Hybrid'
C. 'Jackmanii'
C. 'Lady Betty Balfour'
C. 'Perle d'Azure'
C. *tangutica* and cvs
C. 'Ville de Lyon'
C. *viticella* and cvs

Propagation

CLIMBING plants may be propagated from seed, from stem or root cuttings, or by layering. *Wisteria* is also often propagated by grafting (for further information on this technique, see ORNAMENTAL TREES, "Grafting", p.58).

Propagation from seed is the most cost-effective way of producing large quantities of plants; it is also the only practical method for increasing annuals and the easiest method for propagating herbaceous climbers. Hybrids and cultivars, however, seldom reproduce true from seed, and it is therefore advisable to propagate these by vegetative methods, such as cuttings. Also, woody plants may take several years to reach flowering size if they are raised from seed.

Propagation from stem cuttings that are taken from soft or semi-ripe wood may be carried out successfully for almost all climbers and is the best method for selected cultivars. Propagation from hardwood cuttings is normally applied only to vines (*Vitis*); root cuttings may be used for a small number of plants, such as *Celastrus*. Some climbers produce new plants naturally by self layering. If only a few plants are required, simple and serpentine layering are both straightforward methods of propagating climbers that are difficult to raise successfully from cuttings.

Propagating climbers from seed

Most species produce viable seed without any difficulty. In the case of plants that are not fully hardy, however, a long, hot summer is necessary for the seed to ripen fully. To obtain seed from unisexual plants, such as *Actinidia chinensis* and *Celastrus* species, plants of both sexes must be grown reasonably close together to ensure that they pollinate each other.

The sex of any seedling is unknown until the time that it reaches flowering size. Named, vegetatively propagated male and female clones are, however, available for some plants, such as *Actinidia chinensis*. For sowing and planting annual climbers, see ANNUALS AND BIENNIALS, pp.180–86.

Preparing the seed

For certain climbers it may be necessary to soak the seeds in water before sowing them: *Hardenbergia* and *Lathyrus* seeds should be left in the water for 24 hours, and *Lapageria* for 48 hours. Seeds with a hard outer coating may need to have their dormancy broken by a period of cold, which is best achieved by putting them in a refrigerator for six to eight weeks (for further information, see PRINCIPLES OF PROPAGATION, "Cold stratification", p.536.)

Sowing

If sowing seed in a clay pot, first cover the drainage holes with crocks (this is not necessary when plastic pots, seed trays, or pans are used), then fill the pot, pan, or tray with seed compost, firming with a presser board to ensure that there are no air spaces or hollows. Large seeds should be evenly spaced; press them gently into the compost and then cover to their own depth with a layer of sifted compost that has been mixed with a small amount of fine, horticultural grit. Mix tiny seeds with a little fine, dry sand so that they may be sown evenly and thinly; no extra covering of compost is needed.

Label the pot and water the compost with a fine spray. Then add a thin layer of fine grit or place clear plastic film or glass over the container to prevent the compost from drying out.

The seeds of certain climbers such as *Mutisia* and *Thladiantha* require artificial heat to germinate when grown in a cool climate and so should be placed in a propagator at 13–16°C (55–60°F). *Cobaea*, if grown as an annual, should be sown in late winter with heat so that the young plants are well developed by the time they are planted outside. Most other seeds should be kept in a warm place out of direct sun. Hardy climbers such as most clematis, however, germinate best in cold conditions: plunge the containers in a cold frame outdoors.

Pricking out

As soon as the seedlings emerge, remove the glass or plastic film, if used. When the first pair of true leaves has formed (the seedling's first leaves may differ significantly from the leaves of the adult plant) prick out the seedlings singly into small pots. If they are very small, however, it is best to use a tray, pricking out in rows separated by the space of about one leaf's width.

Inspect the base of the pots or tray at frequent intervals; as soon as the roots are visible through the drainage holes, pot on the seedlings. Seedlings that were germinated in a cold environment should be grown on in warmer conditions under cover.

Planting out

Plant out the seedlings when they are well established. Fast-growing climbers, both annual and perennial, may be planted where they are to flower. If frosts are likely and the climbers are not fully hardy, either plant them under a cloche for protection or delay planting out until all danger of frost has passed.

Slow-growing climbers should be potted on each time the roots begin to appear through the base of the pot. In their first season, grow them on in a sheltered position or in a nursery bed. Provide canes to support the plants in all cases and keep the compost of pot-grown plants moist.

SOWING SEED

1 *Harvest seed (here clematis) from the plant when ripe – it should pull away from the seedhead easily. There is no need to remove the fluffy "tails".*

2 *Sow thinly in a prepared pan or other container of firmed, moist, gritty seed compost.*

3 *Cover the seeds with a thin layer of gritty compost, add a shallow layer of fine grit, and label. Plunge in a sand bed or frame outdoors.*

4 *After germination, prick out the seedlings: loosen a clump with a widger, then lift and replant the seedlings singly, holding each gently by the leaves.*

5 *When the seedlings have developed their first pair of true leaves, pot them on individually in moist potting compost. Label, and place in a cold frame.*

6 *Grow on the seedlings until well established. They are then ready for planting out in their permanent positions.*

Propagation from softwood cuttings

Softwood is the youngest, greenest part of a stem and is produced continuously at the tip. Take softwood cuttings in late spring or early summer, shortly after new growth has started, and before the stems have begun to harden. Prepare a pot, pan, or tray by filling it almost to the brim with moist cutting compost, and firm.

Taking the cuttings

Cut lengths of stem approximately 15cm (6in) long, making cuts above leaf joints or nodes on the parent plant. Then trim the base of each cutting immediately below a node. (Clematis is an exception to this rule: cuttings should be internodal, with a small piece of stem below the node – see "Propagation", p.110.)

Softwood cuttings are particularly vulnerable to water loss, so place them immediately in a clear plastic bag to retain moisture.

Preparing and inserting the cuttings

Remove the leaves from the bottom third of the stems with a sharp knife, and dip the base of each cutting into a fungicide powder to prevent them from rotting. Softwood cuttings root readily and do not need to be treated with hormone rooting powder. Insert each cutting into the compost so that the lowest leaf or pair of leaves is just above the surface.

Label the cuttings, then moisten them with a fine spray. Place them in a propagator, cover trays with sheets of glass, or affix clear plastic bags over pots with an elastic band. Keep the cuttings in good light and check them daily to make sure that they do not dry out.

Potting up

The cuttings generally take four to eight weeks to root, although honeysuckles (*Lonicera*) may take longer. Pot them up in standard, loam-based compost. Alternatively, use a mixture of two parts peat substitute (or peat) to one part sand; as this contains no nutrients, apply a liquid or foliar feed every two weeks.

Cuttings taken in early spring should be ready to plant out in autumn; any taken later should be overwintered under cover and planted out the following spring once there is no danger of frost. In cold areas, all tender cuttings should be overwintered in a frost-free place, gradually hardened off the following spring, and then planted out when all danger of frost has passed.

Propagation from semi-ripe cuttings

From mid-summer to early autumn, take semi-ripe cuttings from healthy shoots. Prepare a pot or pan of moist cutting compost, as for softwood cuttings. Select lengths of about 10–15cm (4–6in) from wood that has not fully hardened, making the cuts above leaf joints or nodes.

PROPAGATION FROM SOFTWOOD CUTTINGS

1 *Fill a 13cm (5in) pot with moist, standard cutting compost. Strike off any surplus with a straight edge to level the surface and firm lightly.*

2 *Select 15cm (6in) lengths from the soft growing tips of healthy shoots (here Solanum crispum). Place the cutting material in a clear plastic bag to prevent drying out.*

3 *Trim the stem of each cutting to approximately 10cm (4in), straight across just below a leaf joint. Remove the lower leaves, cutting flush with the stems.*

4 *Dip each cutting in fungicide powder. Insert two or three to a pot, with the lowest leaves just above the compost. The cuttings must not touch each other.*

5 *Water the cuttings with a fine mist spray, label, and place the pot or pots in a propagator or in clear plastic bags (filled with air so that they do not touch the cuttings).*

6 *After they have rooted, pot on the cuttings into individual pots. Keep the cuttings moist by spraying lightly with a mist spray.*

PROPAGATION FROM SEMI-RIPE CUTTINGS

GOOD EXAMPLE   POOR EXAMPLES

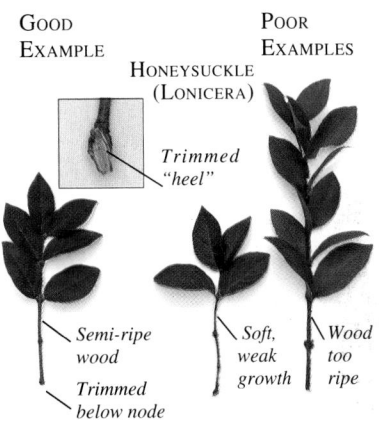

HONEYSUCKLE (LONICERA)

Trimmed "heel"

Semi-ripe wood

Trimmed below node

Soft, weak growth

Wood too ripe

Select 10–15cm (4–6in) lengths from healthy new wood and trim just below a node. Some cuttings are taken with a small heel of bark at the base (see inset). These should be trimmed before use.

Then trim the bases to just below a node, as for softwood cuttings.

Alternatively, make a clean cut through the base of the selected shoot where it is attached to the parent plant. Some cuttings root more readily if taken with a "heel", by gently tugging a shoot away from the parent plant; the shoot peels away with a small triangular section of bark, or heel, at its base. Trim the heel of each cutting and treat with hormone rooting powder, before inserting into the compost and labelling. The pot or pan should then be placed in a propagator. Semi-ripe cuttings generally take eight to twelve weeks, or longer, to root.

When the cuttings have rooted, pot them on, using a standard potting compost and grow on in a cold frame once re-established. The rooted cuttings should be ready for planting out into their permanent positions the following spring, after they have been hardened off.

Propagation from hardwood cuttings

Take hardwood cuttings in autumn and early winter from healthy shoots that have become woody during the growing season. Using secateurs, remove a length of stem, cutting just above a bud. Trim off any sideshoots, then divide the stem into pieces 5–8cm (2–3in) long, using a sloping cut above a bud at the top and a straight cut at the bottom. Alternatively, longer cuttings may be taken with two or more buds.

PROPAGATION FROM HARDWOOD CUTTINGS

Soft, under-ripe wood

Overripe wood

Healthy, woody shoot

1 *Remove a healthy stem from the current year's growth, cutting just above a bud. Do not use overripe and soft, new growth.*

2 *Trim off tendrils and sideshoots. Cut the stem into pieces, with an angled cut above a bud and a straight cut at the base.*

3 *Pare away the outer wood of each cutting, making a clean, downward cut, to reveal the cambium layer (see inset).*

4 *Insert the cuttings into gritty compost so that the top buds just show above the surface. Label, water, and place in a cold frame.*

5 *When the cuttings are well rooted, pot up each one individually. Stake, as required, and grow on before planting out.*

To encourage rooting, wound each cutting at the base by removing a thin sliver of wood with a sharp knife. An application of hormone rooting powder to the wounded section may speed up rooting for climbers that are difficult to root, but is not always needed if suitable stems are taken at the appropriate season.

Inserting the cuttings
Prepare a pot or pan of free-draining cutting compost (add a little extra sand or grit to the compost), filling the pot almost to the brim, and moisten the compost well. Insert the cuttings around the edge of the pot, approximately 5cm (2in) apart. Gently insert the cuttings by up to two-thirds of their length, so that

just the top buds are visible. Firm the compost, then water the cuttings, label the pot, and place it in a cold frame to overwinter. Alternatively, insert the cuttings directly into a cold frame, or in a trench in a sheltered part of the garden (see ORNAMENTAL TREES, "Hardwood cuttings", p.54). Hardwood cuttings of plants that are not fully hardy should be overwintered in a frost-free place.

Hardwood cuttings may take several months to root, but most should be ready for potting up or transplanting by mid-spring of the following year. Either pot them into a standard potting compost, or grow them on in a sheltered place before planting them out in their permanent positions the following autumn.

CLIMBERS THAT MAY BE PROPAGATED BY SEMI-RIPE CUTTINGS (CONT.)

Clematis, some ✽
Clianthus ✽
Clytostoma ✽
Decumaria ✽
Dioscorea ✽
Distictis ✽
Ercilla
Euonymus
Fallopia, syn. *Polygonum*
Hardenbergia ✽
Hedera, some ✽
Hoya ✽
Jacquemontia ✽
Jasminum, some ✽
Kennedia ✽
Lonicera, some ✽
Macfadyena ✽

Mandevilla x amabilis

Mandevilla ✽
Manettia ✽
Mitraria ✽
Mutisia, some ✽
Paederia
Pandorea ✽
Passiflora, most ✽
Petrea ✽
Pileostegia
Plumbago ✽
Podranea ✽
Pyrostegia ✽
Quisqualis ✽
Sarmienta ✽
Schisandra
Schizophragma
Senecio, some ✽
Solandra ✽
Solanum, some ✽
Stauntonia
Stephanotis ✽
Stigmaphyllon ✽
Strongylodon ✽
Tecoma ✽
Tecomanthe ✽
Tecomaria ✽
Thunbergia ✽
Trachelospermum
Tripterygium
Wattakaka

CLIMBERS THAT MAY BE PROPAGATED BY HARDWOOD CUTTINGS

Actinidia kolomikta
Bougainvillea ✽
Lonicera, some ✽
Parthenocissus, some ✽
Vitis, some ✽

Actinidia kolomikta

KEY
✽ *Not hardy*

Root cuttings

A few climbers, notably *Celastrus* and *Solanum*, may be propagated from root cuttings, taken from late winter to early spring.

Taking the cuttings

Dig a hole 45–60cm (18–24in) away from the base of the plant to expose roots that are about 1cm (¹/₂in) thick; these provide the best cutting material. Remove sections of root up to 20–30cm (8–12in) long, depending on how many cuttings are required. Cut straight across the top of the root (nearest the plant) and cut the base of the root at an angle. Place the cutting material in a clear plastic bag to prevent it from drying out.

Preparing and inserting the cuttings

Wash the sections of root to remove any soil, then cut them into smaller pieces and remove the fibrous laterals. Make a horizontal cut at the top and a slanted cut at the base. Insert the cuttings, slanted cut downwards, in a pot filled with a rooting medium of equal parts peat substitute (or peat) and sand. Space them approximately 7cm (3in) apart, with the tips protruding slightly. Cover with a 1cm (¹/₂in) layer of sand. Moisten the compost thoroughly, label the pot, and place it in a cold frame or propagator. Keep the compost moist.

Hardening off and potting on

Buds will appear near the top of the cuttings in spring. Pot up the cuttings individually during early summer, and harden them off gradually, occasionally applying a liquid or foliar feed. Stake the cuttings as they develop. The new plants may be planted in their permanent positions the following autumn.

PROPAGATION FROM ROOT CUTTINGS

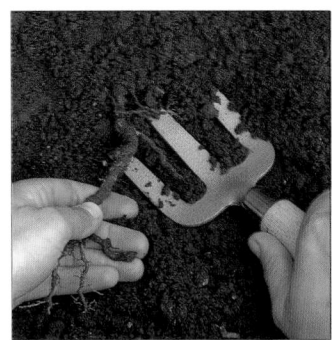

1 *Dig a hole well away from the base of the plant to expose some of the roots.*

2 *Cut off sections of root with secateurs. The pieces should be about 1cm (¹/₂in) thick and at least 10cm (4in) long.*

3 *Wash the roots and divide into pieces 4–5cm (1¹/₂–2in) long, cutting horizontally at the top and obliquely at the base (see inset).*

4 *Insert each cutting vertically into a pot of compost, so that the tips are just protruding above the surface of the compost.*

5 *Cover with a 1cm (¹/₂in) layer of sand. Water, label, and place in a cold frame.*

6 *Pot on into individual pots once the cuttings are well rooted and young shoots are 2.5–5cm (1–2in) high.*

Self-layering climbers

Many climbers have trailing shoots that root naturally where they come into contact with the surrounding soil. A shoot that has self layered may be lifted and severed from the parent plant in autumn or early spring. Choose a healthy-looking, well-rooted layer that has fresh new growth. Lift it carefully and cut it off. Trim back the layered shoot, retaining only the piece or pieces of stem that have produced new roots and that have new buds forming. Strip off any leaves growing near the roots. Pot up the rooted layers individually into standard cutting compost consisting of half peat substitute (or peat) and half sand, and water them in well. Alternatively, if the layer is well developed with strong, vigorous roots and shoots, it may be planted immediately in its permanent position.

PROPAGATION OF SELF-LAYERING PLANTS

1 *Select a low-growing shoot that has rooted into the ground and lift the rooted section with a hand fork.*

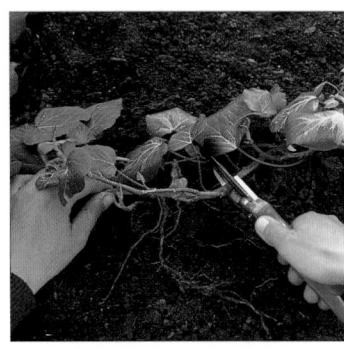

2 *Sever the shoot from the parent plant (here an ivy, Hedera helix), cutting between nodes with secateurs.*

3 *Cut the shoot into sections, each with a healthy root system and vigorous new growth. Remove the lower leaves.*

4 *Replant each section of rooted shoot either into a pot of cutting compost or in its permanent position.*

Simple layering

The long, trailing shoots produced by climbers may often be propagated by simple layering if they do not root naturally. A shoot is wounded and pegged down into the surrounding soil; this induces it to root at a node to provide a young plant.

Layers of many climbers that have been pegged down in spring will develop strong root systems by autumn, at which time they may be separated from the parent plant. *Akebia*, *Campsis*, and *Vitis* should be layered in late winter, however, because, if the stems are wounded in spring, the layers "bleed" sap and are less likely to root.

Soil preparation

If the surrounding soil is poor, fork in some organic compost at least a month before layering takes place. Alternatively, fill a pot with potting compost and plunge it into the ground at the place where the layer is to be pegged down.

Making the layer

Choose a healthy, vigorous, non-flowering shoot or stem that is long enough to trail along the ground. Trim the leaves and any sideshoots from the section of stem to be layered to provide a clear length of stem for about 30cm (12in) behind the tip of the shoot.

Gently bend the stem down to the ground and, to encourage root formation, wound the underside of the stem close to a node, making an angled cut halfway through with a sharp knife. For most climbers apply hormone rooting powder to the wound; vigorous climbers such as *Wisteria*, however, do not require it.

Peg the stem firmly to the ground with one or more "U"-shaped pieces of wire, and cover with not more than 8cm (3in) of soil. Attach the tip of the layered stem to a stake so that it stays upright.

Separating the rooted layer

In autumn, when new shoots and roots have grown from the buried part of the stem, the rooted layer may be severed from the parent plant and potted up or planted out. Trim back the old stem before replanting, and stake the new plant. If the layer is planted in a pot, it should be overwintered in a cold frame. Apply a foliar or liquid feed at regular intervals during spring and summer. Pot on, as necessary, before gradually hardening off and planting out into its permanent position the following autumn.

PROPAGATION BY SIMPLE LAYERING

1 *Select a young, low-growing shoot (here* Akebia quinata). *Trim off the leaves to provide a clear length of stem behind the tip.*

2 *Make an angled cut on the underside of the shoot to form a "tongue" in the centre of the trimmed length of stem.*

3 *Using a clean brush, dust the incision with fresh hormone rooting powder (see inset) and gently shake off any surplus.*

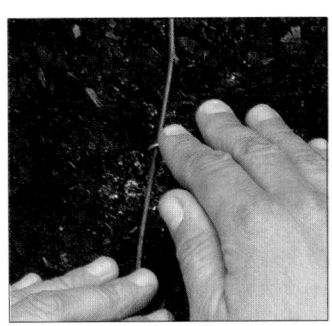

4 *Peg down the shoot firmly in the prepared area, using wire staples. Cover with up to 8cm (3in) of earth.*

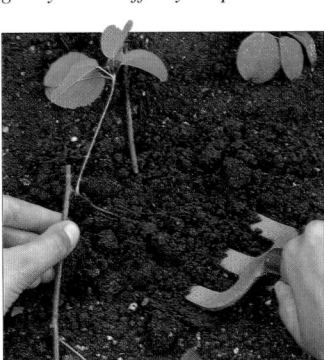

5 *The following autumn, sever the layered shoot close to the parent plant. Lift with a hand fork and trim back the old stem.*

6 *Plant the layer in a 13cm (5in) pot of standard potting compost or into its permanent position. Then water and label.*

Propagation by serpentine layering

Carefully bend a trailing shoot down to the prepared soil and trim off leaves and sideshoots. Make several wounds close to nodes, leaving at least one bud between each incision. Apply hormone rooting powder and peg down the wounded sections, as for simple layering. Separate plantlets in autumn, when roots will have formed from each of the wounds. Trim the old stem from the new plants before replanting and staking.

Several new plants may be produced by serpentine layering. Peg down layers with wire staples (see inset).

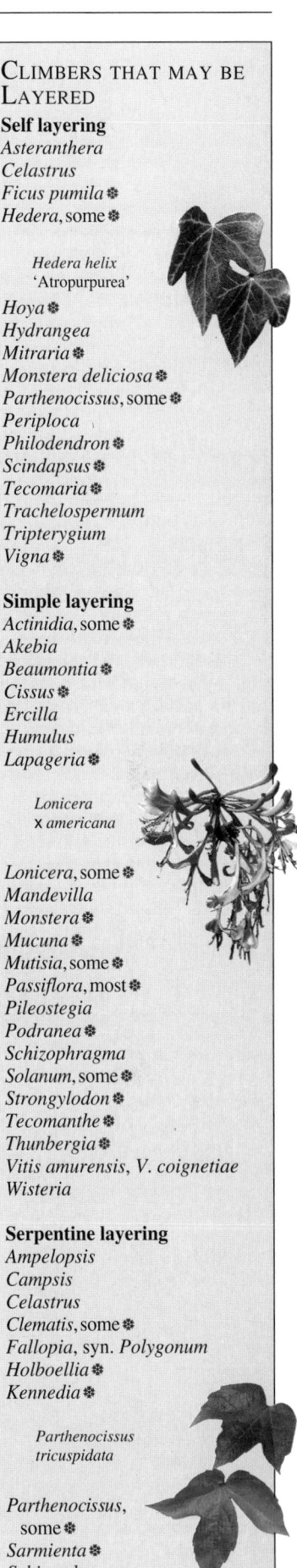

CLIMBERS THAT MAY BE LAYERED

Self layering
Asteranthera
Celastrus
Ficus pumila ❋
Hedera, some ❋

Hedera helix
'Atropurpurea'

Hoya ❋
Hydrangea
Mitraria ❋
Monstera deliciosa ❋
Parthenocissus, some ❋
Periploca
Philodendron ❋
Scindapsus ❋
Tecomaria ❋
Trachelospermum
Tripterygium
Vigna ❋

Simple layering
Actinidia, some ❋
Akebia
Beaumontia ❋
Cissus ❋
Ercilla
Humulus
Lapageria ❋

Lonicera
x *americana*

Lonicera, some ❋
Mandevilla
Monstera ❋
Mucuna ❋
Mutisia, some ❋
Passiflora, most ❋
Pileostegia
Podranea ❋
Schizophragma
Solanum, some ❋
Strongylodon ❋
Tecomanthe ❋
Thunbergia ❋
Vitis amurensis, V. coignetiae
Wisteria

Serpentine layering
Ampelopsis
Campsis
Celastrus
Clematis, some ❋
Fallopia, syn. *Polygonum*
Holboellia ❋
Kennedia ❋

Parthenocissus
tricuspidata

Parthenocissus,
some ❋
Sarmienta ❋
Schisandra

KEY
❋ *Not hardy*

5

THE ROSE GARDEN

GARDENERS AND POETS *since before Roman times have revered the rose as queen of flowering plants for the extraordinary beauty of its blooms. The rose family offers an enormous range of flower colour, shape, and scent, whether it be the simple purity of the wild rose, the soft, pastel charm of the old garden rose, or the jewel-like brilliance of the modern hybrids. Few plants are so* *varied and versatile as the rose in its growth habit, height, foliage, and form; it is possible to clothe the whole summer garden in rose blooms, from the delicacy of a tiny pot rose to the foaming mass of a huge rambler. Whether grown alone in the splendour of a formal garden or heightening the quality of the profusion of a mixed planting, roses epitomize the glory of the garden on a summer's day.*

Designing with roses

WHETHER you choose to grow old garden roses for their grace of habit, foliage, and scent, or modern roses for their long flowering season and showy blooms, the diversity of the rose family makes it possible to find a plant for almost every part of the garden, and to create any style or mood of planting, whether restrained classicism or luxuriant informality.

Roses are adaptable plants that grow happily in almost all parts of the world. They are most vigorous in warm, temperate regions, although some adapt well to subtropical or cold regions. In hot climates, they may flower virtually continuously throughout the year.

Choosing roses

The number of rose cultivars available is bewildering, with many new ones added to the lists each year. Before making a final choice, it is well worth making a visit to some established gardens to observe as many different roses as possible growing in garden conditions. Do this over a period of time to assess the plants' habit, eventual height, health, vigour, fragrance, fastness of flower colour in strong sun, continuity of flowering, and all the other desirable features of a good rose.

Most national rose associations publish listings that give details of where species roses and cultivars stocked by member nurseries may be purchased; these are often invaluable in locating suppliers of more unusual roses.

Fragrance

Roses have long been prized for their scent; most old garden species and some modern roses possess enchanting and diverse perfumes with hints of clove, musk, honey, lemon, spice, and even tea, as well as the "true rose" fragrance. It is not easy to be specific about rose scent as its character and intensity may vary greatly with the time of day, the air humidity, the age of the bloom, and the "nose" of individual gardeners; some will find a particular cultivar fragrant, while others will not.

With most roses one must be quite close to smell them; they are best enjoyed by planting them near a door or a window where their scent may drift into the house on summer evenings, around the patio or along a path, or in a sheltered position in the garden. Other roses, particularly many of the tree-climbing ramblers, are so freely scented that they can perfume the whole garden.

Flower colour

Modern roses embrace virtually every colour of the spectrum, from pale pastels to bold, bright reds and yellows. The blue rose remains the stuff of legend, despite the use of the word "blue" in such cultivars as 'Blue Moon', which is actually pale lilac. The old garden roses range in hue from white, through the palest of blush pinks, deep pink, crimson, and violet, to purple; many are striped pink and white or purple and white.

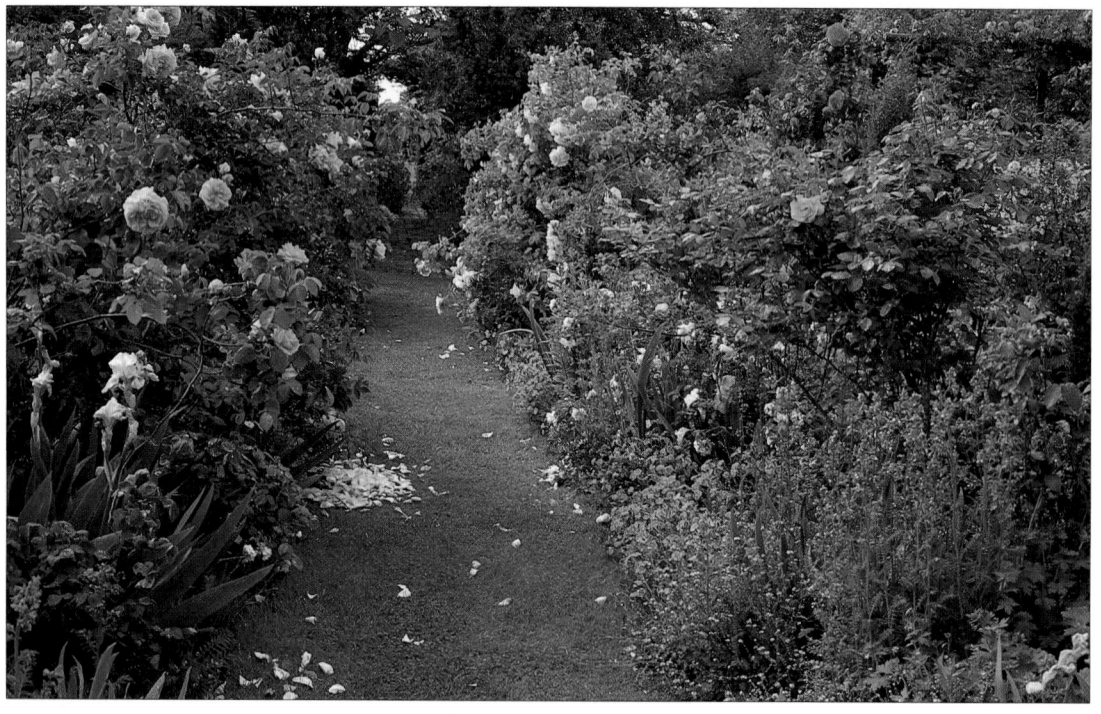

OLD WORLD CHARM
The open blooms and sprawling habit of old garden roses, including 'Constance Spry', 'Céleste', and 'Cerise Bouquet', blend with perennials in a subtle colour theme *to create a mood of informal and restful abundance. The proximity of the beds and the grass walk provides a secluded setting in which to enjoy the heady rose scents.*

The majority of roses co-ordinate well together and with other plants, but combining too many brilliant colours, for instance bright vermilion with cerise pink, may create a discordant effect. Plant white roses or those with softer, pastel hues between groups of strongly toned roses to cool them down and prevent them from clashing.

Flower shapes

The huge rose family comprises a great variety of forms of flower, from the simple, single flowers of the species rose to the elegantly furled blooms of the modern rose and the cabbage-like complexity of many old rose flowers.

The main flower shapes illustrated on this page give a general indication of the shape of the flower when in its perfect state (which in some cases may be before it has fully opened). The flowers may be single (4–7 petals), semi-double (8–14 petals), double (15–20 petals), or fully double (over 30 petals).

Foliage colour

As well as producing a fine flowering display, some groups of roses provide colour in other ways to extend the season of interest. The Alba roses and many of the species (see below) have pleasing foliage, from a soft grey-green to a deep, glossy blue-green, making them attractive even when the bush is not in flower. The bright-green foliage of Rugosa roses has an interesting wrinkled (or rugose) texture and, if the roses are planted as a hedge, it makes a good background for other plantings. The leaves of some species are a dusky plum-purple, as in *R. glauca*, while the foliage of some, such as *R. virginiana*, turns in colour to vivid sunset tints in autumn.

Ornamental rosehips or thorns

Rugosa roses with single or semi-double flowers also develop bright red, decorative hips at the end of the flowering season. Some of the species too, such as *R. moyesii* and its hybrids, produce ornamental hips in

---

FLOWER SHAPES

Flat *Open, usually single or semi-double, with petals that are almost flat.*

Cupped *Open, single to fully double, with petals curving outwards from the centre.*

Pointed *Semi-double to fully double "Hybrid Tea" type, with high, tight centres.*

Urn-shaped *Classic, curved, and flat-topped, semi- to fully double, "Hybrid Tea" type.*

Rounded *Double or fully double, with even-sized, overlapping petals forming a bowl-shaped outline.*

Rosette *Flattish, double or fully double, with many confused, slightly overlapping petals of uneven size.*

Quartered-rosette *Flattish, double or fully double, with confused, uneven petals in a quartered pattern.*

Pompon *Small, rounded, double or fully double, with masses of small petals; blooms are usually borne in clusters.*

Rose classification

There are a hundred or so naturally occurring species roses, as well as many natural hybrids, growing in the wild but, after 2,000 years of being grown as ornamentals, rose cultivars are now numbered in thousands. The ancestry of almost all of them is so mixed, after many centuries of casual and indiscriminate breeding before cross-pollination was understood and proper records of parentage kept, that it is impossible to classify them precisely.

The borderlines between established groups have become blurred; for example the flower size of the cluster-flowered bushes has been increased by crosses with large-flowered bush roses. Similarly, the hybridizing of miniature roses with cluster-flowered bushes has led to recently developed dwarf cluster-flowered bush roses, intermediate in stature between the parents.

Naming rose categories

In 1979, the World Federation of Rose Societies decided that long-established terms such as "Hybrid Tea" and "Floribunda" had lost their original meaning because of the effects of hybridization, and agreed to adopt a new rose classification to clarify the groups so that they could readily be understood.

The system is regarded as the official classification by most rose-growing bodies, including both the Royal National Rose Society in the UK and the American Rose Society. The new classification keeps most of the traditional rose group names. Two changes most likely to affect the gardener are the substitutions of the names "large-flowered bush" for "Hybrid Tea", and "cluster-flowered bush" for "Floribunda". In 1987, the World Federation adopted the category "dwarf cluster-flowered bush" for "Patio" roses. The main groupings are as follows, with previous classification names in parentheses.

Modern garden roses

These are described in sequence according to their growth habit.

Large-flowered bush (Hybrid Tea) Upright, remontant (repeat-flowering) shrubs with large flowers carried one to a stem, or in small clusters, in summer–autumn.

Cluster-flowered bush (Floribunda) Upright, remontant shrubs with better continuity of bloom than large-flowered bushes; the smaller flowers are borne on large sprays or trusses in summer–autumn.

Dwarf cluster-flowered bush (Patio rose) Similar to cluster-flowered bush roses, but with a smaller, neat habit.

Miniature Tiny counterparts of large- and cluster-flowered bushes.

Ground-cover Low-growing, trailing or spreading roses; some flower in summer, other remontant roses flower in summer–autumn.

Climbing Climbing roses with long, strong shoots and large flowers borne singly or in small clusters. Some flower in summer only, but most are remontant and flower in summer–autumn. Climbing roses include a small group of roses (e.g. 'Albertine') which in habit are between a climber and rambler. They used to be classed as ramblers, but in 1987 the Royal National Rose Society reclassified them and they should be treated as climbers.

Rambler Vigorous, climbing roses with long, flexible shoots that bear small blooms in large clusters, mostly in early summer.

Shrub A widely varying group impossible to classify further, ranging from low, mound-forming cultivars to wide-spreading shrubs and giant cluster-flowered bushes.

Old garden roses

Alba Large, freely branching roses with flower clusters borne in mid-summer and abundant foliage.

Bourbon Extremely vigorous, open, fully or partly remontant roses that bear double, fragrant flowers, often three to a cluster, in summer–autumn.

China Small to medium shrubs of twiggy, airy growth, bearing small, mainly double flowers singly or in clusters in summer–autumn.

Damask Open shrubs bearing loose clusters of very fragrant flowers, mainly in summer.

Gallica Fairly dense shrubs that produce richly coloured flowers, often three to a cluster, in summer.

Hybrid Musk Vigorous, remontant shrubs with abundant foliage and fragrant, mainly double blooms borne in trusses, summer–autumn.

Hybrid Perpetual Vigorous, sometimes remontant, shrubs with flowers borne singly or in threes in summer–autumn.

Moss Often lax shrubs with a furry, moss-like growth on stems and calyx; flowers in summer.

Noisette Remontant climbing roses that bear large clusters of flowers, with a slightly spicy fragrance, in summer–autumn.

Portland Upright, dense, and less vigorous but more remontant version of the Bourbon rose.

Provence (Centifolia) Rather lax, thorny shrubs bearing fragrant flowers in summer.

Sempervirens Semi-evergreen climbing roses that bear numerous flowers in late summer.

Tea Remontant shrubs and climbers bearing loose, usually double flowers that have a spicy fragrance.

Species roses

Wild, or species, roses and species hybrids (which share most characteristics of both parent species) are mainly large, arching shrubs bearing one flush of single, five-petalled flowers in spring or mid-summer and decorative hips in autumn.

DESIGN FOR A FORMAL ROSE GARDEN

Here, all is symmetry and order, with clean lines and colour laid out in patterns of geometric simplicity. This design creates a restrained setting in which to enjoy the classic beauty of roses. Formal yew hedges *enclose beds of massed bush roses in pale and deep golds and white, which in turn focus on a graceful, trailing rose in the centre. Red standard roses lift the planting with a bold contrast of colour and form.*

1 Yew (*Taxus baccata*)
2 *Rosa* 'Golden Showers'
3 *R.* 'Suffolk'
4 *R.* 'Korresia'
5 *R.* 'Amber Queen'
6 *R.* 'Harkuun'
7 *R.* 'Margaret Merril'
8 *R.* 'Swany'

autumn that range in colour from yellow and orange, through all the shades of red, to a blackish-purple.

R. sericea subsp. *omeiensis* (syn. *R. omeiensis pteracantha*) has huge, flat thorns which, when young, glow ruby red if the sun is behind them.

The garden setting

One of the best settings for the beds of a rose garden is a smooth, green lawn, but the subtle grey and honey tones of stone paving can be just as attractive. A mellow brick path may complement a rose planting alongside it, especially one of soft, pale tones. Whatever the material, avoid multi-coloured patterns that may compete with the roses. Gravel, although pleasant in appearance and texture, can be troublesome to look after as weeds soon appear and the stones may gradually spread or disappear into the soil.

Edging plants may be used to frame a rosebed. A traditional box hedge makes a formal boundary but many other plants may be used more informally, particularly those that possess grey-green or silver-grey foliage. *Anaphalis triplinervis* var. *intermedia* (syn. *A. nubigena*), with woolly, lance-shaped leaves, or the more dwarf forms of lavender are suitable, as is catmint (*Nepeta*) if there is room for it to sprawl over the path.

Many of the more restrained species and hybrids of *Geranium*, in particular those with blue flowers,

are similarly appealing, and even miniature roses, in contrasting or complementary colours, may be grown on the sunny side of a bed.

Formal rose gardens

The most popular way to grow roses is in a formal rose garden, devoted to displaying the glories of the rose in beds shaped to reflect the plant's classic elegance. Generally, large- or cluster-flowered bushes and standards are used as permanent bedding plants, grouped in blocks of colour. The rather stiff and upright growth of many such bushes lends itself to the formality of bedding and tends not to blend so well with other plants, although roses may be attractively underplanted (see p.119).

Rosebeds may be designed in any shape or size – square, oblong, triangular, or round; at the edges of paths or drives they may be narrow and ribbon-like. Before creating new rosebeds, draw a plan on paper and experiment with different shapes and layouts of beds in order to decide which is the best design for the site that has been chosen. Do not make the beds so wide that access to the roses for spraying, mulching, and pruning becomes difficult.

If mixing rose cultivars in the same bed, plant no less than five or six plants of the same cultivar together in a regular formation for substantial clumps of colour; not all cultivars reach their peak of flowering at exactly the same time. A garden planted

with variations on a colour theme, for instance pale and deep pinks with a touch of white, creates a harmonious effect that is more pleasing than a busy crowd of colour.

When planting, bear in mind the variations in eventual height of different cultivars. For a bed in an open area, choose cultivars of a more or less uniform height. A rosebed that is backed by a wall or hedge is more attractive if the roses at the front are shorter than those behind.

Standard roses may be used to give height to any bedding scheme. Placing a single standard in the centre of a round bed that echoes the shape of the rose creates a graceful symmetry, while several standards placed at intervals of about 1.5m (5ft) along the middle of a long bed help to break up its uniformity.

Informal plantings

The charm of roses may be exploited in a wide range of informal planting schemes, particularly with herbaceous plants or other shrubs. Roses suitable for virtually any site in the garden may be chosen from the multitude of shrub, miniature, climbing, and ground-cover roses of varied stature and habit now available.

Roses combine happily with other plantings; for instance miniature roses give both summer colour and height to a planting of rock plants that are mainly spring-flowering, and a ground-cover rose may clothe a bank with fragrant flowers.

The belief that roses do not mix with other plants probably dates from the days when many commonly used cultivars were large and ungainly and did not suit the Edwardian and Victorian bedding schemes. They were grown in separate walled gardens simply to provide cut blooms for the house. It has, however, long been recognized that roses need not be grown in isolation.

Roses with herbaceous plants
Growing roses in beds or borders with herbaceous plants both highlights the beauties of the rose in flower and provides interest when the rose itself is dormant. The growth habit of many shrub roses, such as the light and airy China roses or the lax and open Damasks, perfectly suits the casual profusion of an informal planting while bringing it height and structure.

Muted drifts of flower or foliage, for example the haze of tiny, white *Crambe cordifolia* flowers, best complement the showy flowers of roses in the summer. At other times of the year, use more flamboyant flowering plants or some with evergreen foliage to extend the season and conceal the bare rose stems.

Many plants may enhance a planting dominated by roses. The tall spikes of purple foxgloves (*Digitalis purpurea*), white *Lilium regale*, or other white and pink lilies pushing up through a planting of lush, old garden roses, for example, make for a striking contrast, both in habit of growth and flower form.

Roses with other shrubs

Both shrub and species roses combine well with other shrubs, as long as they receive enough sunlight. They provide abundant, beautiful, often fragrant flowers to set against the foliage of other spring-flowering shrubs, sometimes right through the summer. Many such roses have almost evergreen foliage and coloured hips in the autumn (see "Ornamental rosehips or thorns", p.117). Smaller shrub roses as well as the Gallicas, most of the Damasks, the Portland roses, and many modern cultivars of similar stature make an excellent ornamental foreground to any planting of shrubs.

Roses that have long, questing branches, such as the freely flowering 'Scarlet Fire' or 'Complicata' with its deep pink blooms, may scramble through and enliven a dull, evergreen shrub. Ramblers may adorn a tree's foliage with their blooms or transform a dead tree into a spectacular feature.

The soft colours of old roses are particularly attractive when planted with subshrubs that combine grey-green leaves with blue flowers, such as the free-flowering *Caryopteris* x *clandonensis*, the ethereal fronds of *Perovskia atriplicifolia*, certain *Hebe* cultivars, and most lavenders.

Underplanting a rosebed

The display in a rosebed may be enhanced and extended beyond the rose flowering season by growing low, shallow-rooted plants between the roses. A wide range of plants may clothe the ground and provide the roses with a background of contrasting colour, texture, and form. Violets (*Viola*) are a favourite choice: the white, soft blue, and mauve cultivars complement roses well. All such ground-cover plants make mulching difficult, however. Take care not to tread on the ground-cover planting when spraying the roses in a particularly wide bed.

When planting between roses, take account of the eventual heights of the various companion plants, and place them so that they will not obscure each other or the roses when they are mature.

The yellow-green of *Alchemilla mollis*, pink and white heads of *Armeria maritima*, and spreading, hardy *Geranium* species also make a fine display under roses.

Spring bulbs brighten up bare rosebeds early in the year: try planting blue or white *Chionodoxa*, daffodils, snowdrops (*Galanthus*), and white, starry *Tulipa turkestanica* to create a gay patchwork of colour. Their only drawback is their dying foliage, which looks untidy until it is removed and may make it difficult to maintain the bed.

Many fragrant, evergreen herbs are good companion plants for roses: use cotton lavender (*Santolina chamaecyparissus*), various thymes (*Thymus*), or sages (*Salvia*) – either the culinary kind or any that have attractive, variegated leaves. Roses always look well when they are contrasted with the silver foliage of perennial plants such as the fern-leaved *Artemisia gnaphalodes* and *A. frigida*, or the grey, woolly-leaved, mat-forming *Stachys byzantina* (syn. *S. lanata*).

Terraces

On a steep hillside, terraces may be used to transform a difficult site into a striking showcase for roses. They provide areas sufficiently level for planting and retain moisture which the roses need while creating eye-catching graduations of height and perspective. The terrace walls look best if made of weathered brick or mellow stone. Bush roses may be grown in the terrace beds, and ramblers or ground-cover roses planted to tumble over the retaining walls, creating curtains of bloom.

Smaller terraced beds are ideal, too, for growing miniature roses. It is much easier to savour the beauty and scent of their tiny, individual flowers if they are raised some way above ground level. Each bed for miniature roses should be approximately 45–60cm (1½–2ft) wide. Place miniature standards along the top bed of the terrace to draw the eye and use some of the smaller and more dainty ground-cover roses to tumble over the walls. This kind of terracing also makes an excellent surround for a sunken rose garden.

Specimen planting

A rose planted on its own makes a handsome specimen plant, perhaps in a lawn or to mark a focal point in a garden, as long as it is an outstanding rose of its type; any defects in a specimen are immediately obvious. Used in this way, weeping standard roses can be especially striking.

INFORMAL STYLE
Large roses, including 'Penelope' in the foreground, clothe the background walls with a fragrant mass of summer colour and provide a magnificent foil for the tall spikes of plants such as Campanula *and delphiniums and the low mounds of the other perennial plants in an informal mixed border of cool blues and whites.*

FLOWERS AND FOLIAGE
Richly coloured rose blooms are set like jewels against an underplanting of herbs with elegant, grey-green foliage, and the golden tones of gravel.

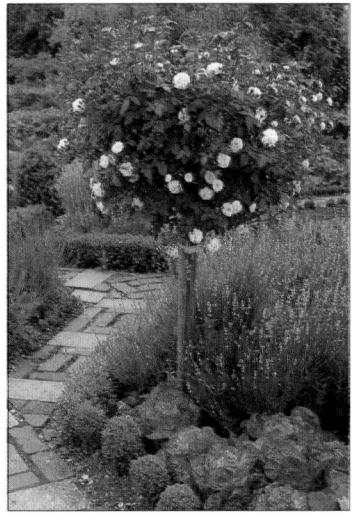

SINGULAR SPLENDOUR
A standard rose, 'Little White Pet', provides a handsome focal point.

These are formed by grafting rambler cultivars onto a 1.5m or 2m (5ft or 6ft) stem, so that their long, flexible shoots, laden with blossom in summer, hang down all round, right to the ground. They usually flower for a limited period, unless a standard grafted from a remontant, ground-cover rose is chosen.

Climbing roses grown as standards may provide a profusion of blooms throughout the entire summer, but their stiff growth does not produce the same, dramatic waterfall effect as weeping standards.

Many of the larger shrub roses, with their graceful, arching habit, almost evergreen foliage, and abundant flowers, are natural choices for planting as specimens in larger gardens. 'Nevada', for example, which can reach 2 x 2m (6 x 6ft) or even more, is smothered with large, cream blooms in early summer, and again in late summer. Other roses, particularly species roses and their hybrids, such as 'Frühlingsgold', have no second blooming.

For a small garden where space for flowering plants is limited, use remontant roses that earn their keep by blooming all summer and well into the autumn, such as the strongly scented 'Roseraie de l'Haÿ'. Smaller shrub roses, such as 'Chinatown' which has masses of gold blooms tinged with pink, and 'Sally Holmes' with large, white flowers clustered

SUMMER RETREAT
A mature rambler rose in full, glorious bloom transforms this trelliswork arbour into an eye-catching feature that is at once intimate and airy. The floral canopy fills the air within the arbour with its delicious perfume, and provides a cool, leafy shelter from which to enjoy the views of the surrounding garden.

above the foliage, are not quite large enough to justify being planted on their own, but are very handsome if planted in specimen groups of three.

Walls, arbours, and pergolas

Most ramblers and climbing species roses are very vigorous, and produce an exuberance of bloom in midsummer. They may clothe structures such as arbours, walls, and fences,

disguise unsightly features, or give height to the summer display in the garden. Be sure to choose a rose with an eventual height that will cover the intended area well without outgrowing it.

Ramblers and climbing roses may be trained on a range of plastic-coated metal bowers, tunnels, arches, and tripod pillars now on the market. Although metal supports may not look so attractive initially as ones made from rustic poles, they have a much longer life and are soon concealed once the roses trained on them become well established. Rustic arches, even if treated, eventually rot at soil level.

Other climbing plants, such as clematis, or wall shrubs may be planted to grow through the rose, to complement the rose blooms as well as to extend the flowering season; climbers with blue flowers are particularly effective. Some of the more vigorous shrub roses, particularly Bourbons, also make excellent short climbers for a pillar or small wall.

Ramblers
Ramblers have more flexible shoots than climbers and are easier to train along complex structures such as pergolas, arches, and trellises to form a great mass of flowering shoots. When grown against walls, however, they may become mildewed as a result of the poor air circulation.

To cover a long pergola, use one of the vigorous, small-flowered, white ramblers such as 'Bobbie James', but remember that they can grow to 10m (30ft) or more and will overwhelm a small structure.

For a picturesque effect, try training roses along chains or ropes that are suspended between uprights to create great swags of bloom.

Climbers
The stiffer shoots of climbing roses are easier to prune than those of ramblers and happily grace walls and fences. Many of the less robust modern climbers may be grown on pillars or as free-standing shrubs with great effect. Pink 'Aloha' is beautifully scented but is too stiff and upright in habit for an arch, although it would suit the pillar supports of a tall pergola.

The Bourbon rose, 'Zéphirine Drouhin', which has pink flowers and repeats well, is an old favourite for growing on arches and pergolas, as it is the only climber that is both thornless and fragrant. It is, however, prone to mildew.

Rose hedges and screens

Roses may, if carefully chosen, provide some of the most colourful and attractive plants for an informal hedge or screen. A few, for example *R. rugosa* and its hybrids, may be shaped to some extent by gentle clipping in winter to make dense hedges while maintaining the natural outline of the shrub. No rose is fully evergreen, so few provide a screen that gives privacy all year, although the thorns make the hedge virtually impenetrable. For further details, see HEDGES AND SCREENS, pp.60–62.

The Hybrid Musk roses, such as the apricot 'Buff Beauty', grow into a thick, thorny screen up to 2m (6ft) in height covered in fragrant flowers all summer long – if their natural unpredictability of growth is curbed by training on horizontal wires or

AUTUMN TINTS
The brilliant scarlet hips of this species rose contrast vividly with its yellowing foliage.

AN ORNAMENTAL ARCH
The old-fashioned, rich pink flowers of Rosa 'Bantry Bay' *festoon this rustic arch to form an enticing and decorative frame to the view beyond.*

DECORATIVE HEDGING
Rosa gallica
'Versicolor', *popularly*
known as Rosa mundi,
is one of the oldest
roses available and has
unusually striped
petals. It forms an
attractive informal
hedge that bursts into
a riot of flower in the
summer to create an
enchanting ribbon of
colour. Here, the line
of the rose hedge
provides a pleasing
contrast of height and
perspective with the
tall spikes of
hollyhocks (Alcea).
The deep pink flowers
in the rose hedge show
reversion to its parent,
R. gallica *var.*
officinalis.

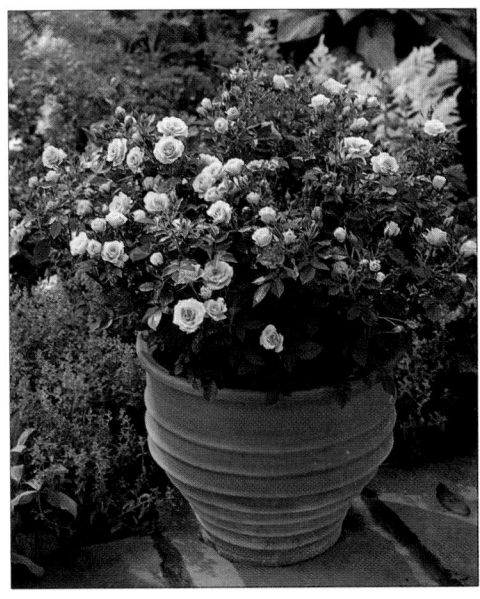

A MOVABLE FEAST
The exquisite, pale
pink flowers of the
miniature rose 'Surrey'
are elegantly offset by
the simple shape of the
terracotta container,
here placed on a low
wall at the edge of
a terrace.

chain-link fencing. If a rose hedge is to line a path, use upright cultivars since those of unpredictable growth may impede the pathway.

For a small garden, a hedge of tall, cluster-flowered bush roses is preferable. These are generally upright plants with little spread and, if planted in two staggered rows (see *Planting Distances for a Rose Hedge*, p.123), cultivars such as the apricot-yellow 'Anne Harkness' rapidly form a pretty screen about 1.2m (4ft) tall. Some shorter-growing old garden roses, such as 'Charles de Mills', have attractive foliage and form hedges of similar height but flower only at mid-summer. Their vulnerability to mildew is, however, increased by close planting.

A delightful way of dividing one part of a garden from another is to train climbing roses or ramblers on decorative screens formed by constructing open, wooden frameworks of the desired height. Ready-made wooden trellis is available but make sure that it is sturdy, since it has to support a considerable weight and to last for years.

Ground-cover roses

Some low-growing roses readily spread along the ground to form a dense and floriferous carpet. These may be used to continue the theme of a rosebed, or as a prettily sprawling edging to a cottage border, as well as to disguise an unsightly feature such as a manhole cover, or scramble down a steep bank that is otherwise difficult to plant.

Some more recently introduced cultivars, such as 'Red Bells', cover the soil very well although, at 1–1.2m (3–4ft), they grow too tall for true ground cover and are not remontant. Others suitable for a small space are 'Rosy Cushion' or those named after English counties.

Ramblers such as 'Grouse' and 'Pheasant', which both have small, pink flowers and glossy foliage, make marvellous ground-cover roses, but their vigour makes them unsuitable for a small garden. They grow naturally along the ground, rooting as they go and covering it very closely, but need strict control to stop them from spreading too far.

If you have a sunken rose garden with fairly low walls, roses such as 'Nozomi' or 'Raubritter' have the right kind of low, spreading growth, if planted along the top, to form waterfalls of flowers over the walls.

Much attention has been given to developing ground-cover roses, but some cultivars that are sold as such are simply low-growing but fairly wide-spreading bushes. They are seldom dense enough in growth to be very effective weed-smotherers, and in winter they shed their leaves, so allowing in air and light which enable weeds to germinate.

A CARPET OF BLOOM
This ground-cover rose, 'Max Graf', *attractively masks an expanse of bare earth with a delightful profusion of dainty, open flowers.*

Roses in containers

Roses are invaluable for their summer colour and fragrance in patio gardens where the surface is mostly paved and there are few or no beds. Containers of many sorts are suitable as long as they are in a position that receives sun for at least half a day. Choose modern cultivars that are bushy and compact, as leggy roses with bare basal stems look unsightly. If grouping a number of roses in a container, make sure it is large enough for the roses to be spaced out to allow for future growth.

Even quite vigorous climbers may, given the support of a wall, be grown in tubs or half-barrels. They should be planted and trained as other climbing roses but as the nutrients in the containers will be quickly exhausted (and the roses difficult to repot), they will require regular feeding.

Miniature roses are ideal plants to use in windowboxes, tubs, troughs, and large pots, whether on their own or with other plants. Try cultivars such as 'Baby Masquerade', whose free-flowering blooms change from yellow to pink and lastly to rose-red, the brilliant orange 'Fire Princess', or dwarf cluster-flowered bush roses such as the soft apricot-peach 'Sweet Dream'. They look especially good in a planting trough built into a low wall bordering one or two sides of a patio or terrace. Even an old sink may be used to display miniature roses as long as it is at least 20–25cm (8–10in) deep to allow for the root growth of the roses.

Roses grown in containers do not have to be confined to a patio garden. They may bring colour to other paved areas, such as the centre of a herb garden, the surrounds of a pool, or even a roof garden.

Soil preparation and planting

GROWING roses in the garden is not difficult if their basic needs are satisfied. They are relatively long-lived flowering plants, so it is worth investing time and effort in choosing a suitable site, properly preparing the soil, selecting cultivars appropriate to the conditions, and planting the roses correctly.

Site and aspect

All roses need a site that is open to the sun and sheltered from strong winds, with good air circulation and a fertile soil. They do not thrive in deep shade, under trees, if crowded by other plants, or in "rose-sick" (see right) or waterlogged soil. Most sites may be improved to meet these needs, for example by erecting windbreaks or by draining heavy, wet soils (see SOILS AND FERTILIZERS, "Improving drainage", p.529). Planting roses in an appropriate compost in raised beds or containers may solve the problem of unsuitable soil.

Evaluate the planting site carefully before choosing a cultivar: the enormous variety of the rose family provides plants that tolerate a range of conditions. Most modern roses do not flourish on chalk, but almost all the old garden roses grow well in alkaline conditions if given large quantities of organic material when being planted and mulched. *Rosa rugosa* and *R. pimpinellifolia* groups do well on sandy soil. These are generalizations since even among modern roses there may be great differences between cultivars: for example on poor soils, 'Grandpa Dickson' and 'Alpine Sunset' suffer but 'Peaudouce', 'The Times', and others thrive if given extra food and moisture. Certain rootstocks may help in some circumstances: for example *R. canina* tolerates and often grows well in heavy, cold soils.

Soil quality

Roses grow in most types of soil, but prefer slightly acid conditions, about pH6.5. If in doubt, use a soil-testing kit to gauge the acidity of the soil. A water-retentive yet well-drained soil is ideal. Always clear weeds when preparing the soil to avoid the young roses having to compete with them for light, moisture, and nutrients.

Improving the soil

The drainage of clay soils, water-retentiveness of light, sandy soils, and pH level of alkaline soils may be improved by incorporating plenty of organic matter. If, on chalk, the topsoil is very shallow, excavate it to about 60cm (24in) when planting, and replace some of the chalk with extra organic matter. For further information on how to influence the soil acidity, and on general soil preparation, see "Soil cultivation", pp.524–7. If possible, prepare the soil approximately three months before planting to allow it to settle.

Rose-sick soil

New roses do not thrive if planted in a rosebed where roses have been grown for two years or more, as they will almost always succumb to "rose sickness" (see "Replant disease/soil sickness", p.569): it seems that the fine feeding roots of new roses are more prone to attack than are the older, tougher roots of roses that are already growing in the bed.

If replacing only one or two roses in an established bed, dig a hole at least 45cm (18in) deep by 60cm (24in) across and exchange the soil with some from a part of the garden where roses have not grown for several years. As this is a daunting task to carry out for an entire rosebed, either locate the bed on a different site, or have the soil chemically sterilized by a qualified contractor.

Choosing roses

Where and how you buy roses will depend to some extent on the particular cultivars that you wish to buy. Many old roses are obtainable only from specialist nurseries, by mail-order if they are not situated locally. Bear in mind that catalogue photographs may not always accurately represent the colour of the flower, nor is it possible to assess the quality of the plant before it arrives, although with a reputable nursery this should not be a problem. Beware of special "bargains", often advertised in the press, that offer bedding or hedging roses cheaply as the plants may be of poor quality.

Nurseries in the UK now generally use *R*. 'Laxa' as a stock, since it is comparatively sucker-free and does well on most soils. Rootstocks may be purchased by those wishing to bud their own roses (see also "Hybridizing", pp.134–5).

Bare-root roses

Mail-order suppliers, stores, and supermarkets sell roses with bare roots, sometimes packaged in plastic. The bare-root roses are in a semi-dormant or dormant state and their roots are virtually clean of soil. Provided that they have not dried out in transit and are planted as soon as possible after arrival, they should establish perfectly satisfactorily.

When buying a bare-root rose in a store, examine it carefully. If the environment in which the rose has been kept is too warm, the rose either dries out or starts growing prematurely, producing blanched, thin shoots that usually die after planting. Do not purchase any roses that display such symptoms.

Container-grown roses

Roses grown in containers may be planted at any time, except during periods of prolonged drought or when the ground is frozen. Many garden centres and suppliers trim the roots of unsold bare-root roses and pot them into containers for convenience of sale; before buying a rose in a container, check that it has not been recently potted up by holding the plant by its main shoot and gently shaking it. If the rose is not firmly rooted and moves about in the compost, it probably has not been grown in its container.

Suppliers whose priority is quick, convenient production tend to select roses that fit into standard-sized containers rather than picking the largest and best plants. These roses are acceptable provided that they are in general good health and do not have spindly, weak growth. Treat them as bare-root roses where

SELECTING HEALTHY ROSES

A BARE-ROOT BUSH ROSE
GOOD EXAMPLE

Strong bud union

Good network of fibrous roots

BAD EXAMPLE

Spindly, damaged shoots

Stunted root system

A CONTAINER-GROWN ROSE
GOOD EXAMPLE

Vigorous, foliage of a good colour

Healthy root system

Sturdy, well-balanced top-growth

Moist compost

BAD EXAMPLE

Spindly shoots

Black spot

Leaf drop

Weeds

A STANDARD ROSE
GOOD EXAMPLE

Strong, healthy shoots, evenly distributed

Stake

Straight stem

Dead wood

Unbalanced, one-sided head

BAD EXAMPLE

PLANTING DISTANCES FOR A ROSE HEDGE

TALL HEDGING ROSES
Plant the roses in a line 1–1.2m (3–4ft) apart, so that, when mature, the branches intermingle to form an effective screen.

MODERN BUSH ROSES
For a denser hedge, plant roses in a staggered formation in 2 rows that are 45–60cm (18–24in) apart.

storage and planting are concerned. If any roots are growing through the drainage holes in the container, knock the plant out of its pot and check that its roots are not thickly coiled around the root ball – a sign that the rose is pot-bound and has been in the container for too long.

Selecting a healthy rose
Whether bare-root or container-grown, the plant should have at least two or three strong, firm shoots and a healthy network of roots in good proportion to the top-growth. Any foliage on container-grown roses should be vigorous. If buying a climbing rose, check that the shoots are healthy and at least 30cm (12in) long. Choose a standard rose with a balanced head since it is likely to be viewed from all sides; a straight stem is best, although a slightly crooked stem is acceptable.

Preparing to plant

Following a few simple principles at the planting stage, such as observing correct planting distances and depths, handling the roots carefully, and providing proper support where necessary, avoids problems with routine care later on. Delay planting for a few days if the ground is too wet, frozen, or too dry for roots to adjust easily to the soil.

When to plant bare-root roses
Bare-root roses are best planted just before or at the beginning of their dormant period, in late autumn or early winter, to lessen the shock of transplanting. Early spring may be better in areas that suffer from bad winters. Plant the roses as soon as possible after purchase. If there is any delay, perhaps because of unsuitable weather, it is best to heel them into a spare piece of ground,

with the roots buried in a shallow trench (see ORNAMENTAL TREES, *Heeling in*, p.41). Alternatively, store the roses in a cool and frost-free place, and keep the roots moist.

When to plant container-grown roses
These may be planted at any time of the year in suitable weather conditions. Container-grown roses, unlike bare-root roses, may be left outdoors in their containers for three weeks or more while awaiting planting, as long as they are kept properly watered. Even though they are frost hardy, do not risk exposing them to prolonged frost as the roots in the containers may suffer some damage in very cold conditions.

Spacing bedding roses
The growth habit determines the planting distances between bedding roses. Close planting makes mulching, spraying, and pruning more difficult and may create stagnant air conditions which allow rapid spread of mildew and blackspot. A narrow, upright cultivar needs less space for healthy growth than a lax, sprawling one and so tolerates closer planting. Plant the bushes 45–60cm (18–24in) apart and about 30cm (12in) from the edge of the rosebed.

If underplanting modern roses or very large species roses, allow more space, about 75–120cm (2½–4ft), depending on their ultimate size and growth habit. Space miniature roses roughly 30cm (12in) apart, according to the varying spread and final height of the plants.

Spacing roses for a hedge
The size and growth habit of the chosen cultivar governs the position of roses in forming a hedge. To gain uniformly dense growth, plant tall, hedging roses such as 'Penelope' and 'Golden Wings', which reach

1.2m (4ft) or more across, in a single line, and modern bush roses such as 'Alexander' in two rows in a staggered formation.

Planting a bush rose

The first stage in planting a rose is to prepare the plant. If the roots of a bare-root rose look dry, soak the plant in a bucket of water for an hour or two until thoroughly moist. Place a container-grown rose in a bucket of water until the compost surface appears moist. If the root ball is wrapped in plastic or hessian, cut away the wrapping carefully. Remove any loose compost, gently tease out the roots, and prune any damaged or diseased roots or shoots; on bare-root roses, remove any buds or hips and most remaining leaves.

Make a planting hole that is wide enough to accommodate the roots or root ball, and deep enough so that, when planted, the bud union of the rose is about 2.5cm (1in) below

ground level or 1cm (½in) for miniature roses. The bud union is easily recognizable as a bulge at the base of the shoots where the cultivar has been grafted onto the rootstock.

Add a planting mixture of garden compost, soil, and a little bone meal to the base of the planting hole. Position the rose in the centre of the hole and check that the planting depth is correct. If the roots of a bare-root rose all point in one direction, place the rose close to one side of the hole and fan the roots out as widely as possible. Then fill the rest of the hole with the soil that was removed from it, shaking the rose a little to allow the soil to settle around the roots or root ball.

Tread the rose in firmly, but not too hard. Use the toe rather than the heel to apply the right amount of pressure, especially on heavy soil that might easily become compacted. Take care not to damage the shoots. Label and water well, but do not mulch until the following spring (see "Mulching roses", p.125).

HOW TO PLANT A BARE-ROOT BUSH ROSE

1 *Remove diseased or damaged growth. Cut out any crossing shoots and thin or straggly stems at the base to produce a balanced shape. Trim any thick roots by about one third.*

2 *Dig the planting hole in a prepared bed and fork half a bucketful of organic compost, mixed with a small handful of bone meal or balanced fertilizer, into the bottom of the hole.*

3 *Place the rose in the centre of the hole and spread out the roots evenly. Lay a cane across the hole to check that the bud union will be 2.5cm (1in) below soil level when the rose is planted.*

4 *Fill in the hole with soil, firming with your hands in stages to ensure that there are no air pockets among the roots. Lightly tread down the surrounding soil. Rake over the soil and water well.*

HOW TO PLANT A CLIMBING ROSE

1 Place the rose in the planting hole, leaning it towards the wall at an angle of about 45° so that the shoots reach the lowest support wire. Place a cane across the hole to check the planting depth.

2 Use canes to guide the shorter shoots towards the wires. Tie all the shoots to the canes or wires with plastic straps (see inset).

Planting a climbing rose or a rambler

Train climbers grown against a wall or fence along horizontal wires that are about 45cm (18in) apart and held in place by tapered vine eyes or strong nails driven into the surface. If the brickwork or masonry of a wall is very hard, drill holes for the vine eyes with a 4.7mm (³/₁₆in) bit. Keep the wires 7cm (3in) away from the wall to allow air circulation and discourage diseases. A rambler has more flexible stems than a climber and may be trained on a hinged trellis that folds away from the wall so that the wall may be maintained without harming the rose.

The ground next to a wall is likely to be dry, since it is in a rain shadow and the masonry absorbs moisture from the soil. Plant about 45cm (18in) from the wall where the soil is less dry and water from any eaves will not constantly drip on the rose.

Prepare the soil and planting hole, and trim the rose as for bush roses. Position the plant, leaning it towards the wall at 45°, and fan out its roots towards moist ground. If necessary, train the shoots along canes pushed into the ground, but keep each cane far enough from the roots to avoid damaging them.

After filling in and firming, as for a bush rose, attach the shoots to the support wires with plastic or hessian ties or with the small, ready-made, plastic straps that are designed for tying in roses. Take care not to tighten the straps too much around the rose's stems as room must be left for the shoots to grow.

Do not prune the main shoots of a climber at this stage: wait until the beginning of the next growing season before lightly pruning, and be prepared to wait a year or two before the rose begins to climb. In the first year, keep the roots thoroughly watered and uncrowded by other plants to help them establish.

Planting a rambler by a tree

Plant a rose that is to scramble up a tree on the windward side of the tree so that the rose's young, flexible shoots blow towards and around the tree, rather than away from it. Dig a planting hole at least 1m (3ft) away from the trunk to increase the amount of rain that reaches the roots of the rose. Train all the new shoots towards the tree along sloping canes, tied at their upper ends to the trunk and inserted just behind the rose. If planting in this way on a boundary, bear in mind that the blooms grow towards, and are visible from, the direction of the strongest sunlight.

Planting a standard rose

Most nurseries bud their standard roses on *Rosa rugosa* stocks which have a tendency to sucker, although a few are experimenting with other rootstocks. To keep suckering to a minimum, plant the rose no deeper than the soil mark: deeper planting will increase sucker growths. If necessary, trim off the top layer of roots so that the bottom layer does not sit too deeply in the soil.

A standard rose needs a stake, placed on the side of the prevailing wind, to support it. Paint the whole stake with a preservative that is not toxic to plants and allow it to dry. Insert the stake very firmly near the centre of the planting hole before positioning the rose, so as to avoid damaging the roots and thereby encouraging suckers. Position the rose next to the stake and check that it just reaches the base of the lowest branches; if necessary, adjust the height of the stake. Use a cane or rake handle to make sure the soil mark and soil surface are level.

Fill in and firm the soil as for a bush rose. Secure the stem to the stake with two rose ties – these should incorporate a buffer to prevent the stake from rubbing the stem – but do not tighten them fully until the rose has settled in the soil. The ties will need to be loosened at least once during the growing season as the diameter of the stem increases.

HOW TO PLANT A STANDARD ROSE

1 Position the stake in the hole so that the rose stem will be in the centre. Drive the stake into the ground and check that the top is just below the head of the rose.

2 Place a cane across the hole to check the planting depth. Use the old soil mark on the stem as a guide and plant at the same depth. Fill in the hole and firm.

3 Use a rose tie (see inset) just below the head of the rose and another half-way up the stem to attach the rose to the stake. Cut out weak or crossing shoots.

Planting roses in containers

The container should be at least 30–45cm (12–18in) deep for bush roses or 23–35cm (9–14in) deep for miniatures to allow for root growth. Place a layer of crocks over the drainage holes in the base of the container and fill it with a standard, loam-based potting compost. Plant the roses in the same way, and at the correct depth, as bush roses (see p.123). Take care to space them correctly.

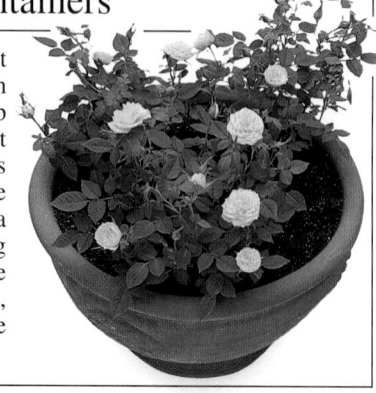

Routine care

ROSES need regular care to produce healthy, vigorous plants that are resistant to pests and diseases. Attention paid to fertilizing, watering, mulching, and general maintenance will be rewarded with a fine display throughout the season.

Fertilizing

Roses are gross feeders and quickly exhaust even a well-prepared rosebed that is rich in nutrients. Many essential mineral salts rapidly leach out in the rain, especially from light soils. If the roses are to flourish, they require regular feeds in a balanced formulation of essential nutrients (nitrogen, phosphates, and potassium) and trace elements. Many suitable proprietary compound rose fertilizers are available, mostly in powder or granular form. For information on how to deal with particular nutrient deficiencies, see PLANT PROBLEMS, pp.545–77.

After pruning in the spring, and when the soil is moist, sprinkle a small handful or 25–50g (1–2oz) of fertilizer around each rose. Hoe or rake it in lightly and evenly, keeping it clear of the stems. Repeat the application about a month after midsummer, when the roses are developing a second flush of bloom. Do not apply a general feed later in the year, because this encourages soft autumn growth that may suffer frost damage. A dressing of sulphate of potash, however, applied at a rate of 75g/sq m (2oz/sq yd) in early autumn, protects late shoots by helping them to ripen.

Foliar feeding (spraying a liquid feed on the leaves and bypassing the roots) is usually only needed to obtain extra-large blooms and leaves on exhibition roses. It may help, however, in a prolonged drought or on chalky soils: in both instances, roses may have difficulty in taking in nourishment through the roots.

Fertilizing roses in containers
Roses in containers soon use up the compost nutrients. Compensate for this loss by top-dressing annually with a balanced fertilizer and foliar feeding once or twice in the growing season to maintain vigorous growth.

Watering

Roses need plenty of water for healthy growth, especially if they are newly planted. Watering too little and too often can be counterproductive since it encourages the roots to grow towards the surface and compete for water and light; give the roses a good bucketful of water to soak the soil thoroughly around their roots instead.

Roses are deep-rooted plants and can flourish even in long, dry summers and near-drought conditions, particularly if they are well established. In such conditions, the flowers may be smaller than usual and may open very quickly. The petals may also be vulnerable to scorching by the sun. During the flowering season, do not water roses in strong light as the blooms may spoil. Water roses in containers every other day, or even daily if the weather is exceptionally hot and dry.

Suckers and how to deal with them

Suckers are shoots that grow below the bud union, directly from the rootstock onto which a cultivar has been grafted. They are usually narrower and a much lighter green than those of the cultivar, often with thorns of a different shape or colour, and the leaves may have seven or more leaflets.

Remove any suckering shoots as soon as they appear. This prevents the rootstock from wasting energy on the sucker's growth at the expense of the cultivar. Some rootstocks produce suckers more readily than others, especially if they have been planted at the wrong depth. Damage to the roots, caused by severe frosts or any accidental nicks from hoes, other implements, or a stake, may also stimulate the production of suckers.

Pull the sucker to detach it from the rootstock: this removes any dormant buds that may be present at the point where it joins the roots. Do not cut it as this is the equivalent of pruning it and only encourages more vigorous growth. It may, however, sometimes be necessary to cut a sucker if it originates from beneath the rose and if pulling it off would mean damaging or lifting the rose.

Shoots on the stem of a standard rose are also suckers, since the stem is part of the rootstock. They normally have the dull, dark green leaves that are typical of *Rosa rugosa* rootstocks. Snap them off or pare them from the stem with a knife.

REMOVING A SUCKER FROM A STANDARD ROSE
Pull away any suckers growing from the rose stem (see inset), taking care not to rip the bark.

REMOVING A SUCKER FROM A BUSH ROSE

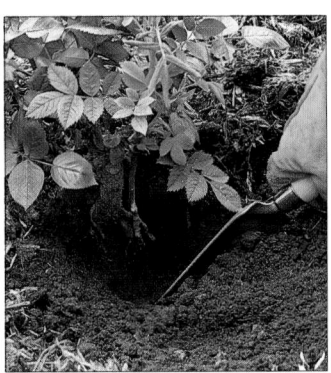

1 *With a trowel, carefully scrape away the soil to expose the top of the rootstock. Check that the suspect shoot arises from below the bud union.*

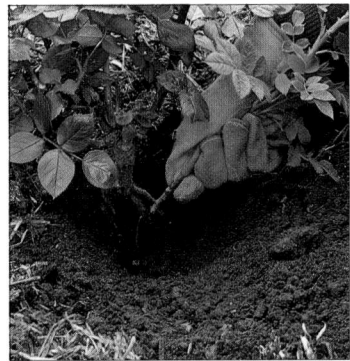

2 *Using a glove to protect your hand, pull the sucker away from the rootstock. Refill the hole and gently firm the soil.*

HOW A SUCKER GROWS

The sucker (right) grows directly from the rootstock. If only cut back at ground level it will shoot again and divert further energy from the rose.

Eradicating weeds

When weeding, the soil around the bases of roses should not be disturbed too deeply to avoid damaging the roots. Control annual weeds by hand or with light use of a hoe and tackle persistent, perennial weeds with a contact weedkiller (see PLANT PROBLEMS, "Weeds", pp.573–7). Mulching roses (see below) or underplanting them with shallow-rooted ground cover also suppresses weeds.

Hygiene

The uncollected fallen leaves, prunings, and any other debris from afflicted plants can spread diseases among roses. Gather up and destroy such material regularly, if possible by burning it; never put it on a compost heap as any diseases present may survive to infect other plants.

Mulching roses

An 8cm (3in) layer of mulch applied in early spring after pruning and feeding helps to smother any weed seeds, and maintain high moisture levels and even temperatures in the soil. Well-rotted stable manure is an ideal mulch, providing many of the nutrients that roses need, but if this proves difficult to obtain, bark chips or cocoa shells are both satisfactory alternatives. For further details, see also SOILS AND FERTILIZERS, "Top-dressings and mulches", p.532.

Dead-heading

The purpose of dead-heading, that is removing faded flowers, is to stimulate the earliest possible development of new, young shoots and further blooms throughout the flowering season. Once a rose flower has been fertilized, it soon fades, and, if left on the plant, may delay the production of new shoots below the old flower cluster.

In some roses, a seed pod or hip forms, and this diverts energy from further flower production; remove the dead flowers regularly unless you require the hips for ornamental purposes. In autumn, even if some roses continue to bloom, stop dead-heading to avoid encouraging new, soft growth which would be damaged by the first frosts.

Moving roses

A rose may be moved at almost any age, but the older it is the greater is the risk that it may resettle badly. It is not difficult to move roses that are up to three or four years old, but do not risk planting in old rosebeds (see "Rose-sick soil", p.122). The roots of older roses are thick and spread deeply, and also have fewer of the fine feeding roots that are essential for re-establishing the plant.

If circumstances allow, move a rose only when it is dormant and always into a well-prepared bed. First loosen the soil by cutting down on all sides with a spade at least 25cm (10in) out from the root ball.

Blind shoots

These are shoots that develop without a terminal flower bud. They divert the plant's energy in the same way as a sucker (see "Suckers and how to deal with them", p.125) so prune out any as soon as they appear.

Cut the blind shoot by about a half to an outward-facing bud to encourage it to grow away and flower. If no bud is visible, cut back to the main stem.

HOW TO DEAD-HEAD ROSES

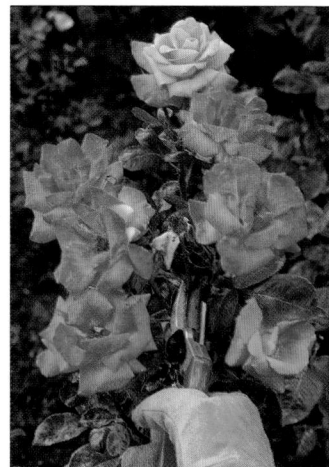

1 CLUSTER-FLOWERED BUSH ROSES *Cut out the central bloom of the truss first to stimulate the other buds into flower.*

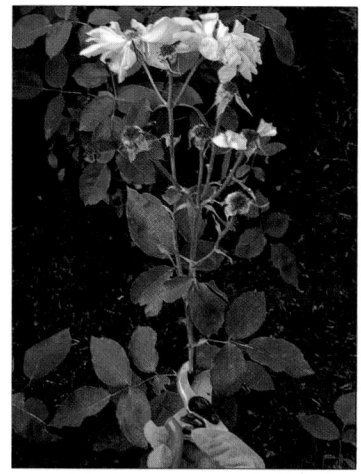

2 *When all the flowers have faded, remove the whole truss by cutting back to an emerging bud or a fully formed shoot.*

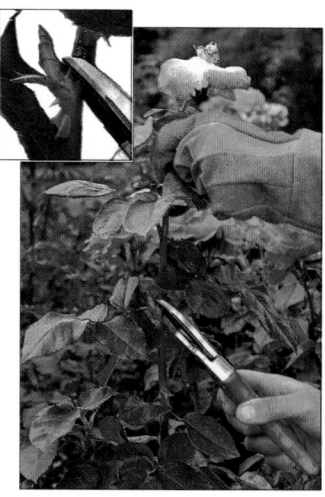

LARGE-FLOWERED BUSH ROSES *Cut back stems bearing faded flowers to an outward-facing bud (see inset) or fully formed shoot.*

Insert a fork well away from the centre of the plant and lift it, taking a good ball of soil with it and disturbing the roots as little as possible; on light soils, use a spade as the soil is likely to fall away from the roots. Trim off any coarse roots and wrap the root ball in plastic or hessian to prevent the roots from drying out before transferring the plant to its new position. Water immediately after replanting and regularly until the rose is established.

Autumn cut-back

Strong winter winds may loosen the roots of roses, making them vulnerable to frost damage. To prevent this, shorten tall, large-flowered or cluster-flowered bushes in autumn.

Winter protection

In temperate climates, roses need protection only in a very bad winter. In heavy soils, the compacted earth may form into a small funnel around the base of the stem and fill up with water that later freezes. The expansion of the water as it freezes may damage the bud union – the most vulnerable part of the rose.

In very extreme climates, severe winters can kill roses outright if they are not protected; any plants that do survive have to make completely new growth each year and will have a very short flowering season.

Large- and cluster-flowered modern bush roses may tolerate temperatures as low as -10° to -12°C

(10–15°F) for a week or so if soil is mounded over the crown. Pack the crowns of standard roses with straw or bracken, loosely tied in place with twine. At colder temperatures, provide greater protection or choose roses that tolerate extreme cold. Roses that are hardy between -20°C and -23°C (-4°F to -10°F) include Bourbon, China, and Provence roses, *Rosa californica*, and *R. wichuraiana*. Grow Alba, Damask, and Gallica roses, and some of the species roses, such as *R. foetida* and *R. palustris*, in areas where the temperature falls to -30°C (-22°F). A few roses, such as *R. virginiana*,

R. blanda, *R. canina*, *R. glauca*, and *R. rugosa*, survive cold as severe as -37°C (-35°F). For full instructions on protecting roses, see FROST AND WIND PROTECTION, pp.520–21.

Pests and diseases

Aphids (p.550), black spot (see "Bacterial leaf spots and blotches", p.552), rose dieback (p.569), powdery mildew (p.550), and rusts (pp.552 and 557) are common problems; spray as a precaution if necessary. Inspect roses regularly and control diseases or pests at once.

CUTTING BACK IN THE AUTUMN

BEFORE *In mid- to late autumn, cut back large- and cluster-flowered bush roses that are over 75cm (2¹/2ft) in height (left) to avoid the effects of wind-rock.*

AFTER *Reduce the entire bush by a half to one third of its height, cutting all shoots above a bud.*

Pruning and training

THE purpose of pruning is to speed up the natural process of new, vigorous, disease-free shoots developing to replace the old, weakened ones, and so produce an attractive shape and the optimum display of blooms. Training a plant on supports stimulates the production of flowering sideshoots and directs new growth into the given space. The severity of pruning depends on the rose type; certain principles of pruning, however, apply to all roses.

Basic principles of pruning roses

A pair of sharp, high-quality secateurs is essential; long-handled pruners and a fine-toothed pruning saw are also useful for removing gnarled, woody stumps and thicker shoots. Wear strong, protective gloves for all pruning tasks.

How to prune

Always make a clean, angled cut above a bud that faces in the direction in which the resultant new shoot should develop. This is usually an outward-facing bud, but it may face inwards on a lax, sprawling rose if the centre of the bush needs filling out. Cut to the appropriate height if a dormant bud is not visible, and cut out any stubs that develop later.

Always remove dead and dying shoots, cutting back to disease-free, white pith, even if this means pruning almost to ground level. Remove any crossing growth that might impede the main shoots, or growth that is thin or twiggy (i.e. matchstick-like twigs that bear only a leaf or two). This concentrates energy in the more vigorous and productive shoots, and allows good air circulation which helps prevent disease.

Applying wound paint to large cuts after pruning is often recommended to prevent entry of disease spores and of pith-boring insects. There is no guarantee that such treatment is effective, however. If pruning is properly carried out, the cut will develop a natural seal, making wound paint unnecessary.

When to prune

Prune roses when they are dormant or semi-dormant, that is between autumn leaf-fall and when the buds are just beginning to break in the spring. Pruning a rose in active growth is sometimes necessary but severely checks growth. Do not prune in frosty conditions as the growth bud below the cut may be damaged and the shoot may die back. Following a very severe winter, cut back frost-damaged shoots in spring to a healthy bud; if the winters are always severe, prune roses in spring, immediately after removing any winter protection material. Conversely, in a climate so warm that the roses flower almost continuously, prune them in the cooler months to induce dormancy and give them an artificial period of rest.

MAKING A PRUNING CUT

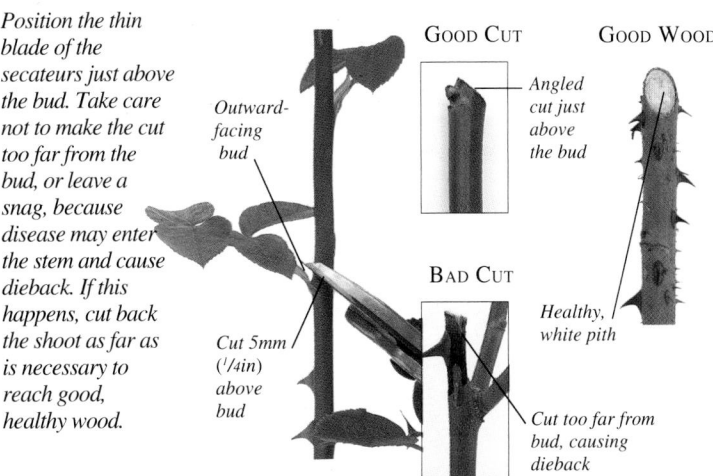

Position the thin blade of the secateurs just above the bud. Take care not to make the cut too far from the bud, or leave a snag, because disease may enter the stem and cause dieback. If this happens, cut back the shoot as far as is necessary to reach good, healthy wood.

Outward-facing bud

Cut 5mm (1/4in) above bud

GOOD CUT

Angled cut just above the bud

BAD CUT

Cut too far from bud, causing dieback

GOOD WOOD

Healthy, white pith

Pruning roses after planting

Almost all newly planted roses should be pruned hard to encourage the development of vigorous shoot and root systems. Climbing roses are the exception to this rule – give them only a light, cosmetic pruning in the first year to remove any weak, dead, or damaged shoots. Remove any weak, dead, or crossing growth from standard roses. Less severe

HOW TO PRUNE A LARGE-FLOWERED BUSH ROSE

Prune the rose fairly hard, in autumn or spring, by trimming off any unproductive growth and then reducing the main shoots to form a strong, balanced framework.

Cut out crossing, congested, and twiggy or spindly growth.

Remove dead wood and any that shows signs of damage or disease.

Prune main shoots to within about 20–25cm (8–10in) of ground level.

Prune a newly planted bush rose to about 8cm (3in) above ground level. Cut back to outward-facing buds and remove any frost-damaged growth.

pruning and regular fertilizing are preferable for roses grown in soils that are deficient in nutrients.

Pruning modern garden bush roses

Modern roses flower on new or the current season's growth, so they are pruned fairly severely to stimulate vigorous, new shoots and to produce a good display of blooms.

Large-flowered bush roses (Hybrid Teas)

Remove completely any dead, diseased, thin, or twiggy shoots. Using long-handled pruners or loppers, cut out stumps from previous prunings that, although healthy, have not produced any worthwhile new growth; they will do no better during the coming season.

Thin out any weak or crossing shoots from the centre of the bush to leave a well-balanced framework and allow free air circulation. It is not as important to produce a balanced framework with bedding roses planted close together as with one that is grown as a specimen, and is seen from all sides.

In temperate climates, the main shoots should then be pruned back to between 20–25cm (8–10in) for general display purposes, but in extremely mild areas, the shoots may be cut down less severely to about 45–60cm (18–24in). To achieve blooms that are of exhibition quality, cut the main shoots hard back to leave only two or three buds.

Cluster-flowered bush roses (Floribundas)

When pruning this type of rose, cut out any unproductive wood as for large-flowered bush roses (see p.127). Reduce any sideshoots by about one third on smaller cultivars and by two-thirds on taller-growing cultivars, such as 'Fred Loads'. Cut back the main shoots to 30–38cm (12–15in), but reduce the shoots of taller cultivars by about one third of their length. Do not prune them any harder, unless growing the roses for exhibition, since this reduces the number of blooms that will be produced in the following season.

Dwarf cluster-flowered bush roses

These are smaller versions of the cluster-flowered bush roses, and should be pruned in autumn or spring following the same principles.

Miniature roses

There are two distinct methods of pruning miniature roses. The simpler of the two is to give them only the minimum of attention: remove shoots that have died back, thin out occasionally the shoots of those cultivars that produce a dense tangle of twiggy growth, and shorten any over-vigorous shoots that may throw the whole plant out of balance.

The second method is to treat the plants as if they were miniature large-flowered or cluster-flowered bush roses. Remove all growth except the strongest shoots, and then cut them back by about one third. This method is used satisfactorily for cultivars introduced from the USA to the UK that do not adapt easily to their new conditions. Such plants benefit from the extra stimulus of a severe pruning and produce strong, new growth.

HOW TO PRUNE A CLUSTER-FLOWERED BUSH ROSE

In autumn or spring, cut out unproductive growth and prune the sideshoots. Reduce the main shoots by a proportion suitable to the height of the cultivar.

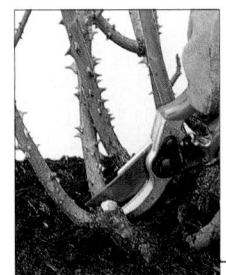

Remove crossing or congested wood and twiggy, spindly growth.

Prune out all dead, damaged, or diseased wood to a healthy bud.

Prune main shoots to 30–38cm (12–15in) from ground level.

Reduce sideshoots by one to two-thirds, cutting to a bud.

Pruning standard roses

The majority of standards are formed from large- or cluster-flowered bush cultivars or from small shrub roses budded onto a straight, unbranched stem, usually 1.1–1.2m (3½–4ft) high. Prune as for the bush or shrub rose equivalents, cutting back the shoots by about one third, so that the shoots are all roughly equal in length. It is especially important to achieve a balanced head that will look pleasing from all sides. If the head is unbalanced, prune the shoots on the thicker side less hard so that they do not produce as much new growth as those on the thinner side.

Weeping standards

These roses are usually formed from cultivars of small-flowered ramblers grafted onto especially tall standard stems of about 1.5m (5ft). The flexible shoots are pendent and require only limited pruning: remove the old, flowered wood when the blooms have faded, leaving growth from the current season intact.

Pruning shrub and old garden roses

Although these vary enormously in their growth habit, most modern and old garden shrub roses, and all the species roses, flower on wood that is two or more years old. They should be pruned fairly lightly to leave the flowering wood intact. Many flower freely for years without any formal pruning if allowed to develop naturally. It is necessary only to cut out any dead, damaged, diseased, or weak wood to keep the roses really healthy. Despite this, some pruning may help to increase the number and quality of the blooms.

Give mature, remontant shrub roses a light renewal pruning each winter by cutting down some of the older, main growths to the base. This encourages the production of vigorous, new basal shoots that will flower the following summer. Over a four-year period of renewal pruning, all the shoots are replaced and, with regular fertilizing, the bushes will remain free-flowering and healthy for many years. Treat non-remontant roses similarly but prune them immediately after flowering.

Rugosa, China, and Hybrid Musk roses may be given similar, annual, renewal pruning.

HOW TO PRUNE A MINIATURE ROSE

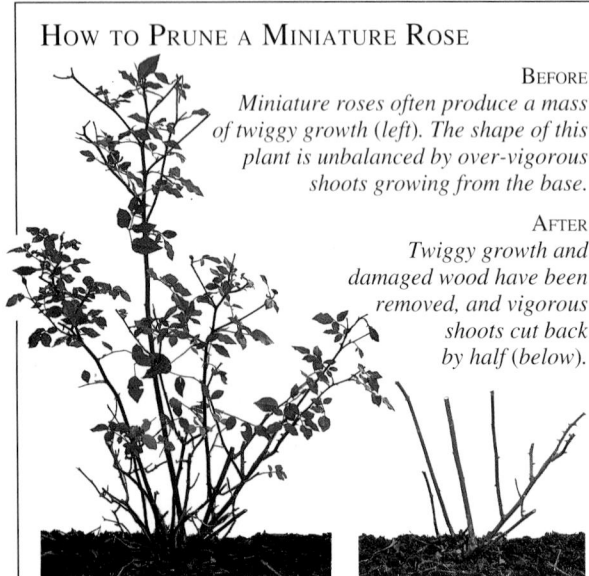

BEFORE
Miniature roses often produce a mass of twiggy growth (left). The shape of this plant is unbalanced by over-vigorous shoots growing from the base.

AFTER
Twiggy growth and damaged wood have been removed, and vigorous shoots cut back by half (below).

HOW TO PRUNE A STANDARD ROSE

BEFORE
In the spring, prune a standard rose to prevent the plant from becoming too top-heavy and to retain an evenly shaped, floriferous head.

AFTER
All dead and damaged wood, and any crossing stems, have been removed to leave healthy shoots. The main shoots have been reduced to 20–25cm (8–10in) and the sideshoots by about one third.

PRUNING A GALLICA ROSE

Throughout the flowering season, thin out the rose to keep it healthy. The annual pruning after flowering involves cutting back sideshoots, unproductive wood, and some older shoots to encourage new growth.

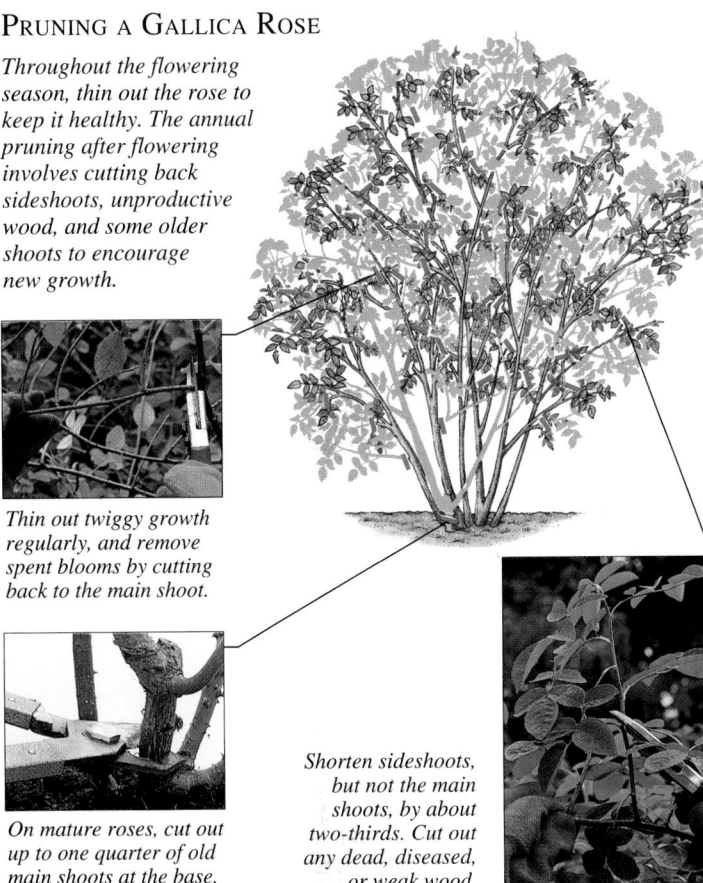

Thin out twiggy growth regularly, and remove spent blooms by cutting back to the main shoot.

On mature roses, cut out up to one quarter of old main shoots at the base.

Shorten sideshoots, but not the main shoots, by about two-thirds. Cut out any dead, diseased, or weak wood.

PRUNING ALBA, PROVENCE, DAMASK, AND MOSS ROSES

Prune after flowering, cutting back both main shoots and sideshoots. If necessary, prune again in late summer to remove any overlong shoots that have developed.

Reduce main shoots that are old and woody by a quarter to one third.

LATE SUMMER

Cut back any overlong, whippy shoots by about one third.

Prune sideshoots to about two-thirds of their length.

Gallica roses

Many of these produce a twiggy tangle of shoots that should be regularly thinned out to improve air circulation. After flowering, shorten the sideshoots only and remove any dead or diseased wood. Gently clip over Gallica roses used for hedging to maintain a tidy shape. Follow their natural outline and do not attempt to shape them into a formal hedge as this would remove many of the sideshoots on which flowers are produced in the following year.

Species roses

Much of the charm of these roses lies in their arching shoots which, in the second and subsequent years, carry flowers all along their length, often on short sideshoots. Formative pruning is needed to establish a balanced framework of strong, new growth. Thereafter these roses need no further pruning other than the removal of dead and diseased wood, unless they become too dense or produce few flowers, in which case renewal prune them in the same way as non-remontant shrub roses.

Severe pruning encourages strong vegetative growth but produces few, if any, flowers until the second year. If the bush becomes lop-sided, reshape it after flowering and trim back all the overlong shoots.

Alba, Provence, Damask, and Moss roses

After flowering, reduce both main shoots and sideshoots. At the end of the summer, cut back any vigorous,

Pruning ground-cover roses

The majority are low-growing, spreading, modern shrub roses so renewal prune them as for shrub roses. Some, mostly related to *Rosa wichuraiana* (a rambler), creep over the ground, rooting as they go. Prune these only to stop them spreading beyond the space available.

Prune shoots to well within the intended area of spread, cutting to an upward-facing bud.

overlong shoots that might whip about in the wind and cause wind-rock damage to the roots.

Bourbon and Hybrid Perpetual roses

These are usually remontant, so prune them, and all hybrids partly derived from *Rosa rugosa*, in early spring as large-flowered bush roses (see p.127), but much more lightly.

Pegging down roses

This technique is an effective, although time-consuming, way of increasing flower production on Bourbon and Hybrid Perpetual roses that tend to send up long, ungainly shoots with flowers only at the tips. Instead of pruning the shoots in late summer or autumn, bend them over gently, taking great care not to snap them. Peg the shoots firmly into the ground. Alternatively, tie the tips to pegs in the ground, to wires strung between pegs, or to a low wire frame placed around the plant. Prune sideshoots on the pegged shoot to 10–15cm (4–6in).

This has much the same effect as horizontally training the shoots of climbing and rambler roses (see p.130) and produces an arching mound covered with a large number of flowering sideshoots in the following season.

Select long, non-flowering shoots and prune the soft tips. Gently bend each shoot over and fasten it to the soil with sturdy wire hoops (see inset).

Climbing roses and ramblers

These roses require minor pruning but regular annual training. Neither climbing nor rambler roses are self-supporting and, if trained incorrectly, may not flower freely and may become bare at their base. Some bush roses that send out large shoots at awkward angles, such as some of the Hybrid Musks, may also be trained against walls, fences, or other supports for an effective display.

Climbing roses

In their first year, and in their second unless they have made exceptional growth, do not prune climbing roses except to remove any dead, diseased, or weak, twiggy growth. Never prune climbing sports of bush roses (roses with the word "climbing" before the cultivar name, for example 'Climbing Shot Silk') in the first two years, since they may revert to the bush form if cut back hard too soon.

Begin training, however, as soon as the new shoots are long enough to reach the supports; train them sideways along horizontal supports to encourage flowering. Where this is not possible, such as on a narrow area between a door and a window, choose a cultivar that is half-way between a tall shrub and a climbing rose. Many of these flower well from the plant base without special training: examples are 'Golden Showers', 'Joseph's Coat', and some of the more vigorous Bourbon roses.

Many climbing roses flower well for years with little pruning, except the removal of dead, diseased, or

HOW TO PRUNE AND TRAIN A CLIMBING ROSE

In the first two years after planting, restrict pruning to cutting out unproductive growth. From the third year, prune in autumn after flowering.

Reduce the sideshoots by about two-thirds or about 15cm (6in), cutting above an outward-facing bud.

Tie all new shoots into horizontal wires 15–20cm (6–8in) apart: the shoots should not cross each other.

Remove any diseased, dead, or twiggy growth, cutting back to healthy wood or the main shoot.

twiggy growth. Prune them in the autumn, after flowering. Leave unpruned the strong main shoots unless they are exceeding their allotted space, in which case shorten them as appropriate. Otherwise simply shorten the sideshoots. Train in all the new season's growth to the supports while it is still flexible.

Occasional renewal pruning may be necessary if the base of a climbing rose becomes very bare. Cut back one or two of the older, main shoots to within 30cm (12in) or so above ground level to encourage vigorous new shoots to develop and replace the older growths. Repeat this as required in subsequent years.

Rambler roses

Like climbing roses, ramblers flower satisfactorily for a good many years without any formal pruning. They produce much more growth from the base than most climbers and, if not carefully trained, grow into a tangle of unmanageable shoots. This results in poor air circulation, which encourages the incidence of disease, and makes it extremely difficult to spray the plants thoroughly.

Prune ramblers in late summer. In the first two years, restrict pruning to cutting back all the sideshoots by about 7.5cm (3in) to a vigorous shoot; also remove dead or diseased wood. In later years, prune the rose

more heavily to maintain its framework. Untie all the shoots from their supports and, if possible, lay them on the ground. Cut no more than a quarter to one third of the oldest, spent shoots to ground level, leaving the new shoots and some older, but still vigorous, shoots for tying in to form a well-balanced framework.

Remove any unripe wood from the tips of the main shoots and cut back any sideshoots. Cut back any wayward shoots that are outgrowing the available space or spoiling the overall shape of the rose. Train in the shoots, as close to the horizontal as possible, to encourage flowering on new, short sideshoots that will develop all along the main shoots.

Training on arches, pergolas, pillars, and trees

Climbing roses or ramblers may be trained up pillars, arches, or pergolas. Twist the main shoots around the uprights to encourage flowering shoots to form low down. Carefully train the shoots in the direction of their natural growth before they have matured and hardened. This is vital for climbers that have stiff, semi-rigid shoots. Tie them in using twine or plastic rose ties; these are easy to undo when pruning or to loosen as the shoots develop. Once the main shoots reach the top of the support, regularly prune them to keep the rose within bounds.

An excess of overlong sideshoots may spoil the appearance of a pillar rose but a little additional pruning soon remedies this. Cut sideshoots back to three or four buds or by about 15cm (6in) in the spring.

HOW TO PRUNE AND TRAIN A MATURE RAMBLER ROSE

After the first two years, prune in late summer as soon as flowering is over, cutting out any dead, diseased, or weak wood. Then train in the new shoots.

Cut sideshoots down to leave between 2 and 4 healthy buds or shoots.

Cut back any old, spent shoots to ground level, using loppers.

Tie all shoots into the wires as close to the horizontal as possible. Secure any loose wires.

Propagation

Roses may be propagated in three main ways: by taking cuttings, by budding onto a rootstock, or from seed. Taking cuttings is the easiest method but it involves the longest wait: it takes about three years, except for miniature roses, for the new plant to become established. Budding needs rootstocks that have grown on in advance, but usually produces stronger and more vigorous plants. Many species roses (*Rosa glauca*, for example) readily breed true from seed. Cross hybrid roses with other hybrids, or sometimes with species, to produce new cultivars.

Hardwood cuttings

Most roses may be propagated from hardwood cuttings, in particular some cultivars that are related quite closely to wild species, such as rambler roses. Cuttings taken from miniature roses root so easily and develop so quickly that they are propagated in this way commercially. Large-flowered bush roses of complex parentage do not root so readily and may not be of sufficient size to sell commercially for two or three years, so they are seldom available on their own roots.

One advantage of roses grown from cuttings is that they do not have a different rootstock and so do not produce suckers. The disadvantages include a loss of vigour with some cultivars (although this may be useful with miniatures), and a tendency towards vigorous but non-flowering growth in the first few years, particularly with species.

In many climates, roses from hardwood cuttings are the most reliable, but success in rooting them is variable; it is therefore sensible to take a good number of cuttings to allow for possible failures.

Preparing the cuttings

In early autumn, select material for cuttings from the current season's growth. Trim any old flowerheads from the chosen shoots and put the shoots into a transparent plastic bag to stop them from drying out. Prepare the cuttings by trimming off their leaves and shortening them to 23cm (9in). Breaking off the thorns will make the cuttings easier to handle. Moisten the base of each cutting, dip it into hormone rooting powder, and shake off the surplus.

Take shorter lengths of stem for miniature rose cuttings, which need be only 5–10cm (2–4in) long.

Preparing the cutting bed

Choose an open site for the cutting bed, preferably one that is sheltered from the midday sun. Single dig the area required, firm, and rake it to produce an even surface.

Inserting the cuttings

Make a series of deep planting holes with a cane or dibber, and trickle a little coarse sand into the bottom of each one to improve the drainage. Alternatively, dig a narrow, slit-like trench to the same depth and trickle sand along the base. On light, sandy soil, it is sufficient to push a spade vertically into the earth along a centre line, working it backwards and forwards to widen the slit.

Insert the cuttings vertically into the holes or trench, leaving about one third of their length above ground. They should be inserted far enough apart so that, once rooted, they may be lifted individually without disturbing adjacent cuttings. Firm and water the soil around the cuttings. In any dry spells that follow, water them again; after frost, which may loosen the roots in the ground, refirm the soil.

Another option is to root hardwood cuttings in deep pots of light, sandy soil. Plunge the pots in soil or sand in a shady outdoor site, and water them as needed. Growing bags or pots in a cold frame or cool greenhouse may be more convenient for miniature rose cuttings.

Development of the cuttings

During the autumn a callus should develop at the base of each cutting, from which the roots will be produced in spring. Once rooted, the young plants should develop strongly, but if flower buds form during the summer, remove them so that the plants can concentrate their energy on the production of new, strong, vegetative growth. The following autumn, if they are large enough, that is about 23–30cm (9–12in), transplant the young roses to their permanent positions; if they are not yet large enough, leave them to grow on for another year.

Semi-ripe cuttings

Semi-ripe cuttings may be more successful than hardwood cuttings in areas that are subject to severe winters. In the late summer after flowering, select mature sideshoots that are still green. Take 15cm (6in) lengths, cutting above a bud where the shoot is beginning to turn woody, and trim off the soft tips. Prepare cuttings about 10cm (4in) long, following the same procedure as for hardwood cuttings.

Insert them into deep pots of sandy compost (equal parts peat substitute, or peat, and sand). Cover the pots with plastic bags, or put them in a propagator, to prevent the cuttings from losing moisture, in a cool, frost-free place. In spring, plant out the rooted cuttings in a nursery bed.

HOW TO PROPAGATE ROSES FROM HARDWOOD CUTTINGS

1 *Select a healthy, well-ripened shoot of roughly pencil thickness (here 'Dreaming Spires'), that has flowered in the summer and is about 30–60cm (12–24in) long. Remove it, cutting at an angle, just above an outward-facing bud. Prepare the cuttings by removing the leaves and soft tip wood.*

2 *Cut into 23cm (9in) lengths, making an angled cut above the top bud and a straight cut below the bottom bud. Dust the base with hormone rooting powder.*

3 *Make a row of planting holes 15cm (6in) deep and the same distance apart. In heavy soil, put a little coarse sand to a depth of about 2.5cm (1in) in each hole.*

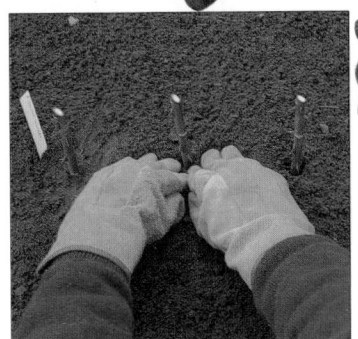

4 *Insert a cutting into each hole: make sure that it reaches the bottom and that about 15cm (6in) of the cutting is buried. Firm the soil, water, and label the cuttings.*

5 *A year later, lift each rooted cutting with a hand fork, taking care not to damage the roots. Plant them in a bed or put them in a cold frame to grow on.*

HOW TO BUD-GRAFT A ROSE

1 Select a flowered shoot about 30cm (12in) long, with 3–4 growth buds. Remove it, making an angled cut above an outward-facing bud on the parent plant.

2 Hold the budwood so that the buds point downwards. Insert the knife 5mm (1/4in) from a bud. With a scooping action, remove the bud with a 2.5cm (1in) long "tail".

3 Holding the scion by the tail between thumb and forefinger, carefully remove the coarse, woody material from behind the bud by pulling it away.

4 Use the blunt side of the knife to remove the thorns from the stem of the rootstock, cleaning a section about 4cm (1½in) long.

5 Cutting just deeply enough to pierce the bark, make a "T"-shaped incision, with the horizontal cut about 5mm (1/4in) long and the vertical cut 2cm (3/4in) long.

6 Insert the tapered end of the budding knife under the flaps of the "T", and ease them outwards to reveal the inner, white cambium layer.

7 Hold the scion by its tail and insert it behind the bark flaps of the rootstock, sliding it well down so that the bud is held firmly in place, just below the cross-stroke of the "T".

8 Using the knife, carefully trim away the surplus tail protruding above the "T", following the line of the horizontal cut. Try to do this without damaging the wood beneath the bark. Discard the tail.

9 Secure a rubber binding tie tightly around the grafted area, pinning it on the side opposite the bud. This binds the stock and scion tightly together.

STANDARD ROSES
Graft 3 buds around the stem (left). Cut back the stock in spring just above the new shoots (right).

BUSH ROSES
If grafting a bush rose, insert only 1 bud or 2, equally spaced on the stem, onto the rootstock (see inset). In the spring, cut back the rootstock just above the new shoots.

Bud-grafting

The budding process involves uniting plant material taken from two different roses in order to combine the virtues of both. A dormant bud (the scion) from the top-growth of one plant, usually chosen for its display, is inserted under the bark and just above the roots of a rootstock, normally a rose species or a specific clone that is selected for its vigour and hardiness. Different rootstocks may be used to suit the soil conditions or climate or to promote the vigorous growth of the scion.

Choosing a suitable rootstock

Many stocks are used to suit varying conditions: the hardy and vigorous *Rosa multiflora* is widely used as a rootstock, particularly where the winters are cold; it is also suitable for use on poor soils although plants budded onto this stock are not long-lived. *R. canina* produces hardy plants and is popular where winters are severe or on heavy soils, but it suckers freely; the crimson climber 'Dr Huey' (at one time known as 'Shafter' when used as a stock) is more frequently used where the dormancy period is shorter. The selected clone 'Laxa' has now largely replaced most other commercial stocks, as it performs reliably in most soils and climatic conditions, is almost thornless, easy to use for budding, and rarely produces suckers. Any commercial supplier of rootstocks, or a local nursery, should be able to advise on the best stock to use for local growing conditions.

Stocks may be obtained from wild hedgerow roses, but their quality is unreliable and it is better to use stocks with more uniform growth characteristics.

Planting the rootstocks

Plant the rootstocks in autumn in a nursery bed, about 30cm (12in) apart and with 75cm (30in) between the rows. For bush roses, the scions are inserted at the point where the shoots and roots join (the "neck"), so for ease of budding, plant the rootstocks at an angle of 45°, with the top of the root just at soil level. Mound soil up to the base of the shoots to keep the bark moist and supple at the point where the scion is to be inserted. Standard rootstocks must be grown on to about 2–2.2m (6–7ft), and any buds rubbed off before they develop to create a straight, bare stem.

When to bud-graft

Budding should be carried out from mid- to late summer, preferably in cool, showery weather, when the air is not too dry. If the weather is very dry in the months that precede budding, water the rootstocks regularly and thoroughly. This ensures a free flow of sap that prevents the wood from drying out, so that it is possible to lift the bark from the wood without bruising the wood underneath. Speed is also important to prevent the wood of both bud and rootstock from drying out before they have been grafted together.

A budding knife, with a single, specially formed blade and a sharp, tapered end (see "Garden knives", p.463) may be used but an ordinary horticultural knife is also suitable. Any knife used for budding must be kept scrupulously clean and sharp.

Selecting the budwood
Prepare scions from well-ripened shoots that have well-formed, dormant growth buds in their leaf axils. These shoots are known as the budwood. Cut off the leaves and leaf stalks; alternatively, leave the stalks as "handles" for inserting the buds later. Place the budwood in a plastic bag to prevent it from drying out before it is used.

Preparing the scion
Hold a piece of budwood upside down and, from just above the base of a bud, use the budding knife to scoop out the bud together with a thin tail. This shield-like piece of bark, about 2.5cm (1in) long, within which the growth bud is contained, is known as the scion. Remove the small sliver of pith behind the bud: if retained, it will prevent the bud from uniting with the rootstock or "taking". It is difficult to do this without damaging the bud if the shield has been cut too deeply from the shoot. The base of the bud should then be visible as a small, circular growth.

Preparing the rootstock
For a bush rose, clear the soil from the rootstock neck, take off the thorns, and wipe the neck clean. Using the blade of the budding knife, make a "T"-shaped cut in the neck, penetrating the bark without cutting into the wood, as this causes damage.

Grafting the bud onto the rootstock
Carefully peel back the cut bark of the rootstock with the blunt side of the knife blade, taking care not to tear the bark or the wood beneath. Gently push the scion into position in the "T" so that the bud faces upwards. Trim off any of the tail that may still be visible and, if necessary, the leaf stalk. Use damp raffia knotted well clear of the bud, or a

special rubber binding tie to hold the bud securely in place and keep the flaps of bark tightly closed to avoid moisture loss. The rubber tie is easily pinned in place and does not inhibit the growth of the bud as it soon rots away. Inserting two scions, opposite one another on the rootstock, is sometimes recommended to produce balanced shoot growth more rapidly but is seldom practised commercially except on standard roses.

Cutting back the rootstock
If the scion takes successfully, the bud will quickly swell and will then produce a shoot, generally by the following spring. Once the shoot develops, cut off the growth of the rootstock above the scion. If the shoot needs support, tie it to a cane, but this is not usually necessary.

Bud-grafting a standard rose
Budding onto a standard rootstock is performed near the top of the stem at the desired height, usually about 1.1–1.2m (3½–4ft); weeping standards are usually budded a little higher, at about 1.5m (5ft). Insert two or three buds around the stem to achieve an evenly balanced head. If using *Rosa canina* rootstocks, insert the buds into equally spaced lateral growths, close to the main stem. It is more usual to place three buds around the main stem of *R. rugosa* stock, staggered vertically.

Layering roses

Any rose which possesses shoots that are long and flexible enough to be bent over and pegged into the ground may be successfully propagated by simple layering.

In late summer after flowering, choose a shoot of healthy, mature wood and trim some of the leaves to create a clear length of stem. Work some peat substitute or peat into the ground where the shoot is to be layered and peg the shoot down into the prepared ground to encourage it to root. The next spring, separate the rooted layer from the parent by cutting the shoot just behind the roots, and plant it out into its destined position to grow on.

Ramblers and climbing roses are ideal for layering, although if they are planted in narrow beds along the base of a wall there may not be a large enough area of exposed soil to peg down the shoots, particularly if other plants are growing around the base of the rose. Many shrub roses, such as Damask, Provence, Bourbon, and most Alba and species roses,

are suitable for layering as they have a lax growth habit and are likely to have more exposed soil around the base into which the selected shoots may be inserted.

Modern shrub roses such as 'Chinatown', which are in fact very tall-growing, cluster-flowered roses, have fairly stiff shoots, so train these shoots horizontally while they are still young and flexible to prepare for layering. Cultivars of ground-cover roses lend themselves to this method of propagation. The shoots of some, such as 'Pheasant' or 'Grouse', root naturally into the soil; simply separate them from the parent and plant them out.

The modern large- and cluster-flowered roses found in the majority of gardens are mostly too stiff and upright in their habit of growth for successful layering and should be increased by taking cuttings. Only a few which are lax, wide-spreading growers, such as 'Europeana', are easily increased by layering.

Propagation by division

If a rose is growing on its own roots, taking rooted suckers and planting them out is an easy method of propagation. Most roses from nurseries are grafted onto rootstocks, so suckers will be from the stock and not the cultivar budded onto it.

Some species grown from seed and other roses grown from cuttings sucker naturally. In the dormant period, detach the rooted suckers or shoots from the parent and plant them out, either in a nursery bed or into permanent positions. Deep planting of budded shrub roses sometimes stimulates the cultivar shoots to produce roots (in effect, a form of layering). Treat such rooted shoots as rooted suckers.

Roses that sucker freely such as the cultivars of *Rosa pimpinellifolia*, *R. rugosa* and some Gallica roses are readily propagated in this way.

HOW TO LAYER ROSES

1 *Make a 2.5cm (1in) slit on the lower side of a long, ripe, but flexible shoot. Dust the cut with hormone rooting powder and then wedge it open with a match (see inset).*

2 *Position the shoot in a small depression in prepared soil and peg it down firmly with a wire hoop. Cover it with soil, firm, and tie in the tip of the layered shoot to a short cane.*

PROPAGATING ROSES BY DIVISION

1 *In late autumn or early spring, select a well-developed sucker. Scrape away the soil to expose its base. Sever it from the rootstock, with as many roots as possible.*

2 *Prepare a hole, wide and deep enough for the roots. Plant the sucker immediately and water and firm the soil (see inset). Trim shoots to 23–30cm (9–12in).*

RAISING ROSES FROM SEED

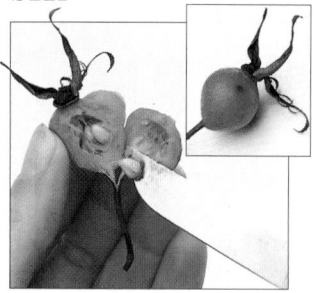

1 Slit open a ripe hip (see inset), taken from the parent plant, with a clean, sharp knife. Take out individual seeds carefully with the back of the knife blade.

2 Place the seed in a plastic bag of moist peat substitute or peat and keep it for 2–3 days at room temperature. Then put it in a refrigerator for 3–4 weeks.

3 Sow the seed singly onto the surface of a sandy compost (1 part sand:1 part peat substitute). Cover with grit, label, and put in a cold frame.

4 When the seedlings have their first pairs of true leaves, prick them out singly into 5cm (2in) pots filled with loam-based potting compost.

Propagating roses from seed

Species roses, unlike cultivars, are self-fertile and may be raised from seed in the same way as other shrubs. Although seeds are not generally available from commercial sources, it is easy to extract them from mature roses in the garden. Hybrid roses do not breed true to type from seed so they are usually propagated by bud-grafting (see p.132).

Extracting and sowing seed

In the autumn, when the rose hips are swollen and ripe, extract the seeds and stratify them in a refrigerator before sowing (see "How to overcome dormancy", p.535). Stratification – the simulation of natural temperature changes – is necessary for all seed of species roses.

Sow the rose seed into seed trays, packs, or into individual pots, which should be at least 6cm (3in) deep. If using a seed tray, place the seeds on the compost about 5cm (2in) apart, and cover them to their own depth with sand or grit. Then leave the tray or pack in a cold frame to protect it from mice and other animals. The seed may take up to a year to germinate. Prick out the seedlings into individual containers as soon as the first true rose leaves have formed; the first pair, the seed leaves, are oval, unlike typical rose leaves. Care is needed in handling the seedlings as they are very fragile at this stage in their development.

Grow on the young seedlings in the cold frame until they have become established in their pots. Then harden them off by moving them out of the cold frame during the day. Once acclimatized, the seedlings may be kept in the open, and potted on as necessary until they are large enough to be planted out.

Hybridizing

New rose cultivars are created by hybridizing, a process by which one cultivar or species is cross-pollinated with another and the new seed sown and grown on. The aim is to create a new rose that inherits the best characteristics of both parents.

Selecting the parents

Most roses are of mixed ancestry, so it is impossible to predict the results of hybridization, and the chances of producing a quality cultivar, with distinct characteristics, are small. Knowledge of the parent roses' genetic characteristics, in particular

their chromosomal number and structure, is important in breeding.

The chromosomes are the parts of plant cells that control the inheritance of characteristics through the genes. Roses may have different chromosome numbers, although the total number per cell in each case is always a multiple of seven. Most of the species roses have 14 (diploid),

28 (tetraploid), 42 (hexaploid), or 56 (octoploid) chromosome numbers. When two roses have been cross-pollinated, equivalent chromosomes from the parents arrange themselves in pairs, which then fuse and count as one in the chromosome number of the new cultivar. Most garden roses are tetraploids and two tetraploids brought together in this

HOW TO HYBRIDIZE ROSES
PREPARING THE SEED PARENT

1 Select an unblemished bloom (here 'Princess Michael of Kent') that has not fully unfolded its petals and should therefore not yet have been pollinated.

2 Remove the petals, taking off the outer ones first. Work gradually towards the centre, taking care not to damage the stigmas as they become exposed.

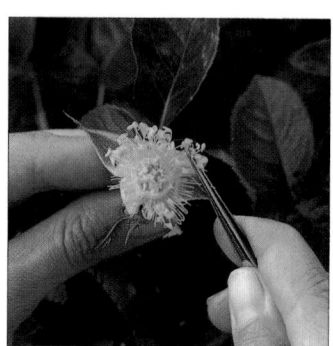

3 Using tweezers or a small pair of scissors, remove the stamens around the stigmas and all fragments of stamens or petals.

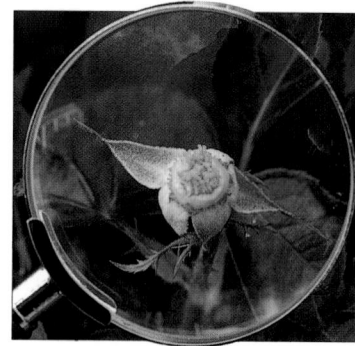

4 Use a magnifying glass to inspect the rose and make sure that no fragments remain. If left they may decay and allow rot fungi to enter the rose hip.

5 Make a paper cone, twisting its point firmly closed (see inset). Holding back the sepals, cover the flower with the cone, and tie securely around the stem.

ALTERNATIVE STEP
Place a clean, dry, plastic bag over the flower and secure it with a firm tie. The flower is thus protected from pollinating insects.

fusion produce another tetraploid rose. A diploid (14) crossed with a tetraploid (28), however, results in 7 + 14 chromosomes, or a total of 21 (triploid) in the new rose. As this is not an even number there are seven chromosomes left without comparable chromosomes with which to pair. Triploids are often sterile and of little or no use in breeding.

Where the chromosome count is known, it is given in the most recent edition of *Modern Roses* (American Rose Society for the International Registration Authority for Roses). This publication also details the pedigree of large numbers of roses.

Heredity is not the only factor influencing the selection of parent plants. Some hybrid roses make good pollen (male) parents, but poor seed (female) parents, and vice versa. Some are completely infertile and others almost so, and in a rose with a very large number of petals, such as a Provence, a proportion of these may have taken the place of the stamens, so that little pollen is available for hybridizing. Crossing a non-remontant rose with a remontant one may be a problem if remontancy is one of the desired characteristics, as the first generation from such a cross is always non-remontant. At least one more cross is needed before remontancy reappears in the offspring.

This is a simplification of a very complex subject and there is a good deal of chance involved in rose breeding. However scientific an approach is taken, the result is still largely unpredictable. As a general principle, choose the healthiest cultivars available as parents, and start with what is perhaps the easiest cross of all, that between two different cultivars of cluster-flowered bush roses.

Controlling the growing environment

Except in a frost-free climate, use pot-grown roses in a greenhouse, as this allows greater control of temperature, humidity, insect pests, and diseases, and gives the hips a better chance of ripening properly. Precise record-keeping is essential: after crosses have been made, carefully identify all the flower stems with a dated label on which is written the names of both parent plants, giving the seed parent first, for example 'Anne Harkness' x 'Memento'.

Preparing the seed parent

First select a bloom of the rose you have chosen for the seed parent, at the stage where it is starting to unfold but before insects could have reached the stamens in the centre and contaminated them with alien pollen. Carefully remove the petals and the stamens (emasculation), and make sure that no tissue is left that could later lead to rot in the hip. Tie a paper cone or plastic bag over the emasculated flower and leave it for one to two days to allow the stigmas to mature.

Preparing the pollen parent

Cut the flower that is to be the pollen parent, which should be at about the same stage as the seed parent. Stand the pollen parent in a vase of water and protect it from insects until the anthers release the tiny, orange pollen grains, usually on the day after being cut. The stigmas of the seed parent should begin to exude a sticky secretion, indicating that they are ready to receive the pollen. Pull off the petals from the pollen parent, leaving the anthers intact.

Pollinating the seed parent

Remove the protective covers and brush the stamens of the pollen parent against the stigmas of the seed parent; their sticky secretion helps the pollen adhere to the stigmas. Replace the cover on the pollinated flower and label the stem.

An alternative method is to cut off the pollen parent's anthers, place them in a small, clean container, such as a plastic pill-box, labelled with the name of the rose, and store it in cool, dry conditions until the released pollen grains are visible in the box. Using a fine brush, dust pollen from the box onto the stigmas of the seed parent. If carrying out more than one cross with different roses, make sure that the brush has been thoroughly cleaned between each operation, preferably with methylated or surgical spirit.

If the cross has not taken successfully, the newly forming hip will shrivel quickly. If it has been successful, the sepals will begin to lift and the hip to swell; once this is evident, remove the protective cone or bag to allow the hip to grow.

The hip will continue to swell; it normally takes about two and a half months to ripen, according to the climate. As it ripens, the hip changes its colour from green to red, to yellow, or possibly maroon, depending on the individual rose.

Harvesting and sowing

Remove the ripened hip from the plant and carefully extract the seeds. Sow and raise the seed (see "Extracting and sowing seed", p.134). Seed resulting from hybridization, however, may be sown fresh without a stratification period.

Selection

The seedlings are likely to flower in the first year – often within a few weeks of germination in a greenhouse – but it is only in the second year that the blooms will be more or less typical of the new hybrid and it is possible to judge whether it should be kept and developed or discarded.

Promising new seedlings can be budded onto rootstocks (see "Budgrafting", p.132) when they have stems of sufficient thickness, that is about 5mm ($^{1}/_{4}$in). Even experienced hybridists, however, find this stage challenging, as it is not easy to detect faults until a selection has been grown in trials for a few years.

PREPARING THE POLLEN PARENT

6 *Select an unblemished bloom that is not yet fully open (here 'Peaudouce'). Cut the stem of the flower at an angle just above a bud.*

7 *Place the chosen flower in water and keep it indoors, free from insects, until it opens fully (usually overnight).*

8 *When the flower is open and the anthers split, revealing the pollen, gently remove all the petals.*

9 *The exposed anthers are now ready to release their tiny pollen grains.*

POLLINATING THE SEED PARENT

10 *Uncover the seed parent and brush the anthers of the pollinator across its stigmas. The pollen grains will adhere to the sticky stigmas of the seed parent.*

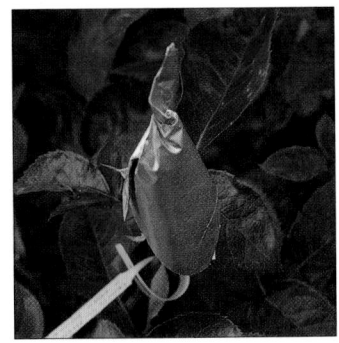

11 *Replace the protective cone over the seed parent and tie securely. Label the rose with the names of the seed parent and pollen parent, and leave it to ripen.*

Roses for display and exhibition

ENTERING roses in a local flower show and, with time, in a town or county horticultural show, can be very rewarding. Higher levels of competition often require much more dedication and time than the average gardener can give.

Rules for exhibiting roses vary from country to country, depending on the requirements of national, and local, rose associations. It is as important for serious exhibitors as it is for judges to be familiar with the details of such rules, so always check with your local association before entering a show.

Cultivating roses for exhibition

Grow several bushes of the same cultivar to ensure a wide choice of blooms. Some bush cultivars are as good in the garden as on the show bench, provided that they are well looked after in the garden and the

DISBUDDING ROSES

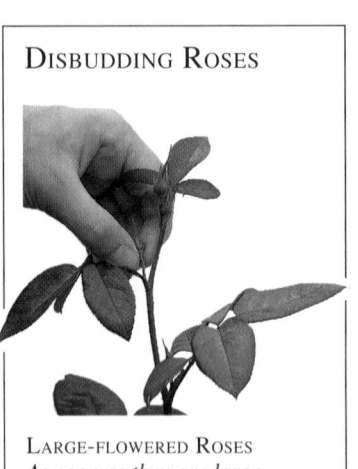

LARGE-FLOWERED ROSES
As soon as they are large enough to handle easily, pinch out all the sidebuds, leaving the main, central bud to grow on.

CLUSTER-FLOWERED ROSES
Pinch out the young, central bud of each smaller spray in the truss for uniform flowering.

CHINESE HATS

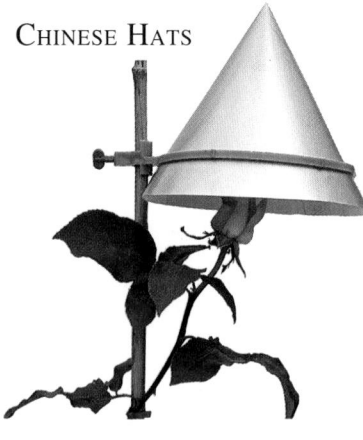

To protect a show bloom from rain damage, insert a stake or cane with a "Chinese hat" by the rose stem and tie the stem in to the stake.

foliage is kept free from disease. Prune cultivars severely to produce a limited number of strong shoots with only eight or nine blooms a season from which to choose exhibition blooms. Maintain vigorous growth with extra fertilizer. Roses are often disbudded to produce exhibition quality blooms. Remove the newly formed sidebuds from large-flowered roses so that the main bud develops strongly. Disbudding the central bloom of cluster-flowered roses ensures that all the other buds open at roughly the same time.

Some blooms are easily damaged by rain, and showing rules permit the use of individual bloom protectors, or "Chinese hats", in the form of plastic cones fixed to canes. They are by no means essential, however, and are not easy to use on the large trusses of cluster-flowered bushes.

Selecting blooms

Timing is crucial in exhibiting. A large-flowered bush bloom should, at the moment of judging, be only three-quarters open, and a cluster-flowered bush truss should have the maximum number of blooms open, although the stamens should not yet have blackened. Blooms should be of average size for the cultivar. Good, healthy foliage is also important.

Preparing for a show

The novice exhibitor should restrict entries in any one show to a maximum of three classes at first. Cut about double the number of roses to be entered, with stems at least 30cm

(12in) long, on the evening before the show. Remove the lower leaves and thorns and plunge them into buckets of cold water, right up to the necks of the flowers. Keep them overnight in a cool place.

Do not be put off if your blooms suffer weather damage. Others are in the same position. If the blooms must be transported any distance, keep each bloom or truss separated, so that they are not damaged.

Staging the blooms

Once at the show, collect your class entry cards from the show secretary and carry your roses straight to the staging table. Use vases or bowls that are as plain as possible. Staging the blooms always takes longer than expected, but greater speed and skill will come with experience.

Arrange the roses symmetrically, placing any larger bloom in the front so it is less noticeable. The blooms should be close together, but not touching; a good blend of colours may win an extra point. Cut out faded cluster-flowered blooms if this does not leave obvious cut stems or gaps. Use a water-colour brush to remove insects or dust specks and sponge off any traces of insecticide deposit with cotton wool. If needed, "dress" large-flowered blooms by gently teasing any petals that are slightly out of place into the correct position. Do not reposition the petals too much, since overdressed blooms may lose points. If the rules allow, support the stems with wires.

When arranging the blooms, check that they conform to the schedule,

A LARGE-FLOWERED ROSE 'VALERIE MARGARET'

High, conical centre

Circular outline

Clean, undamaged leaves of good size

Firm, unblemished petals

Bloom ¾ open

Outer petals evenly reflexed

A CLUSTER-FLOWERED ROSE 'HANNAH GORDON'

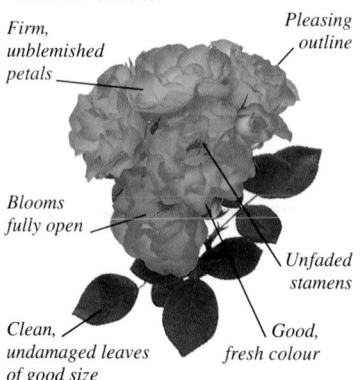

Firm, unblemished petals

Pleasing outline

Blooms fully open

Unfaded stamens

Clean, undamaged leaves of good size

Good, fresh colour

for example "One bloom each of three cultivars of a large-flowered bush rose in a vase"; if there is any deviation, the arrangement will be judged as N.A.S. (Not According to Schedule). Place the class card, and one listing the cultivars, in front of the vase. Tidy away the debris and top up the vases with water.

EQUIPMENT FOR EXHIBITING ROSES

Plain vase

Knife to cut oasis

Wire ties to support staged stems

Florist's wire to position stems

Ruler to measure stems

Soft wool tie to prevent blooms opening in transit

Soft brush to clean petals

Scissors to snip out faded blooms

Block of oasis to arrange the roses

Cotton wool for cleaning leaves

Schedule of shows

Entry card

Variety card

6

PERENNIALS

ITH FLOWERS IN *every colour of the rainbow, a breathtaking range of shapes and textures, and often fine scents, perennials richly deserve their popularity. Their diversity makes them suitable for all sizes and types of garden, while their reliability makes them a lasting source of pleasure. For many people, a traditional herbaceous border in full bloom is the epitome of garden beauty, but perennials can be equally effective in mixed borders, interplanted with shrubs, annuals, bulbs, or even* fruits and vegetables, or grown as ground cover or in containers. There are flowers to suit all tastes from delicate Gypsophila *to sumptuous peonies and spiky delphiniums, and some flowers are followed by attractive seedheads. Foliage ranges from the lacy fronds of many ferns to the umbrella-like leaves of some* Gunnera *species. Perennials can create variety in even a tiny garden, or greater detail in a large one, providing a virtually unlimited palette from which to create a perfect garden picture.*

Designing with perennials

Perennials are non-woody plants that live for two or more years. Most are herbaceous, dying back in autumn to ground level, some to a woody base, and sending up new growth in spring. A few, such as *Helleborus niger*, are evergreen, and so have a valuable winter presence. Most perennial displays occur in summer but some flowers, such as *Liriope muscari* and *Iris unguicularis*, enliven the garden in autumn and winter, while *Helleborus orientalis* and *Pulmonaria* welcome the spring.

Choosing perennials

More than any other group of plants, perennials have an immense variety of shape, form, colour, texture, and scent. Often valued most for their flowers, many also have attractive foliage – from the ribbed, furling leaves of hostas, or the sword-like straps of iris, to the fine tracery of fennel (*Foeniculum vulgare*). In general, the foliage outlasts the floral display so selecting perennials that have ornamental leaves helps to extend the season of interest, a factor that is particularly important in a small garden.

Perennials range in height from the creeping *Lamium maculatum* at just 10–15cm (4–6in) tall, to the statuesque pampas grass (*Cortaderia selloana*), which is 2.5m (8ft) tall or more. Low-growing, ground-cover perennials are ideal for the front of borders or for containers, while tall, stately plants may be better

grown on their own as specimen plants or at the back of a border to give height and structure to the planting design.

Some perennials, such as many carnations and pinks (*Dianthus*) and sweetly scented stocks (*Matthiola*), are worth growing for their fragrance alone, making them ideal for raised beds or windowboxes. Other perennials, especially *Sedum spectabile*, some wallflowers (*Cheiranthus*), and many herbs, have flowers that attract bees and butterflies.

As with all plants, when choosing perennials for a planting scheme, make sure that they are appropriate for the given growing conditions, such as the garden soil, microclimate, and aspect. In the right situation, the plants are much more likely to flourish, and usually need less maintenance than those struggling in an unsuitable position (see also "Site and aspect", p.147).

Herbaceous borders

The most common form of planting with perennials is the herbaceous border, which dates back to late Victorian times. Traditionally, herbaceous borders consisted of long, rectangular plots, usually framed by an expanse of green lawn. They were filled exclusively with summer- and early autumn-flowering perennials, banked according to height, with the shortest at the front and the tallest at the back. Plants characteristic of the border ranged from shasta daisies

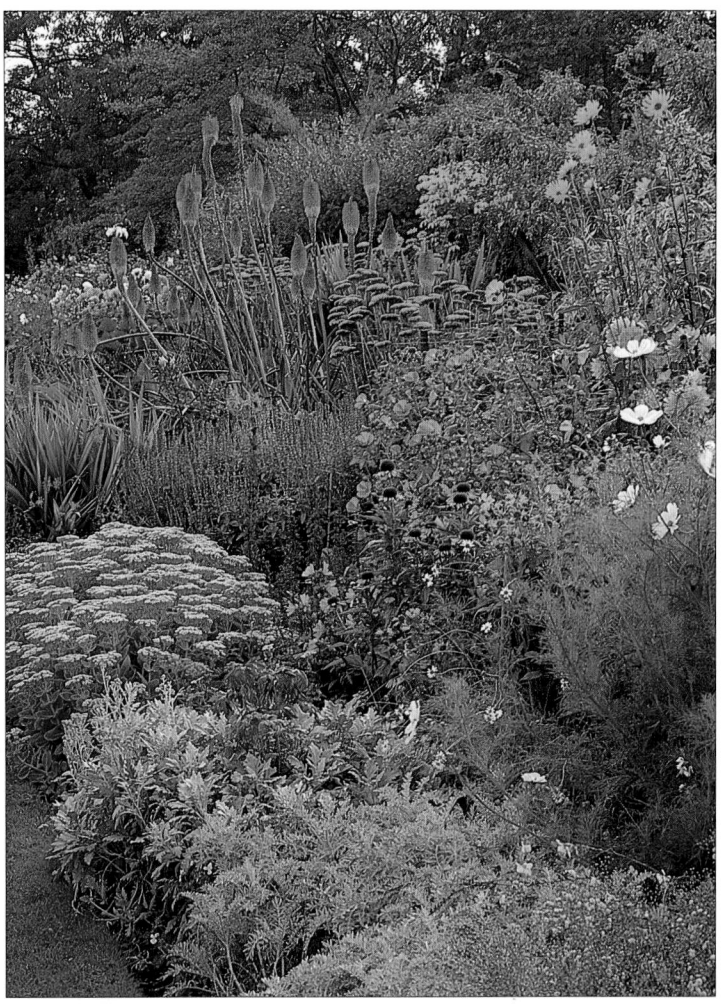

PERENNIAL BORDER
Hot-coloured flowers, such as the poker-headed Kniphofia, *yellow* Achillea, *and pink* Echinacea purpurea, *are offset by the cool, silver-grey foliage of two* Senecio *cultivars; low, rounded plants contrast with tall, upright forms.*

FORMAL BORDERS
In this formal garden, a traditional grass path divides a pair of wide, straight borders. The plants are arranged by height, with low plants such as Sedum spectabile *at the front so that all can be clearly seen. While the planting in each border is not a rigid mirror-image of the other, a number of plants are used in both to provide a balanced, harmonious effect.*

(*Chrysanthemum* x *superbum*), *Scabiosa*, and phlox, traditionally grown in informal, cottage gardens for their charm and pretty colours, to the stately and splendid forms of *Hemerocallis* and *Agapanthus*, which make elegant additions to a formal border.

In the past, depending on the size and style of the garden, a single border might be backed by a wall, fence, or hedge, while a pair of borders might flank a path, allowing the banks of colour and scent to be easily appreciated.

Modern herbaceous borders are usually on a more modest scale than their Victorian counterparts, but they may still exploit some of the same ideas effectively. For a traditional,

formal approach, arrange the plants in large, distinct groups of a single type of plant. If a more informal, fluid effect is desired, form drifts of each plant that flow into each other. This allows you to create impressive swathes of colour and texture with less clearly defined edges.

If a long season of interest is particularly important, perhaps where planting space is very limited, it may be preferable to include shrubs and bulbs in the border as well as perennials (see "Mixed borders", right). In a large garden, however, there may be space to include some traditional, purely herbaceous borders and feature substantial winter and spring planting elsewhere to provide continuing seasonal interest.

Herbaceous borders do certainly provide a dazzling display in summer, when the garden is probably used and enjoyed most, but they often prove to be less attractive at other times of the year. They can, however, always be justified if the pleasure gained from their relatively short-lived beauty outweighs the dormant period between one annual display and the next (see also "Designing beds and borders", p.139).

Island beds

Unlike borders, island beds, which are surrounded by lawn or paving, may be seen from all sides, so the planting design should be effective

from a number of viewpoints. Island bed schemes often include a majority of plants selected for their sturdy, dwarf, or compact habit, as these do not require staking. As with borders, beds that are dedicated solely to herbaceous plants are at their most impressive in summer; for a more enduring display, interplant the perennials with a variety of bulbs and perhaps one or two shrubs.

Geometrical, round, square, or rectangular island beds suit a formal setting; in an informal garden or one with gently undulating ground, loosely curved island beds are more appropriate. Try to avoid intricate shapes and tight curves since they are awkward to maintain and may detract from the planting.

Raised island beds are attractive in paved gardens and can provide improved conditions for growing a greater range of perennials in those gardens where the soil is poor or waterlogged. Their height enables plants to be cared for with minimal stooping, an important factor for disabled or elderly gardeners.

Mixed borders

As their name suggests, mixed borders may contain a combination of small trees, shrubs, climbers, bulbs, annuals, and biennials, as well as perennials. They provide the greatest opportunity for creating year-round interest and imaginative plant associations. Unlike exclusively

MIXED ISLAND BED FOR COLOUR THROUGH THE SEASONS

This island bed, shown here in spring, includes perennials and bulbs to provide colour from early spring through to autumn. Tall, sculptural plants are included to add height at the centre and give the bed a strong impact.

1 *Lamium maculatum* 'White Nancy', interplanted with *Scilla siberica* 'Atrocoerulea'
2 *Iris foetidissima* 'Variegata'
3 *Pulmonaria saccharata*
4 *Heuchera cylindrica* 'Greenfinch'
5 *Galanthus* 'Atkinsii'
6 *Festuca glauca*
7 *Phormium tenax* 'Sundowner'
8 *Anaphalis margaritacea*, syn. *A. yedoensis*
9 *Limonium latifolium* 'Blue Cloud'
10 *Acanthus mollis*
11 *Heuchera* 'Palace Purple'
12 *Euphorbia amygdaloides* subsp. *robbiae*
13 *Oenothera tetragona* 'Fireworks'
14 *Narcissus* 'February Gold'
15 *Libertia grandiflora*
16 *Bergenia* 'Ballawley'
17 *Ophiopogon planiscapus* 'Nigrescens', interplanted with *Galanthus* 'Magnet'
18 *Sedum spectabile* 'Brilliant', interplanted with *Crocus tommasinianus*
19 *Lamium maculatum* 'Roseum'
20 *Achillea* 'Moonshine'
21 *Iberis sempervirens* 'Snowflake'
22 *Chionodoxa forbesii*, syn. *C. luciliae* of gardens

MIXED BORDERS
Colourful tulips provide spring interest, while shrubs such as a golden-leaved Spiraea *and the sculptural mass of* Euphorbia characias *subsp.* wulfenii *add colour and form from spring through to autumn, extending the period of interest beyond the summer burst of colour offered by the hardy* Geranium *species and other perennials.*

MASSED FORM AND COLOUR
Planting in bold groups creates a strong impact. Here, the rounded leaves of a Ligularia *contrast with the pointed swords of red* Crocosmia.

herbaceous borders, well-planned mixed schemes may form an attractive display as the seasons progress from autumn through until spring.

The amount of space given to each type of plant may vary according to taste. A mixed border with a predominance of perennials and only a few non-herbaceous plants usually needs more maintenance than one with a high proportion of shrubs and a small number of perennials. A varied scheme that provides year-round interest may be achieved using shrubs for one third to a half of the planting, including a good selection of evergreens.

A newly planted mixed border may require large groups of bulbs, annuals, and biennials to fill in the gaps between the shrubs and perennials, but these may gradually be decreased as the latter become established and reach their mature size.

Designing beds and borders

When designing a planting scheme, the principles are broadly similar whether planning a herbaceous or mixed border or an island bed. Considerations of height, mass, texture, sequential interest, form, and colour are all variable factors that may be exploited to achieve particular design effects. Imagination and personal taste will inevitably influence your planting schemes, but there are a few basic guidelines to follow.

General principles
Herbaceous borders may be designed in various styles so that they set or strengthen the character and tone of the garden. In a formal setting, straight borders with a restricted colour scheme look elegant and well ordered, while in an informal garden, irregular or curved shapes with a more relaxed and free approach to planting would complement the overall design.

The size of a border or bed can vary but, as a rough guide, the larger the garden setting, the bigger the border or bed should be. The size and shape should be proportionate to and congruous with the house and any other nearby features such as a patio. Generally, 1.5m (5ft) is the minimum width for a bed or border to have any impact in a planting scheme, and to create a layered effect that is well balanced.

When planning which plants to include in the border and how best to position them, remember to allow sufficient room for the plants to spread as they develop and mature, taking account of the different rates at which they grow. If using plants grown in containers, set them out in their positions according to your planting plan and make any adjustments to the scheme at this stage, before planting them out.

Height
In general, site tall plants at the back of a front-facing border, graduating towards the shortest ones in the front, to create a tiered effect in which no

plant is hidden behind another. In an island bed, place the tallest plants in the centre, with the smallest round the outer edge.

This formal regularity may be inappropriate or undesirable in many gardens, however, and the occasional anarchic touch may add greatly to the freshness and individuality of a design. Provided that they are not too dense or spreading, a few tall plants sited towards the front of the border breaks the monotony, while varying the position of the tallest and the shortest plants helps to create a softly undulating effect when the design is viewed from the side.

Generally, the wider the bed or border, the taller the plants may be; very tall plants in narrow borders

may look awkward and the angle from the tallest to the shortest, uncomfortably steep.

Planting in groups
To achieve the greatest impact, mass small and medium-sized plants in groups of one type, rather than planting isolated specimens. Planting in odd-numbered groups, with the plants placed at random rather than in lines, establishes a fluid, natural-looking effect. The smaller the plant, the larger the group should be: *Bergenia* species and hybrids look effective in threes, for example, while London pride (*Saxifraga* x *urbium*) is best planted in groups of seven or more. The huge *Gunnera manicata*, however, is striking enough to be

PLANTING IN DRIFTS
Crimson Rosa moyesii *and yellow* Thalictrum flavum *form counterpoints with soft, purple drifts of* Salvia nemorosa *and catmint (*Nepeta*).*

HARMONIZING
TEXTURES
*A mixture of plants
with airy and feathery
flowers, such as*
Astilbe, Lythrum
virgatum, Filipendula
palmata, *and tall,
yellow* Ligularia
stenocephala *forms
a satisfying pattern
of textures.*

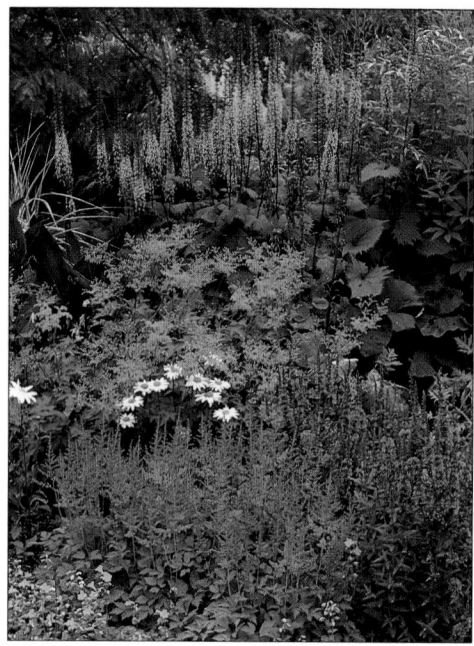

CONTRASTING FORMS
*This grouping of
foliage plants gives
prominence to
differences in form
and texture. The
impressive, jagged
foliage of* Rheum
palmatum *at the rear
contrasts with the
heart-shaped leaves of*
Ligularia dentata *and
the softly arching
straps of an
ornamental grass.*

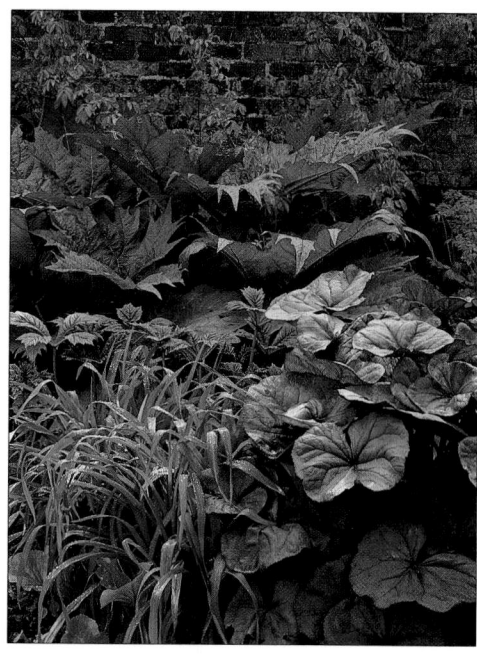

planted singly, as may medium-sized and large shrubs in a mixed border (see "Specimen planting", p.142).

Plants that have strong outlines, such as *Kniphofia caulescens* with its upright poker-head flowers, are effective when planted in smaller groups than those of less distinct forms such as the feathery *Aster ericoides*. Try, too, to plant groups of varying sizes.

Form
Perennials have widely differing forms and silhouettes, including upright, rounded, arching, as well as horizontally spreading. Juxtapose

groups of plants with contrasting forms to create a series of vignettes which build up within a bed or border. The slim spikes of delphiniums or *Eremurus*, for example, act like giant, colourful exclamation marks, when seen against the foaming, cloud-like cushions of *Gypsophila paniculata* or *Crambe cordifolia*.

Some plants are two-tiered, and have their own contrasting form: a fine example is *Rheum palmatum* 'Atrosanguineum', which makes a horizontal layer of reddish-purple leaves that grows 90cm (3ft) tall, above which are held smoky-pink plumes of tiny flowers.

Texture
While flowers and stems contribute to the texture of a planting scheme, it is foliage that provides the strongest impact. Even when seen from a distance, it has the greatest potential for creating striking contrasts and subtle harmonies. The dainty leaves of *Coreopsis verticillata* or the hair-like foliage of *Argyranthemum* 'Chelsea Girl' are very delicate, while large, individual leaves such as those of *Hosta sieboldiana* var. *elegans* create a bold, textural effect.

Texture is also affected by the leaf surface, whether it is the matt, waxy foliage of *Sedum spectabile*, the

glossy, leathery leaves of *Bergenia purpurascens*, or the woolly texture of *Lychnis coronaria*.

As with form, juxtaposing groups of plants that have contrasting textures creates interest; for example, the downy, pleated leaves of *Alchemilla mollis* would contrast well with the spiny stems and jagged foliage of *Eryngium*. Ground-cover perennials such as hardy *Geranium* species and cultivars and *Ajuga reptans* are especially useful for growing as a low foil for other plants, and for filling in the gaps in the planting scheme, to complete the textural tapestry (see GROUND COVER, pp.150–51).

COOL BORDER

*Restful blues, greens, and white combine to form a calm scheme
that is ideal for the cool conditions of a semi-shaded, moist site.*

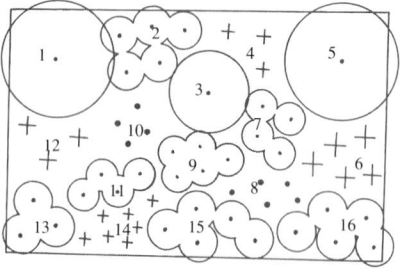

1 *Yucca flaccida* 'Ivory'
2 *Aster turbinellus*
3 *Ferula communis*
4 *Veronica virginica* f. *alba*
5 *Cynara cardunculus*
6 *Iris sibirica*
7 *Amsonia tabernaemontana,*
   syn. *A. salicifolia*
8 *Aster thomsonii* 'Nanus'
9 *Dicentra spectabilis* f. *alba*
10 *Tradescantia* 'Osprey'
11 *Astrantia major* var. *involucrata*
12 *Eryngium* x *oliverianum*
13 *Tiarella cordifolia*
14 *Veronica* 'Crater Lake Blue'
15 *Alchemilla mollis*
16 *Platycodon grandiflorus*

HOT BORDER

A bright colour scheme including vivid reds and yellows looks spectacular in a hot, sunny position.

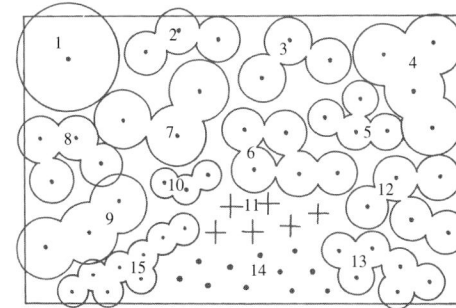

1 *Kniphofia caulescens*
2 *Salvia fulgens*
3 *Euryops pectinatus*
4 *Canna indica*
5 *Mimulus aurantiacus*
6 *Penstemon* 'Garnet'
7 *Hedychium gardnerianum*
8 *Cosmos atrosanguineus*
9 x *Venidio-arctotis* 'Apricot'
10 Yellow form of *Calceolaria*, Bikini Series
11 *Iris* 'Early Light'
12 *Osteospermum* 'Buttermilk'
13 *Hemerocallis* 'Stella d'Oro'
14 *Gazania uniflora*
15 *Verbena peruviana*

Colour

The use of colour in perennial beds and borders may be as daring and experimental or as subtle and restrained as you like. Schemes may be based on a single colour, such as the famous white garden at Sissinghurst, Kent, in England, or on limited bands of colour, for example various shades of pink and red, cream and yellow, or blue and mauve. For a bolder and contrasting scheme, mix striking combinations of reds and blues or yellows and purples. Multicoloured designs offer scope for creating very different effects, depending on whether they are limited to pastel shades, intense hues, or a glorious mixture of the two.

White is a relatively easy monochromatic scheme to plan, since many plants have white-flowered forms or complementary silver or grey foliage, but consider softening

LONG-LASTING DISPLAY
The rich brown seedheads of Sedum spectabile *may be left uncut to provide interest in late autumn and winter long after the succulent leaves have died back.*

the effect by including other pale colours as well. White and pale pink, cream, and grey are invaluable for enlivening a shady border or one in a dark setting, such as a border backed by a yew hedge. These colours may also be used to provide a restful area between strong or clashing colours. By contrast, "hot" colours usually show up best in bright sunlight. Golden or yellow schemes are warming, and particularly welcome in spring and autumn. Adding one or two sparks of contrasting colour can give vitality to a limited colour scheme.

When planning colour schemes, bear in mind that foliage colour is as important as that of flowers. The white- or cream-variegated leaves of plants such as *Hosta crispula* can enhance a white scheme, or the golden foliage of *Filipendula ulmaria* 'Aurea', a yellow one. Generally,

golden foliage colours best in sun, and white in light shade, but very hot, dry conditions may scorch yellow leaves. Plants with silver and grey foliage tend to grow well in hot, sunny beds and counterbalance the "hot" colours of perennials such as Michaelmas daisies (*Aster*), Gaillardia, and *Cosmos*.

Seasonal interest

In a mixed border, it is possible to plan a succession of colour schemes that change with the course of the seasons. For example, a bright and cheerful springtime planting could include a predominance of yellow, from primroses (*Primula vulgaris*) and *Doronicum*, and pale blue, from irises and *Pulmonaria*, interspersed with grape hyacinths (*Muscari*) and daffodils. Summer brings with it the freedom to choose from a more varied palette, perhaps bursting into a joyful riot of colour, with vividly hued, exotic subtropical plants combining with more subtle shades and the rich, warm pinks and reds of roses. The perennials' season ends with the fiery, intense, autumnal colours of chrysanthemums, dahlias, sunflowers (*Helianthus*), Rudbeckia, and *Kniphofia*.

Planning any bed or border involves co-ordinating the timing of each plant's display, so that one feature smoothly follows another and fading flowers pass unnoticed, eclipsed by nearby plants coming into bloom. A scheme that manages to maintain a succession of interest

requires forethought but most mistakes are easily corrected if any "offending" plants are re-sited when they are still young.

It is sometimes possible to extend the effect of a particular plant or group by growing a plant next to it that gives a similar impression. The deep blue flower spikes of *Delphinium* 'Blue Nile', for example, could be followed by those of *Aconitum carmichaelii* var. *wilsonii*, and if the latter is planted in front, the yellowing delphinium foliage will be hidden. Try to front perennials such as lupins (*Lupinus*) that die back early with plants such as *Physostegia* that develop later in the season, to hide awkward gaps or fading leaves.

In mixed borders, bulbs are particularly useful for providing colour in late winter and spring when perennials are starting into growth. Similarly, the new growth of the latter masks the fading foliage of the bulbs once their flowers have finished. For example, the black-purple leaves of the evergreen *Ophiopogon planiscapus* 'Nigrescens' or the soft purplegreen foliage of *Viola labradorica* 'Purpurea' make excellent foils for snowdrops (*Galanthus*) and continue to provide interest after the snowdrops are past their best.

In summer, the perennials are at their peak, creating a rich, full effect, but as they start to die down in autumn, the display created by shrubs is invaluable, maintaining the shape and structure of the design as well as

INFORMAL STYLE
Sprawling plants such as pink Helianthemum *soften the edges of stone steps in an informal, cottage garden, while more sculptural plants such as the variegated* Hosta 'Thomas Hogg' *and the arching, golden* Carex elata 'Bowles' Golden' *add structural interest.*

contributing both colour and texture. The inclusion of deciduous shrubs with attractive autumn foliage (such as *Cotinus*) and those with bright berries (such as many pyracanthas) will help to draw attention away from the perennials as their foliage dies back.

Few perennials are renowned for their winter appeal but some such as *Bergenia* and many hellebores (*Helleborus*) soften the sturdy effect created by a shrub framework, contrasting with the mass of an evergreen shrub or the architectural form of a deciduous one.

Cottage gardens

Traditional cottage gardens are a glorious mixture of plants – herbs, roses, climbers, annuals, fruits, and vegetables, as well as perennials. In the past, cottagers bred plants themselves and produced enchanting perennials such as pansies (*Viola x wittrockiana*), auricula primroses (*Primula auricula*), and scented pinks (*Dianthus*).

Typical plants include peonies (*Paeonia*), lupins (*Lupinus*), and delphiniums, while wild flowers with fragrant, double, extra-large, or unusually coloured blooms are also especially appropriate here. Old-fashioned plants dating back to Victorian times and earlier are often favoured, but they may be combined with modern forms and cultivars for a varied scheme.

Perennials in woodland gardens

Deciduous woodland provides conditions of shelter, light shade, and humus-rich soil suitable for many perennials. A small grove of birches (*Betula*) and other light-foliaged, deciduous trees may provide a suitable setting for a number of shade-loving plants; site the perennials where they will not face too much competition from the tree roots.

Group plants of one type in drifts and intermingling at the edges, or in substantial clumps, to match the scale of the setting. Ferns, in particular, thrive in a woodland setting and add architectural interest when planted in bold swathes.

Some of the most enchanting perennials are the small woodland plants that usher in the spring. Snowdrops (*Galanthus*), primroses (*Primula vulgaris*), wood anemones (*Anemone nemorosa*), and *Ranunculus ficaria* provide colour and interest, while the overhead canopy is still leafless. Combine them with woodland bulbs and shade-loving shrubs.

In cool, dry woodland shade, grow ground-cover perennials such as the superbly scented lily-of-the-valley (*Convallaria majalis*), Solomon's seal (*Polygonatum*), with its pendent, pearly-white flowers, and *Pulmonaria*, which has attractively marked foliage.

Specimen planting

In large areas of lawn or gravel, stately perennials with an architectural form or sculptural foliage, such as *Acanthus spinosus*, may be sited on their own as specimen plants to create a striking effect. In smaller gardens, a specimen perennial, surrounded by low ground cover, could be used to provide a focal point where a border projects into a lawn or hard paving, or in a corner of a garden where two borders meet. The jutting, sword-shaped leaves and arching, fiery-red flower stems of *Crocosmia* 'Lucifer', for example, look spectacular rising from the silvery sea of an ornamental dead-nettle (*Lamium maculatum* 'White Nancy' or 'Beacon Silver').

For year-round interest, evergreen perennials such as *Phormium tenax* are excellent, while the tall, airy plumes of pampas grass (*Cortaderia selloana*) may be left uncut for an impressive feature through autumn and winter. Other perennials that provide a briefer display may also make spectacular specimens because of their form, flowers, or foliage, ranging from the towering, felty stems of *Verbascum olympicum* to the massive leaves of *Gunnera manicata*, or the glorious, pink blooms of *Paeonia* 'Sarah Bernhardt'. As they die down in autumn, it may be desirable to place another feature, such as a container-planted shrub, nearby, to give interest during their dormant period.

Specimen plants are best offset by a plain backdrop, such as a hedge, wall, or stretch of lawn, so that nothing detracts from their impact (see also GARDEN PLANNING AND DESIGN, "Specimen plants", p.23).

POTTED PERENNIALS
A simple, weathered, terracotta pot is the perfect foil for the golden Hakonechloa macra 'Aureola'.

Growing perennials in containers

Perennials are as welcome in containers on a paved patio, courtyard, balcony, or roof garden as they are in open beds and borders. Growing them in this way also makes it possible to include tender plants that must be brought under cover for winter and plants that require a different soil type from the garden soil.

Containers generally look better grouped rather than scattered around the garden, and the plants benefit from the favourable microclimate created by each other's company.

Containerized evergreen perennials such as *Bergenia purpurascens* and *Liriope muscari* can be on display all year round but herbaceous perennials may be better planted with an evergreen shrub to extend the season of interest.

Specimen plants

A clump of one type of perennial in a large container can perform the role of a specimen plant in a paved area. Those with sculptural foliage or flowers, for example *Agapanthus* and *Hosta sieboldiana*, are particularly attractive in appropriate containers and may be left for years to increase in size.

Mixed planting

In large planters, experiment with mixed planting, combining different types of perennial, such as ground-hugging *Stachys byzantina* 'Silver Carpet', shiny, round-leaved species and cultivars of *Bergenia*, and burgundy *Euphorbia amygdaloides* 'Purpurea'. Combining one each of many different types of perennial, however, is liable to appear cluttered and ineffective as well as being difficult to maintain, because the stronger growing plants will swamp the weaker ones.

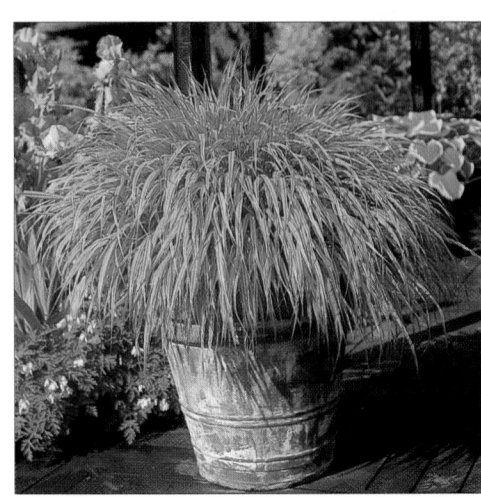

Planter's guide to perennials

EXPOSED SITES

Perennials that tolerate exposed or windy sites; the plant marked � is not suitable for coastal sites

Agapanthus, some ✷
Anaphalis
Anemone hupehensis✎
Artemisia absinthium
Centaurea dealbata, C. hypoleuca
Centranthus ruber
Eryngium variifolium
Euphorbia characias
Festuca glauca
Kniphofia caulescens
Lavatera maritima, L. thuringiaca
Limonium latifolium
Phlomis russeliana
Phormium cookianum, P. tenax
Sedum spectabile, S. telephium
Stachys byzantina
Yucca filamentosa, Y. flaccida

AIR POLLUTION

Perennials that tolerate polluted air

Aconitum napellus
Aquilegia vulgaris
Bergenia cordifolia
Dicentra eximia, D. formosa
Euphorbia amygdaloides
Geranium endressii
Helleborus niger, H. orientalis
Hemerocallis
Heuchera
Hosta
Iris
Lamium
Leucanthemum x superbum
Libertia grandiflora
Polemonium
Polygonatum, some ✷
Pulmonaria

Rudbeckia laciniata 'Goldquelle'

Rudbeckia
Sedum spectabile, S. telephium
Sisyrinchium striatum
Smilacina racemosa
Symphytum
Thalictrum
Tiarella
Veronica gentianoides, V. spicata

DRY SHADE

Perennials that tolerate dry shade

Acanthus mollis
Aconitum carmichaelii, A. napellus
Anemone hupehensis, A. x hybrida
Aquilegia vulgaris
Dicentra
Digitalis grandiflora, D. lutea
Epimedium

Euphorbia amygdaloides
Geranium, some ✷
Helleborus foetidus, H. orientalis
Iris foetidissima
Luzula sylvatica 'Marginata'
Ophiopogon, some ✷
Saxifraga umbrosa, S. x urbium
Symphytum grandiflorum
Tellima grandiflora 'Purpurea'
Vinca minor
Viola labradorica, V. odorata

MOIST SHADE

Perennials that prefer moist shade

Astilbe simplicifolia
Astrantia major
Bergenia
Brunnera macrophylla
Convallaria majalis
Gentiana
    asclepiadea

Hemerocallis 'Marion Vaughn'

Hemerocallis
Hosta
Kirengeshoma palmata
Ligularia przewalskii
Peltiphyllum peltatum
Platycodon
Polygonum bistorta 'Superba'
Primula bulleyana, P. florindae, P. japonica, P. pulverulenta
Rodgersia aesculifolia, R. pinnata
Thalictrum
Trillium grandiflorum, T. sessile

WINTER INTEREST

Decorative flowers

Bergenia 'Ballawley', B. cordifolia
Doronicum
Euphorbia amygdaloides subsp. robbiae, E. characias
Helleborus argutifolius, H. niger
Iris unguicularis
Pulmonaria
Ranunculus ficaria

Decorative leaves

Arum italicum 'Marmoratum'
Bergenia 'Ballawley', B. cordifolia
Euphorbia amygdaloides subsp. robbiae, E. characias
Festuca glauca
Helleborus argutifolius
Heuchera 'Palace Purple'
Iris foetidissima 'Variegata'
Lamium maculatum 'Chequers'
Liriope muscari 'Variegata'
Ophiopogon planiscapus 'Nigrescens'
Phormium (cvs)
Stachys byzantina 'Silver Carpet'
Tiarella polyphylla
Vinca (variegated cvs)

FRAGRANT FLOWERS

Centranthus ruber
Convallaria majalis
Cosmos atrosanguineus ✷
Dianthus 'Brympton Red', D. 'Old Clove Red'
Dictamnus albus
Dracocephalum moldavicum
Filipendula ulmaria
Galium odoratum
Hosta plantaginea var. grandiflora
Iris graminea
Oenothera odorata
Paeonia lactiflora
Petasites fragrans
Phlox paniculata
Viola odorata 'Czar'

FLOWERS FOR CUTTING

Alstroemeria
Aquilegia
Aster, some ✷
Astrantia
Centaurea
Cephalaria
Delphinium, some ✷
Dicentra
Doronicum
Erigeron
Gypsophila
Helenium
Helleborus, some ✷
Kniphofia, some ✷
Monarda
Paeonia
Phlox, some ✷
Primula, some ✷
Rudbeckia
Scabiosa
Solidago
Stokesia
Veronica

FLOWERS FOR DRYING

Acanthus spinosus
Achillea
Alchemilla mollis
Anaphalis
Aruncus dioicus
Astilbe
Catananche
Cynara
Echinops bannaticus, E. ritro
Limonium, some ✷
Phlomis russeliana
Rodgersia
Sedum spectabile, S. telephium
Solidago

DECORATIVE SEEDHEADS

Acanthus
Eryngium
Festuca glauca
Iris foetidissima

Lunaria rediviva
Papaver orientale
Physalis alkekengi
Typha

ARCHITECTURAL PLANTS

Acanthus hungaricus, A. mollis
Angelica archangelica
Arundo donax 'Variegata' ✷
Bergenia 'Ballawley'
Cortaderia selloana
Crambe cordifolia
Cynara cardunculus, C. scolymus
Foeniculum vulgare
Gunnera manicata
Helleborus argutifolius
Heracleum (can be invasive)
Hosta sieboldiana var. elegans
Ligularia dentata 'Othello'
Lysichiton americanus
Melianthus major ✷
Miscanthus sinensis
Phormium tenax
Rheum palmatum 'Atrosanguineum'
Rodgersia

FAST-GROWING PERENNIALS

Artemisia lactiflora
Aruncus sylvester
Arundo donax 'Macrophylla' ✷
Campanula lactiflora
Centaurea macrocephala
Cephalaria gigantea
Crambe cordifolia

Cynara cardunculus

Cynara cardunculus, C. scolymus
Euphorbia characias
Ferula communis
Filipendula rubra
Galega x hartlandii
Gunnera manicata
Helianthus
Kniphofia caulescens, K. uvaria
Lavatera cachemiriana, L. maritima
Ligularia stenocephala
Macleaya cordata
Malva alcea var. fastigiata, M. moschata, M. sylvestris
Miscanthus
Phormium tenax
Rheum palmatum 'Atrosanguineum'
Romneya coulteri
Rudbeckia laciniata 'Goldquelle'
Salvia confertiflora ✷, S. sclarea var. turkestanica, S. uliginosa ✷
Silphium perfoliatum
Solidago canadensis
Thalictrum flavum

KEY

✷ Not hardy

Grasses, bamboos, sedges, and rushes

THESE plants have a variety of elegant and architectural forms which, combined with arching or upright stems, feathery inflorescences, and subtly coloured seedheads, make an outstanding display, whether grown grouped together, as specimen plants, or in borders.

Grasses are often confused with other grass-like ornamental plants, particularly the sedges and rushes, but each of them belongs to a quite separate and distinct family.

The grass family

True grasses (those of the Gramineae family) almost always have hollow, round stems, with solid nodes at regular intervals: the woody-stemmed, perennial bamboos (sub-family Bambusoideae) are good examples with the obvious hollowness of their canes. Grass blades extend in two ranks from a sheath that can be split or peeled back. Grass flowers are borne in panicles, racemes, or spikes.

Grasses
These vary widely in colour and habit. The architectural qualities of the taller grasses make them a striking feature in the herbaceous border, while low-growing grasses provide a contrast at the front of the bed. Do not choose vigorous, creeping grasses, such as *Phalaris arundinacea* var. *picta*, for this purpose, however, because they are likely to engulf any adjacent, weaker plants. More easily managed are the tufted grasses, which slowly build up from a central crown.

Some are suitable for paved areas, such as *Molinia caerulea* subsp. *caerulea* 'Variegata'; for a warm, sunny pocket on the patio, use the taller *Helictotrichon sempervirens*, with slender, blue leaves that are upright and stiffly radiating. For a lawn specimen, good choices include species of *Cortaderia* with tall, nodding plumes in late summer, or *Miscanthus*, with more delicate inflorescences. For the water's edge, species such as *Glyceria aquatica* 'Variegata', which display both attractive form and variegation, provide interesting reflections.

Most grasses prefer full sun, an open position, and well-drained but moisture-retentive soil. Very fertile soil encourages foliage at the expense of flowers. A few species, mainly tall ones such as *Phragmites australis*, need moist soil, growing well alongside stream banks.

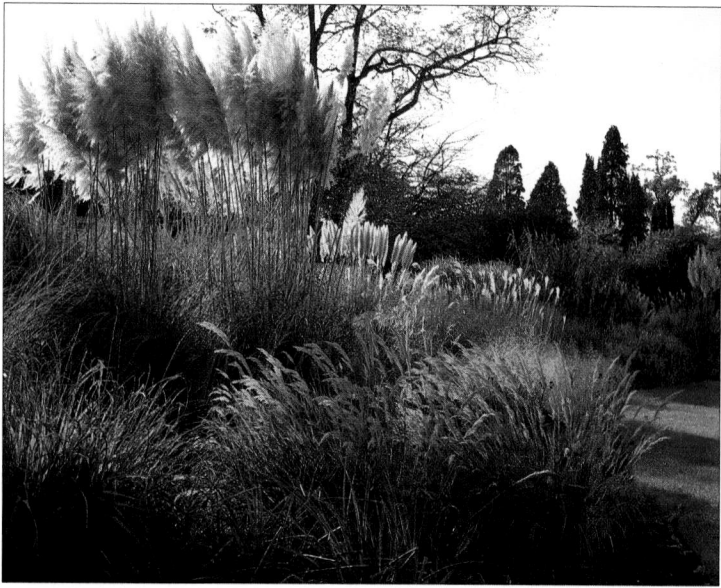

ORNAMENTAL GRASSES
The subtle colours and feathery heads of many grasses (here mostly forms of Cortaderia selloana *and* Miscanthus) *make a striking but informal display.*

Bamboos
Evergreen and woody-stemmed with delicately handsome foliage and architectural outlines, bamboos make ideal specimen plants. A few species flower regularly, but most do not bloom for many years.

Bamboos need ample space since they grow up to 4m (12ft) tall with an arching spread of 6m (20ft), and they often spread quickly. The canes take about three years to mature, although *Phyllostachys nigra* will develop the full beauty of its polished ebony-black stems in its second year. Bamboos grow strongly in most soils once established, and they form excellent screens, hedges, or windbreaks in milder, windswept zones. Many are tropical but a considerable number are hardy in temperate regions.

Sedges and rushes

Sedges (Cyperaceae family) have three-sided stems that are solid and pithy throughout. The leaf blades tightly encase the stem, arising from each side in threes: in cross-section they are concertina-like and cannot readily be split or rolled back.

The family Juncaceae contains two cultivated genera, *Juncus* and *Luzula*, both known commonly as rushes. In *Juncus*, the leaves are cylindrical in cross-section and have a solid pith; in *Luzula*, the leaves are flat and usually edged with hairs.

Woodrushes (*Luzula* spp.) are most appealing when used to provide spreading ground cover in areas of shady woodland. A number of sedges, such as *Carex elata* 'Aurea', and *C. oshimensis* 'Evergold', with their attractive, golden or variegated foliage, also offer fine colour contrasts in the border.

The woodrushes thrive in semishade, but they will also tolerate open conditions. The sedges, although most often found in damp habitats, are usually very tolerant of drier sites, with the exception of moisture-loving species such as *Carex acuta* and *C. riparia*.

LAWN SPECIMEN
*The strong shape and tall, graceful plumes of pampas grass (*Cortaderia selloana) *are most suited to specimen planting.*

Drying grasses for ornamental use

Dried grasses are ideal for indoor decoration. Their bold shapes and neutral colours are effective whether displayed alone or arranged with more colourful dried flowers. To ensure that they are at their best for ornamental use, cut the grasses when the inflorescence is well developed but not open, then stand them in a vase, not too tightly packed together, in a cool, dry place to dry.

Cut the grass, here Miscanthus sinensis 'Silberfeder', *just before flowering (top inset). After a few weeks, the flowerheads will fluff out (bottom inset).*

1 Dig a trench about 20cm (8in) wide, 30cm (12in) from the base of the clump. Make it deeper than the roots of the plant.

2 Insert a barrier made of non-perishable material such as rigid plastic, then fill in the trench and firm the ground well.

Routine cultivation

In general, most ornamental grasses require little care, as long as they are grown in an appropriate, correctly prepared site. Sedges and rushes are largely treated as grasses.

Preparing the soil
On dry soils, incorporate plenty of organic or fibrous matter to ensure adequate moisture retention; this should not be rich in nutrients, however. In mild areas with high rainfall, grasses from the subtropics and very dry regions need a deep, gritty soil with excellent drainage. A top-dressing of stone chippings around the crown in winter helps to disperse surface moisture which, in combination with frost, can kill many plants from warm zones and high altitudes.

Feeding is rarely needed but a dressing of calcium silicate helps to provide tensile strength in bamboo shoots.

CUTTING BACK PAMPAS GRASS

In early spring, cut back the dead foliage and flower stems as far as possible without damaging the new growth (see inset). Wear stout, protective gloves and use shears.

Cutting or burning back
Dead-head annual grasses after flowering to prevent self-seeding, but do not dead-head perennials, since the parchment colours of the fading inflorescence are often an essential part of their winter appeal.

As grasses begin to wither and become unsightly, trim off the old, untidy growth. In early spring, cut back the plant to ground level to encourage vigorous foliage to develop. Grasses from warm climates should be cut back in spring, as the old foliage helps to protect the crown from winter frosts.

Pampas grass (Cortaderia selloana) and Miscanthus species may be cut back using a scythe or shears. Do this in mild areas, or in spring in colder zones. When handling pampas grass, wear stout gloves as the saw-like leaf edges are razor sharp. Alternatively, pampas grass may be burned back, but this demands a controlled burn during a dry period. Always have a hosepipe or bucket of water on hand to dowse any flames that threaten the crown from where new growth will emerge.

Hardy bamboos may occasionally be slightly frost damaged but they usually recover quickly in spring provided that there is ample rainfall. One or two dwarf species, such as Pleioblastus viridistriatus, unlike most other bamboos, perform best if cut back annually to within 15cm (6in) of ground level, to produce fresh young foliage.

Restricting the growth of bamboos
Bamboo root systems are often extremely tough, invasive, and difficult to eradicate. However, you can contain established clumps by digging a trench at least the depth of a spade around the clump, then trimming back the roots and inserting a barrier around them.

Propagation

Perennial grasses may be propagated from seed (see PERENNIALS, "Seed", p.162) or by division. Annuals are increased by seed sown in spring or autumn, depending on the desired time of flowering.

Seed
Collect the seed when it is fully ripe, that is when the inflorescence is dry and fluffy and the seed can be easily pulled away from the spike. Sowing in small pots or cellular trays allows you to pot on without disturbing the young plants. If sown as soon as the seed has ripened, germination is quick, but the young seedlings need some winter protection from frost.

Division
Clump-forming grasses are easily increased by simple division in spring or autumn. Many gardeners prefer division in spring, when new growth is visible, as the plants establish more successfully.

To increase rhizomatous species, lift the clump and cut the rhizome into sections, ensuring that each has at least one growing point. Take care not to damage the fine roots. Insert the sections into individual pots of a free-draining compost and cover the rhizomes to their original depth. Keep them cool and moist, and in good light, but shaded from strong sun until the young plants are established. For further information, see "Dividing perennials", p.164.

Transplanting bamboos
The best time for dividing and transplanting bamboos is spring, just as the shoots are emerging. Transplant when rain is forecast: if the foliage is allowed to dry and wither, which it does very quickly, the transplant is unlikely to survive. Spray water on divided plants regularly and liberally until they are established.

Collect the seed of annual grasses when the inflorescence has fluffed up fully. Pull away the ripe seed from each spike.

1 Dig around the clump to expose the outer rhizomes with new shoots. Separate these from the parent plant.

2 Cut the rhizomes, each with at least one shoot, into pieces. Dust the cut surfaces with fungicidal powder (see inset).

3 Pot up each piece with the rhizome just below the surface of the compost and the shoots exposed. Firm in and water.

PROPAGATING GRASSES BY DIVISION

Cut down the foliage to 15–20cm (6–8in). Lift the clump and divide it, by hand or with two hand forks. Pot up each division in sandy compost in 15cm (6in) pots.

Irises

THE genus *Iris* includes some of the loveliest of flowering plants. Their intricate blooms offer a rich spectrum of colours as well as satin or velvet textures. Species can be selected for diverse situations, ranging from woodland and rock garden, waterside and bog, to herbaceous borders. Botanically, *Iris* is divided into Subgenera, Sections, and Series; these divisions vary in their cultural needs and form a convenient horticultural classification.

Routine care and propagation
Species may be propagated in the autumn or spring by division of offsets or rhizomes, or by seed in autumn (named cultivars by division only). For further information, see PERENNIALS, "Routine care", pp.155–7; BULBOUS PLANTS, "Routine care", pp.234–6, and also "Propagation", pp.237–42.

Rhizomatous irises

Irises in this group have rhizomes as rootstocks, with sword-shaped leaves arranged in a basal fan. Botanically, they are divided into several Subgenera and Series but for horticultural purposes the main groups are bearded, crested, and beardless irises.

Bearded irises
Characterized by a "beard" of numerous hairs along the centre of the falls, this group includes the common irises that are grown in gardens, with many cultivars and hybrids, most flowering in early summer. Suitable for herbaceous and mixed borders, they are easy to grow in rich, well-drained, alkaline soil in sun; many also tolerate poorer soils and partial shade.

Oncocyclus irises are natives of areas with little summer rainfall and need the protection of an alpine house or frame in climates that are subject to summer rains. They have large, beautiful, and sometimes bizarre blooms but are exacting in their requirements and are not easy to grow. They need a fertile, sharply drained soil and full sun, with a dry, dormant period after flowering. If they are grown in pots, the compost must be nutrient-rich, well drained, and preferably alkaline.

Repot before growth begins in early spring, if required. When the foliage dies down after flowering, stop watering, and keep the rhizomes dry while they are dormant. Resume watering in spring.

Regelia irises, with their bearded standards and falls, are related to the Oncocyclus irises and have similar cultural requirements although they are easier to grow. Some species, such as *I. hoogiana*, may be grown outside, given good drainage and a hot, dry site in the summer. The Regeliocyclus group (Regelia x Oncocyclus hybrids) is more easily grown in the open.

Crested irises
These have ridges, or cockscomb-like crests, instead of beards.
Evansia irises are usually found in damp woodland. Larger species, such as *I. confusa* and *I. japonica*, are not fully hardy and need a sheltered position in humus-rich soils, with some shade provided in warm climates. Smaller species, such as *I. cristata* and *I. gracilipes*, are ideal for planting in peaty pockets in a shaded rock garden.

Beardless irises
Irises in this group do not have bearded falls, but usually have crests. Most have similar cultural requirements to bearded irises, but some prefer heavier soil.
Pacific Coast irises, a group that includes *I. innominata* and *I. tenax*, are useful for cutting. Many good, free-flowering hybrids have been produced which are excellent for humus-rich, acid soils, in sun in cool regions or in shade in warmer climates. Others from groups that need similar conditions include: *I. missouriensis*, which is more tolerant of alkaline soils; *I. verna* and *I. prismatica*; and *I. setosa*, which is more tolerant of sun.
Water irises are a group of elegant, moisture-loving plants that thrive in pond margins, bog gardens, or rich, permanently damp soils. They include *I. laevigata*, *I. pseudacorus*, *I. ensata* (syn. *I. kaempferi*), *I. fulva*, *I. versicolor*, and *I.* 'Fulvala'. All need similar damp conditions but can be difficult to establish.
Siberian irises have slender leaves and beautifully formed, delicately marked flowers. This group includes *I. chrysographes*, *I. clarkei*, *I. forrestii*, and *I. sibirica*. They are easily grown in borders in rich soil that does not dry out, and are particularly suited to very moist, waterside soil. The flowers last well when cut.
Spuria irises have narrow, reed-like foliage and elegant blooms. Spurias – *I. orientalis*, *I. graminea*, and *I. spuria* – are suited to sunny herbaceous borders, in well-drained soil; they tolerate drier conditions than the Siberian irises.

Bulbous irises

The storage organs of these irises are bulbs, sometimes with thick, fleshy roots. Subgenera include Reticulata, Juno, and Xiphium irises.

Reticulata irises
Dwarf, hardy bulbs, which flower early. They prefer a sunny position in well-drained, acid or alkaline soil, or may be grown in pots in the bulb frame.

Juno irises
Junos need similar conditions to the Oncocyclus irises and are also difficult to grow. Vigorous species, such as *I. bucharica* and *I. magnifica*, grow well in warm, outdoor sites.

Xiphium irises
These include the brightly coloured Dutch, English, and Spanish irises, often grown for cut flowers. Any alkaline, well-drained soil in full sun is suitable. In cold areas, lift the bulbs in autumn to overwinter in a frost-free place. Replant in spring.

I. 'Bold Print'
(bearded)

I. 'Carnaby'
(bearded)

I. innominata
(Pacific Coast)

I. 'Geisha Gown'
(Japanese)

I. bucharica
(Juno)

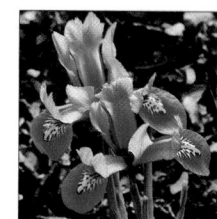
I. 'Joyce'
(Reticulata)

RHIZOMATOUS AND BULBOUS IRISES

INFORMAL ELEGANCE
The colourful blooms of Siberian irises (blue and white), and I. pseudacorus *(yellow) provide a focal point by a garden pond.*

Soil preparation and planting

HERBACEOUS perennials originate from many regions that have widely varying climatic and soil conditions, so whether the proposed site is sheltered or exposed, fertile or stony, there is always a number of plants that will thrive. It is better to select plants that will flourish in the given growing conditions rather than struggle against nature.

Site and aspect

When deciding which plants to grow, take into account climate, aspect, and soil type, as well as the amount of sun, shade, and shelter the site receives at different times of day and from season to season. For example, the shade cast by deciduous trees is most dense in late spring and summer when the trees are in leaf.

Different areas of the garden may provide varying growing conditions: for example, a south-facing border would be ideal for plants that thrive in sun, such as sedums, while a north-facing site or a position beneath a tree would be better for shade-loving species, such as hostas, provided that they can be kept moist.

The ground next to a wall, fence, or hedge is usually fairly dry due to the effect of rain shadow, but since it also tends to be warm and sheltered, it may be a good position for plants that are not fully hardy.

Altering conditions

In small gardens especially, it may be necessary to adapt some elements to create growing conditions that suit a wide range of plants. Heavy, waterlogged soils may be drained or the plants grown in raised beds or containers, while lighter soils may benefit from the addition of organic matter. Shade from trees may be reduced by judicious pruning, and shelter provided by shrubs, hedges, or windbreaks (see also FROST AND WIND PROTECTION, pp.520–21, and HEDGES AND SCREENS, pp.60–62).

Soil preparation

The ideal soil for the majority of perennial plants is a fertile loam that is well drained but retains adequate moisture. Use a proprietary soil-testing kit to find out the degree of acidity or alkalinity of the soil because this partly determines which plants will thrive there.

It is also important to check soil drainage; if much of the ground remains waterlogged in wet weather, then it will be necessary to install soakaways or drains (see SOILS AND FERTILIZERS, "Drainage", p.529).

Clearing the site

All weeds should be cleared from the site prior to planting as once other plants are established, perennial weeds, in particular, are difficult to eradicate. If the ground is infested with weeds, treat the whole area with an appropriate weedkiller during the season before planting. If there are only a few perennial weeds, however, they may be forked out when preparing the soil in winter.

During the first growing season, any remaining perennial weeds should be carefully removed with a hand fork as soon as they are noticed, or treated with a systemic weedkiller, taking care not to harm the newly planted perennials. Annual weeds may be either sprayed or forked out before the site is planted.

Improving the soil structure and fertility

All soils may be improved by the addition of humus or well-rotted organic matter such as manure or compost; this increases the water retention of light, free-draining soils and helps to open up the texture of heavy, clay soils. It also improves the soil's fertility. Before planting (preferably a few weeks in advance), apply a 5–10cm (2–4in) layer of well-rotted organic matter over the site, then fork or rotavate it into the top spit of the soil. Allow the soil to settle before planting. Provided that the soil is fertile and rich in humus, it is usually unnecessary to use fertilizer when planting perennials, although they may require feeding in subsequent seasons (see "Fertilizing", p.155).

CHOOSING PERENNIALS

GOOD EXAMPLE

LUPIN

Strong, healthy top-growth

Moist compost

Established, vigorous roots

POOR EXAMPLES

Weak, woody top-growth

Under-developed root system

Dry compost

Moss and weeds growing on the compost

Pot-bound roots

Selecting plants

Most perennials are sold container-grown, but bare-root plants are also sometimes available from autumn to early spring, when they are dormant. When selecting plants, look for healthy, vigorous specimens with no sign of dieback or abnormally coloured leaves that may indicate a lack of nutrients. If buying herbaceous plants at the beginning of the growing season, check that there are strong, emerging shoots: plants that have a few fat, healthy looking buds are better than those that have a large number of weaker ones.

One or two annual weeds growing in the compost may be removed easily enough, but do not buy any container-grown plants with perennial weeds, moss, or liverworts.

These often indicate that the plant has been in its container for too long and may be starved of nutrients or that the compost is poorly drained, in which case the plant's roots may have rotted or died back.

When possible, remove the plant from its container and inspect the roots: do not choose a plant with a mass of tightly coiling roots or one that has large roots pushing through the drainage holes. The roots should, however, be sufficiently established to retain most of the compost when the plant is removed from its container. For plants growing in flexible plastic bags, check that there is good root growth by feeling them through the bag.

If buying bare-root plants, ensure that the root systems are strong and have not dried out, and that the young shoots are not wilting. Plant them as soon as possible after purchase, protecting them against moisture loss by wrapping them in plastic or wet newspaper until ready to plant.

Dividing large plants

When buying fibrous-rooted plants, choose large examples with a number of healthy shoots that may be divided before planting, rather than a few smaller, cheaper specimens. Divide the plant by prising it apart with your hands or two hand forks used back-to-back, taking care that each division has its own root system and retains as much soil around the roots as possible (see also "Dividing perennials", p.164).

DIVIDING LARGE PLANTS

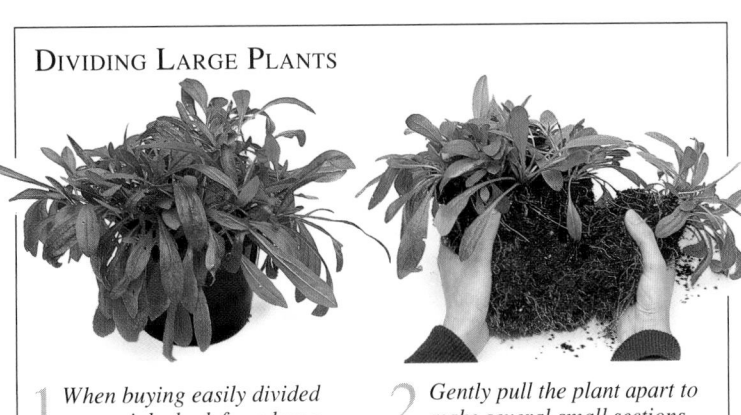

1 *When buying easily divided perennials, look for a large plant with several strong shoots (here Aster tongolensis).*

2 *Gently pull the plant apart to make several small sections, each with its own roots. Keep plenty of soil around the roots.*

When to plant

Perennials grown in containers may be planted out at any time of year when the soil is workable, but the best seasons are spring and autumn. Planting in autumn helps the plants to establish quickly before the onset of winter since the soil is still warm enough to promote root growth yet is unlikely to dry out.

In cold areas, however, spring planting is better for perennials that are not entirely hardy or that dislike wet conditions, such as *Kniphofia*, *Schizostylis*, *Lobelia cardinalis*, and *Scabiosa caucasica*. This ensures that they are fully established before their first winter.

Bare-root specimens should generally be planted in spring or autumn, although a few, such as hostas, may be transplanted successfully during the growing season.

Planting perennials

Plant perennials in prepared ground, taking care to position them at the right depth (see below): for example, those prone to rotting at the base are best planted proud of the soil so that excess water may drain away.

Container-grown plants

First dig a planting hole, then water the plant thoroughly and remove it from its container, taking care not to

HOW TO PLANT A CONTAINER-GROWN PERENNIAL

1 *In a prepared bed, dig a hole 1½ times wider and deeper than the plant's root ball.*

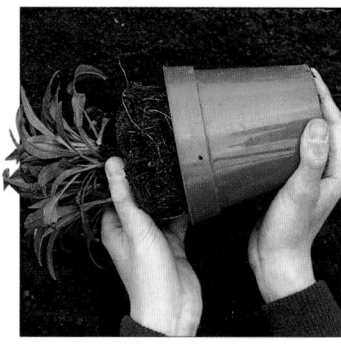

2 *Soak the compost in the pot before sliding out the plant (here an* Aster).

3 *Gently scrape off the top 3cm (1½in) of compost to remove weeds and weed seeds. Carefully tease out the roots around the sides and base of the root ball.*

4 *Check that the plant crown is at the correct depth when planted and fill in around the root ball. Firm in around the plant and water thoroughly.*

Planting depths

SISYRINCHIUM STRIATUM 'AUNT MAY'

ASTER

HOSTA

POLYGONATUM

While most perennials are best planted out at the same soil level as they were in their pots, a number grow better if planted higher or deeper, depending on their individual requirements. Some prefer a raised, well-drained site while others thrive in deeper, moist conditions.

GROUND-LEVEL PLANTING
The majority of perennials should be planted so that the crown of the plant is level with the surrounding soil.

RAISED PLANTING
Set plants that are prone to rot at the base, and variegated plants that tend to revert, with their crowns slightly above the ground.

SHALLOW PLANTING
Plant perennials that require a moist environment with their crowns about 2cm (1in) below ground level.

DEEP PLANTING
Plant perennials with tuberous root systems so that their crowns are about 10cm (4in) below the soil surface.

damage the roots. To help the plant to establish quickly, carefully loosen the sides and base of the root ball, particularly if root-bound, by teasing out the roots with your fingers or a hand fork. Place the plant at the appropriate depth in the prepared hole, backfill with soil, and firm. Loosen the surface of the soil with a hand fork and water in thoroughly.

Bare-root plants

To prevent dehydration, plant bare-root perennials as soon as possible after purchase. Prepare a hole as for container-grown plants, spread out the roots evenly, check the planting depth, and work in soil between the roots as you firm. Water well.

Transplanting self-sown seedlings

A number of perennials, for example *Aquilegia* and foxgloves (*Digitalis*), regularly produce self-sown seedlings that may be transplanted to a nursery bed or moved to another position in the garden.

Before lifting the seedlings, prepare suitable planting holes, spacing them to allow room for the plants to develop. Then gently lift each seedling with a trowel, taking care to retain as much soil around the roots as possible, and replant it immediately. Firm it in well and water it thoroughly. Shade the plants in sunny weather, and water them regularly until they are established.

Raised and peat beds

These beds are often used for growing acid-loving plants in a garden with alkaline soil or for providing a free-draining bed on heavy, clay soil. Plants that thrive in acid soil alone are best planted in a raised bed filled with an ericaceous compost (see also THE ROCK GARDEN, "Raised beds", p.193, and "Peat beds", p.192).

Raised beds may be constructed from a variety of materials including wood, bricks, stone, and logs (see also STRUCTURES AND SURFACES, "Raised beds", p.507). Include a deep layer of coarse drainage material (such as broken bricks) in the base – about one third of the depth of the bed is ideal. Cover this with a layer of fibrous material and fill in with topsoil before planting.

Containers

As well as being a highly attractive way of displaying a number of plants, growing perennials in containers provides an opportunity to include plants that would not flourish in the open garden, either because they are too tender, or because the soil type is not suitable. If growing different plants together in one container, take care to choose those that thrive in similar conditions.

When choosing a container, make sure that it is sufficiently deep and wide to allow room for the plants' roots to develop properly. Consider how the selected plants will look when in full growth in relation to the container to achieve a pleasing balance between them. Tall plants in deep, narrow containers and small plants in large, wide ones may seem out of proportion.

TRANSPLANTING SEEDLINGS

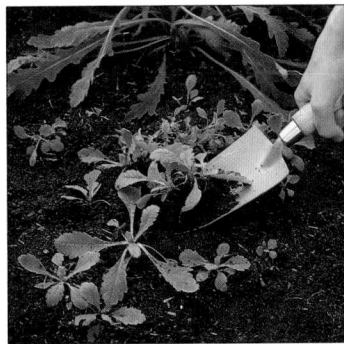

Lift seedlings with soil around their roots so as not to break up the root ball. Plant out and water well.

Planting in containers

If using a heavy container such as a stone urn, lead trough, wooden half-barrel, or large terracotta pot, place it in position before filling and planting since it will be very cumbersome to move afterwards; plastic containers are, of course, considerably lighter, but they are less stable and may be blown over in strong winds. Set the container on a support of blocks or bricks to allow free drainage.

Make sure that the container has drainage holes in the base or low on the sides to prevent waterlogging. Cover the holes with 5–8cm (2–3in) of broken crocks or stones and add a layer of fibrous material, for example upside-down turves or coir fibre; this allows water to filter through freely yet prevents compost from being washed down into the base and blocking the drainage holes.

Most potting composts are suitable, although acid-loving plants must be planted in an ericaceous compost. A prepared, general compost containing a slow-release fertilizer suits most plants; those that need extra drainage (such as *Sedum* or *Achillea*), prefer a compost containing additional grit or sharp sand.

Before planting, arrange the plants on the compost to ensure that they have enough room to develop freely. Plant as for perennials in open ground and keep well watered until established.

Heuchera 'Palace Purple'

Penstemon 'Rich Ruby'

Artemisia 'Powis Castle'

Geranium sanguineum var. *striatum*

1 *When planting in a container, group the plants while still in their pots to determine the spacing and arrangement. Then plant, firm in, and water well.*

2 *A few months later, the plants will have grown and developed to form a well-balanced, attractive display.*

Ground cover

COVERING the ground with a dense carpet of flowering or foliage plants is a fairly recent planting technique designed primarily to reduce the labour of weeding among ornamental plants. Many ground-cover plants are also decorative in their own right, however, adding both attractive pools of colour and contrasting textures, while unifying areas between larger plants and between other garden features.

Once established, ground-cover plants will smother most weed seedlings that attempt to grow beneath their canopy, by depriving them of light, as well as by competing with them for water and nutrients. In the wild, this is frequently a natural process; nature may be imitated in the garden to create attractive, integrated planting schemes requiring very little aftercare.

Selecting ground-cover plants

Choose attractive, vigorous plants that will quickly cover their allotted space with close, dense growth, without becoming unduly invasive. They should be perennial, either remaining above ground all year round for an "evergreen" effect, or re-emerging and developing rapidly in spring. Annuals and biennials are unsuitable except as seasonal fillers while the ground cover is becoming established. Similarly, tender plants, which can form good cover in frost-free conditions, are of only temporary value in cold climates.

Ground cover should be selected to suit its location, for example wet or dry, shady or hot and sunny situations. It should be easy to care for,

routinely requiring only an annual clipping and feed. Choose long-term plants that should remain healthy for five to ten years or more. Finally, look for species, cultivars, and forms that will provide interesting and attractive foliage and habit as well as flowers and fruit.

Benefits and uses of ground cover

Apart from reducing the need for weeding, ground cover can reduce evaporation from exposed, freely draining soils. A dense planting of drought-resistant evergreens, such as *Cistus* x *corbariensis* or the pink-flowered *C.* x *skanbergii*, and most cultivars of rosemary (*Rosmarinus*) and lavender (*Lavandula*) will shade the soil and keep it cool, while their slowly decomposing leaf litter also acts as a mulch.

Steep banks, subject to erosion by rain and wind, may be planted with ground-cover plants such as *Juniperus squamata* 'Blue Carpet', *Cotoneaster dammeri*, or *Hypericum calycinum*. Their low, spreading habit, evergreen foliage, and vigorous suckers and rooted layers combine to form a stable cover that prevents erosion.

In open gardens, shrubby, evergreen, ground-cover plants can act as low, boundary markers. They also trap wind-blown rubbish beneath their branches which can be raked out readily and removed.

In a wildlife garden, ground cover can be used to attract bees and butterflies: the common blue butterfly, for example, lays its eggs on the tight, low, foliage carpets of *Lotus corniculatus* 'Plenus'; and the low,

creeping thymes, such as *Thymus praecox* and its cultivars, are very attractive to bees.

Combining plants

Ground-cover plants with various colours, textures, and forms may be combined to make garden features in their own right, or may provide an attractive linking element in a design.

Backgrounds for bulbs
A low carpet of plants can make an excellent, low-maintenance background for naturalized bulbs, and, unlike grass, will not need mowing as the bulb foliage fades. *Vinca minor* 'Atropurpurea', with dark-green leaves and purple flowers, looks superb as a foil for white daffodils, such as *Narcissus* 'Portrush' or 'Thalia'. Similarly, *Lysimachia nummularia* 'Aurea' is a good foil for crocuses, such as the white 'Snow Bunting', or the copper and yellow 'Zwanenburg Bronze'.

Ground-cover tapestry
A patchwork effect can be created by combining low ground-cover plants of different colour and leaf size. For example, the long, glossy leaves and blue flowers of *Ajuga reptans* 'Atropurpurea' are offset by the matt, heart-shaped leaves of *Tiarella cordifolia*. Both contrast beautifully with the red-flushed *Epimedium* x *rubrum* in spring. Take care not to plant slow growers with small leaves next to large-leaved, vigorous species which can swamp them.

Colour in corners
Ground-cover plants that thrive in permanent shade are useful for brightening dark corners: contrast

ORNAMENTAL GROUND-COVER PLANTS

Hosta fortunei 'Aurea Marginata'
Plant 30–45cm (12–18in) apart.

Houttuynia cordata 'Chamaeleon'
Plant 30–45cm (12–18in) apart.

Lamium maculatum 'Beacon Silver'
Plant 20–30cm (8–12in) apart.

Tanacetum densum
Plant 15–20cm (6–8in) apart.

Tiarella cordifolia
Plant 30cm (12in) apart.

Epimedium x *youngianum* **'Niveum'**
Plant 30cm (12in) apart.

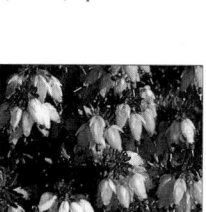
Erica carnea 'December Red'
Plant 30cm (12in) apart.

Vinca major 'Variegata'
Plant 60cm (24in) apart.

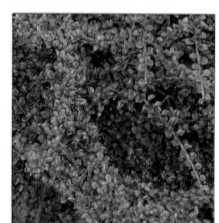
Cotoneaster horizontalis
Plant 1m (3ft) apart.

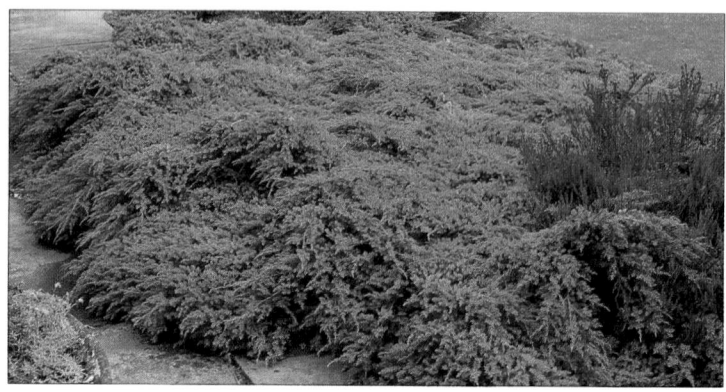
TEXTURAL CARPET
A vigorous dwarf juniper, Juniperus squamata 'Blue Carpet', *provides a spreading mat of colour and texture up to 3m (10ft) wide.*

PLANTING THROUGH BLACK PLASTIC SHEETING

1 Push the edges of the sheeting into the ground with a spade, and make "X"-shaped slits with a knife (see inset) for the plants.

2 Plants with a number of shoots (here Bergenia) may be divided into smaller clumps, each with healthy buds and a root system.

3 Insert a plant through each slit, using a trowel. Firm the soil around the roots of the plants and water them in.

4 Apply a decorative mulch on top of the plastic sheeting to a depth of at least 5cm (2in).

the bold, shining, deep red winter leaves of Bergenia 'Ballawley' with the rough textured and cream-edged leaves of Symphytum x uplandicum 'Variegatum'. Further contrast can be provided by the small, golden-variegated, dark-green leaves of Euonymus fortunei 'Gold Spot'.

An under-canopy

Ground-cover plants are not always low-growing; many of the taller shrubs effectively suppress weeds beneath them. Shrubs are particularly useful in providing medium-height cover, or as an under-canopy below trees. Cotoneaster conspicuus, with bright, scarlet berries, Prunus laurocerasus 'Otto Luyken', with glossy, dark green leaves, and also Fatsia japonica 'Variegata', with deeply lobed leaves edged with white, cover the ground well and provide interest, even in winter.

Planting

It is essential to prepare the soil thoroughly; the ground must be free of weeds before planting, especially creeping, perennial weeds that will later prove difficult to eradicate from established dense cover. This can be achieved by chemical or hand-weeding, or by using a sheet mulch.

There are several ways of planting ground-cover plants to ensure quick cover: plant them at spacings recommended for the species or cultivar concerned and cover the soil with a loose mulch; plant them at recommended spacings through a weed-resistant, black plastic sheet mulch; or plant them more densely than would be usual to provide cover more quickly.

Mulching ground cover

When ground-cover plants have been newly planted at the correct distance, the ground between them will still be bare. Until the plants have begun to spread over the surrounding area, it is advisable to apply a mulch in the gaps around them. This will help to retain moisture in the soil, and will also discourage the growth of weeds. A loose mulch, for example bark chippings, is ideal for the purpose, and should be applied to a depth of about 5cm (2in).

To preserve moisture between new plants (here Erica carnea), apply a loose mulch about 5cm (2in) deep.

The recommended spacing for most plants is just a little less than the approximate spread of a mature specimen. To calculate the number of plants required, measure out the area to be covered and then divide this by the total spread of the chosen plant. For example, an area of 8 sq m (80 sq ft) that is planted with bergenias spaced apart at about 60cm (24in) would require about 30 plants.

The choice of method will depend on the type and cost of plants used, the climate and soil conditions, and how long you are willing to wait for the final effect. Fast-growing plants in favourable conditions and at recommended spacings will generally fill in within two to three years.

Growth is affected by many variable factors, but in general, if plants are spaced at two-thirds of the normal distances, they should join up in 18 months to two years. More plants are needed, of course, but some can be increased by inserting cuttings at close spacing into their final planting positions (see below).

Propagation by cuttings

Some ground-cover plants, such as Euonymus fortunei, Hypericum calycinum, and ivies (Hedera) may be propagated from hardwood cuttings that are inserted directly into their final growing position through holes in a black plastic sheet mulch.

In autumn, when the soil is still warm and moist, take cuttings about 15–20cm (6–8in) long and remove the leaves along the lower two-thirds of the stem. Make holes through the plastic with a dibber and then insert the cuttings so that about two-thirds of their length is in the ground. Space them at about half the normal planting distance for faster cover. The cuttings normally root very

quickly and the young plants develop rapidly during the spring, without competition from weeds.

Pruning

Most ground-cover plants need very little or no regular pruning, although many shrubby plants benefit from an occasional trim to keep them compact. Remove any dead foliage from herbaceous plants.

A few plants need more regular attention. Vinca species and cultivars often produce long, straggling, wiry shoots. In late winter or very early spring, cut them back to near the base with secateurs. Fresh shoots, which produce more compact growth and denser cover, will soon appear and fill the gaps.

Santolina, when one or two years old, tends to open out, revealing its centre. Pruning the plants hard back in the spring encourages rapid new growth, but can leave them looking bare for a period of time. A good way of avoiding this problem is to prune back about one third of the plants by number each year.

Hypericum calycinum may, after a few years, become rather straggly with thin, weak stems. Trim plants annually with shears, a nylon-line trimmer, or a hover mower, in early spring before growth begins.

PRUNING GROUND COVER

SANTOLINA
Some bushy plants need hard pruning. Cut back to the main woody stems, just above where new growth is breaking.

HYPERICUM CALYCINUM
In spring, cut the previous season's shoots hard back.

Chrysanthemums

THE rich colours and luxuriant shapes of their long-lasting flowerheads make the florists' chrysanthemum popular for providing displays in the garden, cutting for the house, and for exhibiting.

Classifying chrysanthemums

The florists' chrysanthemum is derived from a number of species from eastern Asia and is of complex hybrid origin. As a result of this interbreeding, a range of different flower types has been developed. These are grouped according to the type and arrangement of the petals and florets within the flowerheads, as well as by the flowering season.

Chrysanthemums will naturally form a number of flowerheads on the same stem; these are known as "sprays". "Disbudded" chrysanthemums are formed by removing the lateral buds of spray types at an early stage; this leaves a single, terminal bud that produces a much larger flowerhead.

Early-flowering chrysanthemums flower from late summer to early autumn, and are grown outdoors. Late-flowering chrysanthemums are grown in pots outdoors during the summer and are brought into a greenhouse where they flower from autumn until late winter. The cultivation procedures are similar for both early- and late-flowering types, but plants grown for exhibition are given more time and attention.

Early-flowering chrysanthemums

Early-flowering cultivars may be ordered from a reputable specialist supplier for delivery in spring. To be sure of selecting the desired colours, it is best to see the plants at flowering time, or to choose them from an illustrated catalogue.

Once established in the garden, plants that are growing vigorously and that are producing good, healthy blooms should be marked so that they can be used for propagating new plants from cuttings.

Soil preparation and planting
Early-flowering chrysanthemums require a fairly sunny, sheltered site. They prefer a well-drained, slightly acid soil with a pH value of 6.5. For most soils, the ground should be prepared in late autumn or early winter, incorporating plenty of organic matter. Light soils need not be prepared until early spring, with the organic matter applied as a mulch in early summer.

Prior to planting out in late spring, insert 1.2m (4ft) canes about 45cm (18in) apart (a split cane may be tied to the top to support a tall cultivar, if necessary). Plant each chrysanthemum next to a cane, with the root ball just covered with a shallow layer of soil. Tie the stem of each plant to the cane. Water in thoroughly.

Stopping
Soon after planting (refer to a growers' catalogue or specialist publication for precise timing), the plants need to be "stopped". This consists of pinching out the growing tips to encourage lateral shoots, which will eventually bear the flowers.

When the laterals are about 8cm (3in) long, reduce them to the number required: four laterals to each main stem should be sufficient for a general display on cultivars grown as sprays, whereas four to six are required for disbudded plants and those grown for exhibition.

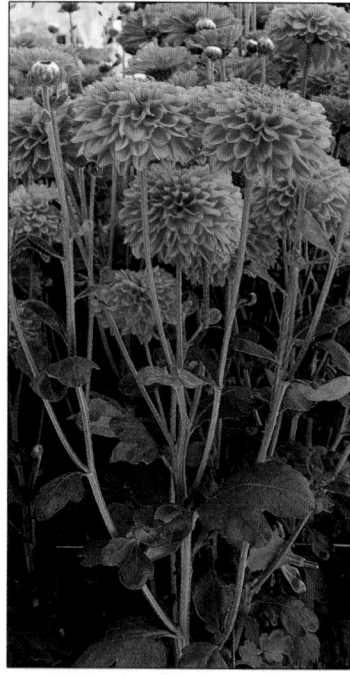

SPRAY CHRYSANTHEMUMS
Chrysanthemums (here C. 'Wendy') naturally form a spray if the laterals are left to develop sideshoots, each bearing a flowerhead.

DISBUDDED CHRYSANTHEMUMS
These (here C. 'Hazy Days') are formed by removing all but one of the flower buds on each lateral, producing large, individual blooms.

TYPES OF CHRYSANTHEMUM FLOWERHEAD

INCURVED
C. 'Alison Kirk'
Fully double flowerheads with incurved petals closing tightly over the crown.

FULLY REFLEXED
C. 'Primrose West Bromwich'
Fully double flowerheads with curved petals reflexing back to touch the stem.

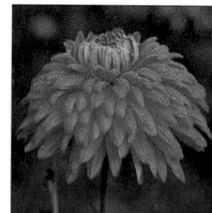

REFLEXED
C. 'Rose Yvonne Arnaud'
Fully double flowerheads with partly reflexed petals and a spiky outline.

INTERMEDIATE (FORMAL)
C. 'Skater's Waltz'
Fully double flowerheads with loosely incurving petals and a regular shape.

INTERMEDIATE (INFORMAL)
C. 'Green Satin'
Fully double flowerheads with irregularly incurving petals.

ANEMONE-CENTRED
C. 'Pennine Oriel'
Single flowerheads each with a dome-shaped disc and flat, or occasionally spoon-shaped, petals.

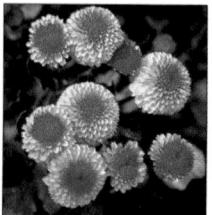

POMPON
C. 'Maria'
Fully double, dense flowerheads bearing tubular florets with flat, rounded petals.

SINGLE
C. 'Rytorch'
Flowerheads with prominent central discs and 5 rows of flat-petalled florets.

SPOON
C. 'Pennine Jewel'
Single flowerheads with tubular florets. Petals open at the tips to form a spoon shape.

About one month after stopping, a light dressing of a balanced fertilizer should be hoed and watered in at a rate of 70g/sq m (2oz/sq yd). Repeat this feed about one month later to encourage strong growth. Remove any sideshoots that develop from the laterals as soon as possible so that all the plant's energy is concentrated on the laterals.

Disbudding

Seven or eight weeks after stopping, trim the laterals to obtain the desired size and distribution of flowerheads. A main, or apical, bud, surrounded by sideshoots, should be visible at the end of each lateral.

If only one flower per stem is required, snap off all the sideshoots from each lateral. The apical buds can then develop unhindered and each lateral will bear a single bloom (the "disbud"). To produce a spray of small, even-sized flowerheads, pinch out the apical bud only; this allows all the sideshoots to develop and produce a spray of flowers.

STOPPING AND REMOVING LATERALS

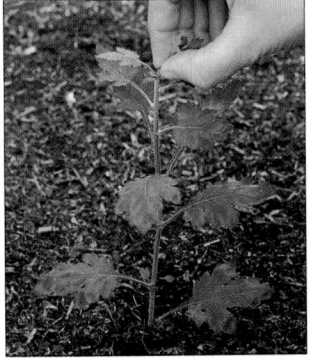

STOPPING
When the cutting is 15–20cm (6–8in) high, pinch out 1cm (^{1}/2in) at the tip to encourage laterals.

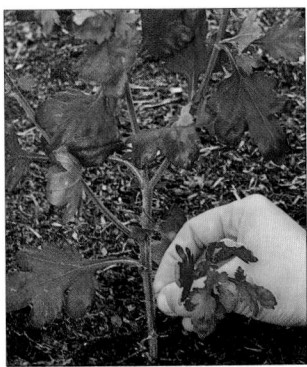

REMOVING EXCESS LATERALS
About 2 months later, select 3 or 4 healthy, evenly spaced laterals and remove any others.

DISBUDDING

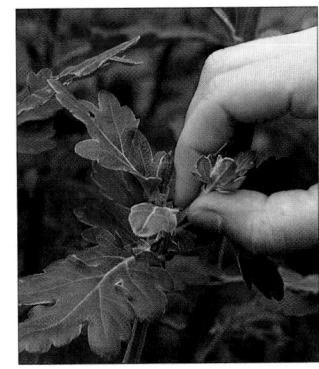

For disbuds, once the side buds around each apical bud have tiny stalks, pinch them out so that only the central bud develops.

Routine care

Water plants regularly, and apply a balanced liquid feed at weekly or 10-day intervals while the buds are developing. Feeding must be discontinued just before the buds show colour, so that the blooms do not become soft and prone to damage.

Overwintering

Early-flowering chrysanthemums may be overwintered in the ground in mild climates that are frost-free, and their stems cut down only in spring. In temperate climates, however, plants are best lifted and stored. After flowering and before the first frosts, cut the stems to about 22cm (9in) and remove all shoots. Keep the plants labelled while in store to identify them the following year.

Lift the plants, wash the roots, and store the stools (rootstocks) in batches of six or eight in a shallow box of loam-based potting compost. Make sure that the compost is slightly moist and that the stocks are not buried too deeply. Do not water them in: keep them almost dry to minimize the risk of rot. Place the containers in a frost-free cold frame or cold greenhouse for two months.

Bring the boxed stools into a greenhouse in mid-winter, water them, and keep them at a temperature of about 7°C (45°F). They will soon produce young shoots.

Taking cuttings

Take cuttings four to six weeks after new shoots have appeared and discard the parent plant. Select close-jointed shoots near the base of the stem, with soft but firm growth, and remove them with a knife or snap them off. Trim them to about 4cm (1^1/2in), cutting just under a node. Dip the base of each cutting in a

OVERWINTERING

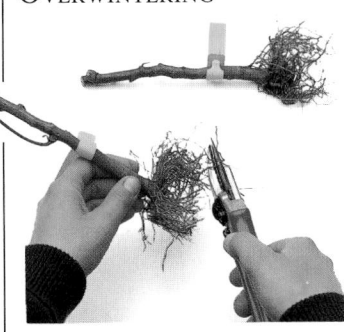

1 *After flowering, cut back the stems, lift the plant (here a young plant is used), and wash the roots. Trim any straggly roots to leave the root ball about the size of a tennis ball.*

2 *Line a 10cm (4in) deep box with paper and place the plants with stems upright on a 2.5cm (1in) layer of damp compost. Fill around them with more compost and firm; store the box in a cool, light place.*

rooting hormone, insert them in standard cutting compost, and then place the pots in a propagator, preferably with gentle bottom heat at 10°C (50°F). Rooting occurs in two to three weeks (see also *How to Propagate by Basal Stem Cuttings*, p.166).

Aftercare

Once rooted, move the cuttings from the propagator to slightly cooler conditions for about a week, then plant them in batches of six to eight to a pot or box, filled with loam-based potting compost. If there are just a few cuttings, pot them up individually. Water well, but then keep them slightly dry for a few weeks, in frost-free conditions. Check regularly for pests and diseases, and treat them accordingly (see PLANT PROBLEMS, pp.545–77). After a month or so, transfer the plants to a cold frame and gradually harden them off; protect them from severe frost and provide ample ventilation.

Late-flowering chrysanthemums

Indoor or "late" chrysanthemums are grown in pots, but their cultivation requirements are similar to early-flowering chrysanthemums.

Planting

Plants may be potted up using loam-based potting compost in late spring and staked as for early-flowering cultivars. The stakes may be tied between straining wires to hold them upright in windy weather. Stand the pots outdoors throughout the summer, in a sunny, sheltered position. Keep well watered and never allow the compost to dry out completely.

Stopping and disbudding

Stop the plants in mid-summer; they will produce their flower buds 10–12 weeks later. Disbud and remove sideshoots in the same way as for early-flowering chrysanthemums.

Routine care

In early autumn, move the pots to a cool greenhouse with the temperature kept to about 10°C (50°F). The greenhouse should be shaded, if necessary, so that the temperature is

LATE-FLOWERING SPRAY
Indoor spray chrysanthemums (here C. 'Win') grown without daylength regulation should be allowed to develop 6–7 flowerheads per stem.

kept low. Continue feeding with a balanced liquid fertilizer until the flower colour just begins to show.

Overwintering

Cut back the plants after flowering to about 22cm (9in). It is not necessary to lift the stools; keep them in their pots in a cool greenhouse or frame at about 5°C (40°F) and in good light for about a month. Then bring them into growth at about 7°C (45°F) to produce shoots for cuttings in late winter, about four to six weeks later.

Taking cuttings

Take cuttings and root them in a propagator, as for early-flowering chrysanthemums. Cuttings of late-flowering spray cultivars do not need to be rooted until early summer.

Once rooted, treat the cuttings as for early-flowering cultivars. In late spring, when the plants' roots have filled their pots, pot them on into their final containers. Use 24cm (9in) pots for incurved and single types; 25cm (10in) pots for intermediate and reflexed ones. Use a loam-based potting compost, with additional slow-release fertilizer. Stake tall cultivars, as well as those with large flowerheads, before final potting.

Growing blooms for exhibition

Blooms grown outdoors for exhibition require protection from the elements. White and yellow blooms may be covered satisfactorily with special grease-proof bags of various sizes. Spray or dust the buds to remove any pests before covering them. The developed blooms are heavy, and care must be taken to support the stems so that the heads do not snap off in high winds.

Blooms of other colours, and any particularly large reflexes, sprays, and plants grown in rows, are better protected by a specially prepared structure, like a small greenhouse with unglazed sides.

It is possible to advance or retard the flowering time of indoor cultivars by regulating the periods of light and darkness. Bud-forming (which usually requires 10 hours of continuous darkness) can be advanced by excluding daylight or, conversely, delayed by extending the period of daylight with artificial light.

Late-flowering spray chrysanthemums intended for exhibition may be subjected to extended hours of darkness for a period of three weeks to encourage bud initiation on the required date. This is achieved by completely blacking out the greenhouse for at least 14 hours a night, or, if only a small number of plants is being grown, by placing black plastic bags over individual plants.

Preparing for exhibition

Blooms for exhibition are cut when fully or virtually fully open; the stems are then plunged immediately into deep water for 24 hours.

Exhibition classes will usually be for sprays with single, three, or five blooms in a vase. A single bloom is staged in the centre and at the top of the vase and held upright with paper.

A group of three is staged with either two blooms at the back and the third slightly lower in front, or one at the back and two slightly lower in front. Five blooms are invariably staged with three flowerheads in an arc at the back and two slightly lower in front.

All the blooms in a vase should match as closely as possible in size and form. If there is any variation between the blooms, stage those with the best outline at the back, and place those with the best developed centres at the front.

There is also a class for charms (dwarf plants that produce hundreds of star-shaped flowers), which are shown in a 30cm (12in) pot, or larger.

EXHIBITION BLOOMS

INCURVED

Not flat-topped

Perfectly round

C. 'DORRIDGE DREAM'

Florets even

SPRAY

With daylight control, late-flowering sprays should develop at least 12 flowerheads per stem.

LARGE EXHIBTION, REFLEXED

Fresh to the tips of the florets

Good clear centre, not blown

C. 'LILAC PRINCE'

Breadth and depth in equal proportion

C. 'RYFLASH'

PROTECTING BLOOMS FOR EXHIBITION

1 *When the blooms are just beginning to open, enclose each one in a 15 x 15cm (6 x 6in) grease-proof bag fastened with a twist tie. Leave this on for 7–10 days.*

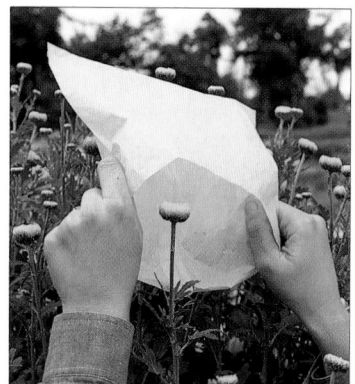

2 *The bud should then be at the "paintbrush" stage with the colour just showing. Remove the bag and replace it with a 30 x 33cm (12 x 13in) bag.*

PROTECTING A ROW OF BLOOMS

Construct a temporary "greenhouse" of wooden supports with a clear plastic roof (do not enclose the sides). The structure should be 2.2m (7ft) at the ridge and 2m (6ft) at the eaves. The slope allows rain to run off, so it is important to keep the soil around the plants moist.

C. 'MORNING STAR'

CHARM CHRYSANTHEMUMS

These are dwarf plants, bearing a mass of single flowers, each with a diameter of about 2.5cm (1in). The star-shaped blooms densely cover each plant to form a rounded head.

Routine care

ALTHOUGH most perennials will thrive with only little maintenance, certain routine tasks help to keep them looking attractive and in the peak of health through the growing season. Occasional watering and feeding is necessary and the surrounding ground should be kept clear of competing weeds. In addition to this, many perennials produce further growth and flowers if deadheaded or cut back, while dividing the plants from time to time renews vigour. Tall, fragile perennials, or those with top-heavy flowerheads, may also require staking, particularly in exposed gardens.

Watering

The amount of water that plants require depends on the site, climate, and the individual species; provided that they are grown in appropriate conditions, established perennials generally need little or no additional irrigation. If there are prolonged dry spells during the growing season, give extra water to the plants to keep them turgid. If they wilt or die back from lack of water they will normally recover fully after heavy rainfall or will become dormant until the following season.

Young plants need to have sufficient water to become established but they should not be watered once they are growing satisfactorily, except in very dry weather. Irrigation, if necessary, is best applied in the evening, when water evaporates less quickly from the soil surface and the sun is no longer strong enough to scorch wet leaves.

Fertilizing

In soil that has been thoroughly prepared before planting, few perennials require more than an annual topdressing of bone meal or a balanced slow-release fertilizer, preferably applied in early spring after rain.

If conditions are dry, first water the soil thoroughly, then work the fertilizer into the soil surface with a hand fork. Do not let the fertilizer touch the leaves since it may scorch them. Plants that are grown primarily for their ornamental foliage, for example *Rheum* and hostas, benefit from an occasional liquid feed during the growing season.

If plant is not growing well, in spite of being in a suitable site, look carefully to see if it has been attacked by pests or disease and treat accordingly. Foliage that is yellowing prematurely may indicate problems with soil drainage or a lack of certain nutrients. If appropriate drainage or feeding does not seem to improve the condition of the plant, sending a soil sample for analysis by a laboratory will determine which elements are lacking (see also "Soil nutrients and fertilizers", pp.530–31).

Mulching

An annual mulch of organic matter, such as spent mushroom compost or bark chippings, helps to suppress weed growth, reduce soil moisture loss, and improve the soil structure. Apply mulch when the ground is moist during spring or autumn by spreading a 2.5–5cm (1–2in) deep layer around the crowns of the plants (see also SOILS AND FERTILIZERS, "Mulches", p.532).

Weeding

Keep beds and borders free from weeds at all times, if practical, as they compete with the ornamental plants for moisture and nutrients in the soil. Underplanting with suitable ground-cover plants (see GROUND COVER, pp.150–51) or mulching in spring helps to reduce problems with annual weeds. Any weed seedlings that do appear from wind-blown seed or seeds that have been dormant in the soil should be removed by hand before they become established.

If perennial weeds appear in the ground after initial cultivation, carefully dig them out with a hand fork. It is usually impractical to apply systemic weedkillers at this time because, to be effective, they must be applied when the weeds are in full growth, usually as they reach the flowering stage. At this point it is virtually impossible to avoid spraying the ornamental plants accidentally at the same time.

If the roots of a perennial weed have grown into those of a border plant, dig up the plant in early spring, wash the roots, and carefully pull out the weed. Then replant the border plant, ensuring that no part of the weed is left in the original site. Do not hoe around perennials since this may cause damage to any surface roots and emerging shoots. For further information on controlling weed growth, see PLANT PROBLEMS, "Weeds", pp.573–7.

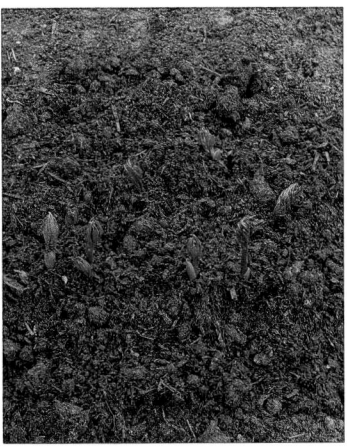

Clear any weeds, and apply a 2.5–5cm (1–2in) layer of mulch to moist soil; do not damage the young shoots of the plant (here a peony).

Improving flowering

Certain perennial plants may be cut back during growth in one of two ways to improve the number or size of their flowers or to extend the flowering season.

Thinning

Although most herbaceous plants produce numerous vigorous shoots in spring, some of these may be spindly and thin; if these weak shoots are removed at an early stage of growth, the plant then goes on to develop fewer, sturdier shoots that usually produce larger flowers. When the plant is about a quarter to a third of its eventual height, pinch out or cut back the weakest shoots. This thinning technique may be used successfully with, for example, delphiniums, phlox, and Michaelmas daisies (*Aster*).

Stopping

It is possible to increase the number of flowers on perennial plants that readily produce sideshoots, such as *Helenium* and *Rudbeckia* species and cultivars, by removing or "stopping" the growing tip of each stem; this also produces sturdier growth and stops the plant becoming too tall and straggly. Stopping should generally be carried out when the plant is about one third of its ultimate height, and in this case 2.5–5cm (1–2in) of each shoot is pinched off with the fingers or cut back with secateurs just above a node. This encourages the buds in the uppermost leaf axils of the shoot to develop.

Individual plants in a group may be stopped a few days apart; this has the added effect of producing a longer flowering season overall. For further information on how to produce fewer but larger blooms, see DAHLIAS, "Stopping and disbudding", p.226.

Dead-heading

Unless decorative seedheads are required or the seed is to be collected to raise further plants, remove the

THINNING
Thin young shoots (here of a phlox) when no more than a third of their final height. Remove about 1 shoot in 3 by cutting or pinching out weaker shoots at the base.

STOPPING
When the shoots (here of an Aster) are one third of their final height, "stop" them by pinching out the top 2.5–5cm (1–2in) to promote bushier growth.

CUTTING BACK TO EXTEND FLOWERING

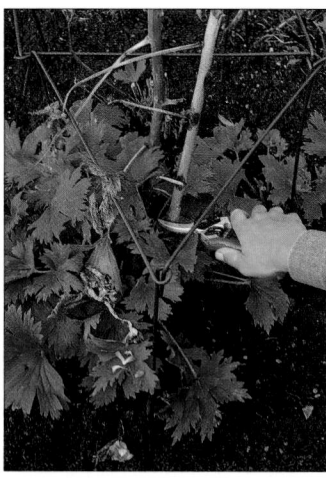

DELPHINIUM
After flowering, when new basal shoots are visible, cut back old stems to ground level.

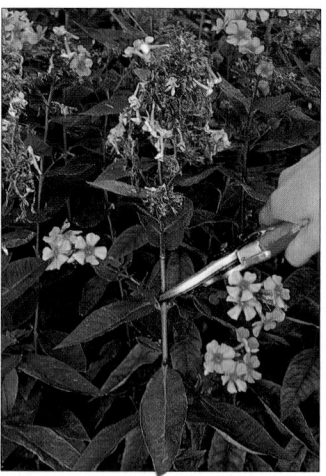

PHLOX
Cut back the central part of the flowerhead as the blooms fade to encourage the sideshoots to flower.

flowers as they begin to fade. Further flowering sideshoots may then develop on the plant and extend the flowering season.

With a number of perennials, for example delphiniums and lupins (*Lupinus*), cutting back the old stems to their base when the first flowers have faded may encourage new shoots to develop that will produce a second display of flowers later in the season.

Cutting back

Shrubby perennials, for example the half-hardy marguerites (*Argyranthemum frutescens*, syn. *Chrysanthemum frutescens*), should be pruned annually in early spring: cut back the main stems with secateurs to reduce the plant to about half its former size. This will remove all twiggy, unproductive shoots and encourage the growth of strong shoots that will produce flowers throughout the summer and autumn.

Autumn clearance
Once perennial plants have finished flowering in autumn, cut down the shoots to the base and remove all dead or faded stems and leaves, as well as any weed growth, so that the beds or borders are tidy. The top-growth of plants that are not fully hardy, however, may be left over winter to provide the crown with some protection from frost; the dead top-growth is then removed in spring. Some perennial plants, such as *Sedum spectabile* and many grasses, have foliage or flowerheads

that remain attractive even when brown, and these may be left on the plant to provide winter decoration if required until early spring.

Transplanting established perennials

Most perennials may be transplanted easily if you wish to change the planting scheme. If possible, move them when dormant in late autumn, or when just coming into growth in spring. Plants that dislike cold, wet conditions, such as *Kniphofia*, and those that are not fully hardy should be moved in spring once the soil has warmed to encourage rapid growth. A few long-lived plants, notably

CUTTING DOWN IN THE AUTUMN

In autumn or early winter, cut dead stems (here of Rudbeckia) *to ground level, or to just above new growth.*

Staking

Tall and fragile perennials may need stakes to support them, particularly in windy situations. Insert stakes early in the season, since staking is harder to do and more likely to damage the plant when growth is more developed. Push the stakes deep into the ground so that they can be raised in stages as the plant grows.

For delphiniums and other tall, single-stemmed perennials, use sturdy canes that are two-thirds of the stem's eventual height: push a cane firmly into the ground near the base of each shoot, taking care not to damage the roots. Secure the stem to the cane with figure-of-eight twine ties as it grows.

To support plants with many stems, it may be easier to use a number of canes placed at intervals in a circle around the plant.

Loop twine around the canes at about one third and two-thirds of the plant's height. Clump-forming plants, such as peonies (*Paeonia*), may also be supported with proprietary devices such as ring stakes and link stakes, or similar home-made supports constructed from large-gauge wire mesh fixed to stakes. Stems grow through the support and eventually hide it.

There are two fairly unobtrusive methods of staking. Push several twiggy hazel stems, or peasticks, into the soil next to the young shoots and bend them inwards at right-angles to form an effective "cage" that is soon covered by the plant as it grows. Alternatively, insert one stout stake in the centre of a small group of plants or stems and radiate ties out to each stem.

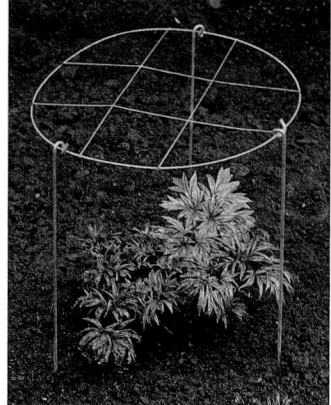

RING STAKE
Stake low, clump-forming plants (here peony) early in the season. Raise the stake as the plant grows.

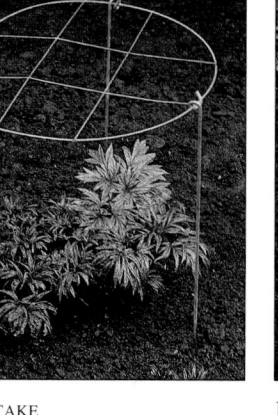

LINK STAKES
For taller plants such as this Aster, *push link stakes deep into the soil, then raise them as the plant grows.*

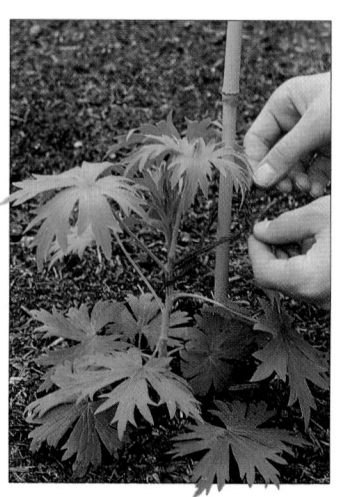

SINGLE CANE
Stake single-stemmed plants (here delphinium) when 20–25cm (8–10in) high. Tie in the stem loosely.

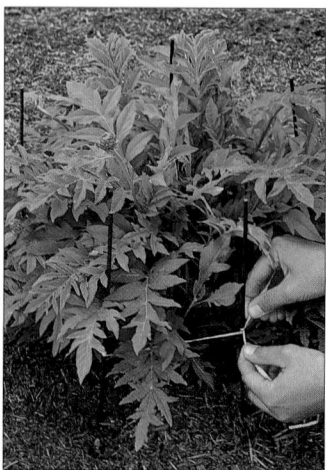

RING OF CANES
Encircle weak-stemmed plants (here Centaurea) *with twine, looped around split canes to secure it.*

peonies (*Paeonia*) and hellebores (*Helleborus*), resent disturbance and take two or more years to establish after transplanting. They should be lifted only if it is necessary to propagate them.

Prepare the new site as for planting, and dig a hole of suitable size. Lift the plant, keeping as much soil around the root ball as possible. It is best to divide the plant at this stage (see "Lifting and dividing", below). Remove any weeds from the clump by hand, then replant the divisions as for container-grown perennials (p.148), firming in and watering well.

Moving plants during the growing season

Occasionally, it may be necessary to move a plant while in full growth; mature plants may not transplant successfully, however, and should be treated carefully if transplanting is essential at this time. To minimize the stress caused to the plant, soak it in a bucket of water for several hours after lifting it. Then cut back the top-growth to within 8–12cm (3–5in) of the base and pot up the plant into a good potting compost. Keep the plant in a cool, shaded position, spraying daily but lightly until there are signs of healthy, fresh growth, then replant it in its new, prepared position.

Storing plants

Perennials may be lifted and stored over winter or if replanting is to be delayed – if transplanting them to a new garden when moving house, for example. The plants should be lifted when dormant and carefully packed in boxes or crates of moist compost or bark so that they do not dry out. Store in a cool, frost-free place.

Lifting and dividing

Where practical, perennials in a bed or border should be lifted, divided, and replanted every three to five years. Fast-growing, vigorous species, particularly those that have a mat-forming habit, such as *Ajuga* and *Stachys*, may need to be divided every other year. Plants that have become woody, with signs of dieback at the centre, or that look congested and flower less freely than in previous years, are in need of being divided.

Lifting plants makes it possible to clear the site of any weeds, and dig over and incorporate well-rotted organic matter or fertilizer as required. Dividing a plant rejuvenates it, keeps it healthy, and checks over-vigorous growth.

In late autumn or early spring, lift the plant, taking care not to damage its roots, and divide it into several portions by gently pulling them away from the main plant. Discard the old, woody centre; each division should contain a number of healthy, young shoots and its own root system (see also "Dividing perennials", p.164). Then dig over and fertilize the original site as necessary and replant the divisions, leaving enough space between each for the plants to develop. Alternatively, replant the divisions in prepared ground in a new position as required.

Pests and diseases

Perennial plants, if grown in fertile soil, are not usually seriously troubled by fungal diseases, insects, or other pests. Damage by slugs and snails (p.548), attack by aphids

PREPARING PLANTS FOR TEMPORARY STORAGE

Lift the plants in winter when they are dormant and place them in a box half-filled with moist bark or compost. Cover the roots with more bark or compost to keep them from drying out.

(p.550), and thrips (p.551) and, with certain plants (such as cultivars of *Aster novi-belgii*), infestations of both powdery and downy mildew (p.550) do occur but seldom give cause for concern. During the growing season, check the plants regularly for any signs of attack, and treat them with an appropriate selection of fungicide as necessary.

Maintaining perennials in containers

Perennials planted in containers require more care than those in open ground as they have limited reserves of food and water. Ensure that the compost does not dry out during the growing season: daily watering may be necessary in hot, dry weather. Plant roots should always remain moist but not wet. Check that the water is able to drain through the container.

Mulching helps to reduce soil water evaporation as well as suppressing weeds; if using an organic mulch, such as bark chippings, replace it periodically when dividing or repotting the plants.

Every year or two in spring or autumn, divide the plants and replant the most vigorous portions using fresh compost, otherwise they soon exhaust the available nutrients and become too large for the container. If using the same container, wash the inside well before replanting, or pot up into a larger container (see "Planting in containers", p.149). Cut back the roots of shrubby perennials by about a quarter before repotting.

In cold areas, bring in half-hardy and tender plants in the autumn, keeping them protected until all frost has passed (see FROST AND WIND PROTECTION, pp.520–21).

1 *In early spring or autumn, rejuvenate perennials in containers by thinning out plants and renewing the compost.*

4 *Plant up the container, fill in with more fresh compost around the plants, and firm them in with your fingers.*

2 *Lift out the plants, separating them carefully, and shake the old compost from their roots. Discard half of the old compost.*

5 *Finally, top-dress with fertilizer and water well until the compost is thoroughly wet and water runs through the drainage holes at the base. The plants grown here are Bergenia cultivars, Pachysandra terminalis, and a hosta (now dormant).*

3 *Refill the container with fresh compost to within 10cm (4in) of its rim. Divide overgrown plants and arrange as required.*

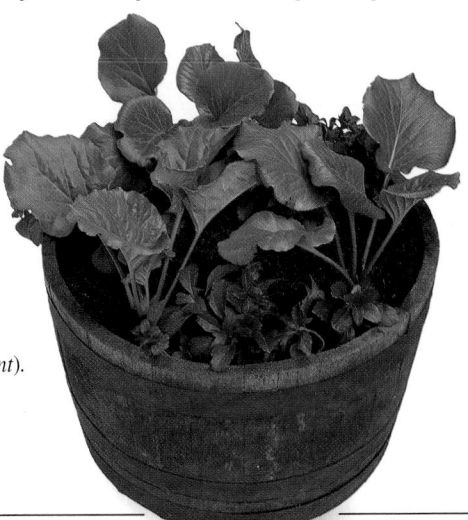

Ferns

AMONG the most popular of the foliage plants, ferns add texture and atmosphere to the house or garden, where they are particularly effective in settings by streams or in damp, shady corners.

Cultivation

Hardy ferns are suitable for growing in the open garden, whereas tender tropical ferns are best cultivated indoors in a greenhouse or conservatory, or as house plants.

Hardy ferns

Most hardy ferns are easily grown and are suitable for shaded, moist conditions. Being very tough, they require the minimum of cultivation and upkeep once they have become established. With the exception of *Thelypteris oreopteris* and all the *Blechnum* and *Cryptogramma* species, which require acid soil, ferns prefer neutral to alkaline conditions. Well-dug garden soil, with added humus, will suit most species.

Planting may be carried out at any time if container-grown plants are used. In dry weather water them regularly until established. Always plant in full or dappled shade; some genera, such as *Dryopteris*, will tolerate dry conditions if they are well shaded, but almost all require damp conditions to thrive.

Many ferns, such as *Athyrium*, *Cryptogramma*, and *Osmunda*, die down at the first touch of frost, but some of the *Dryopteris* retain their fronds well into winter. Leaving the old fronds on the plant until early spring protects the crowns, but these should be removed as the young ones start to uncurl. All species and cultivars of *Asplenium*, *Cyrtomium*, *Polystichum*, and *Polypodium* make good plants for the cold greenhouse, flourishing in the coldest weather under glass without the need for any artificial heat.

Tender tropical ferns

Ferns that will not withstand frost make excellent greenhouse or conservatory foliage plants, grown in pots or hanging baskets. Some also make good house plants. Most require a winter minimum temperature of 10–15°C (50–59°F) but do not like hot, dry conditions and should be shaded from direct sunlight; a north-facing position on a bed of gravel that can be damped down in hot weather is ideal.

Tender ferns are usually sold in very small pots and should then be potted up into 13cm (5in) or 15cm (6in) pots using a soil-less potting compost. For this, use 3 parts peat-substitute- or peat-based potting mixture to 2 parts coarse sand or medium- grade perlite. Add a cupful of charcoal granules to every litre (1³⁄₄ pints) of mixture and, following the pack instructions, a balanced granular or powdered fertilizer.

The root ball should not dry out completely; keep the plant in its pot inside a watertight outer container with about 3cm (1in) of sand or gravel permanently kept damp at its base. Ferns, particularly *Adiantum* species, do not like to be sprayed or overwatered, and *Nephrolepis*, which are probably the easiest to keep as house plants, should be nearly dry before watering. Feed the ferns occasionally with a house plant liquid fertilizer.

Propagation

Ferns are mainly raised from spores, but may be propagated by division or, in some species, by bulbils.

WATER SETTING
Matteuccia *thrives in damp conditions by a stream and provides a striking contrast of form and texture with the* Rodgersia *in the foreground.*

ROCK CREVICE
The lance-shaped fronds of the semi-evergreen Ceterach officinarum *contrast well with the rock behind that provides shade and shelter.*

PROPAGATION BY BULBILS

1 *Select a frond that is drooping under the weight of bulbils. The bulbils may have tiny green fronds emerging from them. Cut off the parent frond close to the base. The plant shown here is* Asplenium bulbiferum.

2 *Peg down the frond onto prepared compost. Make sure the frond's ribs are flat.*

3 *Water thoroughly, label the tray, and put it in a plastic bag. Seal the bag and leave the tray in a warm, light place until the bulbils have rooted.*

4 *Remove the wire pegs and lift each rooted bulbil with a widger or knife; if necessary, cut it away from the parent frond.*

5 *Put each rooted bulbil into a 6cm (3in) pot of moist, soil-less compost. Keep moist in a warm, light place until the plants are large enough to replant.*

Bulbils

Asplenium bulbiferum and some of the hardy *Polystichum* species produce bulbils or small plantlets along the fronds. These may be used for propagation by pegging down that part of the frond with bulbils onto a tray of seed or cutting compost. The bulbils soon produce rooted plantlets which can then be separated and potted up. During the dormant season, it may take up to six months before the new plants are ready for planting out or potting on.

Spores

Ferns produce neither flowers nor seeds, and have a unique way of reproducing. Fronds carry on their undersurfaces very small capsules (sporangia), which release large numbers of powdery spores, which, when sown on damp compost, produce small growths (prothalli). Each prothallus carries both the male and female organs: the male organ (antheridium) produces spermatozoids which swim across the surface moisture of the prothallus to fertilize the "egg cell" lying within the female organ (archegonium). After fertilization, a zygote is formed which eventually develops into a tiny new fern. In this way the normal cycle of growth is continued.

Growing ferns from spores may take 18 to 24 months from sowing the spores to planting out the mature ferns. Collect the spores by removing from the parent plant fronds that are almost ready to shed their spores. Ripe sporangia are plump and vary in colour between species; many are dark brown, some blue-grey, others orange. Immature sporangia are flat and green or pale yellow. If the sporangia are dark brown and rough,

they will probably already have shed their spores. Lay the fronds on a sheet of clean paper and leave them in a warm room. In a day or so the spores will be shed onto the paper, looking like brown dust. Transfer them to a labelled seed envelope.

Fill a 6cm (3in) pot with standard seed compost; firm and smooth the surface. Sterilize the compost by carefully pouring boiling water through a piece of paper towel laid on the surface until water comes through the drainage holes. When the compost has cooled, remove the paper towel and sow spores very thinly over the surface. Cover the pot, or put it in a propagator, and leave it in a warm, light place out of direct sunlight. To keep the surface constantly moist, mist-spray it regularly with previously boiled, luke-warm water. Remove the cover when the top of the pot is covered with a green, velvet-like "moss"; if the compost seems dry, moisten it by standing the pot in a saucer of water for a short time.

Depending on the species, it takes from six to twelve weeks for the young prothalli to cover the compost surface. Prick them out by lifting small pieces of the "moss". Space them evenly, green side up, on the surface of other pots of sterilized seed compost, press them down, and spray with lukewarm water that has been boiled. Cover the pots with clingfilm or return them to the propagator. As the prothalli develop, spray them daily with lukewarm water until tiny plantlets appear. When they are large enough to handle, transplant them separately into pots of soil-less compost and grow them on, potting up as necessary, until they are large enough to plant out.

FORMAL PLANTINGS
The clean, horizontal line of the golden box (foreground) provides a perfect foundation for the striking, shuttlecock shapes of Matteuccia struthiopteris.

PROPAGATION BY SPORES

1 *Examine the undersides of the fronds to find one with sporangia that are ready to release their spores. Cut off the selected frond with a clean, sharp knife and place it carefully on clean, white paper to collect the spores. The plant shown here is* Adiantum fritzluthii.

NOT READY   READY   TOO LATE

2 *Sow a few of the collected spores onto a pot of prepared sterile compost by tapping them from a piece of folded paper. Cover with some clingfilm or place the pot in a propagator.*

3 *Mist-spray twice a week until the surface is covered with a bumpy green "moss". Lift small clumps with a widger or a knife.*

4 *Divide the clumps into small pieces and gently firm them down onto sterile compost. Spray with water and then return them to the propagator.*

5 *When leaf-like plantlets appear, lift them carefully. Firm into packs or small pots of moist compost. Pot on when they have developed small fronds.*

Carnations and pinks

CARNATIONS and pinks belong to the genus *Dianthus*. They have attractive, usually fragrant flowers and grey-green, evergreen foliage. They are grouped according to their growth habit, flower characteristics, and hardiness: the upright, bushy, border carnations and low, spreading pinks are both hardy and prolific. Modern pinks are repeat-flowering and more vigorous than the old-fashioned cultivars.

Perpetual-flowering carnations are similar in habit to border carnations, but are not frost hardy; in the right conditions, they will flower throughout the year.

Flowers may be in a single colour ("self"), in two or more colours ("fancy"), or edged in a contrasting colour ("picotee"). All carnations and pinks provide elegant and long-lasting cut flowers. Border carnations grown outdoors will provide an increasing supply of flowers over three years. Pick flowers with seven nodes on their stems to induce strong sideshoots to develop lower down.

General cultivation

Border carnations and pinks prefer a sunny, airy site and a free-draining soil with a pH of 6–8, but they will grow anywhere except in wet or shaded areas. Perpetual-flowering carnations need to be grown in a greenhouse, and will bloom in minimum temperatures of 10–12°C (50–54°F); at 5°C (41°F) only a few flowers are borne in winter.

In winter, clear away any dead leaves or other debris from around the plants to maintain good plant hygiene and firm any young plants growing outdoors that have been lifted by frost.

Border carnations

For best results, obtain these from specialist growers as rooted layers in autumn or spring. Layers usually establish better than container-grown plants, especially if they are planted outdoors in autumn.

To prepare the bed for planting, single dig in the autumn, incorporating humus-forming material, and the following spring fork in a balanced fertilizer at the manufacturer's suggested rate. Water the young plants before planting them out 38–45cm (15–18in) apart in moist soil. Firm around them, making sure that the lowest leaves are just clear of the soil surface. Stake tall plants with twigs or canes. Water well during the first month after planting; once established, the plants need watering only in very dry weather.

Border carnations are bushy by nature so they do not need pinching out. Disbudding one-year-old plants is not necessary if they are grown for general garden display, but is worthwhile to obtain better-quality blooms. When the buds are large enough to handle easily, hold the brittle, main stem by the node at the base of the bud stalk, and sharply pull the stalk sideways to remove it. To produce larger blooms, leave two or three buds per stem on two-year-old carnations and only the crown buds on three-year-old plants.

Pinks

Pinks are available either as pot-grown plants or as rooted cuttings in spring. Plant them as for border carnations, but space them 22–30cm (9–12in) apart. When growing modern, repeat-flowering pinks from cuttings, pinch out the growing tips of the young plants to leave five or six pairs of leaves; this encourages a bushy habit. Old-fashioned pinks do not usually need pinching out.

Perpetual-flowering carnations

These are best obtained as rooted cuttings or pot plants in spring and early summer. If growing rooted cuttings, break off their growing tips a week or two after potting them up to induce axillary growths (breaks); the plant is then described as "stopped and broken". Such plants with three to five sideshoots may be purchased in spring and are ready

To produce one large bloom on each flower stem of perpetual-flowering carnations, support the stem with one hand and pinch off each bud except the crown bud (left). For spray cultivars, pinch off the crown bud of each flower stem as the colour begins to show (right).

for potting on into 15cm (6in) pots of peat-substitute-based potting compost. Water thoroughly, and support them with 1.2m (4ft) canes.

Stop a few sideshoots a month after potting to boost growth and stimulate flowering. Disbud them gradually over several days so that the calyx (the green petal casing) does not split. Leave only the crown bud and place a calyx band over the bud. For a spray of flowers, remove only the crown bud.

Water the plants only when the compost begins to dry out, preferably early in the day. Feed with a balanced liquid fertilizer, at first fortnightly, then weekly by mid-summer for a good flowering display. In late autumn, change to a monthly, high-potash feed for sturdy foliage, and continue with it throughout winter.

During spring, repot one-year-old plants into 21cm (8in) pots. Then sprinkle one level teaspoonful of ground limestone on the surface to prevent the compost becoming sour through constant watering. A month later, resume feeding the plants as usual for the growing season.

Pests and diseases

Carnations and pinks in the garden are most prone to infestation from caterpillars (p.549), aphids (p.550), thrips (p.560), fungal leaf spots (p.552), and rusts (p.552). In the greenhouse, control aphids, red spider mites (p.550), and thrips; in winter, use insecticidal and fungicidal smokes and dusts, rather than sprays, to discourage fungal diseases.

PERPETUAL-FLOWERING CARNATIONS
Attach wire rings to a single cane to support the stems of carnations grown under cover (here Dianthus 'Manon').

BORDER CARNATIONS
Place a single cane near the centre of the plant (here Dianthus 'Richard Pollak') *to give support. Attach stems to the cane with twine or wire rings.*

1 *About two weeks after potting up a rooted cutting of a perpetual-flowering carnation, when it has 8 or 9 pairs of leaves, snap or pinch out the top 3 or 4 pairs.*

2 *About a month later, snap or pinch out the tops of some of the sideshoots in the same way (see inset), leaving 5 or 6 nodes on each.*

Propagation

Carnations and pinks give a fine display for only two or three years, so propagation is vital to maintain stocks. Pinks and perpetual-flowering carnations are best raised from cuttings, and border carnations by layering. All *Dianthus* may be grown from seed (see PERENNIALS, "Seed", p.162) but do not breed true, apart from some species. Typically, seed-raised plants flower in the first year, give fine blooms in the second, and then begin to deteriorate.

Exhibition plants are normally discarded after one year as blooms in subsequent years are of poorer quality. With successful plants, take cuttings or propagate by layering (as appropriate) before discarding.

Cuttings

Take cuttings from pinks in the summer. Choose healthy shoots with four or five pairs of leaves and break them off cleanly. Trim off the bottom pair of leaves just below a joint. Insert the cuttings about 4cm (1½in) apart into trays or pots of clean, sharp sand, or a mixture of peat substitute and sand or perlite in equal parts; keep the leaves clear of the rooting medium. Put them in a propagator in a well-lit place and spray with a light mist daily for the first two weeks. The cuttings should root after three to four weeks; insert them singly into 6cm (3in) pots of standard potting compost to grow on in a cold frame or greenhouse.

Perpetual-flowering carnation cuttings may be taken at any season, if bottom heat of 20°C (68°F) is provided. Choose strong, axillary shoots that have developed after the flowers have been picked, and prepare

them as for pinks. Dip the base of each cutting into water and then into hormone rooting powder, and insert them into trays or pots of standard cutting compost. Treat them thereafter in the same way as pinks.

Layering

Propagate border carnations after they have flowered by layering the one-year-old plants. Wound the stems of non-flowering sideshoots to encourage new roots to form; then pin the shoots into the prepared soil surrounding the plants. Stake the leafy tip of the layered shoot, if necessary, so that it is held almost vertical and the slit is kept fully open in the soil; this also prevents deformed stems from developing later. When the layered shoots have rooted, detach them from the parent and plant them out into a prepared bed to flower the following year.

To propagate exhibition plants in their pots, remove a ring of compost about 2.5cm (1in) wide and 8cm (3in) deep from the surface around the plant, replace it with equal parts of peat substitute and sand, then layer the plants around the pot rim. In the autumn, once the layers have rooted, insert them singly into 6cm (3in) pots of peat-substitute-based potting compost.

When the roots reach the edge of the compost, pot them on into 15cm (6in) pots with the top of the root ball flush with the compost surface so that the bottom leaves are clear of the compost and do not rot. Firm the compost to about 2.5cm (1in) below the pot rim. Alternatively, insert two layers in a 21cm (8in) pot. Stake them with 1m (3ft) canes and water thoroughly; then water only when the compost is drying out.

LAYERING BORDER CARNATIONS

1 *Loosen the soil around the plant to a depth of about 7.5cm (3in), mix in equal parts of damp peat substitute and sharp sand, and firm. Select a few well-spaced, non-flowering sideshoots and remove all but the top 4 or 5 pairs of leaves on each shoot.*

2 *Pierce each stem with a small, sharp penknife, just below the node with the lowest leaves. Cut downwards through the next node, bringing the blade out sideways below it, to form a tongue (see inset).*

3 *Gently push the tongue of each shoot into the prepared soil, and pin it down securely with a layering pin. Spray the rooting area lightly to keep it moist. After about 5 or 6 weeks, separate and lift the rooted layers. Pot them on or plant them out.*

Exhibiting blooms

Carnations and pinks have been grown as exhibition plants for centuries. Pinks and perpetual-flowering carnations are grown as in "General cultivation" (opposite), but border carnations are usually grown in a light, airy greenhouse to protect the blooms. In summer, the greenhouse must be well ventilated, lightly shaded, and mist-sprayed frequently.

Preparing for a show

When the buds on pinks or carnations begin to form, feed at ten-day intervals with a balanced, liquid fertilizer until they show colour, then give just one high-potash feed. As soon as their buds are large enough to handle, carnations must be disbudded; do this over several days to avoid stressing them. Slip calyx bands over the remaining buds to prevent their calyces from splitting. Pinks, on the other hand, are never disbudded, although exhibitors may remove any spent blooms.

Select blooms for exhibition from well-watered plants in the early

morning or late evening, if possible 48 hours before the show. Trim the stems with a sloping cut just above a node and place them up to their necks in water in a cool, dark place, free from draughts. Use special carnation boxes available from florists to transport the flowers, and stage the blooms as soon as possible after arriving at the show.

CALYX BANDS

Calyx band

Split calyx

When a bud shows colour, put a soft wire ring or a rubber band around it (left) to stop it splitting and forming an untidy bloom (right).

PREPARING CUTTINGS

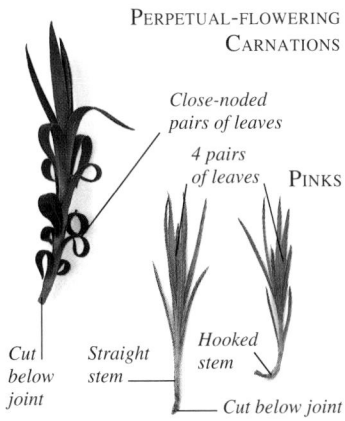

PERPETUAL-FLOWERING CARNATIONS

Close-noded pairs of leaves

4 pairs of leaves

PINKS

Cut below joint

Straight stem

Hooked stem

Cut below joint

Select non-flowering, closely jointed shoots. Remove the bottom pairs of leaves to create small stems and trim them neatly. Cuttings with a hooked stem may also be viable.

BLOOMS FOR EXHIBITION

A good show bloom displays all the characteristics of its class, and reveals no evidence of pests or disease. Calyx bands left on the bloom or a burst calyx invite disqualification.

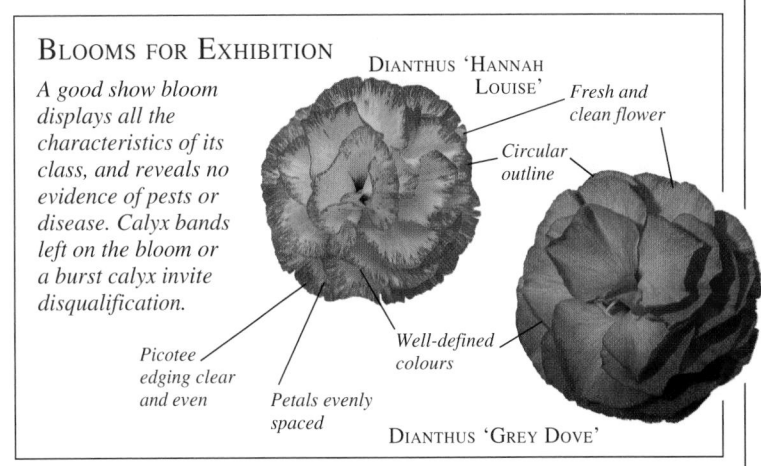

DIANTHUS 'HANNAH LOUISE'

Fresh and clean flower

Circular outline

Picotee edging clear and even

Petals evenly spaced

Well-defined colours

DIANTHUS 'GREY DOVE'

Propagation

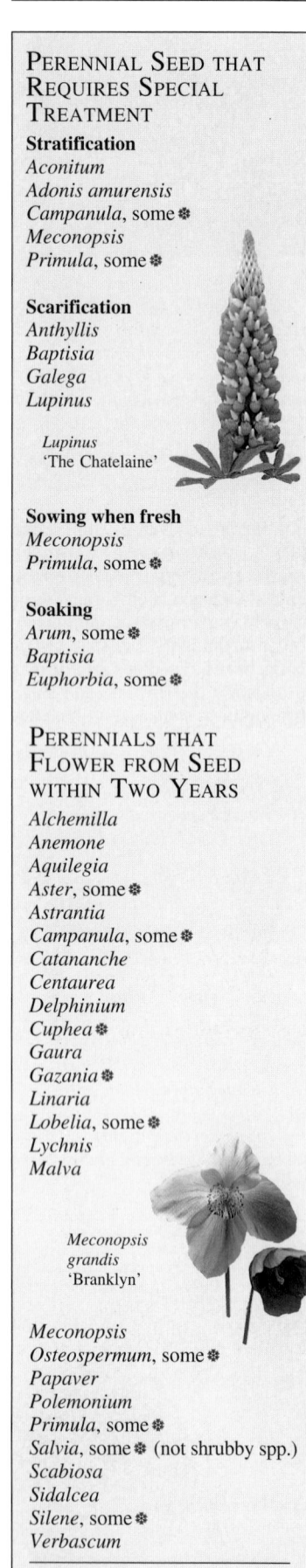

THERE are several ways of propagating herbaceous perennials. Growing them from seed is ideal where a large number of new plants is required. Little experience or expertise is needed to raise the seedlings successfully but this method is generally only suitable for propagating species rather than cultivars.

For many perennials, the simplest and commonest method of propagation is to lift them and divide clumps into separate plants, but others are better raised from seed or by vegetative means, such as cuttings or, more rarely, grafting. Vegetative methods should be used for propagating almost all named cultivars.

Seed

Raising plants from seed is a simple and inexpensive way to propagate many perennials but, apart from a few named cultivars (for example, *Aquilegia* 'Crimson Star'), most cultivars do not come true from seed. Most species also show some variation in habit and flower colour so, if collecting seed yourself, always gather it from plants with the best flower and growth characteristics.

Seed of early-flowering perennials, which ripens on the plant in early to mid-summer, usually germinates quickly if sown as soon as it is ripe, producing young plants that may be overwintered successfully in open ground or in a cold frame. For most perennials, however, sow the seed immediately after it has been gathered in autumn so that it germinates early the following spring. If stored in cool, dry conditions, most seed also germinates well when sown in spring.

Seed of herbaceous plants such as peonies (*Paeonia*) and hellebores (*Helleborus*) usually remains dormant for a considerable period unless suitable conditions are provided or occur naturally to break dormancy and induce germination. Some require a period of exposure to cold or light, while others have hard seed coats that should be weakened by scarification or softened by soaking before sowing (see also PRINCIPLES OF PROPAGATION, "How to overcome dormancy", p.535).

**Pre-germination
treatment of seeds**
Seeds that need to be subjected to a cold period to break dormancy may either be sown outside in autumn or winter (see also *Sowing Seed that Requires Chilling*, p.163) or chilled in a refrigerator for a few weeks before sowing in spring. This method of breaking dormancy is suitable for many genera, including *Aconitum*, *Adonis*, *Campanula*, and *Primula*. Seeds of a few plants, such as those of *Gentiana asclepiadea*, require a period of exposure to light for successful germination.

Scarifying and soaking
A number of perennials, particularly those of the pea family Leguminosae, have seeds with hard coats that impede rapid and even germination. Just before sowing the seeds, scarify them either by rubbing them with sandpaper or by chipping them slightly with a sharp blade to allow water to be taken up and then germination to occur.

Alternatively, many seeds may have their hard coats softened by being soaked in hot, but not boiling, water for 12–24 hours; this allows the seed to absorb water and germination to take place. Soaking is suitable for a number of perennials, for example *Arum*, *Baptisia*, and *Euphorbia*. Once soaked, the seed should be sown immediately.

Double dormancy
Peony and *Trillium* seeds usually require two periods of cold to trigger germination of both roots and shoots. Root development from the germinating seed occurs during the first season but the shoots do not normally start to appear until the seeds have received a second period of cold, usually during the following winter. Sow the seeds in containers in autumn in the normal way.

Sowing seed in containers

Unless a very large number of plants is required, it is easiest to sow seed in containers. A plastic half-tray accommodates as many as two or three hundred seeds, while even a large, square pot is adequate for sowing up to 50 seeds, depending on their size. Square pots fit closely in rows and provide a greater area of compost than round pots of the same width.

Whether using trays or pots, place a layer of broken crocks or grit in the base to provide drainage and fill them with an appropriate seed compost. Loam-based composts are often preferred to peat-based ones if the young seedlings are to be kept in them for more than a short period after germination. Gently press the compost around the edges of the pot or tray, then roughly level the surface and firm it with a presser so that it is about 1cm (½in) below the container rim.

Sowing
The seeds should always be sown thinly – about 0.5cm (¼in) apart; sowing too densely may result in thin, spindly plants that are prone to damping off (see p.564). Fine seeds, and those that require light to germinate, for example some gentians

Collecting seed

Collect the seed as it ripens: shake it from the pods or tie the seedheads into small bunches, enclosed in paper bags, and hang them upside-down so that the seeds fall into the bags. Make sure that the seed is completely dry before storing it in clean paper bags or envelopes labelled with the plant name and harvesting date.

Collect ripened seed pods (here of Meconopsis) *when they have turned brown. Shake the seeds out of each pod onto a piece of paper and store in a cool, dry place until ready to sow.*

(*Gentiana*), may be left uncovered or sprinkled with a shallow layer of fine, sieved compost and then gently firmed with a presser. Larger seeds, such as those of peonies, should be covered with a 0.5cm (¼in) layer of sieved compost.

Aftercare

Label the containers with the seed name and sowing date, then water them using a can with a fine rose, taking care not to dislodge the seeds. Alternatively, if small seeds are being sown, stand the containers in a bowl or tray of water for a short time until they have absorbed enough to moisten the compost throughout; this method prevents the seeds from being washed away. Minimize evaporation by covering the containers with glass, a plastic sheet, or plastic film, and place them in a cold frame or greenhouse. In sunny weather, provide some shade with newspaper or shade netting. Once the seeds have started to germinate, remove the cover and reduce any shading.

Plunging the containers in an outdoor bed

If the containers are to be placed outside unprotected from the weather during autumn and winter to break seed dormancy, add a covering of grit over the sown seeds. This prevents them from being washed out of the containers by heavy rain and, to some extent, deters mosses and liverworts from growing on the compost surface. Cover the containers with fine-mesh chicken wire to protect the seed if rodents or birds are likely to be a problem.

Plunge the pots in an open sand bed as this provides stable, even conditions for germination. Once the seed has germinated and the seedlings are visible, place the containers in a cold frame and care for the seedlings as for those raised under cover.

Pricking out

Once the seedlings are large enough to handle, that is when the first or second pair of true leaves has formed, they may be pricked out. Either space them evenly in seed trays with about 30–40 in each tray or prick them out into individual containers. The latter is advisable for seedlings that do not tolerate much root disturbance. Alternatively, prick out the seedlings into modules (compartmentalized trays). In all cases, a good, loam-based potting compost should be used.

Water the seedlings thoroughly, label them, and then place them in a cold frame or cool greenhouse until they are established. They may then

RAISING PLANTS FROM SEED

1 *Fill a 13cm (5in) pot with moist seed compost. Firm the compost to about 1cm (½in) below the rim, using a presser.*

2 *Using a clean, folded piece of paper, scatter the seeds (here* Chrysanthemum x superbum) *sparingly over the compost.*

3 *Cover the seeds with a shallow layer of fine, sieved compost. Label and then water without displacing the seeds.*

4 *Cover with a glass or clear plastic sheet to retain moisture. Place the pot in a cold frame until the seedlings develop 2 pairs of leaves.*

5 *Prick out the seedlings into pots; degradable pots (inset) allow planting out direct. Handle the seedlings by the leaves since the stems are easily damaged.*

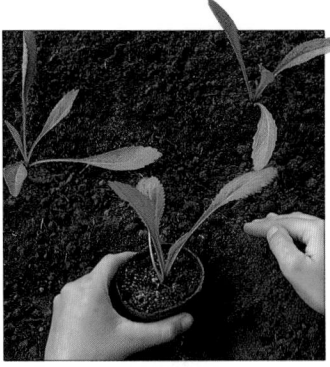

6 *When the seedlings have developed into small plants with a good root system, plant them out or pot them up, as appropriate.*

SOWING SEED THAT REQUIRES CHILLING

1 *In autumn, sow the seed thinly in pots of compost, then cover with a thin layer of fine compost and top-dress with fine grit.*

2 *Label the pots with the seed name and date of sowing, and water thoroughly. Then plunge the pots in an open sand bed outside to encourage the seeds to germinate.*

be potted on individually or planted out in their permanent site in open ground when they are large enough.

Sowing outside in open ground

If large numbers of plants are needed, it may be more convenient to sow seed outside. Prepare an area in fertile, well-drained soil by clearing any weeds and cultivating the soil to a fine tilth. Using a line or a straight-edged board as a guide, make a seed drill using a draw hoe, onion hoe, or the point of a large label.

The depth of the drill depends on the size of the seed to be sown: about 0.5cm (¼in) deep is adequate for small seeds, while large seeds require a drill at least 1cm (½in) deep. If the seedlings are to be transplanted when young, set the drills 10–15cm (4–6in) apart; if, however, they are

to be grown on in rows, allow about 15–22cm (6–9in) between them. Sow small seeds thinly so that they are about 0.5cm (¼in) apart, large seeds such as peonies at intervals of 2.5cm (1in) or more.

After sowing, cover the drills by raking soil lightly over them, then label each drill with the name of the seed and the date. Water carefully, without washing away the soil. For further details, see ANNUALS AND BIENNIALS, *Sowing in Drills*, p.181.

Dividing perennials

This method is suitable for propagating many perennials that have a spreading rootstock and produce plenty of shoots from the base. As well as being a way of increasing stocks, in many cases division rejuvenates the plants and keeps them vigorous, because old or unproductive parts may be discarded (see also "Lifting and dividing", p.157).

Some perennial plants can be divided simply by pulling sections apart by hand, or by using two forks back-to-back; other plants that have fleshy roots are best split apart by using a spade or knife.

When to divide

Most plants should be divided when they are dormant, between late autumn and early spring, but not in extremely cold, wet, or dry weather since these conditions may make it difficult for the divided plants to re-establish successfully.

Fleshy-rooted perennials are usually best left until the end of their dormant season, in spring, before being divided. At this time their buds will be starting to shoot, which will indicate the most vigorous areas of growth, and therefore the best way of dividing up the plant.

Preparation

First lift the plant to be divided by loosening the surrounding soil, taking care not to damage the roots, then levering it up gently with a fork. Shake off as much loose soil from the roots as possible and remove any dead leaves and stems to make it easier to see the best points for division. This also enables you to see which are the healthy parts of the plant to be retained and which are the old, unproductive parts that can be discarded.

Wash most of the soil off the roots and crowns of fleshy-rooted plants, so that all the buds are clearly visible and therefore do not become damaged inadvertently when you are dividing the plant.

Fibrous-rooted plants

Insert two hand forks back-to-back near the centre of each plant so that the tines are close together and the handles apart; then push the handles gently backwards and forwards so that the prongs gradually tease the plant apart and separate the clumps into two smaller portions. Repeat this process with each portion to divide the plant into more sections, each with some new shoots.

Plants that tend to form woody clumps or that have thick, solid roots should be cut into portions with a spade or sharp knife; make sure that there are at least two growth buds or shoots on each piece. Discard the old, weak, and often woody growth from the centre of the plant; the sections containing vigorous, young shoots and healthy roots tend to grow at the perimeter of the plant.

Perennial plants that have loose, spreading crowns and numerous shoots, for example Michaelmas daisies (*Aster*), are easy to pull apart by hand or with two hand forks. Simply separate off single stems growing at the edges of the crown so that each has its own root system.

Fleshy-rooted plants

Plants that have bulky, almost solid, fleshy roots, such as *Rheum*, may need to be divided with a spade as it would be difficult to separate the crowns using back-to-back forks. After cleaning the plant so that the developing buds are clearly visible, slice through between them with a spade, taking care to leave two or more buds on each piece. Then trim each division neatly with a knife, discarding any old, woody material and any damaged or rotting roots.

Plants with numerous, intertwined crowns, such as *Arthropodium* and tufted ornamental grasses, may also be divided with two forks.

Replanting and aftercare

After dividing a plant, dust any cut surfaces with an appropriate fungicide (see PRINCIPLES OF PROPAGATION, "How roots form", p.538). Replant the divisions as soon as possible. It

Dividing hostas

Large hostas with tough rootstocks should be divided using a spade. Include several buds on each division and trim any damaged parts with a knife. Hostas that have looser, fleshy rootstocks may be separated by hand or with back-to-back forks; each division should have at least one "eye" or shoot.

HOW TO PROPAGATE PERENNIALS BY DIVISION

1 Lift the plant to be divided, taking care to insert the fork far enough away from the plant so that the roots are not damaged. Shake off surplus soil. The plant shown here is a Helianthus.

2 Separate plants with a woody centre by chopping through the crown with a spade.

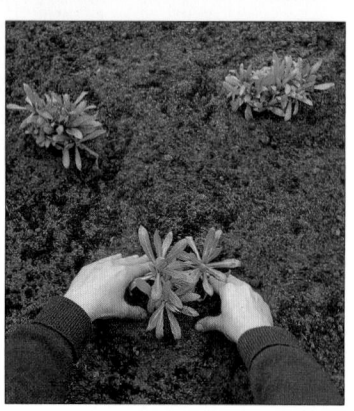

3 Divide the plant into smaller pieces by hand, retaining only healthy, vigorous sections each with several new shoots.

4 Cut back the old top-growth and replant the divided sections to the same depth as before. Firm in and water thoroughly.

ALTERNATIVE METHOD

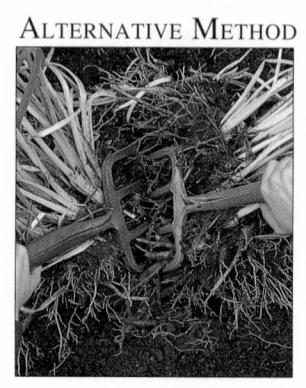

Divide fibrous-rooted, herbaceous plants (here Hemerocallis) using 2 forks back-to-back.

TOUGH, FIBROUS ROOTS
Divide the crown with a spade; each section should include several developing buds.

LOOSE, FLESHY ROOTS
Divide small plants and those with a loose rootstock by pulling the clump apart by hand.

is important that they do not dry out, so if replanting is unavoidably delayed for a couple of hours, dip the plants briefly in water and keep them in a sealed plastic bag in a cool, shady place until you are ready to replant them.

Large divisions, if replanted immediately, may still provide a good show of flowers in the same season although the stems are often slightly shorter than those of more established plants. Very small divisions, however, are best grown on for a season in a nursery bed or in pots in order to become established. In general, the divisions should be replanted at the same depth as the original plant, but those that are prone to rotting at the base are best set slightly proud of the surrounding soil level to keep the crowns of the plants free of excess water (see also "Planting depths", p.148).

When replanting, ensure that the roots are well spread out in the planting hole and the plant firmed in. Water newly planted divisions thoroughly; take care not to expose the roots by washing away any soil.

Division of rhizomatous plants

Divide plants with thick rhizomes, such as *Bergenia* and rhizomatous irises, by splitting the clump into pieces by hand, then cutting the rhizomes into sections, each with one or more buds (see right). Bamboos have tough rootstocks that either form dense clumps with short rhizomes or have long, spreading rhizomes; divide the former with a spade or two back-to-back forks; cut the latter into sections with secateurs, each of which should have three nodes or joints (see also GRASSES, BAMBOOS, SEDGES, AND RUSHES, p.145).

1 *Lift the plant to be divided (here an iris), inserting the fork well away from the rhizomes to avoid damaging them.*

2 *Shake the clump to remove any loose soil. Using your hands or a hand fork, split the clump into manageable pieces.*

3 *Discard any old rhizomes, then detach the new, young rhizomes from the clump and neatly trim off their ends.*

4 *Dust the cut areas with fungicide. Trim long roots by one third. For irises, cut the leaves to a mitre about 15cm (6in) long to prevent wind rock.*

5 *Plant the rhizomes about 12cm (5in) apart. The rhizomes should be half buried, with their leaves and buds upright. Firm in well and water.*

Dividing peonies

Peonies should be divided with particular care as they dislike being transplanted and tend to re-establish slowly. For best results, lift and divide the plants towards the end of the dormant season in early spring, when the swelling, red growth buds are clearly visible. Cut the crown into sections, each with a few buds, taking care not to damage the thick, fleshy roots.

1 *Lift the plant in early spring, when healthy growth buds are visible on the crown. Cut it into sections, each one with several buds.*

2 *Dust all the cut surfaces of the divided sections with fungicide to discourage infection and rot.*

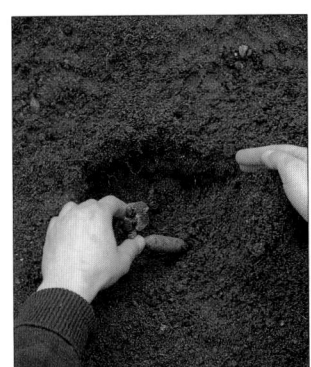

3 *Plant out the divided sections approximately 20cm (8in) apart. The buds should just be visible at the surface. Firm the soil well.*

PROPAGATING PERENNIALS BY STEM TIP CUTTINGS

1 Select short lengths of soft wood about 7–12cm (3–5in) long from the tips of strong, healthy shoots. The plant shown here is a Penstemon *cultivar*.

2 Trim the lower end of each cutting just below a node, with a straight cut, reducing the length to 5–7cm (2–3in). Remove the lower pairs of leaves.

3 Insert the cuttings around the edge of a 15cm (6in) pot of cutting compost and water in. Cover with a plastic bag, held away from the cuttings by canes.

4 When the cuttings have rooted, gently lift them and pot them up individually into 10cm (4in) pots.

Stem tip cuttings

This method of propagation is used most commonly for herbaceous perennials that are difficult to divide successfully and for cultivars that do not come true from seed. Cuttings may be taken at any time during the growing season provided that suitable shoots are available.

Select strong growing tips without flower buds, rejecting any that are thin, weak and leggy, or damaged. If there is likely to be any delay before inserting the cuttings, place them in a sealed plastic bag to protect them from dehydration.

Preparing and inserting the cuttings

Take cuttings with secateurs or a sharp knife, cutting across the stem immediately above a node. Trim the cuttings to just below a node, then remove the leaves from the lowest third of each cutting. Insert the cuttings into prepared pots or trays of an appropriate cutting compost and firm in with your fingers. Leave sufficient space between the cuttings so that the leaves do not touch each other and air can circulate freely. This inhibits the spread of damping off diseases (see p.564).

Aftercare

Water the cuttings using a watering can with a fine rose and treat them with a fungicide to reduce the risk of infection and rot. It is important that the cuttings are maintained at a high humidity level otherwise they will wilt, so, if possible, keep them in a mist unit or propagator. Alternatively, cover the cuttings with a plastic tent or bag; this should be supported on canes or hooped wires to prevent the plastic from touching the leaves since any condensation forming on the foliage could encourage fungal infection.

In hot weather, shade the cuttings with newspaper, proprietary shade netting, or other semi-translucent material to prevent the leaves from scorching or wilting. The shading should be removed as soon as possible to allow the cuttings plenty of light. Inspect them daily, removing any fallen and dead leaves and any material that is infected. Water the compost as necessary to keep it moist but not wet.

After about two to three weeks, the cuttings should produce roots and may be potted on into individual pots. Any healthy cuttings that have not developed roots by this stage should be re-inserted and cared for as before until they have rooted.

Basal stem cuttings

This type of cutting is suitable for a number of herbaceous plants that produce clusters of new shoots at the base in spring. Short, basal cuttings of plants with hollow or pithy stems, such as lupins (*Lupinus*) and delphiniums, as well as those that

HOW TO PROPAGATE BY BASAL STEM CUTTINGS

1 Take cuttings when the shoots (here of Chrysanthemum) are 3.5–5cm (1½–2in) high, each with a small piece of basal wood.

2 Remove the basal leaves from each cutting and trim the lower end, making a straight cut.

3 Insert the cuttings into a prepared pot of moist cutting compost. Place the pots in a propagator or plastic bag to encourage rooting.

4 When the cuttings have rooted, separate them, retaining as much compost as possible around the roots. Pot up the cuttings individually.

have soft tissues, may be rooted successfully from sturdy shoots that are taken from plants in mid-spring.

If required, the plants to be propagated may be lifted and grown in pots or trays in a warm greenhouse to encourage the production of basal shoots earlier than if the plants were growing in the open ground. The cuttings may then be rooted and young plants established earlier in the season. The plants from which cuttings have been taken may then be replanted in the garden.

Preparing and inserting the cuttings

Select strong, sturdy shoots whose first leaves have just unfolded and, using a sharp knife, remove them as close to the base as possible; include part of the woody, basal tissue in the cutting. Do not use any shoots that are hollow or damaged.

Trim off the lower leaves of the cuttings, dip them in hormone rooting powder, and insert them in cutting compost, either individually or several to a pot, or in trays. Firm in the cuttings, water thoroughly, and allow the containers to drain before placing them in a cold frame or propagator. Alternatively, cover each of the containers with a clear, plastic bag supported on wire hoops firmly inserted into the compost. Shade the cuttings from direct sunlight to prevent the leaves from scorching or wilting.

Aftercare

Check the cuttings every few days, removing any dead or decaying foliage as soon as possible to prevent the spread of rot. Ensure that the compost is moist, but not wet, at all times, and wipe away excess water and condensation from the glass or plastic covers. The cuttings should normally be well rooted within a month and they may then be potted on into individual pots filled with equal parts of loam, sand, and peat substitute or peat.

Root cuttings

This is a useful method of propagating perennials that have fairly thick, fleshy roots, such as *Verbascum* and *Papaver orientale* cultivars. It is also the only way of raising new, healthy plants from border phlox cultivars that are affected by eelworm. As the eelworms occur in the top-growth of affected phlox, but not in the roots, taking root cuttings makes it possible to produce healthy, eelworm-free plants. This method is not used for those phlox cultivars with variegated foliage, however, because the resulting plants produce only plain green leaves.

Take care to minimize damage to the parent plant when cutting its roots, and replant it straight after taking the cuttings. Root cuttings are most successful when they are taken during the plant's dormant period, usually in winter.

Preparation

Lift a strong, healthy plant and wash off the soil so that all the roots can be clearly seen. Select roots that are young, vigorous, and fairly thick, as these are more likely to provide successful new plants than those that are weak and thin or old, gnarled, and woody. Cut off the young roots close to the crown and replant the parent plant.

When propagating plants with thick roots, for example *Acanthus*, *Anchusa*, *Romneya*, and *Verbascum*, choose roots that are about the thickness of a pencil and cut them into sections 5–10cm (2–4in) long. With thin-rooted perennials, cut the roots into 7–12cm (3–5in) lengths so there is sufficient food-storage for the developing cuttings.

Cut each section so that the top end (that nearest the plant's stem) is cut straight across and the bottom end (nearest the root tip) is cut at an angle; this makes it easy to insert the cuttings the correct way up. Shoots will develop from the top end of the cutting and roots from the lower end. Trim off any fibrous roots before inserting the cuttings.

Inserting the cuttings

After preparing the cuttings, dust them with fungicide to protect against rot. Then insert them vertically, straight ends at the top, in prepared pots or trays of seed compost about one and a half times their depth; the tops of the cuttings should be level with the surface. Cover the pots with a thin layer of fine sand or grit, label, and place them in a propagator or cold frame. Do not water the cuttings until they begin to root. Once young shoots have developed, pot them up singly into an appropriate compost.

Plants with thinner roots, such as *Anemone hupehensis*, *A. x hybrida*, *Campanula*, phlox, and *Primula denticulata*, are often treated slightly differently as their roots may be too fine to insert vertically. Lay the root cuttings flat on the surface of pots or trays of firmed compost, then cover with more compost. Then treat as for standard root cuttings.

HOW TO PROPAGATE PERENNIALS BY ROOT CUTTINGS

1 *Lift the plant (here* Acanthus*) when dormant and wash the roots. Select roots of pencil thickness and cut them off with a knife, cutting close to the crown.*

2 *Trim the roots and cut each into lengths of 5–10cm (2–4in). Make a straight cut at the upper end of each cutting and an angled cut at the lower end (see inset).*

3 *Insert the cuttings into holes made in pots of moist cutting compost, and firm. The top end of each cutting should be flush with the compost surface.*

4 *Top-dress the pots of cuttings with coarse grit, label them, and place them in a cold frame until the cuttings root.*

5 *When the cuttings have developed young shoots, pot them up into individual pots filled with loam-based potting compost. Water and label the pots (see inset).*

ALTERNATIVE METHOD FOR THIN ROOTS

Place the trimmed cuttings horizontally on moist, firmed compost. Cover with compost and firm lightly.

PERENNIALS THAT MAY BE PROPAGATED BY ROOT CUTTINGS

Acanthus
Anchusa azurea
Anemone hupehensis,
  A. x hybrida
Arnebia
Campanula, some ✿
Catananche caerulea 'Major'
Echinops

Catananche caerulea 'Major'

Erodium,
  some ✿
Eryngium,
  some ✿
Gaillardia
Geranium, some ✿
Gypsophila
Limonium latifolium
Mertensia
Morisia
Papaver orientale
Phlox decussata, *P. subulata*
Primula denticulata
Pulsatilla vulgaris
Romneya
Trollius
Verbascum

KEY
✿ *Not hardy*

Grafting

Although grafting is more commonly associated with trees and shrubs, some *Gypsophila paniculata* cultivars, for example 'Flamingo' and 'Bristol Fairy', are propagated by grafting. This is because they do not root readily from cuttings, so grafting is the only reliable way of increasing stocks. This propagation method should produce vigorous plants that grow well.

Preparing the scion plant

Lift the plants of the cultivar to be propagated in autumn, pot them up, and grow them on in a cool greenhouse. These conditions encourage the plants to produce vigorous, young shoots earlier than usual – in mid- to late winter, which is the optimum time for grafting.

Preparing the rootstocks

For the rootstocks, use one- to two-year-old seedlings of *Gypsophila paniculata*; these should be lifted and prepared in mid- to late winter. Choose roots at least the thickness of a slim pencil and 7–10cm (3–4in) long, cutting them off straight at the top and trimming them with an angled cut at the base. Any small, lateral roots should be cut back and any fibrous roots growing on the stock discarded. Then place the prepared roots in a sealed plastic bag to keep them moist while the scions are being prepared. It is important that the cut surfaces do not dry out as this can prevent a successful union between the stock and scion.

Selecting and preparing the scion material

For the scions, select strong, young shoots 3–7cm (1½–3in) long and detach them from the base of the plant. The lower ends should then be trimmed into a wedge shape.

Uniting the stocks and scions

First prepare the rootstock, by making a small, vertical cut in the top about 1cm (½in) deep. Pot up the rootstock into an individual pot of cutting compost. Then insert the scion, trimming it further if required, so that its lower end fits neatly into the cut in the prepared stock. Bind together the stock and scion using plastic tape or raffia to hold them firmly in place.

Alternatively, the plants may be potted up after grafting. In either case, water thoroughly and allow the pots to drain. Place the grafted plants in a propagator or mist unit, preferably with bottom heat, or cover each one with a clear plastic bag

supported by canes or wires; ensure that the plastic does not touch the foliage, because condensation on the inside of the bag could cause rotting. Secure the bag in place with an elastic band around the pot.

Aftercare

Check the grafted plants regularly to make sure that the compost does not dry out. Water them from beneath, when necessary, by standing the pots in a tray of water; alternatively, remove the plastic bags and mist-spray the plants with water.

The grafts should knit fairly quickly, and new roots form in about four to six weeks; the grafted plants may then be removed from the propagator or plastic bags and kept in cool, but frost-free, conditions until new shoots start to develop.

Once new growth is visible on each grafted plant and the union seems firm, the tape or raffia binding may be removed. When the plants are well established, repot them using a standard potting compost, and grow them on in a cool greenhouse or cold frame. Then plant them out in early summer, either in a nursery bed or in their final positions in the open garden.

PROPAGATION BY GRAFTING

1 *First select and prepare the rootstock. Cut a piece of straight, healthy root about 1cm (½in) thick and 9cm (3½in) long from the parent plant (here Gypsophila paniculata).*

2 *Remove any fibrous roots and cut back lateral roots to within 1cm (½in) of the rootstock. Make a straight cut across the top of the stock and an angled cut at the lower end.*

3 *Using a sharp knife, make a clean, vertical incision, about 1cm (½in) deep, in the top of the rootstock.*

4 *For the scion, select a vigorous shoot about 3–4mm (⅛in) thick and 3–7cm (1½–3in) long. Trim the lower end to make a wedge that will fit into the cut in the rootstock.*

5 *Insert the rootstock into a 6cm (3in) pot of cutting compost and firm in. Carefully insert the lower end of the scion into the vertical incision in the rootstock, so that it fits closely.*

6 *To hold the scion firmly in position, bind the grafted area with plastic tape or raffia. Label the grafted plant, and water thoroughly.*

7 *Cover the plant with a plastic bag supported by canes or wires so that it does not touch the plant. Leave it in light, warm conditions, under cover, until the graft has taken successfully and there are signs of new growth.*

Wild-flower and meadow gardening

WILD-FLOWER gardening stems in part from a wish to conserve native species that are threatened by the erosion of their natural habitats; while it is not possible to re-create such habitats exactly, growing even a small area of wild flowers contributes to their conservation and attracts a variety of insects (often beneficial) and other wildlife into the garden.

Creating a wild-flower area is often the best way of using part of the garden that does not lend itself to more conventional cultivation, perhaps because it is too exposed, sloping, or dry, or has poor soil.

Wild-flower gardens

Wild-flower habitats are extremely diverse but include meadows or flower-rich grasslands (see p.279), alpine meadows, cornfields, wetlands, and woodlands (see p.27).

When planning a wild-flower area, assess the site, taking into account climate, soil type, and drainage, and the degree of sun, shade, and shelter. The growing conditions largely determine the plants that will thrive and look natural in the setting.

An open, sunny site with well-drained soil is ideal for a meadow with field scabious (*Knautia arvensis*) and lady's bedstraw (*Galium verum*) or a cornfield area with poppies (*Papaver*) and cornflowers (*Centaurea cyanus*); a more exposed site may suit an alpine meadow, with short grass and low-growing plants such as gentian (*Gentiana acaulis*) and mountain tassel (*Soldanella montana*) that will not be damaged by wind. Damp or waterlogged ground may be used for a bog garden (see p.245) with plants such as meadowsweet (*Filipendula ulmaria*).

Observe the local wild flora as this will indicate which species to grow, but never take plants from the wild. You may also include some non-indigenous plants that enjoy the same growing conditions and are in keeping with the style of the planting.

Seasonal variation

Depending on the site and the selected plants, the main display may be planned for a particular season or to extend over a longer period. A woodland habitat favours spring-flowering plants, for example, because the tree canopy lets through more light than it does later on. Meadows are at their peak in summer but have a long span of interest, from spring daffodils such as *Narcissus pseudonarcissus* through to autumn-flowering crocuses (*Colchicum autumnale* and *Crocus speciosus*).

Establishing a meadow garden

A meadow garden should preferably be established on soil that is low in fertility, using a mixture of fine grasses such as bents (*Agrostis*) and fescues (*Festuca*) that will not swamp the flowering plants. Typical meadow flowers include perennials such as ragged robin (*Lychnis flos-cuculi*) and clustered bellflower (*Campanula glomerata*). Various seed mixtures are available to suit different sites and soil types.

Sowing and planting

Eliminate vigorous, perennial weeds such as docks (*Rumex*) and dandelions (*Taraxacum officinale*) with a translocated weedkiller. Then strip off any turf and remove the upper layer of fertile topsoil for use elsewhere. Cultivate the soil to a fine tilth, firm by treading or rolling, and rake lightly. In early autumn or spring, sow the wild-flower seed mixture (with fine sand for even distribution) at a rate of 4g/sq m ($^1/_8$oz/sq yd) or as advised by the supplier.

If establishing wild flowers in existing grassland, such as an orchard, reduce the soil fertility over one or two years by mowing regularly and removing the clippings. Then introduce pot-grown plants, using a small bulb planter to remove cores of turf.

Maintenance

In the first year, keep the sward at about 5–8cm (2–3in), removing the clippings to maintain low soil fertility; spot treat any pernicious, perennial weeds. Do not expect flowers in this first season. In subsequent years, cut areas of spring flowers to about 8cm (3in) after they have shed their seed. Continue to cut every three weeks or cut once in late summer. Summer-flowering meadows may be mown or scythed until late spring but should then be left until early autumn, when the flowers have shed their seed. Remove the clippings after each cut.

THE WILD-FLOWER BORDER
Many species bloom profusely in the garden, providing an attractive display and a rich source of nectar for a diversity of bees and butterflies.

STREAMSIDE PLANTINGS
A food plant for the caterpillars of the orange-tip butterfly, the sweetly fragrant Hesperis matronalis *happily colonizes damp soils.*

FLOWERING PLANTS FOR DIFFERENT HABITATS

Leucanthemum vulgare
(meadow)

Geranium pratense
(meadow)

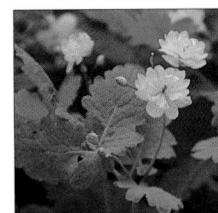

Chelidonium majus
'Flore Pleno'
(wood and hedgerow)

Caltha palustris
(bog)

Galanthus nivalis
'Flore Pleno'
(wood and meadow)

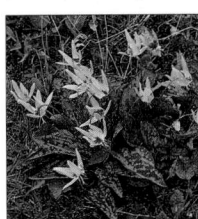

Erythronium dens-canis (wood and alpine meadow)

Pelargoniums

PELARGONIUMS are almost all tender, evergreen, perennial plants of South African origin. When introduced to Britain, they were given the common name geranium because of their botanical similarity to the hardy, herbaceous species of the genus *Geranium*, which was commonly cultivated in Europe at that time. This common name still remains in widespread use today, although almost all the plants usually referred to as geraniums belong to the genus *Pelargonium*.

Types of pelargonium

Pelargoniums may broadly be divided into five groups, according to the main characteristics of the plants. The groups are: zonal, dwarf and miniature zonal, regal, ivy-leaved, and scented-leaved.

Zonal

These pelargoniums have rounded leaves, usually marked with a distinct, dark zone and single, semi-double, or double flowers. Some cultivars, however, do not have a zone and others have gold- or silver-variegated, or tricoloured leaves.

In temperate climates, they grow well in the open garden and are ideal for summer bedding as they bloom continuously from early summer until late autumn. They also thrive in windowboxes, hanging baskets, and containers. Zonals will happily adapt to the growing conditions in a greenhouse or conservatory.

TYPES OF PELARGONIUM

ZONAL
P. 'Dolly Varden'
Rounded leaves, with a darker zone, and single to double flowers.

REGAL
P. 'Purple Emperor'
Deeply serrated leaves and broadly trumpet-shaped flowers.

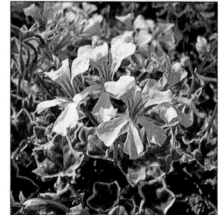

IVY-LEAVED
P. peltatum 'Amethyst'
Trailing plants with lobed leaves and single to double flowers.

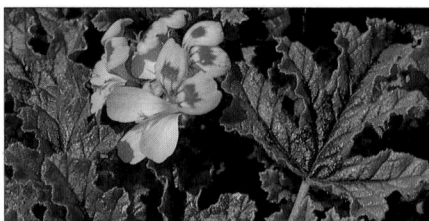

SCENTED-LEAVED
P. 'Royal Oak'
Plants with small, often irregularly star-shaped flowers, grown for their fragrant leaves.

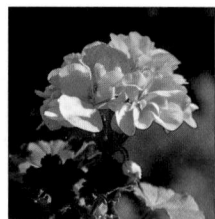

DWARF ZONAL
P. 'Timothy Clifford'
Bushy, free-flowering plants, similar to zonals, up to 20cm (8in) tall.

Dwarf and miniature zonal

Dwarf zonal pelargoniums are 13–20cm (5–8in) tall, bushy, and very free-flowering. They make excellent windowbox plants and pot plants for displaying in greenhouses and conservatories. Miniature zonal pelargoniums have smaller leaves and flowers than the dwarf zonals and are no higher than 13cm (5in). They are very floriferous plants, with double and single blooms in a wide range of colours, and have green to greenish-black leaves.

In recent years, F1 and F2 hybrid zonal pelargoniums have been developed. These are grown from seed and are used mainly for bedding. They are single-flowered and are available in the same range of colours as the cultivars that have been propagated vegetatively.

Regal

These pelargoniums are small shrubby plants with rounded, deeply serrated leaves and wide, trumpet-shaped flowers, often in exotic colours.

They may be grown in the open garden but, in temperate countries, they are much more extensively used as greenhouse, conservatory, and house plants, since the flowers are quickly spoilt by rain. In warmer climates, where they may be planted out permanently, they make splendid flowering shrubs, almost continuously in bloom year round.

Ivy-leaved

These trailing pelargoniums have rounded, lobed, ivy-like leaves, and flowers similar to those of zonals, available in a rich assortment of colours. They are used mainly in hanging baskets and other containers, where their flowers on trailing stems can be displayed to best advantage. They may also be planted so that they spill over the edge of a raised bed or a wall.

Scented-leaved

Scented-leaved pelargoniums have small, delicate flowers with five petals, and fragrant foliage for which they are chiefly grown. They make excellent house and greenhouse plants, and in temperate climates may be grown outside during the summer and autumn, in containers or as bedding plants.

Feeding and watering

All pelargoniums, especially when they are grown in containers, need weekly feeding throughout the summer with a high-potash liquid feed, such as tomato fertilizer. This helps the plants to continue to produce a mass of good-quality blooms without becoming too leafy. Nitrogen-rich fertilizers will produce too much leaf at the expense of flower production and should not be used. Pelargoniums in containers should be watered at regular intervals, as soon as the top of the compost dries out.

Overwintering

Pelargoniums must be kept frost-free, except for *P. endlicherianum*, a rare, hardy species from Turkey. In temperate climates, plants grown outside may be saved for replanting the following season by moving them under cover before there is any frost. Lift the plants before the first frosts are expected, shake as much soil as possible off the roots, trim back the roots and stems, and remove any remaining leaves.

For storing, use a wooden or strong cardboard box with deep sides, and make a few small drainage holes in the bottom. Half-fill the box with seed or cutting compost, which should keep the plants alive but contains insufficient food for them to grow vigorously during storage. Place the prepared stools (old plants) in the box, so that they are close together but not touching. Fill in with more compost around each stool and firm it in stages, finishing level with the top of the box.

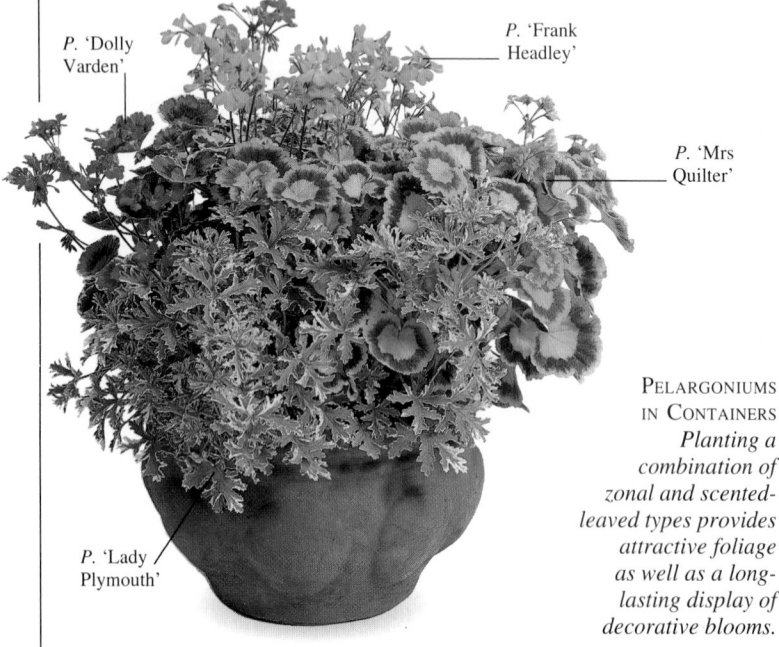

P. 'Dolly Varden'

P. 'Frank Headley'

P. 'Mrs Quilter'

P. 'Lady Plymouth'

PELARGONIUMS IN CONTAINERS
Planting a combination of zonal and scented-leaved types provides attractive foliage as well as a long-lasting display of decorative blooms.

CONTRASTING HABITS
Use trailing, ivy-leaved pelargoniums to spill over the edge of a container. These will make an attractive contrast with upright forms in the centre.

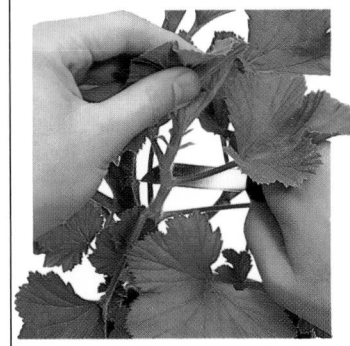

1 *Choose a healthy shoot and cut straight across the stem just above the third joint below the growing tip.*

Water the compost thoroughly and leave the box outside for a day to drain. The plants should be watered again during the winter only if they become very dry. Store the box where it will receive plenty of light and remain frost-free. If no heating is available, protect the plants during very cold weather with newspaper, sacking, or old carpet.

By mid-winter new shoots will be beginning to appear on the stools; these may be used as cuttings in early spring. Alternatively, the stools may be potted up separately and grown on for planting out in the early part of the summer.

Propagation from cuttings

Pelargoniums are easily propagated from cuttings, and the method used is the same for all types. Taking cuttings is an inexpensive way of producing new plants and allows the old plant to remain flowering outside in the garden until the first frosts, thus prolonging the display.

Selecting the cuttings
Although it is possible to take cuttings from spring onwards, the best time is late summer, when light

conditions are good and the weather is still warm. Select strong, healthy shoots (non-flowering ones if from a regal or scented-leaved pelargonium), cutting just above the third joint below the growing tip. Trim each cutting just below the lowest joint and remove the lower leaves.

Inserting the cuttings
Choose the pot size according to the number of cuttings: a 13cm (5in) pot will take up to five cuttings. Fill the pot with standard seed or cutting compost, press down firmly, and place the pot in a container of water until the compost surface becomes moist. Remove the pot and allow it to drain. Insert the cuttings, pressing them down gently to eliminate any air pockets beneath the bases of the cuttings. Do not water them yet.

Aftercare
Place the pot in a light, warm position, but not in full sun. One week after insertion, water the cuttings from below (as above). Water again a week or ten days later, by which time the cuttings should be rooting. If watered from above, the cuttings may suffer from grey mould/*Botrytis* or other damping off diseases. Do not use propagators or cover them with plastic sheeting, for the same reason. Always allow free circulation of air around them. As soon as the cuttings have rooted (when fresh leaves appear) pot them up singly into 6cm (3in) pots.

Growing F1 and F2 hybrids from seed

Seed-sown F1 and F2 hybrids are difficult for the amateur to produce as they require a specialized environment. In hot countries they will flower from seed in six months, but in colder countries it can take 15 months. To shorten this time, commercial nurseries grow on seedlings at high temperatures in artificial light for 14 hours a day over five winter months. They also treat the plants with dwarfing compounds in order to maintain a compact habit and to achieve early flowering.

Sowing the seed
Sow seed in early summer (see ANNUALS AND BIENNIALS, "Sowing in pots or trays", p.182). When the seedlings are 15cm (6in) high, pinch out the growing tips to encourage bushy growth. Grow on as cool greenhouse plants throughout the winter and spring, to flower the following summer.

OVERWINTERING

1 *Lift the plants before the first frosts and shake off any loose soil. Cut down the stems to about 10cm (4in) and remove the leaves. Trim back roots to about 5cm (2in).*

2 *Half-fill a box at least 15cm (6in) deep with seed compost. Put in the plants so that they do not touch each other. Infill with compost; then water and drain.*

3 *Store in a frost-free place until new shoots start to appear, then pot up the plants. Use the new shoots to take cuttings from, as necessary, later in spring.*

2 *Using a sharp knife, remove leaves from each cutting, leaving two at the top. Pinch out any flowers or buds.*

3 *Carefully trim the base of each cutting to just below the lowest joint with a straight cut.*

4 *Make holes 2.5cm (1in) deep in pots of moist, firmed seed or cutting compost. Insert the cuttings and firm.*

7

ANNUALS
AND BIENNIALS

ANNUALS AND BIENNIALS *are traditionally regarded as a quick and inexpensive means of achieving colour in the garden. To restrict their use in this way, however, is to overlook the vast range of foliage, fragrance, texture, and stature they have to offer. Their uses are as varied as their attributes: they can bring to life any garden within just a few months or, as cut or dried flowers, transform the home inside. Annuals and biennials also provide opportunities to experiment in the garden by altering colour schemes and effects during the season. Although short-lived, a large number of these plants flower freely over many weeks and even months. The gardener can use this profusion of colour to create infinite patterns of bedding with plants that are planned to flower in succession. While annuals and biennials are most often used to adorn beds and containers, some varieties with a trailing or climbing habit are particularly striking grown up a support or allowed to sprawl luxuriantly over a bank.*

Designing with annuals and biennials

THE term "annual" describes a plant whose entire lifecycle, from germination to seed production through to death, takes place within one year. Those that are able to withstand frost are known as hardy annuals; those that are not are known as half hardy and must be raised under glass and planted out after all danger of frost has passed.

"Biennials", however, require two growing seasons. During their first season after sowing they produce leaf growth; they then overwinter and flower in the following year.

Several tender perennials prove more vigorous and free-flowering if treated as annuals or biennials.

Annual borders

Whole borders or beds devoted to annuals produce colourful effects. Ideal in a new garden where they quickly provide a vibrant show, annuals may also be used as features in established gardens. The plants may be changed several times in a season to create different displays.

Colour effects

The most effective annual borders are often those that exploit a limited range of colours – dazzling oranges and reds, muted pinks and purples, soft blues and mauves. Plan the planting with a broad sweep of colour, selecting tones that, when adjacent, blend together harmoniously. Greys, greens, and whites are particularly useful for providing a respite from some of the more vibrant reds and blues. Many annuals, such as antirrhinums, pansies (*Viola x wittrockiana*), and petunias, are available in a range of colours, making it possible to select a particular plant whatever the colour range. A bed devoted to pure white flowers looks fresh and crisp, but green-foliaged plants prevent the planting looking cold. Creams should not be substituted for the cleaner whites.

SUMMER-FLOWERING ANNUALS
An exuberant display in a small area is created by the vivid colours of busy lizzies (Impatiens cvs), *shapely clusters of* Schizanthus, *loose masses of* Lobelia, *and petunias. Pelargoniums and fuchsias add to the richness.*

Form and texture

Border compositions are often enhanced by the leaf texture or the overall plant shape as much as by colour alone. Place plants with contrasting textures of either leaf or flower in adjacent groupings. Their differing characteristics will then be

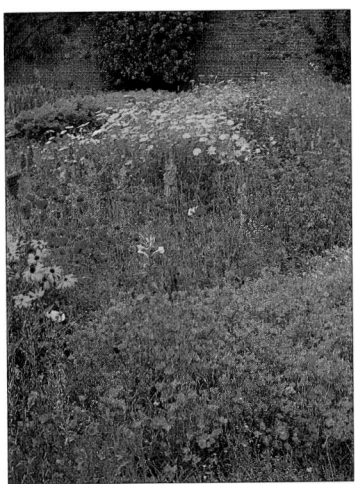

A TAPESTRY OF SUMMER COLOUR
This beautiful display of half-hardy and hardy annuals is attractively offset by the mellow tones of the mature wall in the background.

better appreciated. Form and texture of annuals are often overlooked but they add greatly to the character of a planting, whether it be with the wispy flowers of *Nigella*, the bold spikes of *Salvia*, or the sprawling informality of the poached-egg flower (*Limnanthes douglasii*). A particularly valuable plant is the ornamental maize (*Zea mays* 'Japonica Multicolor'), with its variegated leaves, plume-like flower tassels, and cobs of variously coloured seeds.

Including a variety of shapes and sizes also adds interest to the scheme. Select from, for example, the daisy-like shapes of *Gaillardia*, the golden discs of sunflowers (*Helianthus annuus*), the large bells of petunias, the feathery plumes of *Celosia cristata*, or the tiny pompons of double daisies (*Bellis perennis*) or double-flowered feverfew (*Tanacetum parthenium*, double white).

Grouping the plants
Most annuals look their best when planted in large groups of one cultivar to give a bold block of colour. Single plants can otherwise easily become isolated and weaken the structure of the planting. Sow in irregular patches so that the effect as the plants mature is similar to the interlocking drifts of flowers made by perennials in a traditional herbaceous border. The shapes and sizes of the groups should be varied to create a natural, free-flowing look.

When a border is to be viewed mainly from one direction, perhaps from a path or lawn, or is backed by a fence or hedge, graduate plants according to height. Plant the tallest plants, such as hollyhocks (*Alcea*), *Amaranthus*, and sunflowers, at the back, and naturally low-growing species such as *Ageratum*, sweet alyssum (*Lobularia maritima*), and *Phlox drummondii* to clothe the front of the border. For those that are intermediate in height, juxtapose groups of slightly different heights to achieve variation. This produces a billowing, undulating informality.

Combine plants that flourish in similar conditions. For instance, species or cultivars of *Nicotiana*, which have loose clusters of scented tubular flowers on tall stems, combine well with the low-growing, flower-covered, compact shapes of busy lizzie (*Impatiens* cvs), since both generally prefer cool and shady sites.

Foliage plants
There are several annuals grown chiefly for their foliage to harmonize or contrast with bright flower colour, and to add to the range of textures in a bed or border.

Senecio maritima with its silver-grey leaves is easily grown from seed. Although often treated as a half-hardy annual, it is in fact a perennial, and may be kept for years if it is protected from frost. A clump of castor-oil plants (*Ricinus communis*), another perennial that flourishes in cooler climates when treated as a half-hardy annual, provides an eye-catching feature, with its green or purplish-bronze leaves. The bushy, bright green, cypress-like columns of the annual *Kochia scoparia* f. *trichophylla* contrast well with colourful planting schemes, while selected cultivars of *Coleus* provide a range of foliage colour: reds and purples, yellows and greens.

Other colourful foliage plants include 'Ruby Chard' (a cultivar of *Beta vulgaris*), with its vivid red, upright stalks, and the ornamental cabbages (*Brassica oleracea* forms), which provide low-growing, muted foliage in pinks, greens, and white.

Seasonal display
Plan the planting so that the flowering periods of the annuals coincide as much as possible as this should avoid gaps appearing in the scheme. To provide interest over a long period, use annuals that bloom in succession; for specific colour combinations, make sure that the chosen plants bloom at the same time.

For a spring display choose wallflowers (*Cheiranthus*), forget-me-nots (*Myosotis*), pansies (*Viola* x *wittrockiana*), primroses (*Primula vulgaris*), and polyanthus. For summer and early autumn, the range of plants coming into flower is much greater, and the scope for creating pleasing combinations is limitless.

Petunias have been diversified so greatly that elaborate colour schemes may be created using them alone. Choose from the boldly contrasting, striped blooms, the bright, single colours, or the subtly shaded ones, using them either singly or in combination. Where possible, select hybrids that are not spoiled by rain.

Tagetes also offer a wide range of colours, from cream to deep orange to mahogany-red, and the flowerheads vary from the single daisies of

AN ANNUAL BORDER

A complete border may be devoted to annuals, biennials, and other short-lived plants. In this design, good use has been made of the different growth habits of, for example, the climbing Cobaea scandens *and the spreading sweet alyssum* (Lobularia maritima) *which softens the front of the border. The architectural foliage of the castor-oil plant,* Ricinus communis, *makes a strong focal point in contrast to the more informal flower shapes.*

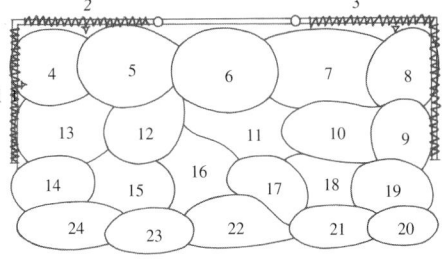

1 *Tropaeolum majus*
2 *Eccremocarpus scaber*
3 *Cobaea scandens*
4 *Chrysanthemum* 'Primrose Gem'
5 *Digitalis purpurea* f. *alba*
6 *Ricinus communis*
7 *Lavatera trimestris* 'Mont Blanc'
8 *Centaurea cyanus*
9 *Tagetes patula* 'Naughty Marietta'
10 *Salvia farinacea*
11 *Nicotiana alata* 'Lime Green'
12 *Nigella damascena* 'Miss Jekyll'
13 *Calendula* 'Orange King'
14 *Arctotis stoechadifolia* var. *grandis*
15 *Gypsophila* 'Covent Garden White'
16 *Rudbeckia* 'Marmalade'
17 *Echium* 'Blue Bedder'
18 *Eschscholzia* 'Monarch Art Shades'
19 *Dimorphotheca*, Sunshine Hybrids
20 *Lobularia maritima* 'Snow Crystal'
21 *Lobelia* 'Crystal Palace'
22 *Convolvulus* 'Royal Ensign'
23 *Tagetes* 'Golden Gem'
24 *Ageratum* 'Blue Danube'

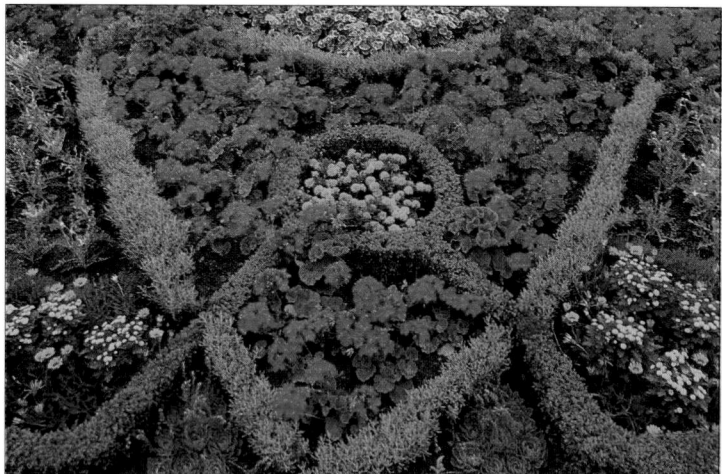

FORMAL BEDDING SCHEME
*Perfect for colouring in a pre-existing pattern, scarlet pelargoniums
and golden marigolds* (Calendula) *make vivid monochrome panels.*

A MIXED BORDER
*Annuals and biennials create a rich tapestry effect when planted among
perennials. Tall, yellow spires of biennial* Verbascum, *golden sunflowers,
and marigolds are interwoven with blue cornflowers and pink* Cosmos.

Tagetes signata to the great globes of the African cultivars. French marigolds (*Tagetes patula*), with single and double flowerheads, display rich crimson or mahogany-red colouring. Their bushy growth may be used to provide an effective display of colourful ground cover.

Formal bedding schemes

The wide variation of colour, shape, and size, as well as the uniformity of growth obtainable in many modern cultivars of annuals, provides opportunities to create long-lasting displays from spring to autumn. One of the glories of annuals is the intensity of colour achieved when a single cultivar of one of the low-growing, floriferous kinds is massed in a bed so that individual plants merge together. A scarlet carpet of pelargoniums or of *Salvia splendens*, for example, makes a vivid display when set into a fresh, green lawn. Patterned designs, using annuals of different colours, may produce similarly bold effects.

The dense growth habit and continuous flowering of many annuals make them ideal candidates for these complex, formal patterns. There is a wide range of dwarf and intermediate cultivars available. Plants may be used to add colour to designs that have been delineated with bricks, gravel, or other architectural materials.

Annuals are excellent for knots and parterres, where small evergreen plants, such as box (*Buxus*), thyme (*Thymus*), or lavender (*Lavandula*), are clipped to create permanent outlines. Vary colour schemes with the seasons: a winter planting of pansies that continues into spring may be followed by a summer one of dwarf zinnias, for example.

Alternatively, annuals, biennials, and other temporary plants can be used alone to create designs that are expressed in the use of contrasting colours and form. An outline of low, mound-forming plants in a single colour will help to define a pattern and contain the infilling plants. White always makes a crisp, clear edging – double daisies (*Bellis perennis*) in spring, sweet alyssum (*Lobularia maritima*) or white *Lobelia* in summer. The fillers may be flowers with a looser, more irregular shape, such as antirrhinums.

Mixed borders

A mixed border, containing shrubs, perennials, bulbs, and annuals, is one of the delights of the garden. With such a diversity of plants, it offers the greatest possible variety in terms of colour, texture, season of interest, and design. Annuals and biennials warrant a place in any permanent planting scheme, in which they can be sown each year or left to self seed. If allowed to self sow they will produce a random effect and a profusion of flowers reminiscent of the traditional cottage garden, where all manner of plants, including salad and vegetable crops, happily jostle for space in the same informal plot.

ANNUALS IN MIXED BORDERS

1 *Onopordum acanthium*
2 *Papaver orientale*
3 *Paeonia* 'Sarah Bernhardt'
4 *Papaver somniferum*
5 *Digitalis purpurea* cvs
6 *Bergenia cordifolia* 'Purpurea'
7 *Monarda didyma* 'Croftway Pink'
8 *Ornithogalum narbonense*
9 *Dianthus* 'Mrs Sinkins'
10 *Allium giganteum*
11 *Dicentra formosa*
12 *Viola tricolor*

In this bed, annuals (represented by grey areas on the diagram) have been planted between the perennials and bulbs to fill the gaps and provide extra interest and wonderful splashes of bright colour throughout the summer months. The sculptural, silvery-grey Scotch thistle and the tall, purple and white spikes of foxgloves appear majestically above the interlocking clumps of perennials. Bright red opium poppies punctuate the planting and, at the front of the border, the delicate Viola tricolor *sprawls out over the path. The pinkish-purple of the* Viola *complements the pink of the peony (*'Sarah Bernhardt'*), the rich purple foxgloves, and the profuse blooms of* Monarda didyma, *helping to create an integrated and effective planting scheme.*

Used as colour highlights among perennials and shrubs, annuals and biennials bring life to established borders. Possible effects range from cheerful mixtures of *Clarkia* (syn. *Godetia*), *Cosmos*, *Eschscholzia*, and corn poppies (*Papaver rhoeas*) to carefully co-ordinated toning schemes. For instance, including flowering annuals such as crimson *Amaranthus caudatus* and *Nicotiana alata*, or scarlet begonias, pelargoniums, and *Verbena* cultivars, will add highlights to a "red" border with a framework of purplish foliage.

Self-sown annuals and biennials may soon become a permanent feature in a mixed border, helping to unify the planting and introducing a pleasing unpredictability. In early summer *Nigella damascena* makes a hazy web of colour, filling gaps and weaving together neighbouring blooms and the young leaves of later-flowering plants. The spire-like stems of certain biennials such as *Verbascum* and foxgloves (*Digitalis*) add a cottage garden informality to an otherwise structured border.

Architectural plants

Handsome leaves, eye-catching flower shapes, and striking habits of growth make certain plants stand out from their companions. Annuals or biennials with such architectural qualities can be key features in a mixed border, enhancing the composition. These plants have the greatest impact when they complement – rather than dominate – the other plants in the vicinity. The large, spiny, grey leaves and tall, widely branched flower stems of the Scotch thistle (*Onopordum acanthium*), for instance, make a statuesque centrepiece in a border that features other types of silver-foliaged plants. The flower spikes of the Excelsior Series foxgloves and larkspur (*Consolida*) rise gracefully above all the neighbouring plants. Shapely blooms, such as those of *Cleome*, will also command attention.

Plants grown primarily for their foliage also play an architectural role. In large borders the green or purple, palmate leaves of castor-oil plants (*Ricinus communis*) add a strong textural quality, as do the bold leaves of the ornamental cabbages (*Brassica oleracea* forms).

Annuals and biennials as fillers

As they grow rapidly and are relatively cheap to raise, use annuals and biennials to fill gaps that occur, either through failure of a plant or between immature perennials and recently planted shrubs in a new border. Sow seed where the plants are to flower, choosing cultivars in a height and colour range to suit the permanent planting scheme.

At the end of the season, plant wallflowers (*Cheiranthus*) in the same gaps for their winter foliage and spring flowers. Multicoloured carpets of winter-flowering pansies (*Viola* x *wittrockiana*), primroses (*Primula vulgaris*), or polyanthus may be interplanted with spring-flowering bulbs, such as daffodils, hyacinths, or late-flowering tulips.

Until alpines become established, gaps in the rock garden may be filled by sun-loving annuals that enjoy the same conditions. To avoid overwhelming their delicate colours and modest stature, however, choose annuals that are on a similar scale, such as *Viola tricolor*, *Lobelia erinus*, and *Portulaca*.

Annuals and biennials for ground cover

Some annuals and biennials may be used as temporary ground cover, creating pools of colour in an otherwise bare space. There are annuals to suit shade as well as sun, poor soil as well as rich. Single-colour cultivars of sweet alyssum (*Lobularia maritima*) or annual candytufts (*Iberis*) may be used to provide dense cover in a sunny spot or busy lizzies (*Impatiens* cvs) in shade, where their spreading growth and colourful, continuous blooms will quickly cover bare ground. For a more textured quality as well as lively colour, sow corn poppies or *Eschscholzia*; both spread quickly. Attractive ground cover is also swiftly created by using cultivars of *Convolvulus tricolor* in blue, purple, or rose, or nasturtiums in red, orange, and yellow, some with variegated leaves.

Climbers and trailers

Vigorous annuals and biennials that climb and trail quickly may transform an expanse of wall or fence with a colourful curtain of foliage and flower, weaving a screen to provide privacy, or embellishing an existing structure. Many annuals have attractive leaves as well as beautiful flowers, and a few, for example sweet peas (*Lathyrus odoratus*), offer the additional pleasure of scent (see SWEET PEAS, pp.178–9).

Plants with a climbing or trailing habit are particularly valuable in restricted spaces such as patios and balconies, where they make use of the vertical space as well as the ground area. Moreover, many annual climbers can be grown in pots, and are ideal for furnishing new gardens, softening bleak surfaces, and disguising or distracting from an unsightly view.

Exuberant climbers that twine around and clothe arches, pergolas, and other architectural features, such as *Ipomoea* and twining cultivars of nasturtium, or half-hardy perennials such as *Cobaea scandens* with its large bell-shaped flowers in purple or greenish-white, may be used to provide an abundance of summer flower in company with more permanent perennial climbers. To create decorative effects quickly, grow *Thunbergia alata* or *Rhodochiton atrosanguineum*, an intriguing plant with curious, deep purple, tubular flowers in dusky maroon calyces.

Climbing annuals are also effective when grown through host plants, such as ivy (*Hedera*) or conifers. Use the twining annual *Tropaeolum peregrinum*, which has pale green, broadly lobed leaves and bright yellow, fringed flowers. Another good choice is the half-hardy *Eccremocarpus scaber*, which climbs by means of tendrils and has a long flowering season, with clusters of tubular flowers that glow yellow, orange, or red among small, tooth-shaped, pinnate leaves. For a dense,

ANNUALS TO TRAIL
With its tumbling form, shapely leaves, and long-lasting, attractive double flowers, this annual nasturtium, Tropaeolum 'Hermine Grasshof', *needs no companion plants to make a vivid and striking focal point in a decorative terracotta pot.*

GROUND-COVER ANNUALS
Busy lizzies (Impatiens *cvs) in contrasting tones form a carpet of intense colour in the cool shade under trees or shrubs.*

leafy screen, plant scarlet runner beans (*Phaseolus coccineus*), which have delicate, scarlet flowers, and the bonus of edible pods.

Annuals in containers

Whether it is a pot, tub, or windowbox, any container is a potential focal point in the garden, and the plants grown in it can make an eye-catching feature. F1 and F2 hybrid annuals, with their even growth habit and consistent flower colours, are specifically bred to provide uniform, long-lasting displays. Most annuals, however, may be used in containers, either on their own or to complement other plants.

The shape, style, and material of the container may be chosen to play a major part in the display or it may be completely subordinate to the planting. A shapely urn or a handsome stone trough may be veiled by wisps of foliage, while a more functional container may be disguised with trailing leaves and flowers.

Increasing the range
The range of annuals suitable for containers or patio beds close to the house may be greater than that in the open garden, as the protection of adjacent buildings often enables plants to be grown that are normally too tender for more exposed sites in the same area. Consider how sunny, shady, or windy the site is before deciding which plants to grow.

Annuals are available for a year-round display. In spring and early summer, winter-flowering pansies, primroses, and polyanthus cultivars continue to provide colour as they thrive in sheltered spots. Protected but sunny sites on patios are also

WINDOWBOX COMPOSITIONS
This restrained cream, blue, and green colouring mixes begonias and pansies with trailing Lobelia, ivy, *and* Lysimachia nummularia.

ideal for petunias, gazanias, zinnias, and busy lizzies (*Impatiens* cvs), which maintain their colour throughout the summer.

Selecting cultivars
Cultivars of compact habit are particularly useful as they will better withstand windy sites and will not need any form of support. Choose dwarf and intermediate antirrhinum cultivars rather than tall ones, and dwarf or multiflowered bedding pelargoniums. Ivy-leaved pelargoniums, which have a long flowering season, may be raised from seed and grown as half-hardy annuals, while new hybrids that are intermediate in habit between the trailing and the bushy pelargoniums, including the Sensation, Breakaway, and Multibloom Series, have been bred specially for production from seed and are ideal for growing in most containers.

Gazanias grow well in hanging baskets and containers positioned in unshaded spots where they open their brightly coloured flowerheads in full sun. Heliotrope is valuable around the house in containers near a window or doorway, where its perfume can be appreciated. Stocks (*Matthiola*) have similar qualities of beauty and scent, particularly the Ten-week Series in summer and the East Lothian and Brompton Series in both autumn and spring.

Hanging baskets and windowboxes
Plants with a trailing habit are ideal for growing in windowboxes and hanging baskets, and effective displays may be created by a mass of foliage and flower. Reliable

performers include sprawling petunias, trailing *Lobelia erinus* such as the Cascade Series, and *Verbena* x *hybrida* cultivars, which are available in a wide range of colours, including pure reds and scarlets as well as deep purples, crimsons, and whites. Trailing and spreading F1 and F2 pelargoniums, renewed annually from seed, are also good value (see PELARGONIUMS, pp.170–71).

Annuals for cutting and drying

Many annuals can provide excellent cut flowers for the house. If space is available in your garden, it is worth growing a number of flowers especially for cutting. They may be either integrated into borders or sown in a separate area. Taller cultivars may be particularly suitable; choose from antirrhinums, cornflowers (*Centaurea cyanus*), stocks, and *Gypsophila*. Sweet peas (*Lathyrus odoratus*) are particularly good as cut flowers and fill the house with their heady fragrance; if the flowers are cut regularly the plants will continue to bloom for many weeks. Larkspur (*Consolida*) is also useful for cutting and is equally attractive whether fresh or dried.

Many annuals may be grown to dry as "everlasting" flowers for decoration indoors throughout the year; they include *Helichrysum*, *Limonium*, and *Amaranthus caudatus*. Others such as honesty (*Lunaria*) and *Nigella* are grown for their decorative seedheads. Annual grasses, such as *Panicum capillare*, are also worth growing for their feathery seedheads.

PLANTING IN THE VERTICAL PLANE
Hanging baskets and windowboxes transform a bare wall. Trailing plants such as ivy-leaved pelargoniums reach down to meet upright, bushy annuals, making a continuous curtain of colour.

Planter's guide to annuals and biennials

EXPOSED SITES

Annuals and biennials that tolerate exposed or windy sites

Borago officinalis
Calendula
Centaurea cyanus
Cheiranthus
Chrysanthemum carinatum,
    C. coronarium, C. segetum
Clarkia
Dianthus barbatus, D. chinensis
Echium vulgare
Eschscholzia
Glaucium flavum
Iberis amara, I. umbellata
Lavatera trimestris
Limnanthes
Linum grandiflorum
Lobularia maritima
Lunaria
Malcolmia
Malope trifida
Oenothera biennis
Papaver rhoeas, P. somniferum
Petunia ✤
Rudbeckia hirta (hybrids)

Rudbeckia hirta

Salvia horminum
Tagetes signata ✤
Vaccaria hispanica

DRY SHADE

Annuals and biennials that tolerate dry shade

Digitalis purpurea
Matthiola bicornis

MOIST SHADE

Annuals and biennials that prefer moist shade

Impatiens walleriana ✤
Matthiola bicornis
Mimulus – seed selections including:
    M., Calypso Series ✤
    M., Malibu Series ✤
Oenothera biennis
Primula vulgaris
Viola x *wittrockiana*

FRAGRANT FLOWERS

Centaurea moschata
Dianthus, Giant Chabaud Series,
    D. chinensis
Exacum affine ✤
Heliotropium, some ✤
Humea elegans ✤
Lathyrus odoratus
Lobularia maritima

Matthiola, Brompton Series,
    M., East Lothian Series,
    M., Ten-week Series
Nicotiana alata ✤, *N.* x *sanderae* ✤
    (some cvs)
Primula, some ✤
Reseda odorata
Viola x *wittrockiana*

FLOWERS FOR CUTTING

Agrostemma githago 'Milas'
Antirrhinum ✤ (tall cvs)
Calendula
Callistephus ✤ (tall cvs)
Centaurea cyanus
Cheiranthus cheiri
Chrysanthemum carinatum ✤,
    C. coronarium, C. segetum
Consolida ambigua
Coreopsis Series
Cosmos ✤
Dianthus barbatus,
    D., Giant Chabaud Series,
    D., Knight Series
Gaillardia pulchella
Gilia capitata
Gomphrena globosa ✤
Gypsophila elegans
Helianthus annuus,
    H., Colour Fashion Series
Helipterum ✤
Lathyrus odoratus
Limonium sinuatum ✤
Lunaria annua
Matthiola, Brompton Series,
    M., East Lothian Series,
    M. incana, M., Ten-week Series
Moluccella laevis ✤
Nigella damascena
Papaver nudicaule, P., Summer
    Breeze Series
Psylliostachys suworowii ✤
Rudbeckia hirta (hybrids)
Salvia horminum
Xeranthemum annuum ✤
Zinnia ✤

FLOWERS FOR DRYING

Ageratum ✤
Amaranthus ✤
Avena sterilis
Briza maxima, B. minor
Calendula
Celosia ✤
Centaurea cyanus
Clarkia
Consolida ambigua
Gomphrena globosa ✤
Helipterum ✤
Hordeum jubatum
Lagurus ovatus
Limonium sinuatum ✤
Lonas ✤
Moluccella laevis ✤
Nigella

Panicum violaceum
Pennisetum villosum
Salvia horminum
Setaria glauca ✤
Stipa pennata

ARCHITECTURAL PLANTS

Alcea rosea, syn. *Althaea rosea*
Amaranthus caudatus ✤,
    A. tricolor ✤
Brassica oleracea 'Cabbage
    Cherry Sundae' (F1),
    B.o. 'Kale Red and White
    Peacock' (F1)
Cleome hassleriana ✤
Digitalis purpurea
Helianthus annuus

Helianthus annuus

Kochia scoparia f. *trichophylla* ✤
Onopordum acanthium
Ricinus communis ✤
Salvia sclarea var. *turkestanica*
Silybum marianum
Verbascum bombyciferum,
    V. densiflorum
Zea mays 'Gracillima Variegata' ✤,
    Z. m. 'Japonica Multicolor' ✤

TRAILING PLANTS FOR CONTAINERS

Ageratum ✤
Arctotis stoechadifolia ✤
Begonia semperflorens ✤,
    B. 'Non-Stop' ✤
Bidens ferulifolia ✤
Brachycome iberidifolia
Convolvulus tricolor
Gazania ✤
Heliotropium, some ✤
Impatiens walleriana ✤
Lobelia erinus ✤
Osteospermum 'Starshine' (and
    other seed selections) ✤
Pelargonium 'Breakaway' ✤,
    P. 'Multibloom' ✤,
    P. 'Sensation' ✤, *P.* 'Summer
    Showers' ✤ (and other F1 and
    F2 Series)
Petunia ✤
Senecio ✤
Tropaeolum majus (semi-trailing
    cvs), *T. m.* 'Empress of India',
    T. m., Gleam Series,
    T. m., Whirlybird Series
Verbena x *hybrida* ✤
Viola x *wittrockiana*

ANNUAL CLIMBERS
See list on p.99.

POT PLANTS

Annuals suitable for growing from seed as (greenhouse) pot plants

Antirrhinum, some ✤
Begonia semperflorens ✤
Campanula pyramidalis ✤
Capsicum ✤ (ornamental fruit cvs)
Centaurea moschata
Coleus ✤
Exacum affine ✤
Humea elegans ✤
Impatiens walleriana ✤ (tall cvs)
Osteospermum ✤
Pelargonium ✤ (F1 and F2 hybrids)
Petunia ✤
Primula malacoides ✤,
    P. obconica ✤, *P. sinensis* ✤
Psylliostachys suworowii ✤
Salpiglossis ✤
Schizanthus ✤
Senecio x *hybridus* ✤ (cvs)
Thunbergia alata ✤
Torenia fournieri ✤
Trachelium caeruleum ✤
Trachymene coerulea, syn.
    Didiscus coeruleus ✤

PERENNIALS THAT MAY BE GROWN AS ANNUALS

Antirrhinum, some ✤
Argemone mexicana ✤

Antirrhinum majus,
Princess Series

Begonia semperflorens ✤
Browallia speciosa ✤
Cobaea scandens ✤
Coleus ✤
Coreopsis, Early Sunrise Series
Eccremocarpus scaber ✤
Gazania ✤
Gomphrena globosa ✤
Heliotropium arborescens ✤
Hesperis matronalis
Impatiens walleriana ✤
Mimulus, Malibu Series ✤ (and other
    seed selections)
Nierembergia rivularis ✤
Pelargonium ✤ (all F1 and F2 seed
    selections)
Ricinus communis ✤
Salvia farinacea ✤, *S. splendens* ✤
Senecio cineraria ✤
Verbena x *hybrida* ✤

KEY
✤ Not hardy

Sweet peas

Sweet peas (*Lathyrus odoratus*) have been dubbed "the queen of annuals" for their beautiful flowers, marvellous scent, and long flowering period. Trained up wigwams, pillars, or canes, they provide long and colourful displays. Grow them among perennials or shrubs or as a decorative contribution to the vegetable garden or potager.

Types of sweet pea

Most familiar are the Spencer and Grandiflora cultivars, which climb a supporting framework by means of leaf tendrils. The large-flowered Spencer cultivars may grow 2–3m (6–10ft) high depending on growing conditions; Grandiflora cultivars have smaller, "old-fashioned" flowers but they are more highly scented.

OLD-FASHIONED SWEET PEAS

Old-fashioned sweet peas are closer to the species than most of the modern cultivars. They have delicately coloured, small, highly scented flowers.

DWARF SWEET PEAS

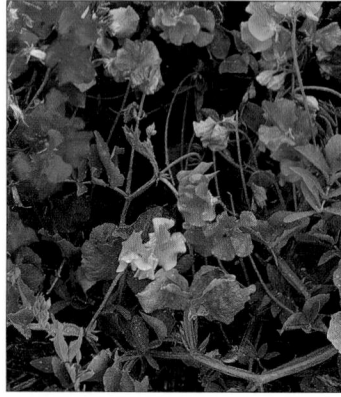

These sweet peas grow to about 90cm (3ft) high and need little or no support. They are ideal for a colourful border display or for planting in tubs.

Hedge cultivars grow to about 90cm (3ft); these include Jet Set Series and 'Knee-Hi'. Dwarf types such as Snoopy Series (with no tendrils) and 'Bijou' grow well in hanging baskets, containers, and windowboxes.

Growing sweet peas from seed

Seeds may be sown in mid-autumn in fairly mild districts, or in late winter or early spring where winters are colder. The process is identical in both cases. Protect seedlings and plants from being eaten by mice.

Sowing

Sweet pea seeds vary in colour from pale buff to black. To help them germinate, nick the darker seeds with a sharp penknife, removing a small piece of seed coat opposite the eye. Do not soak sweet pea seeds as they are susceptible to rotting. Treat with a little fungicidal seed dressing.

Sow in seed trays, root trainers, pots (one, two, or three seeds per pot), or in special sweet pea tubes, 5cm (2in) in diameter and 15cm (6in) deep. Use a soil-less potting compost with 20 per cent grit added or a standard seed compost.

Dark seeds germinate well in fairly damp compost, but pale ones require a compost that is only just moist. Cover the containers with glass and keep them at about 15°C (59°F). When the seedlings appear, transfer them to a cold frame.

Potting on

Seeds sown in trays need pricking out and potting on individually when plants are about 3.5cm (1½in) high. Fill 6cm (3in) pots, or sweet pea tubes, with a similar compost to that used for sowing. Pinch out the root tips and then repot.

Pinch out the growing tips of autumn-sown plants when they are 10cm (4in) high. Stop spring-sown seedlings at the first pair of leaves.

Overwintering autumn-sown plants

Keep the cold frame open as much as possible, during slight frosts, to harden off the plants. In heavier frosts below -2°C (28°F) close the frame and insulate it with matting. Keep the lights on the frame propped open in heavy rain for ventilation. Control aphids (p.550) and give a dilute liquid feed in late winter.

BUSH SWEET PEAS

PEASTICK SUPPORTS
Peasticks are the traditional means of supporting sweet peas. Insert the peasticks when the seedlings are planted out, leaning the sticks in towards the centre of the clump for extra stability.

WIRE RINGS
Bush sweet peas may be grown up wire rings anchored with several bamboo canes. The plants will grow through the wire, hiding their supports.

WIGWAM
A wigwam of canes secured near the top also provides a sturdy support. One seedling beside each cane is usually enough to provide a dense mass of flowers.

Hardening off spring-sown plants

This demands more care as the plants are smaller and growth is softer than on autumn-sown plants. Keep the cold frame well ventilated, but close the lights if frost threatens and protect well with some matting during any very hard frosts.

Planting

Sweet peas thrive in sunny, open sites and well-drained, humus-rich soil (see "Soil structure and water content", p.526). Three weeks prior to planting, carefully rake in a balanced fertilizer at a rate of 85g/sq m (3oz/sq yd). For the best results, trench or double dig the ground in autumn (see "Double digging", p.526). Add well-rotted manure to the lower spit.

Plant out autumn-sown sweet peas in mid-spring, spring-sown ones in late spring. Set plants 23cm (9in) apart just behind and to one side of their support, with the bottom shoot level with the soil. Water during dry spells and when flower buds appear. Apply liquid feed two or three times at fortnightly intervals from mid-summer onwards. Dead-head plants to encourage continuous flowering.

INITIAL TRAINING OF CORDONS

1 *After fixing the wires and posts, insert 2.2m (7ft) tall canes 23cm (9in) apart at a slight angle along the row and attach them to the wires using "V" clips.*

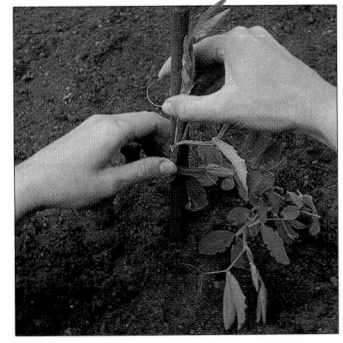

2 *About 2 weeks after planting the young sweet peas, select the strongest shoot of each plant and attach it to the cane with a wire ring loosely fastened beneath a leaf node.*

3 *At the same time, pinch or cut out all the other sideshoots to concentrate the vigour into the main shoot.*

4 *Keep pinching out any sideshoots or tendrils that form and any flower stems carrying less than 4 buds.*

Bush sweet peas

Sweet peas are usually allowed to develop naturally into bushes. Support the plants with peasticks, canes, trellis, or netting. Canes and sticks may be grouped in circles, wigwam-style, or arranged in rows. A double row of peasticks and canes must be well supported, preferably with a post at each end and a strainer wire. Loosely tie young plants to their supports with wire rings; thereafter they need little tying in. Sideshoots are left to grow, producing more flowers on short stems.

Cordon sweet peas

Sweet peas trained into cordons produce top-quality flowers so are usually grown in this way by exhibitors.

Providing supports

At each end of a row, drive in a post with a 45cm (18in) cross-piece near the top, set at 2m (6ft) above ground level. Stretch two parallel wires between the cross-pieces. Place 2.2m (7ft) canes, spaced 23cm (9in) apart, at a slight angle against the wires and secure them with "V" clips. Rows should run north to south to expose plants evenly to sunlight.

Initial training

Leave plants to establish for two weeks. Then pinch out the weaker shoots to leave the strongest shoot on each plant (this may not be the longest, which is often straggly). Train the shoot up the cane, tying it with raffia, tape, or rings at each node. Remove sideshoots and tendrils as they grow. When flower stems form, remove any with fewer than four buds. Sudden weather changes may cause buds to drop.

Layering

When plants reach the top wire, they should be untied and trained up a new cane further along the row (see *Layering Cordons*). Do this on a warm day when plants are not too sappy. They will then continue to grow and flower for several weeks.

LAYERING CORDONS

1 *When the sweet peas have reached a height of 1.2–1.5m (4–5ft), or the top of the canes, they are ready to be layered. This will give them more space to continue growing and flowering.*

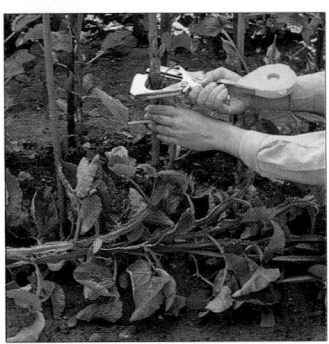

2 *Carefully untie the plants from their canes and lay them on the ground to their full length. If the plants are in double rows, do this for one row at a time.*

3 *Attach the shoot tip to a new cane further along the row, so that it reaches 30cm (1ft) up the cane. Work along the row until all the plants are fixed to new canes.*

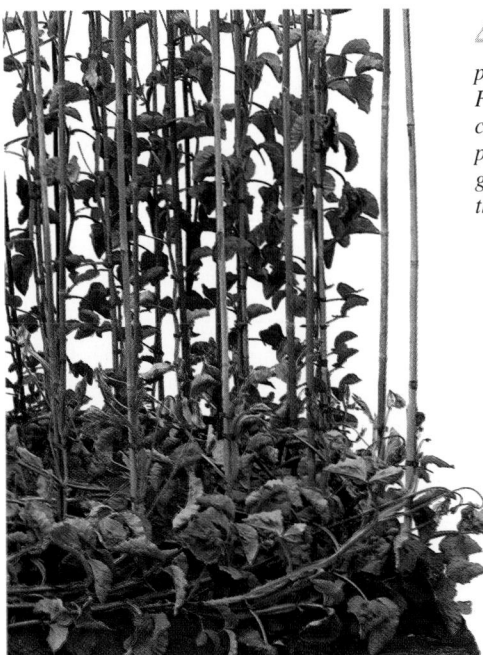

4 *Repeat for the second row of plants, if required. Flowers will then continue to be produced on the new growth stimulated by the layering method.*

Sowing and planting

ANNUALS AND BIENNIALS THAT PREFER SANDY SOIL

Anchusa capensis
Argemone mexicana ❀
Brachycome iberidifolia
Calendula officinalis
Centaurea cyanus
Chrysanthemum segetum
Clarkia amoena
Coreopsis tinctoria
Eschscholzia californica
Glaucium flavum
Helichrysum bracteatum ❀
Impatiens, some ❀
Lavatera trimestris
Limnanthes douglasii
Limonium sinuatum ❀
Linaria maroccana
Lobularia maritima
Mentzelia lindleyi
Oenothera biennis

Papaver rhoeas,
Shirley Series

Papaver rhoeas, Shirley Series,
  P. somniferum
Portulaca grandiflora ❀
Rudbeckia hirta
Schizanthus ❀
Tagetes ❀
Tropaeolum majus
Verbascum bombyciferum
Verbena x *hybrida* ❀

ANNUALS AND BIENNIALS THAT TOLERATE VERY ALKALINE SOIL

Ageratum houstonianum ❀
Antirrhinum majus ❀
Calendula officinalis
Callistephus chinensis ❀
Cheiranthus cheiri
Cosmos
Dianthus, some ❀
Gomphrena globosa ❀
Humea elegans ❀
Lavatera trimestris

*Lavatera
trimestris
'Silver Cup'*

Limonium sinuatum ❀
Lobularia maritima
Matthiola, Brompton Series,
  M. incana
Salvia horminum
Tagetes ❀
Tropaeolum, some ❀
Ursinia anthemoides ❀
Xeranthemum annuum ❀
Zinnia ❀

KEY
❀ *Not hardy*

A
NNUALS and biennials are among the easiest of plants to raise from seed. They may also be obtained as seedlings or young plants from nurseries or garden centres, and will provide an instant display of colour in a garden border or container placed indoors or outside.

Buying seeds

Always buy fresh seeds that have been stored in cool conditions. The viability of seeds of different species varies greatly; while some, such as Leguminosae, may remain viable for a few years if kept cool and dry, most start to deteriorate after a year, especially if they are stored in damp, warm conditions. Seeds in sealed foil packets last for several years; once the packets are opened, however, the seed deteriorates.

F1 and F2 hybrid seeds are available for many annuals and some biennials; these produce plants that are vigorous and true to type with even growth and flower characteristics. These seeds are ideal for the gardener seeking uniformity, but for most ordinary garden purposes well-produced, open-pollinated seeds are equally satisfactory and provide some variation in the plants.

Pelleted and primed seeds

Seeds may be individually coated with a paste, or pelleted, to form a smooth ball. This enables them to be handled separately, so that they may be more easily spaced in containers or the open ground. If pelleted seeds are space-sown at the correct distance for the cultivar concerned they need not be thinned so, although they cost more, fewer are required. The seeds should be watered thoroughly after sowing to ensure that the moisture needed for germination to occur penetrates the seed coat as quickly as possible. Pelleted seeds are normally only available for F1 and F2 hybrids.

Primed seeds have been treated so that they are ready to germinate as soon as they are sown. They are particularly useful for species and cultivars that do not germinate easily.

Seed tapes and gels

Seed tapes are tissue-like, soluble strips with evenly spaced seeds embedded within them. The tapes are laid at the base of a drill, then covered with a thin layer of soil. Gel kits may be purchased for fluid sowing – seeds are added to a paste so that

they are suspended and therefore evenly spaced throughout. The mixture is then squeezed along a pre-prepared drill. It is important not to allow the mixture to dry out. Both these methods distribute the seeds evenly so that less thinning is required than for hand-sown seeds.

Buying small seedlings

Seeds of some plants that germinate less readily are available from some seed firms at the chitting stage – when the seed coat has burst open and roots and seed leaves are starting to emerge. The seeds are usually sown on agar jelly and despatched in a sealed plastic container. Healthy seedlings should have fresh, moist roots and seed leaves; reject any that have pale green leaves or are overcrowded. The jelly contains sufficient food and moisture to sustain them for a few days but the germinating seeds should be transferred to the required growing conditions as soon as possible so that the seedlings have sufficient light to develop.

Seedlings of selected cultivars may be purchased when they have developed at least one pair of true leaves and are ready for pricking out (see p.183). This is useful for plants with very small seeds, such as begonias, which are difficult for many gardeners to germinate successfully. They are sent out in a small plastic

PURCHASING SEEDS AND SEEDLINGS

SEED TAPES

SEED GEL

SEEDLING PLUG

tub to keep them as fresh as possible. If pricked out to 4–5cm (1½–2in) apart within 24 hours of arrival they will usually grow as well as plants from home-germinated seeds.

Small seedlings already well established in wedges or plugs of compost are also available, ready for potting up individually in small pots or for planting in compartmented trays. They should be grown on in an unheated greenhouse or frame, or on a sunny windowsill, until they are at the planting out stage. They are much cheaper than bedding plants.

Sowing

When and where to sow annuals and biennials depends on when they are required to flower and the temperature they need for germination.

Hardy annuals

Sow hardy annuals where they are to flower when the soil has warmed up to at least 7°C (45°F) in the spring. If sown in successive batches until midsummer, hardy annuals provide a long summer display.

Some hardy annuals, if sown *in situ* in the autumn, germinate to produce small plants that overwinter satisfactorily outdoors and flower in late spring or early summer the following year. Candytuft (*Iberis*), marigolds (*Calendula*), and poppies (*Papaver*) are some examples.

Seeds of hardy annuals may also be sown in pots or seed trays and either planted out in their final flowering positions in late autumn or overwintered in a cold frame to be planted out in spring. This is a useful practice in gardens with clay soil that is slow to warm up in spring.

Hardy biennials

Most hardy biennials may be sown outdoors from late spring until midsummer. The optimum time varies

---

Hardy and half-hardy annuals and biennials

Annuals complete their lifecycle in a year, while biennials require two years. Horticulturally, annuals and biennials are termed hardy or half hardy. Hardy annuals are resistant to frosts and so may be sown early in open ground and will be established before more frost-prone annuals. Half-hardy annuals withstand only a limited amount of cold and are killed or badly damaged at freezing temperatures; they need to be maintained in frost-free conditions of 13–21°C (55–70°F) in order to germinate and establish.

Hardy biennials should be sown by mid-summer to allow the plants to become well established by the winter. Overwinter half-hardy biennials in a cool greenhouse or insulated cold frame.

according to what is being grown: forget-me-nots (*Myosotis*) grow rapidly so should not be sown until mid-summer, while Canterbury bells (*Campanula medium*) need longer to develop and should be sown in late spring or early summer.

The young plants may be transplanted to their final flowering position in autumn or, if they are not crowded, the following spring. Premature flowering before winter reduces the spring display, so pinch out any flower buds that form during the first season.

Half-hardy annuals and biennials

In cold regions, sow seed of half-hardy annuals in containers during spring in a temperature of 13–21°C (55–70°F), according to the particular genus. Half-hardy biennials may be sown under the same conditions in mid-summer. In warmer climates, sow half-hardy annuals and biennials directly outside once the soil temperature reaches the optimum for germination.

Frost-tender perennials, for example busy lizzies (*Impatiens* cvs), gazanias, and some *Lobelia* species, may be raised from seed in the same way as half-hardy annuals. Other tender perennials (such as *Argyranthemum* and *Osteospermum*) may be treated as half-hardy biennials: propagate by cuttings taken in autumn, overwinter them in frost-free conditions, then plant them out in late spring to bloom throughout the summer (see PERENNIALS, "Stem tip cuttings", p.166).

Sowing in open ground

There are two main methods of sowing outdoors *in situ*: broadcast and in drills. For both, a seedbed should be prepared first. Dig over the soil to one spade's depth, then rake over the area and firm. Do not sow in soil that is too rich since this encourages leaf growth at the expense of flower production. In soils lacking nutrients, however, a dressing of 70g/sq m (2oz/sq yd) of a balanced fertilizer may be forked in prior to sowing (see "Soil nutrients and fertilizers", p.530–31).

Before sowing a border, prepare a plan showing the position of each cultivar, using any areas likely to be shaded to grow those that are shade-tolerant. Mark the area for each cultivar with grit or a cane so that it is easy to check the balance of colours, heights, and habits of each of the different plants to be used before sowing the seed.

MARKING OUT ANNUAL BORDERS

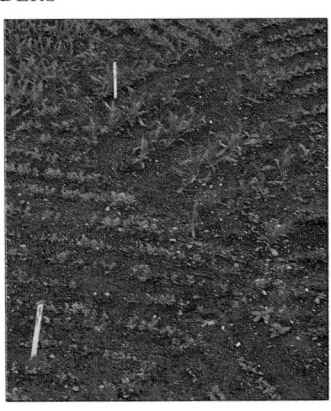

1 *Sprinkle grit or sand on the soil or score the soil with a stick to mark out interlocking areas for sowing seeds.*

2 *The seedlings may appear too sparse at first but will blend together as they grow.*

Sowing broadcast

This method is particularly suitable for annuals that produce deep tap roots such as *Clarkia*, *Gypsophila*, and poppies (*Papaver*), as they are best sown where they are to flower since they do not transplant readily. Sprinkle seeds thinly and evenly on the surface of the prepared seedbed and rake them in lightly. Label, then water the area with a watering can fitted with a fine rose.

Sowing in drills

Seeds sown in drills produce seedlings growing in straight rows at regular intervals so they are readily distinguished from weed seedlings, which are randomly distributed. The seedlings initially look regimented but, once thinned, will form a dense and informal planting.

Using either a trowel tip or the corner of a hoe, mark out shallow drills 8–15cm (3–6in) apart depending on

SOWING SEED BROADCAST

1 *Prepare the soil by raking to produce a fine tilth. Scatter the seeds thinly over the prepared area by hand or from the packet.*

2 *Rake over the area lightly at right angles to cover the seeds so that they are disturbed as little as possible.*

SOWING IN DRILLS

1 *Using a line of string as a guide, make a furrow about 2.5cm (1in) deep with a hoe.*

2 *Holding the seeds in one hand, pick up several at a time and scatter them evenly along the drill.*

ALTERNATIVE STEP

If the seeds are pelleted, place them individually in the base of the drill.

3 *Rake the soil back over the drill without dislodging the seeds. After labelling the row, water the soil using a fine rose.*

THINNING SEEDLINGS

INDIVIDUAL SEEDLINGS
Press on either side of the seedling to be retained (here larkspur, Consolida ambigua) *while pulling out the unwanted ones around it. Refirm and water.*

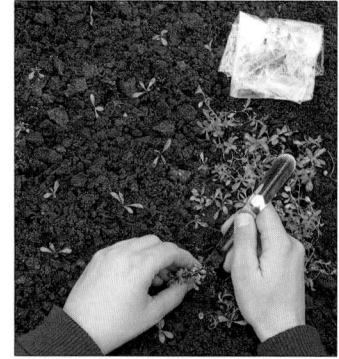

SEEDLING GROUPS
Lift groups of seedlings (here sweet William, Dianthus barbatus) *with plenty of soil around the roots if they are to be replanted. Firm in the remaining seedlings.*

the ultimate size of the plants. Sow seeds thinly and evenly by sprinkling or placing them along each drill at the appropriate depth for the annuals being sown, then carefully draw back the displaced soil with a rake or hoe to cover them. Label each row and water well with a watering can fitted with a fine rose.

Thinning
To prevent overcrowding, the seedlings usually need to be thinned. Do this when the soil is moist and the weather mild, taking care to retain the sturdier seedlings where possible and achieve an even spacing. To minimize disturbance to a seedling being retained, press the soil around it with your fingers as the surplus seedlings are extracted.

If seedlings are very dense, dig them up in clumps, retaining plenty of soil around the roots; disturb as little as possible the other seedlings in the ground. Some biennials such as forget-me-nots (*Myosotis*) and honesty (*Lunaria*) germinate readily and if sown where they are to flower should be thinned appropriately – forget-me-nots to 15cm (6in) and honesty to 30cm (12in), for example.

The thinnings may be used to fill sparse areas caused by uneven sowing or irregular germination, or may be transplanted for use elsewhere in the garden. For transplanting, select the strongest and healthiest among the thinned seedlings, then replant them where needed at the appropriate spacings and water them lightly to settle their roots.

Many annuals and biennials scatter their seeds freely, often producing dense clumps of seedlings; these need to be thinned carefully to the appropriate distances apart, so that the young plants retained may develop without competition.

Sowing in pots or trays

Half-hardy annuals are usually sown in containers so that they may develop under cover and be planted out as young plants when conditions are favourable. Hardy annuals may also be sown in containers left outside, and the seedlings transplanted to their flowering positions when there is sufficient room.

Pots, seed pans, seed trays, and packs are all suitable containers, depending on the number of seeds to be sown and the space they require. Degradable pots are also useful for seedlings that do not transplant well as the whole pot may be planted out without disturbing the roots.

Sowing the seeds
Fill the chosen container to its rim with standard seed compost and press in lightly around the edges with the fingertips to make sure that there are no air pockets. To settle the compost, tap the container against a hard surface and then gently firm the compost level so that the top of the compost is just below the rim of the container. Water with a fine rose and leave for an hour or so to drain.

Sow the seeds thinly on the surface of the compost, tapping them from the seed packet or from a sheath of paper to achieve an even spread. Large or pelleted seeds may be sown individually in compartmented packs or spaced out in trays or pans. Very small seeds are easier to sow if they are mixed first with the same bulk of fine sand; this produces a more even distribution.

Cover the seeds to about their own depth with sieved compost; then water lightly, so as not to disturb the seeds or the surface of the compost. Dust-like seeds, such as those of begonia, should be left uncovered and watered from below: place each container up to its rim in water until the surface of the compost is moist. Do not leave them soaking for too long since waterlogging may cause the seeds to rot before germination or encourage seedling diseases (see "Damping off", p.564).

To maintain even humidity place a piece of glass or clear plastic sheeting over the container; do not

Protecting and supporting seedlings

Support is required for slender-stemmed or tall annuals. Carefully insert peasticks or thin twigs into the soil around young plants; the supports should be slightly shorter than the ultimate height of the plants so that they will be concealed when the plants reach their mature size. These supports will also help protect the seedlings from possible rodent and bird damage.

Alternatively, stretch wire netting, with a mesh no greater than 2.5cm (1in), over the seedbed, bending it down at the edges so it does not touch the seedlings. Secure firmly in the soil, using a stick or wire pin. The plants grow up through the mesh and cover the netting when fully grown.

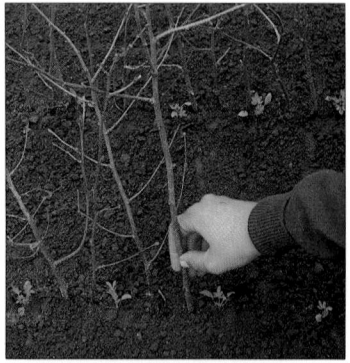

SUPPORTING WITH TWIGS
Peasticks or thin twigs may be pushed into the soil among the seedlings. Tall annuals (here larkspur, Consolida ambigua) *grow to hide the support.*

WIRE PROTECTION AND SUPPORT
Protect seedlings (here Eschscholzia) *with mesh wire netting bent to form a cage. The netting will support the seedlings as they grow through.*

SOWING IN A TRAY

1 Fill the seed tray with a standard seed compost and level with a presser board to 1cm (¹/₂in) below the rim.

2 Sprinkle the seeds thinly over the surface of the compost to achieve an even covering.

3 Cover the seeds with a layer of sieved, moist compost to about the same thickness as the seeds themselves. Water the seeds in lightly.

4 Place a piece of glass or clear plastic sheeting over the tray to maintain even humidity.

5 Shade the tray with netting if the tray is in direct sunlight. Remove both glass and netting as soon as germination starts.

SOWING IN DEGRADABLE POTS

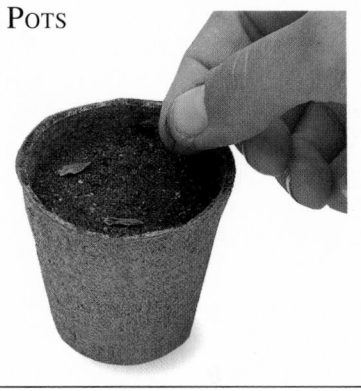

Fill a 5cm (2in) degradable pot with standard seed compost to within 1cm (¹/₂in) of the rim. Sow three seeds on the surface; cover them thinly with compost and water them. These may be thinned to two once they have germinated. The whole pot is planted out when the young plants are well developed.

let it touch the compost surface as this may disturb the seeds. Place the container in a propagator or on a greenhouse bench and shade with fine netting or newspaper if it receives direct sunlight. As soon as the first seedlings germinate, the cover should be removed. Keep them in good light and the compost moist until they are ready for pricking out.

Pricking out

Seedlings raised in trays or pans need to be transplanted into larger containers before they become overcrowded, as they quickly become weak and spindly if deprived of sufficient space or light. This is known as pricking off or pricking out. It enables the seedlings to continue to develop until they are ready for planting out in the garden.

Fill the new containers with a loam-based potting compost and firm gently to eliminate any air pockets. Small pots, no more than 6cm (3in) in diameter, or compartmented plastic packs, are ideal for individual seedlings; larger pots, pans, or trays may be used for several plants.

To prick out, first knock the container of seedlings against a table top or bench to loosen the compost slightly and remove it intact from the container. Then hold each plant gently by the small seed leaves to

avoid bruising the foliage, stems, or growing tips and loosen it with a widger or other small implement. Take care not to damage the roots. Then carefully lift each plant from the soil, retaining some of the moist seed compost around the roots to ensure that there will be little or no check to growth when the seedlings are replanted.

Use a dibber to make holes in the compost 4–5cm (1¹/₂–2in) apart and insert a seedling into each hole. Make sure that all the roots are covered with compost, then gently firm in each seedling using fingers or a dibber, and level the compost. As

Seeds with special requirements

A few seeds need special conditions in order to germinate successfully. Begonia, *Coleus*, and busy lizzie (*Impatiens*) seeds require light and prefer a constant temperature of 21°C (70°F). Primulas prefer light, but need temperatures of no more than 20°C (68°F). Some seeds including *Phacelia*, pansies (*Viola* x *wittrockiana*), and other *Viola* should be germinated in the dark. Seeds of *Thunbergia alata* and pelargoniums require 21–4°C

(70–75°F) to germinate: scarify (break down by scratching) pelargonium seed before sowing (see "Scarifying and soaking", p.162). Pre-scarified seeds are now commercially available. Seeds of *Moluccella* are difficult to germinate unless they have been stratified: the seed pan is set in a refrigerator for a couple of weeks before bringing it into a temperature of 18–21°C (65–70°F) for a further two or three weeks.

PRICKING OUT INTO A PACK

1 When the seedlings (here Tagetes) are large enough to handle, tap the tray on a hard surface to loosen the compost.

2 Carefully separate the seedlings, handling them by their seed leaves. Keep plenty of compost around the roots.

3 Transplant each seedling into a separate section of a pack. Firm the soil around each one with fingers or a dibber, and water.

Annuals in pots

Many annuals make excellent pot plants. Prick out young seedlings into divided trays or individual pots and, when the roots have just filled the container, transfer each seedling to a larger pot prepared with loam-based potting compost. The pot size will vary according to the species or cultivar and time of sowing. Put plants sown in late summer into 9cm (3½in) pots over the winter when growth is slow, and transfer them later to their final pots – either 13cm (5in), or 19cm (7in), or much larger pots for groups of three or five plants per container. Transplant spring-sown annuals directly into their final pots or containers.

Many annuals (here Schizanthus) *are very useful for providing an early, colourful display in a cool greenhouse in spring.*

each container is filled, water it from a can fitted with a fine rose to settle the compost around the roots. Increase the humidity around the seedlings by covering the containers with clear plastic for a few days while the seedlings re-establish, but make sure that the plastic does not touch the leaves because this may encourage rotting. Then return the seedlings to their previous growing conditions to develop further.

If seedlings are ready for planting out, but this is delayed because of a late frost, pot them on into a larger container to ensure that growth is not checked or the long-term success of the plants jeopardized.

Seeds that have been sown singly in packs or space-sown will not need pricking out and may be hardened off before planting out.

Hardening off

All half-hardy annuals that have been raised either under glass or in any other controlled environment before being planted outdoors need to be acclimatized gradually to the natural conditions outdoors. The aim of this is to harden the plants, reducing their dependence on artificial heat and protection without exposing them to sudden environmental changes that might cause damage.

Hardening off is most easily done using a greenhouse and a cold frame. Six or seven weeks before planting the seedlings outdoors, move them to a cooler part of the greenhouse for about a week. Then transfer them to a closed cold frame; increase the ventilation little by little as outdoor conditions improve, eventually dispensing with the frame light (the lid) entirely for the last few days unless frost is forecast.

Keep a close watch on the plants for any indication that the change in temperature is too great or too swift: there may be a check in growth, for example, or the leaves may yellow. A maximum and minimum thermometer placed in the frame records

the daily extremes of temperature, and weather forecasts provide warnings of changes to be expected.

Other equipment ideal for hardening off includes glazed frames, the covers of which may be removed completely when conditions are favourable, and cloches or polytunnels, which may be lifted off and replaced as necessary. Alternatively, the young plants may be placed outdoors in sheltered positions and protected (normally only necessary at night) with plastic or other coverings on temporary wood or bamboo frames. Unless the weather conditions are poor, the covers should be removed during the day to ensure that the plants always receive sufficient light and adequate ventilation.

Planting out

Plant out half-hardy seedlings once all danger of frost has passed. This is particularly important in the case of the more tender plants, such as begonias and *Salvia splendens*. Provided that they have been hardened off, some half-hardy annuals will, however, tolerate cool, but not frosty, conditions for short periods.

Before planting out, prepare the bed (see "Sowing in open ground", p.181), water the young plants thoroughly, and then leave them to drain for an hour or so. To remove a plant from its pot, invert it, supporting the stem with a finger on either side. Then tap the rim against a hard surface to loosen the root ball from the pot. Break apart packs or divided trays to remove each seedling with its root ball undisturbed.

If plants are in trays without divisions, hold the tray firmly with both hands, and tap one side sharply on the ground to loosen the compost. Then gently slide out the contents in one piece. Separate individual plants carefully with the fingers, keeping as much soil as possible around the

roots. Alternatively, remove each plant gently using a widger or other small tool, taking care not to damage the roots.

Make a hole sufficiently large to accommodate the root ball readily. Space the plants so that the leaves will just touch when the plants are fully developed. Normal planting distances range from 15 to 45cm (6 to 18in) depending on the habit of the species or cultivar being grown.

Check that the plants are at the same depth as in the container, then firm the soil around the base of

PLANTING OUT INTO OPEN GROUND

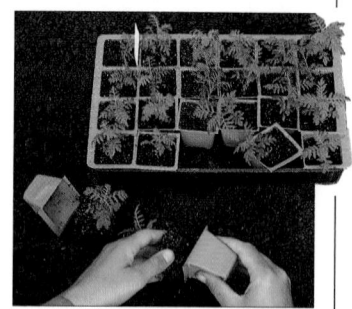

1 *Break the pack apart and carefully remove each seedling (here* Tagetes) *with its root ball intact.*

2 *Place each plant in a hole large enough to take its root ball, ensuring that the plant is at the same level as it was in its container.*

3 *Return the soil around the roots and gently firm so that there are no air pockets. Water the area.*

HARDENING OFF

POLYTUNNEL
Place half-hardy annuals (here Tagetes) *in a polytunnel. Lift the sides for ventilation, as required.*

COLD FRAME
Seedlings may also be placed in a cold frame left open for progressively longer intervals.

FIRST-YEAR GROWTH

Biennials such as Canterbury bells make only vegetative (leafy) growth in their first year. Flowers develop the following summer.

HOW TO BUY ANNUALS
BEDDING PLANTS

GOOD
EXAMPLE

*Compact,
vigorous
growth*

POOR
EXAMPLE

*Healthy,
green
foliage*

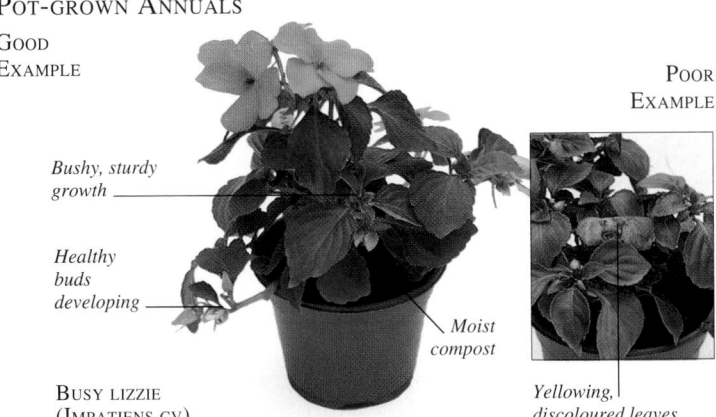

PETUNIAS

*Leggy,
bare stems*

Dead leaves

POT-GROWN ANNUALS

GOOD
EXAMPLE

POOR
EXAMPLE

*Bushy, sturdy
growth*

*Healthy
buds
developing*

*Moist
compost*

BUSY LIZZIE
(IMPATIENS CV)

*Yellowing,
discoloured leaves*

the stem, without compacting the soil too much. After planting, gently break up the soil surface between the plants with a hand fork. To settle them in, water the plants thoroughly using a watering can fitted with a fine rose so that the soil is not washed off the roots.

Stopping or pinching out

As young annuals develop, some may require stopping or pinching out in order to encourage the plants to produce sideshoots and develop a bushy habit. Do not stop plants such as antirrhinums or stocks (*Matthiola*) that have strong terminal shoots, as these develop the main flower spikes and will also produce lateral growths naturally during the summer to continue the flowering display.

Stopping is done by nipping the growing tip off a young plant. Even with annuals that branch naturally it may be necessary when a few plants in a bed produce stronger shoots than others. If an even growth habit of plants is required, stop tall plants when they have reached five or six joints by removing the tip of each long shoot back to the required height.

Stopping delays flower production and so should not be carried out if an early display is preferred.

Bedding plants

Buying more mature annuals and biennials to plant out directly into beds, borders, or containers can save time and may be necessary if no greenhouse is available to grow half-hardy annuals from seed. In addition, whereas seeds of many annuals may be bought only as mixtures, commercial growers are usually able to obtain colours separately, providing gardeners with a much wider range of plant materials with which to plan their bedding schemes.

Judging the quality of bedding plants

Sturdy young plants with evenly balanced, short-noded shoots and healthy foliage are most likely to establish well and give the best results. The plants should have well-developed root systems but must not be pot-bound, with tangled or cramped roots. Do not purchase plants in dry compost or with yellowing or diseased foliage as, although they will usually grow on, they do not always establish well and often produce few flowers.

Half-hardy bedding plants are sold at various stages from seedling to flowering plant, frequently well ahead of the date at which it is safe

Planting in containers

For an immediate display in ornamental containers, use annuals or biennials that are pot-grown. They will flower throughout the season without outgrowing the container. Plan the positions of the plants carefully, arranging trailing plants at the sides or front of the container and taller plants towards the back or centre.

Place crocks in the base of the container to cover the drainage holes and fill it loosely with a loam-based potting compost. Before planting, water the plants well. Remove each from its pot, tease out the roots gently, then place it in position in the container. Firm the compost around each plant, then water thoroughly.

1 Water the chosen plants thoroughly and decide how they are to be arranged before beginning to plant up the container. Begonias, Lobelia, and busy lizzies (Impatiens cvs) are used in this arrangement.

2 Fill the trough half or three-quarters full with moist compost. Invert each pot and support the plant as the root ball slides out. Gently tease out the plant roots.

3 Scoop back the compost and place the plant in position so that the neck of the plant will be 1cm (1/2in) below the rim of the windowbox.

4 Plant up the remaining plants, then firm gently around them, especially at the sides and corners, so that there are no air pockets remaining. Add more moist compost if necessary, and level the surface before watering thoroughly.

to plant them outdoors. Make sure that you have appropriate conditions under cover to grow them on properly if this is necessary. Check also that they have been hardened off if they are for immediate planting outside. Acclimatize the seedlings slowly until the danger of frost is past; sudden exposure to frost or even cold wind may kill them since they may have been produced in heated glasshouses. They may then be planted outdoors.

Planting and supporting annual climbers

Climbing annuals should be planted in positions where they are able to climb naturally through a shrub or small tree or be trained against a fence, wall, or some other support.

If a twining annual is to be grown through a shrub, position the plant at the perimeter of the shrub, on the side where it will receive the most sunlight, with a cane leading the main shoots into the host plant if necessary.

If the climber is intended to be grown up a wall or fence, provide a support that will suit its habit of growth (see CLIMBING PLANTS, "Types of support", p.100); plant it 30cm (12in) from the base of the wall or fence to enable the roots to obtain sufficient moisture.

Twining climbers may also be grown up a wigwam of several canes tied securely near the top; push the canes well into the soil first and plant just outside the canes, then tie in the young seedlings to the canes.

PLANTING OUT CLIMBING ANNUALS

PLANTING BESIDE A HOST
Twining annuals such as Ipomoea *should be planted about 22cm (9in) from the host's stem.*

SUPPORTING WITH CANES
A tripod provides support for twining annuals (here Thunbergia alata*). Tie a seedling loosely to each of the canes.*

Planting annuals to a design

Before starting to plant up a bed or border, assemble all the bedding plants to be used and check them off against the plan. Place the plants, still in their containers, roughly in position on top of the prepared soil to ensure that the bed will be neither too crowded nor too sparsely planted. Now is the time to make any final adjustments to plant positioning – it will be too late once they are in the ground. Keep a few plants in reserve to replace any that may die.

1 *Mark out the design of the whole bed before starting to plant. Work from the centre outwards, or from the back of the bed to the front. Use a plank or kneeler for kneeling on so that the soil does not become compacted, making it difficult to work and inhibiting drainage.*

2 *Plant the seedlings carefully, handling the plants as little as possible. Firm the soil around each. Complete one section of planting before moving on to the next.*

3 *As each section of planting is completed, trim off any damaged, uneven, or straggly shoots to make the patches of plants more compact.*

4 *Water thoroughly section by section so that the seedlings planted first do not dry out while the others are being planted.*

5 *Keep the bed well watered while the seedlings are establishing. Remove any discoloured or damaged foliage that might spoil the display and should any plants fail, replace them to fill gaps.*

Routine care

Annuals generally require little maintenance since they have a relatively short life. They do need to be watered regularly during drought, however, especially if they are grown in containers, and dead-headed to prolong flowering. Tall annuals may require staking when or soon after planting to prevent them from blowing over or toppling under their own weight. When the foliage starts to die down after flowering or at the end of the season, the plants should be cleared away.

SUPPORTING CLIMBING ANNUALS

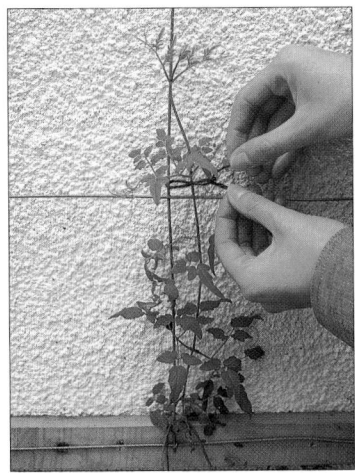

When planting climbers (here Eccremocarpus scaber) *near a wall or fence, support them on pig-wire or trellis. Tie the stems to the support while still supple.*

SUPPORTING TALL ANNUALS

Support tall annuals such as Salpiglossis *by pushing canes into the soil around the pot and twining string around the canes. As the plants develop they hide the canes.*

Watering, feeding, and weeding

Young annuals and biennials that are planted in open ground should be watered regularly with a sprinkler or watering can, soaking the bed thoroughly. Once the plants have become established, water only during prolonged dry weather.

Annuals rarely need extra feeding if the soil has been well prepared. A liquid fertilizer may be applied on very poor soils as flower buds develop. Biennials may benefit from a little food, but only those grown for show purposes need regular feeding. Over-rich conditions produce vigorous vegetative growth at the expense of flowers.

Keep annuals and biennials free from weeds as these compete for light, water, and soil nutrients. Pull out any weeds by hand while they are still small and remove self-sown seedlings in the same way if they are not required or are too numerous.

Providing supports

Many annuals and biennials have rather slender stems, which benefit from some support. Use small, bushy branches, or peasticks, for plants with a mature height of up to 1m (3ft). When the plants are only a few centimetres high, insert the sticks in the soil around them so that they can grow up through the sticks which will quickly be covered and hidden.

Tall annuals in containers may be supported by inserting a few canes around the edge of the pot and tying soft string around the canes – the supports are hidden by the plants as they develop. Very tall plants, such as hollyhocks (*Alcea*) or sunflowers (*Helianthus*), may need to be individually staked. Push the cane into the soil where it will be least visible and, as the plant develops, tie in the stem at intervals as required.

Annuals as dried or cut flowers

Dried or fresh flowers of many annuals and biennials are decorative indoors. Harvest "everlasting" flowers, such as *Xeranthemum*, *Helipterum*, and *Limonium*, when they are about half open, then hang them upside-down in a warm, well-ventilated area. Cut *Helichrysum* flowerheads before they show colour to help keep their shape when dried. Cut fresh flowers as the buds show colour. Dip the ends of Iceland poppies (*Papaver nudicaule*) into boiling water to seal them and avoid air locks that prevent water uptake.

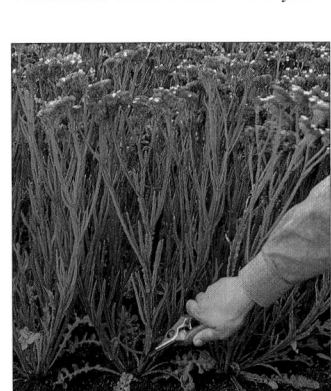

1 *Cut flowers for drying (here* statice, Limonium sinuatum) *as the heads start to open. Use a slightly angled cut as near as possible to the base of the stem.*

2 *Many everlasting flowers may be dried upside-down in bunches fastened with soft string or raffia. Once they have dried, any excess stem may be cut off to suit the flower arrangement.*

Some scrambling annuals that do not twine or have tendrils will need to be tied in to their support. Attach the leading shoots with soft string and continue to tie occasionally as needed to maintain the shape of the plant. Twining annuals and those that have tendrils may need to be guided occasionally.

Maintaining annuals in containers

Plants in windowboxes, hanging baskets, or other containers need little maintenance apart from liberal watering and dead-heading flowers to maintain the display. Check daily during both wet and dry weather to make sure that the compost remains moist (but never waterlogged), and dead-head as the flowers fade.

When a plant has finished flowering, remove it from its container, disturbing the other plants as little as possible, and replace it with a later-maturing plant. Hardy biennials may be overwintered outside; if the plants are likely to be damaged by frost, place the container under cover.

1 *Continue to dead-head flowers in order to keep the display attractive. When plants have finished flowering remove them, taking care not to damage the roots of remaining plants.*

2 *Add fresh, moist compost and fill the gaps with new plants or bulbs that will continue the display. Firm gently and water thoroughly to help the new plants to establish.*

187

DEAD-HEADING

To prolong the flowering period, remove flowerheads as they fade, cutting near the base of the stalk. The plants (here pansies) will produce new blooms for some time.

Dead-heading

In many cases, the flowering season of plants may be extended and their appearance improved by promptly removing any flowerheads that are fading or dead; this prevents a plant from setting seed, and its energy is used to produce additional flowers. Snap off any faded flowers between the fingers and thumb, breaking the stems cleanly; use a pair of sharp scissors or secateurs for tougher stems or where there is a danger of disturbing the plant as the dead flowerheads are removed.

Do not dead-head if the seeds or fruits form part of the ornamental characteristic of the annual or biennial – as they do with honesty (*Lunaria*), *Hibiscus trionum*, and ornamental maize (*Zea mays*), for example. Nor should plants be dead-headed if their seeds are required for growing the plant again during the following season.

A few annuals and biennials, such as poppies (*Papaver*), do not produce any more flowers after dead-heading.

Saving seeds

Seeds may be easily collected from many annuals for sowing the following year. It is, however, often worth saving seeds only from those annuals and biennials that stay true to type, such as *Nigella* or honesty, as seeds saved from most garden-grown cultivars will not produce plants that possess flower or habit characteristics similar to those of their parents.

Dead-head those plants that have poor flowers so that no seeds are formed and later collected for sowing the following season. Such seeds are unlikely to produce plants with good-quality flowers.

Self-sown seedlings are likely to vary to some extent in character and quality but may nevertheless produce quite acceptable plants. Distinct cultivars of *Eschscholzia*, Excelsior Series foxgloves (*Digitalis*), sweet alyssum (*Lobularia maritima*), marigolds (*Calendula*), forget-me-nots (*Myosotis*), and many other annuals and biennials usually vary in flower colour and other characteristics from the original plant.

When seed capsules turn brown and begin to split, cut them off and spread them on paper-lined trays in a warm, sunny place until they are fully dry. Extract the seeds and clean away any debris. Packet, label, and store them in dry, cool conditions until they are required for sowing.

Clearing the bed

In autumn, once the flower display is over, lift and compost all dying plants after any seeds required have been gathered. Burn any diseased plants so that they do not spread infection elsewhere in the garden. Perennials grown as annuals or

AUTUMN CLEARANCE

When annuals have finished flowering, carefully loosen the soil around their roots with a fork and then rake up and compost or burn the old plants.

biennials, such as pansies (*Viola* x *wittrockiana*) and polyanthus, may be lifted and replanted elsewhere, where they may grow and flower satisfactorily for several years. Others, for example wallflowers (*Cheiranthus*) and antirrhinums, seldom grow as well after their first year, so they are usually not worth retaining for future use.

Tender perennials such as begonias and busy lizzies (*Impatiens* cvs) may be lifted and potted up in late summer to continue flowering in the house, conservatory, or greenhouse. Hollyhocks (*Alcea*) and other short-lived perennials may be cut down in autumn and retained since they sometimes survive for several seasons, although the quality and vigour of the plants will deteriorate. Retain a few plants of the new F1 and F2 strains of pelargonium in a frost-proof greenhouse or conservatory since they will usually survive, if kept quite dry, and flower again the following year. *Eccremocarpus scaber*, too, will survive for years in protected positions outside.

Pests and diseases

The pests most likely to be troublesome to annuals and biennials when they are seedlings, as well as when they are more mature, are slugs and snails (p.548), aphids (p.550), and caterpillars (p.549); plants may also be attacked by rusts (pp.552 and 557) and other fungal problems (see "Fungal leaf spots", p.552). Fungicides may prevent or check these diseases but often little can be done beyond pulling out and burning badly affected plants. Young seedlings growing under cover may suffer from damping off (p.568) – a group of soil-borne diseases that causes the plants to rot and collapse.

CUTTING DOWN SHORT-LIVED PERENNIALS

1 Not all seedheads ripen at the same time. To prevent self-seeding, remove flowered stems before any seedheads ripen fully.

2 Short-lived perennials such as hollyhocks may flower for several seasons if cut down immediately after flowering.

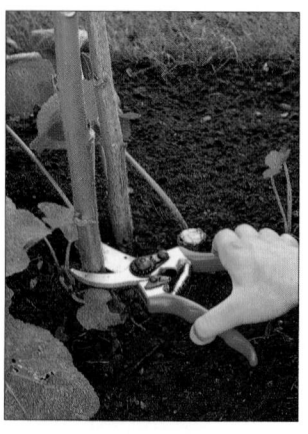

3 Carefully cut each stem at its base, ensuring that the new growth that has been produced during the growing season is not damaged in the process.

SAVING SEEDS

1 Seeds may be collected when the capsules or seedheads (here Nigella) have been dried on blotting paper or newspaper and release their seeds.

2 Once the seedhead has dried, shake the seeds out and separate them from any other debris. Store them in a labelled envelope in a dry place in a constant, cool temperature.

8

THE ROCK GARDEN

SOME OF THE LOVELIEST *garden plants grow wild in the mountain ranges of the world, and have adapted successfully to a surprising diversity of specialized habitats. These range from high alpine rock face niches to aprons of loose scree, and from the short, sparse turf that constitutes high alpine pasture to the richer meadow grasses of lower altitudes. Alpines and rock garden plants provide a garden with a wealth of beautiful species that retain the charm of wild flowers unimproved by the hybridizer's art.*

They often display disproportionately large or prolific numbers of attractive flowers, in an unequalled range of clear, jewel-like colours. Some of these plants are adapted to very specific environments and may therefore present a challenge to even the most experienced gardener; but many more are amenable and undemanding plants that will grow readily in a suitably prepared site in the open garden, and will richly reward a little extra time and attention paid to their cultural requirements.

Designing a rock garden

ALPINES are plants that grow at high altitudes above the tree line, although the term is often loosely used to include a vast range of low-growing rock garden plants, including many bulbs, that may be grown successfully at relatively low altitudes. Their diminutive form and graceful habit make them well suited for grouping together in fascinating, brilliantly coloured collections.

True alpines
Alpines may be deciduous or evergreen woody plants, or they may be herbaceous, or grow from bulbs, corms, or tubers – there are very few annual alpines. They are characteristically hardy, adapted to survive in extremes of climate, and compact, with few over 15cm (6in) tall. In their native mountain habitat, the dwarf or creeping habit of alpines reduces their wind resistance, and helps them to resist the crushing weight of heavy snow in winter.

In alpine regions, plants experience brilliant sunshine and fresh, constantly moving air during their growing season. Their cushion- or mat-forming habit and their small, fleshy, hairy, or leathery leaves, protect them from water loss in high winds and hot sun. Edelweiss (*Leontopodium alpinum*), for example, has its entire surface covered in woolly hairs, which help to conserve moisture, while the leaves of houseleeks (*Sempervivum*) have fleshy, water-retaining tissue.

Although most alpines are adapted to extremes of temperature, few withstand constant wetness at the roots in winter or warm, humid, summer conditions. In their native habitats, they often grow in thin, poor soil that lacks nutrients and has a low organic content but which allows rapid drainage. Most develop extensive, spreading root systems to seek out nutrients and moisture.

Rock garden plants
Rock plants are simply those slow-growing plants of relatively small stature that are suitable in scale for growing in rock gardens. They include dwarf trees and shrubs, which are particularly useful for framework (background) plantings, and many other plants that are not necessarily from alpine regions. Some, such as *Armeria maritima*, originate in coastal habitats while many miniature bulbs are native to sunny, Mediterranean hillsides. In common with true alpines, they share the need for a free-draining soil and are therefore suitable for planting among alpines.

Since many true alpines bloom in the spring and early summer, rock garden plants are especially valuable if they are late blooming, since they may be used to extend the season of interest.

A WELL-FURNISHED ROCK GARDEN
This gently sloping rock garden is studded with a diverse range of alpine plants, from low-growing Dianthus *and saxifrages in the foreground to the dwarf shrubs* Genista lydia, Helianthemum, *and* Potentilla *at the rear.*

Alpines and rock plants in the garden

The usually restricted size of alpines and rock garden plants fits particularly well into the confines of the small, modern garden. Few other types of plant are so characteristically neat and compact and this allows a substantial collection of species and hybrids to be grown in a relatively small space.

Garden-tolerant plants

Many alpine species, and their more showy cultivars, are undemanding in their cultural requirements and may be grown easily in the open garden. They present a wealth of habit and form, from tiny, cushion-forming plants, to spreading mound- and mat-formers; some of the easier alpines bloom well into summer, almost invariably producing a profusion of flowers. The low-growing cultivars of *Aubrieta*, phlox, and *Veronica* form mats of clear, bright colour when in bloom, and may be used to edge beds, their informal, spreading habit gently softening straight lines.

Specialist alpines

Other alpine genera, such as the Aretian *Androsace* and the tight cushion-forming saxifrages, have

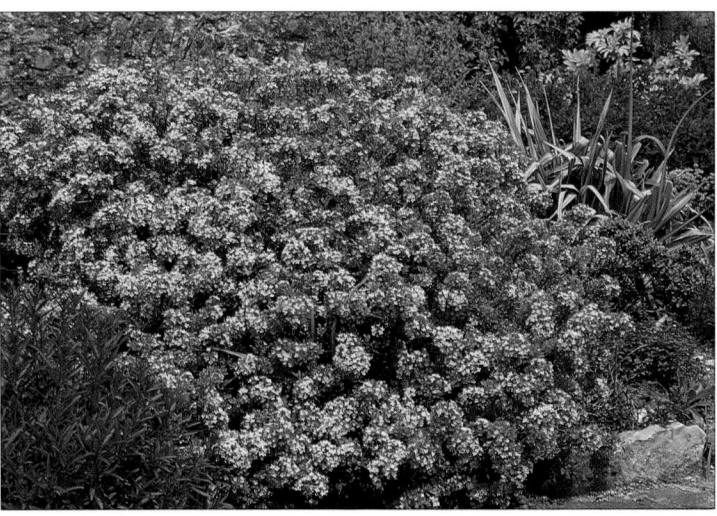

PLANTING IN THE OPEN GARDEN
Daphne x burkwoodii 'Somerset' *has a profusion of pale pink flowers that spill over the edge of a mixed border and drift into the plants on either side.*

special requirements, in particular a need for extremely free-draining soil and protection from excessive winter wet. Most also require plenty of sun but their roots need to be cool; lower-altitude, woodland species often prefer dappled shade and may need moist, acid soil.

The rich and varied colours and diverse forms of many specialist plants may still be enjoyed in the garden, however, as long as well-drained conditions and a suitable

aspect are provided. The best way to fulfil these requirements is to raise the plants in some way from the underlying garden soil by planting them in specially constructed or carefully controlled environments and using prepared, gritty, free-draining soil or composts.

Some alpine plants need a cool root run and shelter, and rock gardens and pockets within stone or brick walls are an ideal way to grow such plants and display them to their best

advantage in natural-looking surroundings. In more formal garden settings or if space is limited, raised beds or troughs and sinks are attractive alternatives, especially when they are constructed from materials that complement any existing hard landscape features. Free-standing troughs and sinks also allow colour to be introduced at a variety of heights and on hard surfaces such as patios and paths.

The rock garden

A sunny, south-, or south-west-facing slope makes an ideal site for the stony outcrops of a rock garden. Well-constructed rock gardens emulate natural rock formations and make strikingly attractive features. They replicate, as nearly as possible, the natural habitat of alpine plants, creating the conditions in which they thrive – the soil beneath the rocks provides the cool, moist, but freely draining root run that they particularly enjoy.

Planning a rock garden

For the greatest visual impact, a rock garden should be constructed on as generous a scale as the site allows. Where possible, choose a naturally sloping, open site that will provide good drainage. A series of rocky outcrops with gullies running in between is highly effective, especially if streams and pools are also included in the design.

A sunny aspect will suit most rock plants, although those that prefer shade may be grown in cooler, shady pockets on the north side of large rocks. Careful placing of the rocks at the construction stage (see p.199) will provide a wide range of planting areas and rock niches to meet the needs of many different alpine plants.

Choosing plants

Several alpine species, such as *Gentiana verna*, with its flowers of intense blue in spring, prefer deep pockets of well-drained, gritty soil, while the mat-forming *Polygonum affine* 'Donald Lowndes', for example, thrives in broader terraces between rock strata. Both *Lewisia* Cotyledon Hybrids and *Saxifraga* 'Tumbling Waters', which has cascades of white flowers over rosettes of lime-encrusted foliage, are most at home in the narrow crevices between vertical stone faces.

Plan the planting scheme to include as much seasonal variation as possible. Alpine bulbs such as *Crocus laevigatus* 'Fontenayi' and *Iris histrioides* 'Major' help to bring

A BLAZE OF SUMMER COLOUR
The brilliant red flowers of Sedum spurium *and* Helianthemum *cascading down the rocky outcrop make a striking contrast with the grey-green stems and leaves* of both Dianthus *and* Hebe pinguifolia 'Pagei' *just behind them. The fresh green foliage of the surrounding plants provides a bright but cool counterpoint.*

A TIERED ROCK GARDEN

In late spring, a collection of alpines and rock plants provides abundant colour and variety of form. Some evergreen dwarf shrubs and early flowering bulbs interplanted among the rocks will extend the season of interest.

1 *Draba rigida*
2 *Anchusa caespitosa*
3 *Saponaria x olivana*
4 *Morisia monanthos*
5 *Dianthus alpinus*
6 *Androsace carnea*
7 *Gentiana verna*
8 *Celmisia walkeri*
9 *Pulsatilla vulgaris*
10 *Saxifraga* 'Southside Seedling'
11 *Berberis x stenophylla* 'Corallina Compacta'
12 *Linum perenne*
13 *Physoplexis comosa*
14 *Helianthemum* 'Wisley Primrose'
15 *Parahebe catarractae*
16 *Helianthemum* 'Wisley Pink'
17 *Armeria juniperifolia*
18 *Chiastophyllum oppositifolium*
19 *Aquilegia alpina*

20 *Anthyllis montana*
21 *Crocus* 'Cream Beauty'
22 *Euryops acraeus*
23 *Iris* 'Joyce'
24 *Viola* 'Haslemere'
25 *Picea mariana* 'Nana'
26 *Narcissus minor*
27 *Diascia rigescens*
28 *Cyclamen coum* subsp. *coum* and *coum* 'Album'
29 *Galanthus nivalis* 'Scharlockii'
30 *Narcissus* 'Tête-à-tête'
31 *Juniperus communis* 'Compressa'

32 *Hebe canterburiensis*
33 *Campanula cochleariifolia*
34 *Phlox douglasii* 'Crackerjack'
35 *Origanum* 'Kent Beauty'
36 *Daphne cneorum*
37 *Phlox* 'Camla'
38 *Androsace lanuginosa*
39 *Gypsophila cerastioides*
40 *Crocus dalmaticus*
41 *Aubrieta* 'Joy'
42 *Aethionema grandiflorum*
43 *Euphorbia myrsinites*
44 *Iberis sempervirens*

the garden to life in winter or early spring, and *Cyclamen hederifolium* and *Sternbergia lutea* add interest in autumn. For year-round colour, include a few evergreens, such as the dwarf *Chamaecyparis obtusa* 'Nana Pyramidalis' and *Juniperus communis* 'Compressa', and dwarf shrubs such as *Hebe buchananii* 'Minor'.

Add texture and structure to the planting by using species with unusual leaves or stems and variation in height and form. Contrasting leaf texture can be particularly striking: bold, fleshy, rosette-forming plants may be used to offset the delicate, feathery leaves and flowers of *Pulsatilla* species, for instance, and a combination of spreading, cushion-forming, and trailing alpines with several dwarf shrubs or trees provides great visual interest. The sword-shaped, silver leaves of *Celmisia coriacea* contrast well with mat-forming plants such as *Polygala calcarea* 'Bulley's Variety', with deep blue flowers in late spring and early summer, and *Campanula cochleariifolia*, with clusters of pale blue or white bells in summer.

A TAPESTRY OF COLOUR
A vivid display in which the rich colours and varied forms of the alpines blend with the evergreen shrubs and dwarf conifers, which form the framework of this attractive rock garden.

A PEAT BED

Alpines that prefer acid soil and damp, woodland conditions are best grown in a specially constructed peat bed. Site the bed in a partly shaded area of the garden, perhaps next to, but not beneath, a light-foliaged tree so that the plants receive dappled sunlight for part of the day.

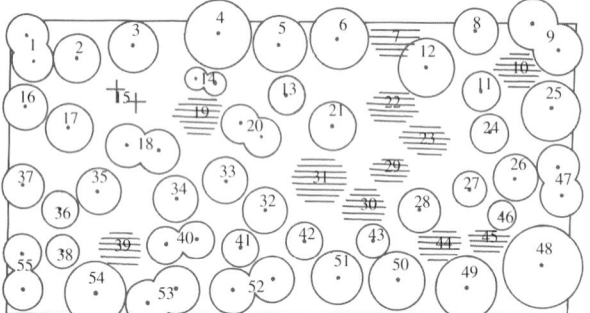

1 *Cyathodes colensoi*
2 *Hacquetia epipactis*
3 *Arctostaphylos uva-ursi* 'Point Reyes'
4 *Rhododendron* 'Curlew'
5 *Anemone nemorosa* 'Robinsoniana'
6 *Trillium grandiflorum*
7 *Erythronium* 'Pagoda'
8 *Betula nana*
9 *Dryas octopetala*
10 *Narcissus bulbocodium* subsp. *bulbocodium*
11 *Jeffersonia dubia*
12 *Phlox* 'Chatahoochee'
13 *Dodecatheon* 'Red Wings'
14 *Dicentra cucullaria*
15 *Celmisia coriacea*
16 *Phlox divaricata* subsp. *laphamii*
17 *Trillium erectum*
18 *Gentiana septemfida*
19 *Erythronium hendersonii*
20 *Phyllodoce empetriformis*
21 *Daphne arbuscula*
22 *Lilium mackliniae*
23 *Erythronium oregonum*
24 *Gentiana acaulis*
25 *Salix reticulata*
26 *Salix* x *boydii*
27 *Polygala chamaebuxus*
28 *Phyllodoce caerulea*
29 *Galanthus nivalis* 'Lutescens'
30 *Nomocharis pardanthina*
31 *Erythronium* 'White Beauty'
32 *Anemonella thalictroides*
33 *Cassiope* 'Edinburgh'
34 *Rhodohypoxis* 'Douglas'
35 *Anemone* x *lipsiensis*
36 *Hepatica nobilis* var. *japonica*
37 *Cassiope lycopodioides*
38 *Trillium rivale*
39 *Scilla siberica* 'Atrocaerulea'
40 *Polygonatum hookeri*
41 *Corydalis solida* 'George Baker'
42 *Rhodothamnus chamaecistus*
43 *Rhodohypoxis* 'Margaret Rose'
44 *Narcissus cyclamineus*
45 *Cyclamen purpurascens*
46 *Calceolaria* 'Walter Shrimpton'
47 *Saxifraga oppositifolia*
48 *Linnaea borealis*
49 *Gentiana sino-ornata*
50 *Vaccinium vitis-idaea* 'Minus'
51 *Andromeda polifolia* 'Compacta'
52 *Gaultheria cuneata*
53 *Polygala chamaebuxus* var. *grandiflora*
54 *Phlox stolonifera* 'Ariane'
55 *Lithodora diffusa* 'Heavenly Blue'

Scree formations

On mountain slopes, the natural weathering of rock outcrops produces a mass of small, broken rocks and stones. These loose, stony slopes, known as screes, are home to many plants that need plenty of moisture at their roots during the growing season, but grow best through an apparently dry 15cm (6in) surface layer of stones. Scree dwellers are among the most beautiful and jewel-like of alpine plants and well worth the extra care needed to grow them.

The scree bed

The scree bed attempts to re-create the highly specialized habitat of natural scree dwellers. A scree is a deep, preferably gently sloping bed of loose rock fragments of varying size, into which is mixed a suitable compost (see p.200). Screes may also be constructed on flat sites, raised from ground level to assist drainage, becoming, in effect, a specialized form of raised bed (see p.193).

Scree dwellers usually form low mats or cushions of dense foliage, and many bear their small, brilliantly coloured blooms in such profusion that the flowers almost completely obscure the leaves. The neutral background of small stones offers an ideal foil for the rich textures and colours of this type of planting.

Specialist plants, for example *Vitaliana primuliflora*, *Anchusa caespitosa*, and *Myosotis alpestris*, thrive in screes. Other rock garden plants which are easier to grow also appreciate the conditions created in a scree bed. Some species, such as *Achillea clavennae* and *Artemisia glacialis*, are grown primarily for their silver foliage, which provides a cool contrast for stronger colours. A number of species, including *Androsace carnea* subsp. *laggeri*, which bears a mass of pink blooms in early summer, naturally self seed. The tiny, blue, bell-shaped flowers of *Campanula cochleariifolia* also spring up around the garden but may become a nuisance if they begin to compete with less robust species.

Integrating the scree bed

Where space is available, one or more scree beds may be integrated with a rock garden on one site to form a bold, unified design and provide a broad range of habitats. A backing of large rocks skirted by scree beds is particularly effective.

Alternatively, pockets of scree mixture may be included in a rock garden to accommodate specialized scree dwellers that need particularly good drainage around their necks. *Dianthus haematocalyx*, for example, is a tightly tufted pink whose deep rose petals have an unusual buff underside; it benefits from a soil surface of loose, dry stones.

The visual effect of a scree bed is enhanced by incorporating just a few, carefully positioned, larger rocks. Plants may then be allowed to skirt their base or to grow over them to soften their outlines.

Peat beds

Alpine plants that require an acid soil or a woodland environment are not always easily accommodated in a rock garden. Acid-loving plants such as *Arctostaphylos*, *Cassiope*, gentians, and most *Vaccinium* species will only thrive in soil with a low pH, and woodland plants prefer moist, shady conditions and leafy, humus-rich soil. Specially constructed peat beds are an excellent way of providing a moist, acidic growing medium and, when sited in dappled shade, closely imitate woodland conditions, extending the range of species that may be grown.

Site and materials

Peat beds may be constructed either as individual garden features or as extensions to a rock garden. The shady, north-facing side of a rock garden provides ideal conditions. Do not place a peat bed beneath trees since the water drip from the leaves after rain may rot the plants. For best results, the site should be in sun for part of the day.

Traditionally, the acidic medium of the peat bed was based on moss peat, which has a naturally low pH, good aeration, and excellent water retention. In view of current anxieties about conserving existing peat reserves, alternative composts based on leaf mould or coconut fibre, which have similar characteristics, should be used wherever possible.

Raised beds

In small gardens, raised beds make highly economical use of limited space. In larger gardens, narrow raised beds may make a useful and attractive boundary feature. The formal appearance of raised beds blends in well with the design and layout of many modern gardens and, in areas where suitable rock is not easily available, or is prohibitively expensive, a raised bed provides a good substitute for a rock garden.

Since drainage in raised beds is entirely independent of the underlying soil, these structures are especially useful in gardens with poorly drained soils (such as wet, heavy clay) that are otherwise unsuitable for the cultivation of alpines. In addition, the dimensions of a raised bed may be planned so that the bed will easily accommodate a frame light to allow cultivation of choice species that require protection from too much winter wet, without restricting airflow around the plants.

Various materials may be used for the construction of a raised bed, including traditional bricks or dry stones and wooden railway sleepers. For further information, see STRUCTURES AND SURFACES, "Raised beds", p.507.

Planting in raised beds

Large raised beds may be divided into separate areas or compartments, and different composts used in each to suit the specific requirements of different plant groups. Rocks may be introduced to the surface of the compost and bedded in to provide textural contrast and vertical niches and crevices for those plants that demand them.

Rectangular raised beds present several aspects so that plants with different requirements may be planted in niches on their sunny or shady side, if required. In addition to growing plants in the bed itself, the walls of the bed may be designed to incorporate planting niches, in the same way as walls that are used for trailing species.

Choose plants that will give successional interest as the seasons progress. The dense, evergreen rosettes of *Haberlea rhodopensis* send up sprays of funnel-shaped flowers in spring, and may be succeeded in summer by *Aquilegia flabellata*, a clump-forming alpine that produces bell-shaped, soft blue flowers, each with fluted petals and a short spur. Both of these plants prefer semi-shade and are small enough to be planted in a raised bed without overcrowding it.

For a sunnier aspect, choose compact species of *Dianthus*, such as *D. alpinus* and *D.* 'Bombadier', with *Erinus alpinus* 'Dr Haenele' trailing from the retaining wall.

Walls

Garden walls may be modified, if required, to provide excellent sites for alpines and rock garden plants. The walls of raised beds and those used to retain banks of earth on a terraced slope may be modified in the same way. If possible, however, leave spaces, crevices, or cracks between the stones or brickwork during the construction of such walls so that these may be planted up when building is complete.

Choosing plants

The most suitable plants to choose are cushion- or mat-forming plants such as *Acantholimon glumaceum*, which forms evergreen cushions that are clothed in pink flowers during summer, or *Dianthus deltoides* and other alpine pinks. Plants that are

A LOW RAISED BED
Here, a raised alpine bed flanks one side of a narrow stone path. The plants draw the eye along the path and entice the visitor to the open lawn beyond.

A DRY-STONE WALL

Crevices in a dry-stone wall provide ideal conditions for a variety of trailing and spreading plants, since drainage between the stones is good. The plants also enjoy the benefit of a cool root run.

1 *Genista sagittalis*
2 *Anacyclus depressus*
3 *Helichrysum selago*
4 *Linum flavum*
5 *Chrysanthemum hosmariense*
6 *Onosma albo-roseum*
7 *Campanula* 'Birch Hybrid'
8 *Achillea* x *kellereri*
9 *Saxifraga* 'Tumbling Waters'
10 *Penstemon newberryi* f. *humilior*
11 *Erinus alpinus*
12 *Gypsophila repens* 'Dorothy Teacher'
13 *Armeria juniperifolia*
14 *Sedum kamtschaticum* 'Variegatum'
15 *Tanacetum argenteum*
16 *Acantholimon glumaceum*
17 *Sedum spathulifolium* 'Cape Blanco'
18 *Erodium corsicum*
19 *Polygonum vacciniifolium*
20 *Arenaria purpurascens*
21 *Tropaeolum polyphyllum*
22 *Arenaria montana*
23 *Saponaria ocymoides*
24 *Jovibarba hirta*
25 *Sedum acre*
26 *Sedum obtusatum*

prone to rotting at the collar, such as *Lewisia* and *Ramonda* species, are well suited to being grown in walls, since the roots enjoy the cool conditions and extra drainage provided by the crevices. The trailing, semi-evergreen *Asarina procumbens*, with its creamy-white, snapdragon-like flowers, and the shrubby *Penstemon newberryi* f. *humilior*, bearing a profusion of flowers on gently arching branches, are also ideal for walls.

Dry-stone walls
These provide ample room for the root systems of many rock garden plants to penetrate, and also allow sharp drainage. Free-standing, single or double dry-stone walls may be used to form boundaries or dividers in the garden and with careful choice of suitable plants make extremely attractive features.

The well-drained tops of dry-stone walls provide an ideal home for mat-forming plants, such as *Gypsophila repens* or *Saponaria ocymoides*, both of which cascade attractively over the edge of the wall. The neat, spreading rosettes of lime-encrusted saxifrages and houseleeks (*Sempervivum*) may be dotted at intervals across the surface, and using both vertical faces of a wall will allow both sun and shade-loving plants to be grown.

Troughs and sinks

Old, stone sinks and troughs for feeding and watering animals make handsome containers for rock plants; unfortunately they are both scarce and expensive. However, troughs made of reconstituted stone or hypertufa, and glazed sinks coated with this material (see p.202) are ideal, inexpensive alternatives. Troughs and sinks may be used as features in patios and courtyards, or on terraces and gravelled areas in larger gardens.

Planting in troughs
The smallest alpine species are often the most intricate. *Antennaria dioica* 'Minima' and other compact alpines and rock plants should be used. By careful selection, a plant community of dwarf and slow-growing species may be planted to make up a rock garden in miniature.

Introduce a few small conifers, such as *Chamaecyparis obtusa* 'Nana Pyramidalis' or *Juniperus communis* 'Compressa', and dwarf trees such as *Ulmus parvifolia* 'Geisha' as framework plants, choosing from others such as *Campanula zoysii*, *Dianthus alpinus*, or

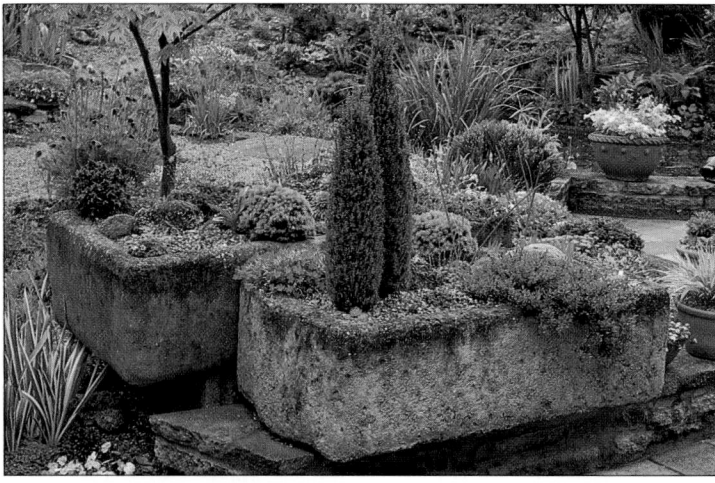

AN ALPINE TROUGH COLLECTION
A collection of troughs makes an appealing feature. Large troughs accommodate dwarf trees and shrubs as well as smaller alpine plants.

D. microlepis for the middle and foreground of the trough. Miniature shrubs may be added to provide contrasting form and colour throughout the year.

Growing plants in other containers

Where containers are selected to complement other hard landscape features of the garden, such as walls and paths, they bring a cohesive element to the overall design of the garden. Containers provide an opportunity to grow alpines in a small garden, and may also be used to flank pathways or steps.

Choosing plants
Containers are especially suitable for cultivating miniature species, and allow plants such as the tiny *Primula scotica*, with its golden-eyed purple flowers, to be appreciated and grown in a situation where they will not be swamped by larger and more vigorous neighbours. Ranging several containers together provides a good opportunity to build up collections devoted to plants of one genus that flourish under similar environmental conditions.

A long season of interest may be achieved by underplanting low growing, mat-forming plants, such as *Raoulia australis* and *Globularia cordifolia*, with late-winter flowering dwarf bulbs, for example *Narcissus asturiensis* or *Iris reticulata* and its many cultivars.

Choosing a container
The range of decorative containers suitable for alpines and rock garden plants is enormous. Make sure

that the container has adequate drainage. If an appropriate compost is then used and the plants are regularly watered and well maintained, almost any container may be used to good effect.

Large flower pots and terracotta tubs are suitable for small collections of the tiniest alpines, and particularly for those that trail over the edges of the pot, such as *Silene schafta*. Small containers are ideal for compact, slow-growing alpines such as *Androsace chamaejasme* and *Sempervivum arachnoideum*, which will provide a display over several years before they start to outgrow their situation.

Old chimney pots make beautiful features if planted up with *Sedum* or *Sempervivum* species. Even windowboxes may be the setting for an attractive, alpine planting.

AN UNUSUAL CONTAINER
Many different types of container may be used for rock plants and alpine species. Here, part of a hollowed-out tree trunk has been planted with Sedum spathulifolium 'Cape Blanco', *valued for its small clusters of tiny, yellow flowers above the rosettes of silvery-green leaves.*

The alpine house

In the wild, many alpines spend their winter dormancy insulated by a deep snow blanket that shields them from excess water, cold drying winds, and severe frosts; temperatures under the snow cover hover at, or just below, freezing point. In gardens at lower altitudes, where conditions are very different, the more exacting alpines need the protection of glass.

A simple, open cloche may be sufficient protection for some plants but a specially designed greenhouse, or alpine house (see GREENHOUSES AND FRAMES, "Alpine house", p.477), greatly extends the range that may be grown, and allows the enthusiastic gardener to try growing some of the most challenging plants.

Using an alpine house
An alpine house will accommodate a huge range of the choicest alpines in carefully controlled conditions. The season of interest in the alpine house may be maintained throughout the early winter months, when colour in the open garden is scarce. Interest increases rapidly in early spring, when the majority of true alpines flower. Where dwarf shrubs, bulbs, conifers, and ferns are also included in the collection, there will be something to attract attention throughout the year.

Although the emphasis is usually on plants that are unsuited for growing in the open, many less demanding alpines, and even robust plants that are strong enough to withstand early spring frosts and rain, may be grown to perfection in the alpine house (see also ALPINE HOUSES AND FRAMES, pp.214–16).

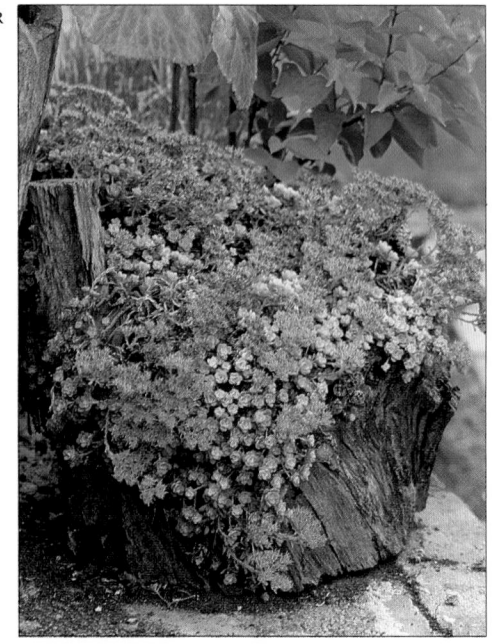

Planter's guide to rock plants

EXPOSED SITES

Rock plants that tolerate exposed or windy sites

Antennaria dioica
Campanula portenschlagiana
Carlina acaulis
Chiastophyllum oppositifolium
Crepis incana
Dryas octopetala
Erigeron karvinskianus
Eryngium, some ❁, ◮
Euphorbia myrsinites
Hebe, some ❁, ◮
Helianthemum
Limonium bellidifolium
Pterocephalus perennis
Sedum, some ❁, ◮
Sempervivum
Silene vulgaris subsp. maritima
Veronica spicata

AIR POLLUTION

Rock plants that tolerate polluted air

Aubrieta
Aurinia saxatilis
Campanula garganica,
    C. poscharskyana
Erinus alpinus
Euphorbia, some ❁, ◮
Sedum, some ❁, ◮
Sempervivum

DRY SHADE

Rock plants that tolerate dry shade

Ajuga pyramidalis, A. reptans
Dianthus carthusianorum,
    D. deltoides
Diascia cordata, D. 'Ruby Field'
Erodium guttatum
Genista sagittalis
Gypsophila dubia, G. repens
Helleborus, some ❁
Lamium maculatum
Saponaria ocymoides
Waldsteinia ternata

Waldsteinia
ternata

MOIST SHADE

Rock plants that prefer moist shade

Adonis amurensis
Cassiope
Cyclamen hederifolium,
    C. purpurascens
Daphne blagayana
Galax aphylla

Hepatica nobilis,
    H. transsilvanica
Hylomecon japonicum
Iris cristata
Meconopsis cambrica
Primula, some ❁ (many spp.
    and cvs)
Sanguinaria canadensis
Shortia uniflora
Stylophorum diphyllum
Trillium

SCREE GARDENS

Acantholimon glumaceum
Aethionema pulchellum,
    A. 'Warley Rose'
Alyssum montanum

Androsace
lanuginosa

Androsace lanuginosa,
    A. sarmentosa,
    A. sempervivoides
Dianthus alpinus, D. anatolicus,
    D. echinacea
Erinus alpinus
Gypsophila aretioides
Hutchinsia alpina
Linaria alpina
Papaver burseri,
    P. miyabeanum,
    P. rhaeticum
Sempervivum
Silene acaulis
Viola cornuta 'Minor', V. jooi

CREVICES AND PAVING

Aubrieta deltoidea (many cvs)
Aurinia saxatilis
Campanula cochleariifolia,
    C. portenschlagiana
Erinus alpinus
Erodium chamaedryoides
Geranium sanguineum var. striatum
Globularia cordifolia
Mentha requienii
Onosma albo-roseum, O. echioides
Pratia pedunculata
Scabiosa graminifolia
Thymus, some ❁

WALL CREVICES

Antirrhinum glutinosum, A. molle
Aurinia saxatilis 'Citrina'
Campanula portenschlagiana
Erinus alpinus
Globularia cordifolia

Haberlea rhodopensis (shade)
Lewisia, Cotyledon Hybrids,
    L. tweedyi
Onosma taurica
Polemonium pulcherrimum
Ramonda myconi (shade)
Saxifraga callosa, S. cochlearis,
    S. longifolia, S. paniculata
Silene vulgaris subsp. maritima
    'Flore Pleno'

PLANTING IN TROUGHS

Anchusa caespitosa
Androsace (small spp. and cvs)
Antennaria dioica 'Minima'
Arenaria purpurascens
Asperula suberosa
Dianthus alpinus, D. freynii,
    D. glacialis
Dryas octopetala 'Minor'
Edraianthus pumilio
Gentiana saxosa, G. verna
    var. angulosa
Helianthemum oelandicum
Linum suffruticosum subsp.
    salsoloides 'Nanum'
Myosotis rupicola
Omphalodes luciliae ❁
Oxalis enneaphylla
Paraquilegia anemonoides
Petrophytum hendersonii
Phlox subulata
Primula farinosa,
    P. marginata

Saxifraga
sancta

Saxifraga, some ❁ (many spp.
    and cvs)
Sedum cauticola
Soldanella alpina, S. montana
Thymus serpyllum 'Minus'
Vitaliana primuliflora

PLANTING IN TUFA

Androsace (small spp. and cvs)
Campanula piperi, C. zoysii
Draba mollissima, D. polytricha
Edraianthus pumilio
Paraquilegia anemonoides
Physoplexis comosa
Potentilla nitida
Saxifraga, some ❁ (many types,
    especially the Kabschias)
Viola cazorlensis, V. delphinantha

RAISED BEDS

Aethionema 'Warley Rose'
Androsace
Antirrhinum molle, A. sempervirens
Aquilegia discolor, A. flabellata

Armeria juniperifolia
Bolax gummifera
Callianthemum anemonoides
Campanula raineri, C. zoysii
Daphne arbuscula, D. cneorum,
    D. petraea 'Grandiflora'
Dianthus, some ❁
Draba bryoides, D. polytricha
Edraianthus dinaricus,
    E. graminifolius
Erinacea anthyllis
Gentiana acaulis,
    G. verna var. angulosa
Globularia meridionalis, G. repens
Haberlea rhodopensis
Leontopodium alpinum, L. nivale
Lewisia (some spp. and hybrids)
Origanum (some spp. and hybrids)
Oxalis adenophylla,
    O. enneaphylla, O. 'Ione Hecker'
Papaver burseri, P. miyabeanum
Paraquilegia anemonoides
Primula auricula, P. marginata
Ramonda myconi
Saxifraga cotyledon, S. longifolia,
    S. paniculata,
    S. 'Tumbling Waters'
Sempervivum
Silene acaulis
Verbascum 'Letitia'

DWARF SHRUBS

Berberis x stenophylla 'Corallina
    Compacta'
Betula nana
Chamaecyparis obtusa 'Intermedia'
Cryptomeria japonica 'Vilmoriniana'
Daphne cneorum, D. retusa,
    D. sericea
Dorycnium hirsutum
Erinacea anthyllis
Euryops acraeus
Genista delphinensis
Hebe buchananii 'Minor'
Helichrysum coralloides

Helichrysum
coralloides

Ilex crenata 'Mariesii'
Juniperus communis 'Compressa'
Picea abies 'Clanbrassiliana',
    P. a. 'Gregoryana', P. glauca
    var. albertiana 'Conica'
Potentilla 'Nana Argentea'
Salix x boydii
Sorbus reducta
Thymus membranaceus

KEY

❁ Not hardy
◮ Rock garden species only

Construction, soil preparation, and planting

Various methods may be used to grow alpine plants in gardens. Planting them in a rock garden is perhaps the best-known method, although this can take up a great deal of space. For a smaller display, screes, raised and peat beds, and the crevices of walls can make very attractive features. Where space is more limited, troughs, sinks, and other containers may also be used for a fine alpine display.

Buying plants

The rock garden should be regarded as a feature that will provide, with careful choice of plants, interest all year round.

Before buying any plants, refer to standard texts to find out the likely range of plants that is suitable for a particular type of locality in terms of climate, soil, and general situation. Visit established rock gardens in parks and botanic gardens, as well as specialist nurseries, to assess the relative merits of various plants for your own requirements. The shape, form, and colour of foliage, fruits, stems, and the overall growth habit are often as important as flowers.

Where to buy plants

Plants are available from a wide range of sources, including garden centres and specialist nurseries. Non-specialist outlets often sell a limited range of colourful cultivars and easily grown species; these may form large, spreading clumps that quickly overwhelm more delicate plants in the rock garden.

The experienced nurseryman is able to advise on the most suitable choice of plants for a particular situation, and often has display beds of mature plants. These give a good indication of the ultimate size, spread, and habit of different plants, and are invaluable at the planning stage. Such specialist outlets may also be consulted for information on composts and suppliers of rock.

A much wider range of plants will be offered by the specialist grower, who is also able to provide detailed advice on cultivation – this is particularly useful for the beginner. Demand for rare or unfamiliar plants sometimes means that general suppliers may carry stocks of plants that are best left to the specialist, since they are often unsuitable for the average rock garden. Such plants may be attractive but are often expensive and may be difficult to cultivate. They offer a rewarding challenge, but only purchase them after obtaining advice on growing them.

Selecting alpine plants

Choose plants that have healthy, compact foliage, and no sign of pests and diseases or water deprivation. Do not buy plants with yellowing or weak growth, since this indicates that they have been kept in poor light. Labels should bear the name of the plant as well as details of flowering times and brief cultivation

ROCK PLANTS THAT REQUIRE ACID SOIL

Arctous alpinus
Cassiope
Corydalis cashmeriana,
   C. flexuosa
Cyananthus
Epigaea repens
Galax urceolata
Gentiana sino-ornata
Glaucidium palmatum
Haberlea rhodopensis
Kalmia angustifolia,
   K. polifolia 'Microphylla'
Leiophyllum buxifolium
Leucopogon fraseri
Leucothöe keiskei
Linnaea borealis
Lithodora diffusa
Menziesia ciliicalyx
Mitchella repens
Epigaea gaultherioides
Ourisia caespitosa,
   O. coccinea, O. 'Loch Ewe'
Paris polyphylla
Pernettya

Phyllodoce caerulea

Phyllodoce caerulea
   P. glanduliflora,
   P. nipponica
Pieris nana
Polygala chamaebuxus,
   P. vayredae
Primula boothii,
   P. edgeworthii,
   P. gracilipes,
   P. sonchifolia
Pyrola rotundifolia
Rhododendron (dwarf spp. and cvs)
Sanguinaria canadensis 'Multiplex'
Shortia soldanelloides
Soldanella villosa
Tanakaea radicans
Vaccinium delavayi,
   V. myrtillus, V. uliginosum

HOW TO SELECT ALPINE PLANTS

GOOD EXAMPLE

SAXIFRAGA

POOR EXAMPLE

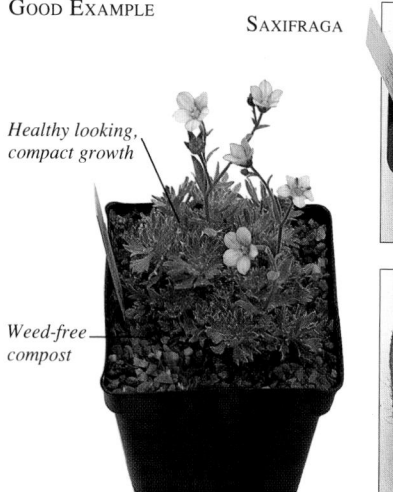

Healthy looking, compact growth

Weed-free compost

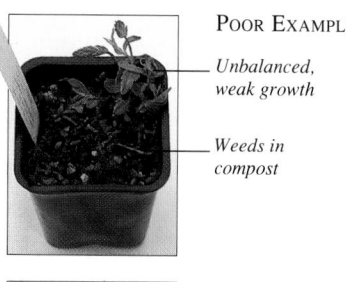

Unbalanced, weak growth

Weeds in compost

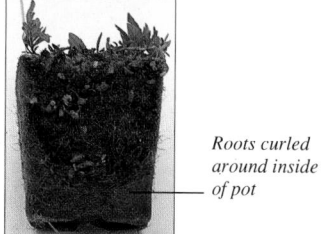

Roots curled around inside of pot

requirements. Plants should not be pot-bound and the roots should either not be visible, or only just, through the hole in the base of the pot. Do not purchase any plants that have rooted into the material on the surface of the display area, since these are almost certain to be pot-bound.

The top-growth of a plant may remain healthy for some time after the root system has been damaged or has actually died, so check that the plant has a healthy root system by sliding it out of its pot and inspecting the root ball carefully.

Large specimens are sometimes available but unless they are grown on correctly, with careful attention to watering, they may take much longer to become established than smaller, vigorous ones.

Select plants that are as weed-free as possible. Before planting, gently scrape off the grit or surface compost so that any weed seeds are removed. Introducing weeds such as pearlwort (*Sagina procumbens*) and hairy

bittercress (*Cardamine hirsuta*), causes problems as, once established, they are difficult to eradicate.

A number of plants that are sold for growing in the rock garden, such as some of the ornamental onions (*Allium*), are over-prolific seeders. Choose plants carefully to avoid introducing such problem plants.

Siting a rock garden or scree bed

Good siting is critical for a rock garden or scree bed because alpine plants require good light and well-drained conditions to thrive. The rock garden or scree should also blend in with the rest of the garden. Before starting construction, draw a rough plan on paper showing the rock garden or scree bed in relation to other garden features. A scree may be integrated into a rock garden or built as a separate feature.

SITING A ROCK GARDEN

Limit of afternoon shade from nearby plants

Sloping ground

Limit of morning shade from hedge

Build a rock garden on sloping ground, if possible, to ensure sharp drainage. Choose an open site that receives full sun, away from the roots and overhanging branches of trees and large shrubs.

Choosing the site

Choose an open, sunny site away from the shade of overhanging trees; trees drip water onto the plants beneath and shed their leaves in autumn, which may also smother plants or create a damp atmosphere that often rots them. Their roots may also compete with the plants for moisture and nutrients. Do not site a rock garden or scree in a frost pocket or on a site exposed to cold, drying winds.

A sloping site is ideal for a rock garden; it will have excellent drainage, and the artificial outcrops of rock may be made to look more natural, and provide different pockets and aspects to suit a variety of plants. Level sites present more difficulties – scree beds (see p.201) or raised beds (see p.204) are usually better for such sites.

It is best to preserve a feeling of space by siting the rock garden or scree so that a distant view is visible beyond it. In small, enclosed gardens, boundary fences or walls that rise behind the rock garden may be concealed with suitable climbers. Plan any water features, such as a pond or stream, into the scheme from an early stage. In large rock gardens, paths or stepping stones are essential to provide access and for ease of maintenance.

Making a natural-looking feature

A rock garden or scree is best sited where it will blend into an informally planted area of the garden, on a slope, by a terrace, or as a natural-looking outcrop from an area of shrubs. If the rock garden or scree is to be next to a lawn, position it so that it does not interfere with cutting and edging the lawn. It is unlikely to

Natural strata

Sedimentary rock, such as chalk and limestone, occurs naturally in distinct layers, or stratum lines, that are clearly visible to the eye. Rocks of this type may easily be split along the stratum lines for use in rock gardens.

Sedimentary rocks that occur in nature always have stratum lines following the same direction; it is important to place the stones in a rock garden to simulate the same kind of effect, otherwise they will look too obviously artificial.

NATURAL STRATUM LINES

look natural if placed next to such features as herbaceous borders, bedding displays, or any other formally planted areas, such as the vegetable or fruit garden. If the main garden is rather formal, it may be better to grow alpines in a rectangular raised bed (see p.204) rather than trying to integrate the informality of a rock garden into the design.

Choosing stone

Use locally available stone for rock garden construction, wherever possible, to harmonize with the local landscape and reduce transport costs. This may not be possible, however, in regions where supplies of natural rock are limited, or where the local stone is unsuitable.

Do not use soft, quick-weathering rock, such as shales and chalk, or hard, featureless, igneous rocks without strata, such as granite and basalt. Hard stone with no clear strata may be inexpensive but is difficult

to use, takes several years to acquire a weathered appearance, and seldom looks natural. Other materials, such as slate, are also used but are sometimes difficult to blend in.

Buying stone

If possible, visit local quarries to inspect the rock and choose suitable pieces, ensuring that the rocks are not too large to handle after being delivered. Choose stone in a range of different sizes, since this makes it easier to construct a natural-looking outcrop. Garden centres may offer a range of stone although there is sometimes a limited choice of size and shape.

Sandstone

The most suitable rocks are the various sandstones, in which the natural strata or layers are clearly visible. One great advantage of using rocks with stratum lines is that they may easily be split.

Limestone

Some types of rock, especially water-washed limestones, are now under great threat in their native surroundings and, for conservation reasons, should not be used. Occasionally, long-quarried, weathered limestone is available second-hand, but do not purchase freshly quarried limestone or rock that has been collected from its natural surroundings or removed from stone walls.

Tufa

Also known as "old horse bone", tufa is a porous, limy rock that is formed as deposits around mineral springs. It is filled with numerous air pockets and its light weight makes it easy to transport and handle. Cavities for plants may be dug or drilled out of its relatively soft surface. It provides ideal conditions for many plants that require free drainage but it is scarce and expensive.

Types of stone

Tufa is an excellent choice for the rock garden because its soft, porous nature means that plants may be grown in cavities on its surface as well as in crevices between the stones. Natural-looking, weather-worn sandstone is also a good choice, as is limestone (if available second-hand).

TUFA

SANDSTONE

LIMESTONE (KENTISH RAG)

HOW TO PREPARE THE SITE AND PLACE THE STONE

1 Place a 15cm (6in) layer of coarse rubble, such as broken bricks, on the proposed site to form a mound and improve drainage in the rock garden.

2 Cover the mound with inverted turves to prevent soil from being washed down to the layer of rubble at the base.

3 Before beginning to lay the stones, use pegs and a length of rope to mark out roughly the shape of each main rock outcrop.

4 Using a spade, dig out hollows for each large piece of stone to make them more stable when placed in position.

5 Use a crowbar to manoeuvre large stones into their final positions. Ensure that the stones are well supported by wedging smaller stones or bricks underneath.

6 Infill underneath and in between the stones with garden soil, making sure that each stone is firmly in place.

7 Build each out-crop of the rock garden in the same way. Tread down the soil gently around the stones (see inset) to eliminate air pockets and to make sure that each stone is firmly seated.

8 When all the stones are in place, fill in around them with further garden soil so they are buried by a third of their depth to ensure complete stability. Prick over the soil between the rocks so that it is not compacted.

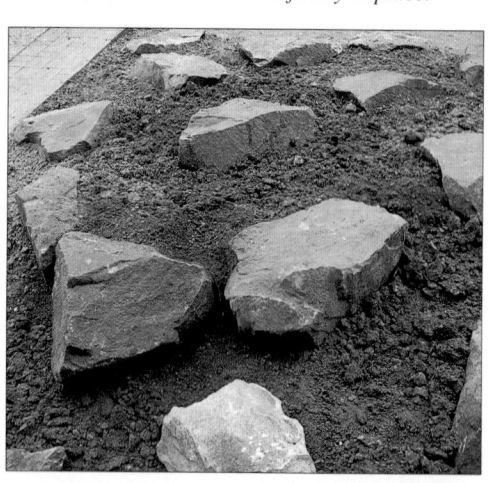

9 Add a layer of specially prepared compost to the surface of the rock garden and around each of the stones. Use a mix of equal parts loam, garden compost or leaf mould, and sharp sand or grit.

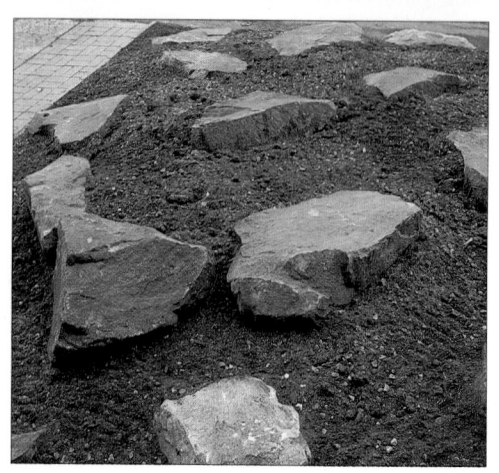

10 The rock garden, once completed, should look as natural as possible. It should also provide a variety of aspects and planting pockets to create environments that suit different types of plant.

Preparing the site for a rock garden

Never attempt to construct rock gardens when the soil is wet, since heavy rocks may compact the soil and severely damage its structure; this interferes with drainage and causes problems with the establishment and growth of the plants. If the site is grassed, cut the turf carefully and remove it for later use when constructing the rock garden.

Clearing weeds

Remove all perennial weeds from the site and, if siting the rock garden near trees or shrubs, remove any suckers that these may have produced. Perennial weeds are very difficult to eradicate from an established rock garden, so it is essential to dig them out or kill them with a weedkiller at this stage. Spray the whole area with a translocated weedkiller several months before construction begins, to kill the deep roots of perennial weeds and clear the site of vegetation.

Drainage

Make sure that the site, particularly if level, is well drained, and if necessary install a soakaway or other drainage system (see SOILS AND FERTILIZERS, "Improving drainage", p.529). This is important on heavy clay soils. Do not simply dig deep holes – these act as sumps in which the water remains, unless they are connected to a drainage ditch. Raising the rock garden above the level of the surrounding ground helps to improve drainage. On naturally sloping sites drainage is not usually a problem, although a drainage ditch may be needed at the lowest point.

If the underlying drainage is good, just dig the soil over and remove any perennial weeds. Then consolidate the soil by treading gently to avoid subsequent sinking; fork over the surface of the soil to maintain good soil structure.

Constructing a rock garden

To visualize the finished rock garden, make a miniature rough scale model, using polystyrene or small stones to simulate rock outcrops. Use different sizes of stone and place them at various levels, linking them, if required, by groups of outlying rocks and small scree areas. On large sites, construct several outcrops, linked by gulleys or scree beds, and incorporate water features, if desired. Outlining the desired shape on site with a hosepipe may help. Aim for a natural effect, with miniature cliffs and valleys, along natural stratum lines. Plan the planting, bearing in mind the relative vigour and ultimate spread of the plants. Once the design is satisfactory, construction of the rock garden may begin.

Building the base

Put down a 15cm (6in) layer of coarse rubble, broken bricks, stones, ballast, angular gravel, or pea shingle. Spread over this a layer of inverted turves, if available; these prevent compost from the rock garden clogging the free-draining layer at the base, without inhibiting normal drainage. If turves are not available, use a polypropylene sheet, with holes punctured at regular intervals to allow water to drain through.

Purchase topsoil or bring in good soil from elsewhere in the garden, ensuring that it is as weed-free as possible; use this for the top layer of the rock garden. Specially prepared, sharply drained compost (see p.200) should be used for filling in between stones where plants are to be grown.

Placing the stone

Rock is heavy and rough on the hands, so wear gloves and protective footwear. Use rollers to move large rocks, and arrange for the consignment to be delivered as close to the site of the rock garden as possible. To manoeuvre large rocks into their final positions, it may be necessary to use a block and tackle, with a steel crowbar as a lever for final adjustments. Mark the approximate positions of larger rocks first, to avoid unnecessary labour.

Select first the large stones that will act as "keystones" – the dominant rocks from which each outcrop is developed. Place the largest of the keystones first, and position the remaining ones so that the strata flow naturally from them to form the outcrops in the required directions.

Further large stones acting as subsidiary keystones may then be used to extend the outcrops. Use enough rock to make the outcrops realistic, while leaving sufficient room for planting. Check progress visually as construction proceeds. If the rocks being used have stratum lines, ensure that these all run in the same direction and at the same angle.

The rocks should be placed to provide the widest range of opportunities for planting. For example, butting rocks together serves to create the narrow crevices in which a variety of plants may thrive. Where space allows, a carefully planned, tiered rock garden may produce a number of useful, broad planting pockets between the rocks.

Bury the rocks to a third of their volume and tip them backwards slightly. This ensures stability and allows water to run back off the rock into the bed rather than onto the plants beneath. Stand on the rocks to make sure that they are stable.

As rocks are positioned, infill planting spaces with prepared compost and firm it in. Any obvious unconformities in the rocks may then be masked by careful planting.

How to plant during construction

To provide a cool, well-drained cavity for growing alpines and other rock plants, plant them between two layers of stone as the rock garden is constructed. Position the plants in the soil close to a stone that has already been firmed in and add a little compost around the roots, firming gently. Use wooden battens to protect the plants as the next stone is placed in position against the first to form a planting pocket or cavity. The battens may then be removed and the second stone firmed in place. Add further compost around the plants and infill with soil between the stones before top-dressing.

1 *Position the plants against a firmed stone. The crowns should face outwards and the roots lie against the rock face. Add compost, and firm to eliminate air pockets.*

2 *Place wooden battens on top of the stone between the plants so that the second stone may be placed in position without crushing the plants.*

3 *When the second stone is in position, remove the wooden battens. Ensure that the stone is stable by firming it well down into the soil.*

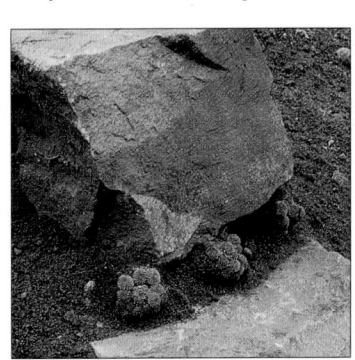

4 *Infill around the stones with topsoil, burying them to a third of their depth. Add prepared compost around the roots of the plants and firm in gently.*

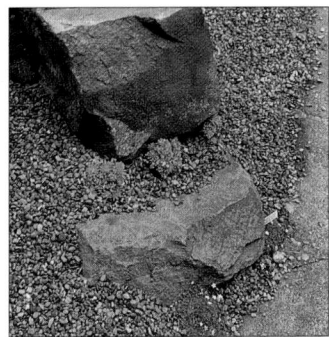

5 *Add a 2.5cm (1in) layer of stone chippings, gravel, or grit as a top-dressing to improve surface drainage and create an attractive and natural finish.*

Soils for rock gardens and scree beds

In nature, many alpines and rock garden plants grow in "soil" that is largely made up of rock fragments and gravel, usually with some accumulations of humus-rich detritus, which retains moisture. Such a growing medium is extremely well drained and it is important to simulate this as closely as possible in a rock garden or scree bed.

Ordinary garden soils may be adapted, to some extent, for cultivating most rock garden plants and alpines by adding peat substitute (or peat) and/or grit, but large quantities of grit are required to provide the rapid drainage needed for the more moisture-sensitive species, such as those grown in scree beds.

Standard mix

A mix of 1 part sterilized garden soil, 1 part peat substitute (or peat), and 1 part sharp sand or coarse grit is suitable for most rock garden plants. The humus-rich materials ensure moisture retention, while the sand or grit maintains good drainage.

Scree mixture

Scree plants require an extremely free-draining compost. Make up a mixture using the same ingredients as for the standard mix, but in different proportions: 3 parts coarse grit or stone chippings (not sand) instead of 1 part. In order to produce a freer-draining compost, increase the proportion of stony material included in the mix. In dry areas, this proportion may have to be reduced to 2 parts; alternatively, use a more retentive mix of 2 parts loam, 2 parts leaf mould, 1 part sharp sand, and 4 parts stone chippings.

Special mix

Some choice alpines, such as the tiny, cushion-forming *Androsace* species and saxifrages, need very free-draining compost. These plants usually come from high altitudes where soil nutrient levels are low. Use a mix of 2 or 3 parts chippings or gravel, to 1 part loam or leaf mould (or peat substitute or peat).

Acid-loving plants

For acid-lovers use a mix of 4 parts lime-free leaf mould, peat substitute (or peat), composted bark, or bracken litter with 1 part coarse sand. On a naturally alkaline soil, however, growing plants in pockets of acid mixture is only effective in the short term, due to the inevitable percolation of lime, which soon kills them. A better solution is to grow these plants in peat beds (see p.206).

Planting a rock garden

Alpines and rock garden plants are almost always purchased as pot plants and may be planted at any time of the year, although it is better not to plant them when the ground is either wet or frozen, or during very warm or dry periods.

Water all the plants thoroughly before planting and allow them to drain. Set the plants out in the planned positions while still in their pots to give an idea of the finished planting. Make any rearrangements at this stage and adjust planting distances, allowing for the vigorous and rapid growth of some types. Slide each plant carefully out of its pot and remove any weeds from the compost. Inspect the roots and top-growth for pests and diseases and treat, as necessary, before planting (see PLANT PROBLEMS, pp.545–77).

Make a planting hole with a trowel or hand fork, ensuring that the hole is big enough to accommodate the roots. Loosen the root ball, position the plant in the hole, and firm in the compost. The plant should sit with the collar slightly above the surface of the compost to leave room for a top-dressing of gravel or chippings.

When all the plants are in place, water them in thoroughly. Keep them moist until they are established and

---

HOW TO PLANT A ROCK GARDEN

1 *Before starting to plant, water all the plants and allow them to drain. To check the planting arrangement, set out the pots on the surface of the bed, taking account of the eventual height and spread of the plants.*

2 *Carefully remove each plant from its pot and loosen the root ball a little to encourage the roots to spread. Remove any moss and weeds before planting.*

3 *Using a trowel, dig a hole large enough to accommodate the root ball. Ease the plant into the hole, and label.*

4 *Fill in around the plant with compost and firm gently, making sure that there are no air pockets between the root ball and the compost.*

5 *Top-dress the compost with a layer of grit or gravel, easing a little around the collars of the plants.*

6 *Continue to plant in the same way until the rock garden is complete. Check that the whole area is properly top-dressed and water in the plants well.*

THE FINISHED ROCK GARDEN
The plants will soon grow away to produce an attractive and mature-looking rock garden.

PLANTING IN A SCREE BED

Pot-grown alpine plants are sometimes slow to establish in scree beds. When planting, remove the bulk of the compost from around the roots and spread out the roots in the scree mixture. This will encourage the roots to spread quickly. Keep well watered until new growth appears.

starting to make new growth. If planting is followed by a dry period, water the plants at approximately weekly intervals until the roots have penetrated the surrounding compost. Thereafter, there should be no need to water except during a drought.

Planting in crevices

Alpines and rock garden plants may be difficult to establish in crevices and need extra care when planting. It is preferable to plant them at the construction stage, although this is not always possible. If planting in the crevices of an established rock garden, use a small tool, such as a widger, to make a planting hole.

Use young, rooted cuttings with vigorous root systems. If only pot-grown plants are available, trim the root balls and top-growth to the appropriate size before planting. Put a small stone in the crevice and place a little compost on top, then ease in the roots with a widger so that the

plant faces outwards. Add more compost around the plant and firm in; place a small stone on top of the root ball for extra support.

Aftercare

Use netting or other deterrents to protect newly planted alpines from birds. Periodically refirm any plants that may have worked loose, adding new compost if necessary. Label the plants or maintain a planting plan to record their names at the time of planting; update planting plans and labelling as plants are added, replaced, or relocated.

Constructing a scree bed

Prepare the site in a similar way to a rock garden, installing artificial drainage, if necessary (see SOILS AND FERTILIZERS, "Improving drainage",

p.529). Sloping sites have naturally good drainage but on flat ground screes are best raised slightly above the ground to assist drainage, and retained within low walls, logs, or old railway sleepers in the same way as raised beds (see p.204).

Scree beds should be 30–40cm (12–16in) deep; about half the depth should be composed of coarse rubble, as for rock gardens, and the upper layer of scree mixture (see p.200). Mark out the site with a rope or hosepipe and on previously grassed areas remove the turf. Lay the rubble foundation and line with thinly cut, inverted turves or a poly-propylene sheet, pierced at regular intervals for good drainage.

Finish off the bed with a 15–20cm (6–8in) layer of scree mixture, and firm by gently treading over the whole area. Water the bed and allow it to settle, then top up with scree mixture any areas that may have sunk before pricking over the surface with a hand fork.

Planting in a scree bed

It may be more difficult to establish plants in a scree bed than in a rock garden, since the freely draining compost tends to dry out before the plants are established. Care during planting and conscientious watering are the keys to success.

The well-developed root systems of pot-grown alpines do not readily penetrate the gritty scree compost, so gently shake off most of the compost (especially if peat-based) from

the roots. Keep the bare roots moist. Place the plant in a planting hole with its roots spread out, and infill carefully with scree mixture. Top-dress with rock chippings and water immediately and thoroughly.

Scree mixes are fast-draining, so water young plants regularly until they are established. In their natural habitats, scree dwellers have deep and extensive root systems to seek out water and nutrients, so when established they will survive for long periods without watering.

Top-dressing rock gardens and screes

After planting is completed, the rock garden or scree bed may then be top-dressed with stone chippings, grit, or gravel. This material should match as closely as possible the rock used at the construction stage.

Top-dressing has a number of advantages: it provides an attractive and natural setting for the plants and blends in better with the rocks than bare soil, creates especially good drainage around the collars of the plants, inhibits weed growth, conserves moisture, and protects the soil surface from compaction during heavy rain or watering.

The layer of top-dressing on a rock garden should be at least 2.5cm (1in) deep, while on a scree bed it may be 2–15cm (^{3}/4–6in) deep, depending on the plants grown; for most screes, a 2–3cm (^{3}/4–1^1/4in) layer is sufficient.

HOW TO PLANT IN A VERTICAL CREVICE

1 *Prepare the crevice for planting by removing the old compost and any debris with a widger or teaspoon. Put a small stone at the base of the crevice.*

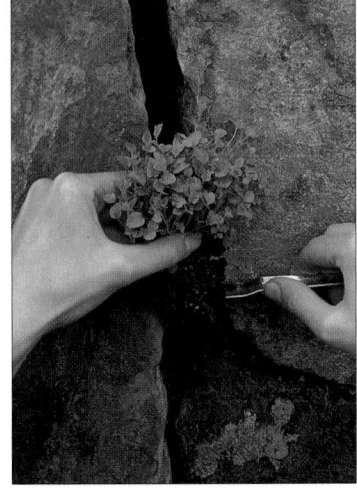

2 *Add 2.5cm (1in) layer of equal parts good soil, coarse grit, and leaf mould. Ease in the roots of the plant (here* Campanula*).*

3 *Cover the roots with another 2.5cm (1in) layer of compost. To keep the plant in place, top the compost with a small stone that slopes down into the rock-face.*

4 *Add more plants, spacing them at least 10cm (4in) apart. Cover the roots of the last plant with compost, then water the crevice to settle the soil.*

Troughs, sinks, and other containers

Alpines and rock garden plants look particularly attractive when grown in troughs and sinks, although most containers are suitable, provided that they allow good drainage and are frost-proof. Choose the correct site at the outset as, once filled, they are heavy and difficult to move. Rocks may be placed in the containers, if desired, to create the effect of a miniature rock garden; this should be done before planting up the container. Select compost to suit the plants to be grown and choose plants that have similar growth rates.

Types of container

Old, stone, animal troughs and stone sinks have traditionally been used to grow alpines and rock garden plants but are now scarce and expensive. Glazed sinks coated in hypertufa, or troughs made entirely of hypertufa or of reconstituted stone are now often used, as are large pottery and terracotta pots and tubs. All should have drainage holes to ensure that there is a free flow of water through the compost. If extra drainage holes are needed, they should be at least 2.5cm (1in) in diameter; if the base of the container is not flat, make the drainage holes at the lowest point.

Covering glazed sinks

Deep, glazed, flat-bottomed sinks may easily be made to resemble stone containers by coating them with hypertufa. Ensure that the sink is clean and dry before coating it, then score the surface with a tile- or glass-cutter to form a key and help the hypertufa to adhere to the sink. To aid adhesion further, paint the surface with a bonding agent before applying the hypertufa.

Make hypertufa from 1–2 parts sifted peat substitute (or sphagnum peat), 1 part coarse sand or fine grit, and 1 part cement. Add sufficient water to form a thick paste. Apply this to the outside of the sink and also inside, down to well below the final level of the compost. Put the hypertufa on by hand (wear gloves); it should be 1–2cm ($\frac{1}{2}$–$\frac{3}{4}$in) thick.

COVERING A GLAZED SINK WITH HYPERTUFA

Glazed sinks covered with hypertufa make fine containers for alpines.

Roughen the surface so that it resembles stone. When the hypertufa is fully dry, after about a week, scrub the surface with a wire brush and coat with permanganate of potash or liquid manure to encourage the growth of algae, mosses, and lichens, for a more natural look.

Hypertufa troughs

Troughs may be made entirely from hypertufa, if required. Prepare the mixture as for coating but increase the proportion of sand and grit to three parts to make a stiffer mix.

Use two wooden boxes that fit inside one another, with a cavity of 5–7cm (2–3in) between them. Stand the larger box on blocks so that it may be lifted once finished; pour two thin layers of the hypertufa mix into the base, with strong wire netting between the layers and parallel to the vertical sides. Press thick dowels or pegs through the hypertufa to make drainage holes. Fit the smaller box inside the larger, with netting between the two, and fill the space with the mix, tamping it down to remove air pockets.

When the cavity is full, cover the trough with a sheet of plastic for at least a week while the mix sets and protect the trough from frost, if necessary. When the mix has set hard, remove the boxes and dowels. If the boxes do not slide off easily, ease them off carefully with a fine chisel and a small hammer. Roughen the surface of the trough with a wire brush and paint on a coat of liquid manure or permanganate of potash to encourage algal growth.

HOW TO MAKE A HYPERTUFA TROUGH

1 *You will need two boxes to make the trough, one slightly larger than the other. Coat the surfaces of the boxes with oil to prevent the hypertufa sticking.*

2 *Place a 2.5cm (1in) layer of hypertufa mix in the base of the larger box and put wire netting on top of this layer and around the sides to reinforce the trough. Then add another layer of hypertufa.*

3 *Press several thick, wooden dowels into the wire and hypertufa base to make the drainage holes for the bottom of the trough.*

4 *Put the smaller box centrally on top of the hypertufa base, making sure the vertical netting is between the two boxes. Fill the cavity with the hypertufa mix, tamping down well as you fill.*

5 *Cover the top of the hypertufa with plastic sheeting until the mix has set (which usually takes about a week). Secure the sheeting in place with a weight and protect the trough from frost.*

6 *When the hypertufa has set, remove the wooden shuttering from the outside of the trough. If the hypertufa has stuck to the box, carefully dismantle the box with a hammer and chisel.*

7 *The surface of the hypertufa will be smooth and straight; for a more natural-looking appearance, scrub the outside of the trough with a wire brush or coarse-grained sandpaper to roughen the surface.*

8 *Remove the smaller box, using a hammer and chisel if necessary. To encourage algal and moss growth, paint the outside surface of the trough with liquid manure.*

Siting containers

An open position, with sun for at least part of the day, is ideal for most plants. Do not place containers in windy sites, unless tough plants are being grown, or on lawns, since it is difficult to maintain the surrounding grass. Avoid slopes, which cause instability, and put containers as close as possible to a tap or hosepipe.

Raise troughs and sinks off the ground, up to a height of about 45cm (18in); the plants may then be viewed comfortably and water will drain away readily. Stone or brick pillars at the corners of a container provide sturdy, stable supports. These must bear the weight of the container without danger of tipping, and should not block the drainage holes. Sinks with single drainage holes should be tilted so that excess water drains off.

Placing rocks and tufa

Virtually any type of rock may be used in troughs and sinks. Rocks give height, and allow a greater depth of compost. A few large rocks are better than many small ones. Niches and crevices in the rocks may also be used to support plants, especially if hard tufa is used. Tufa's light weight and the ease with which planting holes can be excavated in it make it ideal. Roots spread into the porous rock, which is well aerated but also retains water.

Whatever type of rock is used, bury from one third to one half of each stone in the compost to ensure that it is firmly seated.

Filling the container

Most rock garden plants thrive in standard potting compost, preferably with some additional drainage material. Add about one third by volume of 6–9mm ($\frac{1}{4}$–$\frac{3}{8}$in) stone chippings, and mix in some slow-release fertilizer. Acid-loving plants need a lime-free compost, with added granite or sandstone chippings.

Cover the drainage holes with broken crocks or wire gauze and fill the bottom quarter to one third of the container with coarse aggregate, gravel, or stone chippings. Add a layer of fibrous peat substitute (or peat) or inverted, thinly cut turf. Fill up with slightly moist compost, and firm it gently.

Position pieces of rock or tufa on the compost, and bed them in as the container is filled. Place rocks to form crevices and niches, providing both shaded and sunny faces to suit different plants, and add randomly placed smaller pieces of stone to simulate a small-scale rock garden. Water thoroughly and leave to drain completely before planting.

Planting

Choose compact, slow-growing plants that will not swamp their neighbours and quickly exhaust the available nutrients. Do not overplant the container, and replant as soon as it becomes overcrowded (see p.208).

Position container-grown plants, still in their pots, on the compost or make a plan on paper of the planting scheme. Make planting holes, carefully slide the plants out of their pots, and loosen the root balls. Place the plants in the holes, fill in with compost, and firm. When complete, water thoroughly. Then add a layer of top-dressing to help ensure sharp drainage, using chippings or gravel that complement any rocks included.

Planting in tufa

If plants are to be grown in tufa rock, use a drill or a hammer and chisel, and make holes 10–12cm (4–5in) apart. They should be about 2.5cm (1in) in diameter and 5–7cm (2–3in) deep, angled at 30–45° on vertical or sloping surfaces, or straight down on horizontal planes. Soak the tufa, then put a little sharp sand in each hole, and add some compost. Use young, rooted cuttings or small plants, since they establish easily. Wash the roots before planting; ease them into the holes with a small dibber or a pencil and sprinkle in compost until the hole is full. Ensure that the neck of the plant is bedded in and not standing proud of the hole. Firm the compost and wedge small pieces of tufa around the plants to hold them in place. Water thoroughly and keep the tufa moist until the plants are established. In hot, dry weather, soak the tufa regularly.

HOW TO PLANT UP AN ALPINE TROUGH

1 *If planting in tufa, first drill holes in it about 2.5cm (1in) wide, 7cm (3in) deep, and no less than 10cm (4in) apart. Immerse the tufa in water overnight.*

2 *Lay fine-mesh netting over the trough base, cover the holes with crocks, and add 7–10cm (3–4in) of coarse grit.*

3 *Partly fill the trough with a gritty, moist compost, firming it in stages. Set the tufa in place so that at least $\frac{1}{3}$–$\frac{1}{2}$ of it is buried to keep it stable.*

4 *Continue to fill with compost and firm well to allow about 5cm (2in) for top-dressing and watering. Insert a little compost into the tufa holes for planting.*

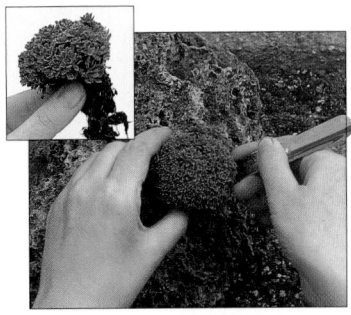

5 *Wash the roots of the plants to go in the tufa, and ease them into the planting holes. Dribble compost into the holes, firm, and put small rock pieces around the plants.*

6 *Set the plants, still in their pots, on the compost to check that the arrangement and spacing are satisfactory, then plant and firm them in. Water well.*

THE FINISHED TROUGH

7 *Water the compost thoroughly, then top-dress the trough with a 2.5–5cm (1–2in) deep layer of coarse gravel or stone chippings.*

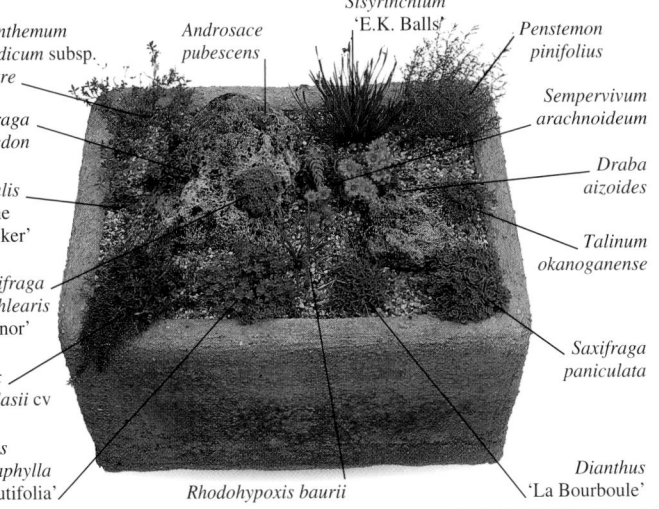

Helianthemum oelandicum subsp. *alpestre*

Saxifraga cotyledon

Oxalis 'Ione Hecker'

Saxifraga cochlearis 'Minor'

Phlox douglasii cv

Oxalis enneaphylla 'Minutifolia'

Rhodohypoxis baurii

Androsace pubescens

Sisyrinchium 'E.K. Balls'

Penstemon pinifolius

Sempervivum arachnoideum

Draba aizoides

Talinum okanoganense

Saxifraga paniculata

Dianthus 'La Bourboule'

Walls

Alpines and rock garden plants may be grown in the crevices of dry-stone walls, including the retaining walls of raised beds and sloping banks. Trailing plants are especially effective when grown in this way. For details on constructing a wall, see "Dry-stone walls", p.506.

If possible, plan for any planting in walls before construction work starts. The most practical approach is to leave planting niches at intervals in the wall and plant them up when the building work is finished.

It is also possible to position the plants as construction proceeds. This produces excellent results, since the plants may be placed at the desired level, and ensures good contact between the roots of the plants and any soil behind the wall. Planting during construction also makes it easier to eliminate air pockets in the compost and firm around the roots.

Planting in existing walls is another option but some of the soil may need to be removed first with a widger or teaspoon before planting. Use young plants or rooted cuttings, since these fit easily in the crevices.

HOW TO BUILD A DRY-STONE RETAINING WALL

MAKING THE FOOTINGS
Dig a trench 38cm (15in) deep; fill it with 25cm (10in) of rubble with a large, sturdy stone on top.

PLACING THE STONES
Slope the stones backwards and downwards for stability and so that water is carried into the compost.

FILLING BETWEEN STONES
As you build, fill crevices between the stones with a compost of loam, leaf mould, and sand or grit.

Filling with compost

For filling the planting crevices in walls, the following mix should be used: 3 parts loam (or good sterilized garden soil), 2 parts coarse fibrous peat substitute or peat, and 1–2 parts sharp sand or grit.

Use extra grit, sand, or stone chippings for plants that are to be grown in the wall itself, since this will help to ensure good drainage.

Planting

Choose plants that grow well in the aspect and conditions available in the wall. Use seedlings or small rooted cuttings, which are easily inserted into the wall crevices. Carefully remove old compost from the roots and ease them into the hole, using a small dibber or a pencil. Do not try to cram roots into too small a space as this damages the plants. Trickle in fresh, moist compost and firm it to remove air pockets. It may be helpful to wedge small stones around the collars of the plants to hold them in place and prevent the compost from being dislodged.

Water thoroughly from the top of the wall and spray the plants regularly until established. After several days, top up any sunken areas with spare compost. Periodically check the plants and firm any that have worked loose.

Raised beds

A wide range of alpine plants may be grown in raised beds, both in the beds themselves and in crevices in the supporting walls. The bed's design should harmonize with the house and garden. Depending on the needs of the chosen plants, a raised bed may be positioned in either sun or shade. Fill the bed with well-drained compost to suit the plants (see p.200). If necessary, plants may be protected in winter with glass or plastic covers placed over the bed.

Siting

For most alpines and rock garden plants, raised beds should be sited in an open, sunny position away from the shade cast by overhanging trees or nearby buildings and fences. Place a raised bed in shade only if woodland or other plants requiring cooler, shadier conditions are to be grown.

To aid mowing, a raised bed that is positioned on a lawn should have a surround of paving slabs or bricks set just below the level of the grass. Raised beds that are constructed for the older or disabled gardener should have wheelchair access, and the beds should be of a height and width to allow the plants to be tended and viewed easily.

HOW TO PLANT IN A DRY-STONE WALL

1 *If planting in an existing wall, check that there is an adequate amount of compost in the crevices to support the plants.*

2 *Use seedlings or small rooted cuttings. Place them on the flat of a stone and, using a widger, ease the roots into the crevices. The plant shown here is a* Sempervivum.

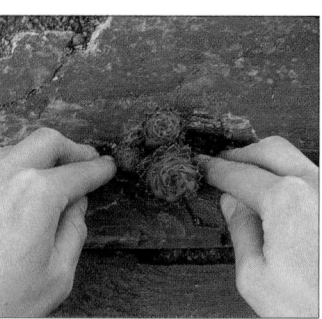

3 *Bed the plants down into compost and pack more compost into the crevices to hold the plants in position. Firm the plants in with your fingers.*

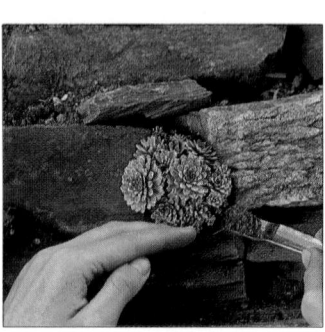

4 *For larger plants, scoop out some compost from the crevices. Ease the roots into the holes and add more compost while holding plants in position.*

5 *When all the plants are in position, water them from the top of the wall or with a mist spray. Keep the plants moist until established and refirm any that work loose. Planted with the* Sempervivum *are 2 saxifrages.*

On sites where the construction of a ground-based scree bed is not possible because of poor drainage, a scree may be placed on the surface of a raised bed instead (see p.201).

Materials and design
Raised beds may be made from stone, brick, old wooden railway sleepers, or any other suitable and attractive material. Stone is the dearest; new or second-hand bricks and sleepers are cheaper and easier to use.

The bed may be almost any shape but it should harmonize with the general design of the garden. Rectangular beds are the most common. The ideal height for a raised bed is 60–75cm (24–30in), although a tiered bed is also attractive and may be more appropriate where space is limited. The width of the bed should be no more than 1.5m (5ft) to allow comfortable access – the centre of the bed should be within arm's reach to allow weeding from all sides.

Large beds may need an irrigation system; install water pipes and inlets before filling the beds with compost.

Construction
Retaining brick walls for raised beds should be vertical; the thickness of one brick is usually adequate. They are built in the same way as a conventional wall and may be mortared but small gaps should be left between bricks at intervals for plants to be inserted. There should also be gaps at the base for drainage. For further information, see STRUCTURES AND SURFACES, "Raised beds", p.507.

Raised beds may also have stone retaining walls. If they are built without mortar they need a slight inward slope for stability (see "Dry-stone walls", p.506). Dry-stone walls are time-consuming to build, since each stone needs to be chosen and positioned carefully. Large crevices may be left between the stones to be planted up with alpines. If wooden sleepers are used, crevice-planting is not possible.

Soil for raised beds
Use a mix of 3 parts loam (or good sterilized garden soil), 2 parts coarse fibrous peat substitute (such as acidic leaf mould or garden compost) or peat, and 1–2 parts grit or sharp sand. For plants that need acid conditions, use lime-free loam and grit. To grow plants that need different soil types in a large bed, divide it into sections with plastic sheeting to keep the sections apart, and fill each with appropriate compost.

Preparing the raised bed
Fill the bottom third of the bed with coarse gravel, stones, or rubble, then place a layer of inverted turves or fibrous peat substitute (or peat) over the top to prevent the drainage material from becoming clogged. Fill the bed with prepared compost, which should be well worked into all the corners and firmed as filling proceeds. Incorporate a slow-release fertilizer. Some settling always occurs, so water the bed thoroughly and leave it for two or three weeks. Top up any sunken areas with spare compost before planting.

Adding rocks gives the effect of a rock garden in miniature and enhances the appearance of raised beds. Set pieces of rock of varying sizes into the compost to provide suitable sites for a range of different plants. Several large pieces of rock arranged together as outcrops are more effective than scattered rocks.

Planting and top-dressing
Make a planting plan or set out the plants on the surface of the bed to see how they will look. Dwarf conifers and small shrubs, tufted and cushion-forming alpines, trailing alpines at the edges of the bed, and some of the smaller bulbs are ideal. Select plants for year-round interest. Plant as for rock gardens (see p.200), with trailing plants near the edges; any crevices in the retaining walls may also be planted up as for dry-stone walls (see p.204).

After planting, top-dress the bed with stone chippings or coarse grit, to match any rocks. Work a 1cm (^{1}/2in) deep layer of the top-dressing carefully around the plants and beneath their collars. This looks attractive, suppresses weeds, and reduces evaporation. Water the bed regularly until the plants are established.

Winter protection
Many alpines dislike excessive winter moisture, even in the well-drained conditions of a raised bed. These may be protected with cloches or sheets of glass or plastic. Use bricks or a wire frame to support the sheets. Fasten down the covering, or it may be blown off.

Such protection should be put in place in late autumn and removed the following spring. If the whole bed needs covering, build a wooden framework for a glass or plastic roof. Plenty of air must circulate around the plants so that they remain as dry as possible, so do not cover the sides of the protective frame.

A RAISED ALPINE BED

A wide range of alpine plants may be grown in a raised bed, both in the bed itself and in crevices in the retaining walls. If rocks are included, these will provide sunny and shady aspects to suit the needs of different plants.

1 *Androsace lanuginosa*
2 *Saponaria* x *olivana*
3 *Origanum* 'Kent Beauty'
4 *Cytisus ardoinii*
5 *Daphne petraea* 'Grandiflora'
6 *Anchusa caespitosa*
7 *Globularia meridionalis*
8 *Penstemon pinifolius*
9 *Dianthus alpinus*
10 *Androsace carnea* subsp. *laggeri*
11 *Edraianthus serpyllifolius*
12 *Saxifraga scardica*
13 *Helichrysum selago*
14 *Morisia monanthos*
15 *Anacyclus depressus*
16 *Erinacea pungens*
17 *Saxifraga* 'Southside Seedling'
18 *Saxifraga burseriana*
19 *Phlox* 'Camla'
20 *Androsace pyrenaica*
21 *Saxifraga grisebachii* 'Wisley Variety'
22 *Parnassia palustris*
23 *Draba rigida*
24 *Euryops acraeus*
25 *Dianthus* 'La Bourboule'
26 *Androsace carnea*
27 *Daphne arbuscula*
28 *Bolax gummifera*
29 *Penstemon newberryi* f. *humilior*
30 *Dianthus pavonius*
31 *Gentiana verna*
32 *Sagina boydii*
33 *Saxifraga* 'Jenkinsiae'

34 *Saxifraga oppositifolia*
35 *Corydalis solida* 'George Baker'
36 *Cyananthus microphyllus*
37 *Phlox stolonifera* 'Ariane'
38 *Soldanella alpina*
39 *Ranunculus alpestris*
40 *Calceolaria* 'Walter Shrimpton'
41 *Gentiana saxosa*
42 *Edraianthus pumilio*

43 *Vitaliana primuliflora*
44 *Daphne cneorum*
45 *Lewisia*, Cotyledon Hybrids
46 *Raoulia australis*
47 *Phlox bifida*
48 *Androsace villosa*
49 *Lewisia* 'George Henley'
50 *Ramonda myconi*
51 *Arenaria balearica*

HOW TO CONSTRUCT A PEAT BED

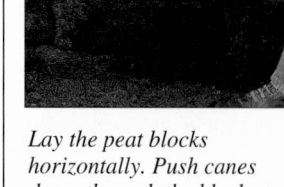

1 *Use a site that is clear of perennial weeds and remove annual weeds. Mark contours with sticks, and terrace the slope with 75cm (30in) wide "steps".*

2 *Soak the peat blocks before use. Make a shallow trench at the base of the lowest step and lay a wall of vertical peat blocks, sloping them inwards. Butt them together and firm.*

3 *Fill the terraces to the top of the blocks with 2 parts peat substitute (or peat), 2 parts acid soil (with slow-release fertilizer), and 1 part lime-free sharp sand or grit.*

Lay the peat blocks horizontally. Push canes down through the blocks to hold them in place.

4 *When all the terraces are filled, allow the peat bed to settle for several days. Water the bed regularly during this period to keep the peat moist and top up with further compost, if necessary, before planting.*

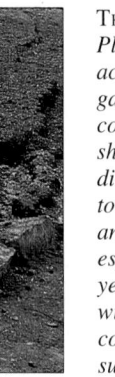

THE FINISHED BED
Plant up the bed with acid-loving rock garden plants and compact, slow-growing shrubs for a fine display. Water often to keep the peat blocks and compost moist, especially in the first year. Top-dress the bed with bark chippings to conserve moisture and suppress weeds.

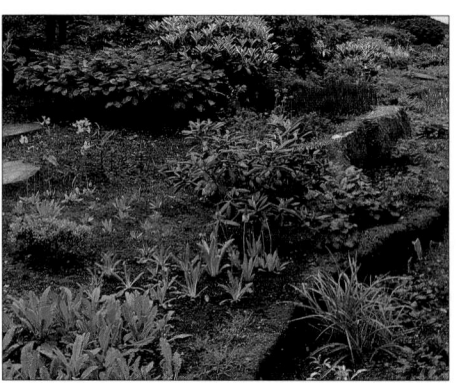

Peat beds

Peat beds provide ideal conditions for a wide range of acid-loving and woodland plants. In gardens with alkaline soils, peat beds should always be isolated from the ground with a plastic or butyl rubber liner so that lime cannot enter.

Consider the needs of the plants when deciding where to place a peat bed, and construct the bed so that it blends in well with the rest of the garden. It is not necessary to use pure peat, since acidic peat substitutes are now available. Plants may be grown on the surface of the bed and in wall crevices to produce an attractive arrangement.

Siting

Choose a site that receives sun and dappled shade, ideally facing away from direct sun. An area next to a rock garden, on a slope, or by the side of a building is appropriate. Peat beds on exposed sites in full sun lose moisture rapidly, and need frequent watering. Dense shade of trees is unsuitable, and the tree roots nearby soon exhaust the moisture and nutrients. Waterlogged sites and frost pockets are not suitable either.

Materials and design

Peat blocks may be used to build the walls of the bed, although these are now less readily available because of concerns about peat conservation. Other suitable materials include logs and railway sleepers.

On a slope, the materials may be arranged in steps to give a terraced effect. The steps may be straight or curved, but it is important to make the finished structure look fairly natural. On flat sites, peat beds may be constructed with retaining walls in a similar way to raised beds.

Constructing the bed

Mark out the shape of the bed with a length of rope or hosepipe. On soils where lime is present, lay a sheet of heavy-duty plastic or butyl rubber to isolate the bed from the underlying soil and prevent any seepage of lime or chalk into the compost. Mound the ground under the sheet so that excess moisture drains off, with a layer of sand on top to prevent stones from damaging the sheet. Tuck its edges into a surrounding trench.

If peat blocks are used, they should be soaked with water and then allowed to drain before building the walls or terraces of the bed. To make

terraces on a sloping site, place the peat blocks, sleepers, or logs in an upright position in a stepped formation. Seat them well into the ground to ensure stability, and backfill with an acidic compost.

If building a bed with retaining walls, set the first layer of peat blocks, sleepers, or logs in a shallow trench about 7cm (3in) deep around the perimeter. Angle the blocks so that the inside edges are a little lower than the outer ones. This gives the wall a slight slope and strengthens the structure. Lay subsequent rows of blocks (to a maximum of three layers) on top of the first, so that the joint between each pair of blocks falls in the middle of the block immediately below.

Butt the blocks tightly together and push sharpened canes vertically down through the blocks at frequent intervals to hold them firmly in place. If desired, leave several gaps between the blocks as niches for planting suitable species.

Filling peat beds

A suitable compost for peat beds consists of 2 parts fibrous peat substitute or moss peat, 2 parts acidic, fibrous, acid loam (preferably

sterilized and with added fertilizer), and 1 part lime-free sand or grit. Peat substitutes include coconut fibre, well-rotted, sieved garden compost, and leaf mould, if they are water-retentive. Check the pH of all of the materials intended for the compost mix and do not use any with a pH close to or above 7, since this indicates alkalinity.

Fill the bed with compost, treading it down lightly. Water the bed thoroughly and leave it for several days to allow the compost to settle. Before planting, top up sunken areas of the bed with additional compost.

Planting and top-dressing

Prepare a detailed planting plan on paper or set out the pots on the surface of the bed. Position trailing plants in crevices in the walls, and small shrubs in the bed itself to provide focal points. Use prostrate shrubs and trailing species to mask the joints between the blocks.

Plant as for rock gardens (see p.200), and insert plants into any crevices as for walls (see p.204). Firm in all the plants and water thoroughly. Top-dress the bed with bark chippings and water regularly during the first season after planting.

Routine care

E VEN when alpines and rock plants are established in the garden, it is essential to care for them regularly. Beds, troughs, and sinks must be kept clean and free of weeds. Although the plants do not usually need nutrient-rich soil, they should be fed at intervals and watered whenever the soil becomes dry. Top-dressings, which improve drainage around the collars of the plants, suppress weed growth, and reduce evaporation of water from the soil, should be replenished occasionally.

Alpines and rock garden plants benefit from periodic removal of dead wood, leaves and flowers, and should be kept trimmed. Troughs, sinks, and other containers should be replanted as soon as they become overcrowded. Check plants routinely for signs of pest infestation and disease, and treat them as necessary. In cold or wet weather, some plants may need winter protection.

Weeding

The use of sterilized compost when planting should minimize problems with weeds, at least for the first years. Always try to remove all weeds as soon as they appear, certainly before they flower and set seed. If perennial weeds do become established and are difficult to remove, paint the foliage carefully with a translocated weedkiller, which is transmitted to the roots and kills them. For further information, see PLANT PROBLEMS, "Controlling weeds", p.573.

When weeding, use a three-pronged hand cultivator to loosen and aerate compacted soil around young plants, if necessary.

Feeding

Newly planted areas should not normally need feeding for some years if the original compost has been correctly prepared and includes slow-release fertilizer. After some time, however, the growth of the plants may begin to slow down and flowering become sparser. This may be remedied by gently scratching in around the plants a dressing of bone meal each spring, combined with a slow-release fertilizer.

Alternatively, carefully remove the top-dressing and a layer of about 1cm (½in) of compost from the surface of the bed and replace it with fresh compost and a further top-dressing of grit.

Top-dressing

The type of top-dressing used for alpines and rock garden plants depends on the plants that are grown, although it should match any of the rocks and stones that feature in beds and rock gardens as closely as possible. Top-dressings used in troughs, sinks, or raised beds should also harmonize well with the container or retaining walls.

Coarse grit or stone chippings are suitable for most situations, but limestone chippings should never be used around lime-hating plants. For plants grown in peat beds, a top-dressing of bark chippings will complement the plantings.

Renewing top-dressings

Top-dressings may need to be renewed from time to time, since grit or stone chippings gradually wash away, especially on slopes, and bark tends to decompose and mix in with the underlying compost. Watch for bare patches throughout the season and top up as necessary. Pay close attention to top-dressings in the autumn, to ensure good soil coverage in winter and avoid compaction by heavy rain. Check again in spring and top up, as necessary. A slow-release fertilizer may be applied at the same time.

Watering

Established plants growing in rock gardens and screes root deeply into the soil and do not usually need more water than is supplied by rainfall. In droughts, however, the area should be thoroughly soaked. Do not water in very frosty conditions or during the heat of the day – early mornings or late evenings are the best times; soak occasionally rather than giving small amounts of water frequently. If the compost is dry at a depth of 3–5cm (1¼–2in), water thoroughly until the water has penetrated to the full depth of the roots. During an average summer this should only be needed two or three times but in very dry summers may be required more frequently.

Watering in containers, raised beds, and under cover

Alpines and rock garden plants that are grown in raised beds, sinks and troughs, under frames, and in the alpine house will need more regular watering, since the soil dries out more quickly than in rock gardens and scree beds.

It is preferable to hand-water troughs and sinks if specialist collections of plants are being grown, so that each plant may be provided with the correct amount of water. This is time-consuming, however, particularly where there are several containers to be watered.

Plants grown in pots in alpine houses and frames should be watered individually. If the pots are plunged in gravel or stone chippings, water both the pots and the surrounding material. Some alpine plants have water-sensitive foliage and therefore dislike overhead watering; if this is the case, regularly soaking only the plunge material should provide sufficient moisture.

RENEWING TOP-DRESSING

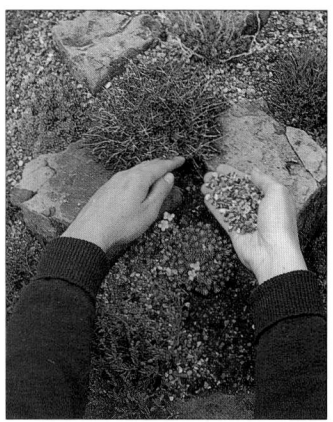

1 Remove the old top-dressing and some compost (see inset). Fill in around the plants with fresh compost (see p.200).

2 Top-dress the bed with a fresh layer of coarse grit or gravel, adding some around and beneath the collars of the plants.

Trimming and pruning

Alpines and rock garden plants need to be cut back periodically to maintain a natural, compact shape and healthy growth, and to restrict them within their allotted space.

Pruning woody plants

To keep rock garden shrubs and woody perennials healthy, any dead, diseased, or damaged wood should be removed. Check the plants regularly and prune them cleanly, using secateurs or sharp scissors.

Severe pruning is unnecessary because most dwarf shrubs are slow-growing and do not outgrow their positions for many years. When

REMOVING DEAD GROWTH

In spring, after all danger of frost has passed, cut out any dieback from plants, trimming carefully to healthy growth with sharp scissors or secateurs.

WEEDING

Weed around young plants with a 3-pronged cultivator, which also loosens and aerates the soil. Remove any top-dressing first and replace it after weeding.

REMOVING DEAD ROSETTES

1 *To remove dead rosettes from plants such as saxifrages, cut out the rosettes with a sharp knife without disturbing the rest of the plant.*

2 *Top-dress the exposed soil to prevent weeds growing through the gaps until the plant produces fresh growth.*

CUTTING BACK AFTER FLOWERING

1 *After flowering, cut back stems (here Helianthemum) to half their length to encourage healthy, new growth.*

2 *The plants will remain compact and produce a good crop of flowers the following year.*

RENOVATING AN ALPINE BED

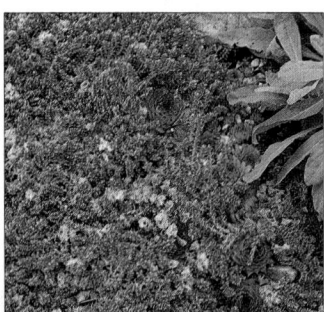

1 *Plants that spread rapidly (here Paronychia kapela subsp. chionaea) may eventually smother less vigorous plants nearby. Cut them back in spring.*

2 *Dig up or pull out clumps of encroaching plants. Straggly plants should be cut back severely. Make sure that plants nearby have plenty of room to grow.*

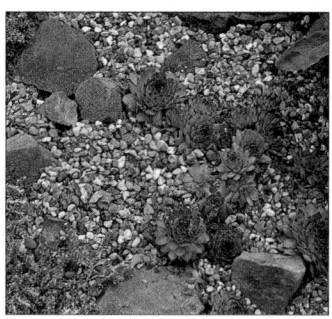

3 *Add a dressing of balanced fertilizer to the bed, before placing a fresh layer of top-dressing on the surface of the compost around the plants.*

pruning, aim to maintain the natural shape of the plant, especially in the case of dwarf conifers.

Removing dead flowers and foliage

Regularly remove all dead flowers and leaves, and any unwanted seedheads, with a sharp knife, secateurs, or scissors.

Pick over small alpine plants by hand, using tweezers, if necessary, to remove dead leaves and flowers. Carefully cut out dead rosettes from plants such as saxifrages; do not pull them off by hand, however, as this may loosen healthy rosettes.

Helianthemum species and cultivars, in particular, need clipping with shears annually after flowering, cutting back the stems by about half their length to encourage growth for flowering the following year. Genera such as *Arabis*, *Aubrieta*, and *Aurinia* also benefit from hard annual pruning (after flowering), which helps to keep them compact and free-flowering. Plants may produce a second flush of flowers if cut back before they set seed.

Encroaching plants

Over-vigorous plants and old, straggly plants that are beginning to encroach on their neighbours should be cut back in early spring. Mat-forming plants may simply be pulled out by hand, others may need to be lifted with a hand fork. Support nearby plants and refirm any that are accidentally lifted. Remove or cut back plants to allow a clear area of bed around all the remaining plants so that they can grow unimpeded.

Hard-pruned plants should be top-dressed with a balanced fertilizer in order to promote strong, new growth.

Winter protection

Plants in troughs, sinks, or raised beds, and some alpine bulbs, may need protection from winter wet. Use a single, propped pane of glass, an open cloche, or, for large areas, a frame light, which will give overhead protection without inhibiting air circulation. Ensure that covers are firmly secured or weighted down. Some protection from severe cold may be provided by placing a layer of evergreen branches or pine boughs over the plants.

Controlling pests and diseases

Few serious problems affect alpines and rock garden plants, but some of the more common pests and diseases may need to be controlled. Regular, basic garden hygiene is often sufficient to control most problems encountered. Aphids (p.550) are likely to be troublesome if alpines are grown in too rich a soil, which induces soft, lank growth.

Coarse top-dressings around plants tend to deter slugs and snails but some control is still necessary, particularly for choice alpines, such as *Campanula zoysii*, which are susceptible to attack from these pests. Control insects such as ants (p.570), which will excavate under cushion-forming plants. Prevent birds from disturbing newly planted specimens by covering the plants with netting.

Fungal diseases may quickly become established in alpine houses and frames (see pp.214–16).

Replanting an alpine trough

Plants in containers eventually need replanting when nutrients in the compost are exhausted. Water thoroughly before carefully removing the plants. Discard the compost and replace it with a fresh, suitable mix (see p.200), containing a slow-release fertilizer. Trim roots and top-growth before returning plants to the container; allow for their eventual spread and top-dress with gravel.

Helianthemum sp.

Iris cristata

Ramonda myconi

Helianthemum sp.

Propagation

MANY alpines and rock garden plants may be propagated from seed, although some plants are sterile and do not produce seed. In addition, cultivars seldom come true from seed and must be increased in other ways. Alternative methods include cuttings (of various types) and division.

Seed

Propagation from seed is the best way to produce large numbers of plants. Since many alpines flower in early spring, ripe seed is often available from mid-summer, and may be sown straight away. Germination will usually occur rapidly and strong seedlings will be produced before winter. Autumn-sown seeds may remain dormant until spring; if germination occurs, overwinter the seedlings in frames. It may sometimes be better to store seed over winter and sow in early spring, although short-lived seed should be sown as soon as it is ripe.

Seed collection and storage
Collect seed as the seedheads become ripe. Remove them while still attached to the stems and place them in paper (not plastic) bags to dry out. Enclose in envelopes any that might split open on drying. Store seeds in a cool, dry, well-ventilated place. Most alpines have seed capsules from which seed may be extracted by rubbing between the fingers. Fleshy fruits may need to be squashed and left on paper to dry.

Separate the seed from the debris by sieving or hand-picking when dry. Put it in sealed, labelled envelopes, and place these in an airtight container in a cool place.

Pre-sowing treatment
Seeds with hard coats need special treatment to allow them to absorb water. Scarify by chipping the seed coat with a sharp knife or rubbing with a file or fine abrasive paper. In some cases, soaking the seed for 12–24 hours will accelerate the take-up of water.

Hard-cased seeds of woody rock garden plants do not respond to scarification alone; they also need exposure to cold (stratification). Store the seeds in boxes of moist sand outdoors for two or three months during winter, and sow in spring; alternatively, sow the seed in pots of seed compost and keep these in the freezer or refrigerator, sealed in plastic bags, for several

weeks before plunging the pots in the ground outside until the seed germinates. Some seeds, such as *Trillium* and peonies (*Paeonia*), need alternating periods of cold and warmth to germinate successfully.

Sowing the seed
Use clean clay or plastic pots, and place broken crocks over the drainage holes. A compost of equal parts sieved peat substitute (or peat) and perlite is suitable, or use loam-based seed compost, mixed with an equal amount of perlite or sharp sand. Fill the pots and firm the compost. Tap out small seeds thinly and evenly and space large seeds by hand, covering them with their own depth of compost. Mix fine seeds with fine, dry, silver sand before sowing but do not cover with more compost.

After sowing, cover all but fine seeds with a 5–10mm (¹/₄–¹/₂in) layer of 5mm (¹/₄in) diameter grit or pea shingle, to deter mosses and liverworts and protect the seed from heavy rain or watering. Label the pots and stand them in water to half their depth, removing them when the compost surface becomes moist. Keep the compost moist at all times.

Germination
Speed of germination depends on the type and age of the seed, and when it is sown. Some seed takes months or even years to germinate.

A cool, sheltered site outdoors is ideal for the seeds of most alpines. Plunge pots in moist sand to maintain an even temperature and reduce the need for watering. When seedlings appear, move the pots to a cold frame. Germination may be speeded up by placing the pots in gentle heat in early spring, but do not expose the seeds to high temperatures.

Pricking out and potting up
Prick out seedlings when they are 5–10mm (¹/₄–¹/₂in) tall and when two true leaves have formed. Knock out the compost and separate the seedlings. Handle only by the leaves or cotyledons to avoid damage to stems and roots. Pot up seedlings individually in small clay pots or plastic pots, or in module packs using low-fertility loam-based potting compost mixed with an equal amount of grit. Fill the container, settle the compost, and make a hole for the roots. Put the seedling in the hole, fill with compost, and firm lightly.

Top-dress seedlings in individual pots with a 5–10mm (¹/₄–¹/₂in) layer of grit. Water them thoroughly with

a fine-rosed watering can and place the containers in a lightly shaded position, until the seedlings are established. Water as required. When the roots are visible through the drainage holes, pot them on.

Seeds that are slow to germinate often do so erratically, and if only a few seedlings appear prick them out as soon as they are large enough to handle. Disturb the rest of the compost as little as possible, and cover it with fresh top-dressing. Put the pot back into the frame in case more seeds germinate.

ROCK PLANT SEED TO BE SOWN FRESH
Anemone
Codonopsis
Corydalis
Cyclamen (alpine spp.)
Dodecatheon
Hepatica
Meconopsis
Primula (alpine spp.)
Pulsatilla
Ranunculus (alpine spp.)

SOWING SEED

1 *Prepare a pot by filling it with equal parts of seed compost and horticultural sand. Firm the compost gently to level the surface and eliminate air pockets.*

2 *Small seed (here Lewisia) should be tapped out evenly over the surface of the compost. Space larger seed by hand.*

3 *Cover the seeds with a fine layer of compost, then top-dress with grit to protect the seeds and prevent the growth of mosses. Water in and label.*

4 *Prick out seedlings when they have 2 true leaves (see inset). Lift the seedlings carefully, handling them by the leaves only.*

5 *Fill pots with equal parts of loam-based potting compost and grit. Pot up the seedlings singly, firming with a dibber.*

6 *Top-dress with grit, water, and place the seedlings in light shade. Pot on the seedlings when the roots fill the pot.*

Aubrieta deltoidea
'Argenteo-variegata'

Viola
'Jackanapes'

Helianthemum
'Fire Dragon'

Softwood and greenwood cuttings

Softwood cuttings are taken from the non-flowering, leafy shoots of a plant during periods of active growth, usually in spring.

Greenwood cuttings are taken in early summer when growth has slowed down; although slightly riper than softwood cuttings, they require the same treatment.

Taking the cuttings

Take the cuttings early in the morning, when the shoots are fully turgid. For softwood cuttings select strong, young shoots that are soft and pliable, with no trace of woodiness or hardening; greenwood cuttings may be just beginning to harden at the base. Cuttings should be about 2.5–7cm (1–3in) long and taken with a sharp knife. Place them immediately in a plastic bag to conserve moisture and prevent them from wilting.

Inserting the cuttings

Trim the base of each cutting cleanly with a sharp knife just below a node (leaf joint) and remove the lower leaves. Pinch off any shoot tips that are soft, particularly if these are showing signs of wilting.

Fill pots with standard cutting compost and make holes for the cuttings with a small dibber. Insert each cutting into the compost by up to half its length so that the lowest leaf is just above the surface.

Label the cuttings and water with a fungicide solution, then place them in a closed propagator with gentle bottom heat, or in a mist propagation unit. Alternatively, seal the pots in plastic bags. Keep the cuttings in good light but out of direct sun, as otherwise the air and soil temperature may become too hot and the cuttings wilt.

Remove with tweezers dead and diseased cuttings, since these may infect their healthy neighbours. Watering is seldom required until after rooting. Look for signs of new growth, and check for rooting by gently pulling at the cuttings. Once they are well rooted, pot them up.

Potting up

Water the rooted cuttings well, and gently slide them out of the pot. Carefully separate them before potting them up individually, using equal parts of potting compost and grit. Top-dress with a 1cm (¹⁄₂in) layer of sharp grit. Water the cuttings thoroughly and return them to the propagator, keeping them out of direct sun. Keep the cuttings well watered. Once fresh growth appears, place the cuttings in a cold frame and harden them off carefully before planting them out.

Semi-ripe and ripewood cuttings

Semi-ripe cuttings are taken in mid- to late summer from non-flowering shoots of the current season's growth; the shoots offer distinct resistance to pressure when bent gently and should be beginning to harden at the base. Ripewood cuttings are taken from evergreen plants during late summer and autumn when the wood has fully ripened.

Taking the cuttings

The cuttings will vary in length with the plant concerned from 1 to 4cm (¹⁄₂ to 1¹⁄₂in) or more. Cut them from the parent plant using a sharp knife or secateurs. Make a clean cut below a node and remove soft tissue at the tips. Remove the lower leaves and dip the ends into hormone rooting powder. Alternatively, take cuttings with a "heel" and trim the heel with a sharp knife to remove any snags.

Potting up

Small cuttings root best in pots of cutting compost, topped with a 1cm (¹⁄₂in) layer of fine sand. Make holes in the sand and insert the cuttings by one third to one half of their length. Label, water with a fungicide, and place in a propagator in a cool greenhouse. Check regularly for disease. Water sparingly and, as growth begins, apply a dilute liquid feed.

If a large number of cuttings is taken, they may be inserted into a cold frame with drainage at the base. Fork over the soil in the frame and then add a mixture of 1 part peat substitute (or peat) and 1 part grit; top with a 2.5cm (1in) layer of sand. After inserting the cuttings, water them and close the frame. Open the frame in mild weather. If there is a danger of frost, insulate the frame.

The following spring, when the cuttings have rooted, repot or pot up those in frames in equal parts potting compost and grit, or plant out in a nursery bed but only after danger of frost is passed. Water well.

Grow on, keeping the rooted cuttings moist and sheltered from direct sun. Give a liquid feed in the growing season. Transplant into their permanent positions in autumn.

SOFTWOOD CUTTINGS

1 *In spring, choose young, non-flowering shoots (here, from* Gypsophila repens) *and take cuttings 2.5–7cm (1–3in) long. Put the cuttings in a plastic bag.*

2 *Trim off the base of the cuttings, and the lower leaves and soft tips (see inset). Fill a pot with moist compost, inserting the cuttings by up to half their length.*

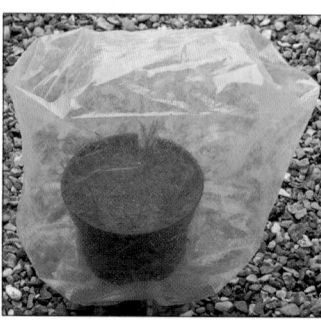

3 *Water and label the cuttings. Place the pot in a sealed plastic bag, keeping it in good light but out of direct sun.*

4 *When rooted, pot up the cuttings singly, holding them by the leaves only. Top-dress the pots, water well, and label.*

Leaf cuttings

This method is suitable for plants with fleshy leaves, such as *Haberlea*, *Ramonda*, and *Sedum*.

Using a sharp knife, cut healthy, strong, and relatively young leaves from the stem at their base. Prepare pots with a mixture of equal parts of standard cutting compost and sand; insert each cutting at a 45° angle, so that it is just held in place by the compost. Enclose each pot in a plastic bag and, when the plantlets appear, pot them up individually.

Basal cuttings

Some plants, such as *Primula marginata* and its cultivars, may be propagated from basal cuttings. These are taken from young shoots at the base of the plant at, or just above, soil level. Basal cuttings are usually taken in spring, but may also be taken in summer or autumn.

Use a well-drained, proprietary cutting compost, or a mix of equal parts of loam and peat substitute (or peat) with 2 parts grit. Fill pots with compost, and firm.

Trim the base of each cutting cleanly just below a node. Make sure that the cutting is not hollow at the base. Remove the lower leaves and dip the base in hormone powder.

Insert one third to one half of each stem into the compost, keeping the leaves clear of the soil. Water well and place the pots in a shaded, closed propagator or cold frame. Rooting takes three to six weeks, after which the cuttings may be potted up individually or lined out in nursery beds or a cold frame to grow on.

BASAL CUTTINGS

Primula marginata

In spring, take cuttings 5–7cm (2–3in) long with new leaves and a short stem. Trim the base and remove the lower leaves, inserting the cuttings to the depth indicated.

Selecting cutting material

For all types of cutting, always choose strong, healthy stems or leaves that show no sign of pests or diseases. Non-flowering shoots that are in active growth should be used. Except for basal cuttings, do not take the cuttings from the base of any plant because this part may be weaker than elsewhere. Do not take all the cuttings from the same area on the parent plant since this may make it look lop-sided.

After taking the cuttings, immediately place them in a clean, plastic bag to prevent any moisture loss. Many cuttings will root readily if they are inserted into pots of cutting compost with added grit. Alternatively, simply use horticultural sand. Insert the cuttings at the depths indicated.

SEMI-RIPE
(Phlox)
In mid- to late summer, select shoots that are just hardening but not woody. Remove 3cm (1¼in) lengths, trimming to about 1cm (½in).

GREENWOOD
(Erodium)
Take cuttings from the soft tips of new shoots in early summer. Remove 2.5–7cm (1–3in) lengths and trim them to about 1cm (½in).

ROSETTE
(Saxifraga)
In early to mid-summer, select new rosettes. Cut the rosettes about 1cm (½in) below the leaves. Trim each cleanly across the base.

RIPEWOOD
(Dryas)
In late summer and autumn, select new shoots and take cuttings about 2.5cm (1in) long. Trim to about 1cm (½in) below the base of the leaves.

LEAF
(Sedum)
Throughout the growing season, select mature leaves that are undamaged, cutting off selected leaves. Trim each cleanly across the base.

Division

Many alpines and rock garden plants may be successfully propagated by division, and in some cases division is the only practicable method of increasing the stock if seed is rarely produced or the plant is sterile.

Plants that are particularly suitable for division include mat-forming species, which produce a mass of fibrous roots, and clump-forming plants that produce clusters of shoots that are readily separated.

ROCK PLANTS THAT MAY BE PROPAGATED BY "IRISHMAN'S" CUTTINGS

Achillea ageratifolia
Arenaria montana,
   A. purpurascens
Gentiana acaulis, G. verna
Primula auricula (and cvs),
   P. marginata (and cvs)
Silene
Veronica peduncularis
Viola cornuta (and cvs)

ROCK PLANTS THAT MAY BE DIVIDED

Achillea ageratifolia
Alchemilla alpina,
   A. ellenbeckii
Allium sikkimense
Antennaria dioica
Arenaria montana
Artemisia schmidtiana 'Nana'
Campanula carpatica,
   C. cochleariifolia
Chiastophyllum oppositifolium
Gentiana acaulis,
   G. sino-ornata

*Gentiana
sino-ornata*

Primula allionii
Sagina subulata 'Aurea'
Viola cornuta

ROCK PLANTS THAT MAY BE PROPAGATED BY ROOT CUTTINGS

Anacyclus depressus
Carduncellus rhaponticoides
Centaurea pindicola
Gentiana lutea
Meconopsis delavayi
Morisia monanthos
Papaver lateritium
Phlox mesoleuca
Primula denticulata
Pulsatilla
Roscoea cautleoides
Weldenia candida ✿

KEY
✿ *Not hardy*

A number of clump-forming plants have a tendency to die out at the centre. These may be divided to rejuvenate them by replanting only the youngest, most vigorous pieces.

When to divide

Most plants are best divided in early spring, when new growth is just beginning; do not divide plants in cold and frosty weather, or when the ground is frozen or waterlogged.

Plants may also be divided in early autumn, which allows new roots to be made while the soil is still warm. Where hard winters are expected, spring division may be safer, since this allows a full growing season for establishment. Some plants, for example primulas and *Meconopsis*, should be divided immediately after flowering, when they enter a period of strong, vegetative growth. They must be well watered after replanting until they are fully re-established.

How to divide

Lift plants and shake off the soil. For large clumps, insert the tines of two garden forks back-to-back into the centre of the clump; lever the plant into two halves. Tease these smaller clumps apart by hand or cut them

HOW TO PROPAGATE BY DIVISION

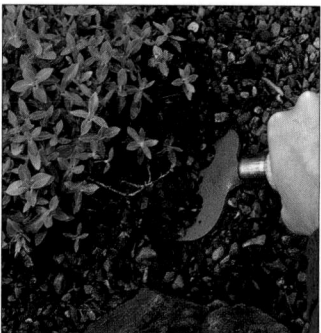

1 *Plants with fibrous roots (here* Gentiana acaulis) *may be divided and replanted to provide new plants. Lift a clump of the parent plant and shake off the soil.*

2 *Using hand forks back-to-back, loosen the root mass and divide the clump into pieces. If necessary, cut away sections from the clump with a knife.*

3 *The plants should have a good root system. Replant them outdoors into their permanent positions, firming around the roots. Add top-dressing around the plants and water thoroughly with a fine-rosed watering can.*

with a sharp knife to produce a number of small pieces with healthy roots and growth buds. The older, woody, central part of the plant should be discarded.

If not replanting or potting up the divisions immediately, wrap them in plastic bags or moist sacking and store them out of direct sun. Divisions of most hardy plants may be

"IRISHMAN'S" CUTTINGS

1 *Lift the rooted shoots close to the base of the plant (here* Veronica) *and remove them with a sharp knife. Trim off sideshoots and straggly roots (see inset).*

2 *Pot up the cuttings individually. Place a little gritty compost in a pot, insert the cutting, then add more compost. Firm gently, water, and top-dress.*

replanted immediately into their permanent positions. If, however, plants are particularly precious, or the divisions are quite small, it may be safer to pot them up and place them in a cold frame until they are established before planting them out. Use 1 part low-fertility, loam-based potting compost and 1 part grit or a lime-free mix for acid-lovers. If replanting in the open ground, make holes large enough to allow the roots to be spread out fully. Firm in and water well. Keep the soil moist until the plants are established.

"Irishman's" cuttings

These are essentially sideshoots that have already rooted. Thymes and other creeping rock plants produce this sort of cutting. The technique is particularly useful for plants with woody rootstocks that are not easily divided, or for those that naturally produce offsets or runners.

Before taking the cuttings, brush away surface soil from the base of the parent plant. Cut rooted pieces from the plant with a sharp knife and pot them up in equal parts of low-fertility, loam-based potting compost and grit. Alternatively, plant them out in a cool, sheltered spot in the garden until well established.

Root cuttings

A limited number of alpines and rock garden plants, such as *Morisia monanthos* and *Primula denticulata*, may be propagated from root cuttings. Take root cuttings from the healthiest-looking roots in either late autumn or winter, when the plants are dormant.

Selecting material

Choose a strong, healthy plant and lift it from the soil. Select young, vigorous roots and cut them from the parent plant. The cuttings should be about 5cm (2in) long. Cut the roots straight across at the top end (nearest the plant's stem) and use sloping cuts at the lower end (nearest the root tips). Wash the cuttings in tepid water and replant the parent stock immediately or, if old and straggly and no longer required, discard it.

Inserting the cuttings

Use pots at least 10cm (4in) deep. Put broken crocks over the drainage holes and place over these a 2.5cm (1in) layer of low-fertility loam-based potting compost. Fill the pots with washed sand, then firm. Make several planting holes in each pot around the edges.

Insert the cuttings into the holes, with the straight ends uppermost and the tops level with the surface of the sand. Cuttings of plants with thin, wiry roots may be laid flat on the surface of the compost. Top-dress with fine grit. Label the pots, water thoroughly, and place them in a cold frame on a layer of grit or gravel or in a propagator. Close the frames in cold weather; otherwise they should be ventilated freely.

Water the pots when new growth appears. When the new shoots are growing strongly, check that the cuttings have rooted before potting them up: gently knock them out of their pots to inspect their roots.

Potting up rooted cuttings

Slide the cuttings out of their pots and separate them carefully. Pot them up singly, using low-fertility, loam-based potting compost mixed with an equal amount of sand. Instead of sand, a mix of peat substitute (or peat) and sand may be used.

HOW TO PROPAGATE BY ROOT CUTTINGS

1 In late autumn or winter, using a hand fork, carefully lift a healthy plant (here Primula denticulata) *with a well-developed root system.*

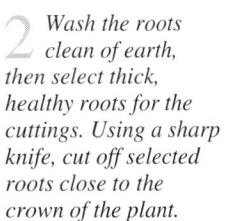

2 Wash the roots clean of earth, then select thick, healthy roots for the cuttings. Using a sharp knife, cut off selected roots close to the crown of the plant.

3 Prepare 5cm (2in) lengths of root, cutting each one straight at the thicker end (closest to the parent plant) and angled at the lower end.

4 Place a layer of compost in the base of a pot, then fill almost to the brim with sharp sand. Insert the cuttings so that straight ends are just level with the sand surface.

5 Cover the sand with a 1cm (¹/₂in) layer of grit. Water and label the cuttings, then place the pot in a propagator or on the greenhouse bench.

Top-dress the pots with 1cm (¹/₂in) of sharp sand or grit. Water and then place outside, out of direct sun. Leave until the new plants are established, watering as required.

Scooping rosettes

Plants that grow quickly or form rosettes, for example *Primula denticulata*, may be propagated *in situ* in mid-winter from root cuttings by scooping out the rosettes with a sharp knife, to expose the top of the root-stock. Select strong-growing rosettes and brush the tops of the roots with fungicidal powder to prevent grey mould/*Botrytis* (see p.557); cover the pots with a thin layer of horticultural sharp sand.

Shoots should soon appear on each root apex. When the shoots are about 2.5–5cm (1–2in) tall, they are ready to be lifted. Separate the clumps into individual, small plants that have healthy-looking, vigorous shoots and roots, pulling them apart by hand or dividing them with a sharp knife.

Pot up the young plants to grow on, using equal parts of potting compost and horticultural sand. Water thoroughly, and place outside in a shady site. Keep moist and plant out the young plants when their roots have filled the pots.

HOW TO SCOOP ROSETTES

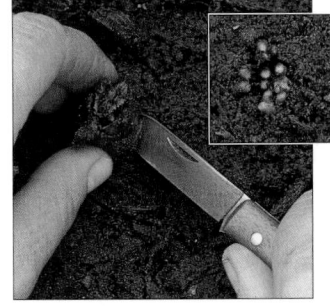

1 Scoop out the live crowns of rosette-forming plants (here Primula denticulata) *with a sharp knife, so that the tops of the roots are visible (see inset).*

2 Dust the exposed roots with fungicidal powder (see inset) to protect them from moulds and fungi. Lightly cover with sharp, horticultural sand.

3 When new shoots appear from the roots, lift the whole clump, using a hand fork or trowel. Take care not to damage the new roots.

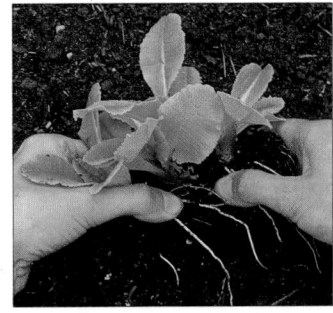

4 Divide the clump into individual plants, each with one shoot and well-developed roots. Pot them up using equal parts potting compost and sand.

Alpine houses and frames

ALTHOUGH some high-altitude alpines grow well in the open garden in temperate climates, provided that their specific requirements of situation and soil are satisfied, most will perform considerably better if they are grown under cover. Many alpines bloom in late winter and very early spring when, if left in the open, their delicate flowers may be damaged by inclement weather, eaten by slugs or snails, or pecked by birds.

In an alpine house, plants are protected from winter wet, cold, drying winds, and sudden sharp frosts, as well as from the attentions of most pests. This enables a far wider range of alpines and rock plants to be grown, either in pots or in ground-level or raised beds, to provide an eye-catching and lasting display.

USING AN ALPINE HOUSE
Part of the house may be used to grow on young plants (foreground) in beds supported by brick pillars.

Using an alpine house

An alpine house is an unheated greenhouse, usually with raised benches, designed for growing and displaying alpines and rock plants under controlled conditions. Often, half of the house is used for growing the plants, and the other half for displaying them. Alternatively, the plants may be grown in cold frames (either attached to or sited very near the alpine house) and brought temporarily into the house for display when they are at their best.

Displaying the plants
Displays may be of plants in pots simply standing on the staging or, more commonly, plunged up to their rims in a layer of sand. Plunging keeps roots cool and moist and reduces temperature fluctuations, while allowing easy irrigation of plants that dislike overhead watering. Specially built display beds are an attractive option. Create miniature rock gardens in the alpine house, either waist-high where staging is strong enough to support the weight, or at ground level. These may have some permanent planting as well as areas of sand or sandy compost into which different plants may be plunged, according to season. Lightweight tufa rocks may be incorporated and planted up to enhance this type of display.

Siting the alpine house
Choose a firm, level site away from the shade of trees, fences, walls, and tall buildings if possible. Siting the alpine house on a north–south axis is ideal but any open, sunny position

AN ALPINE HOUSE DISPLAY
A wide range of rock plants may be grown in pots and attractively displayed in raised sand beds in an alpine house.

is acceptable. Always avoid hollows where cold air forms frost pockets and do not site it in exposed, windy situations. Try to position the alpine house where it will harmonize with other garden features, perhaps even using it as a focal point. For further information on greenhouses, ventilation, shading, and staging, see GREENHOUSES AND FRAMES, pp.483, 484, and 487.

Using frames

Frames should be sited near the alpine house, where they may be used to protect a range of choice plants from climatic extremes, as an "overspill" area, or for storage when plants are not in flower. They are

very useful for bulbs which need to be kept dry when dormant, or for plants that will not tolerate the very hot conditions that may arise in summer. Frames incorporate a top light that must be opened as required to provide good ventilation; a standard Dutch light frame is suitable but other types are available. The lights may be removed in summer if required, but they should be kept on if the frame contains dormant bulbs. Those plants that do not tolerate direct summer sun can be protected by covering the frame with mesh shading (see GREENHOUSES AND FRAMES, "Meshes and fabrics", p.484). Pots in a frame are usually plunged in a material such as washed builder's sand over a layer of rubble to give them good drainage.

CARE OF ALPINES AND DWARF BULBS AFTER FLOWERING

ALPINES INDOORS
After flowering, pots of alpines needing a careful watering regime (here Dionysia *spp.) should be plunged in sand under cover.*

ALPINES OUTDOORS
Alpines that tolerate variable summer weather conditions, such as saxifrages, may be plunged in open cold frames after flowering.

BULBS INDOORS
Pots of dwarf bulbs (here irises) that have finished flowering may be kept dry by plunging in sand or gravel under staging.

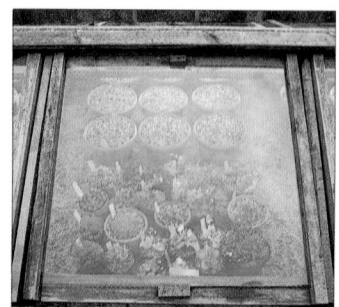

PROTECTING FLOWERING ALPINES
Alpines coming into flower may be grown in outdoor frames before bringing them into the alpine house for display.

Alpines in pots

Growing alpines in pots ensures that special watering, compost, or feeding requirements can be provided for individual plants.

Plastic and clay pots

Although plastic pots are suitable for growing alpines and retain moisture well, clay pots are more attractive – important if the plants are to be exhibited. The compost in plastic pots dries out more slowly than in clay pots so take care not to overwater the plants. Clean and sterilize all pots before use: sterilants based on dilute solutions of sodium hyperchlorite are suitable, but do not use tar-based disinfectants.

Composts

All alpines need a freely draining compost and benefit from a layer of broken crocks in the bottom of clay pots, or grit in plastic pots, since even moisture-loving plants will not tolerate stagnant conditions.

Most species grow well in loam-based potting compost, mixed with an equal amount of grit. Those from high, alpine habitats of scree and rock-face crevices, such as the Aretian *Androsace* species and other cushion-forming plants, need a less fertile and more freely draining mix if they are to retain their neat, natural habit. In rich composts, they quickly become soft and lush and are then more prone to attack by pests and diseases. For these plants use a mix of up to 3 parts grit to 1 part loam-based compost. Introduce plants to these "lean mixes" when they are young, since they may not adapt easily if they have been potted on from a more fertile medium.

A number of species, usually ones from woodland habitats, or those which occur in humus-rich pockets in rocky habitats, such as *Haberlea* and *Ramonda*, prefer well-drained composts that are rich in organic matter. For these, a mix of 1 part each of loam-based compost and grit, with 2 parts leaf mould, peat substitute, or peat will be suitable. Take care to check on the individual needs of each plant before selecting an appropriate compost, and ensure that for lime-hating plants all ingredients are lime-free.

Top-dressings

After planting up the pots (see right), top-dress them with a layer of grit or stone chippings to enhance the plant's appearance, to keep the neck of the plant well drained, and to prevent the growth of mosses and liverworts. Use a top-dressing that is appropriate to the pH requirements of the plant, for example limestone chippings for lime-loving species or granitic grit for lime-hating plants.

Some small, cushion-forming alpines are very sensitive to the presence of water around their necks, so, as well as top-dressing with grit, prop small wedges of rock beneath their cushions in order to keep them clear of the surface.

Repotting

When a plant has outgrown its pot, transfer it carefully into a slightly larger pot, disturbing the root ball as little as possible. Pot on herbaceous and shrubby plants in spring and summer, when they are growing strongly; bulbs should be potted on when they are dormant. Plant to the same level as in the previous pot, firm in fresh compost, and then add a new layer of top-dressing.

Water well after potting by standing the pot in at least 2.5–5cm (1–2in) of water until the top of the compost becomes moist. Then remove the pot to avoid the risk of root rot.

Planting in beds

The beds may be at ground level or raised some 1m (3ft) high. A raised bed allows plants to be tended and

---

REPOTTING A SAXIFRAGE

1 *The roots of this saxifrage can be seen growing through the drainage hole at the bottom of the pot. The plant is pot-bound and should be repotted.*

2 *Choose a pot that is one size bigger than the one that the plant is growing in. Use crocks and gravel to provide drainage at the base of the pot.*

3 *Arrange the crocks carefully over the drainage hole. The crocks should then be covered with a layer of gravel.*

4 *Remove the plant from its pot by tapping gently on the base to loosen the root ball; tease out the roots to encourage fresh roots to penetrate the new compost.*

5 *Cover the crocks in the larger pot with a little compost; position the plant so that the neck is at the same level as in the original pot, and fill in with compost.*

6 *Spread the gravel top-dressing over the surface of the compost, taking care to tuck it under the collar of the plant to keep it sharply drained.*

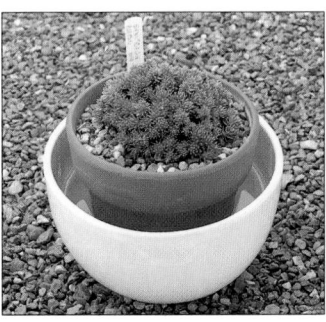

7 *Place the pot in a bowl of water and leave it until the surface of the compost and gravel appears damp.*

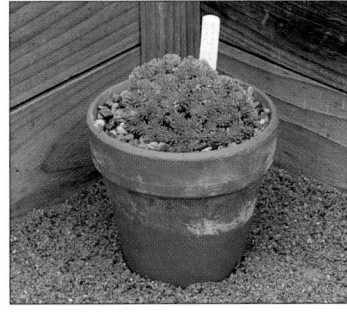

8 *Then remove the pot and place it on a layer of sand in a cold frame, where any excess moisture can easily drain off. This will prevent any risk of root rot.*

9 *The repotted plant may then be plunged in sand in a cold frame or bed to grow on.*

REMOVING DEAD LEAVES

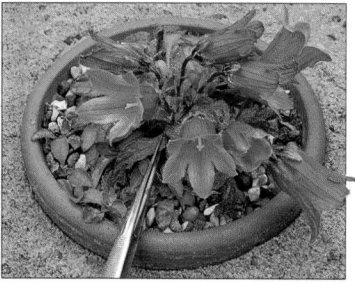

Tweezers should be used regularly to remove any brown or withered leaves from alpine plants such as this Campanula pilosa.

viewed more easily and is especially useful for elderly or disabled gardeners. The staging must drain well and be solidly constructed to bear the weight of the bed (see also GREENHOUSES AND FRAMES, "Raised beds", p.486).

Use a compost of 3 parts loam (or good sterilized garden soil), 2 parts coarse fibrous peat substitute (or peat), and 2 parts sharp sand or grit. Add rocks to the bed to create a miniature rock garden. Tufa is particularly useful because it is lightweight, very moisture-retentive, and as plants can be grown in the rock itself. Plant out alpines in the bed, avoiding species that are invasive and free-seeding, but leave some gaps for plunging a succession of seasonal, pot-grown specimens. Grow ferns and other shade-loving species under a raised bed.

Routine maintenance

As alpines have quite specialized growing requirements, they need considerable attention through the growing season. Plants that are regularly repotted rarely need additional feeding, but where fertilizers are used be sure that they are low in nitrogen – high-nitrogen feed will lead to soft, lush growth that is uncharacteristic of alpines and more prone to pests and diseases.

Ventilation
Ventilating surfaces must occupy at least 25 per cent of the glass area, as the aim is to provide the maximum possible air circulation at all times. In spring and summer, the vents and the greenhouse door can remain open permanently, unless there is strong wind or heavy rain. Use a screen of small-diameter mesh over vents and doors to keep out cats and birds. During heavy rain and windy weather, close the vents on the receiving side to avoid drip on the

foliage and reduce strong draughts that may damage foliage and flowers. In severe winds, it is safest to close all vents and doors.

In winter, open the vents fully (unless it is windy, raining, or snowing) but close them before nightfall to retain any residual warmth. In very cold weather, allow temperatures in the alpine house to rise gradually before ventilating; on bright, sunny days, however, open the vents as soon as possible to prevent the temperature from rising too rapidly. In damp, foggy weather, especially in areas with high levels of atmospheric pollution, close down the house completely to keep out cold, damp air, and use a cool air fan to maintain air circulation.

Temperature
Shading will be necessary during sunny weather, from late spring to autumn, to avoid scorching tender, new growth, and to help reduce temperatures. Do not use heavy shading as this might cause etiolation or lopsided "drawing" of plants towards the available light source. In very hot weather, damp down the house floor to reduce temperatures and maintain atmospheric humidity; plants may be gently misted over with cool water in the evenings.

Heating should be used to stop the pots freezing in severe weather, and a method of heating that does not produce excessive fumes or moisture is best (see GREENHOUSES AND FRAMES, "Heating", p.482).

Hygiene
Remove dead foliage and faded flowers regularly to reduce the risk of fungal attack. Check the plants for pests and diseases and treat any outbreaks promptly (see PLANT PROBLEMS, pp.545–77). Always keep

the floor of the house clean to minimize the risk of diseases, and make sure that the glass is clean so that plants receive maximum light.

Watering
Water regularly throughout the season, especially on sunny spring and summer days, when water loss is rapid. If plants are allowed to dry out between waterings, growth may be severely checked, and flower buds may shrivel. For pots standing on staging, water from above but avoid splashing the foliage. Plunged pots derive moisture from the surrounding material but may need additional watering in warm periods. For plants that are sensitive to moisture on their foliage, water the plunge medium around the pots. As autumn approaches, reduce watering as plants prepare for dormancy. During winter, alpines need to be kept dry but not dust dry (for plunged pots, the plunge medium should be just damp to the touch).

Winter maintenance
A spell of clear, dry weather during late winter is a good time to store the plants in a frame and clean the alpine house (see GREENHOUSES AND FRAMES, "Routine maintenance", p.491). Clean and top up the sand or grit on beds and renew labels. Then transfer pots back from the frame.

Exhibiting

Alpines for showing should be in the best possible condition on exhibition day. No matter how perfect the plant, it will lose marks if poorly presented in a less than scrupulously clean pot, or if top-dressings are thin or show evidence of algal growth. Remove all evidence of weeds, pests,

When transporting fragile plants (here Fritillaria uva-vulpis), *make a "tripod" from split canes bound at the top with twine, and tie in stems.*

and diseases. Check plants for dead, discoloured, or misshapen leaves and faded flowers, and remove these carefully with tweezers.

Clay pots should be scrubbed clean with a wire brush or scourer. Alternatively they may be double-potted: insert the specimen in its pot into a larger, new pot, covering the inner rim with top-dressing. Renew all top-dressings with materials appropriate to the plant's natural habitat, then relabel. Support tall, fragile plants during transport with tripods of split canes. Water plants thoroughly the day before the show and allow to drain before packing for transportation. Carry spare top-dressing to renew any lost in transit.

PREPARING PLANTS FOR EXHIBITION

1 *Use fine sand together with a wire brush or scouring pad to clean the outside of clay pots. This will remove any algae or limescale that may be present.*

2 *Replenish the top-dressing. For this* Dionysia aretioides *the medium is coarse gravel; but stone chippings, grit, or pine needles may be used, depending on the plant.*

3 *Add new, clearly written labels. Pack the pots carefully in a tray using newspaper to hold them steady, and carry extra top-dressing for last-minute renewal.*

9

BULBOUS PLANTS

F ROM THE CHEERFUL, *golden daffodil trumpeting the arrival of spring to the cyclamen, herald of autumn, bulbous plants ring the changes of the seasons throughout the year with glorious displays of flower. Some possess handsome foliage, and others are valued for their fragrance, but it is their blooms that make bulbs essential in a well-planned garden. They offer a wide variety of colour and form, from bright, primary shades to delicate, pastel hues, from the tall grandeur of the gladiolus spike to the dainty bells of the smallest fritillary. Whether they form bold patterns in a formal bed, fill in the detail of a mixed border, provide a splash of colour in a container, or create sweeping highlights beneath trees or in grass, bulbs bring vitality to the more permanent plantings of the garden.*

Designing with bulbs

G ROWING bulbs is an easy way of brightening up the garden with decorative, often flamboyant, and sometimes fragrant displays. The bulbs that are grown in the garden are dominated by hardy favourites, for example crocuses, cyclamen, daffodils, hyacinths, and tulips, of which there is an immense variety of both species and cultivars. Many tender bulbs also deserve a place in the garden, including the starry *Ixia*, *Sparaxis* with its loose, gaudy spikes, and the fiery *Tigridia*.

The key characteristic of bulbs is that they provide visual interest for only one season, remaining dormant and unnoticed for the remainder of the year. This can be an asset with careful planning, making bulbs invaluable as border plants as well as ideal for naturalizing in grass or growing in containers.

In many gardens, bulbs may be left to increase naturally from year to year while their dying foliage is hidden by the developing growth of herbaceous plants or shrubs that provide a succession of interest. Many bulbs, including the popular crocuses, daffodils, and snowdrops (*Galanthus*), increase very rapidly in most sites. Bulbs may also be lifted after flowering and replanted each year to create room for other seasonal plants, making them especially convenient for small gardens or restricted areas.

Seasons of interest
The main bulb season is from early spring to early summer, but many other bulbs flower outdoors or under cover at other times of the year. For colour in winter when most of the

EFFECTIVE USE OF BULBS IN A MIXED BORDER
The dusky, purple-pink globes of Allium sphaero-cephalon *pick up the colour theme of this mixed border,* *providing a strong accent of colour and form amid herbaceous perennials in various shades of pink.*

garden is dormant, early bulbs such as the pink *Cyclamen coum*, the tiny, deep blue *Iris histrioides* 'Major', and white snowdrops may be grown outdoors, and other bulbs forced indoors. Bulbs that flower in summer or autumn are often larger, and of more exotic shapes and hues than spring bulbs.

Where to grow bulbs
If given the well-drained soil that they need to grow and flower well, bulbs are among the easiest of all garden plants to cultivate. There are numerous cultivars and species now available that thrive in all aspects except deep shade.

Many bulbs in cultivation come from areas with a Mediterranean climate, so need to be grown in sunny sites and prefer hot, dry summers – although a huge range of bulbs flourishes in the open garden in regions with summer rainfall.

Bulbs that would normally grow in woodland thrive in moist, light shade. Many others, including some bulbs described as "sun-loving", are happy in light shade cast by nearby shrubs, walls, or trellises. Even dry shade is tolerated by most hardy cyclamen. Bulbs with white or pale flowers appear almost luminous in dusky light, so look very effective when planted in a shaded site.

Whatever the setting, bulbs look best planted in groups of the same species or cultivar, whether jostling shoulders with other plants or forming a single, swaying sea of colour in a formal bed or in grass.

The different types of bulbous plant

BULB (*Hyacinthoides hispanica*)

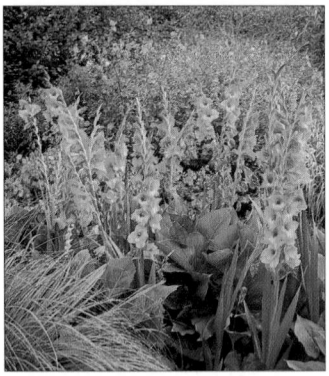

CORM (*Gladiolus* 'Perky')

In this book, the term "bulb" refers to all bulbous plants, including corms, tubers, and rhizomes as well as true bulbs. The terms "corm", "tuber", and "rhizome" are used only in their specific sense throughout. With all bulbous plants, a portion of the plant is swollen into a food storage organ that enables the plant to survive when dormant or when conditions are unsuitable for growth.

Bulbs

True bulbs are formed from fleshy leaves or leaf bases, and frequently consist of concentric rings of scales attached to a basal plate. The outer scales often form a dry, protective skin or tunic, as found in daffodils, Reticulata irises, and tulips. With some lilies (*Lilium*) and *Fritillaria* species, the scales are separate and no tunic is formed. Juno irises are unusual in having swollen storage roots beneath the bulbs.

Corms

Corms are formed from the swollen bases of stems and are replaced by new corms every year. They are common in the family Iridaceae, which

TUBER (*Dahlia* 'Monk Marc')

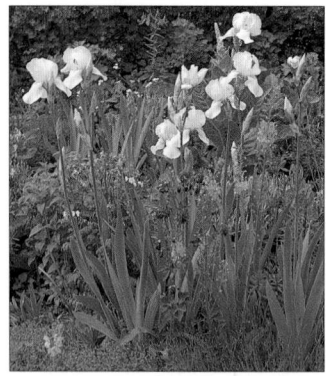

RHIZOME (*Iris* 'White City')

includes crocuses, gladioli, *Romulea*, and *Watsonia*; usually they have a tunic that has been formed from the previous year's leaf bases. In the Liliaceae and related families, they are found in such genera as *Brodiaea* and *Colchicum*.

Tubers

Tuberous is a term applied to many plants with swollen, often irregularly shaped stems or roots used for food storage. It is often misapplied, for example to the tuber-like roots – actually rhizomes – of *Anemone blanda* and the long, thin rhizomes of *A. nemorosa* (for convenience, both are included here as "bulbous plants"). True tubers of various kinds are found in *Corydalis*, in some orchids, such as *Dactylorrhiza*, in cyclamen species (although these are often called "corms"), and in plants such as *Ranunculus asiaticus* where they are lobed or clustered together.

Rhizomes

Rhizomes are swollen, usually more or less horizontal, underground stems, found in the Iridaceae, notably in irises, and in Liliaceae.

Formal beds

Bulbs make a valuable contribution to formal bedding displays. Spring-flowering bulbs are excellent for planting *en masse* in a bed to be occupied by bedding annuals later in summer, since they may be lifted and stored during their dormant season. Classic bedding bulbs are

A PAGEANT OF COLOUR
Serried ranks of tulips parade along these formal beds in bold, bright blocks of contrasting colour, creating an energetic counterpoint to the quiet orderliness of the formal garden. White tulips intersperse those of stronger hue to prevent the colour combinations from appearing too strident.

hyacinths and tulips because of their strong, sculptural forms; in general, the larger, showy flowers of hybrid bulbs best suit a formal position in the garden. Plant in blocks of colour, each of one type of bulb, or in mixed groups that flower at different times to provide a long display of colour during the spring. Bulbs may completely fill the bed or be combined

with companion plants with flowers in complementary or contrasting colours, such as deep blue forget-me-nots (*Myosotis*) or fiery wallflowers (*Cheiranthus*).

There is also scope for effective formal planting with summer- or autumn-flowering bulbs: *Galtonia*, with its elegant, white or green spikes, or the more compact cultivars of gladioli, especially the Primulinus or Butterfly groups, look impressive when planted in large blocks bordered by purple-blue violas, or any similar, low-growing ground cover. *Agapanthus* Headbourne Hybrids, with their large, rounded flowerheads of blue or white, combine well with the graceful, pink blooms of *Nerine bowdenii*.

Mixed herbaceous and shrub borders

Bulbs fill in the permanent planting of a border with a lively variety of seasonal colour. Loose drifts may blend in with the general scheme or draw the eye with splashes of colour. Architectural bulbs, such as *Crinum* x *powellii*, with its huge, pink or white trumpets, punctuate the flow of a border with an arresting contrast

of height and form. Grow some bulbs through low ground-cover plants so that their blooms appear to float above the mat of foliage. For a more informal cottage border, choose species bulbs since florid hybrids may sometimes look out of place.

Mixed plantings for spring flowering

Planting bulbs in a mixed border extends the flowering season, and provides an array of fresh, bright colour from late winter through to early summer. Before the herbaceous perennials and deciduous shrubs in the border begin to grow and spread, bring the front of the border to life with the smaller daffodil species, pale or dark blue Reticulata irises, snowdrops, and the golden cups of winter aconites (*Eranthis hyemalis*).

Plant starry carpets of pink and blue *Anemone blanda*, *Chionodoxa*, and *Scilla bifolia*, or pale yellow drifts of the more freely increasing dwarf daffodil species and hybrids beneath such early-flowering shrubs as *Corylopsis*, forsythia, and witch hazel (*Hamamelis*) to complement their display.

For later in spring, a much wider range of bulbs is available and larger plants, such as the tall daffodils, *Fritillaria* species (for example the

USING BULBS IN A MIXED BORDER

In this border, a variety of bulbs has been planted among shrubs and herbaceous perennials to create a bed that changes in mood with the seasons.

THE BORDER IN SPRING
The border shrubs and perennials are just starting into growth, so bulbs hold the stage. Informal groups of daffodils and tulips fill out the front of the border with fresh, clean colours, creating a bright scene.

THE BORDER IN SUMMER
In the mature border, taller bulbs thrust through the foundation planting to provide pleasing contrasts of height and form. The rich colours and intricate flower shapes of bulbs such as Allium, Crinum, Galtonia, and lilies (Lilium) help create a sumptuous feeling in the summer border.

1 *Campanula lactiflora* 'Prichard's Variety'
2 *Prunus glandulosa* 'Alba Plena'
3 *Echinacea purpurea* 'Robert Bloom'
4 *Crinum x powellii*
5 *Lilium regale*
6 *Galtonia candicans*
7 *Lilium* 'Bright Star'
8 *Allium giganteum*
9 *Tulipa* 'White Triumphator'
10 *Aster frikartii* 'Mönch'
11 *Fritillaria imperialis* 'Lutea'
12 *Knautia macedonica*
13 *Agapanthus* 'Dorothy Palmer'
14 *Tulipa* 'West Point'
15 *Salvia nemorosa* 'May Night'
16 *Narcissus* 'Actaea'
17 *Euphorbia polychroma*
18 *Osteospermum jucundum*
19 *Narcissus* 'Thalia'
20 *Viola* 'Haslemere'
21 *Narcissus* 'Hawera'
22 *Geranium* 'Johnson's Blue'
23 *Diascia vigilis*

purple-black *F. persica* and the regal *F. imperialis*) or tulips, may be used in casual groups to give height among the shrubs and perennials.

Mixed plantings for summer and autumn flowering

A number of bulbs add greatly to the beauty of the garden in summer. Although they are often regarded as only of secondary importance, in fact many summer- and autumn-flowering bulbs are tall and robust enough to hold their own among the surrounding flowering perennials and they offer a dazzling range of colours and flower forms.

Early in the season, try *Camassia leichtlinii* 'Alba' with its creamy-white flower plumes, vivid gladioli, *Triteleia laxa* (syn. *Brodiaea laxa*) for its loose, purple-blue clusters of bloom, and the bold, scarlet goblets of *Tulipa sprengeri*.

Follow them in mid- to late summer with the huge, purple globes of *Allium aflatunense*, arching sprays of blazing red or yellow *Crocosmia*, sun-loving lilies (*Lilium*) and, later, slim pink, red, or white spires of *Schizostylis*. In warmer gardens, greenish-white *Eucomis* with its pineapple-like flowerheads brings an exotic touch to the border planting.

In autumn, continue the display with the fragrant, pink trumpets of *Amaryllis belladonna*, the brilliant yellow funnels of *Sternbergia lutea* or *S. sicula*, and blue to white forms of autumn-flowering crocuses.

Naturalizing bulbs

When left undisturbed, many bulbs readily increase to form flowing drifts of colour. Allowing them to naturalize in this way gives interest to areas of the garden that otherwise might not be given over to flowering plants. Species, which are more delicate in hue and form than most cultivars, create a natural effect when planted in large, informal groups.

Planting with specimen trees

Bulbs make perfect partners for specimen trees with deep roots and light, deciduous canopies. Use bulbs that flower mostly in spring and autumn to form a decorative ground cover when the tree has few leaves to deepen the shade. In spring the soil beneath the tree is moist and sunlit, ideal for anemones, crocuses, daffodils, or *Scilla*. Hardy, autumn-flowering cyclamen, with mottled, silvery foliage and softly folded petals, tolerate the dry summer conditions, and enjoy partial shade.

The flowers of bulbs can complement a tree's habit effectively. White-flowered bulbs, for example, mirror the white blossom of ornamental cherries (*Prunus*), the crisp shape of crocuses echo the chalice form of magnolia blooms, and bulbs with pendent flowers imitate the habit of a weeping tree.

Use dwarf cultivars to naturalize the area around a newly planted tree or shrub, since rapidly increasing bulbs such as daffodils reduce the available food.

Woodland settings

Bulbs are invaluable planted in large, informal pools of colour to enhance the natural beauty of deciduous

BULBS FOR BRIGHT HIGHLIGHTS
Loose drifts of slender tulips bring brilliant colour to this mixed border and contrast with the soft, mounded foliage of the perennials.

woodland. Many relish woodland conditions, blending well with other woodland plants, such as ferns, hellebores (*Helleborus*), and primulas.

Plant bulbs for a succession of flower, and contrast of form and height, with subtle variations on a colour theme to reflect the tranquil mood of woodland. Snowdrops (*Galanthus*) and cyclamen species in pinks and purples make a striking combination, while drifts of *Scilla* and *Chionodoxa* add shades of blue. Spanish bluebells (*Hyacinthoides*

hispanica, syn. *Scilla campanulata*) or many of the more rampant grape hyacinths (*Muscari*) provide swathes of blue, pink, and white, together with tiny, white sprays of lily-of-the-valley (*Convallaria majalis*). These can all colonize considerable areas once established. English bluebells (*Hyacinthoides non-scriptus*) should only be planted on their own because they will rapidly invade other plantings.

A NATURAL PLANTING
Naturally spreading clumps of autumn-flowering Colchicum byzantinum *spring up through a mat of greenery to display their starry blooms. The dark green, velvety moss on the base of the tree provides an attractive foil for the shining, purple-pink flowers.*

Planting in grass

Bulbs can transform grass, whether a bank, a section of a lawn, or an entire meadow, into a gay carpet of spring or autumn colour that spreads more thickly year by year. The bulbs must be robust species that can withstand competition from grass roots. Many of the larger bulbs look best in grass where after flowering their fading foliage is less obtrusive.

Plant earlier-flowering bulbs in grass that is to be mown from spring onwards so that their leaves have time to die down before the grass is cut. Later-flowering bulbs, such as terrestrial orchids (*Dactylorrhiza*), may be grown with grass and wild flowers in "meadows" that are not cut until mid- or late summer. Bulbs that bloom in autumn start into growth and flower before the end of the usual mowing season so the grass must be left unmown after late summer. Alternatively, plant bulbs in irregular but defined areas so that it is possible to mow around them.

Daffodils are the classic choice for grass and a remarkable range – especially the more robust species and hybrids – may be grown in this way. Many crocuses grow well in grass where they are protected to some extent from mice and squirrels. A more delicate effect may be achieved with the pendent bells of the summer snowflake (*Leucojum aestivum*) and the snake's-head fritillary (*Fritillaria meleagris*) that shiver softly in the breeze.

Where the grass is less vigorous, particularly in partly shaded areas, some of the dwarfer bulbs do well: the purple *Crocus tommasinianus*, *Chionodoxa* species, some daffodil

WOODLAND CHARM
Hardy Cyclamen coum *and crocuses in deep and pale shades of pink, lilac, and violet colonize a woodland, clustering prettily around the feet of the trees to provide a show of colour when the trees are bare.*

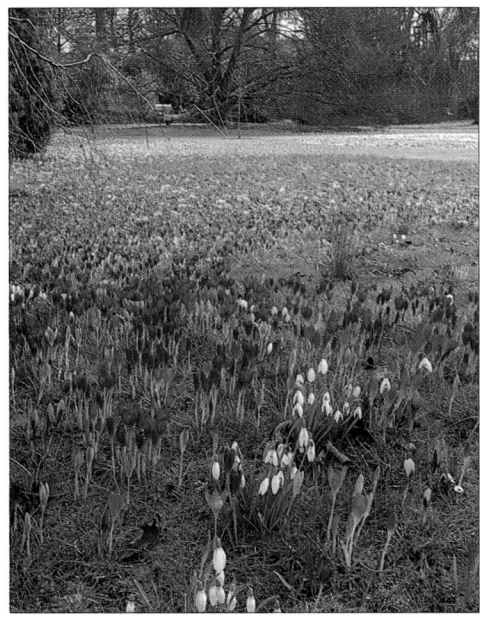

SPRING SPECTACLE
Naturalized crocuses in bloom cover this lawn with vivid pinks, purples, and yellows. The bulbs are planted in great swathes of a single hue, that merge with each other to create a sea of colour. Snowdrops (Galanthus) *planted among the crocuses provide highlights of white.*

species (e.g. *Narcissus cyclamineus*), *Scilla* species, and snowdrops all do well in these conditions.

An area that is naturalized with bulbs on the outskirts of a garden provides a harmonious transition between the flowerbeds of a formal garden and the grassy fields of the surrounding countryside by combining elements of both.

Bulbs with alpines

Using bulbs in the rock garden, trough, or peat bed prolongs the season as most alpines flower in late spring. The erect habit, upright flowers, and spear-like leaves of bulbs contrast well with the low, mounded, or spreading habit of most alpine plants, as well as introducing a greater variety of form. Choose

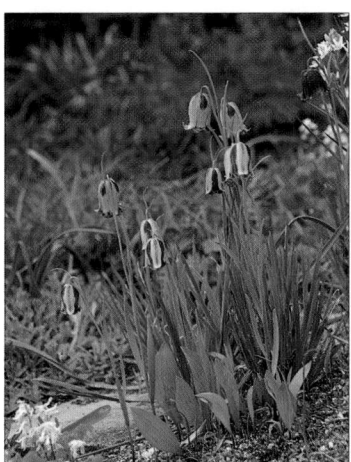

AN ALPINE SETTING
The strange beauty of the bell-like flowers of Fritillaria acmopetala *is best shown off in the small-scale planting of an alpine garden.*

dwarf bulbs with dainty blooms to complement the character of the alpines, and plant some bulbs to grow through and lift the alpine planting. Avoid mat-forming alpines that exhaust the soil around the bulbs and so deprive them of food.

In the rock garden
Many smaller bulbs, especially the more temperamental species for which sharp drainage is essential, thrive in rock gardens, in sun, or partial shade. Dwarf bulbs look attractive when planted in pockets of rock or offset against the grit topdressing of the bed, which also stops their delicate flowers from being muddied during wet weather. If planting very small alpines in the bed, do not use the taller bulb species, which would appear out of proportion to their neighbours.

Bulbs in troughs
Old stone troughs make an attractive setting for a collection of dwarf bulbs and smaller alpine plants where their tiny charms may be appreciated at close hand. The bulbs benefit from the gritty, well-drained soil, and may easily be given the careful watering that they need.

To keep the display in proportion, grow the smallest species and their less robust hybrids; rapidly increasing bulbs may swamp neighbouring alpines. Grow the smaller *Fritillaria* species for their intriguing flowers, whether the purplish-brown and yellow *F. michailovskyi*, or the chequered green *F. whittallii*.

Rhodohypoxis are excellent for troughs, producing pink, red, or white starry flowers through most of the summer. Keep the bulbs moist during the growing season, and give

them an occasional liquid feed. The genus *Cyclamen* includes species that are suitable for troughs in spring and autumn, ranging in hue from pure white to deepest purple-pink.

In a peat bed
A peat garden, with its terraced beds, peat-block "walls", and a compost comprising largely leaf mould and peat substitute, or peat, provides perfect conditions for the dwarfer "woodland" bulbs, whether planted on their own or with ericaceous shrubs or alpines. Try *Corydalis ambigua*, with pretty, purplish-blue flowers, or *Scoliopus bigelovii*, with purple-veined, orchid-like blooms, among many others. The plant choice is determined to an extent by the degree of shade.

Bulbs to associate with water gardens

A few bulbs flourish in damp, poorly drained conditions and provide some of the most striking flowering plants to grow around water. Their strong shapes and colours create pleasing reflections; plant them in clumps to contrast with the flat, open surface of the water. Several handsome rhizomatous irises and the arum lily (*Zantedeschia aethiopica*), with large, white spathes above broad,

BULBS IN POTS
Larger bulbs are naturals for use in containers. Here, Lilium regale *provides the focus of interest in this grouping of pots, which have been arranged on different levels and in gradations of size to draw the eye upwards. The huge, white lily trumpets combine with white pelargoniums and terracotta tones to form an attractive composition that is in harmony with the natural stone wall and greenery behind it.*

arrow-shaped leaves, thrive in pond margins. Both the snake's-head fritillary and summer snowflake (*Leucojum aestivum*) grow naturally in water meadows, so enjoy a moist site or damp beds around ponds.

Other bulbs that enhance water gardens are the magnificent, purple-red *Iris ensata* (syn. *I. kaempferi*), and *Dierama pendulum*, with its wand-like flower sprays, although both of these prefer a soil that is well drained as well as moist.

Bulbs in containers

Growing bulbs in ornamental pots, windowboxes, and other containers provides a varied and spectacular display throughout the season. Careful choice of bulbs may extend the season to include late winter as well as spring and summer. Plant a single species or cultivar in each container to provide a uniform, even effect and then group the containers together for a mass of colour.

Place pots of bulbs with fragrant flowers (e.g. hyacinths or Tazetta daffodils) near the house entrance where they may be fully appreciated. Pots used for spring bulbs may be used for summer-flowering plants later: when the bulbs die down, lift and replant them in the garden (or store them) and replace them with annuals or tender perennials.

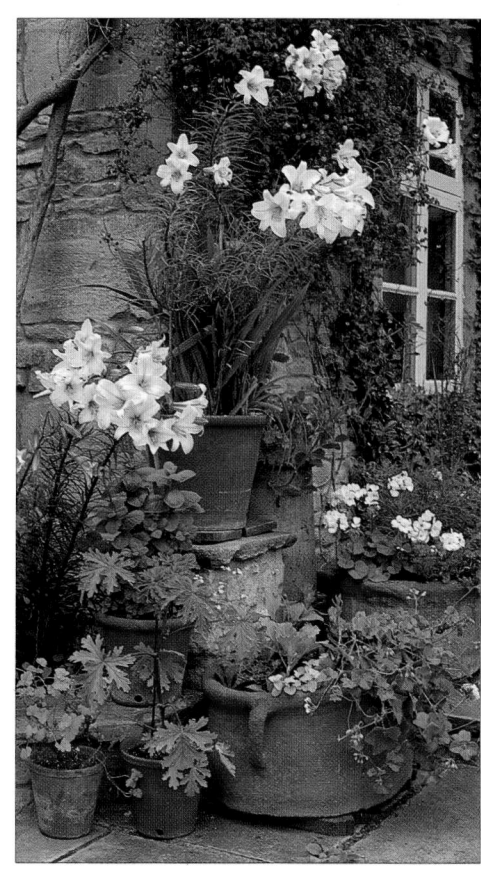

Some larger bulbs are sufficiently striking to be planted on their own in containers. Tall lilies (*Lilium*) or *Crinum* x *powellii*, in pink or white forms, are particularly effective. Any *Agapanthus* species or hybrid provides a long season of showy flower. Alternatively, group several bulbs of varying heights and colours in a large container such as a half-barrel to provide a feature on a patio.

Windowboxes

When planting in windowboxes, choose smaller bulbs that are in proportion to the size of the container. They are excellent for planting in layers below other plants to make best use of limited space; the bulbs thrust through the surface planting to create a pleasing contrast of height and form. Blending the plants with winter-flowering pansies (*Viola* x *wittrockiana*) and ivy (*Hedera*), followed by trailing tender perennials and annuals, gives a prolonged display of colour.

Bulbs under cover

Growing bulbs under cover extends the range that may be cultivated to include many rare species that need particular care. In temperate or cold regions, tender bulbs may be grown that would not survive unprotected in the garden. In regions with summer rainfall, it is the most practical way of growing many of the species bulbs currently in cultivation because they need a dry, summer resting period. Bulbs may be planted in pots or in a greenhouse bed or bulb frame. This allows easier control of the local environment to accommodate the individual needs of a wide range of bulbs, be it a summer drying-off period or protection from excessive winter wet, cold, or frost.

Bulbs in pots

Growing bulbs in pots allows each plant to be grown in conditions that best suit its individual requirements, especially when cultivating small stocks of uncommon bulbs. The pots are easily transferred from outdoors to the shelter of frames or greenhouses when required, or from the greenhouse to the conservatory to enjoy them when in full flower.

Pot cultivation in an unheated greenhouse enables many bulb species that are otherwise of borderline hardiness in temperate climates to be grown. Many are South African and South American bulbs with an exciting diversity of richly coloured blooms, such as *Watsonia* with its dense spikes of deep pink and red. To enjoy tender bulbs, such as *Gloriosa*, and winter-flowering *Veltheimia*, the shelter of a frost-free greenhouse is needed. Overwinter other tender species or cultivars of such genera as begonias, *Canna*, or *Crinum* in a cool greenhouse and bring them out when in bloom to enhance the summer display in the open garden.

If desired, bulbs may be grown in shade and the compost adjusted accordingly to grow small "woodland" bulbs, including *Trillium rivale*, which has finely spotted petals in pink or white, or tender, terrestrial orchids such as the free-flowering *Calanthe* species.

Gardeners with an alpine house may add a little height and splashes of colour to the display by interspersing the plants with pots of dwarf spring bulbs. The alpine house environment is especially suitable for rare or tender bulbs (e.g. ice-white *Narcissus cantabricus* or bright blue *Tecophilaea cyanocrocus*).

Greenhouse beds

Tender bulbs may be planted out directly in prepared greenhouse beds, rather than in pots, for a more natural and vigorous display. The bulbs may be combined in a mixed bed with other plants that flower in summer when the bulbs are dormant. Choose companion plants that tolerate a dry period coinciding with that needed by the bulbs, or that can be plunged in plastic pots and watered without the moisture reaching the bulbs around them.

Spreading, heat-loving plants such as *Osteospermum* or gazanias, and many silver-foliaged plants could be used in this way, and then removed or cut back hard at the end of summer when the bulbs start into growth. Late-flowering *Brodiaea*, *Calochortus*, and *Triteleia* prolong the flowering season still further: group them together and water them separately. Summer-growing bulbs, such as *Eucomis*, some *Gladiolus* species, and the tender *Nerine* species do not need interplanting.

Bulb frames and raised beds

The term "bulb frame" usually refers to a raised bed devoted solely to bulbs; it is covered with a cold frame or Dutch lights during the natural resting period of the bulbs in summer, and also in winter to protect them from excessive rainfall which could cause them to rot. Alternatively, a frame may simply cover bulbs in pots plunged in a sand bed. Such frames may be made more attractive by using stone for the sides.

Bulbs for cut flowers

Many bulbs have flowers that can be cut for the house since their shapely, often solitary, flowers on long stems make them especially suitable for floral arrangement. A few have powerful scents that can fill a room and most are long-lasting if picked before the blooms reach maturity. Some, such as daffodils, are so vigorous and prolific that they may be cut without leaving a gap in the garden display. Alternatively, set aside a separate area to grow bulbs especially for cutting.

Gladioli make fine cut flowers and are often used in this way, since the taller cultivars are difficult to place satisfactorily in an open border.

The pretty, wonderfully fragrant freesias are the only tender or half-hardy bulbs that are commonly grown under cover to provide cut flowers. They have a long flowering season during the winter but make somewhat straggly pot plants that need staking, so they are best cut for display indoors where they will last well.

Schizostylis coccinea 'Sunrise'

Crocosmia 'Lucifer'

Narcissus 'Cheerfulness'

Dahlia 'Early Bird'

Freesia 'Everett'

Gladiolus 'Tesoro'

Zantedeschia aethiopica 'Crowborough'

Nerine bowdenii

Alstroemeria, Ligtu Hybrids

Tulipa 'Clara Butt'

Allium giganteum

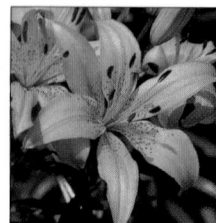
Lilium 'Enchantment'

Bulb frames are the best alternative to the alpine house as a place to grow tender or demanding bulb species without the root restriction of pots, and are used mainly by enthusiasts or collectors. This method of cultivation suits most bulbs, other than those used to some summer rainfall, such as "woodland" and high mountain species. Some crocus, daffodil, *Fritillaria*, and tulip species, Juno and Reticulata irises, and the more difficult *Brodiaea* and *Zigadenus* species tend to be less successful in temperate climates as open garden plants; they may not survive unless they are protected from excess moisture in bulb frames or seasonally covered raised beds during the dormant season.

Forcing bulbs

A good way of bringing colour and fragrance indoors during the winter and early spring is to force bulbs in pots. The bulbs are kept in a cool, dark place for a few months before bringing them into the light to encourage them to flower earlier than they do naturally. *Hippeastrum* with its giant, exotic blooms, scented hyacinths, and daffodils are all suitable. Some hardy bulbs, such as crocuses, may abort their flowers if forced too quickly. A gentler method is to grow bulbs under cover in pots and bring them indoors a week or two before they would normally bloom in the open garden, so that the warmth stimulates them into bloom.

Planter's guide to bulbous plants

EXPOSED SITES

Bulbs that tolerate exposed or windy sites

Anemone
Chionodoxa
Colchicum
Crocus
Cyclamen, some ❀
Fritillaria (dwarf spp.)
Galanthus
Ipheion
Iris reticulata (cvs)
Muscari, some ❀
Narcissus (dwarf spp. and cvs)
Ornithogalum, some ❀
Oxalis, some ❀

Oxalis depressa

Scilla, some ❀
Sternbergia lutea
Triteleia
Tulipa (dwarf spp.)

WALL PROTECTION

Bulbs that prefer the protection of a wall

Agapanthus, some ❀ (most spp.)
Alstroemeria (except Ligtu Hybrids)
Amaryllis belladonna
Anomatheca laxa
Belamcanda chinensis
Bloomeria crocea
Eucomis
Fritillaria persica
Gladiolus ❀ (tender spp.)
Gynandriris sisyrinchium
Habranthus, some ❀ (some spp.)
Hippeastrum advenum
Ixia ❀
Lycoris squamigera
Moraea spathulata
Nerine bowdenii
Scilla peruviana
Sparaxis ❀
Sternbergia lutea, S. sicula
Tulbaghia, some ❀
Watsonia ❀
Zephyranthes candida

DRY SHADE

Bulbs that tolerate dry shade

Anemone nemorosa
Arum italicum 'Pictum'
Cyclamen coum,
  C. hederifolium, C. repandum
Galanthus nivalis (forms)
Hyacinthoides non-scripta
Ranunculus ficaria (cvs)

MOIST SHADE

Bulbs that prefer moist shade

Anemone apennina, A. blanda,
  A. ranunculoides
Arisaema, some ❀ (most spp.)
Arum italicum
Cardiocrinum
Corydalis (some spp.)
Eranthis
Erythronium
Fritillaria camschatcensis,
  F. cirrhosa, F. roylei
Galanthus
Ipheion uniflorum
Leucojum aestivum, L. vernum
Lilium (some spp.)

Lilium hansonii

Narcissus cyclamineus,
  N. triandrus
Nomocharis
Notholirion
Scilla bifolia
Trillium
Tulipa sylvestris

FLOWERS FOR CUTTING

Agapanthus, some ❀
Allium (some spp.)
Alstroemeria (taller spp. and cvs)
Amaryllis belladonna
Anemone, De Caen Series,
  A., St Brigid Series
Camassia
Clivia ❀
Crinum, some ❀
Crocosmia

Cyrtanthus purpureus ❀
Dierama, some ❀
Freesia ❀
Galtonia
Gladiolus, some ❀
Iris, Dutch Hybrids,
  I. latifolia, I. xiphium
Ixia ❀
Lilium
Narcissus
Nerine, some ❀
Ornithogalum, some ❀ (tall spp.)
Ranunculus asiaticus ❀ (forms)
Sparaxis ❀
Tulipa
Watsonia ❀
Zantedeschia, some ❀

ARCHITECTURAL PLANTS

Allium christophii,
  A. giganteum
Canna ❀
Cardiocrinum giganteum
Crinum x *powellii*
Fritillaria imperialis
Lilium (most spp. and cvs)

ROCK GARDENS

Bulbs suitable for planting in rock gardens

Albuca humilis ❀
Allium (dwarf spp.)
Anemone (some spp.)
Bellevalia (some spp.)
Brodiaea (smallest spp.)
Bulbocodium vernum
Colchicum (small spp.)
Corydalis (some spp.)
Crocus
Cyclamen (hardy spp.)
Fritillaria (many spp.)
Gagea, some ❀ (some spp.)
Galanthus
Ipheion
Iris (dwarf spp.)
Leucojum (some spp.)
Merendera
Muscari, some ❀ (non-invasive spp.)
Narcissus (dwarf spp. and hybrids)
Ornithogalum, some ❀ (dwarf spp.)
Oxalis, some ❀ (some spp.)
Puschkinia

Rhodohypoxis
Romulea, some ❀ (some spp.)
Scilla, some ❀
Sternbergia lutea, S. sicula
Tulipa (dwarf spp.)
Zephyranthes candida
Zigadenus

BULBS FOR ALPINE HOUSES

Albuca ❀
Anemone (some spp.)
Anomatheca
Arum, some ❀ (some spp.)
Babiana ❀
Bellevalia
Biarum
Bongardia chrysogonum
Bulbocodium vernum
Calochortus
Colchicum (small spp.)
Crocus
Cyclamen, some ❀
Fritillaria (most spp.)
Gagea, some ❀
Galanthus
Habranthus, some ❀
Hippeastrum, some ❀ (dwarf spp.)

Moraea huttonii

Iris (dwarf spp.)
Leontice
Leucocoryne ❀
Leucojum (some spp.)
Merendera
Moraea, some ❀ (some spp.)
Muscari, some ❀ (some spp.)
Narcissus (dwarf spp.)
Ornithogalum, some ❀ (dwarf spp.)
Oxalis, some ❀ (some spp.)
Pancratium, some ❀
Pinellia
Rhodohypoxis
Romulea, some ❀
Scilla, some ❀
Sternbergia
Tecophilaea
Tulipa (dwarf spp.)
Zephyranthes, some ❀
Zigadenus

KEY
❀ *Not hardy*

Tulips and daffodils

Tulips and daffodils are highly valued for the bold splashes of colour they bring to the garden in spring. Grow them together to extend the flowering season in a mixed border: some daffodils bloom very early in the year, while many tulips last well into late spring. Tulips are excellent for beds or borders, while many daffodils are especially suitable for naturalizing in grass. Dwarf forms are ideal for rock gardens, alpine houses, or containers, where they may be seen at close range.

Tulips

This diverse, versatile genus is horticulturally classified in 15 divisions based on flower form, but may conveniently be grouped by flowering season and garden use.

Early tulips
Single, early tulips have classic, goblet-shaped blooms, some with striped, flushed, or margined petals. Early doubles have long-lasting, open bowl-shaped flowers, often flecked or margined in toning colours. Traditionally used for cutting, in formal bedding, or as border edgings, many can also be grown in pots indoors. In informal schemes their elegant outlines contrast well with spreading or prostrate plants.

Mid-season tulips
This grouping includes Triumph tulips, with their simple, conical blooms, and the Darwin hybrids, with rich and intensely coloured flowers, often with a satiny, basal blotch and dark, velvety anthers. Both types are sturdy, robust, and noted for their weather resistance.

Late tulips
Some of the most vibrant colours and intricate forms are seen in late-flowering tulips. They include the graceful lily-flowered types, vivid and extravagant Parrot tulips, green-tinged Viridifloras, and exuberantly striped and feathered Rembrandts. Peony-flowered forms are suited to informal cottage gardens. All are effective used informally with dark green or grey ground cover or in formal bedding schemes.

Dwarf species and hybrids
The compact Kaufmanniana hybrids produce their brightly coloured blooms very early in the spring while the slightly taller Fosteriana and Greigii tulips usually flower a little later. Many have very attractively marked foliage. The dwarf species are ideal for containers, raised beds, or rock gardens. *Tulipa sprengeri* and *T. sylvestris* tolerate light shade and will naturalize in fine grass.

Cultivation and propagation
Most tulips thrive in fertile, well-drained, humus-rich soils, in sun and with shelter, and in ideal conditions some robust cultivars persist from year to year. Many, however, are best regarded as annual bedding plants, being lifted after flowering and either discarded (if diseased) or replanted until they have died down. The bulbs seldom flower well in the

TULIPS IN A SPRING BORDER
The strong, vertical stems and neat flower-cups of tulips provide height and structure, as well as vivid colour, in an informal spring border.

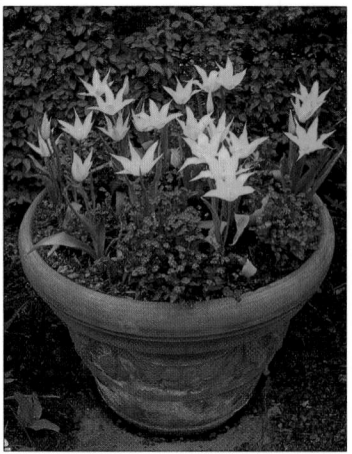

GROWING IN CONTAINERS
The lily-flowered tulips 'West Point' here display their ornate blooms.

Types of tulip

Tulips include an impressive range of flower forms, from the simple, upright goblets of single-flowered tulips to the frilled and twisted petals of Parrot tulips and the open, double blooms of peony-flowered forms. They are available in most colours, except blue, from the purest white to the deepest purple, with many glorious shades of yellow, red, and crimson in between. Many of the dwarf tulips also have attractively marked leaves.

SINGLE

Tulipa 'Dawnglow'
Darwin hybrid

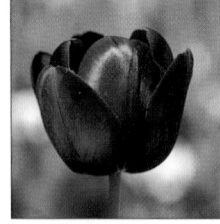

T. 'Queen of Night'
Single, late

T. 'Spring Green'
Viridiflora

DOUBLE AND PARROT

T. 'Peach Blossom'
Double, early

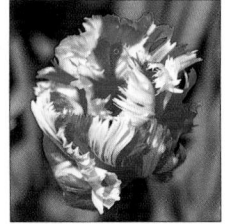

T. 'Estella Rijnveld'
Parrot

DWARF SPECIES AND HYBRIDS

T. tarda
Dwarf species

T. 'Dreamboat'
Greigii hybrid

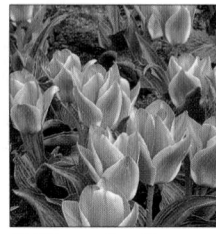

T. 'Giuseppe Verdi'
Kaufmanniana hybrid

T. 'Greuze'
Single, late

EXTENDING THE FLOWERING SEASON
Growing tulips and daffodils together provides a continuous display of colour from early spring until well into summer.

Daffodils

Grown for their cheerful spring blooms, daffodils (*Narcissus*) are among the easiest and most rewarding of bulbs to grow. They are horticulturally divided into 12 groups, based on the form of the flowers.

Daffodils in containers

Most daffodils can be grown in pots, if they are deep enough to allow the bulbs to be covered to 1½ times their own depth. Tazettas, with clusters of up to 12 scented blooms, are often grown under glass or as pot plants to bloom from late autumn to spring. The richly fragrant jonquil hybrids are also useful as container plants for house decoration. Small species, such as *N. cantabricus* and *N. romieuxii*, produce blooms early in the year in the alpine house; they may also then be brought indoors.

Daffodils in the garden

Valuable for formal spring bedding and to give early interest in the mixed border, daffodils are among the most reliable of bulbs for naturalizing: they rarely need lifting in borders or grass. Even tiny species, such as *N. cyclamineus* and *N. minor*, will thrive in fine turf. Dwarf daffodils are ideal for rock gardens and raised beds, some, such as *N. romieuxii*, *N.* 'Tête-à-tête', and *N.* 'February Gold', flowering early in the year.

Cultivation and propagation

Daffodils will grow in almost any soil type, but prefer well-drained, moist, slightly alkaline conditions.

NATURALIZING DAFFODILS IN GRASS
In an informal or wild garden, daffodils may be grown in grass, bringing welcome colour to a dark corner or the ground beneath a tree.

second year but if replanted in autumn may reach flowering size again within two years.

Dwarf tulips generally prefer open, gritty soils, and full sun; lift and replant them only when overcrowded. Propagate by offsets (see p.237) or, for species, by seed (see p.238). Tulips are prone to tulip fire (see p.553) and other bulb problems (see p.236).

They thrive in sun or light, dappled shade. Plant the bulbs 12–15cm (5–6in) deep in late summer or early autumn. When bulbs are naturalized in grass, do not cut the old foliage until at least four to six weeks after they have flowered. Bulbs in pots must be grown in cool conditions, with plenty of fresh air. Temperatures above 7–10°C (45–50°F) usually cause flowers to abort. Place the pots in a cold frame after planting,

and bring them into a cold greenhouse about 12–16 weeks later. Once flower buds have formed, blooming can be advanced by raising the temperature gently although not exceeding 13°C (55°F).

Propagate by offsets (see p.237), or by chipping (see p.241); new hybrids and species may also be raised from seed (see p.238). Daffodils may be affected by both narcissus eelworms (p.567) and bulb flies (p.567).

Types of daffodil

Daffodils provide a wide variety of shapes and forms, from the tiny, exquisite Cyclamineus hybrids, with their swept-back petals, to the tall, trumpet daffodils and the more showy double forms. Modern developments include the split corona and collarette types. In addition to the characteristic bright yellow flowers, cultivars include those with pale butter-yellow blooms or brilliant white petals and fiery orange cups.

DWARF SPECIES AND HYBRIDS

Narcissus triandrus
Dwarf species

N. romieuxii
Dwarf species

N. 'Jumblie'
Cyclamineus hybrid

N. 'Pride of Cornwall'
Tazetta

SINGLE

N. 'Passionale'
Large-cupped

N. 'Fortune'
Large-cupped

N. 'Ambergate'
Large-cupped

DOUBLE

N. 'Irene Copeland'
Double

N. 'Tahiti'
Double

Dahlias

DAHLIAS flower from the middle of summer to the first frosts in autumn, providing bright colour in the garden for several months. All are frost tender. They can be grown in various soil types, providing that they are fertile and well drained, and are excellent border plants.

If grown for exhibition or for cut flowers, they are best planted in rows in specially prepared beds. The dwarf bedding dahlias, usually grown annually from seed (see ANNUALS AND BIENNIALS, "Sowing in pots or trays", p.182), are suitable for planting in containers. Dahlia flowerheads have a diversity of petal forms in a wide colour range, from white to rich yellow through pinks and reds to purples.

Dahlias are classified according to the size and form of their flowerheads. The decorative and cactus types are subdivided by the size of their blooms: miniature under 115mm (4½in); small 115–70mm (4½–7in); medium 170–220mm (7–9in); large 220–60mm (9–10½in); and giant over 260mm (10½in).

Cultivation

Dahlias thrive in well-drained, fertile soils of about pH7. Prepare the soil early in the year. They are gross feeders, so dig in a heavy dressing of manure or garden compost; then add bone meal at 125g/sq m (4oz/sq yd), leaving the bed roughly dug so that frost can break up the soil.

Where and when to plant
Dahlias may be planted as pot-grown plants, as dormant tubers, or as rooted cuttings from tubers. Plants in leaf may be preferable to tubers, as they are often more vigorous. Dormant tubers, however, may be planted directly, about six weeks before the last frosts, whereas plants in leaf should not be planted until all danger of frost has passed.

Choose an open, sheltered site that is not overshadowed. Immediately before planting, top-dress with blood, fish, and bone at 125g/sq m (4oz/sq yd) worked well into the soil. Tie young plants into their stakes to support them as they develop.

Planting pot-grown dahlias
When planting pot-grown dahlias, canes should be positioned at the appropriate spacings. Plants that are 120–50cm (4–5ft) tall are planted 60–90cm (2–3ft) apart, and those that are 90–120cm (3–4ft) tall 60cm (2ft) apart. Water the plants in their pots and leave to drain. Plant with

SELECTING PLANTS

When planting out a pot-grown dahlia or rooted cutting, select young plants with a vigorous root system and disease-free foliage.

PLANTING TUBERS

Insert a 1m (3ft) stake in a planting hole. Place soil around the tuber so that the base of the new shoots is 2.5–5cm (1–2in) below soil level.

care, to avoid disturbing the root ball, and firm gently, leaving a slight depression at the base of the stem. Water thoroughly. The plants will make a tuber by late autumn; this may be lifted and stored for replanting in spring.

Planting tubers
Dormant tubers may be planted directly in the border about six weeks before the last frosts are expected. The ground is prepared as for pot-grown plants. Prepare a planting hole about 22cm (9in) across and about 15cm (6in) deep, place the tuber in the hole, and cover over. Mark the position of the tuber with a labelled split cane placed just to the side; this will indicate the exact position of the tuber when inserting its support stake. The tuber takes about six weeks to develop a shoot above ground.

Planting rooted cuttings
Established tubers may be grown on in the cold frame or greenhouse, to provide cuttings (see "Propagation", p.227). Plant out the rooted cuttings after all danger of frost has passed. As growth develops, water the plants moderately; to retain moisture, mulch when the plants are 30–38cm (12–15in) high with well-rotted compost or manure. Do not place the mulch close to the base of the plants since this may encourage stem rot. If composted grass cuttings are used, ensure that they have not been treated with selective weedkiller.

Stopping and disbudding
When the dahlias have grown to about 38cm (15in), stop the plants by removing the growing points to encourage sideshoots. Insert two more canes to make a triangular

DAHLIA FLOWER TYPES

SINGLE
D. 'Yellow Hammer'
Flowerheads with 8–10 broad florets surrounding an open, central disc.

ANEMONE
D. 'Comet'
Fully double flowerheads with one or more rings of flattened ray florets surrounding a group of shorter, tubular florets.

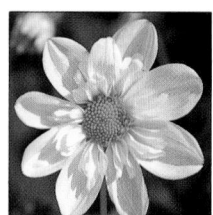

COLLARETTE
D. 'Easter Sunday'
A single yellow disc of stamens in the centre, with a collar of small florets lying between the stamens and the large, outer florets.

WATER LILY
D. 'Vicky Crutchfield'
As their name implies, these flowerheads look like water lilies, and have broad, flat florets.

DECORATIVE
D. 'Frank Hornsey'
Fully double. Florets have broad petals rounded at the ends, usually curling gently inwards along their length, flat, and slightly twisted.

BALL
D. 'Wootton Cupid'
Rounded flowerheads with spirally arranged florets. The petals are rolled for over half their length.

POMPON
D. 'Small World'
Similar to ball dahlias but much smaller, to a maximum diameter of 52mm (2in), and more globular; the petals are rolled for the whole of their length.

CACTUS
D. 'Majestic Kerkrade'
Fully double, with narrow, pointed petals curled backwards or quilled, which are either straight or incurving.

SEMI-CACTUS
D. 'So Dainty'
Fully double. The ray florets have pointed, straight or incurving, broad-based petals that curve backwards.

STOPPING

1 *When the plant is about 38cm (15in) high, pinch out the central shoot to encourage the development of sideshoots.*

2 *When the plant has 6–8 sideshoots, pinch out the top pair of buds. Tie in the stems to stakes.*

support and tie the shoots in, with about 15cm (6in) between ties.

The number of shoots allowed to develop should depend on the size of the blooms required. For giant or large blooms, restrict each plant to 4–6 shoots; for medium and small blooms, allow 7–10 shoots. To produce high-quality blooms, remove the pairs of buds developing in the leaf axils behind the terminal bud. Disbud at least two pairs of these side (wing) buds; for giant blooms, take out three pairs.

DISBUDDING

Pinch out the side (wing) buds growing below the terminal bud on each young plant, so that the bud that remains will develop into a larger bloom.

Summer feeding

Four to six weeks after planting, feed with a high nitrogen and potash fertilizer, either in granular form, or by weekly applications of liquid fertilizer as a root or foliar feed. As flower buds develop, extra potash in the liquid fertilizer gives strong stems and good flower colour, especially in pinks and lilacs; this is important when growing for exhibition.

The tuber's development during late summer and early autumn is stimulated by the shortening day length. During this period, apply a split application of sulphate of potash and superphosphates at the manufacturer's recommended rate. Avoid contact with leaves or stems as this may cause scorch.

Pests and diseases

Dahlias are affected particularly by aphids (p.550), thrips (p.551), red spider mites (p.550), and earwigs (p.548). These may be controlled by spraying regularly. Lift and burn any plants infected with virus.

Lifting and storing tubers

When the foliage has been blackened by the first frosts in autumn, trim back the stems to about 15cm (6in). Carefully lift and clean the tubers of soil, trim off any fine roots, and treat the tubers with fungicide. Place them upside-down for a few weeks to ensure that no moisture remains in the stems and leaves.

Label the tubers and pack them in wooden boxes in vermiculite, coir, or a similar medium. Store in a dry, cool, frost-proof place. Inspect the tubers regularly in winter; if any mildew or rot has developed, cut it out with a clean, sharp knife and dust the cut surfaces with sulphur.

LIFTING AND STORING

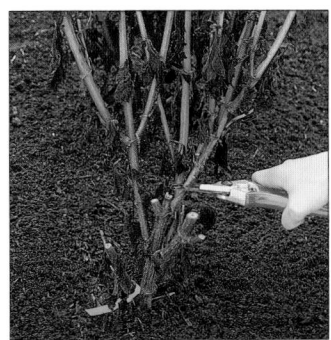

1 *Cut the stems to about 15cm (6in) above ground level. Loosen the soil and ease the tubers out. Remove excess soil.*

2 *Store the tubers upside-down for about 3 weeks in a frost-free place so that the stems dry out thoroughly.*

3 *When the stems have dried out, place the tubers in a cool, frost-free place and cover them with a layer of bark chippings. Keep them dry until spring.*

Propagation

Divide established tubers in spring. First bring them into growth in a cold frame or greenhouse. Press the tubers gently onto the top of a tray of compost, spray with water, and keep warm and damp. As shoots develop, divide the tuber into sections with a sharp knife, ensuring that each piece has at least one growing shoot. Pot up each section separately using a general-purpose compost.

Alternatively, in late winter, force tubers at 15–18°C (60–65°F). When shoots are 7.5cm (3in) long, take basal cuttings, trim at a node, and root in a propagating case with bottom heat. Grow on under glass and harden off before planting out.

Showing dahlias

Cut blooms with a sharp knife in the morning or evening, making sure that the length of the stem is in proportion to the bloom. When exhibiting, blooms should always be well developed with undamaged petals. Read the schedule and present the correct number of stems staged in the vase, with the blooms facing the front.

HOW TO PROPAGATE BY BASAL CUTTINGS

1 *In late winter, force the tubers in the greenhouse. Take cuttings when the young shoots each have 2 or 3 pairs of leaves.*

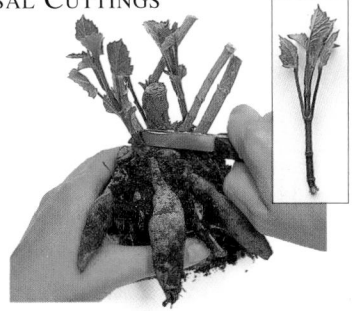

2 *With a knife, remove each shoot, with a thin segment, or heel, from the parent tuber. Trim the basal leaves from each cutting.*

3 *Insert the cuttings in a pot of moist compost. Place in a propagator or plastic bag to root. Then pot up singly to grow on.*

Soil preparation and planting

Most bulbous plants have long, dormant periods underground after flowering and require relatively little attention for much of the year. The initial stages of selecting good stock, preparing the soil, and planting bulbs correctly do, however, contribute significantly to long-term success in cultivating bulbs.

Buying bulbs

There is considerable variation in the quality and size of bulbs available commercially, so examine any bulbs carefully before buying them. Different types of bulb are sold at various times of the year; always buy them when they are as fresh as possible. Select bulbs that are appropriate to the planting site: most enjoy sun, some prefer shade, and others will naturalize in grass.

Conservation

Conservation of bulbs in the wild is of the utmost importance and there are strict rules governing their importation. Wherever possible, check that the bulb stocks on sale at nurseries and garden centres have been obtained from sources of cultivated bulbs, rather than from stocks that have been collected in the wild.

Dry bulbs

Most bulbs are sold in a dry state during their dormant period. Buy these as early as possible before they

HOW TO SELECT BULBS

GOOD EXAMPLES

TULIP

HYACINTH

DAFFODIL (SINGLE-NOSED)

DAFFODIL (TWIN-NOSED)

POOR EXAMPLES

Split tunic

Signs of disease

Diseased tissue

Damaged outer scales

No tunic

Deterioration of bulb tissue

Soft nose

Offset too small to flower

start into growth; most daffodils, for example, normally start producing roots in late summer, and most other spring-flowering bulbs will begin to grow by early autumn. Autumn-flowering crocuses and *Colchicum* species and hybrids especially benefit from early planting: specialist nurseries sell them in mid-summer.

All autumn-flowering bulbs are best bought and planted by late summer. Bulbs tend to deteriorate if kept dry too long; they will have a shorter growing period and will take some time to recover and flower satisfactorily, so buy and plant them as soon as they are available. Some dry bulbs, usually those that have a summer

growing season, such as *Galtonia*, gladioli, and *Tigridia*, are available for purchase in spring.

When buying bulbs, make sure that they are healthy and firm with strong growing points, and no soft or diseased areas or any signs of insect damage. Bulbs that are much smaller than average for their type, and bulb offsets, will not produce flowers in their first season.

Juno irises are unusual in having permanent storage roots beneath the bulb; if these have broken off, do not buy the bulb since it will not develop satisfactorily. Tulips should have intact skins, or tunics, otherwise they will be vulnerable to disease.

Moist bulbs

Although most bulbs may be stored dry, a few are better kept in slightly moist bark, peat substitute, or some similar material. This particularly applies to some of the shade-loving bulb species, such as *Erythronium*, *Anemone nemorosa*, and *Trillium*, that are normally found growing in damp woodland.

When buying cyclamen tubers, look for those with fibrous roots that are stored in moist bark or that are in root growth in pots. Cyclamen that have healthy roots establish much more effectively than dry tubers and so, although more expensive, are a much better buy.

Pot-grown bulbs

Pots of bulbs in active growth, and frequently in flower, are often sold in nurseries and garden centres. These are usually bulbs that were not sold when dormant and have been potted up. They grow satisfactorily and may be planted at once, without disturbing the roots. Alternatively, they may be kept in pots until they have flowered and planted as dry bulbs after they have died down. They are more expensive, however, than dry bulbs.

CHOOSING HEALTHY CORMS AND TUBERS

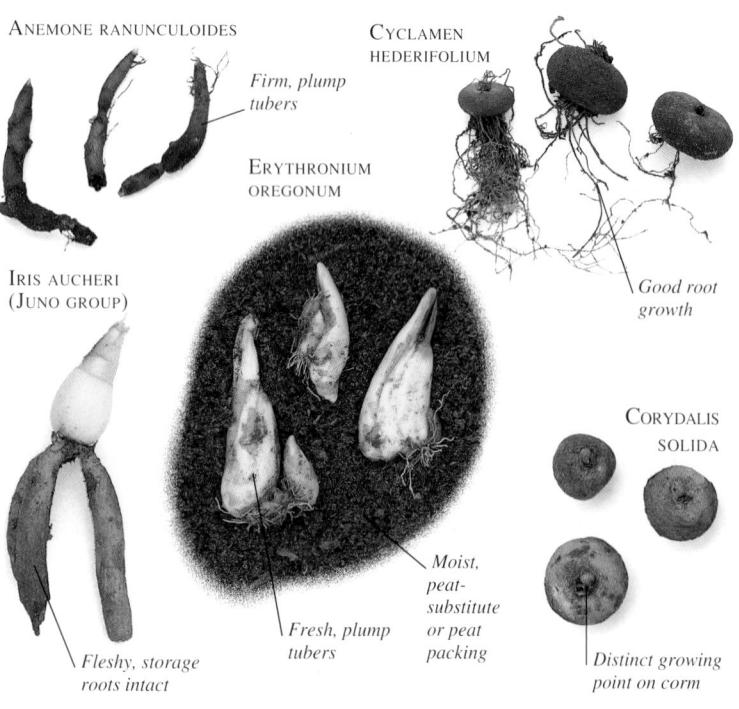

ANEMONE RANUNCULOIDES

Firm, plump tubers

ERYTHRONIUM OREGONUM

IRIS AUCHERI (JUNO GROUP)

Fleshy, storage roots intact

Fresh, plump tubers

Moist, peat-substitute or peat packing

CYCLAMEN HEDERIFOLIUM

Good root growth

CORYDALIS SOLIDA

Distinct growing point on corm

Buying snowdrops "in the green"

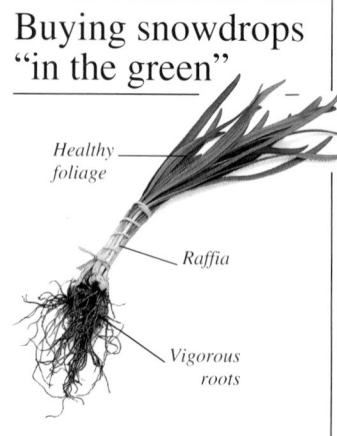

Healthy foliage

Raffia

Vigorous roots

If possible, purchase snowdrops "in the green" (i.e. still in leaf) after flowering, preferably just as the leaves begin to yellow at the tips. Dry bulbs, although much cheaper, often fail to establish well. Specialist nurseries supply snowdrops in the green, bound or packed in moist bark or a similar material.

The influence of different soil types

Bulbs grow in a range of soil types, habitats, and climates throughout the world; the conditions in which they occur naturally indicate their needs in cultivation. Most hardy bulbs are from Mediterranean-type climates and thrive in a warm, sunny site, in freely draining soils that warm up quickly in spring, and become dry in summer. Some species tolerate heavy soils that are moist during the growing season, as long as they are baked dry in summer. If the soil is moderately fertile and humus-rich, many bulbs increase steadily from year to year by seed or vegetative means. Most prefer a near-neutral or slightly alkaline soil.

Good drainage is vital since most bulbs are prone to rot while dormant if the soil is wet and poorly aerated. A few occur in the wild in riverside or swampland habitats; these thrive in moist (or even permanently wet) soils that do not dry out in summer.

Light soils

Sandy or light soils usually warm up rapidly in spring and provide the good drainage that most bulbs need, although they are often deficient in humus and nutrients. Dig in plenty of well-rotted garden compost or manure before planting and, in early spring, top-dress with a balanced fertilizer applied at the manufacturer's recommended rate. Always incorporate manure below the level at which the bulbs are planted to avoid the risk of disease or chemical damage. If using fresh manure, dig it in at least three months before planting. More fertile, sandy soils and loams benefit from extra organic matter, but fertilizer dressing is unnecessary in the first year. In rock gardens, dig in coarse grit to make up at least one third of the top 30cm (12in) of soil for the extra drainage that most dwarf bulbs need.

Heavy soils

Heavy clay soils often need a lot of work to improve their drainage; on very poorly drained soils, a drainage

system must first be installed to grow bulbs successfully. Coarse sand or grit at a rate of at least 1½–2 buckets/sq m (sq yd) dug into the whole planting area will be required to make a significant difference. Heavy applications of well-rotted organic matter also improve the soil structure and therefore the drainage. For further information, see "Soil structure and water content", p.526.

Shady areas

Shade-loving bulbs most often occur naturally in woodland habitats, but grow well in any shady situation, as long as the soil is properly prepared: it should be rich in nutrients and humus and also retain moisture. Incorporate plenty of leaf mould or some other organic matter, such as well-rotted manure or garden compost, before planting. Acid-loving "woodland" bulbs thrive in the peat garden where at least half the soil is leaf mould, peat substitute, or peat.

Planting time

Dry bulbs should be planted as soon as possible after purchase. If the bulbs have been stored over winter (see "Lifting, drying, and storing", p.235), plant them at the end of their dormant period before they start growing. Pot-grown bulbs may be planted after purchase throughout the season, or kept in their pots until after they die down and treated as dry bulbs. Plant summer-flowering bulbs, including those that bloom in late summer under cover, and bulbs in the green, in early to mid-spring.

Planting in the open

Bulbs are usually best planted several to a large hole dug out with a spade. Alternatively, they may be planted singly. Do not make the outline of the planting area or the spacing of the bulbs symmetrical as this will look unnatural and if one or two bulbs fail they leave unsightly gaps.

In a rock garden, remove any top-dressing before planting bulbs and replace it afterwards.

Planting depths and spacing

Plant bulbs with two to three times their own depth of soil above them (deeper in light than in heavy soils) and two to three bulb widths apart. Remove soil to the correct depth, fork some bone meal into the bottom of the hole, and insert the bulbs.

Occasionally it is difficult to identify the "top" of a bulb, especially with rootless cyclamen tubers. The

upper surface is usually flatter than the lower, or sometimes concave. *Corydalis* tubers can be almost globular, but there is usually some sign of shoot growth on the top. If it is impossible to be sure, plant the bulb on its side.

Replace the soil, breaking down any clods. Firm gently so that there are no air spaces around the bulbs.

Bulbs in the green

It may be necessary to plant bulbs in the green if transferring them from another garden, if space is restricted and bulbs are lifted each year to make way for other plants, or if planting snowdrops that have been sold in this state.

Use a trowel or a widger to create randomly spaced holes sufficiently wide to spread out the roots, and plant each bulb individually, at the same level as it was planted before. This is indicated by the colour change between the green top-growth and the chlorotic, yellow-green leaf bases that were underground. Water thoroughly after planting.

Pot-grown bulbs

Bulbs that have been purchased as pot-grown plants may be planted as dry bulbs after they have died down. When planting them, make a hole large enough to accommodate the whole pot, so that the contents may be planted without disturbance.

PLANTING IN THE GREEN

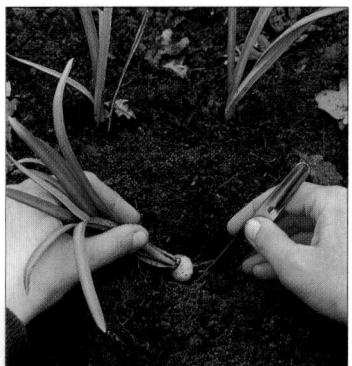

Insert the bulb (here a snowdrop) in a prepared hole that is wide and deep enough to spread the roots and plant the bulb at the same depth as before. Draw the soil over, and firm.

HOW TO PLANT CYCLAMEN IN ROOT GROWTH

1 *Select a planting site where the soil is rich in leaf mould or humus, or prepare the soil as necessary, working in organic matter well below the depth of the planting hole to encourage the roots to grow into the soil after planting. Leave it to settle for a day or two, then make a hole that is deep enough to plant the tuber with its roots spread out below it.*

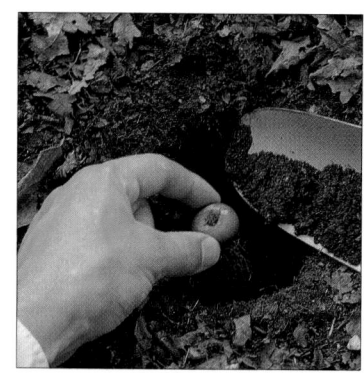

2 *Plant the tuber so that it will lie with its upper surface just visible at soil level. Fill in around the roots with soil, taking care not to damage the roots.*

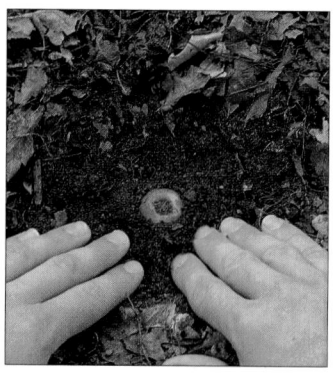

3 *Gently firm the soil around the tuber with your fingers, leaving the growing point just exposed. Lightly cover it with a loose mulch.*

If the bulbs become pot-bound, gently tease out the roots at the base before planting to encourage them to grow out into the soil. If they are growing in a peat-based compost, keep the bulbs under cover in winter. Otherwise the peat acts as a sponge and the dormant bulbs rot in the waterlogged compost.

Planting tubers and corms in root growth

A number of "woodland" species, such as cyclamen, are best planted when they are in root growth, rather than as dry bulbs, as they will then become established more quickly.

They are also more likely to flower in their first season after planting; dry corms or tubers are much less reliable in this respect. Planting in root growth also eliminates any problems in distinguishing between the bottoms and tops of tubers or corms. Work plenty of leaf mould or well-rotted, organic matter into

the soil before planting to create the moist, humus-rich conditions that "woodland" bulbs require, otherwise the bulbs will not thrive.

Planting depth and spacing
Calculate the spacing and planting depth for corms and tubers in the same way as for dry bulbs (see "Planting in the open" and *Correct Planting Depths*, p.229), but allow additional space for the roots.

Cyclamen are unusual in that they grow near the soil surface in the wild, so do not plant the tubers too deeply or they may not flower. Make sure that their tips are at about the same level as the surrounding soil. They may be planted more closely than other bulbs, but they should be spaced at least their own width apart.

Planting
Plant the corms or tubers singly or as a group. It is important for the planting hole to be sufficiently deep and wide to properly accommodate the roots. Spread them out in the hole as this helps the plants to establish more quickly. Fill in the hole and firm it well to remove any air spaces.

The tips of cyclamen tubers may be left exposed or, if preferred, lightly covered with a loose mulch. Use leaf mould or, if the bed already has a top-dressing, coarse grit.

PLANTING LARGE BULBS IN GRASS

1 *Clean the bulbs (here daffodils), removing any loose, outer coatings and old roots. Scatter the bulbs randomly over the planting area, then make sure that they are at least their own width apart.*

2 *Make an individual hole for each bulb, using a bulb planter to remove a circle of turf and a core of soil to a depth of about 10–15cm (4–6in).*

3 *Place a pinch of bone meal, mixed with a little of the soil from the core, into each hole and put in a bulb, making sure that the growing point is uppermost.*

4 *Break up the underside of the core over the bulb, so that it is completely covered with loose soil. Then replace the remains of the core on top of it.*

5 *Replace the lid of turf, and firm it in gently, taking care not to damage the growing point of the bulb. Fill in any gaps in the turf with more soil.*

Naturalizing in grass

When planting bulbs for naturalizing in grass, first cut the grass as short as possible. Random rather than regimented planting achieves a more natural effect; scatter the bulbs by hand over the chosen area and plant them where they have fallen,

PLANTING SMALL BULBS IN GRASS

1 Using a half-moon edger (or spade), cut an "H" shape in the turf. Cut to the full depth of the half-moon blade to make sure that it penetrates the soil below.

2 Undercut the turf and fold back the flaps to expose the area of bare soil beneath. Take care not to crack or tear the turf unduly.

3 Using a hand fork, loosen the soil beneath to a depth of at least 7cm (3in), mixing in a little bone meal at a rate of about 15g/sq m (¹/₂oz/sq yd).

4 Press the bulbs (here crocuses) gently into the soil, taking care not to damage the growing points. Space the bulbs randomly but at least 2.5cm (1in) apart.

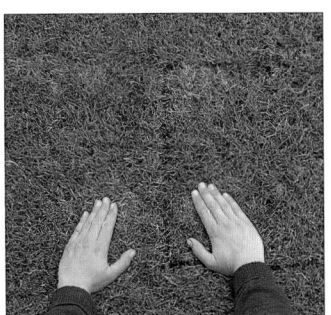

5 Score the underneath of the turf with a hand fork to loosen the soil, so that the bulbs will be able to penetrate the turf easily.

6 Roll the turf flaps back into position, taking care not to dislodge the bulbs or to damage the turf. Firm down the turf, particularly along the joins.

USING A FORK TO PLANT SMALL BULBS

1 Push a garden fork into the grass to the appropriate depth and rock it back and forth. Repeat at random over the rest of the planting area.

2 Thoroughly mix a little bone meal with some garden soil. Trickle a small amount of this mix into the bottom of each hole, using a widger or a small spoon.

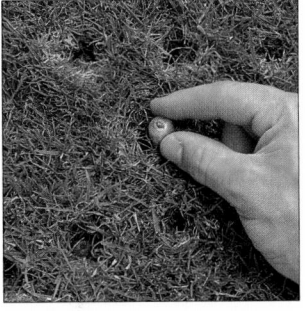

3 Place a single bulb in each hole, growing point upper-most, ensuring that it is buried at twice its own depth. Then cover all the planted bulbs with soil.

NATURALIZING IN GRASS

Allium moly
Anemone apennina,
   A. blanda (and cvs),
   A. pavonina
Camassia
Chionodoxa forbesii
Colchicum autumnale,
   C. speciosum

*Crocus
pulchellus*

Crocus biflorus,
   C. chrysanthus,
   C., Dutch Hybrids,
   C. flavus, C. nudiflorus,
   C. ochroleucus,
   C. pulchellus, C. speciosus,
   C. tommasinianus
Dactylorrhiza fuchsii,
   D. maculata
Eranthis hyemalis
Erythronium dens-canis,
   E. revolutum,
   E. 'White Beauty'
Fritillaria meleagris,
   F. pyrenaica
Galanthus caucasicus,
   G. elwesii, G. nivalis
Gladiolus communis subsp.
   byzantinus
Hyacinthoides hispanica
Leucojum aestivum,
   L. vernum
Muscari, some ✤

*Narcissus
'Fortune'*

Narcissus (some
   dwarf and most large spp.),
   N. bulbocodium,
   N. cyclamineus, N. nanus,
   N. obvallaris, N. poeticus,
   N. pseudonarcissus,
   N. pumilus, N. triandrus
Ornithogalum nutans
Puschkinia scilloides
Scilla bifolia, S. siberica
Tulipa sprengeri

KEY
✤ Not hardy

---

making sure that they are at least one bulb's width apart. Dig planting holes with a trowel or use a bulb planter; this useful implement cuts out neat plugs of turf and soil to a depth of about 10–15cm (4–6in) and is most suitable for larger bulbs.

Check that all the holes are at the correct depth and that the bulbs are the right way up, before inserting them and replacing the turf.

Planting large groups of small bulbs in grass

It is easier and less time-consuming to plant large numbers of very small bulbs, such as crocuses, by lifting a section of turf and planting a whole group of bulbs in the soil beneath rather than planting each bulb individually. Loosen the soil beneath the turf since it may be compacted; fork in a little balanced fertilizer or

some bone meal. Position the bulbs randomly, at least their own width apart. Replace the turf over the bulbs and firm it by hand or by tamping it down gently with the back of a rake.

Alternatively, use a broad-tined garden fork to make a series of holes in the turf, and rock the fork back and forth in the ground to enlarge the holes slightly so that they easily accommodate the bulbs. The tines

should be inserted to three times the depth of the bulb, for example 7cm (3in) for crocuses. Repeat this at random for the entire planting area, so that the final arrangement of holes, in straight but criss-crossing lines, gives a natural effect. Mix a little bone meal with soil and place some in each hole before planting the bulbs singly, then top-dress the whole area with more prepared soil.

BULBS THAT REQUIRE A RESTING PERIOD

Anemone biflora,
  A. tschernjaewii
Bellevalia (some spp.)
Bongardia

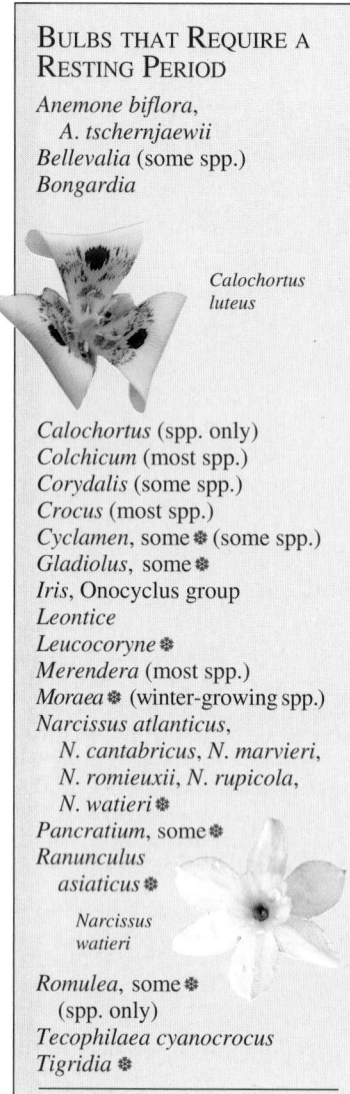

Calochortus
luteus

Calochortus (spp. only)
Colchicum (most spp.)
Corydalis (some spp.)
Crocus (most spp.)
Cyclamen, some ✿ (some spp.)
Gladiolus, some ✿
Iris, Onocyclus group
Leontice
Leucocoryne ✿
Merendera (most spp.)
Moraea ✿ (winter-growing spp.)
Narcissus atlanticus,
  N. cantabricus, N. marvieri,
  N. romieuxii, N. rupicola,
  N. watieri ✿
Pancratium, some ✿
Ranunculus
  asiaticus ✿

Narcissus
watieri

Romulea, some ✿
  (spp. only)
Tecophilaea cyanocrocus
Tigridia ✿

KEY
✿ Not hardy

HOW TO PLANT BULBS IN POTS

Growing tip
uppermost

1 Plant the bulbs (here daffodils) at twice their own depth, and one bulb's width apart.

2 Cover the bulbs with compost to 1cm (¹/₂in) below the rim. Top-dress with grit (see inset), and label.

PREPARING CLAY POTS

Before planting bulbs in a clay pot, place a single crock – or several, according to the drainage requirements of the plant – over the drain-age hole in the base before adding compost.

Composts for bulbs under cover

A good compost mixture with the required humus content and drainage for use in bulb frames and greenhouse beds may be prepared as follows: mix together 2 parts peat substitute or peat, 3 parts coarse grit, and 4 parts loam; then add a base fertilizer or some bone meal at a rate of 25g/5 litres (1oz/1 gallon) and (except for lime-hating plants) garden lime at a rate of 25g/18 litres (1oz/4 gallons).

Make up sufficient compost to create a bulb bed that is at least 30cm (12in) in depth, with a layer, about 5cm (2in) deep, of well-rotted garden compost or manure beneath it.

A similar compost is suitable for most bulbs, whether in pots or other containers. If using a proprietary potting compost, mix in some grit or coarse sand – at least one third, by bulk – because these composts are often not sufficiently well-drained for use with bulbs.

"Woodland" bulbs grown in pots or containers require a well-drained compost with additional organic matter that is rich in nutrients, for example a mixture of 3 parts leaf mould, 2 parts loam, and 1 part grit.

Planting in pots and under cover

It is easy to grow most bulbs under cover in pots because the growing conditions can be precisely tailored to the particular needs of the plant. Suitable composts may be used for different types of bulb, and plants can be given the correct seasonal care, such as a summer drying-off period, restricted winter watering, or plunging in a bed.

Similar control is possible when cultivating bulbs that are planted directly into a greenhouse bed or bulb frame; the planting method is the same under cover as for bulbs grown in the open (see "Planting in the open", p.229).

Choosing clay or plastic pots
Bulbs may be planted in either clay or plastic pots. Clay pots are not so readily available but they are more suitable for bulbs that are unable to tolerate excessive moisture, because the compost dries out more quickly after watering than in plastic pots. Plastic pots are now extensively used and are perfectly satisfactory as long as they are filled with a freely drain-ing compost; water the compost less frequently than with clay pots. For plants that need moist conditions, such as "woodland" bulbs, the greater water retentiveness of plas-tic pots is particularly valuable.

If using clay pots, place one or more crocks over the drainage hole; no "crocking" is necessary for plastic pots as long as the compost itself is well drained. A piece of perforated zinc placed over the drainage hole prevents worms entering the pot.

Planting bulbs in pots
Bulbs should be planted in pots at the same depths as bulbs grown out-doors (see "Planting depths and spacing", p.229). This may not be possible with larger bulbs, in which case make sure that each bulb has at least 2.5cm (1in) of moist compost beneath it in the pot. Plant bulbs of flowering size at a distance of one bulb's width apart. If planting a mixture of larger bulbs with smaller offsets, space the flowering-sized bulbs a little more widely, and scat-ter the small offsets between them.

Cover the bulbs with compost, leaving sufficient room below the rim of the pot for a top-dressing, and firm it well. Top-dress the pot with a generous layer of horticultural grit, which helps to retain moisture and improves the appearance of the pot. Label with the plant name, the date of planting, and source. No watering is necessary until the compost is almost dry. When the roots start into growth, begin watering again.

Lattice pots

Bulbs grown in beds under cover are often planted in pots with open-meshed, or latticed, sides, which allow different types of bulb to be closely planted without mixing them up or restricting their roots. Plant the bulbs in the pots, label them, and plunge them in a bulb bed containing the same compost as the pots. The pots may be lifted from the bed without disturbing their neighbours later. Alterna-tively, but less conveniently, groups of bulbs in beds may be separated by tiles or pieces of slate sunk into the bed between them.

PLANTING IN
LATTICE POTS
Plant up the lattice pots with bulbs in the usual way. Sink the labelled pots up to their rims in a bulb bed so that the compost just covers them. Stagger the rows for economical use of space.

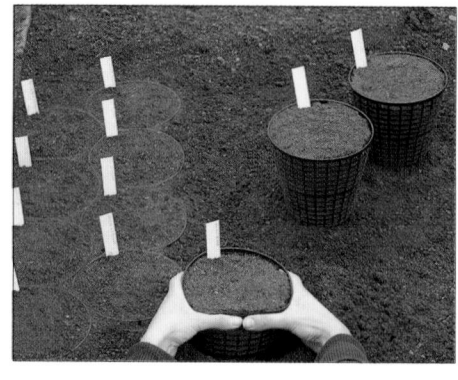

BULBS IN A PLUNGE BED

Plunge the labelled pots up to their rims in a sand bed or cold frame. Check the pots regularly to ensure that the compost does not dry out.

Plunging the pots

After planting, keep the pots in a cold frame or cold greenhouse. Bulbs in pots are more susceptible to frost damage than those in the garden; in severe winters, pots in an unheated greenhouse may freeze solid. Protect them by sinking the pots in a plunge bed of coarse sand or grit, mixed with enough peat substitute to stop the grit collapsing into the hole when pots are taken out. Alternatively, provide minimal heating in very cold periods. Summer plunging is important for bulbs in clay pots which dry out quickly, but is also advisable for plastic pots to prevent overheating.

Planting in ornamental containers

Bulbs may be planted in tubs, troughs, patio pots, or any ornamental container that is clean and has sufficient drainage holes in the base

to allow water to drain away quickly. Place a layer of crocks or another drainage material at least 3cm (1in) deep in the bottom of the container. Raise it off the ground with bricks or special "pot feet". This stops water accumulating in the base and, if the pot is made of ceramic or terracotta, helps guard it against frost damage.

Vary the compost, whether it be loam-based, rich in leaf mould, or very gritty, to suit the requirements of different types of bulb. The compost must be free-draining or it may become waterlogged and the bulbs may rot. Insert them at the same depths and spacing in the compost as for standard pots (see p.232). Do not press the bulbs into the compost too firmly as this may compress the soil just beneath the roots of the bulbs and impede their growth.

Bulbs for forcing

Some bulbs can be planted in bowls and kept in the dark to induce them to flower early. The best way to force most other bulbs for the house is to plant them in ornamental bowls in the same way as for pots (see p.232) and to bring them indoors as they begin to flower. The pots of bulbs are best displayed in a cool room with temperatures only slightly higher than that of the greenhouse or frame where they were grown. In hotter conditions, the flower stems grow very quickly and look out of character, and the flowers do not last as long as in cool conditions. Return the bulbs to the greenhouse or bulb frame as soon as the flowers fade.

Hyacinths

The most popular of all bulbs for forcing is the fragrant hyacinth. Specially prepared bulbs may be

BULBS FOR SUCCESSIONAL INTEREST

Crocuses

Tulips

To provide a display of flowers over a prolonged period, choose two or more types of bulb that come into flower at different times during the season, and plant them together in the same container. Position the early- and late-flowering bulbs in layers, each at approximately twice its own depth. Arrange the bulbs in a random pattern rather than in rows to achieve an informal effect.

purchased and, if they are given suitable treatment, will come into flower by the middle of winter.

Buy the hyacinth bulbs in early autumn and plant them in bowls filled with bulb fibre that has been well moistened beforehand. Plant the bulbs close together, so they are not quite touching one another, with their growing tips protruding just above the top of the compost. Put the newly planted bulbs in a cool, dark place: a closed cupboard in a cool room is suitable. This encourages the flowering stems to develop before the leaves and allows the root systems to become well established. Keep the bulb fibre just moist by carefully watering between the bulbs if it starts to become dry.

Leave the bowls in the dark for about eight weeks, or until the new shoots are about 4–5cm (1½–2in) high; the emerging flower buds that are visible between the tips of the yellow-green leaves should be just starting to show signs of colour.

Once they have reached this stage, bring the bulbs into the daylight, but not into bright sunlight. Do not remove the bowls of bulbs from the dark earlier than this, otherwise the leaves will grow very rapidly and obscure the flowers – a major cause of disappointment with forced bulbs. Once exposed to the light, the leaves will gradually acquire their natural green colour as the plants grow on and begin to flower.

Daffodils

Many daffodils, such as *Narcissus* 'Paper White', may be grown in bulb fibre in the same way as hyacinths. They do require more light, however, and should be placed on a sunny windowsill as soon as the shoots appear above the compost. If the light is inadequate, daffodils may become drawn and excessively tall, and will require staking.

Hippeastrum

The large-flowered *Hippeastrum* hybrids are very popular as indoor flowering plants. Garden centres and stores frequently supply them complete with a suitable bulb compost, ready to be planted in pots and grown in a warm, light room until flowering is over. *Hippeastrum* hybrids are more easily kept from year to year if they are grown for most of the year in a greenhouse and only brought into the house while they are in flower.

FORCING HYACINTHS IN A CONTAINER

1 *Place some moist bulb fibre in the bottom of a container. Position the bulbs and fill in with more fibre, leaving the bulb crowns just visible at the surface. Leave them in a cool, dark place.*

2 *When the flower spikes are visible between the pale leaves, bring the container into bright, indirect light.*

Growing hyacinths in water

Hyacinth bulbs may be forced in water, in special glasses designed to hold one bulb with its base just at water level. Place a bulb in its glass in a cool room away from sunlight and keep the water level topped up to just below the base of the bulb. It rapidly produces roots which grow down into the water.

Wait until the flower buds begin to show colour before moving the rooted hyacinth into a warm, brightly lit room. The flowering shoots then develop and produce blooms. After flowering, discard the exhausted bulb since it is unlikely to provide a good display the following year.

Fill the glass with water up to the "neck" and place the bulb in the top so it sits just above the water. Leave in a cool place. As the roots grow, keep the water topped up.

Routine care

Bulbs do not require a great deal of maintenance if the correct environment is provided. If they flower poorly, the most likely cause is overcrowding: this is easily remedied by dividing them and replanting them in a fresh site. Bulbs are not prone to pests or diseases but any present must be controlled promptly.

Bulbs in grass

Bulbs left to naturalize in grass do not need as much attention as those planted in other sites in the garden, but correct timing in mowing is very important. Dead-heading regularly and feeding very occasionally helps the bulbs to remain healthy and to proliferate steadily over the years.

Fertilizing
Do not feed bulbs in grass regularly, especially with nitrogenous fertilizer because it increases the vigour of the grass at the bulbs' expense. If a feed is needed (e.g. for daffodils that fail to flower freely), use a high-potash fertilizer to aid flower production.

Dead-heading
Regular removal of faded blooms extends the season and improves the vigour of bulbs by stopping them wasting energy on unwanted seed production. After flowering, pinch through the stems below the seed pods. If the seed capsules are to be harvested later or left to seed naturally, leave a number to ripen on the plant and then cut the stems to the ground after harvesting the seed.

CUTTING DOWN BULBS IN GRASS AFTER FLOWERING

Leave clumps of bulbs (here daffodils) planted in grass until the leaves start to turn yellow. Then cut them down to ground level with shears when mowing the grass.

When to mow
If cultivating early-flowering bulbs such as daffodils, do not cut the grass until at least six weeks after they have flowered, or until the foliage is turning yellow. If growing bulbs that increase by self seeding, do not mow the grass until the seed capsules have been able to shed all their seed – usually about three weeks after the leaves begin to die down.

Autumn-flowering bulbs such as *Colchicum* start into growth before the end of the lawn-mowing season. When the first leaves or tips of the flowering shoots appear, mow with the blades set high enough to avoid them; stop mowing when the shoots are too tall to escape the blades.

In a wild-flower meadow that includes late-flowering bulbs, for example hardy orchids, delay mowing until mid- to late summer, when all the foliage has died down.

DEAD-HEADING

Unless the seed is to be used for propagation, cut down all dead flower stems of bulbs in the border (here Allium) with secateurs to ground level.

Bulbs in borders and woodland

The level of maintenance required for bulbs in herbaceous or mixed borders, or in woodland, depends on whether they are intended to be permanent or temporary "fillers". Permanent bulb plantings need little maintenance until the bulbs become overcrowded, when they should be lifted and divided (see p.235).

If the ground is well prepared, no feeding is necessary during the first year, but an application once or twice in a season of a low-nitrogen, high-potash fertilizer, which promotes flowering rather than leafy growth (see SOILS AND FERTILIZERS, "Types of fertilizer", p.530) will encourage a fine display in subsequent years.

Bulbs need adequate moisture during the growing season, especially in woodland, and it may be necessary to water them if there is a prolonged early drought. Dead-head them at regular intervals in the same way as for bulbs in grass.

Care of temporary plantings is the same as for the first-year care of bulbs that are permanently planted. Lift the bulbs for storing at the end of the growing season (see p.235).

Removing dead leaves
After the bulbs in the border have finished flowering, allow their leaves to die down completely before removing them. Do not "tidy" the leaves by tying them together while still green, because this reduces their capacity to photosynthesize and store energy in the bulb in readiness for the next growing season, and therefore the bulb loses vigour. It also makes them die down prematurely.

WHEN TO HARVEST SEED

If seed is required, do not dead-head until the seed capsule (here Fritillaria) is brown and begins to split. The ripe seed is then ready to harvest for sowing or storing.

Staking

A few tall bulbs with slender stems need staking. Stake these plants as soon as they are tall enough for a tie to be put around them; tie in the stems again when the plants are near their full height and are about to flower. Where the bulbs are planted in groups, place bamboo canes on the inward-facing side of the stems so that they are concealed by the growing plants. Insert the stakes well away from the base of the stems so that the bulbs are not damaged.

1 *Support a tall, single-stemmed plant such as a gladiolus with a bamboo cane when the plant is 15cm (6in) tall. Attach the stem to the cane with string or raffia.*

2 *When the flower buds are forming, tie in the stem to the cane just below the buds to prevent the stem from breaking when the buds open.*

STAKING BULBS IN GROUPS

For plants such as lilies that grow in clumps, place one or more canes in the centre of the clump. Tie in surrounding stems to each cane with a figure-of-eight loop so that the stems do not rub against the canes.

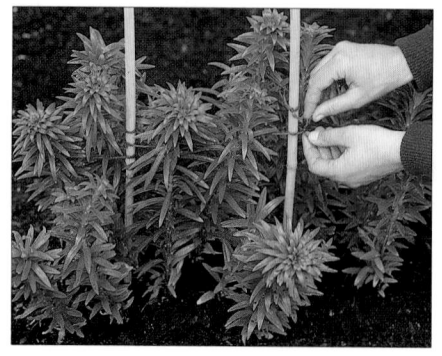

Lifting and dividing overcrowded bulbs

If mature bulbs flower less freely than in previous years, the deterioration is usually due to overcrowding. This may not be obvious unless the bulbs are visible near the soil surface, as is often the case with *Nerine*.

Lift crowded clumps during the dormant season, before the root growth starts. Separate the clumps into individual bulbs and replant them in irregular groups. Insert them separately at two to three times their own depth and two to three bulb widths apart. Plant small offsets or bulblets between bulbs of flowering size. Alternatively, grow them in pots or in a "nursery bed", in a frame or in the garden, in the same way as for two-year-old seedlings (see "Care of seedlings", p.238).

If, on lifting, the bulbs are found not to be overcrowded, but are deteriorating or no longer thriving, inspect them for pests and diseases (see p.236). If there is no obvious explanation for their failure, replant them in a different site that is well drained and has sufficient light and nutrients. Alternatively, grow the bulbs in pots in a cold frame or greenhouse until they recover.

Lifting, drying, and storing

Bulbs planted temporarily in beds or borders should be left *in situ* until the foliage has begun to yellow. Then lift and clean them, lay them out on a tray to dry, and store them in paper (not plastic) bags in a dry place until the next planting season. If there is any sign of fungal disease, dust them with fungicide. Alternatively, lift them in full growth soon after flowering or as the foliage dies down and replant them immediately in another part of the garden so that they may die down naturally.

Dwarf bulbs in the rock garden or raised bed

The principles of routine care of bulbs in borders also apply to dwarf species in raised beds or in the rock garden. Many of the rarer bulbs are slow to increase, however, and do not become overcrowded for several years. Keep them reasonably moist during the growing season, particularly in drought conditions, and feed them regularly with a high-potash, low-nitrogen fertilizer.

If seed is required, harvest the seed capsules when ripe; then clear away the dead leaves to improve the appearance of the bed and reduce the likelihood of disease.

HOW TO DIVIDE AN OVERCROWDED CLUMP

1 *When bulbs planted in the open become overcrowded, use a garden fork to lift the whole clump as the leaves die down. Take care not to damage them.*

2 *Divide the clump of bulbs (here Nerine) by hand, separating it first into smaller clumps and then into individual bulbs. Remove any dead or diseased material.*

3 *Discard any unhealthy bulbs. Clean the good bulbs with care, removing the loose tunics, in preparation for replanting them singly in freshly prepared soil.*

Bulbs in containers outdoors

Bulbs in containers should not be allowed to dry out when in growth and should be fed regularly with a high-potash fertilizer to boost the production of flowers. Wait until the foliage of spring-flowering bulbs has died back naturally, then lift and clean them, and store them in a cool, dry place during summer. Replant the bulbs in a container of fresh compost in early autumn for a display in the following spring. Alternatively, if the container is needed for a summer display, transfer the bulbs while still in the green to a spare bed, and allow them to die back before lifting, cleaning, and drying them in the normal way.

Spring-flowering species such as crocuses, daffodils, and hyacinths may also be transplanted directly into the garden for naturalizing. Store summer-flowering bulbs in a cool, dry place over winter and replant them in spring.

Some bulbs, such as lilies (*Lilium*), do not grow well if allowed to dry out completely after flowering. Keep them moist by plunging them in their pots in a shaded place or in a cold frame to rest. Repot the lilies every year in the spring.

Bulbs in frames and covered raised beds

Bulbs that are grown in frames or under cover need similar treatment after planting to those in borders (see p.234) but require special care with watering and feeding.

Remove the covers to the raised beds or frames during the growing season, but replace them temporarily during excessively cold or wet weather. Keep the bulbs watered in dry periods. When most of the bulbs are beginning to die down, replace the covers until the beginning of the next growing season.

HOW TO LIFT, DRY, AND STORE BULBS

1 *When the leaves are turning yellow, about a month after flowering, gently lift the bulbs (here tulips) with a fork. Put them in labelled containers to avoid confusing different plants.*

2 *Clean the soil off the bulbs and rub off any loose, flaking tunic tissue. Cut or carefully pull off the dying foliage. Discard any bulbs that show signs of damage or of disease.*

3 *Place the bulbs on a wire tray, spaced so that they do not touch, and leave them to dry overnight. Then dust them with fungicide and store them in clean, clearly labelled, paper bags.*

Improve the vigour of the bulbs by feeding them once the nutrients in the original compost are exhausted. Use a granular fertilizer sprinkled on the compost surface as the bulbs come into growth, or apply a liquid feed every two or three weeks. In the latter part of the season, use a high-potash, low-nitrogen feed to produce a good display of blooms.

Bulbs in pots under cover

Bulbs that need a warm, dry summer, and a winter and spring growing period, grow well in an unheated or cool greenhouse, where the bulbs' feeding, watering, and drying off may be controlled to satisfy their needs. Keep such bulbs dry from the time their leaves die down until their natural growing period starts in late summer or early autumn.

During the growing season, give the pots a good soaking when they are nearly dry, but take care not to overwater them, especially in winter. Give them extra water in the growing season up to flowering time, after which gradually reduce watering until the leaves die down. Do not allow some hardy bulbs, such as crocuses from mountainous areas and "woodland" bulbs, to dry out completely; keep the compost slightly moist during the summer.

Bulbs such as *Galtonia* from areas with summer rainfall, for example parts of South Africa and South America, must be watered regularly so that they keep growing during the summer; they should then be allowed to dry out during their natural dormancy in winter.

Renewing compost
Changing the top layer of compost in a pot of bulbs supplies them with enough nutrients for a further year. Before they start to grow, gently scrape away the old compost to expose the tops of the bulbs. If they are healthy and not overcrowded, cover them with fresh, moist compost of the same type that is in the pot. Separate and repot overcrowded bulbs or, if hardy, plant them out.

Repotting
Bulbs may sometimes be kept in the same pot for several years but they eventually become overcrowded and need repotting – usually indicated by a failure to flower well and by undersized or unhealthy foliage. At the end of dormancy, repot the bulbs to encourage them to start into growth. Pot up larger bulbs singly,

as for the initial potting up and in a similar compost (see "Planting in pots and under cover", p.232). Plant small bulbs or bulblets between the adult ones or pot them up separately (see "Care of seedlings", p.238).

In early spring, repot tender bulbs that are dormant in winter when the new growth is about to begin.

Fertilizing
If the bulbs are kept in the same pot for several years, feed them regularly throughout the growing season at alternate waterings with a liquid feed containing a high-potash, low-nitrogen fertilizer. Extra feeding is unnecessary if the bulbs are repotted, or the top layer of compost in the pot is replaced each year.

Care of forced bulbs
When they are ready to be brought into the light, place forced bulbs (see p.233), according to their needs, on a shady windowsill or in a cool, bright room. The bulbs tolerate slightly warmer conditions when their flower buds are well formed. Rotate the bowl periodically if the shoots turn to the light and keep the compost moist.

Forced bulbs are generally in a poor condition after flowering. Discard them or plant them out in the garden where they will eventually, perhaps after two years or more, flower again in their normal season.

Hippeastrum hybrids that have been forced may be kept in a good condition from year to year by replanting them after flowering in a rich, well-drained compost in the same pot. Do not water them from early autumn until mid-winter, and repot them if they are overcrowded.

Bulb problems

Bulbs occasionally fail to flower and are known as "blind" bulbs. In a long-established clump this problem is often due to overcrowding, so the bulbs should be lifted and replanted separately in fresh soil (see "Lifting and dividing overcrowded bulbs", p.235). Shortage of water during the growing season is another possible cause.

Newly planted bulbs that are blind may not have been stored correctly, or they may not yet be fully mature.

Iris danfordiae, *Fritillaria* species such as *F. recurva* and *F. thunbergii*, and some other bulbs do not flower regularly even in nature and so are described as "shy-flowering". Do not dig up such bulbs unless they look unhealthy or seem crowded since they may eventually flower if left undisturbed. It may be helpful to plant the bulbs especially deeply because this discourages them from dividing into bulblets.

Pests and diseases
During the growing season, keep a careful watch for the symptoms of pests and diseases and control any problems as soon as they arise. When planting, repotting, or propagating dormant bulbs, inspect them and destroy any badly afflicted bulbs.

Bulbs may suffer especially from rot or fungal diseases, including ink spot (p.567) which severely affects Reticulata irises. Daffodils may fall prey to narcissus flies (see "Bulb flies", p.567). Aphids (p.550) sometimes infest bulbs and can cause the spread of viruses (p.553). Red spider mites (p.550) occasionally affect bulbs grown under cover.

REPOTTING OVERCROWDED BULBS

2 *Carefully tip out the contents of the pot, and remove the bulbs from the compost. Discard any dead material or any bulbs that show signs of pests or diseases.*

1 *Remove some compost from the pot to inspect the bulbs (here daffodils). If they have become overcrowded in the pot, they should be repotted.*

3 *Separate any pairs or clumps of bulbs with large offsets into individual bulbs by gently pulling them apart.*

4 *Select only healthy bulbs and clean them, rubbing with finger and thumb to remove any loose, outer tunics. Dust the bulbs with fungicidal powder.*

5 *Replant the bulbs in a pot of fresh, moist, bulb compost. Insert them at twice their own depth, and space them at least their own width apart.*

Propagation

MANY bulbs increase naturally by forming offsets or bulblets around the bulb, and may be propagated by separating these from the parent bulbs. Those that do not divide freely may be increased by cutting them into sections and treating these as new bulbs. Some are propagated by other vegetative means, such as scaling or scooping. Seed propagation yields larger stocks but bulbs may take several years to flower.

Dividing bulbs

During the growing season, many bulbs increase by forming offsets from the main, parent bulb, usually within the bulb tunic. Separate them every year or two and plant them out or pot them up individually. If left, they may become too overcrowded and take longer to develop to flowering size. The offsets may be small and numerous as with some *Allium* species or larger and fewer as with daffodils and tulips.

Other bulbs may form bulbils in the leaf axils, as with lilies (*Lilium*) and some *Calochortus* species, or bulblets around the base of the bulb; both may be used for propagation. (Some lilies, such as some American species and hybrid lilies, are rhizomatous and produce small rhizomes. Pot these up, placing them horizontally, to grow on for one or two years before planting out.)

Propagation from offsets
Some bulbs, for example *Crinum*, may be increased by lifting and dividing a clump. Pull the offsets gently from the parent plant or cut the basal plate at the point at which they are attached to the larger bulb. Clean off any loose material or soil, and dust cut surfaces with fungicide.

Replant the larger bulbs in the garden in a well-spaced group. Pot up smaller offsets separately, or insert several in a larger pot or deep tray. Keep them for one or two seasons in a cold greenhouse to grow on; then plant them out in the open.

Propagation from bulblets and bulbils
Bulbs raised from bulblets will generally flower a year or two earlier than those grown from seed. When repotting bulbs, remove the bulblets from around the base of the parent bulb and insert them in rows in trays. Use well-drained cutting compost with a little slow-release fertilizer added. Space the bulblets in the tray as for seed

HOW TO PROPAGATE BULBS FROM OFFSETS

1 In the spring, before active growth begins, lift a clump of bulbs (here Crinum) with a garden fork. Shake excess soil from the roots and pull the clump apart.

2 Select a large bulb with several well-developed offsets. Clean off the soil from the offsets and pull them away from the parent bulb, taking care to preserve any roots.

3 Prepare 15cm (6in) pots with a moist, sandy compost. Insert a single offset into each pot, and cover it with about 2.5cm (1in) of compost. Label, and water.

(see "Sowing the seed", p.238) and cover them with a 2.5cm (1in) layer of compost. Label, and grow them on in a shaded part of the garden. Keep the compost moist; if using clay pots, plunge them in beds to keep them damp. Treat the bulblets thereafter as for seed (see p.238). Bulbils may be removed and treated similarly (see LILIES, *Propagating from Stem Bulbils*, p.243).

Gladiolus cormels
Gladioli often form small cormels at the base of the corm. Remove these from the parent corm and treat them as bulblets. Alternatively, plant them in rows in fertile, well-drained soil, either in a bulb frame in cold areas or in a nursery bed. They may be left until they flower two to three years later, and then may be lifted and planted in their permanent positions.

HOW TO PROPAGATE GLADIOLUS BY CORMELS

1 When the plant has finished flowering and the foliage is dying back, use a hand fork to lift the corm. Cormels should have developed all around the basal plate of the corm. Store all the corms over winter in a cool, dry place.

2 In late winter or early spring, pull off cormels; they should readily come away from the parent corm. The cormels may vary in size but all may be used.

3 Half-fill a tray with moist, gritty compost. Insert cormels, growing points upwards, in rows 2.5cm (1in) apart. Fill the tray with more compost; level, firm, and label it.

BULBOUS PLANTS THAT MAY BE DIVIDED

Offsets
Allium (some spp.)
Alstroemeria
Arum, some ❋
Crinum, some ❋
Crocus
Galanthus
Iris, Juno group,
   I., Reticulata group (some spp.)
Leucojum
Lilium
Muscari, some ❋
   (some spp.)
Narcissus
Nerine, some ❋
Ornithogalum,
   some ❋
Tulipa

Gladiolus
'Deliverance'

Bulblets
Allium (some spp.)
Fritillaria acmopetala,
   F. crassifolia, *F. pudica*,
   F. recurva, *F. thunbergii*
Iris, Reticulata group (some spp.)
Muscari, some ❋ (some spp.)

Cormels
Gladiolus (spp. and hybrids)

KEY
❋ Not hardy

Bulbs from seed

This method of propagation produces a large number of bulbs that initially are free from any viruses (except those specifically transmitted by seed), unlike division which passes on any disease present in the parent bulb to the young plants.

Most bulbs take from three to five years to reach mature flowering size from seed. A few bulbs, for example *Cardiocrinum*, die after flowering but their seed may be collected and sown regularly every year to ensure a steady succession of healthy plants that will mature and provide flowers in each growing season.

Collecting seed

The seed capsules of most bulbs are carried on the old flowering stems, but some plants, mainly crocuses and Reticulata irises, have capsules formed at or just above ground level which are difficult to see.

Watch the ripening capsules carefully for signs of splitting as the seed may be shed very quickly. Remove the capsules as they begin to turn brown and start to split. Extract the seed as soon as possible. A few bulbs, such as *Corydalis*, shed seed when the capsules are still green; cut off and store the capsules in paper bags until the seed is shed. Let the seed dry without artificial heat, and store it until sown in labelled, paper packets in a cool, dry, and airy place. Do not use plastic bags as they seal in the moisture and the seed may rot.

When to sow seed

The following method is suitable for most spring-flowering, hardy bulbs, for example, *Fritillaria*, daffodils, and tulips. The best time to sow is early autumn, but if seed is available earlier, sow immediately. Germination should follow in early spring.

Seed compost for bulbs

Use a proprietary, loam-based seed compost, with a quarter-part coarse sand added if the mixture does not have a sandy appearance. A suitable loam-based compost may be made from 2 parts sterile loam, 1 part peat substitute, and $1\frac{1}{2}$ parts very coarse sand or seed-grade perlite with superphosphate added at a rate of 25g/18 litres (1oz/4 gallons) and lime at a rate of 25g/18 litres (1oz/4 gallons). Proprietary composts containing a peat substitute may also be used, but they contain only enough nutrients for a year.

Sowing the seed

Clay or plastic pots may be used but it is easier to maintain adequate moisture levels in plastic pots. If using a clay pot, place some crocks at the bottom for drainage. Fill the pot with compost and firm it before sowing the seed thinly on the surface. Space large, flat seed of bulbs such as *Fritillaria* or tulips one seed's width apart, and smaller, rounded seed about 5mm ($\frac{1}{4}$in) apart. Sieve a light covering of the compost over the seed so that it is no longer visible, and then cover it with a generous layer of flint grit or aquarium gravel. Label the pots with the plant name, source, and date. Stand them in a shady place in the open garden, or plunge them in a sand frame, and keep them moist.

Care of seedlings

When the seedlings have germinated bring the pots into full light in a cold frame or greenhouse. Keep them moist until they show definite signs of dying down, and then stop watering them. Seedlings of bulbs that are not naturally dry in summer even in their dormant period, such as certain *Crocus* species from mountainous areas, should be kept slightly moist. Start watering again in early autumn, or as soon as there is new growth, and keep the pots watered until the growth dies down.

Leave most bulbs for two growing seasons before repotting, unless they grow very vigorously. It is not

At the end of the growing season, one-year-old bulb seedlings (here Fritillaria meleagris) *are often not vigorous enough to pot on. Let the foliage die back and cease watering.*

essential to feed seedlings in the first growing season, but larger bulbs form if they are fed regularly in the second. Use a proprietary liquid feed as used for tomatoes, but at half the manufacturer's recommended strength.

Removing seedlings from pots

After the seedling bulbs have completed two seasons of growth, or one in the case of very vigorous bulbs, pot them up into the compost recommended for mature bulbs (see "Composts for bulbs under cover", p.232). After the foliage has completely died back towards the end of the dormant period, empty out the whole contents of the pot. Separate out the young bulbs, clean them, and repot them in fresh, moist compost to start them into growth. It is better to grow them in pots for two or three years until they are large enough to establish successfully outdoors.

Keeping seedlings in pots

Seedling bulbs may be grown on in pots and planted out together with the compost to avoid handling the bulbs and disturbing their root growth. Pot on a complete potful of one-year-old seedlings into a slightly larger pot and feed them regularly while they are in growth in the second year. If they are large enough by the end of the season, plant the entire potful of young bulbs in the open garden when they are dormant or just starting into growth. Give them an extra feed after planting to avoid any delay in flowering. If they are too small, keep them in the pot, and feed them regularly for another year.

"Woodland" species

Many shade-loving bulbs grow best in a compost that contains some leaf mould. For seed sowing, use a compost of 1 part sterilized leaf mould, 1 part peat substitute or peat,

---

HOW TO PROPAGATE BULBS FROM SEED

1 *Prepare the pot: fill it to within 1cm ($\frac{1}{2}$in) of the brim with proprietary seed compost mixed with a quarter part coarse sand. Firm it well with a tamper.*

2 *Sow the seed evenly over the compost by tapping the open packet, holding it near the surface so that the seed (here* Fritillaria meleagris) *does not bounce out.*

3 *Use a sieve to scatter a thin layer of fine compost evenly over the seed. There should be just sufficient compost to conceal the seed.*

4 *Top-dress the pot with at least 1cm ($\frac{1}{2}$in) of coarse grit, adding it carefully to avoid disturbing the compost or seeds.*

5 *Label the pot. Place it in a shady situation in the open. Plunge the pot in damp sand and water, as required, to keep the compost moist.*

POTTING UP SEEDLINGS

*1 Carefully knock out the entire pot contents; some of the bulbs (*here* Fritillaria raddeana) *will be visible among the compost. Remove all the bulbs carefully.*

2 Replant the young bulbs in a pot of fresh, gritty bulb compost, placing them at twice their own depth and spaced their own width apart.

and 1 part sterilized loam, with a further 1¹/₂ parts of coarse, horticultural sand or seed-grade perlite.

The growth of many of these bulbs, for example *Erythronium* and *Trillium*, is slow. Planting the whole panful of seedlings after two or three years' growth into a well-prepared peat bed is better than regular repotting over several years which repeatedly disturbs the roots.

TWO-YEAR-OLD BULB SEEDLINGS

*After two years, seedling bulbs (*here* Calochortus tolmiei) *may vary noticeably in size but all should develop satisfactorily.*

Cyclamen

Seed of hardy cyclamen germinates most readily if it is sown as soon as it is ripe, usually in mid-summer. If using dry seed, soak it for about 24 hours before sowing to aid germination. Sow as described opposite.

The seedlings generally grow strongly in their first year and the young tubers may then be repotted in seedling compost (see opposite), preferably while they are still in growth. Add 1 part leaf mould to 3 parts of the compost to encourage vigorous growth. The tubers usually develop well if planted several to a pan, rather than singly. Insert them with their roots spaced out and cover the tops with surface grit.

Place the pans in a shaded cold frame to grow on for a second year. In spring of the third year, repot the tubers singly using the same compost mix and leave them until they are approaching flowering size. Plant them out in the garden in late summer.

Growing lilies from seed

Sow the seed in pots about 10cm (5in) deep filled with peat substitute, peat, or seed compost based on loam or peat, preferably as soon as they are ripe (in late summer or early autumn). Sow the seed thinly to avoid the need for pricking out, cover it with fine grit, and place the pots in a cold frame or cold greenhouse.

In some lilies, the seedlings germinate two to six weeks after sowing. Others may take several months to germinate. Lily seeds differ in the way they germinate. With hypogeal lilies, root formation occurs initially; a cold period is then needed to stimulate leaf production. Seed of epigeal lilies usually (but not always) germinates fairly rapidly with both root and shoot development occurring almost together (see also PRINCIPLES OF PROPAGATION, *How a Seed Germinates*, p.536).

EXTRACTING CYCLAMEN SEED

Harvest the seed capsules in early summer when they are beginning to split. Shake out the seeds and soak them in a bowl of tepid water overnight to assist germination.

PLANTING OUT "WOODLAND" BULBS

*1 Plant out "woodland" species without separating the young bulbs. Invert a pot of two-year-old bulbs (*here* Erythronium). *Slide out the mass of bulbs and compost.*

2 Plant the entire potful of compost and bulbs, so that the top of the bulb mass is at least 2.5cm (1in) below the surface. Firm, label, and water lightly.

Overwinter the pots in a cold frame or sheltered place outdoors, then bring the pots into a cold greenhouse in spring. Do not discard the containers even if no seedlings appear after the first year; germination can take up to two or occasionally more years, depending on the species.

Leave the germinated seedlings in their pots for their first growing season and liquid feed them regularly. Alternatively, prick them out when they have two true leaves into a loam-based potting compost. Repot them regularly or transfer them to nursery beds until they are large enough to be planted out in the garden. This process takes from one to three years, depending on the species.

Tender bulbs

Sow the seed of tender bulbs as described above, but keep the pots at a temperature above freezing point during the winter, plunged in bulb frames or beds under cover. Seed of many tender species, for example *Hippeastrum*, germinates more quickly if bottom heat is used (this is usually supplied by soil-warming cables; see GREENHOUSES AND FRAMES, p.488) and a temperature of 21°C (70°F) is maintained.

If the germination characteristics of a particular plant are uncertain and there is plenty of seed available, sow half with bottom heat and half in normal greenhouse temperatures. If germination has not taken place within six to eight weeks in heat, move the pots to a cooler place. Some genera, notably *Alstroemeria*, germinate rapidly when a warm period is followed by a cool period.

Sow fleshy seeds of bulbs such as *Amaryllis* fresh, directly from the seed capsule while it is still green. If left in the capsule, the seed may germinate *in situ*, and it should then

be removed and sown in the normal way. Grow on the seedlings (see "Care of seedlings", p.238). Seedlings of some genera, for example some *Hippeastrum* species, remain in active growth for more than one season; if so, keep them moist, and they may grow until they flower without going dormant.

Seeds with erratic germination

Seed of certain bulbs, for example Juno irises, germinates very erratically, sometimes over several years. If, after two seasons, only a few seedlings have appeared, repot the entire potful without disturbing the compost; late-germinating seedlings often appear a year or so later.

Germination in plastic bags

Seed of some genera may be germinated in plastic bags rather than pots; this is most frequently done with lilies (*Lilium*) but is applicable to most bulbs with large seeds, for example *Fritillaria*, tulips, and tender genera such as *Hippeastrum*.

Mix the seed with three or four times its bulk of moist peat substitute, peat, vermiculite, or perlite. The medium used should not exude water when squeezed. Add a little fungicide, place the mixture in small, plastic bags, then seal and label them.

For seed that benefits from an initial warm period, such as that of the smaller *Hippeastrum* species, keep the bags at approximately 21°C (70°F), for example in an airing cupboard or near a central heating boiler. When the seed has germinated, prick out the seedlings into pots or trays of well-drained cutting compost and keep them in cooler conditions. If the seed has not germinated after six to eight weeks, transfer the bags to a cold frame or cool greenhouse until germination occurs.

HOW TO SCALE LILIES

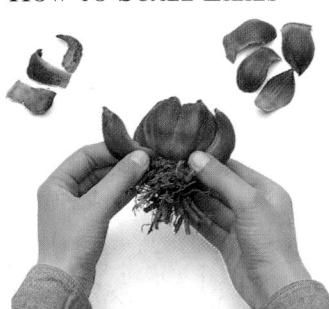

1 Clean the lily bulb; remove and discard any damaged, outer scales. Gently snap off about 6 good scales, as close as possible to the base of the bulb.

2 Place some fungicidal powder in a plastic bag and add the scales. Shake the bag gently so that all the scales are thoroughly coated with the fungicide.

3 Remove any surplus fungicide from the bag. Place the coated scales into a second bag containing a 50:50 mix of peat substitute, or peat, and perlite.

4 Blow up the bag, then seal and label it. Store at 21°C (70°F) in a warm, dark place.

5 When small bulblets have developed on the scales, remove the scales if they are soft. If they are fleshy and firm, leave them attached to the bulblets.

6 Plant the groups of bulblets either singly in small pots or several in a pan. Top-dress the pots with grit, label them, and leave them in a warm, light place.

7 The following spring, harden off the young bulbs by placing the pots in a cold frame.

8 In the autumn, when the bulbs have grown on, remove them from the pots and separate them. Pot them up individually or plant them in their permanent positions.

Scaling

Scaling is an important method of propagating lilies (*Lilium*) but it may also be used for other genera that have bulbs consisting of scales, for example some species of *Fritillaria*. The bulbs of most lilies are composed of concentric rings of scales attached at their lower ends to a basal plate. If these scales are detached from the parent bulb close to the base, so that they retain a small piece of basal tissue, they may develop bulblets, often near the base of the scale. Portions of scales lacking this tissue seldom form bulblets.

Remove lily scales for propagation in late summer or early autumn before root growth starts. Lift the dormant bulbs, then remove a few of the scales. Usually only a few are needed and the parent bulb may be replanted to flower the following season. If many new plants are required, scale the whole bulb. Alternatively, without lifting the parent bulbs, remove the soil from around them and snap off a few scales.

Select only disease-free, plump, unblemished scales. If using only a few scales for propagation, coat them with fungicide, then mix them together with some damp peat substitute and perlite or vermiculite in a plastic bag. Seal the bag and place it in a warm, dark place at about 21°C (70°F) for approximately three months. Then place the bag in a cold place, such as a refrigerator (but not a deep-freeze), for six to eight weeks to encourage bulblets to develop. When these form, fill some pots with a free-draining potting compost. Insert one or more scales, with their small bulblets attached, so that the tops of the scales are just below the compost surface.

Keep the pots in a shaded cold frame or cool greenhouse in hot weather. During the summer, plunge the pots of hardy bulbs in a frame or sheltered position in the open garden. At the end of the first growing season, separate the bulblets and repot them individually in a freely draining compost suitable for mature bulbs (see "Composts for bulbs under cover", p.232). Grow them on in a cold frame or a cool greenhouse until the following spring when they

HOW TO PROPAGATE BULBS BY TWIN-SCALING

1 Remove the brown, outer scales of a bulb (here a daffodil). With a sharp knife, trim off the roots without damaging the basal plate, and slice off the nose.

2 Place the bulb upside down on its cut end. Cut downwards through the basal plate to divide it into small sections, each piece having a section of basal plate.

3 Divide the sections into pairs of scales by peeling back the layers. Use a scalpel to cut each pair away with a piece of the basal plate attached (see inset).

may be repotted into a container or planted in their flowering position in the garden.

Alternatively, after dusting with fungicide, insert the scales in trays filled with 2 parts damp vermiculite, perlite, or peat substitute mixed with 1 part coarse sand. Keep them moist and shaded, preferably in a warm greenhouse at about 21°C (70°F), for two months. In spring, move them to a cool place to promote good leaf growth; the bulblets may then be repotted singly and grown on for a year before being planted out.

Twin-scaling

This is used to build up stocks of genera such as daffodils, hyacinths, and snowdrops (*Galanthus*). Cut up the bulbs into pairs of scales, with each pair retaining a small section of the bulb's basal plate. Be sure to keep your hands, the knife, and the cutting surface scrupulously clean so that no disease has the opportunity to infect the cut scales. After dusting the twin-scales with fungicide, treat them in the same way as single scales (see p.240).

Cutting bulbs into sections

Sectioning bulbs is not widely used by amateur growers but it is useful for plants that do not divide freely or set seed. Bulbs may be sectioned near the end of the dormant period: parts of the basal plate may be cut through, or the entire bulb may be cut into pieces.

Chipping

Many bulbs may be propagated at the end of the dormant period, for example in the early autumn, by cutting them into several segments

HOW TO PROPAGATE BULBS BY CHIPPING

1 *When the foliage has died down, lift the dormant bulbs and select a healthy, undamaged specimen (here* Hippeastrum). *Trim off the growing tip and the roots, taking care not to cut into the basal plate.*

2 *Place the bulb on a clean cutting surface, with its basal plate uppermost. With a clean, sharp knife, carefully cut down into the bulb, dividing it into halves.*

3 *Cut each half of the bulb again in the same way, making sure that the basal plate is divided equally between the individual segments.*

4 *Repeat until the bulb has been cut into about 16 chips. Soak them in fungicide for 10–15 minutes, occasionally agitating the container. Drain off any excess moisture.*

5 *Half-fill some plastic bags with 11 parts vermiculite, moistened with 1 part water. Put several chips in each bag. Seal the bags with rubber bands or plastic twist-ties. Store in a warm, dark, airy place.*

6 *When bulblets appear around the basal plate of the chips, plant the chips individually into 6cm (3in) pots filled with a well-drained potting compost. Place in a sheltered position to grow on.*

or "chips". Chipping allows more rapid propagation of bulbs that do not increase rapidly by offsets; it also serves to build up stocks of new cultivars. Large bulbs, such as daffodils or *Hippeastrum,* may be cut into as many as 16 chips; smaller daffodil bulbs and others, such as snowdrop bulbs, are usually chipped into four or eight segments.

Good hygiene is essential to avoid disease infecting the chips through their exposed, cut surfaces. Wear gloves for cleanliness and protection as some people are allergic to the sap the bulbs release when cut. Clean and sterilize the bulbs with methylated spirit to help stop them rotting. Use a knife or scalpel that has been sterilized in methylated spirit to cut the bulbs on a clean, disinfected surface. Soak the chips in a fungicide such as benlate after cutting. Alternatively, dust the cut surfaces with flowers of sulphur.

Store the chips in the dark for 12 weeks in plastic bags of vermiculite that contain plenty of air. A temperature of 20–25°C (68–77°F) gives good results for most genera. Separate the young bulblets that develop on the chips, and pot them on into pans of freely draining potting compost. They generally reach flowering size in two or three years.

Cutting up bulbs that have growing points

Some cyclamen species, particularly *C. hederifolium* and *C. rohlfsianum,* form multiple growing points on the

BULBS THAT MAY BE PROPAGATED BY CHIPPING

Erythronium
Fritillaria
Galanthus
Hippeastrum,
  some ✽ (spp.
  and hybrids)
Hyacinthus
Iris
Narcissus
Nerine, some ✽
Scilla, some ✽
Sternbergia

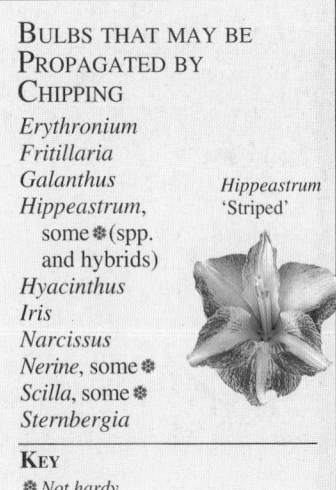

Hippeastrum 'Striped'

KEY
✽ Not hardy

surface of the tubers. The corms of several genera, such as *Crocosmia* and *Gladiolus*, do the same. Such tubers and corms may be propagated by cutting them up, as long as each section has a growing point.

Prepare 5–6cm (2–3in) pots with a few crocks at the bottom for good drainage and almost fill them with well-drained potting compost. Dust

CUTTING UP BULBS FOR PROPAGATION

1 *Take a large, healthy bulb (here* Cyclamen hederifolium) *and cut it into 2 or 3 pieces with a clean knife. Each piece must have at least one growing point. Dust the cut surfaces with fungicide.*

2 *Leave the pieces on a wire tray in a warm, dry place for 48 hours, until the cut surfaces form a callus (see inset). Pot them up individually into pots containing sharply drained compost.*

the pieces with fungicide, and insert them singly, growing points uppermost, in the compost. Cover the tubers with more compost. Top-dress the pots with grit, label, and leave them in a cold greenhouse until they begin to grow. Keep the compost moist enough to sustain the sections until growth starts.

Grow them on in well-lit conditions in a cold frame, and shade them from the hot summer sun. Water with care; do not let the young plants dry out when in growth. Plant them out the next autumn.

Simple cutting

Make cuts 0.5cm (¹/₄in) deep with a sharp knife through a bulb's basal plate; the number of cuts depends on the bulb's size. Dust the cuts with fungicide. Keep the bulb in a plastic bag of damp perlite or vermiculite, and some fungicide, in a warm place.

The damage to the basal plate induces bulblets to form along the cuts. When these have formed, insert the bulb upside-down in a gritty compost made of 1 part peat substitute to 1 part perlite or coarse sand. The bulblets will develop above the old bulb. A year later, carefully separate the bulblets, and plant them in trays in a cool greenhouse to grow on.

How to Propagate Hyacinths by Scooping

1 Use a clean, sharpened teaspoon, or a knife, to scoop out the inner part of the bulb's basal plate, leaving the outer rim intact. Discard the basal plate.

2 Dip the cut surfaces in fungicide, then lay the bulbs, with their scooped areas uppermost, on a tray of sand. Place the tray in an airing cupboard.

3 Water the sand lightly as needed to keep it moist. When bulblets form around the edge of the scooped base, separate them from the parent and pot them up.

Scooping hyacinths

Scooping is a technique used for the commercial propagation of hyacinths. The centre of the basal plate of the bulb is scooped out and discarded, the exposed surface dusted with fungicide, and the bulb kept upside down in warm, dark conditions. Numerous small bulblets eventually form on and around the cut surface. They may then be separated from the parent bulb and grown on in the same way as bulblets (see "Propagation from bulblets and bulbils", p.237) in individual pots.

Basal cuttings

The sprouting tubers of a few bulbs may be used in late winter for basal cuttings – young shoots that retain a piece of the parent tuber from which new roots develop. The cuttings are placed in a pan of moist compost until they root and are then potted up. For details of the technique, see DAHLIAS, *How to Propagate by Basal Cuttings*, p.227. Grow on rooted cuttings in a warm greenhouse until danger of frost is past. Harden them off in a cold frame and plant out in early summer. Propagate tuberous begonias and gloxinias (*Sinningia speciosa*) in this way in spring.

Scooping and scoring *Trillium*

Various cutting techniques may be used to propagate *Trillium* rhizomes in late summer, after the leaves have died down.

One method that avoids lifting the parent plant is to remove sufficient soil to expose the tops of the rhizomes and to score lightly a shallow cut around the growing point of each rhizome. Dust the cuts with a fungicide and cover the rhizomes with a top-dressing of peat substitute and coarse sand in equal parts, or cover them with soil if it is light and well draining. Small rhizomes should form along the cut surfaces and in time become large enough to propagate.

Alternatively, lift the rhizomes and scoop out their growing points. Make concave "scoops", rather than cutting across the base of the growing points, to ensure that no soft tissue remains that could rot. Dust the cut surfaces with fungicide and replant the rhizomes. Small rhizomes should then form around the excised growing tip.

One year later, expose the rhizomes, remove the young ones, and grow them on in pots as described for young seedlings (see "Care of seedlings", p.238).

How to Propagate Trilliums by Scoring

1 Carefully scrape away the topsoil to expose the rhizome. Score a shallow incision around it with a sharp, clean knife, just below the growing point (*see inset*).

2 Use a clean, soft brush to dust the cut surface of the rhizome with fungicidal powder.

3 Carefully cover the scored rhizome with a mix of peat susbstitute and coarse sand in equal parts to the same level as before. Gently firm it with your fingers.

4 A year later, remove the topsoil to expose the rhizomes and remove any young ones that have formed. Pot them up individually and grow them on.

Cutting out Growing Points

1 Remove the growing point of the rhizome entirely by making a cut in the form of a concave "scoop" with the tip of a clean, sharp knife.

2 Dust the cut surfaces of the parent rhizomes with fungicide. Cover them up again with soil and firm the soil down lightly.

Lilies

LILIES are among the most graceful of summer-flowering plants – their tall, slim stems bear flowers with an enormous variety of dazzling colours and exotic shapes. There are a great many to choose from – more than 80 species lilies and thousands of hybrids, which are more tolerant of different conditions and so are often easier to grow.

Lily classification

Lilies are classified into nine different divisions based on their origin, parentage, and flowers:

Div.I Hybrids of Asiatic species such as *L. cernuum*, and *L. davidii*.
Div.II Hybrids of *L. martagon* and *L. hansonii*.
Div.III Hybrids of *L. candidum* and *L. chalcedonicum*.
Div.IV Hybrids of American species lilies.
Div.V Hybrids of *L. longiflorum* and *L. formosanum*.
Div.VI (Aurelian hybrids): Trumpet lilies and *L. henryi* crosses.
Div.VII (Oriental hybrids): From Japanese species.
Div.VIII All other hybrids.
Div.IX All species and cultivars.

Where to grow lilies

Lilies are excellent border and woodland plants and make superb companion plants for roses. A few of the smaller lilies may be used to add summer colour to the rock garden when most alpine plants have already finished flowering. Lilies look splendid planted as specimens in containers, especially on terraces and patios. Div.V lilies are not hardy, but make excellent pot plants for the cold greenhouse and conservatory.

Planting and care

Always buy fresh bulbs and plant them immediately. Do not buy dried and shrivelled bulbs. Most lilies grow well in a range of soils. Div.III lilies prefer alkaline soils and full sun; Div.VII hybrids must be grown in lime-free soil or ericaceous compost in containers; Div.IV hybrids are best suited to damp, woodland conditions. Plant lilies in autumn at two and a half times the depth of the bulb in well-prepared, free-draining soil; *L.candidum* needs only 2.5cm (1in) of soil above the bulb and should be planted in late summer. The routine care of lilies is similar to that of most bulbs (see pp.234–6); stake the plants well so that their flowering stems do not snap.

Propagation

Lilies may be propagated easily by stem bulbils, scaling, seed, or by simple division for *L. pardalinum* and Div.IV hybrids. Always propagate from healthy stock.

Bulbils and bulblets
Species such as *L. lancifolium* (syn. *L. tigrinum*), *L. bulbiferum*, and their hybrids produce stem bulbils in the leaf axils and bulblets at the base of the old flowering stem. Remove these and pot them up to grow on. The following autumn, either plant out the whole pan of young bulbs or pot them up individually.

Seed, scaling, and division
Seed sowing produces vigorous, virus-free bulbs (see "Growing lilies from seed", p.238), but is slow; Div.V lilies are easy to propagate in this way. For details of division and scaling, see pp.237 and 240.

LILY FLOWER SHAPES

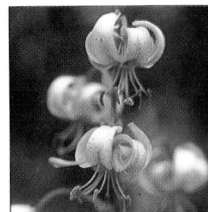
Lilium martagon (scented, nodding, turkscap flowers)

L. bulbiferum* var. *croceum (chalice-shaped)

L. monadelphum (scented trumpets)

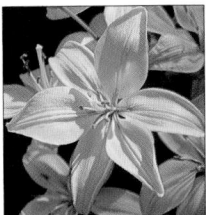
***L.* 'Connecticut King'** (upward-facing, cup-shaped blooms)

L. regale (fragrant, outward-facing trumpets)

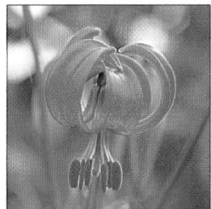
L. chalcedonicum (scented turkscaps)

Pests and diseases

Lilies are particularly vulnerable to several viruses (p.553) transmitted by aphids. Visible symptoms are mottled and twisted leaves. *L. lancifolium* and some of its hybrids are carriers but show no symptoms; keep them away from other lilies to minimize infection. Grey mould/*Botrytis* (p.550) may cause problems in damp, windless conditions. Red lily beetles (p.548) destroy stems and flowers.

PROPAGATING FROM STEM BULBILS

1 *Throughout late summer, as soon as the bulbils loosen and are ripe, collect them from the leaf axils of the lily stems by carefully picking them off.*

2 *Insert the bulbils in pans of moist, loam-based potting compost, pressing them gently into the surface. Cover with grit, and label (see inset). Place in a cold frame until young bulbs develop.*

RAISING LILIES FROM BULBLETS

1 *After flowering, lift the bulb and dead stem, pick off the bulblets, and replant the main bulb. Alternatively, leave the bulb in the ground, cutting the stem above it to remove the bulblets.*

2 *Plant the bulblets, at twice their own depth, into 13cm (5in) pots of moist, loam-based potting compost. Cover with a layer of grit, label, and place in a cold frame until the spring.*

THE WATER GARDEN

10

A WATER FEATURE *is an irresistible attraction in any garden; whether it is a formal pool graced by water lilies and the bright gleam of goldfish, a trickling stream bordered by ferns, or a simple pond reflecting the sculptural silhouette of a clump of irises, there is a style to suit every setting. Even the smallest and quietest courtyard garden can be brought to life by the murmur of running water and the dancing patterns of light. Creating a water* garden *provides habitats for a specific range of plants as well as attracting a host of wildlife, including newts, frogs, toads, dragonflies, and perhaps even water birds. Water may be either restful or exciting: still water is valued for its properties of reflection and tranquillity, while moving water – whether in the form of a classical fountain or a rushing waterfall – adds a delightful sound and a dynamic vitality to the garden.*

Designing a water garden

U NLIKE any other element in the garden, water brings an ever-changing pattern of reflections, sound, and movement that is particularly appealing. Even when frozen, its surface provides contrasts of colour and texture. A pond is a popular form of water feature but there are others: a waterfall, fountain, or watercourse, for instance.

A garden water feature allows you to grow many plants that do not thrive in any other conditions, from the floating frogbit (*Hydrocharis morsus-ranae*) and water hyacinth (*Eichhornia crassipes*) to the bog garden candelabra primulas.

When deciding which type of water feature to create, bear in mind the size and style of the garden. If large and informal, a meandering watercourse may be effective, while in an enclosed town garden, a raised formal pool might be appropriate. Water may even be included in a garden for children in the form of an attractive "bubble fountain" – in which the water splashes over stones and is recirculated without forming an area of any depth.

A NATURALISTIC WATER GARDEN
In an informal or semi-wild garden, a gently meandering stream provides a lush, cool area by which to sit and relax. Clouds of pink rhododendrons add both height and colour to the scheme, while marginal plantings of bright yellow Iris pseudacorus, *ferns, and rushes form a transition between the stream and the garden.*

Siting a pond

Exploit the reflective quality of water by siting a pond where it mirrors an eye-catching feature – a specimen plant or statue, perhaps. It may help to lay a reflective sheet in the proposed site to give an idea of reflections to be seen during the day and evening; check it from major viewpoints such as the house and patio.

An open, sunny position, away from overhanging trees, provides the best conditions in which to grow most water plants.

If planning to create a pond on wet land that is prone to flooding, check that there is no danger of fertilizer or pesticide residues leaching into the water from an adjacent vegetable garden or farmland. These substances invariably affect pond life adversely. Direct potential overflows to a suitable drainage system. Land with a high water table may cause problems because, in very wet periods, water pressure from below may push a pond liner out of shape.

Do not site a pond in a frost pocket or in a very exposed position, since this restricts the range of plants that may be grown and protection may have to be provided in winter.

Informal ponds

In an informal garden, a natural, sunken pond may look most effective. Usually, this is in an irregular, curved shape, bordered with natural materials such as turf or stones to link it with the garden. The water surface is, however, only part of the total scheme: the inclusion of marginal and moisture-loving plants

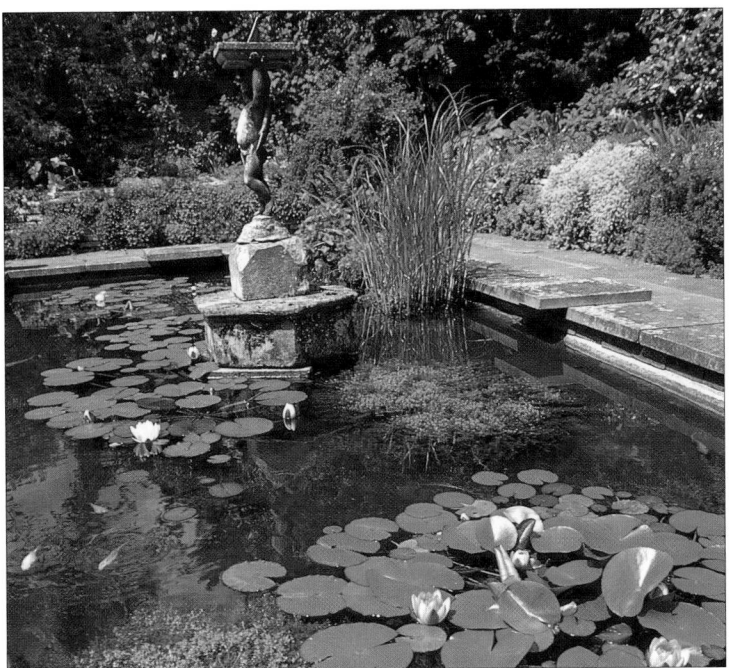

A FORMAL POOL
Water lilies (Nymphaea) *bring elegance and colour to a rectangular pond. A sundial links the informality of the plants to the pool's formal margins.*

around the pond, to soften or hide its outline completely, helps to create a lush and refreshing effect.

As when planting in a border or bed, consider how the plants will combine to create complementary and contrasting associations of colour, texture, and form.

Formal ponds

In contrast to the natural effect of an informal pond, a formal pool makes a much bolder feature. It may be raised or sunken and is usually of a regular, geometric design. As a rule, less space is devoted to planting than in an informal pond, although plants with floating leaves and flowers (e.g. water lilies) are often included; sculptural plants such as certain ferns, grown next to the pool, provide attractive reflections. A fountain or water spout to complement the style of the pond can be an ornamental and dramatic addition.

Far from being disguised, the edge of the pond may form an important feature, perhaps made of attractive paving or, if the pool is raised, wide enough or, to form a seat; this type of design is particularly suitable for elderly or disabled people.

In many cases formal ponds are sited so that they form a striking focal point in the garden, at the main axis of paths, for example, or where they may be conveniently viewed and enjoyed from the windows or terrace of the house.

Fountains

The style and size of a fountain should be considered in the context of the surrounding pool and the overall design of the garden. Often used in a formal garden as a focal point, a fountain is also invaluable for adding height to a design, and for its dynamic contribution of sound and movement and the scattering of light. In addition, a fountain is particularly effective if lit at night.

A cobble or bubble fountain, in which water bubbles over stones into a small underground reservoir, looks more informal than a standard fountain and is ideal in a garden that is used by children.

As well as being ornamental, fountains also provide a practical function: the splashing action introduces oxygen into the water and this is beneficial to any fish. Most water plants do not flourish in disturbed water, however, so they should not be grown close to a fountain.

Water spouts

While a fountain or waterfall might be too large in an average garden, a water spout provides all the pleasure of running water scaled down for the smallest garden or even a conservatory. There are many styles, from the classical lion's head or gargoyle above a pool to the simplicity of an oriental bamboo pipe trickling water over stones.

A water spout is usually fixed to a wall, with a pump and pipe similar to those used for a watercourse; the pump circulates water from a pool or reservoir to the rear of the spout and out through the "mouth".

Streams, watercourses, and waterfalls

Few gardens have a natural stream or waterfall, but it is possible to create a circulating watercourse spilling out into a pool or underground reservoir. Making a watercourse or waterfall is an attractive way of exploiting a change of level in the garden. It may be used to link parts of the garden as well as providing points of interest between levels.

In an informal garden, a watercourse may be made to look more natural by being edged with rocks or stones and moisture-loving plants such as ferns and irises. Ornamentals that have large leaves, for example *Rheum palmatum*, are particularly valuable for watercourses made from liners or preformed units since they help to disguise the edges.

Bog and wildlife areas

In an informal or naturalistic design, a bog garden makes an attractive and unconventional feature. Usually most appropriate next to ponds, bog gardens provide a gradual and

TRADITIONAL WATER SPOUT
A water spout is attractive even in a tiny garden. Here, mellow stone complements this traditional spout.

natural transition from aquatic to moisture-loving plants and ideal conditions for wildlife.

Bog gardens

Creating a bog garden is a better way of using waterlogged land than struggling against nature by trying to drain it. While the ground next to a man-made pool is unlikely to be wet enough to provide suitable conditions for growing bog plants, using a liner under the soil will retain sufficient moisture.

Bog gardens bring a freshness of growth in late summer when many other plants are showing the effects of drought; most bog plants, however, die back naturally after frost, so they do not provide great interest in winter months.

AN INFORMAL
WATERCOURSE
A terrace of weirs formed from thick slabs of stone creates cascades of water that spill into a shallow, cobble-lined pool. Overhanging plants such as ivies (Hedera), *Japanese maple* (Acer palmatum), *and primulas help to break up the rigid line of the stone, while the meandering path of the watercourse gives the scheme an appealing informality and charm.*

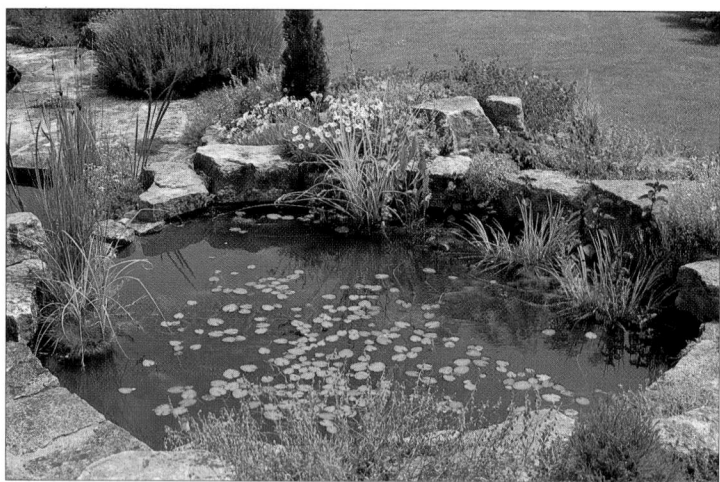

LINKING THE POOL WITH THE GARDEN
Rugged pieces of stone form a practical yet pleasing edging to this semi-formal pool. Rock plants provide a colourful link with the garden beyond.

Wildlife ponds

A water feature increases diversity in a wildlife garden, providing a habitat for waterfowl, frogs, newts, and an enormous range of insects. Limiting the planting to native species only will attract more wildlife, although many native plants can prove invasive; the inclusion of some exotic ornamentals creates a greater opportunity to make the pond a highly decorative feature as well. Informal ponds with muddy bottoms and shallowly sloping edges interspersed with large, flat stones are particularly suitable, providing ideal conditions for amphibians.

Container water gardens

In a small garden or patio, or where major construction work is impractical, it is still possible to have a pool by using an appropriate ornamental

CONTAINER POOL
A decorative, sealed metal cauldron provides the perfect place to cultivate one or two miniature water lilies, for example Nymphaea pygmaea 'Helvola'.

container, such as a sealed and lined half-barrel. A container is suitable for growing only a few selected plants, however, and remember that fish probably will not be able to survive in it outdoors over winter. If using a metal container, it should be sealed with a rubber paint or liner, otherwise it may be harmful to both plants and fish.

Plants for the water garden

In any water garden, plants are vital to the scheme. Lush foliage and flowers enhance the pool and link it with the rest of the garden, while certain plants help to maintain clear water and, in the case of oxygenators, good conditions for fish.

Plants suitable for a water garden range from those that thrive in deep water to those requiring moist soil only around their root tips. They are usually grouped into six categories: oxygenators, deep-water plants, surface floaters, marginals, bog plants, and moisture-loving plants.

Oxygenators

Lagarosiphon major (syn. *Elodea crispa*) and *Myriophyllum* species are examples of oxygenators: submerged, fast-growing plants that will help to clean and oxygenate the water. In sunny weather, submerged algae may turn a new pond green within a week or two of installation. Oxygenating plants, however, compete for the dissolved mineral salts on which algae thrive and starve them out so that the water eventually becomes clear once more. Such oxygenators are essential if you are planning to keep fish in the pool.

Deep-water plants

These flourish in a depth range of 30–90cm (12–36in). This category includes plants such as *Aponogeton* and *Hydrocleys*, with water lilies (*Nymphaea*) forming the largest group (see pp.248–9). Apart from their ornamental value, their floating leaves also help to reduce algae by cutting down the amount of light allowed to reach the water.

Surface floaters

Floating plants, such as *Trapa natans* and *Azolla caroliniana*, perform a similar function to the deep-water plants, especially during the establishment phase. It is vital not to let them cover too much water, however, since oxygenators may suffer if there is not enough light.

Marginals

Marginal plants are grown at the edges of pools in shallow water usually about 7–15cm (3–6in) deep, but occasionally up to 30cm (12in). Many of these plants are extremely attractive, such as *Iris laevigata* 'Variegata' with fans of green- and cream-striped leaves and lavender-blue flowers, and they are valuable in an informal pond for breaking up the outline. In a wildlife pool, marginals provide cover for wildfowl and other small creatures. Some species such as *Mentha aquatica* and *Veronica beccabunga* also help to oxygenate the water.

Bog plants

Bog-loving plants such as *Lysichiton* or some *Caltha* species thrive in waterlogged soil and can withstand occasional flooding. Under a bog-plant heading, nursery catalogues may include plants that grow in moist or even wet soil but do not tolerate

a waterlogged soil; when ordering, ensure that any plants chosen tolerate high water levels around the roots.

Moisture-loving plants

These thrive in soils that contain extra moisture without being waterlogged. Moisture-lovers include many herbaceous perennials, such as *Astilbe*, *Ligularia*, and *Primula florindae*. They all associate well with marginal plants in the areas surrounding natural, informal pools where the growing conditions are ideal for them.

Planting associations

Create a varied and attractive display by mixing plants with different heights and growth habits around the pool. Similar design principles should be applied as for planting in the rest of the garden to develop a successful scheme with a diversity of shapes and forms (see also "Principles of planting", pp.21–6). Site *Gunnera manicata*, for example, so that its immense, platter-like leaves tower over the jutting swords of *Acorus calamus*. Use plants at the edge of the pond to act as a foil for floating plants or deep marginals – an island of water lilies such as *Nymphaea alba* with its pure white blooms would be beautifully offset by a drift of ostrich-feather ferns (*Matteuccia struthiopteris*).

Plants with contrasting colours and textures also provide the potential for some spectacular combinations. For example, the upright, scarlet flower spikes of *Lobelia cardinalis* would form a fine contrast with the heart-shaped, blue-grey leaves of *Hosta sieboldiana*.

Plan the planting to supply interest throughout the seasons. Including evergreen foliage plants such as

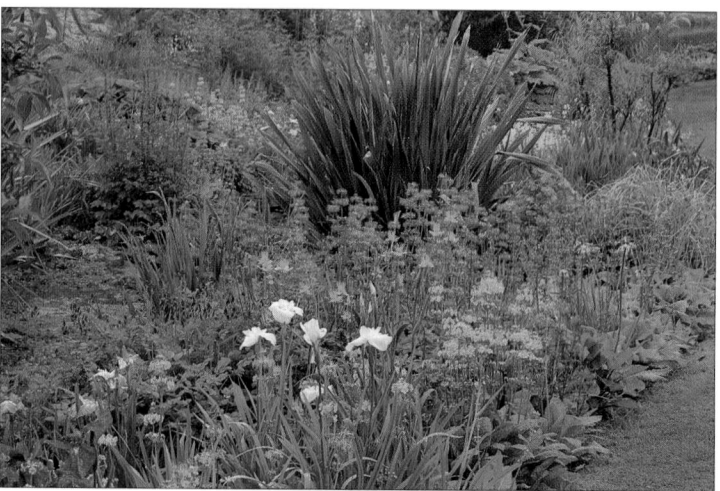

BOG GARDEN
The boggy ground next to a pond is ideal for plants such as Primula bulleyana *and* Iris laevigata. Phormium tenax *gives the design its focus.*

Bergenia at the pool edges provides continuity of form and colour, while other types of plant – ranging from the golden flowers of the marsh marigold (*Caltha palustris*) in spring to the summer-long display of the water forget-me-not (*Myosotis scorpioides*) with its delicate, blue flowers – may be used to create a changing, seasonal display.

Fish

While most ornamental fish live in harmony with aquatic plant life, the inclusion of larger specimen fish necessitates certain precautions in pond design and planting. Oxygenating plants provide oxygen only in daylight, and fish may suffer from stress during warm, sultry nights unless additional oxygen is provided – for example, from the water agitation created by the splashing of a fountain.

If planning to keep large koi carp, remember that they may disturb the roots of water lilies and other deep-water plants, so cover the soil over the roots with large stones. Pools for these fish should be at least 1m (3ft) deep and have vertical sides projecting above the surface so that the carp cannot leap out. Goldfish and orfe are easier to manage, the latter being ideal decorative fish that enjoy shallow water and feed on any insect larvae present. In the wildlife garden, native species such as tench may be suitable and less damaging to tadpole populations.

Planter's guide to water plants

SHALLOW MARGINALS
(6in/15cm depth of water)

Acorus gramineus,
  A. g. 'Variegatus'
Alisma parviflora
Calla palustris

Calla palustris

Caltha leptosepala,
  C. palustris, C. p. 'Alba',
  C. p. 'Flore Plena'
Carex elata 'Aurea',
  C. pendula, C. riparia
Colocasia esculenta✤
Cotula coronopifolia
Cyperus 'Haspan',
  C. involucratus✤, *C. longus*
Damasonium alisma
Decodon verticillatus
Eriophorum angustifolium,
  E. latifolium
Houttuynia cordata,
  H. c. 'Chamaeleon' (syn. *H. c.*
  'Variegata'), *H. c.* 'Plena'
Hydrocleys nymphoides✤
Iris laevigata, I. versicolor

Hydrocleys nymphoides

Juncus effusus, J. e. f. *spiralis,*
  J. e. 'Vittatus', *J. ensifolius*
Lobelia paludosa
Lysichiton americanus,
  L. camtschatcensis
Mentha aquatica
Mimulus cardinalis,
  M. cupreus, M. guttatus,
  M. ringens
Myosotis scorpioides,
  M. s. 'Mermaid'
Peltandra alba
Polygonum amphibium
Sagittaria latifolia, S. sagittifolia,
  S. s. 'Flore Pleno'
Sparganium minimum
Typha minima
Zizania aquatica✤

DEEP MARGINALS
(12in/30cm depth of water)

Acorus calamus,
  A. c. 'Variegatus'
Alisma lanceolatum,
  A. plantago-aquatica
Butomus umbellatus
Cyperus papyrus✤
Glyceria maxima 'Variegata'
Hottonia palustris
Iris pseudacorus
Nelumbo lutea✤, *N. nucifera* 'Alba
  Grandiflora'✤, *N. n.* 'Alba
  Striata'✤, *N. n.* 'Rosa Plena'✤
Phragmites australis,
  P. a. 'Variegata'
Pontederia cordata, P. lanceolata
Ranunculus lingua 'Grandiflora'
Saururus cernuus
Scirpus lacustris,
  S. l. subsp. *tabernaemontani*
  'Albescens', *S. l.* subsp. *t.* 'Zebrinus'
Sparganium erectum,
  syn. *S. ramosum*
Thalia dealbata✤, *T. geniculata*✤
Typha angustifolia, T. latifolia
  'Variegata', *T. stenophylla,*
  syn. *T. laxmannii*
Zantedeschia aethiopica
  'Crowborough'

DEEP WATER PLANTS

Aponogeton distachyos
Euryale ferox✤
Nuphar advena, N. lutea
Nymphaea, some ✤ (most spp.)
Nymphoides indica, N. peltata
Orontium aquaticum
Victoria amazonica, V. regia

SUBMERGED OXYGENATORS

Callitriche hermaphroditica,
  syn. *C. autumnalis*
Ceratophyllum demersum
Ceratopteris thalictroides✤
Egeria densa✤
Fontinalis antipyretica
Hydrocleys parviflora✤
Lagarosiphon major,
  syn. *Elodea crispa*
Myriophyllum aquaticum,
  syn. *M. proserpinacoides*✤

Potamogeton crispus
Preslia cervina
Tillaea recurva

FLOATING AQUATICS

Azolla caroliniana✤, *A. filiculoides*
Ceratopteris pteroides✤
Eichhornia azurea, E. crassipes✤
Hydrocharis morsus-ranae
Lemna trisulca
Limnanthemum lacunosum
Limnobium spongia,
  L. stoloniferum
Phyllanthus fluitans
Pistia stratiotes✤

Pistia stratiotes

Riccia fluitans
Salvinia auriculata✤, *S. natans*✤
Stratiotes aloides
Trapa natans
Utricularia minor, U. vulgaris
Wolffia arrhiza✤

BOG AND MOISTURE-LOVING PLANTS

Alnus glutinosa, A. incana
Anemone rivularis
Aruncus dioicus 'Kneiffii'
Arundo donax 'Variegata'
Astilbe x *arendsii, A. chinensis,*
  A. simplicifolia
Astilboides tabularis
Cardamine pratensis
Cimicifuga americana,
  C. racemosa
Cornus alba
Eupatorium purpureum
Euphorbia palustris
Filipendula rubra, F. ulmaria
Gunnera chilensis, G. manicata
Hemerocallis (most spp.)
Hosta (most spp.)
Iris ensata, I. sibirica
Leucojum aestivum
Ligularia clivorum, L. przewalskii
Lobelia cardinalis, L. fulgens✤

Lythrum salicaria
Osmunda regalis
Parnassia palustris
Peltiphyllum peltatum
Phalaris arundinacea
Phragmites communis
Polygonum amplexicaule,
  P. bistorta, P. campanulatum
Primula alpicola, P. denticulata,
  P. florindae, P. helodoxa,
  P. japonica, P. pulverulenta,
  P. rosea, P. secundiflora,
  P. sikkimensis
Rheum alexandrae, R. palmatum,
  R. p. 'Atrosanguineum'
Rodgersia aesculifolia, R. pinnata,
  R. podophylla
Salix alba, S. babylonica,
  S. daphnoides, S. matsudana
  'Tortuosa'
Scrophularia auriculata
  'Variegata'
Senecio smithii
Taxodium distichum
Trollius x *cultorum,*
  T. europaeus,
  T. ledebourii

Trollius europaeus

RECOMMENDED PLANTS FOR AQUARIUMS

Alternanthera philoxeroides✤
Anubias barteri✤
Aponogeton crispus✤,
  A. madagascariensis✤
Bacopa monnieri
Cabomba caroliniana✤
Cryptocoryne ciliata✤
Echinodorus bleheri✤, *E. maior*✤
Hemigraphis alternata✤
Hygrophila polysperma✤
Ludwigia arcuata✤
Luronium natans
Myriophyllum hippuroides✤
Potamogeton crispus
Salvinia natans✤
Utricularia exoleta✤, *U. vulgaris*
Vallisneria gigantea✤

KEY
✤ *Not hardy*

247

Water lilies

THE elegant, floating cups and lush foliage of water lilies (*Nymphaea*) are a graceful addition to any water garden, whether it is in a natural, rural setting or a formal, city courtyard. The flower forms vary from open and star-like to goblet-shaped, peony blooms, with colours ranging from the simple purity of white or cream to striking shades of red, yellow, or even blue. Some are offset by dark purplish-green leaves, while others have foliage that is attractively mottled. Certain species have richly perfumed flowers; these are best grown in a raised pool where their scent may be easily enjoyed.

While most water lilies bloom in the daytime, some tropical cultivars such as 'Missouri' and 'Red Flare' open at dusk – these are best enhanced by complementary lighting to create a bold display after dark. Native to tropical and subtropical zones, these lilies may be grown in temperate regions in a conservatory pool or outdoors in hot summers.

Water lilies need several hours of full sun each day, otherwise they develop a mass of leaves but few blooms, so they should be grown in an open, sunny part of the pool. They also prefer calm water; if there is a fountain or waterfall, grow the lilies well away from it so that they are not disturbed by the movement. Tropical species usually grow more quickly than those that are hardy and require high light intensity, an ample food supply, and warm water at a minimum of 20°C (68°F).

As well as being decorative, water lilies help to keep the water clear because their large, spreading leaves create shade, thereby helping to control the growth of algae.

HARDY AND TROPICAL WATER LILIES

Nymphaea 'Attraction'

N. pygmaea 'Helvola'

N. 'Fire Crest'

N. marliacea 'Chromatella'

N. 'American Star'

N. 'Blue Beauty'

N. 'Escarboucle'

N. 'Virginalis'

N. marliacea 'Carnea'

15–19cm (6–7¹/₂in) deep, depending on the size and vigour of the cultivar. Alternatively, plant in submerged beds 30–45cm (12–18in) deep and 45–60cm (18–24in) square.

Prepare the plant by trimming back long roots and cutting off old or damaged leaves and flower buds. The older leaves make the plant more buoyant and difficult to anchor under water and they produce little food for the plant. New leaves will quickly replace them. When planting tropical water lilies, insert a sachet of slow-release fertilizer.

If the planted container is not too heavy, water well before placing it in the pond so that any soil shrinkage can be rectified. Lower the basket into place with strings as for planting deep water plants (see p.257).

In a new pool, the containers may be positioned on the bottom before the pool is filled. Cover them with only 8–15cm (3–6in) of water initially; raise the containers on blocks if necessary so that they have the correct depth of water above them. As the plants grow, gradually lower the containers in stages until they finally rest on the bottom. Tropical water lilies may be planted at their permanent depth immediately, however, as they grow quickly and prefer shallower water than most hardy cultivars.

Feeding

Water lilies usually benefit from limited additional feeding; insert a proprietary sachet of slow-release fertilizer into the soil or compost approximately every six weeks during the growing season. This gradually releases small quantities of plant food without discolouring the water or encouraging algae.

Care and cultivation

Most water lilies have thick tubers which grow roughly vertically, with fibrous roots beneath; cultivars of *N. odorata* and *N. tuberosa* have longer, fleshy rhizomes which grow horizontally near the soil surface.

Planting

Plant between late spring and late summer so that the plants will be well established before winter; do not plant out tropical water lilies until the risk of frost has passed.

For planting, use containers that are 30–35cm (12–14in) across and

PLANTING A TUBEROUS WATER LILY

1 Using secateurs or a sharp knife, trim back to within 5cm (2in) of the tuber any roots that are damaged or excessively long.

2 Cut off any dead or damaged leaves, or those with broken stalks. Retain new, young leaves and flower buds.

3 Line the basket and partly fill it with dampened soil. Position the tuber so that the crown is within 4cm (1¹/₂in) of the rim.

4 Pack soil firmly around the tuber, ensuring that the crown remains 4cm (1¹/₂in) above the level of the soil.

A FLOATING GARDEN
The strong, straight lines of a wooden deck bridge offset the plate-like leaves and colourful blooms of an island of water lilies.

PROPAGATION BY BUD CUTTINGS

1 *Remove the plant from its container and wash it. Using a sharp knife, remove strong-growing buds from the root by cutting flush with the tuber.*

2 *Fill 10cm (4in) pots with soil or aquatic compost, firm, and press a single cutting into the surface. Top-dress with grit.*

3 *Immerse the pots in water and keep them in a greenhouse or cold frame, partially shaded; plant out the following spring.*

Division

To maintain healthy growth, divide water lilies when the foliage is crowding the water surface, or when the roots have outgrown the container. Cut off pieces from the crown, each with a young, strong shoot and about 15cm (6in) of attached tuber, and replant these in fresh soil. The old crown may be discarded.

Propagation

Most tuberous water lilies may be propagated by means of bud cuttings; rhizomatous types may have their rootstocks divided (see p.260). Some water lilies may be raised from seed, or by separating plantlets.

Bud cuttings

Some tuberous water lilies produce sideshoots or "eyes" that may be used to propagate new plants. Cut the eyes from the roots and dust them with charcoal or sulphur. Press each cutting into a prepared pot, top-dress, and immerse in water; leave the pots in a greenhouse or cold frame at 15–18°C (60–65°F). As the plants develop, pot them on and gradually increase the water depth until they are ready to plant in the pool the following spring.

Seed

With the exception of *N. odorata* and *N. tetragona*, hardy water lilies do not readily set seed but tender or tropical water lilies set large quantities. Before collecting seed, enclose the ripening capsules in muslin bags to prevent them from floating away. Sow hardy seed at once before it dries out; tropical water lily seed should be washed and allowed to dry, then stored in bags at room temperature. Tropical water lily seed is best sown in spring.

Sow the seed evenly, still attached to its jelly-like bladders, in pans of seed compost. Sprinkle with compost, water, then place the pans in a container and cover with 2.5–5cm (1–2in) of water. Hardy water lily seed requires a minimum temperature of 13°C (55°F) to germinate, tropical seed 23–7°C (73–81°F).

When the seedlings are large enough to handle, carefully lift, rinse, and plant them in pans submerged in 5–7.5cm (2–3in) of water. Pot on later into 6cm (3in) pots in 8–10cm (3–4in) of water.

After overwintering, the tubers produce young plants that may be detached and potted on.

Plantlets

Certain day-blooming, tropical water lilies produce plantlets that may form and bloom while still attached to the parent leaf. Alternatively, they may be transplanted into shallow pans in water and then grown on at a temperature of 15–18°C (59–64°C); gradually increase the water level, then pot them up into aquatic containers.

Aquariums

Small, submerged tropical plants may be easily grown in the controlled environment of an aquarium. As well as being attractive, these plants provide shelter for fish. Choose small, gregarious fish, avoiding any that eat or disturb plants. Landscaping with suitable rocks and wood will also help to increase the interest.

As in a garden pool, a good water chemistry balance is maintained by achieving the correct levels of light, temperature, stocking, and organic matter. Aquariums should not be placed too near a sunny window, as the high light intensity encourages algal growth. Use lime-free, washed sand or shingle to cover the base of the aquarium, in a layer 8cm (3in) deep at the front, rising to 10–12.5cm (4–5in) at the back.

Heating the water to 23–6°C (73–9°F) by means of thermostatically controlled cables in the sand enables a wide range of plants to be grown. Provide artificial lighting for approximately 12 hours each day; gro-lux fluorescent tubes emit the necessary ultra-violet light. For pristine water clarity, circulate the water through a decanting filter with a small electric pump.

FRESHWATER AQUARIUM
This tank provides a fine setting for plants such as Baldellia ranunculoides *with upright, oval leaves and the feathery* Hygrophila difformis, *while tropical fish add colour and movement.*

Constructing ponds and watercourses

For many years, man-made ponds were generally constructed from heavy materials such as stone, concrete, or brick. Since the advent of plastics and fibreglass, however, it has become easier to install your own pond and also to create a more naturalistic design, if desired.

The best shape, size, and material for the pond depends to a large extent on the size and style of your garden, the preferred method of construction, and cost. Flexible liners allow you maximum freedom of shape and size, and are ideal where a natural look is required since the edge may be easily concealed and the lining material itself is relatively unobtrusive; they are the best choice for large ponds. Rigid, preformed pools are easier to install, but there is only a limited range of shapes and sizes. While they are excellent for small ponds, larger units are difficult to manoeuvre and very large sizes are not available. Hard materials such as concrete provide the strongest and most long-lasting pools but they are also the most difficult and slowest to construct.

There are several methods of constructing watercourses. Flexible liners are versatile and particularly suitable for naturalistic designs. Where strength and durability are more important, or where the design incorporates a series of shallow cascades, preformed, rigid units may be more appropriate. Liners and rigid units may be used in combination.

Flexible liners

Most new garden pools are constructed using a flexible lining sheet of synthetic rubber or plastic, which provides a waterproof barrier between the soil and the water. These flexible liners are available in a wide range of sizes and can be cut to fit any shape of pool. Before buying a liner, decide on the site and size of the pond: marking out the desired shape with string and pegs makes it easier to check the effect.

Butyl rubber is the most widely used pond lining material. It is much stronger than either polythene or PVC, with a life expectancy of about 40–50 years, but it is also more expensive. Butyl is very pliable, and is tough enough to resist tearing or deterioration caused by ultraviolet light, bacterial growth, and temperature extremes. To line an informal pool, particularly if part of the material may be exposed to sunlight,

it is best to use a top-quality butyl liner that is 7mm ($\frac{1}{4}$in) thick.

PVC liners are reasonably strong and tear-resistant, and some come guaranteed for ten years. They are resistant to both frost and fungal attack, but after several years of exposure to sunlight they may harden and crack. These liners are usually blue or black in colour, or black on one side and beige on the other; it is usual to place them with the dark side uppermost since darker colours absorb light and heat and look more natural than lighter colours.

Polythene is the cheapest of all the lining materials; it is easily torn and cracks after constant exposure to sunlight. Where it can be protected from light or from accidental damage, it is an economical material to use. It is particularly suitable as a lining for bog gardens, where it is covered by a layer of earth.

Measuring the liner
To calculate the size of liner required, first determine the maximum length, width, and depth of the pool. The liner should measure the maximum width of the pool plus twice its depth, by the maximum length plus twice its depth. Add 15cm (6in) on both width and length to allow for a flap at the edge to prevent leakage. A pool measuring 2 x 2.5m (6 x 8ft) and 60cm (2ft) deep would require a liner 3.5 x 4m (11 x 13ft).

Installation
First spread out the liner away from the site, in the sun if possible as the warmth will make it more flexible and easier to handle. Mark the required shape of the pond on the site with string and pegs, hosepipe, or a length of rope, then mark the soil just inside this line. Dig to a depth of approximately 23cm (9in), making the pool sides slope inwards at an angle of 20° from the vertical; this slope prevents the sides from caving in, makes it easier to install the liner, and ensures that if the pool freezes in winter the ice can expand upwards without causing damage.

If planning to grow marginal plants, cut a shelf about 23cm (9in) wide to provide adequate planting positions, and then continue digging at a slight angle until the desired depth – normally 50–60cm (20–24in) – is reached. Check that the rim of the pool is level all round by using a straight plank and spirit level across both the length and the width of the hole. This is extremely important, as if the pool is not level

INSTALLING A FLEXIBLE LINER

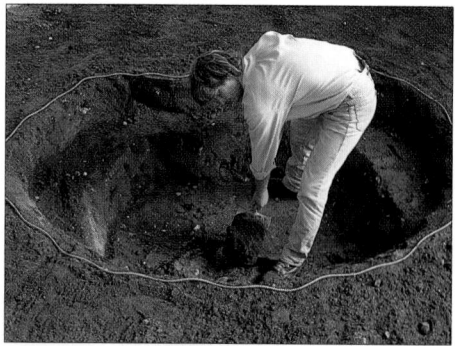

1 Mark out the proposed shape of the pond using string and wooden pegs or a hosepipe, and then start to excavate the hole. Form marginal planting shelves where required about 23cm (9in) broad and 23cm (9in) deep.

2 Use a plank and spirit level to check that the hole is level. Remove from the hole all tree roots and sharp stones that might otherwise pierce the liner when it is installed.

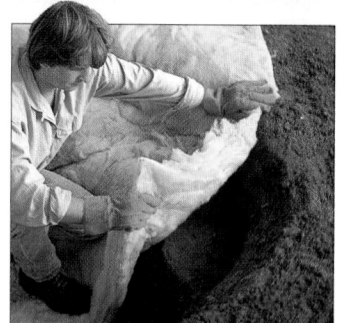

3 Spread fibreglass, loft insulation material over the base and sides to act as a cushioning bed for the flexible liner. Trim the material level with the top of the hole.

4 Drape the liner evenly across the hole and weight the edges. Slowly fill the pool with water, tugging at the liner edges to eliminate creases. Trim off any excess liner, leaving an overlap of about 15cm (6in).

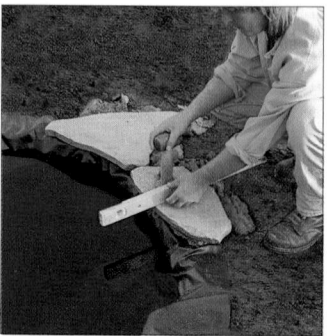

5 Provide an edging round the rim of the pond with paving slabs or stones, bedded on mortar, or with turf. Check that the edging stones or slabs are level and then tamp them into place.

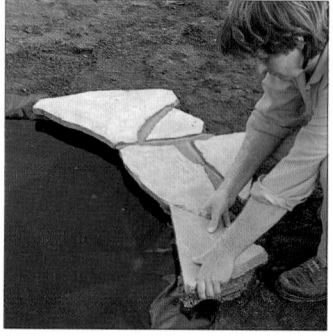

6 The edging stones should overhang the pool by about 5cm (2in) so that the liner cannot be seen. Do not drop mortar into the water or the pond will have to be emptied and refilled.

water may spill over the edge. If including edging stones, remove 5cm (2in) depth of soil to a width of 30cm (12in) all around the pool, so that the stones can be firmly bedded in later.

Once the hole is excavated, remove any roots and sharp stones that could puncture the liner, and tamp the soil firmly. To protect and cushion the liner, spread an undersheet of polyester matting or fibreglass insulation, or a 2.5cm (1in) layer of damp sand in the hole. Undersheets are preferable as they are both stable and durable; sand may eventually shift, leaving part of the liner exposed to damage from stones that may have been missed.

Drape the liner over the hole, so that the centre touches the base, leaving an overlap on all sides. Anchor it all the way round before starting to fill the pool slowly with water. Weighed down by the water, the liner will stretch and sink to mould itself into the contours of the pool. As more liner is required, remove some anchoring stones and tug the edges of the liner to ensure that it is straight, forming neat folds at the sides if it starts to crease.

When the pool is filled, remove the remaining stones and check again that the rim is level all round; add or take away soil if necessary until it is level. Cut off any excess liner, leaving a 15cm (6in) flap all around the edge; this surplus may be hidden beneath rocks, turf, or paving stones bedded on mortar. The stones should protrude slightly over the pool edge to hide the liner from view. Take care not to let any mortar slip into the water; if this happens you should empty the pond and refill it.

Making planting beds

If including vigorous water plants in a large pool, it may be better to plant them in permanent beds or containers such as concrete pipes or half-dustbins rather than in planting baskets. These larger beds allow a greater root run and tall plants are less likely to be displaced by wind. Beds may be sited on the marginal shelves or on the pond base for growing deep-water aquatics.

Retaining walls of mortared bricks or building blocks may be built on top of a pond liner before the pond is filled, first protecting the liner with a cushioning strip of surplus liner offcuts. You should allow a minimum depth and width of compost of 23cm (9in). Apply pond sealant to the bed before planting. With a concrete pond, planting beds may be incorporated during construction.

PREFORMED MOULDS

Preformed fibreglass or plastic pools are available in a wide range of sizes and shapes. Most designs include planting shelves for marginal plants.

Preformed pools

The simplest pools to install are those preformed from fibreglass or plastic. These are available in a variety of shapes and are often contoured to provide ledges on which to grow marginal plants. Fibreglass ponds are more expensive than those made of plastic, but they are tough and weather resistant, with a life expectancy of at least ten years.

Installation

Level the site as much as possible and clear away any debris. If the mould is symmetrical in shape, invert it and mark out its outline using pegs and string. For asymmetrical shapes, stand the mould the right way up, supporting it on bricks if necessary to keep it stable and level; mark out the contours with long canes, pushed vertically into the ground, and string or rope.

To dig a hole that matches the mould, first remove soil down to the level of the marginal shelf. The topsoil may be reserved for use in the garden, while the subsoil should be set aside for backfilling around the pond later. Place the pool in the prepared hole, and press it down firmly onto the earth to leave a clear impression of the shape of the base. Lift out the mould, then dig out the central, deeper area that has been marked out by the pool base, allowing approximately 5cm (2in) extra depth all over the entire hole for the cushioning material.

Clear the hole of any sharp stones, tree roots, or debris, tamp the soil firmly, and line it with a 5cm (2in) layer of polyester matting, fibreglass insulating material, or damp sand. Put the mould in place and check that it is level all the way round, otherwise the water will run to one end when the pool is filled.

Ensure that the pool sits firmly on the bedding layer, then add about 10cm (4in) of water. With sand or sifted soil, backfill around the sides to the same depth as the water, ramming the soil firmly under the shelf; ensure that there are no gaps and that the pool remains absolutely level. Continue this process of adding water, backfilling, and checking the level until the pool is full. Finally, firm the earth around the pool and mask the edges with paving stones bedded on mortar or turves.

INSTALLING A PREFORMED POND

1 *Firmly support the fibreglass or plastic mould with bricks to keep the pond level and upright, and then mark out its shape by pushing a series of canes into the ground all around the edges. Lay a length of rope around the canes to mark out the precise outline that will need to be excavated.*

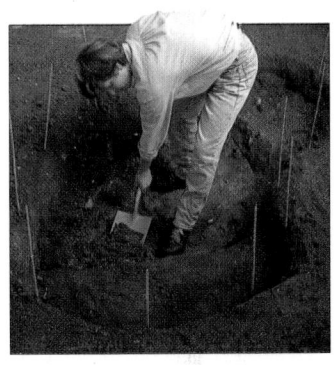

2 *Excavate the hole 5cm (2in) deeper than the mould, following its profile of shelves and base as accurately as possible.*

3 *Use a plank of wood, laid across the width of the pond, and a tape measure to check that the depth of the hole is correct, and use a spirit level to check that the base is flat.*

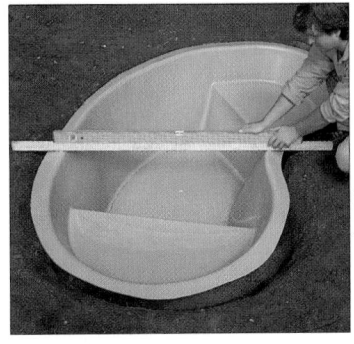

4 *Remove any tree roots and sharp stones, and then line the hole with a 5cm (2in) layer of sand. Lower the mould into place and check with a spirit level and plank that the mould is set level.*

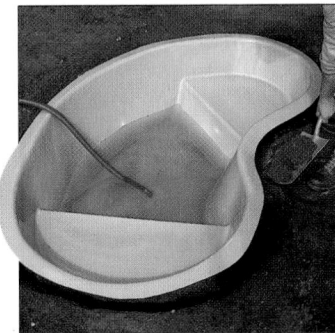

5 *Fill with water (here pond water) to a depth of 10cm (4in). Backfill around it to the same depth with sifted soil or sand. Tamp firmly. Continue to add water, backfill, and tamp.*

Concrete ponds

The rigidity of concrete is an advantage when creating formal ponds. It is durable and is suitable for ponds of almost any size. Construction does, however, require more skill and expertise than is needed for installing a liner or preformed pool.

In areas prone to long periods of severe frost, concrete ponds should be constructed with walls that slope outwards at an angle of 30–45°; this minimizes the risk of cracking since the ice can expand upwards and outwards as it freezes. Ponds of the same size that have vertical walls provide a larger area of deep water, which may be important if you plan to keep fish. Construction is more laborious than for a pond with sloping sides as the wet concrete has to be supported with timber shuttering until it hardens (see below).

Construction

When digging the hole for a concrete pond, add an extra 15cm (6in) to all dimensions to allow for the volume occupied by the cement; if there is to be a shelf for marginal plants, see "Flexible liners, Installation", p.250. Line the hole with 500 gauge plastic sheeting, then spread 5cm (2in) of concrete over the base. For added strength, place a sheet of galvanized wire reinforcing mesh over this and cover with a second 5cm (2in) layer of concrete. When the concrete has slightly hardened, roughen the surface around the edge to a width of 15cm (6in) to form a firm grip for the side walls.

After about 48 hours, or when the base is dry, install vertical wooden shuttering 10cm (4in) in from the sides, bracing it at the corners. Thoroughly soak the shuttering with water, slide a piece of galvanized wire mesh between the shuttering and the sides of the hole, then pour in the concrete. If a walled, marginal shelf is required, this shuttering will need to be higher (see below). Leave the shuttering for about two days to allow the concrete to dry out thoroughly. For a marginal shelf, repeat the procedure with another two stages as for the main body of the pool. Remove a band of soil around the pool edge to a depth of 8cm (3in); lay hardcore in this area as a base for the edging stones.

A few days later, apply a sealant that prevents lime in the concrete from leaching out into the water and harming the plants and fish. Finally, fill the pool and check the alkalinity of the water with a pH test kit. If close to neutral (pH7) it is safe to introduce plants, and, after a further two weeks, fish. If alkaline, this may be due to hard mains water or ineffective sealant. In either case, delay planting water lilies and marginals for a few weeks as the pH will gradually become more neutral. Oxygenators and surface-floaters generally tolerate alkaline water, and may therefore be included sooner.

Raised pools

The walls of raised pools must be strong enough to resist the pressure of the water; if necessary, seek professional help. They are more vulnerable to frost damage than sunken pools, and a minimum depth of 60cm (24in) is needed for fish.

Construction

The best way to construct a raised pool is with double walls, similar to house cavity walls. The exterior wall

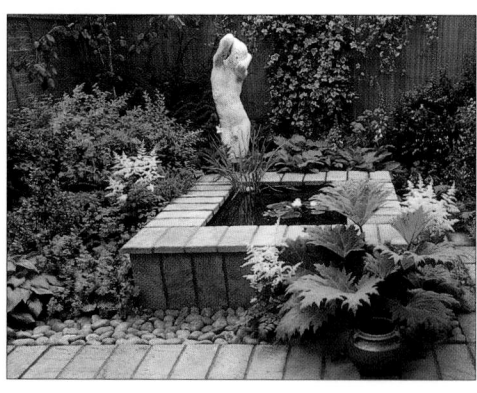

can be made from walling stones or bricks. The interior wall, which will be hidden, can be constructed with a cheaper brick or walling stone. The walls need to be close enough together to be linked with proprietary, wire wall ties. A flexible liner is used inside the interior wall.

Mark out the required shape with string and pegs, then construct concrete footings (see *How to Make a Concrete Footing*, p.504) 10–15cm (4–6in) deep and 38cm (15in) wide for the walls. Rake over the base, remove sharp stones, and cover with a layer of fine sand or polyester matting. Then construct the double side walls, incorporating wire ties at intervals to link the walls.

Lining a raised pool

The liner may be fitted so that an attractive stone or brick surface is exposed above the water on the inner wall. Extra liner will be needed (about 1m/1yd on width and length). Before laying the top two courses, fit the liner in the pool then over the inner wall and into the cavity of the double wall. The top two courses should then be mortared in place, securing the liner; the surplus liner is then taken around behind the top

two courses and tucked back under the coping. No liner is visible at the water's edge, and therefore no white "tide lines" appear on black liners when the water level drops in summer; it also ensures that no leakage occurs through the stone. Cut off any surplus liner and mortar the coping stones on top of the double wall.

Using a liner to make a watercourse

Watercourses may be constructed to meander over small changes in level, or to be faster moving over a steeper gradient with several falls and a pool at the bottom. The proposed route of the watercourse should be marked out and the position and depth of the height changes noted. Use flexible liners for a natural appearance.

If the water movement is powered by a pump, the outlet for the proposed watercourse, usually a header pool, must contain enough water not to show major variations in level when the pump is turned on and off. One unobtrusive way of creating an outlet is with an underground header pool lined with a flexible liner. Cover

---

CONSTRUCTING A CONCRETE POND WITH VERTICAL WALLS

MAKING THE POND
Line the pond area with plastic sheeting. Build the pond in stages, allowing the concrete to set at each stage. Lay the base first, using reinforcing wire mesh between 2 layers of concrete. Once set, install vertical shuttering braced at the corners, insert mesh between the pond wall and shuttering, and pour in concrete. Repeat the process for a marginal shelf.

Galvanized wire reinforcing mesh

Concrete

Polythene

Concrete

Hardcore base for edging stones

Shuttering

MAKING A WALLED MARGINAL SHELF
A walled marginal shelf allows direct planting. Proceed as before, making the vertical shuttering higher to retain at least 23cm (9in) of soil (left). Once set, concrete the base of the shelf as before and then the outer shelf wall. After the concrete has set, lay the edging stones so that they will overlap the water by about 5cm (2in). Apply sealant and fill the marginal shelf with soil. Plant up and then fill the pool with water (right).

the pool with a sturdy mesh and place a layer of rocks and cobbles on top of it; the water pours out between the rocks into the watercourse.

As well as the flexible liner, non-porous rock is needed to mask the watercourse edges and to create the waterfalls, while small pebbles or cobbles make an attractive addition to the base of the watercourse.

Amount of liner required for the watercourse

The route, dimensions, and changes of level in the watercourse are the factors that determine how much lining material will be required.

If the route is fairly straight, one piece of liner may be used. This should be the maximum width plus twice the depth by the length of the watercourse, allowing for any changes in height between the top and bottom, plus about 15cm (6in) at either end of the course so that it can overlap into the header and base pools. A twisting watercourse is best made from a succession of liner pieces, each overlapping the next by 15cm (6in) to avoid unwieldy folds and excessive wastage. Allow for these overlaps when calculating the amount of liner needed.

Construction

Make a bank of soil slightly larger than the dimensions of the watercourse, with the highest point where the header pool or water source will be and the lowest point adjacent to the base pool. Then mark the outline on the soil. Starting from the lowest point, cut steps into the bank to form the falls and cascades; the flatter sections – the "treads" of the steps – should be made with a slight fall in the opposite direction to the water flow so that they are covered by water even when the water supply is turned off. For the header pool, dig a hole at the uppermost point at least 60cm (24in) square and 40cm (16in) deep. Rake the base and remove any sharp stones, then compact the soil with the back of a spade. Spread a layer of polyester matting or similar material over the course. The flexible liner may then be fitted into the channel, allowing approximately 30cm (12in) of liner on either side, which will later form the vertical side walls. If using more than one piece of liner to form the length of the watercourse, overlap the pieces by 15cm (6in). Place the higher piece so that it overlaps the lower one where there is a fall or downwards slope so that water flows away from the join. Dig a channel next to the watercourse for the pipe that will circulate water from the base pool to the header pool (see *Recirculating Water in a Watercourse*, p.254).

Set rocks in place to form the steps and sides of the watercourse, arranging them until the grouping is satisfactory. Lift the liner at the sides behind the rocks and pack soil in to just above the waterline. If plants at the edge are to be included, plant them at this stage in the soil behind the rocks. To provide increased stability, mortar the rocks into position using a waterproof cement.

Using rigid units to make a watercourse

Preformed modular units may be combined in various ways and installed to incorporate falls of different heights. Strong, interlocking units are unlikely to move should any future subsidence of the underlying soil or sand occur. Installation by two people is recommended, as final adjustments in levels may require lifting one side of a unit while sand is backfilled underneath.

Mark out the proposed area with string and dig out the watercourse to accommodate the units. Allow extra depth for a level layer of sand beneath them. Work from the bottom upwards, positioning the lowest unit so that the lip overlaps the base pool

---

MAKING A WATERCOURSE WITH A FLEXIBLE LINER

1 Build a soil bank to the required height and mark the shape of the watercourse. Working from the bottom, shape the steps and header pool.

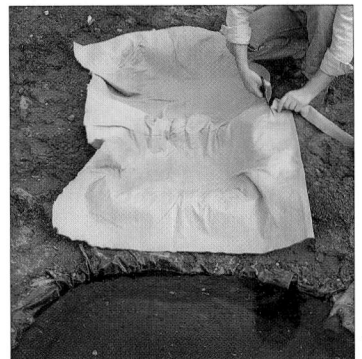

2 When complete, compact the soil with the back of a spade. Remove sharp stones and line the course with a cushioning layer of polyester matting, cutting it to fit.

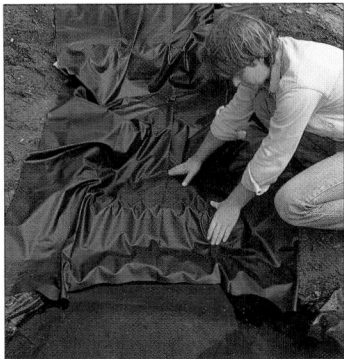

3 Lay the liner in place with the bottom edge overlapping the pool. Cut to fit, leaving 30cm (12in) on each side. Smooth the liner into the contours of the channel.

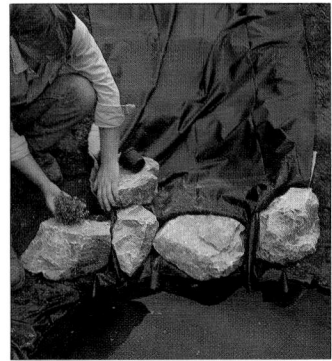

4 Starting at the base, set rocks in place to form the steps. To prevent water escaping, tuck in the edges of the liner behind the rocks. Backfill firmly with soil.

5 Continue working upwards, arranging rocks and pebbles to form the falls and sides of the watercourse. Ensure that the sides are sufficiently steep to prevent water escaping.

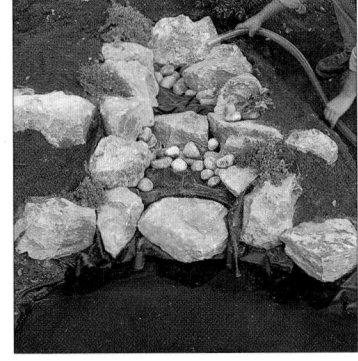

6 Position plants in the crevices between rocks to soften the edges of the watercourse. Bury the water pipe alongside so that it overhangs the header pool.

7 Disguise the end of the pipe with strategically placed pebbles. Finish off the construction with a 2.5cm (1in) layer of decorative gravel around the edges of the watercourse to create an attractive, natural setting. Check that the water flows at the correct rate and with the desired effect. Adjust the position of the rocks if necessary before finally cementing them in.

and ensuring that it is level. Remove it and bolt on a vertical plate that determines the height of the water-fall. To ensure watertight joins, use a silicon sealant around each bolt. Install the linked units, making any final adjustments by backfilling or removing excess sand so that they are level. Once the first unit is level, a small amount of water may be added to increase stability.

The following units, and the final header pool, are then bolted on in the same way. Once each is attached and the levels checked, partially fill it with water and backfill with sand around the outside edges as before. Conceal the edges of the watercourse with rocks and plants.

Circulating the water

To circulate water from the bottom pool to the header pool in a water-course, link the two pools with a flexible pipe attached to a pump. The pipe may be pushed well down into the header pool to hide it; in this case, a non-return valve should be fitted. Alternatively, keep the end of the pipe above the water surface and disguise it at the pool edge with an overlapping stone or slab. Sink the pipe in a trench alongside the stream and cover it with thin pieces of stone to protect it from being pierced.

Pumps and filtration

Two types of pump are available for garden use: surface-mounted and submersible models. For most small installations involving a fountain or watercourse, a submersible pump is quite adequate. Larger installations may require a surface-mounted pump that is housed in a separate, ventilated chamber.

If using a submersible pump, place it in the base pool, raised on bricks or blocks to help prevent debris from being sucked into the inlet strainer.

RECIRCULATING WATER IN A WATERCOURSE

Raise a submersible pump on blocks on the pond base. Attach a flexible pipe; bring it out to one side and bury it in a trench 25cm (10in) deep and 7cm (3in) wide, next to the pool. Push the other end into the header pool.

Rocks placed to hide pipe

Non-return valve

Water pump

Header pool

Flexible pipe

Cushioning liner

Base pool

If circulating water through a watercourse, connect a pipe to the pump to carry water up to the header pool (see diagram). Only use approved water-proof connectors with pumps and other electrical fitments. Protect outdoor cables with armoured sleeving and always include a residual current device.

Usually there should be no need for filtration. If there are large numbers of fish or if it is difficult to maintain submerged plants, physical or biological filtration may be needed. Filter kits that fit onto the suction inlet of submersible pumps are available, but larger installations may need a biological filter.

MAKING A WATERCOURSE WITH RIGID UNITS

1 *Mark out the watercourse perimeter, prepare the base pool, then remove soil to the dimensions of the units, allowing extra depth for a level base of sand beneath.*

2 *Spread a 1cm (1/2in) layer of sharp sand over the base, then put the first unit in place so that it overlaps the main pool. Check that it is level and backfill with sand around it to provide a firm base.*

3 *Remove the unit and bolt it to a plate that forms the fall. Seal the joins, then install the unit, adding or removing sand as necessary so that it is level. Backfill behind the base of the plate.*

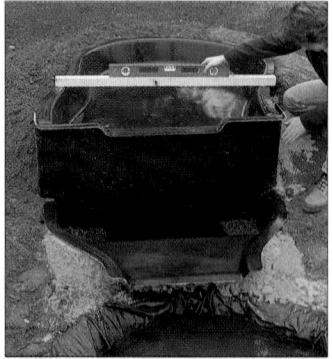

4 *Prepare the base for the header pool, covering it with sand. Bolt the base to the upper part of the plate and seal the joins. Backfill the base with sand so that it is firm and level.*

5 *Install a submersible pump in the main pool, connect a flexible pipe and lay it in a trench alongside the watercourse. Push the other end down into the header pool.*

6 *Fill in the trench with soil. Snap into place the pebbledash cladding. Place stones around the watercourse and pool edge, hiding the pipe where it leaves the main pool and enters the header pool.*

7 *If desired, place stones under the lip of the lowest unit to mask the pool edge. Add plants around the watercourse to enhance and soften its rigidity. Some units include integral shelves to accommodate marginal plants. Fill the header pool with water, then turn on the pump.*

Planting and stocking

W HILE most plants are grown for their ornamental features, some also help to maintain the quality and appearance of water by keeping down algae (see "Plants for the water garden", p.246). There is a wide range of planting containers available, allowing flexibility when planting and making routine maintenance relatively simple.

Selecting water plants

When selecting plants, look for clean, fresh-looking, and vigorous specimens, growing in tanks that are free from algae and duckweed (*Wolffia*). Check that the undersides of the leaves are free from jelly-like deposits of snail or whelk eggs, and that there are no strands of blanket-weed in the foliage. Vacuum-packed plants should appear plump and green; if they look weak and limp they are unlikely to grow well.

If buying plants by mail order, use a specialist supplier. It is worth paying a slightly higher price since the plants are more likely to be clean and disease-free, and to have been propagated in the nursery. Reputable suppliers should also pack the plants with care, and despatch them on the same day that they are lifted.

When buying oxygenators for a new pool, allow at least five bunches for every square metre or yard of water surface. They are generally sold as bunches of unrooted cuttings about 23cm (9in) long, and they should be weighted at the bottom with a piece of lead to keep the plants anchored, in case they become loosened after planting.

Since oxygenators are extremely susceptible to drying out, they should be kept moistened in a plastic bag or submerged in water until they are ready for planting in the pond.

PLANTING BASKETS

Planting baskets are available in various sizes to suit different plants. All except those with a very close-weave mesh should be lined.

STANDARD MESH   CLOSE-WEAVE MESH

SELECTING PLANTS FOR THE WATER GARDEN

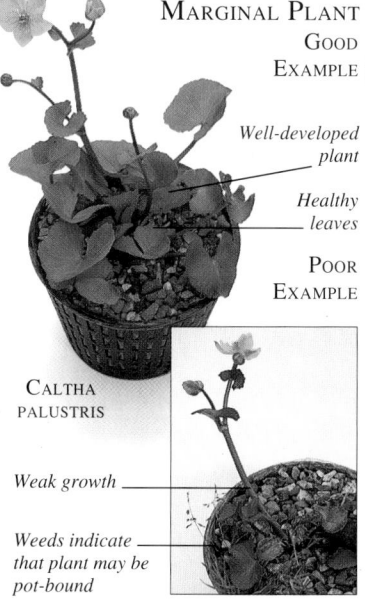

MARGINAL PLANT
GOOD EXAMPLE

Well-developed plant

Healthy leaves

POOR EXAMPLE

CALTHA PALUSTRIS

Weak growth

Weeds indicate that plant may be pot-bound

OXYGENATOR
GOOD EXAMPLE

POTAMOGETON CRISPUS

POOR EXAMPLE

Healthy, vigorous growth

Limp, tired stems

SURFACE-FLOATER
GOOD EXAMPLE

Young, fresh growth

POOR EXAMPLE

STRATIOTES ALOIDES

Damaged growth

Old, rotting foliage

Containers and planting beds

The most convenient way of growing aquatics is in purpose-made baskets or crates. This makes it easy to lift and divide or replace the plants when necessary, and it is also a relatively simple matter to alter the planting arrangement when desired.

Proprietary containers
Aquatic containers have wide, flat bases to provide stability in the water, which is important for tall marginals on narrow shelves. Containers have open lattice walls, allowing water and gases to circulate through the soil. Most should be lined with close-weave polypropylene sheeting or hessian to prevent the soil from seeping out, although very fine-mesh containers that eliminate the need for a liner are also available.

Crates and containers range in size from 28cm (11in) in diameter with a 10 litre (2¼ gallon) capacity, suitable for medium-sized water lilies, down to 4cm (1½in) in diameter with a 50ml (2fl oz) capacity, for aquarium planting. Larger, circular tubs without lattice walls are also available for vigorous water lilies.

Planting directly in soil beds
In wildlife ponds, aquatics may be planted directly into a layer of soil on the bottom of the pool and on marginal shelves. In most pools, however, this is inadvisable since the vigorous species spread rapidly, swamping their slower-growing neighbours. In addition, subsequent removal or thinning out of plants can be extremely difficult.

Permanent beds
A good compromise is to build permanent planting pockets or beds on the base of the pool and around the edges during construction, which are easily planted up before the pool is filled (see also "Making planting beds", p.251). This makes it possible to maintain a natural appearance while controlling the plants' spread.

Planting

The pool should be filled with water a few days before planting to allow the water temperature to reach that of the surrounding air, and to "mature". During this period the water in the pool may become populated with micro-organisms that disperse impurities in the water and create an environment most beneficial to plants, fish, and other pond life.

Unlike the majority of terrestrial plants, aquatics should be planted while in active growth, preferably between late spring and mid-summer when water temperatures are warm and there is plenty of sunlight. If planted in late summer and early autumn, the plants have little time to become established before they die down. Water lilies must have time to build up food reserves before winter if they are to survive and grow satisfactorily the following season.

The planting medium
Aquatic plants grow quite happily in good garden soil, preferably a heavy loam; if possible, use soil that has not been fertilized or manured recently. Sieve out any loose organic matter as this will rot or float when the planting crate is submerged.

Proprietary composts made for terrestrial plants should not be used for aquatics; as well as peat, which tends to float, they contain added fertilizers, which will encourage the growth of algae (see p.258). A handful of coarse bone meal mixed into the soil in a large planting crate is all the fertilizer required. If the suitability of the garden soil is in any doubt, use a prepared aquatic compost from a specialist supplier.

Planting depths
The ideal planting depth varies, depending on the type of plant, and can differ even within a given group of plants. Planting depths should be

measured from the top of the soil in the crate or planting pocket to the water surface (see right).

It is important not to plant too deeply: without adequate sunlight for photosynthesis, plants will die. When planting young specimens, it may be necessary to stand the containers on bricks or blocks at first so that the plants are not completely submerged. As the plants grow, gradually lower the crates until they reach the appropriate depth.

Bog and moisture-loving plants

The area bordering a natural pool is ideal for bog and moisture-loving plants, but correct growing conditions can be supplied next to a man-made pond by creating special beds.

Mark out the planting beds, then dig out at least 45cm (18in) depth of soil, removing any roots of perennial weeds such as couch grass. Form sloping sides at the edges. Drape a flexible liner (thick-gauge plastic sheeting is suitable for this purpose) into the hole, ensuring that the top edge of the liner finishes just below the existing soil level.

Although a number of vigorous, moisture-loving plants tolerate saturated soil, most of them will grow better if the liner is pierced to allow some slow seepage of water from the bed. This slight movement of water through the soil also helps to prevent stagnant conditions from developing. Cover the drainage holes with gravel so that they do not become clogged up with soil.

Simplify watering in summer by sinking a perforated, rigid pipe into the bed. The pipe should be blocked at the far end and covered with a layer of gravel or stones to prevent the holes from becoming blocked with soil. Fit the end of the pipe to a hose connector, which should remain above the soil surface.

Refill the bed with soil, and then mulch with a deep layer of coarsely sieved organic matter to help prevent moisture loss. Do not incorporate bulky additives throughout the whole bed as sufficient moisture is retained by the liner.

Planting, which is best done in spring, is carried out in the same way as in ordinary soil, although the whole bed should be thoroughly soaked afterwards. Plants which enjoy these moist conditions will grow vigorously, so very invasive

PLANTING DEPTHS

Place plants at the appropriate depth for the species, measured from the top of the soil to the water's surface. When planting young water lilies (Nymphaea), raise the crates on bricks. Lower the crates as the plants grow.

species are best confined to sunken containers to prevent them from crowding out other plants.

Marginal plants

Primarily included for their ornamental flowers or foliage, marginal plants are grown at the pool edges with their roots in shallow water. Ornamental pools usually include a shelf to accommodate marginal plants, which may either be grown in baskets or in pockets built directly onto the shelf (see also "Making planting beds", p.251).

Most marginals require approximately 8–15cm (3–6in) of water above their crowns; it may be necessary to raise the planting baskets to ensure that the plants are at the correct depth until they are established. The more vigorous species, known as deep marginals, should be planted in 30cm (12in) or more of water, either on a deeper shelf or on the bottom, away from the margin.

When planting marginals, take into account their height, spread, and vigour. Plant rampant growers singly in containers to stop them smothering slower-growing plants. If planting in containers, always make sure that there is sufficient

room for root development; for most marginals, a container at least 23cm (9in) in diameter is necessary. Plant marginals in prepared containers or planting beds of loam and top-dress with pea shingle; if using containers, place them on the marginal shelf or the bottom of the pond, as appropriate, so that the plants are at the correct depth.

Deep-water plants

As with marginals, these plants are usually grown in aquatic containers or planting beds. Most of them are best planted fairly shallowly at first so that their leaves are able to float on the surface of the water and photosynthesize in the sun.

Whether planting in beds or free-standing containers, settle the plants firmly in the soil as they are very buoyant and may be dislodged. Always plant in moist soil, and soak containers well before immersing them in the pool. A top-dressing of small gravel or pea shingle to a depth of 2.5cm (1in) prevents soil from floating out and clouding the water and discourages fish from disturbing the plant roots.

When submerging the containers in deep water, thread string through

PLANTING A BOG PLANT

1 *In the prepared bed, dig a hole sufficiently wide and deep to accommodate the root ball of the plant.*

2 *While supporting the plant (here Caltha palustris) with one hand, gently ease the root ball out of the container, taking care not to damage the roots.*

3 *Place the plant in the hole so that it is at the correct depth; the soil should always reach the same level as it was in the container.*

4 *Using your hands, thoroughly firm the soil all around the crown of the plant. Soak the whole area with water.*

Surface floaters

With a new planting, include some surface-floating plants to discourage the growth of algae. When the ornamental plants become more established, some of the floaters should be removed. In a large pond, a line may be drawn across the pond from both ends to bring plants within reach. Duckweeds in particular are very persistent, so choose less vigorous species.

Surface-floating plants have no anchorage as their roots obtain nutrients directly from the water. Their initial positioning is unimportant as the groups are moved around on the surface by wind.

Surface-floating plants (here Stratiotes aloides) may be placed on the water's surface; in warm weather they multiply rapidly, giving valuable surface shade.

Planting oxygenators

Incorporating oxygenating plants is one of the first priorities when planting in a new pool. This is because their cleaning and oxygenating properties are vital to the health of the fish population and the oxygen content of the water.

Keep the plants wet after purchasing them and until they are ready to plant. Even during the planting process, they should not be left exposed to the air longer than is absolutely necessary.

Species vary in the effectiveness with which they oxygenate the water, depending on the time of year and the pH of the water, so plant a selection of four or five species to ensure that enough plants thrive to maintain correct oxygen levels throughout the year. Keep only a single species in each container to prevent stronger-growing plants from crowding out less vigorous species.

Prepare a planting crate and make planting holes in the soil, then insert bunches of cuttings into the holes and firm them in. Cover the soil with grit or pea shingle, water thoroughly, and place the crate on the bottom of the prepared pond at a depth of 45–60cm (18–24in).

1 Line a crate and almost fill with damp compost, then firm. Make planting holes and insert bunches of cuttings (here Lagarosiphon major).

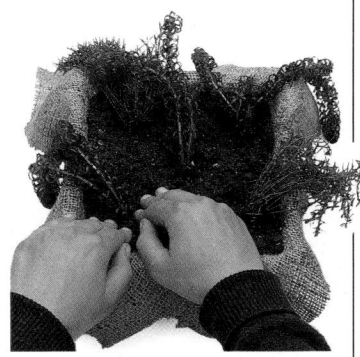

2 Firm in the plants. Trim off excess liner, top-dress with 1–2.5cm (¹/₂–1in) pea shingle, and lower the crate into the pond.

the sides to form handles; this makes it much easier to position the crate, as it may then be gradually lowered onto the bottom.

Stocking with fish

Like water plants, fish are best introduced to the pool during the warmer months. In cooler temperatures, fish become semi-dormant and are more prone to stress when moved. Allow at least two weeks after planting before stocking with fish to allow plant roots to establish.

Unless there is supplementary filtration, overstocking with fish may encourage algae which feed on excess waste. As a guide, calculate a maximum of 50cm (20in) of fish body length (when fully grown) per square metre or yard of water surface or 5cm (2in) per 1,000sq cm (1sq ft). It is advisable to stock the pool in two stages, introducing half the fish eight to ten weeks before the rest. This allows the bacteria that feed on the fish waste products to multiply to a sufficient level to deal with the waste. If too many are introduced at once, the water may become polluted and the fish starved of oxygen. Leaving a fountain or waterfall on overnight to agitate the water will provide temporary relief.

Fish are usually supplied in a large, clear plastic bag containing a small amount of water and inflated with oxygen. On arrival, do not release the fish straight into the pond: they are very sensitive to sudden changes in temperature, and the water in the pond is likely to be colder than that in the bag. Float the bag unopened on the water until the water temperature in the bag is the same as in the pool. In hot, sunny weather, shade the bag with newspaper. A small amount of pool water may be gradually introduced into the bag before the fish are released. Do not lift the bag to examine the fish closely as this causes them extreme stress.

Other water creatures

As well as fish, a number of other aquatic life forms may be introduced to the pond as scavengers. Ramshorn snails are often sold specifically for this purpose, and in the USA *Viviparus maniatus* performs the same function. Ordinary pond snails are likely to be a nuisance as they eat water lily leaves. Mussels, and in particular the swan mussel, are excellent scavengers, cleaning up where ornamental fish have been overfed. Mussels require deep water that remains cool even in the height of summer.

PLANTING DEEP-WATER AND MARGINAL PLANTS

1 Choose a planting crate to accommodate the plant roots and line it with hessian or close-weave polypropylene.

2 Fill the crate with heavy, moist loam to a depth of at least 5cm (2in). Set the plant (here Aponogeton distachyos) in the centre of the crate.

3 Fill with more loam to within 1cm (¹/₂in) of the rim of the crate, firming the plant in well to give it good anchorage.

4 Top-dress the container with washed gravel or pea shingle to a depth of 2.5cm (1in).

5 Trim away any surplus liner with scissors. Tie string "handles" to the rim of the crate on opposite sides.

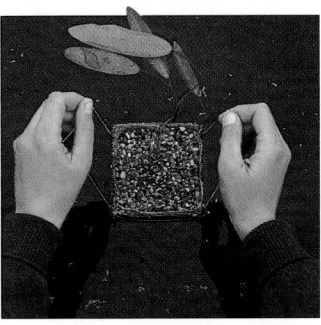

6 Hold the crate by the string handles and gently lower it onto blocks or the marginal shelf. Release the handles.

ADDING FISH TO A POND

Float the unopened bag until the water temperature in the bag matches that of the pond. Slowly introduce some pond water to the bag before gently releasing the fish.

Routine care

Good construction and siting and ensuring the right balance of water, plants, and fish should help to keep a pond relatively trouble-free, but occasionally structural repairs may be necessary, if the pool is damaged or leaks, for example. Algae and weeds must also be kept in check, while many plants will benefit from periodic division.

Structural repairs

Any sudden or persistent loss of water is likely to indicate a leak. If a pool is leaking, it will be necessary to drain and inspect it. Accommodate the fish and plants in a suitable container, such as a paddling pool.

Most ponds may be drained either with an electric pump or by siphoning off the water. Check first that the pond's edges are level; water may be overflowing at the lowest point. With a watercourse, switch off the pump and check the level in the base pool: if constant, the leak is in the watercourse.

REPAIRING A FLEXIBLE POND LINER

1 *Dry the area of damaged liner and then clean it carefully with methylated spirits and a soft cloth.*

2 *Apply special double-sided adhesive sealing tape over the tear and allow it to become "tacky".*

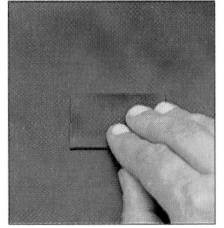

3 *Cut out a patch from spare liner and press it firmly onto the adhesive, ensuring that the edges are stuck down flat.*

Flexible liners
If the water level in a lined pool drops or the flow of water in a watercourse decreases, check that no part of the edge of the liner has slipped below water level. Leaks may also be caused by punctures. The simplest way to repair a butyl liner is with double-sided adhesive tape obtainable from water garden suppliers. This is used to secure a patch of butyl liner over the hole. The pool may be refilled after one hour.

Preformed pools and units
If a pool or watercourse unit is inadequately supported or the ground underneath it is not properly consolidated, it may eventually crack under the weight of the water. Repair cracks with a fibreglass repair kit as used for car bodies and boat hulls. Allow the compound to harden thoroughly as it may be toxic when fluid. Before refilling with water, ensure that the base is firmly bedded down and that soil is compacted around the sides to support the water pressure.

With rigid, interlocking units, check the sealant around the bolts and reseal if necessary.

Concrete pools
The most common cause of leaking is through cracks created by frost damage or subsidence. Inspect the pool carefully as water can escape through even a hairline crack. If the crack is very fine it is usually necessary to widen it slightly and brush clean any loose debris before sealing it with mortar. Leave the mortar to dry, then paint it with sealant.

Water quality

Once a balance of plants and animal life is established, the water should remain clear without needing further attention. If there are marked changes in the numbers of fish or plants, or if there is a sudden introduction of mains or flood water, however, the water balance may be upset and a surge of harmless, but unsightly, algal growth may result.

Algae
Algae depend on sunlight, carbon dioxide, and dissolved mineral salts for their survival. Reduce the amount of light that they receive by growing sufficient plants (water lilies, deep-water aquatics, and floaters) so that their floating leaves cover between 50 and 70 per cent of the water surface. The introduction of oxygenating plants, which are efficient at absorbing minerals and carbon dioxide, helps starve out the algae. In addition, take care to keep down the amount of organic matter in the pool by regularly removing dead and decaying leaves and flowers.

Green water due to algal growth may occur in a newly planted pool, or one that has recently been cleaned out. Normally this problem clears itself within a short time.

If the water is persistently cloudy, even with adequate populations of surface and submerged leaves, it may be necessary to use an algicide or, in very acid water, to alter the pH; the latter should be done gradually, adding small quantities of ground limestone weekly until the water is neutral. For a small pond with a surface area of 4 sq m (40 sq ft) or less, introduce no more than 110 g (4 oz) of ground limestone at any one application.

Blanketweed
A filamentous form of algae called blanketweed (*Spirogyra*) is sometimes found in pools with otherwise clear water; if left unchecked, it chokes the plants and restricts the free movement of fish. Remove periodically by winding it onto a stick or lifting it out with a garden rake; in severe cases use an algicide.

REMOVING BLANKETWEED

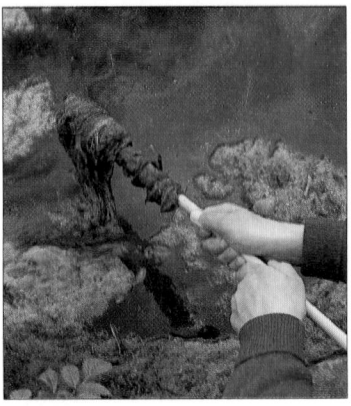

Insert a stick into the mass of blanketweed (Spirogyra) and twist it. The weed wraps around the stick and may then be pulled free.

REPAIRING A CRACK IN A CONCRETE POND

1 *If a crack is very fine, use a club hammer and chisel to widen it slightly.*

2 *Clean off any algae and debris from the surrounding area with a wire brush.*

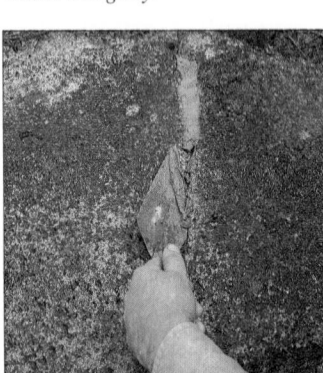

3 *With a trowel, fill the crack with mortar or a proprietary sealing compound. Allow it to dry.*

4 *Brush with a pool sealing compound to prevent any toxins leaching out into the water.*

THINNING OUT AN OVERGROWN OXYGENATOR

1 In spring or autumn, thin out overgrown submerged plants, either by "combing" them off the water's surface with a rake, or by lifting out the basket and trimming back with a sharp knife.

2 Thinning out oxygenating plants prevents them from becoming congested. Do not remove too much growth, however, since this may leave the pond's surface area too exposed to sunlight, and allow algae to proliferate. Oxygenators are best thinned little and often.

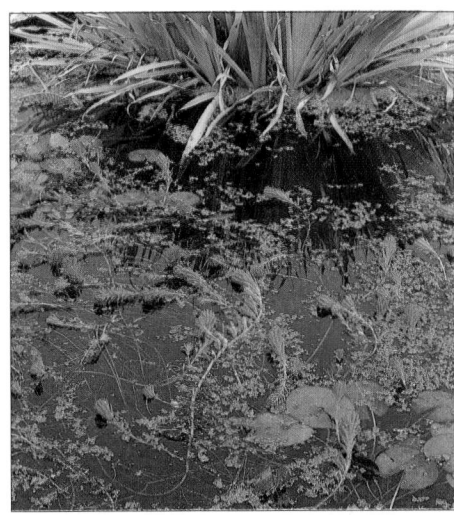

Clear out the dead material quickly, since decaying matter will reduce the water's oxygen content.

Pond cleaning
If the water is kept clear of fallen leaves and the plants are regularly trimmed, it should only be necessary to clean the pond every few years to remove decaying organic matter from the base. After cleaning, the water chemistry must again be carefully balanced.

Plant care and control

Water plants do not require much attention, but periodic division and repotting helps to keep them healthy and attractive. Their overall vigour normally makes it necessary for them to be kept in check rather than

encouraged, although certain water lily cultivars will require some feeding (see p.248).

Thinning out and division
In late spring or early autumn thin out or divide plants that are overgrown or crowding their neighbours. Lift container-grown plants and check whether they have become root-bound. If so, remove the plants from their containers and divide them with back-to-back forks or by hand. Tight and thick roots may need to be split with a spade or a knife. Replant the divided clumps singly.

After the first growing season, submerged oxygenating plants may become overgrown and entangled with weeds. In small pools, the oxygenators are easily thinned by pulling out a few handfuls; in larger ponds, use a garden rake to comb out

excess growth. Alternatively, lift the container from the pool and cut back the plants by one third to a half. Do not thin out all the plants drastically at any one time since this causes a sudden change in the water balance and encourages algal growth.

Autumn maintenance

The most important task in autumn is to keep the water free from decaying vegetation. When the waterside plants begin to die down, remove dead and dying foliage regularly and prune back the excess growth of submerged plants. If there are deciduous trees and shrubs nearby, cover the surface of the pool with a fine-mesh plastic net to catch fallen leaves, and keep it in place until the trees are bare of foliage.

In winter, float a ball on the water. When ice forms, pour boiling water over the ball and remove it, then cover the hole with a sack. In a thaw, remove the sack and replace the ball.

In cold areas, protect tender plants by removing them from the pool and placing them in a bucket of water in a frost-free place to overwinter. Cut off the ripe seed pods of invasive plants to prevent them from setting seed. Feed the fish before they go into hibernation for the winter.

If a pump is fitted, remove it from the pool and clean it thoroughly. Replace any parts that may be worn, and store it in a dry place until spring.

Winter care

In winter, ice may form, trapping methane gas released by submerged, decaying vegetation, with potentially lethal effects on the fish. Ice also exerts pressure on the sides of concrete pools as it expands and may cause them to crack. Ensuring that a small area of the pool remains ice-free prevents this and allows methane to escape into the air. Either float a ball on the surface or use a floating electric pool heater. This gives out just enough heat to maintain a small area of open water.

Pests and diseases

Pests are less of a problem in a pool stocked with fish, since the fish eat the insect larvae. Any infestations can be cleared by hand or washed off plants with a hosepipe; insecticide sprays are unsuitable for water gardens and are highly toxic to fish. In late summer, aphids (p.550) often attack the aerial parts of water lilies and other aquatics, causing discoloration and decay. Dislodge them with a jet of water or submerge the leaves for 24 hours, weighting down affected parts with sacking.

Diseases affecting aquatic plants are relatively few, and mostly concern water lilies. Fungal disease is indicated by the premature yellowing or spotting of the leaves. If the symptoms persist, treat the plant with copper fungicide in a separate tank.

REPOTTING A MARGINAL

1 Plants that are growing in containers will eventually become root-bound and need thinning out. Roots protruding through the container wall indicate that a plant should be divided and repotted. The plant shown here is Iris pseudacorus.

2 Remove the plant from its container and divide it into smaller clumps, teasing the roots out by hand. Very tightly packed roots may be prised apart with hand forks used back-to-back.

3 Repot each clump in a separate container filled with damp soil. Water well and top-dress with grit or pea shingle before placing in the pool. Trim off surplus hessian with scissors.

259

Propagation

Most water plants, especially marginals, may be propagated by division. Other methods are also used, depending on the type of plant: many submerged oxygenators and some creeping marginals, for example, are propagated by cuttings, while a number of floating plants naturally produce runners, plantlets, or turions, which grow into new plants. Moisture-loving species that grow around the pool edge, as well as some aquatics, may be raised from seed or increased by division.

Cuttings are best taken and plants divided in spring or early summer, when high temperatures and long daylight hours provide excellent conditions for new plant growth.

WATER PLANTS THAT MAY BE PROPAGATED BY SOFTWOOD CUTTINGS

Bacopa monnieri
Cabomba caroliniana ✸
Callitriche hermaphroditica
Ceratophyllum demersum
Decodon verticillatus
Egeria densa ✸
Hydrilla verticillata
Hydrocleys parviflora ✸
Hygrophila polysperma ✸
Lagarosiphon major
Limnophila heterophylla
Ludwigia arcuata
Myriophyllum, some ✸
Potamogeton crispus
Tillaea recurva
Trapa natans

WATER PLANTS THAT MAY BE DIVIDED

Tubers
Aponogeton distachyos
Colocasia esculenta ✸
Nelumbo nucifera ✸
Zantedeschia, some ✸

Rootstock
Acorus calamus
Butomus umbellatus
Calla palustris
Caltha palustris

Caltha palustris 'Flore Plena'

Cryptocoryne ciliata ✸
Damasonium alisma
Decodon verticillatus
Eriophorum angustifolium

KEY
✸ *Not hardy*

Division

A large number of marginal plants may be readily propagated by division. The exact technique that should be used depends on both the plant's root system and its pattern of growth. For further information, see "Dividing perennials", p.164.

Plants with fibrous or creeping roots

Plants that have extensive fibrous or creeping roots, such as *Typha latifolia*, may be divided by levering apart the rootstocks. Simply pull the rootstocks apart with your hands; if the roots are tightly compacted, use two garden forks positioned back-to-back and lever apart.

Each divided portion should include a growing point (a horizontally placed, terminal shoot). Cut off the old, brown roots and remove any dead leaves. Trim the new roots before replanting the divided portions in individual containers. Level the soil with the base of the shoots. Firm them in, then top-dress lightly with a layer of gravel. Cover the container with approximately 5–8cm (2–3in) of water.

Butomus umbellatus may be divided but may also be propagated from bulbils that form in the axils of the leaves. These are separated and then grown on individually (see LILIES, *Propagating from Stem Bulbils*, p.243).

Rhizomatous plants

For plants with strong, rhizomatous roots, such as irises, pull apart the root mass and divide it into sections with a sharp knife, each containing at least one bud and preferably some young roots. Cut off any long roots and trim back the foliage, if needed. Do not trim the foliage back to below the water line since the newly cut surface tissue may begin to rot.

Plant the division in a suitable container, firming the soil around the roots but leaving the rhizome itself almost exposed. Cover the soil with a layer of gravel and immerse the crate in the pool so that the roots are covered by about 5–8cm (2–3in) of water. Rhizomatous plants with creeping, surface stems, such as *Calla palustris*, may be lifted and divided into sections, each containing a bud. Replant the sections individually in the same way as other rhizomatous plants.

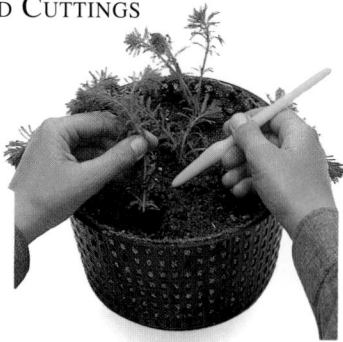

1 *In spring and summer, cut off healthy young shoots (here of* Myriophyllum). *Tie with wire into small bunches of three to six cuttings 10–15cm (4–6in) long.*

2 *Using a dibber, make holes in damp soil in a prepared planting crate lined with hessian. Insert the bunches of cuttings to a depth of about 5cm (2in).*

DIVIDING FIBROUS ROOTSTOCKS

Remove the plant from the container or lift it from the soil with a fork. Insert two forks, placed back-to-back, into the root mass and lever them apart, dividing the plant. Repeat to divide further, then trim and replant the divisions. The plant shown here is Acorus calamus.

DIVIDING RHIZOMATOUS PLANTS

1 *Lift the plant (here* Acorus calamus). *Split the root mass into sections with your hands. Each part should have a good root system and several healthy shoots.*

2 *Use a sharp knife to trim back long roots and foliage by approximately one third to a half of their original length.*

3 *Line a container with hessian and part-fill with damp soil. Plant each division so that the rhizome is just covered with a thin layer of soil.*

Cuttings

Most submerged oxygenating plants may be quite easily propagated by softwood cuttings taken in spring or summer; this process also helps to keep plants in check. Fast-growing oxygenators, for example *Elodea canadensis* and *Potamogeton crispus*, should be regularly replaced by young stock.

Prepare the cuttings by pinching or cutting off healthy, young shoots, inserting them into pots or trays of loam, and submerging them. The cuttings may be inserted individually or tied into small bunches of six. Cuttings of some creeping marginal plants, for example *Mentha aquatica* and water forget-me-nots (*Myosotis scorpioides*), should be inserted singly rather than in bunches. The cuttings establish quickly and may be potted up and planted in position after two to three weeks.

Some tuberous water lilies may also be propagated by cuttings, although a different method is used (see "Bud cuttings", p.249).

Runners and plantlets

Many of the floating plants that are invasive in tropical lakes and rivers propagate themselves by means of runners or plantlets produced on long, adventitious shoots. The water hyacinth (*Eichhornia crassipes*) and *Pistia stratiotes* can populate vast areas of warm water in this way. In shallow water, the young plantlets quickly root into the rich mud at the bottom, drawing up fresh nutrients and sending out yet more runners. The plantlets may simply be snapped off and replaced on the water surface to grow separately.

A dwarf form of the Egyptian paper reed, *Cyperus papyrus* 'Nanus' (syn. *C. papyrus* 'Viviparus'), forms young plantlets in the flowerhead. If the head is bent over and immersed in a container of soil and water the plantlets root and develop; these can be divided and potted up separately.

Turions

Some water plants, for example *Hydrocharis morsus-ranae*, produce swollen buds known as turions that become detached from the parent and survive the winter at the bottom of the pool. In spring these turions rise to the surface of the water again and develop into new plants.

The turions of *Hottonia palustris* develop from the mud in spring without floating to the surface. Since

PROPAGATION OF RUNNERS OR PLANTLETS

1 Some floating plants (*here water hyacinths,* Eichhornia crassipes) *form offsets. In spring, remove an offset from the parent by snapping the connecting stem.*

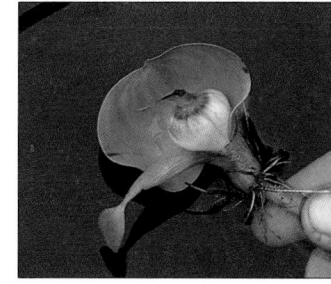

2 *Place the offset directly on the water surface, supporting it gently with your hand until it floats upright.*

these are difficult to collect, wait for them to develop into young plants before lifting and replanting them in their new positions.

The turions may also be collected in autumn and stored in loam in a submerged seed tray covered with 15cm (6in) of water throughout the winter. In spring, when the emerging buds float to the surface, they may be collected and potted up into prepared containers of loam.

Seed

Most moisture-loving plants, and certain of the aquatics, including *Aponogeton distachyos, Euryale ferox, Orontium aquaticum, Trapa natans,* and tropical water lilies (see *Hardy and Tropical Water Lilies,* p.248) may be grown from ripe seed collected in summer or autumn.

Keep the seeds cool and moist until ready to sow. If using dried seeds, germination will be delayed or the seeds may lose viability. Aquatic plant seeds should be grown in submerged or partially submerged

conditions, similar to their natural habitat. When sowing seed, first prepare containers such as seed trays or pans by filling them with an appropriate aquatic compost or garden loam passed through a 7mm (^{1}/$_4$in) sieve. The growing medium should not contain any fertilizers, since they encourage algae, which could smother germinating seedlings.

Sow the seeds on the surface of the growing medium, and then cover them with a shallow layer of fine grit before placing the tray in a large watertight container, such as a plastic bowl or an aquarium. Fill the container with water until the pan is just covered, and leave it on a greenhouse bench in partial shade, or on a well-lit windowsill, at a minimum temperature of 18°C (64°F). The following spring, the seeds should start to germinate.

When the first pair of true leaves appears, carefully prick out the seedlings into individual pots and leave them immersed in water in the greenhouse for another year. Transfer the plants to the pool when the water warms up in spring.

SOWING SEED

1 *Sow the seeds evenly by tapping them from paper onto a pan of firmed aquatic compost or sieved garden loam.*

2 *Cover the seeds with a shallow layer of fine grit. Then place the pan in a large plastic bowl.*

3 *Gradually add water to the bowl so that the pan is just covered. Place in a well-lit position at about 18°C (64°F) until germinated.*

11

CACTI AND OTHER SUCCULENTS

CACTI AND OTHER *succulents display a unique variety of sizes and shapes, and a wealth of colour and texture. Some have plump, smooth surfaces, while others have curved or straight, sometimes colourful spines or a covering of silky hair. Their forms range from the symmetrical rosettes of* Echeveria *to the squat, globular* Echinocactus *and the fluted columns and candelabra of some desert cacti. Many bloom only briefly and bear large, brightly coloured flowers, while others flower for longer* periods, *producing a profusion of exquisite blooms. In cool-temperate climates, most cacti and other succulents are grown in the greenhouse or as house plants, but the hardier species also make beautiful garden displays. In warmer climates, there is scope to create an outdoor desert garden. Whether grown as single specimens or grouped for contrast of form and texture, the diversity of cacti and other succulents, and their tolerance of dry conditions, make them ideal for containers, both indoors and out.*

Designing with cacti and other succulents

MANY cacti are native to the desert regions of the southern USA and Mexico, where rainfall is low and intermittent, and there are great extremes of temperature. In contrast, some of the most floriferous cacti originate in the warm, humid rainforests of Central and South America. These plants are usually epiphytic, which means that they grow on other plants, either weaving through host trees or lodging in niches in their branches.

Other succulent plants occur in a far greater range of habitats than cacti, and, since they are found in at least 20 different plant families, show a wide diversity of characteristics. Their natural habitats include the semi-arid regions of Central America, Africa, and Australasia, as well as the more temperate and cold climates of Asia, and northern parts of Europe and America.

Characteristics of succulents

Cacti and other succulents show a number of adaptations, such as reduced leaf size and loss of leaves in very dry weather, that are designed to conserve water by reducing transpiration. The distinguishing feature that is common to all, however, is the presence of water-storing, fleshy tissue in the stems, leaves, or roots. It is this tissue that allows succulent plants to withstand long periods of drought.

Cacti are easily distinguished from other succulents by structures called areoles – the cushion-like growths on their stems from which the spines, hairs, flowers, and shoots develop.

Succulent plants may be loosely divided into three groups, depending on which part of the plant contains the moisture-retaining tissue. Some genera, for example *Euphorbia*, may be represented in more than one group. Most cacti are stem succulents, as are some succulent plants from the Asclepiadaceae and Euphorbiaceae families. Others, including *Aloe, Echeveria, Lithops,* and *Sedum,* are leafy succulents. Plants in the third group are known as caudiciform succulents and have the water-storing tissue in a swollen rootstock (the caudex), although this often extends into the stem, as in *Adenium obesum.* Plants that belong to this group are mostly found in the families Apocynaceae, Cucurbitaceae, and Convolvulaceae.

Form and habit

The diverse forms and growth characteristics of cacti and other succulent plants may be used to create a range of effects. The tall

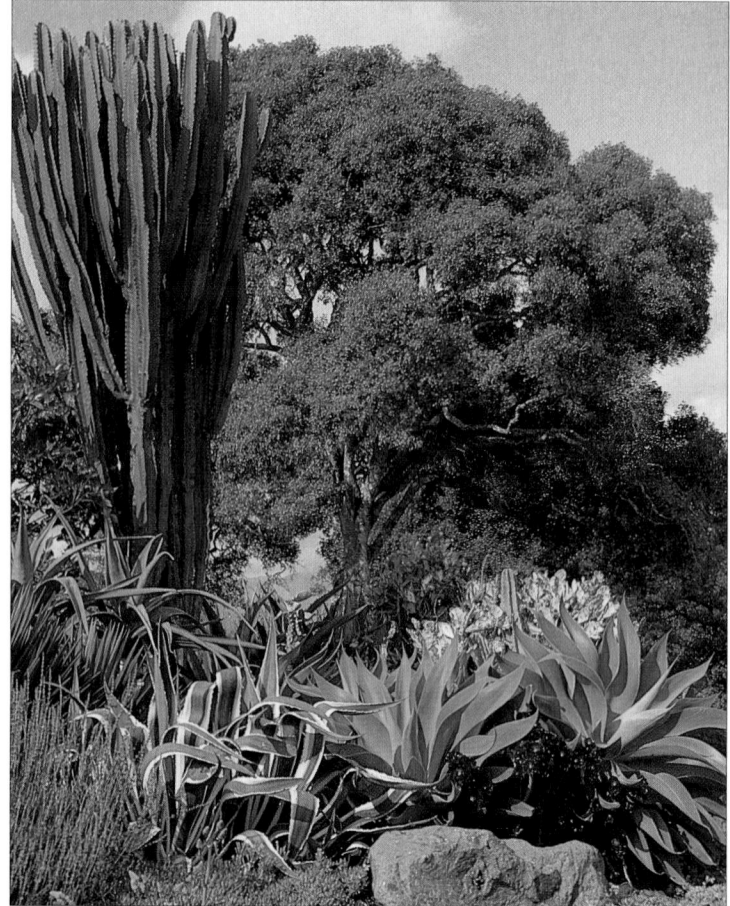

A NATURAL GROUPING
Collections of succulent plants make an impressive sight. Here Euphorbia canariensis *towers above* Agave americana 'Variegata' *and* A. attenuata.

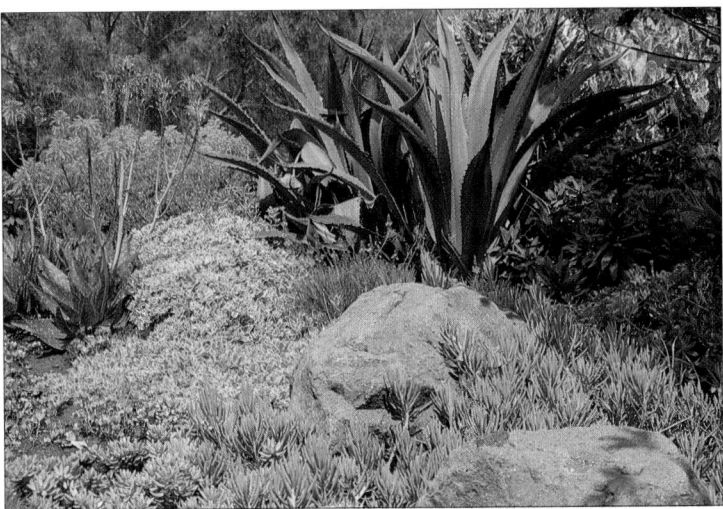

VARIETY OF FORM
The strong, architectural leaves of Agave americana *(centre) make a fine contrast with the orange flower spikes of the* Aloe *species (left) and the prostrate, blue-grey leaves of a* Senecio *cultivar in the foreground.*

FLOWERING SUCCULENTS

Ferocactus setispinus

Oroya neoperuviana

Parodia chrysacanthion

Strombocactus disciformis

Lithops pseudotruncatella* var. *pulmonuncula

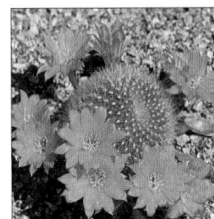

Rebutia muscula

columns of *Cleistocactus strausii*, for example, make strong, vertical lines that contrast with foreground plantings of smaller, spherical forms, such as *Echinocactus grusonii*, or the characteristically flattened segments of some *Opuntia* species.

Several species have a creeping habit that adds a horizontal element to the design. *Carpobrotus edulis*, for instance, as well as *Lampranthus* and *Ruschia* species, make dense carpets of growth that provide excellent ground cover.

Trailing succulent plants, for example *Ceropegia woodii* and *Schlumbergera* and *Rhipsalis* species, produce cascades of slender stems or leaves that are seen to best effect in hanging baskets. A number are scrambling climbers: *Aloe ciliaris* and *Selenicereus* species add height to mixed plantings if given the support of trellis or the branch of a tree. In warm, frost-free climates, the jointed and climbing stems of *Hylocereus* species are most effective when sprawling over walls.

Flowering cacti and other succulents

Cacti and other succulents often produce exquisite blooms and will flower regularly once they reach maturity, although this may take between one and 40 years. Most are day-blooming, with individual blossoms sometimes lasting for several days. Some epiphytic cacti are winter-flowering and have blooms that are carried in succession over long periods.

Others bloom only briefly, however, the flowers sometimes appearing soon after sunset and fading as evening advances. Many of the large, columnar cacti produce buds that gradually unfold during the evening and then fade in the early morning hours.

The flowers, often of delicate appearance and silken texture, are usually exceptionally large in comparison with the size of the plant, and their colour range is mainly at the warm end of the spectrum with a profusion of rich yellows, hot scarlets, and vivid carmines. A number of genera, often those of the family Mesembryanthemaceae, and some of the epiphytes, have sweetly scented blooms. Some species, especially members of the Agavaceae, are monocarpic, that is they die after flowering and setting seed. A number of small, non-flowering offsets are often formed around the flowering rosette, however, and these flower in subsequent years.

Outdoor display

With careful selection and skilful arrangement, attractive collections of cacti and other succulents may be grown outdoors even in relatively cool conditions. Few succulents, however, tolerate excess moisture; even the hardy species require good drainage – these grow well in raised beds where water drains away freely. Among the hardiest are *Opuntia humifusa*, *Sedum*, and houseleeks (*Sempervivum*), along with some *Crassula* and *Umbilicus* species.

With sharp drainage and a good baking in summer, a number of desert cacti, particularly some *Lampranthus* and *Opuntia* species, withstand surprisingly low temperatures – although not the combination of cold and wet.

In mild areas that have few frosts, the range of plants is extended to include the spectacular rosettes of *Agave americana* and its cultivars, *A. filifera*, and *Beschorneria yuccoides*. Half-hardy species need a freely draining site with the shelter of a warm, sunny wall for additional protection. Where temperatures are unlikely to fall much below 7–10°C (45–50°F), such as in the southern and south-western USA and the more southerly parts of Europe, there are few restrictions when choosing succulents for outdoors.

Mixed plantings

When growing non-succulent and succulent plants together, it is important to choose plants that have similar needs for light, soil type, and watering regime. In frost-free gardens, compatible non-succulents include *Fuchsia*, *Nerium*, *Gazania*, and *Rehmannia* species, all of which provide additional colour and variety. Bulbs and rhizomes such as *Clivia*, *Cyrtanthus*, and *Sprekelia*

HARDY AND HALF-HARDY SUCCULENTS

Beschorneria yuccoides (half hardy)

Maihuenia poeppigii (hardy)

***Sedum spectabile* 'Brilliant'** (hardy)

Agave filifera (half hardy)

Opuntia humifusa (hardy)

Sempervivum montanum (hardy)

species are also good choices in mixed plantings.

In cooler regions, annual species and plants that are grown as annuals, such as *Lampranthus* species and *Portulaca grandiflora*, are suitable for planting outdoors among groups of perennial cacti and succulents.

Desert gardens

In arid climates where temperatures seldom fall below 10°C (50°F), the complete range of cacti and other succulents may be grown in a desert garden to create a fine landscape feature. Where the subsoil is particularly heavy, collections of plants may be grown in raised beds to ensure the excellent drainage that these plants require.

Use smaller species at the front of the bed, so that their delicate beauty is not obscured by taller plants. Allow clump-forming plants, such as *Echeveria*, *Haworthia*, and *Mammillaria* species, sufficient space to develop fully. These low-growing, cluster-forming species flower at different periods from spring to autumn, to give colour during the warmer months.

For background planting, erect, columnar cacti and other succulents are ideal. Choose plants such as the tall, single-stemmed *Cephalocereus senilis*, the branching *Cleistocactus strausii*, or the towering, tree-like form of *Euphorbia candelabrum*.

Containers outdoors

Most cacti and succulents have shallow roots and respond well to being grown in containers. Select containers that enhance the shape and

A DESERT GARDEN
The branching arms of Euphorbia candelabrum *balance the surrounding globular and columnar cacti to complete this striking collection.*

form of the plants – a wide, shallow bowl, for example, is the natural choice for displaying low-growing and creeping species, whereas those with stronger form, such as *Agave attenuata*, are much better suited to large pots or urns.

Troughs are particularly useful for creating imaginative combinations of plants of quite different sizes and habits, and hanging baskets are suitable for displaying trailing and pendent species.

Choosing and siting the plants

In cool regions, but where temperatures seldom fall below freezing, many species will thrive outdoors in troughs and pots, provided that these

are raised above the ground to allow water to drain away freely. A warm, sheltered position such as a corner of a covered patio or balcony, where the plants can more easily be protected from rain, will provide the ideal environment.

The foliage shapes of *Sedum* and neat rosettes of *Sempervivum* may be used to form a contrast with the leafy forms and brilliant blooms of *Lewisia* species and cultivars, or with the green-flowered *Echinocereus viridiflorus* and the scarlet, early summer blooms of *Lobivia silvestri*. Other species, such as *Agave parryi*, which has symmetrical rosettes of plump, grey-green leaves, or *Opuntia polyacantha*,

with its brilliant display of yellow flowers, make striking focal points if they are planted on their own in large bowls.

In warmer climates, there is much greater scope for growing cacti and other succulents outdoors in containers. In large pots, group plants that flower at different periods and have striking foliage forms: the purple-leaved *Aeonium arboreum* 'Schwarzkopf', *Aloe barbadensis*, which has yellow flowers, and the red-flowered *Crassula falcata* will provide structural interest all year round, and give a succession of attractive blooms throughout the warmer months.

Where temperatures do not consistently fall below 13°C (55°F), many dwarf cacti, such as species and cultivars of *Gymnocalycium*, *Mammillaria*, and *Rebutia*, make fascinating displays of form and texture in outdoor bowls and troughs in the garden. These dwarf, cluster-forming species also give a magnificent display of vibrant colour that will last for many weeks on end during the summer.

Indoor display

The protected environment of the greenhouse or conservatory, which allows almost complete control of light, temperature, humidity, and water, provides ideal conditions for an extensive range of cacti and other succulents – most of the plants recommended for outdoor cultivation in warm climates will thrive under cover in cooler regions. The adaptations these plants have made to help them to survive in harsh, arid

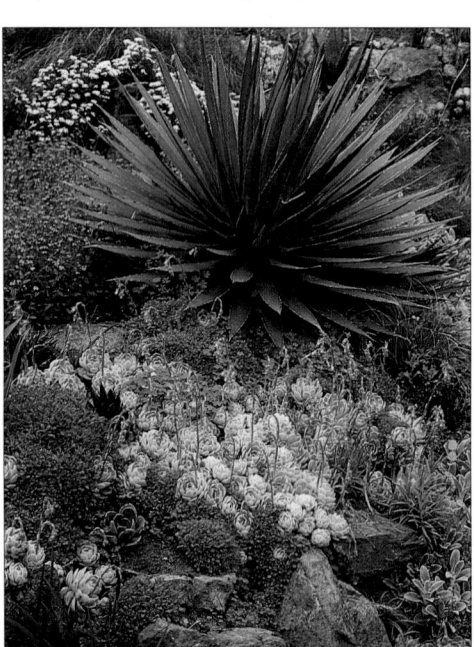

MIXED PLANTING
The neat rosettes and delicate, nodding flowerheads of Echeveria *provide a dainty contrast with the strap-like leaves of* Agave filifera (centre), *the focal point of this attractive arrangement.*

AN OUTDOOR CONTAINER
This varied collection of tall, spreading, and pendent cacti and other succulents creates a highly decorative and unusual feature on a balcony outdoors.

AN INDOOR BED
The bright foliage of Agave americana 'Variegata'*, offset by the rosettes of* Orostachys chanetii, *is a fine centrepiece in this greenhouse bed.*

environments in the wild also make them well suited to the warm, dry conditions of the centrally heated home, where many other plants may fail to thrive.

The variation in shape and habit, and their beautiful flowers, ensure that these plants provide interest throughout the year, and, since different species are adapted to a variety of environmental conditions, they may be selected to suit a number of situations in the home.

Providing the right conditions

The great majority of cacti and other succulents need high light levels, warmth, and good ventilation to thrive, although some, the leafy succulents in particular, may need protection from direct sun in summer to avoid leaf scorch.

There is an important group, however, that requires shady conditions, or at least filtered light: these are epiphytes that come from the humid and shaded rainforests of Central and South America.

Epiphytic plants are among the most floriferous of cacti and other succulents, and they can be used to great effect to add bold splashes of colour and interest to shady corners of the home or garden. The best known of this group are the Christmas cactus (*Schlumbergera bridgesii*), *Rhipsalidopsis gaertneri*, and *R. rosea*. Some of the loveliest are the magnificent hybrids created by crossing *Epiphyllum* species with those of *Echinopsis, Heliocereus, Hylocereus,* and *Nopalxochia*. These hybrids produce extraordinarily beautiful, and sometimes fragrant, flowers in spring and summer, in colours ranging from pure white, through cream, yellow, and orange to red and deepest purple.

Plants for the greenhouse and conservatory

Plants in a greenhouse or conservatory may be grown in pots or open beds, either at floor level or raised on benches. Planting in open beds offers potential for growing larger species and even for creating a miniature desert garden.

When in growth, many species from warm habitats need bright light, a fairly dry atmosphere, and a temperature of 18°C (64°F) if they are to develop to their full potential and bear flowers. These conditions are more easily provided under glass than in the home, and many cacti grow and flower most successfully in the greenhouse.

Some, notably *Rhipsalis* species, require fairly high levels of humidity (80 per cent) to thrive, and nearly always perform best in the humid atmosphere of a conservatory. Other groups that are well suited to the conservatory and greenhouse are those that need space to grow and

GREENHOUSE DISPLAY
The rich colour and diverse forms of, among others, Crassula, Echeveria, Echinocactus, *and* Mammillaria *species provide a sumptuous collection of plants for the greenhouse bench.*

flower well. These include the clambering *Selenicereus* (the most outstanding species is Queen-of-the-night, *S. grandiflorus*) and several *Hylocereus* species, all preferring filtered light.

When drawing up planting plans for a greenhouse or conservatory, combine groups of cacti and other succulents that have similar cultural needs, to make maintenance easier.

Container-growing indoors

If provided with warm, bright, and draught-free conditions, many cacti and other succulents will thrive in indoor containers. Use small pots for displaying individual plants, or large bowls for planting a variety of compatible species together.

Wear gloves when handling spiny plants such as *Agave, Aloe,* and *Opuntia*, because their sharp spines may easily become embedded in your fingers if you brush against them, causing a painful injury.

Bowl gardens

If planted with different species that have the same cultural requirements, bowl gardens are particularly effective for growing succulent plants indoors. One or two plants with an erect habit, for example young specimens of *Cephalocereus, Cleistocactus*, or other columnar genera, may provide the focal point of the bowl. Alternatively, use a leafy succulent such as *Crassula ovata* as the main plant. Fill the rest of the bowl with smaller plants, such as *Echeveria* and *Lithops*. Free-flowering cacti such as *Mammillaria, Notocactus*, and other globular cacti are also good choices for planting in a bowl garden indoors.

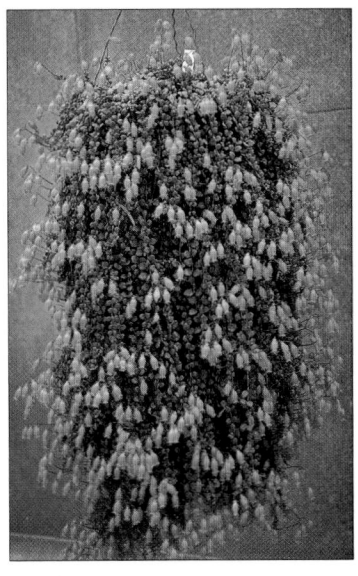

A HANGING BASKET
The graceful stems and flowers of Kalanchoe manginii *cascade like a waterfall against the house wall.*

Hanging baskets

Succulents in hanging baskets make colourful displays in the home or conservatory. Pendent cacti such as *Aporocactus flagelliformis*, and trailing succulent plants such as *Kalanchoe, Rhipsalidopsis gaertneri*, and *Schlumbergera* species and cultivars are the most suitable plants to choose, since they will trail attractively over the edge of the basket. *Sedum morganianum* and other semi-trailing species are also effective in hanging baskets.

Plant hanging baskets with just one specimen, or use several species for a harmonious but varied arrangement of shape and texture. In general, non-epiphytic plantings require bright light, but epiphytes need partly shaded conditions or bright but filtered light, so position the baskets accordingly.

Planter's guide to cacti and other succulents

DAMP CONDITIONS

Succulents that tolerate damp conditions
Crithmum maritimum
Salicornia europaea
Suaeda fruticosa, S. maritima
Umbilicus intermedius, U. rupestris

SHADE

Succulents that tolerate shade
Lewisia, Cotyledon Hybrids,
　L. leeana
Orostachys chanetii ❀ , *O. spinosus* ❀
Rhodiola crassipes
Sedum dasyphyllum, S. montanum,
　S. rosulatum, S. sediforme,
　S. spectabile, S. ternatum,
　S. villosum
Sempervivum arachnoideum,
　S. ruthenicum

BOWLS AND TROUGHS

Sun
Adenium obesum ❀
Aeonium arboreum ❀ ,
　A. nobile ❀
Agave filifera ❀ , *A. stricta* ❀ ,
　A. victoriae-reginae ❀
Aloe humilis ❀ , *A. longistyla* ❀ ,
　A. rauhii ❀
Astrophytum myriostigma ❀ ,
　A. ornatum ❀
Cephalocereus senilis ❀
Cereus forbesii ❀ , *C. peruvianus* ❀
Cleistocactus strausii ❀
Cotyledon teretifolia ❀ ,
　C. undulata ❀
Crassula falcata ❀ , *C. ovata* ❀ ,
　C. rupestris ❀ , *C. socialis* ❀
Echeveria agavoides ❀ ,
　E. derenbergii ❀ , *E. pilosa* ❀
Echinocactus grusonii ❀
Echinocereus blanckii ❀ ,
　E. pentalophus ❀

Echinocereus pentalophus

Echinopsis eyriesii ❀ ,
　E. multiplex ❀ , *E. oxygona* ❀
Espostoa lanata ❀
Euphorbia flanaganii, E. milii ❀ ,
　E. obesa ❀
Faucaria felina ❀
Ferocactus acanthodes ❀ ,
　F. latispinus ❀
Gasteria batesiana ❀ ,
　G. liliputana ❀
Glottiphyllum linguiforme ❀
Gymnocalycium baldianum ❀ ,
　G. gibbosum ❀ , *G. mihanovichii* ❀

Haworthia cooperi ❀ ,
　H. limifolia ❀ , *H. reinwardtii* ❀
Jatropha podagrica
Kalanchoe blossfeldiana ❀
Lithops bella ❀ , *L. dorotheae* ❀
Lobivia densispina ❀ ,
　L. jajoiana ❀ , *L. pentlandii* ❀ ,
　L. silvestri ❀
Mammillaria bocasana ❀ ,
　M. compressa ❀ , *M. gracilis* ❀ ,
　M. hahniana ❀ , *M. mystax* ❀ ,
　M. rhodantha ❀
　M. spinosissima ❀ ,
　M. zeilmanniana ❀
Opuntia microdasys ❀
Orbea variegata
Pachypodium geayi ❀ , *P. lameri* ❀
Parodia leninghausii ❀ ,
　P. mutabilis ❀
Rebutia albiflora ❀ , *R. aureiflora* ❀ ,
　R. heliosa ❀ , *R. marsoneri* ❀ ,
　R. minuscula ❀ , *R. senilis* ❀
Sansevieria trifasciata 'Hahnii' ❀ ,
　S. t. 'Laurentii' ❀
Sulcorebutia glomeriseta ❀ ,
　S. steinbachii ❀
Thelocactus bicolor ❀ ,
　T. nidulans ❀

Thelocactus bicolor

Trichocereus pachanoi ❀ ,
　T. pasacana ❀ , *T. spachianus* ❀

Partial shade
Epiphyllum oxypetalum ❀
　(and hybrids)
Hoya australis ❀ , *H. carnosa* ❀
Rhipsalidopsis gaertneri ❀ ,
　R. rosea ❀
Schlumbergera bridgesii ❀ ,
　S. truncata ❀ (and hybrids)

HANGING BASKETS

Aporocactus flagelliformis ❀
Ceropegia haygarthii ❀ , *C. woodii* ❀
Epiphyllum oxypetalum ❀
　(and hybrids)
Hatiora salicornioides ❀
Hoya bella ❀ , *H. linearis* ❀ ,
　H. polyneura ❀
Kalanchoe jongsmanii ❀ ,
　K. manginii ❀ , *K. pumila* ❀
Rhipsalidopsis gaertneri ❀ ,
　R. rosea ❀
Rhipsalis cereuscula ❀ ,
　R. mesembryanthemoides ❀ ,
　R. pachyptera ❀
Schlumbergera bridgesii ❀ ,
　S. truncata ❀ (and hybrids)
Sedum morganianum ❀

SUCCULENTS THAT TOLERATE TEMPERATURES DOWN TO 0°C (32°F)

Agave americana ❀ , *A. lophantha* ❀ ,
　A. parryi ❀ , *A. utahensis* ❀
Echinocereus viridiflorus ❀
Lobivia silvestri ❀
Opuntia humifusa, O. hystricina ❀
Sedum anglicum ❀ , *S. cyaneum* ❀ ,
　S. dasyphyllum, S. formosanum ❀ ,
　S. hispanicum ❀ , *S. lanceolatum* ❀ ,
　S. rupestre ❀ , *S. spectabile*
Sempervivum (most spp.)
Umbilicus ❀ (spp. only)

SUCCULENTS THAT TOLERATE TEMPERATURES DOWN TO 7°C (45°F)

Agave attenuata ❀ , *A. parviflora* ❀
Aloe arborescens ❀ , *A. aristata* ❀ ,
　A. barbadensis ❀ , *A. brevifolia* ❀ ,
　A. distans ❀ , *A. spinosissima* ❀ ,
　A. variegata ❀
Bulbine frutescens ❀ , *B. latifolia* ❀ ,
　B. mesembryanthemoides ❀
Caralluma europaea
Carpobrotus acinaciformis ❀ ,
　C. edulis ❀
Cereus chalybaeus ❀ , *C. jamacaru* ❀
　(and other columnar spp.)
Conicosia communis ❀ , *C. muirii* ❀
Crassula sarcocaulis ❀ ,
　C. sarmentosa ❀
Echeveria cuspidata ❀ , *E. elegans* ❀ ,
　E. gibbiflora ❀ , *E. pubescens* ❀
Echinocereus chloranthus ❀ ,
　E. enneacanthus ❀ ,
　E. pentalophus ❀
Gasteria angulata ❀ , *G. distichia* ❀ ,
　G. verrucosa ❀
Kalanchoe marmorata ❀ ,
　K. tubiflora ❀

Kalanchoe tubiflora

Lampranthus falcatus ❀ ,
　L. multiradiatus ❀
Lewisia, Cotyledon Hybrids ❀
Lobivia silvestri ❀
Maihuenia poeppigii ❀
Opuntia exaltata ❀ , *O. fragilis* ❀ ,
　O. polyacantha ❀ , *O. rastera* ❀ ,
　O. robusta ❀ , *O. subulata* ❀
Orostachys chanetii ❀ , *O. spinosus* ❀
Pelargonium acetosum ❀ ,
　P. echinatum ❀ , *P. tetragonum* ❀
Rosularia modesta ❀
Senecio haworthii ❀ ,
　S. macroglossus ❀

FLOWERING CACTI

Day-flowering
Aporocactus flagelliformis ❀
Astrophytum myriostigma ❀

Astrophytum myriostigma

Echinocereus engelmannii ❀ ,
　E. triglochidiatus ❀ , *E. viereckii* ❀
Echinopsis aurea ❀ ,
　E. kermesina ❀ , *E. multiplex* ❀
Epicactus ❀
Gymnocalycium bruchii ❀
Hatiora salicornioides ❀
Heliocereus speciosus
　var. *superbus* ❀
Lobivia famatimensis ❀ ,
　L. silvestri ❀
Mammillaria blossfeldiana ❀ ,
　M. bocasana ❀ , *M. hahniana* ❀ ,
　M. microcarpa ❀ , *M. nana* ❀ ,
　M. spinosissima ❀ ,
　M. zeilmanniana ❀
Matucana aureiflora ❀
Nopalxochia phyllanthoides ❀
Opuntia lanceolata ❀ ,
　O. paraguayensis ❀
Parodia brevihamata ❀ ,
　P. graessneri ❀ , *P. haselbergii* ❀ ,
　P. leninghausii ❀ ,
　P. mammulosa ❀ , *P. mutabilis* ❀
Rebutia aureiflora ❀ ,
　R. marsoneri ❀ , *R. senilis* ❀
Rhipsalidopsis gaertneri ❀ ,
　R. rosea ❀
Schlumbergera x *buckleyi* ❀ ,
　S. truncata ❀ , *S. t.* var. *delicata* ❀
Sulcorebutia glomeriseta ❀
Thelocactus bicolor ❀
Weingartia lanata ❀

Night-flowering
Cephalocereus senilis ❀
Cryptocereus anthonyanus ❀
Echinopsis eyriesii ❀
Epiphyllum cartagense ❀
Eriocereus bonplandii ❀
Espostoa lanata ❀ , *E. melanostele* ❀
Haageocereus acranthus ❀ ,
　H. setosus ❀ , *H. versicolor* ❀
Harrisia gracilis ❀
Hylocereus ocamponis ❀
Pachycereus pringlei ❀
Selenicereus grandiflorus ❀ ,
　S. macdonaldiae ❀
Setiechinopsis mirabilis ❀
Trichocereus fulvilanus ❀ ,
　T. spachianus ❀ , *T. terscheckii* ❀

KEY
❀ *Not hardy*

Soil preparation and planting

Many cacti and other succulents grow naturally only in desert or jungle conditions, but they also make striking displays out of doors in cooler climates. Whether grown indoors or outside, specially prepared, well-drained soil or compost is essential. A sunny site with adequate protection from frost is also required for most species.

Buying cacti and other succulents

When buying cacti and other succulents, choose healthy, unblemished plants that show new growth or have flower buds forming. Do not buy damaged or slightly shrivelled specimens, or any with dull, dry, or flaccid segments. Also reject plants that have outgrown their pots.

Planting in a raised bed or desert garden

Cacti and other succulents require well-drained conditions, so they benefit from being planted in a bed

RAISED BED CONSTRUCTION

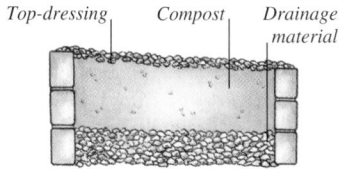

Top-dressing Compost Drainage material

A raised bed has a deep gravel base and free-draining compost.

SELECTING CACTI AND SUCCULENTS

GOOD EXAMPLE

REBUTIA SPECIES

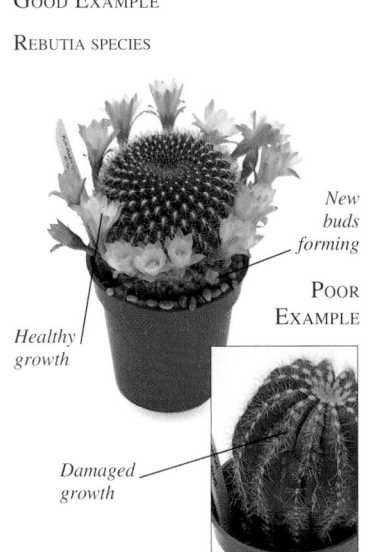

New buds forming

POOR EXAMPLE

Healthy growth

Damaged growth

GOOD EXAMPLE

Plump, fleshy leaves

Healthy, new growth

POOR EXAMPLE

CRASSULA OVATA

Shrivelled leaves

Handling cacti

Most cacti have sharp spines. When moving or planting them, either wear gloves or take other protective measures.

When handling spiny cacti, such as this Ferocactus, *wrap a loop of folded paper around the plant.*

---

that is raised at least 25cm (10in) above ground level. To ensure good drainage make the bed slightly sloping and provide a thick base of gravel or crocks that is at least one third of the total height of the bed.

Never construct the bed on a concrete or other impermeable base as this impedes drainage. Choose a bright, sunny site with a minimum temperature of 5°C (41°F). In cooler areas, provide adequate protection for tender species (see FROST AND WIND PROTECTION, pp.520–21).

Preparing the soil and compost mix

Cacti and other succulents do not usually thrive in ordinary garden soil, because it is not sufficiently

well drained; it needs to be replaced by or supplemented with a carefully prepared growing medium. Good garden loam that has a pH level of 4–5.5 may be used as the basis of a home-made compost. It must be sterilized first, however, to kill pests or weed seeds that might be present, and to eliminate diseases.

To prepare the compost, mix 2 parts sterilized garden loam with 1 part peat substitute or fine shredded sphagnum or sedge peat, 1 part sharp sand or washed grit, and a little slow-release fertilizer.

If the garden loam is alkaline, use a loam-based proprietary compost mixed with sharp sand or grit in a ratio of 1 part sand or grit to 3 parts compost.

Placing the plant in the bed

Water the plant, and carefully remove it from its pot. Check the root ball for disease or pest infestation (see also p.269), and treat any infections before planting.

Dig a hole of appropriate size and place the plant so that its base is at the same level in the soil as it was in its container. Fill in around the roots with compost, and firm, making sure that the stems and leaves are above soil level. Top-dress with grit, to protect the plants from excess moisture and reduce soil water evaporation. Allow the plants to settle, then water, lightly at first, gradually increasing the amount until the plants are well established and producing new growth.

PLANTING IN A BED OUTDOORS

1 *To plant out a succulent (here* Espostoa lanata), *moisten the compost in the pot, then dig a hole large enough to accommodate the root ball in a prepared, well-drained bed. Allow space for the development of the plant and those around it.*

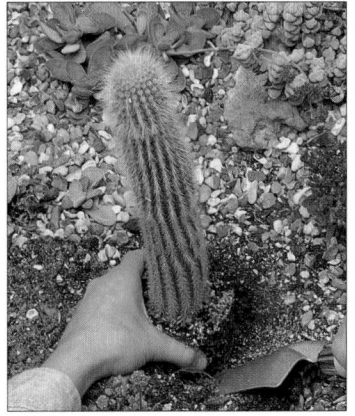

2 *Remove the cactus from the pot and place it in the hole at the same depth as it was in the pot. Firm the compost around the root ball.*

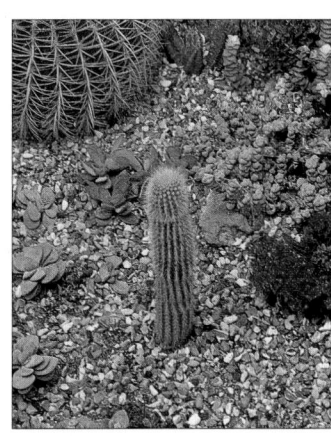

3 *Top-dress with a 5mm (¼in) layer of clean 3mm (⅛in) grit. Water after 2–3 days when the plant has settled.*

Succulents in containers

A collection of cacti and other succulents grown in pots, bowls, or troughs provides an attractive focal point on a patio or windowsill.

Preparing the compost
The compost used should be well-drained and preferably slightly acid with a pH of 4–5.5. Use 1 part sand or grit to either 3 parts loam-based compost or 2 parts loamless compost.

A slightly more acid compost may be required for epiphytic succulents, such as certain *Hoya* species, and cacti – *Rhipsalis* and *Schlumbergera* in particular – native to forest areas. Mix 1 part humus (such as peat substitute, sphagnum peat, or leaf mould) with 2 parts standard potting compost; add sand or grit to ensure adequate drainage.

Choosing the pot or container
Both clay and plastic containers are suitable for growing cacti and other succulents. Compost in plastic pots retains moisture longer than that in clay pots, which means that the plants need less frequent watering, but clay pots provide better aeration around the roots. Choose containers that have one or more drainage holes in the base to ensure that water drains away quickly. The size of pot or container should always be proportionate to the size of the plant but never less than 10cm (4in) deep; for tuberous-rooted species such as *Wilcoxia* species, a pot with a depth of at least 15cm (6in) is preferable.

Planting in containers
Always wash thoroughly all containers before use to remove possible sources of infection. Place a layer of drainage material (washed gravel or broken crocks) in the base, to approximately one third of the depth of the container; large troughs as well as deep bell- or urn-shaped pots need at least an 8cm (3in) base of gravel or crocks to ensure sufficiently sharp drainage. Fill the container with compost to within 1cm (1/2in) of the rim.

Carefully remove the plant from its pot, discarding any top-dressing, and insert it into the new container so that the top of the root ball is at the same level in the compost as it was in the original pot. Firm the plant into the compost, and then top-dress with coarse gravel or with grit.

When planting several cacti or other succulents in one container, space the plants so that there is room for them to develop. To create a more natural effect, decorative pieces of rock or pebbles may be added to the composition.

Allow the plants to settle for a few days before watering; water routinely (see p.269) only when the plants are well established.

Hanging baskets
To create an attractive and slightly unusual feature, plant trailing succulent species in a hanging basket. Make sure that the basket is completely clean. Wire baskets should be lined with a proprietary liner or a layer of sphagnum moss. Do not line the basket with plastic sheeting, since this restricts drainage. If using a plastic basket that has a fixed drainage tray, place a layer of small pebbles or gravel in the base instead of sphagnum moss.

Fill the basket with an appropriate potting compost, without disturbing the moss or pebbles, then insert the plants in the same way as for other containers. Do not overcrowd the basket, as most suitable species have a naturally spreading or pendent habit; one plant is often sufficient to fill an average-sized basket. Top-dress with gravel or grit if extra drainage is required; allow to settle for a few days before watering. Once the plant is established and showing new growth, routine watering may be applied (see p.269).

PLANTING IN A BOWL

Crassula ovata
Cereus peruvianus
Mammillaria muehlenpfordtii
Aloe 'Black Gem'
Mammillaria polythelle

1 *Select a group of plants that have similar cultivation requirements and moisten the compost in the pots. Arrange the group by positioning the pots in the container, placing the taller plants at the back.*

2 *Prepare the container, placing a 5cm (2in) layer of drainage material – gravel or crocks – in the base and covering this with a layer of compost (1 part sharp sand, 3 parts loam-based potting compost).*

3 *Remove the plants from their pots, place them in the container, and infill with compost.*

4 *Top-dress the planted container with a 5mm (1/4in) layer of 3mm (1/8in) gravel.*

PLANTING IN A HANGING BASKET

1 *Line a wire hanging basket with a layer of moist sphagnum moss. The layer should be 3cm (1 1/4in) thick when compressed.*

2 *Fill the basket almost to the brim with a mix of 1 part sharp sand to 3 parts loam-based potting compost. Prepare a hole for the plant in the centre of the basket.*

3 *Insert the plant (here a* Schlumbergera), *spreading out the roots. Infill with compost so that there are no air pockets around the roots.*

4 *Wait for 2–3 days after planting before watering the finished basket.*

Routine care

CACTI and other succulents need little maintenance in order to thrive, but they must have adequate light, warmth, and ventilation. Feed and water as appropriate for the particular species, and check regularly for signs of diseases or pests. Repot plants in containers as soon as they outgrow them, to prevent them from becoming pot-bound.

The right environment

Place cacti and other succulents in a position appropriate to their cultural needs. Most species need full sun, although some prefer dappled shade. The maximum daytime temperature in spring and summer should be 27–30°C (81–6°F), and the night-time temperature 13–19°C (55–66°F). During the dormant season, most plants should be kept at a temperature of at least 7–10°C (45–50°F), although species from the tropics and equatorial regions may require a warmer environment, with a minimum temperature range of 13–19°C (55–66°F).

Ventilation

Good ventilation is essential, although cacti and other succulents should not be exposed to draughts. For plants grown in a greenhouse it may become necessary to use blinds or to apply proprietary shading paint to the outside of the glass, if ventilation is insufficient to keep the temperature below 27–30°C (81–6°F) (see "Shading", p.484). In exceptionally hot weather, watering the greenhouse floor will help to reduce the temperature. Occasionally, plants grown in the open may need some shade to protect them in conditions of extreme heat.

Watering and feeding

Water only when the plants are in active growth (not during their resting period). For most cacti and other succulents this is in summer, but epiphytes and succulents from forested areas bloom principally between late autumn and early spring. In the dormant season, do not water unless temperatures remain high, and then only enough to prevent complete dehydration.

Watering

During the growing season, moisten the soil or compost thoroughly with tepid water, allowing it almost to dry out before watering again. Provided that the plants are grown in free-draining soil, surplus moisture drains away quickly.

Water early in the day or in the late evening, as the plants may scorch if they are covered in water droplets in bright sunshine. Alternatively, plants that are grown in pots may be watered by placing the container in a shallow pan of water, so that the water permeates the compost but does not touch the stems or leaves. Remove the container from the water to drain as soon as the surface of the compost appears moist; the plants will rot if left standing in water.

Epiphytic plants and those that need shaded conditions should be kept moist but not wet: an occasional, light mist-spray maintains a reasonable level of humidity.

Feeding

During the growing season, feed cacti and other succulents to help maintain healthy, vigorous growth and to encourage flowering. Several proprietary fertilizers are available but a standard, well-balanced liquid fertilizer containing all the major nutrients is satisfactory. Apply in accordance with the manufacturer's instructions at four-weekly intervals. Never apply fertilizer when a plant is dormant or the soil is dry as this may damage the stems and foliage.

Hygiene

Cacti and other succulents may need occasional cleaning, as dust sometimes accumulates on the leaves or between the spines. During the growing season, house plants may be sprayed lightly with water; succulents in the greenhouse or garden may be hosed down carefully, provided that they are not in direct sun.

Pests and diseases

Check cacti and other succulents routinely for pests and diseases. The most prevalent pests are mealybugs (p.550), scale insects (p.552), red spider mites (p.550), root mealybugs (see "Mealybugs", p.550), and sciarid flies (see "Fungus gnats or sciarid flies", p.570).

Diseases of cacti and succulents are rare, although poor cultural conditions or excess nitrogen in the soil may encourage the development of black rot, which principally affects epiphytic cacti and *Stapelia* species. The plants become disfigured and may die. There is no treatment, so, if it appears that a plant is likely to die as a result of infection, take healthy shoots or sections as cuttings and grow them on to replace the diseased plant.

Repotting

Cacti and other succulents should be repotted as soon as the roots begin to show through the drainage holes – usually every two to three years for fast-growing species. Repot slow-growing plants every three to four years. Always water a plant before repotting so the roots do not dry out.

Carefully remove the plant from its original pot. Inspect the roots, looking for signs of pests or disease, and treat if necessary. Cut out any roots that are dehydrated or dead, and dust with fungicide. Choose a new container one size larger than the original, and repot, ensuring the planting depth is the same.

REPOTTING SUCCULENTS

1 When a succulent (*here* Aloe arborescens) *has outgrown its container, repot it, selecting a container that is at least one size larger than the current one. Moisten the compost before sliding the plant out of its pot.*

2 *Gently tease out any roots that have become coiled or compressed.*

3 *Place some crocks and a little compost in the new pot. Position the plant at the same depth as it was in the previous container.*

4 *Carefully infill around the root ball with more compost. As you add the compost, firm it in stages to eliminate any air pockets between the roots. Wait until the plant is settled in the new pot before watering.*

Propagation

CACTI and other succulents may be propagated from seed, from leaf or stem cuttings, by division, or by grafting. Division and cuttings are the easiest methods. Raising plants from seed is slower and more difficult but provides the opportunity to obtain selected variants from within species, and to raise new hybrids by hand pollination. Grafting is useful for rare species and hybrids, and for those slow-growing succulents that are difficult to propagate by other methods.

Propagating plants from seed

Seeds of cacti and other succulents vary widely in shape and size, and some have special requirements. Some fine seeds are slow to germinate, while some of the larger ones have a thick coating (e.g. those of several *Opuntia* species) and seldom germinate unless they have been stratified – they should be placed in a refrigerator for 48 hours.

Sowing
Sow seed under cover between late winter and late spring. Place a layer of coarse gravel, combined with a sprinkling of charcoal chippings, in the base of a seed tray or pot. Fill almost to the top with seed compost, then smooth over and firm lightly.

Sprinkle fine seeds evenly over the surface, water lightly, and barely cover with sterilized, sharp sand or a sand and grit mix. Larger seeds should be pressed into the compost, allowing ample space between them, and covered with coarse sand or grit. Stand pots or trays of larger seeds in tepid water and leave them until the

upper surface of the soil is moist, then remove the containers and let the surplus moisture drain.

Place the containers in a propagator, maintaining a temperature of 21°C (70°F). Alternatively, seeds in pots may be sealed in a clear plastic bag. Keep the seeds in partial shade until they have germinated.

Care of seedlings
When the seedlings appear, remove the pots from the plastic bags or the propagator and provide additional ventilation. Spray the seedlings with fungicide to discourage damping off. Maintain a temperature of 21°C (70°F), giving further light and air as the seedlings develop.

Pricking out
After six to twelve months (depending on the species), when the seedlings are large enough to be handled without damaging them, prick them out singly into 6cm (3in) pots. Prepare the pots with a layer of crocks and fill almost to the brim with moist compost, then firm gently.

PROPAGATION FROM SEED

1 Cover the base of the pot with crocks, then add at least 1cm (¹/₂in) of coarse gravel mixed with a little charcoal.

2 Fill the pot to within 1cm (¹/₂in) of the brim with moist seed compost, and firm. Sprinkle fine seeds evenly over the surface.

3 Apply a fine, light mist-spray to the surface of the compost. Take care not to overwater.

4 Cover the seeds with a top-dressing of sterilized, fine gritty sand – only a very thin layer is required.

5 Label and place the pot in a plastic bag. Keep in partial shade, at a minimum temperature of 21°C (70°F).

SOWING LARGE SEED
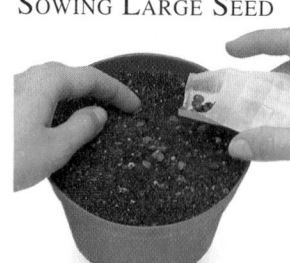
Press each seed into the compost, sowing at twice the seed's own depth. Space seeds about 1cm (¹/₂in) apart, so that they have room to develop.

PRICKING OUT SEEDLINGS

1 When the seedlings are large enough to handle, lift a clump from the pot, taking care not to damage the roots.

2 Divide the clump into individual small plants, retaining as much compost as possible around the roots (see inset).

3 Insert each seedling into a pot containing 3 parts cactus compost to 1 part gritty sand. Keep the top-growth clear of the compost.

4 Top-dress with a 5mm (¹/₄in) layer of 3mm (¹/₈in) gravel, and label. Do not water the seedlings for 3 or 4 days.

Remove a group of seedlings and separate them out carefully. Plant out the seedlings singly, top-dress them with a thin layer of gravel, and then label each pot. Keep the young plants at a minimum temperature of 15°C (59°F). After a few days, water them, sparingly at first, but then gradually increasing the amount until, after three weeks, the normal watering routine may be followed (see p. 269).

Leaf cuttings

Some succulent plants, for example many species of *Crassula* and *Echeveria*, may be propagated from leaf cuttings. These should be taken from the parent plant in spring or early summer when there is plenty of new growth.

Choose firm, fleshy leaves and remove them carefully from the parent plant. Sever them with a sharp knife or pull them gently downwards, ensuring that a small piece of stem remains attached to the base of each. Put the severed cuttings on a clean piece of paper and place them in partial shade at a temperature of 10°C (50°F). Leave them for a day or two until each one has formed a noticeable callus.

PROPAGATION FROM LEAF CUTTINGS

1 *Remove a healthy leaf by carefully pulling it away from the parent plant. It should break off at the base, with a small piece of stem attached.*

2 *Allow 24–48 hours for the wound to callus (see inset). Fill a pot with equal parts fine peat substitute (or peat) and sand. Insert the cutting so that the base is just held in the compost.*

3 *Top-dress with gravel or grit, and label. When new growth has been developing for about two weeks (see inset), the rooted cutting is ready to pot up into loam-based potting compost.*

Fill pots almost to the brim with equal parts of fine peat substitute (or peat) and sharp grit or sand. Each cutting should be inserted in an upright position in a pot so that the stem of the leaf is just held in place in the top of the compost. Firm the compost around the cuttings with your fingers.

Cover the surface with a light top-dressing of gravel or grit to help keep the cuttings in position. Label the pot, and place it in dappled shade,

making sure that you maintain a regular temperature of 21°C (70°F). Keep the young cuttings moist by watering them every day with tepid water. Use a fine mist-spray to cause least disturbance to the cuttings.

Rooting does not take long, and normally occurs within a few days. Approximately two weeks after new growth appears, pot up the rooted cuttings into suitably sized pots, filling them with standard, loam-based potting compost.

Producing hybrids

When growing cacti and other succulents in a mixed collection, cross-pollination may occur, i.e. pollen from the flowers of one species or variety may pollinate those of another to produce hybrid offspring. Sometimes these hybrids are improvements on other types raised and may be worth propagating. More frequently, however, they are not worth keeping.

To be sure of raising plants with the desired characteristics, it is

necessary to control the pollination process. Controlled pollination may be used to produce further plants of the same species, which retain the parental characteristics, or purposely to produce hybrid offspring from different species (which combine the characteristics of the parent plants).

To produce a new hybrid, choose the parent plants (usually species of the same genus) in an attempt to combine the best characteristics (e.g. leaf shape or flower colour) of both

parents. To prevent open pollination by insects occurring, just before the stigma appears receptive or the anthers are ready to dehisce, tie a small paper bag loosely over the flowers that are to be used. Transfer the pollen from the anthers of one parent flower to the stigma of the second parent by hand, using a soft, fine brush. Then re-cover the hand-pollinated flower with a paper bag.

Many cacti and other succulents are not self-fertile, and it is essential to cross-pollinate in order to obtain seed. If a species is self-fertile, however, cover the flowers with a bag, as above, to prevent cross-pollination by insects. A gentle tap on the bag is usually sufficient to spread pollen onto the stigmas within the flower and effect self-pollination.

As the fruits ripen from green to red they become soft and fleshy and may release seed. If not, slice the fruits open and leave them for two or three days in a partially shaded but warm position so that the pulp dries out. Then wash the seed to remove the pulp and dry it on blotting paper before sowing.

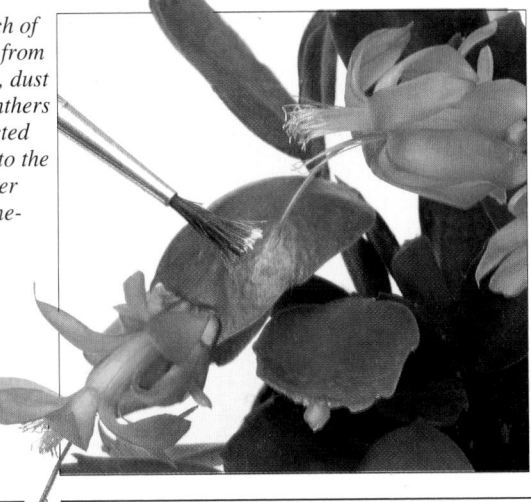

To produce a batch of hybrid seed (here from a Schlumbergera)*, dust pollen from the anthers of one of the selected parent flowers onto the stigmas of the other parent, using a fine-haired brush.*

SUCCULENTS THAT MAY BE PROPAGATED BY LEAF CUTTINGS

Adromischus cooperi❋ , *A. festivus*❋
Aeonium arboreum❋
Begonia incana❋ , *B. venosa*❋
Cotyledon ladismithiensis❋ , *C. undulata*❋
Crassula ovata❋ , *C. perfoliata*❋
Dudleya ingens❋ , *D. rigida*❋
Echeveria agavoides❋ , *E. elegans*❋
Fenestraria aurantiaca❋
Gasteria batesiana❋
Glottiphyllum linguiforme❋
Graptopetalum amethystinum❋
Haworthia attenuata❋ , *H. planifolia*❋
Hoya australis❋ , *H. carnosa*❋
Kalanchoe beharensis❋ , *K. tomentosa*❋
Lenophyllum pusillum❋ , *L. texanum*❋
Orostachys chanetii

Pachyphytum oviferum

Othonna dentata
Pachyphytum oviferum❋ , *P. viride*❋
Peperomia dolabriformis❋
Sedum hintonii, S. sempervivoides❋
Senecio fulgens❋ , *S. jacobsenii*❋
Streptocarpus saxorum❋
Thompsonella platyphylla❋
Umbilicus chloranthus❋
Xerosicyos danguyi❋

KEY
❋ Not hardy

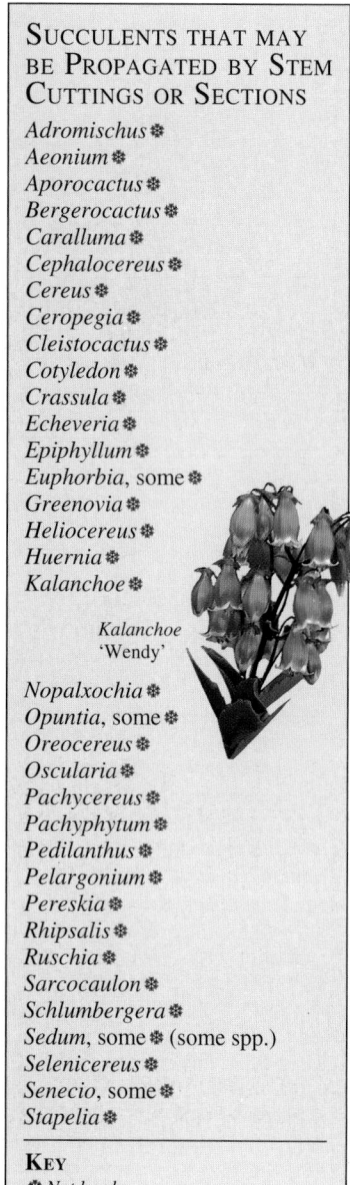

Kalanchoe 'Wendy'

KEY
❀ *Not hardy*

Stem cuttings and stem sections

Stem cuttings may be used to propagate many species of succulent, including *Euphorbia*, *Stapelia*, and most columnar cacti.

Take stem cuttings or sections in early to mid-spring. The amount and type of stem material that is removed depends on the plant. Some cacti, such as *Opuntia*, consist of a series of rounded pads or sections that may be severed with a sharp knife at the joint or base for propagation. For plants that have flattened, leaf-like stems, for example *Epiphyllum*, make a cut across a stem to remove a short length. To avoid disfiguring the plant, remove a complete "leaf" at the point where it joins the main stem, and treat this as the cutting or cut it into several sections (see below). Most columnar cacti, and some species of *Euphorbia*, may have sections of stem removed to provide cuttings (see below).

All *Euphorbia* and some Asclepiads produce a milky latex when cut; to stop the flow, dip the cutting into tepid water for a few seconds. Seal the cut on the parent plant by holding a damp cloth against the wound. Avoid getting the sap on your skin, since it can cause irritation.

Leave stem cuttings in a warm, dry place for approximately 48 hours to allow a callus to form, before potting them up in suitable compost.

Inserting the cuttings

Insert one stem cutting centrally into a prepared pot, or place several small ones around the edge of the container. The cuttings should be inserted just deep enough to stay upright but not too deeply, as otherwise the base of the cuttings may rot before they have rooted. Stem cuttings from succulents that bear true leaves, such as *Pereskia* species, need to have the lower leaves removed before they are inserted, in the same way as non-succulent plants. Apply a mist-spray of tepid water occasionally, but do not overwater, as this may cause the cuttings to rot. Rooting normally takes place after approximately two weeks, although cuttings from some genera such as *Selenicereus* may take a month or more.

STEM CUTTINGS

2 *Trim the stem (see inset) to about 1cm (¹/₂in). Remove the lower pair of leaves, if necessary.*

1 *Choose a healthy, vigorous stem (here from* Kalanchoe *'Wendy'). Make a straight cut, severing the stem as close to the base as possible.*

3 *Insert each cutting into a compost of equal parts fine peat substitute (or peat) and sharp grit or sand. The leaves should be just clear of the compost surface.*

PROPAGATION FROM PAD SECTIONS

1 *Sever a pad, making a straight cut across the joint, and leave it in a warm, dry place for about 48 hours to allow the wound to callus (see inset).*

2 *Insert the cutting into a pot containing equal parts fine peat substitute (or peat) and sharp grit or sand, and label. Once rooted, pot on into standard potting compost.*

Propagation from stem sections

Many cacti and other succulents may be propagated from a small section of stem rather than using a complete one. Use lengths of about 5–10cm (2–4in), depending on the species. For columnar cacti, remove a section of stem (below), cutting it off at the appropriate point; for cacti with flattened, leaf-like stems, cut the stem laterally into pieces (right). Then treat each section as a stem cutting.

LEAF-LIKE STEM SECTION
Remove a stem (here Epiphyllum*) and cut it into sections.*

INSERTING A STEM SECTION

COLUMNAR STEM SECTION
Sections of stem taken from some columnar cacti may be treated as cuttings.

Cutting just inserted into the compost

Crocks and gravel

Division of offsets

A large number of clump-forming cacti and other succulents, such as *Conophytum*, *Mammillaria*, and *Sedum*, may be propagated from offsets early in the growing season.

Clump-forming offsets

Scrape away the top layer of soil from around the parent plant to reveal the base of the offsets, and carefully detach one or more from the parent plant, as required, with a sharp knife. Treat any wounds on the offsets with fungicide, leaving them to dry for two to three days to allow a callus to form. Pot up undamaged offsets immediately.

Rootless offsets should be inserted into compost made up of equal parts fine peat substitute (or peat) and sand. If the offsets have already developed roots, use a standard potting compost. Use appropriately sized containers with a layer of crocks at the bottom. Pot up offsets separately and water them in lightly.

Keep the potted offsets in semi-shade for about two weeks at a minimum temperature of 15°C (59°F), and water them again after the first week. Once new growth appears, the plants should be potted on into a standard potting compost and the normal watering routine applied (see p.269).

Offset tubers

Some tuberous-rooted succulents, such as *Ceropegia*, produce small, offset tubers around the main tuber of the parent plant. These may be treated as divisions and grown on to produce new plants. During the dormant season, remove some compost to reveal the offsets and separate them from the parent plant using a clean, sharp knife. Treat the cut surfaces of rootless offsets with fungicide and allow a callus to form. Insert each offset tuber in a clean pot that contains a mix of equal parts peat substitute (or peat) and coarse sand.

If the offsets have roots, place them directly into a standard potting compost. Top-dress with a thin layer of washed, sharp grit, and label. Place the pots in semi-shade and maintain a temperature of 18°C (64°F).

Allow the tubers to settle for three or four days and then water them regularly with a fine mist-spray. As soon as growth starts and some young shoots begin to appear, follow the normal watering routine (see p.269). Pot on into a standard potting compost as soon as the young plants have several shoots and have become well established.

DIVISION OF CLUMP-FORMING OFFSETS

1 *Gently scrape away the top surface of compost around an offset. Cut straight across the joint and allow the wound to callus (see inset).*

2 *Using a compost mix of equal parts coarse sand and peat substitute (or peat), insert the offset just below the surface of the compost.*

3 *Top-dress with 5mm (¼in) of grit, label, and place in semi-shade. Water after 3–4 days.*

4 *When new growth appears pot on into standard potting compost, top-dressing as before.*

DIVISION OF OFFSET TUBERS

1 *Scrape away some compost from around the main tuber and carefully detach offset tubers. Lift them without damaging the roots, if present (see inset).*

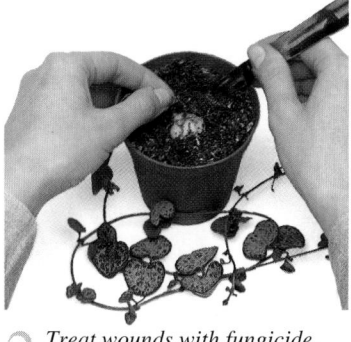

2 *Treat wounds with fungicide, and allow to callus. If roots are present, insert into potting compost, otherwise use equal parts of fine peat substitute (or peat) and sand.*

3 *Top-dress with a 5mm (¼in) layer of 3mm (⅛in) sharp grit. Label the pot but do not water for several days.*

SUCCULENTS THAT MAY BE PROPAGATED BY DIVISION OF OFFSETS

Agave, some ❁
Aloe ❁
Aloinopsis ❁
Caralluma ❁
Carruanthus ❁
Conophytum ❁
Copiapoa ❁
Coryphantha ❁
Crassula ❁
Dactylopsis ❁
Delosperma ❁
Dinteranthus ❁
Dracophilus ❁
Duvalia ❁
Ebracteola ❁
Echidnopsis ❁
Echinocereus ❁
Echinopsis ❁
Epithelantha ❁
Erepsia ❁
Escobaria ❁
Faucaria ❁
Gasteria ❁
Glottiphyllum ❁
Greenovia ❁
Gymnocalycium ❁
Haworthia ❁
Huernia ❁
Juttadinteria ❁

Lithops karasmontana

Lithops karasmontana ❁
Lobivia ❁
Mammillaria ❁
Meyerophytum ❁
Mitrophyllum ❁
Orbea ❁
Orostachys ❁
Parodia ❁
Pleiospilos ❁
Pterocactus ❁
Pygmaeocereus ❁
Rebutia ❁
Rhombophyllum ❁
Sarcozona ❁
Sedum, some ❁
Semnanthe ❁
Sempervivum
Stapelia ❁
Stomatium ❁
Sulcorebutia ❁
Tephrocactus ❁
Thelocactus ❁ (a few spp.)
Weingartia ❁
Wigginsia vorwerkiana ❁

Wigginsia vorwerkiana

KEY
❁ *Not hardy*

273

SUCCULENTS THAT MAY
BE PROPAGATED BY
DIVISION OF ROOTSTOCK

Agave, some ❁
Aloe ❁
Argyroderma ❁
Caralluma ❁
Carpobrotus ❁

Aloe variegata

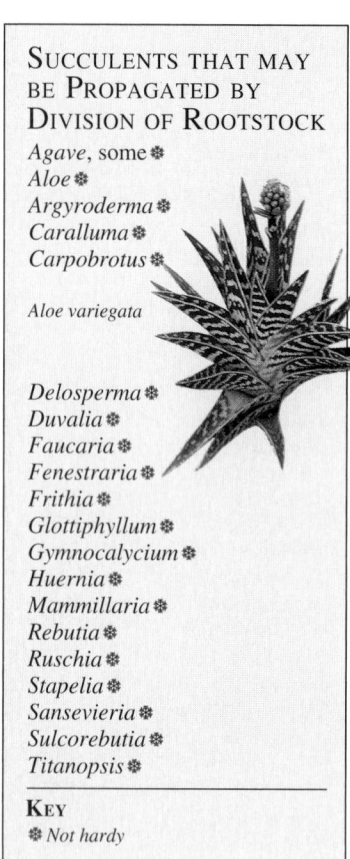

Delosperma ❁
Duvalia ❁
Faucaria ❁
Fenestraria ❁
Frithia ❁
Glottiphyllum ❁
Gymnocalycium ❁
Huernia ❁
Mammillaria ❁
Rebutia ❁
Ruschia ❁
Stapelia ❁
Sansevieria ❁
Sulcorebutia ❁
Titanopsis ❁

KEY
❁ *Not hardy*

Division of rootstock

Many species of Aizoaceae such as *Delosperma* and *Frithia*, some clump-forming cacti, and genera such as *Aloe* are readily propagated by division. For some cultivars of *Sansevieria*, division is the most reliable method of retaining the variegation, as leaf cuttings may produce plants that revert. Divide clump-forming cacti and other succulents in the early stages of the growing season.

Lift the whole plant from its pot, and carefully pull apart or cut the rootstock into a number of smaller pieces, each with a healthy bud or shoot and well-formed roots. Treat all cut areas with fungicide and pot up each section separately into standard potting compost. Label, water, and place in a semi-shaded position until well established.

Alternatively, cut away a piece of the rootstock without lifting the plant, and ease a section out of the soil with a hand fork. Dust the cut surfaces with fungicide and pot up as for offset tubers (see p.273). Fill any gaps that are left around the parent plant, using a standard compost, and water lightly.

DIVISION OF ROOTSTOCK

1 *Lift the plant (here* Sansevieria trifasciata). *Divide it into sections by cutting straight through the rootstock.*

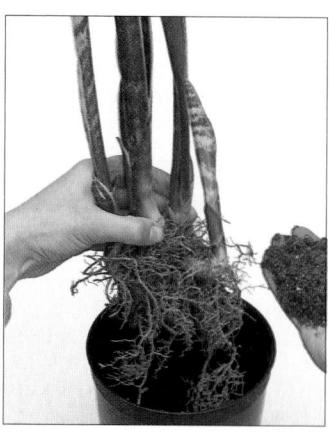

2 *Discard old, woody material and any soft or damaged roots before replanting each new section.*

Grafting

Some cacti and other succulents, notably certain members of the Asclepiadaceae, such as *Edithcolea* and *Pseudolithos*, are slow to mature and flower when grown on their own roots. By grafting them onto established specimens of related species that are quicker to mature, they can be induced to flower in a comparatively short space of time. During the growing season the topgrowth, or scion, of the required

APICAL-WEDGE GRAFTING

1 *Prepare the rootstock by trimming off the tip, making a straight cut through the stem with a clean, sharp knife.*

2 *Make a slender "V"-shaped cleft (see inset) in the stock, to a depth of about 2cm (³⁄₄in).*

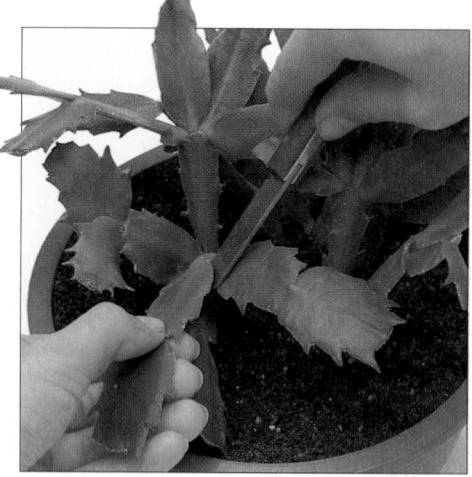

3 *Select the scion material and remove from the parent plant (here a* Schlumbergera), *cutting straight through at a node with a sharp knife.*

4 *Trim the lower end of the scion to a narrow wedge shape to match the "V"-shaped cleft in the stock plant.*

5 *Insert the scion wedge into the cleft in the stock plant (see inset), making sure that they are in close contact.*

6 *To secure the scion in place in the clefted stock, insert a cactus spine through the grafted area.*

ALTERNATIVE METHOD
Bind the graft firmly, but not tightly, with raffia.

plant is grafted onto the rootstock of one of the more vigorous species. Three methods of grafting may be used: apical-wedge grafting, flat grafting, and side grafting.

Apical-wedge grafting

Epiphytic cacti are often propagated by apical-wedge grafting in order to create an erect "standard" or tree-like plant. Use *Pereskiopsis* or *Selenicereus*, which are sturdy but of slender growth, as the rootstock.

To produce the rootstock, take a stem cutting (see p.272) of the selected plant. When this has rooted and shows evidence of new growth, it is ready to be used for grafting. Slice off the tip and then make two slanted, downward cuts into the top of the rootstock stem to produce a narrow, vertical, "V"-shaped slit approximately 2cm (³/₄in) long.

Select a healthy shoot from the scion plant and prepare it by trimming the lower end into a wedge shape to match the cleft in the stock. Insert the prepared scion "wedge" into the cleft so that the cut surfaces match as closely as possible. Secure the stock and scion firmly in position either by pushing a cactus spine

horizontally through the graft or, alternatively, by binding with raffia.

Place the grafted plant in partial shade at a temperature of 21°C (70°F). The stock and scion should unite within a few days; once this has happened, remove the spine or raffia, dusting any holes made by the spine with fungicide. When fresh growth appears, water and feed, as for established plants (see p.269).

Flat grafting

This method of grafting may be used to propagate crested variants – succulents with tufts of hair or soft bristles – and also *Gymnocalycium mihanovichii* and *Lobivia silvestri* as their seedlings may lack chlorophyll. Genera for use as rootstocks include *Echinopsis*, *Harrisia*, *Hylocereus*, and *Trichocereus*.

Make a straight, horizontal cut through the stem of the rootstock at the required height. Then remove the rib margins with a sharp knife to form a bevelled edge, and trim off any spines near the cut.

Prepare the scion in a similar way, and position its base on the cut surface of the stock plant. Place elastic bands over the top of the scion and

under the base of the pot to keep the scion securely in place; make sure the bands are not too tight, otherwise they may damage the plant.

Leave the grafted plant in a well-lit position, but not in full sun. Keep the compost barely moist until the scion and the stock have united (normally in one to two weeks), when the elastic bands may be removed. Thereafter, water and feed as for established plants.

When grafting asclepiads, the fleshy tubers of *Ceropegia* or the robust stems of *Stapelia* may be used as rootstocks. The former, in particular, make excellent stock plants for some of the Madagascan and Arabian asclepiads, which may otherwise be difficult to propagate.

Side grafting

This method is useful if the scion is too slender to be grafted onto the top of the stock. It is very similar to side-veneer grafting, used for woody plants. Prepare the stock by slicing off the top at an oblique angle, then trim the base of the scion to match the stock as closely as possible. Secure them together with a spine or raffia and treat as for flat grafting.

FLAT GRAFTING

1 *Slice off the top of the rootstock with a sharp knife, to produce a flat surface.*

2 *Trim the cut surface to produce a slightly bevelled edge; hold the stem without touching the wounded area.*

3 *Cut the scion material, slicing through at the base. Bevel the edge of the scion (inset) so that it will fit closely onto the stock.*

4 *Place the scion on the stock and secure firmly, but not tightly, with elastic bands. Label with the name of the scion plant.*

5 *Place the pot in good light at a minimum temperature of 16°C (61°F). Remove the elastic bands when new growth appears.*

SIDE GRAFTING

If the scion plant is slender it may be grafted onto the side of the stock. Make a slanted cut in both stock and scion, place the cut surfaces together, and fasten with a cactus spine and raffia. Leave in good light at 16°C (61°F) until new growth appears.

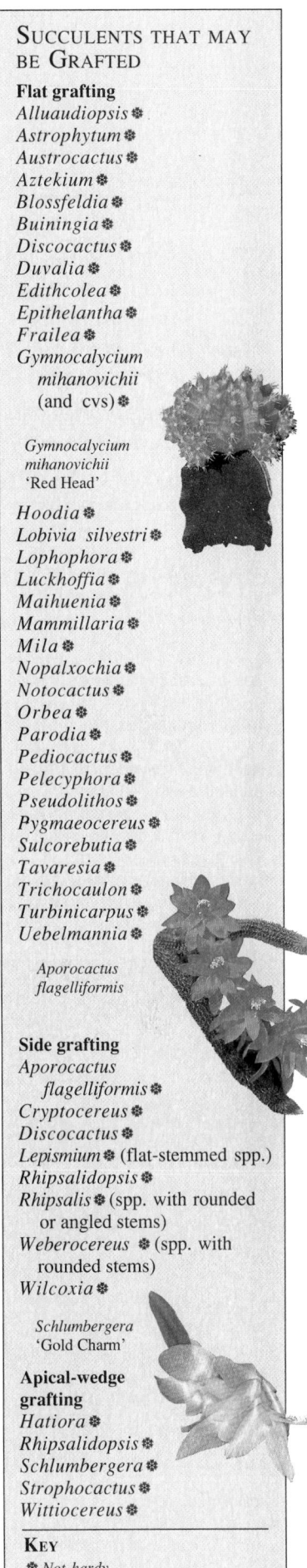

SUCCULENTS THAT MAY BE GRAFTED

Flat grafting
Alluaudiopsis ❋
Astrophytum ❋
Austrocactus ❋
Aztekium ❋
Blossfeldia ❋
Buiningia ❋
Discocactus ❋
Duvalia ❋
Edithcolea ❋
Epithelantha ❋
Frailea ❋
Gymnocalycium mihanovichii (and cvs) ❋

Gymnocalycium mihanovichii 'Red Head'

Hoodia ❋
Lobivia silvestri ❋
Lophophora ❋
Luckhoffia ❋
Maihuenia ❋
Mammillaria ❋
Mila ❋
Nopalxochia ❋
Notocactus ❋
Orbea ❋
Parodia ❋
Pediocactus ❋
Pelecyphora ❋
Pseudolithos ❋
Pygmaeocereus ❋
Sulcorebutia ❋
Tavaresia ❋
Trichocaulon ❋
Turbinicarpus ❋
Uebelmannia ❋

Aporocactus flagelliformis

Side grafting
Aporocactus flagelliformis ❋
Cryptocereus ❋
Discocactus ❋
Lepismium ❋ (flat-stemmed spp.)
Rhipsalidopsis ❋
Rhipsalis ❋ (spp. with rounded or angled stems)
Weberocereus ❋ (spp. with rounded stems)
Wilcoxia ❋

Schlumbergera 'Gold Charm'

Apical-wedge grafting
Hatiora ❋
Rhipsalidopsis ❋
Schlumbergera ❋
Strophocactus ❋
Wittiocereus ❋

KEY
❋ Not hardy

12

THE LAWN

ROM THE STRIPED, *velvety, green sward in a formal, traditional garden to the closely mown turf of a sports area or the rough grassland under a grove of fruit trees, there are many different types of lawn. Whether it is viewed as a showpiece in its own right, a foil for colourful beds and borders, a playing surface for children, or simply a relaxing haven, the lawn can be both a functional and attractive part of the garden. For centuries, grass has been chosen to create lawns because it* is visually appealing, pleasant to walk on, tolerates wear, and may be cut very low without being damaged. A few other species, such as chamomile and thyme, may also be used for lawns, but they are generally much less hard-wearing than grass. Frequently undervalued as merely a flat surface underfoot, the lawn may make a much more important contribution to the garden – it may be used to complement planting, soften hard surfaces, separate and define distinctive features, and unify the garden as a whole.

Creating lawns

HEALTHY, well-maintained lawn is an attractive feature that also provides a clear area in which to walk, play, and relax. For some gardeners, the lawn is primarily ornamental while for others its function is paramount and wearability is the most important consideration. In addition to such formal and utility lawns, grass may be used for other areas such as sports or games lawns, in orchards and wild gardens, for wide paths and gently sloping banks.

Some broad-leaved plants, for example chamomile (*Chamaemelum nobile*), may also be used to form lawns; they should, however, be considered primarily as ornamental, to be admired rather than extensively used, because they are less tolerant of wear than grass (see "Non-grass lawns", p.279).

When deciding on the type and shape of the lawn as well as where to site it, consider how it will link to the rest of the garden – to other plants, features, and the overall layout – so that it forms a congruous, unifying part of the design.

Grass

Grass is the plant most commonly chosen for a lawn because it is hard-wearing and usually attractive all year. It may also be repeatedly cut low without damage as the growing point is at the base of the plant.

Mown lawns

Mown areas of grass include high-quality lawns, utility lawns, and sports lawns. A primarily ornamental, high-quality lawn is suitable where a perfect, even appearance is paramount; it stands some wear but requires a considerable amount of maintenance to keep it in pristine condition. If the grass is likely to be subject to heavier wear – by being used as a play area, for example – opt for a utility lawn; this should also be attractive but may contain minor imperfections and requires less maintenance.

Sports areas, such as for lawn tennis or bowls, demand a particularly hard-wearing surface that can be cut very low. To stop unnecessary additional wear, they are best sited separately from the main lawn.

Long grass and grassland

As part of a wild garden or orchard, unmown grass or flower-rich grassland is very attractive, but as the grass is relatively long, it is not practical for a utility lawn. It needs very little maintenance, however, so may be suitable for an area such as a slope or a stream bank where mowing is difficult. Flower-rich grasslands often thrive on impoverished soils, so this may be a good way of using a part of the garden where little else grows.

In informal or semi-wild gardens, bulbous plants such as daffodils look very attractive when naturalized in grass. The bulbs are best planted in an established area of medium or

A FORMAL LAWN
Here, the close-clipped, pristine expanse of a high-quality, formal lawn provides a uniform, fine-textured foil for an elegant planting of white Agapanthus, *silver-grey* Senecio, *and other complementary plants and a platform to offset an ornamental garden seat and pots of marguerites* (Argyranthemum frutescens).

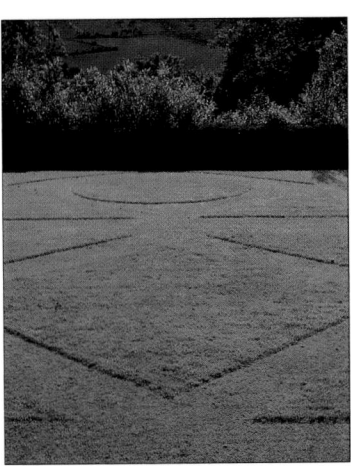

CONTRASTING TEXTURES
Create low-relief, geometric patterns and provide definition or interesting textures in an area of lawn by altering the height of cut.

could be included at the far end of the garden. Mixing grasses in this way is both practical and attractive, providing contrasting but complementary ornamental, wildlife, and play areas; mowing time is also reduced as part of the area requires cutting only infrequently.

Form and position

The lawn may well be the largest single area in the garden so it is important to plan its shape and position carefully within the context of the overall design. Take into account both practical and aesthetic considerations so that the lawn will be pleasurable to use, convenient to maintain, and an enhancing, integral part of the garden plan.

Shape
The shape of the lawn may harmonize with the garden style or be used to dictate it. A symmetrical layout of geometrically shaped lawns bordered by paths would be elegant and appropriate in a highly stylized, formal garden. In a small garden, a simple shape such as a circle could be visually striking and might be echoed imaginatively by the introduction of a circular pool or patio and containers packed with ornamental plants.

A curved, irregular design lends the garden an appealing fluidity, linking the different elements with a sweeping plane of even colour. Broad, flowing curves can be created to set off the planting in a border, and to lead the eye to a focal point, such as an architectural plant or a fountain. Steer clear of fussy, scalloped edges or awkward angles,

INFORMAL LAWN
The bold, curving sweep of an informal lawn is echoed by a winding, gravel path beyond and a ribbon of gold-leaved plants in an adjacent border.

long grass that does not need frequent mowing, such as on a bank (see also BULBOUS PLANTS, "Planting in grass", p.220).

Mixing long and short grass
Using different grasses in various parts of the garden, or varying the height of cut, helps to define separate areas and adds textural contrast. For example, a closely mown path running through long, flower-rich grassland provides an eye-catching shift in height, colour, and texture, and also encourages people to walk only on the path.

In large gardens, consider having a small, low-cut, high-quality lawn sited near the house where its fine appearance may be easily enjoyed; a path or steps could then lead to a utility lawn farther away, while an area of long grass and wild flowers

GRASS PATHS
Including a closely mown grass path through the garden allows a clear view of adjacent plants; here, a broad, straight path contrasts with the informal planting of daffodils and shrubs and clearly indicates where people are expected to walk.

however, as they may detract from the impact of any planting and make mowing difficult.

Space permitting, it may be more effective to have more than one lawn: for example, two or more of similar or complementary shapes could be linked by paths or archways. The farther lawn could be partially screened so that it provides an intriguing, half-glimpsed reflection of the nearer one.

Design functions
As well as being attractive in its own right, the lawn may fulfil different design criteria for both plants and hard features. Uniform areas of grass create a natural bond between otherwise disparate elements, leading the eye from one part of the garden to another. A statue or specimen tree sited in a lawn has maximum impact since the surrounding sea of plain colour separates it from other, more

distracting elements. In a large lawn, one or two flower beds or trees may be extremely effective if they are positioned so that they break up the green expanse, but resist the temptation to dot the entire lawn surface with eye-catching features: as well as making maintenance more time-consuming, the overall effect may be cluttered and disjointed.

The uniform texture and colour of grass form a neutral background that enhances other planting particularly well. The level surface acts as a foil for more sculptural plants – the strong silhouette of a columnar tree, the jutting spread of a prostrate shrub – as well as the variety of shapes, colours, and textures found in a mixed or herbaceous border.

Paths and access
Narrow areas of grass are usually subject to concentrated wear and are difficult to mow; for these reasons, paths narrower than about 1m (3ft) may be impractical. For a frequently used route across a lawn, such as from the house to the shed, consider laying a hard path or stepping stones to prevent uneven wear.

If possible, leave at least one side of the lawn open for access; if there are only one or two narrow openings, the grass may become damaged at these points.

Edging
Edging the lawn with a band of paving stones or bricks helps to define its shape and that of the borders, and also has practical advantages. It makes it easier to cut the lawn right to its edge while avoiding the risk of damaging other plants. Sprawling or trailing plants may be allowed to overhang the edge, breaking up any effect of rigidity, but without depriving the grass beneath of light. In

addition, ornamental containers may be set on the hard edging as focal points or to provide an interesting change of level. Alternatively, a narrow "mowing strip" of bare earth may be created at the edge of a lawn; this is particularly useful if the lawn is adjacent to a wall or fence since the grass may be more easily mown up to the edge.

Climatic considerations

Turf grasses are commonly divided into two main groups depending on their temperature tolerance. Those that grow mainly in a temperate climate, preferring temperatures of 15–24°C (59–75°F), are known as cool-season grasses, while those that grow best in subtropical or tropical climates, thriving in temperatures of 26–35°C (79–95°F), are known as warm-season grasses.

In large countries that cover a number of climatic zones, local advice can be sought on the best grass species to use. In temperate regions, warm-season grasses are not normally used for lawns, although some can be grown satisfactorily, because they turn brown during winter as they become dormant.

Cool-season grasses
Temperate or cool-season grasses are widely used for lawns throughout the UK, Northern Europe, North America, and other regions with similar climates (see "Climate zones", p.514). The grasses that are most commonly found in cool-season lawns are bents (*Agrostis*), fescues (*Festuca*), meadow grasses (also known as blue grasses, *Poa*), and perennial ryegrass (*Lolium perenne*).

Bents are low-growing and, of all grasses, are the most tolerant of close mowing. Fescues are fine-leaved and may be cut low; they are quite hard-wearing and some species grow in poor soils. Meadow grasses are more resistant to wear but cannot be mown very low, and some have quite coarse leaves. Ryegrass is extremely hard-wearing and tolerates most soils, including heavy clay, but is coarse-textured and does not like to be closely mown. Annual meadow grass (*Poa annua*) is also found in many lawns, but is often considered a weed grass by gardeners as it quickly runs to seed and forms coarse patches among fine-leaved grasses.

Cool-season grasses are usually sown as mixtures of more than one species, although in some areas of temperate North America, smooth-stalked meadow grass, which is also known as Kentucky blue grass (*Poa pratensis*), is grown on its own. If sowing a single species lawn, however, it is common to mix several cultivars together as this improves the lawn's disease resistance and the overall colour (see also "Choosing the right cultivars", p.279).

Warm-season grasses
These grasses occur naturally in tropical and subtropical regions, including South America, Africa, and Asia, especially southern China, and they are therefore adapted to grow successfully in a wide range of warm climatic zones.

The major warm-season grasses that are planted in lawns and other areas of intensive use are the various species and cultivars of Bermuda grass (*Cynodon*), St Augustine grass (*Stenotaphrum secundatum*), and zoysia grasses (*Zoysia*).

The Bermuda grasses include common Bermuda grass (*Cynodon dactylon*), African Bermuda grass (*C. transvaalensis*), Bradley Bermuda grass (*C. incompletus* var. *hirsutus*), and Magennis Bermuda grass (*C. x magennisii*).

Three species of zoysia grass are appropriate for use as lawns: Japanese lawn grass (*Zoysia japonica*), Manila grass or Japanese carpet grass (*Z. matrella*), and also Mascarene grass (*Z. tenuifolia*). Zoysia grasses grow particularly well in areas that have very warm summers combined with cool winters.

Warm-season grasses are usually grown as a single species turf as they have a strong, creeping habit and do not mix well together. If other grasses are included, they tend to form unsightly, distinct patches of differing colour and texture. Warm-season species become dormant and lose their colour at temperatures below 10°C (50°F), which can be problematic where conditions are ideal only during summer. In these areas, cool-season grasses, such as ryegrasses and fescues, may be oversown in autumn to improve the colour of the lawn in winter.

Selecting the right grass

Before selecting seed or turf, assess the relative importance of the lawn's appearance, wearability, and maintenance needs. Of the many different grass mixtures available, some are particularly good for areas of heavy use while others may give attractive colour and texture. The grass seed should also be suitable for the growing conditions such as the soil type and drainage, and the degree of shade.

High-quality lawns
To create formal, high-quality lawns, where a perfect appearance is the prime consideration and very heavy wear is not anticipated, select grass species that create an attractive, uniform texture and colour.

Cool season For the highest quality lawns, a grass mixture of fine-leaved bents and fescues is used. Browntop and highland bent (*Agrostis tenuis* and *A. castellana*) are mixed with Chewing's fescue and slender, creeping red fescue (*Festuca rubra* var. *commutata* and *F.r.* var. *rubra*).

Warm season Cultivars of the common Bermuda grass are excellent for high-quality lawns. There

PLAY AREAS
If the lawn is to include an area for games or play, as in this garden, use a particularly hard-wearing grass mixture in order to prevent the lawn from becoming patchy.

are several improved cultivars that tolerate heat, drought, and heavy wear. Zoysia grasses also form a high-quality, slow-growing turf.

Utility lawns
Lawns that are primarily functional, perhaps providing a play area for children or a space for outdoor entertaining, need to be relatively hard-wearing but they must still provide an attractive, even surface; grasses for this purpose do not usually create the perfect texture and colour of a high-quality lawn, as this is inevitably of secondary importance.

Cool season For hard-wearing lawns, the major grass is perennial ryegrass; it is usually mixed with red fescue (*Festuca rubra* var. *rubra*), smooth-stalked meadow grass, and browntop or highland bent (*Agrostis tenuis*, *A. castellana*). Lawns of only smooth-stalked meadow grass are quite widely planted in temperate regions of North America.

Warm season The Bermuda grasses (see "High-quality lawns", left) are tough enough for most utility lawns but may need frequent mowing. St Augustine grass has a less fine texture but is also suitable, particularly for shady areas. For a low-maintenance lawn, choose a grass such as bahia grass (*Paspalum notatum*), carpet grass (*Axonopus*), or centipede grass (*Eremochloa ophiuroides*). These require less frequent mowing, but since they have coarse-textured leaves, they do not provide a very fine finish.

Games and sports areas
Areas of grass used for playing ball games or sports require particularly wear-tolerant species and selected cultivars. In addition, some sports lawns must be able to tolerate a very low cut and have a fine finish to

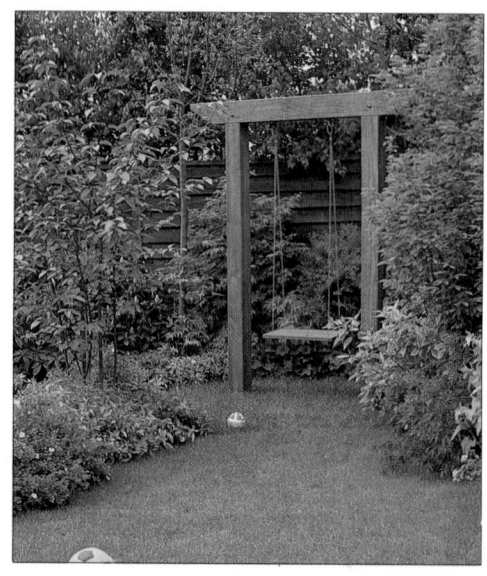

minimize the effect of the grass on the run of the ball.

Cool season A mixture of bents and fescues as for high-quality lawns (see p.278) tolerates some wear and is suitable for areas such as croquet lawns, bowling greens, and golf putting greens; very heavy use, however, soon damages the grasses. If a more hard-wearing surface is needed, such as for lawn tennis, it is better to opt for a mixture containing perennial ryegrass (see "Utility lawns", p.278).

Warm season The Bermuda grasses (see "High-quality lawns", p.278) should provide a reasonably hard-wearing, attractive surface. Some cultivars are more tolerant of wear than others, so take care to select those recommended as suitable for games areas.

Flower-rich grassland

For flower-rich areas, whenever possible use grass species that are native to the area: as well as being more likely to flourish, they do not look incongruous or artificial (see also WILD-FLOWER AND MEADOW GARDENING, p.169). Usually a flower-rich seed mixture consists of slow-growing grasses and various native, broad-leaved flowering species. As well as climate, factors such as soil type, soil moisture, and aspect may affect the choice of species sown; some prefer extremely dry, well-drained conditions, while others grow well on marshy ground.

Cool season Bents and fescues are usually included, while a short-lived grass, such as Italian ryegrass (*Lolium multiflorum*), may be added for initial, fast ground cover. If mown, the Italian ryegrass will die out within two years, leaving behind the fine-leaved grasses and broad-leaved flowering plants. Some species need an overwintering or cold period before they will germinate, and so may not appear in the first year after sowing.

Warm season In areas where warm-season grasses are grown, it is rare for flower-rich grassland to be cultivated: as warm-season grasses grow vigorously they tend to smother the flowering plants.

Problem areas

For lawns in difficult sites, such as shady, wet, or dry areas, choose a grass mixture that is specially designed for such conditions. If the problem is extreme, it may be better to grow ground-cover plants instead (see GROUND COVER, pp.150–51).

Cool season In wet, shady areas, grass does not readily grow into a dense, vigorous sward. There are some species, however, that are more tolerant than others: wood meadow grass (*Poa nemoralis*) is often sown along with rough-stalked meadow grass (*P. trivialis*), although neither survives close mowing or heavy wear. Fescues may also be included because they grow reasonably well in these conditions and take a lower height of cut when mowing. Turf timothy (*Phleum pratensis* subsp. *bertolonii*) is sometimes used in place of perennial ryegrass in moist areas that are not too shady.

In very dry regions, use grasses native to such areas, such as western wheatgrass (*Agropyron smithii*) which grows naturally on the great plains of North America, or fairway crested wheatgrass (*A. cristatum*) which is native to the dry, cold plains of Russia and Siberia. The wheatgrasses generally produce medium- to low-quality lawns; couch grass or quackgrass (*Elymus repens*) may become a weed in lawns that are left to grow over 2.5cm (1in).

Warm season For shady areas, St Augustine grass is a good choice; it is also salt-tolerant and so is valuable for coastal gardens. It is coarser than the various forms of either Bermuda grass or zoysia grass, however, so is generally only used where finer species do not thrive.

Choosing the right cultivars

Many modern grass cultivars have been specially bred to provide qualities particularly valued in lawns, such as even colour, disease resistance, wear tolerance, and compact growth. When selecting grass seed, therefore, make sure that the mixture includes not only the correct species (such as *Festuca rubra* var. *commutata*) but also a modern cultivar of that species, for example 'Frida', 'Lobi', or 'Atlanta'. New cultivars are introduced each year, so check with the retailer which cultivars are the best available for your particular lawn requirements. The grass mixture should not contain agricultural cultivars; these are bred to produce vigorous, vertical leaf growth for grazing and need frequent mowing. They also tend to spread less, and so do not always produce a dense, uniform cover.

Non-grass lawns

Although lawns are usually established with grasses, other evergreen species are sometimes used. These

FLOWERS IN GRASS
The grass in this informal orchard is dotted with bright yellow buttercups (Ranunculus) *and the vivid red, white, and purple cups of naturalized tulips.*

include chamomile (*Chamaemelum nobile*), *Cotula* species, *Dichondra micrantha*, and even various species of moss. Unlike grasses, these ground-cover plants do not stand up to heavy, continual wear, so they are rarely the best choice for the main lawn; they may, however, be used for primarily ornamental areas. Grow them in a patio or courtyard garden to provide a welcome patch of green, as a living surround at the base of a fountain, raised pond, pedestal urn, or statue, or next to a patio or path to creep over the edges and relieve the rigidity of the hard surface.

Chamomile leaves release a sweet, apple-like fragrance when crushed underfoot but they do not tolerate heavy wear; the non-flowering clone, 'Treneague', is naturally low-growing and especially suitable for lawns. *Cotula*, which has fern-like leaves, is considerably more hard-wearing as it forms a thick carpet of creeping stems; it also flourishes in moist conditions. *Dichondra* grows most successfully in warm areas and does not survive temperatures lower than -4°C (25°F).

Another option is to create a "tapestry lawn" with a patchwork effect by growing a number of low, mat-forming plants together. It is best to use plants that grow at a similar rate, such as the various creeping thymes (*Thymus praecox* var. *arcticus* 'Coccineus', *T. p.* var. *a.* 'Doone Valley', *Thymus caespititius*, etc.), otherwise one species may gradually predominate and so upset the balance of the original design. As for other non-grass lawns, tapestry lawns should not be heavily used.

CHAMOMILE LAWN
The soft, spreading cushion of a chamomile lawn provides a central focal point in a herb garden or a patio and softens the hard effect of the gravel edging and formal sundial.

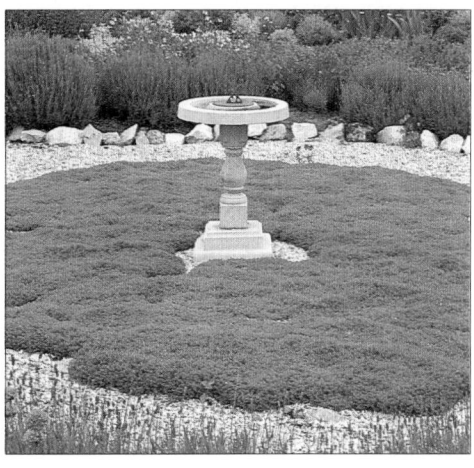

Soil and site preparation

THOROUGH site preparation is the key to establishing a successful new lawn. Although this may be time-consuming and expensive, in the long run it is easier and cheaper to prepare the site properly at the outset than to try to alleviate problems later. The general principles of preparation apply to all sites, but decisions on drainage, soil improvement, and irrigation should depend on the individual site and the climate.

Clearing the site

It is important to clear the site completely, removing any large stones and rubble, and all plant growth, including any tree stumps or roots. If the site is already partially turfed but in too poor a condition to be worth renovating, then remove all the turf (see also "Renovating a neglected lawn", p.289).

Eradicating weeds
Take particular care to eliminate any perennial weeds that have underground rhizomes or deep tap roots, such as couch grass or quackgrass (*Elymus repens*), dandelion (*Taraxacum officinale*), docks (*Rumex*), and the perennial stinging nettle (*Urtica dioica*), as they regenerate rapidly from small pieces of root or rhizome. It is difficult to dig these out entirely so, before cultivating the soil, spray with a systemic weedkiller and leave the weeds to die back completely before raking them away. Once the lawn grass is established, broad-leaved weeds may still be controlled using selective weedkillers, but weed grasses will be more difficult to eliminate, so it is sensible to use a weedkiller to clear the ground initially.

Annual weeds, such as fat-hen (*Chenopodium album*) and shepherd's purse (*Capsella bursa-pastoris*), may be controlled by mowing after the grass has germinated. It is preferable, however, to remove annual weeds before sowing as part of the site preparations.

Preparing the soil

The ideal topsoil for a lawn is a well-drained, sandy loam at least 20cm (8in) and preferably 30cm (12in) in depth, overlying a well-structured and free-draining subsoil. In these conditions the grass becomes deep-rooted and obtains ample water and nutrients from the soil.

Other soils may also be suitable, but if the soil does not drain freely and the lawn is likely to be heavily used, even in wet conditions, then the drainage should be improved. If the topsoil is very shallow or poor, it may be necessary to add new topsoil; this may be moved from other parts of the garden or bought, although for large areas the latter is very expensive.

If the soil has a naturally high sand content, and is, therefore, too free-draining, incorporate some well-rotted, organic matter to help retain nutrients and water (see "Soil structure and water content", p.526). Be careful, however, not to add too much because organic matter quickly rots down, and this may result in soil sinkage and an uneven surface.

After clearing the site, plough, rotavate, or dig over the whole area, removing any large stones that are brought to the surface, then rake the ground to produce a fine tilth. Breaking up the soil in this way makes subsequent levelling easier, as well as relieving compaction and improving the soil structure. On heavy, clay soils, however, rotavating or ploughing may create a compacted layer below the soil surface which could impede drainage: if necessary, break it up, using a subsoiling machine or by double digging. For further information, see "Soil cultivation", pp.524–7.

Drainage
Lawns on free-draining soils, and those in regions with low rainfall, are unlikely to require draining. In heavy, clay soils, drainage may be improved by incorporating approximately two parts of sand to every one part of soil by double digging, but this is expensive and laborious. In any soil that is not free-draining, it is preferable to install a drainage system during the preparation stage to avoid continual and expensive attempts to alleviate the problem after the lawn has been established.

The best type of drain for lawns consists of a row of pipes laid in a trench, which is backfilled with gravel. The ideal depth of the drain, and the distance between drains, will vary from site to site depending on the type of soil and the rainfall. For most loamy soils receiving moderate rainfall, one drain every 5–8m (15–25ft) is needed. Heavier, clay soils or sites in areas with a high rainfall will need drains laid at closer intervals (see also SOILS AND FERTILIZERS, "Improving drainage", p.529).

Adjusting the soil pH
For new lawns, the pH is unlikely to need adjusting, unless previous use has left the site in extremely poor condition. Most grasses grow satisfactorily at pH levels of 5.5–7. Fine fescues and bents grow best at pH 5.5–6.5, while perennial ryegrass, the meadow grasses, and many warm-season grasses grow better at pH 6–7. Soil-testing kits for measuring pH are available from most garden centres.

If the soil is very acidic (below pH5), dig or rotavate lime into the soil, the exact amount depending on the degree of acidity (see "Liming", p.531). Then leave the site for about a week before applying fertilizer. Lime may be added once the lawn is established but, as large amounts spread on grass may encourage certain diseases, only use a small quantity and repeat the following year if necessary. If uncertain about what to do, seek advice from an agricultural or horticultural college, or an agricultural advisory service.

Levelling the site

In gardens that have only minor undulations and deep topsoil, the site may be roughly levelled by raking soil from the high spots to fill the hollows, firming at intervals to consolidate the ground. Although it is not essential for the ground to be precisely level, awkward bumps and

HOW TO LEVEL THE GROUND

1 Firm the site well, especially at the edges, by tamping with the back of a rake or by treading. Mark some pegs at the same distance from the top of each. Insert a row of pegs at the site edge. If next to paving, the marks should be level with its surface.

2 Add a second, parallel row of pegs about 1m (3ft) from the first row. Place a spirit level on top of these to check that they are level with the previous row. Adjust the pegs as necessary.

3 Repeat the process to create a grid of pegs all at the same level. Rake up the soil to the top of the marks on the pegs, adding topsoil to fill any hollows. Once the ground is level, the pegs may be removed.

ACCURATE LEVELLING

To level the ground, first create a grid of pre-marked pegs and knock them into the soil at the same depth. Add or remove soil until it is level with the marks on the pegs.

hollows may cause problems when mowing. In some instances – for example, for a paddock or an area of rough grass – levelling by eye is sufficient. But if a perfectly level surface is required, such as for a formal lawn, a more accurate method should be used.

Achieving an accurate level

After levelling the ground roughly, an exact level may be achieved by knocking pegs into the ground all at the same depth to form a grid.

Start from a straight edge such as a path or patio, or create a taut line with string. Then take a number of identical pegs and make a mark on each one at the same distance from the top. Starting from the straight edge, knock the pegs into the ground at equal intervals so that the marks are at the required level of the lawn or approximately 2cm (³/₄in) below this if turfing. Add a second row of pegs and then further rows until the site is covered by a grid of pegs.

Use a spirit level – placed on a straight plank of wood if necessary to span across the rows – to check

that the pegs within the rows are all at the same height. Then adjust the level of the soil so that it is aligned with the mark on each peg.

Substantial levelling

If the site needs more substantial levelling or the topsoil is very shallow, the subsoil must be levelled first. To do this, remove the topsoil, rotavate or dig over the subsoil, then rake, level, and firm it roughly before replacing the topsoil in an even layer at least 20–30cm (8–12in) deep. To prevent the filled areas from sinking later, firm them thoroughly at intervals, adding more topsoil if necessary, and allow the site to settle before preparing the surface.

Creating a slope

Making the lawn slope gently away from the house or patio improves drainage and ensures that water does not drain into the foundations. A method similar to levelling is used, but each successive row of pegs is marked farther up or down to form a sloping grid. For example, to create a gradient of 1:100, make the marks

on each row of pegs successively lower by ¹/₁₀₀ of the distance between the rows. If sloping the lawn down towards the house, install a drain or soakaway to prevent water from reaching the house.

Final site preparations

Once the soil has been drained and levelled, the final surface may be prepared so that the site is ready for establishing a lawn.

Firming and raking

Tread the soil evenly all over to firm it and to ensure there are no soft spots which might later sink, making the turf vulnerable to scalping during mowing. It may be necessary to tread the area about three times before the soil is sufficiently consolidated, but take care not to compress the soil too much, and do not firm wet soil as it will become compacted. Even after firming, the soil may settle further over the course of a year or two, leaving small hollows. These should be levelled by applying a sieved, sandy top-dressing (see p.288).

After firming, thoroughly rake the surface to produce a fine tilth. The soil should be level, without humps or hollows, and with a fine crumb texture. If sowing seed, remove any stones larger than about 1cm (¹/₂in) across during raking; if turfing, it is only necessary to remove stones over 2.5cm (1in).

Leave the prepared site for about three to four weeks to allow any weed seeds to germinate; any emerging weeds should then be either hoed off carefully or treated with a contact weedkiller and gently raked off two or three days later once they have died, taking care not to disrupt the levelled soil unduly.

Fertilizing

A few days before establishing the lawn, and once the surface has been prepared, apply fertilizer to the site. This should contain the three major nutrients to ensure good growth: nitrogen (N), phosphorus (P), and potassium (K). Sites that have not been fertilized for many years may be deficient in all three. Phosphorus is especially important during the early stages of growth. Either use a simple fertilizer such as superphosphate, or, preferably, a compound granular or micro-granular fertilizer that contains all three of the nutrients; apply it according to the supplier's instructions at a rate of 150–200g/ sq m (4–6oz/sq yd).

PREPARING THE SOIL SURFACE

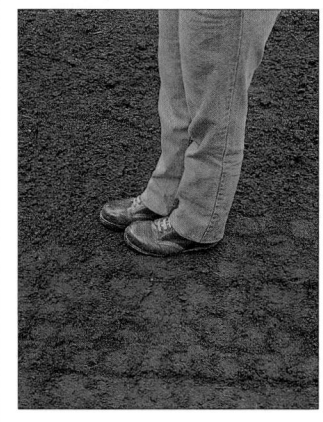

1 Firm the surface by treading it evenly, or by tamping it with the back of a rake. Repeat, if necessary, until the entire site is well firmed.

2 Rake the soil to a fine tilth and leave it to allow any weeds to germinate. Apply a weedkiller and, after about 2–3 days, rake off the weeds, making sure that no roots remain.

3 Apply a base dressing of a compound granular or micro-granular fertilizer and lightly rake it into the surface. Leave the site for a few days before turfing or seeding.

CREATING A SLOPE

Decide how many rows of pegs will be used and mark the pegs for each row at different heights in order to achieve the desired gradient (see left). Using a spirit level, create a grid of pegs as for levelling, and rake soil up to the marks.

INSTALLING A DRAIN

Position the drain at the lowest point, sloping the ground away from the house. Dig a trench, lay pipes in the base, and cover with hardcore. Add topsoil then turf or seed.

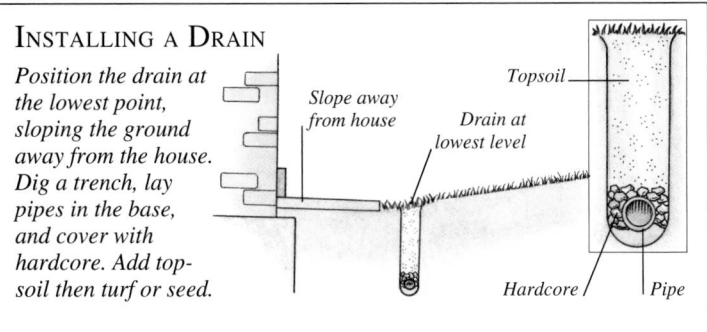

Slope away from house

Topsoil

Drain at lowest level

Hardcore

Pipe

Establishing a lawn

THERE are various methods of establishing a lawn. For cool-season grasses in temperate areas, the gardener may choose between seeding or turfing; for warm-season grasses in subtropical and tropical regions, vegetative propagation methods may also be used.

Seeding a lawn is usually the cheapest method, but it takes up to a year before the lawn can be subjected to heavy wear. Establishing a lawn by vegetative means takes longer and is more costly than seeding. Turfing, although more expensive, gives an immediate visual effect, and the lawn may be used within two to three months; it is advisable to use turf if you have pets that may disturb grass seedlings before they are established.

Turfing

There is a wide range of turf types available, including purpose- and custom-grown turf, meadow and treated meadow turf, and sea-marsh turf; the type chosen largely depends on considerations of site and expense. Always buy turf from a reputable garden centre or turf farm.

If possible, inspect the turf before buying it to make sure that it is in good condition, of the right quality (see "Selecting the right grass", p.278), and that the soil is a free-draining loam rather than a heavy clay. Check that there are no weeds, pests, or diseases, nor an excessive amount of thatch (the organic matter consisting of decaying grass, stolons, and rhizomes that accumulates on the soil surface); there should, however, be enough organic matter to hold the turf together.

Purpose-grown turf
Purpose-grown turf is widely available and contains different grasses for various uses. It is raised from the newest grass cultivars and treated to make it free from weeds and disease. Turf that is guaranteed free of annual meadow grass (*Poa annua*) is also available from the top producers, although at a high price. If you need a very large quantity of special turf, and are prepared to wait 18 months for it to be grown and harvested, it may also be grown to order, but this is expensive.

Meadow turf
This is usually grown for agricultural purposes and therefore is less fine in texture; it may have been

1 Lay the first row of turves alongside a straight edge such as a patio or path. Place each new turf exactly flush with its neighbour.

2 Place a plank on the first row of turves. Use this to kneel on. Then lay the next row with the turf joints staggered, as in a brick wall. Proceed in exactly the same way for the rest of the lawn.

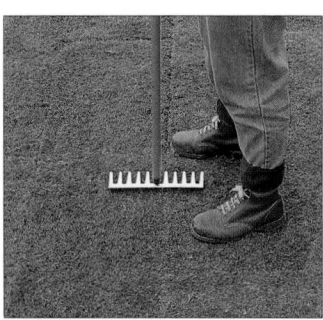

3 Tamp down each turf with the back of a rake to make sure that there are no air pockets. Alternatively, roll the lawn with a light roller.

4 Apply a light top-dressing of sieved, sandy loam and brush this in well, filling any gaps between the turves.

5 If no rain is forecast, water the turves well. Take care to keep them moist until they have rooted into the topsoil or they may shrink and gaps will appear.

either sown recently or grown in a long-established field. It is usually the cheapest turf, as it may contain coarse, vigorous, agricultural grasses and broad-leaved weeds such as daisies (*Bellis perennis*). The quality varies greatly, however, so it is especially important to buy meadow turf from a reputable supplier to ensure that it is of reasonable quality. If the weeds are eliminated by the use of selective weedkillers, the improved turf is described as treated meadow turf. Lawns established with meadow turf may have a coarse appearance and need more frequent mowing, but are perfectly adequate for utility or family use.

Sea-marsh turf
Once considered the finest turf available, sea-marsh turf contains fine fescues and bents. As it frequently grows in river estuaries where there are silt and clay deposits, however, it may contain a silty layer, which restricts drainage, thus reducing its wear-tolerance. Purpose-grown turf, containing new cultivars of fine

fescues and bents, is often preferred, since it is usually grown on better soil and is readily available.

Turf sizes
Turf is available in a range of sizes and shapes. High-quality turf is often sold in 30cm (1ft) squares and lower quality turf in lengths of 90 x 30cm (3 x 1ft). Major producers usually supply turf of all qualities in units of 1sq m (1sq yd).

STORING TURF

Lay the turves as soon as possible; if it is essential to store them, spread them out flat – grass side up – so that they receive enough light, and keep them watered.

Storing turf
Turf is best lifted and relaid in its new position within the same day. If there is an unavoidable delay, lay the turf flat on paving or plastic sheeting, preferably in a slightly shaded area, and keep it watered; in hot weather, it may dry out very quickly, so check it regularly. If the turf is left rolled up, it will not receive enough light, so the grass will turn yellow and eventually die.

Laying turf

Turf may be laid at almost any time of the year except during prolonged spells of extreme temperatures. If possible, choose a time when rain is expected in the next day or two. Turf should be laid on moist, but not wet, soil to encourage rapid rooting.

Starting at the edge of the site, lay the first row of turves in a straight line. Standing on planks placed on the turf, rake over the soil on which the next row is to be laid. Lay this next row so that the turves form an alternate bond, like bricks in a wall.

Do not finish a row with a small segment of turf beside the edge, as it will be vulnerable to damage and drying out. If necessary, lay the last complete piece of turf at the edge, and fill the gap behind with the trimmed segment. Lay further rows until the site is covered.

Shaping the edge

When all the turf has been laid, cut the edges to shape. For a curved edge, lay a hose or rope along the curve required, and cut just inside it. For a straight edge, use a string

TRIMMING THE LAWN EDGE

CURVED EDGE
Lay a hose or rope to the required shape and secure with wire hoops. Standing on a board, cut just inside the hose.

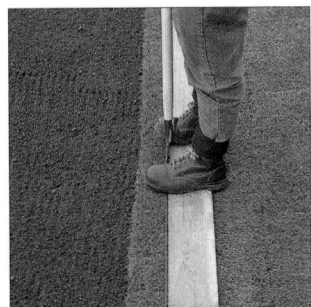

STRAIGHT EDGE
Stretch a taut string along the required line and align a plank with this. Then, standing on the plank, cut along its edge.

LIFTING TURF FOR RELAYING

1 *Cut the turf to be lifted into strips: insert 2 short canes a little way apart, 30cm (12in) in from the turf edge, and lay a plank flush against them. Stand on the plank and cut along its edge.*

2 *Cut each strip into turves about 45cm (18in) long, then undercut the turves to a depth of at least 2.5cm (1in). To stack them, lay grass to grass, soil to soil, on a path or piece of plastic sheeting.*

3 *Trim the lifted turves so that they are all the same depth: place each turf upside down in a prepared box and slice off any soil above the correct level. Relay the turves as required.*

drawn between pegs to mark the proposed lawn edge. Align a plank with this guideline and cut along it using a half-moon or powered edger. Move the plank along the guideline and repeat the procedure until the entire edge has been cut.

Aftercare

Either tamp down the turves with the back of a rake or roll the lawn with a light roller to ensure that there are no air pockets between the turf and the soil. In wet conditions, however, do not roll until the turves have rooted and knitted together. Brush or lute a light top-dressing (see p.288) between the turves to encourage the roots to spread.

Do not allow the turf to dry out before the grass has rooted through. It is essential to water the turf thoroughly so that it reaches the soil below, otherwise the turves may shrink in dry or hot weather, leaving large gaps between them.

Moving turf

Sometimes it may be necessary to lift and relay an area of turf. It should be cut and lifted in uniformly sized pieces so that they fit together easily when they are relaid.

Cutting

First, divide the turf to be lifted into lengths 30cm (12in) wide by cutting along the edge of a plank with a half-moon edger. Move the plank 30cm (12in) in from the previous cut to form each new length. Then cut each length at right angles to form pieces about 45cm (18in) long. Alternatively, a mechanical turf lifter may be hired; this cuts the turf to the size and depth required and also lifts it.

Lifting

Once cut, lift the turves with a flat spade or turf float, carefully severing them from the underlying soil and roots. Remove a wedge of turf next to the first piece to be lifted, then insert the spade under the turf without damaging the edge. Undercut each turf to a depth of at least 2.5–3cm (1–1¼in). Stack the lifted turf grass to grass, soil to soil, on a hard surface such as paving.

Trimming

After the turves have been lifted, trim them all to the same depth using a specially constructed shallow box the same size as the cut turves. Leave one of the shorter sides open and, if possible, cover the remaining top edges with a smooth metal strip. Place each turf upside down in the box and, using a sharp blade, remove the excess soil by slicing along the top of the box.

Establishing a non-grass lawn

To create a new lawn from broad-leaved species, such as chamomile (*Chamaemelum nobile*), prepare the site as for a grass lawn, including a dressing of fertilizer on the base. Plant pot-grown specimens, rooted cuttings, divisions, or seedlings at 15–30cm (6–12in) intervals. They may be planted closer together or farther apart – the closer they are, the faster they will form a lawn and, of course, the greater the expense. Keep the site well watered during dry periods. Once the plants have covered the site, trim the lawn with a rotary mower, nylon-line trimmer, or hand shears when necessary. If growing chamomile, it is best to use the non-flowering cultivar 'Treneague' which is naturally very low-growing. Flowering forms may be grown from seed but they require more frequent trimming and the dead flower-heads may be unsightly.

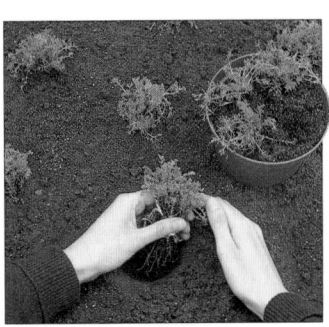

1 *Plant rooted cuttings or divisions (here chamomile) 15–30cm (6–12in) apart in prepared ground. Keep the area well watered and free from weeds.*

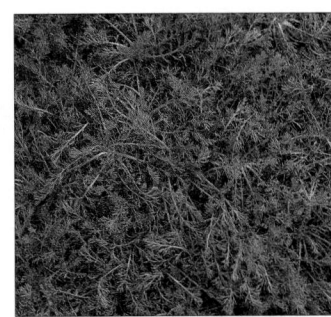

2 *After several weeks, when the plants have grown together to form a lawn, lightly trim them with a nylon-line trimmer or garden shears.*

Seeding

Grass seed is best sown in warm, moist conditions so that it will germinate and establish quickly: early autumn is usually best. Spring-sown grass is also successful but the soil is colder than in autumn and there is more competition from weeds. Seed may be sown in summer if irrigation is available, but in hot conditions young grass seedlings suffer heat stress and may wilt or even die.

Sowing rates

Grass sowing rates vary, depending on the mixture or species (see chart, below). Although there is some leeway to allow for factors such as depletion caused by birds eating the seeds, it is important not to sow seed in much greater or smaller quantities than the recommended rate. Sowing too little seed may allow weed seedlings space to compete with the grass, and the lawn will take slightly longer to establish. Sowing too much seed may cause more problems by producing humid conditions among the seedlings. This encourages damping off (p.568), which can damage the young lawn in a very short time, particularly in warm, humid weather (see also "Lawn problems", pp.571–2).

Sowing seed

Seed may be sown either by hand or, faster and more evenly, by a machine. First calculate the amount of seed needed by multiplying the size of the area to be sown (in square metres or yards) by the recommended sowing rate (the amount of seed per square metre or yard). Before sowing the seed, shake the container to mix the seeds thoroughly and ensure that small seeds do not settle to the bottom and thus give an uneven distribution of grass types.

Sowing by machine

This is the best way to sow grass seed over a large area. Measure out the correct amount of seed for the lawn and divide it in half. For even coverage, sow half of the seed in one direction and half at right-angles to this. A well-defined lawn edge may be achieved by laying plastic sheeting or hessian at the site edge and running the machine just over it; this also prevents the uneven distribution that may occur when stopping the machine at the end of a strip.

Sowing by hand

If sowing by hand, first divide the area into small, equal-sized sections, using string and canes or pegs; this makes it easier to sow the seed evenly. Then measure out the correct amount of seed for one section and accurately divide the batch of seed in half. Transfer one half-batch into a measure, such as a small cup, to make it easier and faster to measure out each subsequent amount. Work on one section at a time, scattering half the seed of a batch in one direction, then sowing the other half at right angles to this before moving on to the next section.

Aftercare

After sowing, lightly rake over the surface. Unless rain is forecast, water the site with a sprinkler. Germination will occur in one to two weeks, depending on grass species, soil and air temperature, and moisture. Protect the site from birds by covering it with netting or brushwood until the seedlings have established.

ESTABLISHING A LAWN BY SOWING SEED

1 If using a machine, sow half the seed in one direction and half at right angles to this. For a defined edge, lay down plastic sheeting and push the machine just over it at the end of each row.

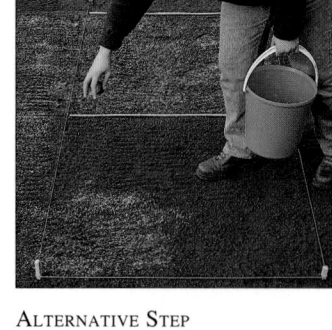

ALTERNATIVE STEP
If sowing by hand, mark the site into equal areas. Weigh out enough seed for a single area, then scatter it evenly, half in one direction and half at right angles to this.

2 After sowing, lightly rake over the surface. In dry conditions, water the site regularly to encourage the seeds to germinate.

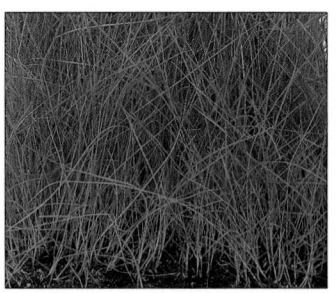

3 The grass seedlings should take 7–14 days to emerge. Once the grass is about 5cm (2in) high, cut it to a height of 2.5cm (1in) with a rotary mower.

Water the site regularly in dry weather since young grasses are very susceptible to drought. Once the seedlings have emerged, the surface may be gently firmed with a light-weight roller (100kg/220lb), although this is not essential.

Cutting

When the grass has reached approximately 5cm (2in), cut it to a height of 2.5cm (1in). For the first two or three cuts, use a rotary mower, because a cylinder mower with a roller may tear the vulnerable young leaves. Then carefully rake up and remove all excess clippings. If the lawn was sown in late summer or early autumn, continue to mow when necessary through late autumn in order to maintain it at about 2.5cm (1in) high. During the following spring, gradually lower the height of the cut until the desired height is reached, depending on the type of grass used (see also "Frequency and height of cut", p.285). Young grasses are particularly vulnerable to damage by wear, so try to use the lawn as little as possible during its first full growing season.

Vegetative propagation

Lawns grown from warm-season grasses, or the cool-season creeping bentgrass (*Agrostis stolonifera*), which produce vigorous stolons and rhizomes, may also be established by vegetative means such as stolonizing, sprigging, or plugging. The best time of year for creating a lawn by one of these methods is late spring or early summer, on a site prepared as for sowing grass seed. It will take about two months for the material to root and spread over the soil. As for grass seedlings, regular irrigation is essential.

To establish a lawn by stolonizing, spread stolons evenly over the soil at the supplier's recommended rate, top-dress with a light, sandy soil, roll, and water. Alternatively, for sprigging, stolons and rhizomes are planted in holes or furrows 2.5–5cm (1–2in) deep and 8–15cm (3–6in) apart, then firmed in and watered. For plugging, small pieces of turf, or plugs, are planted at intervals of 25–45cm (10–18in).

SOWING RATES

MIXTURES	g/sq m	(oz/sq yd)
Fescues and bents	25–30	($^3/_4$–$^7/_8$)
Perennial ryegrass and other species	35–40	(1–1$^1/_8$)
Flower-rich mixtures (depending on mixture)	2.5–5	($^1/_{16}$–$^1/_8$)
SINGLE SPECIES		
Bents (*Agrostis*)	8–10	($^1/_4$–$^5/_{16}$)
Carpet grass (*Axonopus*)	8–12	($^1/_4$–$^3/_8$)
Common Bermuda grass (*Cynodon dactylon*)	5–8	($^1/_8$–$^1/_4$)
Centipede grass (*Eremochloa ophiuroides*)	1.5–2.5	($^1/_{24}$–$^1/_{16}$)
Red fescue (*Festuca rubra* var. *rubra*)	15–25	($^1/_2$–$^3/_4$)
Perennial ryegrass (*Lolium perenne*)	20–40	($^5/_8$–1$^1/_8$)
Bahia grass (*Paspalum notatum*)	30–40	($^7/_8$–1$^1/_8$)
Smooth-stalked meadow grass/Kentucky blue grass (*Poa pratensis*)	10–15	($^5/_{16}$–$^1/_2$)

Routine care

ONCE the lawn is well established, regular maintenance is needed to ensure its health and attractive appearance. The amount required depends on the lawn's size and type as well as the site and climate. In general, the most frequent tasks are mowing and watering, but annual maintenance may also include such things as fertilizing, top-dressing, aerating, and, where necessary, controlling moss, weeds, pests, and diseases. For large lawns, using mechanical or powered tools, which may be hired, often makes maintenance tasks faster and easier (see "Lawncare tools", pp.466–7).

Mowing

In addition to making the lawn a pleasure to walk on, regularly cutting the grass helps to create a dense, healthy sward with an even, attractive finish. Mowing is needed most frequently in the warm, moist conditions of early and late summer; during drought conditions, however, it is best either not to mow at all or to set the mower to a higher cut. Delay mowing during very wet or frosty weather: wet grass can clog the mower or the mower may slip, and mowing in frost damages the grass. If mowing a fine lawn, brushing with a besom beforehand raises the grass and so achieves a better cut. Brushing the lawn in the morning also helps to remove dew and dry the grass surface, making it considerably easier to mow.

Mowers
For most lawns, a cylinder or reel mower, or a rotary (including the hover type) mower is suitable. A

BRUSHING AWAY DEW

To remove excess moisture and raise the grass before mowing, brush away the dew with a besom; for large areas, drag a piece of hessian over the lawn.

cylinder mower that incorporates a roller provides the finest finish for a lawn and creates stripes, but a rotary mower gives a perfectly acceptable surface for a utility lawn. The type of mower selected should depend on the size of the lawn and the finish required. For more information, see "Lawnmowers", p.465.

Frequency and height of cut
The frequency of mowing and the height of cut depends on a number of factors, including the type of grasses grown, how the lawn is used, and the time of year, but little and often is a good general rule to follow. Try to remove no more than a third of the leaf growth at any one time. If the grass is cut sporadically and drastically, it will struggle to recover after each mowing and there will be a noticeable decline in the lawn's quality. Frequent mowing is necessary in summer when the grass grows quickly; during spring and autumn, the rate should be reduced and, in winter, occasional "topping" – removing just the tips of the grass – may be all that is required.

High-quality lawns may be cut even as low as 0.5cm (¼in) but they need to be mown frequently – every two or three days in summer – to maintain their appearance. Utility lawns should be left to grow slightly longer than this as the grasses do not tolerate such a low cut; this also helps to protect the surface against heavy wear and tear.

It is not necessary to mow all areas to the same height. Try two or three heights of cut for different grass areas to add texture and interest to the garden. For practical reasons, cut the main area to be used for walking or playing to a height of about 1–2.5cm (½–1in). Keeping the grass at this length protects the surface against wear. Mow the areas under trees less frequently – every one or two weeks in summer – to a height of 5–10cm (2–4in). Leave any

MOWING STRIPES

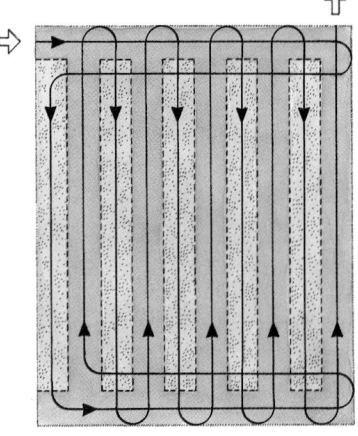

REGULAR SHAPE
First mow a wide strip at each end of the lawn for turning space, then mow up and down the lawn in slightly overlapping runs.

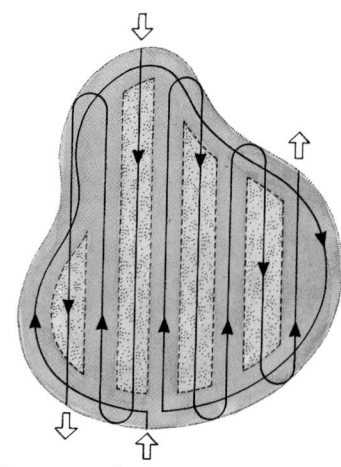

IRREGULAR SHAPE
Mow a strip around the lawn edge, then mow a straight strip up the centre. Mow up and down one half of the lawn, then the other half.

areas of flower-rich grassland at 10cm (4in) or more; they will need no more than three cuts per year and should not be cut until the flowering species have shed their seed in mid-summer (see WILD-FLOWER AND MEADOW GARDENING, p.169). Since they are mown infrequently, these areas produce much more growth and debris which should be raked up and removed after mowing.

Mowing stripes
Use a mower fitted with a roller to achieve a classic, striped finish to the lawn. If the lawn is square or rectangular, first mow a wide strip at either end of the lawn to provide turning space. Then mow up and down in straight strips, slightly overlapping the previous run to make sure that all the grass is mown.

If the lawn is of an irregular shape first mow all around its edge. Then, starting at the centre of one end, mow a straight line down the middle by picking out an object or tree beyond the end of the lawn and then

pointing the mower directly towards it. Mow straight strips up and down one half of the lawn, then return to the centre and mow the other half in a similar fashion.

Mowing sports lawns
On areas to be used for ball games, such as croquet, bowls, or putting, vary the direction each time you mow to prevent a "grain" from developing. Grain is produced by grass growing in one direction and affects the run of the ball.

Grass clippings
On fine lawns where a high-quality finish is required, use a mower that collects grass clippings as it cuts or rake them up afterwards and add them in layers to the compost heap. Removing grass clippings tends to discourage earthworms and lessens the spread of annual meadow grass and weeds such as speedwell. It may also help to prevent a build-up of thatch and thus maintain a finer finish to the lawn.

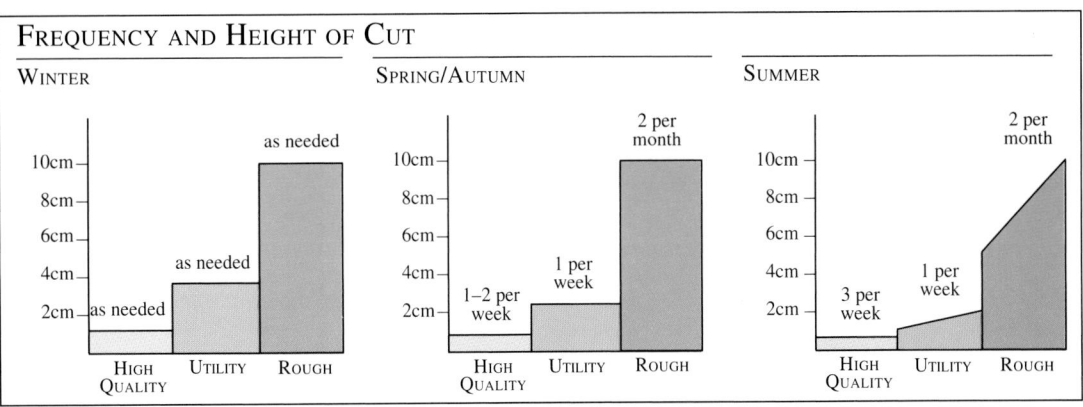

FREQUENCY AND HEIGHT OF CUT

WINTER — High Quality: as needed; Utility: as needed; Rough: as needed

SPRING/AUTUMN — High Quality: 1–2 per week; Utility: 1 per week; Rough: 2 per month

SUMMER — High Quality: 3 per week; Utility: 1 per week; Rough: 2 per month

Utility lawns containing earthworms may benefit from a light layer of clippings left on the lawn as they will be recycled by the worms, thereby returning plant nutrients to the soil. The majority of the clippings should be raked up, however, as excessive amounts may cause damage to the turf beneath as they rot down. In general, it is better to remove grass clippings and replace the nutrients lost by feeding.

Removing fallen leaves

In autumn and winter, clear away any fallen leaves from the lawn by brushing or raking them up and removing them; a layer of leaves left on the lawn reduces evaporation, and the resulting humidity can encourage turf diseases.

Trimming edges

After mowing, create a neat finish by trimming the lawn edges with long-handled edging shears, a mechanical edging machine, or a nylon-line trimmer with an adjustable head for edging (see "Lawncare tools", pp.466–7). If the lawn edges become irregular, recut them once or twice a year with a half-moon edger, cutting against a plank for a straight line; for very large lawns, it is faster and less laborious to use a powered edging machine for this task.

CLEARING LEAVES

Remove any fallen leaves and debris by brushing the lawn briskly with a besom or a spring-tined rake. For large lawns, use a leaf-sweeper or blower to speed up the task.

Watering

Grass generally resists drought well once established, but growth slows down and the turf turns brown in prolonged dry spells. To maintain growth and colour, it is essential to water the lawn thoroughly in very dry periods. The best time to water is either in the early morning or in the evening to minimize evaporation.

Start to water as soon as you notice that the grass does not spring back up after the lawn has been walked on – a state known as "footprinting". It is vital to give the lawn enough water; after watering, the soil should be moistened to a depth of 10–15cm (4–6 in). Shallow watering encourages plant roots to remain near the surface, making the lawn more susceptible to drought. Dig a small hole to check that the soil is damp to the required depth; make a note of the time that it took to water the lawn sufficiently to guide you in future. Alternatively, an electric moisture meter may be used, pushed into the soil to register the moisture level.

On heavy soils, where the drainage is restricted, it is important not to apply too much water as this restricts oxygen and mineral intake by the grass roots. If pools of water remain on the lawn for some time after heavy rain or watering, the lawn may need additional drainage (see "Improving drainage", p.529).

Areas of grass that need regular watering are best served by a built-in, pop-up sprinkler system installed underground. When the water is turned on, the pressure lifts the sprinkler heads from below ground and water is released. When turned off, the heads return underground and out of sight. Such systems may also be set to operate automatically but, of course, are much more expensive than a sprinkler or hose pipe, which is perfectly satisfactory for most lawns. For more information, see "Watering aids", pp. 468–9.

Fertilizing

As with all plants, grasses require nutrients to grow, and regular applications of fertilizer help ensure a vigorous, healthy lawn. Most of the nutrients essential for growth are plentiful within the soil, but four – nitrogen (N), phosphorus (P), potassium (K), and iron (Fe) – are often applied as a supplement. Nitrogen is the nutrient most commonly added: it is removed in grass clippings and is essential for producing further growth that is stimulated by mowing. Nitrogen-deficient grass is generally yellow-green in appearance and lacking in vigour.

Fertilizers are the easiest and most usual way to apply nutrients to the lawn; both organic and artificial products are available (see also "Soil nutrients and fertilizers", pp.530–31). The exact amount of fertilizer that is required depends on how quickly water drains from the soil, how much rainfall or irrigation is received by the lawn, whether or not the grass clippings are removed, and on the type of grasses grown. On heavy, clay soils that are rich in nutrients, and where rainfall or irrigation rates are low, only light fertilizing is necessary. However, light, sandy soils that are well watered and that lose nutrients quickly by leaching need greater amounts.

Types and constituents of fertilizer

For most lawns, two applications of fertilizer a year are sufficient (see chart, opposite). Apply a spring/summer fertilizer at the beginning of summer, and an autumn/winter one after routine maintenance in early autumn. Both contain nitrogen, phosphorus, and potassium, but in differing proportions, because nitrogen, applied too late in the year, may stimulate soft, lush growth and encourage diseases such as snow mould/*Fusarium* patch (p.571). Select a fertilizer that contains a mixture of both slow- and fast-release nitrogen; this helps the lawn to "green up" within two to three days and stay green for several weeks.

Iron (Fe), although not generally used on its own, is a constituent of lawn sand, which is used to control moss. Some complete fertilizers also contain iron. "Weed and feed" compounds are available to control moss and broad-leaved weeds and to fertilize the lawn all in one operation. Iron darkens the grass, making it appear greener without stimulating growth. It is especially useful in autumn when the grass may lose some of its colour but excessive growth is undesirable.

How to apply fertilizer

It is essential to apply fertilizer evenly to avoid variations in growth and the risk of damaging or even

CUTTING THE EDGE OF THE LAWN

EDGING BY MACHINE
Periodically recut the lawn edge to retain the lawn's shape and create a well-defined finish. For large lawns, use a powered edger: align the cutting blade along the required new edge and guide the machine forward.

TRIMMING THE EDGE
After mowing, trim the grass overhanging the lawn edge with long-handled edging shears; or use a nylon-line trimmer adapted to work vertically.

EDGING BY HAND
If recutting the edge manually, use a sharp half-moon edger, cutting along the line of a plank for a straight edge.

WATER PENETRATION

Shallow watering may make the lawn vulnerable to drought (right); apply enough water to moisten the soil to a depth of about 10–15cm (4–6in) (far right).

HOW TO APPLY FERTILIZER

Weigh out the correct amount of fertilizer for the area and divide it in half. Apply the first half in one direction, working up and down the lawn in adjoining but not overlapping runs. Apply the second half at right angles to this. Close off the supply when you turn the machine at the end of each run.

killing the grass. Any variation in the rate of application will generally be more than obvious within a week, and excessive doses may leave a bare patch behind. Although fertilizer may be spread manually, it is both easier and more accurate to apply it by machine.

Probably the simplest method is to use a continuous belt or drop spreader. This is pushed up and down the lawn, as if mowing, but so that each pass abuts the previous one, without overlapping it. To ensure even coverage, it is best to divide the fertilizer into two batches and apply half in one direction, the rest at right angles to it.

Alternatively, a spinning disc or broadcast spreader may be used to apply the fertilizer over a larger area; the spread may be uneven, however. To reduce the risk of fertilizer being distributed unevenly, set the machine to half the application rate and make adjacent runs at half the distance apart of the machine's spread. For example, if the extent of spread is 2m (6ft), make the runs 1m (3ft) apart. After using either type of machine, be certain to wash it out thoroughly because fertilizers are corrosive and may, therefore, damage any metal parts.

UNEVEN DISTRIBUTION

Take care to apply fertilizer evenly as uneven distribution may make the lawn patchy; it may even damage or kill areas of grass.

Before applying fertilizer, calibrate the spreader to obtain the correct distribution rate. To calibrate a spreader, first find a dry, flat area of concrete or asphalt, and chalk out a measured area of 4sq m (4sq yd), for example. Set the spreader to medium and fill it a quarter full. Using the machine, spread the fertilizer as evenly as possible over the marked area, as if over the lawn, then brush up all the fertilizer within the area and weigh it. Divide this weight by the area, in this case 4sq m (4sq yd), to give the application rate in grams per square metre (ounces per square yard). Adjust the machine setting accordingly, and then check the application rate again over the same measured area. Continue this process until the rate is correct.

Annual maintenance

In addition to routine tasks such as mowing and watering, regular maintenance is required to keep a lawn healthy and to reduce the risk of serious pest or disease problems (see chart, below). A maintenance programme should involve aeration (including thatch removal, or scarifying), fertilizing, and the control of weeds, moss, pests, and diseases (see "Lawn weeds", p.290, and "Pests and diseases", p.290).

It is also important for the continued good health of the lawn to top-dress the grass as well as to rake or brush it regularly to clear away leaves and other debris (see "Removing fallen leaves", p.286). Tasks that may be necessary at least once a year include recutting any edges that have become uneven or jagged and repairing any damaged or worn patches of grass by returfing or reseeding (see "Repairing lawn damage", p.289). Winter, when the lawn is no longer in need of quite such regular attention, is the most convenient time to check all equipment carefully. Sharpen all cutting edges, oil tools where necessary, and send the mower for servicing, so that it will be in peak condition for the first cut of the new season.

Aerating the turf

Aeration is vital since it allows deep root growth and so helps the turf to become established as well as reducing soil compaction. It is also important to reduce excessive thatch, the organic matter consisting of decaying blades of grass, rhizomes, and stolons that accumulates on the soil surface. A certain amount of thatch – up to about 1cm ($\frac{1}{2}$in) deep – is beneficial as it reduces evaporation and helps to protect the lawn from wear. In excess, however, it prevents water from reaching the soil beneath and may itself become saturated, interfering with drainage. The removal of thatch also encourages new grass growth and so promotes a healthy, vigorous sward.

There are several ways of aerating the soil and removing thatch. These include scarifying, slitting, hollow tining (also known as coring), and spiking. It is preferable not to undertake these tasks in dry conditions, however, as they make the lawn more vulnerable to drought. Autumn is often the best time since the warm, moist conditions allow the grass to recover quickly from

ANNUAL MAINTENANCE PROGRAMME							
MAINTENANCE PROCEDURE	EARLY/ MID SPRING	MID/LATE SPRING	EARLY/MID SUMMER	MID/LATE SUMMER	EARLY/MID AUTUMN	MID/LATE AUTUMN	WINTER
Mowing	Roll before mowing if turf is lifted by frost	Mow weekly. Adjust mower to summer cut height	Mow 1–3 times a week as required	Mow 1–3 times a week (set mower higher in dry periods)	Raise height of cut as growth rate slows	Set mower to winter cut height	Lightly mow if there is new growth
Watering		May be needed in dry regions	Water as necessary	Water well in dry periods	Occasionally water if dry		
Fertilizing		Apply spring fertilizer	Summer fertilizer		Apply autumn fertilizer		
Aerating and scarifying		Lightly scarify		Spike or slit areas subject to heavy wear	Scarify and aerate lawn, or hollow tine to remove thatch	Aerate lawn if not done in early autumn	
Weed and moss control		Apply lawn sand in place of spring feed if moss present	Apply weed-killer	Apply weed-killer if not applied in early summer	Apply weed-killer; treat moss with lawn sand		
Worm, pest, and disease control		Treat lawn with a wormicide			Apply wormicide/ pesticide/ fungicide		
Other procedures	Recut edges if required. Carry out any restoration work				Top-dress after autumn renovation	Remove fallen leaves	Remove leaves. Service tools

SCARIFYING

BY MACHINE
For large areas of lawn, use a mechanical or powered scarifier. Work the machine back and forth across the lawn as if mowing.

BY HAND
Pull a spring-tined rake vigorously across the lawn to remove thatch and dead moss. Ensure that the tines of the rake reach well down into the soil surface.

these renovation procedures. Whichever the aeration technique, first mow the lawn to its normal summer height. After maintenance work, apply a low nitrogen feed and avoid using the lawn for one to two weeks to encourage recovery.

Scarifying
This technique helps to remove thatch and permits air to enter the surface of the lawn. These processes

are important as the soil organisms that naturally break down thatch require air to live. For small areas, scarifying may be done manually by vigorously raking the lawn with a wire or spring-tined rake. This is hard work, however, so it may be worth hiring a mechanical or powered scarifier instead. To remove the maximum amount of thatch, scarify the lawn in two directions, one at 30° to the other. Any moss should be killed prior to scarifying so that it will not spread to other parts of the lawn (see "Moss", p.290).

Slitting
For slitting, a special machine is used that penetrates the soil with flat, knife-like blades to a depth of 8–10cm (3–4in). The blades cut slits through the thatch which allow air into the soil thereby encouraging a dense, healthy sward.

Hollow tining or coring
This removes thatch, aerates the soil, and relieves soil compaction, all in one operation. A mechanical or hand tiner removes a core of grass, thatch, and soil, making a series of holes across the lawn, about 10cm (4in) apart. Remove the cores, then fill the holes with a sandy top-dressing (see below) to prevent them from closing and to allow air and water into the lawn. Hollow tining may take longer to do than spiking and slitting because soil is removed rather than simply pushed sideways.

Spiking
This allows air into the soil, thereby encouraging root growth; it can also relieve soil compaction. Use a mechanical or hand spiker, or, for small areas, a garden fork. Angle the spikes back slightly to raise the turf gently without breaking it up. This encourages deep root growth by creating fissures in the soil.

AERATING

AERATING BY MACHINE
For large lawns, use a mechanical or powered aerator; work the machine in slightly overlapping runs.

SLITTING
Slitting, which must be done with a special machine, allows air into the soil; push the machine back and forth across the lawn.

HOLLOW TINING
Use a purpose-designed tool, working methodically across the lawn to lift out cores of grass and soil 0.5–2cm (¼–¾in) wide.

SPIKING
For small lawns, spiking using a garden fork is adequate; insert the fork straight, then lean it back slightly to let in more air.

Top-dressing
Immediately after autumn maintenance work, apply a top-dressing, on a dry day if possible. This helps break down thatch by keeping the lawn open and aerated, fills core holes, and helps to level the surface. For most lawns, a sandy mixture of six parts medium-fine sand, three parts sieved soil, and one part peat substitute, peat, or leaf mould is

suitable. After scarifying, apply the top-dressing mixture at a rate of 1kg/sq m (2lb/sq yd), but if the lawn has been both scarified and hollow tined, apply the dressing at the rate of 3kg/sq m (6½lb/sq yd).

Ensure that the top-dressing does not smother the grass by luting or brushing it into the surface and any core holes. Luting also helps level any slight surface irregularities.

TOP-DRESSING

Medium-fine sand

Sieved soil

Peat

1 *Prepare the top-dressing by mixing medium-fine sand with topsoil and peat substitute, peat, or leaf mould. Pass the mixture through a 5mm (¼in) mesh sieve.*

2 *Weigh out the correct amount of top-dressing for the lawn area and apply it on a dry day. For a large lawn, it is best to use a machine.*

ALTERNATIVE STEP
For small areas, the top-dressing may be applied by hand; spread it evenly over the lawn with a shovel or spade.

3 *Use a lute or besom to work in the dressing, keeping a steady pressure to distribute it evenly, and water thoroughly.*

Rolling

Rolling is not essential, but if done in spring it may help to resettle the surface after any maintenance work carried out the previous autumn and any possible upheaval caused by frost. A roller or, alternatively, a cylinder mower may be used; if using the latter, raise the blades to prevent damaging the lawn. The traditional practice of rolling lawns frequently is unnecessary and could cause problems of compaction, particularly on heavy soils.

Renovating a neglected lawn

In some cases, a neglected, patchy lawn may be improved by renovation; if, however, it is dominated by weeds and moss, it may be preferable to remove the old turf and establish a new lawn instead. The best time to start renovation work is in spring because the grass will grow well during spring and summer and should therefore be well established by the end of the season.

A renovation programme involves a series of procedures that restore the lawn to a good condition. First, in early spring, cut the grass to about 5cm (2in) using a rotary mower, and remove any clippings. After one week, mow again, but this time with a cylinder mower set to its highest cut. Over the next couple of weeks gradually reduce the height of cut until it reaches the correct level. At this stage, feed the lawn with a liquid or granular fertilizer and, two weeks later, apply a weedkiller. If there are any bare or uneven patches, they may be reseeded after one or two weeks. At the beginning of autumn, aerate the lawn, top-dress, and apply an autumn feed. A regular maintenance programme should then be followed so that the lawn is kept in tiptop condition (see "Annual maintenance programme", p.287).

Repairing lawn damage

If an area of the lawn becomes damaged or patchy, perhaps because of uneven wear, it may usually be repaired by removing the affected part, then turfing or seeding. It is important to use turf or seed that is the same type as the rest of the lawn; if this is unknown, use a piece of turf from a less prominent part of the lawn to replace the damaged area. If the problem of lawn damage occurs repeatedly, it may be necessary to consider introducing a completely different and more hard-wearing surface, such as gravel or paving (see STRUCTURES AND SURFACES, pp.492–513).

Repairing a damaged edge

Edges that have been damaged in only one or two small areas may be repaired quite simply. Using a half-moon edger and a straight edge, such as a short plank of wood, mark out a small section of turf containing the damaged part. Slice under the section of turf with a turf float or spade and push it towards the lawn edge until the poor area is outside the lawn. Then trim off the damaged part to align the turf with the existing lawn edge. This leaves a gap within the lawn, which should be gently forked over and a granular or liquid fertilizer added. Then returf or add a little soil and reseed with an appropriate grass mixture. Ensure that the repair will be flush with the rest of the lawn.

Alternatively, lift the turf, then turn it around and replace it so that the damaged area is within the lawn. Repair the damage by turfing or seeding, taking care to ensure that any new turf is laid level with the surrounding lawn.

Repairing a damaged patch

If there is a damaged patch within the lawn, first cut out and lift a piece of turf containing the damaged area. Fork over the soil then fertilize it, if required, and lightly firm the soil.

HOW TO REPAIR A DAMAGED EDGE

1 Using canes and string, mark out a small, straight-sided section of turf containing the damaged part; cut out the area with a half-moon edger.

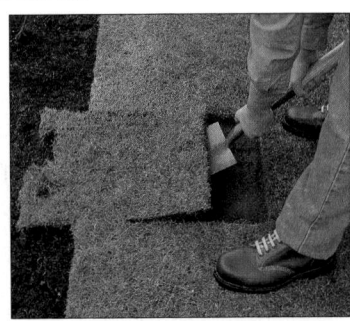

2 Carefully undercut the turf with a spade, then slide it forward until the damaged part is beyond the lawn edge.

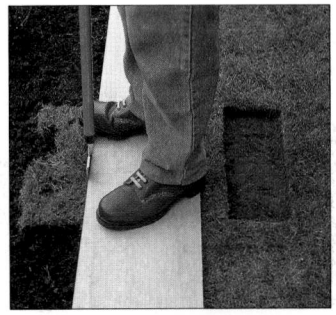

3 Align a plank with the lawn edge, then cut along it to trim off the damaged section so that the turf is level with the rest of the lawn edge.

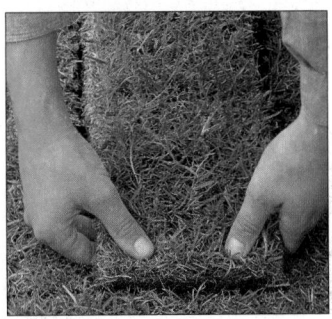

4 Cut a new piece of turf to fit the resulting gap and ease it into the hole; if it is too large, trim it so that it forms an exact fit.

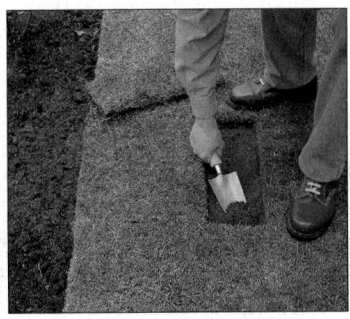

5 Adjust the soil level beneath the new turf, if necessary, by adding or removing soil until the new piece sits level with the rest of the lawn.

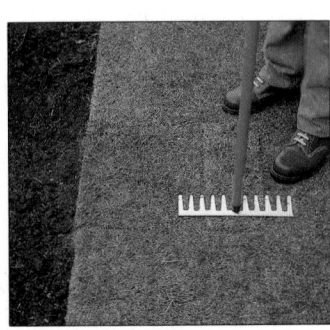

6 Once the level is correct, tamp the new piece firmly into place with the back of a rake or a medium-weight roller.

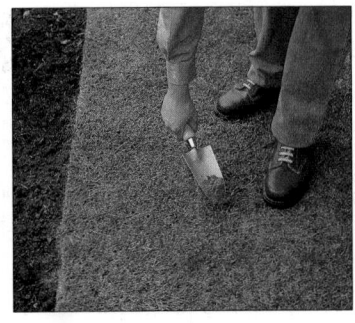

7 Sprinkle some sandy top-dressing over the repaired area, particularly into the joins, and water thoroughly.

ALTERNATIVE METHOD

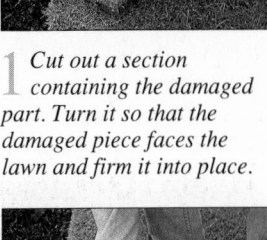

1 Cut out a section containing the damaged part. Turn it so that the damaged piece faces the lawn and firm it into place.

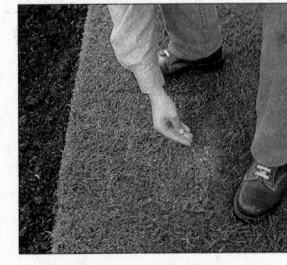

2 Add a little sandy loam, if necessary, so that the damaged part is level with the rest of the lawn, then sow grass seed over the damaged section, and water well.

HOW TO REPAIR A DAMAGED PATCH

1 *Using a half-moon edger and the edge of a plank, cut around the damaged area, then undercut the turf with a spade and remove it.*

2 *Lightly fork or rake over the area of exposed soil to loosen it, and then apply a liquid or granular fertilizer if required.*

3 *Carefully tread over the soil to consolidate it and firm the surface before returfing.*

Lay a new piece of turf to fit the exposed space, raising or lowering the soil level beneath, if necessary, so that the new turf is level with the rest of the lawn, and tamp it down in position with the back of a rake or your hands. Top-dress and water the repaired surface well.

Levelling a hump or hollow
Small humps or hollows within the lawn may be easily levelled. First cut a cross through the turf on the affected area and peel back the cut turf. To level a hollow, fork over the soil beneath and fill in with topsoil, then lightly firm the ground. For a hump, remove the excess soil until the ground is level, and firm. Fold back the cut turf and tamp it down with the back of a rake before top-dressing and watering.

On larger areas, it may be necessary to remove complete sections of turf entirely, level the soil beneath (see "Levelling the site", p.280–81), and then carefully relay the turf over the original area.

4 *Place a new piece of turf in the hole, cutting it to fit with a half-moon edger.*

5 *Check that the new turf is level with the rest of the lawn; if necessary adjust the soil level beneath the turf. Then firm in the turf and water well.*

Lawn weeds

Although some weeds, such as slender speedwell (*Veronica filiformis*) and daisies (*Bellis perennis*), may look attractive in utility lawns, they are generally considered undesirable in high-quality, closely mown lawns. Many broad-leaved weeds can survive in grass that is mown, but excessive numbers may make the grass suffer so, even in a utility lawn, control may be needed. Unless the lawn clippings are collected, mowing may even spread certain types of weed that can root from small pieces of stem. On small lawns, daisies and plantains (*Plantago*) may be cut out individually by hand, but for a large lawn, the simplest method is to use a "weed and feed" mixture. This may be applied with a fertilizer spreader or by hand, according to the instructions given.

Moss
Almost always undesirable, moss may be found in lawns for many reasons, including soil compaction, poor drainage, low fertility, insufficient light, mowing too closely, and extremes of soil pH; it can be a problem even in the best-kept lawns. If the lawn is occasionally affected by moss, treat it with a chemical moss killer or lawn sand, then remove it by scarification (see p.288). If the problem continually recurs, identify and correct the possible causes; this may involve improving soil aeration, drainage, and fertility and, on light soils, top-dressing to assist water retention. Adopting an annual maintenance programme should help to control the problem. For further details see PLANT PROBLEMS, "Lawn weeds", pp.576–7.

Pests and diseases

Most high-quality lawns are treated to remove earthworms because, although their tunnelling improves soil texture and aeration, some create worm casts, providing ideal sites for the germination of weed seeds.

Several turf diseases, including brown patch (see "Drought", p.571), dollar spot, fairy rings, snow mould/*Fusarium* patch, and red thread attack lawns, particularly in hot, humid countries; *Fusarium* patch is a problem in cold regions too and may even occur under snow. Preventive sprays may be necessary, but in cooler temperate and maritime climates it is usual to spray only in serious cases. For treatment of pests and diseases, see "Lawn problems", pp.571–2.

LEVELLING A HOLLOW OR HUMP

1 *Cut a cross right through the hump or hollow in the turf, using a half-moon edger; the cross should reach just beyond the affected area.*

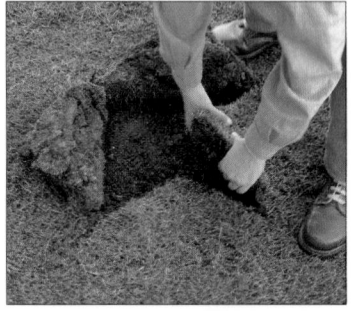

2 *Fold back the cut sections of turf, taking care not to pull them too harshly or they may crack.*

3 *For a hollow, fill in the ground beneath with a good, sandy topsoil; for a hump, remove some of the soil until the entire surface is level.*

4 *Replace the folded back turf and lightly firm to check that the level is correct. Adjust the soil level beneath, if necessary, firm, top-dress, and water well.*

13

THE HERB GARDEN

WHETHER GROWN ON *their own as an ornamental feature, with other plants in a border, or among the ordered ranks of a vegetable plot, herbs are an invaluable addition to any garden. They have always been prized for their culinary, cosmetic, or curative uses, but they also make highly decorative garden plants. Although few have spectacular or showy flowers, many are graced* *by attractive foliage and almost all are worth growing for their scent alone – ranging from the fresh, citrus tang of lemon balm to the aniseed aroma of fennel and the sweet apple perfume of chamomile. Their heady fragrance is hard to resist and their nectar-filled flowers tempt bees and butterflies, so adding the drowsy hum of insects to complete the restfulness of a herb garden.*

Designing with herbs

HERB growing combines the delights of the flower garden with the productivity of the vegetable plot. The results are decorative, excellent in aroma and flavour, and inexpensive to produce. By definition, a herb is any plant that has culinary or curative uses, so the range is surprisingly wide. Herbs include annuals, perennials, shrubs, and trees, not just herbaceous plants.

Historically, herbs have been used for flavouring and preserving food, and, in addition, for making medicines and toiletries. Their aesthetic appeal has always been important, too, and their ornamental qualities, as well as their practical uses, are of equal value today.

STRUCTURED INFORMALITY
Growing a rich profusion of herbs brings a wealth of fine scents and contrasting textures to the garden. In this herb garden, clipped dwarf hedges add structure while bold blocks of herbs such as golden marjoram contrast with casual plantings of feathery fennel and low alpine strawberries.

Herbs in the home

Although fresh and dried herbs are widely available, they rarely have as fine an aroma or flavour as those harvested from your own garden. Enjoy their scents indoors as well as outside by using them fresh in flower arrangements or dried to make pot-pourri or to fill herb pillows. All over the world, herbs are considered invaluable in cooking to enhance and enliven other foods, elevating even the simplest meal to the level of *haute cuisine*. The curative and cosmetic properties of herbs are also renowned: for thousands of years, they have been used in many medicines and beauty products.

Culinary uses
Freshly harvested herbs are an important ingredient in many classic combinations, such as tomato and basil salad, potato mayonnaise with chives, and Pimm's with borage. In some cases, the flowers may be used as an edible decoration: borage, chives, elder, and marigold are all simple to grow and produce attractive flowers. Stalks, such as angelica for crystallizing, or branches of rosemary for barbecues, are also easily grown but are rarely available otherwise. Aromatic seeds, or spices, are easier to obtain but again are mostly cheap and easy to produce.

Certain herbs, such as lemon balm and peppermint, may be infused in boiling water to make herb teas, which are a good alternative to ordinary tea and coffee since they do not contain tannin or caffeine. Most are made from dried leaves, flowers, or seeds, although they may also be made from fresh herbs.

Medicinal herbs
In many parts of the world herbal medicine is commonplace and the herb garden is a source of home-grown treatments for all sorts of ailment; mint, for example, is a mild local anaesthetic, a powerful antiseptic, and a remedy for digestive problems. Herbs are also grown for processing into drugs by the pharmaceutical industry. In general, it is inadvisable to use herbs for medicinal purposes without specialist knowledge or advice.

Cosmetic and scented preparations
A number of herbs have beneficial effects on the condition of skin or hair, and are included in beauty products: rosemary, chamomile, and mint are used in shampoos and conditioners, thyme as an antiseptic for mouthwashes, and marigold and elderflower in skin lotions.

Aromatic herbs may be enjoyed all year round if they are made into scented household articles such as pomanders and linen sachets. Commercially, they are also used in perfumery; extracting oils and essences is, however, usually too complex to undertake at home.

Herbs in the garden

The majority of herbs grown today are still the wild species, but many cultivars are also now available, differing in habit or in the colour of their foliage or flowers. This diversity makes them more valuable as decorative garden plants, while their scent and other properties are usually similar, if not identical, to the species.

The appeal of herbs lies largely in their fragrance which, in contrast to other plants, usually derives from the foliage rather than the flowers. Essential oils are released when the leaves are warmed or crushed: on a sunny day, the scent of a herb garden fills the air.

A few herbs have brightly coloured flowers which may be used to great effect: the orange of marigolds (*Calendula officinalis*) offset by bronze fennel (*Foeniculum vulgare* 'Purpureum'), or the brilliant blue of borage (*Borago officinalis*) with silver-grey wormwood (*Artemisia absinthium*), for example.

Certain herbs are reputed to benefit other plants: some pungent plants such as southernwood (*Artemisia abrotanum*) are considered to repel insects if crushed or infused, while growing chamomile (*Chamaemelum nobile*) in the garden is said to increase the health and vigour of other plants nearby.

Where to grow herbs

As for other plants, herbs should be grown in conditions that are similar to their natural habitat to ensure that they are healthy and vigorous. Many herbs are Mediterranean in origin, and these usually prefer plenty of sunshine and a free-draining soil.

Some herbs tolerate a damp, partially shaded site, however, provided that they are not waterlogged or in dense or permanent shade. Most variegated and golden cultivars

---

HERBS THAT TOLERATE MOIST SHADE

Angelica (*Angelica archangelica*)
Chervil (*Anthriscus cerefolium*)
Chives (*Allium schoenoprasum*)
Elder (*Sambucus nigra*, *S.n.* 'Aurea', *S.n.* 'Marginata')
Feverfew (*Tanacetum parthenium*, *T.p.* 'Aureum')
Lemon balm (*Melissa officinalis*, *M.o.* 'All Gold', *M.o.* 'Aurea', *M.o.* 'Variegata')
Lovage (*Levisticum officinale*)
Mints (*Mentha*)
Parsley (*Petroselinum crispum*)
Sorrel (*Rumex acetosa*)
Sweet cicely (*Myrrhis odorata*)
Tansy (*Tanacetum vulgare*)
Woodruff (*Asperula odorata*)

---

thrive in light shade. Pineapple mint (*Mentha suaveolens* 'Variegata') and golden forms of lemon balm (*Melissa officinalis*) and feverfew (*Tanacetum parthenium*) retain their colour best in a position that is lit by morning or evening sun but shaded at midday.

Herbs may be grown in a variety of situations, the choice largely depending on personal preference and convenience. A separate herb garden in an attractive design provides an appealing feature and need not take up much space, but it may be preferable to have a culinary herb patch, or herbs in containers, within easy reach of the kitchen. Some herbs are decorative enough to be grown with other plants in a bed or border, while others may be better sited in the vegetable garden. Culinary herbs should always be sited away from possible contamination by pets or roadside pollution.

Herb gardens

If there is space, it is worth creating a separate herb garden and growing many different herbs together for a strong impact and to reap the benefit of their combined scents in one place. Making a special feature of the plants allows plenty of opportunity to create an interesting pattern or design using blocks of complementary or contrasting colours. As well as being a highly ornamental way of displaying the herbs, it makes harvesting easier. Traditionally, herb gardens have been bordered by low, clipped hedges of box (*Buxus sempervirens*), but a less formal edging of hyssop (*Hyssopus officinalis*) or lavender (*Lavandula*) would also be suitable.

Beds and borders

Herbs may also be grown with other ornamental garden plants. This is useful where there is no space for a separate herb garden, or for herbs that are border plants in their own right, such as bergamot (*Monarda didyma*) and rue (*Ruta graveolens*). Grey-leaved species are especially fine in a silver border or as a contrast to plants with blue, purple, or pink colouring, such as purple sage (*Salvia officinalis* 'Purpurascens').

Stately, architectural plants are valuable as focal points on their own or at the back of a border. Fill any gaps in borders with colourful annuals, such as poppies (*Papaver*), blue borage, and dark opal basil (*Ocimum basilicum* 'Purpurascens').

Planting aromatic herbs next to doorways, paths, and seats makes it easy to enjoy their scents to the full. Low, spreading herbs, such as wild

---

thyme (*Thymus serpyllum*), lawn chamomile (*Chamaemelum nobile* 'Treneague'), and creeping savory (*Satureja spicigera*), are suitable for rock gardens or *en masse* to form a fragrant carpet. These and other, more upright, herbs such as chives (*Allium schoenoprasum*) make an unusual and attractive edging to a border or path.

Herbs in the vegetable garden

For culinary herbs that are used in large quantities, such as parsley (*Petroselinum crispum*), the vegetable plot may be the best site. This may also be the most convenient place for fast-growing herbs, such as chervil (*Anthriscus cerefolium*) and dill (*Anethum graveolens*), that are sown in succession and do not transplant successfully. The herbs may be grown in straight rows among the vegetables or as an ornamental border around the edge of the vegetable garden.

Growing herbs in containers

Many herbs grow well in containers. From a hanging basket to a chimney pot, almost any container is suitable, provided that it has drainage holes and that a layer of porous material is added before planting in it.

In small gardens or on balconies, the entire herb garden may consist of containers, imaginatively positioned on walls, steps, shelves, and windowsills, as well as at ground level. If space is at a premium, using a strawberry planter (a pot with planting pockets) offers an attractive and functional way of growing a number of different plants together. Even if you have a separate area for herbs or grow them with other ornamentals or vegetables, it is often convenient to have one or two pots of commonly used herbs near the door.

Some of the best herbs to grow in containers are chervil, parsley,

CARTWHEEL BED
A cartwheel design provides a decorative and practical way of growing a small range of herbs.

CONTAINER GARDENING
Even in the smallest garden, there is room to grow a variety of aromatic herbs in a group of pots.

chives, compact marjoram (*Origanum vulgare* 'Compactum'), rock hyssop (*Hyssopus officinalis* subsp. *aristatus*), and thymes (*Thymus*). Large plants, such as rosemary (*Rosmarinus officinalis*) and bay (*Laurus nobilis*), often look good grown as single specimens in pots or tubs. Growing slightly tender herbs, such as myrtle (*Myrtus communis*), lemon verbena (*Aloysia triphylla*), and rose-scented geranium (*Pelargonium graveolens*), in containers is convenient because they may be brought inside during winter; they also make good conservatory plants.

Paving and patios

Planting herbs in the gaps between paving stones is an attractive option for those herbs that prefer well-drained conditions, such as thymes and creeping savory; allow the plants to spread onto the paving so that an occasional light tread may release their fragrance.

Patios are often ideal for displaying a variety of tender or Mediterranean herbs that enjoy warmth and shelter, while an exotic touch may be added by including plants such as lemon trees (*Citrus limon*), cardamom (*Elettaria cardamomum*), or ginger (*Zingiber officinale*) grown in ornamental containers.

Raised beds

Growing herbs in raised beds makes it easier to enjoy their fragrance at close quarters as well as being practical for the disabled or elderly, providing easy access for planting, maintenance, and harvesting. Raised beds must have strong retaining walls and should be no more than approximately 75cm (30in) wide and at a comfortable height for working (see also STRUCTURES AND SURFACES, "Raised beds", p.507).

Raised beds are also a good option on paved areas against a wall (but not above the damp course in a house wall) and in any site where the soil is not free-draining. Choose small, compact herbs for raised beds, and control their spread by regular pruning and dividing.

Designing a herb garden

Whether informal or formal, a herb garden should be designed so that it is congruous with the style of the rest of the garden and the house. Take into account maintenance resources when planning: in general, informal herb gardens need less initial structural work than formal ones, and routine care may be less time-consuming, depending on the plants used and the size and complexity of the design. It is also possible to combine elements of both formal and informal designs; for example, a well-defined, symmetrical pattern of paths could form a framework for a free planting of herbs of different heights, habits, and colours.

Informal designs

An informal design largely depends for its success upon the complementary habits and colours of the herbs. Variegated and coloured-leaved forms, such as golden marjoram (*Origanum vulgare* 'Aureum') and purple sage, are especially effective in such a scheme. Try green- and gold-leaved plants together, for example, or those with purple and silver foliage.

There is greater freedom to use plants of different heights and habits than in a formal scheme: tall ones

FORMAL HERB GARDEN
This well-planned layout is divided by brick paths, which provide a formal framework for a number of geometric herb beds.

may be used to striking effect without upsetting the balance and impact of the design, and the overall impression of colourful harmony and rich abundance allows greater flexibility for experimenting with bold combinations.

Formal designs

These designs are usually based on geometric patterns and framed by low hedges or paths. Each small bed created by the pattern is then planted with one kind of herb, giving bold blocks of colour and texture. At its simplest, the design may take the form of a cartwheel bedded into the soil with a different herb planted in each segment. These designs often look particularly impressive when viewed from above, so consider siting the herb garden where it may be overlooked from an upper

window or a slope. When choosing plants, do not include tall, invasive, or sprawling herbs that may spoil the rest of the design when fully grown.

A formal garden with paths is labour-intensive initially but soon looks mature and needs little structural maintenance. One that includes a framework of dwarf hedges that require regular clipping may be considerably more demanding. The hedging may outline the design or

take on the complex shapes of a knot garden (see "Knot gardens", p.31). Suitable plants for dwarf hedges include hyssop, shrubby germander (*Teucrium fruticans*), lavenders, box, and winter savory (*Satureja montana*) planted about 22–30cm (9–12in) apart.

Making a plan

To draw up a plan, first measure the site and surrounding features accurately, taking account of any changes in level. Also note where shadows fall at different seasons as well as at different times of day.

Whether the garden is to be formal or informal in style, remember that herbs should be within arm's reach for convenient harvesting; for beds or borders in open ground, provide access by paths or stepping stones so that the soil is not walked on as this could lead to compaction.

Transfer the measurements to squared paper, working to scale; in order to compare a number of different designs, draw each scheme on a sheet of tracing paper laid over the master plan.

Finally, decide on which herbs to grow, taking into account their cultivation requirements, habit, colour, eventual height and spread, and the amounts that will be required for harvesting, then mark them on the plan. Herbs in containers may also be included in the design to provide focal points.

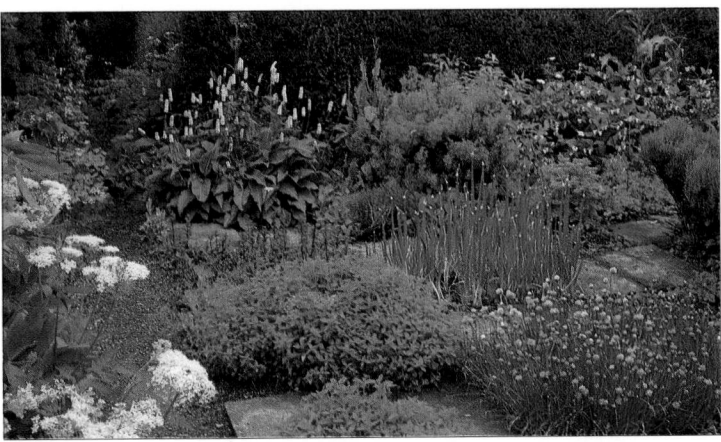

HERBS IN A PATIO GARDEN
Enliven a patio or courtyard, and soften the effect of the hard materials, by planting herbs directly into the gaps between paving or in gravel.

PLANNING A FORMAL HERB GARDEN

There are many possible formal designs, although imagination should be restrained by considerations of balance and proportion. Cartwheel and chessboard schemes are popular but unusual geometric patterns also provide plenty of opportunity to create an eye-catching feature.

Directory of common herbs

Chives
(Allium schoenoprasum)

Hardy, herbaceous, clump-forming perennial with hollow, grass-like leaves and mauve flowers. Good as a low edging for borders. May be forced for winter use (see p.298). Use the leaves, which have a mild onion flavour, as a garnish and flavouring in salads, dips, soft cheeses, and soups; the edible flowers make a decorative addition to salads.
Harvesting and storing Cut leaves and flowers as available to use fresh. For freezing and drying, cut leaves before flowering and chop finely.
Propagation By seed sown in spring (see p.162) or by division in autumn (p.164).
Related species and variants Variations in height, flower colour, and flavour are available; Chinese or garlic chives (*A. tuberosum*) have a mild garlic flavour and white flowers.

Lemon verbena
(Aloysia triphylla)

Half-hardy, upright, deciduous shrub with pointed, oval leaves. Plants may be cut back by frost but usually grow again from the base. The leaves have a strong, clean, lemon scent and are used in herb teas, desserts, and, dried, in pot-pourri and teas.
Harvesting and storing Pick leaves during the growing season for using fresh or drying.
Propagation By softwood cuttings (see p.83).

Dill
(Anethum graveolens)

Hardy, upright annual with flat heads of greenish-yellow flowers and feathery, blue-green leaves. Do not plant dill near fennel as this may result in cross-pollination and the loss of its distinctive flavour. Runs to seed quickly. Use the leaves or, for a stronger flavour, the aromatic seeds in soups, sauces, potato salad, pickles, and fish dishes.
Harvesting and storing Pick leaves in spring and summer before flowering. Cut seedheads as they ripen in summer.
Propagation By seed sown in spring and early summer (see p.180); may not transplant well.

Angelica
(Angelica archangelica)

Hardy biennial with large, divided leaves and large flowerheads. A bold, architectural plant. Unless seeds are required, remove seedheads

before ripening to prevent unwanted seedlings. The young stalks may be candied; the leaves are used in cooking, especially in fruit desserts and fish dishes.
Harvesting and storing Gather fresh leaves in spring and summer. Cut young stalks for crystallizing in spring or early summer. Cut seedheads as they ripen in summer.
Propagation By seed sown in autumn (see p.180); seeds lose viability within three months of ripening.

Chervil
(Anthriscus cerefolium)

Hardy annual with bright green, fern-like leaves. Runs to seed quickly in hot, dry conditions. The leaves have a fine, subtle flavour, reminiscent of parsley and anise. Use the leaves in egg dishes, salads, soups, and sauces.
Harvesting and storing Gather leaves before flowering. Freeze or dry them gently to preserve their delicate flavour.
Propagation By seed sown at monthly intervals from spring to early autumn (see p.180); do not transplant. May also be sown in trays under glass in early autumn for winter use.

Horseradish
(Armoracia rusticana)

Hardy perennial with large, coarse leaves. Plants are persistent and difficult to eradicate. The stout, white-fleshed roots have a pungent flavour and are grated into coleslaw, dips, and sauces, especially in horseradish sauce. Young leaves are used in salads or sandwiches.
Harvesting and storing Pick the young leaves in spring. Harvest the roots in autumn when the flavour is at its peak, or as required.
Propagation By division (see p.164) or 15cm (6in) root cuttings (p.167), or by seed (p.162).

Southernwood
(Artemisia abrotanum)

Hardy, semi-evergreen subshrub with finely divided, grey-green foliage. May be used to form a low hedge, trimmed in summer; it is also attractive in mixed borders. Flowers are rarely produced in cool climates. Use the aromatic leaves in pot-pourri and as an insect repellant.
Harvesting and storing In summer, pick leaves as required for using fresh or for drying.

Propagation By softwood cuttings in summer, semi-ripe heel cuttings in late summer, or by hardwood cuttings in autumn (see pp.83–5).

Wormwood
(Artemisia absinthium)

Hardy, deciduous subshrub with deeply divided, greyish-green leaves. Good as a border plant or informal hedge. Prune to within 15cm (6in) of the ground in spring. The aromatic leaves are intensely bitter; they were formerly used to flavour alcoholic drinks but are now regarded as toxic. The foliage is attractive in herbal decorations and posies.
Harvesting and storing Pick foliage in summer for use fresh or dried in arrangements.
Propagation By softwood cuttings in summer (see p.83) or by semi-ripe heel cuttings in late summer (p.85).
Variants 'Lambrook Silver' is a cultivar with silver-grey foliage.

French tarragon
(Artemisia dracunculus)

Half-hardy perennial with upright stems and glossy, narrow leaves. In cold areas, may need winter protection, but may be forced for winter use. The leaves are commonly used in sauce *béarnaise*, *fines herbes*, tartare sauce, in egg and chicken dishes, and to flavour vinegar.
Harvesting and storing Cut sprigs of foliage throughout the growing season, leaving two-thirds of the stem to regrow. The leaves are best frozen but may also be dried.
Propagation By division of rhizomes in spring (see p.165) or by stem tip cuttings in summer (p.166). Seed is not available: that sold as tarragon is the Russian species.
Related species A hardier species is Russian tarragon (*A. dracunculoides*), but it unfortunately has an inferior flavour.

Woodruff
(Asperula odorata, syn. Galium odoratum)

Hardy, creeping perennial with star-shaped, white flowers that appear above the whorls of narrow leaves in spring and early summer. An excellent ground-cover plant in damp shade. The dried leaves are used in pot-pourri and herb tea.
Harvesting and storing Gather the leaves for drying just before the flowers open in spring.
Propagation By division in autumn or spring (see p.164) or by seed sown in early autumn (p.162), but germination may be slow.

Borage
(*Borago officinalis*)

Hardy, upright annual with hairy foliage and intense blue flowers. Add the cucumber-flavoured leaves, and the flowers, to cold drinks (such as Pimm's) and salads. Crystallize the flowers for use in cake decoration.

Harvesting and storing Pick young leaves and use fresh. Gather the flowers (without calyces) in summer to use fresh, freeze in ice cubes, or crystallize.

Propagation Sow seed from spring to early autumn (see p.180). Self-sows in light soils.

Variants There is also a form with white flowers, *B.o.* f. *alba*.

Marigold
(*Calendula officinalis*)

Bushy, hardy annual with bright orange flowers. A colourful plant for borders and containers. Dead-head to prolong flowering. Use the petals to flavour and colour rice, soft cheese, and soups, and to garnish salads. Chop the young leaves into salads. Dried petals may be used to add colour to pot-pourri.

Harvesting and storing Pick open flowers in summer and remove petals for drying. Gather leaves when young.

Propagation By seed sown in autumn or spring (see p.180). Self-sows freely.

Variants Double-flowered forms in shades of cream, orange, and bronze are widely available.

Caraway
(*Carum carvi*)

Hardy biennial with feathery leaves and, in the second year, flat heads of tiny, white flowers. Aromatic seeds are used in baking, confectionery, cheeses, and meat stews such as goulash. Add the leaves to soups and salads.

Harvesting and storing Gather leaves when young. Collect the ripe seedheads in summer.

Propagation By seed in autumn (see p.180).

Chamomile
(*Chamaemelum nobile*)

Hardy, creeping, evergreen perennial, forming a dense mat of finely cut, feathery leaves. Good at the edge of paths and borders, or between paving stones. May be planted as an ornamental lawn (see p.283). Use the apple-scented leaves in pot-pourri; the aromatic flowers are used in pot-pourri and herb teas.

Harvesting and storing Pick leaves at any time as required. Gather flowers when fully open in summer and dry whole.

Propagation By division in spring or autumn (see p.164), or by stem tip cuttings of sideshoots in summer (p.166).

Variants 'Treneague' is a dwarf, non-flowering form that is particularly suitable for lawns and gaps in paving. *C.n.* var. *flore-pleno* has attractive double flowers.

Coriander
(*Coriandrum sativum*)

Hardy annual with divided foliage and small, white or pale mauve flowers. The plants have an unpleasant smell and should not be grown indoors. The lobed, lower leaves are used in curries, chutneys, sauces, and salads. The seeds, which have a sweet, spicy flavour, are used in baking, chutneys, and sausages.

Harvesting and storing Pick young leaves for using fresh or for freezing. Gather seedheads as they ripen.

Propagation By seed sown in autumn or early spring (see p.180).

Cumin
(*Cuminum cyminum*)

Tender annual with delicate leaves and white or pale pink flowers. Requires heat for the seeds to ripen. The aromatic seeds are used in curries, pickles, yoghurt, and Middle Eastern dishes.

Harvesting and storing Gather seedheads as they ripen.

Propagation By seed sown in late spring in a warm situation or under cover (see p.181).

Fennel
(*Foeniculum vulgare*)

Hardy perennial with fine, filigree leaves and clusters of yellow flowers. A tall, graceful plant for borders. Use the leaves and leaf sheaths for their aniseed flavour in salads, and meat and fish dishes. Seeds are used in baking, fish dishes, and herb teas.

Harvesting and storing Cut leaves and leaf sheaths when still young. Gather seedheads as they ripen.

Propagation By seed sown in spring (see p.162) or by division in autumn (p.164).

Variants 'Purpureum' is an attractive bronze cultivar; Florence fennel (*F.v.* var. *dulce*) is grown as an annual for use as a vegetable (see p.350).

Hyssop
(*Hyssopus officinalis*)

Hardy, semi-evergreen subshrub with spikes of small, dark purple-blue flowers. Suitable for growing as a low hedge. The aromatic leaves are used sparingly in soups, bean dishes, stews, game, and pâté.

Harvesting and storing Gather leaves any time for fresh use; pick young leaves in early summer to dry.

Propagation By seed (see p.86), division (p.90), or by softwood cuttings in spring (p.83).

Variants Pink- and white-flowered varieties are available. Rock hyssop (*H.o.* subsp. *aristatus*) is a dwarf form especially suitable for containers.

Orris
(*Iris* 'Florentina', syn. *I. florentina*)

Hardy perennial with off-white flowers and sword-shaped leaves. Plant so that the rhizomes are exposed to full sun. The thick rhizome is bitter when fresh but develops a violet scent after drying and prolonged storage. It is ground for using as a perfume fixative in pot-pourri and linen sachets.

Harvesting and storing In autumn, dig up rhizomes at least three years old. Peel, split, and dry, leaving for up to two years before grinding.

Propagation By division of rhizomes in late spring or early autumn (see p.165).

Related species *I. pallida* is also grown as orris in the same way.

Bay
(*Laurus nobilis*)

Hardy, evergreen tree or shrub with dark, leathery, pointed leaves. Makes an excellent container plant. May be clipped for topiary or pruned hard to restrict size. In cold areas, it may need protection from frost and wind. Use the leaves in *bouquet garni*, and for flavouring stock, marinades, sauces, milk desserts, and meat and fish dishes.

Harvesting and storing Pick leaves any time for using fresh. Dry mature leaves in summer.

Propagation By semi-ripe heel cuttings of sideshoots in late summer (see p.55) or by layering in summer (p.57).

Variants 'Aurea' has yellow-flushed leaves.

Lavender
(*Lavandula angustifolia*)

Hardy, evergreen, bushy shrub with narrow, grey-green leaves and upright, mauve flower spikes. Good for low hedging. The flowers are used in pot-pourri, linen sachets, herb pillows, and tea. They may also be crystallized or used to flavour oil or vinegar.

Harvesting and storing Gather flowering stems in summer, and air-dry.

Propagation By cuttings of semi-ripe, non-flowering shoots in summer (see p.84).

Related species There are several other species

and cultivars, varying in habit, foliage, flowering time, and flower colour. They include dwarf cultivars, such as 'Hidcote', and white-flowered forms, for example 'Nana Alba'; French lavender (*L. stoechas*), which is half hardy, has purple flowers crowned by purple bracts.

Lovage
(*Levisticum officinale*, syn. *Ligusticum levisticum*)

Hardy perennial with divided leaves and clusters of pale green flowers; a tall plant, suitable for the back of a border. The leaves have a strong flavour, resembling celery and yeast, and are used in soups, stocks, and stews; add the raw, young leaves to salads. The aromatic seeds are used in baking and vegetable dishes, and the young stalks may be crystallized. Blanch plants under pots in spring for use as a vegetable.
Harvesting and storing Pick young leaves in spring and freeze or dry. In spring, gather young stalks for crystallizing. Cut stalks after two to three weeks of blanching in spring, leaving central shoots to grow.
Propagation By seed sown as soon as ripe in late summer (see p.162) or by division in spring or autumn (p.164).

Lemon balm
(*Melissa officinalis*)

Hardy, clump-forming perennial with oval, toothed leaves. Add the lemon-scented leaves to cold drinks, sweet and savoury dishes, or infuse them to make herb tea.
Harvesting and storing Pick leaves before flowering for using fresh or for drying.
Propagation By seed sown in spring (see p.162) or division in spring or autumn (p.164).
Variants Yellow-variegated cultivars, such as 'Aurea', are available; grow them in partial shade to avoid leaf scorch.

Mint
(*Mentha spicata*)

Hardy, herbaceous perennial with tiny, mauve flowers in summer. May be invasive (see p.298). Use the leaves to make mint sauce, in salads, drinks, and with potatoes or peas.
Harvesting and storing Pick leaves before flowering and dry or freeze, or chop and infuse in vinegar.
Propagation By stem tip cuttings rooted in spring or summer (see p.166), or by division in spring or autumn (p.164).
Related species There are numerous species and cultivars with slightly differing foliage and scents. Some, such as pineapple mint (*M. suaveolens* 'Variegata'), have variegated leaves. Peppermint (*M. x piperita*) has purplish-green leaves used in peppermint tea and in syrups and desserts, while

eau-de-cologne mint (*M. x piperita* 'Citrata') has purple-flushed foliage and a fine perfume. Bowles' mint (*M. x villosa* 'Alopecuroides') has rounded leaves with a fresh, spearmint aroma and purplish-pink flowers.

Bergamot
(*Monarda didyma*)

Hardy, herbaceous perennial with heads of red, claw-shaped florets in summer. An excellent border plant for moist soil. Infuse the aromatic leaves in tea for an "Earl Grey" flavour, and add them to summer drinks, salads, pork dishes, or pot-pourri. Use the attractive florets to add colour to salads and pot-pourri.
Harvesting and storing Pick leaves in spring or just before flowering in summer for using fresh or drying. Gather flowers in summer.
Propagation By seed in spring (see p.162), stem cuttings in summer (p.166), or division in early spring (p.164).
Related species and variants Cultivars with red, pink, white, or purple flowers are available. *M. fistulosa* has lavender flowers.

Sweet cicely
(*Myrrhis odorata*)

Hardy, herbaceous perennial with flat heads of tiny, white flowers in summer. The fern-like leaves, which have an aniseed flavour, are used mainly in fruit dishes to reduce acidity but may also be added to salads. The thick taproot can be eaten raw or cooked as a vegetable. The large seeds are added to fruit dishes.
Harvesting and storing Pick leaves in spring and early summer for drying. Collect unripe seeds in summer and dry or pickle them. Dig up roots in autumn for using fresh.
Propagation By seed sown outdoors in autumn (see p.163). Self-sows readily.

Basil
(*Ocimum basilicum*)

Half-hardy annual with toothed, pointed oval leaves. In cold regions, basil must be grown under cover or in a warm position. Grows well in pots on a sunny windowsill. The highly aromatic leaves are used in salads, vinegars, pesto, and tomato pasta dishes.
Harvesting and storing Pick leaves when young in summer and freeze, dry, or use to flavour herb oil or vinegar; or pack leaves in jars of oil to preserve them.
Propagation By seed sown in warmth in late spring (see p.181).
Related species and variants 'Purpurascens' is an attractive, purple-leaved cultivar with pink flowers. The compact bush basil (*O. minimum*) is hardier but has less flavour.

Marjoram
(*Origanum vulgare*)

Hardy, herbaceous perennial with tiny, white or mauve flowers in summer. Needs warmth and full sun for its flavour to develop. The aromatic leaves are used widely in cooking, especially in pizzas and pasta sauces.
Harvesting and storing Pick leaves for immediate use during the growing season. For drying or freezing, pick just before flowers open.
Propagation By seed sown in spring (see p.162), division in spring or autumn (p.164), or by root or stem cuttings of non-flowering shoots in summer (pp.166–7).
Variants There are various species and hybrids, differing in hardiness, flavour, and flower and foliage colour, for example golden marjoram (*O.v.* 'Aureum'). The low-growing 'Compactum' is ideal for containers and edging.

Parsley
(*Petroselinum crispum*)

Hardy biennial with bright green, crinkled leaves and, in its second summer, flat heads of tiny, greenish-yellow flowers. Good for growing in pots. Use the leaves whole or chopped as a garnish and in *bouquet garni*, sauces, and egg and fish dishes.
Harvesting and storing Pick leaves of plants in their first year and use fresh or freeze.
Propagation By seed sown at intervals from early spring to late summer (see p.180).
Variants *P.c.* 'Neapolitanum' is a flat-leaved parsley with a stronger flavour.

Aniseed
(*Pimpinella anisum*)

Half-hardy annual with deeply divided leaves and, in late summer, heads of tiny, white flowers. In cold regions, it must have a sunny, sheltered position for the seed to ripen. Add the leaves to fruit salads. The aromatic seeds are used in baking, confectionery, and both sweet and savoury dishes.
Harvesting and storing Pick lower leaves in spring for immediate use. Collect seedheads as they ripen in autumn.
Propagation By seed sown in late spring in its final position as it is difficult to transplant successfully (see p.181).

Rosemary
(*Rosmarinus officinalis*)

Hardy, evergreen shrub with dense, needle-like leaves and pale blue flowers in spring and summer or, in mild regions, all year round. Not reliably hardy in cold areas. May be grown as an informal hedge. The leaves, which have a strong,

resinous aroma, are used in meat dishes, especially with lamb, and to make pot-pourri and hair rinses. The flowers may be added to salads.
Harvesting and storing Pick leaves and flowers as required for immediate use. Gather sprigs for drying during the growing season.
Propagation By seed sown in warmth in spring (see p.86), semi-ripe cuttings in late summer (p.84), or layering in autumn (p.88).
Variants Cultivars with flowers in various shades of blue, pink, and white are available. The vigorous, erect cultivar 'Miss Jessopp's Upright' is suitable for hedging; 'Severn Sea' has bright blue flowers and a dwarf, arching habit ideal for containers.

Sorrel
(*Rumex acetosa*)

Hardy, upright perennial with dock-like leaves. Remove the flower spikes to prolong leaf production. Protect with cloches for a winter supply. The young, tender leaves, which have a sour taste, are used in salads, soups, and sauces.
Harvesting and storing Pick young leaves before flowering for using fresh or freezing. May be frozen for use in cooked dishes.
Propagation By division in either spring or autumn (see p.164), or by seed sown in spring (p.162).
Related species The low-growing species, French, shield, or buckler-leaf sorrel (*R. scutatus*), has small, fine-flavoured leaves.

Rue
(*Ruta graveolens*)

Hardy, evergreen subshrub with divided, grey-green foliage and greenish-yellow flowers in summer. An excellent plant for borders or low hedges. Handling rue on sunny days may cause a skin rash. Use the pungent leaves with discretion in salads, sauces, and to flavour cream cheese.
Harvesting and storing Pick leaves as required for immediate use, protecting hands with rubber gloves on sunny days.
Propagation By seed sown in spring (see p.86), or cuttings of semi-ripe sideshoots in late summer (p.84).
Variants There are cultivars that have cream-variegated and blue leaves, for example, 'Variegata' and the compact 'Jackman's Blue'.

Sage
(*Salvia officinalis*)

Hardy, evergreen subshrub with grey-green foliage and, in summer, purplish-blue flowers. An excellent plant for shrub borders and rose gardens. The aromatic leaves are used in stuffings, meat

dishes, to flavour cheese, and in herb teas.
Harvesting and storing Pick leaves as needed to use fresh. Gather leaves before the flowers open for drying.
Propagation By seed sown in spring (see p.86), softwood cuttings in summer (p.83), or semi-ripe heel cuttings in early autumn (p.85).
Variants Cultivars include purple sage (*S.o.* 'Purpurascens') with strongly flavoured, purple leaves, and the half-hardy 'Tricolor', with white-margined, pink-flushed leaves.

Cotton lavender
(*Santolina chamaecyparissus*)

Hardy, evergreen subshrub with narrow, divided, silver-grey leaves on upright stems. In summer, it bears masses of yellow, button flowerheads. It is good as a low hedge, especially to provide a contrasting colour in knot gardens (see p.31). Add the aromatic leaves to pot-pourri, and dry the flowers for decorative purposes.
Harvesting and storing Pick leaves for drying in spring and summer. In summer, gather flowers as they open for drying.
Propagation By cuttings of semi-ripe sideshoots in late summer (see p.84).
Variants 'Lemon Queen' has bright green foliage and cream flowers; the cultivar 'Nana' is a dwarf form, only 15cm (6in) tall.

Winter savory
(*Satureja montana*)

Hardy, evergreen subshrub with tiny, white to pink flowers in summer, and small, narrow, aromatic leaves. Use the leaves in bean and cheese dishes.
Harvesting and storing Pick any time for using fresh. Gather leaves to dry or freeze as flower buds form.
Propagation By seed sown in spring (see p.86), division in spring or autumn (p.90), or by softwood cuttings taken between late spring and early summer (p.83).
Related species Creeping savory (*S. spicigera*) is a low species ideal for containers, edging, and rock gardens. Summer savory (*S. hortensis*) has lilac flowers and a fine flavour.

Alecost
(*Tanacetum balsamita*)

Hardy perennial with small, daisy-like flowers in late summer and oval, grey-green leaves. The leaves have a citrus-mint fragrance; use them sparingly in cooking and also in pot-pourri.
Harvesting and storing Gather fresh leaves in spring and summer for using fresh or for drying.
Propagation By division (see p.164).

Feverfew
(*Tanacetum parthenium*, syn. *Chrysanthemum parthenium*)

Hardy, semi-evergreen perennial with light green, chrysanthemum-like leaves; in summer and autumn it is covered with long-lasting, daisy-like flowers. An easy-to-grow, attractive plant for borders and containers. Use the pungent leaves in sachets to deter clothes moths. The aromatic flowers are added to pot-pourri.
Harvesting and storing Pick leaves and flowers in summer for drying.
Propagation By seed sown in spring or autumn (see p.162), division in autumn (p.164), or basal stem cuttings in summer (p.166). Self-sows freely.
Variants There are cultivars varying in height and foliage, with single or double flowers. Highly recommended is the golden-leaved 'Aureum'.

Thyme
(*Thymus vulgaris*)

Hardy, evergreen, low-growing subshrub with tiny leaves and, in summer, pale lilac flowers. May be grown as an edging for borders, between paving stones, and in containers. Add the aromatic leaves to *bouquet garni*, stuffings, sauces, soups, stocks, and meat dishes.
Harvesting and storing Pick leaves at any time to use fresh. Gather flowering tops for drying, stripping leaves and flowers from the stalks when quite dry. Fresh sprigs may also be infused in oil or vinegar.
Propagation By seed (see p.86) or division in spring (p.90), layering in spring or autumn (p.88), or by semi-ripe heel cuttings in early summer (p.85).
Related species and variants There are many species and cultivars, varying in height, foliage, and flower colour. Wild thyme (*T. serpyllum*) is a low, mat-forming plant with mauve flowers; *T. praecox* var. *arcticus* 'Coccineus' and 'Snowdrift' have, respectively, magenta and white flowers and 'Doone Valley' has scented foliage with gold markings. *T. x citriodorus* has lemon-scented leaves and lilac flowers; *T. vulgaris* 'Silver Posie' has silver-margined leaves.

Ginger
(*Zingiber officinale*)

Tender, deciduous perennial with tall, cane-like stems and lance-shaped leaves. The thick, tuberous rhizome is highly aromatic and is used in baking, preserves, confectionery, chutneys, sauces, and many oriental dishes.
Harvesting and storing Dig up young rhizomes and peel them for using fresh or preserving in syrup. For drying, dig up the rhizomes as the leaves turn yellow.
Propagation By division of rhizomes as they start to sprout (see p.165).

Soil preparation and planting

THE ideal site for a herb garden is sunny, open but sheltered, with neutral to alkaline soil, and good drainage. These conditions suit the majority of common herbs such as lavender (*Lavandula angustifolia*), winter savory (*Satureja montana*), sage (*Salvia officinalis*), marjoram (*Origanum vulgare*), rosemary (*Rosmarinus officinalis*), and thyme (*Thymus vulgaris*), most of which are Mediterranean in origin.

Preparing the site

If possible, prepare the ground well in advance, preferably in autumn. First, remove all weeds, taking care to eliminate any persistent, perennial weeds such as couch grass, using a weedkiller if necessary. Then dig over the soil, leaving it in a rough state over the winter to be broken down by frost.

In early spring, remove any weeds that have appeared subsequently, fork in well-rotted organic matter (such as garden or mushroom compost), and rake the soil to a fine, level tilth. The aim is to provide a free-draining and reasonably fertile soil. Feeding with manure or artificial fertilizers is not recommended, especially for Mediterranean herbs, since it produces soft growth with little aroma or resistance to frost.

On heavy, clay soil, it may be necessary to improve the drainage (see SOILS AND FERTILIZERS, "Improving drainage", p.529); alternatively, grow the herbs in raised beds or containers. Most herbs tolerate a slightly acid soil; if the pH is below 6.5, however, add a dressing of lime when preparing the soil (see SOILS AND FERTILIZERS, "Liming", p.531).

Planting invasive herbs

If planting invasive herbs, such as mints (*Mentha*), tansy (*Tanacetum vulgare*), or woodruff (*Asperula odorata*, syn. *Galium odoratum*), in open ground, restrict their spread by growing them in sunken containers. Old buckets, large pots, or even heavy-duty plastic bags are suitable, although it is usually necessary to make drainage holes. For best results, lift and divide the plants each spring and replant young, vigorous pieces in the containers using fresh compost; if not replenished, nutrients are quickly depleted and the herbs may deteriorate and become more prone to disease, such as rusts (see p.552).

1 *Dig a hole large enough to accommodate a large pot or old bucket. Make drainage holes in the pot, then place it in the hole and fill with a soil and compost mixture.*

2 *Plant the herb (here mint), firming in well; add enough compost to conceal the pot's rim, and water thoroughly. Each spring, replant and replace the compost in the pot.*

Herbs in winter

Although herbs are harvested mainly in spring and summer, the availability of many can be extended almost all year round.

Sown in late summer or early autumn, a number of herbs such as chervil (*Anthriscus cerefolium*), coriander (*Coriandrum sativum*), and parsley (*Petroselinum crispum*) continue to grow throughout the winter if they are protected from frost by a cold frame or cloches. They also grow well in pots placed on a sunny windowsill.

Herbaceous perennials that die down in winter, such as chives (*Allium schoenoprasum*), French tarragon (*Artemisia dracunculus*), and mints, may be forced for winter use. In early autumn, dig up mature plants, divide them, and replant in containers of loam-based potting compost. If kept in a light place that is free from frost and draughts, they produce fresh shoots throughout the winter that may be harvested regularly. Discard forced plants in spring or plant them out; if planted out, do not pick their leaves for at least a season to allow them time to recover vigour.

Evergreen herbs, such as winter savory, thyme, and rosemary, may be gathered throughout the year, but limit winter harvesting as there is no new growth at this time.

Planting container-grown herbs

Container-grown herbs may be planted throughout the year, but the best time is in spring when they establish rapidly. If they have been kept in a heated greenhouse during the winter, gradually harden them off in a cold frame before planting them out.

Water well before planting, as dry root balls are difficult to wet once below ground. To avoid trampling and compacting the soil in a bed, it is best to stand on a plank in order to reach the planting positions. Set out the herbs, while still in their pots, according to your planting plan and check that each has sufficient room to develop, depending on its growth rate and spread.

Whatever the weather, water thoroughly after planting in order to settle the soil around the plants and provide even moisture for new root growth. After planting, pinch out the tips of clump-forming herbs and trim back shrubby herbs to encourage new sideshoots and to develop a bushy habit.

HOW TO GROW HERBS FOR FRESH WINTER USE

1 *Choose a dry day in early autumn to lift a clump of herbs (here chives) from the garden using a fork.*

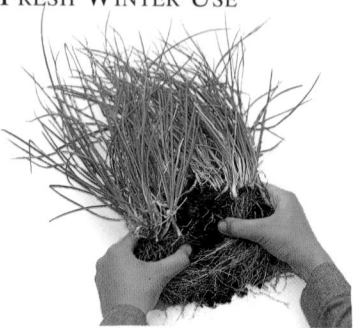
2 *Divide the clump into smaller pieces with your hands or a hand fork. Shake loose as much of the soil from the roots as possible.*

3 *Plant up the divided pieces into pots or trays of potting compost; water well and cut back the top-growth.*

4 *Place the plants in a light, frost-free place. Once they are about 10cm (4in) high, harvest the leaves regularly to mcintain a supply of new growth.*

Planting a herb garden to a design

Whether creating an intricate, formal design or a simple, informal one, careful planning, both on paper and on site, is essential for success. Make plans well in advance: start in the winter for planting in the spring, or as early as the preceding summer if you are raising the plants yourself.

As for all planting, thoroughly prepare the ground, clearing any weeds and raking the surface of the soil to a fine tilth (see "Preparing the site", p.298).

Once you have determined the design and the planting scheme on paper, mark the basic outline of the herb garden, including any paths, on the prepared site. Make any adjustments to the layout at this stage if required. It is most convenient to use container-grown herbs, since they can easily be set out according to the plan and the arrangement checked before actual planting begins.

If using turf or heavy materials such as paving, bricks, or stone, lay them before planting, while paths made of lighter, loose materials, such as grit, gravel, or bark chippings, may be laid before or after planting. When making paths of grit or gravel, provide retaining battens or edging tiles to prevent the material from spreading onto the plants in the beds.

1 First prepare the soil for planting. Then, using string and canes, or grit, mark out the planned design for the herb garden, including any paths or paved areas, on the site.

2 Lay out the plants, still in their pots, to check the overall effect and spacing. If using grit or gravel for the paths, sink battens at the edges to keep the material in place.

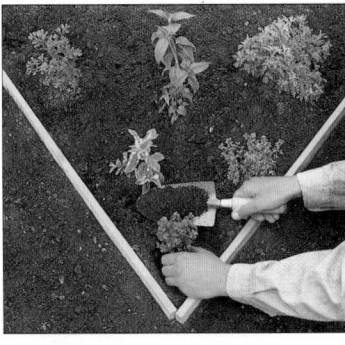

3 Once the design is finalized, plant the herbs and water them; you may prefer to plant them densely to achieve the desired effect quickly.

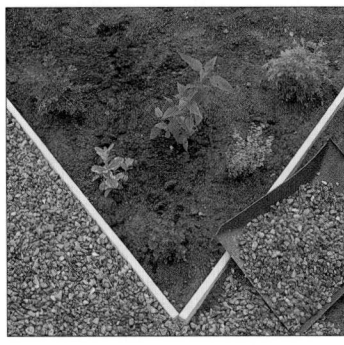

4 Lay the paths, adding grit or gravel evenly in between the battens; level the surface.

5 Keep the herb garden watered and weeded. Pinch out growing tips to promote bushy growth and prune as necessary.

DESIGN FOR A HERB GARDEN

1 Chives (*Allium schoenoprasum*)
2 Compact marjoram (*Origanum vulgare* 'Compactum')
3 Bergamot (*Monarda didyma*)
4 Wormwood (*Artemisia absinthium*)
5 Hyssop (*Hyssopus officinalis*)
6 Wild thyme (*Thymus serpyllum*)
7 Silver-variegated thyme (*Thymus vulgaris* 'Silver Posie')
8 Marjoram (*Origanum vulgare*)
9 Pineapple mint (*Mentha suaveolens* 'Variegata')
10 Chamomile (*Chamaemelum nobile*)
11 Buckler-leaf sorrel (*Rumex scutatus*)
12 French tarragon (*Artemisia dracunculus*)
13 Variegated sage (*Salvia officinalis* 'Icterina')
14 Parsley (*Petroselinum crispum*)
15 Sweet cicely (*Myrrhis odorata*)
16 Cotton lavender (*Santolina chamaecyparissus*)
17 Creeping savory (*Satureja spicigera*)
18 Golden lemon balm (*Melissa officinalis* 'Aurea')
19 Chinese chives (*Allium tuberosum*)
20 Orris (*Iris* 'Florentina')
21 Borage (*Borago officinalis*)
22 Pink hyssop (*Hyssopus officinalis*)
23 Purple sage (*Salvia officinalis* 'Purpurascens')
24 Pink lavender (*Lavandula* 'Loddon Pink')
25 Common thyme (*Thymus vulgaris*)
26 Opal basil (*Ocimum basilicum* 'Purpurascens')
27 Rosemary (*Rosmarinus officinalis*)
28 Summer savory (*Satureja hortensis*)
29 Southernwood (*Artemisia abrotanum*)
30 Sweet marjoram (*Origanum majorana*)
31 Alecost (*Tanacetum balsamita*)
32 Golden feverfew (*Tanacetum parthenium* 'Aureum')
33 Chervil (*Anthriscus cerefolium*)
34 Marigold (*Calendula officinalis*)
35 Bronze fennel (*Foeniculum vulgare* 'Purpureum')
36 Woodruff (*Asperula odorata*)
37 Cotton lavender (*Santolina chamaecyparissus* 'Lemon Queen')
38 Sorrel (*Rumex acetosa*)
39 Lemon thyme (*Thymus* x *citriodorus*)

This small garden includes a wide range of aromatic and culinary herbs; they have been grouped in beds of restricted colour and divided by symmetrical paths for a traditional, formal effect, softened by the informal plant groupings within the beds.

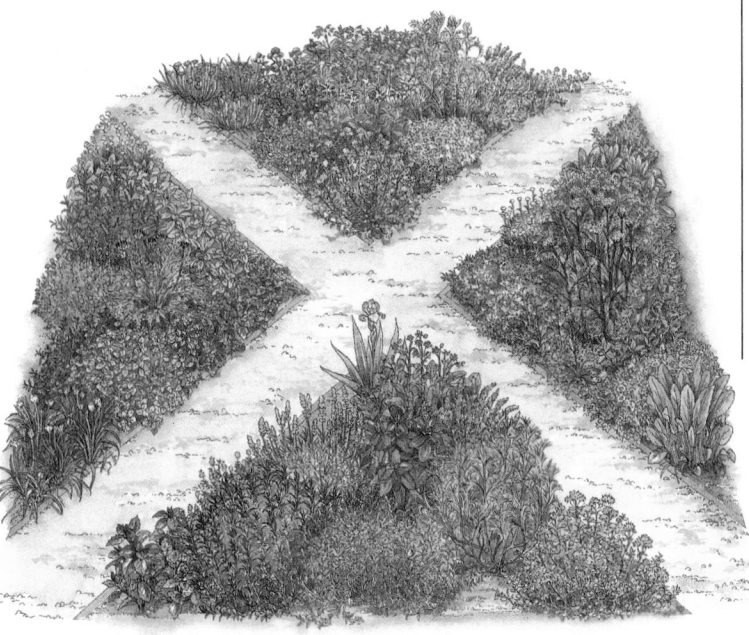

Routine care

Most herbs flourish and require little attention once established. Maintenance largely consists of cutting back plants in spring and summer to encourage healthy growth, and tidying up dormant plants in winter. Herbs in containers usually need routine watering and feeding during the growing season, while periodic repotting or top-dressing is also necessary. Growing herbs in the right conditions should minimize any pest or disease problems; take action as necessary (see PLANT PROBLEMS, pp. 545–77) but then wait one or two weeks after treatment before using the herbs.

Cutting back

Herbs that are valued for their fresh, young foliage may be cut back to produce a regular supply of leaves. Remove the flowering stems of sorrel (*Rumex acetosa*) as they appear; chives (*Allium schoenoprasum*) and marjoram (*Origanum vulgare*) may be left until after flowering as the flowers are attractive and useful as flavourings; variegated forms of marjoram, mint (*Mentha*), and lemon balm (*Melissa officinalis*) produce bright new foliage if the plant is cut right back shortly before flowering as its colours fade.

The growth of invasive herbs should be checked regularly: even when planted in sunken containers, they produce surface runners which must be removed before they spread too far. Remove any reverted, plain shoots from variegated herbs as soon as they appear.

Dead-heading and pruning

Unless planning to save the seed, remove the dead flowerheads from most herbs so that energy is channelled into growth. Dead-heading annuals such as borage (*Borago officinalis*) lengthens the flowering season. Certain herbs such as angelica (*Angelica archangelica*) self-sow prolifically; these may become a nuisance if they are left to set seed.

Dead-head and prune shrubby herbs, such as lavender (*Lavandula*) and thyme (*Thymus*), by trimming lightly with shears after flowering. Hard pruning in spring encourages sideshoots and new growth from the base; thyme, however, is best pruned little and often during the growing season.

Mulching

It is recommended to mulch only established herbs that thrive in moist soil, such as mint and bergamot (*Monarda didyma*). In summer, mulch after rain to retain moisture and to improve the soil as it breaks down. Use an inorganic mulch such as grit around Mediterranean or grey-leaved plants in heavy soil to reduce the risk of rotting.

Autumn clearance

The extent to which herbs are cut back in autumn partly depends on personal preference. In cold areas, leaving the dead foliage of herbaceous perennials until spring helps to protect them against frost and wind. Remove any dead leaves that have fallen on thyme and other low-growing, evergreen herbs as they may encourage fungal attack.

Winter protection

In cold weather, tender herbs should either be brought under cover or otherwise protected (see FROST AND WIND PROTECTION, pp.520–21). In spring, cut them back and plant them out again, or propagate new plants from cuttings. The hardiness of a number of herbs, such as sage (*Salvia officinalis*) and lavender, varies according to the species or cultivar; check this when buying.

Herbs in containers

Most herbs are easy to grow in containers and require little maintenance; they are, however, more prone to drying out than plants in the open ground so, in hot weather, check soil moisture daily and water thoroughly when dry. During the growing season, feed the herbs every two weeks with a liquid fertilizer.

In cold periods, bring herbs in containers under cover in good light.

Frost-proof pots may be left outdoors, but insulate them with sacking to protect the herbs' roots.

Repotting

Inspect herbs periodically to check that they are not becoming pot-bound. Look out for such signs as roots protruding through the base of the pot, rapid drying out, pale foliage, and weak new growth. Repot during the growing season to encourage new root growth.

If repotting is impractical, renew the top 2.5–5cm (1–2in) of compost, incorporating well-rotted organic matter or a slow-release fertilizer. It will then be unnecessary to feed the herbs for about a month.

PRUNING LAVENDER

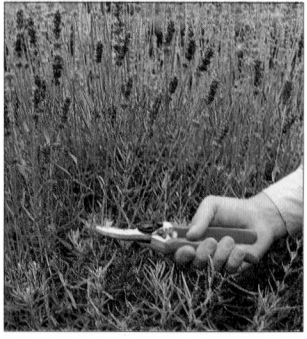

1 *In late summer or early autumn, cut off all the dry flower stalks with secateurs and lightly clip the shrubs to maintain a neat finish.*

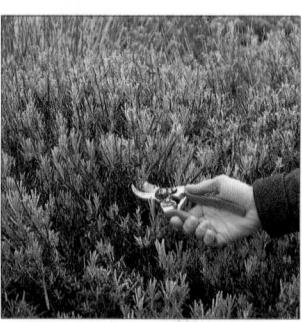

2 *Early the following spring, cut back shoots by 2.5cm (1in) or more of the previous year's growth, making sure that some green growth remains.*

REPLANTING A STRAWBERRY PLANTER

1 *Each spring, replace or divide and replant the herbs in a strawberry planter if they have outgrown the pot or need rejuvenating.*

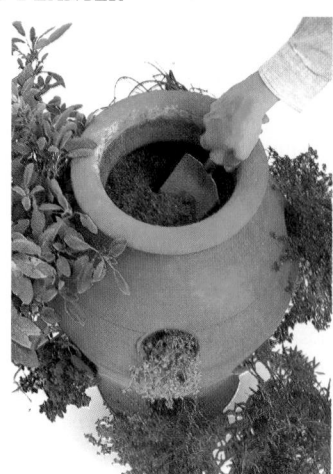

2 *First lift the plants from the top, then dig out the compost, carefully removing the plants from the pockets. Tip out any remaining compost. Replace the drainage material.*

3 *Add fresh compost up to the level of the lowest pockets. Divide or replace the old plants. Place each plant at the inside of a pocket, then gently pull the foliage through the hole.*

4 *Pack compost around the roots and up to the next level, firming well after each addition. Water the compost thoroughly.*

Propagation

Herbs may be propagated by a wide variety of methods, depending on the type of plant and the quantity of new plants required. Sowing seed is a simple, inexpensive way to raise a large number of plants and is necessary for annuals and biennials, although it may also be used for other plant groups. Cuttings are used to propagate various perennials as well as shrubs and trees, while division is suitable for a number of perennials and layering is a good method for some shrubby herbs. For further information on propagating individual species and cultivars, see "Directory of common herbs", pp.294–7.

Raising new plants from seed

Most herbs are easy to grow from seed; they may be sown in containers or, where large quantities are required, in drills in the open ground. Seed may also be sown direct into the cracks between paving stones where it would be difficult to insert plants. Prepare a fine seedbed for any seedlings that you intend to transplant outside from containers.

Spring is generally the best time for sowing seed, although some annual herbs may also be sown in early autumn.

Annuals and biennials

Hardy annuals such as borage (*Borago officinalis*) and marigolds (*Calendula officinalis*) may be sown in the spring or – to provide flowers late in the next spring – in autumn. Sow biennials, such as caraway (*Carum carvi*) and angelica (*Angelica archangelica*), outdoors in late summer or early autumn for flowering the following summer. Thin out the seedlings twice: once after germination so that two or three remain at each position, and again after a few weeks so that only the strongest is left in place.

Short-lived, hardy herbs that are used regularly in large quantities, such as parsley (*Petroselinum crispum*), coriander (*Coriandrum sativum*), and chervil (*Anthriscus cerefolium*), may be sown at intervals of three to four weeks from early spring to early autumn. This provides a succession of foliage for harvesting throughout the year, although in some areas it may be necessary to provide protection from frost with cloches. Annual herbs of the Umbelliferae family – chervil and dill (*Anethum graveolens*) for example – are difficult to transplant successfully and are best sown directly in their ultimate positions.

Basil (*Ocimum basilicum*) is one of the more difficult herbs to grow from seed. In cold areas, sow basil seed very thinly in late spring, and keep it at a minimum temperature of 13°C (55°F). Prick out the seedlings once they are large enough to handle and keep them in a sunny, well-ventilated place. In cold, damp conditions, basil seedlings are prone to damping off (p.568) and grey mould/*Botrytis* (p.557). Plant out the seedlings once all danger of frost is past or, in poor summers, grow them in containers under cover. In warm climates, basil may be sown directly into an outdoor seedbed (see ANNUALS AND BIENNIALS, "Sowing in open ground", p.181).

Perennials

If raising perennial herbs from seed, sow the seed in warmth in spring and grow on the seedlings in pots until they are large enough to be hardened off and planted out. Plant and care for them as for container-grown herbs (see p.298).

Most cultivars of perennial herbs do not come true from seed, however, and must be propagated by either cuttings or layering; an exception to this is variegated rue (*Ruta graveolens* 'Variegata'). Non-flowering forms, such as lawn chamomile (*Chamaemelum nobile* 'Treneague'), cannot be raised from seed; new plants should be propagated by cuttings or division.

Mound layering

This method is particularly suitable for propagating shrubs such as sage (*Salvia officinalis*), rosemary (*Rosmarinus officinalis*), lavender (*Lavandula*), and thyme (*Thymus*) that tend to become woody at the base or centre with little or no new growth. In spring, mound free-draining soil over the base of the plant, leaving just the top exposed. This stimulates new shoots to develop roots in a manner similar to stooling (see ORNAMENTAL SHRUBS, p.89). Leave the soil in place, replenishing it if it is washed away by heavy rain, until new roots have grown in late summer or autumn. Then cut off the shoots from the parent plant and treat them as rooted cuttings.

SOWING PARSLEY SEED IN CONTAINERS

1 Soak the seed in warm water for several hours, then dry it. Tap seeds from a piece of paper onto firmed seed compost. Lightly cover with sieved compost.

2 Once the seedlings are large enough to handle, carefully lift them with a widger, holding them by the leaves not the stems.

3 Prick out the seedlings individually into prepared modules or pans of firmed compost. When they are approximately 5–6cm (2–2¹⁄₂in) high, transplant them outside into prepared ground.

MOUND LAYERING SHRUBBY HERBS

1 To stimulate rooting, mound 7–12cm (3–5in) of sandy loam over the crown of the plant (here thyme) so that just the tips of the shoots are visible.

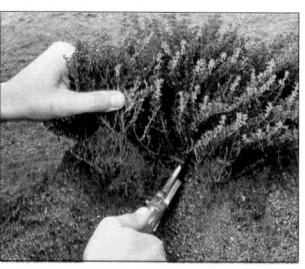

2 Once the layered stems have established new roots, remove them with a knife or secateurs. Pot up the rooted layers individually or plant them out.

HERBS THAT MAY BE PROPAGATED BY MOUND LAYERING

Cotton lavender (*Santolina chamaecyparissus, S. pinnata, S. rosmarinifolia*)
Hyssop (*Hyssopus officinalis*)
Lavender (*Lavandula angustifolia, L. stoechas*)
Rosemary (*Rosmarinus officinalis* 'Prostratus')
Sage (*Salvia lavandulifolia, S. officinalis*)

Salvia officinalis

Southernwood (*Artemisia abrotanum*)
Thyme (*Thymus cilicicus, T. x citriodorus* and cvs, *T. vulgaris* and woody cultivars)
Winter savory (*Satureja montana*)
Wormwood (*Artemisia absinthium*)

Harvesting and preserving

THE flavour of herbs may vary according to the growing conditions, the season, and the time of day. As the level of essential oils fluctuates with light and temperature, it is important to harvest herbs at the right time to ensure that they are at their peak. There are various methods of preserving herbs so that their scents and flavours may be enjoyed all year round. For advice on specific herbs, see the "Directory of common herbs", pp.294–7.

Harvesting

Herbs should be harvested on a fine, dry day after the dew has dried but before the plants are exposed to hot sunshine, which evaporates the essential oils. Always try to harvest herbs in a way that helps to maintain the plant's shape and vigour: choose straggly or invasive shoots, and with clump-forming herbs, such as chives (*Allium schoenoprasum*) and parsley (*Petroselinum crispum*), pick the outer leaves to encourage new growth in the centre. Only use foliage free from damage and insects.

Leaves and shoots may be picked at any time during the growing season but are at their best before flowering. Evergreen herbs may be harvested in winter but this should be limited. Handle aromatic leaves gently as bruising releases the essential oils. Use or preserve herbs as soon as possible after harvesting.

Collecting flowers, seed, and roots

When harvesting flowers, pick them on a warm, dry day, when they are fully opened. Collect seed by cutting off whole seedheads in summer or early autumn as they turn brown but before they are completely ripe and starting to shed. Roots may be lifted at any time of year, but the flavour is best in autumn.

Preserving

The main methods of preserving herbs are drying and freezing. In addition, a number are suitable for flavouring vinegars, oils, or jellies, while a few may be crystallized (candied) for decorating cakes and desserts. Store dried herbs in dark glass or ceramic containers, as exposure to light speeds the deterioration of their aromas.

Air-drying

Do not wash herbs as this may encourage moulds to develop. Dry herbs by hanging them upside-down in a warm, dry place such as an airing cupboard. Alternatively, place leaves, flowerheads, or petals in a single layer on a rack covered with muslin, netting, or kitchen paper. Leave them in a warm, dark, well-ventilated place until crisp.

Microwave drying

Wash the herbs and pat them dry, then place sprigs or leaves in a single layer on kitchen paper. Microwave them for two to three minutes, checking every 30 seconds and rearranging them if necessary to ensure even drying. Cool, then crumble and store as for air-dried herbs.

Drying seedheads

Cut seedheads in summer or early autumn as they turn brown, then place them in a paper bag or hang them upside-down and cover them with muslin to hold the seeds as they fall. Keep them in a warm, dry place to ripen; when dry, remove the seeds and store them. Seed for sowing should be kept in a cool, dry, frost-free place.

Drying roots

Most roots are best used fresh, but some may be dried and ground. First wash the roots thoroughly, then peel, chop, or slice them, before spreading them out on absorbent paper. Dry them in either a cool oven or a warm airing cupboard at 50–60°C (122–40°F) until brittle, then crush or grind them before storing.

Freeze-drying

Many soft-leaved herbs, such as parsley and basil, retain their colour and flavour better when frozen than when dried. Simply pack whole sprigs into labelled plastic bags, and freeze them; they crumble easily for use once frozen. For long-term storage, blanch them before freezing by dipping them first in boiling water, then in iced water. Pat dry and freeze.

Freezing in ice

Herbs may be frozen in water to form ice cubes; this is a good way of preserving borage flowers and mint leaves to use as a decorative addition to drinks, and the ice also protects the herbs from damage during storage. Herbs for cooking should be chopped before freezing since this is difficult to do once they have thawed. Place the ice cubes in a sieve and drain the water before use.

Making herb oils and vinegars

Many herbs, such as French tarragon, thyme, oregano, and lavender, may have their flavours preserved by being steeped in oil or vinegar.

To make flavoured oil, loosely fill a clear glass jar with the fresh herb, pour over a good, flavourless oil, such as sunflower, and seal; for a sweet oil, such as lavender, use almond oil as the base instead. Leave the jar in a sunny spot for two weeks, shaking or stirring daily. Strain and bottle, adding a fresh sprig of the herb for identification. For a stronger flavour, replace the herbs and leave the oil for a further two weeks. Basil leaves may be preserved by being packed in jars of oil; the leaves themselves may be used in pasta sauces and other cooked dishes and the oil in salad dressings.

Herb vinegars are made in a similar way, using wine or cider vinegar, but the herbs should be lightly crushed before steeping. Warm the vinegar, pour it over the herbs, and proceed as above.

14

THE VEGETABLE GARDEN

MORE AND MORE *people are discovering the deep satisfaction of growing their own vegetables. They do so for many reasons: for some gardeners it is the joy of a freshness and flavour rarely to be found in shop-bought produce, while for others it is a chance to grow exotic crops or some of the more unusual varieties that they cannot otherwise obtain. Another motive, for those who favour organic methods, may be the knowledge that their produce is untainted with potentially harmful chemicals.*

Then again, there are gardeners who find a well-tended vegetable patch, with its variety of leaf colour and texture, just as beautiful as a herbaceous border. Modern science and methods of cultivation, coupled with the outstanding vigour and resistance to disease of many of today's vegetable cultivars, enable even newcomers to vegetable growing to experience the considerable satisfaction of bringing to the table fine vegetables that they have sown, tended, and harvested in their own gardens.

Designing a vegetable garden

A HEALTHY, productive area for growing vegetables may be created in a garden of any size, from a large, sunny area to a few containers on a patio. The vegetables may be grown in a separate vegetable plot or integrated with flower beds.

Good growing conditions are essential if vegetables of quality are to be produced. Virtually any site can, however, be made suitable, perhaps by erecting windbreaks if it is exposed, or taking the necessary steps to improve soil fertility and drainage. This cannot be done overnight, but within a year or two very satisfactory results may be obtained.

Choosing the site

Most vegetables lead short but pampered lives so the ideal situation for a vegetable garden provides warmth, sunlight, shelter, and fertile, well-drained, loamy soil with an adequate water supply. The chosen site should be open but not exposed, and not overshadowed: trees shade and drip on plants and remove nutrients and moisture from the soil, while buildings may create shade and funnel damaging winds across the plot.

Shelter from wind
Providing shelter from wind is one of the most important factors in vegetable growing. Wherever possible,

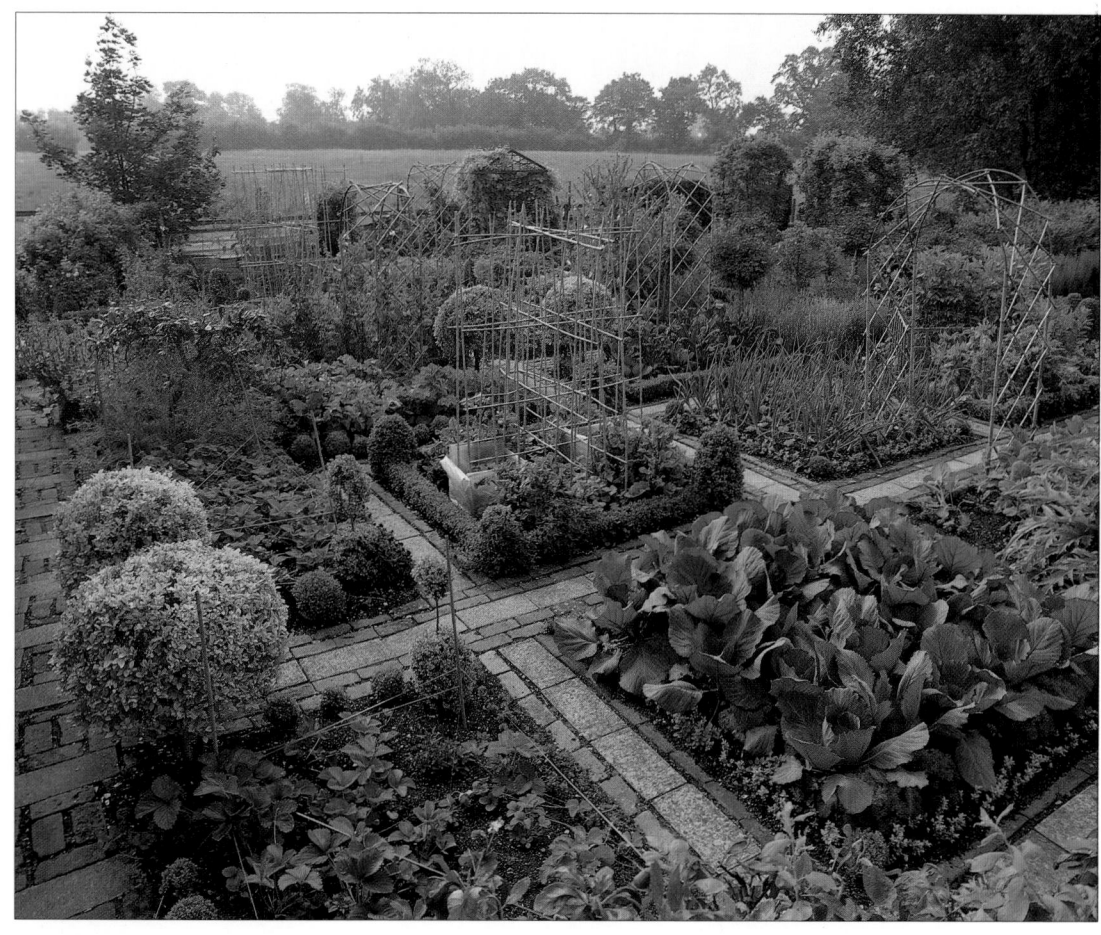

A WELL-DESIGNED GARDEN
This thriving vegetable garden is both well designed and effectively maintained, with an open, but not exposed,
aspect. The beds all contain different crops, and a network of paths allows easy access to each bed.

THE IDEAL VEGETABLE GARDEN

*This vegetable garden is shown
in mid-summer. The east and west
boundaries are marked by sturdy
screens of windbreak netting to shelter
the garden. To the north is a brick wall
with a warm, south-facing border at
its base. This is used for sun-loving
crops such as tomatoes and
courgettes. The south is marked by
rows of Jerusalem artichokes which
act as a hedge or windbreak
during the summer and autumn.*

*The four main beds are laid out
on the narrow bed system; they are
1.2m (4ft) wide so that the centre
of each bed is easily reached
from the surrounding paths.
Each is planted with veg-
etables from one of the
four main rotation groups.
From mature spring
cabbages to salad
rocket seedlings, the
beds are planned
to provide a
succession of crops.
At the southern
end of the garden,
the beds are perm-
anently planted
with perennial
vegetables such
as rhubarb and
asparagus.*

1 Courgettes	23 Garlic
2 Cucumbers	24 Bulb onions (autumn-planted)
3 Tomato cordons	25 Shallots
4 Bush tomatoes	26 Bulb onions (spring-planted)
5 Sweet peppers	27 Spring onions
6 Spring cabbages	28 Leeks (for autumn harvesting)
7 Summer cauliflowers	29 Summer purslane
8 Calabrese	30 Leeks (for winter harvesting)
9 Brussels sprouts	31 Winter purslane
10 Lettuces (as a main crop)	32 Endive (curly type)
11 Purple sprouting broccoli	33 Salad rocket
12 Corn salad	34 Pak choi
13 Globe artichoke	35 Salad bowl lettuces
14 Broad beans	36 Spinach
15 Scarlet runner beans	37 Potatoes (early)
16 Dwarf scarlet runner beans	38 Potatoes (maincrop)
17 Swiss chard	39 Parsnips
18 Peas	40 Radishes
19 Dwarf French beans	41 Carrots
20 Beetroot	42 Self-blanching celery
21 Sweet corn	43 Celeriac
22 Mizuna greens	44 Asparagus
	45 Jerusalem artichokes
	46 Rhubarb

avoid windy sites: even light winds may decrease vegetable yields by 20–30 per cent, while strong winds are often devastating. Vegetables in coastal gardens may be damaged by desiccating wind-borne, salt spray.

Windbreaks

In gardens exposed to wind, windbreaks should be erected; they should be about 50 per cent permeable, allowing the wind to filter through, rather than solid structures which force the wind over them, creating an area of turbulence on the other side (see also FROST AND WIND PROTECTION, pp.520–21, and CLIMATE AND THE GARDEN, "Wind", p.518).

Effective windbreaks may be either a living barrier, such as a hedge, or a structure such as a fence or a screen of windbreak netting. Hedges are attractive but take time to become established, require maintenance, take up considerable space, and compete for soil, water, and plant nutrients; they are therefore only appropriate in quite large gardens. For further information, see HEDGES AND SCREENS, pp.60–62. A windbreak of trees should be considered only in a very large garden. In smaller gardens, fences, hurdles, or windbreak netting battened to posts or stakes are more practical.

A windbreak gives shelter at a distance roughly five times its height. A very exposed garden may need a windbreak approximately 2m (6ft) high. In this case, nets and posts must be strong, as they will be subjected to great strain in high winds. Alternatively, erect lower, short-term windbreaks between rows of plants or beds; netting windbreaks

no more than 45cm (18in) high and 3–4m (10–13ft) apart, attached to canes, are very effective for this.

If gaps in buildings or trees create a wind funnel across the garden, erect a barrier extending 1m (3ft) beyond the gap in each direction. Deciduous shrubs or a hedge may be planted in the gap, with an artificial windbreak to shelter the plants until they are established.

Slopes

A sloping site is less easy to work than a flat one and soil erosion after heavy rain may be a problem on steep slopes; setting the beds across the slope may help. A site on a south-facing slope is an advantage in cool-temperate climates because it warms up rapidly in spring. In hot climates, site beds on a north-facing slope because here they will have relief from intense sun.

Positioning

The orientation of vegetable beds often makes little difference to open-ground crops, although greenhouses and frames must be orientated correctly to maximize their efficiency. Position tall crops, such as climbing beans, carefully: in temperate climates, place them where they will not shield dwarf-sized plants from the sun, and in hotter climates use them to provide some shade.

Sites below garden walls

In temperate and northern climates, the ground at the foot of a south-facing garden wall is a warm, sheltered place that is useful for growing early spring and late autumn crops and, in summer, tender, sun-loving

ALLOCATING SPACE
Each element in this garden has been sited to produce optimum growing conditions for the crops. The greenhouse and frame are positioned to receive maximum light, the hedge filters the prevailing wind, and tall plants, such as the runner beans, do not overshadow the smaller vegetables.

crops such as tomatoes and aubergines. Keep these beds fertile and well watered so that the soil does not dry out. North-facing walls may be used to provide some shade for plants such as lettuces and peas that suffer in high temperatures.

Maintaining soil fertility

A friable loam is ideal for growing vegetables: it is rich in plant nutrients, and supports a population of earthworms and micro-organisms to break down organic matter. It has a good structure, and remains workable even in adverse conditions: it

does not become sticky during wet weather or dusty in dry periods, but always retains a crumbly texture, so that the soil is well aerated; this is important for both the living organisms in the soil and the roots of the vegetables themselves. An ideal soil is both well drained and moisture retentive, and should be slightly acid (pH6–6.5). In such a soil, most vegetables grow well, and need little extra feeding.

Soil types

Vegetables may be grown successfully on a range of different soil types. At one extreme are the porous, sandy soils, which warm up quickly in spring and are ideal for early crops. Nutrients are washed out rapidly, however, from these soils and crops that are planted in them often need extra feeding.

At the other extreme are heavy clays. Naturally sticky and cold (and sometimes waterlogged), clay soils warm up slowly in spring, but are rich in nutrients, and, once their structure has been improved by incorporating organic matter (and if necessary, drainage), they are fertile and retain moisture well. Hungry crops, such as the cabbage family, grow well on clay soils. For further information, see "Soil and its structure", pp.522–3.

In practice, most soils are a mixture of different types, and although few of us start with perfect soil it can usually be improved by working in organic matter regularly.

Using organic matter

Crops continuously remove nutrients from the soil and from naturally decomposing organic matter. In

ALTERNATING ROWS
Provided that the fertility of the soil is maintained, rows of vegetables may be arranged to maximize yields by alternating rows of fast- and slow-growing crops (here different types of lettuce and a range of brassicas). The fast-growing lettuces will have been harvested by the time the brassicas have reached maturity.

almost all soils fertility must be maintained by replenishing the supplies of organic matter. The main forms available to gardeners are animal manures (preferably with a high straw content but little sawdust or woodshavings), spent mushroom compost, seaweed, or home-made garden compost.

A layer of organic matter 8–10cm (3–4in) deep, applied over most of the ground each year, should maintain structure and fertility. It may be spread on the surface or dug into the soil. If organic matter is spread on the soil surface in the autumn, it may be left for the worms to work in. This is particularly beneficial on light soils where heavy winter rainfall can cause nutrients to be washed out. Any organic matter remaining on the surface in spring should be forked in. Well-rotted organic matter is a useful mulch and can be used at any point in the growing season.

Dig organic matter into heavy soils in the autumn, or into light soils in the spring, spreading it evenly throughout the soil as deeply as possible (see also "Mulching", p.312).

Green manuring

This is the practice of growing crops specifically to dig into the soil to improve its fertility. In the vegetable garden a green manure may be grown and dug in between crops or over the winter to augment plant

VEGETABLES IN ROUND BEDS
In addition to providing easy access to the vegetables grown, round beds may be used as part of the design of a garden or as a link between ornamentals and vegetables. Here, rhubarb is surrounded by chicory which may be substituted by other annual crops in subsequent plantings.

nutrients and avoid leaving the soil bare (see SOILS AND FERTILIZERS, "Green manures", p.531).

Drainage

Good drainage is essential; where there is a serious problem, it may be necessary to lay land drains (see SOILS AND FERTILIZERS, "Improving drainage", p.529). In most cases, working in organic matter improves drainage markedly, since this will encourage earthworms which improve the soil structure by forming a network of drainage channels.

Preserving soil structure

Good soil structure is easily destroyed by physically damaging the soil, for example by walking on it or cultivating it when it is either very wet or very dry, or from heavy rain beating down on the surface. Laying out the garden in narrow beds (see "The bed system", below) to minimize the need to tread on the soil, and keeping the surface continuously mulched (see "Mulching", p.312) will help to preserve the soil structure.

Planning the vegetable garden

The layout of a vegetable garden is determined by the size, shape, and nature of the garden and the demands of the household. The quantity and choice of vegetables to be cultivated depends on the aims of the gardener. These may be to achieve self-sufficiency, to produce gourmet vegetables and well-flavoured, unusual cultivars that are unavailable locally, to grow produce for the freezer, or to save money.

The following are a few guidelines that give an indication of the main factors to be considered.

A place for perennials

Most vegetables are grown as annuals on a different piece of ground each year. The few perennial vegetables, such as rhubarb, asparagus, and globe artichokes, should be grouped in a permanent bed at one side or end of the garden, separated from the annual vegetables. If there is space, they may be intercropped with other, fast-growing vegetables.

Vegetables in containers

Gardeners who are limited to terraces, concreted yards, patios, roofs, or balconies often grow vegetables in containers to provide an attractive and productive display. Although vegetables are more difficult than flowers to grow successfully in containers, they are still worth the effort involved. Place containers on paths and low walls to make the best use of the space available, and plant them up with dwarf and the more decorative cultivars. Suitable containers range from terracotta pots and tubs to proprietary makes of growing bag filled with compost.

Growing vegetables in rows

A traditional vegetable garden consists of a number of rectangular plots each several metres wide, in which vegetables are grown in widely spaced rows. This method allows easy access between individual rows.

The bed system

Although the traditional layout of vegetable plots is still used, the modern trend is to grow vegetables in smaller, narrower beds, with the plants evenly spaced in all directions. This is known as the "bed system". In practice, the beds may be of any shape or size: square, round, or even crescent-shaped, as long as the centre of the bed is reached easily from the path, so that all sowing, planting, routine care, and harvesting can be done without walking on the soil. The paths between the beds may be of soil, grass, concrete, bark, stones, brick, sawdust, or any other suitable material.

The main benefit of growing vegetables in narrow beds is that the soil structure is preserved by using the access paths between the beds rather than walking on them. Also, organic matter and manure are concentrated on areas where the crops grow, rather than being wasted on pathways and working areas where they are not used by the plants.

High yields may be obtained from narrow beds by growing plants in patches at equidistant spacing, which makes the best use of available space and minimizes competition between plants. Even spacing also helps to suppress weed germination by allowing fully grown broadleaved vegetables to make a canopy over the soil.

A PATCHWORK OF CROPS
Square beds with soil paths between them provide a neat framework for manageable rows of vegetables. A plot laid out like this allows a variety of crops to be grown, and is designed for a simple method of crop rotation.

A place for herbs

For practical purposes, it is best to grow herbs as near the kitchen as possible, and within easy access of paths. Compact herbs such as chives, marjoram, and parsley make neat, attractive edgings to vegetable beds; the larger perennials such as mint, sage, and rosemary are often best grown in a separate bed. For further information, see THE HERB GARDEN, "Where to grow herbs", p.292.

Vegetables in flower beds

As many gardens are no longer spacious enough to allow a complete area to be devoted to vegetables, there has been a move towards integrating vegetables into flower beds, or planting them in groups of beds designed in an attractive pattern. Wherever possible, vegetable cultivars are selected for their decorative qualities, and then grouped to display them to maximum effect.

This approach is known as "potager gardening" in Europe and "edible landscaping" in the USA. There is enormous scope for gardeners to develop their own ideas.

The only requirement for growing vegetables in flower beds is ensuring that the soil fertility is maintained at the level necessary for the chosen vegetables.

Climatic factors

Most vegetables grow only when the average daytime temperature rises above about 6°C (43°F) between spring and autumn. The number of "growing days" with suitable daytime temperatures that occur between these seasons is governed by factors such as latitude, altitude, and degree of exposure, and largely determines what may be grown outdoors in any locality.

Temperature requirements

Vegetables are sometimes classified as warm- or cool-season crops, depending on their physiological needs, particularly those relating to temperature. Most brassicas and several bulb and stem vegetables cannot withstand intense heat, whereas more tender vegetables, such as tomatoes,

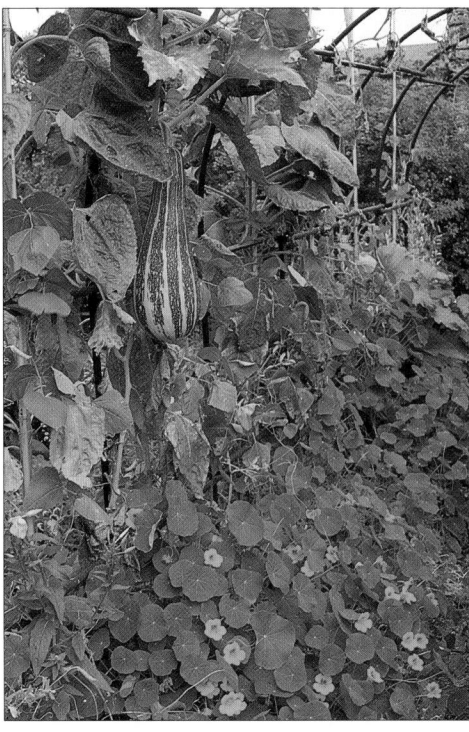

A PRODUCTIVE DISPLAY
This example of potager planting groups marrows climbing a supporting arch with a profusion of yellow and red nasturtiums beneath. All thrive in warm, sunny conditions.

are damaged or killed by freezing temperatures. Cultivars of some vegetables have been bred to resist cold, and the growing season of many vegetables may be extended by growing them under cover (see p.315). See individual vegetables for specific requirements.

Daylength

The number of daylight hours, or daylength, differs according to the latitude and season, and vegetable cultivars have a varying response to daylength at different stages of growth. Short-day plants grow and seed only if the daylength is less than 12 hours; long-day plants only if it is more than 12 hours.

This affects the sowing time, particularly of crops that are grown for their seeds, such as beans; others must be harvested before flowering. Onions, for example, are naturally long-day plants: when the daylength is 16 hours or more, onions stop making leafy growth and start to develop a bulb. The more leafy

growth that has been made up to this point, the larger the bulb that forms; onion seeds should therefore be sown early in the year so that the plant will develop as much leafy growth as possible before the daylength increases.

Cultivars are available that have been adapted to long or short days or that are daylength neutral. Examples are mentioned under individual vegetables later in the chapter; the safest course is to choose cultivars recommended for your area.

Rotation

Rotation is a system by which vegetable crops are grown on different areas of the plot in succession in consecutive years.

Advantages of rotation

The principal reason for rotating crops is to prevent a build-up of soil-borne pests and diseases specific to one group of crops. If the same type

COMBINING VEGETABLES AND HERBS
This informal garden has vegetables intermingled with herbs. Runner beans climb up an arch, parsley and chives ring red and green "Salad Bowl" lettuces at the edge of the centre bed, and sweet corn develops among feathery dill.

VEGETABLES IN A WINDOWBOX
Vegetables can thrive in small containers, such as this window-box. Here shallow-rooted lettuces, young cabbages, tomatoes, and strawberries have been chosen not only for their culinary uses, but also for their decorative qualities.

of "host" crop is grown every year in the same soil, its pests and diseases increase rapidly in number and often become a serious problem, whereas in the absence of their host they gradually die out. Various types of potato and tomato eelworm (nematodes), clubroot which attacks almost all brassicas (crucifers), and onion white rot are some of the common garden problems that may be alleviated by rotation.

Other benefits stem from rotating vegetables. Some crops, for example potatoes, blanket the soil so well that they smother most weeds, so it is useful to follow them with crops that are difficult to weed, such as onions. Most vegetables in the legume family, including peas and beans, fix nitrogen in the soil by means of nodules on their roots and make it available for the next crop. Therefore nitrogen-hungry crops, such as leafy brassicas, potatoes, or spinach, should follow legumes.

Several vegetables, including perennial types and many salad plants, do not fall into a principal rotation group. Salad plants stay in the ground for a short time and are therefore useful for intercropping or to fill temporary gaps in vegetable beds. As with the other vegetables, they should not be grown in the same patch of ground year after year. Perennial vegetables are best grown in a permanent bed of their own and so are not rotated. For the most important vegetable groups, see *Rotation of Vegetable Crops*, right.

Drawbacks of rotation

A weak point in the rotation theory is that to be completely effective rotation should take place over a much longer timescale than the usual three or four years: clubroot and white rot infections can stay in the soil for up to 20 years. Rotations on that scale are out of the question in small gardens. Another shortcoming is that, in practice, the distance between beds is often so small that soil-borne pests and diseases can easily spread from one to the next.

Planning for rotation

Despite the disadvantages, rotation is a sensible practice, and gardeners should try to build it into their garden plans, taking care at the least to follow a crop of one vegetable type with a vegetable from another group.

Draw up a list of the main vegetables that you want to grow, with a rough indication of the quantities required. Growing vegetables that are climatically unsuited to the area is usually unsatisfactory, particularly in small gardens. Neither is it sensible to grow crops that are likely to be cheap to buy when your own crop is ready. List the various beds in the vegetable garden. Group the selected vegetables in their rotation groups (e.g. all legumes and pod crops, or all brassicas), with a miscellaneous category for vegetables not in the main groups (see *Rotation of Vegetable Crops*, right).

Month-by-month planning

Make a chart with a column for each month of the year, and for every vegetable on your list fill in the months during which it will be in the ground. Remember that this period may be shortened by raising plants in containers (see "Sowing indoors", p.311) for transplanting later, and lengthened by the use of some form of cover early and late in the season (see "Growing under cover",

ROTATION OF VEGETABLE CROPS

LEGUMES AND POD CROPS

Okra
Dolichos beans
Scarlet runner beans
Lima beans
French beans
Peas
Broad beans

ALLIUMS

Bulb onions
Pickling onions
Spring onions
Shallots
European Welsh onions
Oriental bunching onions
Leeks
Garlic

BRASSICAS

Kales
Cauliflowers
Cabbages
Brussels sprouts
Purple sprouting broccoli
Calabrese
Oriental mustards
Chinese broccoli
Pak choi
Mizuna greens
Chinese cabbages
Komatsuna
Kohl rabi
Swedes
Turnips
Radishes

SOLANACEOUS, ROOT, AND TUBEROUS CROPS

Sweet peppers
Tomatoes
Wonderberries
Aubergines
Celery
Celeriac
Beetroot
Cocoyams
Carrots
Sweet potatoes
Parsnips
Scorzonera
Salsify
Potatoes

p.315). Some crops are sown once a year (parsnips and winter cabbages, for example), but with others, such as lettuces and radishes, repeat sowings may be made to provide a continuous supply throughout the year.

Planning a layout

Allocate each bed (or several beds if needed) to a different rotation group of vegetables, and write in the most important crop that each bed will grow. Refer to your month-by-month chart, and indicate a suitable crop to precede or follow it. For example, if Brussels sprouts are cleared in mid-spring, they may be followed by carrots, lettuces, or peas. Assume that most pieces of ground will bear only two crops a year. Use this basic plan in subsequent years and move the crops to different beds.

Look on the overall plan as a rough guide only. Many factors – not least unpredictable weather – have a bearing on the success and failure of crops. The key to success lies as much in flexibility as in strict adherence to the plan.

Keeping records

Every vegetable garden is unique, both in its site and in the requirements of the household it supplies. Detailed records of the cultivars grown, sowing and planting dates, treatment given, problems encountered, and results enjoyed, provide an invaluable guide to improving performance in future seasons.

Intercropping

For maximum yield over a given area, crops of vegetables may be combined in a single bed. A fast-growing crop, such as radishes, is planted at the same time as a slow-growing crop, such as parsnips. A chequer-board pattern gives maximum efficiency, but alternate rows also work well. Fast-growers make almost immediate use of the available space, but reach maturity before the slow-growing crops need the room. Make sure that the short-term crop is not shaded by more slowly maturing vegetables.

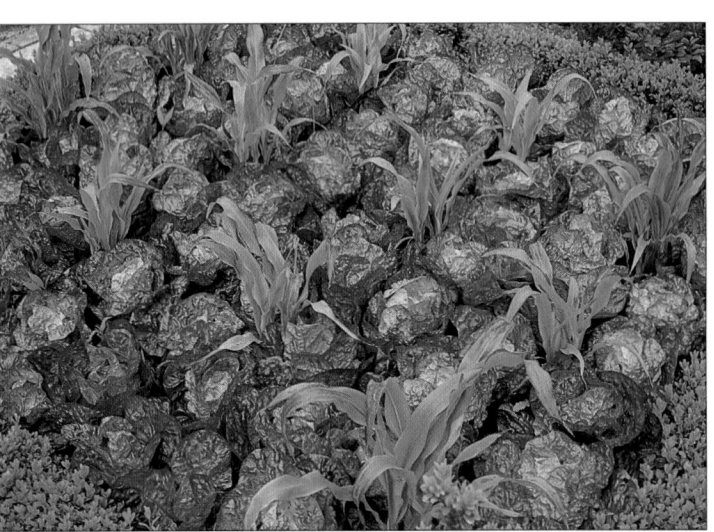

INTERCROPPING
Lettuces and sweet corn planted together mature at varying rates. The fast-growing lettuces are ready to harvest before the sweet corn is fully grown.

Sowing and planting

THE most common method of raising vegetables is from seed. There are several methods for sowing outdoors or under cover; use the most suitable for the chosen cultivar and the space available. Care in the early stages ensures healthier, more productive crops. Thin or transplant seedlings to their final position in a bed, greenhouse, or container before they become overcrowded.

Choosing seed

In the past, seed was sold only as ordinary, "naked" seed, but it is now also available prepared in a variety of ways to make sowing and germination easier. Seed can also be purchased pre-germinated.

Purchasing seed
Always buy good-quality seed, preferably vacuum-packed to preserve viability. Many of the best cultivars are F1 hybrids, bred by crossing two selected parents. Although expensive, they are very vigorous and productive. Vegetable seeds differ widely in their viability: to be safe, use seed under three years old, or test a sample before sowing.

Prepared seed
Pelleted seeds are individually coated with clay to form tiny balls which are easier to sow evenly than naked seed. This is useful for handling small seeds such as those for carrots. Pelleted seeds should be carefully placed in a drill one by one, which saves transplanting later. They are sown in the normal way, but the clay coating must be kept moist until after germination.

Seed is also available embedded, evenly spaced, in paper sheets or tapes, which disintegrate in the soil after sowing. The tapes are laid in a drill and covered with soil, as for ordinary seed. The backing gives protection in the early stages of germination and reduces thinning.

Sometimes seeds are marketed in a gel in small tubs. They grow to the seedling stage in the tub, and may then be pricked out into a pot or directly into the ground. This saves the initial thinning after sowing.

Pre-germinated seed
Chitted or pre-germinated seed is purchased and sown just after germination, when the first root is emerging. Chitted seed is despatched in small plastic containers; the gardener then sows each seed carefully in a pot or seed tray. This is a good method if germination is unreliable, or if seed needs temperatures that are difficult to maintain without an electric propagator.

To start ordinary seed early, it may be pre-germinated at home. This is useful for seed that germinates slowly in cold soil and may rot before germination. Space seeds on damp, paper towelling and put them in a warm place. Keep them moist until germination, then sow them carefully in containers or in open ground. This method may also be used to test a sample of old seed for viability before sowing.

Sowing outdoors

Vegetables are either sown *in situ*, where they grow to maturity, or in a seedbed from where they are transplanted to their permanent position. *In situ* sowing is used for crops that are harvested young, such as spring onions and radishes, or vegetables that do not transplant well, such as carrots and parsnips. Most other vegetables may be sown in a seedbed, in rows up to 15cm (6in) apart.

Successful sowing outdoors requires warm and well-prepared soil. Germination occurs for most vegetables once temperatures are over 7°C (45°F), so do not sow seed in cold soil. In several cases, lettuces for example, germination is poor at high temperatures. Particular temperature requirements for germination are given under individual vegetables. Soil temperature may be measured with a soil thermometer but most gardeners use their own knowledge of the soil to assess if it is warm enough for germination to occur.

Preparing the ground
Before sowing, dig the soil, then rake the surface until it has a fine texture or tilth, removing stones and large clods of earth. Rake when it is neither very wet and heavy nor very dry. If soil sticks to your shoes, delay until it has dried out a little, but not so much that it is dusty.

If sowing in wet soil, standing on a board prevents damaging the structure of adjacent soil. This is not necessary with the bed system (see p.306) since the seed may be sown from the surrounding path.

Guidelines for sowing
Seeds are sown at different depths according to their size. Unless otherwise directed, sow small seed, such as onions, about 1cm (½in) deep, brassicas 2cm (¾in) deep, peas and sweet corn about 2.5cm (1in) deep, and beans up to 5cm (2in) deep. The most important requirement is to sow thinly so that seedlings are not crowded in the early stages. Various methods of sowing are described below; whichever is used, it is vital to preserve surface moisture. In dry weather, cover the soil after sowing with plastic sheeting or newspaper. Remove any covering when the first seedlings appear.

Sowing in a drill
This is the most common method of sowing vegetables. Mark a row with a string line and make a small, even channel (a "drill") in the soil to the required depth. Take pinches of seed to scatter along the drill. Either space the seeds evenly, or station sow at intervals in groups of three or four seeds to be thinned later to one seedling per station. If the seed is sown *in situ*, space the stations half the required distance between the mature plants to allow for losses; stations may be closer if seedlings are to be transplanted. Consider station sowing fast-growing crops such as radishes between slow-growing crops such as parsnips: the radishes are pulled before the intervening space is needed by the parsnips. After sowing, cover the seed with soil, drawing it back lightly with a hoe or rake, firm the area gently, and water with a can fitted with a fine rose.

If sowing in unavoidably wet conditions, line the drill before sowing with dry, light material such as sand or vermiculite. If conditions are very dry, water the drill before sowing, lightly press each seed into the soil

---

SOWING IN A DRILL

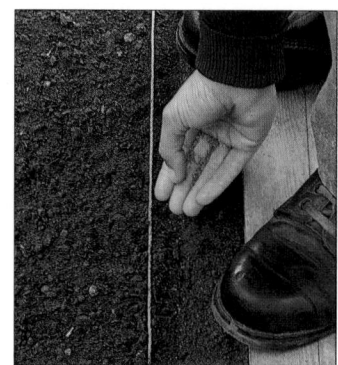

1 Mark out the drill using pegs and string. Use the corner of a hoe or a trowel to make the drill, ensuring that it is the depth required for the seed.

2 Sprinkle the seeds thinly and evenly along the drill. Stand on a plank placed parallel to the drill to prevent compaction of adjacent soil. Cover the seeds without dislodging them.

ALTERNATIVE METHODS

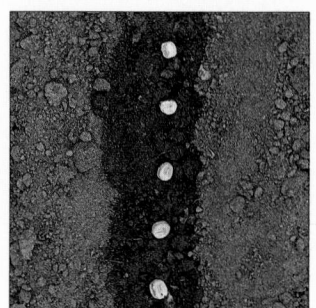

WET CONDITIONS
If the soil drains slowly or is very heavy, sprinkle a layer of sand at the base of the drill, sow the seed, then cover it.

DRY CONDITIONS
When the soil is very dry, water the base of the drill, then sow the seeds and lightly press them in before covering with dry soil.

SOWING IN A WIDE DRILL

1 Use a draw hoe to mark out parallel drills 15–23cm (6–9in) wide and flat at the base.

2 Sow seeds the required distance apart in the drill.

3 Cover the seeds with soil using the hoe. Take care not to dislodge them.

4 Protect them from birds or animals by pegging wire netting over the drill.

then cover them with dry soil. This slows down the rate of evaporation and helps the seeds to stay moist until they germinate.

Wide drills

Use wide, flat drills for plants that are grown closely together, such as peas, early carrots, and seedling crops. Make each drill up to 23cm (9in) wide and to the required depth. Space the seeds evenly in the drill, and cover carefully.

Large seed

The seed of beans and pumpkins may be sown individually by placing a seed in a hole made by a small dibber or a finger. Make sure that each seed is at the base of the hole and in contact with the soil. Sowings of tender plants, such as marrows, may be covered with glass jars or cut-off plastic bottles which are removed once the seedlings emerge.

Broadcasting seed

In this method, the soil is first raked to produce a fine tilth; the seed is then scattered as evenly as possible either by hand or from a packet. Rake the soil lightly again afterwards to cover the seed.

Cut-and-come-again seedling crops

Many leafy or salad vegetables may be sown for harvesting at the seedling stage when they are at their most nutritious. Once cut, they often resprout to produce a second and third crop. This method is a very productive way to make use of a small area, and such crops are ideal for sowing under or between other, slower-maturing vegetables.

BROADCASTING

1 Prepare the area to be sown by raking carefully in one direction to produce a fine tilth. Sprinkle the seed thinly and evenly over the surface.

2 Rake lightly at right angles to the original direction to cover the seed, then water thoroughly with a can fitted with a fine rose.

To obtain seedling crops, sow seed either broadcast or in wide drills or rows about 8cm (3in) apart; seedlings do not need thinning and are often ready for their first cut in a few weeks.

Successional crops

Vegetables that grow fast, but rapidly pass their prime or run to seed, for example lettuces, should be sown little and often. To avoid both gluts or gaps in cropping, wait until one sowing has emerged before making the next.

Thinning

Young seedlings need to be thinned to prevent overcrowding. Thin to the final spacing in stages, rather than immediately, to allow for any loss from pests and diseases; at each stage, aim to leave a seedling just clear of its neighbours. If the seeds have been sown *in situ*, continue to thin until they are at the spacing required for mature plants. Very small seedlings should be thinned by nipping them off just above ground level so as not to disturb the roots of adjacent plants. Clear thinnings away as their scent may attract pests. Seedlings of plants such as lettuces, cabbages, and onions may be lifted for transplanting, and the soil refirmed around the remaining seedlings.

Planting

Plant or transplant vegetables into their final position when they are as young as possible so that they can grow without further check. Exceptions to this are plants that have been raised in containers or modules (see p.311). Do not transplant root vegetables once the tap root has started to form as this may distort its shape.

THINNING SEEDLINGS

To thin small seedlings, nip them out at ground level so that the roots of the remaining seedlings are not disturbed.

Before taking plants from a seedbed, water around their roots; if the ground into which they are being planted is dry, water it lightly. Pick up a plant by a leaf rather than the stem or roots, which are easily damaged. Make a hole slightly bigger than the roots and position the plant in the hole, replacing the soil so that the lower leaves are just above soil level. Firm around the stem to anchor the plant. In hot weather, water seedlings,

TRANSPLANTING SEEDLINGS

Lift seedlings gently, keeping as much soil around the roots as possible. Before replanting, place the seedlings in a clear plastic bag to retain moisture.

PLANTING DEPTH

Plant vegetable seedlings so that their lowest leaves are just above soil level. Planting too high exposes the stalk, which may not support the weight of the mature vegetable.

and then shade them with fine-mesh netting or newspaper cones until they are established. Keep the soil moist for a few days after planting (see "Critical watering periods", p.312).

Spacing

Different vegetables have individual spacing requirements, which sometimes determine their final size. Traditionally, vegetables are grown in rows with a recommended spacing between the plants, and between the rows.

They may alternatively be grown with equidistant spacing between the plants – the average of the recommended spacing between plants and rows; so plants 15cm (6in) apart, in rows 30cm (12in) apart, may alternatively be grown 23cm (9in) apart each way. This method probably gives the best results: plants have an equal share of light, air, moisture, and soil nutrients, and as they mature they form a canopy over the soil which suppresses weeds (see also "The bed system", p.306). Vegetables may also be grown close together within widely spaced rows.

Sowing indoors

Vegetable seed may be sown indoors, in a cool greenhouse, or on a windowsill. This is helpful in climates with cool or short summers, for tender vegetables, and for those that need a long growing season. It is also a way of producing healthy seedlings and overcoming problems with germination, since the temperature is more easily controlled.

After germination, keep most seedlings at a lower temperature in a spacious, light, protected environment until they are planted out. Where this is not possible, it may be practical to buy more mature plants.

Seed trays

Sow seed in a small pan or seed tray, in standard seed compost (for details see ANNUALS AND BIENNIALS, "Sowing in pots or trays", p.182). When the seedlings have two or three small leaves, prick them out into a seed tray of potting compost, spaced 2.5–5cm (1–2in) apart. Seedlings usually need to be kept slightly warm. Put them in a well-lit, draught-free place to grow fast and evenly. Transfer larger plants to individual pots before planting them out.

Modules and small containers

Modules are individual units or small cells in which seeds are sown and plants grown for planting out directly. This produces plants of high quality

SOWING AND TRANSPLANTING

1 *Fill the module with seed compost and make a hole 5mm (¼in) deep in each section. Sow one or two seeds per section. Cover with compost, then water.*

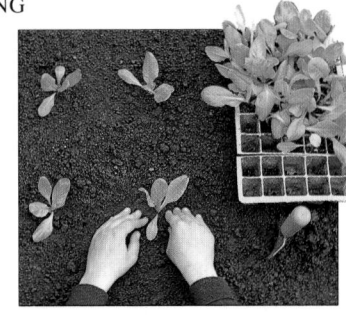

2 *Remove each plant from the module. Make a hole to take its rootball. Place the plant in the hole with its lower leaves just above the surface; firm and water.*

that grow on well: seedlings have no competition and so develop a healthy root ball which is hardly disturbed when planted out in their final position. They do, however, need more space and compost in the early stages than those that are planted in trays.

Many types of module are available, the cheapest being plastic or polystyrene cellular trays. Small containers include clay or plastic pots, degradable pots, and soil blocks made of compressed compost. The compost may be enclosed in netting, which roots can penetrate.

Sow two or three seeds per unit; then thin the seedlings to leave the strongest. In some cases, such as onions and leeks, several seeds are sown and grown together, planted out as a unit at a wider spacing than usual, and grown on to maturity.

Hardening off

Plants raised indoors must be acclimatized to lower temperatures and wind before being planted in the open. Harden them off in cloches or cold frames over 10–14 days. Increase ventilation gradually during the day and then at night, until the seedlings can be left out all the time.

Vegetative propagation

A few vegetables are usually raised vegetatively, from offsets, tubers, corms, bulbs, or cuttings. This may be because they rarely set seed or, if raised from seed, are variable, or because vegetative propagation is faster. Details are given under individual vegetables (pp.317–58).

Growing vegetables in containers

Containers are useful for growing vegetables where space is limited, or to extend the vegetable garden into a paved area. They are also used in the greenhouse, especially if the soil is infected with soil-borne diseases and it is impractical to sterilize or replace it. Vegetables need a richer growing medium and more consistent and thorough watering than flowers and so are hard to grow well in containers unless they are carefully maintained.

Choosing the vegetables

The best vegetables for containers are compact, quick-maturing plants, such as lettuces, radishes, and beetroot, or robust, undemanding, leafy vegetables, such as spinach beet; fruiting vegetables, such as peppers, aubergines, and tomatoes, also flourish. Fast-maturing, seedling crops also grow well. Dwarf cultivars are excellent since they do not need support. Do not use vegetables that are deep-rooting, slow to mature, very tall or large, or gross feeders, such as brassicas, parsnips, or celery. Raise plants for containers in modules; sow cut-and-come-again seedling crops directly in the container.

Preparing the container

The larger the container, and the greater its volume of soil or compost, the better. Large vegetables

and gross feeders, such as potatoes and tomatoes, generally need a container at least 25cm (10in) deep and wide. For large or top-heavy vegetables, the container must be strong and stable.

Good drainage is essential. If there are no drainage holes, make several of at least 1cm (½in) diameter in the base; cover them with crocks to prevent blockage. For growing bags, follow the maker's instructions; drainage holes are not usually made since they would allow infection to enter when laid on diseased soil.

The soil or compost must be light and well aerated, since frequent watering will compact it. Lighten garden soil with well-rotted compost mixed with coarse sand and peat substitute or peat.

In hot and windy weather containers dry out rapidly by evaporation through the top and, if not made of plastic, the sides. To minimize this do not put them in exposed sites or at the foot of a hot wall. Line non-plastic containers with plastic sheeting perforated with drainage holes.

Dwarf broad beans

Fast-maturing, compact lettuces

Stable plastic container to retain moisture

Peas supported by peasticks

Routine cultivation

THE best vegetables are produced when the plants are maintained in the optimum conditions for growth. Keep them free from weeds and water them thoroughly as required. Mulches may be used to retain moisture and to suppress weeds. The level of nutrients needs to be maintained as the crop grows.

Watering

Most vegetables need reasonably moist soil; they vary, however, in the amount of water they require as well as when they most need it (see "Critical watering periods", below). Overwatering may lead to loss of flavour in tomatoes and carrots, and, in root crops, to the development of leaves at the expense of root.

How to water
It is more effective to water heavily and occasionally rather than frequently and lightly; very young plants, however, should be watered lightly and frequently so that they never dry out. Light watering evaporates rapidly without reaching the plants' roots, and encourages shallow surface rooting rather than the deep rooting that enables plants to withstand drought. Direct the water at the base of each plant. Water in the evening when less moisture will evaporate, and allow time for the plants to dry before nightfall.

Watering equipment
Use a can fitted with a fine rose to water young plants. For general watering in small gardens, a can may be adequate; in larger gardens, use a hand-held hose, regulating the flow with a fixture attached to the end.

A practical choice in vegetable gardens is either a seep hose or a porous hose laid among the plants (see also TOOLS AND EQUIPMENT, "Seep hoses", p.469). Water seeps through the holes or pores, usually watering a strip about 30cm (12in) wide. The tubing can be easily moved from crop to crop, and some types of porous hose may be buried shallowly in the soil.

Critical watering periods
There are periods in the growing cycle of vegetables when water is particularly beneficial; these vary according to the individual vegetable. In prolonged, dry weather confine watering to these periods.

Germinating seeds, seedlings, and newly transplanted plants should never be allowed to dry out, so water frequently and lightly.

Leafy and salad vegetables, such as spinach, chard, most brassicas, and lettuces, require frequent watering to help them crop heavily. The most critical period is between ten days and three weeks before maturity; during this period, but only in very dry conditions, apply a single, heavy watering of 22 litres/sq m (5 gallons/sq yd). Outside this period, give half this amount weekly during dry weather.

The critical point for fruiting crops such as tomatoes, peppers, beans, courgettes, cucumbers, and peas is when the flowers are forming and fruits or pods are developing. If conditions are dry during this time, water weekly at the rate for leafy crops (above). Do not water heavily before the critical period since this produces leafy growth at the expense of fruit.

Root crops such as carrots, radishes, and beetroot need moderate watering during the growing period. In the early stages, water at a rate of 5 litres/sq m (1 gallon/sq yd) if the soil is dry. Increase this rate fourfold when the roots start to swell, watering every two weeks if dry conditions persist.

Minimizing the need to water
To conserve soil moisture, particularly in dry areas, dig the soil deeply, working in plenty of organic matter to improve soil structure and moisture retention and to encourage deep rooting. Keep the soil surface mulched (see "Mulching", below), and keep down weeds, which compete for moisture. Do not hoe in dry weather since this encourages moisture to evaporate from the soil. Erect windbreaks to protect from desiccating winds (see "Shelter from wind", p.303). In areas prone to drought, adopt slightly wider spacing so that the roots can spread further to take moisture from a larger area.

Controlling weeds

A vegetable garden should be free of weeds. They compete for water, nutrients, and light, may physically suffocate plants, and may harbour pests and diseases (see PLANT PROBLEMS, "Weeds", pp.573–7).

Perennial weeds
Wherever possible, clear a vegetable garden of perennial weeds before starting to grow crops. Dig out

A seep hose laid between rows of vegetables ensures that the water reaches the roots of the plants and penetrates deeply into the soil.

deeply rooted and spreading perennials, taking care not to leave in the soil small pieces of root that will sprout again. Where a weed problem is very serious, either use appropriate weedkillers or smother the weeds with a light-proof mulch, such as old carpet or heavy, black, plastic sheeting. Most (except very persistent weeds) will die if covered for six to twelve months. While crops are growing, take care to prevent or control perennial weeds.

Annual weeds
These germinate and grow very rapidly and become a nuisance if they are allowed to seed freely in the vegetable garden. Pay particular attention to weeding in the first three weeks after crops germinate, when they are most affected by competition. Pull up weeds by hand or hoe shallowly to avoid bringing deeper weed seeds to the surface. Remove the weeds to prevent rerooting.

Minimizing weed growth
During the growing season weed growth may be greatly reduced by mulching crops (see below) and also by growing vegetables at equidistant spacing (see "Spacing", p.311). Once they have reached a reasonable size, most form a canopy over the ground, which suppresses weeds.

Stale seedbeds
Spring sowings or plantings are the most vulnerable to annual weeds. Where the soil has not been cultivated recently and may be full of weed seeds prepare the soil in advance; allow the first flush of weeds to germinate, and hoe them off before sowing or planting (see also SOILS AND FERTILIZERS, "The stale seedbed technique", p.526).

Mulching

A mulch is a layer of organic or inorganic material laid on the soil around plants. Where the surface is kept mulched, the need to cultivate is lessened or even eliminated.

Organic mulches
Bulky organic mulches add nutrients to the soil and improve the soil structure. They may be in the form of well-rotted, straw-rich, animal manures, garden compost, spent mushroom compost, dried lawn clippings, or seaweed. Do not use any materials derived from wood, such

Vegetables such as runner beans drop their flowers if the soil around their roots dries out. Water the crops well, then apply a mulch by forking it onto the border. A mulch prevents soil-moisture evaporation, and also insulates the soil, suppresses weeds, protects the surface from heavy rain and erosion, and reduces damage to soil when it is trodden on.

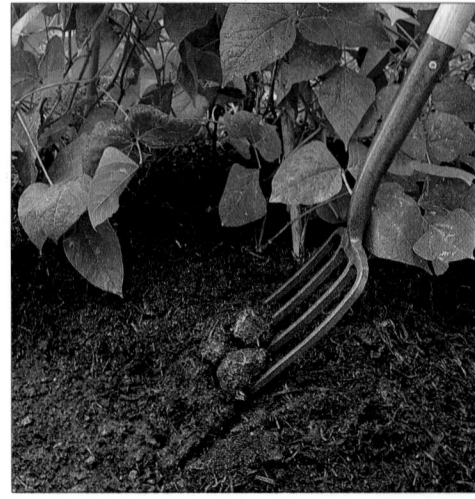

as sawdust and pulverized or shredded bark, unless they are at least two years old because their decomposition uses up soil nitrogen.

Organic mulches are best applied to growing crops in spring and early summer when the soil is moist. They maintain the temperature and moisture levels of the soil once they are applied so, if possible, mulch after the soil has warmed up in spring but before it starts to dry out. Never mulch cold, wet, or very dry soil. In areas with high rainfall and on heavy soil, however, an organic mulch is best spread on the ground in autumn to allow the worms to work it in.

In practice, it is often easiest to apply organic mulches when planting, watering plants first if necessary. Alternatively, mulch young seedlings that are already planted and growing strongly and are at least 5cm (2in) high. A mulch may be 2.5–7cm (1–3in) deep or more; aim for a deep mulch if the purpose is to keep down weeds.

Plastic film mulches

These are sheets of plastic that may be black, white, or transparent. Depending on which kind is used, they raise soil temperatures to bring on crops early, suppress weeds, reflect heat up to ripening fruit, and keep fruiting vegetables clean and free from soil splash. Shiny film mulches help deter flying pests.

Black films are mainly used to suppress weeds, although they also raise the soil temperature. Early potatoes may be grown under black films instead of being earthed up (see "Potatoes", p.357).

White films are mainly used to reflect light and warmth onto ripening fruit such as tomatoes and melons. Some films are made with the lower side black to suppress weeds, and the upper side white to reflect light. These films raise soil temperatures about 7°C (12°F) more than black films. Transparent films are used mainly to warm up the soil in spring, or to prevent soil splash.

It is simpler to lay films before planting or sowing crops. If desired, lay seep or porous hoses in position first, then lay the film on the ground or over the bed to be covered. Make slits 7–10cm (3–4in) deep in the soil around the bed, and anchor the mulch by tucking the edges into the soil, using a spade (see *Sheet Mulch*, p.532). This is simpler on slightly mounded beds. To plant, cut cross-shaped slits in the film with a knife, make a hole in the soil beneath, then carefully ease the plants through into the soil, and firm. Sow large seeds such as sweet corn by making holes

PLANTING THROUGH A BLACK-AND-WHITE PLASTIC MULCH

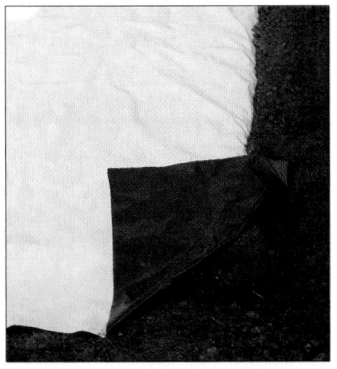

1 *Dig a trench around the area to be planted, lay down the mulch with the white side upwards, and secure its edges firmly into the earth.*

2 *Make cross-shaped slits in the plastic the required distance apart and dig a hole in the soil large enough to take the plant's root ball.*

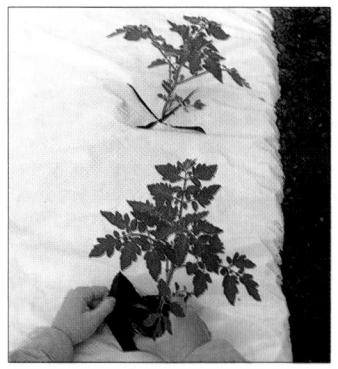

3 *Remove the plant (here a tomato) from its pot, and place it in the hole. Firm the soil around the root ball and water. Stake if necessary.*

in the plastic and pushing the seeds through. When seedlings appear, guide them through the holes so that they are not trapped.

When necessary, water carefully through the planting holes. Slugs may be attracted to films: lift the film edges carefully and remove them or use a proprietary slug killer.

Feeding

In fertile garden soils, into which plenty of organic matter is regularly worked, most vegetables will grow satisfactorily without the use of additional fertilizers. As it takes a few years to build up soil fertility, however, supplementary feeding will be necessary on poor soils or to correct deficiencies and, in some cases, to obtain higher yields.

Soil nutrients

Plants need a range of nutrients; the three most important for vegetables, and those most commonly in short supply, are phosphorus (P), nitrogen (N), and potassium or potash (K). For further information, see "Soil nutrients and fertilizers", pp.530–31.

Maintain adequate levels of phosphorus and potassium with an annual application of garden compost at 2–5kg/sq m (5–11lb/sq yd) or manure at 5.5kg/sq m (12lb/sq yd). Alternatively, use artificial fertilizers such as triple phosphate or superphosphate (for P) and potassium sulphate (for K) at levels recommended by the manufacturer, or apply them in compound fertilizers containing N, P, and K.

Potassium is washed out of the soil only slowly, so reserves last into the following season. Phosphorus is not lost through leaching, but may be "locked up" in insoluble forms and not available to plants; reserves may need replenishing if soil analysis indicates that they are low. Nitrogen is constantly leached out and reserves need to be replenished continually, by adding either organic matter (which releases nitrogen as it breaks down) or artificial fertilizers.

Vegetables vary in their need for nitrogen. For further information, see *Nitrogen Requirements*, p.314. This indicates the broad requirements of different groups using a fertilizer with 21 per cent N content. Rates therefore vary according to which fertilizer is used; nitrogenous fertilizers include ammonium nitrate and nitrate of potash.

Applying fertilizers

Fertilizers are sold in dry forms (dusts, granules, and pellets) and as concentrated liquids (see "Types of fertilizer", p.530). They can be applied either as a base-dressing before sowing or planting, or as a top-dressing to give a boost during growth (see "Applying fertilizers", p.531).

Apply nitrogenous fertilizers in spring, a month before sowing or planting; additional applications may be made later in the growing season. Never apply nitrogen in the autumn or it will be washed out of the soil before most vegetables are planted. Phosphate and potassium fertilizers are applied at any time, often in the autumn, or, where compound fertilizers are used, at the same time as nitrogen, in spring.

Feeding in organic systems

If extra feeding is necessary, use slower-acting organic fertilizers. These include fish, blood, and bone meal, a general fertilizer applied as a base- or top-dressing, and dried blood (relatively fast-acting) and hoof and horn (slower-acting), both of which provide a source of nitrogen.

Various proprietary and general-purpose liquid feeds are available, some based on animal manures and others on seaweed extracts. The latter appear to be particularly beneficial to growth, even though their nutrient levels are not very high. They are either watered in or applied as a foliar feed.

Container-grown vegetables

The compost in containers can dry out very rapidly in hot weather. To conserve moisture, keep the upper surface mulched with up to 5cm (2in) of organic material, stones, or a sheet mulch. Be prepared to water thoroughly twice a day.

Occasional feeding may be necessary; use an organic or artificial fertilizer at diluted strengths, according to the manufacturer's instructions. Top-dress the compost in the container in spring, and change the compost completely every two or three years when it becomes compacted and less productive.

Pests and diseases

Healthy plants can resist most pest and disease attacks. Therefore good basic care of plants will keep problems caused by pests and diseases to a minimum. Learn to recognize the most common pests and diseases in your garden, and take the appropriate preventive measures wherever feasible. Avoid using chemicals in the vegetable garden as far as possible. Apart from their inherent danger and the risk of residues in the soil as well as on the plants, they may kill the natural enemies of many pests and diseases. If using chemical controls seems unavoidable, try to use organically approved products at least. In a few cases, biological control – the introduction of a pest's natural enemy – may be used. For general information and details about specific pests and diseases, see PLANT PROBLEMS, pp.545–77.

Healthy practices

To reduce problems with pests and diseases, keep the soil fertile and well drained, work in plenty of organic matter, and rotate crops regularly (see p.307). Grow suitable crops for the climate, choosing, wherever possible, cultivars with pest and disease resistance or tolerance (see the lists of recommended cultivars for individual vegetables, pp.317–58). Always purchase disease-free plants. Raise plants in modules wherever feasible and harden off plants raised indoors. If growing plants under cover, always use clean seed trays and pots and sterilized potting compost.

Common pests

Animals and birds that may attack vegetables include deer, rabbits, mice, moles, and pigeons. In cases of persistent attack, erect wire fences or nets around the garden or over crops, use humane animal traps, and deter large birds with humming wire and small ones with strands of black cotton. In damp climates slugs and snails may be the most serious of all pests. They are mainly night-feeders – collect them after dark by torchlight and discard them. Where chemical controls are used, they must be handled carefully.

Soil pests, such as slugs and cutworms, commonly attack young plants, sometimes biting through the stems of plants at ground level. They tend to be worse in newly cultivated ground. Thorough digging exposes them to the birds. Many soil pests are night-feeders and may be easily caught by torchlight.

Microscopic soil pests known as eelworms or nematodes attack certain groups of plants, including potatoes. Rotate crops to prevent the pests from becoming established, and grow resistant cultivars where they are available.

Sucking insects, including many species of aphid, as well as carrot flies, cabbage root flies, and thrips or thunderflies, damage a range of plants by sucking the sap; they may spread virus diseases in the process. Knowledge of the pests' habits may help to prevent attacks – by earlier or later sowings, for example. Use sticky, yellow traps to catch aphids, collars (see *Collaring Seedlings*, p.317) to deter cabbage root flies, and film barriers against carrot flies (see p.354). Chemical or organic sprays may control outbreaks.

Various caterpillars attack a wide range of plants. Pick them off by hand or use the biological control *Bacillus thuringiensis*, or organic or chemical sprays. Fine nets placed over vegetables prevent the adult butterflies or moths from laying eggs on the plants. Small beetles, such as flea beetles, nibble seedling leaves of brassicas. They may be controlled with sprays, and plants may be protected with fine nets. Large beetles, such as Colorado beetles, pose serious problems in affected areas.

Pests may multiply very rapidly in the high temperatures under glass. The most serious are greenhouse whiteflies and red spider mites, both of which attack a wide range of crops. They have become very resistant to most standard chemical sprays. Discourage them with maximum ventilation and by damping down to increase humidity. As soon as these pests are noticed, introduce some form of biological control to restrict their numbers (see "Biological control", p.546).

Keep vegetable beds (here of ornamental cabbages and carrots) and paths free of weeds and debris; remove and burn diseased plant material. Water and feed carefully – excess can be as damaging as insufficiency. Thin seedlings early to avoid overcrowding, and remove the thinnings. Encourage rapid germination of home-grown plants by sowing indoors if conditions are adverse outside.

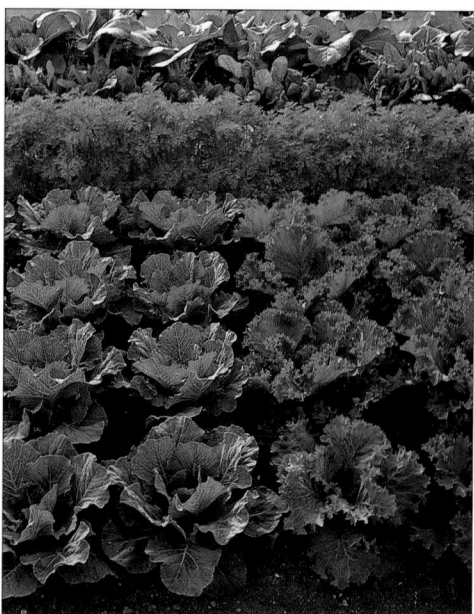

Common diseases

Diseases are caused mainly by fungi, bacteria, and viruses. Infected plants develop a range of symptoms which in some cases merely disfigure plants, but in others will kill them. Damping off diseases, for example, infect and usually kill young seedlings; dig up and burn affected plants.

Diseases spread very rapidly in conditions that are favourable to their development and once established are difficult to control. Preventive measures and good garden hygiene are vitally important to prevent diseases from spreading and becoming established. A few sprays may be used in anticipation of an attack. Choose disease-resistant cultivars.

Clubroot, a soil infection, is one of the most serious problems affecting members of the cabbage family. Raising the soil pH by applying lime (see "Liming", p.531), and raising plants in sterile soil in modules so that they are vigorous, may help to control this infection.

Physiological disorders

Some problems experienced with growing vegetables are due to incorrect cultural conditions. Most common among these problems is premature bolting (flowering and setting seed), which may be caused by sudden low or high temperatures, drought, or sowing at the wrong time. Fruits failing to set may be due to lack of pollination, erratic watering, or drought. If there are mineral deficiencies in the soil, cauliflower curds may fail to grow. Further details are given under individual vegetables (see pp.317–58), with advice on how to create healthy growing conditions.

NITROGEN REQUIREMENTS (using fertilizer with 21 per cent N content)				
VERY LOW 12g/sq m (¹/₂oz/sq yd)	LOW 25–35g/sq m (1–1¹/₃oz/sq yd)	MEDIUM 45–55g/sq m (1¹/₂–2oz/sq yd)	HIGH 70–100g/sq m (2¹/₂–3¹/₂oz/sq yd)	VERY HIGH 110g/sq m (4oz/sq yd)
Carrots Garlic Radishes	Asparagus Beans (all) Celeriac Chicory (all) Courgettes Cucumbers Endive Florence fennel Gherkins Globe artichokes Kohl rabi Marrows New Zealand spinach Okra Onions (all) Parsnips Peanuts Salsify Scorzonera Swedes Tomatoes Turnips (and turnip tops)	Amaranths Aubergines Broccoli raab Cabbages (for storage) Calabrese Cauliflowers Cocoyams Hot peppers Jerusalem artichokes Kales Lettuces Potatoes (early) Pumpkins Rhubarb (young) Spinach Sprouting broccoli Sweet corn Sweet/chilli peppers Sweet potatoes Watermelons Wonderberries	Beetroot Brussels sprouts Celery Ceylon spinach Leeks Potatoes (maincrop) Spinach beet Sweet melons Swiss chard	Cabbages (spring, summer, winter) Chinese broccoli Chinese cabbages Komatsuna Oriental mustards Mizuna greens Pak choi Rhubarb (cutting years)
(Peas do not require any extra nitrogen)				

Growing under cover

THE productivity of a vegetable garden may be increased greatly in climates with a short growing season by growing plants under cover in a protected environment for some or all of their lifecycle. The shorter the growing season, the more effective cover will be.

Under cover, air and soil temperatures are increased, and crops are sheltered from chill winds. This lengthens the growing season by up to two months. The quality and yields of many crops are improved by higher temperatures and shelter.

Cover may be used to start crops early in spring for planting outside when temperatures rise. Half-hardy summer vegetables that would not mature outdoors during the growing season may ripen under cover; in cool climates, okra and aubergines, for example, only ripen fully under cover. The winter cropping period of many vegetables may be extended; for example lettuces, peas, Oriental brassicas (see p.323), and spinach all stop growing in the open but continue under cover.

Make the most of cover by ensuring that the soil underneath is fertile and weed-free. Vegetables require extra watering under cover – mulch them where practical to cut down watering. Plants started under cover may be set back if abruptly exposed to the elements. Harden them off gradually where appropriate.

Greenhouses and frames

Cover may be provided by anything from a greenhouse to a cold frame or a plastic polytunnel. For full details, see GREENHOUSES AND FRAMES, pp.474–91.

Greenhouses

A permanent, glazed greenhouse provides an excellent growing environment. It is easily ventilated and retains heat at night better than plastic film. Diseases may build up in soil if crops such as tomatoes are grown for several consecutive years, and the soil must then be changed or sterilized, or crops grown in containers. Supports may be required for tender, climbing vegetables.

Walk-in polytunnels

These are made of heavy-duty, clear plastic sheeting on metal supports. They are cheaper and easier to erect than greenhouses, and may be moved

LOW POLYTUNNEL

Use wire hoops pushed into the ground 90cm (3ft) apart to support plastic film, which is tied at each end to a stake. Tie strings over the plastic and secure them at the base of each hoop.

to a different site if required. Ventilation is hard to control, however, increasing the risk of pests and diseases if temperatures rise rapidly; holes may be cut in the film in summer and taped over in winter. The film needs to be renewed every two or three years.

Low polytunnels

These are cheap, mobile, and flexible; the lightweight plastic film may be rolled back for ventilation and watering. They provide shelter from wind and are useful in most gardens, especially for the final stages of hardening off seedlings and protecting vegetables in unsettled spring and autumn weather. Low polytunnels are limited by their height and flimsiness, however, and give little protection from low temperatures. They also need to be well anchored in windy situations.

Garden frames

Being relatively small, frames are most beneficial in gardens lacking space for a greenhouse or polytunnel. Some types are portable. They are easily ventilated, and may be heated by electric soil-warming cables. They are useful for raising and hardening off seedlings; their low height limits the range of crops grown, although the lids may be removed to allow semi-hardy crops to mature. Garden frames may be blacked out for forcing crops such as Witloof chicory and endive.

Cloches

Although individual cloches only cover a small area, when placed end to end they can be used to cover an entire row. To make maximum use of cloches, move them from one crop to another during a season; for example protect overwintering salads, start tender early potatoes or dwarf beans in spring, then ripen melons in mid-summer.

Floating mulches

These are various types of film, including perforated plastic film, fine netting film, and non-woven fleecy film. All may be laid over low polytunnel hoops or directly over crops after sowing or planting, and anchored shallowly in the soil or weighted down. The mulches are lifted by the crops as they grow.

Floating mulches promote earlier crops and higher yields by raising temperatures and protecting plants from wind as well as, in some cases, insect pests. All give better ventilation than unperforated plastic films.

Weed beds carefully before laying floating mulches, since they are awkward to lift for weeding later.

Perforated plastic films

These are perforated with tiny slits or holes. They are generally used in the early stages of growth. Disadvantages include overheating in hot weather, minimal frost protection, and the risk of plants being chafed. To "wean" plants, slit plastic films down the centre a few days before removing them completely.

Netting films

Fine netting films are strong and last for several seasons. They are well ventilated so may usually be kept on until plants mature. They have little effect on temperature, but protect against wind. Provided that they are well anchored at the edges, they protect against many insect pests.

Fleecy or fibrous films

These light, soft, non-woven films usually last one season. Depending on the film's weight, it may protect against frost and flying insect pests; the films are more permeable to light and air than plastics. Many vegetables may be grown under fleecy film until they are nearly mature.

USING FLOATING MULCHES

PERFORATED PLASTIC FILM *Floating mulches are spread over a bed of seedlings and earthed in at the edges so that they are loose enough to allow for growth. Perforated plastic film protects the seedlings but allows ventilation.*

NETTING FILM
This protects plants against insect pests and wind damage.

FLEECY FILM
This is effective against frost as well as deterring insect pests.

Harvesting and storing

How and when vegetables are harvested, and whether they are used fresh, stored, or both, depends on the nature of the vegetable and the climate. The shorter the growing season and the more severe the winter, the greater the incentive to store vegetables, either naturally or by freezing. For details, see individual vegetables (pp.317–58) and *Vegetables that Freeze Well*, below.

Harvesting

Follow the guidelines under individual vegetables for how to harvest. Most vegetables are harvested

VEGETABLES THAT FREEZE WELL

Asparagus 1
Aubergines 1 2
Beetroot 1 3
Broad beans 1
Broccoli raab 1
Brussels sprouts 1
Calabrese 1
Carrots 1 3
Cauliflowers 1 2
Cabbages 1 2
Celery 2
Chinese broccoli 1
Chinese cabbages 1 2
Courgettes 1
Dolichos beans 1
French beans 1
Hot peppers 1 2
Kales 1
Kohl rabi 1 2
Lima beans 1
Marrows 1 2
New Zealand spinach 1
Okra 1
Parsnips 1 3
Peas 1
Potatoes (small and new potatoes only) 1
Pumpkins 2
Rhubarb 2
Scarlet runner beans 1
Spinach 1
Spinach beet 1
Spring onions 2
Sprouting broccoli 1
Swedes 1 2
Sweet corn 1
Sweet peppers
Swiss chard 1
Tomatoes 1
Turnips 1 2 3
Wonderberries 1

KEY
1 Blanch
2 Dice, slice, purée, or shred
3 Freeze only when young

at maturity, but some, notably leafy plants and brassicas, may be cut at various stages, and will often resprout for a second and third crop.

Cut-and-come-again harvesting

This method of harvesting is suited to vegetables that resprout after an initial cut has been made, enabling them to be used fresh over a fairly long period. Crops may be harvested at the seedling stage, or later when they are semi-mature or mature.

Harvest seedling crops when they are 5–10cm (2–4in) high, cutting about 2cm (^{3}/4in) above soil level. Some, for example salad rocket, salad rape, and cress, may be cut and left to resprout several times in succession. See also "Cut-and-come-again seedling crops", p.310.

Some semi-mature or mature crops, if harvested by cutting 2.5–5cm (1–2in) above soil level, will resprout and after a few weeks produce more leaves and, in some cases, edible flowering shoots (see "Cultivating Oriental brassicas", p.323).

The technique is suited to certain types of lettuce, endive, sugar loaf chicory, Oriental greens, and Swiss chard. It is useful in cool climates in autumn and early winter as plants treated this way survive lower temperatures than they would otherwise and may be very productive, especially under cover.

Storing

The length of time that vegetables may be stored depends on the storage conditions and on the vegetable or cultivar. For details, see individual vegetables. The main cause of deterioration after harvesting is water loss, so aim to keep this to a minimum. Do not store damaged or diseased specimens since they may rot.

Vegetables often freeze well; almost all need to be blanched either in steam or boiling water and cooled quickly before freezing. The only exception to this is sweet peppers, which may be frozen without any initial preparation.

Leafy vegetables and brassicas

Leafy vegetables and various types of brassica, such as calabrese and cauliflower, have such a high water content that few of them store well. An exception is the winter storing cabbage, which may be stored either hanging in nets or on a bed of straw, in a frost-free shed or cold frame.

STORING STRINGS OF ONIONS
Plait together the dried onion leaves to form strings of bulbs. These may be hung outside in warm weather to dry further, and then brought indoors to be stored in frost-free conditions.

Several brassicas freeze well: some cultivars are bred for the purpose. Freeze only top-quality produce.

Fruiting vegetables

Vegetables such as tomatoes, aubergines, and cucumbers usually have an optimum time for harvesting, although fruits may also be harvested immature. If they are to be stored for winter use, they are best made into preserves or deep frozen.

Sweet peppers keep in good condition for many months if whole plants are pulled up and hung in a dry, frost-free place. Certain cultivars of marrow and squash may be stored for several months. Leave the fruit on the plant until it is mature, then pick and "cure" it in the sun to harden the skin so that it forms an effective barrier to water loss, and store it in a dry, frost-free environment (see also "Pumpkins", p.335).

Bulbs

Certain cultivars of onion, shallot, and garlic will keep for many months. Lift the crop when mature or nearing maturity, and dry it in the sun (or under cover in wet climates), until the outer skins are papery. Handle the bulbs carefully to avoid bruising. Hang them as plaited strings, in nets, or spaced out on trays, in well-ventilated, frost-free conditions (see also *Storing Onions*, p.345).

Root vegetables

Some root vegetables, such as carrots and potatoes, may be either harvested young and eaten immature or left to mature and lifted and stored at the end of the season. A few, such as parsnips, are extremely hardy

and, except in severe winters, may be left in the ground until required.

Prepare vegetables carefully for storing, removing any foliage since this will rot. Store only healthy, unbruised specimens. Potatoes are susceptible to frost; store them packed in light-proof sacks in a frost-free place.

Root vegetables such as beetroot and carrots easily lose moisture, so store them in layers in boxes of moist sand, peat substitute, or peat in a cool shed or cellar (see *Storing Carrots*, p.354). They may also be stored in outdoor clamps: pile them on straw and cover with more straw, and, in cold areas, a layer of soil to give protection against frost (see *Making a Swede Clamp*, p.353).

STORING RED CABBAGES

Lay the cabbages on slats covered with straw in a cool, well-ventilated, frost-free place. Leave gaps between them to allow free air circulation and discourage rotting.

Western brassicas

WESTERN brassicas include kales, cauliflowers, cabbages, Brussels sprouts, sprouting broccoli, calabrese, turnip tops, broccoli raab, kohl rabi, swedes, and turnips. For kohl rabi, swedes, and turnips, see pp.350, 352, and 353 respectively.

Western brassicas are naturally biennial but are cultivated as annuals for their leaves and roots, and as biennials for flowerheads and shoots. Each type displays considerable variation, and there is often a range of cultivars for different seasons. They are usually cooked, but some are used raw. Western brassicas are

COLLARING SEEDLINGS

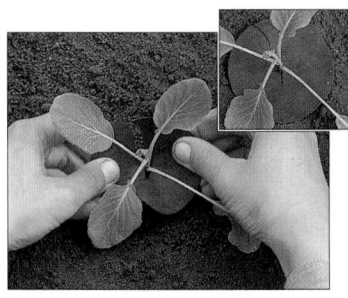

Where cabbage root flies are a problem, place a collar around the stem of each seedling. Make sure that it is flat on the ground to prevent the adult flies from laying their eggs at the base of the stem.

cool-season crops with varying degrees of frost tolerance; most perform poorly at high temperatures, so in warm climates grow them in winter. In temperate climates, they may provide crops for much of the year.

Siting Western brassicas
An open situation with fertile, well-drained, moisture-retentive soil is required. Rotate brassicas (see p.307) to avoid a build-up of clubroot. If this is a problem, lime the soil (see p.531) to bring the pH to 6.5–7 and discourage the disease. Most Western brassicas need high levels of nitrogen (see p.314), but they should not be planted on freshly manured ground since this causes overlush, leafy growth that is prone to pests and is more tender. A base-dressing may be applied to the area before planting (see "Applying fertilizers", p.313).

Sowing and planting Western brassicas
Western brassicas prefer firm soil; they may be planted after a previous vegetable crop without forking the soil. Sow *in situ*, or in a seedbed, or indoors in trays or modules for transplanting. If the soil is infected with clubroot, sow in modules, transferring to pots before planting out, so that the plants have a healthy

Calabrese

Cauliflower

Winter cabbage

Curly kale

Savoy cabbage

Brussels sprouts

start and are more likely to mature without infection. Tall, top-heavy brassicas, such as Brussels sprouts or sprouting broccoli, should be planted 10cm (4in) deep. Earth up the stem as it grows by building a small mound of soil around it to a depth of about 10cm (4in); in windy sites, support the stem with a stake 1m (3ft) high. Plant brassicas firmly, with the lower leaves just above soil level. In some cases, spacing may be varied to determine the size of the brassica. If plants are widely spaced, they may be intercropped with salad seedlings or radishes.

Cultivating Western brassicas
Mulch after planting to suppress weeds. In dry weather, water as for leafy vegetables (see "Critical watering periods", p.312). Apply a nitrogenous fertilizer during growth.

Flea beetles (p.548), slugs and snails (p.548), damping off (p.548), cabbage root flies (p.564), white blister (p.550), whiptail (p.556), and cutworms (p.564) all affect young plants. Caterpillars (p.549), cabbage whiteflies (p.550), mealy aphids (see "Aphids", p.550), clubroot (p.553), and birds (p.561) attack plants at all stages of growth.

Kales (*Brassica oleracea* Acephala Group)

Grown as annuals or biennials depending on the type, dwarf kales are 30–40cm (12–16in) tall, with a 30cm (12in) spread; tall types grow to 90cm (3ft) and spread up to 60cm (24in). Some American kales are known as collards. Plain (such as the tall 'Thousandhead') and curly-leaved types (such as the medium-sized 'Fribor'), and curly-broad

CURLY KALE

hybrids (such as the tall 'Pentland Brig') usually produce leaves from a central stem. The leaves of all kales, and the spring-flowering shoots and young leaves of broad-leaved types, are used cooked or raw. Kales are the hardiest brassicas, some surviving at -15°C (5°F); many also tolerate high temperatures. All prefer fertile, well-drained soils and need medium nitrogen levels (see p.314).

Sowing, planting, and routine cultivation
Sow seed in early spring for summer crops, and in late spring for autumn and winter crops. Sow *in situ* or in seedbeds or seed trays for transplanting; dwarf forms should be spaced 30–45cm (12–18in) apart, tall forms 75cm (30in) apart.

Give overwintering types a nitrogenous top-dressing in spring to encourage growth. In severe winters, grow dwarf cultivars under cloches or low polytunnels. Kales are usually unaffected by pests and diseases.

Growing under cover
For very early, tender kales, sow seed in early spring in rows 15cm (6in) apart, or in wide drills. Either harvest them as large seedlings, or thin the seedlings to 7cm (3in) apart and cut when they form plants 15cm (6in) tall, leaving the stumps to resprout for a second harvest.

Harvesting and storing
Some cultivars mature seven weeks after sowing, but plants can stand a long time in the ground. Snap off the leaves as required in autumn and winter to encourage new growth. Pick the shoots in spring when they are about 10cm (4in) long, before the flowers open. Kales freeze well.

ORNAMENTAL KALES

Ornamental kales are grown mainly for winter decoration in the garden or for garnishing salads. Leaves are variegated green, red, white, or purple.

Cauliflowers (*Brassica oleracea* Botrytis Group)

Grown as annuals or biennials, cauliflowers form an average head (or curd) of about 20cm (8in) in diameter; the plants are 45–60cm (18–24in) tall, with a spread of up to 90cm (3ft). They are classified by the main season of use, usually winter (with a distinction between those for frosty and frost-free areas), early summer, and summer/autumn, although these groups overlap (see *Cauliflower Types*, below). Most types of cauliflower have creamy or white curds, but there are attractive, distinctively flavoured types with green or purple curds. The curds, and in some cases the young green leaves surrounding them, are cooked or used raw in salads. Smaller curds, or mini-cauliflowers, about 5cm (2in) in diameter, may be specially grown from early summer cultivars.

Cauliflowers are a cool-season crop and do not usually grow well in areas with high summer temperatures. Several cultivars are frost hardy, but cauliflowers may only be harvested all year round in areas with frost-free winters. For soil and site see "Siting Western brassicas", p.317; overwintering cauliflowers need a sheltered situation outside,

and are not usually grown to maturity under cover. All cauliflowers need a moisture-retentive soil, with medium nitrogen levels (see p.314), and a pH of 6.5–7.5.

Sowing and planting

Success with cauliflowers depends on sowing the correct cultivar at the appropriate time, and allowing plants to develop with as few checks to growth (from transplanting or dry soil, for example) as possible. Where drought is likely in summer, grow spring-heading types, which will benefit from autumn rainfall, or fast-maturing mini-cauliflowers.

The main sowing times and spacings are given in the chart below. Cauliflowers are usually sown in seed trays, modules, or a seedbed for transplanting, but may be sown *in situ* and thinned to the correct spacing. Generally, the later the planting, the larger the cauliflower will grow and the wider the spacing required. Seed germinates best at a temperature of about 21°C (70°F).

For a very early summer supply, sow seed in autumn, in modules or seed trays, then pot up seedlings in small pots. Put the pots into a well-ventilated frame or under cloches for the winter. Alternatively, sow *in situ* in frames or under cloches, thinning to 5cm (2in) apart. Harden off seedlings before planting them out in spring. For a later crop, sow indoors in gentle heat in early spring, and prick out into small pots.

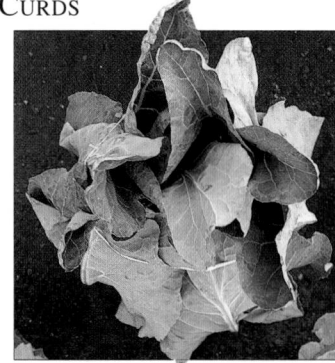

1 *In winter and early spring, mature curds of overwintering types may need protection from severe frost.*

2 *Wrap the leaves up around the central curd, securing them with soft string.*

For summer/autumn and winter groups, sow the first batch indoors in seed trays or modules, or *in situ* in frames or under cloches. Successive sowings may be made in a seedbed outdoors, or in modules for transplanting later on.

To obtain mini-cauliflowers, select an early summer cultivar to be sown in spring or early summer; sow several seeds per station, 15cm (6in) apart, thinning to one seedling after germination. Alternatively, raise plants in modules and plant them out 15cm (6in) apart. For a continuous supply, make successive sowings.

Routine cultivation

Cauliflowers need regular water throughout the growing period. In dry conditions, water at a rate of 22 litres/sq m (5 gallons/sq yd) every two weeks. Overwintering cauliflowers require low nitrogen levels when planted or they will be too soft to survive the colder conditions. A nitrogenous fertilizer or organic liquid feed may be applied in spring.

To prevent white curds from discolouring in sunny weather, tie the leaves over the curds. This may also be done in winter and spring to protect curds of overwintering types from the elements; most modern cultivars, however, have leaves that naturally tend to cover the curds.

Pests and diseases

For cauliflower pests and diseases, see "Cultivating Western brassicas", p.317. Cauliflowers are also attacked by pollen beetles (p.561).

Harvesting and storing

The time from sowing to maturity varies from approximately 16 weeks for summer/autumn cauliflowers to about 40 weeks for winter ones. Cut the curds while they are still firm and tight. Mini-cauliflowers mature about 15 weeks after sowing and should be picked immediately since they deteriorate quickly. All cauliflowers, and in particular the mini-cauliflowers, freeze well.

MINI-CAULIFLOWERS

PURPLE-HEADED CAULIFLOWER

CAULIFLOWER TYPES

Group	When to Sow	When to Plant	Spacing	When to Harvest
Winter (frost-free areas)	Late spring	Summer	70cm (28in)	Winter/very early spring
Winter	Late spring	Summer	63cm (25in)	Early spring
Early summer	Autumn/early spring (sow under glass)	Spring	52cm (21in)	Early to mid-summer
Summer/autumn	Mid- to late spring	Early summer	55–63cm (22–5in)	Late summer to late autumn

Cabbages (*Brassica oleracea* Capitata Group)

Most cabbages are grown as annuals. Plants are generally 20–25cm (8–10in) tall, with a spread of up to 70cm (28in). The average head is about 15cm (6in) in diameter.

They are grouped according to their season of maturity, although there is some overlap between the groups. Leaves are dark or light green, blue-green, white, or red, and smooth or crinkled (savoy). Cabbage heads are pointed or round, and vary in their density. Spring greens are either loose-leaved cultivars or standard spring cabbages harvested before the head forms. Cabbage leaves are eaten either cooked or raw and sliced in salads. They may also be pickled. If they are tender enough, stems and stalks may be sliced finely and cooked. Some types of winter cabbage may be stored.

Cabbages grow best at 15–20°C (59–68°F). Do not plant in temperatures over 25°C (77°F). The hardiest cultivars may survive temperatures as low as -10°C (14°F) for short periods. Cabbages are not usually grown under cover.

To grow well, cabbages need soil that is fertile, moisture-retentive, and humus-rich with a pH level above 6. Spring, summer, and fresh winter cabbages require very high nitrogen levels, and winter storage cabbages medium nitrogen (see p.314). Do

MATURE SPRING CABBAGES

not give spring cabbages a nitrogenous base-dressing at planting, since the nitrogen will probably be washed from the soil over the winter; top-dress in spring instead.

Sowing and planting
Sow the chosen cultivars at the correct time for their group (see *Cabbage Types*, below). Sow seeds in seedbeds or modules and transplant seedlings to their final position on average five weeks later. Appropriate spacing varies according to type (see chart below) and it may be

modified to vary the size of the head; adopt closer spacing for smaller heads, and wide spacing to produce larger heads. A collar may be placed around each seedling stem when transplanting to protect against cabbage root flies (see *Collaring Seedlings*, p.317). Ensure that young seedlings have sufficient moisture until they are well established.

For spring greens either grow a greens cultivar, spacing the plants about 25cm (10in) apart, or use a heading spring cultivar and space plants 10–15cm (4–6in) apart. Cut

AUTUMN CABBAGE

RED SUMMER CABBAGE

SAVOY CABBAGE

CABBAGE TYPES

GROUP (TIME OF MATURITY)	DESCRIPTION	MAIN SOWING PERIOD	AVERAGE SPACING
Spring	Small, pointed or round heads	End of summer	30cm (12in)
	Loose-leaf greens	End of summer	25cm (10in)
Early summer	Large, mainly round heads	Very early spring (sow under glass)	35cm (14in)
Summer	Large, round heads	Early spring	35cm (14in)
Autumn	Large, round heads	Late spring	50cm (20in)
Winter (for storage)	Smooth, white-leaved, winter white types	Spring	50cm (20in)
Winter (to use fresh)	Blue, green, and savoy leaf types	Late spring	50cm (20in)

Plant spring cabbages 15cm (6in) apart. When they have grown on, but before they start to form a compact heart, harvest alternate plants, cutting them at the base. Use these as spring greens.

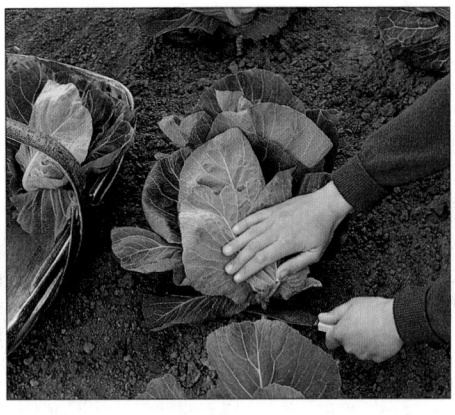

HOW TO OBTAIN A SECOND CROP

1 *To produce a second crop of greens, make a cross-shaped cut in the stalk after harvesting the cabbage head.*

2 *A few weeks later, several miniature heads should have sprouted, ready for a second harvest.*

them young as loose greens; every second or third plant may be left to heart up if a heading cultivar is used.

Routine cultivation
To increase their stability, earth up winter cabbages as they grow. Protect spring cabbages under cloches or floating mulches, and apply a liquid feed or a nitrogenous top-dressing in spring; feed others in the growing season. Keep cabbages moist throughout growth (see "Critical watering periods", p.312).

Pests and diseases
For pests and diseases that may affect cabbages, see "Cultivating Western brassicas", p.317. Seedling blight (p.558) may also occur.

Harvesting and storing
Spring and summer cultivars vary in their ability to stand in good condition once the head has matured; modern cultivars often stand longer than traditional ones. Normally the plant is dug up once the head has been cut, but spring and early summer cultivars may produce a second crop if the head is cut to leave a 10cm (4in) stalk in the ground. Using a sharp knife, make a shallow cross in the top of the stem to encourage new growth. Provided that the soil is fertile and moist, three or four more heads may develop together on the stalk.

Storage cabbages (winter white cultivars and appropriate red cabbages) should be lifted before heavy

PREPARING CABBAGES FOR STORING

Before storing cabbages, carefully remove any loose or discoloured, outer leaves without damaging the head (see inset). Inspect the cabbages regularly while they are in store and remove leaves that are rotting.

frost. Dig them up and carefully remove any loose, outer leaves. Place them on slatted supports or straw on the floor of a shed, or suspend them in nets. Store the heads at just above freezing point, with relatively high

humidity. They may also be stored in a cold frame, provided that it is ventilated on warm days to discourage rotting (see also *Storing Red Cabbages*, p.316). Cabbages may keep for four or five months.

Brussels sprouts (*Brassica oleracea* Gemmifera Group)

These are biennials grown as annuals, and vary in height from about 35cm (14in) for the dwarf forms to 75cm (30in) for the tall forms, with a spread of up to 50cm (20in) in both cases. Brussels sprouts are loosely divided by their time of maturity into early, mid-season, and late groups. The earlier types tend to be dwarfer and less hardy. The modern

F1 cultivars are an improvement over older, open-pollinated ones; they perform better on fertile soils, are less prone to lean (as they have a stronger root system), and have more compact, even sprouts. The tight sprouts that develop on the stem are cooked but may also be shredded raw into salads. The mature leaves at the top of the plants may also be eaten. There is a well-flavoured, but less productive, red cultivar, 'Rubine'.

Brussels sprouts are typical cool-season brassicas; the hardiest cultivars survive temperatures of -10°C (14°F). If sown in succession, Brussels sprouts provide a constant crop from early autumn to late spring. A general base-dressing may be applied shortly before planting; high nitrogen levels are needed (see p.314). Avoid using freshly manured ground as this encourages blown and loose, rather than firm, sprouts. For soil and site requirements, see "Siting Western brassicas", p.317.

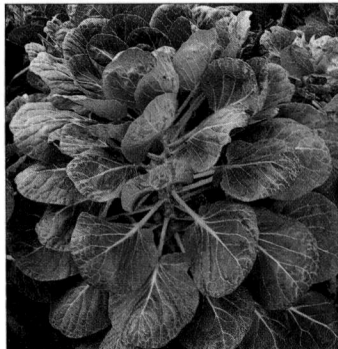

DWARF BRUSSELS SPROUT PLANT

EARTHING UP BRUSSELS SPROUTS

About a month after planting out, earth up Brussels sprouts by drawing the soil around the base of the stem to increase stability. At this stage they may also be staked if they are in an exposed site.

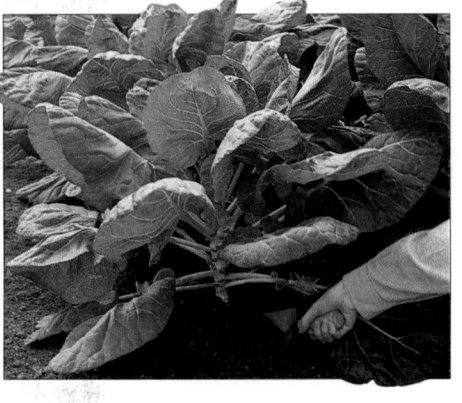

Sowing and planting
Sow in succession from mid- to late spring as the soil begins to warm up, starting with the early-maturing cultivars. For a very early crop, sow in gentle heat under cover in early spring. Sow either in seed trays or in

a seedbed for transplanting, or *in situ* in firm ground; most Brussels sprouts do not grow well in modules.

Thin out or transplant to the required spacing in early summer, generally four to five weeks after sowing. Plant dwarf cultivars about

45cm (18in) apart, and tall cultivars about 60cm (2ft) apart. Use closer spacing to produce smaller sprouts of a more uniform size, and wider spacing for large sprouts that mature in succession and so may be picked over a longer period. Wide spacing also encourages good air circulation, which keeps plants healthy and disease-free. Plant tall cultivars deeply and earth up the stems as they grow to provide extra stability. Keep young plants moist until they are well established.

REMOVING LEAVES

Snap off any yellowing or diseased leaves that develop as these may carry fungal diseases that could spread to the whole crop. This also improves air circulation.

Brussels sprouts, with their slow rate of growth, may be intercropped in the first few months with fast-maturing vegetables.

Routine cultivation

Keep beds weed-free. Since plants are widely spaced, extra watering is required only in very dry conditions, when they should be watered at the rate for leafy crops (see "Critical watering periods", p.312). A top-dressing of a nitrogenous fertilizer or an organic liquid feed may be applied in late summer if the plants are not growing vigorously. Remove any withered or diseased leaves from the stems as they appear.

If sprouts are wanted for freezing, grow an early cultivar that matures in autumn, and nip off the sprout top or growing point in late summer, when the lower sprouts are roughly 1cm ($\frac{1}{2}$in) in diameter. All the sprouts will then mature for picking together, rather than in succession.

Pests and diseases

The most common problems are mealybugs (p.550), which can colonize the individual sprouts, and downy mildew (p.550). For other diseases likely to affect Brussels sprouts, see "Cultivating Western brassicas", p.317.

Harvesting and storing

Brussels sprouts are ready to harvest about 20 weeks after sowing. Their flavour is improved after they have been exposed to some frost. Pick the lowest sprouts first by snapping them off at the base; the upper sprouts will continue to develop. If the sprouts are intended for freezing, pick them before the outer leaves become damaged by winter weather; freeze only top-quality sprouts. Sprout tops may be harvested by cutting them off at the end of the season.

After harvesting, dig up the plants and break up the stems with a hammer. This deters the build-up and spread of brassica diseases, and enables the stems to rot down more quickly when composted.

Where winters are very severe, uproot the whole plants before the ground freezes and hang them in a cool, frost-free place; the sprouts will remain fresh for several weeks.

F1 AND OPEN-POLLINATED SPROUTS

Modern F1 hybrids produce sprouts that are compact, evenly spaced, and of uniform size. Traditional, open-pollinated cultivars are more likely to produce blown sprouts widely varying in size.

F1 HYBRID   TRADITIONAL CULTIVAR

RECOMMENDED BRUSSELS SPROUTS

Early
'Lancelot' F1
'Oliver' F1
'Peer Gynt' F1

'Peer Gynt'

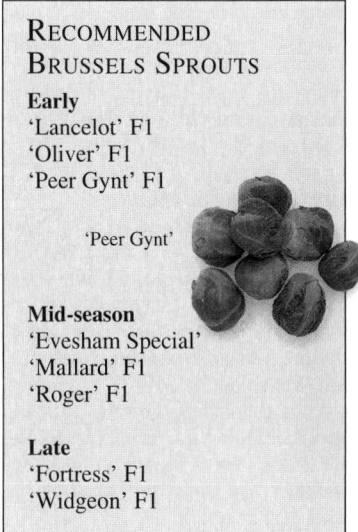

Mid-season
'Evesham Special'
'Mallard' F1
'Roger' F1

Late
'Fortress' F1
'Widgeon' F1

Sprouting broccoli (*Brassica oleracea* Italica Group)

These large, biennial plants may reach a height of 60–90cm (2–3ft) and a spread of 60cm (2ft). There are purple and white forms; the purple is more prolific and hardier. The flowering shoots that develop in spring are eaten cooked.

PURPLE SPROUTING BROCCOLI

Sprouting broccoli is grown mainly in the British Isles, where it is considered one of the hardiest winter vegetables, surviving temperatures of about -12˚C (10˚F). Because it is a slow-maturing vegetable that occupies the ground for up to a year, broccoli requires a fertile soil and medium nitrogen levels (see p.314). Avoid shallow and sandy soils and sites exposed to strong, winter winds.

Sowing, planting, and routine cultivation

Sow in spring, either in a seedbed or in modules. Transplant from early to mid-summer, spacing plants at least 60cm (2ft) apart, and planting them deeply for stability.

Plants may need staking in the autumn. If wood pigeons (p.549) eat leaves, cover the plants with netting for the winter. For further cultivation requirements, see "Cultivating Western brassicas", p.317.

Pests and diseases

Sprouting broccoli is, in theory, affected by the common brassica pests, but in practice is fairly trouble-free. Pollen beetles (p.561) attacking the flowering shoots are an increasing problem in some areas.

RECOMMENDED SPROUTING BROCCOLI

'Minaret'
'Nine Star Perennial'
'Purple Sprouting'

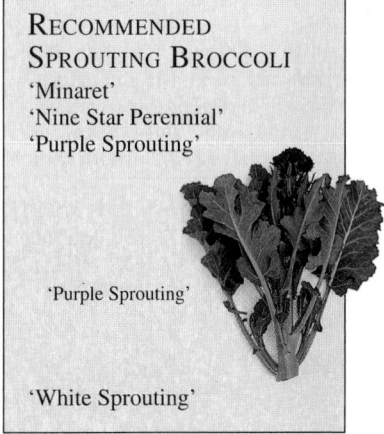

'Purple Sprouting'

'White Sprouting'

Harvesting and storing

Pick shoots from early to late spring. Snap them off when they are about 15cm (6in) long, while the flowers are in bud. Pick regularly to encourage the production of more shoots; plants may crop for up to two months. Sprouting broccoli freezes well.

Calabrese (*Brassica oleracea* Italica Group)

Also known as American or Italian broccoli, calabrese is grown as an annual or biennial, and produces compact plants about 45cm (18in) tall, with a spread rarely over 38cm (15in). Cultivars are classified as early, mid-season, and late, with the earliest maturing the fastest. F1 hybrids are more productive than the original cultivars. The compact, terminal head and the young sideshoots are eaten lightly cooked.

Calabrese is a cool-season crop and should not be grown in areas where the average mean temperature is above 15°C (59°F). Young plants tolerate some frost, but it may damage embryonic and young heads once they start to develop. Calabrese needs an open site in moisture-retentive, fairly fertile soil with medium nitrogen levels (see p.314).

Sowing and planting

Sow in succession from spring to early summer for a crop during summer and autumn. Calabrese seedlings do not transplant well, so either sow two or three seeds per station *in situ*, or sow in modules and transplant seedlings to moist ground, disturbing the roots as little as possible. For an early crop, make the first sowings indoors; these are, however, especially prone to bolting when transplanted.

HARVESTING CALABRESE

1 *Just before the flower buds open, harvest the first central head by cutting through the stalk.*

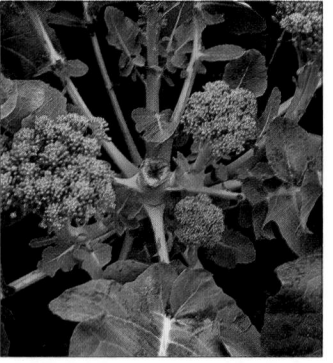

2 *This encourages sideshoots to develop; these can also be harvested and more sideshoots will be produced.*

Calabrese plants grow well at various spacings. For the highest overall yield, space plants 22cm (9in) apart each way, or 15cm (6in) apart in rows spaced at 30cm (12in). Closer spacing produces smaller terminal shoots, which mature together and are suitable for freezing.

Routine cultivation

Keep the bed weed-free. Calabrese plants need plenty of water to crop well – 11 litres/sq m (2 gallons/sq yd)

every two weeks. In very dry conditions, water as for leafy crops (see "Critical watering periods", p.312). A nitrogenous top-dressing or an organic liquid feed may be applied once the terminal heads have been cut in order to encourage additional sideshoots to develop.

Pests and diseases

For pests and diseases that may affect calabrese, see "Cultivating Western brassicas", p.317. Problems

may also be caused by pollen beetles (p.561) and downy mildew (p.550).

Harvesting and storing

Calabrese is a fast-maturing brassica, ready 11–14 weeks after sowing. The main head should be cut when it is 7–10cm (3–4in) in diameter, while still firm and before the flower buds open. Sideshoots will subsequently develop; cut these when they are about 10cm (4in) long. Calabrese freezes well.

RECOMMENDED CALABRESE

Early
'Emperor' F1

'Emperor'

'Green Belt'
'Green Comet' F1
'Mercedes' F1

Mid-season
'Citation' F1
'Stolto' F1

Late
'Corvet' F1
'Shogun' F1

Turnip tops and broccoli raab (*Brassica rapa*)

Over the centuries different brassicas have been grown for cutting in the immature stages for use as quick-maturing greens. The two types commonly used for this purpose today are turnip tops (*Brassica rapa* Rapifera Group) and broccoli raab (*Brassica rapa* Utilis Group), which

is also known as turnip rape and by a number of Italian names such as *cime di rapa*, *rapini*, and *broccoletti*.

They are grown as annuals or biennials, generally with single stems that reach a maximum height of about 30cm (12in). The leaves, young stems, and sweetly flavoured

young flowerheads are eaten cooked as spring greens, or raw in salads.

Turnip tops and broccoli raab are cool-season brassicas. Grow them in spring and autumn in hot climates, or all year where summers are cool. All turnip cultivars are suitable; broccoli raab has no named cultivars. Both grow best in fertile, moisture-retentive soil and require low to medium nitrogen levels (see p.314).

Sowing, planting, and routine cultivation

Sow thinly broadcast or in rows about 10cm (4in) apart. For larger plants only, thin to 15cm (6in). For an early crop in cold areas, make the first sowing indoors in early spring. Plants need little attention subsequently.

Harvesting and storing

Harvest plants within seven to eight weeks of sowing. Make the first cut when they are leafy and 10cm (4in) tall, or wait until the immature flowering shoots appear and the plant is

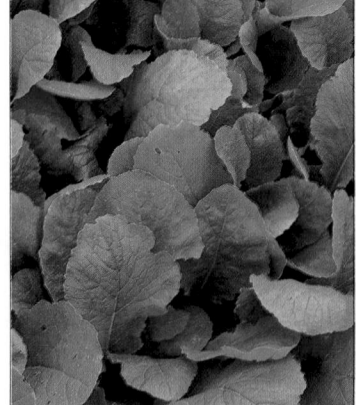

TURNIP TOPS

20–25cm (8–10in) tall. Cut about 2.5cm (1in) above ground level. In cool weather, the plants resprout to give two or three further cuttings over a period of four or five weeks. Cut as long as the stems are tender. Use turnip tops and broccoli raab fresh as they do not store well.

BROCCOLI RAAB

Oriental brassicas

SEVERAL Oriental brassicas are now being introduced to the West. They have many features in common with Western brassicas but tend to be faster growing and have a wider range of uses than Western brassicas. If they are given the right conditions they are highly productive. They are grown as annuals or biennials.

Oriental brassicas are cultivated mainly for the leaves and leafy stems, but also for the young, sweetly flavoured flowering shoots. Leaf shape and colour vary from the glossy, white-ribbed leaves of some pak choi cultivars, and the feathery green leaves of mizuna greens, to the purplish-green of Oriental mustards. Oriental brassicas are nutritious, succulent, and crisp, and are mild to peppery in flavour. Cook them, preferably by stir-frying or steaming, or use young leaves and shoots raw in salads.

Oriental brassicas are best suited to climates with cool summers and mild winters, although many cultivars are available that are adapted for hotter climates. Most will withstand light frost, especially if harvested when they are semi-mature as a cut-and-come-again crop (see p.316). A few Oriental brassicas, such as komatsuna and some of the mustards, are extremely hardy.

In temperate climates, Oriental brassicas grow best in late summer and autumn. Where winter temperatures fall several degrees below freezing, they may be grown as a winter crop under cover in unheated structures; if planted late in the summer, they may crop from autumn to spring, although they will stop growing at low temperatures.

Oriental brassicas require similar conditions to Western brassicas (see "Siting Western brassicas", p.317) but, being fast-growing, hungry, and thirsty plants, the soil must be rich in organic matter, moisture-retentive, and fertile. They never develop well in poor, dry soil. Most of them have very high nitrogen requirements (see p.314).

Sowing and planting Oriental brassicas

All standard methods of sowing may be used; where there is a risk of plants going to seed prematurely (bolting), sow seed in modules or *in situ*. Many have a tendency to bolt when days are lengthening, particularly when this is combined with low spring temperatures. In these cases, in northern latitudes, delay sowing until mid-summer, unless plants are started off in heat or cultivars with bolting resistance are used. If bolting continues to be a problem, grow Oriental brassicas as seedling crops, and harvest the leaves before the plants start to bolt.

Their rapid rate of growth makes Oriental brassicas ideal for intercropping among slower-maturing vegetables, especially for cutting as a cut-and-come-again seedling crop, when their flavour is superb.

Loose-leaved Chinese cabbage

Tight-headed Chinese cabbage

Pak choi

Pak choi

Cultivating Oriental brassicas

Oriental brassicas are generally shallow-rooting and so need regular watering. In very dry conditions, water at the rate for leafy crops (see "Critical watering periods", p.312). They should also be kept mulched.

Oriental brassicas are susceptible to the same pests and diseases as Western brassicas (see "Cultivating Western brassicas", p.317). Those with tender leaves are very prone to slugs and snails (p.548), caterpillars (p.549), and flea beetles (p.548). They may be grown under fine nets to provide some protection.

Harvesting and storing Oriental brassicas

Most Oriental brassicas mature within two to three months after being sown. They may be harvested at four different stages from seedling to mature plant.

At the seedling stage they may be harvested using cut-and-come-again techniques (see "Cut-and-come-again harvesting", p.316), or left a few weeks longer and cut as semi-mature plants. When the plants are fully mature they may be either harvested all at once or alternatively cut about 2.5cm (1in) above ground level so that they sprout again for a second crop. The flowering shoots that develop naturally from mature plants may also be harvested before the flowers open.

In the West, Oriental brassicas are mainly used fresh, although most will keep for a few days if refrigerated. In the Orient, leaves are pickled and dried, and Chinese cabbages are stored for off-season supplies.

Oriental mustards (*Brassica juncea*)

The mustards are a varied group of annuals and biennials, forming large, often coarse-leaved plants. Leaf texture may be smooth, blistered, or deeply curled (for example 'Art Green'). Some cultivars are purple-leaved. The mustards are naturally very robust and less prone to pests and diseases than most Oriental brassicas. Several, including the purplish-green 'Miike Giant', 'Osaka Purple', and 'Xue Li Hong' survive at least -10°C (14°F). The distinctive flavour may be piquant in some cultivars, becoming stronger as they run to seed. The leaves are used cooked but may also be eaten raw in salads when young or if sliced.

Sow from mid- to late summer in temperate climates, and until early autumn in warm climates, for harvesting from autumn to spring. The seed is small and is sown in shallow soil *in situ* or in modules. Thin or plant out seedlings 15cm (6in) apart for harvesting young, and 35cm (14in) apart for larger plants. If they are planted under cover in autumn, plants are more tender, but will run to seed earlier the following spring.

Oriental mustards mature in 6–13 weeks, depending on the cultivar. Cut single leaves as required.

PURPLE-LEAVED ORIENTAL MUSTARD

Chinese broccoli
(*Brassica rapa* var. *alboglabra*)

These annuals, also known as Chinese kale, form stout plants with thick, blue-green leaves, growing up to 45cm (18in) tall. The succulent, fine-flavoured, chunky flower stems, which may be 2cm (³/₄in) thick, are generally cooked.

Chinese broccoli tolerates higher summer temperatures than many other brassicas, and withstands light frost. In warm and temperate climates, sow from late spring to late summer. For a very early crop, make the first sowings under cover in spring to transplant outside. For a protected early winter crop, plant under cover in autumn. In cool climates, delay sowing until mid-summer since sowings earlier than this may bolt.

Sow seed *in situ* or in modules. For small plants, to be harvested whole as soon as the flowering shoots appear, grow plants 12cm

CHINESE BROCCOLI

(5in) apart with 10cm (4in) between rows. For large plants, to be cropped over a longer period, space plants 30cm (12in) apart each way. Cut the main shoot first, as for calabrese (see p.322); further sideshoots will continue to develop for harvesting later. Large plants take nine to ten weeks to mature.

Pak choi
(*Brassica rapa* var. *chinensis*)

PAK CHOI

Pak choi is a biennial usually grown as an annual, forming a loose head of fairly stiff leaves with wide mid-ribs that broaden out markedly and overlap at the base. There are many types, the most common being white-ribbed or green-ribbed, available as F1 cultivars 'Joi Choi' (white) and 'Shanghai' (green). They vary in size from squat forms about 10cm (4in) tall to large plants about 45cm (18in) tall. Pak choi is succulent and mild in flavour, and may be eaten either cooked or raw.

Pak choi grows best at cool temperatures of 15–20°C (59–68°F). Most cultivars will tolerate some frost in the open but survive lower temperatures under cover grown as winter cut-and-come-again crops. A few are suited to hotter climates.

In temperate climates, sow seed throughout the growing season. There is some risk of premature bolting with spring sowings, so confine these to cut-and-come-again seedling crops. Sow seed *in situ* or in modules. Spacing depends on the cultivar and size of plant required, ranging from 10cm (4in) apart for small cultivars to about 45cm (18in) apart for the largest cultivars. In late summer, transplant pak choi under cover for an autumn crop.

Pak choi may be harvested at any stage from seedlings to the young flower shoots of mature plants.

HARVESTING SEEDLINGS

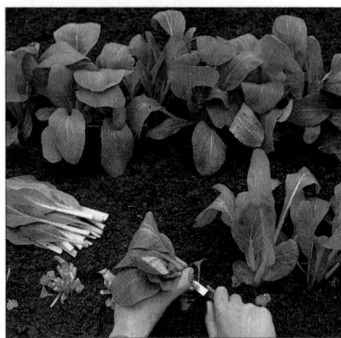

Pak choi may be harvested at the seedling stage. If they are cut about 2.5cm (1in) from the ground, new leaves will sprout.

Seedling leaves will be ready for harvesting in three weeks. They may be cut 2.5cm (1in) above ground level and will resprout. Mature plants may be cut higher and will also resprout for a second harvest.

Mizuna greens (*Brassica rapa* var. *nipposinica*)

Annuals or biennials, depending on climatic conditions, mizuna greens have dark green, glossy, deeply serrated, almost feathery leaves and slender, white, juicy stems forming a rosette up to 45cm (18in) in diameter and about 23cm (9in) tall. They are highly decorative, especially when grown as an edging or in blocks. Mizuna greens are eaten cooked, or raw when leaves are harvested young and tender.

MIZUNA GREENS

They are very adaptable, capable of tolerating both high summer temperatures (provided that they are in moisture-retentive soil) and winter temperatures down to -10°C (14°F).

They may be sown throughout the growing season. Bolting resistance is good and seed may therefore be sown in seed trays or modules, in a seedbed for transplanting, or *in situ*. For an extra, tender, winter crop, sow in late summer to transplant under cover. Space plants 10cm (4in) apart for small plants harvested young, up to 45cm (18in) apart to obtain large plants. Mizuna greens are useful for intercropping if cut at the seedling stage.

Mizuna greens mature eight to ten weeks after sowing and may be harvested at all stages; seedling leaves may be ready within two or three weeks (see "Harvesting and storing Oriental brassicas", p.323). The plants are vigorous, and are capable of resprouting several times after they have been cut initially.

Chinese cabbages (*Brassica rapa* var. *pekinensis*)

These are annuals or biennials usually grown as annuals. Chinese cabbages have dense, upright heads. The leaves are marked by prominent white veins, the broadened midribs overlapping at the base rather like pak choi. The barrel type forms a stout head about 25cm (10in) high, the cylindrical type a longer, less compact head up to 45cm (18in) high. Leaf colour ranges from dark green to almost creamy white, especially in the centre. There are also some very attractive, loose-headed types. Mild-flavoured with a crisp texture, Chinese cabbages are excellent in salads and lightly cooked.

For preferred climatic conditions, see "Pak choi" (left). Most headed types are likely to bolt if they are sown in spring, unless a temperature of 20–25°C (68–77°F) is maintained during the first three weeks of growth. It is safer to delay sowing until early summer. Some loose-headed types may be sown in spring. If they start to bolt, treat them as cut-and-come-again crops, although the leaves of some cultivars may be rough-textured and hairy when young. Sow seed in modules or *in situ*; thin or transplant seedlings to 30cm (12in) apart. Plenty of moisture throughout growth is vital. Chinese cabbages have soft leaves which are susceptible to pests (see "Cultivating Oriental brassicas", p.323).

Chinese cabbages mature eight to ten weeks after sowing, and can be harvested at any stage since they respond well to cut-and-come-again treatment both after the main heads have been cut, and during growth, as semi-mature plants.

HARVESTING CHINESE CABBAGES

1 *Harvest Chinese cabbage (here a loose-leaved cultivar) by cutting about 2.5cm (1in) above soil level.*

2 *After a few weeks, new leaves will have formed and may be cut. Stumps may resprout several times.*

Komatsuna (*Brassica rapa* var. *perviridis*)

The komatsuna group, also known as spinach mustard, is extremely diverse; its members form large, productive, robust, healthy plants, often with glossy leaves that may be up to 30cm (12in) long and 18cm (7in) wide. The flavour of the leaves resembles cabbage, with a touch of spinach, and they are eaten cooked, or raw, finely sliced in salads.

Komatsuna plants tolerate a wide range of temperatures and will survive -12°C (10°F). Some cultivars are suitable for tropical climates.

Plants are less likely to bolt from early spring sowings than most Oriental brassicas and are more drought-tolerant. For sowing and spacing, see "Mizuna greens" (left). Komatsuna makes a useful and successful winter crop under cover.

KOMATSUNA

Leaves may be harvested at all stages (see "Harvesting and storing Oriental brassicas", p.323). Mature plants are usually ready to be harvested eight weeks after sowing.

Leafy and salad vegetables

THIS group of vegetables is grown for the great variety of leaves that it produces, which may be eaten raw in salads, or cooked. The freshly picked leaves are delicious and highly nutritious. The range of leaf colour also gives them decorative value. Careful choice of cultivar and the right growing conditions ensure a year-round supply. If seeds are sown in succession, gluts of crops maturing together may be avoided. Due to the high moisture content of the leaves, many store for only two or three days; a few are suitable for freezing, however.

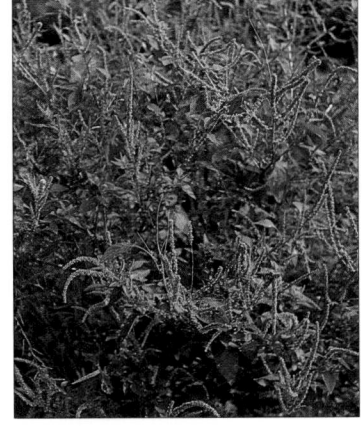

Butterhead lettuce

Loose-leaf lettuce

Spinach

Cos lettuce

Witloof chicons

Amaranths (*Amaranthus* spp.)

These rapidly growing annuals reach a height of about 60cm (24in) and a spread of 30–38cm (12–15in). *Amaranthus cruentus*, the most commonly grown as an edible crop, has oval, light green leaves; amaranth cultivars are mostly local – they include 'Fotete', 'Green Spinach', and 'Stubby'. *A. tricolor*, or Chinese spinach, has red, yellow, or green leaves and greenish-white flowers; cultivars include 'Lal Sag Rouge', 'Tampala', 'Banerjee's Giant', and 'Crystal'. *A. caudatus* has pale green leaves and is often grown as an ornamental plant for its vivid red, tassel-like flowers. Amaranth species are also known as African or Indian spinach. The leaves of the plants and immature flower buds are cooked and eaten in the same way as spinach.

Amaranths are tropical and subtropical plants that require temperatures of 22–30°C (72–86°F) with a humidity of above 70 per cent to crop well. They may also be grown in temperate climates in greenhouses or outdoors in a sunny, sheltered site. Moderately deep, well-drained, fertile soil with a pH of 5.5–7 and medium to high nitrogen levels are required (see p.314).

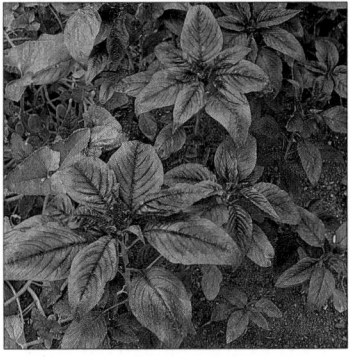

AMARANTHUS CRUENTUS

Sowing and planting
Sow outdoors in spring, once the temperature is high enough, in rows 20–30cm (8–12in) apart. Thin seedlings to 10–15cm (4–6in) apart when they are about 5–7cm (2–3in) high. Protect with plastic covers or under cloches until the young plants have become established.

In cool areas, or for an earlier crop, seed may be sown in trays in a greenhouse; prick out seedlings into 6 or 9cm (3 or 3½in) pots when they are large enough to handle. Transplant them outdoors when they are 7–9cm (3–3½in) tall, spacing them 10–15cm (4–6in) apart.

Routine cultivation
Keep amaranth beds weed-free, and water regularly. Apply a balanced fertilizer or organic liquid feed every two to three weeks. Give additional dressings of nitrogen and potassium every three weeks on less fertile soils. Apply an organic mulch around the base of the plants to retain moisture and warmth. When the plants are 20cm (8in) tall, pinch out the growing point to encourage lateral shoots and to produce a heavier crop.

Pests and diseases
Downy mildew (p.550), powdery mildew (p.550), caterpillars (p.549), and aphids (p.550) may affect amaranths outside, and thrips (p.551) and damping off (p.568) under cover.

Growing under cover
When seedlings are 7–9cm (3–3½in) tall, transplant them to 21cm (8in) pots, growing bags, or beds, spacing them 38–50cm (15–20in) apart each way. Keep them at a minimum temperature of 22°C (72°F). Water, and maintain 70 per cent humidity by damping down in hot weather.

Harvesting and storing
Amaranths are ready to harvest eight to ten weeks after sowing. Using a sharp knife, cut young shoots up to 10cm (4in) long when the plants are about 25cm (10in) tall; they will produce further shoots over several months. Continue picking them as required. Amaranths are best eaten fresh; alternatively, they may be stored for up to one week at 0°C (32°F) and 95 per cent humidity.

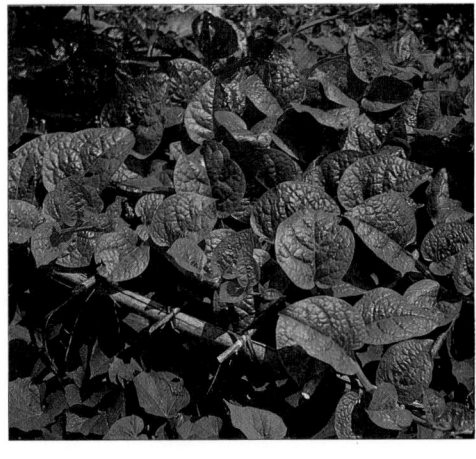

AMARANTHUS TRICOLOR

Ceylon spinach (*Basella alba*)

Also known as Indian or vine spinach, these short-lived, twining perennials may grow to 4m (12ft) tall if supported. Var. *alba* has dark green leaves; var. *rubra* has red leaves and stems. The oval or round leaves are eaten cooked; the purple berries are not normally eaten.

Ceylon spinach is a tropical and subtropical plant that requires a temperature of 25–30°C (77–86°F). Lower temperatures reduce the growth rate, resulting in smaller leaves. Larger leaves are, however, produced in light shade. Well-drained and highly fertile soil with a pH of 6–7.5 and high nitrogen levels (see p.314) is required for good growth.

Sowing and planting
Sow in seed trays or 6 or 9cm (3 or 3½in) pots, maintaining the required temperature range. When the seedlings are 10–15cm (4–6in) tall, transplant them to well-prepared beds, spacing the plants 40–50cm (16–20in) apart each way.

Routine cultivation
Support plants by staking or by tying in the stems to a vertical or horizontal trellis. Keep plants weed-free and water as necessary. Mulch with organic material. Apply a balanced fertilizer or liquid feed every two to three weeks during the growing period. When the seedlings reach a

SUPPORTING CEYLON SPINACH

Ceylon spinach may be supported on a trellis parallel to the ground, raised about 30cm (12in) above soil level. The stems should be evenly spaced on the trellis so that they do not become overcrowded.

height of about 45cm (18in), remove the growing point to encourage branching. Remove flowering shoots to encourage leaf production.

Propagate plants by taking cuttings 10–15cm (4–6in) long; insert these in small pots until rooted and then transplant as described for seedlings.

Pests and diseases
Ceylon spinach is generally free of pests and diseases. Root-knot nematodes (p.564) may, however, affect plants, and, under cover, aphids (p.550), whiteflies (p.550), and glasshouse red spider mites (p.550) may also be troublesome.

Growing under cover
Transplant seedlings to growing bags or to 20–25cm (8–10in) pots. Remove the growing tips when the seedlings are about 30cm (12in) tall to encourage branching, and damp down regularly to maintain high humidity. Tie in developing shoots.

Harvesting and storing
Harvest 10–12 weeks after transplanting by cutting young terminal shoots that are 15–20cm (6–8in) long; this encourages further shoots to develop over several months. Eat leaves within two days of picking, or refrigerate them for a few days.

Swiss chard and spinach beet (*Beta vulgaris* Cicla Group)

These spinach-like biennials belong to the beet family. Swiss chard, also known as seakale beet, forms large, glossy-leaved plants. Individual leaves may be up to 45cm (18in) long and 15cm (6in) wide. The midribs widen into broad leaf stalks up to 5cm (2in) in diameter that may be white, red, creamy-yellow, or pink. Leaf colour varies according to cultivar, from deep green ('Fordhook Giant') to greenish-yellow ('Lucullus') and reddish-green ('Rhubarb Chard'). Leaves and midribs are normally cooked; the latter require longer cooking

WHITE-STEMMED SWISS CHARD

and are often treated as a separate vegetable. Spinach beet, or perpetual spinach, forms smaller-leaved plants, with narrow, green leaf stalks. It is eaten lightly cooked or raw.

Although chard and spinach beet are essentially cool-season crops, growing best at 16–18°C (61–4°F), they tolerate higher summer temperatures than spinach (see p.329) without bolting, and survive winter temperatures of -14°C (7°F). They may be grown in a wide range of soils other than acid ones, provided that the soil is moisture-retentive and fertile, containing plenty of organic matter. Plants may remain in the ground for up to 12 months, and so need high nitrogen levels (see p.314).

Sowing and planting
For a continuous supply, sow seed in spring (plants may crop until late spring the following year), and again in mid- to late summer (for plants cropping until the following summer). Sow *in situ* in rows 38cm (15in) apart for spinach beet or, for Swiss chard, 45cm (18in) apart; thin seedlings early to 30cm (12in) apart. Plants may be grown closer

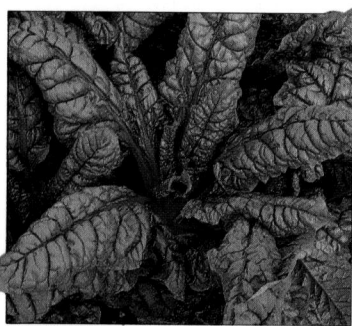

RED-STEMMED SWISS CHARD

together in more widely spaced rows, but avoid overcrowding, since this may encourage downy mildew.

Alternatively, seed may be sown in seed trays or modules for transplanting. Germination is usually rapid. Spinach beet may be sown closely for use as a cut-and-come-again seedling crop (see p.310).

Routine cultivation
The chards and spinach beet are naturally healthy and vigorous and usually require little attention. Give an organic mulch to keep down weeds and preserve moisture; apply

a nitrogenous fertilizer or organic liquid feed during the growing season if plants are not developing well.

Pests and diseases
Birds (p.561) may attack seedlings. Fungal leaf spots (p.552) and downy mildew (p.550) may also be problems.

Growing under cover
In cool climates, the chards and spinach beet are excellent winter crops under cover. Sow seed in modules in late summer and transplant under cover in early autumn, or broadcast spinach beet for cut-and-come-again seedling crops. They often crop throughout winter and early spring.

Harvesting and storing
Leaves are ready to be harvested 8–12 weeks after sowing. Cut the outer leaves first and continue picking as required; alternatively, harvest the whole plant by cutting the leaves about 2.5cm (1in) above ground level. Further leaves are then produced from the base over many months. Both Swiss chard and spinach beet may be frozen.

Endive (*Cichorium endivia*)

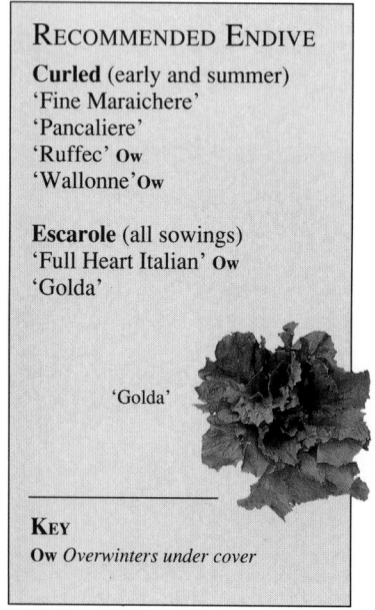
Endive is an annual or biennial plant that forms a flat or semi-upright rosette of leaves 20–38cm (8–15in) in diameter. The two most distinct types of endive are the serrated- or curled-leaved endive, and the broad-leaved escarole, but there are also intermediate types. Outer leaves are dark to light green and the more tender, inner leaves creamy-yellow. Endive is slightly bitter and is blanched to make it sweeter. Used mainly in salads, it is shredded to reduce bitterness, or may be cooked.

Endive is a cool-season crop that grows best at 10–20°C (50–68°F), but withstands light frost in the open; the hardier cultivars survive -9°C (15°F). Bitterness generally increases at high temperatures. Some curled types are quite heat-tolerant, while escarole types tend

to withstand greater cold. There is a risk of premature bolting from spring sowings if temperatures fall below 5°C (41°F) for an extended period. Endive performs much better than lettuce in the low light levels of northern winters and therefore makes a useful winter greenhouse crop.

For soil and site requirements, see "Lettuces", p.328. Summer crops may be grown in light shade; always grow autumn crops on well-drained soil to avoid the risk of rotting. Endive has a low nitrogen requirement (see p.314).

Sowing and planting
Choose appropriate cultivars for each season. Sow in late spring for a summer crop or in summer for an autumn crop, either *in situ* or in modules or seed trays. Thin or plant out

the seedlings 25–38cm (10–15in) apart, using the widest spacing for spreading cultivars. Curled types may be sown as cut-and-come-again crops (see p.310), most usefully in late spring and late summer.

Routine cultivation
To blanch leaves, choose nearly mature plants with dry leaves and blanch a few at a time since they deteriorate rapidly after blanching.

For complete blanching *in situ*, cover each plant with a bucket. For partial blanching, lay a large plate or piece of cardboard over the centre. With escarole types bunch up the leaves and tie them together. Protect the plants against slugs until they are ready for harvesting, which is after about ten days. In autumn, plants for blanching should be lifted before

BLANCHING ENDIVE

1 *Ensure that the endive is dry, then lay a plate over the centre to blanch the leaves partially.*

2 *The centre should have turned white and be ready for harvesting after about 10 days.*

severe weather disfigures them; transplant them into a darkened frame or dark area under greenhouse staging, then blanch as for Witloof chicory (see below).

Pests and diseases

Slugs (p.548) and aphids (p.550) are the most common problems. For other pests and diseases that affect endive, see "Lettuces", p.328.

Growing under cover

Protecting plants under cover provides a year-round supply. For use in winter and early spring, transplant seedlings in early autumn from seed trays or modules under cover. Sow as a cut-and-come-again seedling crop under cover in spring for harvesting early, and in early autumn for a late crop.

Harvesting and storing

Harvest endive between 7 and 13 weeks after sowing, depending on the cultivar and season. Pick individual leaves as needed, or cut across the crown, leaving the plant to resprout. Mature plants respond well to cut-and-come-again treatment (see "Cut-and-come-again harvesting", p.316). Endive leaves do not store well, so should be eaten fresh.

Chicory (*Cichorium intybus*)

There are many types of chicory, all with a distinctive, slightly bitter taste. Nearly all are hardy and are useful crops in the winter months. Their diverse colours make them attractive in salads, and some types may also be cooked. All types have low nitrogen requirements (see p.314).

Witloof or Belgian chicory

Similar in appearance to dandelions, these biennials have pointed leaves about 20cm (8in) long, with a spread of about 15cm (6in). Their "chicons" (the whitened, compact, leafy shoots obtained from lifting the roots and forcing and blanching them to make them sweeter) are eaten raw or cooked. The green leaves may also be used, but taste more bitter.

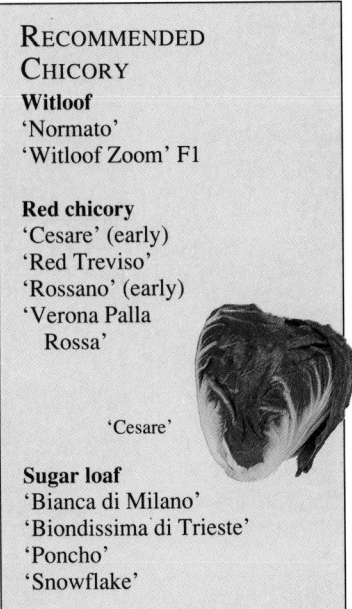
Witloof chicory grows best at 15–19°C (59–66°F). It is generally forced for winter use. Grow the plants in an open site in reasonably fertile – but not freshly manured – soil.

The plants require a fairly long growing season. Sow seed outdoors *in situ* in spring or early summer, in rows 30cm (12in) apart. Thin the seedlings to about 20cm (8in) apart. Keep plants weed-free. Water the plants as necessary, to prevent the soil from drying out.

Witloof chicory may be forced *in situ* in light soils and areas with mild winters. In early winter, cut the green leaves about 2.5cm (1in) above ground level. Cover the stumps with soil, making a ridge about 15cm (6in) high; the chicons will grow and force their way through.

Force indoors if the garden soil is heavy or winters are severe, or if an earlier crop is required. Dig up the plants in late autumn or early winter. Cut the leaves to 2.5cm (1in) and trim the roots to about 20cm (8in); reject any that are very thin. The roots may be forced immediately or stored for forcing a few at a time in succession during the winter and early spring. To store the roots, lay them flat in boxes with moist sand between each of the layers and keep them in a frost-free shed or cellar until they are required.

To force indoors, plant several of the prepared roots in a large pot or box filled with compost or garden soil, and cover with an inverted pot or box of the same size. Block any drainage holes to keep out light. Keep the soil moist, and maintain a temperature of 10–18°C (50–64°F). Roots may also be planted under greenhouse staging, or in a garden frame. Make a light-proof area by stretching black plastic sheeting over wire hoops or attaching it to a

wooden support. Do not use plastic sheeting in spring if temperatures soar, since aphid damage and rotting may occur. Witloof chicory is normally free of pests and diseases.

Harvest chicons forced outside after 8–12 weeks when about 10cm (4in) high by moving the soil and

cutting the heads 2.5cm (1in) above the neck. Plants forced indoors should be ready after three to four weeks. Stumps may resprout to give a second crop of smaller chicons. Keep chicons wrapped or refrigerated after cutting since they become green and bitter on exposure to light.

FORCING AND BLANCHING CHICORY

1 *In late autumn or early winter, lift the mature plant carefully. The central leaves may be tender enough to eat.*

2 *Using a sharp knife, trim the leaves to 2.5cm (1in) from the crown and slice off the base of the root and any side roots, leaving a 20–22cm (8–9in) length.*

3 *Put a layer of moist potting compost or garden soil into a 24cm (9in) pot. Place three trimmed roots in the mixture and firm so that they stand upright, then fill the pot to within 2.5cm (1in) of the rim and firm, leaving the crowns exposed.*

4 *Line another pot with cooking foil or black plastic to cover the drainage holes and place it over the roots to block the light. Keep at 10–18°C (50–64°F). Harvest the chicons 3–4 weeks later by cutting just above soil level.*

Red chicory

This is a varied group of perennials usually grown as annuals. The typical red chicory, also known as radicchio, is a low-growing plant with bitter, reddish-green outer leaves and a compact heart. It is eaten raw in salads, shredded to reduce bitterness, or may be cooked.

Red chicory tolerates a wide range of temperatures and soil conditions, but is mainly grown for use in the cooler months. Cultivars vary in their frost tolerance. 'Treviso' is exceptionally hardy; it may be forced in the same way as Witloof chicory (see p.327). The new F1 hybrids produce more solid heads than traditional cultivars. Sow in early and mid-summer, *in situ* or in seed trays for transplanting. Plant 24–35cm (10–14in) apart depending on the cultivar. Transplant summer-sown crops under cover in autumn.

Eight to ten weeks after sowing, pick single leaves or harvest the whole head. Chicory stands a long time after maturing; in cold climates, protect with low tunnels in late autumn so that the plants develop more solid heads.

Sugar loaf chicory

Sugar loaf chicory is green-leaved, forming a conical head not unlike cos lettuce in both shape and size. Its inner leaves are naturally blanched and slightly sweetened. For use, and for climate, soil, and cultivation requirements, see "Red chicory" (left).

Sugar loaf chicory may be sown in spring as a cut-and-come-again seedling crop (see p.310); harvest the seedlings before temperatures rise, causing leaves to coarsen. For mature plants, thin seedlings to 25cm (10in) apart, and harvest in late summer to autumn. The plants tolerate light frost, and provide winter crops if grown under cover.

Harvest leaves as needed, or cut the heads when mature. The heads keep for a few weeks in cool, dry, frost-free conditions. They may also be piled up, turned inwards and covered with straw to form clamps (see *Making a Swede Clamp*, p.353).

SUGAR LOAF CHICORY

Lettuces (*Lactuca sativa*)

Lettuces are annual, low-growing plants; they usually have green leaves, although some cultivars have red or reddish-green leaves.

There are several distinct types. Cos (romaine) lettuces have long, substantial, well-flavoured leaves with fairly loose hearts; semi-cos are shorter with very sweet, crunchy leaves. Butterhead lettuces have smooth, soft leaves, forming a rounded, compact heart; crispheads (known as icebergs when marketed with the outer leaves removed) have crispy leaves forming a heart. Loose-leaf lettuces, typified by the "Salad Bowl" types, do not form hearts so are slow to bolt and may be cut over a long period; their leaves are often indented and are very decorative. They are the most nutritious form of lettuce and may also be used for cut-and-come-again seedling crops (see p.310).

Lettuces vary from 10cm (4in) to over 30cm (12in) in spread. The cos types are about 25cm (10in) tall, others about 15cm (6in) high. Lettuces are primarily used as salad vegetables, but outer and older leaves may also be cooked or used in soups.

Lettuces are cool-season crops, growing best at 10–20°C (50–68°F). Cool nights are essential for good results. Some cultivars are tolerant of heat or frost. Germination is poor above 25°C (77°F); at these temperatures, plants tend to bolt rapidly and may become bitter, although loose-leaf lettuces are slower to bolt than other types.

Grow in an open site, or in light shade in very hot weather. Lettuces need fertile, moisture-retentive soil and, although they fall into none of the rotation groups, should not be

LOOSE-LEAF LETTUCES ('LOLLO ROSSA')

grown in the same patch of soil for two years in a row to prevent the build-up of fungus disease. They require medium nitrogen (see p.314).

Sowing and planting

Cultivars appropriate for the season must be sown. For a year-round supply in cool climates, sow from early spring to late summer at two- to three-week intervals. At the end of summer or in early autumn, sow hardy cultivars that overwinter outdoors or under cover for a spring crop. In warm climates, only heat-tolerant cultivars should be sown during the summer.

In cool climates, sow seed *in situ*, in a seedbed, or in trays or modules for transplanting. Sowings in summer are best made *in situ*, since seedlings wilt when transplanted unless they have been raised in modules. Seed may become dormant in high temperatures; this is most likely to occur several hours after sowing and may be overcome by watering after sowing to cool the soil, by putting seed trays or modules in a cool place to germinate, or by sowing seed in the afternoon so that the critical period occurs at night when temperatures are lower.

HARVESTING LOOSE-LEAF LETTUCES

Loose-leaf lettuces may be harvested by cutting across the leaves 2.5cm (1in) above ground level. Leave the stump to resprout.

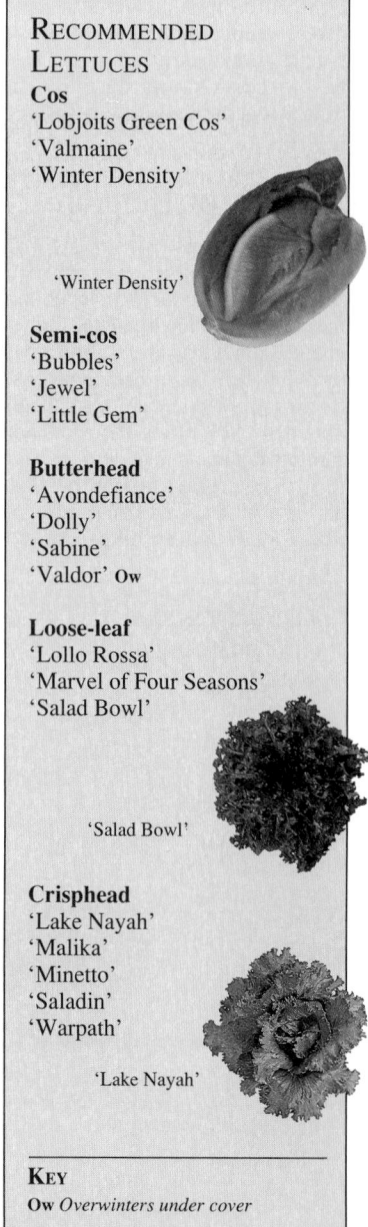

Transplant lettuces in moist conditions when they have five or six leaves, with the base of the leaves positioned just above soil level. In hot weather, shade young plants until they are established. Space small cultivars 15cm (6in) apart, and larger ones about 30cm (12in) apart.

Sow hardy cultivars for overwintering outdoors *in situ* or under cloches or in frames; thin to about 7cm (3in) apart in autumn and to the full distance apart in spring. Floating mulches or cloches put over the plants in spring improve their quality, and help them to mature earlier.

Most types of lettuce may be grown as cut-and-come-again seedling crops, especially loose-leaf types, including the traditional European "cutting" cultivars, and some cos types (see "Cut-and-come-again seedling crops", p.310).

Routine cultivation
Keep lettuce beds weed-free. Apply a nitrogenous fertilizer or organic liquid feed if growth is slow. In dry conditions, water the plants at a rate of 22 litres/sq m (5 gallons/sq yd) per week. The most critical watering period is about seven to ten days before maturity (see also p.312). In late autumn or early winter, protect lettuces with cloches to improve the quality of the crop.

Pests and diseases
Problems include greenfly and root aphids (see "Aphids", p.550), cutworms (p.559), leatherjackets (p.564), slugs (p.548), mosaic virus (see "Viruses", p.553), downy mildew (p.550), boron deficiency (p.558), and grey mould/*Botrytis* (p.557); birds may attack seedlings (p.561). Some cultivars show aphid resistance and

Protecting seedlings with perforated film helps them mature more quickly early in the season.

others show some tolerance to mosaic virus and downy mildew.

Growing under cover
In cool climates, earlier lettuce crops may be obtained by sowing

or planting in early spring in an unheated greenhouse, beneath cloches or perforated fleecy films, or in cold frames. Some cultivars may also be grown under cover in winter for early spring cropping; for mid-winter crops, gentle heat is usually required.

Harvesting and storing
Loose-leaf lettuces should be ready about seven weeks after sowing, butterheads after 10 or 11 weeks, and cos and crispheads after 11 or 12 weeks. Cut cos, butterhead, and crisphead types soon after maturing to prevent bolting. They may be stored for a few days in a refrigerator. Pick the leaves of loose-leaf types a few at a time, as required, since they do not store well, or cut across the plants 2.5cm (1in) above soil level, leaving the stumps to resprout within a few weeks.

Spinach (*Spinacia oleracea*)

Spinach is a fast-growing annual that reaches a height of 15–20cm (6–8in), with a spread of about 15cm (6in). The highly nutritious leaves are smooth or crinkled, and round or pointed, depending on the cultivar. They are eaten lightly cooked or, when young, raw in salads.

A cool-season plant, spinach grows best at 16–18°C (61–4°F), although it will grow well at lower temperatures. Small plants and seedlings may survive -9°C (15°F). Grow cultivars recommended for the area; for example, many are prone to bolt in long days (see "Daylength", p.307), especially after a cold period or in hot, dry conditions. Recommended cultivars that may be used as seedling crops or mature plants include 'Jovita', 'Norvak', and 'Sigmaleaf'.

Spinach tolerates light shade in summer, and needs a soil with medium nitrogen levels (see p.314). For other soil requirements, see "Swiss chard and spinach beet", p.326.

Sowing and planting
Sow in cool seasons as spinach will not germinate in temperatures above 30°C (86°F). Sow *in situ*, placing individual seeds about 2.5cm (1in) apart in rows spaced about 30cm (12in) apart. For a continuous crop, sow in succession, after seedlings of the previous sowings have appeared. Thin early as for Swiss chard (see p.326), to about 7cm (3in) for young plants, or to 15cm (6in) apart for large plants.

Spinach may also be grown as a cut-and-come-again seedling crop

for use in salads (see p.310). For this, sow in early spring and early autumn under cover, and also in late summer for an overwintering crop in the open. For routine cultivation, pests and diseases, and growing under cover, see "Swiss chard and spinach beet", p.326.

Harvesting and storing
Cut leaves between five and ten weeks after sowing at any stage once the plants are about 5cm (2in) tall. Either cut individual leaves, or cut the heads about 2.5cm (1in) above the ground and leave them to resprout; alternatively, pull up whole plants. In warm areas, harvest plants young, before they start to run to seed. Use the leaves fresh soon after picking, or store by freezing.

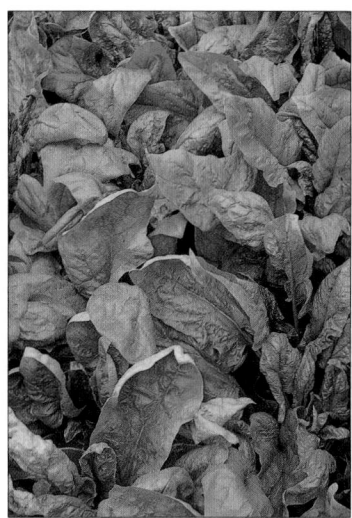

SPINACH

New Zealand spinach (*Tetragonia tetragonioides*, syn. *T. expansa*)

A half-hardy, creeping perennial, New Zealand spinach is also grown as an annual. The plants have thick, triangular leaves about 5cm (2in) long with a spread of 90–120cm (3–4ft). The leaves are used in the same way as spinach (see above).

New Zealand spinach tolerates high, even tropical, temperatures, and drought, but cannot withstand frost. It grows best in an open site on reasonably fertile and moisture-retentive soil, and needs low nitrogen (see p.314). It is generally less prone to bolting than spinach.

Seeds may be slow to germinate, so to aid germination soak them in

water for 24 hours before sowing. In cool climates, sow seed indoors and plant out at 45cm (18in) each way after all risk of frost has passed. Otherwise sow seed *in situ* outdoors after the last frost, thinning in stages to the final spacing. Keep seedlings weed-free (mature plants cover the soil, suppressing weeds). Pest or disease problems are rare.

Start picking the young leaves and the tips of the stems six or seven weeks after sowing. Pick frequently to encourage further young growth for three or four months. New Zealand spinach should be used fresh immediately after cutting, or frozen.

Pick the young leaves and tips of stems of New Zealand spinach before seedheads start to form. Plants will continue to make new growth that may be harvested until the first frosts.

Minor salad vegetables

THERE are many lesser-known vegetables worth cultivating to use raw in salads, either on their own or mixed with other vegetables. They are suitable for growing in small gardens and containers. The leaves are distinctly flavoured and nutritious, especially if used young. Apart from summer purslane and iceplants, all tolerate a few degrees of frost, or even lower temperatures on well-drained soil with wind protection. In cool climates, most may be grown under cover in winter for higher yields. Most salad plants are fast-maturing but make lusher growth in nitrogen-rich soil. Many are best sown as cut-and-come-again crops (see p.310). They are usually free of pests and diseases.

Land cress (*Barbarea verna*)

This biennial, low-growing plant has a spread of 15–20cm (6–8in); land cress is also known as upland cress. The glossy, deep green leaves have a strong flavour similar to watercress, and are used as a watercress substitute, either raw or cooked. Land cress is very hardy, remaining green in winter. It grows best in the shade; in heat it runs to seed rapidly, becoming coarse and very hot-tasting. It may be intercropped between taller vegetables or used to make a neat edging for beds.

Grow land cress in fertile and moisture-retentive soils. Sow seed in spring for an early summer crop, or in late summer for an autumn and overwintering crop. It may be grown in unheated greenhouses in winter. Sow *in situ*, thinning to 15cm (6in) apart, or in seed trays to transplant. Pick leaves seven weeks after sowing when they are 7–10cm (3–4in)

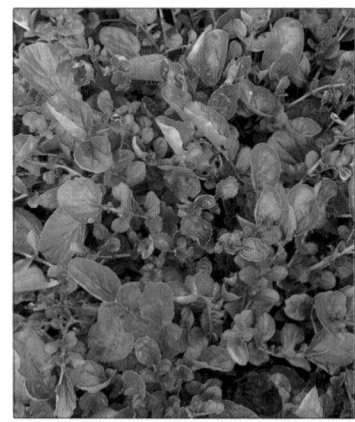

LAND CRESS

long. If a few plants are left to run to seed in spring they seed freely, and the seedlings may be transplanted where they are needed. Flea beetles (p.548) may affect young plants.

Mustard (*Brassica hirta*)

Mustard is similar to cress in its habit and is often partnered with it. It is grown for the sharply flavoured seedling leaves which may be used raw in salads. It is a cool-season crop that runs to seed very rapidly in hot weather; its leaves tend to become coarse if it is grown in areas with heavy rainfall.

In temperate climates, outdoor sowings are most successful in spring and autumn *in situ*, using any of the methods suggested for cut-and-come-again seedlings (see p.310).

Mustard, like cress, is a useful crop for growing under cover from autumn to spring. It may be sown without soil either on moist paper towelling in a saucer placed on a windowsill, or in a sprouter; alternatively it may be sown in a seed tray of potting compost or soil. These methods may be used all year round. Mustard germinates faster than cress, so if the two are required together, sow the mustard two or

MUSTARD

three days later than the cress. A sowing every seven to ten days ensures a continuous supply.

Harvest mustard by cutting as required when the seedlings are about 3.5–5cm (1½–2in) tall. It runs to seed much more rapidly than cress, and will normally provide no more than two or three cuts.

Salad rape (*Brassica napus*)

This annual plant has light green, mild-flavoured leaves and is often used as a substitute for mustard in mustard and cress packs. It is fast-growing but slower to run to seed than mustard or cress. The leaves are used raw as seedlings, while larger leaves may be cooked as greens.

Salad rape survives temperatures of -10°C (14°F), and tolerates moderate heat. The plants grow in a wide range of soils. In temperate climates, sow under cover in early spring and late autumn; sow in succession outdoors until early autumn. Indoors, grow on a windowsill as for mustard (below, left). Outdoors, sow broadcast, or in rows or wide drills. Make the first cut after ten days; when plants reach 60cm (24in), harvest small leaves over several months.

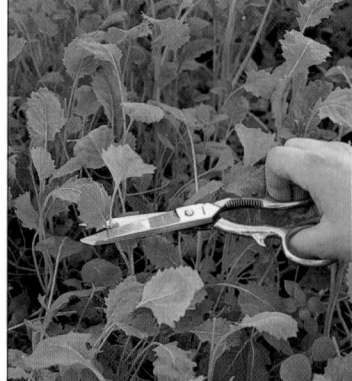

Cut leaves of salad rape at any stage from seedling to 7cm (3in) long. In good conditions, three cuts of seedling leaves may be possible.

Salad rocket (*Eruca vesicaria*)

This hardy, spicy-leaved Mediterranean plant is used in salads; older plants may be cooked. Salad rocket is also known as rucola, erugala, Mediterranean rocket, or roquette. It grows best in cool weather in moisture-retentive soil; in cool climates, it is excellent under cover in winter, and as a cut-and-come-again crop. Sow broadcast or in rows to cut as seedlings, or thin to 15cm (6in) to cut when larger. Seedlings are ready in three weeks. Flea beetles (p.548) may attack salad rocket.

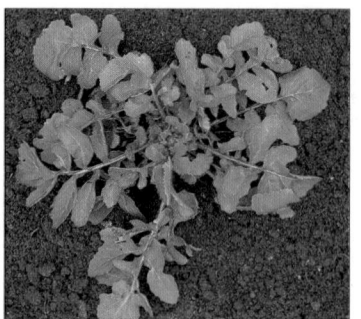

SALAD ROCKET

Cress (*Lepidium sativum*)

This fast-growing plant is grown for its seedling leaves, which are used raw. Cress is also known as garden cress, curly cress, or peppercress. There is a fine-leaved and a broad-leaved form. It is a moderately hardy, cool-season crop, running to seed rapidly in hot weather, unless sown in light shade. In cool climates, cress grows well under cover in the winter months. It may stop growing at very low temperatures, but starts again when temperatures rise. It is useful for inter- and undercropping.

Except in very cool areas, cress is best sown in spring and late summer or early autumn; avoid sowing in hot weather. Either sow on moist paper in a saucer and place on a windowsill or sow in a sprouter; this will give one cut. To obtain several consecutive cuts, sow in a seed tray of light soil, or in the ground, broadcast, in

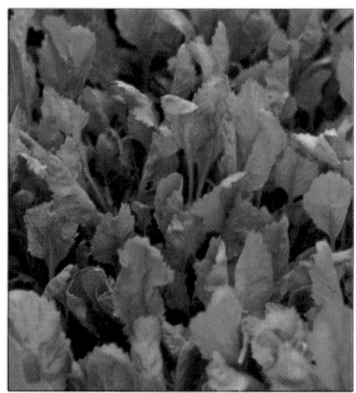

BROAD-LEAVED CRESS

single rows, or in wide drills. Cut ten days after sowing when seedlings are up to 5cm (2in) high. If sown in the ground, up to four successive cuts may be made.

Iceplants (*Mesembryanthemum crystallinum*)

Grown as perennials in warm climates and as tender annuals elsewhere, iceplants have a sprawling habit, succulent stems, and thick, fleshy leaves, covered with sparkling bladders. The leaves and young stems taste refreshing and slightly salty. They are used raw in salads or cooked like spinach.

Iceplants need a sunny position in light, well-drained soil. In warm climates, sow *in situ* outdoors; in cool climates, sow indoors in the spring, transplanting to 30cm (12in) apart after all risk of frost has passed. Slugs (p.548) may attack seedlings. Plants may be propagated by means of cuttings (see PERENNIALS, "Stem tip cuttings", p.166). The first picking of the young leaves and tender pieces of stem may be made about

ICEPLANTS

four weeks after planting. Harvest plants regularly to encourage further growth, and remove any flowers that appear. Leaves and stems keep fresh for several days.

Winter purslane (*Montia perfoliata*)

This is a hardy annual with heart-shaped leaves and dainty flowering shoots. The mildly flavoured, slightly succulent leaves, stems, and flowering shoots are used raw in salads. Also known as miner's lettuce or claytonia, it thrives in cool weather. It prefers well-drained conditions but grows well even in poor, light soil. Once established, it self-seeds rapidly; invasive seedlings are shallow-rooted and easily pulled up.

Make the main sowing in late summer for an autumn to early winter crop outdoors. Sow in spring for a summer crop. Grow either broadcast as a cut-and-come-again seedling crop, or in rows, or 10cm (4in) wide drills; seed may be sown *in situ*

WINTER PURSLANE

or in seed trays. Transplant or thin seedlings to 15–23cm (6–9in) apart. Start cutting 12 weeks after sowing, leaving the plants to resprout.

Summer purslane (*Portulaca oleracea*)

This half-hardy, low-growing plant has slightly succulent leaves and stems that are used raw or cooked. There are green- and yellow-leaved forms; the green type has thinner leaves, is more vigorous and possibly better flavoured, but the yellow or golden form is attractive in salads. The plants need a warm, sheltered site with light, well-drained soil.

Grow summer purslane either as a cut-and-come-again seedling crop or as single plants. In cool climates, sow in a seed tray in late spring, planting out 15cm (6in) apart, after all risk of frost. Make earlier and late summer sowings under cover as a cut-and-come-again seedling crop. In warm climates, sow *in situ* outside throughout the summer. Cut the seedlings, or young shoots of single

GOLDEN SUMMER PURSLANE

plants, from about four to eight weeks after sowing. Cut regularly, always leaving two basal leaves, and remove any flowers that develop. Slugs (p.548) may attack plants.

Watercress (*Rorippa nasturtium-aquaticum*)

A hardy aquatic perennial, watercress (also known as *Nasturtium officinale*) has nutritious, sharply flavoured leaves that are used in salads and soups. Its natural habitat is fresh running streams, with slightly alkaline water at about 10°C (50°F).

Root cuttings by placing stems in fresh water; they will soon root and may be planted at the edge of a stream in spring, spaced 15cm (6in) apart. Watercress may be grown in moist garden soil, but it is easier to grow in 15–21cm (6–8in) pots. Put a layer of gravel or moss in each pot, fill with rich soil, and stand it in a dish of cool, clean water. Plant three or four rooted cuttings per pot,

WATERCRESS GROWN IN A POT

and stand it in a sheltered position in good light. Change the water at least daily in hot weather. Cut leaves as needed.

Dandelions (*Taraxacum officinale*)

Hardy, perennial weeds, dandelions spread up to 30cm (12in). Wild and cultivated forms are grown for the young leaves, which are used raw. The cultivated forms are larger and slower to run to seed. Dandelion leaves are slightly bitter but blanching sweetens them. The flowers and roots are also edible. Dandelions tolerate a range of well-drained soils.

Sow in spring, in seed trays for transplanting, or *in situ*, spacing 35cm (14in) apart. Blanch in succession from late summer, covering dry plants with a large, light-proof bucket. Harvest the leaves when they are elongated and creamy-yellow. Dandelions die back in winter, but reappear in spring; the plants will continue to grow for several years.

BLANCHING DANDELION

When the plant has several leaves, cover it with a bucket 30cm (12in) tall. Harvest the creamy-yellow, elongated leaves after several weeks.

Corn salad (*Valerianella locusta*)

Grown for autumn and winter salads in cool climates, these hardy annuals form small, mild-flavoured plants. Corn salad is also known as lamb's lettuce or mache. There are two types: the floppy, large-leaved type, and the smaller, upright type with darker green leaves, which is reputedly the hardier. They tolerate a wide range of soils. In cold climates, grow them under cover in winter to obtain more prolific and tender-leaved plants. Corn salad is a useful crop for inter- or undercropping vegetables such as winter brassicas.

Corn salad may be grown as a cut-and-come-again seedling crop, or as individual plants. Sow from midsummer onwards *in situ*, broadcast, in rows, or in wide drills. Keep the seeds moist until they have germinated. Thin seedlings to 10cm (4in) apart. Corn salad is slow-growing

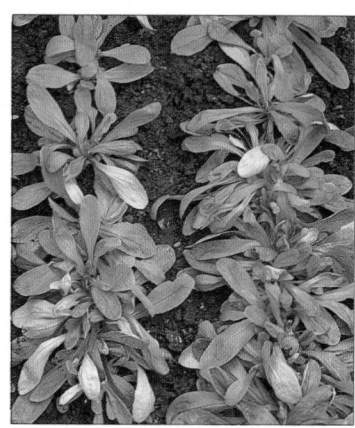

LARGE-LEAVED CORN SALAD

and may take 12 weeks to mature. Harvest leaves individually or cut across the plants, leaving them to resprout for a second cut.

Fruiting and flowering vegetables

Honeydew melon

Aubergines

Marrow

Sweet peppers

Courgettes

Cherry tomatoes

Musk melon

Plum tomatoes

Greenhouse cucumber

Sweet peppers

Sweet corn

Some of the most exotic and succulent vegetables fall into the fruiting and flowering group of vegetables. Many – tomatoes, peppers, aubergines, and melons, for example – are tropical or subtropical in origin; in cooler areas these may need to be grown under cover or in a warm situation. In temperate climates, others such as marrows, sweet corn, and pumpkins need to be germinated indoors but may be planted outdoors to grow to maturity. All need a warm, sheltered situation to ripen their fruits and for pollination to be successful.

Sweet peppers (*Capsicum annuum* Grossum Group)

Also called capsicums, or bell peppers, these annuals have a bushy habit and may grow up to 75cm (30in) tall with a spread of 45–60cm (18–24in). The fruits are usually oblong, ranging in size from 3–15cm (1¹/₄–6in) long and 3–7cm (1¹/₄–3in) in diameter, and may be green, cream, yellow, orange, red, or dark purple. The mature fruits are eaten cooked or raw, whole or sliced.

Sweet peppers are tropical and subtropical plants needing a minimum temperature of 21°C (70°F) with a humidity of 70–75 per cent. Temperatures over 30°C (86°F) may reduce fruit set and cause buds and flowers to drop. In temperate climates, plants may be grown under cover or outside in a sunny, sheltered site. Moderately deep, fertile, well-drained soil with medium nitrogen levels (see p.314) is required.

Sowing and planting
Sow seed in spring in the greenhouse in trays of compost with a pH of 5.5–7. Prick out the seedlings into

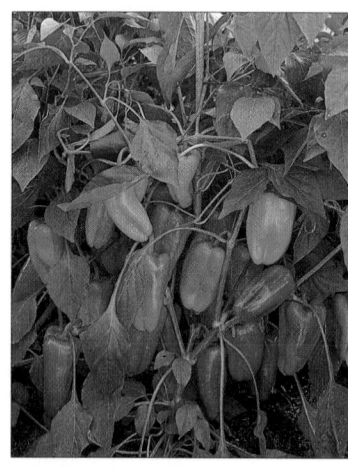

SWEET PEPPERS

6–9cm (3–3¹/₂in) pots and plant out 10–12 weeks after sowing in well-prepared beds, spacing the plants 45–50cm (18–20in) apart each way. In temperate climates, pot on seedlings and do not plant out until all risk of frost has passed.

Routine cultivation
Pinch out the terminal growing point of established plants to encourage a bushy habit and stake cultivars over 60cm (24in) tall. Water regularly to prevent leaf and bud drop, and mulch with organic material. Apply a balanced fertilizer or liquid feed every two weeks during the growing season. Protect plants outdoors with plastic covers, if necessary.

Pests and diseases
Plants may be attacked by aphids (p.550); under cover they may also be affected by glasshouse red spider mites (p.550), whiteflies (p.550), blossom end rot (see "Calcium deficiency", p.562), and thrips (p.551).

Growing under cover
Sow as above in early spring. When the seedlings are 8–10cm (3–4in) tall, pot them into 21cm (8in) pots or transplant into growing bags or well-prepared greenhouse beds. Space plants at least 50cm (20in)

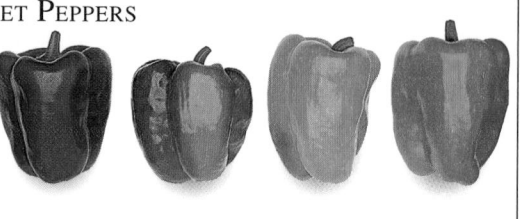

RIPENING SWEET PEPPERS

As they ripen, the fruits change colour from green to red, yellow, or dark purple, and the flavour becomes sweeter.

apart and stake taller cultivars. Maintain the recommended temperature and a humidity of 70–75 per cent by regularly damping down.

Harvesting and storing
Harvest the peppers 12–14 weeks after transplanting and before the first frost if the plants are growing outside. Some cultivars are best used when the fruits are green, but others may be left on the plants for two to three weeks until they change colour to red or creamy-yellow. Cut off individual peppers; they may be stored in cool, humid conditions for up to 14 days at 12–15°C (54–9°F). Entire plants may also be stored (see "Fruiting vegetables", p.316).

HARVESTING SWEET PEPPERS

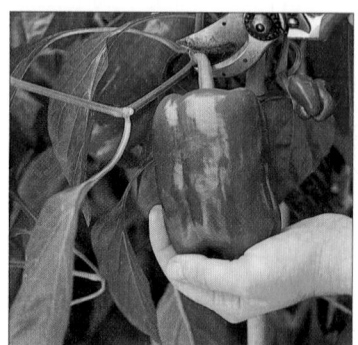

Some peppers are best harvested when green; others may be left to turn red or yellow. Cut the stalk about 2.5cm (1in) from the fruit.

RECOMMENDED SWEET PEPPERS

'Ace' F1
'Bell Boy' F1
'Californian Wonder'
'Canape' F1

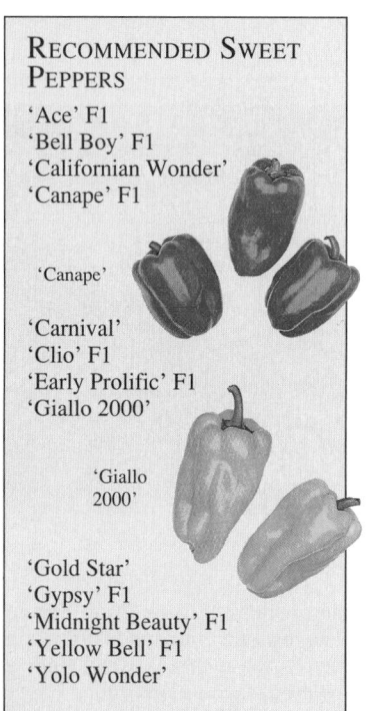

'Canape'

'Carnival'
'Clio' F1
'Early Prolific' F1
'Giallo 2000'

'Giallo 2000'

'Gold Star'
'Gypsy' F1
'Midnight Beauty' F1
'Yellow Bell' F1
'Yolo Wonder'

Chilli peppers (*Capsicum annuum* Longum Group)

This form of *Capsicum annuum* has pointed fruits up to 9cm (3¹/₂in) long. Popular cultivars include 'Chili Serrano', 'Hot Gold Spike', 'Red Chili', and 'Apache'.

The plants are cultivated in the same way as sweet peppers (see above); chilli peppers are slightly more tolerant of high temperature levels, however. They may be picked for use at any stage when the colour is green to red. If they are growing outside, they should be harvested before the first frost is expected.

The hot flavour increases with the maturity of the chilli fruit and comes from the white pith and seeds inside. If the flavour is too hot, the pith and seeds may be removed and discarded.

RIPENING CHILLI PEPPERS

RED CHILLI PEPPERS

Hot peppers (*Capsicum frutescens*)

These plants, also known as cayenne peppers, are branching perennials that grow to 1.5m (5ft) tall and bear small, narrow, orange, yellow, or red fruits which may hang from the branches or be carried upright, depending on the cultivar. They are highly pungent and are used in sauces and as a general flavouring.

Hot peppers are tropical and subtropical plants and therefore cannot tolerate frost. Plants should be spaced 60cm (24in) apart in each direction, and cultivated in the same way as sweet peppers (see p.332), although they generally require more water. Staking is not normally necessary.

Hot peppers need a long growing period, and the first fruits are usually produced about 15–18 weeks after planting. They should be allowed to ripen fully before being picked. They may be frozen or dried and stored for several months.

HOT PEPPERS

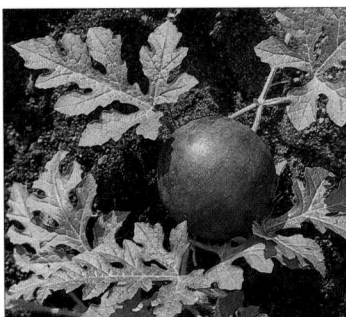

WATERMELON

Watermelons (*Citrullus lanatus*)

Watermelons are annual, tropical or subtropical plants with spreading stems that grow to 3–4m (10–12ft). Their fruits are rounded or oblong, green or cream, striped or mottled, and may grow to 60cm (24in) in length; they are eaten raw. Plants need a temperature of 25–30°C (77–86°F) and may be grown outdoors only in sunny, sheltered areas, but may also be grown under cover. Well-drained, sandy loam soils with medium levels of nitrogen (see p.314) and a pH of 5.5–7 are needed. Incorporate well-rotted manure and a general-purpose fertilizer into the soil before planting.

Sowing and planting
Sow in early spring under cover, in trays or 6–9cm (3–3½in) pots, at a temperature of at least 22–5°C (72–7°F). When the seedlings are 10–15cm (4–6in) tall, harden them off. Plant them out after all risk of frost has passed, spaced at least 1m (3ft) apart. Protect from wind and cold weather with plastic screens.

Routine cultivation
Mulch to retain moisture and apply a balanced fertilizer or liquid feed every two weeks until the fruits begin to develop. Pinch out the growing points of the main shoots when they are 2m (6ft) long and train sideshoots between other plants in the row. To assist formation of fruits, hand-pollinate the flowers (see "Marrows and courgettes", p.336). Reduce sub-lateral growths from the sideshoots to two or three leaves after fruits start to develop, and place a pad of dried grass or a block of wood beneath each fruit to protect it from soil-borne pests and diseases.

Pests and diseases
Humidity levels over 75 per cent encourage leaf diseases, particularly powdery mildew (p.550) and mosaic virus (see "Viruses", p.553). Likely pests include aphids (p.550), root-knot nematodes (p.564), and fruit flies (p.563).

Growing under cover
Watermelons are extremely vigorous and are not normally grown in a greenhouse. They may be grown under plastic covers, spaced 1m (3ft) apart; remove covers at flowering time to reduce humidity and encourage insect-pollination.

Harvesting and storing
Harvest 11–14 weeks after sowing; mature fruits give a hollow sound when tapped. They may be stored for 14–20 days at 10–12°C (50–54°F).

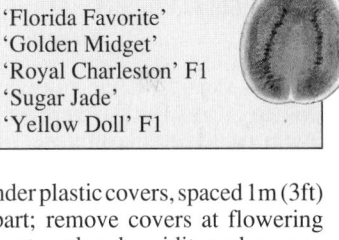

Sweet melons (*Cucumis melo*)

These climbing annuals, normally trained as cordons, reach a height of about 2m (6ft) with laterals extending to 60cm (24in). The three major types are cantaloupe, winter or casaba, and musk (including honeydew) melons. Cantaloupe melons have grey-green, thick, rough skins with deep grooves; individual fruits weigh up to 750g (1lb 11oz). Winter melons have smooth, yellow, or yellow and green striped skin, and weigh up to 1kg (2lb 2oz). Musk melons vary in size but are usually smaller than cantaloupe and winter melons and often have fine reticulated markings on smooth skins. Winter melons and some cultivars of cantaloupe melons are suitable for growing in a greenhouse.

Sweet melons are tropical plants requiring a minimum temperature of 18°C (64°F) for germination, rising to 25°C (77°F) during the growing period. In very sunny, sheltered sites, growing in the open is possible but in temperate climates plants are grown in cold frames or in a greenhouse. They need a well-drained, fertile soil with a pH of 6.5–7, a high humus content, and high nitrogen levels (see p.314). Add a general-purpose fertilizer and well-rotted compost or manure.

Sowing and planting
Sow seed under cover in early spring in trays or in 6–9cm (3–3½in) pots (two seeds per pot), removing the weaker one if both germinate. After about six weeks, and when risk of frost is passed, harden off and plant out the seedlings, spaced 1m (3ft) apart with 1–1.5m (3–5ft) between rows. Plant each seedling on a slight mound and protect young plants until they are established from wind and cold weather with plastic tunnels.

MUSK MELON

STOPPING SWEET MELONS

Allow 1 flower per lateral to set, and then pinch or cut out the growing tip of each lateral at 2–3 leaves beyond the developing fruit.

Routine cultivation

After five leaves have developed, pinch out each growing point to encourage further shoots. When these are well developed, reduce them to about four of the most vigorous shoots. Train two shoots on either side, between adjacent plants in the row. Remove any protective covering when the plants begin to flower to encourage insect-pollination. Hand-pollinate if required (see "Marrows and courgettes", p.336).

Thin to one fruit per shoot when the fruits are 2.5cm (1in) in diameter, and stop all sub-laterals at two to three leaves beyond the developing fruits. Pinch out the main shoots when they are 1–1.2m (3–4ft) long and remove any further sub-laterals that form. Place a pad of dried grass, a tile, or a piece of wood beneath each developing fruit to protect it from soil-borne diseases.

Water regularly and feed every 10–14 days with a liquid feed as the fruits begin to develop; reduce watering and feeding as the fruits ripen.

Pests and diseases

Aphids (p.550) and powdery mildew (p.550) may be troublesome. Under cover, the plants may be affected by glasshouse red spider mites (p.550), powdery mildew (p.550), whiteflies (p.550), and *Verticillium* wilt (p.557).

Growing under cover

To raise sweet melons in a cold frame, plant seedlings singly in the centre of the frame. Train the four laterals to grow towards the corners. As the plants develop, increase ventilation and gradually reduce humidity. Once the fruits start forming, remove the lights, replacing them at night only in cold weather. In hot weather, shade lightly.

Sweet melons may be grown in a greenhouse if the distance from the base of the side walls to the ridge is at least 2m (6ft). Plant seedlings onto well-prepared mounds (see "Cucumbers and gherkins", below). Grow as single or double cordons, training on canes tied to horizontal wires up to the ridge. Space plants 38cm (15in) apart for single cordons, 60cm (2ft) for double cordons. They may also be grown in growing bags or 24–5cm (9–10in) pots placed on greenhouse staging.

For a single cordon, pinch out the growing point when the main shoot is 2m (6ft) long to encourage lateral growth. Stop laterals at five leaves and sub-laterals at two leaves beyond the flowers. For a double cordon, pinch out the main shoot and let two shoots develop vertically; train as above. Support developing fruits in 5cm (2in) mesh slings or nets fixed to the ridge. To aid pollination do not damp down during flowering. Maintain a temperature of 24°C (75°F) at night and 30°C (86°F) in the day.

Harvesting and storing

Harvest 12–20 weeks after sowing. Cantaloupe and musk melons are sweet-smelling when mature, and the fruit stalks crack. Separate the fruits gently from the stalks. Store for 14–50 days at 10–15°C (50–59°F), depending on the cultivar.

Cucumbers and gherkins (*Cucumis sativus*)

Most are annual, trailing vines that grow to 1–3m (3–10ft); there are a few compact bush cultivars. The immature fruits are eaten raw, pickled, or cooked in soup.

Outdoor or ridge cucumbers are characteristically rough-skinned, spiny, and 10–15cm (4–6in) long. Modern, improved cultivars, many of Japanese origin, are smoother and up to 30cm (12in) long, with improved cold tolerance and disease resistance. They are mainly grown outdoors or in frames and are insect-pollinated. Gherkins are ridge cucumbers with short, often stumpy fruits up to 7cm (3in) long, harvested young, and used mainly for pickling. Apple and lemon cucumbers are round, yellow-skinned, ridge cucumbers that grow up to 6cm (2½in) in diameter. European or greenhouse fruits are smooth and over 30cm (12in) long. They do not require pollination to set fruit and, if pollinated, may produce bitter, swollen fruits; use the modern all-female cultivars to remove the risk of accidental pollination.

Cucumbers are warm-season vegetables, growing best at a mean temperature of 18–30°C (64–86°F). They have no frost tolerance and most are damaged at temperatures below 10°C (50°F). In northern latitudes, ridge types may produce male flowers alone early in the season; female flowers, then fruits, occur later. Grow cucumbers in a sheltered site in fertile, humus-rich soil that is well drained but moisture-retentive: the roots must not be allowed to dry out. Lime very acid soils. The plants need low nitrogen levels (see p.314). Rotate indoor crops.

Greenhouse types must be grown with minimum night temperatures of 20°C (68°F) and in high humidity. Never grow ridge types in the same greenhouse as all-female cultivars since cross-pollination will occur.

Sowing and planting

Cucumbers transplant badly, so seed for outdoor varieties should be sown *in situ* after all risk of frost has passed or alternatively in small pots or modules. If sowing outside, prepare holes at least 30cm (12in) wide and deep, working in plenty of well-rotted compost or manure as you backfill. Cover with about 15cm (6in) of manured soil made into a small mound to ensure sharp drainage. Place seeds on their side about 2cm (¾in) deep, sowing two to three per pot or site.

Seed germinates at a minimum soil temperature of 20°C (68°F). Thin to one seedling after germination. Seed sown in pots needs a minimum temperature at night of 16°C (60°F)

GHERKIN

until the seedlings are planted out, about four weeks after sowing. Space climbing types 45cm (18in) apart; bush types, and climbing types if trailing over the ground, should be spaced about 75cm (30in) apart. In cool climates, protect plants with cloches or fleecy film after planting.

Routine cultivation

Grow trailing types up supporting fences, nets, or canes, or allow them to twine up strings. Nip out the growing point after five or six leaves have appeared, and train the resulting stronger growths up the support, tying them in if necessary. When these shoots reach the top of the support, nip them out two leaves beyond a flower; laterals will develop on which more fruits will form. As fruiting continues, feed plants every two

SOWING AND PLANTING OUT

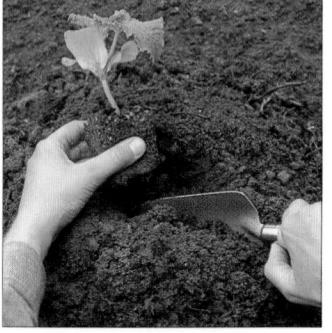

1 *Fill a 5cm (2in) pot with seed compost to within 2.5cm (1in) of the rim. Place 2 or 3 seeds on their sides in the compost, then cover them to a depth of about 2cm (¾ in). Water well and label.*

2 *Prepare a hole 30cm (12in) wide and 30cm (12in) deep, and fill with well-rotted compost. Pile the soil on top to make a mound about 15cm (6in) high. Plant the cucumber on top of this mound. Firm in and water.*

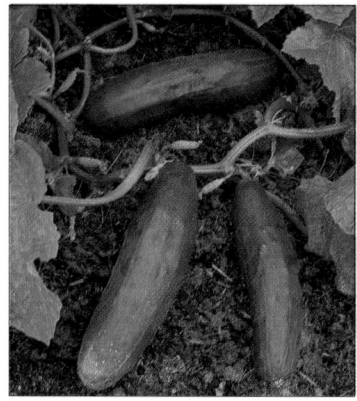

BUSH CUCUMBERS

weeks with a high-potash fertilizer or equivalent organic liquid feed. Regular watering is essential during the growing period, particularly after transplanting so that plants establish quickly, and during flowering and fruiting (see "Critical watering periods", p.312).

Pests and diseases
Cucumbers may be affected by snails (p.548), aphids (p.550), powdery mildew (p.550), cutworms (p.559), glasshouse red spider mites (p.550), whiteflies (p.550), cucumber mosaic virus (see "Viruses", p.553), and foot and root rots (p.558).

Growing under cover
Grow as in the open using appropriate cultivars – the all-female selections are recommended. Stop the main shoot of each plant at the top of the supports and nip off sideshoots beyond the first leaf. Damp down greenhouses to control pests.

Harvesting and storing
Harvest cucumbers regularly from about 12 weeks after sowing when the sides of the fruits are parallel and they are about 15–20cm (6–8in) long. Harvest gherkins when they are 2.5–7cm (1–3in) long or when they have reached pickling size.

CLIMBING CUCUMBERS

RECOMMENDED CUCUMBERS AND GHERKINS

Ridge cucumbers
'Burpless Tasty Green' F1
'Bush Champion' F1

'Bush Champion'

Smooth cucumbers
'Brunex' F1
'Diana'
'Pepita' F1

Japanese cucumbers
'Tokyo Slicer' F1
'Kyoto'

Gherkins
'Bestal' F1
'Conda' F1
'Hokus'

'Hokus'

Pumpkins (*Cucurbita maxima, C. moschata, C. pepo*)

This is a very diverse group of annuals, also known as winter squashes, with fruits weighing from 450g (1lb) to over 30kg (66lb). The skin may be smooth, warted, or ridged, and green, cream, blue-green, yellow, orange, red, or striped, the colour often changing with maturity. Their shapes vary considerably and may be round, long, squat, onion-shaped, or a two-layered, "turban" shape. Most form very large, trailing plants with huge leaves; some are compact and bushy. Both young and mature fruits may be eaten cooked, either fresh or after storage. Shoots and young leaves may be cooked and flowers may be eaten raw or cooked. Some cultivars have edible seeds.

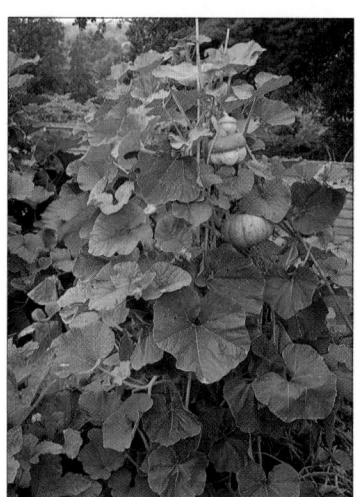

PUMPKINS ON A TRIPOD

For climate, site, and soil preparation requirements, see "Cucumbers and gherkins", p.334. Pumpkins require medium to high nitrogen levels (see p.314).

Sowing and planting
Seed may be soaked overnight before sowing to hasten germination. Sow as for cucumbers (see p.334). Space plants 2–3m (6–10ft) apart, depending on the cultivar. For large cultivars, prepare holes up to 45cm (18in) deep and 60cm (24in) wide. Insert a marker cane when planting so that the centre of the plant can be found if watering is necessary. Protect and mulch after planting.

Routine cultivation
A top-dressing of a general fertilizer may be applied soon after planting. Shoots may be trained in circles on the ground using bent wire to hold down the stems, or grown on supports, such as tripods, which for vigorous cultivars must be very strong. Where only a few large fruits are needed, remove all but two or three of the fruits while still young.

Hand-pollinate as for marrows (see p.336), if necessary. Pumpkins are deep-rooting so watering should only be needed in very dry weather.

Pests and diseases
The most serious pests and diseases are slugs (p.548) in the early stages and cucumber mosaic virus (see "Viruses", p.553).

Harvesting and storing
Cut away any foliage shading the fruits to encourage them to ripen. Harvest pumpkins 12–20 weeks after planting. Leave fruits for storing on the plant to mature as long as possible: the stem starts to crack and the skin hardens when the fruit is ripe. Pick before the first frosts, cutting each fruit with a long stalk.

After harvesting, most storage types must be exposed to the sun for ten days to "cure" or further harden the skin so that it forms a barrier, slowing the rate of water loss. Cover the fruits at night if frost threatens, or cure indoors at 27–32°C (81–90°F) for four days. 'Acorn' may be stored without curing. Store pumpkins in a well-ventilated place at about 10°C (50°F) with a humidity of 95 per cent. They may be kept from four to six months, and, in some cases, even longer, depending on the conditions and the cultivar grown.

CURING PUMPKINS
When it is ripe, cut the pumpkin off the plant with as long a stalk as possible. Leave the pumpkins in the sun for about 10 days so that the skin hardens.

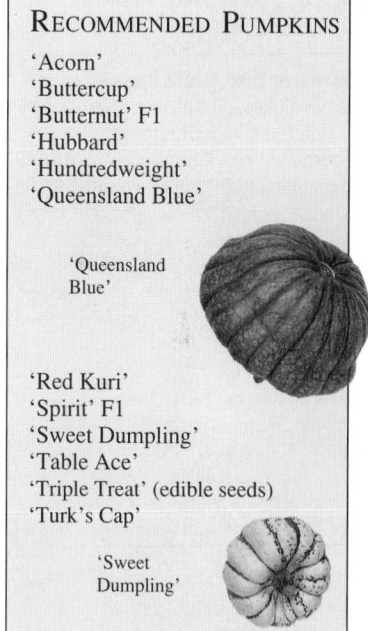

RECOMMENDED PUMPKINS
'Acorn'
'Buttercup'
'Butternut' F1
'Hubbard'
'Hundredweight'
'Queensland Blue'

'Queensland Blue'

'Red Kuri'
'Spirit' F1
'Sweet Dumpling'
'Table Ace'
'Triple Treat' (edible seeds)
'Turk's Cap'

'Sweet Dumpling'

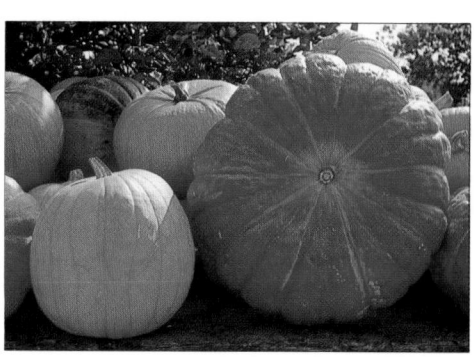

Marrows and courgettes (*Cucurbita pepo*)

Also known as vegetable marrows or summer squashes, marrows are annuals that trail for several metres or form compact plants of 90cm (3ft) spread. They commonly have cylindrical fruits about 30cm (12in) long and 13cm (5in) in diameter. Courgettes are marrows harvested young; only tender-skinned cultivars are suitable. Marrows are usually trailing, while courgettes are bushy. The skin of marrows may be green, yellow, white, or striped. Custard marrows have flattish, fluted-edged fruits; crook-neck squashes have swollen fruits with a bent neck. There are also round-fruited cultivars. Spaghetti marrows are marrow-like in shape, but with hard skins; their flesh resembles spaghetti when cooked. All the fruits are generally cooked. Young leaves and shoot tips may also be cooked, and flowers eaten raw or cooked.

Marrows and courgettes are warm-season crops, needing temperatures of 18–27°C (64–81°F). Frost tolerance, soil, and soil preparation are as for cucumbers (see p.334). They need low nitrogen levels (see p.314).

Sowing and planting
Sow as for cucumbers (see p.334) when the soil temperature is at least 15°C (59°F). Place each seed about 2.5cm (1in) deep or a little deeper in light soils. Sow seed *in situ* after all risk of frost has passed, or germinate in pots indoors. Space bush types 90cm (3ft) apart, and trailing types 1.2–2m (4–6ft) apart. In cool areas, protect young plants with cloches or floating mulches. In hot areas, floating mulches will protect young plants against insects. Mulch after planting.

Routine cultivation
Trailing types may be grown up strong supports. The shoots may also be trained in circles, using bent wire to peg down the stems. Towards the end of the season, nip off the ends of the shoots. Feed and water as for cucumbers (see p.334).

Pests and diseases
Slugs (p.548) may attack in the early stages; cucumber mosaic virus (see "Viruses", p.553) and pollen beetles (p.561) may also be a problem.

Growing under cover
This is only appropriate in cool climates when a very early crop is required. Use bush cultivars.

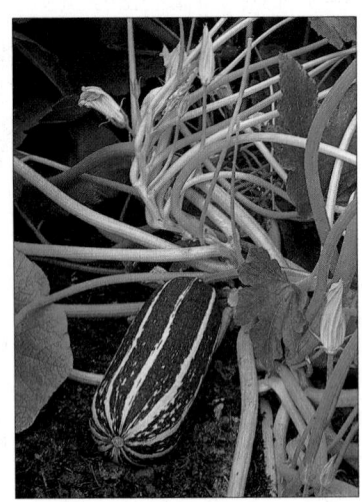

BUSH MARROW

Hand-pollinating

Marrows and courgettes are generally insect-pollinated but in cold seasons, if fruits are not setting, it may be necessary to hand-pollinate. The female flower has a tiny bump (the embryonic fruit) behind the petals which the male flower lacks (see below); this makes it easy to distinguish between them.

To hand-pollinate, take a male flower, remove all the petals and press it against the female flower. Alternatively, use a fine paintbrush to transfer the pollen from the stamens of the male flower to the stigma of the female.

MALE FLOWER

FEMALE FLOWER

Embryonic fruit

Harvesting and storing
Harvest marrows seven to eight weeks after planting. Some types may be stored for a few weeks if they are kept well ventilated at about 10°C (50°F) with a humidity of 95 per cent. Spaghetti marrows may be stored for several months. Pick courgettes when they are about 10cm (4in) long, preferably with the flower attached as this indicates freshness. Harvest shoots from the top 15cm (6in) of stem; new growth is soon made. If harvesting flowers, pick male ones after the females have set.

HARVESTING COURGETTES

Cut courgettes when they are 10cm (4in) long, with a short stalk. Handle the fruits carefully to avoid bruising them. Regular harvesting will encourage more fruits.

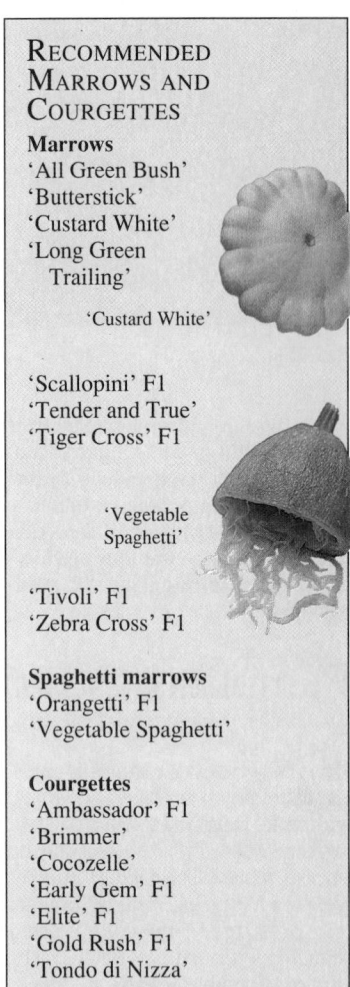

RECOMMENDED MARROWS AND COURGETTES
Marrows
'All Green Bush'
'Butterstick'
'Custard White'
'Long Green Trailing'
'Custard White'
'Scallopini' F1
'Tender and True'
'Tiger Cross' F1
'Vegetable Spaghetti'
'Tivoli' F1
'Zebra Cross' F1
Spaghetti marrows
'Orangetti' F1
'Vegetable Spaghetti'
Courgettes
'Ambassador' F1
'Brimmer'
'Cocozelle'
'Early Gem' F1
'Elite' F1
'Gold Rush' F1
'Tondo di Nizza'
'Zucchini' F1

Globe artichokes (*Cynara scolymus*)

These perennial plants have blue-grey leaves and thistle-like flowers. Globe artichokes may grow up to 1.2–1.5m (4–5ft) tall with a 90cm (3ft) spread. They are grown for the green and purple flower buds, which have edible, fleshy pads (the "hearts") at the base of the outer scales and the top of the flower stem; the hearts are cooked or pickled. A reliable cultivar is 'Vert de Laon'.

Globe artichokes grow best in cool climates at 13–18°C (55–60°F) and tolerate light to medium frosts. They need an open but not exposed site, with fertile, well-drained soil into which plenty of compost or well-rotted manure has been dug, and low levels of nitrogen (see p.314).

Sowing and planting
Globe artichokes are normally increased by division. Using a sharp knife, two hand forks, or a spade, divide healthy, established plants in the spring; each division should have at least two shoots with a tuft of leaves and a good root system. Plant these divisions 60–75cm (24–30in) apart and trim the tips of the leaves to 13cm (5in). Globe artichokes may be raised from seed either indoors or

DIVIDING GLOBE ARTICHOKES

In spring, lift an established plant and divide it using two hand forks, a spade, or a knife. Each division should have at least two shoots, and strong roots.

outdoors in spring, but the results are variable; thin or plant out seedlings at the correct spacing. In future years, divide the most productive plants to build up a good stock. Named cultivars can only be raised from divided offsets. Plants should be replaced every three years to maintain vigour and cropping levels.

Routine cultivation
Keep the planting area free of weeds and well mulched to conserve soil moisture. Do not allow the roots of globe artichokes to dry out in summer or become waterlogged in winter. If heavy frosts are expected,

earth up the base of each plant, covering with a thick layer of straw; remove the covering in spring.

Pests and diseases
Lettuce root aphids (see "Aphids", p.550) may cause problems.

Harvesting and storing
In favourable conditions, some heads may be cut in the late summer of the first season. More flowering stems will be produced in the second season. Pick before the scales open, when the buds feel plump. Remove the hairy choke and stalk before freezing; the hearts may be pickled.

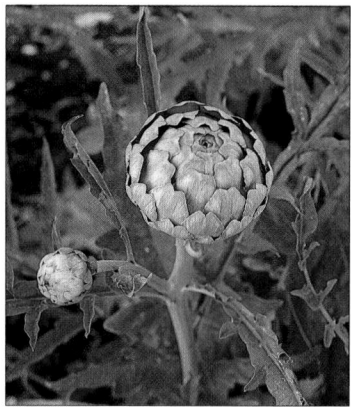

GLOBE ARTICHOKE

Tomatoes (*Lycopersicon esculentum*)

These are annual plants in temperate areas and short-lived perennials in the tropics. The main trailing stem of the indeterminate (mid-size, non-bushy) types grows to over 2.5m (8ft) long in warm climates, with vigorous sideshoots. The shorter (semi-determinate) types and the bush (determinate) types stop growing earlier than the indeterminates, with the stems ending in a fruit truss. Compact dwarf types may grow up to 23cm (9in) across and as tall.

Ripe tomato fruits are red, yellow, orange, pink, or white, and round, flat, plum- or pear-shaped. The tiny currant tomatoes (*Lycopersicon pimpinellifolium*) are 1cm (¹/₂in) in diameter, cherry types 2.5cm (1in), the ribbed Marmande and giant beefsteak types up to 10cm (4in). All are eaten raw or cooked.

Tomatoes grow best at 21–4°C (70–75°F), but do not grow well below 16°C (61°F) or above 27°C (81°F) and do not tolerate frost. They need high light intensity. In cool climates, grow them in a sheltered site outdoors or under cover; they are often grown in containers. Tomatoes tolerate a wide range of fertile and well-drained soils, with a pH of 5.5–7; lime very acid soils (see "Liming", p.531). Crops need to be rotated (see p.307).

Prepare the ground by working in plenty of well-rotted manure or compost at least 30cm (12in) deep, since tomatoes are deep-rooted and gross feeders. Apply a basic fertilizer before planting: tomatoes need high levels of phosphorus (see "Soil nutrients", p.313) but low levels of nitrogen (see p.314).

Sowing and planting
In warm climates, sow seed *in situ* in spring and thin seedlings to the correct spacing. In cool climates, six to

BUSH TOMATOES

eight weeks before the last frost, sow seed 2cm (³/₄in) deep, at about 15°C (59°F), in seed trays or modules. Transplant into 5–6cm (2–3in) pots at the two- or three-leaf stage; give the seedlings ample ventilation, space, and light. They can stand short periods of low temperatures if day temperatures rise to compensate. Harden off before planting out

when night temperatures are over 7°C (45°F) or soil temperatures at least 10°C (50°F) and the risk of frost is over. Plant when the flowers on the lower truss are visible.

Cordons Train indeterminate and semi-determinate types as cordons with 38–45cm (15–18in) between plants in single rows 45cm (18in) apart, or in double rows with 90cm (3ft) between the pairs of rows.

Bush and dwarf types Bush types sprawl on the ground; space them 30–90cm (12–36in) apart, depending on the cultivar. Dwarf types may be more closely spaced than this. Cover with cloches or floating mulches in the early stages. Bush types grow well when mulched with plastic film (see "Mulching", p.312).

Routine cultivation
All types of tomato should be watered and mulched heavily once the soil is warm. In dry conditions, water tomatoes weekly at a rate of 11 litres

(2 gallons) per plant. Plants in containers need more frequent watering and supplementary feeding with a tomato fertilizer. Take care not to overwater or overfeed as this may reduce flavour.

Cordons Tie in cordons to the support canes or wires as they grow, and remove all sideshoots when they are about 2.5cm (1in) long. In late summer, remove the terminal shoot two leaves above a truss to allow the remaining fruits to develop and ripen before the first frost. In cool climates, remove supports at the end of the season, bend over the plants *in situ* on straw, and cover with cloches to encourage ripening (see p.338).

TRAINING CORDON TOMATOES

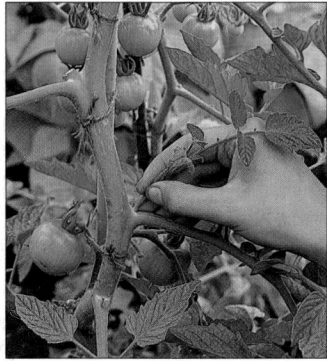

1 *On cordon tomatoes, regularly pinch out sideshoots as they develop to concentrate the plant's energies into swelling the fruits.*

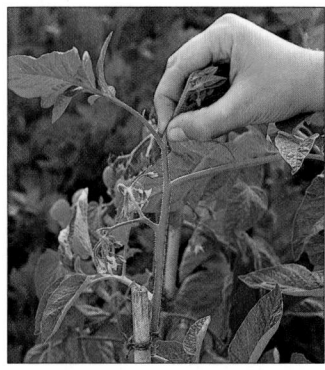

2 *When the cordon has reached the required height in late summer, nip out the tip of the main shoot 2 leaves above the top flower truss.*

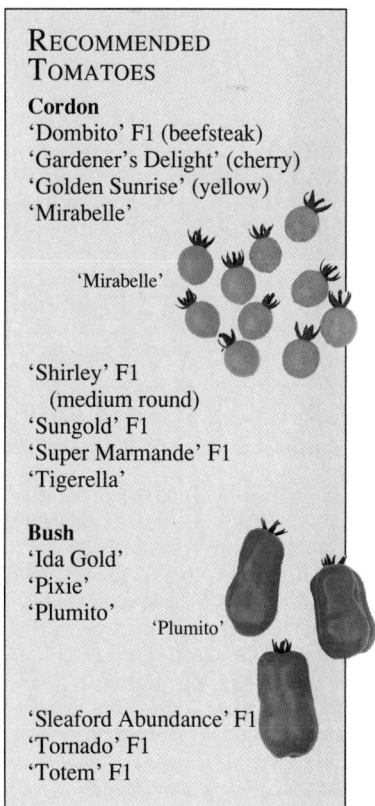

RECOMMENDED TOMATOES

Cordon
'Dombito' F1 (beefsteak)
'Gardener's Delight' (cherry)
'Golden Sunrise' (yellow)
'Mirabelle'

'Mirabelle'

'Shirley' F1
   (medium round)
'Sungold' F1
'Super Marmande' F1
'Tigerella'

Bush
'Ida Gold'
'Pixie'
'Plumito'

'Plumito'

'Sleaford Abundance' F1
'Tornado' F1
'Totem' F1

TOMATOES RIPENING UNDER A CLOCHE

In cool climates, tomatoes will continue to ripen at the end of the season if they are cut down from their supports, leaned over horizontally on a bed of clean, dry straw, and covered with cloches. The roots stay in the ground.

Pests and diseases

Outdoor tomato plants are affected by damping off in seedlings (p.564), leafhoppers (p.551), potato cyst eelworms (p.570), and tomato blight (p.562). Tomatoes under cover are affected by whiteflies (p.550), potato mosaic virus (see "Viruses", p.553), tomato leaf mould (p.552), grey mould/*Botrytis* (p.562), magnesium deficiency (p.555), boron deficiency (p.558), seedling blight (p.558), foot and root rots (p.565), and blossom end rot (see "Calcium deficiency", p.562). Use disease-resistant cultivars where possible. Interplanting with French marigolds may deter whiteflies.

Growing under cover

In cool climates, tomatoes may be grown in greenhouses or poly-tunnels. Polytunnels, which can be moved to a fresh site, are better than greenhouses, where soil-borne diseases may develop unless the soil is replaced every three years. Alternatively crops may be grown in containers or by ring culture (plants are grown in "rings" or bottomless pots filled with compost, resting on shingle or gravel). Cultivars may also be grafted onto disease-resistant rootstocks. After the first truss has set feed weekly with a high-potash fertilizer or an organic liquid feed.

Harvesting and storing

Pick fruits as they ripen. Harvest the earliest bush types seven to eight weeks after planting; before the first frosts, these may be pulled up by the roots and hung upside-down indoors to ripen. Harvest cordon types after 10–12 weeks. Tomatoes freeze well.

GROWING BAGS

Tomatoes may be planted in growing bags outdoors or in greenhouses. Growing in bags prevents the plants from being infected by soil-borne diseases.

Wonderberries (*Solanum* x *burbankii*)

These annual plants grow to about 75cm–1m (30in–3ft) tall with a spread of 60cm (24in). Several cultivated forms of the wonderberry, or sunberry, are grown; all have oval, light green leaves as well as round, purple berries up to 1cm ($\frac{1}{2}$in) in diameter. The leaves and young shoots are used like spinach. The unripe fruits contain a poisonous alkaloid, so pick only ripe berries and cook them thoroughly.

Wonderberries are tropical and subtropical plants requiring temperatures of 18–25°C (64–77°F) with a humidity of at least 70 per cent. They may be grown in the open in sunny, sheltered sites, but in temperate areas, greenhouse cultivation is recommended. A fertile, well-drained soil with a pH of 5.5–7 is preferable; medium nitrogen levels are required (see p.314).

Sowing and planting

Sow seed in spring in trays in the greenhouse. Prick out the seedlings when they are large enough to handle, into 6–9cm (3–3$\frac{1}{2}$ in) pots. When they are 8–10cm (3–4in) tall, harden them off and transplant them; space plants 40–50cm (16–20in) apart, with about 60cm (24in) between rows.

Routine cultivation

Wonderberries need high levels of soil moisture; mulch well and water regularly. Apply a general-purpose fertilizer or an organic liquid feed every 10–14 days during the growing period. Pinch out the growing point when plants are 30cm (12in) tall to encourage lateral branching, and stake plants that grow higher than 60cm (24in). Keep the ground around plants free from weeds.

Pests and diseases

Aphids (p.550) are the major pest. Under cover, glasshouse red spider mites (p.550) and thrips (p.551) may also attack plants.

Growing under cover

When seedlings are about 10–15cm (4–6in) tall, transplant into 21cm (8in) pots or growing bags, leaving at least 50cm (20in) between plants, or transplant into well-prepared greenhouse beds, spacing plants 50–60cm (20–24in) apart each way. Reduce the level of humidity during flowering to promote pollination.

Harvesting and storing

Harvest shoots 9–11 weeks after transplanting; continue removing shoots 10–15cm (4–6in) long to encourage lateral growths. To produce berries, do not remove shoots

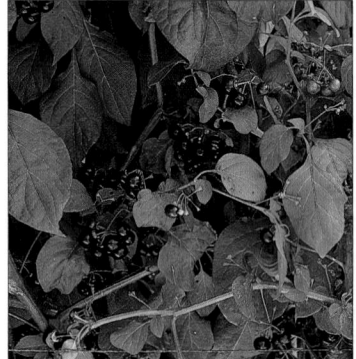

WONDERBERRIES

but allow the plants to become bushy and to flower. Harvest the fruit about 14–17 weeks after sowing, removing bunches with a sharp knife. Ripe berries may be stored for 10–14 days at 10–15°C (50–59°F).

Aubergines (*Solanum melongena*)

Short-lived perennials normally cultivated as annuals, aubergines form small bushes about 60–70cm (24–8in) tall with a spread of about 60cm (24in). Also known as eggplants or garden eggs, cultivars differ mainly in the shape, size, and colour of the fruits, which may be oval, pear-shaped, or round, dark purple, yellowish-green, or white, and weigh 200–500g (7–18oz). The fruits are generally sliced and cooked.

Aubergines are tropical and subtropical plants requiring temperatures of 25–30°C (77–86°F), with a minimum humidity of 75 per cent. Below 20°C (68°F) growth may be checked, although many cultivars may be grown in temperate areas in greenhouses or outdoors in a sunny, sheltered site, with protection.

Aubergines require a deep, fertile, well-drained soil and medium nitrogen levels (see p.314).

Sowing and planting

In spring, sow seed under cover in trays using a light, slightly acid (pH 6–6.5) compost: soak the seed in warm water for 24 hours first to aid germination. Prick out into 6–9cm (3–3$\frac{1}{2}$in) pots. In warm climates, plant out the seedlings into well-prepared beds when they are 8–10cm (3–4in) tall, spacing them about 60–75cm (24–30in) apart each way. Pinch out their terminal growing

RECOMMENDED AUBERGINES

'Black Beauty'
'Black Bell' F1
'Black Prince' F1
'Easter Egg'
'Long Purple'

'Easter Egg'

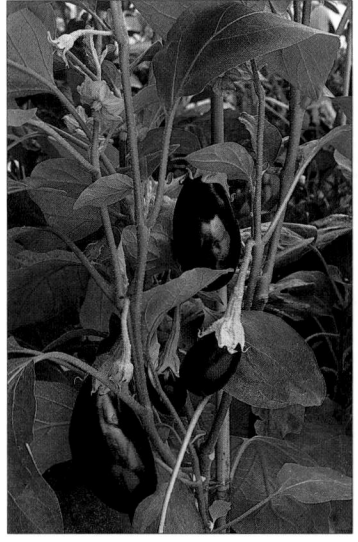

AUBERGINES

points to promote a bushy habit. In temperate climates, pot up singly into 15cm (6in) pots; plant out after risk of frost has passed. Protect from heavy rain, wind, and low temperatures.

Routine cultivation
Stake cultivars over 60cm (24in) tall. Keep plants well watered, otherwise leaves and buds are liable to drop, and mulch to preserve moisture. Apply a balanced fertilizer or liquid feed every two weeks during the growing season. Prune back mature plants to stimulate growth. To produce large fruits, restrict the number per plant to five or six.

Pests and diseases
Aubergines may be attacked by aphids (p.550). Under cover, red spider mites (p.550), mealybugs (p.550), caterpillars (p.549), thrips (p.551), and powdery and downy mildew (p.550) may be troublesome.

Growing under cover
Sow seed in early spring at 20–30°C (68–86°F). When the seedlings are 8–10cm (3–4in) tall, transfer them to 20cm (8in) pots or growing bags, and pinch out the tips. Maintain the temperature above the minimum required during the growing period. Damp down greenhouses to help discourage red spider mites.

Harvesting and storing
Harvest 16–24 weeks after sowing, when fruits reach full colour and are unwrinkled. Cut the fruit stalks close to the stem. Aubergines may be stored for up to two weeks in humid conditions at 12–15°C (54–9°F).

HARVESTING AUBERGINES

Cut aubergines while their skin is still purple and shiny; once it loses its shine, the flesh will taste bitter. Cut the stalk at least 2.5cm (1in) from the fruit.

Sweet corn (*Zea mays*)

Sweet corn is an annual that grows to at least 75cm–1.7m (30in–5½ft) and has an average spread of 45cm (18in). Male tassels and female ears (cobs) are borne on the same plant. The cobs are golden, white, or bicoloured white and yellow, and cooked or eaten raw when young. New, "supersweet" (sugar-enhanced) cultivars are available.

Sweet corn needs a long growing season of 70–110 frost-free days after planting. It requires temperatures of 16–35°C (61–95°F), but pollination is poor in hot, dry conditions; in warm climates, grow in an open site. In cool climates, grow early-maturing cultivars in a frost-free, sheltered site. Sweet corn is shallow-rooting and grows on a wide range of fertile, well-drained soils with medium nitrogen (see p.314).

Sowing and planting
Seed does not germinate at soil temperatures below 10°C (50°F). In warm climates, sow seed in spring *in situ*, 2.5cm (1in) deep and 7cm (3in) apart, thinning to the correct spacing after germination. Seed may be sown through plastic mulches. In cool climates, sow indoors in modules and plant out seedlings when the soil temperature reaches 13°C (55°F), or sow *in situ* after all risk of frost has passed. In wet soils, use treated seed that will not rot.

To ensure good pollination and full cobs, plant corn in blocks of at least four plants each way. The average spacing is 30cm (12in) apart; short cultivars may be closer, tall ones further apart. In cool climates, cover with floating mulches or cloches after sowing or planting, removing them at the five-leaf stage. Fine-net floating mulches will protect the plants against frit flies. Supersweet types need higher temperatures to germinate and grow and should not be planted with other types as the sweetness will be lost if they are cross-pollinated. Mini-corn is obtained by planting early cultivars about 15cm (6in) apart and harvesting them when the cobs are about 7cm (3in) long.

Routine cultivation
Hoe shallowly when weeding to avoid damaging the roots. In exposed areas, earth up the stems to 13cm (5in) to increase stability. Watering is not necessary, except in very dry conditions, until flowering starts and again later when the grains are swelling. Water at a rate of 22 litres/sq m (5 gallons/sq yd).

Pests and diseases
Mice (p.566), slugs (p.548), and birds are the most serious pests. The maggots of frit flies may attack the bases of seedlings, causing the growing points to wilt and die. Raise seedlings in pots, or under fine nets, until past the five- or six-leaf stage.

Harvesting and storing
Plants normally produce one or two cobs. Pick just before required, as the sweetness soon deteriorates; supersweet types retain their flavour for about a week. Sweet corn freezes well.

SWEET CORN PLANTED IN A BLOCK

Male and female flowers are carried on the same plant. The male flowers (inset, top), which release pollen, are produced in tassels up to 40cm (16in) in length at the tip of the plant. The female flowers (inset, bottom) are silky strands under which each cob forms. The strands are sticky to collect pollen. The female flowers are wind-pollinated so plant in a block rather than a row to ensure good pollination.

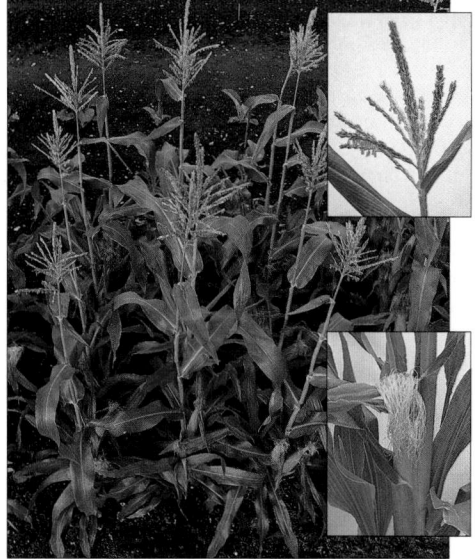

RECOMMENDED SWEET CORN

Early
'Butter Imp' F1
'Earliking' F1
'Sunrise' F1

'Sunrise'

Late
'Pilot' (bicolour)
'Reward' F1
'Silver Queen'
'Sundance' F1

Supersweet
'Butterscotch' F1
'Candle' F1
'Sweet 77' F1 (late)
'Sweet Nugget' F1

TESTING SWEET CORN FOR RIPENESS

Once the silks have turned brown, peel back the sheath and press into a kernel with a fingernail. If the liquid that appears is milky, the cob is ripe; if watery, it is underripe, and if doughy, overripe.

Podded vegetables

VEGETABLES in this group all produce seed pods. Some are grown for these pods, which may be cooked and eaten whole, while others are grown for the seeds, which are extracted and cooked or eaten raw. The seeds of some may be dried; most may be frozen. Several of the plants are decorative as well as functional and may be used for screening, or trained over arches. Podded vegetables often need sheltered conditions at specific temperatures for pollination; they generally require a rich soil to which organic matter has been added before planting.

French beans

Scarlet runner beans

Dried French beans

Peas

Mangetout peas

Haricots

Broad beans

French beans

Sugar peas

Peanuts

Shelled peanuts

Okra (*Abelmoschus esculentus*)

These tender, annual plants are also known as ladies' fingers. The fast-maturing cultivars may grow to 1m (3ft) with a spread of 30–40cm (12–16in); the slow-maturing ones (mainly grown in tropical areas) are up to 2m (6ft) tall. The pods are 10–25cm (4–10in) long and white, green, or red. Recommended cultivars include 'Clemson Spineless', 'Green Velvet', and 'Tender Pod'. Immature pods are eaten as a cooked vegetable; mature pods may also be dried and powdered for use as a flavouring.

In warm-temperate and subtropical areas, plants may be grown in the open only in very favourable, sunny conditions. Seeds germinate only at soil temperatures of at least 16°C (61°F); after germination a stable temperature in the range 20–30°C (68–86°F) is needed for optimum growth. Most modern cultivars are daylength-neutral (see "Daylength", p.307). Plant in well-drained soil, adding plenty of organic material. Okra plants need low to medium nitrogen levels (see p.314).

Sowing and planting
Soak seed for 24 hours before sowing to aid germination. When soil temperatures reach 16–18°C (61–4°F), sow seed *in situ* in rows 60–70cm

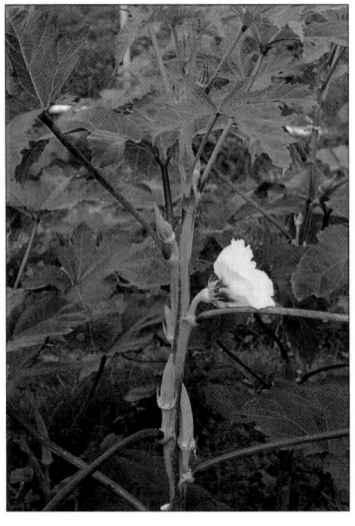

OKRA

(24–8in) apart, leaving 20–30cm (8–12in) between plants. In warm-temperate areas, sow in spring under cover at 20°C (68°F) or above, in trays or 6–9cm (3–3¹/₂in) pots. When seedlings are 10–15cm (4–6in) tall, harden off and transplant to well-prepared beds, spacing as above.

Routine cultivation
Stake tall plants and protect from strong winds with plastic covers or screens, if necessary. Remove all weeds, water regularly, and apply an organic mulch to retain soil moisture. Pinch out the growing points when seedlings are about 60cm (24in) tall to promote branching. Apply a general-purpose fertilizer or liquid feed at two-week intervals to encourage rapid growth. Do not overfeed with nitrogen since this delays flowering.

Pests and diseases
Plants are likely to be damaged by aphids (p.550), caterpillars (p.549), and powdery mildew (p.550); whiteflies (p.550), glasshouse red spider mites (p.550), thrips (p.551), and fungal leaf spots (p.552) may also be troublesome under cover.

Growing under cover
Seedlings may be transplanted into well-prepared beds in the greenhouse or in growing bags, spacing the young plants at least 40cm (16in) apart. Maintain a temperature above 20°C (68°F) and a humidity of over 70 per cent. Spray the plants as necessary to control pests and diseases, and apply an organic liquid feed or a general-purpose fertilizer.

Harvesting and storing
Four to six pods per plant are produced. They may be harvested approximately 8–11 weeks after sowing, depending on the cultivar. Sever the pods from the plant with a sharp knife when they are bright green; overmature pods may become fibrous. Pods may be stored in perforated bags at 7–10°C (45–50°F) for up to ten days.

Peanuts (*Arachis hypogaea*)

These tender, annual plants, also known as groundnuts and monkeynuts, originate from South America. Plants grow to a height of 60cm (24in) with a spread of 30cm (12in) for the more upright Spanish-Valencia types, or up to 1m (3ft) for the less common, prostrate, Virginia types. The Spanish-Valencia types are often divided into Spanish, with two seeds per pod and light brown seed coats, and Valencia, with up to four seeds per pod and dark red seed coats. The stems of the Valencia types are usually thicker than those of the Spanish. The Virginia forms have two seeds per pod, with dark brown seed coats.

The fertilized flowers produce shoot-like structures that penetrate the soil where the immature fruits develop into peanuts. Removed from their pods, the nuts are eaten fresh or roasted, or used in cooking.

Peanuts are tropical plants that need average temperatures of about 20–30°C (68–86°F) and a relative humidity of 80 per cent, although some forms grow well in the warmer subtropics. A frost-free site is essential. Rainfall at flowering time may adversely affect pollination.

Peanut cultivars are generally daylength-neutral (see "Daylength", p.307). Sandy, well-drained loams with a pH of 5.5–6.5 containing calcium, potassium, and phosphorus are preferable. The plants also need low nitrogen levels (see p.314).

Sowing and planting
Sow seeds *in situ*, removed from their shells, in spring or when soil temperatures exceed 16°C (61°F). In temperate climates, sow under cover in trays or 9cm (3¹/₂in) pots, keeping temperatures over 20°C (68°F).

When the seedlings are 10–15cm (4–6in) tall, harden them off and transplant them to well-prepared beds. Whether directly sown or transplanted, the plants should be spaced 15–30cm (6–12in) apart with about 60–70cm (24–8in) between the rows. Protect them with cloches or polytunnels where necessary.

Routine cultivation
Earth up around the roots when the plants are 15cm (6in) tall, and hoe regularly to encourage the fertilized flowers to penetrate the soil. Remove all weeds, and water well in dry periods. Do not water plants during the flowering period, however, as this may lead to poor pollination.

SPANISH-VALENCIA PEANUT PLANT

Pests and diseases
Plants may be affected by aphids (p.550), thrips (p.551), and caterpillars (p.549); under cover, glasshouse red spider mites (p.550) and whiteflies (p.550) may be a problem. Fun-

leaf spots (p.552), root and stem rot (see "Seedling blight", p.558), and rosette virus (see "Viruses", p.553) may also be troublesome.

Growing under cover
Sow seed as described above. Transplant the seedlings when they are 10–15cm (4–6in) tall into growing bags, or well-prepared greenhouse beds. Maintain a temperature over 20°C (68°F), reducing humidity at flowering time to aid pollination.

Harvesting and storing
Harvest the pods 16–20 weeks after sowing for the upright types, and three to four weeks after this for the prostrate types. Virginia types, which produce two seeds per pod, may require up to 25 weeks from sowing to harvesting. Assess the stage of maturity by uprooting one or two pods; they keep for several months. Dry the pods in the sun, then remove the peanuts for storing in cool, dry conditions.

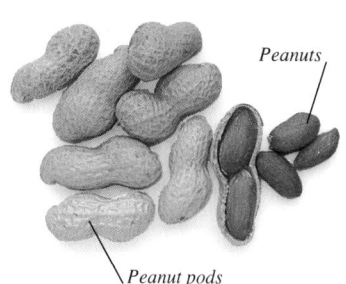
Peanuts

Peanut pods

Dolichos beans (*Lablab purpureus*)

These dwarf or climbing, short-lived, tender perennials are also known as hyacinth beans and lablab beans. Both long- and short-podded cultivars occur. Climbing forms may grow to 4–6m (12–20ft), while dwarf forms reach 1m (3ft) with a spread of about 60cm (2ft). The pods range in colour from green to purple. Young pods and mature seeds are eaten cooked; the latter should be cooked thoroughly. Young seedlings, raised in the dark, may be used as bean sprouts.

Dolichos beans may be grown in subtropical and warm-temperate regions in very favoured, sunny sites with protection. The plants require a temperature of 18–30°C (64–86°F) with a minimum humidity of 70 per cent; cool weather may adversely affect pollination since it discourages pollinating insects. Daylength-neutral cultivars are available (see "Daylength", p.307).

Most soils are suitable for dolichos beans, particularly those containing plenty of organic matter; good drainage is essential. Some cultivars respond well to applications of superphosphate. Dolichos beans need low nitrogen levels (see p.314).

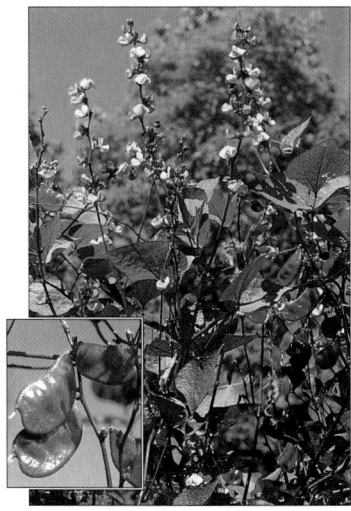
DOLICHOS BEANS

Sowing and planting
Sow *in situ*, in spring or at other times of the year if temperatures are high enough. In temperate areas, sow seeds under cover, in trays, or in 6–9cm (3–3½in) pots at a depth of 2.5cm (1in). When the seedlings are 10–15cm (4–6in) tall, harden them off and transplant into well-prepared beds. Space climbing cultivars 30–45cm (12–18in) apart, allowing 75–100cm (30–36in) between rows; space dwarf cultivars 30–40cm (12–16in) apart with a distance of 45–60cm (18–24in) between rows.

Routine cultivation
Climbing cultivars should be supported by stakes, at least 2m (6ft) high. Water the plants regularly, and mulch to conserve moisture. Protect as necessary with plastic screens or covers and remove all weeds. Apply a general-purpose fertilizer or liquid feed every 10–14 days until flowering. Pinch out the growing points of dwarf cultivars to encourage them to develop a bushy habit; the shoots of climbing cultivars should be trained or tied in to the stakes.

Pests and diseases
Aphids (p.550), thrips (p.551), caterpillars (p.549), root-knot nematodes (p.564), powdery mildew (p.550), fungal leaf spots (p.552), and some viruses (p.553) may be troublesome; under cover, whiteflies (p.550) and glasshouse red spider mites (p.550) may also affect plants.

Growing under cover
Transplant seedlings to growing bags or well-prepared beds in the greenhouse, spacing the plants at least 50–60cm (20–24in) apart. Alternatively, seedlings may be grown on in 21–5cm (8–10in) pots (two plants may be grown in the larger pots). Maintain a temperature of at least 20°C (68°F) and reduce humidity by providing adequate ventilation at flowering time to improve pollination. Dolichos beans may also be propagated from softwood cuttings (see PRINCIPLES OF PROPAGATION, "Stem cuttings", p.538), taken early in the growing season, which root readily in high humidity.

Harvesting and storing
Harvest the young pods six to nine weeks after sowing, when they are fully grown but before the seeds develop; the mature pods containing seeds may be harvested after 10–14 weeks before they become fibrous. If the plants remain healthy after the first crop, cut back the main stems to about half their length to encourage a second crop. Dolichos beans freeze well.

Scarlet runner beans (*Phaseolus coccineus*)

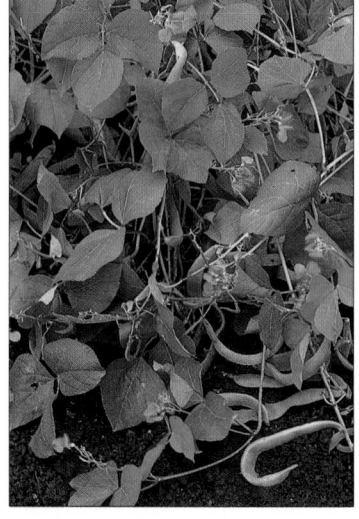
SCARLET RUNNER BEANS

These perennial climbers are grown as annuals in temperate and cool climates. Plants grow to over 3m (10ft) tall, with a spread of about 30cm (12in); some naturally dwarf cultivars form bushes about 38cm (15in) tall. They have pink, red, white, or bicoloured flowers.

The flat pods, over 25cm (10in) long and up to 2cm (³/₄in) wide, are eaten cooked; immature seeds and mature, dried seeds may also be cooked. With some cultivars, it may be necessary to remove the "strings" along the pods.

Scarlet runner beans are a temperate or cool-season crop that does not withstand frost. Plants need a growing season of about 100 frost-free days and they grow best at 14–29°C (57–84°F). At higher temperatures, especially if combined with high humidity, the pods may not set unless the plants are in light shade. In cool climates, choose a sheltered situation to encourage pollinating insects. Plants are deep-rooting and need fertile, moisture-retentive soil. Prepare the soil by digging a trench one spade deep and 60cm (24in) wide, working in well-rotted straw or compost. Runner bean crops should be rotated (see p.307), and need low nitrogen levels (see p.314).

Sowing and planting
Before planting climbing types, erect a strong support system of poles or canes over 2.5m (8ft) long, tied to a horizontal pole or to each other to form a "wigwam". Commercial supports or towers are available. Plants

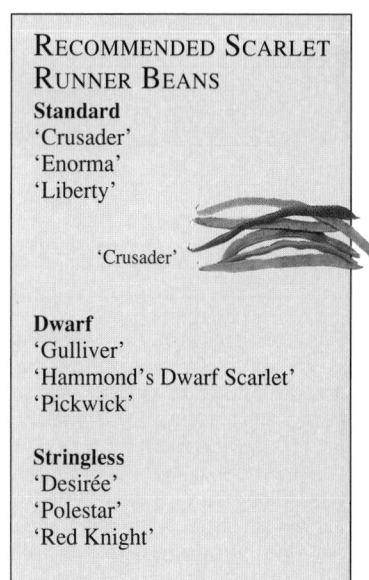

RECOMMENDED SCARLET RUNNER BEANS

Standard
'Crusader'
'Enorma'
'Liberty'

'Crusader'

Dwarf
'Gulliver'
'Hammond's Dwarf Scarlet'
'Pickwick'

Stringless
'Desirée'
'Polestar'
'Red Knight'

may also be twisted up nylon netting, strings, or wires pegged to the ground; do not use plastic-coated netting since the plants do not cling onto it. Sow seed *in situ* 5cm (2in) deep, after all risk of frost has passed bearing in mind that a minimum soil temperature of 12°C (54°F) is needed for germination. In cool areas, sow seed indoors in seed trays and harden off seedlings before transplanting outside. Grow climbers in double rows 60cm (2ft) apart or in circular "wigwams", spacing the plants 15cm (6in) apart. Bush forms may be grown in groups at the same spacing. Mulch well to retain moisture after germination or planting out.

Bean Supports

There are various ways to support climbing beans, depending on the space available. Mature plants will obscure the support structure beneath.

CROSSED CANE ROW

Two rows of 2.5m (8ft) canes, crossed and secured to a horizontal bar

WIGWAM

2.5m (8ft) canes tied near the top

NETTING SUPPORT

10cm (4in) square nylon net fixed to a pole frame

RUNNER BEANS ON A WIGWAM

Routine cultivation

Protect seedlings with cloches or floating mulches. To convert climbing forms into bushes, nip out the growing shoots when plants are 23cm (9in) high. Such plants crop earlier but have lower yields.

Watering is especially important when the flower buds appear and pods are setting (see "Critical watering periods", p.312). At these times water at a rate of 5–11 litres/sq m (1–2 gallons/sq yd) twice a week.

Pests and diseases

Slugs (p.548) in the early stages, pollen beetles (p.561), bean seed flies (p.570), anthracnose (see "Fungal leaf spots", p.552), foot and root rots (p.558), halo blight (see "Bacterial leaf spots and blotches", p.552), seedling blight (p.558), and viruses (p.553) may be troublesome.

Harvesting and storing

Harvest after 13–17 weeks. Pick pods when they are at least 17cm (7in) long and tender; continue picking to prolong the cropping period. Runner beans freeze well.

Lima beans (*Phaseolus lunatus*)

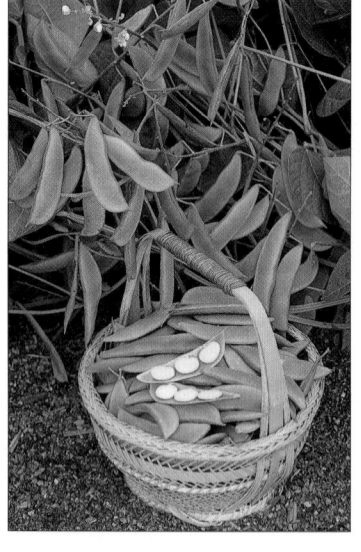

DWARF LIMA BEANS

Also known as butter beans, lima beans are tender annuals and short-lived perennials. Some forms of lima bean climb while others are dwarf and branching. Climbing cultivars may grow to a height of 3–4m (9–12ft), dwarf cultivars to 90cm (3ft), spreading to 40–45cm (16–18in). The young pods and mature seeds are eaten cooked; the seeds may also be dried or germinated in the dark for use as bean sprouts.

The lima bean is a tropical plant that requires a minimum temperature of 18°C (64°F) for germination. Temperatures above 30°C (86°F) may adversely affect pollen formation. In subtropical and warm-temperate areas, growing in the open is possible only in full sun, using plastic screens or covers for protection until the plants are fully established.

Small-seeded cultivars flower only in short daylengths of about 12 hours but the large-seeded cultivars are normally daylength-neutral (see "Daylength", p.307). Most cultivars thrive in a wide range of soil types, but a sandy, well-drained loam with a pH of 6–7 is preferable. Lima beans require low to medium nitrogen levels (see p.314). The procedures for sowing, planting, routine cultivation, and growing under cover are as described for dolichos beans (p.341).

Pests and diseases

Aphids (p.550), thrips (p.551), caterpillars (p.549), whiteflies (p.550) and glasshouse red spider mites (p.550) may be troublesome. Diseases include powdery mildew (p.550), fungal leaf spots (p.552), and viruses (p.553).

Recommended Lima Beans

Climbing
'Challenge'
'Florida Butter'
'Wilber'

Dwarf
'Fordhook 242'
'Henderson'

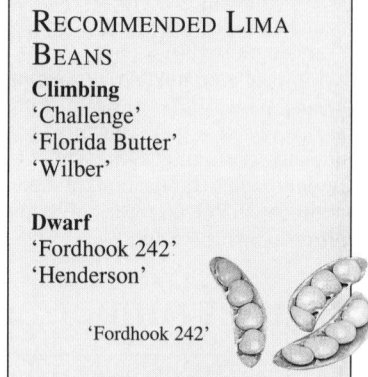

'Fordhook 242'

Harvesting and storing

Harvest whole pods young, mature seeds about 12–16 weeks after sowing. Store both above 4°C (39°F) at 90 per cent humidity for up to two weeks. Lima beans may be frozen.

French beans (*Phaseolus vulgaris*)

These tender annuals have climbing, dwarf, and intermediate forms. They are also known as kidney, snap, or string beans. Height and spread are as for scarlet runner beans (see p.341). The pods are 7–20cm (3–8in) long. They may be round, flat, or curved in shape; diameter ranges from pencil-thickness (for the filet types) to about 2cm (³/₄in); they may be green, yellow, purple, red, or green flecked with purple. The yellow, waxpod types have a waxy texture and excellent flavour. Types vary in the stringiness of the pods; stringless cultivars are available. Never eat the pods raw as the seeds inside contain toxins that must first be destroyed by cooking. Use the immature pods, the half-ripe, shelled bean seeds (flageolets), or the dried, mature bean seeds (haricots). Special cultivars are grown for drying.

French beans grow in similar conditions to scarlet runner beans (see p.341) but the seeds need a minimum temperature of 12°C (54°F) to germinate. The optimum growing temperature is 16–30°C (61–86°F); seedlings do not tolerate temperatures below 10°C (50°F). The plants are self-pollinated, and grow best in rich, light soil. Good drainage is essential to prevent root rot. Work plenty of well-rotted compost or manure into the soil before planting, and always rotate crops (see p.307). Seed may be dressed with the appropriate rhizome inoculant, or rhizobium granules may be applied to the soil at planting; this treatment increases current and subsequent yields by encouraging the formation of nitrogen-fixing root nodules. French beans usually need low nitrogen levels (see p.314).

PRE-GERMINATING FRENCH BEANS

1 *Spread the beans out on moist tissue paper in a tray without drainage holes. Keep damp, at a minimum of 12°C (54°F).*

2 *When the delicate shoots begin to appear and before they turn green, carefully pot up the beans or sow them directly in their final position outside.*

Sowing and planting
Seed may be pre-germinated before sowing. Sow seed or pre-germinated seeds 4cm (1¹/₂in) deep *in situ* or indoors as for scarlet runner beans (see p.341), and make successive sowings throughout the summer. If necessary, warm the soil beforehand with cloches. Space climbing forms as for scarlet runner beans. Dwarf types may be grown at an equidistant spacing of 22cm (9in) in staggered rows for the highest yields. In cold climates, protect after planting with cloches or floating mulches.

Routine cultivation
Support climbing types as for scarlet runner beans; use twigs to support intermediate types. Stems may also be earthed up to keep plants upright. Mulch and do not allow plants to dry out completely; extra watering at a rate of 22 litres/sq m (5 gallons/sq yd) may be necessary in dry conditions at flowering time.

Pests and diseases
Slugs (p.548), bean seed flies (p.570), root aphids and black bean aphids (see "Aphids", p.550), anthracnose (see "Fungal leaf spots", p.552), foot and root rots (p.558), halo blight (see "Bacterial leaf spots and blotches", p.552), and viruses (p.553) may affect French beans.

Growing under cover
In cold climates, dwarf French beans may be grown to maturity in a greenhouse or polytunnel, or under cloches. Space plants as in the open.

EARTHING UP

Plant out the beans 15cm (6in) apart, and once they have formed several pairs of leaves earth them up to support them.

Harvesting and storing
Harvest after 7–13 weeks. Pick young beans regularly to use fresh or freeze. For shelled beans, see below; store in an airtight jar.

DRYING FRENCH BEANS

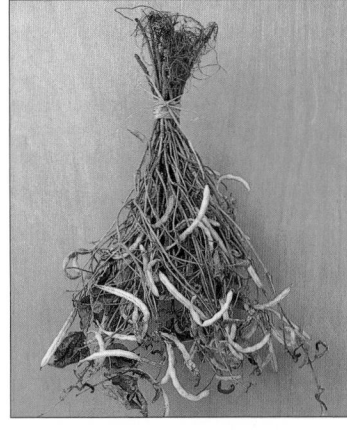

In damp climates, pull up plants and hang them by the roots in a dry, frost-free place. Once dried, remove the pods and extract the beans.

RECOMMENDED FRENCH BEANS
Dwarf
'Aramis' (filet)
'Chevrier Vert' (for flageolets and drying)
'Delinel' (filet)
'Dutch Brown' (for drying)
'Kinghorn Wax' (waxpod)
'Loch Ness' (stringless)
'Pros' (stringless)
'Purple Queen' (purple podded)
'Purple Teepee' (purple podded)
'Tendergreen' (stringless)

'Purple Podded'

Climbing
'Blue Lake'
'Marvel of Venice'
'Purple Podded'

Peas (*Pisum sativum*)

Peas are annuals that grow from 45cm (18in) to over 2m (6ft) tall, with an average spread of 23cm (9in). Plants cling to supports with tendrils; modern semi-leafless types are almost self-supporting. Peas are grouped according to the time taken to mature. The early groups are dwarfer and lower yielding. Pods are usually green but there are purple-podded cultivars.

Shelling-pea types are grown for the fresh peas in the pods; some may be dried. Petit pois are small, fine-flavoured peas. Wrinkle-seeded cultivars are usually sweeter but less hardy than the smooth-seeded types. Edible-podded types (mangetout, sugar peas) are eaten before the peas mature. Mangetout types are flat-podded and eaten young; the round-podded sugar types are used when semi-mature. Peas and pods are usually cooked, but may be eaten raw.

SEMI-LEAFLESS PEAS

Peas are a cool-season crop, growing best at 13–18°C (55–64°F). The flowers and pods cannot withstand frost. Grow peas in an open site, in reasonably fertile, moisture-retentive, well-drained soil; they will not tolerate cold, wet soil, or drought. Work plenty of well-rotted compost or manure into the soil before planting. Peas should be rotated (see p.307). The plants have nitrogen-fixing nodules on their roots, and do not require any extra nitrogen during growth.

Sowing and planting
Make the first outdoor sowings as soon as the soil is about 10°C (50°F). Germination is much slower at lower temperatures. The first sowings may be made under cloches or floating mulches using dwarf cultivars. For successive crops, either sow seeds at 14-day intervals or sow cultivars from different groups at the same time so that they mature in succession. Avoid mid-summer sowings in warm areas, as high temperatures also affect germination. If sowing an early type late, allow about ten weeks before frost is expected for the pods to ripen. Where winters are mild, sow hardy, early-maturing cultivars in late autumn to overwinter. There is a high risk of loss to mice, but surviving plants crop very early.

Sow the seed 3cm (1¹/₄in) deep in patches so that plants can support each other, spacing individual seeds 5–7cm (2–3in) apart. Alternatively, make a flat-bottomed drill up to 23cm (9in) wide, spacing seeds 5cm (2in) apart each way (see "Wide drills", p.310). The drills should be 60–90cm (24–36in) apart, using wider spacing for tall cultivars. Seed may also be sown in double rows 23cm (9in) apart, spacing seeds 1cm (¹/₂in) apart.

Routine cultivation
Protect seedlings against birds with horizontal netting as pea guards. Once the tendrils have developed, remove the pea guards and erect supports: use wire netting, pea nets, or brushwood on either side of a drill. Semi-leafless

and dwarf types need less support. When the peas have several leaves mulch them to keep the roots cool.

Once plants are flowering and forming pods, water every week (unless rainfall is high) at a rate of 22 litres/sq m (5 gallons/sq yd).

Pests and diseases
Jays (p.563), wood pigeons (p.549), pea moths (p.563), and pea thrips (p.563) are the most common pests; mice (p.566) may also be troublesome since they eat seeds. Damping off (p.564), foot and root rots (p.558), seedling blight (p.558), and *Fusarium* wilt (p.558) are occasional problems.

Growing under cover
Early spring and late autumn sowings may be made under cover; grow dwarf peas to maturity under cloches for early or overwintering crops.

Harvesting and storing
Harvest early types 11–12 weeks after sowing, and maincrop peas after 13–14 weeks. Pick edible-podded

SUPPORTING PEAS

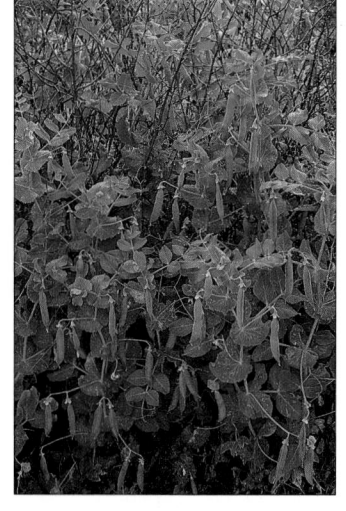

When seedlings have developed tendrils, push peasticks into the ground, as upright as possible, all around the outside of the patch (above). As the peas grow, the tendrils wrap around the peasticks and the peas grow up them (right).

types when the immature peas are just forming inside the pods, shelling peas and sugar snap types when the pods have swollen. Edible-podded

types may be left to mature and shelled normally. All may be frozen. For storing pods on plants, see *Drying French Beans, p.343.*

RECOMMENDED PEAS

Early
'Douce Provence'
'Early Onward'
'Feltham First'
'Hurst Beagle'

Maincrop
'Dark-skinned Perfection'
'Hurst Green Shaft'
'Poppet'
'Tristar'

Sugar and mangetout peas
'Carouby de Maussane'
'Oregon Sugar Pod'
'Sugar Bon'
'Sugar Dwarf
   Sweet Green'

'Sugar Bon'

'Sugar Rae'
'Sugar Snap'

Broad beans (*Vicia faba*)

These annual plants are also known as fava beans. They range in height from 30cm (12in) for dwarf cultivars to about 1.5m (5ft), with an average spread of 45cm (18in). Broad beans are grouped according to the time they take to mature. The broad pods are up to 2.5cm (1in) wide and 7–15cm (3–6in) long, with green, white, or pinkish-red seeds 2–2.5cm (^{3}/$_4$–1in) long. The immature bean seeds, as well as the young pods and leafy shoot tips, may be cooked. The shelled beans freeze well.

Broad beans are a cool-season crop, growing satisfactorily only at temperatures below about 15°C (59°F). Some cultivars are very hardy, the immature plants surviving -10°C (14°F) on well-drained soil. Some that are adapted to higher temperatures have recently been bred. Grow spring and early summer sowings in an open site, and autumn sowings for overwintering in a sheltered site, in reasonably fertile, well-manured soil. Rotate broad bean crops (see p.307). The plants need low nitrogen levels (see p.314) because their root nodules fix atmospheric nitrogen.

Sowing and planting
Sow seed *in situ* in spring and early summer as soon as the ground is workable. Seed germinates at fairly low temperatures. For an early crop, sow seed in late autumn to early

DWARF BROAD BEANS

winter of the previous year – the plants need only be 2.5cm (1in) high before winter. In very cold areas seed may be sown indoors in winter and transplanted outside in spring after the risk of frost has passed.

Sow seed about 4cm (1^1/$_2$in) deep, spaced about 23cm (9in) apart each way. Grow either in double rows, with 90cm (3ft) between the pairs of rows or evenly spaced in blocks across a bed. The taller cultivars may be supported with strands of wire attached to strong canes or poles placed around the rows or blocks of plants. If necessary, dwarf cultivars may be supported with twigs to keep their pods clear of the ground. Overwintering crops and those sown in

early spring may be protected with cloches or floating mulches in the early stages of growth.

Routine cultivation
Do not allow the plants to dry out; water as for French beans (see p.342). Once flowering starts, pinch out the growing tips to encourage pods to form and to combat blackfly. Earth up overwintering plants to protect them against the elements.

Pests and diseases
Mice (p.566), jays (563), wood pigeons (p.549), tropical root rots

PINCHING OUT

When the beans are in full flower, pinch out the growing tip of each plant. This will remove any blackfly and concentrate the plant's energy into producing beans.

(p.565), blackfly (see "Aphids", p.550), chocolate spot (p.553), and foot and root rots (p.558) may affect broad beans.

Harvesting and storing
Harvest broad beans that were sown in spring after 12–16 weeks, and those sown in autumn after 28–35 weeks. Pick them while the pods are plump with the swelling beans and before they become leathery. The beans may be frozen, or dried at the end of the season for use during the winter months as for French beans (see p.342).

RECOMMENDED BROAD BEANS

Dwarf
'Bonny Lad'
'Sutton'

'Red Epicure'

Early
'Aquadulce Claudia' (autumn sowing only)
'Express'
'Red Epicure'
'Witkiem Major'

'Witkiem Major'

Late
'Hylon'
'Jubilee Hysor'
'Relon'
   (longpod)

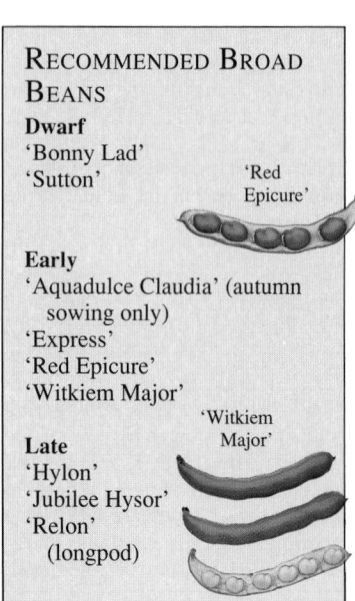

Bulb and stem vegetables

VEGETABLES grown for their bulbs or stems include members of the onion family as well as a varied group of other plants that, with the exception of Florence fennel, are mostly hardy and slow-maturing. Celeriac, kohl rabi, and Florence fennel form swollen stems just above ground level, rather than true bulbs. The onion family should be rotated as one group; for rotation groups for the other vegetables, see p.307. Both asparagus and rhubarb are perennial vegetables that should be planted in permanent beds that have been specially prepared for them.

Leeks · Garlic · Spring onions · Bulb onions · Florence fennel · Celery · Red bulb onions · Asparagus · Shallots

Bulb onions (*Allium cepa*)

These are grown as annuals. The bulbs may be rounded, flattened, or have a long, torpedo shape. They normally have brown or yellow skins with white flesh, although some have red skin and pinkish-white flesh; the leaves grow 15–45cm (6–18in) long. Immature and mature bulbs are eaten either raw or cooked. Some cultivars are suitable for storage. The green-leaved thinnings may be used as spring onions (see p.346).

Bulb onions are a cool-season, frost-tolerant crop, growing best at 13–24°C (55–75°F). Cool temperatures are required in the early stages of growth. Cultivars need different daylengths in order for the bulbs to swell; long-day types should be chosen for northerly latitudes, and short-day types for southerly latitudes (see also "Daylength", p.307).

Grow them in an open site, on fertile, medium to light soil that is well drained. Prepare the soil by digging in a good deal of well-rotted manure, preferably the autumn before planting. Do not plant on newly manured ground. A general feed may be worked into the seedbed before sowing. They have low nitrogen requirements (see p.314).

Sowing and planting
Onions may be raised from seed or sets (small bulbs specially grown and harvested immature the previous year). Seed is cheaper but slower to develop; sets are easier to grow but usually only available for certain cultivars. Bulb onions require a long growing season, particularly if large bulbs are required or if they are to be stored.

Sow in spring when the soil is workable, on a firm seedbed, sowing seed very thinly 1cm (½in) deep, in rows 23–30cm (9–12in) apart. Thin out the seedlings in stages. For the highest yield of medium-sized onions, space 4cm (1½in) apart; for larger onions, thin seedlings to 5–10cm (2–4in) apart.

To extend the growing season in northern latitudes, start under cover in seed trays or modules at temperatures of 10–15°C (50–59°F) from late winter to early spring. Harden off seedlings at the two-leaf stage and plant out at the appropriate spacing. Modules may also be multi-sown with five seeds per section and each section planted out as a unit, with 25cm (10in) between units (see also *Transplanting Leeks*, p.347).

Certain cultivars may be sown in summer or autumn to overwinter for earlier crops the following year. This is inadvisable where winters are very severe or very wet since seeds may rot before germination. Traditional, summer-sown cultivars are reasonably hardy and may be sown *in situ* in late summer, thinning to 2.5cm (1in) apart in autumn and in stages to the final spacing in spring. Japanese overwintering onions are also suitable for sowing at this time; they are hardier than other bulb onions, but are unsuitable for storage. The precise sowing date for these is critical. Sow during the summer at the recommended date for the area, spacing and thinning as above.

Most sets are planted in the early spring. If using heat-treated sets, consult the suppliers for planting times. Plant at the above spacing in shallow furrows so that the tips protrude just above the soil. Recently introduced sets for planting during autumn may be available.

Routine cultivation
Keep the site weed-free, especially when the onions are young and susceptible to competition from weeds. Onions are fairly shallow-rooted and need little water once established, except in very dry conditions. Overwintering onions may be given a nitrogenous fertilizer or organic liquid feed if necessary in spring.

Pests and diseases
Onion flies (p.567), bean seed flies (p.570), onion white rot (p.567), downy mildew (p.550), and, in storage, onion neck rot (p.567) are common problems that affect onions.

Harvesting and storing
Spring-sown bulb onions will take 12–18 weeks to mature; summer-sown onions up to 42 weeks. Pull or lift them as needed to use fresh.

For storage, wait until the leaves have died back naturally (do not bend them over by hand), and then carefully uproot all the onions. In sunny conditions, leave them in the sun to dry for about ten days, either hung in nets or supported off the ground on an upturned seed tray to allow maximum ventilation. In wet conditions, hang them in a greenhouse. The outer skins and leaves must all be thoroughly dry before the bulbs are put into storage.

Handle the bulbs gently since any bruises may encourage storage rots. Do not store onions that are bull-necked; these should always be used first. Store onions either hanging in nets or plaits (see *Storing Strings of Onions*, p.316) or packed carefully in layers in boxes. They must be kept at 0–7°C (32–45°F) and in low humidity (i.e. below 40 per cent). Average storage life is three to six months, depending on the cultivar.

RECOMMENDED BULB ONIONS

Onions for autumn harvesting
'Giant Fen Globe'
'Rijnsburger Balstora'
'Rijnsburger Robusta'
'Sturon'
'Stuttgarter Giant'

Red onions (use fresh or store)
'Long Red Florence'

'Long Red Florence'

'Mammoth Red Onion'
'Red Baron'

Traditional and Japanese overwintering onions
'Express Yellow'
'Imai Early Yellow'
'Kaizuka Extra'
'Reliance'
'Southport Red Globe'

Sets for autumn planting
'Unwin's First Early'

STORING ONIONS IN A BOX

Prepare onions carefully for storing. Bull-necked onions (those with thick necks above the bulbs, see far right) should be rejected. Be careful not to damage any onions for storing as this encourages rot. Place them in layers in a box and store them in a place that is well ventilated and frost-free.

Spring onions

Traditional European spring onions, or bunching onions, are cultivars of bulb onions suitable for using young when the green leaves are 15cm (6in) tall, with a whitened shank and tiny bulb. A widely grown cultivar is 'White Lisbon'. For climate, soil requirements, and pests and diseases see "Bulb onions", p.345. Lime acid soil (see p.531).

In spring, sow thinly *in situ*, in rows 10cm (4in) apart, or bands 7cm (3in) wide and 15cm (6in) apart. For continuous crops, sow every three weeks in summer. Overwintering cultivars (e.g. 'White Lisbon Winter Hardy') may be sown in late summer for an early spring crop; protect them in winter with cloches. Water the onions in dry conditions. Spring onions are ready for pulling after two months.

THINNING SPRING ONIONS

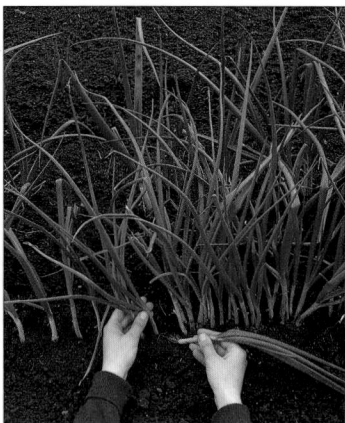

If densely sown, harvest seedling spring onions to leave the others spaced 2.5cm (1in) apart. Those remaining will continue to grow and may be harvested when required.

Pickling onions

These bulb onion cultivars produce small, white bulbs (also known as mini-onions) in northerly latitudes, and larger bulbs in southerly latitudes. They may be used when they reach about thumb-nail size, either fresh or for pickling. Cultivars include 'Barletta' and 'Paris Silver Skin'. They prefer fertile soil, but tolerate fairly poor soil. For climate, cultivation, and pests and diseases, see "Bulb onions", p.345.

In spring sow seed *in situ*, either broadcast or in bands about 10cm (4in) wide, spacing seeds 1cm ($\frac{1}{2}$in) apart. Thin them only if larger onions are required. Harvest them after about eight weeks when the foliage has died back; use them fresh, or dry and store as for bulb onions (see p.345) until required for pickling.

PICKLING ONIONS

Shallots (*Allium cepa* Aggregatum Group)

These distinctly flavoured, onion-shaped bulbs form clumps of about a dozen bulbs. There are yellow- and red-skinned forms; all may be used fresh or after storing, and are eaten raw or cooked. The leaves of young shallots may be used fresh as spring onions.

Climate and soil requirements, routine cultivation, and pests and diseases are as for bulb onions (see p.345). Shallots are very hardy. Buy virus-free sets that are ideally about 2cm ($\frac{3}{4}$in) in diameter. Plant in early spring or during winter in

mild areas. Plant as for bulb onion sets (see p.345), spacing the sets about 18cm (7in) apart each way. Each set will develop into a clump, maturing in early summer. For an early crop of green leaves, plant small sets in autumn, spacing them in the ground, or in seed trays under cover about 2.5cm (1in) apart.

Harvest green leaves as needed. For good-sized bulbs, do not pick the leaves; lift the bulbs once the foliage has died down. To store them, dry as for bulb onions (see p.345); good stocks store for up to a year.

PLANTING SHALLOTS

Make a drill 1cm ($\frac{1}{2}$in) deep. Push the sets into the drill about 18cm (7in) apart so that the tips show above the soil.

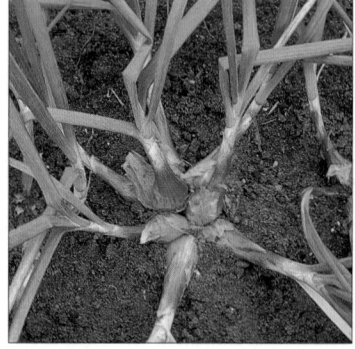

SHALLOTS

European Welsh onions (*Allium fistulosum*)

These onions are very hardy perennials. They have hollow leaves up to 45cm (18in) tall and 1cm ($\frac{1}{2}$in) in diameter, growing in clumps of 23cm (9in) diameter on average; the bases of the leaves are thickened at and below ground level. The leaves remain green all year, even at temperatures as low as -10°C (14°F), so they are a useful winter vegetable. The leaves and tiny bulbs may be eaten either raw or cooked.

Climate and soil requirements, cultivation, and pests and diseases are as for bulb onions (see p.345). Sow seed *in situ* in spring or summer in rows about 30cm (12in) apart. Thin the seedlings in stages until they are about 23cm (9in) apart, or propagate by dividing established clumps and carefully replanting the younger, outer sections of the clumps to the above spacing. Leaves may be

WELSH ONIONS

harvested from 24 weeks after sowing; cut individual leaves as required, or pull up part or all of the clump. Established clumps can become very thick and should be divided every two or three years. Welsh onions do not store well.

Oriental bunching onions

These have been developed from European Welsh onions. They are perennials usually grown as annuals or biennials for harvesting at any stage from seedlings to large plants. Mature plants have thickened, white shafts 2.5cm (1in) in diameter and 15cm (6in) high. All parts are edible. There are cultivars for planting and harvesting year-round, and for a wide range of climatic conditions.

For soil requirements, see "Bulb onions" (p.345). Sow seed *in situ* in spring and summer, in rows 30cm (12in) apart. Thin out in stages up to 15cm (6in) apart, depending on the size required. Seed may also be sown in trays and planted out. Sow the hardiest cultivars, such as 'White

Evergreen' or 'Ishikura', in autumn and overwinter to use in early spring. Some cultivars, such as 'Ishikura', may be earthed up several times during growth to obtain long, white shafts. Young leaves may be picked four weeks after sowing.

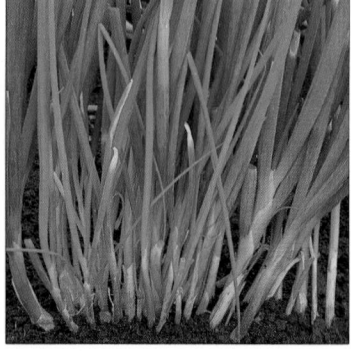

ORIENTAL BUNCHING ONIONS

Leeks (*Allium porrum*)

These are biennials, grown as annuals, reaching 45cm (18in) tall and 15cm (6in) across. The edible part is the sweetly flavoured, thick, white shank that forms below long, blue-green leaves. This may be blanched by earthing it up or by deep planting. Leeks with short, thick shanks are called pot leeks. All types are used cooked, as a vegetable or in soups.

Leeks are a cool-season crop, and grow best below 24°C (75°F), but will tolerate higher temperatures if kept moist. Cultivars range from early and moderately hardy to late and very hardy. Grow in open sites on fertile, moisture-retentive soil, working in plenty of manure or compost and a nitrogenous fertilizer if the soil is low in nitrogen (high levels are needed; see p.314). Do not plant on compacted soils. Leeks must be rotated (see p.307).

Sowing and planting

Leeks need a long growing season; start them as early in the year as possible, sowing in succession. Sow 1cm (^{1}/$_2$in) deep in an outdoor seedbed for transplanting when 20cm (8in) tall. Alternatively sow *in situ* in rows 30cm (12in) apart. Thin or

LEEK PLANTS

Fill a module with seed compost to within 1cm (^{1}/$_2$in) of the top. Sow 4 leek seeds in each module on the surface of the compost. Cover with a thin layer of compost, and water.

transplant the seedlings at the three-leaf stage to 15cm (6in) apart. Use closer spacing if smaller leeks are preferred. For well-blanched stems, make holes 15–20cm (6–8in) deep with a dibber and drop a seedling in each, making sure that the roots reach the soil at the base. Water gently, then allow soil to fall in around the plants as they grow. Leeks may also be planted on the flat and blanched by hoeing up soil around the stems, 5cm (2in) at a time, as they grow.

To extend the growing season, sow under cover as for bulb onions (see p.345). Leeks respond well to being multi-sown in modules with up to four seeds per cell. Plant out the groups of seedlings at an even spacing of 23cm (9in).

Routine cultivation

Water thoroughly until the leeks are well established, and thereafter only in exceptionally dry conditions. Keep beds weed-free. Mulch to retain soil moisture if necessary.

Pests and diseases

Stem and bulb eelworms (see "Eelworms", p.556), onion flies (p.567), rusts (p.552), and onion white rot (p.567) may be troublesome.

Each section of a module may be planted out as a whole; plant the clumps 23cm (9in) apart.

Leeks sown outdoors may be transplanted to their final position in holes 15–20cm (6–8in) deep and 10–15cm (4–6in) apart.

Harvesting and storing

Leeks may be harvested 16–20 weeks after sowing but can stand for many months. Lift them as required from summer onwards; the hardy cultivars may be lifted throughout

To store outdoors, lift the leeks and lean them against one side of a "V"-shaped trench. Cover the roots and white stems with soil and firm lightly. Lift and use as required.

winter into spring, except in very severe climates. Leeks do not store well out of the ground. If the site they occupy is required, prolong the season by digging them up and heeling them in elsewhere.

RECOMMENDED LEEKS

'Autumn Mammoth – Argenta' l
'Autumn Mammoth – Goliath' e, m, l
'Autumn Mammoth – Pancho' e
'Blauwgroene Winter – Alaska' l
'Cortina' m
'Gennevilliers – Splendid' e
'King Richard' e
'Swiss Giant – Albinstar' e, m
'Swiss Giant – Pancho' e
'Tilina' e
'Wintra' l
'Zorba' e

KEY
e *early*
m *mid-season*
l *late*

'Zorba'

Garlic (*Allium sativum*)

Biennials grown as annuals, garlic plants grow up to 60cm (2ft) tall with a spread of about 15cm (6in). Each produces an underground bulb up to 5cm (2in) in diameter. There are pink- and white-skinned forms and many selections are available that are adapted to different climatic zones. Garlic is grown mainly for the strongly flavoured cloves that form the bulb and may be stored for a year-round supply. The cloves are

used either fresh or after storing for seasoning, and may be eaten both cooked and raw.

Garlic tolerates a wide range of climates, but needs a period of one to two months at about 0–10°C (32–50°F) in winter. Some variants are extremely hardy; use those recommended for your area. Garlic grows best in an open, sunny position on light soil that does not have to be very fertile, so do not grow it

on freshly manured ground. Good drainage is vital. Garlic needs very low levels of nitrogen (see p.314).

Sowing and planting

For planting, split off individual cloves at least 1cm (^{1}/$_2$in) in diameter from a mature bulb. Always use healthy, virus-free stock. To produce large bulbs, garlic needs a long growing season, so wherever possible plant cloves in the autumn. In

very cold areas and on heavy soils, delay planting until the early spring, or plant the cloves in modules in winter, one per section. Then place the modules in a sheltered position outdoors to provide them with the necessary cold period. Plant them out in the ground after they have started to sprout in spring.

Plant the cloves upright with the flat base-plates downwards, at about twice their own depth. Space them

PLANTING GARLIC CLOVES IN MODULES

Plant one clove 2.5cm (1in) deep in each section of a module. Cover the cloves with more compost.

about 18cm (7in) apart each way or 10cm (4in) apart in rows 30cm (12in) apart. The bulbs tend to push themselves upwards as they grow.

Routine cultivation

Little attention is required during growth other than keeping the beds free of weeds. For pests and diseases that may affect garlic, see "Bulb onions", p.345.

Harvesting and storing

Garlic takes between 16 and 36 weeks to mature, depending on the variant and when it has been planted.

Uproot the plants as soon as the leaves have started to fade so that the bulbs do not resprout; if they are allowed to resprout they are much more likely to rot when stored.

Dry them thoroughly after lifting as for bulb onions (see p.345). Handle the bulbs very carefully when preparing them for storage to avoid bruising. Store the bulbs hanging in bunches or plaits made with the dried leaves or place them loose on trays kept in dry conditions at 5–10°C (41–50°F). Garlic may be stored for up to ten months, depending on the variant and storage conditions.

STORING GARLIC

After harvesting the garlic, tie the leaves loosely together with raffia or plait them. Then hang each bunch in a cool, dry place.

Celery (*Apium graveolens*)

A biennial plant, celery grows to 30–60cm (12–24in) tall, with a spread of 30cm (12in). Traditional trench celery has large, white, pink, or red stems that are blanched before use. Self-blanching types have creamy-yellow stems that may be partially blanched. American green types have green stems. Intermediates are also available. Celery stalks are eaten raw or cooked and the leaves used as a seasoning or garnish.

As a temperate-climate crop, celery grows best at 15–21°C (59–70°F). Depending on the cultivar and conditions, it tolerates light or moderate frost; trench cultivars with red stems are hardiest. Some have improved resistance to bolting. Grow celery in an open site in fertile, moisture-retentive, but well-drained soil; lime acid soil (see p.531). Rotate celery (see p.307), but do not plant it near parsnips since both are susceptible to celery flies. Dig plenty of well-rotted organic matter into the soil before planting. For trench celery,

CELERY SEEDLINGS IN A BLOCK

prepare a trench 38cm (15in) wide and 30cm (12in) deep in autumn before planting; work in manure or compost, and replace the soil to ground level. Celery needs high nitrogen levels (see p.314).

Sowing and planting

Sow in spring *in situ* after all risk of frost is past, or indoors in seed trays or modules at 15°C (59°F) no more than ten weeks before the last expected frost. Use seed treated with a

fungicide to avoid celery leaf spot. Sprinkle it onto the compost or cover it shallowly as light is needed for germination. Do not sow too early; plants may bolt if the temperature falls below 10°C (50°F).

Thin out seedlings with four to six true leaves; plant out indoor-sown seedlings after all risk of frost is past. Reject any with blistered leaves. Plant self-blanching types 23cm (9in) apart in blocks to increase natural blanching. Young plants may be covered with cloches or floating films which should be removed after a month. Plant trench celery seedlings 38cm (15in) apart in single rows. They may be planted in trenches, or on the flat.

Routine cultivation

Celery requires steady growth, with no checks from water shortage or sudden drops in temperature. Apply a nitrogenous fertilizer or organic liquid feed about a month after planting. Once the plants are established, water them weekly at a rate of 22 litres/sq m (5 gallons/sq yd).

To sweeten self-blanching types, tuck a thick layer of loose straw around the plants when they are 20cm (8in) tall. To blanch celery in a trench, tie the stems loosely together with soft string and fill in the trench gradually, earthing up the stems as they grow. If planted on the flat, wrap purpose-made collars or 23cm (9in) strips of heavy, light-proof paper around the stems when the plants are 30cm (12in) tall. To extend the blanched area, add a second collar three weeks later. In winter, cover trench celery with straw or bracken to protect against frost.

Pests and diseases

Slugs (p.548), celery flies (see "Leaf miners", p.551), carrot flies (p.564), boron deficiency (p.558), fungal leaf

RECOMMENDED CELERY

Self-blanching
'Celebrity'
'Ivory Tower'
'Lathom's Self Blanching'

Trench
'Giant Pink'
'Giant White'
'Martine' (red)

American green
'Hopkins Fenlander'
'Tall Utah'

'Tall Utah'

LIFTING CELERY

Lift self-blanching celery plants before the first frosts. Clear the straw from around the stem and use a fork to uproot the whole plant.

spots (p.552), and violet root rot (p.565) are the most common pests and diseases.

Harvesting and storing

Harvest self-blanching and green celery 11–16 weeks after planting and trench celery in late autumn. Cut the stalks before they become pithy. Before frost threatens, lift and store the remaining plants in high humidity in a cool, frost-free place. They will keep for several weeks.

BLANCHING CELERY

Light-proof collar fastened with string

Second collar added as stems develop

1 When the celery is about 30cm (12in) tall, wrap the stems loosely with light-proof paper so that the leaves are still exposed to the light.

2 As the stems continue to grow, a second collar may be added to blanch the new growth.

Celeriac (*Apium graveolens* var. *rapaceum*)

This is a biennial plant that grows about 30cm (12in) high with a spread of 38cm (15in). The swollen "bulb" at the stem base is cooked and also grated raw in salads. The leaves are used for seasoning and garnishing.

Celeriac is a cool-temperate crop, withstanding temperatures of -10°C (14°F) if the crowns are protected with straw. Plants tolerate light shade

PLANTING OUT CELERIAC FROM A MODULE

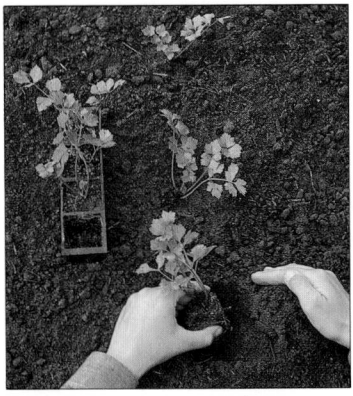

Plant out celeriac from a module when it is 8–10cm (3–4in) high with 6 or 7 leaves. Space the young plants 30–38cm (12–15in) apart; take care not to bury the crowns.

if the soil is moist. For soil requirements, see "Celery", p.348; celeriac needs low nitrogen levels (see p.314).

Sowing and planting

Celeriac needs a six-month growing season for the bulb to develop. Germination may be erratic. Sow seed indoors in early spring, preferably in modules. If using trays, prick out the seedlings to 5–7cm (2–3in) apart or pot them singly into small pots or modules. Harden off the young plants before planting out when they are about 7cm (3in) tall. Space them 30–38cm (12–15in) apart with their crowns at soil level, not buried.

Routine cultivation

Mulch after planting, and water well, especially in dry conditions. Plants may be fed during the growing season (see "Celery", p.348). Towards the end of the summer, remove some of the coarse, outer leaves to expose the crowns; this encourages the bulbs to develop. To protect from frost, tuck a loose layer of straw 10–15cm (4–6in) thick around the crowns.

Pests and diseases

Celeriac may be affected by the same pests and diseases as celery (see p.348), but is normally healthy.

CULTIVATING AND PROTECTING CELERIAC

1 *Towards the end of the summer, as the swollen stem bases develop, remove a few of the outer leaves to expose the crowns.*

2 *Before the first frosts, mulch around the base of the plants with a 15cm (6in) layer of straw to protect the crowns.*

Harvesting and storing

Celeriac may be harvested from late summer until the following spring. The bulbs are ready for use when they are 7–13cm (3–5in) in diameter.

The flavour is best and the bulbs will keep longer if the roots are left in the ground over winter. Where winters are very severe, dig up the plants in early winter without damaging the bulbs; trim off the outer leaves, leaving a central tuft, and store the plants in boxes of damp soil in a cool, frost-free place.

RECOMMENDED CELERIAC

'Balder'
'Marble Ball'
'Monarch'
'Snow White'
'Tellus'

'Monarch'

Asparagus (*Asparagus officinalis*)

Asparagus is perennial and may be productive for up to 20 years. Its light, fern-like foliage grows over 90cm (3ft) tall, with a spread of about 45cm (18in). It is cultivated for the delicious young shoots or spears that push through the ground in spring. Male and female plants are available; the females produce berries. Male plants are higher yielding; very productive, all-male,

F1 hybrid cultivars are now also readily available. Asparagus is normally eaten cooked.

Asparagus is a cool-season crop, growing best at 16–24°C (61–75°F) in regions with cool winters that provide the necessary dormant period. Choose an open site, avoiding exposed situations and frost pockets. Asparagus tolerates a very wide range of moderately fertile soils

although acid soils should be limed (see p.531). Good drainage is essential. Do not make a new asparagus bed where asparagus has been grown before, since soil-borne diseases may persist. Remove all perennial weeds from the site and prepare the ground by digging it over and working in manure or compost. Asparagus may also be grown in raised beds to improve drainage. It has low nitrogen requirements (see p.314).

Sowing and planting

Asparagus is traditionally grown by planting one-year-old purchased plants or "crowns" in spring. The crowns are fleshy and must never be allowed to dry out before planting.

Grow them about 38cm (15in) apart, either in single or double rows, with the rows spaced 30cm (12in) apart. Plant the crowns about 10cm (4in) deep by first making a small trench with a central, mounded ridge along the flat base. Spread out the roots evenly over the ridge and cover them with soil to the level of the crowns. Fill in the rest of the trench

RECOMMENDED ASPARAGUS

Traditional
'Connover's Colossal'
'Giant Mammoth'
'Martha Washington'

All-male cultivars
'Angela'
'Cito'
'Franklin'
'Lucullus'
'Sorbonne'

'Lucullus'

with soil gradually as the stems grow, always leaving 8–10cm (3–4in) of the stems exposed.

Raising asparagus from seed is cheaper, but the results are more variable. Sow seed 2.5cm (1in) deep *in situ* in spring, and thin out to about 7cm (3in) apart. Plant out the

PLANTING ASPARAGUS CROWNS

Dig a trench about 30cm (12in) wide and 20cm (8in) deep with a central, mounded ridge that is 10cm (4in) high. Place the asparagus crowns on the ridge about 38cm (15in) apart. Spread the roots out evenly and cover them with about 5cm (2in) of soil to the level of the crowns.

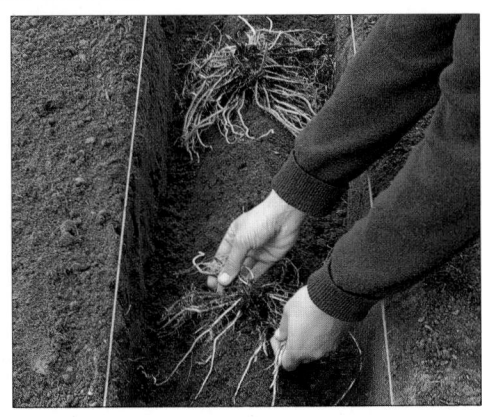

CUTTING BACK ASPARAGUS STEMS

Using secateurs, cut back the stems in autumn to within about 2.5cm (1in) of ground level.

largest the following spring. Alternatively, sow seed indoors in modules in early spring at 13–16°C (55–61°F). The seedlings grow rapidly, and may be planted out in permanent positions in early summer.

Routine cultivation

Asparagus requires little attention other than keeping the beds weed-free. Hoe shallowly to avoid damaging the roots. When the foliage turns yellow in autumn, cut the stems back to about 2.5cm (1in) above the soil.

Pests and diseases

Slugs (p.548) at an early stage and asparagus beetles (p.548) on more mature plants are the most serious

pests. The soil-borne fungal disease violet root rot (p.565) may destroy plants in long-established beds.

Harvesting and storing

Asparagus must be allowed to build into a strong plant before it is harvested in mid-spring. Good, modern cultivars may be cut lightly in the second season. The following year, limit cutting to a six-week period; subsequently, cutting may continue over eight weeks if the plants are growing well. Harvest the spears when they are about 15cm (6in) high and fairly thick. Cut at an angle, taking care not to damage other nearby spears. Remaining spears will continue to grow. Asparagus freezes well.

HARVESTING ASPARAGUS

When the spears are 12–15cm (5–6in) high, cut each stalk 2.5–5cm (1–2in) below soil level.

Kohl rabi (*Brassica oleracea* Gongylodes Group)

These annual plants from the brassica family are grown for the white-fleshed, turnip-like, swollen stem or "bulb" that forms just above ground. Kohl rabi reaches 30cm (12in) high and has an average spread of 30cm (12in). The outer skin is green (sometimes described as "white") or purple. The bulbs are nutritious, well flavoured, and used cooked or raw.

Kohl rabi is a cool-season crop, growing best at 18–25°C (64–77°F). Young plants tend to bolt prematurely in temperatures below about 10°C (50°F). For soil requirements, see "Siting Western brassicas", p.317. Kohl rabi grows well in light soils and withstands drought better than most brassicas. It has low nitrogen requirements (see p.314).

Sowing and planting

In mild climates, sow seed outdoors in succession from spring through to late summer, using the hardier pur-

ple forms for late sowings. In hot climates, sow in spring and autumn. Sow *in situ* either in rows about 30cm (12in) apart, thinning seedlings to about 18cm (7in) apart, or space the seeds about 25cm (10in) apart in

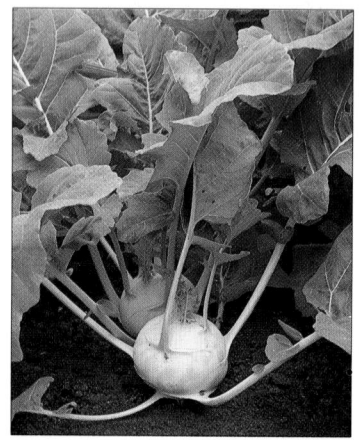

GREEN KOHL RABI

each direction. Under cover, sow earlier in gentle heat in trays or modules. Plant out seedlings when they are no more than 5cm (2in) high. Protect early outdoor crops with cloches or floating mulches.

Routine cultivation

Kohl rabi is fast-maturing; little attention is required during growth other than keeping beds weed-free.

Pests and diseases

Flea beetles (p.548), cabbage root flies (p.564), and clubroot (p.564) may affect kohl rabi. See also "Cultivating Western brassicas", p.317.

Harvesting and storing

Depending on the cultivar and season, kohl rabi may be ready for cutting between five and nine weeks after sowing. Traditional cultivars should be eaten when they are no larger than tennis balls or they will

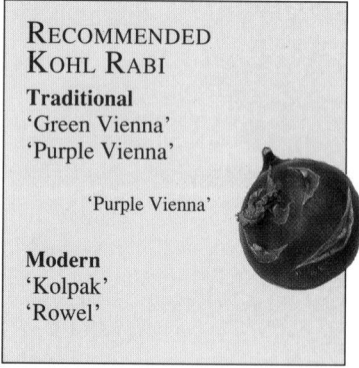

RECOMMENDED KOHL RABI

Traditional
'Green Vienna'
'Purple Vienna'

'Purple Vienna'

Modern
'Kolpak'
'Rowel'

become woody; improved, modern cultivars are still tender at a diameter of about 10cm (4in).

Leave later crops in the earth until heavy frost threatens, since the flavour deteriorates once lifted. In cold areas, lift in autumn. Leave a central tuft of leaves on each bulb to help keep them fresh; store them for up to two months in boxes of moist sand.

Florence fennel (*Foeniculum vulgare* var. *dulce*)

Grown as an annual, Florence, or sweet, fennel is distinct from the perennial herb fennel. The plants grow up to about 60cm (2ft) high and have a spread of about 45cm (18in). The anise-flavoured, flattened "bulb" of overlapping scales that develops at the base of the leaf stalks is eaten cooked or raw. The highly decorative fern-like foliage may be used as a flavouring or garnish.

Florence fennel tolerates a wide range of climates, from temperate to subtropical. It thrives at a warm, even temperature, but mature plants can withstand a light frost. Grow it in an open situation, in very fertile,

moisture-retentive, but well-drained soil into which plenty of humus has been worked. Florence fennel grows well in light soils but must not be allowed to dry out. It has low nitrogen requirements (see p.314).

Sowing and planting

In cool, northern latitudes, sow seed from early to mid-summer; traditional cultivars are likely to bolt if sown in spring, so use modern, bolt-resistant cultivars for earlier sowings. In warmer climates, sow in spring for a summer crop and again in late summer for an autumn crop. Florence fennel does not transplant

well and may bolt prematurely if checked, so either sow seed *in situ* or in modules for transplanting when the seedlings have no more than four leaves. Space the young seedlings about 30cm (12in) apart each way. Early and late crops may be protected from the frost by covering with cloches or floating mulches.

Routine cultivation

Little attention is required; keep beds weed-free. Florence fennel needs to be kept moist, so water thoroughly and mulch. When bulbs start to swell, earth them up to half their height to make them whiter and sweeter.

FLORENCE FENNEL

HARVESTING FLORENCE FENNEL

1 *Cut the fennel bulb about 2.5cm (1in) above soil level. Leave the base in position.*

2 *Feathery leaves will usually sprout from the base of the stem within a few weeks.*

Pests and diseases

Florence fennel rarely suffers from any pests or diseases. Most problems stem from lack of water, fluctuating temperatures, or from transplanting, all of which may cause bolting.

Harvesting and storing

Harvest the bulbs when they are well rounded, about 15 weeks after sowing or two to three weeks after earthing up. Pull them up whole, or cut across the bulbs about 2.5cm (1in) above ground level. The stump will normally resprout to produce small sprigs of ferny foliage that may be used for flavouring or as a garnish. Florence fennel does not store well; eat it as fresh as possible.

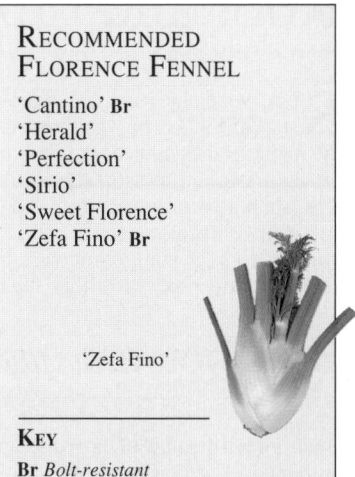
Rhubarb (*Rheum* x *cultorum*)

This perennial lasts over 20 years in good conditions. Rhubarb grows about 60cm (24in) or more high and up to 2m (6ft) across. The leaves may be 45cm (18in) wide. The pale-green or pinkish-red leaf stalks, which may be 60cm (2ft) long, are harvested young and used cooked.

Rhubarb is a temperate-climate crop and does not thrive at high temperatures; the roots survive at least -15°C (5°F). Recommended cultivars include 'Champagne', 'Timperley Early', and 'Victoria'. It grows on a wide range of soils, as long as they are rich and well drained. Before planting, dig in plenty of manure or compost. Rhubarb needs medium nitrogen levels when young and very high nitrogen once it is mature (see p.314).

Sowing and planting

Rhubarb is normally propagated by planting "sets", each consisting of a fleshy rootstock with at least one bud. Sets are about 10cm (4in) in diameter. Plant them in the dormant season from autumn to spring, preferably autumn. Either buy virus-free sets, or separate a set from a healthy, two- or three-year-old plant, once its leaves have died back, by lifting the plant and slicing through the crown; replant the parent. On light soils, plant the set so that 2.5cm (1in) of soil covers the buds; on heavy or wet soils, plant with the buds just above ground level. Space the plants 90cm (3ft) apart.

Rhubarb may also be raised from seed, although the results are variable. Sow seed in spring, 2.5cm (1in) deep in rows 30cm (12in) apart, in a seedbed outdoors. Thin the seedlings to 15cm (6in) apart, and plant out the strongest-looking ones in their permanent positions in autumn, or in spring the following year.

Routine cultivation

Mulch the plants heavily, and water them in dry weather. Apply a heavy dressing of manure or compost every

DIVIDING RHUBARB

1 *Lift or expose the crown. Cut through it carefully using a spade, ensuring there is at least 1 main bud on each section. Prepare the soil by digging in manure.*

2 *Replant the sections (sets) 75–90cm (2¹/₂–3ft) apart. Fill in around each root so that the bud is just above the surface. Firm, and rake around the bud.*

autumn or spring and a nitrogenous dressing or organic liquid feed in spring. Remove any flowering stems.

Rhubarb may be forced in the dark to obtain very tender sticks. Cover the dormant crowns in late winter with a 10cm (4in) layer of straw or leaves, then a forcing pot, or a large bucket, at least 45cm (18in) high; leave this on for about four weeks until stems are large enough.

Pests and diseases

Honey fungus (p.565), crown rot (p.569), and viruses (p.553) may attack established plants.

Harvesting and storing

Harvest in spring and early summer. With set-raised plants, start pulling lightly the first year after planting; with seed-raised plants, wait until the second year. In subsequent years, pull heavily until the quality starts to deteriorate in summer. Forced stems are ready to harvest about three weeks earlier than unforced ones.

FORCING RHUBARB

For an earlier, tender crop, cover the dormant buds (see upper inset) in winter with straw or leaves inside a forcing pot or any large container that excludes the light. The plant will produce tender, pink stems a few weeks later (see lower inset).

HARVESTING RHUBARB

When the rhubarb stems are ready, they may be harvested by gripping each stem at the base and twisting it while pulling it upwards and outwards.

Root and tuberous vegetables

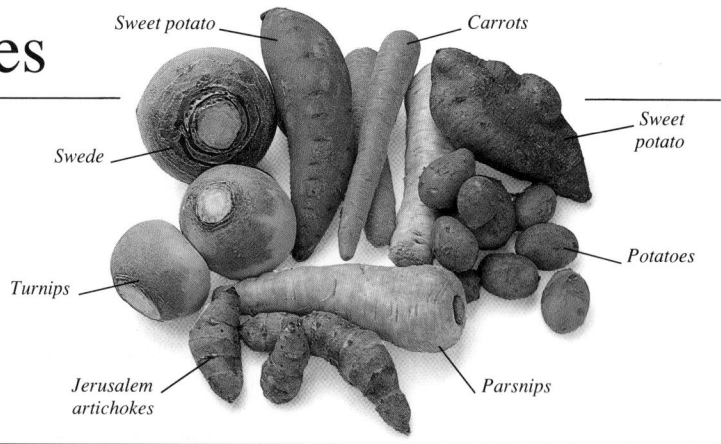

Sweet potato — Carrots

Swede

Sweet potato

Turnips

Jerusalem artichokes

Parsnips

Potatoes

Root vegetables are the mainstay of the kitchen garden. As the name suggests, most are grown for their swollen roots or tubers. A few, such as turnips, beetroot, and cocoyams, are also used for their young, leafy growth; some radish cultivars also produce edible seed pods. A variety of root vegetables may be grown and harvested in succession for a steady supply; many store quite easily, sometimes still in the ground, for use throughout the winter. Salsify and scorzonera may both be overwintered for their flowering shoots, produced in the spring.

Beetroot (*Beta vulgaris* subsp. *vulgaris*)

Beetroot is a biennial plant grown as an annual. It grows to about 15cm (6in) tall and about 12cm (5in) across. The swollen root forms at ground level and may be round, flat, or cylindrical. It is on average 5cm (2in) in diameter, and about 10cm (4in) or more deep in the long forms. The flesh is normally red but may be yellow, white, or even have concentric pink and white rings. The skin is similarly red, yellow, or off-white. The sweetly flavoured roots are mainly used cooked, either fresh or stored, but may also be pickled. The fresh, young leaves (tops) may be used as greens.

Beetroot grows best and develops the deepest colours in cool, even temperatures, ideally of 16°C (61°F). Grow it in an open site on rich, light soil with high nitrogen levels (see p.314). Apply half the nitrogen before sowing. Lime very acid soils.

THINNING SEEDLINGS

When the beetroot seedlings have produced 3 or 4 leaves, thin clumps growing close together to the required spacing by nipping off the top green leaves at soil level without disturbing the remaining seedlings.

Sowing and planting

Beetroot "seeds" each contain a cluster of two or three seeds, the seedlings of which must be thinned out early. Some cultivars, such as 'Cheltenham Mono' and 'Monopoly', have been bred to produce single, or monogerm, seed, which needs little or no thinning.

To overcome slow germination, soak seed in warm water for 30 minutes before sowing. Some cultivars may bolt if sown early or in unfavourable conditions so choose bolt-resistant cultivars for early sowings.

In spring, sow seed *in situ* outdoors when the soil is workable and has warmed up to at least 7°C (45°F). Sow seed 1–2cm (^{1}/$_2$–^{3}/$_4$in) deep, with the spacing determined by the type of beetroot and the size required. Grow maincrop beetroot in rows 30cm (12in) apart, thinning to 7–10cm (3–4in) apart. For pickling beetroot about 2.5cm (1in) in diameter, space rows 7cm (3in) apart, thinning seedlings to 6cm (2^1/$_2$in).

For earlier crops, sow in early spring under cloches, in frames, or indoors in seed trays or modules, transplanting outside when the seedlings are 5cm (2in) tall. Sow three monogerm or ordinary seeds per module (see "Modules and small containers", p.311), thinning as necessary. Early beetroot needs plenty of space, so plant indoor-sown seedlings in rows 23cm (9in) apart, then thin them to 9cm (3^1/$_2$in) apart. For continuous supplies of young beetroot, sow seed at intervals of two to three weeks throughout summer. Sow cultivars intended for storage in late summer, at least ten weeks before the first heavy frost is expected.

HARVESTING BEETROOT

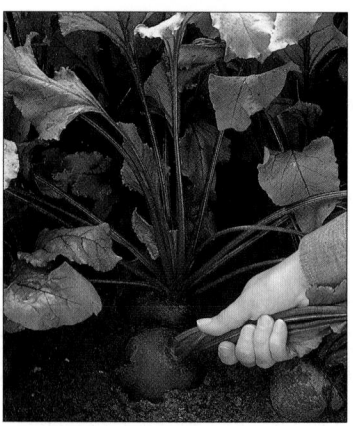

Grip the stems and pull the beetroot from the soil; it should lift easily since it is shallow-rooted. Avoid damaging the roots, which will bleed if they are cut.

Routine cultivation

Water only to prevent the soil from drying out, at a rate of 11 litres/sq m (2 gallons/sq yd) every two weeks. Apply the remaining nitrogenous fertilizer during active growth.

Pests and diseases

Beetroot may be affected by sparrows (see "Birds", p.561), cutworms (p.559), aphids (p.550), damping off (p.564), fungal leaf spots (p.552), and boron deficiency (p.566).

Harvesting and storing

Harvest beetroot at any stage from small, immature roots 2.5cm (1in) in diameter to fully mature roots; this will be from 7 to 13 weeks after sowing, depending on the cultivar, the season, and the size required. In mild areas, beetroot may be left in well-drained soil in winter, protected with a layer of straw up to 15cm (6in) deep, but they eventually become rather woody. Otherwise lift them before severe frost. Twist off the leaves (cutting causes "bleeding") and store the roots in moist sand in a frost-free place. Beetroot normally keeps until mid-spring.

Swedes (*Brassica napus* Napobrassica Group)

Biennials from the brassica family, swedes are grown as annuals and reach a height of 25cm (10in) with a spread of 38cm (15in). The root flesh is usually yellow, but sometimes white, and the skin generally purple, buff, or a combination of both. The large, often irregularly shaped, underground roots, which may be 10cm (4in) in diameter and as long, are sweetly flavoured and used cooked. This hardy, cool-season crop grows best on light, fertile soil with low nitrogen levels (see p.314). For climate and soil requirements, see "Siting Western brassicas", p.317.

Sowing and planting

Swedes need a growing season of up to 26 weeks to mature fully. Sow seed from early to late spring *in situ*, 2cm (^{3}/$_4$in) deep in rows 38cm (15in) apart, thinning early and in stages until the seedlings are about 23cm (9in) apart.

Routine cultivation
Keep beds weed-free and if conditions are very dry, water at a rate of 11 litres/sq m (2 gallons/sq yd).

Pests and diseases
Downy mildew (p.550), powdery mildew (p.550), boron deficiency (p.566), and violet root rot (p.565) may affect swedes. Some cultivars are resistant to mildew. For other pests and diseases, see "Cultivating Western brassicas", p.317.

Harvesting and storing
Swedes generally mature in autumn and, being hardy, may be left in the soil until the end of the year, when they should be lifted carefully to prevent them from becoming woody; except in very cold climates, covering with a thick layer of straw provides sufficient protection until the swedes are lifted. Store swedes in clamps outdoors or in wooden boxes under cover (see *Storing Carrots*, p.354) for up to four months.

MAKING A SWEDE CLAMP

Choose a sheltered, well-drained site and stack the roots on a 20cm (8in) layer of straw in a pyramid, with their necks facing outwards. Cover with a layer of longer straw. In very cold climates, protect further with a 10cm (4in) layer of soil.

Turnips (*Brassica rapa* Rapifera Group)

These are biennials from the brassica family grown as annuals. The plants are about 23cm (9in) high with a spread of about 25cm (10in). The underground roots swell to 2.5–7cm (1–3in) in diameter and are round, fairly flat, or long. The flesh may be either white or yellow and the skin white, pink, red, or yellow. The young leaves, known as turnip tops, may be eaten as greens (see "Turnip tops and broccoli raab", p.322). Turnip roots are used either fresh or stored and are normally cooked.

Turnips are a temperate-climate crop, growing best at about 20°C (68°F). They are reasonably hardy, tolerating light frost. For general climate and soil requirements, see "Siting Western brassicas", p.317. Grow turnips in moist soil as they bolt prematurely in dry conditions. Early types, many of which are small and white, are fast-growing and excellent for early spring and summer crops; the hardier types are used fresh during summer and winter and for storage. They require low to medium nitrogen levels (see p.314).

Sowing and planting
Start sowing seed of early turnips in spring as soon as the ground is workable, or sow under cover. Make

HARVESTING TURNIPS

Harvest turnips by pulling them from the soil by their leaves. Do not leave them in the ground too long or they may become woody.

successive sowings at three-week intervals until early summer. Sow maincrop types from mid- to late summer *in situ*, 2cm (³/₄ in) deep. Space early types in rows that are 23cm (9in) apart, thinning seedlings to 10cm (4in); space maincrop types in rows 30cm (12in) apart, thinning to 15cm (6in).

Routine cultivation
Keep beds weed-free. In dry conditions water at a rate of 11 litres/sq m (2 gallons/sq yd).

Pests and diseases
Flea beetles (p.548) may affect seedlings; other problems include violet root rot (p.565) and boron deficiency (p.566). Turnip gall weevils cause hollow swellings on the roots that may be mistaken for clubroot but are rarely serious; discard all affected plants. For other pests and diseases, see "Cultivating Western brassicas", p.317.

Harvesting and storing
Harvest early turnips after about five weeks, maincrop types after six to ten weeks. Pull them before they become woody. Lift turnips for storage before the first frost, then store them for up to three or four months in outdoor clamps covered with straw.

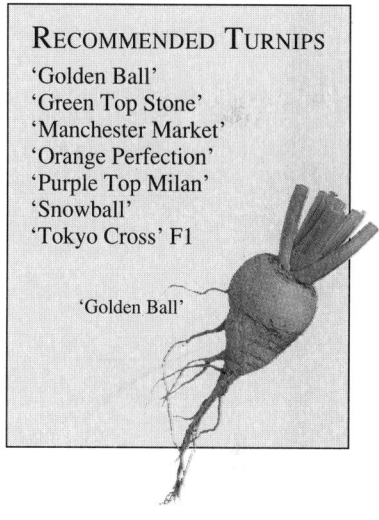

RECOMMENDED TURNIPS
'Golden Ball'
'Green Top Stone'
'Manchester Market'
'Orange Perfection'
'Purple Top Milan'
'Snowball'
'Tokyo Cross' F1

'Golden Ball'

Cocoyams (*Colocasia esculenta*)

These herbaceous, frost-tender perennials grow to about 1m (3ft) tall, with a spread of 60–70cm (24–8in). The plants have large, long-stalked leaves, which may be green or greenish-purple. Cocoyams, sometimes known as taro, are grown for their large, swollen tubers, which

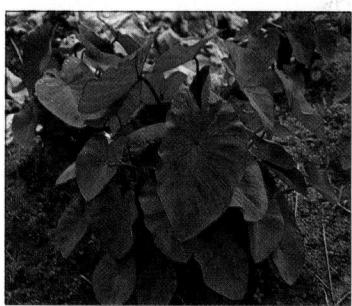

COCOYAM PLANT

are eaten cooked. The young leaves and shoots are also edible, and may be cooked and used as greens.

Cocoyams are tropical and subtropical plants that require temperatures of 21–7°C (70–81°F), with humidity levels over 75 per cent. In temperate areas they need a very sheltered, sunny site, or they may be grown under cover. Cocoyams are adapted to short daylengths of about 12 hours (see "Daylength", p.307); they rarely produce flowers. Some forms are tolerant of light shade. Moisture-retentive soil is essential because many forms of cocoyam are sensitive to dry soil conditions. Fertile soil that has a high organic content and a slightly acid pH level of 5.5–6.5 is recommended. Cocoyams require medium to high levels of nitrogen (see p.314).

Sowing and planting
Seeds are rarely available, so propagation is usually from existing tubers. Plant mature tubers or portions of tubers with dormant buds *in situ* in well-prepared beds. Space the tubers about 45cm (18in) apart with 90cm (3ft) between rows.

Cocoyams may also be propagated by cuttings. Sever the tops of tubers with a horizontal cut; each cutting should consist of several leaves 10–12cm (4–5in) long, a central growing point, and a small portion of the tuber. Plant the cuttings in their final positions at the above spacing; if the temperature is below the optimum 21°C (70°F), plant them in 21–5cm (8–10in) pots of standard compost to grow on under cover until the temperature is high enough for transplanting outside.

Routine cultivation
Cocoyams need a constant supply of water for the highest yields, so water regularly. Apply an organic mulch to conserve moisture, and feed with a general-purpose fertilizer at two- to three-week intervals. Keep beds free of weeds. The plants should be earthed up around the stems once they are established to encourage the tubers to develop.

Pests and diseases
These are rarely serious for cocoyams that are grown in the open, but aphids (p.550), thrips (p.551), red spider mites (p.550), and fungal leaf spots (p.552) may reduce tuber yields. Under cover, cocoyams are liable to the same pests and diseases as those grown outside; whiteflies (p.550) may also be troublesome.

Growing under cover

Propagate from tubers (see p.353). When these have rooted, transfer them to well-prepared greenhouse beds, 21–30cm (8–12in) pots, or growing bags, ensuring that the roots are disturbed as little as possible.

Water and feed the plants regularly, maintaining a temperature of 21–7°C (70–81°F) and humidity of more than 75 per cent by damping down. Tubers that are cultivated under cover tend to be smaller than those grown outdoors.

Harvesting and storing

Cocoyams are slow to develop and reach maturity. Harvest the tubers 16–24 weeks after planting when the leaves start to turn yellow and plants die down. Lift cocoyams grown in the open carefully using a fork; plants under cover may be lifted gently out of their pots or growing bags. Try not to damage the tubers since this encourages rotting.

Healthy tubers may be stored for about eight to twelve weeks at a temperature of 11–13°C (52–5°F), with humidity of 85–90 per cent.

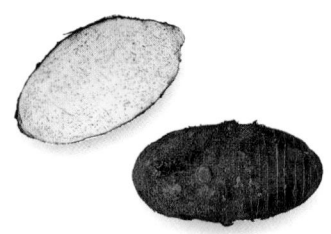

COCOYAM TUBER

Carrots (*Daucus carota*)

These are biennials grown as annuals. Their swollen, orange tap roots may be up to 5cm (2in) in diameter at the neck and up to about 20cm (8in) in length. The feathery, green foliage grows to about 23cm (9in), with a 15cm (6in) spread. Carrots are normally long and tapered but may be rounded. There are many types: early ones are usually small and slender and used young; maincrop types are larger and are used fresh or stored. Carrots are eaten either cooked or raw.

Carrots are a cool-season crop, tolerating the same temperatures as beetroot (see p.352). Grow in an open site on light and fertile soil. Deep-rooted types require reasonably deep, stone-free soil. Work in plenty of organic matter, preferably in the autumn before sowing. The fertile, loose soil of established raised beds is particularly suitable for growing carrots. Rake the soil into a fine tilth before sowing. Carrots should be rotated (see p.307). They need very low nitrogen levels (see p.314).

Sowing and planting

Sow early types in spring *in situ* as soon as the soil is workable and has warmed up to 7°C (45°F). Earlier sowings may be made under cloches, in frames, or under floating mulches; remove these after a few weeks. Sow maincrop types from late spring until early summer. A second sowing of early types may be made in late summer and protected with cloches.

Sow seed sparingly about 1–2cm (½–¾in) deep, either broadcast or in rows 15cm (6in) apart. Thin early carrots to 7cm (3in) apart; maincrop carrots should be thinned to 4cm (1½in) to obtain medium-sized carrots or farther apart if large carrots are needed. Carrots do not transplant well unless sown in modules:

RECOMMENDED CARROTS

Early

'Amsterdam Forcing – Amstel'

'Amsterdam Forcing – Amstel'

'Amsterdam Forcing – Sweetheart'
'Early French Frame' (round-rooted)
'Nairobi'

'Early French Frame'

'Nanco' F1
'Nandor' F1
'Nantes – Express'
'Nantes – Tiptop'
'Parmex' (round-rooted)
'Suko'
'Sytan'

Maincrop

'Autumn King – Vita Longa'
'Berlicum – Berjo'
'Camberley'

'Favourite'

'Cardinal' F1
'Chantenay Red Cored Supreme'
'Favourite'
'Liberno'
'Narman'

PROTECTION AGAINST CARROT FLY

Surround the patch of young carrots with a protective barrier 60–90cm (2–3ft) high. The barrier may be made either of fine mesh netting or stiff, clear, plastic, both of which also help to warm the soil inside.

sow seed of deep-rooted cultivars singly, those of round-rooted ones, several together. Round-rooted carrots sown in modules do not need thinning and should be planted out as a group at slightly wider spacing than for maincrop carrots.

Routine cultivation

Remove weeds regularly once the carrots have germinated and until the foliage hinders further weed growth. Water at a rate of 16–22 litres/sq m (3–5 gallons/sq yd) every two or three weeks.

Pests and diseases

Carrot flies (p.564) may be a serious problem. The egg-laying, adult flies are attracted by the smell of carrot foliage; thin in the evening, nipping off the seedlings at ground level and removing the tops from the site. Root and leaf aphids (see "Aphids", p.550), carrot motley dwarf virus (see "Viruses", p.553), violet root rot (p.565), and boron deficiency (p.566) may be troublesome.

Harvesting and storing

Harvest early cultivars about seven to nine weeks after sowing, maincrop cultivars after 10–11 weeks. Pull them by hand or fork them out. On well-drained soils in areas with mild winters, carrots may be left in the soil in winter (see *Protecting Parsnips*, p.356). Otherwise lift them before heavy frost, cut or twist off the foliage, and store healthy roots in boxes in a cool, dry place for up to five months.

THIN SOWING

Sow carrot seeds about 2.5cm (1in) apart so that the seedlings will need little thinning later. The seed should be 1–2cm (½–¾in) deep.

HARVESTING YOUNG

Early cultivars may be harvested when they are very young. Pull them up in a bunch when they are 8–10cm (3–4in) long.

STORING CARROTS

Twist the foliage off the carrots; place them on a layer of sand in a box. Cover them with more sand and continue in layers.

Jerusalem artichokes (*Helianthus tuberosus*)

These are perennial plants, also known as sunchokes or girasoles. The distinctively flavoured tubers are 5–10cm (2–4in) long, about 4cm (1½in) in diameter and, in most cultivars, very knobbly. 'Fuseau', however, produces smooth tubers. The plants may grow up to 3m (10ft) tall. The tubers are normally cooked but may be eaten raw. Jerusalem artichokes grow best in temperate climates and are very hardy. They

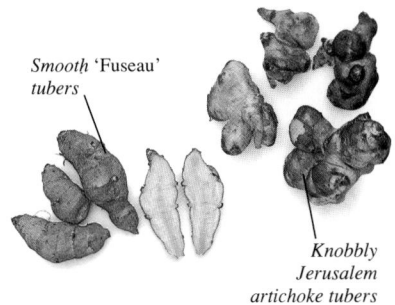

Smooth 'Fuseau' tubers

Knobbly Jerusalem artichoke tubers

tolerate a wide range of soils and require medium nitrogen levels (see p.314). They may be planted as a windbreak screen.

Sowing and planting
Plant tubers as soon as the ground is workable in spring. Those the size of a hen's egg may be planted whole; cut large ones into pieces, each with several buds. Make a drill, planting about 12.5cm (5in) deep and 30cm (12in) apart. Cover with soil.

Routine cultivation
When the plants are about 30cm (12in) tall, earth up the stems to half their height for stability. In late summer, cut the stems back to 1.5m (5ft), removing any flowerheads at the same time. In very exposed sites, stake or support the stems. Water in very dry conditions. When the leaves start to yellow, cut the stems back to just above ground level.

PLANTING

Make a drill 10–15cm (4–6in) deep. Place the tubers in the drill 30cm (12in) apart with the main bud facing upwards. Cover carefully so the tubers are not dislodged.

Harvesting and storing
Harvest the tubers 16–20 weeks after planting. Lift them only when required, since they keep best in the ground, and take care not to damage the roots. Save a few tubers to replant or leave some in the soil for the

CUTTING DOWN

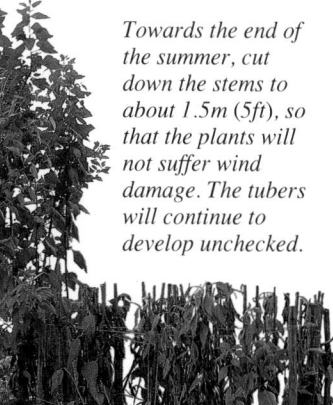

Towards the end of the summer, cut down the stems to about 1.5m (5ft), so that the plants will not suffer wind damage. The tubers will continue to develop unchecked.

following year. Otherwise, remove even small tubers since they rapidly become invasive. In severe climates or on heavy ground, lift in early winter and store in a cellar or in clamps outdoors (see *Making a Swede Clamp*, p.353) for up to five months.

Sweet potatoes (*Ipomoea batatas*)

These tender perennials are grown as annuals. They have trailing stems that grow to 3m (10ft) or more if unpruned. Cultivars vary considerably in leaf shape and tuber size, shape, and colour. Tubers are eaten cooked; the leaves may be used in the same way as spinach (see p.329).

Sweet potatoes are tropical and subtropical plants, requiring a temperature of 24–6°C (75–9°F). In warm climates, they need a sunny aspect; in temperate climates, they should be grown under cover, but tuber yields are smaller. Most cultivars are short-day plants (see "Daylength", p.307).

Highly fertile, well-drained, sandy loams with a pH of 5.5–6.5 and medium to high nitrogen levels (see p.314) are required.

Sowing and planting
In the tropics and subtropics, plant sweet potatoes at the start of the rainy season. In warm and temperate climates, plant in spring. Make raised ridges about 75cm (30in) apart, then plant the tubers 5–7cm (2–3in) deep in the ridge, spacing them 25–30cm (10–12in) apart. Alternatively, take 20–25cm (8–10in) long stem cuttings from mature plants and insert them to half their length just below the apex of the ridge.

Cultivars raised from seed will provide reasonable crops. Sow indoors in trays or 21–5cm (8–10in) pots at a temperature of at least 24°C

(75°F). When seedlings are 10–15cm (4–6in) high, harden them off and transplant outside.

Routine cultivation
Water and weed regularly, and mulch to conserve moisture. Train shoots to spread around the plant. Apply a general-purpose fertilizer at two- to three-week intervals until the tubers have formed. Protect from winds.

Pests and diseases
Aphids (p.550), caterpillars (p.549), root-knot nematodes (p.564), fungal leaf spots (p.552), *Fusarium* wilt (p.565), seedling blight (p.558), and various viruses (p.553) affect sweet potatoes growing outdoors. Under cover, whiteflies (p.550), thrips (p.551), and glasshouse red spider mites (p.550) may be troublesome.

Growing under cover
Sow seed, as described above, transplanting seedlings to growing bags or prepared beds. Alternatively, take cuttings and insert three or four into 15cm (6in) pots. Maintain a minimum temperature of 25°C (77°F) and a humidity of over 70 per cent by damping down regularly. When roots develop, transfer plants to greenhouse beds or growing bags. Water regularly and remove the growing points of shoots longer than 60cm (2ft) to encourage lateral shoots. Keep the temperature below 28°C (82°F), and the growing area well ventilated.

Harvesting and storing
Harvest 12–16 weeks after planting, when the stems and leaves turn yellow. Crops from seed are ready three

SWEET POTATO PLANT

or four weeks later. Lift the tubers, using a fork, without damaging them. In order to store sweet potatoes they must first be cured for four to seven days at temperatures of 28–30°C (82–6°F) and humidity of 85–90 per cent (see "Pumpkins", p.335). They may be stored in shallow trays at 10–15°C (50–59°F) for several months.

STEM CUTTINGS FOR GROWING UNDER COVER

1. *Select healthy, vigorous shoots and cut them off the parent plant with secateurs.*

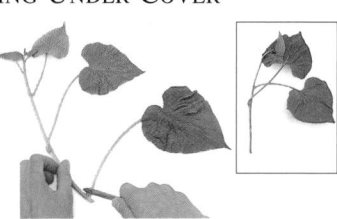

2. *Remove the lower leaves and trim each shoot below a node to 20–25cm (8–10in). Insert in pots and grow on under cover.*

RECOMMENDED SWEET POTATOES

'Centennial' (orange-fleshed)
'Eland' ✱ (orange-fleshed)
'Gem' (white-fleshed)
'Gold-rush' (orange-fleshed)
'Jewel' (white-fleshed)
'Nemagold' ✱ (orange-fleshed)

KEY
✱ *Resistant to root-knot nematodes*

Parsnips (*Pastinaca sativa*)

Parsnips are biennials grown as annuals. The tap root grows to 5cm (2in) across at the neck and about 10cm (4in) long in short forms and up to 23cm (9in) in long types. The leaves are about 38cm (15in) long and 30cm (12in) wide. The roots are eaten cooked.

Parsnips are a hardy, cool-season crop, and prefer light, deeply cultivated, stone-free soils. On shallow soils, grow the shorter forms. Lime very acid soils and rotate crops (see p.307). Parsnips have low nitrogen requirements (see p.314).

RECOMMENDED PARSNIPS

'Avonresister' (short)
'Cobham Improved Marrow' (medium)
'Gladiator' F1 (long)
'Tender and True' (long)
'White Gem' (long)
'White Spear' (long)

'White Gem'

Sowing and planting

Always sow fresh seed. Parsnips need a long growing season and so should be sown as soon as the soil is workable in spring, but not in cold or wet soil. Sow seed *in situ* 2cm (¾in) deep in rows 30cm (12in) apart. Thin the seedlings to 10cm (4in) apart to produce large roots, or 7cm (3in) for smaller roots. A faster-germinating crop such as radishes may be intersown; to allow for this, station sow several parsnip seeds at intervals of 10cm (4in), and thin to one seedling per station. To start parsnips earlier, sow seed in modules with gentle heat under cover and transplant seedlings before the tap roots develop.

Routine cultivation

Always keep beds free of weeds. In very dry conditions water the plants as for carrots (see p.354).

Pests and diseases

Parsnips may be attacked by celery flies (see "Leaf miners", p.551), lettuce root aphids (see "Aphids", p.550), and carrot flies (p.564). Use cultivars resistant to parsnip canker

(p.565) where possible; of those recommended, all but 'Tender and True' are resistant. Boron deficiency (p.566) and violet root rot (p.565) may occasionally be troublesome.

Harvesting and storing

Parsnips mature in about 16 weeks. Their flavour is improved by frost and, except in very severe climates,

INTERSOWING

In a prepared drill, sow 3 parsnip seeds every 10cm (4in) and then sow radish seeds between them, about 2.5cm (1in) apart.

they may be left in the soil during winter and lifted as required. The leaves die back in winter, so mark the ends of the rows with canes so that the plants are easily found to harvest. Where winters are very severe, cover the rows with 15cm (6in) of straw to keep the soil from freezing and to make lifting easier. Young parsnips may be lifted and frozen.

PROTECTING PARSNIPS

In severe climates, cover the plants with layers of straw or bracken, to a depth of 15cm (6in). Hold in place with wire hoops and mark each row.

Radishes (*Raphanus sativus* and *Raphanus sativus* Longipinnatus Group)

There are several types of radish, some biennial and others annual; all are grown for the swollen roots. Small, round types have roots up to 2.5cm (1in) in diameter; small, long types up to 7cm (3in) long. The leaves of both may grow to about 13cm (5in) high. Large forms include oriental radishes (Longipinnatus Group), known as mooli or daikon, and the large, overwintering, winter radishes. Roots of large, round cultivars may be over 23cm (9in) in diameter, those of large, long cultivars up to 60cm (24in) long, while the plants grow 60cm (24in) tall with a spread of 45cm (18in).

Radish skin colour is red, pink, white, purple, black, yellow, or green; the flesh is normally white. Small roots are used raw when fresh, and large roots are used raw or cooked, fresh or stored. Immature seed pods from cultivars such as 'Münchner Bier' and young seedling leaves from most cultivars are edible raw.

Radishes are mainly a cool-season crop, but there are cultivars suited to a wide range of growing conditions. Some mooli and all overwintering types are frost-tolerant. Grow radishes in an open site, although midsummer crops tolerate light shade.

Radishes prefer light, rich, well-drained soil, preferably manured for the previous crop, and very low nitrogen levels (see p.314). Radishes should be rotated (see p.307).

Sowing and planting

Sow standard, small types outdoors throughout the growing season, starting when the soil is workable. Sow at 15-day intervals for a continuous crop. Very early and late sowings may be made under cover, using small-leaved cultivars bred for growing under cover. Delay sowing most oriental mooli until summer to prevent bolting. Some bolt-resistant cultivars may be sown earlier. Sow overwintering radishes in summer.

Radishes are normally sown *in situ*. Small types grow very fast and may be used for intercropping (see "Parsnips", above). Broadcast seed very thinly, or sow 1cm (½in) deep in drills 15cm (6in) apart. Thin the seedlings to at least 2.5cm (1in) apart, never allowing them to become overcrowded. Alternatively, seeds may be spaced 2.5cm (1in) apart so that no thinning is needed. Sow large types about 2cm (¾in) deep, in rows about 23cm (9in) apart, thinning to 15–23cm (6–9in), depending on the

cultivar. Small types may be used for cut-and-come-again seedling radish leaves (see "Cut-and-come-again seedling crops", p.310).

Routine cultivation

Radishes should never be allowed to dry out. In periods of dry weather, water the crop every week at a rate

HARVESTING

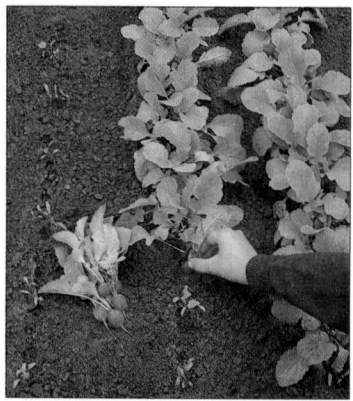

Radishes are ready to harvest 3–4 weeks after sowing. If the radishes are being used for intercropping, pull them up carefully without disturbing the roots of the other seedlings in the row.

RECOMMENDED RADISHES

Small
'Crystal Ball'
'French Breakfast'

'French Breakfast'

'Long White Icicle'
'Pink Beauty'
'Red Prince', syn. 'Prinz Rotin'
'Sparkler'

For sowing under cover
'Helro'
'Robino'
'Saxa'

'Black Spanish Round'

Mooli
'April Cross' F1 (slow bolting)
'Minowase Summer Cross' F1

Overwintering
'Black Spanish Round'
'Cherokee' F1
'China Rose'

of 11 litres/sq m (2 gallons/sq yd). Overwatering, however, encourages leaf rather than root development.

Pests and diseases
Radishes may be attacked by flea beetles (p.548), cabbage root flies (p.564), and slugs (p.548).

Harvesting and storing
Small radishes mature three to four weeks after sowing, most large types after eight to ten weeks. Pull small types soon after they mature, since most will become woody if they remain in the ground for long. Large types, however, may be left in the ground for several weeks with no risk of deterioration. Overwintering radishes may be left in the soil for lifting when required, except in severe winter weather or if they have been grown in heavy soil. In these cases, lift the roots and store them in boxes of moist sand in a frost-free place, or outside in clamps for three or four months (see *Making a Swede Clamp*, p.353). Where radish seed is required for propagation, leave a few plants to produce seed. Harvest the pods while they are still young and green, then dry them, and collect the seeds.

Scorzonera (*Scorzonera hispanica*)

This hardy perennial is normally grown as an annual. Plants grow to about 90cm (3ft) tall and have yellow flowerheads. The black-skinned, white-fleshed roots are 20cm (8in) or more long, and about 4cm (1½in) across at the neck. They have an unusual flavour and are eaten cooked. The young leaves and shoots (chards) of overwintered plants are edible, and the young flower buds and their flower stalks are also delicious cooked. For soil, climate,

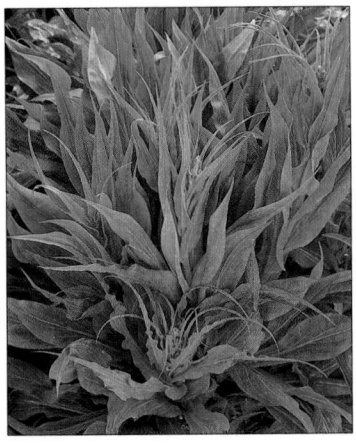

SCORZONERA PLANTS

and manuring requirements, see "Carrots", p.354. A fertile, deep, light soil is essential for good roots to develop. Scorzonera has low nitrogen requirements (see p.314).

Sowing and planting
Sow fresh seed *in situ* in spring about 1cm (½in) deep, in rows about 20cm (8in) apart, thinning out seedlings to 10cm (4in) apart. Water at a rate of 16–22 litres/sq m (3–5 gallons/sq yd) in dry spells. For routine cultivation, see "Carrots", p.354. Pests and diseases rarely affect scorzonera.

Harvesting and storing
The roots need at least four months to develop. They may be left in the soil throughout the winter (see *Protecting Parsnips*, p.356), or lifted and stored in boxes in cool conditions. Start lifting the roots for use in the autumn and continue into spring. If they are only pencil-thin, leave the remaining plant roots to thicken for harvesting the following autumn.

For chards, cover the plants with about 13cm (5in) of straw or leaves in early spring. The young, blanched leaves will push through this layer. Cut them when about 10cm (4in) tall.

For flower buds, leave a few roots in the soil during winter with no covering; these will flower the following spring or early summer. Pick the unopened buds with about 8cm (3in) of stem.

SCORZONERA ROOTS

Salsify (*Tragopogon porrifolius*)

A hardy biennial with purple flowers, salsify is known as vegetable oyster or oyster plant, due to its taste. It is similar to scorzonera in appearance and use, and has the same climate, soil, cultivation, harvesting, and storage requirements. Salsify roots need to be eaten in their first winter.

SALSIFY ROOTS

If the roots are overwintered, the flower buds may be eaten the following spring. Pick the buds with short stalks, preferably in the morning before they open.

Potatoes (*Solanum tuberosum*)

Potatoes are tender perennials that grow to an average height of 60cm (2ft), with a similar spread. There are numerous potato cultivars, displaying enormous variation in their underground tubers.

A typical mature tuber is about 7cm (3in) long and 4cm (1½in) wide with white or pinkish-red skin and white flesh, but there are yellow- and blue-fleshed cultivars, often used in salads. Potatoes are eaten cooked, fresh or after storing.

Potatoes are a cool-season crop, growing best at 16–18°C (61–4°F). Neither plants nor tubers tolerate frost. Depending on the cultivar, they require a growing season of 90–140 frost-free days. They are divided into early, second early, and maincrop groups, depending on the number of days required to mature. The earlies grow fastest but are generally lower-yielding. Potatoes need at least 500mm (20in) of rainfall or irrigation during the season.

Grow potatoes in an open, frost-free site; they need well-drained, fertile soil at least 60cm (2ft) deep that is rich in organic matter. Although tolerant of a wide range of soils, acid soils (pH5–6) are preferred.

Potatoes are subject to several soil-borne pests and diseases, and so crops must always be rotated (see p.307). Prepare the ground well by digging in plenty of organic matter. A general fertilizer may be worked in just before planting. Early potatoes need medium nitrogen; high nitrogen is required for maincrop potatoes (see p.314).

Planting
Grow cultivars recommended for the area. Plant small tubers (known as "seed potatoes") that have been specially raised and are certified disease-free. In northern latitudes with a short growing season, potatoes (especially the earlies) are sprouted, or chitted, indoors to start them into growth about six weeks before planting. Place the tubers in a shallow tray, with the eyes or buds uppermost, in even light in a cool but frost-free room. Planting is easiest when the sprouts are about 2cm (¾in) long, but they may be planted with sprouts of any length. For large, early potatoes, leave only three sprouts per plant, rubbing off the others. Otherwise, the more sprouts per tuber, the higher the yield.

SPROUTING SEED POTATOES FOR PLANTING

To sprout seed potatoes, place them in a box or tray in a single layer with the end of the potato containing the most "eyes" uppermost. Store in a light, frost-free, but well-ventilated place until the sprouts have grown to about 2cm (¾in) in length.

Plant outside when there is no longer risk of heavy frost and once the soil temperature has reached 7°C (45°F). Make drills 7–15cm (3–6in) deep or make individual holes, and place tubers upright with the eyes or sprouts at the top, covering them with at least a 2.5cm (1in) layer of soil. Plant early potatoes 35cm (14in) apart in rows 43cm (17in) apart, second early and maincrop potatoes 38cm (15in) apart in rows 68cm (27in) and 75cm (30in) apart respectively.

In cool areas, cover early potatoes with cloches, clear plastic sheeting, or floating film mulches (see p.315). When shoots emerge, cut holes in the film and ease the foliage through. Remove floating films about a month later, cutting them down the centre first to acclimatize the potatoes to cooler conditions for a few days.

Early potatoes may also be planted under black plastic sheeting, which excludes light and makes earthing up unnecessary; this is not recommended for maincrop potatoes since watering is difficult. Lay the plastic on the ground, anchor the edges in the soil, and plant the potatoes through cross-shaped slits in the plastic. Alternatively, plant the potatoes, cover them with plastic, make slits, and pull the stems through when the plants start to push up the plastic.

Potatoes are sometimes grown from seedlings, plantlets, or eyes. These are planted in seed trays and transferred outside, after hardening off, once all risk of frost has passed.

Routine cultivation

If frost threatens after the leaves have appeared, cover them at night with a light layer of straw or newspaper. Plants normally recover from light frost damage. Unless grown under black plastic, potatoes need to be earthed up to prevent tubers near the surface from becoming green and unpalatable and sometimes toxic. When the plants are about 23cm (9in) tall, hoe up soil around the stems to a depth of about 13cm (5in). This may be done in stages.

In dry conditions, water early potatoes every 12 days at a rate of 16 litres/sq m (3 gallons/sq yd). Delay watering maincrop potatoes until the young potatoes are the size of marbles – check the size of the tubers by scraping back the soil beneath one plant – then give one watering of at least 22 litres/sq m (5 gallons/sq yd). Potatoes may be given an organic liquid feed or a nitrogenous top-dressing during growth.

Pests and diseases

Cutworms (p.564), snails (p.548), potato cyst eelworms (p.570), millipedes (p.548), blackleg on potatoes (p.568), and violet root rot (p.565) may be troublesome. For full details of potato blight (including resistant cultivars) and other pests and diseases affecting potatoes, see "Potato tuber problems", p.566.

Harvesting and storing

Harvest early potatoes when, or just before, the flowers open. Potatoes under black plastic may be harvested by lifting the sheeting – they should be on the surface. Leave healthy maincrop potatoes in the soil for as long as possible; in autumn, cut the haulm (the stems) of each plant to about 5cm (2in) above ground level, and leave the potatoes

for another two weeks, to harden the skins, before lifting. In areas with warm, wet summers where potato blight is prevalent, cut the haulm in late summer and burn the foliage; lift the potatoes two weeks later.

Lift potatoes for storage on a dry, sunny day and leave them in the sun for two hours, then store them in the dark in paper sacks in a cool, frost-proof place. Give extra protection if frost threatens. Potatoes may also be stored for up to six months outdoors in well-insulated clamps (see p.353) or in a cellar. Young or new potatoes may be frozen. For new potatoes to be eaten during winter, plant a few tubers in the middle of summer and cover with cloches in autumn.

Planting Potatoes

1 *Make a drill 7–15cm (3–6in) deep, using a draw hoe. If planting maincrop potatoes, place them in the drill 38cm (15in) apart with the sprouts upwards. Cover carefully once planted.*

2 *Draw up the soil around the stems when the foliage is about 23cm (9in) high. Earthing up prevents tubers that form near the surface from turning green and being unfit to eat.*

Alternative Method

1 *To plant under black plastic, unroll the plastic and anchor it by burying the edges. Make a cross-shaped cut where each potato is to be planted. Place each potato 10–12cm (4–5in) deep in the soil under each cut.*

2 *Once the haulm has been cut, the plastic can be pulled back and the crop of potatoes will be lying on the soil surface, ready to harvest.*

Harvesting Potatoes

In autumn, cut the haulm (stems) cleanly with a knife just above ground level. Leave the potatoes in the ground for another 2 weeks before lifting.

Salsify (*Tragopogon porrifolius*), see Scorzonera, p.357

15
THE FRUIT GARDEN

T*he satisfaction of growing, harvesting, and tasting your own fresh fruits is one of the great pleasures of gardening. A fruit garden may be highly decorative as well as productive: some plants have attractive, fragrant blossom or fine foliage while, in many cases, the fruits themselves are as ornamental as they are edible, from the bright gleam of cherries to the downy bloom of peaches. In most areas, a wide range of fruits may be grown, while in cool regions, growing under cover makes it possible to* cultivate an even greater variety. In a large garden, there *may be room to devote an area exclusively to fruit – whether in a formal layout with neat rows of trees, bushes, and canes, bordered by trained fans or cordons, or in an informal orchard. If space is limited, incorporate fruits into the rest of the garden, perhaps edging a bed with alpine strawberries or growing a grape vine over a pergola; even in a small, patio garden, there should be space for one or two citrus trees in pots or wall-trained apples or pears.*

Planning the fruit garden

FRUITS have traditionally held a prominent place in the garden, and today, with a wide range of cultivars and many dwarf fruit trees available ideal for the average garden, fruit growing is increasing in popularity. There are always some fruits that will thrive in the given climatic and growing conditions, although the majority prefer a good loam and a sunny situation. In warm climates, a wide range of fruits may be cultivated outdoors although some fruits that require periods of cold dormancy before flowering will not usually be successful.

Where only a few fruit plants are required, the gardener may prefer to grow them within the ornamental garden rather than in a specialized fruit garden; many fruit trees are suitable for growing as specimens in a lawn. Alternatively, if space is very limited, most fruits may be cultivated in containers either free-standing or trained against a support.

If planning to grow plants in large numbers, however, it is best to create a separate fruit area within the garden; this makes it possible to grow fruits with similar requirements together, and to protect them against birds and frost damage. This is possible even in a small garden, as long as suitable rootstocks are chosen and trees are carefully trained. If grown as espaliers, fans, or cordons around the borders of a garden, fruit

trees may be both ornamental and a source of fresh crops. Thoughtful planning as well as careful selection of cultivars and methods of training make it possible to provide fresh fruit supplies over several months, and if there is some storage and freezing space available, the produce from a fruit garden may be enjoyed all year round.

In cool areas, the range of fruits that may be grown is even wider if some protection under cover is available. Reliable crops of peaches, nectarines, figs, grapes, or more tender fruits may be obtained by growing plants in a greenhouse, although ample room is needed for even a single tree. Protection and shelter is required by many of these fruits if they are grown outdoors.

The range of fruits

The different groups of fruit plants may be categorized according to their stature, their growth and fruiting habit, and their frost-hardiness.

Tree fruits (top fruits) include apples, peaches, and figs. The term embraces both pome fruits (those containing a core with pips, such as apples, pears, and medlars) and stone fruits (those containing stones, such as cherries, peaches, and plums), as well as a few other fruits, including mulberries and persimmons.

WALL-TRAINED PEACH TREE
A sunny, south-facing garden wall is ideal for accommodating a fan-trained peach tree, providing warm and sheltered ripening conditions and a high yield of fruits from a limited space.

The term "vine" is used to describe woody, fruiting climbers, such as grapes and kiwi fruits; in some countries, the term is usually applied only to *Vitis vinifera*, the grape vine.

The category soft fruits includes bush fruits, cane fruits, and strawberries, which are herbaceous. Bush fruits are naturally shrubby, forming a compact, bush shape, although they may also be trained into other forms. Blackcurrants, redcurrants, whitecurrants, and gooseberries are the most commonly grown bush fruits. Plants described as cane fruits produce cane-like shoots that bear the fruits; raspberries, blackberries, and hybrid berries, such as loganberries, are in this group. Most develop their canes in one season, and bear fruit on these the next, while producing new canes that will fruit in the following year.

Certain fruit-bearing plants cannot withstand frost and need warm, subtropical temperatures to develop and ripen fully; these may be categorized as tender fruits. Tender fruits include citrus, pomegranates, pineapples, tree tomatoes, and prickly pears. Some are also tree fruits, but have been grouped here with tender fruits because of their need for consistently warm temperatures.

Nuts include all plants that produce fruits with a hard outer shell around an edible kernel, for example cobnuts, almonds, and pecans.

FRUIT FOR FROST-FREE AREAS
Oranges grow well in warm, virtually frost-free regions such as Mediterranean countries, South Africa, and California. They often produce two crops a year and may bear flowers at the same time as an earlier orange crop is maturing.

Unrestricted and trained forms

Many fruits, particularly tree fruits, and to a lesser extent vines and some soft fruits, may be trained into a variety of forms. When deciding which forms to grow, bear in mind the space available, the relative ease of harvesting, and the degree of pruning and training needed to produce a plant that crops well. The choice of rootstock for fruit trees also determines their ultimate size (see "Rootstocks and tree size", p.363).

With the correct technique, trees and bush fruits may be trained almost as desired. The principle is to train young shoots into the required shape while they are still pliable; the branches then retain this form with regular, basic pruning.

Unrestricted tree forms
These forms develop, with limited pruning, in much the same way as a natural tree; they include the bush tree, standard, half-standard, and spindlebush. The bush and spindlebush are more compact than the standard and half-standard, and are suitable for small gardens.

A bush tree has a trunk up to 90cm (3ft) tall, with branches radiating out from the top third. It has an open centre, thus allowing the branches maximum light and space. Bush trees are small to medium sized, that is 1.5–4m (5–12ft).

The half-standard is similar to the bush but the trunk measures 1–1.5m (3–5ft) and the overall height is 4–5m (12–15ft). The standard is similar in form, but with a trunk measuring 1.5–2.2m (5–7ft) and an overall height of 5m (15ft) or more.

The spindlebush is a small tree growing up to 2.2m (7ft) tall with branches that are trained to radiate out from the central leader at a wide angle. It has fewer branches than other lightly pruned forms, but each branch is pruned to be as productive as possible. The lowest branch is usually about 45cm (18in) from ground level.

Trained forms
Some fruit trees and bushes are suitable for growing in trained (or restricted) forms. These include cordons, fans, and espaliers. They need careful training initially, and are then maintained by regular summer pruning, to restrict vegetative growth, with a minimum of winter pruning. Most require support wires, either secured to free-standing posts or against a wall or fence. Wall-trained forms are often favoured in temperate climates for fruits such as peaches because the fruits receive maximum sun and also benefit from the reflected heat of the wall. All the trained tree forms are ideal for small gardens as they make it possible to cultivate a variety of fruits in a restricted space. Maiden plants that have been grafted onto dwarfing rootstocks are usually used for training restricted forms.

A cordon is restricted to a single stem 1.5–2m (5–6ft) long, clothed with fruiting spurs to produce a high yield in a small area. It is usually planted at an angle of about 45° but may also be grown vertically or horizontally. Most commonly used for apples and pears, it is also useful for red- and whitecurrants and gooseberries. Double (sometimes known as "U"), triple, or multiple cordons may be formed by pruning a maiden plant so that it forms two or more parallel stems. Cordons that have more than a single stem are usually trained vertically.

A fan is trained with the main branches radiating in a fan shape from a short 24cm (10in) trunk and is suitable for tree fruits that are grown against walls and fences.

TRAINED CORDONS
Apple cordons make good use of a fence, while alpine strawberries make an edging to the border.

TREE FORMS

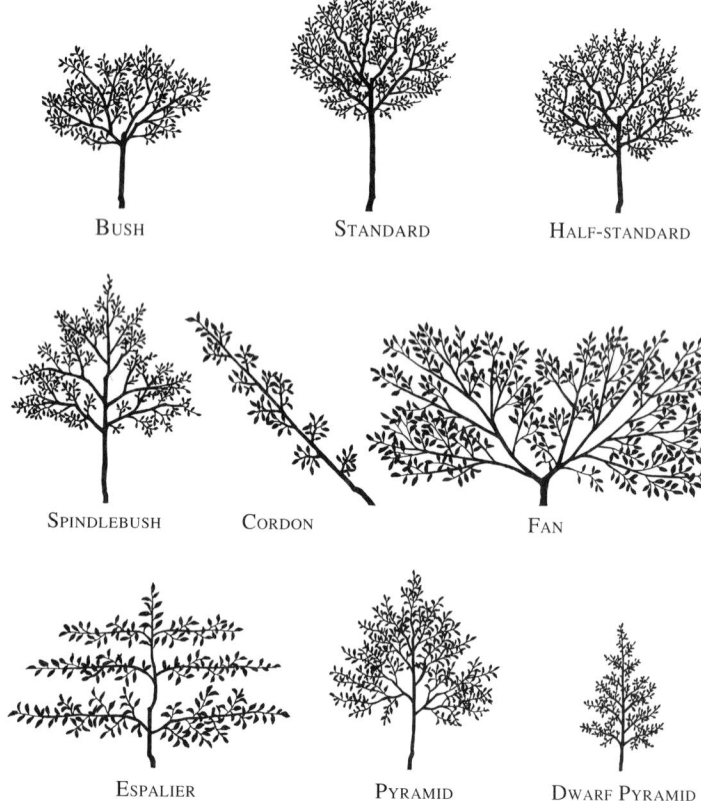

BUSH   STANDARD   HALF-STANDARD

SPINDLEBUSH   CORDON   FAN

ESPALIER   PYRAMID   DWARF PYRAMID

An espalier is trained with matching pairs of horizontal branches extending at regular intervals from a central stem. Each branch is clothed in short, fruiting spurs. The number of pairs of branches is variable depending on space and tree vigour. This method is particularly suitable for apples and pears grown against walls or fences.

Unlike the other trained forms, the pyramid is free-standing; its branches radiate from a central trunk, with an overall pyramidal form that is maintained by regular summer pruning to produce trees of small to medium size. Dwarf pyramids are similar but are grown on a more dwarfing rootstock.

Integrating fruits into the garden plan

Fruits may be grown either in a separate area on their own or intermingled with other, ornamental plants; the choice depends on space, personal preference, and the range of fruits to be included. In either case, assess the impact that the fully grown fruit plants will have on the adjacent or surrounding plants. Planning and siting are particularly important because most fruits are long-term plants that require consistently good conditions to flourish and crop well over many years; in addition, with the exception of a few fruits such as strawberries, it is seldom practical or worthwhile transplanting them to other positions.

The planned fruit garden

Where a range of different fruits is required, it is well worth growing the plants together in a single area. When planning a fruit garden, take into account the preferred growing conditions of each type of plant and recommended planting distances; for example, site tall fruit trees where they will cast least shade on smaller bushes nearby. Also make sure that the space allocated for each plant is sufficient for it to develop naturally to its mature size.

Plants that have similar cultivation requirements may be grouped together to simplify practical operations such as applying fertilizer: for example, redcurrants and gooseberries need more potassium than other fruits. Grouping plants also

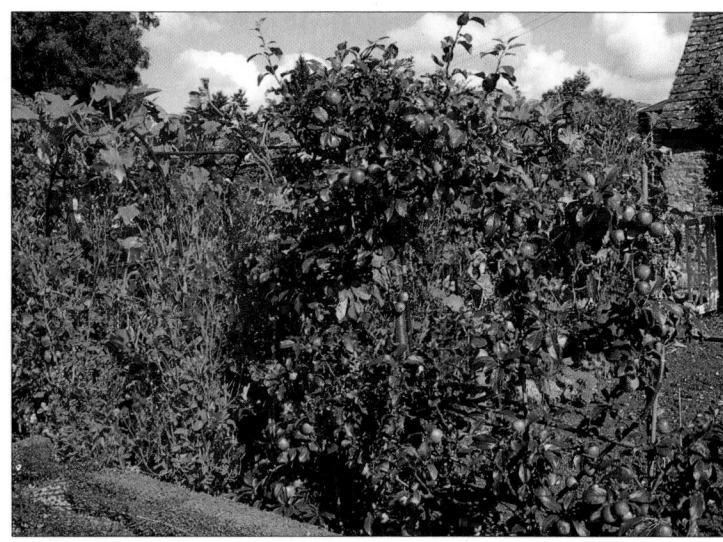

ORNAMENTAL DIVIDER
Apple espaliers form an attractive screen providing a fine display of spring blossom followed by handsome fruits in autumn.

makes it easier to protect them from birds (with a fruit cage) or wind damage (with a windbreak).

For an ornamental border, edge the fruit garden with a row of trained trees; cordons or dwarf pyramids are especially suitable because they need a minimum of support and occupy comparatively little space.

In planning the position of fruit trees (particularly apples, pears, sweet cherries, and some plums), remember that a self-sterile cultivar should be sited near a cultivar with

PLAN FOR A LARGE FRUIT GARDEN

A large plot, 11 x 17m (35 x 54ft), provides space for a range of fruit. Here, the chosen apple and pear cultivars will crop over a long period, and the soft fruit has been grouped for easier maintenance. The more tender peaches and grapes thrive in a lean-to greenhouse.

1 Apple 'Discovery' (on 'M6'/'MM106')
2 Apple 'Epicure' (on 'M6'/'MM106')
3 Apple 'St Edmund's Pippin' (on 'M6'/'MM106')
4 Apple 'Sunset' (on 'M6'/'MM106')
5 Apple 'Cox's Orange Pippin' (on 'M6'/'MM106')
6 Apple 'Ashmead's Kernel' (on 'M6'/'MM106')
7 Plum 'Czar' (on 'Pixy')
8 Plum 'Victoria' (on 'Pixy')
9 Damson 'Prune' (on 'Pixy')
10 Pear 'Onward' (on 'Quince A')
11 Pear 'Concorde' (on 'Quince A')
12 Pear 'Doyenné du Comice' (on 'Quince A')
13 Pear 'Joséphine de Malines' (on 'Quince A')
14 Blackcurrant 'Boskoop Giant'
15 Blackcurrant 'Ben Lomond'
16 Blackcurrant 'Ben Sarek'
17 Redcurrant 'Red Lake'
18 Gooseberry 'Careless'
19 Gooseberry 'Leveller'
20 Raspberry 'Autumn Bliss'
21 Acid cherry 'Morello'
22 Raspberry 'Malling Jewel'
23 Loganberry (thornless)
24 Tayberry
25 Blackberry 'Merton Early'
26 Grape 'Black Hamburgh'
27 Peach 'Peregrine' (on 'St Julien A')
28 Strawberry 'Elsanta'
29 Sweet cherry 'Stella' (on 'Colt')
30 Fig 'Brown Turkey'

which it will cross-pollinate (see "Pollination requirements", p.364), or it will produce few if any fruits.

For many fruits there is a wide choice of cultivars that ripen at different times; this makes it possible to plan for a succession of fruits that may. be regularly harvested rather than a single glut. Some fruits, late-ripening apples and pears for example, may be stored for long periods, so if a steady supply is required more space should be devoted to these than to earlier-ripening cultivars.

Fruit in the small garden

There are various ways to make the most of a limited area for fruit growing so that it provides a high yield and is an attractive feature. Whenever possible, choose trees grafted on dwarfing rootstocks (see p.363) and use training methods that make the best use of the available space. Train trees and soft fruits such as redcurrants and gooseberries as cordons against the house or garden wall, rather than as bushes, since cordons need less room for a comparable fruit yield than fans or espaliers. Grow grape vines over a sturdy pergola or ornamental arch as part of the garden design. Cane fruits may also be trained in a variety of ways depending on space. Strawberries may be grown in vertical growing bags attached to a stake, fence, or other structure.

If there is room for only a single tree then it is essential to choose a self-fertile cultivar (see "Pollination compatibility", p.363). It is also worth selecting plants with a prolonged cropping season, unless there is ample storage and freezer space.

Mixed planting

In a garden that is largely ornamental or where there is insufficient space for a dedicated fruit garden, fruits

FRUIT IN A BORDER
The compact, rounded shape of a lemon tree laden with fruit punctuates an informal planting, providing a pleasant contrast to the colourful display of roses and double daisies.

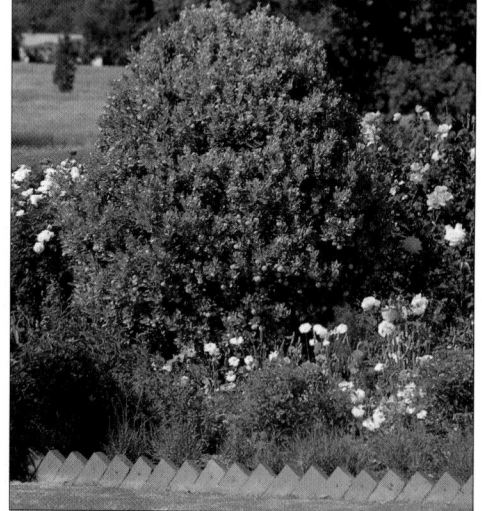

SMALL FRUIT GARDEN

This small, fenced area supports no fewer than 17 fruit cultivars, providing abundant crops from early summer through to autumn. The plot measures only 4 x 9m (12 x 28ft) with a 2m (6ft) fence surrounding it; careful choice of cultivars and rootstocks coupled with correct training of the trees allows a wide range of fruits to be accommodated. The apple and pear cordons provide especially good yields from a limited space.

1 Sweet cherry 'Stella' (on 'Colt')
2 Pear 'Beth' (on 'Quince C')
3 Pear 'Concorde' (on 'Quince C')
4 Pear 'Doyenné du Comice' (on 'Quince C')
5 Raspberry 'Leo' (summer-fruiting)
6 Plum 'Victoria' (on 'Pixy')
7 Raspberry 'Autumn Bliss' (autumn-fruiting)
8 Peach 'Rochester' (on 'St Julien A')

9 Gooseberry 'Careless'
10 Gooseberry 'Leveller'
11 Whitecurrant 'White Grape'
12 Redcurrant 'Red Lake'
13 Apple 'Epicure' (on 'M9')
14 Apple 'Lord Lambourne' (on 'M9')
15 Apple 'Sunset' (on 'M9')
16 Blackcurrant 'Ben Sarek'
17 Acid cherry 'Morello' (on 'Colt')

may be planted among other plants. One or more fruit trees may make attractive specimens in the lawn, or grown in containers on a sunny terrace or patio. Fruit cordons or dwarf pyramids look effective when used as an ornamental divider, providing an unusual and productive screen, with attractive blossom in spring and ripening fruits in late summer to autumn. Trained forms of bushes or trees may be grown on almost any type of garden structure such as a pergola, fence, or shed, provided that the aspect is suitable.

When fruits are planted with ornamentals, make sure that all the plants' needs are compatible. If, for example, the fruits need protection from birds with netting, this may impede the growth of surrounding plants and look out of place. Particular care is also needed to ensure that fruit tree sprays do not adversely affect any nearby ornamental plants.

Strawberries are often grown among other plants either in the vegetable garden or – a popular use of alpine strawberries – along the edge of a border or raised bed.

Choosing a site

A sunny, sheltered position, where the plants will produce fruits of good quality and flavour, is ideal. Sites with some light shade are also acceptable but provide fewer ripening hours, so are best used for soft fruits or early-ripening cultivars of apples, pears, and plums. Plants on a south-facing slope may produce crops earlier than elsewhere but, as they also flower earlier, they are more likely to suffer frost damage.

Growing against supports

Walls, fences, pergolas, and arches all provide an ideal site for growing trained trees, especially if they are exposed to maximum sun. These structures make good use of space and allow the fruits to develop and ripen well; fruits trained on supports are also easier to protect from birds and frost than fruits in the open garden. The wall or fence must be high enough to accommodate the chosen fruits: 1.2m (4ft) would be enough for soft fruits, or apples or pears trained as cordons or espaliers, but a height and spread of 2m (6ft) or more are required for a fan-trained apple, pear, cherry, plum, or peach. Pergolas and arches are likely to provide sufficient height, but ensure that there is enough space for the plants to spread as they mature. The structure must be able to support heavy crops, even in strong winds.

Frost and wind

Avoid planting in frost-prone sites because flowers, unopened buds, and fruitlets are all susceptible to frost damage. The coldest air collects where the ground is lowest, and a frost pocket will form in a valley-floor or at the foot of a sloping garden. Shaded areas remain frost-covered for longer than sunny ones – the duration of the frost is often as critical as its severity.

Exposure to wind discourages pollinating insects and therefore greatly reduces the regularity of cropping. Strong winds also cause considerable crop damage. Draughty sites, such as between two buildings, are not recommended, but a suitable, well-placed windbreak may be very effective in diverting or filtering wind to improve the conditions. Trees or large shrubs are preferable to solid barriers as they filter wind that would otherwise swirl over the barrier and damage plants on the other side (see also CLIMATE AND THE GARDEN, "How a windbreak works", p.519).

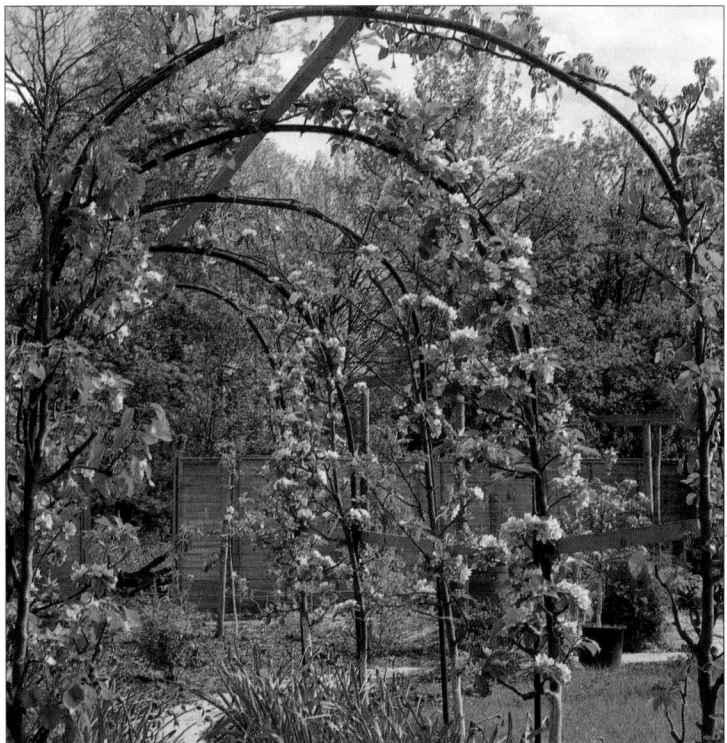

A CORDON ARCH
Fruit trees trained as vertical cordons over a series of arches provide an attractive, architectural feature as well as abundant crops of fruit. The structure must be sufficiently strong to support the weight of trees heavily laden with fruit in autumn.

Growing fruits under cover

Crops native to warm climates, such as peaches, nectarines, and grapes, are ideal for greenhouse cultivation in cooler climates, but skill and attention to detail are required to maintain them in good condition and obtain satisfactory crops. If fruits are to be grown with other plants in the same greenhouse, ensure that their temperature, humidity, and ventilation requirements are compatible. It is important that the greenhouse has the maximum possible number of side and top vents to provide a free flow of air. As for planting in open ground, the soil needs to be fertile and well-drained for the plants to thrive.

A number of tender fruits such as tree tomatoes and pomegranates may be grown successfully under cover; in temperate climates, they are often grown as ornamental plants as they seldom crop heavily, even under glass.

Trained fruits
Tree and soft fruits that are suitable for training may also be treated in this way when grown in a greenhouse. Check that there is enough space for the chosen cultivar to develop and grow to its mature size, and ensure that suitable fittings for training the plant in the chosen form are in place before planting.

Fruits in pots
Strawberry plants that are grown in individual pots in a greenhouse or under a cloche will produce ripe fruits earlier than those in the open, thereby prolonging the fruiting season if both cultivation methods are used. Tender fruit trees such as citrus may be grown in pots that are placed outdoors during summer and returned under cover for winter.

Growing fruits in containers

Container-growing is useful for cultivating fruits where space is limited. The pots should be placed in sunny, sheltered sites and may be used on paved areas such as patios to provide ornamental features as well as crops of fruits. It is also a way of controlling the root growth, and therefore the vigour, of plants such as figs that (particularly in temperate climates) may make excessive vegetative growth at the expense of the crop.

Most fruits may be grown successfully in a large pot, half barrel, or similar container with a diameter of at least 30cm (12in). Strawberries may be grown either singly in 10cm (4in) pots or in strawberry planters (containers with side planting pockets). Fruits need more regular care in containers than when in the open ground, particularly with watering and feeding, because the root systems are confined and easily dry out.

Deciding which plants to grow

Whether planning an entire fruit garden or choosing just two or three trees, it is vital to select plants that will thrive in the given soil and climatic conditions without growing too large for their allotted space.

Check the compatibility of different cultivars for pollination purposes before deciding which to grow (see "Pollination requirements", p.364). The final choice should also depend on the size of the crop required and the harvesting time.

Rootstocks and tree size
Tree size is determined largely by the rootstock onto which the tree has been grafted. Choose rootstocks that are of appropriate vigour for the planting area or training space available. Apple trees grown on dwarfing rootstocks such as 'M27' or 'M9', for example, are likely to suit most gardens; their relatively small size makes picking, pruning, and spraying easier. If a large tree is required, select one that is grown on a more vigorous rootstock. For further details, see pp.364 and 375.

Pollination compatibility
Most cultivars of apples, pears, sweet cherries, and some plums, are not satisfactorily self-fertile, and therefore need to be planted close to one or more suitable cultivars of the same fruit that are in flower at about the same time so that insects are able to cross-pollinate all the trees. For example, the apple cultivars 'Cox's Orange Pippin', 'Bramley's Seedling', and 'Lord Lambourne' need to be planted together for all to be successfully cross-pollinated. When planning a fruit garden, take account of the minimum number of trees required for pollination to occur and position compatible cultivars adjacent to each other to ensure satisfactory cropping.

Crop size and timing
Within the limits of space available, the amount of fruits that are required will determine the number of plants that should be obtained, bearing in mind that crop levels inevitably vary from year to year. The amount of storage or freezer space available may govern the size of crop that can be handled. Try to balance the numbers of early-, mid-, and late-ripening cultivars of each fruit grown in order to provide a consistent supply over a long period rather than a brief glut.

Early-ripening apples and pears do not keep well for more than a day or two, so do not grow more than can be consumed quickly: one or two cordons yielding 2–5kg (5–11lb) per tree should suffice. If you have plenty of storage space, plant a high proportion of late-ripening cultivars, the fruits of which can be stored for several months. Plums are also liable to produce gluts and the fruits must be used quickly unless they are frozen or otherwise preserved.

When deciding whether to plant early- or late-ripening cultivars, remember to take climatic factors into account: for example, late-ripening apples or pears are not a good choice for a region with a short summer or if the proposed site is shady, because there will not be enough time or sun for the fruit to ripen fully.

GRAPE CANOPY
A grape vine thrives in the warm but well-ventilated atmosphere of a conservatory or greenhouse. Care must be taken to prevent the ripening bunches from becoming scorched by the sun.

Site, soil preparation, and planting

A LL fruits require soil that is well-structured, adequately drained, and fertile to thrive. Before planting fruits, therefore, choose and prepare a suitable site so that it provides the necessary conditions.

Preparing the site

Prepare the site at least two months before planting. Remove all weeds, especially perennial ones, before any soil preparation takes place (see PLANT PROBLEMS, "Weeds", pp.573–7).

Soil types
A loam soil is ideal and produces high yields of good-quality fruits. Clay soils may produce very good crops if drainage is good but are slow to warm up in spring; growth and therefore cropping may be later. On sandy soils, plants come into growth earlier since the soil warms up quickly in spring. Heat is lost equally rapidly, however, which creates a greater risk from frost; sandy soil is also prone to drought. Sandy soils are usually less fertile than others, so the quality and flavour of fruits grown on these may be inferior to those produced on more fertile soil.

On chalk soils, lime-induced chlorosis caused by manganese and iron deficiencies (see p.355) may be severe, causing the leaves of plants to turn yellow and adversely affecting the quality and yield of fruit. In extreme cases, it will prove impossible to grow certain fruits satisfactorily; pears and raspberries, in particular, suffer badly. The use of sequestered iron alleviates the problem, but regular treatment may be necessary and is expensive. Annual mulches of farmyard manure and compost help by providing some of the trace elements required.

Improving the soil
For soft fruits, dig in generous amounts of well-rotted manure or garden compost and fertilizer to improve water retention and fertility. In preparation for planting tree fruits, fertilizers should not be used unless the soil is very poor and infertile, since it may produce excessive, soft growth rather than fruiting wood.

Drainage problems
Although poor drainage is more likely on heavy, clay soils, it may occur in many types of soil. Improve the soil structure where possible (see "Soil structure and water content",

p.526), and install a drainage system if necessary (see SOILS AND FERTILIZERS, "Installing drains", p.529). Where drains cannot be installed, plant fruits in raised beds (see STRUCTURES AND SURFACES, "Raised beds", p.507).

Adjusting the pH level
Soil with a pH level of 6–6.5 is ideal for all fruits except blueberries, which need an acid soil of pH4–5.5. Soils below about pH5.8 will need liming (see p.531). If planting in soil with a pH level over 7, top-dress regularly with sulphate of ammonia and mulch with acid compost to reduce the pH in the short term.

Preparing the support for a trained fruit tree or bush
If a fruit tree or bush is to be trained against a solid support such as a wall or fence, fix horizontal, parallel wires to the support with vine eyes and a tightener to keep the wires taut as the fruits develop. The vine eyes should hold the wires 10–15cm (4–6in) from the support to allow air to circulate around the branches and leaves of the plant. The spacing of the wires will vary, depending on the type of fruits grown. If using a free-standing post-and-wire support, secure the wires firmly to the posts. Just before planting, attach bamboo canes to the wires at the appropriate angles, and tie in the young plants to begin the training process.

Buying plants

Always choose fruits that will thrive in the conditions in your garden. Check that the ultimate size of the plant or tree will fit the available space and that there is room to train it into the desired form. Pollination needs must also be considered before deciding which cultivars to buy.

Specialist fruit nurseries are often the best and most reliable source of supply. They offer a wide range of old and new cultivars and will also advise about suitable rootstocks. Wherever possible, buy fruits that are certified free from disease.

It is best to buy young plants, since these become established quickly and may be shaped and trained to your own requirements. Plants are available bare-root or in containers. Container-grown plants are available all year round, but bare-root plants only in late autumn and winter when the plants are dormant and may safely be lifted. Reject plants

BUYING FRUIT TREES

BARE-ROOT TREE

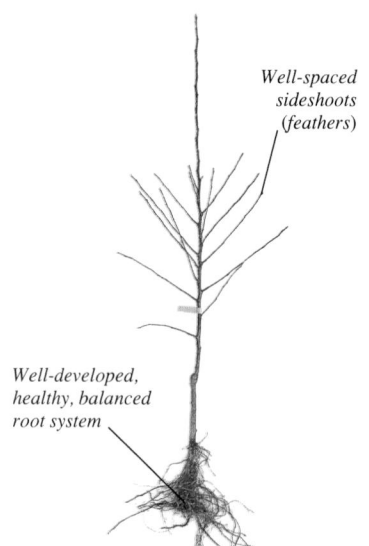

Well-spaced sideshoots (feathers)

Well-developed, healthy, balanced root system

CONTAINER-GROWN TREE

Vigorous, healthy roots that have not become congested and pot-bound

Moist, weed-free compost

with a pot-bound root system, since they seldom develop well. When buying bare-root plants, make sure the roots have not dried out and select plants with balanced main and fibrous roots.

Choose fruit trees that are healthy with sturdy growth and, if two or three years old, with well-spaced laterals. Inspect plants carefully and do not buy any with signs of pest infestation, damage, disease, or those that are lacking in vigour.

Pollination requirements
Most soft fruits and some tree fruits are self-fertile, that is they produce a crop without needing a pollinating cultivar nearby, and may therefore be grown singly. Apples, pears, nearly all sweet cherries, and some plums are not reliably self-fertile, however. To produce a successful crop, self-sterile cultivars need to be cross-pollinated by another cultivar

ROOTSTOCK

A graft union between rootstock and scion is identifiable by a noticeable kink in the stem 10–30cm (4–12in) above the soil mark, especially on young fruit trees that have only recently been propagated. When planting, make sure that the graft union is not below soil level.

of the same fruit. Usually, one pollinating cultivar is sufficient but some apples and pears must be grown close to two other cultivars for all trees to produce good crops.

For cross-pollination to occur, the flowering periods of the different cultivars must overlap. Cultivars are therefore divided into flowering groups, from early to late, which are indicated by numbers under the individual fruit entries. Cultivars for cross-pollination should be in the same, preceding, or following group. A cultivar in group 3, for example, is compatible with others in groups 2, 3, and 4.

Certain cultivars of some fruits, however, will not cross-pollinate, although they may flower at the same time. For sweet cherries and pears, these are classified in incompatiblity groups, which are indicated in the lists. Seek advice, if in doubt. A few sweet cherry cultivars will pollinate all other cultivars in flower at the same time; these are known as universal pollinators.

Selecting rootstocks
Many tree fruit cultivars offered for sale will have been grafted onto a compatible rootstock, since cultivars do not breed true from seed, and cannot be raised consistently from cuttings. The rootstock controls the growth rate and size of the mature tree, while the scion determines the cultivar of fruits produced. Some rootstocks have a dwarfing effect (useful for a small garden) and induce early fruiting. A few rootstocks are resistant to certain diseases.

Selecting fruit trees

Young fruit trees may be purchased at several stages of growth – choose the one most appropriate for the form that the tree is to take. Maiden whip trees (with sideshoots) take at least one year longer than other forms to train and fruit. One-year-old feathered maidens are popular with experienced growers since their sideshoots enable the earliest possible training. Two-year-old trees fruit more quickly, and good specimens are easily trained. Three-year-old, trained trees are more expensive and can be harder to re-establish.

Planting in open ground

Container-grown plants may be planted at any time of year except when the ground is frozen or water-logged, or during drought. Plant bare-root plants from late autumn to early spring while they are dormant; soak the roots well before planting. In frosty periods, heel them in temporarily in moist, frost-free soil until conditions are suitable for planting.

Planting fruit trees

If planting a number of trees, measure the site and mark out the planting positions with canes. Dig a hole for each tree at least one third wider than the tree's root system; firm the base of the hole and slightly mound it.

Insert a stake into the hole 7–8cm (3in) away from the centre to allow for the tree's growth in girth as it matures. The height of the stake depends on the form into which the tree is to be trained (for details, see under individual fruits). Fruit trees on dwarfing rootstocks need permanent staking; remove the stake of those on other rootstocks after three years.

Place the tree in the hole, making sure that the soil mark on the stem is at ground level, and spread out the roots. Do not cover the union between rootstock and scion, since this encourages scion-rooting and the rootstock's influence will be lost.

Backfill in stages with soil, while another person holds the tree upright, shaking it gently from time to time so that the soil settles in between the roots. Firm the soil; when the hole is nearly full, break up the soil around the edges to obtain a uniform soil firmness over a greater area. Firm and level the area, and attach the tree to the stake using a soft, pliable, plastic tie with a firm cushion between tree and stake to prevent chafing. Protect the tree from rabbits and other animals with a wire netting surround.

Fruit trees to be planted against a wall or fence should be positioned 15–22cm (6–9in) away from the support, with the branches sloping gently inwards. This ensures that the roots are in good soil and allows for future expansion of the trunk.

Planting soft fruits and vines

Bush and cane fruits are planted as for fruit trees, but no staking is needed. Plant only up to the soil mark: planting too deeply inhibits the plants' growth. For vines, make the planting holes or trench wide enough for the roots to be fully extended, and train the vines against a support.

Planting in containers

Water the young plant thoroughly before planting. Use a moist, soil-based potting compost, leaving 2.5cm (1in) between the compost surface and the rim of the pot for watering. Water again after planting and keep the compost moist until growth begins, then water regularly.

PLANTING CORDONS

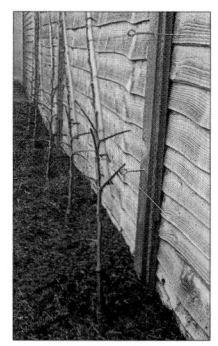

IN THE OPEN GROUND
Space trees 75cm (2¹/₂ft) apart (top). Attach a cane at an angle of 45° to horizontal wires (bottom left) stretched between sturdy posts. Tie each tree securely to a cane (bottom right).

AGAINST A FENCE
Fix wires 10–15cm (4–6in) away from the fence to allow for the growth of the trees and to promote good air circulation. Plant the trees 15–22cm (6–9in) from the fence.

PLANTING A FRUIT BUSH

1 *Dig a hole large enough to accommodate the roots of the bush when spread out. Place a cane across the hole to check that the level of the surrounding soil is the same as the soil mark on the main stem.*

2 *Backfill the hole with soil; tread in the soil gently to ensure that no air pockets remain between the roots. Rake over the soil lightly to level the surface.*

PLANTING A FRUIT TREE

1 *Dig a hole one third wider than the tree's root system. Drive in a stake to a depth of 45cm (18in) about 7cm (3in) from the centre of the hole.*

2 *Slightly mound the soil at the base of the hole and place the tree in the centre. Use a cane to check that the soil mark on the stem is level with the soil surface.*

3 *Spread out the tree's roots, then gradually fill the hole with soil. Firm to ensure that the tree is well anchored and that there are no air pockets between the roots.*

4 *Attach a buckle-and-spacer to the top of the stake and then to the tree so that the cushion is between the stem and the stake (see inset). Adjust as necessary.*

Routine care

Most fruit plants need regular maintenance to ensure that they are healthy and produce high-quality crops. Routine operations vary, depending on the type of fruit, growing conditions, and season.

Fruit thinning

Fruit thinning is necessary for a number of tree fruits, particularly apples, pears, and plums, to provide good-sized, high-quality fruits. It also prevents branch breakages by ensuring balanced crop distribution. In addition, thinning helps to prevent biennial bearing (to which some fruit cultivars are prone), that is bearing heavy crops one year and little or none the next.

Thin initially by hand or with scissors to remove disfigured fruits; later, thin again to leave the fruits room to develop fully and receive enough sun and air to ripen. Details of how and when to thin are given under each fruit.

Fertilizing, mulching, and watering

Apply manures and fertilizers when needed, observing crop performance and checking for any leaf discoloration that may denote nutrient deficiencies. In hot, dry summers, watering will usually be necessary; a trickle watering system (see p.469) uses water most efficiently.

Care of tree fruits

In early spring, mulch newly planted trees and any that are not thriving with manure or compost. First check

HOW TO THIN FRUIT

1 *Thinning of some fruits is required to obtain fruit of a good size and quality; if it is left unthinned, the fruit is usually small and of poor flavour.*

2 *Remove unhealthy or disfigured fruits first, then reduce the remainder to at least 5–8cm (2–3in) apart, depending on the type of fruit.*

that any problem is not caused by a pest or disease; if it is, treat as recommended in PLANT PROBLEMS, pp.545–77. Once the trees reach flowering size, apply a balanced fertilizer at a rate of 105–140g/sq m (3–4oz/sq yd) in early spring. Do not overfeed, particularly with nitrogen, as this may produce soft, disease-prone growth.

If a particular nutrient is needed, use specific fertilizers: potassium sulphate to correct potassium deficiency; ammonium nitrate to supply nitrogen; superphosphate to provide

phosphorus. Apply these in spring at a rate of 35g/sq m (1oz/sq yd), except superphosphate, which is normally applied at three times this rate every three or four years. Correct magnesium deficiency (p.555) by spraying the foliage, after flowering, with a solution of Epsom salts. In severe cases, repeat the treatment after three weeks.Other deficiencies, especially of manganese and iron (p.555), may also arise. If, more rarely, deficiencies of zinc, copper, or other elements are suspected, seek specialist advice.

Apply fertilizers evenly over an area just beyond the branch spread. Where trees are grown in grass, mow regularly and leave the mowings *in situ*; they rot down and return nutrients to the soil, helping particularly to avert potassium deficiency.

Care of soft fruits

Mulch soft fruits regularly in spring with rotted farmyard manure. Use fertilizers as indicated for tree fruits; nitrogen and potassium are the most essential nutrients. Apply fertilizer over the whole area; in the case of raspberries, spread the dressing at least 60cm (2ft) either side of the row. With strawberries, dig in manure before planting.

Fruit in containers

Although soil-based potting composts contain nutrients, plants should be fed in the growing season in order to replace the nutrients as they are used; nitrogen and potassium in particular are often needed. Fruit plants in containers require watering

more frequently than those planted in open ground. Check the compost regularly – at least once a day in hot, dry weather – and keep it moist.

Each winter, fruit trees and bushes in pots should be top-dressed or repotted. To top-dress, remove the top 2.5cm (1in) of compost with a hand fork and replace with fresh compost. In alternate winters, where possible, repot the plant. Remove the plant from its container, and gently comb away some of the old compost from the root ball, using a hand fork or wooden stick. Cut out any coarse roots, taking care not to damage the fibrous roots, and repot into a larger, clean container (see also "Planting in containers", p.365).

Stakes and ties

The stakes and ties of both free-standing and trained fruits should be checked regularly. When the cushioning or ties are weak or worn out, the tree may rub against the stake, and *Nectria* canker (p.568) on apples, or bacterial canker (p.569) on stone fruits may develop. Check the base of the stake: this may rot and then topple with the tree in high winds, particularly just before a heavy crop is to be gathered. On trained trees, ensure that branches are not tied too tightly to canes or wires since this will restrict growth. Loosen any ties if necessary.

Supporting branches

Tree fruits grown in unrestricted forms may need to have their branches supported when the tree is heavily laden with fruit, even if the

FERTILIZING FRUIT TREES

Using string and a peg, mark a circular area around the tree, slightly beyond the spread of the branches. This indicates where fertilizer should be applied – over the whole span of the tree's root system.

SUPPORTING LADEN BRANCHES

Tie several pieces of nylon string to a centrally placed pole attached to the main trunk. Use a nail to stop the string slipping down the pole. Tie at least one string to each heavily laden branch (away from the fruits) to support it.

fruits have been correctly thinned. If only one or two branches are affected, support them on forked stakes or rope them in to stronger branches. If several branches are overloaded, secure a sturdy stake either to the trunk or to the main stake and tie a rope to each branch and to the top of the stake; this technique is known as "maypoling".

Protecting plants

Fruit trees and bushes may need to be protected from bad weather or frost with windbreaks or insulation. Protection against birds and animals may also be necessary.

Wind protection
Maintain windbreaks (see p.519) properly so that they remain effective, and prune natural barriers such as trees or shrubs if they become thin to encourage bushier growth. Check that posts supporting windbreak netting or fences are secure and repair them as necessary.

Frost protection
Most frost damage is caused by spring frosts that kill or injure buds, flowers, or fruitlets overnight. Severe winter frosts may cause bark splitting and dieback, but in areas where low temperatures are common, select cultivars that are bred to withstand the conditions. In subtropical regions, there should be few problems; if necessary, cover small trees and bushes with polyester fabric or spun polypropylene sheets.

A very slight frost seldom causes any serious damage: -2°C (28°F) is frequently the danger point. The duration of the frost is usually more important than the temperature alone: -3°C (27°F) for a quarter of an hour would cause little or no damage whereas, sustained over three hours, it could cause substantial losses.

If frost is forecast, protect strawberries, bushes, and even small trees by using old curtains, hessian, or layers of newspaper to cover the plant completely and trap warm air around it. Remove the covers each day once the temperature has risen above freezing point. For further information, see FROST AND WIND PROTECTION, pp.520–21.

Protection from birds
In winter, bullfinches and tits damage fruit buds by feeding on the nutritious centre of the buds and discarding the outer bud scales. This damage is much more serious than the loss of ripe fruit because it denudes whole branches permanently,

making it necessary to prune them back to obtain new, young shoots, which will not fruit for two or more seasons. The best protection is to place nets over the trees or bushes. If snow is forecast, support the net or remove it temporarily because the weight of the snow on the net may damage branches underneath.

Ripening fruit should also be protected against birds; small areas may be temporarily covered with netting but for large areas it is preferable to erect a fruit cage instead. It is impractical to protect large fruit trees, although those trained against

supports may be enclosed by attaching netting to the support. The mesh of any net used must be small enough to exclude tiny birds. Protect strawberries in a patch with a low, temporary cage.

Pest, disease, and weed control

It is advisable to check plants once a week for signs of pest and disease problems; they may then be treated at an early stage before extensive

damage has been caused (see PLANT PROBLEMS, pp.545–77). If virus diseases (pp.553 and 563) are suspected, seek professional advice to ensure that this is the problem; strawberries, raspberries, loganberries, blackberries, and blackcurrants are especially vulnerable. The only practical solution is to dig up infected specimens with their roots and burn them, otherwise the virus may spread to adjacent plants.

Weed control is also essential. Remove seedling weeds and mulch to inhibit germination of weed seeds. Perennial weeds should be dug out or spot-treated as soon as they are noticed. For further details, see "Weeds", pp.573–7.

Plants under cover

In cool-temperate climates, some fruits may need to be grown under cover. These include all the tender fruits, and a number of other fruits which either have flowers that are vulnerable to damage by spring frosts or require a long ripening period, for example peaches and many late-ripening grapes.

In subtropical climates, fruit trees are rarely grown under cover, since the only climatic problems encountered are exceptionally cool periods and heavy rainfall, which most are able to tolerate.

Plants that need to be under cover all year are best grown in greenhouses; walk-in polytunnels are of limited use because temperature levels and adequate ventilation are hard to maintain (see also GREENHOUSES AND FRAMES, "Choosing a greenhouse", pp.476–9).

Particular care is needed to maintain free air circulation around plants grown in greenhouses to discourage diseases that may be caused by the increased heat and humidity. Support wires for trained fruits should be secured at least 30cm (12in) away from the glass or plastic of the greenhouse. Control any pests and diseases and apply fertilizer as recommended under individual tree fruit entries. For details of pruning fruits grown in a greenhouse, see "Pruning under cover", p.370.

Growing tender fruits (for example citrus, guava, pomegranate, and olive) in containers makes it possible to bring them under cover when necessary. In cool areas, place tender plants grown in pots outside in a sunny position in spring and bring them under cover again in autumn. Overwinter the plants in the greenhouse at a temperature of at least 10–15°C (50–60°F).

PROTECTING AGAINST BIRD AND ANIMAL DAMAGE

BUD-STRIPPING
Birds stripping buds from branches over winter cause permanent damage, leading to unproductive, bare wood.

NETTING STRAWBERRIES
Protect fruit by erecting a frame 1.2m (4ft) high and draping and tying 2cm (³/4in) mesh netting over it. Secure the base so that birds and squirrels cannot get underneath.

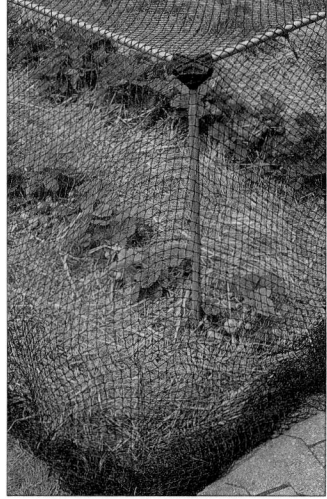

FRUIT CAGE
Fruit bushes or small fruit trees may be protected by a cage constructed from metal supports covered with wire or plastic netting.

PROTECTING TRAINED TREES
Fruit trees trained against supporting wires may be protected with a 2cm (³/4in) mesh net fixed at the top and secured firmly to the support.

Pruning and training

Fruit trees and bushes need correct, regular pruning and, in many cases, training to yield a good crop. The degree and method required depend on the desired shape and the fruiting time and habit as well as on the individual type of fruit. Relatively limited pruning is needed to produce an open-centre bush tree, for example, while extensive, formative pruning and training are required for a fan or espalier to produce a symmetrical network of well-trained branches.

Aims of pruning and training

Initially, young trees and bushes should receive formative pruning and training to produce the desired shape (such as a cordon) and to develop a strong, balanced framework. With established plants, the aim of subsequent pruning is to maintain the health and shape of the plant and ensure a good yield of fruit.

Pruning
This is the cutting out of unwanted shoots and branches, either because they spoil the plant's framework or because they are unproductive. Correct pruning maintains an open, uncrowded structure to allow the maximum amount of sun to reach the ripening fruits and to simplify spraying and harvesting. It also includes the removal of dead, diseased, damaged, or old, unfruitful wood.

On young plants, pruning may be combined with training to form a particular shape; unwanted shoots are removed completely while those retained may be cut back to stimulate the growth of sideshoots. The established, cropping tree, bush, or plant is pruned to encourage optimum growth and fruit production.

Training
The selection and, in many cases, the tying in of shoots to create a specific shape is known as training. Forms close to the natural shape, such as the bush, require much less training than, for example, a fan, which is produced by precise selection, spacing, and tying in of individual shoots onto a supporting framework of canes and wires.

Over- and underpruning
Take care not to over- or underprune as this restricts fruitfulness and may encourage disease. Repeated, severe pruning results in increased, vigorous, vegetative growth, and little or no fruit since few fruit buds are able to develop. This is especially damaging on a plant that is already vigorous. Underpruning leads to overcrowded branches that will receive less sun, which is essential to ripen the fruit; the branches may also rub together, exposing the tree to the risk of diseases such as *Nectria* canker (p.568). Pruning a young tree too lightly may also cause early overcropping that could stunt the tree and even break branches by overloading them.

When to prune

The time of pruning depends both on the specific treatment and on the kind of fruit. In the pruning procedures described here and under the individual fruits, "year one" refers to the first twelve months after planting, "year two" to the following twelve months, and so on.

Winter pruning is standard practice on all untrained apple, pear, quince, and medlar trees, on vines, and on black-, red-, and white-currants, gooseberries, and blueberries. Pruning of untrained trees of stone fruits (plum, cherry, peach, nectarine, and apricot) must be delayed until spring for young trees or summer for established ones, to minimize the risk of silver leaf infection (p.551). Summer pruning is essential on trained forms of tree fruits, grape vines, currants, and gooseberries. This reduces their vigour and contains them within the restricted space they occupy; it also concentrates the plants' energies on fruit production. Many tender fruits are pruned directly after fruiting.

How to prune

When deciding on the extent of pruning, always take into account the vigour both of the individual shoot and of the whole tree. Vigorous growth should be pruned lightly; this usually involves thinning out a percentage of shoots completely and leaving the remainder unpruned. Prune weak growth more severely, but check first that no disease, such as canker, is causing the weakness.

Where to cut
It is important always to prune to just above a healthy bud and to make a clean cut; cutting midway between buds or leaving a ragged end may cause dieback and increase the shoot's vulnerability to disease. If removing a shoot or branch completely, cut it back to the point of origin but leave the bark ridge and branch collar intact rather than cutting flush with the parent stem.

WHERE TO MAKE A PRUNING CUT

CUTTING TO A BUD
Cut just above a bud at a 45° angle, sloping the cut away from the bud. Do not cut too close or the bud may be damaged, nor too far away, or the stem may die back.

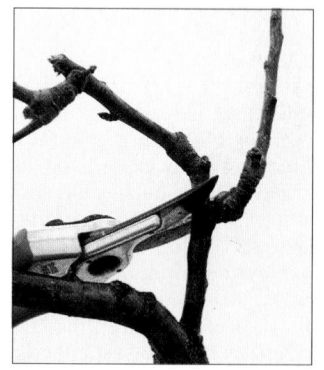

CUTTING TO A REPLACEMENT SHOOT
As when cutting to a bud, make an angled cut sloping away from the replacement shoot.

CUTTING BACK TO A MAIN BRANCH
Make a clean cut, leaving the branch collar intact (inset, top). The tree is then less susceptible to disease and the wound heals faster (inset, bottom).

REMOVING A BRANCH

1 Using a pruning saw, make the first cut approximately 30cm (12in) away from the trunk. Saw at right angles to the branch from underneath, to about a quarter of the way through.

2 Start the second cut at the top of the branch, slightly further out than the first cut. Saw right through the branch; if it breaks away, the bark will tear only as far as the first cut.

3 When making the final cut, take care not to damage the bark ridge at the top of the branch or the collar at the base. If necessary, start the cut from below and cut down from above to meet it.

4 Pare away rough edges with a sharp knife. The exposed area will seal itself more quickly with the bark ridge and collar left intact. This also reduces the risk of disease entering the wound. Do not apply wound paint, as it might seal in an existing infection.

To prevent the branch or bark from tearing before cutting is completed, undercut first before finishing the cut from above. Cut back to the point of origin or to a well-placed, healthy branch as a suitable replacement. Do not leave a stub or the cut end will die instead of healing. Pare away any rough edges with a sharp knife.

Fruiting habits

How a plant is pruned depends on its fruiting habit. For example, sweet cherries form fruit mainly on spurs on two-year and older wood, so many of the older shoots must be retained. Acid cherries, however, fruit on one-year-old shoots; when pruning, leave most of the young shoots but remove some of the old, unproductive wood.

Training for shape

A young tree is usually bought as a "feathered maiden" (a one-year-old tree with sideshoots). Initial pruning consists of selecting shoots to be retained, shortening them as required, and removing unwanted shoots. If a young tree is bought as a

maiden whip (a one-year-old tree without sideshoots), it should be cut down to a bud after planting, the height depending on how the tree is to be trained. This encourages the growth of sideshoots. When these develop, the tree, now two years old, is equivalent to a feathered maiden. Formative pruning continues for the first two or three years until the desired shape has been obtained.

Training for fruitfulness

The vigour and fruitfulness of shoots may be adjusted by raising or lowering selected laterals or, with oblique cordons, the whole tree. Horizontal growths are more fruitful than vertical ones, so tying a lateral closer to the horizontal makes it produce more fruit. If one lateral is less vigorous than another and more sideshoots are needed, raising it will stimulate vegetative growth. For an established, cropping tree or bush, pruning is more important than training; even on an untrained tree, less fruitful or unbalanced shoots may be tied down in summer to increase their yield.

PRUNING A MAIDEN WHIP TO FORM A FEATHERED TREE

WINTER, YEAR 1
To produce vigorous "feathers" (sideshoots) on a maiden whip tree, cut it back with an angled cut just above a bud at the required height.

WINTER, YEAR 2
By the following winter, a number of new sideshoots should have been produced below the pruning cut.

TRAINING ON CANES

1 The vigour of laterals of trained trees may be altered by adjusting the angle at which they are trained. This technique corrects uneven growth on either side of the same tree.

2 Lower a young, strong-growing lateral, with its cane, at the start of or during the summer to reduce its vigour; raise a lateral to encourage it to grow more quickly. Retie the canes to the wires.

3 By the end of the summer, the branches may be returned to their original positions; they should be more even in length.

Curbing excessive vigour

Extremely vigorous trees that produce rapid vegetative growth at the expense of cropping may benefit from root pruning. On apples and pears only, bark-ringing (see p.377) may also be used as a last resort to curb vigour; it should not be used on stone fruits as it may kill them. Both methods will induce the formation of fruit buds, so the beneficial effects will be seen in increased blossom and fruiting one or possibly two years later.

Root pruning

Trees may be root pruned at any age, but only when they are dormant. When pruning the roots of a young tree, first lift it by digging around it, then remove soil carefully from around the fibrous roots, taking care not to damage them. Cut back a few of the thick roots in the process. Then replant the tree firmly and stake it.

Larger trees need to be root pruned *in situ*, pruning one side of the root system one winter, and completing the other side a year or two later. To do this effectively, make a trench 45cm–1.2m (18in–4ft) wide, depending on the size of the tree, to expose the main roots. These should be severed and a section of each root removed. Then fill in the trench, firm, and mulch; in some cases, staking may be required to provide support until the tree is fully stable.

Pruning under cover

Prune back branches and shoots of plants grown in a greenhouse so that they do not touch the glass or plastic surfaces, as otherwise they may suffer sun scorch and growth will be constricted or damaged. Regular pruning also allows more light to reach the developing fruits and helps them to ripen.

Renovation

If a tree is too old to crop well, and has rotten or severely diseased branches or trunk, it should be grubbed out and burnt. If the trunk and the main branches are sound, however, and the tree is merely overcrowded, it can be rejuvenated by means of renovative pruning followed by correct, routine care.

Renovative work should be carried out in spring or summer on stone fruits and in winter on apples, pears, and other pome fruits. Cut out any branches that are dead, damaged, or diseased, or so low that they may trail on the ground when laden with fruit. Also remove crowded or crossing branches, as these will shade the developing fruits, and, if they rub together, may become prone to diseases such as canker. On a vigorous tree, it is advisable to stagger this pruning over more than one year; pruning too severely on a single occasion may only induce more vigorous, vegetative growth.

Once this initial thinning has been achieved, more precise pruning, such as spur thinning, may be carried out (as described for routine pruning under individual fruit entries). Chemical inhibitors are available to curb the regrowth of water shoots around the cuts, but wound paints are not recommended as they may seal in any infection.

ROOT PRUNING TO IMPROVE FRUITING

1 *Mark out the position for a trench around the tree using string and a peg. The trench should be at the same distance from the tree all the way round, just below the outermost spread of the branches.*

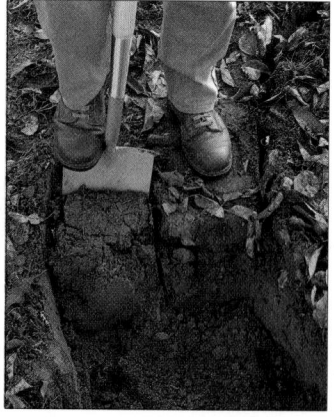

2 *Dig out a trench around the tree at the marked line; it should be at least 45cm (18in) wide and approximately 60cm (24in) deep.*

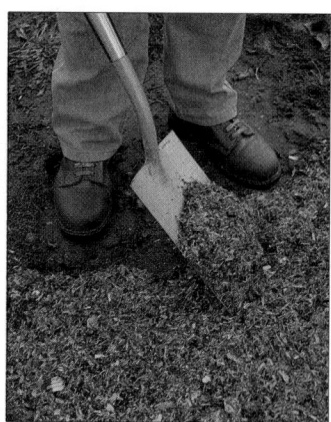

3 *At the base of the trench, use a fork to remove soil from around the thick roots without damaging the fibrous roots.*

4 *Sever each woody root on either side of the trench with a pruning saw, discarding the central section. Leave the fibrous roots unpruned.*

5 *Backfill the trench with soil, firm well, then cover the area with an organic mulch to retain moisture and help the tree re-establish. Stake if necessary.*

RENOVATING A NEGLECTED TREE

1 *Remove overcrowded, rubbing, or crossing branches to let in light and air by cutting them back to their point of origin, or to a vigorous sub-lateral facing the required direction.*

2 *Any branches that are damaged or affected by a disease such as canker (shown above) should be removed completely, or cut back to a healthy shoot.*

Harvesting and storing

MANY home-grown fruits may be enjoyed long after their normal harvesting time if correctly harvested and stored. While most are at their best eaten fresh, a number keep their flavour well even after prolonged storage. For details on harvesting and storing specific fruits, see the individual fruit entries.

Harvesting

Most fruits are best picked when fully ripe for using fresh. Fruits for storing are usually harvested slightly earlier, however, when they are mature but not yet completely ripe and still firm. Since not all the fruits on a single plant ripen at the same time, it is usually necessary to harvest over a period and this provides a succession of fresh supplies.

For tree fruits such as apples and pears, test for ripeness by holding a fruit in the palm of the hand, then gently lift and twist. If ripe, the fruit will come away easily complete with its stalk, otherwise it should be left for a day or two.

When harvesting, discard any damaged, diseased, or bruised fruits as they will quickly become infected with rot, which then spreads rapidly to adjacent fruits when in storage.

Soft fruits must be picked completely dry otherwise many may be affected by rot unless the fruits are used immediately. Regular picking,

at least every other day, is advisable for strawberries, raspberries, blackberries, and hybrid berries.

Always take care not to damage the plant when harvesting – by pulling fruit off sharply, for example. Some types of fruit, such as cherries, grapes, and mangos, should be cut off the plant to avoid the risk of accidental damage.

Storing

There are various ways of keeping fruits for later use, including cool storage, freezing, and preserving; the most suitable method depends on the type of fruit. Some fruits, especially those such as apples, apricots, and figs that have a high acid and sugar content, may also be oven-dried at 120–40°F (49–60°C) but this is difficult to do successfully at home.

FREEZING SOFT FRUITS

Spread out soft fruits, such as raspberries, on trays so that they are not in contact with each other, then freeze them. Once they are frozen, they may be packed into suitable containers and kept in the freezer until they are required for use.

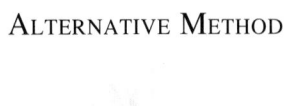

When preparing fruits for storage, handle them carefully to avoid bruising. Always store different cultivars in separate containers that are free from any residues or aromas that may taint the fruits.

Cool storage

Apples and pears in particular may be kept for several weeks, or even months in the right conditions – consistently cool, dark, and slightly damp. Various other tree fruits, such as lemons, may also be stored this way although they do not usually keep for such a long period, while most nuts keep well for up to a few months. Soft fruits cannot be stored in this way. The required temperature and degree of humidity vary for different fruits, but most should be stored in slatted trays and boxes to allow free air circulation. Some apple and pear cultivars, however, tend to

shrivel and are better kept in clear plastic bags. Check unwrapped fruits regularly and remove any that show signs of disease or rotting.

Freezing

This is ideal for most soft fruits, except strawberries, and for a number of tree fruits. Small fruits such as raspberries are usually frozen whole, while large fruits such as apples are best chopped or sliced beforehand to ensure even and thorough freezing. Remove any stalks (and "strigs" of currants) then open-freeze whole fruits spread out on trays. Once they are frozen – after two to four hours – transfer the fruits to plastic boxes or bags, excluding as much air as possible, and keep them frozen until needed. Strawberries and some soft-fleshed tree fruits such as plums are often puréed before being frozen.

Preserving and bottling

All soft fruits and a number of tree fruits such as apricots and damsons may be made into preserves. In most cases, the entire fruit is used, while some such as grapes and blackberries are better strained and only the juice used to make a sweet jelly.

Citrus fruits, pineapples, and most stone fruits such as cherries may be bottled in sugar syrup with alcohol (such as rum, brandy, or *eau de vie*) if desired to preserve them. Citrus peel may also be candied or dried for use in baking.

STORING APPLES

1 *Wrap each fruit individually in greaseproof paper to prevent rot and keep it in good condition.*

2 *Carefully fold the greaseproof paper around the fruit, holding it lightly so that you do not bruise it.*

3 *Place each wrapped fruit on its folded end in a wooden slatted box, or other well-ventilated container, and store in a cool place.*

ALTERNATIVE METHOD

Store fruits of cultivars that tend to shrivel quickly in a plastic bag. Make several holes in the bag before filling it with no more than 3kg (6lb 8oz) of fruit. Seal the bag loosely.

FRUITS THAT FREEZE WELL

Apples Sl
Apricots Sl
Blackberries and all hybrid berries Sk
Blackcurrants Sk
Blueberries Sk
Cherries (acid) Sk
Cherries (sweet) Sk
Damsons Sk (with or without stones)
Gages Sk
Gooseberries Sk
Grapes Sk
Nectarines Sl
Peaches Sl
Plums Sk, Sl
Raspberries Sk
Redcurrants Sk
Whitecurrants Sk

KEY

Sk *Remove stalks (and stones where applicable)*
Sl *Remove cores or stones and slice and peel if required*

Propagation

TREE fruits (except figs) are usually propagated by grafting; figs, vines, and many soft fruits by cuttings, although if *Phylloxera* (see p.401) is a problem, grape vines should be grafted. Some fruits produce runners, layers, or suckers, all of which may be used to produce new plants. Several tender fruits and some nuts may be grown from seed but hardy fruits seldom come true.

Bud-grafting

Both chip-budding and T-budding are used to increase the stock of fruit trees. They are economical methods of propagation, since a new tree is produced from a single bud. Grafting should be carried out in mid-summer, using as the rootstock an established plant with a stem that is at least 1cm (¹/₂in) thick. A bud from the scion plant is cut from a ripe shoot (the budstick) of the current season's growth, and grafted onto an incision in the rootstock.

Propagating by chip-budding

Select a healthy budstick and carefully remove a bud (the bud chip), taking care not to damage the cambium layer. Remove a sliver of rind from the rootstock and place the bud chip onto the exposed wood of the rootstock so that the cambium layers are in close contact. Bind the bud chip tightly onto the rootstock to hold it in place. When the bud and rootstock have united the bud will start to swell and the binding may be removed. The following winter, trim the rootstock just above the grafted bud to encourage a strong shoot to develop from the graft in spring.

CHIP-BUDDING

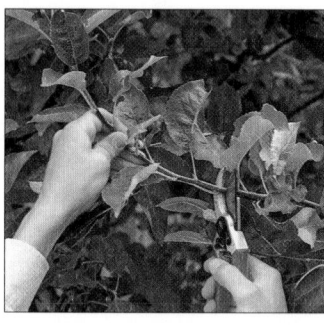

1 *Choose a vigorous shoot of the current season's ripened wood as the budstick. The shoot should be approximately pencil thick and have well-developed buds.*

2 *Hold the budstick firmly and, using a clean, sharp knife, slice off the soft tip and remove all the leaves to produce a clear length of stem.*

3 *To remove a bud chip, first slice into the budstick about 2cm (³/₄in) below a bud. Cut down to a depth of about 5mm (¹/₄in), slanting the blade at an angle of 45°.*

4 *Make another incision about 4cm (1¹/₂in) above the first. Slice downwards behind the bud towards the first incision, taking care not to damage the bud.*

5 *Remove the bud chip, holding it by the bud to keep the cambium layer clean. Place the bud chip in a plastic bag to stop it drying out.*

6 *To prepare the rootstock, stand astride the plant and, using a sharp knife, remove all the shoots and leaves from the bottom 30cm (12in) of stem.*

7 *Make a shallow cut in the stock. Remove a sliver of rind to reveal the cambium layer (see inset), leaving a "lip" at the base. Do not touch the exposed wood.*

Bud chip in position on rootstock

8 *Place the bud chip onto the prepared lip of rind, offset if necessary, so that the exposed cambium layers of bud chip and rootstock match and touch.*

9 *Bind the bud chip to the rootstock with plastic tape. Carefully remove the tape after a few weeks when the bud chip has united with the rootstock.*

10 *The following late winter, remove the top of the rootstock. Cut cleanly with secateurs just above the grafted bud, using an angled cut.*

11 *During the summer, a shoot from the grafted bud will develop. The new tree is then at the maiden whip stage (see "Selecting fruit trees", p.365).*

Propagating by T-budding

In this technique the rootstock and scion bud are prepared in a similar way to chip-budding, except that two slits are made in the rootstock, to form the shape of a "T". This allows the bark of the rootstock to be lifted slightly so that the scion bud may be tucked behind it. Removing the scion bud with a leaf stalk attached makes it easier to handle; the stalk is removed before the bud is bound to the rootstock. The rootstock should be cut back the next winter.

For this technique to be successful, the bark of the rootstock must lift smoothly: in dry weather, rootstocks need to be watered for up to two weeks before T-budding takes place.

Whip-and-tongue grafting

This is a common method of grafting for tree fruits. It may be used as an alternative to budding but it is usually more successful with pome than with stone fruits. Use well-established rootstocks that have been planted either the previous winter or, preferably, two winters before grafting takes place.

The scion material should have at least three buds and should be taken in mid-winter from a healthy shoot of the previous season's growth. Heel it in until ready for grafting. In late winter or early spring, prepare the stock by cutting off the top of the stem and removing any sideshoots.

Using a sloping cut, slice off a small piece of bark from the top of the remaining stem; make a further shallow incision in the exposed cambium layer, to create a tongue.

Trim the scion to a length of three or four buds then, using a sloping cut, slice off a small piece of bark close to a bud but on the opposite side to it. Make a further, shallow incision, to match that in the stock, and hook the resulting tongue onto the one on the rootstock. Make sure that the two cambium layers are in

---

T-BUDDING

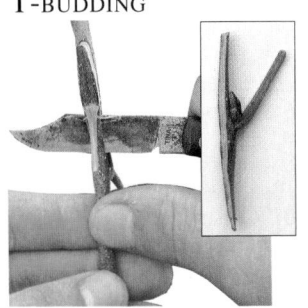

1 Select a ripened shoot as the scion from the current season's growth and remove the leaves. Remove a bud by slicing underneath it (*see inset*).

2 Make a "T"-shaped cut in the stock about 22cm (9in) above ground level and prise open the flaps of bark.

3 Place the bud behind the flaps of bark, trimming the top level with the horizontal cut on the stock. Bind the bud as for chip-budding.

WHIP-AND-TONGUE GRAFTING

1 In mid-winter, remove healthy, vigorous hardwood shoots from the scion tree. Cut lengths of about 22cm (9in), cutting obliquely just above a bud.

2 Make bundles of 5 or 6 scions. Choose a well-drained, sheltered site and heel them in to keep them moist but dormant, leaving 5–8cm (2–3in) above the soil surface.

3 In late winter or early spring, prepare the rootstocks just before bud break. Cut off the top of each rootstock about 20–25cm (8–10in) from ground level.

4 Trim off any shoots from the rootstock with a sharp knife, then make a 3.5cm (1¹/₂in) upward-sloping cut on one side to receive the scion.

5 Make a slit 1cm (¹/₂in) deep about one third of the way down the exposed cambium layer, to form a tongue into which the scion may be inserted (*see inset*).

6 Lift the scions, cut off any soft growth at the tips, and trim to 3 or 4 buds. For each, cut off a piece of bark behind a bud that is about 5cm (2in) from the base.

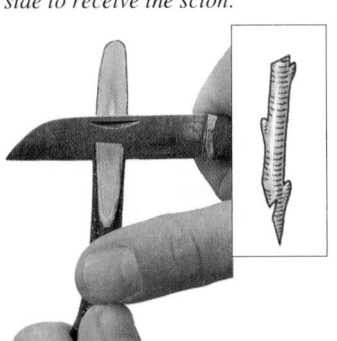

7 Without touching the cut surface with your hand, cut the cambium layer (*see inset*) to match the tongue in the rootstock.

8 Place the scion into the tongue on the stock (*inset, top*). Use the arches of the cambium layers as a guide (*inset, bottom*) to ensure the exposed surfaces fit together well.

9 Bind together stock and scion with clear plastic tape. When the cut surfaces start to callus, remove the tape by carefully scoring it downwards.

close contact, then bind the graft firmly. Remove the binding carefully when a callus has formed around the graft union. By spring, buds on the scion will have started to grow. Select the best shoot that develops (keeping others pinched back) to form a maiden whip tree (see "Selecting fruit trees", p.365).

Cuttings

Hardwood, softwood, and leaf-bud cuttings may used to propagate certain fruits. Cutting material should always be selected from a healthy parent plant that crops regularly.

Hardwood cuttings
Figs, vines, currants (white, red, and black), and gooseberries may be propagated from hardwood cuttings, usually taken in autumn.

Select a well-ripened shoot of the current season's growth and trim off the leaves and soft tip. Remove some or most of the buds, depending on the fruit being propagated, and trim off the top and base. The exact preparation and length of the cuttings vary slightly; details are given under individual fruit entries.

If the soil is well cultivated and not too heavy, the cuttings may be inserted into a narrow trench in the open ground. If the soil is heavy, however, place the cuttings in a pot of moist, sandy compost. The cuttings should be ready for transplanting one or two years later.

Softwood cuttings
Guavas, pomegranates, tree tomatoes, and blueberries are propagated from softwood cuttings (where the climate is warm enough for the wood to ripen sufficiently, blueberries may also be propagated from hardwood cuttings). Take the cuttings in mid-summer and place them in pots of cutting compost (see p.418). Harden off the young plants before transplanting to their permanent positions.

Leaf-bud cuttings
Stocks of blackberries and hybrid berries may be increased quickly by leaf-bud cuttings (see p.412). Take the cuttings in late summer: remove short lengths of stem, each with a bud and leaf attached; insert them in compost with the buds just above the surface. Once rooted, the cuttings may be potted up or planted out.

Runners, layers, and suckers

Some fruits send out runners, layers, or suckers, which root naturally at stem nodes while still attached to the parent plant. This process may be exploited to increase fruit stocks.

Runners
Strawberries (but not all alpine strawberries) produce creeping horizontal stems, or runners, which root where they come into contact with the ground and may be used for propagation. As the runners are produced, spread them out evenly. Allow them to root, and then lift and sever them (see p.410).

Layers
Blackberries and hybrid berries may be propagated by layering, although some hybrids are slow to root. The tip of a shoot is induced to root by carefully pegging it down in the soil or in a pot of moist compost (see "Tip layering", p.411). A year later, when the tip has rooted and produced new growth, it may be severed from the parent plant and transplanted to its permanent position.

Suckers
Established cane fruits such as raspberries naturally produce suckers that are usually hoed off. If retained, rooted suckers may be lifted and severed in autumn, when the plants are dormant but the soil is still warm. Transplant the rooted suckers directly to their permanent positions (see *Propagating by Suckers*, p.414). Figs, cobnuts, and filberts also produce suckers: if the suckers have good root systems, sever them with a spade and replant in the same way.

Seed

Propagation from seed is the usual method of increasing stock of many tender fruits, including avocado (see p.426), guava, and papaya.

The alpine strawberry is one of the few hardy fruits that may be raised successfully from seed (see p.410). Cobnuts, filberts, walnuts, and sweet chestnuts may also be raised from seed with a reasonable chance of success, although cultivars selected for the quality of their fruit need to be propagated vegetatively. For details, see ORNAMENTAL TREES, "Raising trees from seed", p.56.

HARDWOOD CUTTINGS

1 Dig a narrow trench 15cm (6in) deep. If the soil has a high clay content, sprinkle a little sand into the base of the trench to improve drainage.

2 Choose a ripened stem from the current season's growth (here, from a fig tree). Remove lengths of at least 30cm (12in), cutting flush with the main stem.

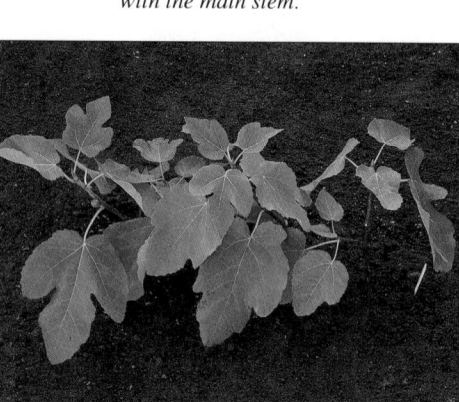

Cut off all the leaves and the soft growth at the tip of each cutting, then trim to about 23cm (9in): make an angled cut above the top bud and a straight cut at the base.

4 Place the cuttings in the prepared trench, spacing them 10–15cm (4–6in) apart and burying two-thirds of the stems. Firm the soil, and label.

5 The cuttings will take several months to root. Towards the end of the following growing season, they should have developed sturdy new growth.

6 After leaf-fall in autumn, carefully lift the rooted cuttings, wrapping the roots in plastic to stop them drying out. Transplant the cuttings to their permanent positions to grow on.

Tree fruits

The fruits in this group, known also as "top fruits", are the largest-growing forms in the fruit garden. They may be divided into two main categories: "pome fruits", such as apples and pears, have a pip-containing core; "stone fruits", such as cherries and apricots, have a hard, central stone. There are also certain other fruits within this group that fit into neither of the above categories, such as figs, mulberries, and persimmons.

Cultivating tree fruits is a long-term undertaking that requires careful planning. The size and shape or form of the trees are important considerations. Left to grow naturally, many tree fruits would become impracticably large for the average-sized garden. Smaller forms grown on dwarfing rootstocks have been developed, however; fruit trees may also be trained and pruned as fans, espaliers, or cordons and grown flat against walls or fences, making it feasible to grow them successfully in even the smallest of spaces.

Another factor to consider is the number of trees required. Many fruit trees are self-sterile and, to produce fruit, need at least one other tree of the same type to act as a pollinator. Even self-fertile trees crop more heavily if pollinators are present.

Some tree fruits such as figs prefer a long, hot growing season and are difficult to cultivate in cooler climates; growing them under cover provides protection and improves fruit and crop size, as well as flavour.

Once a tree fruit has been selected and planted, it is important to follow the correct pruning methods. Good pruning not only builds a strong framework of branches, but also encourages and maintains maximum cropping for many years.

Apples (*Malus sylvestris* var. *domestica*)

Apples are one of the most widely grown, hardy fruits and both dessert and culinary cultivars offer a great variety of flavours and textures.

Tree size may be considerably reduced now that dwarfing rootstocks are more widely available, which allows a number of different apples to be grown in small gardens where only one large tree could have been accommodated before. Apple trees may readily be trained into almost any shape. Cordon-, espalier-, and fan-shaped forms are particularly useful for growing against walls and fences.

The extensive choice of cultivars covers a period of ripening from midsummer to late winter, and fruit may be stored until mid-spring, given suitable conditions. There are cultivars and rootstocks suitable for most climates, including those with severe winter temperatures. For flowering to occur, the trees must be subjected to at least 900 hours below 7°C (45°F): the chilling requirement. Apples are not grown successfully in tropical or subtropical regions, as they do not receive adequate chilling.

Site and planting

When planting, make sure that each tree has sufficient space to develop to its full size. Select the most appropriate size of tree (largely determined by the rootstock) for your garden. In most cases, more than one apple tree will be required for pollination.

Site
A sunny, sheltered site is essential for consistently good crops. Walls for trained fruit should not be shaded and should preferably be in full sun. For shaded gardens or those in a region with short summers and cool temperatures, choose cultivars that ripen early. Where late frosts occur, select late-flowering cultivars so that the blossom will not be damaged.

Apples will grow in most well-drained soils, given adequate preparation (see "Preparing the site", p.364). The more dwarfing the rootstock, however, the more fertile the soil should be.

Rootstocks
Choice of rootstock depends on the tree size required and the soil type. Apple rootstocks are prefixed by M or MM, which stand for Malling and Malling Merton respectively, the research stations where the rootstocks were developed. A wide range of rootstocks is available, from 'M27', which is very dwarfing, to the extremely vigorous 'M25'. For normal garden purposes, 'M9' is recommended for dwarf trees, 'M26' for larger ones, and 'MM106' for medium-sized trees (see *Planting Distances*, p.376). Cultivars on 'M27' bear fruit within three years of being grafted but require good growing conditions to maintain high yields. Where the soil is poor, use a more vigorous rootstock to compensate: for example, where a dwarf tree is required use 'MM106' instead of 'M9' or 'M26'. The vigour of the chosen cultivar also determines the size of the mature tree. Triploid cultivars grow larger than diploids (see below); use a more dwarfing rootstock for a triploid than for a diploid cultivar to attain a tree of similar size.

Pollination
No apples are reliably and consistently self-fertile: diploids must be planted near a second, compatible cultivar; triploid apples, which will not pollinate other cultivars, require two compatible cultivars nearby to pollinate them. Cultivars are divided into flowering groups according to their time of flowering; a cultivar from one group may be cross-pollinated by another from the same group or one in the group before or after it if flowering times overlap (see also *Recommended Dessert Apples*, p.376, and *Recommended Culinary Apples*, p.377). Some cultivars are incompatible: of those listed on pp.376 and 377, 'Cox's Orange Pippin' will not pollinate 'Kidd's Orange Red' or 'Suntan' and vice versa. If in doubt about compatibility, ask a fruit nursery for advice.

Planting
Bare-root trees are best planted when dormant, preferably in autumn as the soil is then still warm; they may be planted until late winter (except when it is frosty) but keep them moist in spring so that they establish well. Container-grown trees may be planted at any time, unless the ground is frozen or very wet; water before planting so that the roots are moist. Using the soil mark as a guide, plant each tree at its original planting depth (see also *Planting a Fruit Tree*, p.365).

If the tree is to be trained, fit the supports and wires securely in place before planting (see under individual tree forms for details). For all untrained trees, staking when planting is essential and should be permanent for those on dwarfing rootstocks.

Planting distances (see p.376) depend upon how the trees are to be trained, as well as on the vigour of the chosen rootstocks and cultivars.

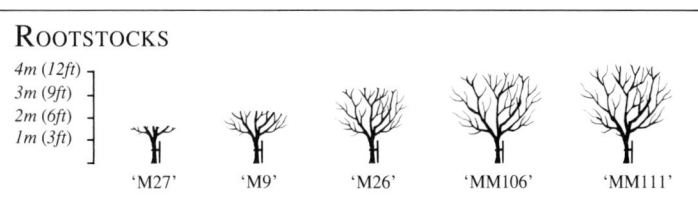

ROOTSTOCKS

4m (12ft)
3m (9ft)
2m (6ft)
1m (3ft)

'M27' 'M9' 'M26' 'MM106' 'MM111'

Routine care

Establish a regular maintenance programme to ensure that trees stay healthy and crop well. Feed and mulch periodically as required. Blossom and fruit thinning are annual tasks required to ensure satisfactory cropping. Check trees regularly for signs of pests and diseases and damage from rubbing stakes and ties.

Blossom thinning and biennial bearing

Certain cultivars, such as 'Laxton's Superb', tend to produce heavy crops in alternate years, with little or no blossom or fruit in intervening years. This is known as biennial bearing.

Blossom thinning can largely correct this; it involves removing nine of every ten blossom clusters by pinching them out, leaving the rosette of young leaves around each intact. The tree then produces a moderate, rather than heavy, crop and its resources are channelled into producing fruit buds for the following year, which would otherwise have been fruitless. On large trees, where it would be impractical to thin blossom over the entire tree, biennial bearing can be corrected by blossom-thinning a few branches.

If trees that normally crop regularly start to crop biennially, this may be due to the loss of blossom from frost and hence the crop; this may then induce a tree to overcrop the following year. The tree may not have sufficient resources to develop adequate fruit buds for the third year and a biennial tendency is set in motion. Disease or pest infestation causing a setback in one year may have a similar effect.

Fruit thinning

Thinning is essential where heavy crops have set, to improve fruit size, quality, and flavour, and to help prevent branches from breaking. On young trees, over-heavy cropping strains the tree's resources and slows the growth of new buds. Some thinning is possible on the young fruitlets, but it is simpler to carry out the whole task in early summer, after the "June drop", when the tree naturally sheds imperfect and infertile fruits.

Use secateurs to remove the centre (or "King") fruit of each cluster, which is sometimes abnormally shaped; then cut out any fruits that are damaged. In about mid-summer, thin the clusters again so that there is one good fruit per cluster. Fruit of dessert cultivars should be spaced 10–15cm (4–6in) apart, and that of culinary cultivars 15–22cm (6–9in) apart; these distances may vary according to the individual cultivar and the size of fruit required.

Fertilizing, watering, and mulching

Water trees in spells of hot, dry weather, apply fertilizer annually, and mulch as necessary (see "Care of tree fruits", p.366). If growth is poor, apply ammonium sulphate in spring at a rate of 35g/sq m (1oz/sq yd).

Stakes and ties

Inspect stakes and ties regularly to check that they are not rubbing against the bark of trees and that ties are not too loose; adjust them as necessary. Trees grown on dwarfing rootstocks such as 'M9' and 'M26' produce few tap roots and therefore need permanent staking to provide support and compensate for their lack of anchorage.

Pests and diseases

Common pests that may be troublesome include birds (p.561), wasps (p.563), codling moths (p.563), and red spider mites (p.550). Diseases that can affect apples include, scab (p.562), powdery mildew (p.562), brown rot (p.562), bitter pit (see "Calcium deficiency", p.562), and *Nectria* canker (p.568).

PLANTING DISTANCES

TREE FORM	ROOTSTOCK	DISTANCE BETWEEN TREES	DISTANCE BETWEEN ROWS
Bush	'M27'	1.2–2m (4–6ft)	2m (6ft)
	'M9'	2.5–3m (8–10ft)	3m (10ft)
	'M26'	3–4.75m (10–14ft)	5m (15ft)
	'MM106'	3.5–5.5m (11–18ft)	5.5m (18ft)
Half-standard	'MM111'	7.5–9m (24–28ft)	7.5–9m (24–28ft)
Standard	'MM111', 'M25' (or Seedling crab)	7.5–10.5m (24–32ft)	7.5–10.5m (24–32ft)
Spindlebush	'M9' or 'M26' (and triploids on 'M27')	2–2.2m (6–7ft)	2.5–3m (8–10ft)
	'MM106'	2–2.2m (6–7ft)	3.5m (11ft)
Cordon	as bush	75cm (30in)	2m (6ft)
Fan/espalier	'M9'	3m (10ft)	
	'MM106'	4.75m (14ft)	
	'MM111'	5.5m (18ft)	
Dwarf pyramid	'M27'	1.2m (4ft)	2m (6ft)
	'M9' or 'M26'	1.5m (5ft)	2–2.2m (6–7ft)
	'MM106'	2m (6ft)	2.2m (7ft)

APPLE THINNING

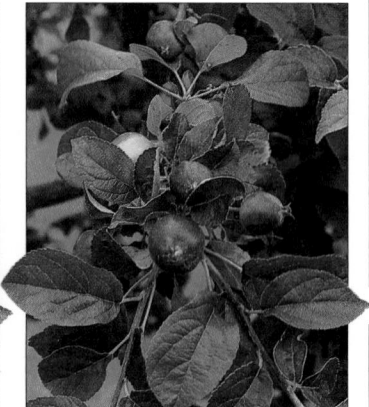

1 *Thinning is essential if the apple tree is carrying a heavy crop. After the "June drop", which is a normal occurrence, the remaining fruits will require further thinning if the crop is still heavy.*

2 *Remove sufficient small fruitlets (especially any that are malformed or very small) to leave about 10–15cm (4–6in) between each and only one fruitlet per cluster.*

Pruning and training techniques

Apple trees produce flowers and fruit mainly on two-year-old and older shoots and on short spurs produced on the older wood. Two-year-old shoots carry both large fruit buds and smaller, pointed growth buds. Fruit buds produce flower clusters and then fruit, while growth buds form into fruit buds for the following year or into sideshoots or fruiting spurs. One-year-old shoots may also carry fruit buds but these flower later than those on older wood. Tip-bearing cultivars produce markedly fewer spurs (see below).

Once their branch framework is established, trained trees need to be pruned (mainly in summer) to maintain shape, curb vegetative growth, and stimulate the production of fruit buds. Untrained trees require moderate pruning in winter to stimulate growth for the next season's fruit and to maintain an open, well-balanced structure so that they crop well and the fruit is of good quality.

FRUIT BUDS AND GROWTH BUDS

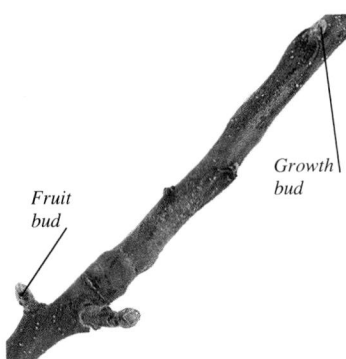

Fruit bud

Growth bud

Large fruit buds develop on 2-year-old and older wood. The smaller buds are growth buds, and are found mainly on one-year-old wood.

NICKING AND NOTCHING

NICKING
To weaken bud growth, make a nick in the bark just below the bud and into the cambium layer.

NOTCHING
To stimulate bud growth, make a notch through the bark into the cambium layer just above the bud.

Tip bearers and spur bearers

Cultivars differ in the way they bear most of their fruit. Tip bearers carry much of the crop at, or near, the shoot tips, whereas spur bearers carry it along the whole shoot on short-jointed spurs from which further growth develops each year.

Tip bearers are not easily trained as cordons, espaliers, or fans because on each shoot there is bare, unproductive wood that limits the cropping capacity of the tree. They are best grown as standard, half-standard, or bush forms; once they are established, they need renewal pruning only (see p.378).

Nicking and notching

Sometimes it may be necessary to correct the balance of the branch framework of a trained tree; this may be achieved by nicking, which weakens the growth of a particular bud, or notching, which strengthens it. Notching may also be used to stimulate the production of sideshoots on bare lengths of stem.

Nicking and notching are most effective in spring when the sap is rising. Make a nick or a small incision with a sharp knife just below a bud to inhibit its growth; make a notch just above it to increase its vigour and stimulate new growth.

Bark-ringing

On excessively vigorous apple and pear trees (but not on stone fruits) that produce unsatisfactory crops, bark-ringing may be used as a last resort to curb vegetative growth and induce a greater fruit set. In late spring, remove a narrow band of bark from around the trunk through to the cambium layer at a height of about 1m (3ft). This reduces the flow of nutrients and hormones back to the roots, so that they are concentrated in the upper part of the tree.

Bark-ringing must be carried out carefully or the tree may die. First measure out the width of the band, which must be only 3mm ($^1/_8$in) on a small tree, graduating to no more than 1cm ($^1/_2$in) on a very large tree, then score the band with a knife. Cut through the bark and the cambium layer and remove the bark within the band down to the hardwood all the way round. Seal the wound at once with several layers of water-proof adhesive tape – it must cover the wound without touching the cambium layer.

RECOMMENDED CULINARY APPLES

Early
'Early Victoria', syn. 'Emneth Early' **Fg3, B, Sb**
'George Neal' **Fg2, Sb,☆**
'Grenadier' **Fg3, Sb**
'Lord Grosvenor' **Fg3, Sb**
'Lord Suffield' **Fg1, Sb,☆**

Mid-season
'Arthur Turner' **Fg3, Sb**
'Bismarck' **Fg2, Sb**
'Blenheim Orange' **Fg3, T, Sb, Vg,☆**
'Cox's Pomona' **Fg4, Sb**
'Golden Noble' **Fg4, Tb,☆**
'Lord Derby' **Fg4, Sb**
'Norfolk Beauty' **Fg2, Sb**

'Rev. W. Wilks'

'Peasgood Nonsuch' **Fg3, Sb,☆**
'Rev. W. Wilks' **Fg2, Sb,☆**
'Royal Jubilee' **Fg5, Sb**
'Warner's King' **Fg2, T, Sb**

Late
'Annie Elizabeth' **Fg4, Sb**
'Bountiful' **Fg3, Sb,☆**
'Bramley's Seedling' **Fg3, Tb, T, Vg**
'Crawley Beauty' **Fg7, Sb**
'Dumelow's Seedling', syn. 'Wellington' **Fg4, Sb,☆**
'Edward VII' **Fg6, Sb**

'Edward VII'

'Encore' **Fg4, Sb,☆**
'Howgate Wonder' **Fg4, Sb, Vg**
'Lane's Prince Albert' **Fg3, Sb**
'Monarch' **Fg4, B, Sb,☆**
'Newton Wonder' **Fg5, B, Sb, Vg**
'Woolbrook Russet' **Fg4, Sb**

KEY
Fg *Flowering group (numbers indicate period of flowering)*
T *Triploid (unsuitable as pollinator)*
B *Biennial bearing*
Sb *Spur bearer*
Tb *Tip bearer or partial tip bearer*
Vg *Vigorous growth*
☆ *Excellent flavour*

BARK-RINGING

1 *Stick tape around the trunk as a guide for 2 parallel cuts. The ring may be 3mm–1cm ($^1/_8$–$^1/_2$in) wide, depending on the age and size of the tree.*

2 *The parallel cuts should be made through both the bark and the cambium layer. Carefully remove the ring of bark with the blunt side of the knife blade.*

3 *Wind water-proof tape around the ring so that it covers the wound without touching the cambium layer. Remove the tape when the wound has healed.*

The wound should heal over by the autumn, when the waterproof tape may be removed. The following year, the tree should produce much more blossom and, consequently, a much heavier crop of fruit because the reaction of any wounded plant is to reproduce.

Winter pruning

There are three main techniques for winter pruning, all of which stimulate new growth. Spur pruning and thinning should be carried out only on cultivars that produce plenty of spurs, not on tip bearers. Renewal pruning is appropriate for spindle-bushes and all tip bearers, as well as for vigorous cultivars that would be overstimulated by hard pruning. Regulated pruning is suited to cultivars that are naturally very vigorous, particularly triploids such as 'Bramley's Seedling', 'Blenheim Orange', and 'Jonagold'.

It may be necessary to vary the degree and type of pruning from year to year depending on the extent of growth, the quantity of fruit produced, and the age of the tree.

Spur pruning involves cutting back branch leaders and young laterals to stimulate the growth of sub-laterals and fruiting spurs. The extent of pruning required depends on the tree's vigour – the greater the vigour, the lighter the pruning, since pruning stimulates growth.

Shorten branch leaders on vigorous trees by no more than a few buds but on weaker ones by up to one third to stimulate new sub-laterals to form. Shorten young laterals to three or six buds where growth is good but to three or four buds on weaker trees so that spurs form. On a stronger tree, shoots up to 15cm (6in) long may be left unpruned.

Spur thinning is necessary as a tree ages to prevent fruits from becoming overcrowded. If left unthinned, the spurs become entangled and carry inferior fruit. When spur systems become congested, remove the older wood in favour of the younger. In time, it may be necessary to saw off whole spur systems to allow room for new ones to develop.

Renewal pruning involves the annual cutting back of a proportion of older, fruited shoots to their base to stimulate the growth of new, young wood. Keep the centre of a bush tree open by pruning out any vigorous growth that is crossing or shading other laterals so that all the branches are well spaced. Remove only a little of the tip from branch leaders and none at all on vigorous trees.

Regulated pruning consists of removing shoots and sometimes long sections of large branches that are crowded or crossing, particularly in the centre of the tree, to keep the branch framework open. Remove old wood to make room for young shoots. Do not tip prune the branch leaders.

Summer pruning

This is carried out to keep trained trees within their allotted space. It involves removing a large proportion of the new growth each summer to slow down vegetative growth.

The Modified Lorette System is the standard method of summer pruning in temperate climates with cool, unpredictable summers. It is carried out once the young shoots have become woody at the base. Maiden (new) laterals more than 22cm (9in) long that grow directly from the main stem or a main branch should be reduced to three leaves above the basal cluster. Prune back sideshoots arising from spurs and existing laterals to one leaf above the basal cluster. Continue to prune in this way as shoots mature.

WINTER PRUNING
SPUR PRUNING

1 *Cut back young laterals to between 3 and 6 buds of the current growth, depending on the vigour of the shoot.*

2 *Prune back the current season's growth on branch leaders by a quarter to one third.*

SPUR THINNING

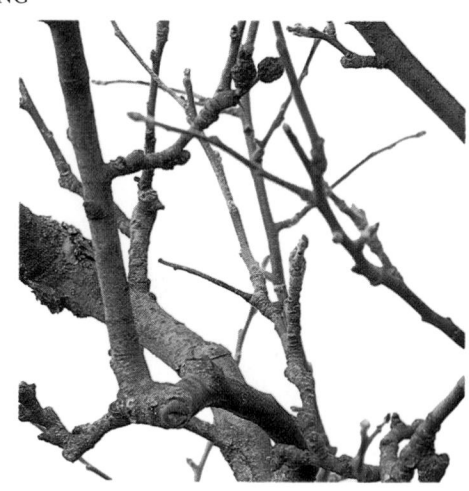

On older trees, spur systems may become too dense. Thin these out by removing weak spurs and any on the undersides of the branches.

RENEWAL PRUNING

Prune out a good proportion of the older shoots that have already borne fruit (left). This will encourage new shoots to develop (right).

REGULATED PRUNING

On this tree there is congested growth; correct this by removing any branches that are crossing or touching each other, and thinning out any sub-laterals or laterals that are overcrowded.

SUMMER PRUNING (MODIFIED LORETTE SYSTEM)

Prune trees when the lowest third of all new growth has become woody.

Cut back laterals on the main stems to 3 leaves above the basal cluster.

Basal cluster

BEFORE PRUNING

Trim any sideshoots to 1 leaf.

AFTER PRUNING

To help prevent sideshoots, or secondary growths, from developing behind the pruning cut, leave a small number of the longer shoots unpruned; tie these shoots securely to other branches so that they are roughly horizontal and draw the sap down. Do not shorten any of them until after fruiting. Then, in mid-autumn, cut back any secondary growth shoots to one bud.

The Full Lorette System should be used in warmer climates. Prune back new laterals to about 5cm (2in), repeating at intervals through the summer. Shorten the laterals to 2cm (^{3}/4in) once they are woody at the base. Prune any secondary growths in late summer in the same way.

APPLE BUSH
YEAR 1, WINTER PRUNING

Prune back the leader to a selected lateral, leaving 2 or 3 strong laterals below it.

Cut back each of these laterals by two-thirds to an upward-facing bud. Remove all other laterals.

YEAR 2, WINTER PRUNING

Sub-laterals that are not needed for secondary branches should be pruned back to 4 or 5 buds.

Prune back branch leaders and well-placed sub-laterals by half to outward-facing buds.

Bush

The open-centre or goblet-shaped bush is comparatively simple to maintain; it is ideal for larger gardens where there is plenty of space.

Formative pruning
Start with a well-feathered maiden tree; the laterals will form the first branches. After planting, while the tree is dormant, cut back the leader to a strong lateral 60–75cm (24–30in) above ground level, leaving at least two or three well-spaced laterals below it radiating out like the spokes of a wheel. These form the basis of the branch system; shorten them by two-thirds, cutting to an upward-pointing bud. Remove all other laterals.

If a maiden whip is used, or a feathered maiden tree that has few or no suitable laterals, cut back the leader in winter to a strong bud 60–75cm (24–30in) from the base, then make a small nick under the top two buds; this depresses their growth and encourages shoots from the lower buds to grow. Remove any unwanted laterals completely.

By the end of the following summer, three or four strong, healthy laterals should have developed to produce a plant equivalent to a pruned, feathered maiden.

Strong growth should develop the following summer. If one lateral grows faster than the others, tie it down nearly horizontally to slow its growth. Remove weak, inward-, and downward-growing shoots.

In the second winter, select several well-spaced growths arising from the original laterals to build up the branch framework, and shorten them by half, cutting to outward-facing buds. If any are not needed for the framework, shorten them to four or five buds, and remove altogether any shoots crossing the

ESTABLISHED BUSH, SPUR PRUNING IN WINTER

Prune vigorous branch leaders, leaving two-thirds of the previous season's growth. Weaker branch leaders should be cut back by two-thirds.

Cut back to 5 or 6 buds any young sideshoots growing from permanent branches to form spurs.

open centre. As growth continues in the second summer, remove any vigorous, upright shoots that unbalance the shape of the tree. By the third winter, the final branch formation should be established, with eight to ten main branches as well as several subsidiary ones.

Routine pruning
Only winter pruning (see p.378) is necessary for bushes once the framework is established; the pruning required will depend on the amount of growth made by the tree and on whether it is a tip or spur bearer. A tip bearer requires renewal pruning. Spur bearers require spur pruning and thinning.

Standard and half-standard

Few gardens are large enough to accommodate a standard or half-standard tree, but they make fine specimen trees where there is space.

Two or three years' training and pruning is needed to produce a clear stem of 1.2–1.35m (4–4^1/2ft) for a

ESTABLISHED BUSH, RENEWAL PRUNING IN WINTER

Thin out crowded sub-laterals to leave the centre of the tree open.

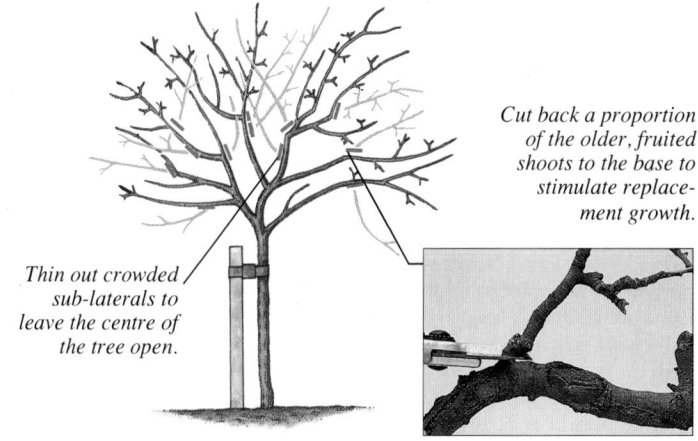

Cut back a proportion of the older, fruited shoots to the base to stimulate replacement growth.

half-standard, or 2–2.1m (6–6^1/2ft) for a standard. After planting a feathered maiden or maiden whip, tie in the leading shoot to a cane and cut any laterals hard back to 2.5cm (1in) in winter. In spring and summer, periodically pinch or cut back any feathers to a few leaves; this helps to thicken the main stem. Repeat this procedure in the second year.

In the following winter, remove most of the laterals and cut back the

leader to the desired height, either for a half-standard or standard; if the tree is not of the required height, grow it on for a third year. Several laterals should then develop below the cut; select and retain three or four well-spaced laterals to form the basic branch framework. Then train as for an open-centre bush (above).

Subsequent pruning of the tree is also as for a bush, but growth will be much stronger because the tree is grafted on a vigorous or a very vigorous rootstock. Carry out regulated pruning on the established tree; it is only necessary to prune hard if the tree is not growing satisfactorily.

Spindlebush

A spindlebush is trained into the shape of a pyramid or cone, to a height of 2.2m (7ft); once it is established, only renewal pruning and pruning to keep the shape are required.

Numerous variations of the spindle bush have been developed but the basic aim is to keep the three or four lowest branches dominant by removing shoots that would otherwise develop in the centre of the tree. Any shoots that do develop higher in the tree are allowed to fruit and are then pruned hard back, to be replaced by fresh growth.

Formative pruning
Plant a strong feathered maiden, supporting it with a 2m (6ft) stake. Cut back the leader in the winter to about 1m (3ft), or to just above the top-most lateral if this is higher. Select three or four vigorous and evenly spaced laterals that are about 60–90cm (2–3ft) from the base. Prune back each lateral by half to a downward-pointing, healthy bud and remove all other laterals.

If growth is strong, tie down any upright laterals towards the end of the first summer, in order to suppress growth and encourage the tree to fruit. If growth is weak, the upright laterals do not need to be tied down until the next summer.

Tie down the laterals with strong string secured to wooden or hooked metal pegs driven into the ground at an angle around the tree. If using wooden pegs, hammer a large "U" staple into the top of each one so that a string may be secured to it. Tie each string loosely to the branch so that it pulls down the branch to a 30° angle. Long branches may need to be tied in two places.

Remove any excessively vigorous shoots growing upwards from the main stem or laterals; do not attempt to tie them down as they may break. Train the central stem vertically by tying it to the stake.

The second winter after planting, shorten the central leader by one third of the new growth, cutting to a bud on the opposite side of the pruning cut made the previous winter. This helps to maintain a straight stem. Make sure that the strings are not constricting the tied-down shoots; once the growths have hardened and will remain in a more

or less horizontal position, remove the strings. The following summer, tie down some of the vertical shoots and remove completely any that are exceptionally vigorous or too close to the main stem, or that unbalance the branch framework.

By the third winter, laterals higher in the tree should have developed and been tied down to form further tiers of branches. They should be nearly horizontal, as this encourages early fruiting, and should not overshadow the lower framework branches if this can be avoided.

In the third summer, when the tree should produce fruit for the first time, tie down selected new side-shoots in late summer and remove any excessively strong shoots.

Routine pruning
From the fourth or fifth year onwards, renewal pruning (see p.378) is necessary in winter: shorten some of the old, fruited wood. Some of the shoots, particularly those that are higher in the tree, should be pruned hard back close to the trunk to encourage the development of replacement growths.

If the central leader is too vigorous, it may be cut back a little to a weaker lateral that will replace it. This concentrates vigour in the lower branches and helps to retain the pyramid shape, allowing maximum light to reach the fruits. In summer, continue cutting out completely any excessively vigorous and strongly upright-growing shoots.

Cordon

A feathered maiden may be trained as an oblique cordon on wires that are secured to posts or to a wall or fence. Space three horizontal wires about 60cm (24in) apart; the lowest wire should be 75cm (30in) from the ground. Fix the wires about 10–15cm (4–6in) clear of the supporting wall or fence to allow free air circulation. Attach a cane to the wires at an angle of 45°, then plant a feathered maiden by it (see p.365) and tie in the main stem to the cane.

Formative pruning
In the winter immediately after planting, shorten to three or four buds all lateral shoots that are over

APPLE SPINDLEBUSH
YEAR 1, WINTER PRUNING

Prune the leader by making an angled cut just above a suitable bud about 1m (3ft) from the ground.

Cut back 3 or 4 strong laterals by half to downward-facing buds. Remove other laterals.

YEAR 1, SUMMER PRUNING

Tie down each of the 3 or 4 main laterals to pegs in the ground so that the branches are at a 30° angle.

Cut to the base any vigorous upward-pointing laterals or sub-laterals.

YEAR 2, SUMMER PRUNING

Repeat summer pruning as for Year 1, concentrating on removing any upright growths.

ESTABLISHED SPINDLEBUSH, WINTER PRUNING

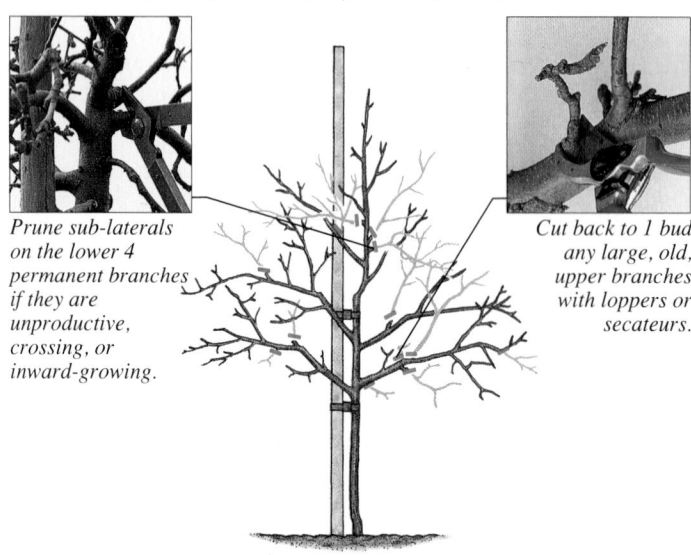

Prune sub-laterals on the lower 4 permanent branches if they are unproductive, crossing, or inward-growing.

Cut back to 1 bud any large, old, upper branches with loppers or secateurs.

10cm (4in) in length. For tip-bearing cultivars, shorten the leader by about one third; do not attempt to prune the cordon further.

From the first summer onwards, prune the new shoots in mid- to late summer, once they have become woody at the base. Not all shoots ripen together, so pruning should continue over several weeks. Use the Modified or Full Lorette System (see "Summer pruning", p.378). The time of pruning depends on climate, and on which system is used.

Routine pruning

Winter pruning is essential to prevent congestion: reduce overgrown spur systems and remove completely those that are overcrowded. If the cordon is not producing enough well-spaced laterals, shorten the leader by about a quarter of its length to encourage strong growth.

Once a cordon has extended beyond the top wire, lower its angle of growth slightly to provide space for the leader to extend. When it reaches the top wire, trim it back to 1 leaf of new growth in late spring. Alternatively, if the leader is vigorous, cut it back in late spring to a sideshoot near the top wire to curb its growth.

Continue pruning on the Modified or Full Lorette System; on an established cordon, this largely involves cutting sideshoots to one leaf.

Double cordon

A double cordon is usually grown vertically, but may be grown at an angle if desired. Feathered maidens and maiden whips may be trained as double cordons. The process is similar in each case, except that maiden whips must form sideshoots before training can begin (see "Forming a double cordon", right).

If using a feathered maiden, prune the leader to two sideshoots of equal vigour, one on either side, about 24cm (10in) above soil level; do this during the winter immediately after planting. Tie the sideshoots to canes at an angle of 35°. Train the new growth upwards in summer while it is still supple, with at least 45cm (18in) between the vertical arms of the "U"; each arm is subsequently treated as a single cordon.

Fan

A wall or fence is an ideal support against which to grow a fan-trained apple tree; select a cultivar on a dwarfing rootstock so that it may be comfortably accommodated in the available space. Fix horizontal support wires about 15cm (6in) apart,

APPLE CORDON
YEAR 1, WINTER PRUNING

Cut back laterals that are over 10cm (4in) to 3 or 4 buds. Do not prune laterals that are shorter than this.

YEAR 1, SUMMER PRUNING

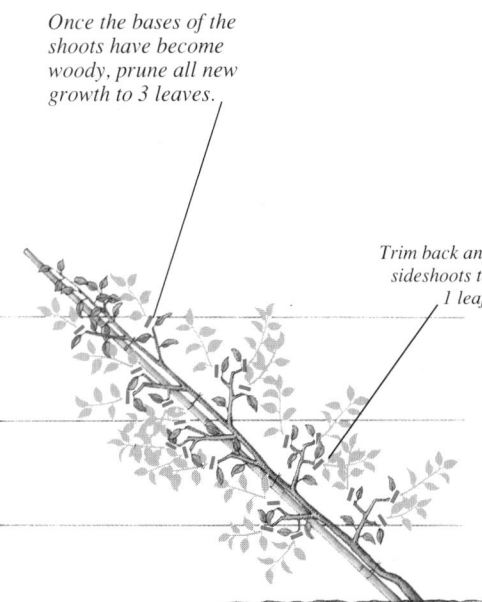

Once the bases of the shoots have become woody, prune all new growth to 3 leaves.

Trim back any sideshoots to 1 leaf.

ESTABLISHED CORDON, WINTER PRUNING

Thin spurs as they become congested on older cordons.

ESTABLISHED CORDON, SUMMER PRUNING

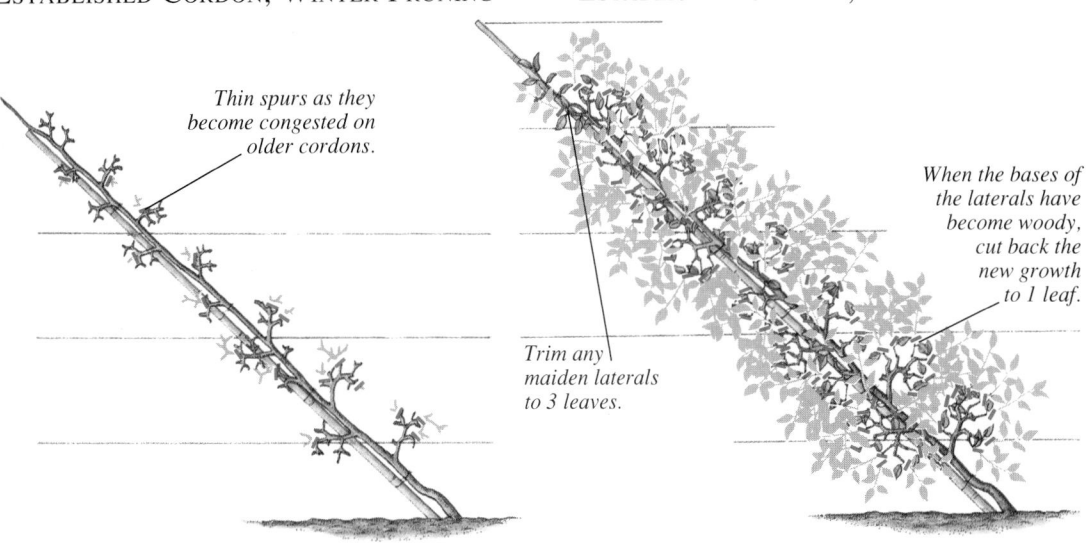

When the bases of the laterals have become woody, cut back the new growth to 1 leaf.

Trim any maiden laterals to 3 leaves.

Forming a double cordon

To train a maiden whip as a double cordon, cut back the newly planted tree to about 24cm (10in) from soil level during the first winter, leaving a strong bud on either side below the cut. The following summer, when new shoots have been produced, tie the two uppermost shoots to canes at an angle of 45°, lowering them to 30° later in the season. When the tips of these shoots are more than 45cm (18in) apart, train them upwards by tying them to vertical canes.

Once the basic "U"-shape of the double cordon has been formed, the two vertical arms should each be pruned in the same way as a single cordon.

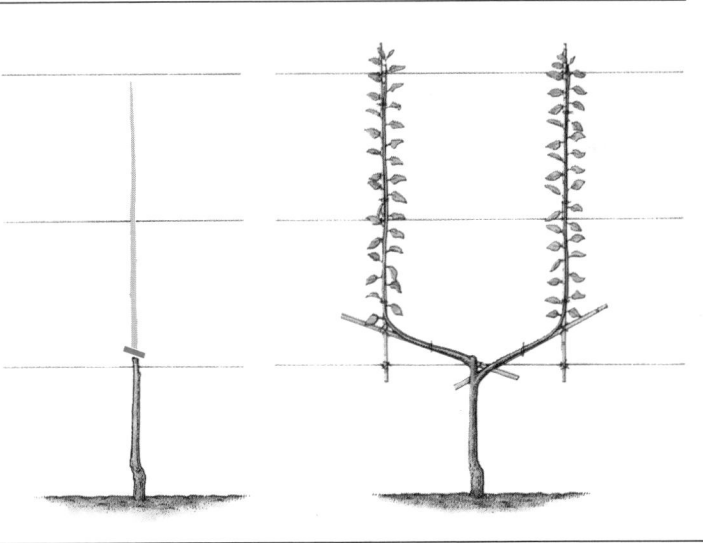

starting at 38cm (15in) from soil level. The initial development of the framework is as for peaches (see p.393); once established, it should be pruned on the Modified Lorette System (see p.378) with each arm being treated like a single cordon. This encourages fruiting spurs to develop along the arms.

Espalier

For this tree form, one or more pairs of opposite shoots are trained at right angles to the main stem onto support wires 38cm (15in) apart. An espalier usually has two or three tiers but more are possible with trees of sufficient vigour and where there is room to accommodate them. If a maiden whip is used, the first tier of branches may then be trained more readily at the required height.

Formative pruning

After planting a maiden whip, prune back the leader to a bud just above the lowest wire. The following summer, train the uppermost shoot vertically to form a new leader; as the two strongest laterals below this develop, tie each to a cane at an angle of 45° to form the first branch tier. Cut or pinch back all other, lower shoots to two or three leaves.

Tie down the laterals of the first tier into their horizontal position towards the end of the first growing season. If the two main arms develop unevenly, lower the more vigorous shoot to check growth and raise the weaker shoot to induce vigour. Once the two are balanced, tie them into their horizontal positions (see also *Training on Canes*, p.369).

The following winter, remove completely any laterals that have developed other than the main arms. To create the second tier, first look for two strong buds about 38cm (15in) above the first tier, then cut back the central leader to the bud above these. Shorten each first tier arm by one third to a downward-facing bud; where growth is very vigorous, leave the arm unpruned.

The bud to which each arm is cut back will produce a shoot that should be trained horizontally during the second summer after planting. Cut back other sub-laterals according to the Modified Lorette System (see p.378). The second pair of arms will form and these should be trained in the same way as the first pair. Repeat this process as necessary to obtain the required number of tiers.

Routine pruning

Once the arms of the top-most tier are well established, prune back the

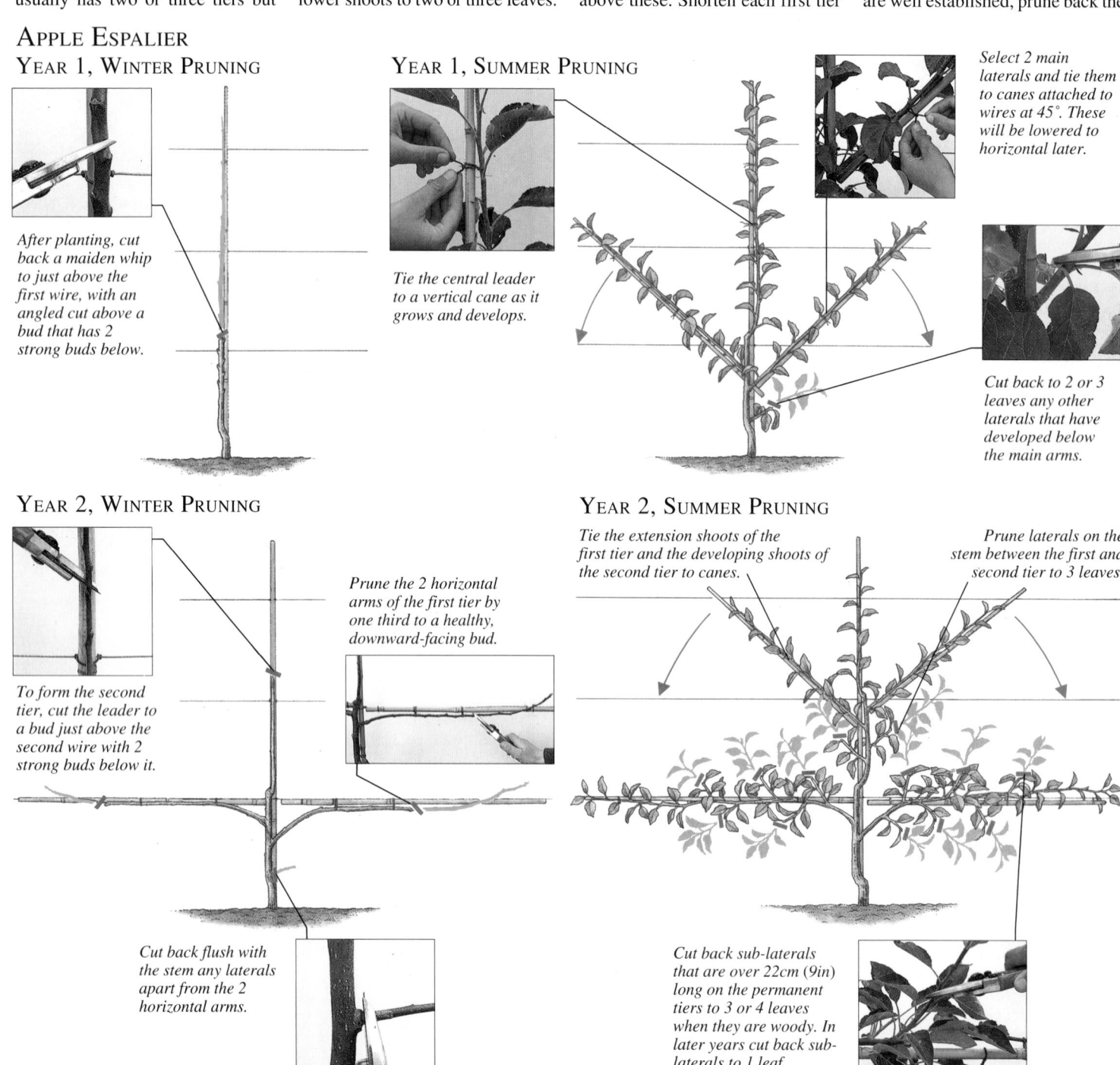

APPLE ESPALIER

YEAR 1, WINTER PRUNING

After planting, cut back a maiden whip to just above the first wire, with an angled cut above a bud that has 2 strong buds below.

YEAR 1, SUMMER PRUNING

Tie the central leader to a vertical cane as it grows and develops.

Select 2 main laterals and tie them to canes attached to wires at 45°. These will be lowered to horizontal later.

Cut back to 2 or 3 leaves any other laterals that have developed below the main arms.

YEAR 2, WINTER PRUNING

To form the second tier, cut the leader to a bud just above the second wire with 2 strong buds below it.

Prune the 2 horizontal arms of the first tier by one third to a healthy, downward-facing bud.

Cut back flush with the stem any laterals apart from the 2 horizontal arms.

YEAR 2, SUMMER PRUNING

Tie the extension shoots of the first tier and the developing shoots of the second tier to canes.

Prune laterals on the stem between the first and second tier to 3 leaves.

Cut back sub-laterals that are over 22cm (9in) long on the permanent tiers to 3 or 4 leaves when they are woody. In later years cut back sub-laterals to 1 leaf.

PICKING

Support the apple in the palm of the hand and twist it slightly. If the apple comes away easily from the spur, it is ready for picking.

central leader in winter to just above this tier. The espalier should thereafter be pruned in summer following the Full or Modified Lorette System (see p.378).

Dwarf pyramid

The dwarf pyramid is a compact tree form suitable for a small garden or for a container. It needs permanent staking if grown on an 'M27' or 'M9' rootstock; cultivars on other rootstocks need staking for four or five years. For pruning details, see "Pears: Dwarf pyramid", p.385.

Secondary growth often develops after summer pruning. These unwanted shoots inhibit the formation of fruit buds, so prune two or three weeks later than usual to help retard their growth if this is a problem. If secondary growth continues to appear, leave one or two shoots unpruned to act as sap-drawers (see "Summer pruning", p.378).

Harvesting and storing

Early-ripening apples should be gathered just before they are fully ripe or they soon become mealy. Late-maturing cultivars must not be picked too soon, however, or the fruits will shrivel in store.

Wrap fruits individually in greaseproof paper and, keeping different cultivars separate, store them in slatted boxes or crates in a cool place (see p.371). Fruits from young or overvigorous trees store less well than those from more mature trees and should therefore be used first. For further information on harvesting and storing, see p.371.

Propagation

Apple trees may be propagated by chip-budding or T-budding in summer (see pp.372 and 373) or whip-and-tongue grafting in early spring (see p.373). If possible, use certified scions and rootstocks.

Grafting over

Grafting over is a technique used to graft scions of a selected cultivar onto an established apple or pear tree to replace the original cultivar. This is usually done to introduce a new pollinator for adjacent trees or to try a new cultivar; as the roots and main branch system are already established, the new cultivar should bear fruit quickly. There are two methods: top-working and frame-working.

Top-working

Initially, this entails heading (cutting) back most of the main branches to within 60–75cm (24–30in)

of the main branch fork in spring. Leave one or two smaller branches unpruned to act as sap-drawers to reduce the number of new shoots that may form around the pruning cuts. Trim the cuts where branches have been sawn off. Two or three scions are used per branch but only the most vigorous one is grown on; the presence of the others may initially help to stop canker developing in the cut surface. These may be either rind- or cleft-grafted (the latter is rarely used by amateurs and is not described here).

For rind grafting, take dormant scions from the previous season's growth of the desired cultivar and prepare them with angled top cuts and tapering basal cuts. Cut away a sliver of bark on the other side of the tapering cut to prevent the bark from being damaged when inserted into the branch. When rind grafting branches of about 2.5cm (1in) in diameter, place two scions opposite each other. Larger branches can accommodate three, evenly spaced scions. Make a vertical cut for each

scion in the bark of the prepared branch. Carefully lift the bark and slide the scion into position underneath. Bind the graft firmly into position and seal the cut surfaces with grafting wax. Scion growth is rapid and ties must be released.

Retain the most vigorous scion and remove the others. Frequently, more than one shoot will develop from the selected scion; allow the best one to grow unchecked as the basis for the new branch. Shorten any others if they are less vigorous than the retained shoot but remove them completely if they are of equal vigour. After three or four years the new cultivar should start to crop regularly. Subsequently prune the new branch, according to the individual tree form.

Frame-working

In this method, most of the branch framework is retained and many scions are grafted onto different parts of the tree. Frame-working is preferred by commercial growers as trees crop more quickly than if top-worked.

HOW TO RIND GRAFT

1 *In early spring, cut off most of the main branches to within 60–75cm (24–30in) of the trunk. Leave 1 or 2 branches uncut to draw the sap.*

2 *Make a vertical cut 2.5cm (1in) long through the bark of one of the trimmed branches. If it is 2.5cm (1in) in diameter, make 2 evenly spaced cuts; if larger, make 3 cuts.*

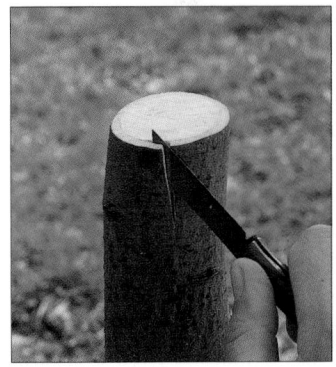

3 *Use the blunt side of the knife blade to ease the bark away from the cambium layer.*

4 *Prepare scions 3 buds long, each with an angled cut at the top and a 2.5cm (1in) tapering cut at the base. Insert them with the tapering cut facing inwards.*

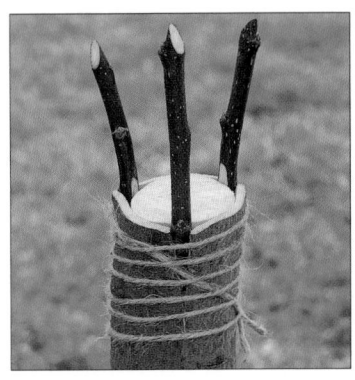

5 *When 2 or 3 scions have been inserted into the branch, bind the grafts tightly with strong string, winding it round the whole branch to hold the scions in place.*

6 *Apply grafting wax to the exposed areas. When the scions have united with the branch, retain the most vigorous and remove the others.*

Pears (*Pyrus communis* var. *sativa*)

Pears need more consistently warm conditions than apples to crop reliably. Late-ripening cultivars require dry and warm conditions throughout late summer and early autumn. They have a winter chilling requirement of 600–900 hours below 7°C (45°F).

Pears may be trained in a similar way to apples; bush, dwarf pyramid, cordon, and espalier forms are the most suitable for small gardens. They are usually grown on quince, rather than pear, rootstocks as this produces smaller trees. Some new rootstocks are under trial.

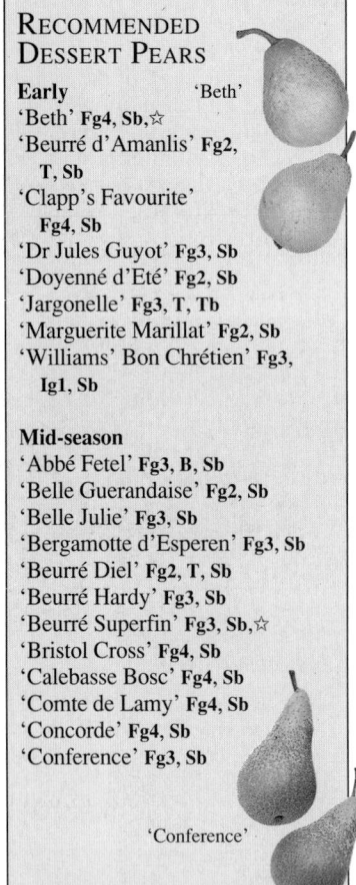

RECOMMENDED DESSERT PEARS

Early

'Beth' **Fg4, Sb,**☆
'Beurré d'Amanlis' **Fg2, T, Sb**
'Clapp's Favourite' **Fg4, Sb**
'Dr Jules Guyot' **Fg3, Sb**
'Doyenné d'Eté' **Fg2, Sb**
'Jargonelle' **Fg3, T, Tb**
'Marguerite Marillat' **Fg2, Sb**
'Williams' Bon Chrétien' **Fg3, Ig1, Sb**

Mid-season

'Abbé Fetel' **Fg3, B, Sb**
'Belle Guerandaise' **Fg2, Sb**
'Belle Julie' **Fg3, Sb**
'Bergamotte d'Esperen' **Fg3, Sb**
'Beurré Diel' **Fg2, T, Sb**
'Beurré Hardy' **Fg3, Sb**
'Beurré Superfin' **Fg3, Sb,**☆
'Bristol Cross' **Fg4, Sb**
'Calebasse Bosc' **Fg4, Sb**
'Comte de Lamy' **Fg4, Sb**
'Concorde' **Fg4, Sb**
'Conference' **Fg3, Sb**

'Cosica' **Fg3, Tb**
'Doyenné Bussoch' **Fg3, T, Sb**
'Doyenné du Comice' **Fg4, Ig2, Sb,**☆
'Fertility' **Fg3, Sb**
'Fondante d'Automne' **Fg3, Ig1, Sb,**☆
'Louise Bonne of Jersey' **Fg2, Ig1, Sb**
'Marie Louise' **Fg4, Sb**
'Merton Pride' **Fg3, T, Sb**

KEY

Fg *Flowering group (numbers indicate period of flowering)*
Ig *Incompatibility group (pears within each group will not pollinate each other)*
T *Triploid (unsuitable as pollinator)*
B *Biennial bearing*
Sb *Spur bearer*
Tb *Tip bearer or partial tip bearer*
☆ *Excellent flavour*

Site and planting

Pears flower earlier than apples, in mid- to late spring, and may be damaged by frosts. Pears are not fully self-fertile; cross-pollination is needed for a good crop.

Site

Pears require a warm, sheltered, and sunny site. The soil should retain moisture but must be well drained, particularly for trees on quince rootstocks (see below); pears tolerate wetter conditions than apples. Trees on poor or sandy soils produce fruits of inferior flavour, while those on shallow soils overlying chalk may suffer from lime-induced chlorosis, a nutritional problem caused by deficiencies of manganese and iron (see p.555). Such sites may be improved by regularly mulching with large amounts of organic matter and occasionally applying chelated iron and manganese.

Rootstocks

As well as producing relatively small trees, growing pears on quince rootstocks induces early fruiting. 'Quince A' is moderately dwarfing (similar to 'M26' in apple); 'Quince C' is more dwarfing (similar to 'M9' in apple). A few cultivars, however, do not make a good union with quince rootstocks and may need double-working (see p.386).

Pollination

Provision for cross-pollination should always be made by planting two compatible cultivars. Some cultivars are triploid, and a very few are male sterile: these require two pollinators nearby. Incompatible cultivars are indicated in the lists *Recommended Dessert Pears*, left and p.385, and *Recommended Culinary Pears*, p.385.

Planting

Plant pears in autumn when the soil is still warm or by mid-winter at the latest. This allows trees to establish

ROOTSTOCKS

4m (12ft)
3m (9ft)
2m (6ft)
1m (3ft)

'Quince C' 'Quince A'

before coming into growth, which may occur very early in a mild spring. Planting distances (see below) depend on the choice of rootstock and the form in which the trees are grown (see "Pruning and training", right).

Routine care

Regular maintenance including fruit thinning, feeding and watering, and checking for pest and disease problems, is similar to that required for apples (see p.376). For general information, see pp.366–7.

Fruit thinning

After the natural shedding of fruitlets at or soon after mid-summer, thin out to leave one fruit per cluster if the crop is heavy, but two if cropping is lighter.

Feeding, watering, and mulching

Water and fertilize trees as needed (see p.366). It is particularly important to give pears adequate nitrogen: in spring, apply light dressings of up to 35g/sq m (1oz/sq yd) of ammonium sulphate to maintain levels during the growing season. Mulch around newly planted trees in spring.

Pests and diseases

Pears may be affected by birds (p.561), rabbits and hares (p.570), wasps (p.563), aphids (p.550), winter moth caterpillars (p.549), fireblight (p.553), pear midges (p.562), scab (p.553), and brown rot (p.562). Pear leaf blister mites produce pustules in the leaves. Remove and destroy affected leaves in the summer. Some

pears, especially 'Conference', may develop parthenocarpic fruits. These have a cylindrical shape and may be produced when partial fertilization has occurred; the fruit continues to grow but is misshapen. Treat by providing a suitable pollinator and giving shelter to encourage more pollinating insects.

Pruning and training

Pruning requirements and techniques are similar to those for apples, but pears tolerate harder pruning once they have started to crop. Fruiting occurs predominantly on two-year-old and older wood. On pears, spur production is usually more prolific than on apples, and spurs should be thinned regularly on established trees. Very few pear cultivars are tip bearers.

Training and pruning to develop a cordon or an espalier are as for apples. Both are pruned by the Modified Lorette System in temperate areas or, in warmer climates, by the Full Lorette System (see "Apples: Summer pruning", p.378). A fan is formed in the same way as for peaches (see p.393) but, once established, prune as for an apple fan (see p.381). Pears are normally pruned two or three weeks earlier than apples, soon after mid-summer.

Where excessive vigour occurs at the expense of cropping, root pruning (see p.370) where practicable or, as a last resort, bark-ringing (see p.377) may be carried out.

Bush

Initial training and pruning of a bush are as for apples (see p.379). Several pear cultivars (for example 'Doyenné du Comice') have an upright growth habit; when pruning branch leaders of these cultivars, cut to an outward-pointing bud. Shoots that are upright should be tied down before they ripen fully at the base, as part of the initial training process, to encourage a wider angle of growth. Pruning on very vigorous trees should be much lighter after the second year. Where vigour is lacking, shorten new laterals to five or six buds or fewer.

The few tip bearers (for example, 'Jargonelle' and 'Joséphine de Malines') need to be renewal pruned as described for tip-bearing apples (see p.378). Established spur-bearing trees need considerable spur shortening and thinning, and occasional branch thinning, in winter.

PLANTING DISTANCES			
TREE FORM	ROOTSTOCK	DISTANCE BETWEEN TREES	DISTANCE BETWEEN ROWS
Bush	'Quince C'	3.5m (11ft)	5.5m (18ft)
	'Quince A'	4.75m (14ft)	5.5m (18ft)
Cordon	'Quince A' or 'C'	75cm (30in)	2m (6ft)
Espalier	'Quince C'	3.5m (11ft)	
	'Quince A'	4.75m (14ft)	
Fan	As espalier	As espalier	
Dwarf pyramid	'Quince C'	1.2m (4ft)	2m (6ft)
	'Quince A'	1.5m (5ft)	2m (6ft)

Dwarf pyramid

Prune back the leading shoot of a feathered maiden after planting to 50–75cm (20–30in) from the ground, and reduce any laterals to 15cm (6in); remove weak or low laterals. In the first summer, prune extension growth on the laterals, and any new laterals, to five or six leaves to downward-facing buds. This encourages horizontal growth and induces early fruiting. Cut back sub-laterals to three leaves. The following winter, prune the leading shoot to leave 25cm (10in) of the new growth, cutting to a bud on the opposite side to that of the previous year's pruning. In each subsequent year, prune the leader to buds on alternate sides. When the leader reaches the required height, prune back in late spring to leave one bud of the new growth.

Once the initial framework has been formed, nearly all pruning is carried out in mid- to late summer, depending on season and location. It is important that shoots have become

PEAR, DWARF PYRAMID

YEAR 1, WINTER PRUNING

Cut back the leader with an angled cut just above a bud, 50–75cm (20–30in) from the ground.

Prune back each lateral to a downward-facing bud about 15cm (6in) from the main stem.

Cut back entirely any low laterals on the main stem.

YEAR 1, SUMMER PRUNING

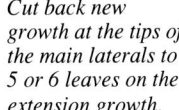

Cut back new growth at the tips of the main laterals to 5 or 6 leaves on the extension growth.

Prune new laterals growing directly from the main stem to 5 or 6 leaves.

Cut back any sub-laterals growing from the main laterals to 3 leaves. These will start to form spurs for the following summer.

YEAR 2, WINTER PRUNING

Prune the previous season's growth on the leader to about 25cm (10in).

YEAR 2 AND ROUTINE SUMMER PRUNING

Trim sub-laterals from existing laterals or spurs to 1 leaf beyond the basal cluster.

Cut back new growth at the ends of the permanent branches to 5 or 6 leaves.

Cut back laterals growing from the main branches to 3 leaves.

ESTABLISHED DWARF PYRAMID, WINTER PRUNING

When the leader reaches the required height, prune it to 1 bud of the previous season's growth.

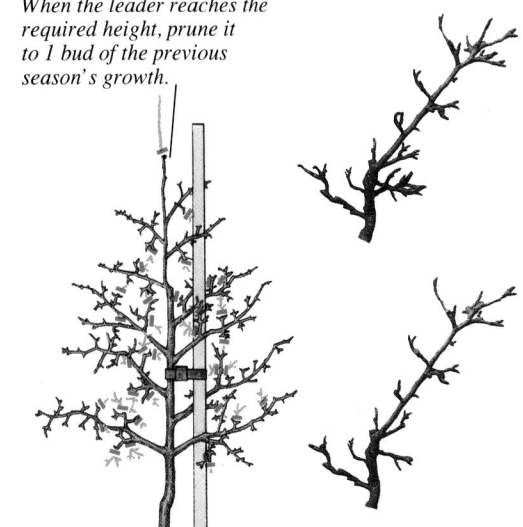

BEFORE
The spurs on the darker wood at the base of this shoot are congested and require thinning.

AFTER
Thin by removing any unproductive or overlapping spurs. Trim out excess fruit buds to leave 2 or 3 evenly spaced buds per spur.

RECOMMENDED DESSERT PEARS (CONT.)

Mid-season (cont.)
'Onward' **Fg4, Ig2, Sb**,☆
'Packham's Triumph' **Fg2, Sb**
'Pitmaston Duchess' **Fg4, T, Sb**
'Santa Claus' **Fg4, Sb**
'Seckle' **Fg2, Ig1, Sb**,☆
'Thompson's' **Fg3, Sb**

Late
'Beurré d'Anjou' **Fg2, Sb**
'Easter Beurré' **Fg2, Sb**
'Glou Morceau' **Fg4, Sb**
'Joséphine de Malines' **Fg3, Tb**
'Olivier de Serres' **Fg3, Sb**
'Passe Crasanne' **Fg2, Sb**
'Winter Nelis' **Fg4, Sb**,☆

'Joséphine de Malines'

RECOMMENDED CULINARY PEARS

Mid-season
'Beurré Clairgeau' **Fg2, Sb**

Late
'Bellissime d'Hiver' **Fg2, Sb**
'Black Worcester' **Fg3, Sb**
'Catillac' **Fg4, T, Sb**
'Double de Guerre' **Fg4, Sb**
'Uvedale's St Germain' **Fg2, T, Sb**
'Vicar of Winkfield' **Fg2, T, Sb**

'Catillac'

KEY
Fg *Flowering group (numbers indicate period of flowering)*
Ig *Incompatibility group (pears within each group will not pollinate each other)*
T *Triploid (unsuitable as pollinator)*
Sb *Spur bearer*
Tb *Tip bearer or partial tip bearer*
☆ *Excellent flavour*

woody at their base before they are pruned; the operation is therefore spread over three or four weeks and a few shoots may not be ready to prune until early autumn. Do not shorten shoots that are 15cm (6in) or less in length. Cut back branch leaders to six leaves of new growth and prune any sub-laterals to one leaf above the basal cluster. Any shoots arising directly from the main branches should be shortened to three leaves. If secondary growth develops, leave a few shoots unpruned as for apples (see "Summer pruning", p.378) to draw the sap.

The only major operation for winter pruning is the shortening of the central leader already described plus, in later years, some spur thinning and shortening. If the spur systems are allowed to become congested, the tree loses vigour and small, overcrowded fruits are produced.

Harvesting and storing

Time of picking is most important, especially for cultivars that ripen in late summer and early autumn. If left on the tree too long, the fruits will have turned "sleepy" and brown at the centre. Gather them at the first sign of a change of ground colour on the skin from dark to slightly lighter green. If in doubt, gently lift and twist

a fruit: if it comes away easily, it is almost ripe and will be at peak flavour in a few days. If the stalk breaks, wait for some days longer. Several harvests need to be made because all fruits do not ripen simultaneously. Fruits of late-ripening cultivars and those grown in cool climates must be left on the tree until mature to develop their full flavour.

Store pears in cool conditions, laying them in slatted boxes; do not wrap otherwise the flesh discolours. The fruits of later-ripening cultivars should be conditioned before eating: keep them at room temperature for a day or two and eat when the flesh gives under gentle pressure by the thumb near to the stalk. The flavour should then be at its fullest.

Propagation

For most pear cultivars, whip-and-tongue grafting or chip- or T-budding (see "Propagation", p.372) onto a 'Quince A' or 'Quince C' rootstock is usually successful. Grafting over may also be used to change the cultivar of an existing tree to another, preferable cultivar (see p.383).

Double-working pear cultivars

The few pear cultivars that are incompatible with quince rootstocks need to be double-worked: a cultivar that is compatible with both the quince rootstock and the selected scion cultivar is used as an "interstock" between the two. The cultivar 'Beurré Hardy' is the most widely used interstock; 'Vicar of Winkfield', 'Pitmaston Duchess', and 'Beurré d'Amalis' may also be used for all pear cultivars that require double-working. These include 'Dr Jules Guyot', 'Souvenir de Congrès', 'Marguerite Marillat', 'Williams' Bon Chrétien', 'Marie Louise', 'Packham's Triumph', and 'Thompson's'. Two methods of double-working may be used: double chip-budding and double grafting.

Double chip-budding entails carrying out chip-budding two years in succession: in the first

DOUBLE BUDDING
Insert the bud chip 5cm (2in) above the first graft and on the opposite side, so that the resulting stem will grow out straighter when the bud develops. Cut off the interstock above the new bud once the scion shoot has developed. Remove any shoots on the interstock.

year, a scion of the interstock is budded onto a quince rootstock; in the second year, a scion of the selected cultivar is budded onto the interstock on the opposite side. The method is as for chip-budding (see p.372).

For double grafting the same principle is followed. Graft the interstock onto the quince rootstock in early spring using the whip-and-tongue

DOUBLE GRAFTING
This follows the same principle as double budding: cut back the interstock a year after it is grafted, once the sap starts to rise, and graft on the required scion. Leave 5cm (2in) between grafts; position the scion graft on the opposite side from the previous one.

method (see p.373). In late winter or early spring, cut back the grafted interstock and graft the incompatible cultivar scion onto the interstock. Alternatively, it may be budded onto the interstock in summer, following the grafting of the interstock in spring. Remove shoots from the interstock but retain those from the cultivar scion.

Quinces (*Cydonia oblonga*)

Quinces are fruits grown mainly in temperate regions. As bushes, they reach 3.4–5m (10–15ft); they may also be trained as fans. The fruits are apple- or pear-shaped and are covered with greyish-white down. The most widely grown cultivars are 'Meech's Prolific' and 'Vranja'. Quince trees have a chilling requirement of 100–450 hours below 7°C (45°F) in order to flower.

Site and planting
Quinces require a reasonably sunny, sheltered site. The protection provided by a wall may be beneficial in cold areas. Moisture-retentive, slightly acidic soils are preferred; marked alkalinity usually causes lime-induced chlorosis.

'Quince A' is normally used as a rootstock. Where trees are grown on their own roots, suckering may be difficult to control. Quinces are generally self-fertile but the provision of pollinators is claimed to improve cropping levels. Plant quinces in

autumn or winter if bare-root, or throughout the year if container-grown, spacing them approximately 4–4.5m (12–15ft) apart.

Routine care
Cultivation requirements are as described under "Care of tree fruits", p.366. Once established, quinces need little attention. Occasional feeding at the standard rate may be necessary, particularly on poor soils, while watering and mulching may also be required. Quinces are comparatively easy to grow but fungal leaf spots (p.552) may be troublesome.

Pruning and training
Quinces fruit on spurs and on the tips of the previous summer's growth. Bushes may be left to grow into multi-stemmed trees or pruned in the early stages as for apple bushes (see p.379) with an open-centred, well-spaced branch framework.

Pruning of established trees is minimal, with occasional thinning in

winter of old, overcrowded growth. Not every lateral should be pruned, however, since this removes too many fruit buds.

Harvesting and storing
Pick the fruits when the skins have turned from green to gold, usually in late autumn. Store in boxes in a cool, well-ventilated, dark place. Do not wrap the fruits: quinces stored in plastic bags will discolour internally.

QUINCE TREE
Leave a generous grass-free area around young quinces, so that all the nutrients are absorbed by the trees and not shared with the grass.

Because quinces have a strong aroma, they should be stored separately, so that they do not contaminate other fruits. They are often used in preserves.

Propagation
Quince trees may be propagated either by chip-budding onto 'Quince A' rootstocks in summer (see p.372) or by taking hardwood cuttings in autumn (see p.374).

Medlars (*Mespilus germanica*)

Medlars are decorative, spreading trees with golden autumn colour and large, white or pinkish-white flowers in mid- to late spring. Medlar trees are most commonly grown as bushes, or as half-standards where larger specimens are required. They are self-fertile and have a chilling requirement of 100–450 hours below 7°C (45°F). The fruits are apple-shaped and somewhat flattened with prominent, horny calyces. Their flavour is an acquired taste; the fruits are used to make preserves.

RIPENING MEDLARS
The small, brown fruits ripen in autumn and measure 2.5–5cm (1–2in) across.

Site and planting
A sunny, sheltered site is preferable, although medlars tolerate partial shade. They may be grown in a wide range of soils, with the exception of those that are very chalky or badly drained. Adequate moisture is essential to obtain strong growth and a good crop of fruits.

Trees grown for the quality of their fruits are usually grafted on 'Quince A' rootstocks, although half-standards are sometimes available on seedling pear rootstocks.

Medlar trees are best planted in late autumn to winter. Half-standards should be spaced at a distance of 8m (25ft), and bushes at 4.5m (14ft).

Routine care
Cultivation requirements are generally as for apples (see p.376). Medlars may sometimes be affected by leaf-eating caterpillars (p.549) and fungal leaf spots (p.552).

Pruning and training
Train a bush tree as for apples (see p.379). For half-standards, pruning is initially as for apples. Once the main framework is established, occasionally thin branches in winter to maintain an open framework, removing overcrowded, diseased, or dead growth.

Harvesting and storing
Leave fruits on the tree for as long as possible so that they develop their full flavour. Pick them in late autumn

MEDLARS

when the stalk parts easily from the tree, preferably in dry weather. The fruits are unpalatable immediately after picking, and must be stored before use. Dip the stalks in a strong salt solution to prevent rotting, then store the fruits, calyces downwards, on slatted trays, so that the fruits do not touch. Use when the flesh has become soft and brown.

Propagation
Propagate by chip- or T-budding (see pp.372 and 373), or whip-and-tongue grafting (see p.373).

Plums, gages, damsons, and bullaces (*Prunus domestica*)

Various kinds of plum are grown for their fine fruits. These include: European plums (selections of *Prunus domestica*); gages (*P. domestica* and *P. insititia*); damsons, Mirabelles, and bullaces (*P. insititia*); cherry plums (*P. cerasifera*); and the Japanese or Salicine plums (*P. salicina*, syn. *P. triflora*).

Regions with cool-temperate climates are ideal for European plums, damsons, and bullaces; in warmer areas with earlier springs, Japanese plums and Mirabelles are more widely grown. All types of plum prefer areas that have plenty of sun and relatively low rainfall. Cherry plums, or myrobalan, are rarely grown for their fruit, but are often used as vigorous rootstocks for a number of fruiting plums, and for some ornamental trees.

There is a wide range of cultivars adapted to different climates and, with more dwarfing rootstocks now available, plums are ideal for even small gardens; damsons usually make smaller trees than plums. The compact pyramid tree and dwarf bush forms are particularly suitable for small gardens; for the choicest fruit in cool climates, grow fan-trained trees on warm, sunny walls. European plums and damsons have a chilling requirement of 700–1,000 hours below 7°C (45°F), and the Japanese plum one of 500–900 hours.

Site and planting

Plums need a warm, sheltered site to ensure that the flowers are pollinated successfully. Their pollination requirements are complex – some cultivars are self-fertile while others require suitable pollinators planted nearby. Make sure that there is enough room on the proposed site for the required number of trees, allowing for their mature height.

Site
All plums flower early in spring, Japanese plums markedly so and cherry plums earlier still, so that spring frosts are always a hazard. They are, therefore, best planted in a relatively frost-free site. Plums need to be sheltered from wind to avoid damage to the trees and also to encourage pollinating insects.

Most soils are suitable, but avoid those that are very chalky and badly drained. Plums on poor, sandy soils need extra feeding and watering to maintain good growth and cropping (see "Feeding, watering, and mulching", p.388).

Rootstocks
'Pixy' (dwarfing) and 'St Julien A' (moderately vigorous) are best for small to medium-sized plum trees, 2.2–4m (7–12ft). For trees up to 4.5m (13ft), choose 'Myrobalan B'

ROOTSTOCKS

4m (12ft)
3m (9ft)
2m (6ft)
1m (3ft)

'Pixy'   'St Julien A'   'Brompton'   'Myrobalan B'

(incompatible with some cultivars) or 'Brompton' (universally compatible). 'Marianna' is excellent for Japanese plums, but is incompatible with some European plums. Plum trees tend to produce suckers, but this is less common with modern rootstocks.

Pollination
European plums and damsons may be self-fertile, partially self-fertile, or self-sterile. Fortunately, some very popular cultivars, such as 'Victoria', are self-fertile, but planting suitable pollinators nearby will ensure more consistent cropping. Cultivars that are not self-fertile must

always be planted with compatible pollinators nearby. Cherry plums are self-fertile. Some Japanese plums are self-fertile, but most give better results when planted near a suitable pollinator. Plum cultivars that will not pollinate certain others are indicated in the lists of recommended cultivars on pp.388 and 389, which also give details of flowering times. Seek advice about pollination of individual trees when buying.

Planting
This should be completed as early as possible in late autumn or early winter as growth starts early in

PLANTING DISTANCES			
TREE FORM	ROOTSTOCK	DISTANCE BETWEEN TREES	DISTANCE BETWEEN ROWS
Bush	'St Julien A'	4–5m (12–15ft)	5.5m (18ft)
Half-standard	'Brompton' or 'Myrobalan B'	5.5–7m (18–22ft)	7m (22ft) minimum
Fan	'St Julien A'	5–5.5m (15–18ft)	
Pyramid	'St Julien A' or 'Pixy'	2.5–4m (8–12ft)	4–6m (12–20ft)

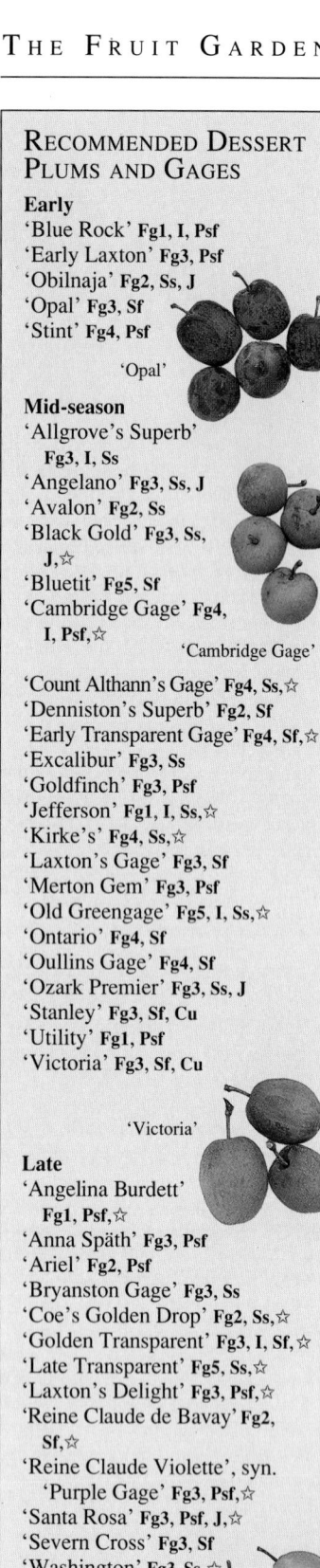

spring. All trees are best staked for two years; stake those on 'Pixy' rootstocks permanently. Planting distances (see p.387) are determined by the chosen tree form and by the vigour of the rootstock.

Routine care

Feed and water trees regularly, and check for pests and diseases. Fruit thinning should be carried out as necessary. If spring frosts are likely, protect wall-trained trees in bloom with a hessian cover (see FROST AND WIND PROTECTION, pp.520–21).

Fruit thinning
This is an important procedure both to give larger, better-flavoured fruits and to reduce the risk of branches breaking from the heavy weight of too many fruits. Fruitlets may be thinned early if the set is heavy. After the stones have formed and natural fruit drop has occurred, thin the remaining fruit to about 5–8cm (2–3in) apart for small fruits and 8–10cm (3–4in) for larger cultivars (such as 'Victoria'). Scissors are best for this job since they are quicker to use than secateurs.

Feeding, watering, and mulching
Plums require plenty of nitrogen; apply a spring dressing at the rate recommended under "Care of tree fruits", p.366. Mulch annually with well-rotted manure or compost, and water as required, particularly in prolonged spells of hot weather. Plums planted against walls or fences will need more regular watering than those grown in the open.

Pests and diseases
Plums may be attacked by rabbits and hares (p.570), wasps (p.563), aphids (p.550), and winter moth caterpillars (p.549). Diseases that

may affect plums include silver leaf (p.551), bacterial canker (p.569), and brown rot (p.562). Any trees that are badly infected with silver leaf, bacterial canker, or (less commonly) with viruses (p.553) should be dug up and burnt without delay.

All stone fruit trees may be affected by the physiological disorder known as gumming. Trees that have this problem exude a translucent, amber-coloured, gum-like substance from the trunk and branches, while plums may also form gum around the stone within the fruit. The gum is produced by the trees as a result of stress caused by disease, adverse soil conditions, or physical damage caused by, for example, strong winds or a heavy crop. If gumming is noticed, try to identify the cause and alleviate the problem if possible.

Birds may also be troublesome; if they attack the fruit buds, it may be necessary to place fine mesh nets over the trees during the winter to prevent damage (see also p.561).

PLUM BUSH
YEAR 1, EARLY SPRING PRUNING

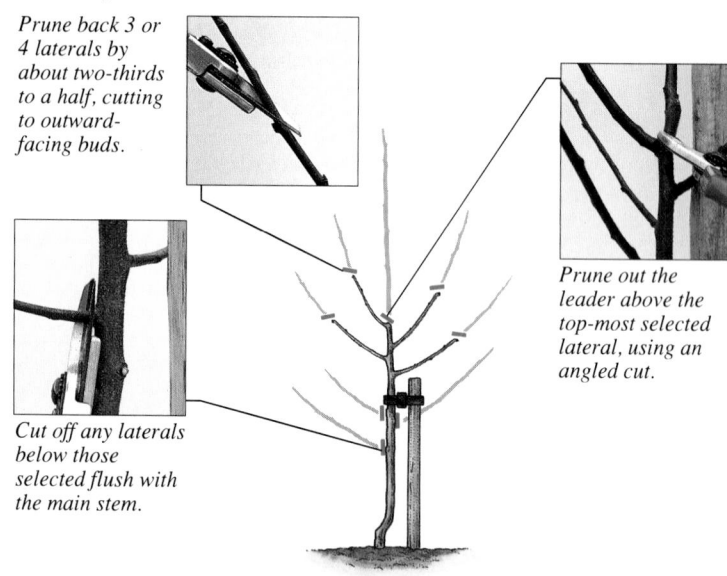

Prune back 3 or 4 laterals by about two-thirds to a half, cutting to outward-facing buds.

Cut off any laterals below those selected flush with the main stem.

Prune out the leader above the top-most selected lateral, using an angled cut.

Pruning and training

Plum trees produce fruit at the base of one-year-old shoots, as well as on two-year-old wood and spurs. Once initially trained, they require less pruning on unrestricted forms than apples or pears. In cool-temperate climates it is essential to prune in summer (after training) to minimize the risk of silver leaf (p.551). Trained trees require routine summer pruning to maintain their restricted shape. Remove any damaged or diseased branches immediately, cutting back to healthy wood.

Bush
In early spring when the buds are breaking, start training a newly planted feathered maiden. Select three or four strong, evenly spaced laterals, the highest at about 90cm (3ft) from ground level, and prune them by about two-thirds or a half, to healthy, outward-facing buds. These laterals will form the basic

YEAR 2, EARLY SPRING PRUNING

Prune back 3 or 4 of the strongest sub-laterals that develop from each of the framework laterals by about half.

Remove other weak, badly placed, or narrow-angled laterals completely.

PRUNING A MATURE BUSH

If sub-laterals are unproductive, damaged, or dead (as here) cut them back in summer to the point of origin or to a suitable replacement shoot.

framework of branches. Then prune out the leader, making an angled cut above the highest of the selected laterals. Cut back to the main stem unwanted laterals below those selected.

The following early spring, choose three or four of the strongest sub-laterals that have developed on each of the pruned laterals and shorten them by half. To achieve a balanced framework, trim off weak or badly placed laterals and pinch out any shoots growing from the main stem. Subsequently, restrict pruning of young trees to the removal in summer of excessively vigorous or awkwardly placed growths. With older trees, thin some branches in summer to avoid overcrowding, and seal wounds with bituminous paint.

If using a maiden whip, prune it to about 90cm (3ft). The following spring, laterals should have developed, and it may then be trained as a feathered maiden.

Half-standard

Choose three or four well-spaced laterals on a feathered maiden; cut back the leader just above the uppermost lateral at 1.35m (4¹/₂ft), then prune each of the chosen laterals by one third to a half. Remove any lower laterals. Subsequent pruning of the sub-laterals and training to form an open-centre head is the same as for a bush. Half-standard trees are less easy to manage than pyramid or bush plums when mature because of their greater size.

Spindlebush

Similar in shape to a plum pyramid (see p.390), the spindlebush requires a little more space but does not need the same annual summer pruning. Pruning and training are as for apple spindlebushes (see p.380) but prune in early spring when the buds break.

Tie down upright shoots and keep the top of the tree in check by removing the more vigorous shoots and retaining the less vigorous ones to produce fruit. In this way the conical shape is maintained.

Fan

Train a plum fan initially as for a peach fan (see p.393) to produce main branches or ribs to train against horizontal support wires. When

ESTABLISHED PLUM FAN

SPRING PRUNING

Thin new sideshoots to about 10cm (4in) apart.

Cut out any sideshoots that are growing towards the centre of the fan or are badly placed.

SUMMER PRUNING

Tie in any laterals needed to extend the framework or replace older wood.

Cut back sideshoots that are not needed for the permanent branch framework to 5 or 6 leaves.

Cut back wrong-pointing or awkward shoots to shoots facing in the required direction or flush with the stem.

AFTER FRUITING

In the autumn, after the fruit has been harvested, prune back to 3 leaves all the sideshoots that were shortened to 5 or 6 leaves earlier in the summer.

training the young fan, retain some sideshoots to fill in gaps and pinch back others to one bud. Remove any very vigorous sideshoots or those growing at an awkward angle.

On an established fan, in spring or as soon as they appear, remove sideshoots growing inwards towards the wall or fence, or the centre of the fan. Thin the remainder to 10cm (4in) apart and pinch or cut them back to six leaves during the summer unless they are required to fill spaces in the fan framework. After the crop has been picked, shorten these shoots to three leaves.

Pyramid

Plant a feathered maiden against a strong stake and, in early spring, cut back the central leader to a healthy bud at a height of about 1.5m (5ft). Remove any laterals growing below 45cm (18in) from the ground. Shorten the remaining laterals over 22cm (9in) long by half their length. When the bases of the young shoots are turning woody later in the summer, cut back extension growth on the main branches and new (maiden) laterals, to about 20cm (8in); at the same time, reduce sub-laterals to about 15cm (6in). To start forming the pyramid shape, cut main branches and sub-laterals back to downward-facing buds so that growth is more or less horizontal. Remove any laterals that are very vigorous or upward-pointing. Tie in the central leader to the stake, but do not prune it until the following spring, then shorten it by two-thirds of its new growth. Once the tree has reached a height of about 2m (6ft) on 'Pixy' or 2.5m (8ft) on 'St Julien A', cut back the central leader. This should be delayed until late spring, however, as this reduces its subsequent growth; cut it back to a bud about 2cm (1in) from the old wood. Continue annual summer pruning as previously described, cutting branch leaders to downward-pointing buds and removing any excessively vigorous, upright shoots, especially those growing in the upper parts of the tree, to maintain the pyramid shape.

On mature pyramids, overcrowding will develop; in summer, trim off any badly placed, old wood as necessary. Maintain the pyramid shape by keeping any vigorous or dominant upper branches in check.

Harvesting and storing

For the best flavour, allow fruits to ripen fully; for freezing or preserving, pick them when ripe but still firm. In wet weather, gather the ripening crop before brown rot or wasps spoil it. Split skins may occur with some cultivars in moist conditions. Keep the fresh fruits in a cool, dark place and use within a few days.

Propagation

Chip- or T-budding is most usual (see pp.372 and 373); whip-and-tongue grafting (see p.373) is less reliable for plums than for apples and pears.

PLUM PYRAMID

YEAR 1, EARLY SPRING PRUNING

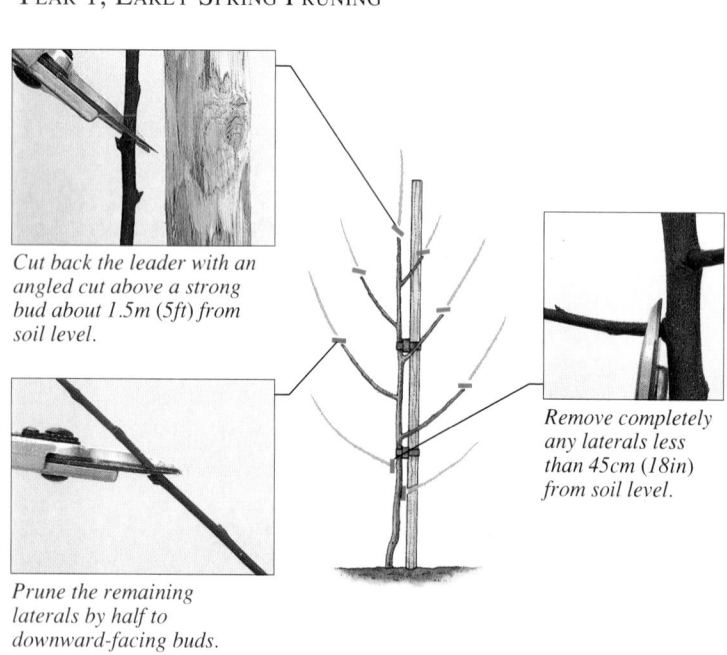

Cut back the leader with an angled cut above a strong bud about 1.5m (5ft) from soil level.

Prune the remaining laterals by half to downward-facing buds.

Remove completely any laterals less than 45cm (18in) from soil level.

YEAR 1, SUMMER PRUNING

Any new laterals forming too narrow an angle with the main stem should be removed. Do not prune the central leader.

Cut back any sub-laterals to 15cm (6in) with an angled cut just above a leaf.

Cut back new growth at the tips of the main branches to about 20cm (8in).

YEAR 2, EARLY SPRING PRUNING

Just before bud burst, shorten the central leader by two-thirds of its new growth.

ESTABLISHED PYRAMID, SUMMER PRUNING

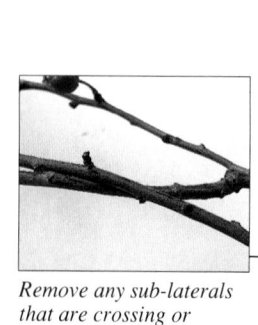

Remove any sub-laterals that are crossing or overcrowded.

Repeat the routine summer pruning of main branches and sub-laterals.

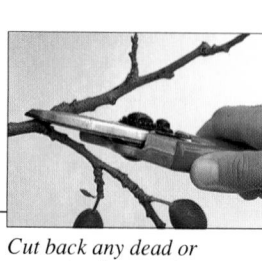

Cut back any dead or unproductive wood to a healthy shoot or to the point of origin.

Peaches and nectarines (*Prunus persica* and *P.p.* var. *nectarina*)

Peaches and nectarines are grown in many temperate regions. They have a chilling requirement of 600–900 hours below 7°C (45°F). Sunny, reasonably dry summers are essential to produce good crops; in cooler climates, peaches may be grown under cover. A range of cultivars is available for different climates (see *Recommended Peaches*, right, and *Recommended Nectarines*, p.392); they are yellow-, pink-, or white-fleshed. On cling peaches the flesh tends to cling to the stone; other peaches are known as freestone. The nectarine is a smooth-skinned form of the peach and requires very similar treatment, although it prefers warmer growing conditions.

Peaches and nectarines are usually grown in bush form, but fans are popular in temperate climates since they allow the fruits to receive maximum sunlight for ripening. Some naturally compact (genetic dwarf) cultivars are ideal for growing in pots.

Site and planting

Peaches flower early in the year and so should be protected from frost; a south-facing wall is an ideal site.

Site

Maximum sun is necessary, in a sheltered site that is not susceptible to spring frosts. In cooler climates, a sunny wall or a greenhouse is needed. Peach trees in areas with high rainfall may be badly affected by peach leaf curl (p.555) unless given some protection (see "Routine care", right).

Deep, fertile, slightly acid soils (pH6.5–7) are ideal for growing peaches. If grown on sandy soils they need extra feeding and watering; shallow, chalky soils often give rise to lime-induced chlorosis.

Rootstocks

The plum rootstock 'St Julien A' is used to provide a moderately vigorous tree, while 'Brompton' is used if more vigour is required. In some areas, peach seedling rootstocks are preferred, using vigorous selections resistant to root-knot nematodes.

HAND-POLLINATION

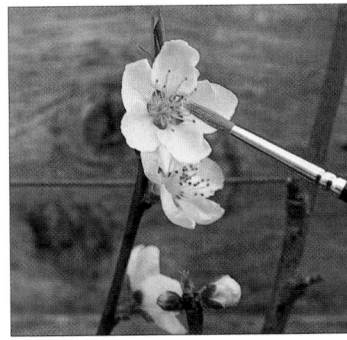

Peaches may be hand-pollinated once the blossom is fully out. On a warm, dry day, use a small, soft brush to transfer the pollen from the anthers of one flower to the stigmas of another.

Pollination

Nearly all cultivars are self-fertile. An exception is 'J. H. Hale', which requires a nearby pollinator that flowers at the same time (seek advice when buying). In areas with wet or uncertain weather, pollination may be erratic or poor but this can be improved by hand-pollination.

Planting

Plant peach trees by mid-winter if possible, as growth starts very early. Stake bush trees for the first two years. Planting distances vary depending on the tree form and choice of rootstock (see chart, below).

Routine care

For details of maintenance and cultivation requirements, see "Care of tree fruits", p.366. Lime-induced chlorosis may lead to manganese/iron deficiency (p.555), which must be treated as soon as possible. Protect

ROOTSTOCKS

4m (12ft)
3m (9ft)
2m (6ft)
1m (3ft)

'St Julien A'   'Brompton'

PROTECTING PEACH FANS

In the autumn, at leaf fall, cover the tree with a polythene shelter open at both ends for ventilation. This keeps the leaf buds dry and inhibits peach leaf curl spores from germinating.

the developing foliage of fan-trained peaches against peach leaf curl, and frost to some extent, with a polythene lean-to in winter and early spring.

Fruit thinning

To produce large fruits, thinning will be needed. When the fruitlets are the size of hazelnuts, thin them to one fruit per cluster. Later, when they are walnut-sized and some fruitlets have been shed naturally, thin to a spacing of 15–22cm (6–9in); in warm climates closer spacing may be used.

Feeding, watering, and mulching

In dry areas, watering is necessary to support growth and fruiting. Mulching in spring once the soil has

RECOMMENDED PEACHES

Early
'Adriatica' **W, C, Wh**
'Amsden June' **Wh**
'Duke of York' **Wh,☆**
'Earliglo' **Y**
'Early Alexander' **Wh**
'Flavorcrest' **W, Y**
'Iris Rosso' **W, Wh**
'J. H. Hale' **Y**
'Maycrest' **W, Y**
'Saturne' **P**
'Springcrest' **W, Y**
'Spring Lady' **W, Y**
'Suncrest' **W, Y**
'Waterloo' **Wh,☆**

'Earliglo'

Mid-season
'Bonanza' **Gd, Y**
'Crimson Galande' **Wh,☆**
'Elegant Lady' **W, Y**
'Garden Lady' **Gd, Y**
'Glohaven' **W, Y**
'Maria Bianca' **W, Wh**
'Peregrine' **Wh,☆**
'Redhaven' **Y**
'Rochester' **Y**
'Royal George' **Y,☆**

Late   'Peregrine'
'Andross' **W, C, Y**
'Barrington' **Y,☆**
'Bellegarde' **Y,☆**
'Cresthaven' **W, Y**
'Dymond' **Y,☆**
'Fayette' **W, Y**

KEY
W *Warm climate needed*
Gd *Genetic dwarf (good for pot culture)*
C *Cling*
Y *Yellow flesh*
Wh *White flesh*
P *Pink flesh*
☆ *Excellent flavour*

PLANTING DISTANCES

TREE FORM	ROOTSTOCK	DISTANCE BETWEEN TREES	DISTANCE BETWEEN ROWS
Bush	'St Julien A'	5–5.5m (15–18ft)	5.5m (18ft)
	'Brompton' or seedling peach	5.5–7.5m (18–24ft)	7.5m (24ft)
Fan	'St Julien A'	3.5–5m (11–15ft)	

THINNING

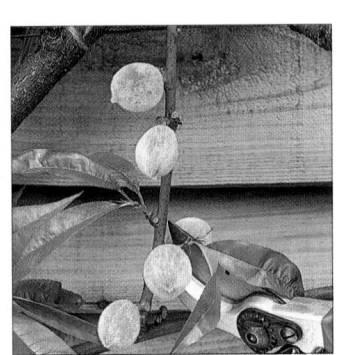

1 *As they form, thin peaches to one fruit per cluster, removing first any fruits growing towards the wall or fence.*

2 *These remaining fruits will need thinning again later, in order to leave one fruit every 15–22cm (6–9in).*

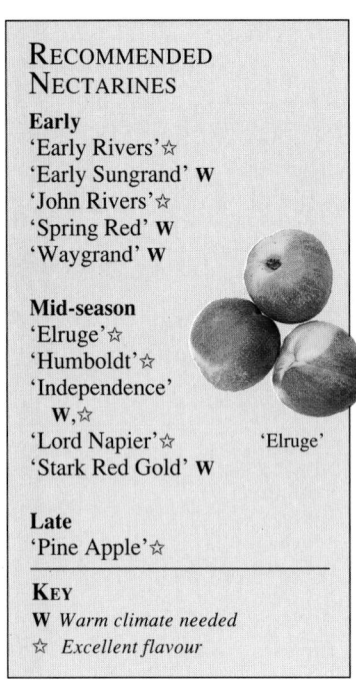

'Elruge'

warmed up helps the soil to retain its moisture. Adequate nitrogen is essential to promote new growth for cropping and potassium is needed to enhance hardiness and fruit quality.

Pests and diseases

Peaches may be attacked by aphids (p.550), birds (p.561), red spider mites (p.550), earwigs (p.548), and root-knot nematodes (p.564); diseases include peach leaf curl (p.555), bacterial canker (p.569), grey mould/*Botrytis* (p.550), and gumming (see "Plums: Pests and diseases", p.388).

Growing under cover

Peach trees under cover are best fan-trained so that the fruits receive maximum sun. The greenhouse must be able to accommodate a minimum span of 2.75m (9ft). Fertile, moisture-retentive soil is essential.

A trained tree should be grown against suitable support wires spaced at 15cm (6in) intervals, starting at 38cm (15in) from the ground. Secure the wires so that they are held about 22cm (9in) away from the glass. Full ventilation is essential in winter to allow adequate chilling.

In early spring, but not too early if no heat is available, reduce ventilation to start the tree into growth. Keep the temperature at 8–10°C (40–50°F) for up to two weeks and then raise it to 20°C (68°F).

Trees under cover grow rapidly; always feed and water them well. Occasional, copious watering is preferable to frequent, light applications. Syringe the foliage with a mist of tepid water and damp down the greenhouse floor on bright days.

Pollinate the trees by hand when in bloom (see *Hand-pollination*, p.391). Do not syringe or damp down during the flowering season as this

may prevent pollination, but start again once the flowers have dropped in order to help control red spider mites and mildew; stop syringing and damping down when the fruits begin to ripen.

Fruit thinning is essential to ensure that the fruits develop to their full size (see p.391).

Pruning and training

Peach and nectarine trees bear fruit only on shoots produced the previous year. The first fruits usually develop the third year after planting. Pruning is aimed at encouraging new growth and replacement shoots to maintain a well-balanced, open branch framework. There are three different kinds of bud: plump fruit buds; small, pointed growth buds; and triple buds that have a plump, central fruit bud with growth buds

PEACH BUSH
YEAR 1, EARLY SPRING PRUNING

Select 3 or 4 strong laterals. Cut back each by two-thirds to an outward-facing bud.

Trim back to the stem any unwanted laterals.

Prune back the leader to the top-most lateral.

YEAR 1, SUMMER PRUNING

Cut back flush with the stem any sideshoots below the main laterals.

Remove any shoots that are growing inwards or downwards.

YEAR 2, EARLY SPRING PRUNING

Prune weak sub-laterals to about 10cm (4in).

Before bud-break, cut back the strongest laterals and sub-laterals by a half to form the main branches.

ESTABLISHED BUSH, EARLY SUMMER PRUNING

Cut back to a replacement bud or shoot up to a quarter of shoots that have fruited.

Remove old, unproductive wood, as well as any crowded and crossing branches.

on either side. On branches where extension growth is required, prune back to a growth bud, or, failing this, to a triple bud.

Bush

Plant a feathered maiden between late autumn and late winter. In early spring select three or four strong, well-spaced laterals with the topmost one about 75–90cm (2½–3ft) from the ground; prune back the leader to just above the top lateral. Prune back each of the selected laterals by two-thirds and remove all other unwanted laterals. During summer, remove any badly placed or low shoots that have developed.

The following early spring, before bud-burst, select strong laterals and sub-laterals to form the basic framework. Cut these back by about half to a bud; prune any other sub-laterals to about 10cm (4in).

Once the tree is well established, keep the centre open by removing some of the older, fruited shoots each summer; occasionally, unproductive branches may need to be cut out.

Fan

Partially trained fans are sometimes available; if buying one of these, make sure that it has been correctly trained (as shown below). A fan should be developed from two branches trained out approximately 30cm (12in) above the ground at 40°. The central leader immediately above them should have been removed to channel vigour equally to both sides of the tree. A fan that retains its long, central leader and has side branches radiating out at an angle along its length will produce excessive growth at the top of the fan, leaving the base bare.

Formative pruning
Set up support wires as for an apple fan (see p.381). After planting a feathered maiden, choose two laterals about 30cm (12in) above the ground and remove the leader above them. Prune the selected laterals to about 38cm (15in) to form the first two "arms" and tie them to canes at 40°. Prune back all other laterals to one bud as a reserve until the two main shoots have developed.

In summer, tie in the leader and selected sideshoots to canes as they develop, to start forming the framework "ribs". Select and train in two equally spaced shoots on the upper side of each branch and one underneath. Pinch back any other shoots on the stem to one leaf, and remove any shoots on the ribs that are badly placed. Before bud-burst in the second spring, cut back the extension growth on the two main arms by one third to a strong bud to promote growth and the fan's development.

In early summer, continue tying in the selected developing shoots. Pinch back weak shoots and remove any that are very vigorous or pointing in the wrong direction.

The following early spring, shorten these new ribs by a quarter. During the third summer, select further shoots to complete the main ribs or branches of the fan. Any space in the centre of the tree is soon filled in by sideshoots. Thin sideshoots produced from the main branches early in the season to 10–15cm (4–6in) apart; retain those that lie naturally along the plane of the fan but remove any that are awkwardly placed and

growing straight outwards or inwards towards the wall or fence. Tie in the retained shoots; they should produce fruit the following year. Pinch back any overlapping shoots to four to six leaves.

Routine pruning
The aim of pruning in spring is to ensure a constant supply of well-placed, young shoots each year. At the base of each flowered shoot that will carry fruit in the forthcoming summer, there are usually two buds or young shoots; pinch out (disbud) one of these to prevent growth from becoming congested. The remaining one will carry fruit the following year. A second bud about half-way up the shoot may also be retained as a reserve in case the other one becomes damaged. After harvesting, remove the fruited wood, and tie in a replacement shoot at the base of each shoot that is cut out.

Continue this process annually; retain two replacement shoots if there is space in the framework. Without rigorous pruning, a peach tree soon becomes congested with old wood that bears no fruit.

PEACH FAN

YEAR 1, EARLY SPRING PRUNING

Choose 2 laterals, one on either side, 30cm (12in) from the ground to form the main arms. Cut out the leader just above the higher lateral.

Prune back each arm to about 38cm (15in) to a strong bud to encourage sideshoots or "ribs" to form.

Tie each main arm to a bamboo cane attached to the wires at 40°.

Cut back other, lower laterals to 1 bud.

YEAR 1, SUMMER PRUNING

Choose 2 sideshoots on the top of each arm and 1 underneath and tie them to well-spaced canes attached to the wires. Pinch back other shoots to 1 leaf.

YEAR 2, EARLY SPRING PRUNING

In early spring, cut back the extension growth on the two main arms by one third to strong buds facing in the required direction.

YEAR 2, EARLY SUMMER PRUNING

Train in developing sideshoots by tying them to canes to extend the permanent framework.

Cut back any wrong-pointing sideshoots to the point of origin, and remove any shoots emerging below the two main arms.

YEAR 3, EARLY SPRING PRUNING

Cut back each of the
main ribs by a quarter
to stimulate further
growth and extend
the framework.

YEAR 3, SUMMER PRUNING

Pinch back any shoots
that overlap the ribs
to 4–6 leaves as they
develop.

As the remaining
sideshoots
develop, tie them
to canes to fill in
the framework.
These shoots
should fruit the
following year.

YEAR 3, EARLY SUMMER PRUNING

Thin young sideshoots to 10–15cm (4–6in)
apart by pinching out unwanted shoots. Pinch
out any shoots that are growing towards the
wall or fence or in the wrong direction.

ESTABLISHED FAN, PRUNING AFTER FRUITING

Cut back each fruited
shoot to a suitable
replacement near
its base.

Tie in the replacement
shoot to fill the gap.
These shoots should be
evenly distributed over
the whole fan.

Harvesting and storing

Harvest the fruits when they are
fully ripe. Rest them in the palm of
the hand and apply gentle pressure
with your thumb on the part of the
fruit nearest to the stalk. If the flesh
"gives" slightly, the fruit is ready
for picking. For the finest flavour,
peaches and nectarines are best eat-
en as soon as possible after picking.
If necessary, they can be stored for a
few days by placing the fruits in
a container lined with soft material
and keeping it in a cool place.

Propagation

Peaches and nectarines are usually
propagated by chip- or T-budding
(see pp.372 and 373) in summer.
Seedling peaches are variable in
quality, but are often vigorous and
may produce excellent crops.

Apricots (Prunus armeniaca)

Apricots are more difficult to grow
than many other fruits. Not all
cultivars thrive in certain areas, so
always seek advice when selecting
trees. The chilling requirement for
apricots is 350–900 hours below
7°C (45°F), most cultivars being at
the lower end of this range. They
flower extremely early in the year.

Although dry, sunny summers are
needed for successful cropping,
drought conditions may cause serious bud drop late in the season. In
cool climates, apricots may be grown
under cover or fan-trained against a
warm wall. In warm areas, the bush
form is popular.

Site and planting

Apricot trees should be planted in
a sunny, sheltered, and frost-free site
in order to produce good crops of
fruit. In cool areas, it is essential to
grow them against a sunny wall or in
a greenhouse to protect the flowers
from frost and low temperatures in
late winter and early spring.

A deep, slightly alkaline loam is
the most suitable soil. Apricots are
least likely to thrive on sandy and
chalky soils. It is also best to avoid
planting them on heavy soils, particularly in areas that have cool, wet
winters, since this may make them
prone to dieback.

For rootstocks, both seedling apricots and peaches are widely used. A
seedling peach rootstock tolerates
wetter conditions than a seedling
apricot rootstock and produces a
smaller tree. The plum rootstock
'St Julien A' is also often used; this
is moderately vigorous.

Apricots are self-fertile; in cool
areas, however, flowers should be
pollinated by hand.

Plant in late autumn or very early
winter (see Planting Distances,
p.395) before bud-break. Stake bush
trees securely for the first two years.

PLANTING DISTANCES

TREE FORM	ROOTSTOCK	DISTANCE BETWEEN TREES	DISTANCE BETWEEN ROWS
Bush	'St Julien A'	4.5–5.5m (15–18ft)	5.5m (18ft)
	Seedling peach or apricot	5.5–7m (18–22ft)	7m (22ft)
Fan	'St Julien A'	4.5–5.5m (15–18ft)	

Routine care

In general, maintenance and cultivation requirements are as for other tree fruits (see "Care of tree fruits", p.366).

In warm regions where heavy cropping is common, blossom may need thinning to counteract biennial bearing (see p.376). Remove badly placed fruitlets and carry out the main thinning after any fruits have dropped naturally and the stones have started forming. Thin so that there is a single fruit on each truss, to leave about 7cm (3in) between fruits.

In cool areas, branch dieback occurs quite frequently; cut back affected branches to clean wood as soon as possible. Birds (p.561), earwigs (p.548), bacterial canker (p.569), brown rot (p.562), and gumming (see "Plums: Pests and diseases", p.388) may be troublesome.

Pruning and training

Fruits are borne both on one-year-old shoots and on older spurs. Pruning is aimed at maintaining the shape of the tree and removing any old, unproductive wood. If young trees are too vigorous, they may be root-pruned (see p.370). Prune and train an apricot bush as for plums (see p.388).

The initial training of a fan is as for peaches (see p.393). On an established fan, thin young shoots to 10–15cm (4–6in) apart as they develop in the spring, and remove any shoots that are pointing downwards, towards the centre of the fan, or inwards to the wall. Retain growths that are needed to fill gaps in the framework. Pinch back sub-laterals to six leaves if they are not required to fill gaps and any sideshoots to one leaf later in the season. After fruiting, prune sub-laterals to three leaves.

Harvesting

Pick the fruit when it is fully ripe and comes away easily from its stalk. Use immediately because fresh apricots do not store well; alternatively they may be frozen, used in preserves, or dried (see p.371).

Propagation

Apricots may be propagated by chip- or T-budding (see pp.372 and 373), using seedling peach or 'St Julien A' rootstocks.

RECOMMENDED APRICOTS

Early
'Antonio Errani' **W**, ☆
'Beliana' **W**
'Bella di Imola' **W**
'Cafona' **W**
'Early Moorpark'
'Hemskerk' ☆
'New Large Early'
'Priana' **W**
'Tyrinthos' **W**

Mid-season
'Alfred'
'Boccuccia' **W**
'Breda'
'Canino' **W**
'Farmingdale'
'Hargrand' **W**, ☆
'Mariem' **W**
'San Castrese' **W**

'Hemskerk'

Late
'Bergeron' **W**
'Helena du Rousillon' **W**
'Moorpark'
'Polonais' **W**
'Portici' **W**, ☆
'Reale d'Imola' **W**, ☆
'Rouge du Rousillon' **W**, ☆
'Shipley's', syn.
'Blenheim'

KEY
W *Warm climate needed*
☆ *Excellent flavour*

ESTABLISHED APRICOT FAN, EARLY SUMMER PRUNING

To fill gaps in the framework, tie in young sideshoots once they have hardened at the base.

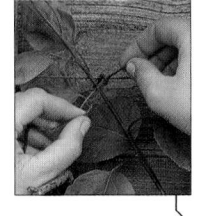

Cut or pinch out altogether any shoots pointing downwards or towards the wall or fence.

Cut or pinch back to 5 or 6 leaves any sub-laterals not needed as replacement shoots.

THINNING

Thin out the young shoots to leave them 10–15cm (4–6in) apart. Tie them in to the wires as they develop.

AFTER FRUITING

Using secateurs, cut back to 3 leaves the shoots that were reduced to 6 leaves earlier in the summer.

Sweet cherries (*Prunus avium*)

Sweet cherry trees may grow to a height and spread of 7.5m (25ft) or more and, as most cultivars are self-sterile, two trees are often necessary to produce a crop. There are as yet no reliable dwarfing rootstocks (see p.396) so sweet cherries are best suited to an orchard or large garden. For an average garden, choose a self-fertile cultivar; ideally, this should be fan-trained on a wall or fence, since this restricts its growth and makes it easier to protect the tree from attack by birds and from rain just before picking, which may cause the fruits to split. Sweet cherries have a chilling requirement of 800–1,200 hours below 7°C (45°F).

Duke cherries are thought to be hybrids between the sweet cherry and the acid cherry. They are not very widely grown but where chosen require similar treatment and spacing to sweet cherries. Some Duke cherry cultivars are self-fertile and combinations of acid cherries and Duke cherries are compatible.

Site and planting

Sweet cherries need a warm, sheltered site to produce a good crop. It is important to choose cultivars carefully to make sure that they will pollinate each other; this should be checked before buying trees (see "Pollination requirements", p.364).

ROOTSTOCKS

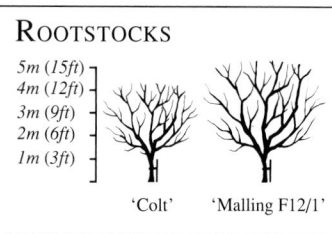

5m (15ft)
4m (12ft)
3m (9ft)
2m (6ft)
1m (3ft)

'Colt' 'Malling F12/1'

RECOMMENDED SWEET CHERRIES

Early
'Early Rivers' **Fg1, Ig1, Ss,**☆
'Waterloo' **Fg2, Ig2,**☆

Mid-season
'Merton Bigarreau' **Fg3, Ig2,**☆
'Merton Glory' **Fg2, Up, Ss,**☆
'Sunburst' **Fg4, Sf**

Late
'Bigarreau Gaucher' **Fg5, Up, Ss**
'Lapins' **Fg4, Sf**
'Merton Favourite' **Fg2, Ig2**
'Napoleon Bigarreau' **Fg4, Ig3**
'Noir de Guben' **Fg1, Up, Ss,**☆
'Stella' **Fg4, Sf,**☆

'Stella'

KEY
Fg *Flowering group (numbers indicate the period of flowering)*
Up *Universal pollinator*
Ig *Incompatibility group (cherries within each group will not pollinate each other)*
Sf *Self-fertile*
Ss *Self-sterile*
☆ *Excellent flavour*

Site

Choose an open, sunny, and sheltered site. If the cherry is to be grown as a fan, the support must be at least 2.5m (8ft) high and 5m (15ft) wide, with a reasonably sunny aspect; a tree grown on a cold wall will produce fruit of poor quality and flavour. A good, deep, well-drained soil is essential, as trees grown on shallow, poor soils produce small fruits and are less long-lived.

Rootstocks

'Colt', a semi-dwarfing rootstock, is suitable for bush or fan-trained trees in small gardens. 'Malling F12/1', which is very vigorous, is used where there is space. Two new dwarfing rootstocks, 'Inmil' and 'Camil', are under trial; their longevity and cropping potential are as yet unproven.

Pollination

The pollination requirements of sweet cherries are complex. The majority are self-sterile and they fall into distinct groups within which any combination is incompatible. Unless a self-fertile cultivar is obtained, it is important to choose a pair of trees that are from different groups and that flower at the same time. A few sweet cherries are universal pollinators, that is they will pollinate any cherries that flower at about the same time (see *Recommended Sweet Cherries*, left).

Planting

Sweet cherries should be planted in late autumn or winter if bare-root, or at any time if container-grown.

Construct the necessary supports and wires before planting fan-trained plants. Allow 5–5.5m (15–18ft) between trees that are to be fan-trained and between half-standards.

Routine care

Fruit thinning is unnecessary. Little or no feeding should be needed, apart from mulching as described under "Care of tree fruits", p.366. If growth is poor, apply ammonium sulphate at the standard rate of 35g/sq m (1oz/sq yd). Sweet cherries need thorough watering in dry conditions, but sudden watering on dry soils may cause the fruits to split.

As the fruits begin to colour, protect them from birds by draping netting over fan-trained trees. Bush and half-standard trees are difficult to net, however, so pick fruits as soon as they ripen.

The most likely pests and diseases to afflict sweet cherries are birds (p.561), cherry blackfly (see "Aphids", p.550), winter moth caterpillars (p.549), brown rot (p.562), silver leaf (p.551), and bacterial canker (p.569); cut out any branches with signs of silver leaf or bacterial canker as soon as they are noticed.

Pruning and training

Sweet cherries fruit on spurs on two-year-old and older wood. Mature trees should be pruned in summer to restrict vegetative growth and induce the formation of fruit buds.

Train and prune half-standards and bushes as for plums (see p.388).

Fan

Sweet cherry fans are established as for peaches (see p.393). If there are conveniently placed laterals on a feathered maiden, however, it may be possible to select four rather than two laterals to speed up the development of the fan. Tie these laterals to canes (attached to wires), which radiate out at 35–45° from the stem. In the spring following planting, prune back the selected shoots to 45–60cm (18–24in) and remove all other laterals that have developed.

During the summer, select two or three well-placed shoots from each branch and tie them in to fill the available space; remove the remainder. All branches or ribs on the young tree may be tip pruned at bud-burst (but never earlier) to reduce the risk of silver leaf and bacterial canker.

On older fans, spurs may be thinned or shortened in spring (see "Winter pruning", p.378) and branch leaders pruned to shorter replacement laterals to reduce height. In summer, pinch back all shoots not needed for the framework to six leaves, then to three after fruiting. Upright or very vigorous growths should be removed or tied horizontally to prevent the fan from becoming unbalanced.

Harvesting and storing

Pick fruits when fully ripe, complete with stalks, and eat or cook them immediately. If the fruits are to be frozen (see p.371), pick when firm.

Propagation

Chip- or T-budding are the usual methods of propagation (see pp.372, 373). 'Colt' rootstocks are compatible with all cultivars, as is the more vigorous 'Malling F12/1' rootstock.

ESTABLISHED SWEET CHERRY FAN, SUMMER PRUNING

Tie in sideshoots that are needed to replace old wood or fill bare spaces.

Cut back to 5 or 6 leaves any new growth not needed to extend the fan framework.

AFTER FRUITING

After the crop has been harvested, cut back all the laterals that were pruned to 6 leaves in early summer to 3 leaves.

Acid cherries (*Prunus cerasus*)

Acid or sour cherry trees are much smaller than sweet cherries and most cultivars are self-fertile so they are more suitable for the average garden. The fruiting habit also differs in that the crop is mostly borne on one-year-old shoots produced the previous summer. The fruit is not usually eaten raw but is prized for preserves and other culinary uses. Acid cherries have a chilling requirement of 800–1,200 hours below 7°C (45°F).

Site and planting

Site and soil requirements are generally as for sweet cherries (see p.395) except that acid cherries may also be grown successfully against a north- or east-facing wall or fence.

The recommended rootstock, as for sweet and Duke cherries, is 'Colt'. It is best to obtain cultivars such as 'Morello' (the most popular) from a specialist fruit supplier since inferior, less fertile selections

ROOTSTOCK

4m (12ft)
3m (9ft)
2m (6ft)
1m (3ft)

'Colt'

exist. Plant trees to be trained as bushes and fans 4–5m (12–15ft) apart and for fans provide a minimum support height of 2.1m (7ft).

Routine care

Acid cherries have the same cultivation requirements as sweet cherries (see p.395). Greater attention to feeding, particularly with nitrogen, may be necessary to encourage young, replacement shoots, but do not overfeed. Irrigation is important in dry areas. Netting is essential to protect the fruits from birds (see p.367); since acid cherries may be

trained into small tree forms, such as the bush or dwarf pyramid, they may be grown in a fruit cage. Acid cherries are affected by the same pests and diseases as sweet cherries (see "Routine care", p.396).

Pruning and training

Acid cherries are pruned on a renewal system to produce a constant supply of one-year-old wood on which fruit is produced. A proportion of the older wood should be removed each year. Prune trees in spring and summer since this reduces the risk of silver leaf (p.551).

Fan

This is trained as for a peach fan (see p.393). Renewal pruning to encourage young growth once cropping starts is important because of the restricted space. In spring, on an established fan, pinch out badly placed or overcrowded new shoots

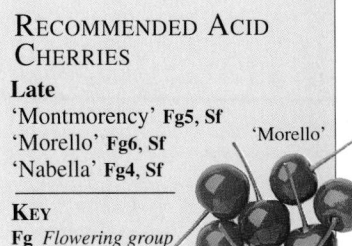

RECOMMENDED ACID CHERRIES

Late
'Montmorency' **Fg5, Sf**
'Morello' **Fg6, Sf**
'Nabella' **Fg4, Sf**

'Morello'

KEY
Fg *Flowering group (numbers indicate the period of flowering)*
Sf *Self-fertile*

and thin the rest to leave them 10cm (4in) apart. Tie these into support wires as they develop. Retain one or, where space permits, two developing shoots low down on each fruiting shoot. Tie in one of these to replace each fruiting shoot that is cut out after harvesting. The second shoot may be used as a reserve in case the first is damaged, or to fill a gap in the fan. To rejuvenate older fans, prune back to young shoots on older wood in spring and autumn.

ESTABLISHED ACID CHERRY FAN

SPRING PRUNING

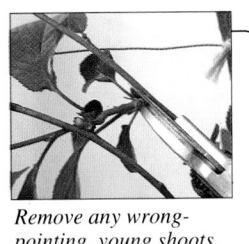

Remove any wrong-pointing, young shoots, cutting them back flush with the stem.

Thin the young, developing shoots to about 10cm (4in) apart, if necessary.

SUMMER PRUNING, AFTER FRUITING

Cut back each fruited shoot to a suitable replacement near its base.

Tie in the replacement shoots to maintain even spacing. These should fruit the following year.

Remove any wrong-pointing shoots that have developed and were not removed in the spring, cutting them back flush with the stem.

ESTABLISHED ACID CHERRY BUSH, PRUNING AFTER FRUITING

Cut back a quarter of the fruited shoots to replacement shoots near the base of each.

Each year, cut back a few older, crossing, or unproductive laterals to replacement shoots.

Bush

The bush is built up as for peach (see p.393). After the third or fourth year, once the bush is established, renewal pruning is essential. In early autumn, after fruiting, cut out a quarter of the fruited shoots, preferably to replacement shoots, to maintain even spacing and leave room for the young growth that will carry the next year's crop. Remove old or unproductive wood at the same time. If pruning is neglected, fruiting will decrease and be restricted to the tree's outer edge.

Harvesting

Cut the stalks with scissors as hand picking may injure the shoots and encourage infection. Cook, freeze, or preserve soon after picking (see "Harvesting and storing", p.371).

Propagation

The usual methods are chip- or T-budding (see pp. 372 and 373). All cultivars are compatible with 'Colt' and 'Malling F12/1' rootstocks.

HARVESTING ACID CHERRIES

Harvest by cutting each stalk close to the lateral, not by pulling as this may damage the bark and increase the risk of bacterial canker.

Persimmons (*Diospyros kaki*)

Persimmons are deciduous, slow-growing trees that will eventually reach a height of 10–15m (30–50ft) and a spread of about 10m (30ft). The fruits are usually globular, and they may be yellow, orange, or red when fully ripe; some cultivars produce seedless fruits.

Outdoor cultivation in subtropical areas with a minimum temperature of 10°C (50°F) is possible, but a range of 16–22°C (61–72°F) during autumn is preferable. Most cultivars have a low chilling requirement of 100–200 hours below 7°C (45°F); in addition, during the active growing season they need at least 1,400 hours of sunshine to fruit successfully.

Site and planting

A sheltered and sunny site is preferable; provide protection with windbreaks, if necessary. A well-drained and fertile soil is essential, with a pH of 6–7; mature trees are relatively drought-resistant, but they require irrigation if there is inadequate rain in the growing season.

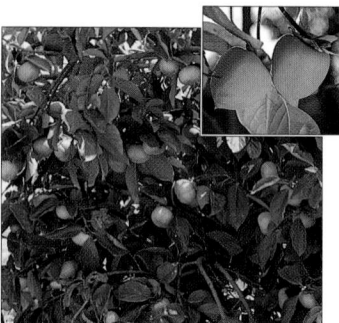

PERSIMMON

Vigorous seedlings of *Diospyros kaki* are suitable as rootstocks, but *D. virginiana* is most frequently used for this purpose.

Although some persimmon cultivars have both male and female flowers on the same tree, a number have only one or the other. The most widely grown cultivars have only female flowers; these will produce fruit without pollination but the fruits are small and astringent. A pollinator cultivar, with male flowers, must therefore be grown nearby. A ratio of one pollinator plant to eight or ten female-flowering plants is usually adequate.

In well-manured ground, prepare planting holes; add organic material and general-purpose fertilizer. Trees should be spaced at about 5m (15ft).

Routine care

Apply fertilizer around the trees every three to four months, using a general-purpose mixture with medium nitrogen levels. Conserve moisture in the soil by mulching with organic matter, and water regularly in the dry season. Keep the ground around the trees weed-free.

The major pests that affect persimmons grown in the open are thrips (p.551), mealybugs (p.550), scale insects (p.552), and fruit flies (p.563). Common diseases that may cause problems include crown gall (p.559) and anthracnose and other fungal leaf spots (p.552).

If cultivating persimmons under cover, pests such as red spider mites (p.550) and whiteflies (p.550) may also be troublesome.

Growing under cover

If growing persimmons in a greenhouse, plant them in prepared beds or in large containers with a minimum diameter of 35cm (14in); use a very fertile compost incorporating a general-purpose fertilizer with medium nitrogen levels. Maintain a temperature of at least 16°C (61°F) and a humidity of 60–70 per cent. Water regularly during the growing season and apply a general-purpose fertilizer every three to four weeks.

It is necessary to pollinate the flowers by hand for a successful fruit set (see *Hand-pollination*, p.391). During the summer, move plants in containers into the open; leave them until the autumn until their chilling requirement has been met.

Pruning and training

Cultivars vary greatly in vigour. Dwarf and semi-dwarf cultivars are usually trained in a similar way to an apple spindlebush (see p.380). Prune trees for the first three years during the dormant season to form a framework. Subsequent pruning should be relatively light: restrict it to the removal of crowded, crossing, or unproductive branches, and to cutting back branch leaders annually by about one third of their new growth.

Harvesting and storing

Pick fruits when they are fully ripe. Cut fruits from the tree, leaving the calyx and a short fruit stalk attached. Seal the fruits in clear plastic bags and store them at 0°C (32°F); they should remain in good condition for up to two months.

RECOMMENDED PERSIMMONS

'Fuyu'
'Gailey' (pollinator)
'Hachiya'

'Hanafuyu'

'Hanafuyu'
'Hayakume'
'Jiro'
'Tamopan'
'Zenjimaru' (pollinator)

Propagation

Persimmon trees may be propagated by seed, by grafting, from cuttings, or from rooted suckers.

Sow seed taken from mature fruits immediately in containers; kept at 28°C (82°F), it usually germinates in two to three weeks. In 12 months, the seedlings provide stocks suitable for grafting. Handle seedlings carefully when transplanting.

Cultivars may be propagated by chip- or T-budding (see pp.372 and 373), or by whip-and-tongue grafting (see p.373). Softwood cuttings (see p.55) taken in summer and treated with hormone rooting powder should root in a mist unit with basal heat.

Rooted suckers may be detached from the base of the parent tree (provided that it has not been budded or grafted). Establish them in containers before planting them out in their final positions.

Figs (*Ficus carica*)

Figs are among the oldest fruits in cultivation, and belong to the family Moraceae. They have a low chilling requirement of 100–300 hours below 7°C (45°F) and thrive in regions with a long, hot growing season.

Site and planting

Figs require a sunny position and in cool areas need a wall or fence for more warmth and protection from frost; this should be at least 3–3.5m (10–11ft) wide by 2.2m (7ft) high.

Figs prefer slightly alkaline, deep, rich, moisture-retentive soils, and a warm, dry climate. Cooler, wetter conditions induce too much growth, with poorer crops. When the pH is less than 6, lime the soil (see p.531).

Where space is limited, a concrete or brick "pit", or box, may be built below soil level to restrict the root system and produce a smaller tree. The pit should be 60cm (2ft) square and have a base that is not solid but filled with broken bricks or stones to a depth of 25–30cm (10–12in); this will provide drainage and restrict root growth downwards.

In cool climates, figs may also be grown in pots placed in a sunny, sheltered site and transferred to cold but frost-free conditions in winter. Use a container 30–38cm (12–15in) in diameter, with several large drainage holes, and filled with a loam-based potting compost.

No specific rootstocks have yet been introduced, and trees are grown on their own roots. Modern cultivars are self-fertile.

Select two-year-old, pot-grown specimens and plant these in winter, teasing the roots gently loose from the soil ball before planting. Unrestricted trees need to be spaced 6–8m (20–26ft) apart; those planted in a pit need only half this spacing.

Routine care

To protect branches carrying the embryo figs from frost, tie a dense layer of bracken or straw around

FRUIT PLACEMENT

Ripening fruits

Embryo fruits

them (see also FROST AND WIND PROTECTION, *Hessian and Straw Cover*, p.520). At the same time, remove any unripe figs from the previous summer. It may be necessary to protect the ripening fruits against birds and wasps.

Feeding, watering, and mulching

A spring mulch of well-rotted manure is all that is normally required, but trees with restricted roots need extra nutrients. This may be in the form of a balanced fertilizer applied at a rate of 70g/sq m (2oz/sq yd), and supplemented during the summer with occasional liquid feeds. Avoid overfeeding fig trees.

Watering is essential in hot, dry weather, especially where the roots are restricted. Pot-grown figs need regular watering throughout the growing season. Repot and root-prune them every two years.

Pests and diseases

Figs in the open are usually problem-free, but wasps (p.563) and birds (p.561) may attack fruits. Under cover, red spider mites (p.550), mealybugs (p.550), whiteflies (p.550), wasps, (p.563), mice (p.566), and *Nectria* canker (p.568) may be troublesome.

Growing under cover

In cool areas, fan-trained figs may be grown under glass and will crop more regularly than in the open. The roots must be contained to restrict growth. Once growth starts, water regularly but reduce watering as the fruits ripen to prevent the skins splitting. Prune as for figs grown outdoors but leave a more open tree to allow as much light as possible to reach the leaves and fruit.

Pruning and training

In warm climates, figs need only light pruning and are usually grown in bush form. Two crops per season are normally produced, an early one from embryo figs (about the size of small peas) formed late in the previous season, followed by the main crop which is both formed and ripened during the same summer. Meanwhile, further embryo fruits develop to repeat the process.

In cool climates, figs are trained either as open bushes or fans. Only the first crop from embryo figs will have time to ripen. Remove those

ESTABLISHED FIG BUSH
SPRING PRUNING

Cut back frost-damaged shoots to healthy wood and thin out wrong-pointing shoots and any that are overcrowded.

Cut out a proportion of the remaining shoots or, on older trees, branches to 1 bud to promote new growth.

SUMMER PRUNING

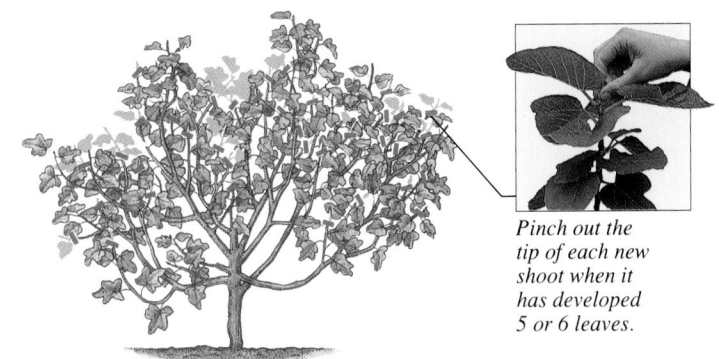

Pinch out the tip of each new shoot when it has developed 5 or 6 leaves.

that do not ripen to concentrate the tree's energies into producing new embryo fruits.

Bush

Purchase a tree with three or four branches arising about 60cm (2ft) above ground. Prune these back by half their length in the first winter to encourage further branches to form and establish a basic framework. Pot-grown trees should branch at 38cm (15in) from the base so that they are compact and not top-heavy.

Pruning of established trees differs with the climate. In warm climates in spring, shorten spreading branches to more vertical shoots and leave some growth in the tree's centre to protect the bark from sunscorch. In cooler climates, remove all crowded, crossing, or frost-damaged branches; keep the centre open by taking out all upright shoots and pruning to buds on the lower sides of branches.

Lengths of bare wood should be cut back to one bud to promote new growth. In the summer, pinch out new shoots or sideshoots to five or six leaves to encourage fruit to form.

Fan

Plant a two-year-old tree with two or three strong shoots. Tie down the two best-placed as for peach fans

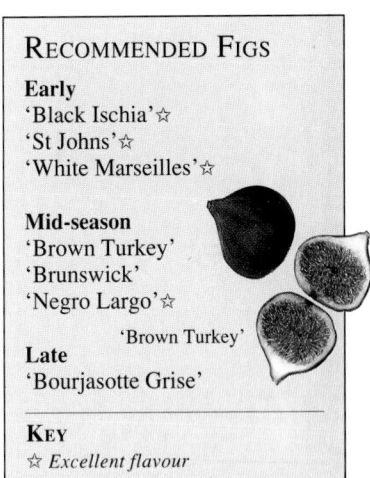
(see p.393) and tip prune lightly. Prune back trees without suitable sideshoots to about 40cm (15in) to encourage lateral growth. The fan is then developed as for peaches but with greater space between branches to allow for the fig's larger foliage.

Prune the established fan in early spring to remove old, fruited wood and any that is frost-damaged or badly placed, and leave the younger wood. Also prune back a proportion of younger shoots to one bud to induce fresh growths close to the main branches. Wherever possible, tie in the unpruned shoots to fill any spaces and remove all others. Pinch out the tips of new growths to five leaves in mid-summer. The resulting new shoots should then develop embryo fruits for overwintering.

Harvesting and storing

Pick the fruits when fully ripe. Ripe fruits tend to hang down, are very soft to the touch, and may have slight splits in the skin. Figs are best eaten fresh, but may also be dried.

Propagation

Seed-raised plants vary in fruit quality. Hardwood cuttings of one-year-old wood from selected cultivars should be used. Take cuttings (see p.374) 30cm (12in) long and insert them in well-prepared, well-drained ground. Protect them from frost with cloches. Figs may also be propagated by rooted suckers, severed from the parent tree and transplanted.

ESTABLISHED FIG FAN
SPRING PRUNING

Once all risk of frost has passed, cut all frost-damaged shoots back to their point of origin.

Cut back a proportion of young shoots to 1 bud to encourage replacement growth that will produce embryo fruits.

Tie in the shoots so that they are evenly spaced over the fan.

Cut off wrong-pointing shoots to the point of origin or to a well-placed sub-lateral.

Cut back a proportion of old, bare wood to 1 bud or node to promote new growth.

SUMMER PRUNING

Pinch back new shoots to 5 leaves to encourage embryo fruits to form in the leaf axils.

Mulberries (*Morus nigra*)

Mulberries belong to the Moraceae family. Black mulberries reach a height of 6–10m (20–30ft), and are grown for their fruit. White mulberries (*M. alba*) are not usually grown for their fruit.They grow up to 3m (10ft) tall. The chilling requirement is high and the trees begin growth late in the season.

Site and planting
Moist, slightly acid soils are preferable. Mulberries are usually grown on their own roots, and are self-fertile. Plant in late autumn to winter, 8–10m (25–30ft) apart; in cold areas, plant in spring.

Routine care
Cultivation is similar to that of apples (see p.376). Mulch and water in dry weather. Mulberries are mainly untroubled by pests and diseases.

Pruning and training
Mulberries are grown as either half-standards or standards. Prune only to establish a strong framework of four to five branches, and thereafter only remove branches if they are badly placed or crowded. The trees should be pruned when fully dormant in winter since shoots and roots bleed profusely if cut or damaged between early spring and autumn. If bleeding

does occur, cauterize the wounds as quickly as possible with a hot poker or other iron implement.

Harvesting and storing
Pick the fruit when fully ripe in late summer, or allow it to drop onto a suitable temporary surface (such as a sheet of plastic) to keep it clean. Eat mulberries fresh, or freeze them.

Propagation
Mulberries may be propagated by simple or air layering (see p.88) or by hardwood cuttings about 18cm (7in) long, taken with a heel (see p.85), known as "truncheons".

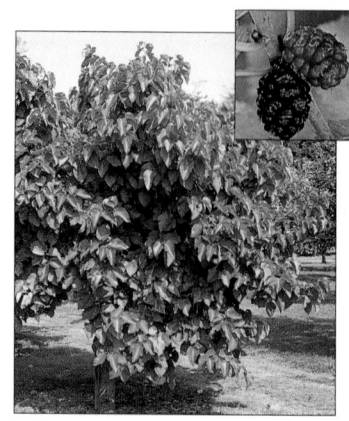

BLACK MULBERRY

Vines

VINES require warm, sheltered positions for successful fertilization, and to ripen their fruits. Grapes, kiwi fruits, and passion fruits all belong to this group. In cool areas, they should be given a sheltered environment or they may be grown under glass. Vines fruit on long, flexible stems of one-year-old wood and need to be pruned after fruiting each year to encourage them to produce a supply of new shoots; these grow rapidly and need to be carefully trained into their supports so that they receive the maximum amount of light and air.

Black dessert grapes

White dessert grapes

Kiwi fruits

Grapes (*Vitis vinifera*)

Through the ages grapes have traditionally been one of the choicest fruits for eating or for wine-making. The European grape (*Vitis vinifera*) and its cultivars are generally considered to be of the highest quality. The American grape (*V. labrusca*) tolerates colder climates and has been hybridized with *V. vinifera* to widen the choice in cooler climates of cultivars for dessert and wine grapes. Many cultivars are suitable for both dessert and wine use.

The fruits need a hot, dry summer to ripen. Warm-temperate regions suit a wide range of cultivars; many may be grown successfully in cooler climates, however, in protected sites or in greenhouses. Decorative pergolas, arches, or other suitable structures may support vines. Pruning methods vary: vines grown for dessert grapes are pruned to produce fewer, higher-quality fruits; vines grown for wine grapes are pruned to obtain the greatest quantity of fruits.

Dessert grapes

It is comparatively easy to produce high-quality dessert grapes in warm areas. In cooler climates, they may be grown against a sunny, warm wall or, preferably, in a greenhouse. For details of greenhouse cultivation, see "Growing under cover", below. Dessert grapes are usually divided into sweetwater, muscat, and vinous groups. Sweetwater are sweet grapes, ripening earliest; muscats have the finest flavour and are second to mature; vinous grapes tend to have less flavour, but are strong-growing and crop late. Vines are usually self-fertile and wind-pollinated.

Site
A warm, sheltered, sunny site free from frosts at flowering time is ideal. Vines need a reasonably fertile, well-drained soil, with a pH of 6–7.5. Avoid planting them on very rich soil as this encourages excess growth at the expense of fruits. Sharp drainage

is essential as grapes will not tolerate wet soils; improve the soil or install a drainage system if necessary (for details, see SOILS AND FERTILIZERS, "Improving drainage", p.529).

In cool climates, vines grown on a warm, sunny wall give reasonably good results but will not match the quality of vines grown under glass. Early-ripening cultivars should be used for wall cultivation to obtain dessert fruits by late summer. Support vines with horizontal wires, held in place by vine eyes, 2.5–5cm (1–2in) from the wall.

Vines are usually grown on their own roots, except in areas where *Phylloxera* is a hazard (see "Pests and diseases", right); in this case, seek local advice on which rootstock to use. The use of a rootstock may have other advantages, too, such as greater tolerance of a high pH or wet soil conditions, and control of overvigorous growth.

Planting
Cultivate the soil thoroughly before planting. In poor or sandy soils, incorporate upturned turves at the foot of the planting trench, adding well-rotted manure or compost, then firm the area and water well. The soil by a wall is often dry and thorough preparation, with the addition of ample organic matter, is usually required to improve water retention. Plant bare-root vines in winter but containerized specimens may be planted at any season. Space single cordons at least 1.2m (4ft) apart, double or "U" cordons at twice that spacing; the arms of multiple cordons should be 60cm (24in) apart.

Routine care
Water thoroughly during the growing season whenever conditions are dry, reducing watering as the fruit ripens. Particular care is needed with grapes grown on a wall, since they may be in a rain shadow. Mulch to retain moisture. Once vigorous young shoots develop, feed with a high-potash fertilizer every two or

three weeks; if growth is poor, give high nitrogen instead. Stop feeding as soon as the fruits start to ripen.

If using the cordon system, retain no more than one bunch per 30cm (12in) of vertical stem, or rod, for best-quality grapes; remove intermediate bunches at an early stage. Thin the fruits to obtain both well-shaped bunches and large, evenly sized grapes (and to discourage mildew). Use grape-thinning scissors and a small, forked stick to expose portions of the bunch so that small fruits in the centre may be removed. Do not touch the fruits themselves since this may spoil their bloom. Some cultivars need a second thinning as the fruits develop further.

Pests and diseases
Vines are affected by problems such as scale insects (p.552), vine weevils (p.549), wasps (p.563), downy mildew (p.550), and grey mould/ *Botrytis* (p.562). Under cover, red spider mites (p.550), whiteflies (p.550), mealybugs (p.550), and powdery mildew (p.562) may also be troublesome.

Vine *Phylloxera* is a serious pest in warmer climates, where this aphid-like insect attacks the roots of European vines; galls may also form on the leaves. The attack causes severe stunting and is often fatal. Little treatment is available, although the use of resistant rootstocks and resistant hybrids of American grape cultivars has greatly reduced its incidence. Net vines to protect them against birds (see "Protection from birds", p.367).

Growing under cover
In cool climates, grow vines in a greenhouse, preferably with heating. Other crops with compatible temperature and humidity requirements may also be grown in the greenhouse. In a lean-to greenhouse, the warmth from the back wall is particularly beneficial, especially if there is little or no direct heating. Greenhouses with both top- and side-ventilation give the best results.

The soil must be fairly fertile, weed-free, and well drained, with a pH of 6–7.5. Any drainage must be 75cm (2½ft) deep as vines are deep-rooted. Plant as for vines in the open. Hand-pollinate by tapping the rod around midday, or drawing the hand gently down the flower truss.

Either train vines directly onto the back wall or plant them at the foot of the glass wall, training them on support wires that are 22cm (9in) or

THINNING GRAPES

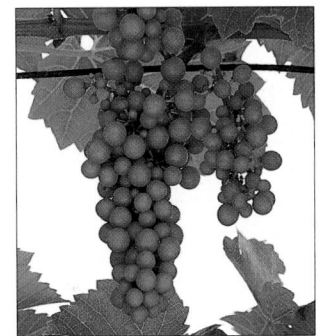

1 *Once the bunches have been thinned to 30cm (12in) apart, the fruits will need thinning as they swell to increase the size of individual grapes and allow air circulation between them.*

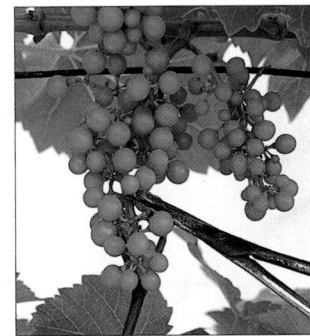

2 *Use a forked cane and vine scissors to expose portions of the bunch and snip off unwanted grapes. The thinned bunch should be wide at the top and tapering towards the base.*

more from the glass. In free-standing houses, plant vines at one end, then train up and along the roof on wires. For details of cultivation, see "Routine care", p.401. A soil auger may be used to gauge levels of moisture in the soil; use tepid water for the first waterings of the season.

Control ventilation carefully; keep it at a maximum in winter to ensure adequate winter chilling of the vines. Reduce to a minimum in late winter to induce growth. Vary the amount according to the weather to maintain even temperatures. Slight ventilation is always advisable and adequate warmth is needed at flowering to aid pollination. After fruit set, good air circulation is needed to control grey mould/*Botrytis* and mildew.

Damping down and mist-spraying help control red spider mites. Do not damp down on dull days, or during flowering or ripening periods.

Fork over the bed carefully in late winter, avoiding the root area; remove 1cm (¹/₂in) of soil from the surface and replace it with loam-based compost. After the first watering, mulch with well-rotted manure or compost around the base of the vines.

Once the fruits ripen, they need a "finishing period" during which they remain on the vine to attain maximum colour and flavour: allow two to three weeks for early cultivars, and longer for late-ripening ones. Provide good ventilation, netting ventilators to exclude birds if these are a problem.

Pruning and training
The usual method for dessert grapes is to develop single or double ("U") cordons or rods on which permanent fruiting spurs are formed. These produce high-quality fruits.

Vines fruit on the current season's growth. Spring and summer pruning, therefore, is aimed at restricting new growth from the rods so that one bunch of grapes develops from each spur. It also restricts the growth of foliage enough to expose the developing fruit to sun, particularly in cool climates. In hot climates, take care that sun scorch does not occur. Carry out winter pruning before mid-winter to restrict sap-bleeding.

Single cordon After planting, while the vine is dormant, shorten the stem to a strong bud a few inches above the ground. In summer, train one leading shoot onto a vertical bamboo cane and pinch or cut back any laterals to five or six leaves. Shorten all the sub-laterals (shoots that are

GRAPE, SINGLE CORDON
YEAR 1, WINTER PRUNING

At planting, cut back the main stem by two-thirds to a strong bud not far from ground level.

YEAR 1, SUMMER PRUNING

Pinch back to 1 leaf any sub-laterals that form from the laterals.

As the main leader develops, tie it in to the vertical cane.

Cut back each of the main laterals to 5 or 6 leaves.

YEAR 2, WINTER PRUNING

Cut back the leader by about two-thirds of the new growth.

Prune back the laterals that have formed to 1 strong bud.

YEAR 2, SUMMER PRUNING

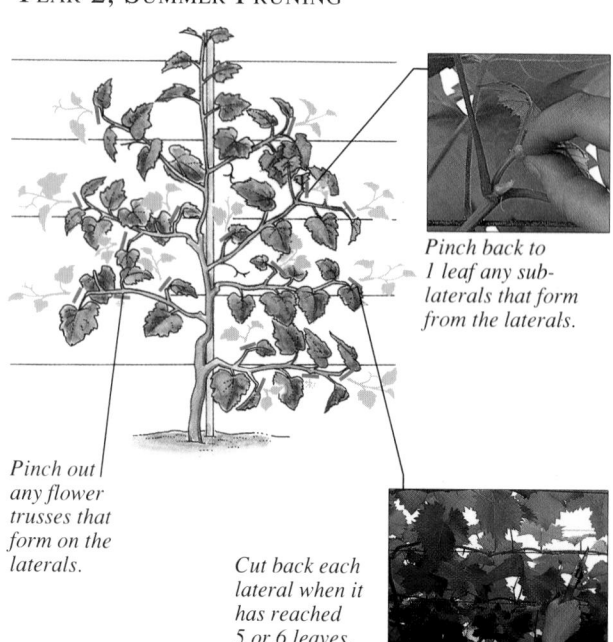

Pinch out any flower trusses that form on the laterals.

Pinch back to 1 leaf any sub-laterals that form from the laterals.

Cut back each lateral when it has reached 5 or 6 leaves.

growing from the laterals) to one leaf. Remove any shoots that develop from the base.

During the second winter, reduce the leader by two-thirds of the new growth to well-ripened wood and laterals back to one bud. In the second summer, tie in the leading shoot as it extends. Pinch or cut sideshoots to five or six leaves and sub-laterals to one leaf as for the first summer. Remove any flower trusses; do not allow the vine to fruit until the third year.

In the third winter, shorten the leading shoot by two-thirds of its new growth and cut back all the laterals to one strong bud to create spurs that will bear fruiting shoots.

Routine pruning Carry out routine pruning from the third year onwards. In spring, let two shoots grow at each spur and pinch out others. Retain the stronger of the two for fruiting, and pinch back the weaker to two leaves, keeping it as a replacement in case the fruiting shoot breaks. In summer, as flower trusses develop, retain the best, pruning out the others to leave one per lateral. Stop laterals at two leaves beyond the chosen flower trusses. Pinch out laterals not carrying flowers at about five leaves and any sub-laterals at one leaf.

Each winter continue to remove two-thirds of the new growth from the leader, but when it has reached the top of its support cut it back annually to two buds. Cut laterals to one strong bud. If spur systems become congested in later years, either remove part of the system with a pruning saw or, if there are too many spurs on the rod, remove some of them completely. The spurs should be 22–30cm (9–12in) apart. The rod should be untied from its wires to about half-way down its length and bent over until nearly horizontal for a few weeks during winter to encourage the even development of shoots the following spring; then retie the rod vertically.

Double cordon This may be formed by training in two shoots horizontally in the first summer. Prune each back to 60cm (2ft) the following winter. The next year, train the extension growths vertically. These form two vertical arms; prune each arm as a single cordon.

Multiple cordon Train in two shoots in the first summer and in winter prune each back to 60cm (2ft). Train the extension growths horizontally, and choose a strong shoot every 60cm (2ft) to train vertically in order

HARVESTING DESSERT GRAPES

Avoid touching the fruits and spoiling the bloom. Cut each bunch complete with a "handle" consisting of 5cm (2in) of woody stem from either side of the bunch.

YEAR 3, WINTER PRUNING

Cut back the leader, removing about two-thirds of the new growth.

Cut back laterals to 1 strong bud.

SPRING PRUNING

When shoots form at each spur, thin to 2 shoots, one to form the main lateral, the other as an insurance shoot.

ESTABLISHED SINGLE CORDON, SUMMER PRUNING

If any lateral is not fruiting, cut back the tip to 5 or 6 leaves.

Cut all fruiting laterals back to 2 leaves beyond the flower truss.

Pinch back any sub-laterals that form on the laterals to 1 leaf.

Pinch out any weak flower trusses to leave no more than 1 per lateral.

ESTABLISHED SINGLE CORDON, WINTER PRUNING

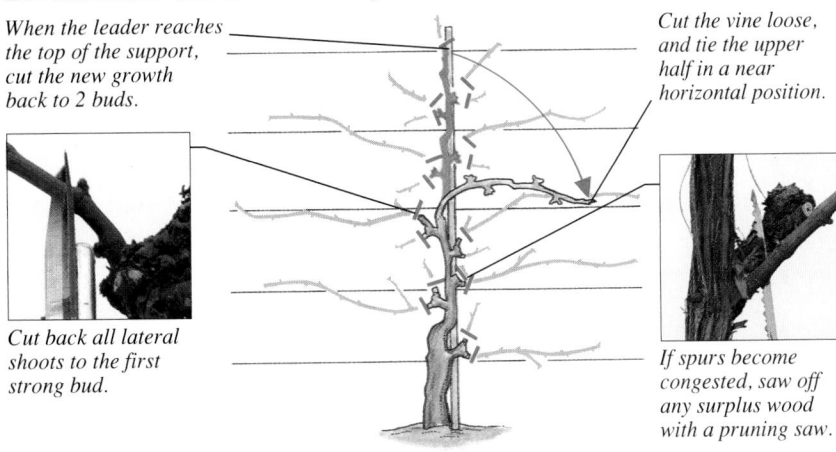

When the leader reaches the top of the support, cut the new growth back to 2 buds.

Cut back all lateral shoots to the first strong bud.

Cut the vine loose, and tie the upper half in a near horizontal position.

If spurs become congested, saw off any surplus wood with a pruning saw.

MULTIPLE CORDON

A multiple cordon may be trained with as many vertical rods as space allows. Once established, each arm is pruned in the same way as a single cordon.

RECOMMENDED WINE GRAPES

Early
'Dunkelfelder' (black)
'Findling' (white)
'Huxelrebe' (white)
'Madeleine Angevine 7972'
 (white) **Du**
'Madeleine Sylvaner' (white) **Du**
'Melon' (white)
'Ortega' (white) **Du**
'Regner' (white)
'Reichensteiner' (white)
'Siegerrebe' (golden) **Du**

'Siegerrebe'

Mid-season
'Auxerrois' (white)
'Bacchus' (white)
'Dornfelder' (black) **Du**
'Kernling' (white)
'Léon Millot', syn. 'Kuhlmann'
 (black) **Du**
'Müller Thurgau',
 syn.'Riesling
 Sylvaner',
 'Rivaner'
 (white) **Du**

'Müller Thurgau'

'Pinot Meunier', syn. 'Meunier',
 'Müllerrebe', 'Schwarzriesling',
 'Wrotham Pinot' (black)
'Pinot Noir', syn.
 'Spätburgunder' (black)
'Schönburger' (white)
'Seibel 13053', syn. 'Cascade'
 (black)

Late
Late-ripening cultivars ripen
outside only in areas with
reliably warm summers.

'Black Hamburgh', syn.
 'Trollinger'
 (black) **Du**

'Black
Hamburgh'

'Chardonnay', syn. 'Pinot
 Chardonnay' (white)
'Chenin Blanc' (white)
'Gewürztraminer' (white)
'Pinot Gris', syn. 'Grey
 Burgunder', 'Ruländer' (white)
'Riesling' (white)
'Sauvignon Blanc', syn. 'Blanc
 Fumé', 'Quinechon',
 'Sauvignon Fumé', 'Sauvignon
 Jaune' (white)
'Scheurebe' (white)
'Seyval Blanc', syn. 'Seyve-Villard
 5276' (white)

KEY
Du *Also for dessert use*

to form the number of arms required. Once established, prune each arm as a single cordon.

Alternative pruning methods Some cultivars will not produce adequate fruit-bearing shoots from the basal buds left by spur pruning. In such cases, longer lengths of ripened wood, or canes, are retained when winter pruning the buds from which fruit-bearing shoots will be produced. Other canes are cut back to three or four buds to produce strong new growths to replace the old fruiting canes the following winter. This process is repeated annually. Many other renewal systems may also be used to train dessert grapes (for details on the double Guyot system, see "Pruning and training: Guyot system", p.405).

Harvesting and storing

Tie back or remove some of the foliage to allow more sun to reach the ripening fruits. Cut ripe bunches from the vine with a short piece of woody stem – the "handle" – and place in a container with soft lining so that the fruits are not damaged and their bloom is not spoiled.

Bunches may be stored for a week or two at room temperature by cutting a longer handle and placing this in a narrow-necked container of water, with the fruit hanging down on the outside of the container.

Propagation

Vines may be propagated by hardwood cuttings or grafting (for details, see "Wine grapes: Propagation", p.406, and "Bud-grafting", p.372).

GRAPE, DOUBLE GUYOT
YEAR 1, WINTER PRUNING

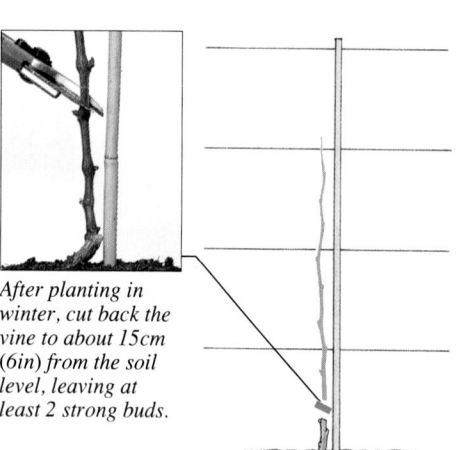

After planting in winter, cut back the vine to about 15cm (6in) from the soil level, leaving at least 2 strong buds.

YEAR 2, WINTER PRUNING

Prune the leader back to about 38cm (15in) from soil level, just below the bottom wire, to leave 3 good buds.

YEAR 1, SUMMER PRUNING

As it develops, tie in the leader to a vertical stake with a loose figure-of-eight knot.

Prune any laterals that develop back to 5 leaves.

Remove any competing shoots developing below the main leader.

YEAR 2, SUMMER PRUNING

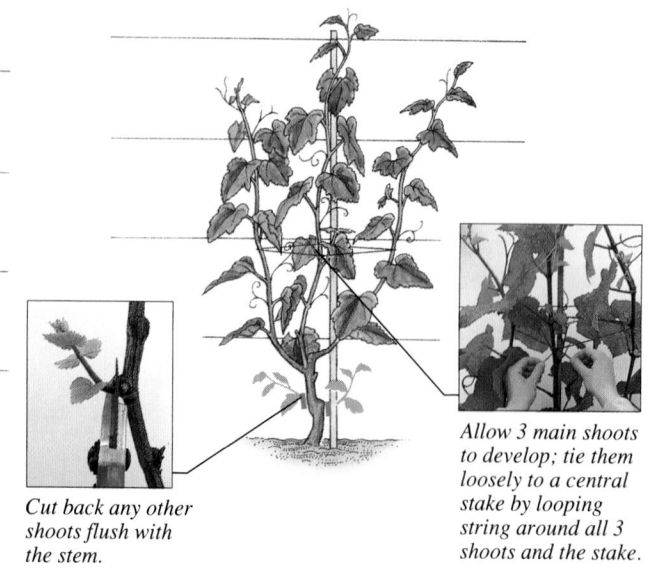

Cut back any other shoots flush with the stem.

Allow 3 main shoots to develop; tie them loosely to a central stake by looping string around all 3 shoots and the stake.

Wine grapes

Grapes may be grown for wine in areas with long, dry, sunny summers and adequate soil moisture. In cooler climates, early- and mid-season cultivars grown on warm walls or under cover give good results.

Site and planting

Most well-drained soils with a pH of 6–7.5 are suitable. Clear weeds before planting. Rootstocks are as for dessert grapes (see "Dessert grapes: Site", p.401). The flowers are usually self-fertile, and are wind-pollinated. Before planting, erect a row of support posts. Fix a single wire 38cm (15in) above the ground and double wires at 75cm and 1.2m (30in and 4ft). Each of the double wires is looped round the posts to form a figure of eight. Plant one- or two-year-old vines in winter, 1.5–2m (5–6ft) apart, in rows 2m (6ft) apart.

Routine care
Remove any weeds, and water to establish young vines in dry conditions; water cropping vines only in drought conditions since too much water reduces grape quality. Give a light, annual, early spring application of a balanced fertilizer, and apply sulphate of potash in alternate years. Use a foliar spray of magnesium sulphate to correct deficiencies of magnesium (see p.555). Mulch every other year with plenty of well-rotted compost, or annually if the soil quality is poor. Fruit size is not important for wine quality so thinning is only necessary in cold areas, to improve sugar levels.

Pruning and training
Some cultivars need spur pruning (see "Dessert grapes: Pruning and training" p.402); many, however, require annual replacement of old canes to fruit regularly.

Guyot system This is widely used for wine grapes, since it produces a prolific crop in a limited space. It involves annual training of horizontal rods from which fruiting shoots are trained vertically. In the double

YEAR 3, WINTER PRUNING

Gently bend down the 2 strongest sideshoots and tie them to the bottom wire, one on either side. As shoots develop from these, train them vertically.

Prune these shoots back to 8–12 buds, to leave 60cm (2ft) of strong growth.

Prune the third, central shoot back, leaving at least 3 or 4 good buds to encourage the formation of new shoots during the following season.

YEAR 3, SUMMER PRUNING

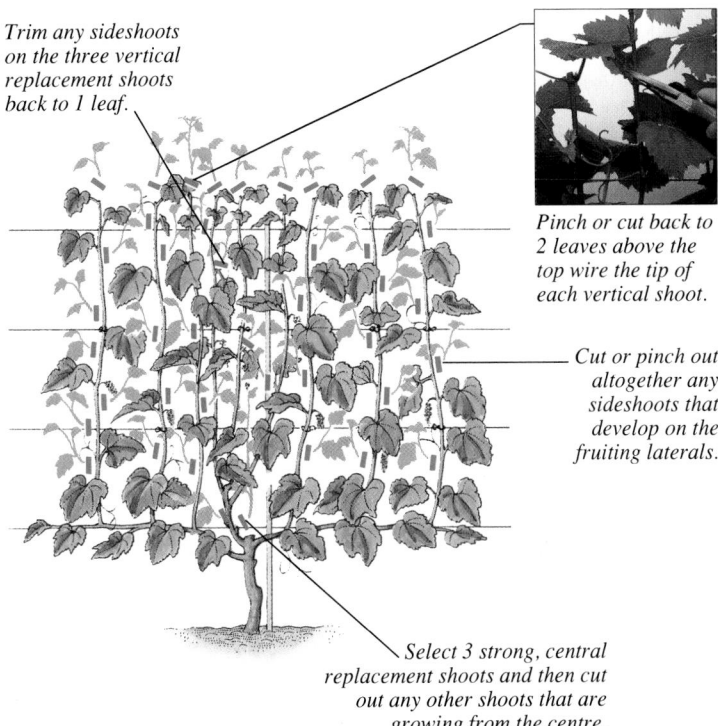

Trim any sideshoots on the three vertical replacement shoots back to 1 leaf.

Pinch or cut back to 2 leaves above the top wire the tip of each vertical shoot.

Cut or pinch out altogether any sideshoots that develop on the fruiting laterals.

Select 3 strong, central replacement shoots and then cut out any other shoots that are growing from the centre.

ESTABLISHED DOUBLE GUYOT, WINTER PRUNING

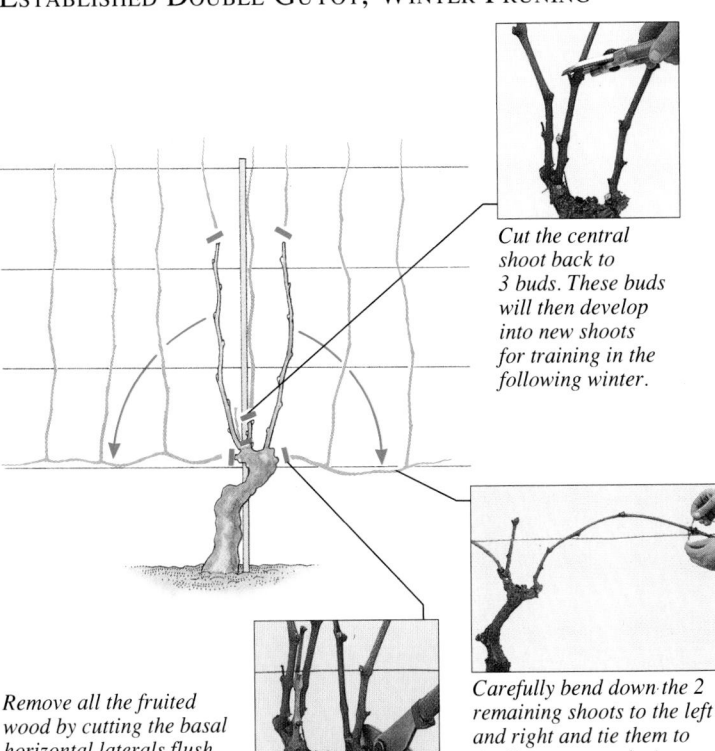

Cut the central shoot back to 3 buds. These buds will then develop into new shoots for training in the following winter.

Remove all the fruited wood by cutting the basal horizontal laterals flush with the main stem, leaving the 3 replacement shoots.

Carefully bend down the 2 remaining shoots to the left and right and tie them to the first or second wires. Tip prune to 8–12 buds.

ESTABLISHED DOUBLE GUYOT, SUMMER PRUNING

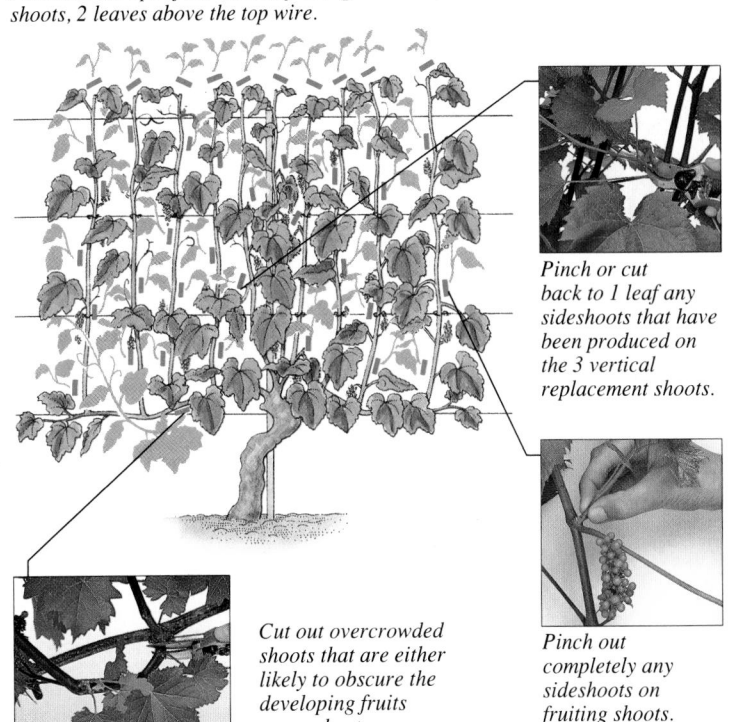

Pinch out the tips of the vertical fruiting shoots, 2 leaves above the top wire.

Pinch or cut back to 1 leaf any sideshoots that have been produced on the 3 vertical replacement shoots.

Cut out overcrowded shoots that are either likely to obscure the developing fruits or surplus to requirements.

Pinch out completely any sideshoots on fruiting shoots.

Guyot two rods on each plant are trained in this way, in the single Guyot system only one.

To train a vine by the double Guyot system, cut it back during the first winter to two strong buds above ground level. In the first summer, let one shoot develop and tie it to a vertical cane or wires. Remove other

REMOVING FOLIAGE

When the grapes are developing, cut off any leaves that shade the ripening fruit directly. Do not remove too many as this may cause scorch from excess sunlight.

HARVESTING WINE GRAPES

Bunches of wine grapes may be harvested simply by cutting the stalk with secateurs.

low shoots and cut any laterals to five leaves. In the second winter, cut back to just under the lowest wire, making sure that there are at least three strong buds remaining.

The next summer, let three strong shoots develop and tie them in vertically. Remove low shoots. In the third winter, tie down two of the shoots to the bottom wire, one on either side. Tip prune these to eight to twelve buds; they will produce fruiting shoots the following summer. Cut the third shoot back to three or four buds to produce replacement shoots, so that the whole process may be repeated. (For the single Guyot system allow two shoots to develop; tie down one and cut back the other.)

During the third summer, select three of the best central shoots growing from the rod and tie loosely to a central post or cane; cut out other, weaker, central shoots. Pinch back to one leaf any sideshoots that form on the three replacements. Train the shoots from the two arms vertically through the parallel wires. If growth is strong, allow a few bunches of grapes to develop on them. Pinch or cut out shoot tips at two leaves above the top wire; remove any sideshoots on the fruiting shoots.

Routine pruning For winter pruning, cut out all old, fruited wood leaving only three replacement shoots. Tie two of these down, one on either side, and tip prune as for the third winter. Prune the third shoot to three strong buds. Routine summer pruning and training of replacement shoots is as for the third summer. Cut out any overcrowded shoots obscuring the fruits. Remove any leaves shading the grapes six weeks before they are expected to ripen.

Harvesting
Cut the bunches from the vines with secateurs; the grapes should be fully ripe and completely dry.

Propagation
Propagate from hardwood cuttings prepared in winter when pruning, using wood from the hardened base of one-year-old shoots. To plant in the open, take sections about 20cm (8in) long, trimming above and below a bud, and insert the cuttings 15cm (6in) deep in sandy soil.

Under cover it is possible to use shorter one- or two-bud cuttings. Grow these singly in 9cm (3½in) pots or insert five cuttings in a 21cm (8in) pot. Place the pots in a cold frame. Pot on each young rooted plant the following summer.

HARDWOOD CUTTINGS

Trim the stems into lengths of about 20cm (8in), making an angled cut above a bud at the top and a flat cut below a bud at the base. Insert the cuttings to two-thirds their length into a trench in sandy soil.

TWO-BUD CUTTINGS

1 *While pruning at leaf fall, trim off a long section of ripened wood from the current season's growth. Then remove any leaves or tendrils remaining.*

2 *Divide the stem into cuttings with 2 buds, with an angled cut above the top bud and a horizontal cut between 2 nodes below the lower bud. Remove a 1cm (½in) length of rind above the lower cut.*

3 *Insert cuttings in a compost of 2 parts peat, 1 part loam, and 1 part sand, the lower bud just below the surface. Label, water, and place in a greenhouse.*

4 *When the cuttings have rooted, they should be potted on individually into 10cm (4in) pots to grow on.*

Kiwi fruits (*Actinidia deliciosa*)

Deciduous trailing climbers, kiwi fruits were originally known as Chinese gooseberries. The vines will grow up to 9m (28ft) in length. The berries have a hairy, brown skin and green pulp, with small, black seeds.

Warm, moist conditions are preferable during the growing season, the optimum temperature range being 5–25°C (41–78°F). Dormant plants will, however, tolerate several degrees of frost and require chilling for a period of at least 400 hours below 7°C (42°F) to encourage good flower production.

Site and planting
Kiwi fruits can only be grown in the open in sunny, sheltered areas, since plants in growth are sensitive to adverse weather conditions. The soil should be well-aerated, deep, and rich in organic matter, with a pH of 6–7. Incorporate a general-purpose fertilizer into the site at a rate of 50–110g (2–4oz) per plant.

Kiwi fruits are dioecious, with plants bearing either male or female flowers. One male is needed for every eight or nine female plants to ensure adequate fertilization.

Erect a post and wire support, with wires at 30cm (12in) intervals. Plant either rooted cuttings or grafted plants 4–5m (12–15ft) apart in rows 4–6m (12–18ft) apart, staking the vines until they are tall enough to reach the supporting wires.

Routine care
Mulch the plants heavily and apply a general-purpose fertilizer rich in phosphate and potassium. Water regularly, particularly in prolonged dry periods. Keep rows weed-free. Fruit thinning is rarely necessary.

RECOMMENDED KIWI FRUITS

'Abbot' **F**
'Allison' **F**
'Bruno' **F**
'Hayward' **F**
'Montgomery' **F**
'Saanichton' **F**
'Tomuri' **M**
'Vincent' **F**

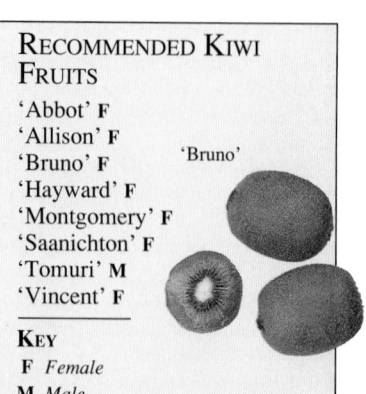

'Bruno'

KEY
F *Female*
M *Male*

HOW TO SUPPORT KIWI FRUIT

A common method is to train the plants as espaliers on horizontal wires with two main laterals per plant arising from the main stem, with fruiting laterals (see inset) at intervals of about 50cm (20in).

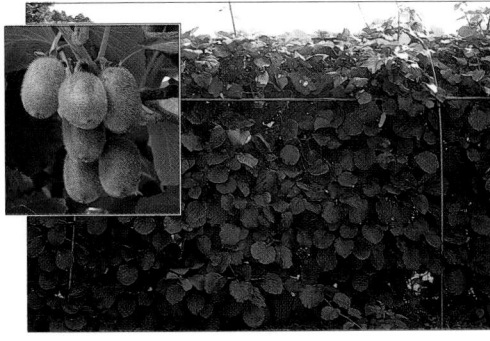

Plants grown in the open may be liable to root rot (see *Phytophthora* root rots, p.565). Under cover they may be infested with thrips (p.551), scale insects (p.552), and root-knot nematodes (p.564). Fruit rot may also occur as a result of infection of the petals. Infection spreads to the fruits, which then drop early. The spread of the disease is promoted by high humidity. Spraying flowers at petal fall with thiram or a similar fungicide gives reasonable control.

Growing under cover
This is rarely practicable due to the long, trailing growth of the plants; in exposed conditions, however, plants grown in the open may be protected from excessive wind and hail by a light plastic screening material.

Kiwi fruits may be grown in walk-in polytunnels if the appropriate environmental conditions can be provided. Soil preparation and cultivation details are the same as for plants grown in the open.

Pruning and training
Commercial crops are often grown on a "T" bar or overhead pergola structure. Another commonly used system is to train plants as espaliers on horizontal wires: each plant then has two main laterals arising from the main stem, and fruiting branches at intervals of 50cm (20in). For details, see "Apple: Espalier", p.382.

The fruits are produced on one-year-old wood only, so all fruited sideshoots should be cut back to two to four buds in the dormant season.

Harvesting and storing
Kiwi fruits start to bear fruit three to four years after planting. Harvest them as they soften. Snap or cut them from the branch, with the calyx attached; keep them cool. If wrapped in plastic film, fruits store for several months at 0°C (32°F).

Propagation
Both soft- and hardwood cuttings may be rooted successfully. Softwood cuttings should be taken in spring; trim to 10–15cm (4–6in) and insert in cutting compost (see p.374). Hardwood cuttings are taken in late summer; these should be 20–30cm (8–12in) long and inserted in sandy compost (see p.374).

Selected cultivars may also be grafted onto vigorous seedling stocks; the most common methods are T-budding and whip-and-tongue grafting (see p.373).

Passion fruits (*Passiflora* spp.)

Passion fruits are climbing plants, with individual stems reaching many metres in length. The globular fruits are either purple or yellow when ripe, and may be up to 7cm (3in) in diameter. The two species most commonly grown for their fruits are the yellow-fruited *P. edulis* f. *flavicarpa* and the purple *P. edulis*.

The optimum temperature range for the purple passion fruit is about 20–28°C (68–82°F). The yellow passion fruit prefers temperatures over 24°C (75°F) and does not tolerate frost; purple types may withstand frost for short periods. Moderate to high humidity is required for satisfactory growth.

Site and planting
Select a sunny site, protected by windbreaks, if necessary. Soils may vary in type but must be well drained, with a pH of about 6.

Cross-pollination by insects, normally bees, is usual, but hand-pollination may be necessary in wet weather; hand-pollination has been found to increase the yield of plants that are grown in the open.

Passion fruits require support, in the form of a wire trellis. Before planting, insert stout uprights, 3m (10ft) long, at intervals of 4m (12ft) each way. Link adjoining uprights in rows by tying with one or two strands of wire.

Take care to prepare the planting holes thoroughly, adding both organic material and a general-purpose fertilizer with medium to high levels of nitrogen. Establish the plants at about 3–4m (10–12ft) apart each way, or less if only a few plants are grown. The yellow form is usually planted 3m (10ft) apart each way.

Routine care
Apply a general-purpose fertilizer that has a medium to high nitrogen content at a rate of 0.5–1kg (1–2lb) per plant per year, preferably in equal dressings at intervals of three to four months. Apply an organic mulch in spring, and weed and water regularly during the dry season.

Pests affecting plants in the open as well as under cover include fruit flies (p.563), aphids (p.550), red spider mites (p.550), and various scale insects (p.552). Root-knot nematodes (p.564) and *Fusarium* wilt (p.558) may also be serious in some subtropical areas. "Woodiness" is caused by cucumber mosaic virus (see "Viruses", p.563), which is transmitted by aphids. As passion fruit vines are susceptible to nematodes and various wilt diseases, replace the plants every five or six years with healthy seedlings, rooted cuttings, or grafted plants.

Growing under cover
This is possible in temperate areas, but fruits may not be produced unless the optimum temperatures and conditions are provided; hand-pollination is generally necessary. Provide wire supports as for outdoor plants. Grow plants either in prepared beds or in large containers at least 35cm (14in) in diameter. Use a well-drained, fertile compost with

PASSION FRUITS

a high organic content and incorporate a general-purpose fertilizer into the compost before planting. Maintain a minimum temperature of 20°C (68°F) and humidity of 60–70 per cent. Apply a liquid feed or a general-purpose fertilizer at monthly intervals, and water regularly.

Pruning and training
Train two main growing stems along the wires to form a permanent framework. If these have not produced laterals by the time they are 60–90cm (2–3ft) long, pinch out their tips. Allow the lateral shoots, on which the fruits will be produced, to hang down as they develop each spring. Prune these laterals so that they are never less than 15cm (6in) from the soil. Once the plant is established, each winter cut back the current season's fruited shoots as these will not bear fruit again.

Harvesting and storing
Pick fruits when they begin to change colour, from green to either purple or yellow. The fruits should be ripe 8–12 weeks after fruit set depending on the cultivar. Fruits may be stored for up to 21 days if maintained at an even temperature of at least 6–7°C (43–5°F) and at a constant humidity level of 85–90 per cent.

Propagation
This is usually by sowing seed or raising cuttings; passion fruits may also be propagated by bud-grafting.

Seed may be extracted from the fully ripe fruits, and should be fermented for three to four days, then washed and dried. Sow the seed under cover in trays or 6–9cm (3–3½in) pots of seed compost, and keep at a temperature of at least 20°C (68°F). When the germinated seedlings are 20–35cm (8–14in) tall, transplant them to open ground, after hardening off, or grow them on under cover.

Cuttings 15–20cm (6–8in) long should be prepared and inserted into a tray or pot filled with cutting compost. Apply bottom heat and mist-spray to encourage rooting.

For details of bud-grafting, see p.372. Healthy bud-grafted plants should be transplanted into their permanent positions to grow on when approximately 15cm (6in) tall.

If nematodes or wilt diseases are a serious problem, the purple cultivars may be grafted onto resistant rootstocks. Vigorous seedlings of the yellow-fruited type are normally used for this purpose.

Soft fruits

ALL the usually cultivated soft fruits are bush or cane fruits, except for strawberries, which are herbaceous perennials. Bush fruits include blueberries, gooseberries, and black-, red-, and whitecurrants. Cane fruits include blackberries, hybrid berries, and raspberries. All produce succulent fruits that are eaten fresh, or preserved, bottled, or frozen. Most soft fruits grow best in cool climates. They prefer a well-drained, moisture-retentive, and fertile soil. A sunny site is best and gives fine-quality fruit, but in most cases a little shade is tolerated. Almost all cultivars are self-fertile. Pruning methods depend on whether fruit is produced on one-year-old wood, on older wood and spurs, or on both.

Blackberries

Yellow raspberries

Blueberries

Strawberries

Boysenberries

Redcurrants

Raspberries

Strawberries (*Fragaria* x *ananassa*)

Strawberries are low-growing, herbaceous plants that may be grown in most gardens, either in the open ground or in containers. There are three distinct types of strawberry plant: summer-fruiting, perpetual-fruiting, and alpine.

Summer-fruiting strawberries produce nearly all their fruit in an intensive two- to three-week period in mid-summer. Some cultivars also give a smaller, autumn crop.

Perpetual-fruiting (ever-bearing) strawberries crop briefly in summer, cease for about two months, and then produce a succession of fruits in autumn. They grow best in regions with mild, frost-free autumn weather.

Alpine strawberries, which are raised from seed, produce small, delicately flavoured fruits.

Variations in daylength (see THE VEGETABLE GARDEN, p.307) affect the formation of flowers in some cultivars. It is therefore important to choose those appropriate for the latitude of the particular garden: nearer the tropics, for example, the cooler temperatures that are essential for growth and cropping may be found only at high altitudes.

Site and planting

Strawberries are best grown where new plantings may be made regularly on fresh ground, since cropping, fruit size, and plant health deteriorate if the same ground and plants are used after the third year. If you have room, grow one-, two-, and three-year-old plants in succession, discarding the oldest plants and planting new runners in fresh ground each year.

Site
Sunny, warm sites give the best-flavoured fruit. Sandy soils produce the earliest crops, loams and well-drained clays the heaviest and most finely flavoured; chalky soils do not produce good results. Slightly acid conditions with a pH of 6–6.5 are ideal. Good drainage is vital to avoid soil-borne diseases. Planting strawberries after potatoes can be risky, since the ground may be infected with *Verticillium* wilt (p.557).

To prolong the fruiting season, plantings may be split – choose a warm, sheltered position for the earliest crops, sunny, open ground for the main crop, and a less sunny site for late-ripening fruits.

Pollination
Most cultivars are self-fertile. The cultivar 'Pandora', however, fruits well only if several plants of a different cultivar that flowers at the same time are planted nearby.

Planting
The planting time for strawberries depends on geographical location. Seek expert advice if in doubt. In cool-temperate regions, late summer to early autumn planting is best and ensures the heaviest crops the following summer. For later plantings, remove flowers in spring to allow plants to become well established before they begin to bear fruit.

Use plants of certified stock, if possible, and plant in fresh ground, where strawberries have not been grown for at least three years. Replace plants every two or three years and grub out and burn any old plants nearby to prevent the spread of virus diseases. Clear all weeds and apply generous amounts of well-rotted farmyard manure, unless plenty remains in the soil from the preceding crop. On hungrier sandy or chalky soils, rake in a dressing of a balanced fertilizer as well, at a rate of

BUYING HEALTHY STRAWBERRY PLANTS

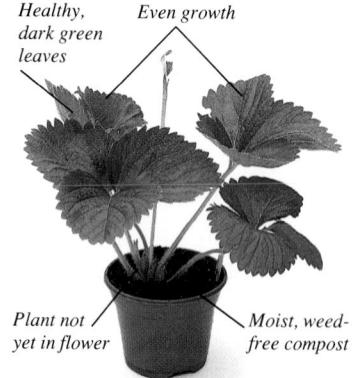

Healthy, dark green leaves

Even growth

Plant not yet in flower

Moist, weed-free compost

105g/sq m (3oz/sq yd), just before planting. Space strawberries at 45cm (18in) intervals in slightly raised rows, 75cm (2¹/₂ft) apart, so that rainwater runs off. Plant with the base of the central crown at soil level, firm in the plants, and water well. On wet sites, plant in raised beds (see STRUCTURES AND SURFACES, "Raised beds", p.507).

Strawberries may also be planted through sheets of black plastic, which smother weeds, retain soil moisture, and encourage early cropping by

PLANTING STRAWBERRIES UNDER A PLASTIC MULCH

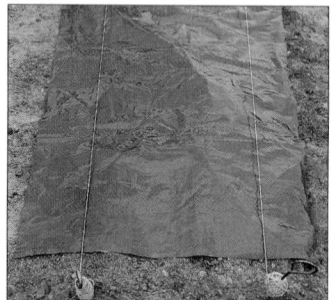

1 In moist soil, mark out a 90cm (3ft) wide bed with string. Mound the soil in the centre, and cover the bed with a length of black plastic 1.2m (4ft) wide.

2 Dig a narrow trench on either side of the bed and, using a spade, anchor the edges of the plastic sheet firmly in the trenches to stop it blowing away.

3 Make cross-shaped cuts in the plastic (see inset) at 45cm (18in) intervals. Plant the strawberries through the slits and firm the soil around their crowns.

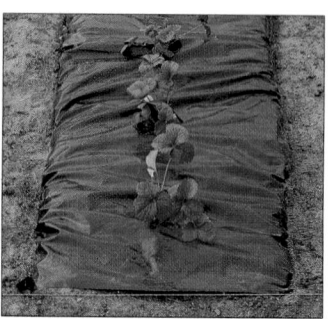

4 Tuck in the cut plastic around the crowns of the plants. The finished row of strawberries should be slightly raised so that rain drains away from the plants.

warming the soil. Anchor the plastic firmly, then make planting slits at the required intervals.

Routine care

Strawberries need regular watering. Ripening fruits should be netted against pests, and kept off the soil to keep them clean. Remove surplus runners, weed, and regularly check for pests and diseases. Flowers may need protection from frost in spring: double-thickness sheets of newspaper are very effective.

Protecting the fruits

Before the fruit trusses develop fully, lay clean, dry straw or proprietary mats beneath them to prevent soil splash on the fruits; this is unnecessary for plants grown through plastic. Protect the fruits from birds before they redden, using posts to support fruit nets (see p.367).

HOW TO KEEP STRAWBERRIES CLEAN

When the strawberries are in flower or the fruits are forming, put a thick layer of straw underneath and between the plants to prevent the ripening fruits from touching the soil.

ALTERNATIVE METHOD

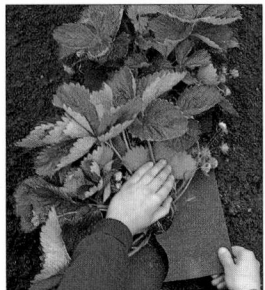

Alternatively, strawberry mats may be laid carefully around the crowns to protect the developing fruits.

REMOVING RUNNERS

Remove excess runners as they develop. Pinch them out close to the parent plant, taking care not to damage any other foliage.

Controlling runners

Pinch out runners as they appear, unless they are needed to help form matted rows (see "Growing under cover", below).

Watering and weeding

Water strawberries when newly planted, then regularly during the growing season, especially after flowering to promote the development of quality fruits. Water plants under plastic only in very dry weather, watering through the planting slits. Keep beds free of weeds.

Pests and diseases

Strawberries may be eaten by birds (p.561), grey squirrels (p.563), and slugs (p.548), and are vulnerable to aphids (p.550), viruses (see p.563), grey mould/*Botrytis* (p.562), fungal leaf spots (p.552), and red spider mites (p.550). Dig up and burn diseased or stunted plants. Red core and strawberry beetles are not widespread, but are serious where they occur. Red core is a soil-borne disease, more prevalent in heavy soils, causing the foliage to collapse and die. The only remedy is to change the site. Strawberry beetles take seeds from the outside of the fruits, encouraging rotting. They feed on weed seeds, so weed beds well; control them with methiocarb slug pellets.

Growing under cover

Strawberries grown in a heated greenhouse fruit up to one month earlier than those grown outdoors, but have less flavour. Establish runners in 6cm (3in) pots of seed compost as early as possible (see p.410). Before the roots fill the pots, transplant into 15cm (6in) pots of potting compost; keep the plants outside until mid-winter, protected from heavy rain, then place them in the

PICKING FRUITS

Pick dessert strawberries by the stalk to avoid bruising the fruit. Strawberries for jam may be picked without the stalk.

greenhouse in a position of maximum light. When new leaves form, maintain minimum temperatures of 7°C (45°F) at night and 10°C (50°F) during the day.

Adjust the ventilation to maintain these temperatures. Water and damp down frequently to keep a moist atmosphere and reduce the risk of red spider mite infestation. Increase the temperature by about 3°C (5°F) when flower trusses start to develop; during flowering, raise the temperature again by the same amount and stop damping down. Pollinate flowers by hand with a soft brush; do this around midday on a bright day. Remove late-forming flowers to improve the size of the ripening fruits. To enhance their flavour, lower the temperature as they begin to ripen.

For plants grown in the open, cloches placed over plants in late winter advance ripening by about three weeks, and polytunnels by one to two weeks (see p.490). Both should be well ventilated on warm days. Under cloches or plastic tunnels, strawberries may be grown in "matted rows", in which the planting distance is halved to give maximum yield. Runners may be retained to increase the density of the planting. Revert to the usual spacing after the first year by removing every other plant, otherwise fruit quality deteriorates and routine care becomes difficult.

Harvesting and storing

Harvest dessert strawberries when fully ripe, complete with stalks, and use them at once for the best flavour. Pick strawberries for jam when ripe but still firm. Pick the fruit every other day and remove and burn diseased or damaged fruit. Strawberries

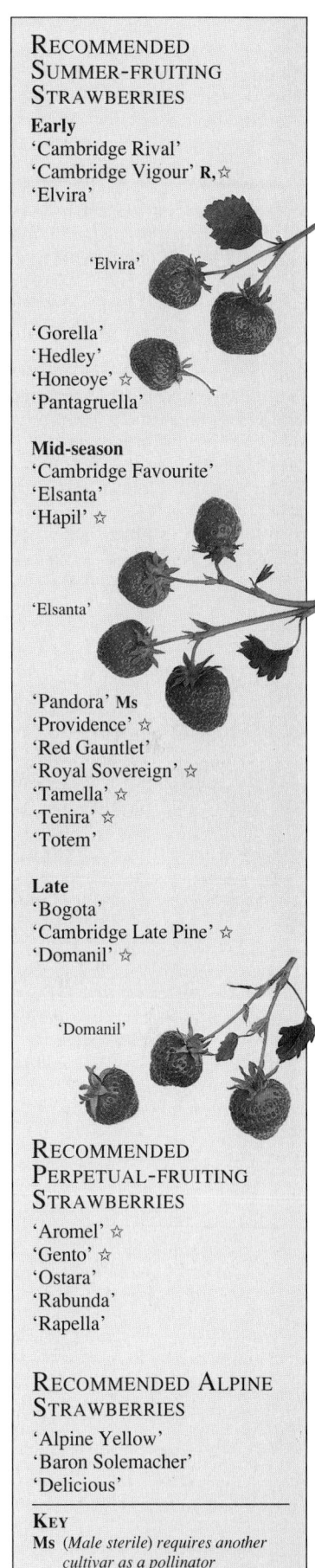

RECOMMENDED SUMMER-FRUITING STRAWBERRIES

Early
'Cambridge Rival'
'Cambridge Vigour' **R,**☆
'Elvira'

'Elvira'

'Gorella'
'Hedley'
'Honeoye' ☆
'Pantagruella'

Mid-season
'Cambridge Favourite'
'Elsanta'
'Hapil' ☆

'Elsanta'

'Pandora' **Ms**
'Providence' ☆
'Red Gauntlet'
'Royal Sovereign' ☆
'Tamella' ☆
'Tenira' ☆
'Totem'

Late
'Bogota'
'Cambridge Late Pine' ☆
'Domanil' ☆

'Domanil'

RECOMMENDED PERPETUAL-FRUITING STRAWBERRIES

'Aromel' ☆
'Gento' ☆
'Ostara'
'Rabunda'
'Rapella'

RECOMMENDED ALPINE STRAWBERRIES

'Alpine Yellow'
'Baron Solemacher'
'Delicious'

KEY
Ms *(Male sterile) requires another cultivar as a pollinator*
R *Ripens mid-season when two years and older*
☆ *Excellent flavour*

may also be bottled or preserved. If frozen, the fruits, except those of the cultivar 'Totem', lose their firmness.

After harvesting, clear surplus runners, weeds, and straw from the site. Cut off the old foliage from plants, taking care not to damage the young leaves. Apply a balanced fertilizer and water it in if the soil is dry. Where plants are growing through a plastic mulch, make a fresh planting unless they are thriving.

Propagation

Each year plant one or two certified virus-free young plants well away from established fruiting beds. Control aphids and remove all flowers. The plants will produce a healthy supply of runners for up to two years; then start afresh with new, certified stock. Some perpetual-fruiting cultivars produce few runners.

CLEARING THE FOLIAGE AFTER HARVESTING

As soon as the crop has been picked, remove the old foliage to leave 10cm (4in) of stem above the young leaves and crown. Clear away and burn straw, foliage, and other debris from around the plants to minimize the risk of pests and diseases.

HOW TO PROPAGATE BY RUNNERS

1 *Plant certified virus-free plants especially to produce runners. As they form, spread them out evenly around the parent plant.*

2 *Once a runner has rooted and is making vigorous new growth, lift it carefully, using a hand fork, without damaging the roots.*

3 *Sever the rooted runner from the parent plant. Transplant it to well-prepared soil or pot it up singly for planting out later.*

Alpine strawberries

Alpine strawberries (*Fragaria vesca* 'Semperflorens') have small, fragrant, sweetly flavoured fruits and make a neat and attractive edging for flower borders or

ALPINE STRAWBERRY

vegetable plots. They tolerate cooler conditions than most other strawberries and prefer partial shade in the summer in warm areas. Their fruiting season lasts from midsummer through to late autumn.

Plants deteriorate after about two years, so should be propagated regularly from either runners or seed.

HOW TO PROPAGATE FROM SEED

To separate seed from the fruits, leave the strawberries to dry and squash them between finger and thumb. Sow the seed in pots of standard seed compost and maintain them at 18–24°C (64–75°F). Prick out seedlings when they have two true leaves. Plant out young strawberries in early summer.

1 *Use dried fruits, squashing them gently between finger and thumb so that the seeds fall off. Hold the fruits over a clean container to collect the seeds.*

2 *Fill a 6cm (3in) pot with seed compost. Sprinkle the seeds thinly on the surface, then cover them with a thin layer of compost and a layer of fine grit.*

Blackberries and hybrid berries (*Rubus fruticosus* and *Rubus* hybrids)

The fruits of cultivated blackberries and hybrid berries such as loganberries and boysenberries are borne on canes in late summer. The hybrids have arisen from crosses between different *Rubus* species or cultivars.

Site
Before planting, the ground should be well prepared and fertilized, as for raspberries (see p.412). Buy blackberries and hybrid berries from specialist nurseries and, if possible, choose plants that are included in a certification scheme to ensure healthy, virus-free stock. Thornless cultivars are usually less vigorous than prickly ones. Blackberries and

hybrid berries are all self-fertile and consequently may be grown singly.

Blackberries and hybrid berries need a sunny or partially shaded position. Do not plant them in exposed sites.

Provide support for the canes: walls and fences, with horizontal wires set up at 30cm (12in) intervals, are ideal.

A post 3m (10ft) long sunk 60cm (2ft) into the ground may also be used as a basic support, but for vigorous cultivars erect a post-and-wire fence. Position the posts at 4–5m (12–15ft) intervals with four horizontal wires running between them, the lowest at 90cm (3ft) from the ground, the highest at 2m (6ft). On light, sandy soils,

you should provide extra support for the end posts by bracing them with diagonal wooden props. This will help to prevent the wires from sagging under the weight of the canes.

Planting
Plant during winter; if the weather is severe, delay until late winter or early spring. Some hybrids may be killed in very cold areas so seek local advice. Plant shallowly, spreading out the roots well and firming the soil at the base of the plants. Space more vigorous cultivars 4–5m (12–15ft) apart, less vigorous ones 2.5–3m (8–10ft) apart. After planting, shorten the canes to 22cm (9in).

BUYING HEALTHY BLACKBERRY PLANTS

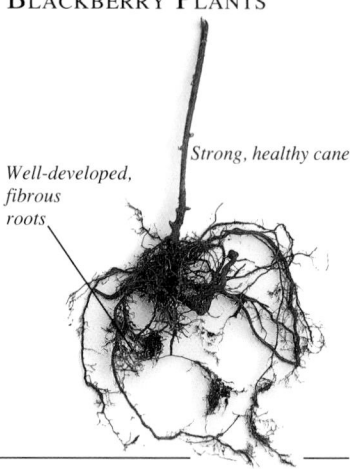

Strong, healthy cane

Well-developed, fibrous roots

METHODS OF TRAINING

ALTERNATE BAY
*Train new canes to one side of the plant,
while the older ones fruit on the other side.*

ROPE
*Train fruiting canes in groups along wires,
leaving new canes to grow centrally.*

FAN
*Fan-train fruiting canes individually to the left
and right, and train new canes centrally.*

WEAVING
*Weave fruiting canes through the lower wires.
Train new canes centrally and along the top wire.*

RECOMMENDED BLACKBERRIES

Early
'Bedford Giant' **Rg**
'Himalaya Giant' **Rg**
'Merton Early'
'Merton Thornless'

Late
'Ashton Cross'
'John Innes'
'Oregon Thornless'
'Smoothstem'
'Thornfree'

'Bedford Giant'

RECOMMENDED HYBRID BERRIES

Boysenberry
Kings Acre Berry
Loganberry
Sunberry **Rg**
Tayberry
Tummelberry
Veitchberry

Tayberry

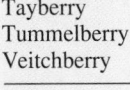

KEY
Rg *Rampant growth*

PRUNING ESTABLISHED BLACKBERRIES
AFTER FRUITING

*Cut down all the fruited
canes to ground level near
the base of the stem.*

*Tie the new canes
securely to the
horizontal wires
according to the
training system used.*

TIP PRUNING FROST-DAMAGED STEMS

*Inspect the canes for
signs of frost damage
in early spring and, if
necessary, cut back the
tips of affected canes to
healthy wood.*

Routine care
Maintenance requirements are as for raspberries (see p.412).

Pests and diseases
Problems may be caused by raspberry beetles (p.562), birds (p.561), grey mould/*Botrytis* (p.562), and viruses (p.563), although resistance varies from one hybrid to another.

Pruning and training
The plants fruit on one-year-old wood, so training needs to separate fruiting canes from newly developing ones. For small gardens, the rope and fan methods (see above) are best. The alternate bay and weaving systems use much more space, but weaving is the best method for vigorous plants.

After cropping, cut out the fruiting canes at ground level. Retain and tie in those canes that have grown during the current season but remove any that are weak or damaged. In early spring, cut back the tip of each cane if it shows any signs of dieback resulting from frost.

Harvesting and storing
Pick the fruits regularly; unlike raspberries, the central plug stays within the picked fruit. For exhibiting, pick fruits complete with their stalks. Blackberries may be stored by bottling, preserving, or freezing.

Propagation
To provide a few new plants, use tip layering (see p.411). In summer,

TIP LAYERING

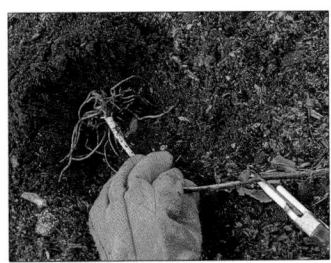

1 *Bend over the tip of a healthy, vigorous shoot and place it in a hole 10cm (4in) deep. Fill the hole with soil and firm down well.*

2 *Once the tip has rooted in late autumn or winter, cut the old stem close to the young, rooted plant to sever it from the parent. Pot it up, if required, or transplant in spring.*

bend a shoot to ground level and place the tip in a hole dug in the soil. Cover it with earth and firm. Once the tip has rooted in late autumn or winter, sever it from the parent plant. Transfer the young plant to its final growing position in spring.

To produce a larger number of young plants, remove shoots, 30cm (12in) long, of the current season's growth in late summer; take leaf-bud cuttings from them, with a leaf and a piece of stem. Place several cuttings in one 14cm (5¹/₂in) pot in a moist atmosphere or cold frame; they should root in six to eight weeks. Harden them off and plant them out in late autumn or, where winters are harsh, in early spring. Transplant the young canes to their final positions a year later.

HOW TO PROPAGATE BY LEAF-BUD CUTTINGS

1 *Select a strong, healthy shoot from the current season's growth, taking at least 30cm (12in) of stem with plenty of well-developed leaf buds.*

2 *Make a cut 1cm (¹/₂in) above a bud: slice downwards to remove the bud and a portion of stem about 2.5cm (1in) long, with a leaf attached.*

3 *Place 3 cuttings in a 14cm (5¹/₂in) pot, with the stem portions at an angle and growth buds just above the soil. Water, label, and place in a cold frame.*

Raspberries (*Rubus idaeus*)

A number of raspberry cultivars have been produced by crossing the European wild red raspberry (*Rubus idaeus*) with the American raspberry (*R. idaeus* var. *strigosus*) and the North American black raspberry (*R. occidentalis*).

Raspberries are a cool-season crop, growing best where there is plenty of moisture. Fruits vary in colour from dark red through to yellow. There are two main types of raspberry: summer-fruiting, which has a short season of heavy cropping in high summer, and autumn-fruiting, which has a protracted cropping period beginning in late summer and continuing until the start of winter frosts.

Site and planting

The site needs thorough preparation before planting, since raspberries do not crop well on poor soils, particularly if in competition with weeds. Raspberries are self-fertile.

Site
Raspberries should be planted in a sheltered, sunny position. They tolerate partial shade, and in hotter regions some shade may be a positive advantage.

The soil should be rich in humus and moisture-retentive but also well drained, as raspberries do not tolerate poor drainage. Sandy, chalky, and poor, stony soils need an annual, heavy dressing with humus-rich material, and regular watering. In addition, if raspberries are grown on lime-rich soil they may suffer from chlorosis (see "Manganese/iron deficiency", p.555).

Preparation
Clear all perennial weeds before planting as they are extremely difficult to deal with later. Prepare an area at least 90cm (3ft) wide and dig in plenty of well-rotted manure.

Construct permanent supports. For a post-and-wire support, set a single row of stout posts 3m (10ft) apart. Run three lengths of wire or nylon string between the posts setting them at heights of 75cm (30in), 1.1m (3¹/₂ft), and 1.5m (5ft). Keep the wires or strings taut and tie in the canes with twine by "continuous lacing" (weaving between the canes and wires) to prevent the canes from being blown along the row.

The parallel wires method requires two rows of posts, with posts at the above spacing and rows 75cm (30in) apart. Run two pairs of parallel wires along the posts, one pair at 75cm (30in), the other at 1.5m (5ft), then criss-cross between them with wire or strong string. The canes are supported by the cross-wires and do not need to be tied in.

For the Scandinavian system, erect two rows of posts, as above, but with 90cm (3ft) between rows, then run a single wire along each row at a height of 90cm (3ft). Twist fruiting canes along the wires, allowing new canes to grow in the open, central space.

Obtain certified virus-free canes; otherwise use suckers taken from established plants of known good health and cropping performance.

Planting
Plant dormant canes in well-manured ground at 38–45cm (15–18in) intervals, in rows 2m (6ft) apart. Plant in autumn or early winter, as this

SUPPORTING AND TRAINING METHODS

The post-and-wire method is useful if space is limited. The parallel wires method gives the canes more room, but is not suitable in windy conditions. The Scandinavian system bends young canes around each other and the wire; the canes are not tied in or tip pruned. This method needs more space than the others.

SCANDINAVIAN SYSTEM

POST AND WIRES

PARALLEL WIRES

HOW TO PLANT RASPBERRIES

1 *Prepare a trench 5–8cm (2–3in) deep in well-manured ground. Plant the canes 38–45cm (15–18in) apart. Spread out the roots carefully and backfill the trench with soil.*

2 *Firm the soil around the bases of the canes, ensuring that they remain vertical. Prune canes back to a bud, about 25cm (10in) from the ground. Rake over the soil lightly.*

encourages the canes to establish quickly. Spread out the roots evenly at a depth of 5–8cm (2–3in), and gently firm them in. Prune the canes to 25cm (10in) from the ground.

Routine care

In spring, mulch with well-rotted manure. Apply this on either side of the row, taking care not to bury the canes. If manure is unavailable, apply regular dressings of a balanced fertilizer (see "Care of soft fruits", p.366) and mulch with compost or leaf mould to conserve moisture.

Flowers usually appear too late to be damaged by frost so do not need protection. Remove weeds and water the plants regularly and thoroughly. Remove any suckers more than 22cm (9in) from the main row.

Pests and diseases
Raspberry beetles (p.562) and birds (p.561) are the main pests. Grey mould/*Botrytis* (p.562), spur blight/cane blight (p.557), and viruses (p.563) may also be a problem.

Pruning and training

As soon as new canes are established, by about mid-summer, cut out the canes that were shortened at planting time.

Summer-fruiting raspberries should have all fruited canes removed at ground level after cropping. Tie in the new canes (see *Supporting and Training Methods*, p.412), spacing them evenly 8–10cm (3–4in) apart. Cut out damaged and weak canes so that those remaining

receive as much light and air as possible. Loop over and tie in tall canes to prevent wind damage.

Autumn-fruiting raspberries (see p.414) should have all canes cut to ground level in late winter. The new canes grow, then fruit in the autumn.

The following spring, trim canes to 15cm (6in) above the top-most wire, cutting back any tips with frost damage. Remove dead, diseased, or crowded canes or any growing more than 22cm (9in) from the row.

Harvesting and storing

Pick the fruit when it is firm to ripe for preserves and freezing, and when it is fully ripe for eating fresh, harvesting every other day, if possible.

HOW TO REMOVE UNWANTED SUCKERS

If suckers become overcrowded or are growing too far outside the row, as here, lift them and sever from the parent plant.

PRUNING AT THE END OF THE FIRST SEASON

1 *By about mid-summer, cut down to ground level the old canes that were shortened when planting was carried out.*

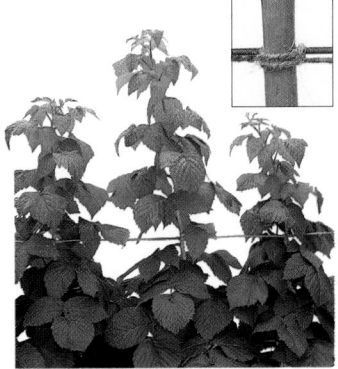

2 *Tie the current season's strongest canes to the support wires (see inset) when they reach about 90cm (3ft). Remove weak shoots and those growing more than 22cm (9in) from the row.*

ESTABLISHED RASPBERRIES, PRUNING AFTER FRUITING

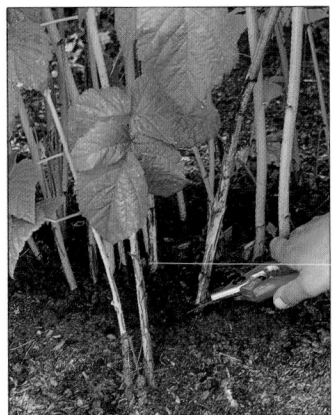

1 *When all the fruit has been picked, cut back all the fruited canes to ground level.*

2 *Tie the current season's strongest canes to the support wires when about 90cm (3ft) tall, spacing them 10cm (4in) apart: here the continuous lacing method is used.*

3 *At the end of the growing season, loop any tall canes over the top wire and tie them in.*

SPRING PRUNING

Before the growing season begins, tip prune all the canes to a healthy bud. Wherever possible, the cut should be made about 15cm (6in) above the top supporting wire.

Detach the fruit from the central plug and the stalk; fruits for exhibiting should be picked complete with stalk, however. Remove and burn diseased or damaged fruits promptly to prevent the spread of infection to healthy fruits.

Propagation

In late autumn, select strong suckers that are growing away from the main fruiting row, and lift and replant them while they are dormant. Ensure that they are from plants that are known to be healthy and free-cropping; where doubt exists, use certified virus-free canes from specialist nurseries instead.

PROPAGATING BY SUCKERS

Lift suckers carefully in autumn and sever them from the parent plant. Remove any remaining foliage. Ensure that the suckers are healthy and replant where new stock is required. Water in thoroughly.

Autumn-fruiting raspberries

These should be sited in a sunny, sheltered position where the plants will quickly become established and the fruits should ripen in as short a time as possible. The fruits are borne freely on the upper part of the current season's canes. Planting and cultivation requirements are as for summer-fruiting raspberries.

Pruning of autumn-fruiting raspberries is carried out in late winter before growth starts; the fruited canes are all cut down to the ground to stimulate new canes, which will fruit in the autumn.

LATE WINTER PRUNING
Before new growth starts, cut down all the canes to ground level. Fruit will be produced in autumn on the new season's canes.

Blackcurrants (*Ribes nigrum*)

Blackcurrants thrive only in cool-temperate regions. The bushes flower early, so are prone to frost damage on exposed sites. They fruit in mid-summer. In parts of the USA their cultivation is prohibited because they are hosts for a rust disease on white pine. Jostaberries, a hybrid between blackcurrants and gooseberries, are cultivated in the same way.

Site and planting

The ground should be well prepared before planting to provide the best conditions for the continual production of new fruiting shoots. Remove all weeds from the site before planting and dig in plenty of manure.

Site

Choose a sunny site, sheltered from cold winds; some shade is tolerated. Protect blackcurrants from spring frosts if necessary (see FROST AND WIND PROTECTION, pp.520–21). Blackcurrants grow in a range of soils but deep, moisture-retentive soil is most suitable; avoid wet, poorly drained ground. A pH of 6.5–7 is preferable; lime very acid soils (see p.531). Blackcurrants are self-fertile.

Planting

Plant disease-free bushes from certified stock. Bushes sold under certification schemes are normally two years old, but one-year-old plants from disease-free stock are also ideal. Planting in late autumn is preferable but blackcurrants may be planted throughout the winter. Handle the plants carefully to avoid damaging the basal buds. Space

the bushes 1.2–1.5m (4–5ft) apart, with the same distance between the rows. After planting, cut down all the shoots to one bud to encourage strong, new growth.

Routine care

In spring, apply a mulch of well-rotted manure as well as nitrogen and potassium fertilizers at a rate of 35g/sq m (1oz/sq yd). If manure is not available, increase the amount of fertilizer (see "Care of soft fruits", p.366) and mulch around the base of bushes with compost or leaf mould to conserve soil moisture.

Water in dry weather, but not as the fruits ripen, since this may cause the skins to split. Net bushes to protect ripening fruits from birds.

Pests and diseases

Aphids (p.550), gall mites (p.556), big bud mites (p.559), winter moth caterpillars (p.549), and birds (p.561) may affect blackcurrants. Grey

mould/*Botrytis* (p.562), powdery mildew (p.562), and fungal leaf spots (p.552) may also be troublesome.

Pruning and training

Regular pruning is essential to maintain high yields. Most of the fruits are borne on shoots produced the previous season. Pruning, together with adequate feeding, encourages strong, new shoots to develop.

Cut all stems to one bud above ground level after planting. The following year, remove any weak or down-pointing shoots. Thereafter, prune established bushes before late winter by cutting to the base a quarter to one third of two-year-old wood, and any older, weak wood. No tip pruning is required. New shoots are a pale tea colour, two-year-old wood is grey, and older wood black.

If a bush needs rejuvenating cut out a greater proportion of the old wood, retaining only those branches from which strong, young shoots have

NEW AND FRUITED SHOOTS

Pale, new shoot

Dark, fruited wood

developed. If few shoots develop yet the bush is healthy, cut down the whole plant to just above ground level in winter. Most bushes then rejuvenate well if fed and mulched, but one year's crop is sacrificed. The new shoots that develop may need thinning, retaining the strongest. After ten years or so it is better to replace a bush than to try to rejuvenate it.

BLACKCURRANT BUSH
YEAR 1, WINTER PRUNING

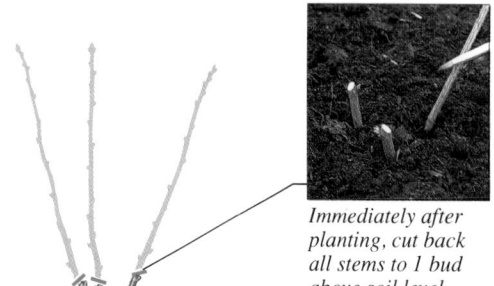

Immediately after planting, cut back all stems to 1 bud above soil level.

YEAR 2, WINTER PRUNING

The bush should develop 7 or 8 strong, new shoots. Cut back any weak or low-growing shoots to about 2.5cm (1in) above soil level, to encourage new growth from the base.

ESTABLISHED BUSH, PRUNING AFTER FRUITING

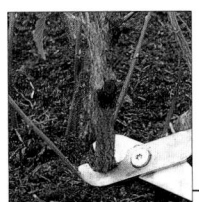

Cut out the old wood and a quarter to one third of two-year-old stems to stimulate new growth.

Remove any weak, damaged, or low-growing shoots, cutting close to the main stem.

Harvesting and storing

Blackcurrants are borne on "strigs" in bunches. Harvest the fruits when dry and ripe but still firm. Remove the whole bunch, not the individual fruits, which may otherwise be damaged. Early-ripening cultivars soon shed their fruits but late-ripening cultivars retain their fruits much longer. Fruits may be either eaten fresh or stored by bottling, preserving, or freezing.

Propagation

Blackcurrants are propagated from hardwood cuttings (see p.374) taken from healthy bushes in autumn. Retain all buds on the cuttings to encourage basal shoots to grow.

HARDWOOD CUTTINGS

Insert 20–25cm (8–10in) cuttings in a trench, leaving two buds exposed.

Red- and whitecurrants *(Ribes sativum)*

Red- and whitecurrants require a cool climate. Whitecurrants are simply a colour variant of redcurrants; both fruit in mid-summer and need the same growing conditions.

Site and planting

Red- and whitecurrants need a sunny site but tolerate some shade; in hot climates some shade may be necessary. Protect plants from winds to prevent stems breaking, and in high temperatures to prevent scorching.

Prepare the soil well before planting, as for blackcurrants (see p.414). Heavier, moisture-retentive, but well-drained soils are preferable. Potassium deficiency may occur on very sandy soil. All cultivars are self-fertile.

When buying young bushes, ensure that the plants are from healthy stock that crops well. There is no certification scheme, however. Plant in autumn or winter: space bushes 1.2–1.5m (4–5ft) apart, cordons at 30cm (12in), and fans at 1.6m (6ft).

Routine care

For details of maintenance, see blackcurrants (p.414). Maintain high potash levels by applying potassium sulphate if necessary (muriate of potash may scorch the foliage).

Pests and diseases

Net the plants throughout the winter to prevent birds from damaging the buds. If the buds are damaged, delay winter pruning until just before bud-burst and then prune to healthy buds. Aphids (p.550), sawfly larvae (p.549), grey mould/*Botrytis* (p.562), and coral spot (p.569) may affect plants.

Pruning and training

Red- and whitecurrants are normally grown as open-centre bushes but may be trained on supporting wires as cordons, double cordons, or fans. Fruits develop on spurs produced by pruning back the sideshoots.

Bush

A one-year-old bush should have two or three strong, young shoots; shorten these by half in late winter. Remove any that are less than 10cm (4in) from the ground to produce a short leg.

The following winter, shorten new growth by half to form the main branches, pruning to an outward-pointing bud. Prune sideshoots

REDCURRANT BUSH
YEAR 1, WINTER PRUNING

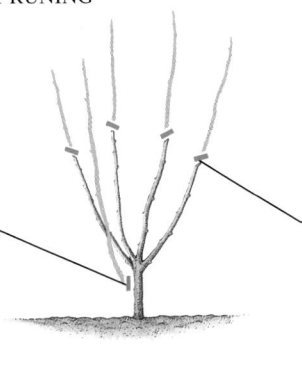

Remove any side-shoots growing within 10cm (4in) of soil level by cutting flush with the stem. This will form a short leg at the base.

Prune each stem to an outward-facing bud (or to an upright shoot) about half-way along its length.

YEAR 2, WINTER PRUNING

To form the permanent branches, shorten leaders and sideshoots by half of the new growth, cutting to outward-facing buds.

Cut back to 1 bud any sideshoots crowding the centre or growing downwards.

ESTABLISHED BUSH, WINTER PRUNING

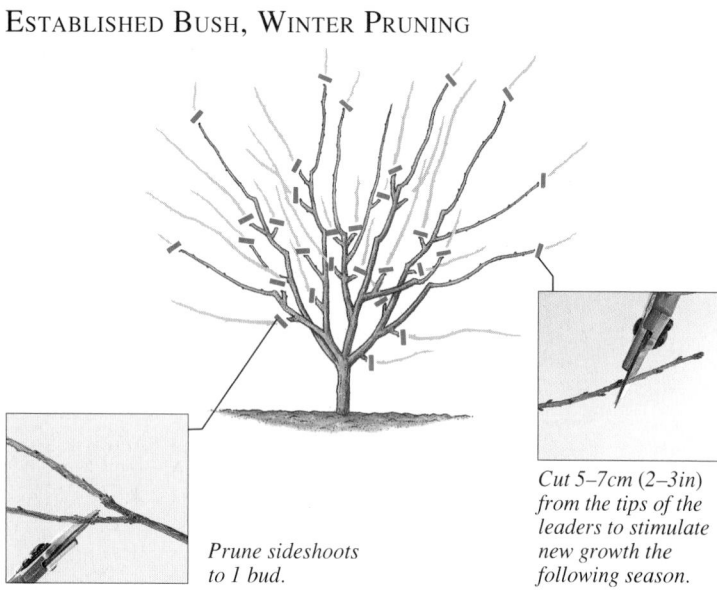

Prune sideshoots to 1 bud.

Cut 5–7cm (2–3in) from the tips of the leaders to stimulate new growth the following season.

growing in- or downwards to one bud. Prune established bushes by cutting back sideshoots to one bud and tip pruning main branches.

Cordon

Single cordons are usually trained vertically. Set up wires at 60cm (24in) and 1.2m (4ft) from the ground. Select a main shoot on a one-year-old plant and train it against a cane; prune back the shoot by half, then cut back all other shoots to one bud.

In summer, prune sideshoots to five leaves of new growth. Shorten these sideshoots to one or two buds in winter, and prune the leader by a quarter of the new growth. When the leader reaches the top of its support, trim it to one bud. A double cordon is developed by training two shoots at about 30° to the ground as for apples (see "Forming a double cordon", p.381); they are subsequently trained vertically when 30cm (12in) apart. Each branch is then pruned as for a single cordon.

Fan

Fan-trained red- and whitecurrants are established as for a peach fan (see p.393). Each branch should then be pruned as a cordon.

Harvesting and storing

Harvest red- and whitecurrants as for blackcurrants. The plants tend to retain their ripe fruits a little longer than most blackcurrants. They may be bottled, preserved, or frozen.

Propagation

Take hardwood cuttings in early autumn. Use young shoots 30–38cm (12–15in) long, and remove all but the top three or four buds, to produce a plant with a short stem.

Insert the cuttings in moist, fertile soil, burying them by about half their length, and firm well. Once rooted, transplant the young plants to their final positions.

RECOMMENDED RED- AND WHITECURRANTS

Early
'Jonkheer van Tets' (red)
'Laxton's No.1' (red)
'Jonkheer van Tets'

Mid-season
'Red Lake' (red)
'Rondom'(red)
'Stanza' (red)
'White Dutch' (white)
'White Grape' (white)
'White Versailles' (white)
'White Grape'

Late
'Wilson's Long Bunch' (red)

HARDWOOD CUTTINGS

Cuttings should be 30cm (12in) long. Retain only the top few buds.

REDCURRANT CORDON
YEAR 1, WINTER PRUNING

Cut back the leader by half of its new growth to stimulate new sideshoots.

If there are any sideshoots at planting, cut them back to 1 bud.

YEAR 1, SUMMER PRUNING

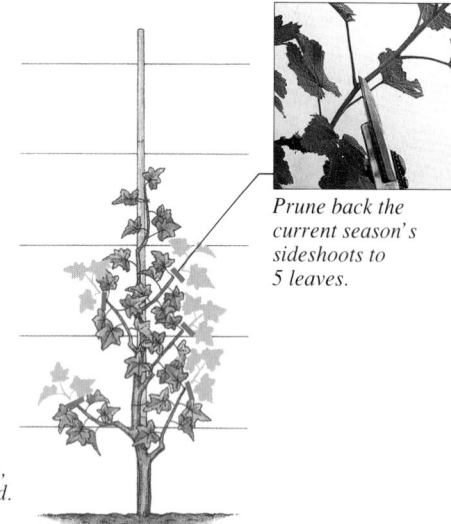

Prune back the current season's sideshoots to 5 leaves.

ESTABLISHED CORDON, WINTER PRUNING

If the leader has reached the top wire, prune to 1 bud, otherwise prune it back by a quarter of the summer's growth.

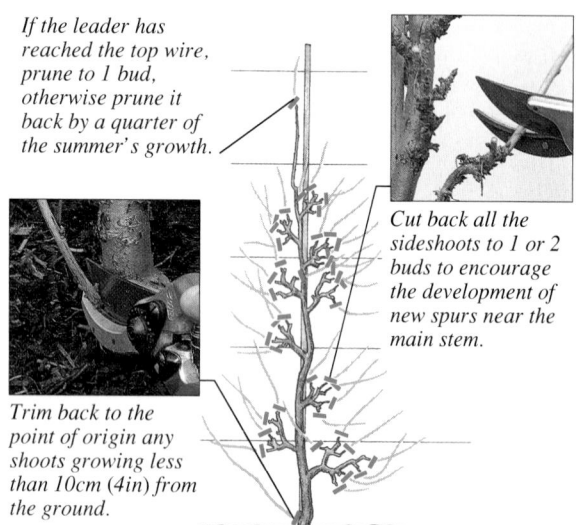

Trim back to the point of origin any shoots growing less than 10cm (4in) from the ground.

Cut back all the sideshoots to 1 or 2 buds to encourage the development of new spurs near the main stem.

Gooseberries (*Ribes uva-crispa*)

Gooseberries are easy to grow but like currants (also *Ribes*) need cool conditions and, if summer temperatures are high, adequate shade. Fruits ripen yellow, red, white, or green, depending on the cultivar. Methods of cultivation, pruning, and training are similar to those used for redcurrants.

Site and planting

Growing conditions and planting distances are as for redcurrants (see p.415). You may often find that there is only a limited range of certified cultivars available, but specialist nurseries may offer a wider selection. All cultivars are self-fertile.

Routine care

General maintenance is largely as for blackcurrants (see p.414). Gooseberries require high potassium levels and regular mulching, ideally with well-rotted manure. New shoots on young bushes are vulnerable to breakage and need protection from strong winds. If the crop is heavy, thin the fruits in late spring.

Pests and diseases

Birds (p.561) may cause severe bud loss, so cover plants with netting. If the buds have been attacked, delay winter pruning until bud-burst, then prune to live buds. Gooseberry plants may be affected by powdery mildew (p.562), which attacks the tips of shoots, sawfly larvae (p.549), and bacterial or fungal leaf spots (p.552).

Pruning and training

Young plants may be trained as bushes, cordons, or fans as for red-currants. A number of gooseberry cultivars, such as 'Leveller', have a natural drooping habit, however; to prevent stems from trailing to the ground, prune to upward-pointing buds, particularly when training young bushes.

GOOSEBERRY BUSH
YEAR 1, WINTER PRUNING

Prune back all the shoots by a half to three-quarters to an outward-facing bud.

ESTABLISHED BUSH, REGULATED PRUNING, WINTER

Cut out older branches to prevent overcrowding and to maintain an open centre.

The bush should have mainly young shoots, evenly spaced, pointing up- or outwards.

ESTABLISHED BUSH, SPUR PRUNING, WINTER

Prune all new sideshoots to a bud about 8cm (3in) from their base.

Tip prune the branch leaders to 3 or 4 buds of the new growth. This encourages the formation of spurs.

Bush For initial pruning, see red-currants (p.415); aim to create an open-centre bush on a stem 10–15cm (4–6in) long. Established bushes may be pruned by regulated or spur pruning in winter.

Regulated pruning is the simpler method: remove low, crowded, and crossing shoots to maintain well-spaced growth at the centre of the bush; also remove any old, unproductive branches and select new, young shoots to replace them.

Spur pruning is more labour-intensive: all the sideshoots are shortened to a suitable bud 8cm (3in)

GOOSEBERRY STANDARD

from the main branches. The branch leaders also need to be tip pruned.

Standard Cultivars to be trained as standards are grafted onto *Ribes odoratum* or *R. divaricatum* stock. Select one shoot of the rootstock and train it vertically, keeping any sideshoots short. It will take about three years to grow to a suitable height. When the stem has thickened and reached about 1.1–1.2m (3½–4ft), trim off the sideshoots and graft on the selected cultivar using whip-and-tongue grafting (see p.373). Use a strong stake to support the stem. The scion will develop and branch naturally the following summer. The next winter establish the framework as for a bush and then prune and train in the same way.

Cordon and fan These are trained as for redcurrants (see p.416). Once established, prune in summer, reducing new sideshoots to five leaves. In winter, shorten shoots to 8cm (3in) and tip prune leaders.

Harvesting and storing

Fruits should ripen by mid-summer. Gooseberries for cooking should be picked while still green, but allow dessert-quality cultivars to ripen fully on the bush for the best flavour, ensuring that they are protected from

birds. Yellow-, white-, and red-berried cultivars should be left to ripen to their full colour before they are picked. Gooseberries freeze well.

Propagation

Take hardwood cuttings in early autumn. Gooseberry hardwood cuttings may be difficult to root; retaining all the buds often improves the success rate. Remove all low buds and sideshoots when the rooted cutting is lifted. If this is not done, troublesome suckers will develop.

RECOMMENDED GOOSEBERRIES

Early
'Broom Girl' (yellow)
'Golden Drop' (yellow)
'May Duke' (red)

'Invicta'

Mid-season
'Bedford Red' (red)
'Careless' (white)
'Crown Bob' (red)
'Invicta' (green) **Rm**
'Keepsake' (green)
'Langley Gage' (white)
'Leveller' (yellow)
'Whinham's Industry' (red)
'Whitesmith' (white)

'Whinham's Industry'

Late
'Captivator' (red) **Th**
'Lancashire Lad' (red) **Rm**
'Lancer', syn. 'Howard's Lancer' (green)
'London' (red)
'Lord Derby' (red)
'White Lion' (white)

KEY
Rm *Some resistance to mildew*
Th *Nearly thornless*

HARDWOOD CUTTINGS

1 *In early autumn, take cuttings of well-ripened young shoots. Trim to 30–38cm (12–15in), with an angled cut above a bud at the top and a straight cut at the base. Insert in a trench to half their length.*

2 *The following autumn, carefully lift the rooted cuttings. Remove basal buds or shoots less than 10cm (4in) from the base (see inset), before transplanting the young plants.*

417

Blueberries (*Vaccinium corymbosum*)

Highbush blueberries are derived from the American wild blueberry. They produce clusters of fruits that are a dark, hazy purple-blue with a grey bloom; their flavour is enriched by cooking or preserving. They require a cool, moist climate, needing 700–1,200 hours below 7°C (45°F) and very acid soil (pH4–5.5). Highbush blueberries grow to a height of 1.3–2m (4½–6ft) and are deciduous, with white flowers in spring, and striking gold and scarlet autumn colour.

Rabbit-eye blueberries (*Vaccinium ashei*) are grown in the same way as the highbush group, but tolerate less acid soils and drier conditions; they are cultivated mainly in Australia and the USA. The fruits are smaller and more gritty than highbush blueberries.

Cropping, in mid- to late summer, is light at first but after five or six years yields of 2.25kg (5lb) of fruit per bush may be obtained, and on older bushes considerably more. Blueberries are self-fertile, but crop better when two or more cultivars are planted close together.

Site and planting
Blueberries need a sunny location, although they tolerate some shade. The soil must be well drained. Clear all perennial weeds from the site before planting and, if the soil is alkaline, correct this by mixing a 15cm (6in) layer of acidic compost with the existing soil to a depth of at least 60cm (2ft). Alternatively, apply flowers of sulphur at a rate of 50–120g/sq m (2–4oz/sq yd).

Blueberries may also be grown in large pots or tubs with a diameter of 30–38cm (12–15in), filled with ericaceous compost.

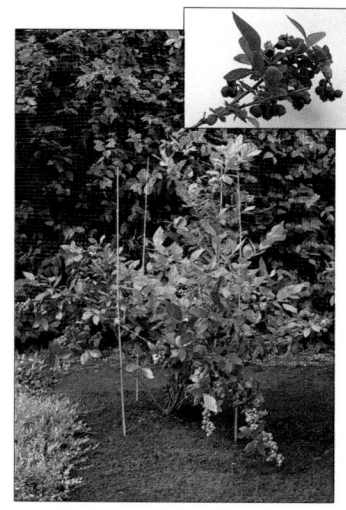

HIGHBUSH BLUEBERRY BUSH

Plant from late autumn to late winter, spacing bushes 1.5m (5ft) apart. Cover the roots with 2.5–5cm (1–2in) of soil, and mulch with acid compost or leaf mould. Growing a mixture of cultivars results in better fertilization and heavier crops.

Routine care
To promote growth and cropping and to maintain acidity, apply a dressing each spring of sulphate of ammonia at 35g/sq m (1oz/sq yd), sulphate of potash at 35g/sq m (1oz/sq yd), and bone meal at 105g/sq m (3oz/sq yd). Keep plants mulched with acid compost, and water with rainwater. Avoid root disturbance when weeding.

Pests and diseases
The fruits may be eaten by birds, so provide protection by netting the bushes (see "Protection from birds", p.367). Other pests and diseases rarely cause any trouble.

ESTABLISHED BLUEBERRY BUSH, WINTER PRUNING

Cut weak or unproductive shoots back to where a strong new shoot can take over.

Cut to ground level older, non-fruiting branches to stimulate new basal shoots.

Cut back any low or downward-pointing branches to their point of origin or to a branch growing in the required direction.

Pruning and training
Blueberries fruit on two- or three-year-old wood. New bushes need little pruning for two or three years, but cut out weak shoots to provide a strong basic framework.

Thereafter, prune to ensure regular production of new shoots from the base, as for blackcurrants (see p.414), by cutting out some of the oldest wood each year.

Harvesting and storing
The fruits ripen over a period of several weeks. Pick over the bushes carefully, harvesting only the ripe fruits, which part easily from the cluster. Blueberries may be successfully stored for later use by preserving, bottling, or freezing.

Propagation
Take 10–15cm (4–6in) softwood cuttings in mid-summer, dip them in hormone rooting powder, and then insert them in an acidic, peat/sand rooting medium. Place the cuttings in a propagator until rooted, then transplant to a larger pot. Harden off before planting out.

RECOMMENDED HIGHBUSH BLUEBERRIES

Early
'Bluecrop'
'Bluetta'
'Earliblue'
'Patriot'

'Bluetta'

Mid-season
'Berkeley'
'Herbert'
'Ivanhoe'

Late
'Coville'
'Darrow'
'Goldtraube 71'
'Jersey'

BLUEBERRY SOFTWOOD CUTTINGS

1 Select suitable softwood material and take cuttings at least 10cm (4in) long. Cut just above a leaf joint.

2 Trim the base of each cutting just below a node with a sharp knife, and remove the leaves from the lower third of the cuttings. Dip the ends of the cuttings in hormone rooting powder.

3 Prepare a pot of acid cutting compost. Make holes with a dibber and insert each cutting so that the basal leaves are just above the compost. Water, label, and place the pot in a propagator.

Tender fruits

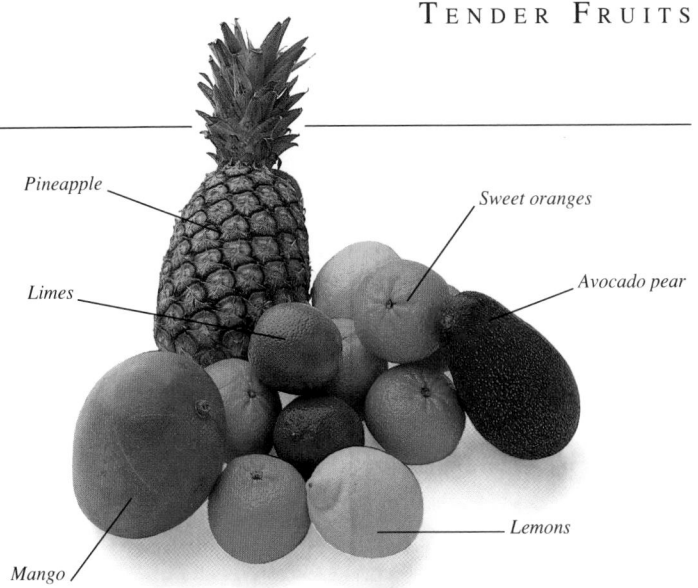

Pineapple

Sweet oranges

Avocado pear

Limes

Lemons

Mango

Most tender fruits originate from tropical and subtropical regions, where they thrive in the warm, dry conditions. Apart from olives, which need to be treated to remove their bitterness, many may be eaten straight from the tree, or stored for a short period of time in suitable conditions. Members of the citrus family that are too acid for eating, such as lemons and limes, are grown either for their juice or for use in preserves and marmalades. Since tender fruits are generally grown in hot climates, where the soil may be lacking in nutrients, it is important to prepare the site adequately when planting: an extra 110–80g (4–6oz) of slow-release fertilizer forked into the base of the planting hole will help the plants to establish quickly.

In cool-temperate climates, some tender fruits may still be grown, in containers or under cover, as long as the correct temperature and humidity levels are provided. Although many do not consistently ripen their fruits under cover, they nevertheless make attractive ornamentals.

Pineapples (*Ananas comosus*)

Pineapples are tropical perennials that produce terminal fruits each composed of up to 200 seedless fruitlets. For best results they need full sun and temperatures of 18–30°C (64–80°F) with humidity of 70–80 per cent. Cultivar groups include the Cayenne Group, the Queen Group, and the Spanish Group, of which the Spanish has the sweetest flavour.

Site and planting
Select a sunny site that is sheltered from strong winds. Pineapples tolerate a wide range of soils, but prefer a sandy, medium loam with a pH of 5–6.5. Plant "slips" or suckers about 30cm (12in) apart, with 60cm (24in) between rows, or at a spacing of 50cm (20in) each way.

Routine care
Use a general-purpose fertilizer with medium potassium and high nitrogen levels at intervals of two to three months, at a rate of 50g (2oz) per plant. Correct any iron and zinc deficiencies by spraying with a 2 per cent solution of ferrous or zinc sulphate. Water pineapples regularly in dry weather and apply an organic mulch to conserve soil moisture.

Pests and diseases
Pests that may affect pineapples include mealybugs (p.550), root-knot nematodes (p.564), scale insects (p.552), red spider mites (p.550), and thrips (p.551).

The most serious disease affecting pineapple plants in the open is heart-rot, caused by *Phytophthora cinnamoni* and *P. parasitica*, fungi that often affect pineapples grown in wet conditions. Since this is difficult to treat, it is advisable to guard against infection by planting resistant cultivars where these are available; all suckers that are required for propagation should be dipped in a fungicide, since the fungus enters through wounds.

Growing under cover
Plant rooted pineapple "slips" or cuttings in well-prepared beds with good drainage, or use pots at least 30cm (12in) in diameter. Use compost with a high organic content and apply a liquid feed every three to four weeks. Maintain a temperature of at least 20°C (68°F) and humidity of about 70 per cent. Water regularly and thoroughly, particularly while young plants are establishing.

Harvesting and storing
Harvest the fruits when they begin to turn yellow by cutting the stem 2.5–5cm (1–2in) below each fruit. Pineapples may be stored for up to three weeks at 8°C (46°F) and at 90 per cent humidity.

Propagation
The terminal crown shoot may be used as a cutting; remove it with about 1cm (1/2in) of the fruit attached. Pineapples may also be propagated

PROPAGATING PINEAPPLES FROM SUCKERS

Sever basal shoots or suckers and leave to dry before inserting in a sandy cutting compost (see inset).

by "slips" or suckers that arise from the leaf axils, the base of the stem, or from below the fruit; these may be detached with a sharp knife. Dip the cut surfaces of shoots or slips in a fungicide, then leave them to dry for several days. Remove the lower leaves and insert the cuttings in pots of sandy compost. Pot them on into 15cm (6in) pots when rooted.

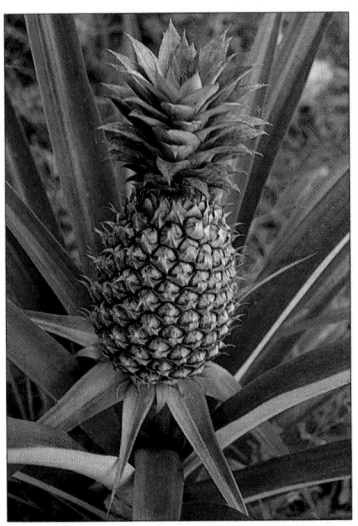

PINEAPPLE

PROPAGATING PINEAPPLES FROM THE CROWN SHOOT

1 *Scoop out the crown shoot of a ripe pineapple with a sharp knife, ensuring that you do not cut through the base of the shoot. Dip the wound in fungicide and leave for several days to dry.*

2 *Insert the prepared cutting into a pot of cutting compost and maintain at a temperature of at least 18°C (64°F). The cutting should be rooted and ready to pot on within a few weeks.*

RECOMMENDED PINEAPPLES

Cayenne Group
'Baronne de Rothschild'
'Smooth Cayenne'
'Sugar Baby'

Queen Group
'Natal Queen'
'Ripley Queen'

Spanish Group
'Red Spanish'
'Singapore Spanish'

Papayas (*Carica papaya*)

Papayas (or paw-paws) are slender, generally single-stemmed, tropical trees, growing up to 4–5m (12–15ft) with a spread of 1–2m (3–6ft) at the crown. The fruits may be up to 20cm (8in) long when mature. A temperature range of 22–8°C (72–82°F) with humidity of 60–70 per cent is normally required; some cultivars will withstand temperatures as low as 15°C (59°F), although flowering and fruiting may then be poor.

Site and planting

Choose a warm, sunny site with protection from strong winds. Papayas require fertile, well-drained soil,

with a pH of 6–7; good drainage is essential, since the trees are sensitive to waterlogging.

Many cultivars of papaya are dioecious, with male and female flowers produced on separate plants, but hermaphrodite cultivars are sometimes available. One male tree is usually sufficient to pollinate five or six female trees. Pollination is normally by insects and wind. Plant at a spacing of 2.5–3m (8–10ft).

Routine care

Apply a general-purpose, balanced fertilizer, 1–1.5kg (2lb 3oz – 3lb 6oz) per tree per year, in two or three separate dressings during the growing season. Water regularly in dry conditions and conserve moisture with an organic mulch. Papayas may be affected by viruses and nematodes after three or four years; if this happens, they should be replaced with either young plants of named cultivars or seedlings.

Pests and diseases

Common pests in the open are root-knot nematodes (p.564); papaya diseases include anthracnose (see "Fungal leaf spots", p.552), bunchy top virus (see "Viruses", p.553), and damping off of seedlings (p.568). Papaya trees grown under cover may also be attacked by aphids (p.550), thrips (p.551), whiteflies (p.550), and mealybugs (p.550).

Growing under cover

In temperate areas, papayas may be grown successfully under cover, if adequate light and temperature levels are provided. Raise seedlings or cuttings as described under "Propagation", below. Transplant them when they are 20–25cm (8–10in) tall into prepared beds, or pots with a minimum diameter of 35cm (14in). Use a fertile compost, to which a slow-release fertilizer has been added. Maintain a temperature of at least 22°C (72°F) and humidity of 60–70 per cent. Apply a liquid feed or light dressings of fertilizer with medium to high nitrogen content every three to four weeks. The plants should be watered regularly.

Pruning and training

Remove any lateral branches, since these are unproductive. After fruiting, prune to 30cm (12in) from the ground; of the new shoots that arise, select the strongest as the new leader and cut back the others.

Harvesting and storing

Harvest the fruits when they are orange to red. They may be stored at 10–13°C (50–55°F) with 70 per cent humidity for up to 14 days.

Propagation

Seed is the usual method of propagation. Sow the seed under cover in trays or, preferably, in bottomless

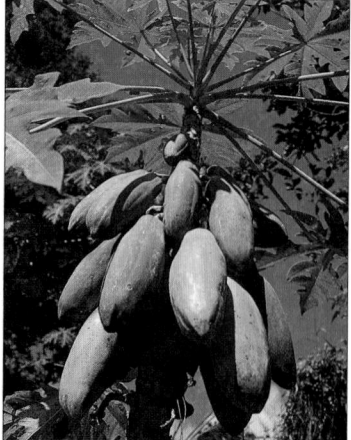

PAPAYA TREE

pots 6–9cm (2½–3½in) in diameter. Handle the seedlings carefully, since papayas are sensitive to root disturbance. Harden them off, then plant them out when they are 30–45cm (12–18in) tall. To obtain adequate numbers of female plants when dioecious cultivars are used, plant seedlings in clumps of three or four, thinning to one female plant after flowering begins. Hermaphrodite seedlings may be planted singly.

Cuttings are usually obtained by pruning mature trees to 30–40cm (12–16in) from the ground and using the new shoots as cuttings. Dip their bases in hormone rooting powder and grow them on under cover.

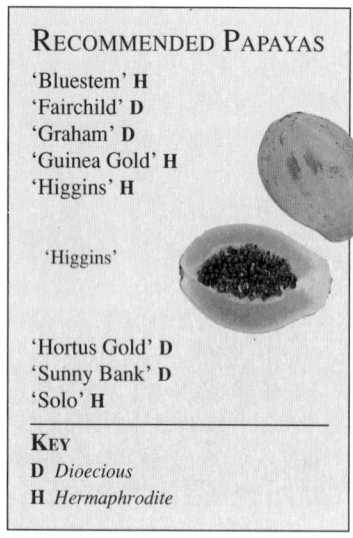

RECOMMENDED PAPAYAS

'Bluestem' **H**
'Fairchild' **D**
'Graham' **D**
'Guinea Gold' **H**
'Higgins' **H**

'Higgins'

'Hortus Gold' **D**
'Sunny Bank' **D**
'Solo' **H**

KEY
D *Dioecious*
H *Hermaphrodite*

Citrus (*Citrus* spp.)

The genus *Citrus* includes oranges, lemons, and a number of other edible species (see p.421). Citrus form small, widely branching trees on trunks of 50–60cm (20–24in) in circumference. The trees will reach a height of 3–10m (10–30ft) and a spread of 5–8m (15–25ft). Limes are the most compact, grapefruits the largest and most vigorous. Lemon trees have a more upright habit than the other species. Also discussed here is the kumquat, formerly included within the genus *Citrus* but now classified as *Fortunella*. Its cultivation requirements are similar to those of *Citrus*.

Citrus is a subtropical genus. All species and hybrids are evergreen and have aromatic leaves. For optimum growth, they require a temperature of 15–30°C (58–86°F), although most species will survive short periods at 0°C (32°F). They thrive at altitudes of 100m (320ft)

or above, with humidity levels of 60–70 per cent, unless otherwise stated. Flowering is not seasonal but occurs during warm periods with regular rainfall; flowers and fruits may coincide. Many species of citrus make excellent plants for growing in containers under cover in temperate areas.

Site and planting

Citrus prefer a sunny aspect and should be protected by windbreaks in exposed areas. They tolerate a wide range of soils but do best in fertile, well-drained, slightly acid soils (pH 6–6.5). Young citrus respond well to a high soil fertility.

Rootstocks

Sweet orange may be used, since it is compatible with all widely grown citrus species and cultivars. Rough

lemon rootstocks produce early-bearing, vigorous trees resistant to tristeza (quick decline) viruses, but their fruits may have thick rinds and a low acid and sugar content. Sour orange is also a good universal rootstock, but it is susceptible to tristeza viruses.

Trifoliate orange is a dwarfing rootstock that is suitable for cooler areas. It has some resistance to nematodes but is not compatible with certain cultivars of lemon. Cleopatra mandarin and Rangpur lime are also used as rootstocks. Seedling rootstocks may also be raised – for details, see "Propagation", p.421.

Pollination

Most citrus, including sweet orange, are self-fertile, so a pollinator is not normally required; many, for instance the 'Washington' sweet orange, also produce seedless fruits.

Planting

Planting distances vary between 5m (15ft) and 10m (30ft) each way, depending on the vigour of the species or cultivar chosen, so seek specialist advice from the nursery when

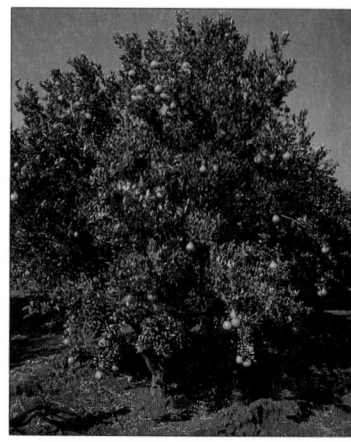

SWEET ORANGE TREE

purchasing a tree. Citrus are sensitive to waterlogging, so on a site where the soil is not sufficiently well drained, plant each tree on a slight mound, 5–7cm (2–3in) high, to allow excess water to run off.

Routine care

During the first few years, feed citrus trees with a balanced fertilizer that has a high nitrogen and medium potassium level at a rate of 1kg (2lb 3oz) per tree per year. The fertilizer should be given in two or three doses, applied at regular intervals around the base of each tree, when the trees are in active growth. Double the quantity of fertilizer after five years. A mulch helps to retain moisture.

Remove all weeds around the bases of the trees, and water thoroughly in dry weather, particularly when the flowers or fruits are developing. The non-seasonal habit of fruiting makes fruit thinning unnecessary. Remove any suckers.

Pests and diseases

Various mealybugs (p.550), scale insects (p.552), thrips (p.551), red spider mites (p.550), aphids (p.550), root and crown rots (see "*Phytophthora* root rots", p.558), anthracnose (see "Fungal leaf spots", p.552), and scab (p.562) may affect citrus grown in the open and under cover. Root-knot nematodes (p.564) may be serious pests on some soils. In the tropics and subtropics, fruit flies may be a problem (p.563).

Many citrus species and cultivars may be infected with tristeza virus, which is spread by aphids and causes stem pitting on grapefruits, limes, and citrons. Infected trees will lose vigour and produce small fruits. The virus is most likely to affect cultivars that are budded onto sour orange rootstocks. Spray against aphids, or use alternative rootstocks.

Growing under cover

In temperate areas, several cultivars of sweet orange, tangerine, lemon, and lime, as well as the Seville orange and kumquat, may be grown under cover, although they may not be relied on to bear fruit. Prepare the beds well, or use large containers, at least 60cm (2ft) in diameter, filled with a nutrient-rich compost. Maintain a minimum temperature of 20°C (68°F) with at least 75 per cent humidity, and water the plants regularly. Apply a liquid fertilizer each month once the young trees are well established.

Pruning and training

Shorten the main branches of newly planted trees by one third in the first year. This encourages lateral growth and produces a rounded shape. After fruiting, prune only to remove dead, diseased, or crossing branches and any that touch the soil. Citrus may also be trained as standards or half-standards (see p.379), particularly if grown as ornamentals.

Harvesting and storing

Citrus fruits may take from six to eight months, or even longer, from fruit set to ripen, depending on the climate (the lower the temperature, the longer the period required). In areas of low sunshine, mature citrus fruits may remain green.

Harvest the fruits when they have ripened by cutting them at the fruit stalk with secateurs or a sharp knife or by pulling the fruit stalk from the tree with a slight twist. Undamaged fruits may be stored for several weeks at 4–6°C (38–42°F).

Propagation

Some citrus may be raised from seed. Most citrus seeds are polyembryonic and therefore "clonal", reproducing characteristics of the parent tree. The quality of fruits from non-polyembryonic cultivars is variable. For named cultivars the usual means of propagation is by budding.

To raise citrus trees from seed, use fresh seed, sowing it in trays or pots of seed compost at a depth of 3–5cm (1¼–2in). Water the seeds frequently and maintain a temperature of 25–32°C (77–90°F). When the seedlings are large enough to handle, prick them out into 10 or 12cm (4 or 4½in) pots. When they are 20–30cm (8–12in) high, transplant them into 21–30cm (8–12in) pots, or plant them out, after hardening them off. Alternatively, repot them into 25–38cm (10–15in) pots and plant in the open when they are 60–90cm (2–3ft) tall.

T-budding (see p.373) is the usual method of propagating citrus vegetatively. Use seedling citrus stocks with stems 1cm (½in) in diameter. After three to four weeks, remove the budding tape and cut the stock growth above the budded area halfway across. When the bud shoot is 2.5cm (1in) long, the stock growth above the budded shoot may be removed entirely.

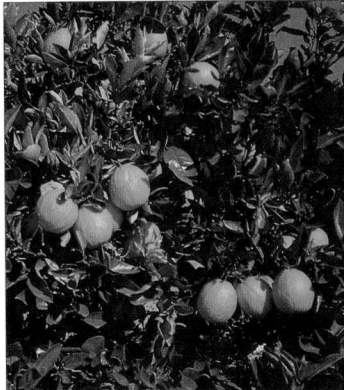

RIPE SWEET ORANGES

Species of citrus

Limes (*Citrus aurantiifolia*)
There are two main groups of lime. One has an acidic taste, the other is fairly sweet and is often used as a rootstock. One of the acidic cultivars grown most commonly is 'West Indian'. Its fruits are round, small, and thin-skinned, with few seeds; the skin and pulp are green.

Most limes are grown as seedlings but may also be reproduced by budgrafting onto rough lemon rootstock.

Sour, Seville, or bitter oranges (*Citrus aurantium*)
The sour, or bitter, orange is mainly used as a rootstock. The fruits, which are used for making marmalade, are about 7cm (3in) in diameter, rounded, with thick peel. They are fairly acidic, but some forms of the species bear fruits of lower citric acid content.

Lemons (*Citrus limon*)
Most lemon cultivars produce seeded fruits that may remain green, rather than turning yellow, even when fully mature. To grow successfully in the open, they require an altitude of 300–500m (960–1,600ft), with little variation in temperature, and need a minimum temperature of 20°C (68°F).

An interesting hybrid between lemon and lime is the "lemonime"; this may be grown in the open in subtropical areas or as an ornamental under cover in temperate areas.

Citrons (*Citrus medica*)
The fruits of the citron are ovoid and yellow, with a thick rind and a rough surface, and may be up to 15cm (6in) long; the pulp is acid with little juice.

No specific citron cultivars have been recorded; citrons are grown mainly for their peel, which is usually candied for use in the confectionery

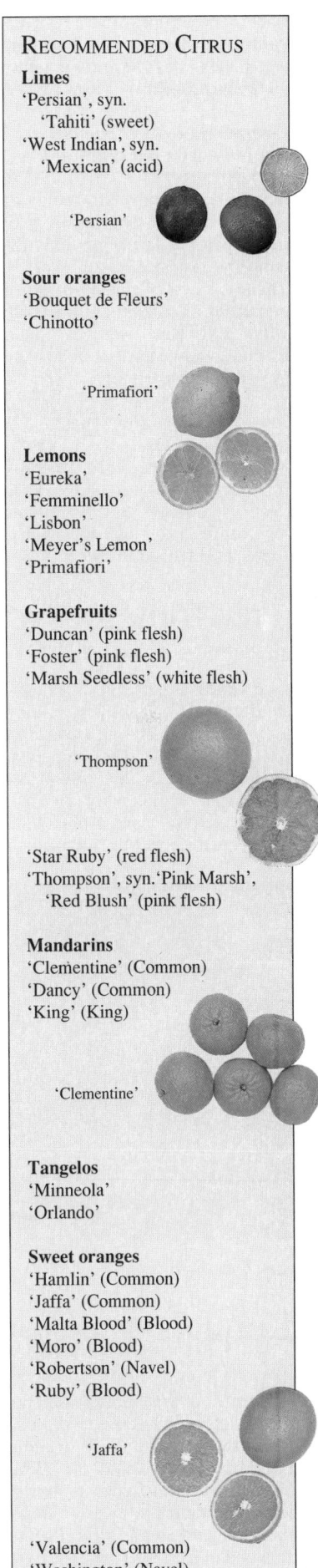

RECOMMENDED CITRUS

Limes
'Persian', syn. 'Tahiti' (sweet)
'West Indian', syn. 'Mexican' (acid)

'Persian'

Sour oranges
'Bouquet de Fleurs'
'Chinotto'

'Primafiori'

Lemons
'Eureka'
'Femminello'
'Lisbon'
'Meyer's Lemon'
'Primafiori'

Grapefruits
'Duncan' (pink flesh)
'Foster' (pink flesh)
'Marsh Seedless' (white flesh)

'Thompson'

'Star Ruby' (red flesh)
'Thompson', syn. 'Pink Marsh', 'Red Blush' (pink flesh)

Mandarins
'Clementine' (Common)
'Dancy' (Common)
'King' (King)

'Clementine'

Tangelos
'Minneola'
'Orlando'

Sweet oranges
'Hamlin' (Common)
'Jaffa' (Common)
'Malta Blood' (Blood)
'Moro' (Blood)
'Robertson' (Navel)
'Ruby' (Blood)

'Jaffa'

'Valencia' (Common)
'Washington' (Navel)

trade. Citrons make attractive ornamentals, however; in temperate areas they may be grown under cover (see p.421).

Grapefruits (*Citrus paradisi*)
The fruits of the grapefruit are large, rounded, up to 10–15cm (4–6in) in diameter, and yellow. Most cultivars are well adapted to growing at or just above sea level, provided the temperature exceeds 25°C (77°F). There are two principal groups of grapefruit in cultivation, one with white pulp, the other with pink; seeded and seedless cultivars are available in both groups.

Mandarins or tangerines
(*Citrus reticulata*)
Mandarins, or tangerines, generally require temperatures above 18°C (64°F), but very high temperatures may result in loss of fruit quality. Cross-pollination between trees

frequently occurs; this gives rise to fruits with many seeds.

The Satsuma Group is the one most frequently cultivated; the fruits of cultivars in this group are mainly slightly flattened and seedless, with a well-developed orange colour and sweet flavour. Some cultivars have a "navel", a miniature fruit that develops at the end of the fruit. The other three groups are the Cleopatra Group, which is widely used as a rootstock but has unpalatable fruits itself, the King Group, and the Common Mandarin Group (which includes the cultivar 'Clementine').

Tangelos or ugli fruits (*Citrus reticulata* x *C. paradisi*)
This hybrid between the grapefruit and the mandarin inherits some characteristics from each of its parents; the orange fruits are larger than those of the mandarin but have a relatively thin, easily peeled skin.

They may be grown under cover in temperate areas, where they may occasionally bear fruit.

Sweet oranges (*Citrus sinensis*)
Most sweet oranges, including the widely grown 'Jaffa' orange, belong to the Valencia (or Common) Group. The fruits are medium to large and spherical to ovoid, with few or no seeds. Oranges in this group may have a slightly acid taste but have an excellent flavour.

Sweet oranges are usually grown from seed, but a few specific cultivars are propagated vegetatively by budding. Seedlings are also widely used as rootstocks for grafting with other species. Sweet orange cultivars are usually classified into three groups: Navel oranges, Blood oranges, and Valencia oranges.

Navel oranges have a small secondary fruit at the main fruit apex and are usually seedless. They grow

well in slightly cooler climates, peel and separate easily, and have excellent flavour. Blood oranges are similar but their pulp, juice, and rind are red (except when they are grown at high temperatures).

Two sweet orange crops at different stages of development may be borne on a tree at the same time.

Kumquats (*Fortunella japonica*, *F. margarita*)
Originating in China, kumquats are hardier than the citrus fruits described above: they can withstand temperatures down to -5°C (23°F) for short periods. The fruits, which may be eaten unpeeled, are small and yellow. Those of *Fortunella japonica* are rounded in shape, while those of *F. margarita* are ovoid.

The Calamondin (x *Citrofortunella microcarpa*) is a mandarin-kumquat hybrid; it is grown as an ornamental in temperate regions.

Tree tomatoes (*Cyphomandra betacea*)

Also known as tamarillos, tree tomatoes are subtropical trees growing to 3–5m (10–15ft), with a spread of 1.5–2.5m (5–8ft). They are most productive at 20–28°C (68–82°F) with 70 per cent humidity. The red, orange, or yellow fruits are ovoid and may be 7.5cm (3in) long.

RIPE TREE TOMATOES

Site and planting
Tree tomatoes require a sunny situation and need protection from the wind in exposed sites. Fertile, loam soils produce the best results. Allow a planting distance of about 3m (10ft) each way.

Routine care
A general-purpose fertilizer with medium to high nitrogen should be applied every two to three months at a rate of 110g (4oz) for each tree. Water well during dry periods, and use an organic mulch around the base of the plants to prevent loss of moisture from the soil.

Pests and diseases
Tree tomatoes in the open may be affected by aphids (p.550). They are susceptible to cucumber mosaic virus and potato virus "Y" (see "Viruses", pp.553 and 563); *Phytophthora palmivora* and *P. infestans* (see "Tomato/potato blight", p.553) may also cause problems. Under cover,

plants may be attacked by thrips, (p.551), whiteflies (p.550), and red spider mites (p.550).

Growing under cover
Tree tomatoes may be grown in containers with a diameter of at least 35cm (14in) or in well-prepared beds. Use fertile compost, to which a general-purpose fertilizer has been added. Maintain the correct temperatures and humidity, water regularly, and apply a liquid feed every three to four weeks.

Pruning and training
When plants reach a height of 1m (3ft), remove the growing point to encourage branching. Little pruning is needed apart from removing crowded and crossing branches, and diseased or dead wood.

Harvesting and storing
Tree tomatoes usually fruit one to two years after planting. Detach the fruits using a sharp knife when they

TREE TOMATOES

start to change colour. They may be stored for up to two weeks at a temperature of 4–6°C (39–43°F).

Propagation
Sow seed under cover; pot the seedlings individually into 10cm (4in) pots when they are 3–5cm (1¼–2in) tall. When they reach 15–25cm (6–10in), harden them off and plant them out in the open. Propagation is also easy from softwood cuttings: select shoots 10–15cm (4–6in) long and use a sandy (but not acid) compost. Follow the procedure as for blueberries (see p.418).

Loquats (*Eriobotrya japonica*)

A member of the family Rosaceae, the loquat is an attractive, evergreen tree growing to 7m (22ft) or more tall, with a spread of about 5m (15ft). Loquats are best suited to a subtropical environment and need a minimum temperature of 15°C (59°F) to flower and fruit regularly. They are widely grown in the Mediterranean

region. In cooler climates loquats may be successfully grown under cover, since they are able to withstand relatively low temperatures for short periods. Some cultivars have a low chilling requirement.

Loquats bear clusters of fragrant, cream-coloured flowers, followed by bunches of round, yellow fruits

3–8cm (1¼–3in) long with tough skins. The pulp is soft and sweet.

Suitable rootstocks for loquats include quince (*Cydonia oblonga*), hawthorns (*Crataegus* spp.), and vigorous loquat seedlings. Most loquat cultivars are self-pollinated, but cross-pollination by insects may also occur.

Site and planting
Select a warm, sunny situation. Windbreaks should be erected to reduce wind damage and moisture evaporation. Loquats tolerate a wide range of soils, but a well-drained, fertile loam is most suitable. The trees should be planted at a distance of 4–5m (12–15ft) each way.

Routine care

Apply a top-dressing of general-purpose fertilizer at a rate of about 450g (16oz) per tree every three to four months. Loquats must be regularly watered to keep the roots moist during dry periods; regular applications of organic mulch help to reduce water loss. Keep the surrounding area free of weeds.

To ensure the production of large fruits, thin the bunches at an early stage of their development. Remove any that are weak or damaged, leaving healthy, evenly spaced fruitlets.

Pests and diseases

Plants in the open have few problems. Under cover, however, loquats may be attacked by thrips (p.551), mealybugs (p.550), red spider mites (p.550), and whiteflies (p.550).

Growing under cover

Young, seed-raised plants may be grown in containers or planted out in well-prepared beds when they are about 45cm (18in) tall. Use a loam-based compost, with a slow-release fertilizer incorporated, and maintain a temperature of at least 18°C (64°F) during the summer. Water them regularly, and apply a liquid feed every month.

Pruning and training

Minimal pruning is required for loquats other than tip pruning all over-vigorous shoots and removing wayward branches; any crossing, damaged, dead, or diseased branches should also be removed.

Harvesting and storing

Harvest when the fruits soften and begin to turn rich yellow or orange. Short-term storage is possible at temperatures of 5–10°C (41–50°F).

Propagation

Loquats may be propagated by seed, sown 2–3cm (³/₄–1¹/₄in) deep in containers filled with a sandy seed compost, and maintained at not less than

RIPE LOQUATS

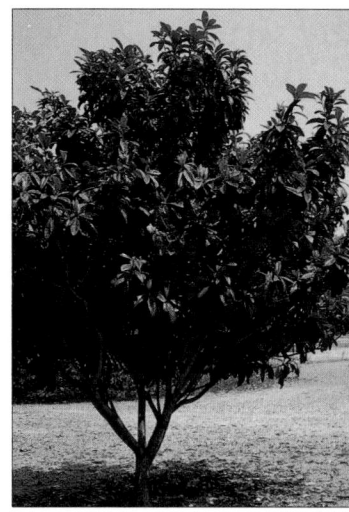

LOQUAT TREE

18°C (64°F). Transplant the seedlings to their final positions when they are 7–10cm (3–4in) high. Other techniques that may be used for propagating loquat cultivars

include T-budding (see p.373), side-veneer grafting (see *Propagating Trees by Side-veneer Grafting*, p.58), and air layering (see THE INDOOR GARDEN, p.456).

Mangos (*Mangifera indica*)

Mangos are tropical, evergreen trees that often reach 30m (100ft) when grown from vigorous seedlings. If dwarfing rootstocks and compact-growing clones are used, the trees' height may be restricted to 7–10m (22–30ft). The spread is about 8m (25ft) for dwarf types.

Mango fruits vary from 5 to 30cm (2 to 12in) in length and may weigh from 100g (3¹/₂oz) up to about 2kg (4lb 6oz). They have a leathery skin and may be orange, yellow, green, or red, depending on the cultivar. The single seed may comprise 25 per cent of the total volume of the fruit. Cultivars are available that are adapted to growing in subtropical areas with a temperature range of

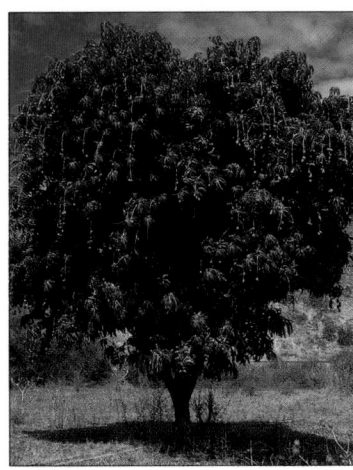

MANGO TREE

21–5°C (70–77°F) with humidity above 60 per cent; the higher temperature is regarded as the optimum for most cultivars. For successful flowering and fruit set, mangos require a high light intensity and a dry period.

Site and planting

Select a warm, sunny aspect. If necessary, provide protection from strong winds, since high moisture loss may seriously affect the growth of the trees; very low humidity may worsen the situation, and lead to leaf scorch, seed abortion, and fruit drop.

Soil type is less important for mangos than it is for most other tree crops, and both sandy loams and medium clays are suitable, provided they are well drained. Mangos need a pH of between 5.5 and 7.5.

Dwarfing rootstocks are rapidly becoming available; these are often more suitable, particularly for small gardens, than non-selected local cultivars. If dwarfing rootstocks are not available, polyembryonic seedlings produced from parent trees selected for their high quality of fruit and yield are to be preferred.

Pollination is only successful in relatively dry weather, since high humidity and heavy rainfall limit fertilization (flowering usually begins after a period of cool or dry weather). A solution of potassium nitrate, applied as a spray, may promote flowering. Pollination is

mainly by insects, although some mango cultivars are self-fertile.

Space compact and dwarf cultivars 8m (25ft) apart each way; more vigorous cultivars require a spacing of 10–12m (30–40ft).

Routine care

Feed with a general-purpose fertilizer with medium potassium and high nitrogen levels, at a rate of 1–1.5kg (2lb 3oz–3lb 5oz) per tree, per year. This should be applied in three or four doses during the growing season; after the fourth year of growth, double the amount.

Water mangos well during dry periods, particularly in the first three years of growth, since plenty of moisture is essential for root development. An organic mulch retains moisture and suppresses weeds. Fruit thinning is rarely necessary.

Pests and diseases

In the tropics, mangos are liable to attack by fruit flies (p.563) and mealybugs (p.550); various types of scale insect (p.552) may also be a problem. Diseases that may affect trees in the open include anthracnose (see "Fungal leaf spots", p.552) and powdery mildew (p.550).

Mangos grown under cover may also be subject to damage by aphids (p.550), whiteflies (p.550), thrips (p.551), red spider mites (p.550), and certain forms of powdery and downy mildew (p.550).

MANGOS

Growing under cover

Mangos grown from seed are likely to be too vigorous for growing under cover unless they have been grafted onto a dwarfing rootstock, when they will form attractive, ornamental trees. They may be grown in large containers or well-prepared beds. In temperate regions, flowering will generally occur under cover only towards the end of the growing season, and only if the optimum growing conditions have been provided. Fruiting cannot be guaranteed, however, and is dependent on successful pollination.

Transplant young plants when they are about 1m (3ft) tall. They will require a compost containing a slow-release fertilizer with a medium potassium and high nitrogen content. Ensure a minimum temperature of 21–5°C (70–77°F) and humidity of about 75 per cent are maintained. Mangos grown under

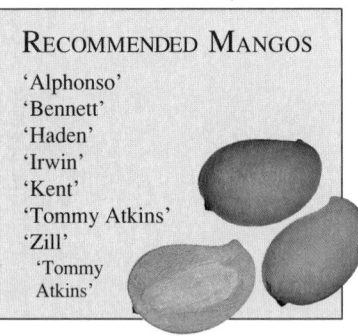

cover should be watered regularly and given a liquid feed every month. Supplement this with sprays of a nitrogenous fertilizer if the leaves turn yellow due to lack of nitrogen.

Pruning and training

Restrict pruning to tip pruning the leading shoot when it is about 1m (3ft) long to encourage lateral branching. Remove overcrowded or very vigorous growth during the early years to ensure an evenly spaced, rounded tree canopy. Once the tree is established, pruning is limited to the removal of diseased, dead, or crossing branches, or those that are congested.

Harvesting and storing

Mangos fruit three to four years after planting. The fruits should be picked when they begin to change colour. Handle them carefully to avoid any damage by bruising.

Any mangos that are slightly immature may be stored at 10°C (48°F) for two to four weeks, maintaining humidity of 90–95 per cent; they should ripen during this time.

Propagation

Propagation from seed is possible for polyembryonic cultivars, or various methods of grafting may be used instead. For seed propagation, remove the pulp of ripe fruits; to hasten germination, soak the seed in water for 48 hours and carefully remove the seed coat. Sow immediately in beds or containers, using well-prepared compost, and with the convex side of the seeds uppermost, lightly covering them with compost, and water.

The resulting seedlings may be polyembryonic and similar to the parent tree, but they are also likely to be very vigorous and take five to eight years to bear fruits that may prove variable in quality. A mango seed usually produces at least one such vigorous seedling resulting from self- or cross-pollination; any such seedlings should be discarded. The remaining seedlings are ready for transplanting to containers at least 15cm (6in) in diameter within six to eight weeks and may be used for rootstocks. Alternatively, they may be grown on as fruiting trees.

Mangos may also be propagated vegetatively, although stem cuttings often fail to root successfully. "Approach" grafting is a recommended alternative. Take a container-grown rootstock that is about one year old. Place the container near the scion branch still growing on the parent tree. Using a sharp knife, take a shallow, vertical slice 5–6cm (2–2¹⁄₂in) long from the side of the rootstock and scion, thus exposing the cambium layers. Place the matching cut surfaces together and bind them firmly. After two or three months the two should have united; cut the top off the rootstock, and sever the scion from the parent plant.

Other successful methods of propagating mangos are by T-budding (see p.373) and air layering (see THE INDOOR GARDEN, p.456).

Olives (*Olea europaea*)

Olives are evergreen trees, growing 9–12m (28–40ft) tall, with a spread of 7–9m (22–8ft). The fruits may be gathered while they are still green, or when they are fully ripe and have turned black. They may measure up to 4cm (1¹⁄₂in) long.

Olives grow well in subtropical areas with an optimum temperature range of 5–25°C (41–77°F). They need long, hot summers for the fruits to ripen fully, followed by winter temperatures that are low enough to meet the chilling requirement of the specific cultivar, so seek specialist advice on which cultivars grow best in your area. Very low winter temperatures may result in frost damage. Hot, dry winds and cool, wet weather during the flowering period reduce fruit set. In temperate areas olives are occasionally grown as ornamental trees in warm gardens, but seldom flower or fruit. Given suitable growing conditions, an olive tree may attain a great age.

Site and planting

A wide range of soils is suitable, although low to medium fertility is preferable, since soils that are very fertile are likely to result in excessive vegetative growth. The site must be well drained. Olives grow well on alkaline soils, including those with a high level of salts, provided that the pH level does not exceed 8.5. Windbreaks should be used in exposed areas.

Most cultivars are self-fertile but pollinators may be necessary to increase fruit yield in cooler climates. Olives are pollinated by insects and also by wind; high humidity levels inhibit pollination.

The usual planting distance varies from 7m (22ft) to 12m (40ft) each way, depending on the habit of the cultivar; all olives should be staked to avoid wind damage. Closely planted trees may be thinned by removing alternate trees when the canopies begin to overlap.

Routine care

Top-dress with a general-purpose fertilizer with medium to high levels of nitrogen at a yearly rate of about 0.5–1kg (1–2lb) per tree, applied in two or three doses when the trees are in active growth. Applications of potassium and, possibly, boron supplements may be necessary on some soils. Water olives regularly during dry periods, particularly for the first two to three years after planting. Mulching with organic material is also beneficial. Keep the planting area free of weeds.

OLIVE TREE

OLIVES

Fruit thinning may be necessary, if the trees show signs of biennial bearing (see "Apples: Blossom thinning and biennial bearing", p.376). Thinning is generally done by hand, but applications of a spray containing alpha naphthalene acetic acid 4–18 days after flowering may also be effective.

Pests and diseases

Olives grown in the open may be affected by various types of scale insect (p.552) and root-knot nematodes (p.564). Olive diseases include *Verticillium* wilt (p.557). Trees grown under cover may be affected by whiteflies (p.550), thrips (p.551), and red spider mites (p.550).

Growing under cover

Rooted cuttings or budded plants should be grown either in prepared beds, or in containers no smaller than 30–35cm (12–14in) in diameter; use a fertile compost that incorporates a slow-release fertilizer with medium levels of potassium and nitrogen. Apply a liquid feed every three to four weeks and water the trees regularly.

Maintain a high temperature – above 21°C (70°F) – in summer and as low a temperature as possible in winter. Olives grown in containers may be placed in the open during the summer months.

Pruning and training

Prune newly planted olives by removing the leading shoot when it is about 1.5m (5ft) tall; select three to four strong laterals to provide the basic branch framework. Subsequent pruning consists of removing older branches to encourage the growth of new shoots, since fruits are produced on one-year-old wood mostly at the edges of the tree canopy.

Harvesting and storing

Olive trees grown in the open are likely to flower and fruit in three to four years from planting; yields generally increase until the tree is 15 years old, after which they remain fairly constant.

Olives are processed to remove their bitterness. Fruits used for fermenting should be harvested when they are fully ripe but still green. Olives for eating without being processed may be harvested when black and firm, then packed in dry salt. When thoroughly dehydrated, the olives are stored in oil.

Fruits that are required for oil production should be left on the tree until they are fully ripe. They are harvested by shaking the tree so that the olives fall onto a cloth or fine netting placed on the ground below the tree canopy.

Propagation

Olives are usually propagated by stem cuttings, but selected cultivars may also be increased by bud-grafting.

Cuttings may be either hardwood (from one- or two-year-old wood) or leafy, semi-ripe cuttings from the current season's growth.

Hardwood cuttings, which are taken during winter, should be about 30cm (12in) in length. Remove the leaves from the lower half of each cutting, and soak its base for 24 hours in hormone rooting solution. Insert the cuttings to half their length in cutting compost, leaving them for

about 30 days to root while maintaining a temperature of 13–21°C (55–70°F). Transplant the cuttings singly into pots, and raise them in greenhouse conditions.

Alternatively, take semi-ripe cuttings 10–15cm (4–6in) long (see ORNAMENTAL TREES, p.55). Named olive cultivars may be propagated by T-budding (see p.373), always budding onto vigorous, olive seedling rootstocks.

Prickly pears (*Opuntia ficus-indica*)

This member of the cactus family is grown mainly in the subtropics. Although many of its forms are relatively low-growing and spreading in habit, some may eventually attain a height of 2m (6ft).

Most prickly pears will tolerate semi-arid conditions, with an optimum temperature range of 18–25°C (64–77°F); they will survive at lower temperatures, with a minimum of 10°C (50°F). Full sunlight is essential for satisfactory growth.

The stems of prickly pears consist of flattened, elliptic sections, 30–50cm (12–20in) long, which

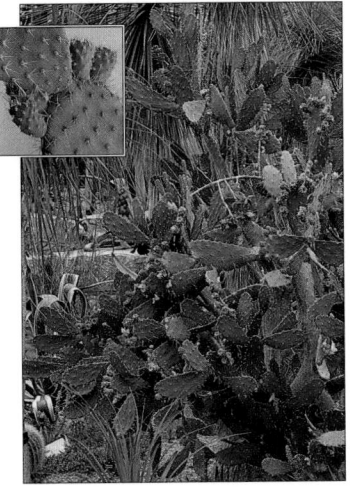

PRICKLY PEAR

are almost spineless in many of the cultivated forms but very spiny on wild and naturalized plants.

Prickly pear fruits, which are produced from the upper part of the sections, are purple or red when ripe, and about 5–10cm (2–4in) long. They contain a soft, juicy pulp with many seeds. Prickly pears are pollinated by insects.

Site and planting

Prickly pears thrive in subtropical regions, where they are able to tolerate lengthy periods of drought. They are sensitive to poor drainage and saline conditions, however, and prefer sandy, well-aerated soils, with an ideal pH of 5.5–7.

Rooted sections are usually established 2–2.4m (6–7¹/₂ft) apart, with a spacing of 2–3m (6–10ft) between each row.

Routine care

Fertilizers are not normally required, unless the soil is particularly poor. Keep the planting site weed-free. Pests are rarely serious. Some forms of *Pythium* spp. (see "Damping off" p.564), however, may affect prickly pears in humid conditions.

Growing under cover

Use a sandy compost to which a slow-release fertilizer has been added. Maintain the temperature at

PROPAGATING PRICKLY PEARS FROM STEM SECTIONS

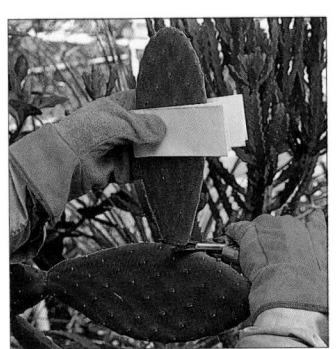

1 Using a sharp knife, cut a whole section away from the parent plant. It is advisable to wear gloves, since the spines irritate the skin.

2 After allowing the section to dry out for a few days, place it in a sandy compost, and firm it in. The section should have rooted in 2–3 months.

18–25°C (64–77°F) with humidity of 60 per cent or below. Little watering is required once the plants have become established.

Harvesting and storing

Prickly pears produce fruits three to four years after planting. Detach them carefully from the stem sections using a sharp knife. They are best eaten within a few days after they have been harvested, but may be stored for short periods in cool conditions, if necessary.

Propagation

Detach whole stem sections from the parent plant; if these are very large, cut them horizontally into two or three pieces. Allow them to callus in a sunny, sheltered place for several days before inserting them into a sandy compost. The sections should take two to three months to root; they may then be potted on into 15–20cm (6–8in) pots, or transplanted to their final positions. Water the new plants regularly until they are established.

Avocado pears (*Persea americana*)

The avocado pear is a subtropical, evergreen tree that may grow to a height of 10–15m (30–45ft), with a similar spread. Its fruits are pear-shaped, with a large, central, rounded seed. Fruit size and skin texture vary with the cultivar and colours range from green to russet. The three main types of avocado are Guatemalan, Mexican, and West Indian.

The optimum temperature range for growth and fruit development is

20–28°C (68–82°F) with humidity of over 60 per cent; some Mexican and Guatemalan cultivars are able to withstand temperatures as low as 10–15°C (48–58°F), but they do not usually produce flowers at such low temperatures.

Site and planting

Avocado trees may be grown in the open in subtropical areas, provided the temperature is within the range

given above. Their branches are brittle, so it is necessary to provide windbreaks in exposed areas to prevent them from being seriously damaged by the wind.

Select a site with maximum exposure to sun if possible. Avocados need a well-drained soil, since their roots are extremely sensitive to waterlogging. Medium loam soils with a pH of 5.5–6.5 are preferable, but sandy or clay loams may

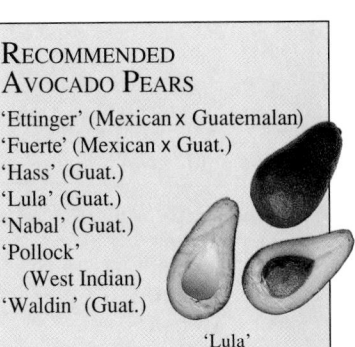

RECOMMENDED AVOCADO PEARS

'Ettinger' (Mexican x Guatemalan)
'Fuerte' (Mexican x Guat.)
'Hass' (Guat.)
'Lula' (Guat.)
'Nabal' (Guat.)
'Pollock'
   (West Indian)
'Waldin' (Guat.)

'Lula'

weeds. It is not normally necessary to thin the fruits on avocado trees.

Pests and diseases
Avocados may be affected by avocado root rot (see "*Phytophthora* root rots" p.558), and *Cercospora* spot or blotch (see "Fungal leaf spots", p.552). They may be attacked by such pests as whiteflies (p.550), thrips (p.551), red spider mites (p.550), and mealybugs (p.550).

Growing under cover
Establish young plants either in well prepared beds or in containers with a minimum diameter of 21cm (8in). Maintain temperatures of 20–28°C (68–82°F) and humidity of 70 per cent. For container-grown plants, pot on into containers at least 30cm (12in) in diameter, taking care not to disturb the plants' root systems.

Water containerized avocados regularly, and apply either a general-purpose fertilizer with a medium level of both potassium and nitrogen at intervals of two to three weeks, or a liquid feed. In temperate climates, flowering and fruiting are rare under cover, due to the trees' daylength and light intensity demands.

Pruning and training
Avocado trees need little pruning beyond shaping the tree during its early growth to ensure that an evenly spaced, rounded canopy develops. Once the tree is established, remove any diseased, damaged, or crossing branches after fruiting.

Harvesting and storing
Seed-raised trees start to bear fruit when they are between five and seven years old; budded or grafted plants are productive at three to five years after planting. The fruits may remain on the tree for up to 18 months without maturing, but they usually ripen rapidly after harvesting.

Cut the fruits from the tree using secateurs. Handle them carefully to avoid bruising. Store them at temperatures above 10°C (48°F) and at 60 per cent humidity. Any damaged fruits should be discarded.

Propagation
Avocado trees are easily grown from seed and reproduce virtually true to type. Select healthy, undamaged seeds and soak them in hot water for 30 minutes at 40–52°C (106–30°F) to inhibit infection from avocado root

RIPE AVOCADOS

rot. Cut a thin slice from the pointed end, then dip the wound in a fungicide. Sow the seed in sandy compost with the cut end slightly above the soil surface; germination usually takes about four weeks. The seedlings may be grown on in containers until they are about 30–40cm (12–16in) tall. They should then be ready for transferring to their final positions.

To propagate named cultivars onto disease-resistant rootstocks, side-wedge grafting (see PRINCIPLES OF PROPAGATION, p.542) or saddle grafting (see ORNAMENTAL SHRUBS, p.90) may be used.

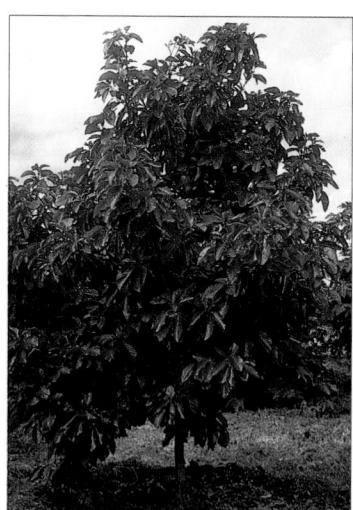
AVOCADO TREE

also be suitable, if the drainage is good, or has been improved (see also "Preparing the site", p.364).

If grafted plants are to be used, those on rootstocks that are known to be both vigorous and resistant to avocado root rot (*Phytophthora cinnamoni*) are preferable. Avocados may be self-pollinated, but the best crops are produced if at least two cultivars are planted near to each other. Choose cultivars whose flowering periods coincide or overlap. When planting, allow 6m (20ft) each way between the trees.

Routine care
Apply a general-purpose fertilizer with a medium potassium and nitrogen content, when the trees are in active growth. The recommended rate is 1.5–2kg (3lb 4oz–4lb 6oz) per tree every year, preferably in two or three doses. Use an organic mulch around the base of each tree, leaving 25cm (10in) clear around the stems.

Water avocado trees during dry periods, particularly during the first three years when they are becoming established. Keep the area around the base of the trees free from all

GROWING AVOCADOS FROM SEED

1 Soak the seed in hot water and then prepare it by cutting about 1cm (1/2in) off the pointed end with a sharp knife. Dip the wound in fungicide.

2 Place the seed in a 15cm (6in) pot of moist seed compost so that the cut top of the seed is just above the soil surface.

3 Several weeks later the seed will have germinated to produce a shoot and roots.

Guavas (*Psidium guajava*)

Guava trees grow to a height of up to about 8m (25ft) and have a spread of 7m (22ft). They are widely grown in both tropical and subtropical regions and thrive in temperatures ranging from 22–8°C (72–82°F). The preferred humidity level is 70 per cent or less: a higher level may affect the quality of the fruits produced.

Guava fruits are 5–10cm (2–4in) in diameter, with either white or pink flesh. The flowers are normally pollinated by insects.

Site and planting
A sheltered site is preferable, protected by windbreaks if necessary. Guavas tolerate a wide range of soils, but a well-drained loam is ideal. The pH may range from 4.8 to 8, but a pH of approximately 6 is most desirable.

When planting, allow a spacing of 5m (15ft) in each direction between the trees. The young trees should be securely staked in areas that are exposed to strong winds.

Routine care
Guavas respond well to applications of a general-purpose fertilizer with a medium potassium and nitrogen content. Use this at a rate of 1–2kg (2lb 3oz–4lb 6oz) of fertilizer for each tree per year, divided into two or three top-dressings during the growing season. Weed the area around the bases of the trees, keep them well watered, and apply a mulch of organic matter, which helps to retain soil moisture.

GUAVAS

GUAVA TREE

Pests and diseases
Pests are rarely a serious problem, but in the open, aphids (p.550), fruit flies (see p.563), and scale insects (p.552) may require control. Plants under cover may also be infested by whiteflies (p.550), and thrips (p.551). Guava seedlings are sensitive to damping off (p.508).

Growing under cover
Guavas may be grown in either well-prepared beds or large containers at least 30–35cm (12–14in) in diameter, using a fairly rich, proprietary compost to which a slow-release fertilizer has been added. Maintain a minimum temperature of 22°C (72°F) with humidity of 70 per cent. Water plants regularly, and apply a liquid feed every three to four weeks. To improve the chances of fruiting, cross-pollination by hand may be necessary. A relatively dry atmosphere should be maintained during the flowering period.

Pruning and training
When the young trees are about 1m (3ft) tall, cut back the leading shoot by about two-thirds, to encourage branching. Subsequent pruning can be limited to the removal of any dead, crossing, or diseased branches, and any low branches that droop down and touch the soil.

Harvesting and storing
Guavas cultivated in the open generally fruit after one to three years, depending on cultivar and environmental conditions. The fruits ripen about five months after fertilization and may be picked when they begin to turn yellow. Handle them carefully, since they bruise easily. They may be stored for up to three or four weeks at a temperature of 7–10°C (45–50°F), with relative humidity of 75 per cent.

Propagation
Guavas are usually propagated from seed; for the increase of specific cultivars, air layering, cuttings, or bud-grafting may be used.

Sow seed in a fertile, sterile compost in trays or 6cm (3in) containers; germination normally occurs in two to three weeks. The seedlings may vary in quality: pot the strongest ones on into 15cm (6in) pots when they are 20cm (8in) tall. Harden the young plants off and transplant them when they are 30cm (12in) tall.

Selected guava cultivars may be chip-budded (see p.372) onto vigorous seedling guava rootstocks, the stems of which should have a diameter of at least 5mm (^{1}/4in). No specific rootstocks are recommended; select only strong, healthy plants, preferably self-pollinated, as parents for rootstock seeds.

Guavas may also be increased by softwood cuttings 12–16cm (5–6in) long (see p.538). Plants produced by these buddings or cuttings may be planted out when they are about 30cm (12in) tall. In the open, guavas may be increased by simple layering (see ORNAMENTAL TREES, p.57) or by air layering (see THE INDOOR GARDEN, p.456). With the latter, hormone rooting powder applied to the girdled sections increases the success rate.

RECOMMENDED GUAVAS

'Beaumont' (pink flesh)
'Malherbe' (pink flesh)
'Miami White' (white flesh)
'Parker's White'
  (white flesh)

'Parker's White'

'Patillo' (pink flesh)
'Patnagola' (white flesh)
'Pink Acid' (pink flesh)
'Red Indian' (pink flesh)
'Ruby' (pink flesh)
'Supreme' (white flesh)

Pomegranates (*Punica granatum*)

Pomegranates form small, ornamental trees or bushes 2–3m (6–10ft) tall with a spread of 1–1.5m (3–5ft). They are evergreen in the subtropics but deciduous in cooler climates. The globular fruits are up to 10cm (4in) in diameter with leathery, yellow or red skins. The optimum temperature range is 18–25°C (64–77°F), but temperatures just below freezing are tolerated for short periods. Dry weather and a high temperature, ideally 35°C (96°F), are required for fruiting. In temperate climates, therefore, pomegranates are usually grown for their orange-red summer flowers and autumn colour; a dwarf variant of the species, *Punica granatum* var. *nana*, fruits freely under cover in temperate areas.

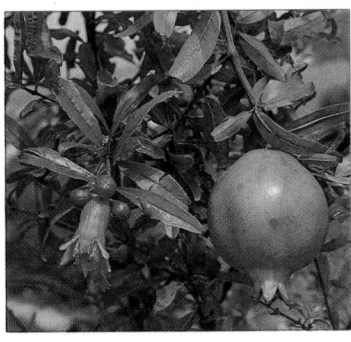

POMEGRANATE FLOWER AND FRUIT

Site and planting
Select a sunny aspect, sheltered by windbreaks in exposed conditions. Heavy loam soils with a pH level of about 7 are generally suitable, if they are well drained. Most cultivars are self-fertile. Plant seedlings, rooted cuttings, or suckers 4–6m (12–20ft) apart each way.

Routine care
Once plants are established, apply a general-purpose fertilizer every two to three months at a rate of 110g (4oz) for each tree per year. Mulch the site and keep it free of weeds; water the trees regularly during dry weather. Cut out all suckers.

Pests and diseases
Pomegranates grown in the open are generally trouble-free; under cover, they may be affected by whiteflies (p.550), aphids (p.550), red spider mites (p.550), and thrips (p.551).

Growing under cover
Plant pomegranates in well-prepared beds or containers with a minimum diameter of 35cm (14in), using a fertile compost with slow-release fertilizer added. Maintain a temperature range of 18–25°C (64–77°F) and humidity of 60–70 per cent. Apply a liquid fertilizer every three to four weeks, and water the plants regularly. Plants in containers may be moved into the open in summer.

Pruning and training
Select three or four main branches to form a framework and remove any crowded, crossing, or diseased branches. Cut out any suckers not required for propagation.

Harvesting and storing
Fruiting should start about two to three years after planting. Harvest the pomegranates when they turn yellow or red; they may then be stored for several weeks at 4–6°C (39–43°F).

Propagation
Pomegranates are usually propagated from cuttings or root suckers. Insert hardwood cuttings (see p.374) in sandy compost, and give bottom heat until they have rooted. Softwood cuttings (see *Blueberry Softwood Cuttings*, p.418) require bottom heat and mist (use compost with neutral pH). Pot on both types into 10–15cm (4–6in) pots when they have rooted. Root suckers may be carefully separated from the parent plant and re-planted. Alternatively, dry off the seed; sow it in pots or trays of seed compost, maintaining a temperature of 22°C (72°F).

POMEGRANATE TREE

POMEGRANATES

Nuts

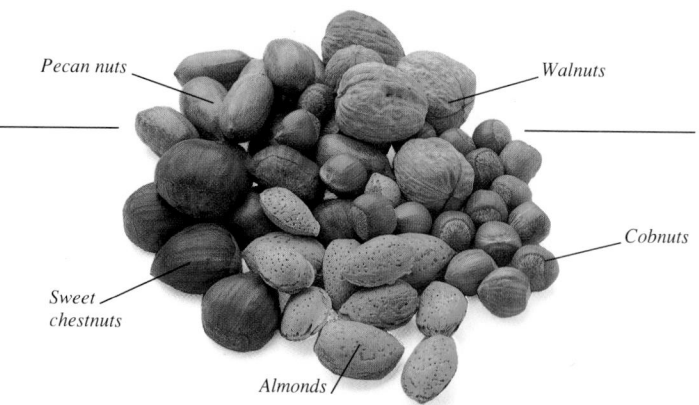

Pecan nuts

Walnuts

Cobnuts

Sweet chestnuts

Almonds

SEVERAL nut-bearing trees and bushes are suitable for gardens; they prefer a sunny, open situation. Some, such as sweet chestnuts, walnuts, and pecans, eventually form large trees and make handsome specimens. In small gardens, an almond tree may make a fine feature, although it may produce nuts only in warm climates. Cobnuts and filberts may be pruned as compact bushes in a fruit garden or planted in informal groups in a wild garden. Most nuts (but not almonds) are monoecious, having separate male and female flowers on the same plant.

Pecan nuts (*Carya illinoensis*)

Pecans are deciduous trees that may grow to 30m (100ft) high with a spread of 15–20m (50–70ft), so they are suitable only for large gardens. They grow best in warm-temperate climates: temperatures over 38°C (100°F) may lead to bark damage and the production of low-quality nuts; flowers may be damaged if the temperature drops below 1°C (34°F). Pecans have a chilling requirement of 150–250 hours below 7°C (45°F) in order for flowering to occur.

Pecans are monoecious but the male flowers are often open before the females on the same tree, so it is best to grow two or more cultivars near to each other to ensure that fertilization takes place. Since pecans are wind-pollinated, heavy rainfall when the trees are flowering may adversely affect pollination; after such conditions, crops may be poor. The nuts are ovoid, 2–2.5cm (³/₄–1in) long, and have a relatively thin shell.

Site and planting
Choose selected cultivars that have been grafted onto pecan seedling stock as trees raised from seed may not produce fruit of good quality. Pecans quickly develop a long tap root, so plant young trees: older, pot-grown plants with congested roots are seldom successful. Pecans need a site that is sheltered from strong winds and thrive on deep, fertile soils with a pH of 6–6.5.

Plant the trees when they are dormant (see *Planting a Fruit Tree*, p.365), spacing them 8m (25ft) apart.

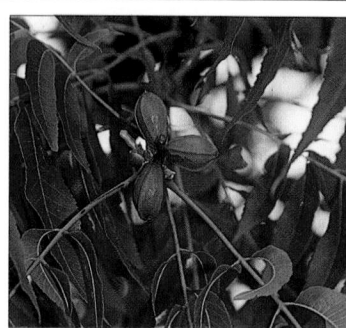

PECANS

Routine care
Apply a top-dressing of a balanced fertilizer at a rate of 70–140g/sq m (2–4oz/sq yd) annually. Keep the planting site weed-free, and water the trees during dry periods until they are established. Pecans are moderately resistant to drought but require plenty of water during the summer months.

Pecan trees are seldom affected by pests and diseases; *Phytophthora* root rots (p.565) and aphids (p.550) may sometimes be a problem.

Pruning and training
Train pecans with a central leader initially (see "Central-leader standard trees", p.48). Once the trees are established, pruning is restricted to removing crossing and congested branches and any dead wood.

Harvesting and storing
The first crop may be produced after five years; full production is reached after 15–20 years. The nuts are usually harvested by hand. They may be stored, in cool, dry, airy conditions, for several months.

Propagation
Whip-and-tongue grafting of selected cultivars onto vigorous pecan seedling rootstocks is the most usual method of propagation (see p.373). The seedlings to be used as stock plants should be raised in deep pots or plastic sleeves, since their long tap roots are sensitive to damage during transplanting.

RECOMMENDED
PECANS

'Desirable'
'Elisabeth'
'Elliot'
'Mohawk'
'Moore'
'Moreland'
'P 22'
'P 24'
'P 176'

Sweet chestnuts (*Castanea sativa*)

Sweet or Spanish chestnuts are deciduous, summer-flowering trees up to 30m (100ft) tall with a spread of 15m (50ft). They are monoecious and wind-pollinated. Some cultivars may need a pollinator. The shiny, rich brown nuts are borne most consistently in areas with cold winters and warm summers. Two or three kernels are usual, but in some cultivars, such as 'Marron de Lyon' and 'Paragon', a single kernel is formed.

Site, planting, and routine care
A fertile, moisture-retentive soil with a pH of 6 is preferred; allow 10–12m (30–40ft) between trees (see *Planting a Fruit Tree*, p.365). Water young trees and keep the site weed-free. On well-prepared sites, applications of fertilizer are unnecessary. Trees may be affected by honey fungus (p.569).

Pruning and training
Train as central-leader standards (see p.48). On established trees, remove congested, crossing, or dead branches.

SWEET CHESTNUTS

Harvesting and storing
Nuts are borne after about four years. Harvest them in the autumn. Hull the nuts, soak them for 48 hours, discarding any that darken, then dry and store them in a cool, airy place.

Propagation
Propagate from selected cultivars by bud-grafting or whip-and-tongue grafting onto seedling stock of sweet chestnut (see pp.372 and 373).

Cobnuts and filberts (*Corylus avellana* and *C. maxima*)

Cobnuts (or hazels) and filberts are valued for their winter catkins and their nuts. Unpruned, they reach a height and spread of 4–5m (12–15ft). They are deciduous and monoecious, and crop best in cool, moist summers. The chilling requirement is 800–1,200 hours below 7°C (45°F). Winter temperatures below -10°C (13°F) may damage the male flowers (catkins), although the female flowers are usually less vulnerable. The outer husk or calyx of the cobnut does not completely envelop the nut. The filbert has a husk that is longer than the nut and often completely encloses it; a sub-group of filberts has frilled husks and is known as frizzled filberts. Cobnuts and filberts are wind-pollinated; many are self-fertile. For cobnuts, recommended self-fertile cultivars include

COBNUTS

FILBERTS

'Cosford' and 'Nottingham' (syn. 'Pearson's Prolific'); a recommended self-fertile filbert is 'Kentish Cob'. The nuts of cobnuts and filberts are brown and egg-shaped.

Site and planting
A partially shaded, sheltered position is preferable. A soil pH of 6 is best; very rich soil may cause excessive soft growth at the expense of cropping. Adequate moisture with good drainage is important. Plant in autumn or early winter, 4.5m (15ft) apart (see *Planting a Fruit Tree*, p.365).

Routine care
Weed and mulch regularly; water in dry spells. On poor soils apply a balanced fertilizer in spring at a rate of 105g/sq m (3oz/sq yd). Trees are usually trouble-free, but may be attacked by nut weevils unless sprayed in late spring and again in early summer, with fenitrothion or permethrin.

Pruning and training
Cobnuts and filberts are usually grown as open-centre bushes, each with a 45cm (18in) stem and eight to twelve main branches. On young plants, prune the leaders in winter to 55cm (22in); good laterals should then develop. Remove any shoots growing low down on the main stem and all but the best-placed, strongest shoots needed to develop the framework. Shorten these by a third in winter. The following winter remove any excessively strong, upright growth and, if necessary, tip prune sideshoots to form a well-balanced framework.

Established bushes bear heavier crops if pruned in late summer using

BRUTTING COBNUTS

In the late summer, strong shoots of the current season's growth that are about 30cm (12in) long are broken and left hanging. This helps the formation of flower buds.

a technique known as "brutting". Break the longer sideshoots halfway along their length, and let them hang. This opens up the bush and encourages more female flowers to form. In winter, when the catkins release pollen, shorten the brutted shoots to three or four buds; remove old or overcrowded shoots.

Harvesting and storing
Nuts are borne after three or four years. Gather them when the husks begin to yellow. Dry, then store.

Propagation
Suckers produced from tree roots may be used for propagation. In winter, remove them, each with a root ball, and grow on in a nursery bed or plant directly in their final positions. Trees may also be propagated by simple layering (see p.88) in autumn.

Walnuts (*Juglans regia*)

English walnuts (strictly speaking Persian) are deciduous trees that may reach a height of 18m (60ft) with a similar spread; they are suitable only for large gardens. Named cultivars should always be planted for fruit, since seedlings may produce poor-quality nuts. Walnuts are monoecious and wind-pollinated. Most are self-fertile but some cultivars produce male catkins and pollen before the female flowers are receptive. To overcome this problem, plant nearby a reliable pollinator such as the old French cultivar 'Franquette'. Walnuts have a chilling requirement of 500–1,000 hours below 7°C (45°F). The gnarled nuts develop within a pitted shell.

Site, planting, and routine care
A well-drained, moisture-retentive soil is best. Walnuts prefer a pH of

> ### RECOMMENDED WALNUTS
> **All cultivars listed are self-fertile.**
> 'Broadview'
> 'Buccaneer'
> 'Franquette'
> 'Granjean'
> 'Lara'
> 'Marbot'
> 'Parisienne'

6.5–7 but tolerate some alkalinity. Since flowers and young shoots are susceptible to frost damage, avoid cold sites. Walnuts have a long tap root, so select young plants rather than older, pot-grown ones whose roots may be congested. Plant in late autumn or winter (see *Planting a Fruit Tree*, p.365), with 12–18m (40–60ft) between trees.

Walnuts may be slow to establish, but after two or three years, once the root system is well developed, stronger growth occurs. Bacterial leaf blotch and blight may be a problem (see "Bacterial leaf spots and blotches", p.552).

Pruning and training
Walnuts should be trained as central-leader standards (see p.48). Prune in mid-winter since the trees do not bleed when they are dormant. Remove any strong shoots that make a narrow angle with the stem, to leave a well-balanced framework of evenly spaced branches. Thereafter, little pruning is required apart from cutting out overcrowded, crossing, or congested branches in winter and removing dead wood as required.

Harvesting and storing
Walnut trees may need many years before they start bearing. Walnuts for pickling should be picked in summer before the hulls and shells harden. In early autumn, the hull or casing cracks to release the nut, still in its shell.

Almonds (*Prunus dulcis*)

Unpruned, sweet almonds grow about 5–6m (15–20ft) tall, with a similar spread. They crop regularly only in areas with warm, dry summers and frost-free winters. The chilling requirement is 300–500 hours below 7°C (45°F). In cool areas they are often grown as ornamentals. Almonds are insect-pollinated. Most cultivars are partly self-fertile, but crops will be better if a pollinator is planted nearby. The nuts are flattened and pointed, with a pitted shell.

Site, planting, and routine care
Almonds require a sheltered, frost-free site and a well-drained soil, preferably with a pH of 6.5. Plant them 6–7m (20–22ft) apart (see *Planting a Fruit Tree*, p.365).

Cultivation of almonds is as for peaches (see p.391). Peach leaf curl (p.555) and bacterial canker (p.569) may affect almond trees.

Pruning and training
Almonds are usually pruned and trained as bushes, as for peaches (see p.392). Nuts are borne on one-year-old wood. In summer, on established trees, remove a quarter of the old shoots that have cropped in previous seasons to encourage fresh growth.

Harvesting and storing
The nuts are borne after three to four years. Gather them as their hulls

WALNUTS

Gather the crop before the shells become discoloured. Clean, then gently dry the nuts. Store them in cool, airy, slightly humid conditions.

Propagation
The usual methods are whip-and-tongue grafting (see p.373) or chip-budding (see p.372) cultivars onto seedlings of the American black walnut (*Juglans nigra*). In cool climates keep a grafted tree under glass until the graft has taken, then move the container to a protected site in the open. Plant young trees in their final positions in autumn or winter.

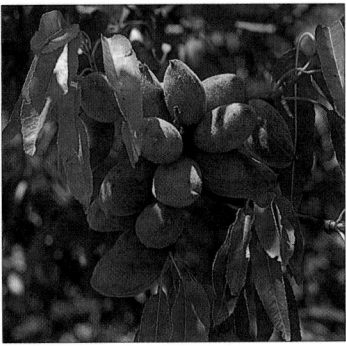

ALMONDS

start to crack. Clean and dry the almonds before storing them.

Propagation
Almonds are usually propagated by chip-budding (see p.372). Rootstocks vary according to soil type: almond seedlings are often used for dry regions while peach seedlings are more suitable for heavier soils.

> ### RECOMMENDED ALMONDS
> 'Ayles' **Sf**
> 'Ferraduel' **Psf**
> 'Ferragnes' **Psf**
> 'Guara' **Sf**
> 'Steliette' **Sf**
>
> **KEY**
> **Sf** *Self-fertile*
> **Psf** *Partly self-fertile*

16

THE INDOOR GARDEN

THE GARDEN MAY *be enjoyed in comfort despite the vagaries of the seasons by bringing it indoors or under cover – into the house, a garden room, or a greenhouse. Flowering pot plants may be grouped together in a wicker basket for an ornamental, table-top display, a sunny windowsill may become a garden in miniature, and a lush, small-scale jungle may be created in a conservatory. The palette of leaf and flower colours, forms, and textures is as rich as that of outdoor plants. Equally, the approach may vary, from using plants as interior design accessories that are bought at the height of their perfection, displayed, enjoyed, and then discarded, to growing collections of rare plants that demand long-term enthusiasm and attention to detail. In regions subject to frost, the evergreen foliage and exotic blooms of tropical or subtropical plants that would not survive in the open garden thrive in their protected environment, to brighten even the dullest of days with an ever-changing, living decor of foliage and flower.*

Displaying plants indoors

THE range of plants that may be grown in the home and the greenhouse offers a wealth of form, colour, and texture. Plants may be chosen for their handsome foliage, or the beauty of their blooms, from the exuberant hues of *Bougainvillea* to the cool elegance of *Zantedeschia aethiopica*. Others, such as *Solanum capsicastrum*, are valued for their brightly coloured fruits.

The choice of plants depends on whether the display is to be permanent, when plants with interesting form and foliage are the best choice for a year-round display, or temporary, when the seasonal interest of plants such as *Cyclamen persicum* may be used to give spots of colour.

Plants may reinforce or contrast with the style of the indoor setting, whether it is a rustic cottage kitchen or a formal and sophisticated urban living room. The plants may dominate the scene and give a room its essential character, create pockets of interest, or simply add to the detail. Whatever effect is desired, select plants that will both thrive in and enhance their intended position.

Foliage and form

Plants that have attractive foliage are invaluable for long-term indoor display. They may have huge leaves, as does *Fatsia japonica*, or a mass of dainty ones, such as those of *Soleirolia soleirolii*, syn. *Helxine soleirolii*. Leaves may have subtle or striking patterns and colours, as do *Calathea* species, or interesting shapes, for example the Swiss-cheese plant (*Monstera deliciosa*).

Foliage also has different textures, from the high gloss of the rubber plant (*Ficus elastica*) to the corrugated surfaces of *Pilea involucrata*, and the soft velvet of *Gynura aurantiaca*. Some plants are chosen for their strong forms, whether they are spiky bromeliads, graceful palms and ferns, or pebble-like *Lithops*.

Grouping plants

When planning an arrangement, choose plants with strongly coloured flowers or patterned leaves carefully so that they do not detract from each other. Experiment with contrasts by placing plants together in shops, nurseries, and garden centres before making a purchase.

Architectural plants such as palms make very fine specimen plants or striking focal points in a group. Smaller plants have impact when arranged together on a tiered stand, but may be used singly as a dainty finishing touch. A tight group of identical plants, for example a bowl of white hyacinths, makes a strong yet simple statement.

A GARDEN ROOM
Yellow Abutilon, *blue* Agapanthus, *purple and white* Streptocarpus, *and lush foliage create a garden-like setting in which to relax.*

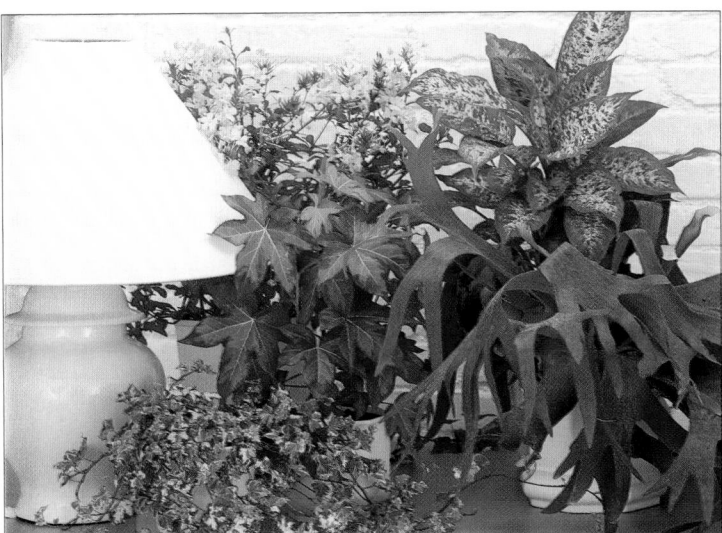

A CONTRAST OF STRONG SHAPES
Variegated ivy (Hedera), Dieffenbachia, Fatsia japonica, *and the sculptural fronds of* Platycerium bifurcatum *complement the pale blue* Plumbago.

The indoor environment

The specific temperature and light requirements of plants are the most important factors in deciding where to position them indoors (see "Planter's guide to indoor plants", p.435). If the conditions are incompatible with the plants' needs, they will soon become stressed and unhealthy. Newly purchased plants that have just come from controlled conditions are especially vulnerable.

Temperature

Although most modern houses are kept warm during the day in winter, the temperature is often allowed to drop markedly at night – a problem for many house plants of tropical origin. Place these plants where they are protected from draughts and are not subject to wide fluctuations in temperature. Do not leave tender plants on windowsills at night, especially if the drawn curtains close off residual warmth from the room, or place plants directly above radiators or heaters that are in use. To flower, indoor plants need warmth, but if the temperature is too high for the individual species the blooms quickly fade and die.

Light

Most plants thrive in bright, filtered sunlight or in a well-lit position that is not in direct sun. Plants that have variegated leaves need more light than those with plain, green leaves, but over-strong sunlight will damage the foliage. Flowering plants such as *Hippeastrum* need good light if they are to flower well, but excessive light can shorten the life of the blooms. Indeed, few indoor plants can tolerate direct sunlight.

Insufficient light results in plants with pale, stunted, new leaves, and drawn-out, or etiolated, growth with long, thin, weak stems. Some variegated plants may begin to produce plain leaves. In time, the mature leaves will turn yellow and fall. A plant thus weakened is especially vulnerable to pests and diseases.

The amount of natural light in a room depends on the number, size, height, and aspect of the windows. Light levels fall quickly as the distance from the window increases. In winter, there is far less natural light than in summer, and some plants may need to be moved in response to the seasonal light variation – a plant trolley is ideal for this purpose.

If plants start to grow lopsidedly towards a source of light, turn them slightly when watering them. If light levels are too low for healthy growth (most plants need 12–14 hours of daylight per day) supplementary "grow-lights" are effective.

Positioning the plants

With a little forethought and planning, it is possible to find a handsome house plant that flourishes in almost every site indoors, from a brilliantly lit room to a dim passage or alcove.

The indoor setting

Give careful consideration to the impact of plants within a room. Are they in proportion to the room? A tiny pot plant is lost in a large space. Is the background suitable? Plain, pale walls show flowering plants to advantage. Does the flower or foliage colour blend with the decor?

High-level hanging baskets and shelves suit trailing plants, while eye-level positions are best for plants with delicate flowers or foliage. Train climbing plants, such as *Cissus antarctica*, *Philodendron scandens*, and ivy (*Hedera*), on a trellis or freestanding support to create a screen.

Use plants to enliven empty corners or space, such as an unused fireplace which provides an instant frame for a display. Large plants or groups may play an architectural role as room dividers or as a link between the house and the garden.

Plants for various light levels

Bright, sunny conditions suit succulent plants as well as plants with woolly, waxy, or grey leaves. *Hoya carnosa*, pelargoniums, and *Ananas comosus* 'Variegatus' will also appreciate direct sunlight. In positions with indirect or filtered light, grow foliage begonias such as *Begonia rex*, epiphytic orchids such as *Phalaenopsis*, and *Spathiphyllum* with their striking, white spathes.

For corners that are remote from a window, choose ferns and tough-leaved plants such as *Chamaedorea*, *Fatsia japonica*, and ivy. Expose the plants to slightly brighter light occasionally, if only for a few days.

Kitchens and bathrooms

Temperatures and humidity in kitchens and bathrooms, especially small ones, can fluctuate, so choose plants that can tolerate extremes. Smooth, hard bathroom surfaces contrast well with the soft, feathery forms of ferns and grasses, and some *Cyperus* species. Bathrooms often have low levels of light, ideal for *Episcia*, *Nephrolepis*, or *Pilea*. Fill high-level bathroom space with trailing plants such as *Philodendron scandens*. Do not put trailing plants on top of kitchen cabinets since they may interfere with the cupboard doors. In brightly lit positions, use hanging baskets to grow a selection of herbs or tiny tomato cultivars, such as 'Tumbler', an F1 hybrid. Herbs are also ideal for growing on a sunny kitchen windowsill.

Tolerant plants

Attractive foliage plants that are tolerant of a wide range of conditions include *Aspidistra*, *Chlorophytum*, *Cissus antarctica*, and *Sansevieria*. Flowering plants are more exacting, but potted chrysanthemums (see pp.152–4) or forced bulbs (see p.223) may give short-term floral colour.

Containers

Choose a container whose material, colour, and shape blends with the decor and shows the individual plant

HAZARDS OF A WINDOWSILL

Too much sunlight, excessive heat from radiators, and draughts through the frame can weaken or kill house plants that are placed on a windowsill.

VARIATION OF LIGHT LEVELS WITHIN A ROOM

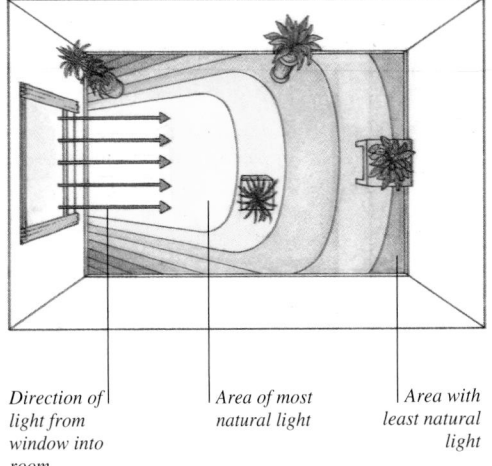

Direction of light from window into room

Area of most natural light

Area with least natural light

The farther away from a window a plant is sited, the less natural light it will receive. If the plant is 2m (6ft) away, the light level may be as little as 20 per cent of that by the window. Plants that are placed close to a window but to one side of it derive little benefit from the position, especially if the windowsills are very deep.

A HANGING GARDEN
This temporary planting creates an instantly attractive, high-level feature.

Stephanotis floribunda

Ficus 'Starlight'

Coleus blumei

Gardenia jasminoides

Parthenocissus quinquefolia

or group to its best advantage. The choice is vast, both in style and materials, allowing a range of effects from rustic to ultra modern. Some plastic containers are available with an integral reservoir, which reduces the need for watering; other types are specially manufactured for hydroculture (see *Cross-section of a Hydroculture Pot*, p.449). The most unlikely household objects, such as birdcages, coal scuttles, cooking utensils, kettles, and urns, can make unusual and striking plant holders.

Hanging baskets

Hanging baskets are a popular feature on porches, balconies, patios, and terraces, but may also be an attractive way of growing indoor plants. Hang them in stairwells, from rafters, by windows, or from free-standing supports for an economical and colourful use of space. A group of baskets suspended at varying heights makes a fine display.

Arching fern fronds, the rosettes of epiphytes, and cascading habit of many foliage plants lend themselves perfectly to hanging baskets. Vary the planting during the year to take advantage of seasonal displays. In a winter arrangement, Christmas cactus (*Schlumbergera bridgesii*) provides a mass of bright colour as do fuchsias in summer. Temporary arrangements may be created by planting up a basket with pot plants, but they will need replanting each year. Permanently planted baskets are easier to manage, especially if devoted to a single, large plant.

Choosing a hanging container

Hanging baskets are available in various materials and designs. When choosing and positioning them, take into account the fact that most plants require frequent watering. Plastic-coated wire hanging baskets are practical indoors only in rooms that have water-resistant floors; some rigid, plastic baskets have drip saucers which are a practical solution. Also available are attractive, although heavy, pottery and terracotta hanging pots, and wooden, wrought iron, or wicker baskets.

A planted basket is heavy, especially when just watered, so it must be supported by strong rope or chain from a hook or bracket fixed securely to a ceiling joist or a solid wall.

Terrariums and bottle gardens

Terrariums are enclosed glass containers, often decorative in their own right, used to display small plants in the home. They were popular in the 19th century as a way of providing a suitable microclimate for ferns, but any slow-growing ornamental plants that need a humid atmosphere thrive in a terrarium. A selection of plants with contrasting leaf textures and colours is the most effective – avoid flowering plants because the dead blooms rot in the moist conditions. Terrariums may be built permanently into a window to house a lush arrangement of larger plants.

Bottles may also be used to create a diminutive landscape of foliage plants. As long as the neck is sufficiently wide to allow the insertion of the plants and routine aftercare, any shape or colour of bottle may be used, but bear in mind that tinted glass cuts out some of the light.

Indoor lighting

A display may be enhanced by ordinary floodlights or spotlights, or given dramatic contrasts of light and shade with uplighting or downlighting. Do not place plants too close to the light source since the heat may damage them. Ordinary, incandescent bulbs do not significantly improve food production (photosynthesis) or growth.

Plants for the office

Introducing plants into an office not only brightens it visually, but may help to deaden noise, refresh the air,

and create a less stressful ambience. In a modern, open-plan office that is air-conditioned and fully glazed, temperatures are constant, air pollution is minimized, and space and light are plentiful – almost ideal growing conditions. Older buildings with smaller windows and little climatic control present more challenging conditions.

Use self-watering containers, especially if the plants are sited near electrical equipment, or plunge several plants into a large container. Unless maintenance contractors are employed, ensure that responsibility for care is clearly assigned.

Suitable plants

Evergreen, shiny-leaved plants are as tough and tolerant in an office as they are in the home. The popular genus *Ficus* includes plants of every shape and size, from the lustrous, huge-leaved *F. lyrata* (stand it in solitary splendour in a large space) to the small-leaved, creeping, leathery leaved *F. deltoidea*.

Another large and impressive genus with handsome leaves is *Philodendron*, which includes climbers and trailers. The tenacious, long-lived Swiss-cheese plant (*Monstera deliciosa*) climbs slowly but will eventually reach several metres in height and spread.

Garden rooms and conservatories

The garden may be brought indoors, either into a garden room, which is a living space furnished with container plants, or into a conservatory, which is devoted principally to planting. In temperate climates, both may be used to give winter shelter to container-grown plants that spend the summer months outdoors; a conservatory may also provide the warm, humid environment needed by tropical and subtropical plants.

The high light levels usually found in conservatories encourage coloured leaves to assume intense hues, and plants to flower well. Scented flowering plants, for example *Jasminum polyanthum,* are especially welcome in a confined space, where fragrance lingers in the air.

Select plants that suit the conservatory's aspect and temperature, bearing in mind that glass structures can be costly to heat in winter and very hot in summer.

Create a lush profusion of planting by taking full advantage of all the available space: grow plants at different levels in raised and ground-level soil beds, in pots on the floor, on windowsills and shelves, and

SEASONAL COLOUR
In this room, a white poinsettia (Euphorbia pulcherrima)*, carmine azalea* (Rhododendron)*, and Calamondin orange* (x Citrofortunella microcarpa) *add winter interest to a permanent framework of evergreen foliage plants.*

COOL CONSERVATORY

The foliage and flowering plants shown here are among the many that thrive in the cool, but frost-free, conditions of a lean-to conservatory to create a fine display.

1 *Plumbago auriculata* (syn. *P. capensis*)
2 *Chlorophytum comosum* (syn. *C. capense* of gardens)
3 *Campanula isophylla*
4 *Saxifraga stolonifera* 'Tricolor' (syn. *S. sarmentosa*)
5 *Pelargonium* 'Mini Cascade'
6 *Camellia japonica*
7 *Sedum morganianum*
8 *Streptocarpus* 'Heidi'
9 *Ceropegia woodii*
10 *Callistemon citrinus* 'Splendens'
11 *Correa pulchella*
12 *Calceolaria* 'Sunshine'
13 *Nierembergia hippomanica* var. *violacea* 'Purple Robe'
14 *Prostanthera rotundifolia*
15 *Polygala myrtifolia* 'Grandiflora'
16 *Rehmannia elata*
17 x *Citrofortunella microcarpa* (syn. *Citrus mitis*)

MULTI-LEVEL DISPLAY
Staging, shelves, and floor space are used to maximum advantage in this cool greenhouse. Busy lizzie (Impatiens cvs), Plumbago, and Streptocarpus flowers are complemented by a variety of foliage plants, including ivy (Hedera), scented-leaved pelargoniums, Hypoestes, Pellaea, and Tolmiea.

hanging baskets. Large tropical or subtropical plants and climbers that are free-standing are useful for training on trellis or wires affixed to the walls; grape vines will grow over and clothe the wall and roof. Use plants in the conservatory that complement those in the open garden; this will create a visual link between the two as well as a sense of space.

Indoor water features
A sunken or raised pool or a half-barrel may accommodate tropical water lilies or other tender aquatic and marginal plants. A simple and elegant water spout will provide the restful murmur of falling water and help to maintain humidity (see also THE WATER GARDEN, pp.244–61).

Growing plants in a greenhouse

The control of light, temperature, and humidity in a greenhouse will allow a much wider range of plants to be grown than in a garden that is subject to frost. It also extends the season of display and cropping from early spring until late autumn, or even all year round if desired.

Uses of a greenhouse
A greenhouse is very useful in cool temperate climates, where there is frost, strong winds, or excessive rain: it may be used for propagation; raising and growing tender plants or flowers for cutting; or for crops such

as salads, early vegetables, and even fruit. Many plants grow faster under cover and fruit or flower more profusely than they would outdoors. Half-hardy plants may be grown in containers outdoors and transferred to temporary shelter in the greenhouse when needed.

The greenhouse may hold a specialized collection of plants, such as alpines (see pp.214–16), cacti (see pp.262–75), ferns (see pp.158–9), and orchids (see pp.442–5). Alternatively, a mixed collection of foliage and flowering plants that enjoy similar conditions may provide a display throughout the year.

The greenhouse layout
The traditional, free-standing greenhouse interior comprises a central path with waist-high staging at the sides and far end; wider greenhouses may also have staging in the centre. Staging (see also p.487) is essential; even if removed in summer for border crops, it may be used at other times of the year for raising seedlings, propagating cuttings, and displaying pot plants. Slatted or meshed staging is used for pot plants, to avoid pools of standing water and ensure that air circulates freely, particularly in winter.

For extra display space, use tiered staging, bench beds, or soil borders. If the glass begins at ground level, ferns and other shade-loving plants, and dormant plants, may be grown or rested under the staging. Raised beds are useful for displaying small

plants, such as alpines and cacti, that are planted directly in the beds or in pots plunged into gravel or sand.

The ornamental greenhouse
Although a greenhouse is often more practical in use than a conservatory, part or all of it may be devoted to ornamental displays. Groups are usually more attractive than widely spaced plants. Feature a single genus, for example *Streptocarpus*, or mixed plants and display them in a random pattern or as a landscape in miniature. Try to include contrasts of leaf form, size, and texture and control the use of colour, whether from flowers or foliage, to create a harmonious arrangement.

A lean-to greenhouse against a house wall may double as a conservatory. Make the most of the back wall by growing climbers, which need only a 30cm (12in) wide bed or pot. Paint the wall white to help to reflect light and provide a contrasting background for the plants.

The greenhouse environment

Essential requirements for success are adequate ventilation and heat, as well as shading in summer; piped water and electricity are also useful.

The temperature range of a greenhouse depends on its purpose, but there are four basic types of greenhouse: cold or unheated, cool or

AN INTERIOR GARDEN
Where space allows, a naturalistic landscape may be created within a greenhouse. Here, foliage plants, including Cordyline, Eucomis, Justicia, *and* Phormium, *provide a lush framework that is offset by the colourful blooms of flowering plants such as blue* Agapanthus, *pink fuchsias, and white and salmon pelargoniums.*

frost-free, temperate, and warm. For further information, see GREENHOUSES AND FRAMES, "Creating the right environment", pp.481–5; see also "Planter's guide to indoor plants", p.435.

The cold greenhouse

An unheated greenhouse protects against any extremes of wind and rain and is significantly warmer, even in summer, than outdoors. It extends the growing season by providing the plants with an artificially early spring and late autumn.

Most hardy annuals, biennials, and shrubs may be overwintered in an unheated greenhouse, and half-hardy annuals, bulbous plants, and shrubs grown on to plant out in summer when the garden soil has warmed up and danger of frost is past. A cold greenhouse is also useful for raising seed and enabling an early start to be made with fruit or vegetables. As an alpine house it may be used to provide the specialized conditions needed for growing alpines and rock plants in pots (see ALPINE HOUSES AND FRAMES, pp.214–16).

An unheated greenhouse does not exclude frost for more than an hour or two, so it is not suitable for overwintering plants that are not frost hardy. Sunlight, or even bright light, raises the temperature during the day, but night temperatures can drop almost as low as those in the open garden. In temperate climates, most greenhouses built against a warm house wall give conditions similar to those in a cool greenhouse (see below), but this will not prevent tender plants from being killed by a few days of really sharp frosts.

The cool greenhouse

Freedom from frost increases the range of plants that may be grown. A frost-free greenhouse is also easier to manage, since protective measures become unnecessary. Daytime temperatures of 5–10°C (41–50°F) and a minimum at night of 2°C (36°F) allow ornamentals to be enjoyed throughout the year.

In a cool greenhouse, hardy bulbous plants, particularly those with delicate blooms that are not noticed in an open garden, flower earlier, providing colour in late winter and early spring. Here tender patio plants may be raised and overwintered; house plants may be revived and propagated in warmer months; and winter-flowering plants such as the aromatic *Prostanthera* may be grown in bench beds or in pots. Grown under cover, chrysanthemums and perpetual-flowering carnations (*Dianthus*) provide a good supply of cut flowers, while hardy annuals raised from seed sown in late summer sowings give early flowers.

The cool greenhouse requires heating capable of excluding frost and maintaining a minimum temperature in all weathers (see GREENHOUSES AND FRAMES, "Heating", p.482). Even if the entire greenhouse is not heated, an electrically heated propagator, or a propagating bench, will enable an early start to be made on raising new plants in the spring.

AN ORNAMENTAL COLLECTION
A warm greenhouse may be devoted to displaying a collection of plants from a particular group such as orchids or cacti. Tropical plants such as these forest cacti thrive in the heat and high humidity provided by the greenhouse. A luxuriant show is provided by the richly hued flowers and cool, fleshy foliage of Epiphyllum, Heliocereus, Pfeiffera, *and other forest cacti at the height of their summer glory.*

The temperate greenhouse

Raising the temperature to 10–13°C (50–55°F), with a night-time minimum of 7°C (45°F), widens the scope still further. If kept in a temperate greenhouse, plants associated with the essentially frost-free climates of California, the Mediterranean, South Africa, and parts of Australia and South America may be enjoyed in harsher climates than they could normally bear. These include genera such as *Brunfelsia*, *Jacaranda*, and *Strelitzia*, and orchids such as *Cymbidium* species and hybrids. If zonal pelargoniums are kept at 9°C (48°F) they will flower all the year round.

The warm greenhouse

A minimum temperature of 13°C (55°F) to 18°C (64°F) in a warm greenhouse allows cultivation of subtropical and tropical plants, as well as year-round propagation or flowering displays. Tender plants, for example many bromeliads (see pp.436–7) and a number of orchids (see pp.442–5), may be grown to bring indoors when at their best.

The warm greenhouse needs controllable heating throughout the year, even in summer in cooler climates. This incurs considerable heating costs in temperate zones. Equipment such as thermostats, double glazing, fans, and automatic ventilation, an automated watering and damping-down system, and shading help to control conditions and facilitate routine care. A warm section in a cool greenhouse is a useful, cheaper option; a warm conservatory, or plant room, is another possibility.

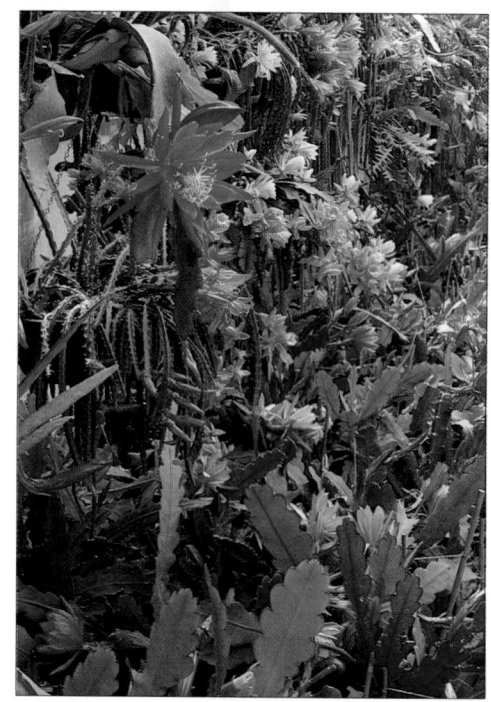

Planter's guide to indoor plants

WARM GREENHOUSE

(Minimum 13–18°C/55–64°F)

Flowering plants
Aeschynanthus ❁ ◉
Anthurium ❁
Aphelandra ❁ ◉
Brunfelsia ❁ ◉
Columnea ❁ ◉
Euphorbia fulgens ❁,
    E. pulcherrima ❁
Hibiscus rosa-sinensis ❁
Hoya bella ❁
Justicia ❁
Kohleria ❁ ◉
Medinilla ❁ ◉
Pachystachys ❁
Ruellia ❁ ◉
Saintpaulia ❁ ◉

Sinningia
'Red
Flicker'

Sinningia ❁ ◉
Smithiantha ❁ ◉
Spathiphyllum ❁ ◉

Foliage plants
Aechmea ❁ ◉ (and most bromeliads)
Aglaonema ❁ ◉
Begonia rex ❁ ◉ (and other spp.)
Calathea ❁ ◉
Chamaedorea ❁ ◉ (and most palms)
Codiaeum ❁ ◉
Dieffenbachia ❁ ◉
Dracaena ❁ ◉
Ficus, some ❁
Fittonia ❁ ◉
Maranta ❁ ◉
Peperomia ❁ ◉
Philodendron ❁ ◉
Tradescantia, some ❁, ◉

TEMPERATE GREENHOUSE

(Daytime 10–13°C/50–55°F; night minimum 7°C/45°F)

Flowering plants
Achimenes ❁
Begonia ❁ ◉
Catharanthus ❁
Cyclamen, some ❁, ◉
Exacum ❁ ◉
Haemanthus ❁
Impatiens, some ❁, ◉

Impatiens,
Novette Series
'Red Star'

Schlumbergera ❁ ◉
Strelitzia ❁
Streptocarpus ❁ ◉

Foliage plants
Asparagus, some ❁
Coleus ❁ ◉
Jacaranda ❁

COOL GREENHOUSE

(Daytime 5–10°C/41–50°F; night minimum 2°C/36°F)

Flowering plants
Abutilon, some ❁
Bougainvillea ❁
Browallia ❁
Calceolaria, some ❁, ◉
Callistemon, some ❁
Cestrum, some ❁
Chrysanthemum, some ❁, ◉
x *Citrofortunella* ❁
Cuphea ❁
Datura, some ❁
Freesia ❁
Fuchsia, some ❁
Gerbera ❁
Hippeastrum, some ❁
Hoya ❁
Jasminum, some ❁
Lachenalia ❁
Lantana ❁
Lapageria ❁
Nerium ❁
Passiflora ❁
Pelargonium ❁
Plumbago, some ❁
Primula, some ❁
Schizanthus ❁
Senecio, some ❁

Senecio articulatus
'Variegatus'

Sprekelia ❁
Streptosolen ❁
Tibouchina ❁ ◉
Veltheimia ❁
Zantedeschia, some ❁
Zephyranthes, some ❁

Foliage plants
Aspidistra ❁
Chlorophytum ❁
Cissus rhombifolia ❁
Rhoicissus ❁
Ricinus ❁

COLD GREENHOUSE

Flowering plants
Agapanthus (hardy spp.)
Anemone
Antirrhinum (hardy spp.)
Camellia (hardy spp.)
Cheiranthus (hardy spp.)
Crocus
Cyclamen (hardy miniature spp.)
Dicentra
Erica
Hyacinthus
Jasminum (hardy spp.)
Narcissus
Rhododendron (hardy azaleas in shady greenhouse)

Foliage plants
Adiantum ◉ (hardy spp.)
Euonymus
Fatsia ◉
Hedera ◉ (hardy spp.)
Laurus nobilis
Phormium
Tolmiea

PLANTS THAT PREFER DIRECT LIGHT INDOORS

Warm room (18°C/64°F and over)
Ananas ❁ ◉
Bougainvillea ❁
Euphorbia pulcherrima ❁
Hibiscus rosa-sinensis ❁
Hippeastrum, some ❁
Justicia ❁
Opuntia, some ❁
Senecio, some ❁
Solanum capsicastrum ❁ ◉

Cool room (5–18°C/40–64°F)
Billbergia ❁
Browallia ❁
Campanula isophylla ❁ ◉
Capsicum ❁ ◉
Chlorophytum ❁
Clivia ❁
Coleus ❁ ◉
Crassula, some ❁
Cyclamen; some ❁, ◉
Cyrtanthus ❁
Echeveria ❁
Gerbera ❁
Hyacinthus
Jasminum, some ❁
Kalanchoe ❁
Nerine, some ❁

Pelargonium
'Caligula'

Pelargonium ❁
Streptocarpus ❁ ◉
Veltheimia ❁

PLANTS THAT PREFER INDIRECT LIGHT INDOORS

Warm room – medium light (18°C/64°F and over)
Adiantum, some ❁, ◉
Aechmea ❁ ◉ (and all bromeliads)
Caladium ❁
Codiaeum ❁ ◉
Cryptanthus ❁ ◉
Dieffenbachia ❁ ◉
Howea ❁
Hypoestes ❁
Kohleria ❁ ◉
Mandevilla ❁ ◉
Maranta ❁ ◉
Neoregelia ❁ ◉
Peperomia ❁ ◉

Pilea ❁ ◉
Saintpaulia ❁ ◉
Sansevieria ❁
Schefflera ❁
Sinningia ❁ ◉
Spathiphyllum ❁ ◉
Stephanotis ❁ ◉
Streptocarpus ❁ ◉
Syngonium ◉
Thunbergia ❁
Tradescantia, some ❁, ◉

Pilea cadierei

Warm room – poor light (18°C/64°F and over)
Asplenium, some ❁
Calathea ❁ ◉
Chamaedorea ❁ ◉
Cissus ❁
Dracaena ❁ ◉
Episcia ❁ ◉
Fittonia ❁ ◉
Hedera, some ❁, ◉
Philodendron ❁

Cool room – medium light (5–18°C/40–64°F)
Epiphyllum ❁ ◉
Epipremnum ❁
Fatsia ◉
Grevillea ❁ ◉
Monstera ❁
Platycerium ❁ ◉
Primula malacoides ❁, *P. obconica* ❁
Schefflera ❁ ◉
Sparmannia ❁ ◉

Cool room – poor light (5–18°C/40–64°F)
Aspidistra ❁
x *Fatshedera* ◉
Hedera, some ❁, ◉
Pteris ❁ ◉
Rhoicissus ❁

HYDROCULTURE

Anthurium ❁
Chamaedorea ❁ ◉
Cissus ❁
Codiaeum ❁ ◉
Dieffenbachia ❁ ◉
Dracaena ❁ ◉
Euphorbia milii ❁
Ficus benjamina ❁
Hedera, some ❁, ◉
Monstera ❁
Nephrolepis ❁ ◉
Saintpaulia ◉
Schefflera ❁
Spathiphyllum ❁ ◉
Streptocarpus ❁ ◉
Yucca, some ❁

KEY
❁ *Not hardy*
◉ *Requires high humidity*

Bromeliads

BROMELIADS, the 2,000 or so members of one of the most diverse and exotic families, the Bromeliaceae, are a fascinating group of plants that can make curiously beautiful specimens for the home, the warm greenhouse, or conservatory. Most are tropical epiphytes growing naturally on tree branches and rock faces, clinging by means of anchorage roots. These plants obtain moisture and nutrients via their leaves directly from the atmosphere, often from mists and low, moisture-laden cloud. Others are terrestrial, growing in the earth.

Almost all bromeliads are rosette-forming, frequently with strikingly coloured or variegated foliage, and many produce flamboyant blooms. Their forms range from the long and graceful, silvery strands of Spanish moss (*Tillandsia usneoides*) to the imposing *Puya alpestris*, which holds its massive spike of tubular, metallic-blue flowers above a rosette of arching, spiny foliage.

Displaying epiphytes

Most epiphytes are displayed to their best advantage if attached to a tree or branch, simulating the way that they grow in nature; the "Bromeliad tree" also avoids the risk of basal rot, which may occur if plants are grown in compost. Old, branched sections of trees cut to size are ideal.

METHODS OF DISPLAY

BINDING WITH MOSS
Wrap moistened sphagnum moss around the roots of large plants (here a Tillandsia purpurea) *and attach them to the mount by binding the roots to it with wire or raffia. The moss must be kept moist at all times.*

USING ADHESIVE
Place adhesive onto the mount and plant roots (see inset), then gently press the plants (here Tillandsia argentea. *above, and* T. ionantha) *into position.*

Bromeliad trees
If using an upright branch, secure it firmly in a deep container with cement or, if small, a strong adhesive. Alternatively, an artificial tree or branch may be constructed from a metal or wire framework covered in bark. There is a wide range of epiphytes suitable for displaying in this way, including many species from the genera *Aechmea*, *Catopsis*, *Guzmania*, *Neoregelia*, *Nidularium*, *Tillandsia*, and *Vriesea*. Use young plants if possible as they are easier to mount and tend to become established more quickly.

Prepare the plants by gently removing any loose compost from around the roots, then wrap the roots in moistened sphagnum moss and bind them to the support. Soon the plants will root onto their support and the binding may be removed. Some small plants may be lodged securely in crevices without being bound, or attached with adhesive, as described for *Tillandsia*, below.

Displaying *Tillandsia*
Tillandsia species may be mounted individually or in groups on pieces of driftwood or cork bark, on rocks,

or even on natural crystal. Position each plant with a small amount of adhesive. Make sure that the base of the rosette is free from adhesive so that new root growth is not inhibited. Press the plant onto the mount and secure it with an elastic band, twine, or wire, until the glue has set.

Epiphytes as pot plants
A number of naturally epiphytic genera, particularly those with coloured foliage, and the usually epiphytic species and cultivars of *Aechmea*, *Billbergia*, *Neoregelia*, *Nidularium*, and *Vriesea* may also

BROMELIADS SUITABLE FOR GROWING INDOORS

Ananas bracteatus 'Tricolor'

Tillandsia stricta

Tillandsia caput-medusae

Aechmea fasciata

Neoregelia carolinae f. *tricolor*

Cryptanthus bivittatus

Bromelia balansae

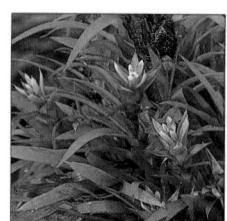

Guzmania lingulata

Guzmania lingulata var. *minor*

Vriesea splendens

be grown as pot plants, provided that an appropriate compost is used. It must be an extremely open, porous mixture, high in humus and almost lime-free. For this, use half coarse sand or perlite, and half peat substitute (or peat). To ensure that any extra moisture drains away swiftly, add pieces of partly composted tree bark to the potting medium.

Growing terrestrials

There are several hundred terrestrial bromeliads belonging to the genera *Abromeitiella*, *Ananas*, *Dyckia*, *Hechtia*, *Portea*, and *Puya*. In regions where temperatures never fall below 7–10°C (45–50°F), a wide variety of terrestrials may be grown outdoors. *Fascicularia bicolor* may even be grown without protection in temperatures as low as 0°C (32°F).

Terrestrial bromeliads often have stiff, spiny leaves and a spreading habit. While they may be grown in pots as houseplants, they perform much better if given more space in a greenhouse or conservatory border or, where conditions permit, out of doors. With their eye-catching foliage and strong outlines, they make a distinctive addition to the garden, particularly if combined in schemes either with cacti and other succulents or with subtropical plants.

Routine care

As most bromeliads originate from tropical rainforests, they need warm, humid conditions in order to thrive; most need a minimum temperature of 10°C (50°F). In the right conditions they require little maintenance but, indoors, attention is needed to maintain the necessary humidity.

Watering

As epiphytes draw moisture from the air, they should be mist-sprayed once every day rather than watered conventionally; use soft water or rainwater when possible, particularly for genera that do not tolerate lime, such as *Aechmea*, *Neoregelia*, *Nidularium*, *Tillandsia*, and *Vriesea*. In spring and summer, add a dilute quarter-strength liquid feed of an orchid fertilizer to the spray every four to five weeks to keep the plants healthy and vigorous (see ORCHIDS, "Feeding", p.444).

Where plants are growing with sphagnum moss around their roots, keep the moss moist by regularly spraying it with tepid water and also mist-spray the foliage occasionally. Bromeliads whose rosettes form a

DIVIDING ROOTSTOCKS

Gently tease or cut the offset away from the parent plant (here Billbergia nutans) so that the root system remains undamaged.

natural well or "urn" in the centre should be kept filled with water, particularly in hot, dry conditions. Change the water and apply a dilute foliar feed to the leaves occasionally.

Propagation

Bromeliads may be propagated by vegetative methods or by seed. Most epiphytic plants produce offsets that may be removed and grown on separately, while stoloniferous terrestrial kinds may be divided at the start of the growing season.

Offsets of epiphytes

Many epiphytic bromeliads are monocarpic, meaning that the rosettes flower only once and then die. Before they flower, however, they form offsets around the base of the mature rosette. The offsets should

be left in place until they are about one third the size of the parent plant. In many cases, the offsets may be removed by hand, but some will have to be cut off with a sharp knife, as close to the parent plant as possible. Replant the parent plant.

Once removed, the offsets should be transferred immediately into prepared containers of free-draining compost, with their bases just held firm in the compost (see "Epiphytes as pot plants", p.436). Keep the young plants slightly shaded at about 21°C (70°F), and lightly mist-spray them with tepid water daily.

Offsets of the non-monocarpic species may be detached from the parent plant and attached to mounts in the same way as for adult plants. The offsets may have no roots, but these will soon develop if the plants are regularly mist-sprayed and if a few strands of moist sphagnum moss are fixed at the base of the rosettes to retain moisture.

Offsets of terrestrials

Some terrestrial bromeliads, for example some *Ananas* and *Hechtia*, have stoloniferous rootstocks that also produce offsets. At the start of the growing season, lift the parent plant from the ground, or remove it from its container, so that the offsets may be cut off without injuring the parent plant. Then replant the parent and pot up the young offsets in a compost of 1 part shredded peat substitute (or peat), 1 part leaf mould, and 3 parts coarse sand.

Raising plants from seed

Most bromeliad seeds are sown like other seeds, although it is important to sow them when they are fresh because, with a few exceptions, they do not remain viable for long.

A less conventional method is used for *Tillandsia* seeds. These are sown on bundles of conifer twigs, such as *Thuja*, that are packed with well-moistened sphagnum moss and then bound together. Hang the bundles in a slightly shaded position, mist-spray them regularly, and ensure that there is free air circulation but no draughts. If kept in a temperature of about 27°C (81°F), seeds will germinate in around three to four weeks. Young plants may then be transferred to branches or other types of support and grown on.

HOW TO PROPAGATE TILLANDSIA BY SEED

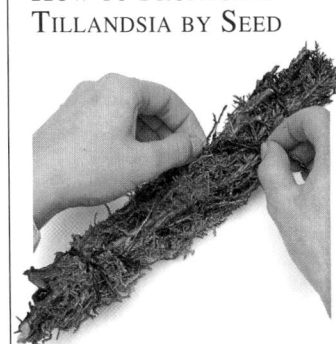

1 *Make a bundle of* Thuja *twigs interspersed with moist sphagnum moss, binding it with string, raffia, or wire.*

2 *Sprinkle the seed evenly over the prepared bundle; it will adhere readily to the moist moss.*

3 *Water the seeds with a light mist-spray and then hang up the bundle in position (see inset). Continue to mist-spray on a regular basis.*

HOW TO PROPAGATE BY DIVISION OF OFFSETS

1 *When the offsets are about one third of the size of the parent plant (here* Aechmea*), sever them at the base with a knife. Retain any roots that they may have.*

2 *Pot each offset into a mix of equal parts shredded peat, decomposed leaf mould, and sharp, gritty sand, inserting it so that the base stays on the surface.*

Soil preparation and planting

STRONG, healthy plants, suited to an indoor environment, are vital for success. Since pot plants grow in a limited amount of soil, it is important to use appropriate composts and to maintain the level of nutrients in the compost with correct feeding.

Choosing plants

Most indoor plants are container-grown. If possible, check their date of delivery at the point of sale and buy those that have recently arrived. Each plant should be labelled with its full name and cultivation details.

Look for sturdy plants with strong stems, healthy foliage, and vigorous growing points; reject any that have weak growth, dieback, or discoloured, wilting, or brown-edged leaves. Choose younger plants, which should adapt more easily than larger specimens to new conditions. Do not buy pot-bound plants or those with dry, weedy, or moss-covered compost – they have been starved of nutrients and seldom recover fully. Make sure that the growing tips and leaves are free of pests and diseases.

Flowering plants should have plenty of buds that are just starting to colour. Climbing plants should be correctly pruned and trained. Do not

SELECTING A HOUSE PLANT

GOOD EXAMPLE

Label

POOR EXAMPLE

Vigorous, healthy top-growth

Strong stems

Leaves of good colour

Moist, weed-free compost

COLEUS

Spindly, unbalanced top-growth

Pallid leaves

Dry, weed-infested compost

buy tropical plants in winter, since sudden fluctuations in temperature may have damaged them. If transporting plants in cold weather, wrap them in plastic for insulation.

Positioning a plant

Place each plant in a room that provides the levels of temperature, humidity, and light that it requires.

Flowering house plants that are of subtropical or tropical origin flower poorly or not at all if kept too cool or in poor light, whereas many foliage plants tolerate cool and shady areas. Cacti and other dry atmosphere plants need light, airy, and dry conditions; plants such as *Begonia rex* require more humidity. If conditions in your home are not ideal for a particular plant, a different cultivar of the same genus may be more suitable.

Potting mixtures

Always use good-quality, prepared potting composts for indoor plants. Loam-based composts are generally most suitable, because they contain and retain more nutrients, dry out less quickly, and are easier to re-wet than peat-substitute- or peat-based mixes. They are also heavier, providing stability for big pot plants.

Composts based on peat substitute or peat are often used for short-lived plants, for example *Primula malacoides*. They have little inherent fertility compared with loam-based mixes, and plants grown in them require careful, regular feeding. These composts tend to lose their structure in time, causing poor aeration and watering difficulties.

Lime-haters such as camellias need special lime-free or ericaceous composts. Other groups of plants such as orchids (see pp.442–5) need specialized composts. For further information, see SOILS AND FERTILIZERS, "Composts", pp.533–4).

Grouping plants

For ease of management, group together plants with similar needs for water, humidity, temperature, and

Plant supports

Various supports are available for house plants. Choose one that is suitable for the growth habit of the plant, taking into account its speed of growth and eventual size.

Plants with aerial roots grow well up a moss pillar; tie in the shoots until the roots penetrate it; keep the pillar damp by misting. Trailing or climbing plants with several stems may be trained onto wire hoops. Use a single hoop or several, depending on the plant's vigour. A balloon shape of up to eight wires is attractive, allowing good air circulation and access to light for plants with many stems.

Many climbers support themselves by means of twining stems, leaf stalks, or tendrils, and grow readily up bamboo tripods; they may need tying in at first. Single-stemmed plants need only a bamboo cane for support; insert the cane before planting to avoid damaging the roots. For details of support aids, see TOOLS AND EQUIPMENT, "Ties and supports", p.472.

PHILODENDRON SCANDENS

Moist moss

Natural direction of growth

Shoot pinned to moss pillar

Wire hoops tied together at the top

JASMINUM OFFICINALE

FICUS BENJAMINA 'VARIEGATA'

Cane

Plastic twist-tie

TRACHELOSPERMUM JASMINOIDES

Tripod formed by tying 3 canes together with twine

MOSS PILLAR
Twine stems with aerial roots round a pillar, tying them in so that they are in contact with the moss.

WIRE HOOP
Train trailing plants around wire hoops inserted into the potting compost. Tie them in regularly as they grow, adding extra hoops if necessary.

STAKE
Insert a cane into the compost before planting. Tie in the stem of the young plant.

BAMBOO TRIPOD
Encourage stems or tendrils of climbing plants to twine around the canes by tying them in.

light. If planting into the same container, make sure that the potting compost suits all the plants. In permanent arrangements, use plants that have similar growth rates, otherwise vigorous specimens may swamp their more delicate neighbours.

To increase the humidity level in a dry, centrally heated building, group individually potted plants on wet gravel in shallow bowls or trays. Alternatively, place plants on upturned pots in a tray of water, with their roots above water level.

Plunging pot plants

Plants arranged in large containers may be plunged in their individual pots into water-retentive material, such as clay pellets, to reduce water loss and improve the local humidity. (Clay can absorb up to 40 per cent of its own weight in water, so use a watertight outer container.) Any plant that is past its best or too big may then be easily removed. Alternatively, divide (see "Propagation by division", p.451) and replant it.

Coconut fibre, bark, and peat are used as plunge materials, but plants may root into the medium, making them difficult to remove. Overwatering peat may result in waterlogging, which can rot the roots. Moisture indicators are useful in gauging when the plants need water.

Planting a hanging basket

For the balcony, conservatory, or greenhouse, use slatted or plastic-coated wire baskets with a 5cm (2in) mesh. Insert plants through the sides to form a ball of flowers and foliage. Indoors, where dripping water would cause damage, use solid baskets, with integral drip trays or an outer container that has no drainage holes. Water such hanging baskets with care to avoid waterlogging.

While planting the basket, sit it on a bucket or large pot to keep it stable and clear of the ground. Wire baskets tend to dry out very quickly but a lining of green florist's foam, or plastic sheeting, reduces moisture loss. It is unattractive initially, but is soon obscured by the growing plants. Alternatively, line the basket with sphagnum moss; a plant saucer placed between the moss and the compost forms a small reservoir of moisture. Multi-purpose composts based on loam, peat substitute, or peat are suitable, although loam-based composts are easier to re-wet.

Plant the basket in stages from the base. If necessary, cut the plastic to insert plants through the sides; a roll of paper around their top-growth protects them during this process.

SINKING PLANTS INTO A LARGE CONTAINER

Schefflera arboricola 'Gold Capella'

Cordyline australis 'Purpurea'

Ficus benjamina 'Reginald'

Hibiscus rosa-sinensis

Begonia rex

Fatsia japonica 'Variegata'

Fill the container to about half of its depth with clay pellets and position the plants in their pots on the surface. Fill in with more pellets around the pots, making sure that each pot is sunk up to its rim.

HOW TO PLANT A HANGING BASKET

1 *Line the bottom of the basket with a layer of moist, live sphagnum moss, packed tightly to a thickness of at least 3cm (1¼in). Add moist, loam-based potting compost to a depth of approximately 5cm (2in). Firm the compost.*

2 *Insert the trailing plants by carefully guiding their root balls through the sides of the basket from the outside, so that the root balls are level with the compost. Add more compost around the roots and firm them in.*

3 *Keep adding moss and compost, while inserting more plants at various levels around the sides of the basket to produce a balanced display. Firm the compost as you add the plants. Continue until the compost is within 2.5–5cm (1–2in) of the rim.*

4 *Edge the top with moss. Insert plants of a more upright habit in the top of the basket. Fill in with compost. Firm it around the plants so that the surface slopes slightly towards the centre for efficient watering.*

Asparagus densiflorus 'Sprengeri'

Petunia

5 *Water the planted-up basket thoroughly and leave it to drain. Place it in a greenhouse to grow on for 4–6 weeks. Do not put a basket of tender plants out on a balcony or terrace until all danger of frost is past. Then hang it from a suitable, sturdy support.*

Ivy (*Hedera*)

Lobelia

RECOMMENDED PLANTS FOR TERRARIUMS

Acorus gramineus 'Pusillus'
Adiantum raddianum ❁
Asparagus densiflorus
  'Sprengeri' ❁
Asplenium nidus ❁
Begonia 'Tiger Paws' ❁
Callisia ❁
Chamaedorea elegans ❁
Cissus discolor ❁
Codiaeum ❁
Cryptanthus acaulis ❁,
  C. bivittatus ❁,
  C. bromelioides ❁, C. zonatus ❁
Dracaena sanderiana ❁
Episcia ❁
Ficus pumila ❁
Fittonia verschaffeltii ❁
Hedera (miniatures)
Hypoestes phyllostachya ❁
Maranta leuconeura ❁
Nertera granadensis
Pellaea rotundifolia ❁
Pellionia daveauana ❁

Peperomia caperata ❁
Pilea cadierei ❁, P. spruceana ❁
Plectranthus oertendahlii ❁
Pteris cretica ❁
Saintpaulia (miniatures) ❁
Sansevieria trifasciata 'Hahnii' ❁
Schefflera elegantissima
  (seedlings) ❁
Selaginella ❁
Soleirolia soleirolii

Fittonia
verschaffeltii

Strobilanthes dyerianus ❁
Syngonium hoffmannii ❁
Tradescantia cerinthoides ❁,
  T. fluminensis ❁, T. spathacea ❁

Planted baskets are heavy, so ensure that supporting chains and fixings are sound. A universal hook fixing allows the basket to be rotated to receive an even amount of light.

Planting in a terrarium

Before planting, clean the terrarium thoroughly to avoid contamination with algae and fungal diseases which thrive in enclosed and humid environments. Choose a mixture of tall, upright plants and smaller, creeping ones and decide how to arrange them before starting to plant.

Since a terrarium is self-contained, it must have a layer of drainage material, such as clay pellets, gravel, or pebbles, as well as some horticultural charcoal which absorbs any gaseous by-products and helps keep the compost fresh. A lightweight, free-draining, but moisture-retentive potting compost is the most suitable planting medium. Extra peat substitute or peat may be added to keep the soil well aerated.

Use young plants with root systems that are sufficiently small to establish easily in shallow compost. Soak them thoroughly before planting, and remove dead foliage that might encourage rot. Insert the plants into the compost, allowing space for them to spread. If the terrarium is too small to accommodate a hand easily, attach a split cane to a widger to assist planting, and a cork or cotton reel to another cane to make a firming implement. Cover bare areas with moss or pebbles to stop the compost drying out, and water lightly before replacing the lid.

Once established, terrariums require very little or no watering (see "Maintaining terrariums and bottle gardens", p.447). If excess condensation appears on the glass, ventilate it a little until there is only a slight misting of the glass in the morning.

PLANTING A TERRARIUM

1 Plan the arrangement with taller plants either at the back (as here) or in the centre, depending on whether the terrarium will be viewed from the front only or from all sides. The plants used here are:

Asparagus densiflorus 'Sprengeri'
Maranta leuconeura
Ficus pumila 'Variegata'
Selaginella martensii
Soleirolia soleirolii
Selaginella kraussiana 'Aurea'

2 Cover the terrarium base with a 2.5–5cm (1–2in) deep layer of pebbles and a few pieces of horticultural charcoal. Add 2.5cm (1in) of moist potting compost.

3 Remove each plant from its pot and shake off any loose compost. Gently tease out the roots, reducing the size of the root ball, to help the plant establish.

4 Use a widger or other small implement to make hollows for the plants, and insert them carefully, allowing space between them for further growth.

5 Fill in around the plants with more moist compost and firm the surface. A cork fixed to the end of a split cane provides a tamper of suitable size.

6 Using tweezers, place a layer of moss (or pebbles) over any bare areas of compost between the plants. This will prevent the compost from drying out.

7 Spray the plants and the moss lightly with a fine mist of water and replace the lid. The terrarium is now ready for display.

GROWING PLANTS IN A SOIL BENCH

Zonal pelargonium

Streptocarpus

Ficus benjamina

Fittonia argyroneura

Surface level with greenhouse window

Loam-based potting compost, about 30cm (12in) deep

38cm (15in) deep bench

7cm (3in) layer of coarse gravel for drainage

Drainage holes

Strengthened timber frame

Prepare the soil bench for planting by placing a layer of drainage material in the bottom and then filling the bench with loam-based potting compost. Plant a selection of ornamentals for a fine display in the greenhouse.

Soil preparation and planting under cover

Conservatories and greenhouses allow control of the environment, and extend the range of plants that can be grown in temperate or cool climates.

Soil beds and bed benches

Although conservatory and greenhouse ornamentals may be grown in pots, a large number, particularly climbers and woody shrubs, may be planted permanently in soil borders. For a new conservatory, consider at the planning stage if soil borders are needed. Raised and well-drained soil beds provide a good method of display. Prepare soil beds well since ornamentals will be in place for some years. Make the beds about four weeks before planting to allow the soil to settle, and at least 30–45cm (12–18in) deep, with 7–15cm (3–6in) of drainage material at the base.

A bench bed is useful for propagating and raising different plants, and for specialized plant collections. Bench beds are shallow raised beds, usually at waist height, on supporting frames or pillars. They are ideal for small plants and for use with soil-heating cables (see p.488), mist units (see p.488), and automated watering systems (see p.485). Site the bench to make maximum use of available light.

Bench beds are usually built from aluminium or wood, lined with wire mesh or perforated plastic. They should be at least 15–22mm (6–9in)

deep and no more than 1m (3ft) wide for easy access. A 7cm (3in) layer of drainage material is sufficient.

Composts under cover

For soil beds, use a well-drained, loam-based compost enriched with organic matter at a rate of about 10 litres/sq m (2.2 gallons/10 sq ft). Do not use unsterilized garden soil as it can harbour pests, diseases, and weeds. No safe chemical soil sterilization methods are readily available to amateurs and heat-sterilizing units, although effective, are expensive.

In general, use loam-based composts under cover as they contain their own nutrients and trace elements that do not leach out as readily as in less rich peat-substitute- or peat-based composts; loam-based composts are also easier to re-wet.

It is important to select the appropriate compost for specific purposes and for groups of plants with special needs. Most container-grown plants require a good-quality, loam-based compost that is free-draining and of approximately neutral pH. Tropical plants prefer more humus-rich, leafy soils, so incorporate additional leaf mould in the compost before filling containers or soil beds. Most ferns, heathers, and many lilies (*Lilium*) need an ericaceous compost, as do hydrangeas in order to produce blue flowers rather than pink ones.

Ornamental plants grown in borders need a dressing every year of 2–3 oz/sq yd of a balanced fertilizer with a mulch of well-rotted compost in spring to maintain strong growth.

Planting a bottle garden

Bottle gardens provide an attractive way of growing very small, slow-growing plants in an enclosed microclimate. Many of the smaller plants grown in terrariums are suitable (see *Recommended Plants for Terrariums*, p.440).

Use any clean, plain, or slightly coloured, glass bottle, as long as the neck is wide enough to allow plants to be inserted easily. If the neck is too narrow to take a hand, make special tools, from split canes, loops of wire and common household utensils such as a dessert fork and teaspoon, to help with planting and routine care.

With the aid of a wide funnel or cardboard tube, pour clay pellets into the bottle to provide a 3cm (1¼in) layer of drainage material and add a handful of horticultural charcoal to keep the compost sweet. Cover it with a 5–7cm (2–3in) layer of dampened, peat-substitute-based potting compost.

If the bottle is to be viewed from the front, use a widger to bank up the compost at the back. Level the compost if the bottle is to be viewed from all sides.

Begin planting at the sides of the bottle and work in towards the centre. Remove the plants from their pots, and shake off any excess compost. Carefully lower each plant into a planting hole, using tweezers, tongs, or a length of wire twisted into a noose. Space the plants at least 3cm (1¼in) apart to allow room for growth. Cover the roots with compost, and use a cork tamper to firm it gently.

Trickle a cupful of water down the sides of the bottle interior to dampen the compost, and cover bare areas with sphagnum moss to keep it moist. Clean the inside of the glass with a sponge fixed to a length of cane or stiff wire. If the bottle garden is not sealed after planting, water occasionally.

Hypoestes phyllostachya 'Purpuriana'

Dracaena sanderiana

Hedera helix 'Eva'

Hypoestes phyllostachya 'Splash'

Asplenium nidus

Saintpaulia cv

Selaginella kraussiana

Sphagnum moss

If the planting needs renewal after several years, remove and dispose of the plants, having propagated them first. Then dig in some well-rotted compost or manure and incorporate a slow-release fertilizer or base dressing prior to replanting.

In beds of ornamental plants, there is seldom such a build-up of pests and diseases that it is necessary to change or sterilize the soil. With crop plants grown in borders where pests and diseases may increase rapidly, the soil usually has to be replaced annually or sterilized if a suitable method is available. Crop plants are better cultivated in growing bags or containers, where the compost can be disposed of if problems occur. Always ensure that the

bases of containers with drainage holes do not come into contact with the border soil. This avoids cross-contamination by pests and diseases.

Planting

Always select plants that grow well in the range of temperatures provided (see "Planter's guide to indoor plants", p.435). Make sure that ornamentals or crop plants are planted at spacings that allow free air circulation and so inhibit the spread of pests and diseases. Position the plants to receive optimum light and ventilation for their growing requirements. Make full use of temperature, light intensity, humidity, and air-circulation controls that are provided in a well-built and fitted-out greenhouse.

Orchids

INCLUDED in the orchid family are some 750 genera, nearly 20,000 species, and many thousands more hybrids. Their exotic blooms and intriguing habit make them very desirable ornamental plants, mostly for indoor display, although there are a significant number of beautiful terrestrial species that are hardy. When choosing which to grow from the vast range of types available, consider the conditions and care that you are able to provide. Some orchids have fairly rigorous demands as to growing conditions, but many hybrids are specially bred for ease of cultivation, and can be successfully grown and propagated in the home.

Terrestrial orchids

As the name suggests, these orchids grow in the ground, in widely varying habitats. Most of those that inhabit temperate to cold regions die down after flowering and exist in a resting state as tubers or similar underground storage organs during the winter. These hardy and near-hardy terrestrials often have flowers that, although individually small, are borne in dense spikes. Many are attractive plants for the rock garden or alpine house (see pp.214–16).

Some terrestrials, such as the slipper orchids belonging to the genus *Paphiopedilum*, come from warmer regions, where they inhabit sheltered sites such as the forest floor. Never having to face harsh weather conditions, these remain evergreen throughout the year, but – because they are delicate – they need to be cultivated in a greenhouse.

Epiphytic orchids

Epiphytic orchids, which form a very large proportion of those grown by enthusiasts, are fundamentally different in their structure and habit of growth. As implied by their name (derived from the Greek *epi*, upon, and *phyton*, plant), they make their homes in the branches of trees.

They are not parasites (because they do not feed off the tree) but "lodgers": they take their nourishment from substances dissolved in the rainwater and from debris accumulated around their roots. A few orchids known as lithophytes live in a similar manner on rocks. In temperate climates, epiphytes need to be grown under glass.

Sympodial and monopodial

Epiphytes have two methods of growth: sympodial and monopodial. Sympodial orchids, such as *Cattleya* and *Odontoglossum* species and hybrids, have creeping rhizomes. Each season new growths arise from growing points on the rhizomes, and these develop into swollen stem structures known botanically as pseudobulbs. Flowers of the different sympodial species vary greatly, and may appear from the top, base, or side of the pseudobulbs.

Monopodial orchids grow in what is called an indeterminate manner. The stem continues to elongate indefinitely, growing taller and taller as new leaves and stem are produced at the apex. Monopodials include many of the most spectacular orchid genera, such as *Phalaenopsis* and *Vanda*. These come originally from the warmer regions of the world, climbing their way upwards towards the light through dense, jungle foliage. Most monopodials bear their flowers in branched, often gracefully arching, flowerheads from axillary points along their stems, from which aerial roots are also often produced to give new growth.

Choosing plants

If you are a beginner, it is best to obtain plants from a specialist orchid nursery, where they will have enjoyed an ideal environment and not suffered any setbacks. Specialists are also a valuable source of advice on suitable species for the conditions you have at home. Hybrid orchids are generally the easiest to grow, being themselves bred partly for vigour and ease of care. The species thrive best in environments similar to those in which they grow naturally, and these conditions are not always easy to re-create.

Owing to commercial techniques of mass production, orchids are no longer prohibitively expensive. For a modest price, plants that are attractive but have not yet won an award may be bought when you visit specialist nurseries and see them in flower. Least expensive of all are the unflowered seedlings that may take several years to come into bloom; the result is uncertain, but there is always the exciting possibility that one of the seedlings may be a future award-winner.

RECOMMENDED ORCHIDS

Dendrobium nobile

Cymbidium Strath Kanaid

Vanda Rothschildiana

Paphiopedilum callosum

Cattleya bowringiana

Miltonia candida var. *grandiflora*

Cultivation

The unusual structure and growth habit of epiphytic orchids give them a reputation for being very delicate, and therefore difficult to grow. With a knowledge of a few guidelines and careful preparation, however, most of the difficulties are easily remedied or avoided.

Compost

Although most epiphytes can be grown in pots, their roots are specially adapted to open conditions on trees or rocks (lithophytes), so they cannot endure the close-textured composts suitable for most other plants. Orchid composts must drain very freely after watering; if they remain wet for long the roots are likely to rot. Chopped pine or fir bark makes an excellent potting medium, with some additions to keep the mixture open and prevent it from becoming sour. A suitable compost mix is as follows: 3 parts medium-grade bark (dust-free), 1 part coarse grit or perlite, 1 part charcoal pieces, and 1 part broken dry leaves or fibrous peat substitute or peat. Specialist mixes can usually be obtained from orchid nurseries.

Terrestrial orchids also require a much more free-draining potting mixture than most plants. A suitable compost can be made up of 3 parts fibrous peat substitute or peat, 3 parts coarse grit, and 1 part perlite, with the addition of 1 part charcoal.

COMPOST FOR EPIPHYTIC ORCHIDS

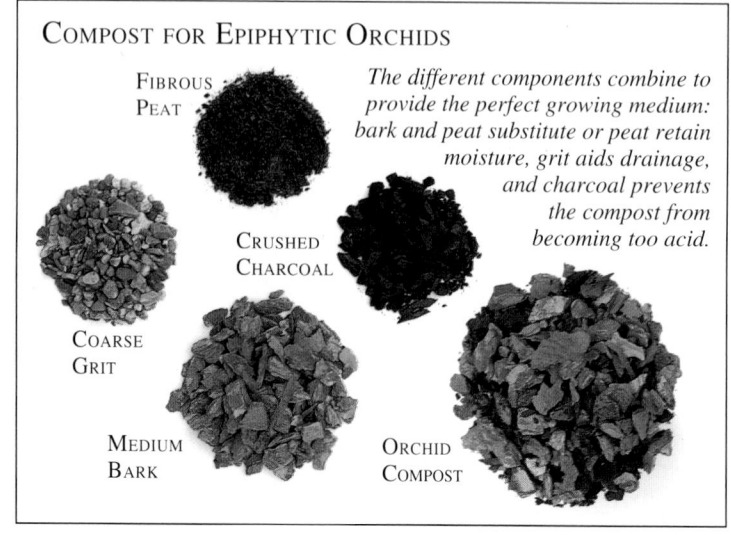

FIBROUS PEAT

The different components combine to provide the perfect growing medium: bark and peat substitute or peat retain moisture, grit aids drainage, and charcoal prevents the compost from becoming too acid.

CRUSHED CHARCOAL

COARSE GRIT

MEDIUM BARK

ORCHID COMPOST

Potting

When a plant has filled its container, it should be transferred to a new pot a size or two larger to provide space for further growth. Choose a pot that will accommodate the roots and allow for one or two years' growth but no more; a pot that is too large for the root system is likely to lead to stagnant conditions in the compost. To assist drainage, many growers fill the bottom quarter of the pot with broken crocks, pieces of polystyrene, or large grit. This also adds extra weight to plastic pots, making them less likely to be knocked over.

Hold the plant with one hand so that the crown is just below the rim of the pot and place the compost around the roots, tapping the pot sharply in order to settle the compost. Use relatively dry compost, which should be thoroughly watered after repotting. The plant, especially the roots, should be disturbed as little as possible.

Some epiphytes do well in containers that allow more air to reach the roots, such as hanging baskets made of wire or wooden slats. Such containers are essential for species of *Stanhopea* because their flowers grow down through the compost to emerge on the underside.

When potting on sympodials, old pseudobulbs of two to three seasons' growth that have lost their leaves (usually called "back-bulbs") may be removed and used for propagating (see p.445). Place the rear of the plant against one side of the pot, leaving space on the opposite side for the new growth to develop.

Support

Many orchids are sturdy enough not to need support. Others, however, require careful staking to look their best, particularly those with long flowering stems that carry many heavy blooms. Use upright canes or stout wires, to which the stems may be tied as unobtrusively as possible. Do this as the stems are growing and before the flower buds open. Avoid changing the position of the plants or the effect will be spoilt because the flowers will face in different directions.

Growing on bark

Some orchids that do not grow successfully in containers will thrive if mounted on pieces of either bark or tree-fern with moss at their roots, although they do then require a constantly humid atmosphere. Initially they must be tied firmly to the slab; nylon thread is ideal for this purpose. New roots will appear which will adhere to the slab and thus secure the plant.

Routine care

For successful cultivation, it is vital to provide orchids with their particular care requirements; these vary according to the species.

Temperature

While the hardy terrestrials (notably *Cypripedium* species) do well in the rock garden or alpine house, others (usually described as half hardy) may also be grown in these unheated conditions in mild areas. They include the cool-growing genera *Pleione* and *Bletilla*, which need only enough heat to ensure frost-free conditions.

A cool greenhouse, with a minimum night temperature in winter of 10°C (50°F), is suitable for a large number of different orchids, including some *Brassia, Coelogyne, Cymbidium, Dendrobium, Laelia, Odontoglossum, Oncidium*, and *Paphiopedilum* species and hybrids.

The intermediate house, with a minimum winter night temperature of 13–15°C (55–60°F) will greatly extend the range of possibilities, to include species and hybrids of *Cattleya* and its relatives, and a wider selection of the *Odontoglossum* group and of *Paphiopedilum* species and hybrids, as well as many other attractive and beautiful orchids.

The warm house, with a minimum night temperature of at least 18°C (65°F), provides the necessary conditions for species and hybrids of *Phalaenopsis* and *Vanda* and their many relatives, as well as the heat-loving species and hybrids of *Dendrobium*, and many orchids from the hot and humid lowlands of the tropics and subtropics.

Watering and humidity

These are perhaps the most important factors in orchid cultivation. Watering should be frequent enough to avoid drying, but not so frequent that the compost becomes soggy – once or twice a week for most of the year is usually sufficient. In the summer months plants may need watering every day and during the period of short winter days only once every two or three weeks.

Rainwater is usually recommended, but drinkable tapwater is quite safe. Water plants in the early morning. Do not let water remain too long on

HOW TO DISPLAY EPIPHYTIC ORCHIDS

Most epiphytes may be grown in pots, although they may also be successfully cultivated in a hanging basket or on bark. Keep the plants in a constantly humid atmosphere until established.

GROWING ON BARK
Tie moistened moss to a piece of bark then attach the roots of the orchid (here Dendrobium 'Happiness') *with nylon thread.*

POT-GROWN
Choose a pot that will allow for no more than 2 years' growth, place crocks or grit in the base, and fill with standard orchid compost. Plant the orchid (here Zygopetalum mackayi) *and firm in.*

HANGING BASKET
Plant the orchid in standard orchid compost in a hanging basket lined with sphagnum moss. The flower stems of some orchids (here Stanhopea tigrina) *grow through the compost to emerge below.*

the foliage, or it may cause leaf scorch if the plants are exposed to hot sun. Overwatering must be avoided, but water thoroughly, so that the compost is evenly moist. Allow the compost to become nearly – but not quite – dry before watering again; if in doubt, delay watering.

During the growing season, orchids need a high level of humidity. This may be achieved by damping down the orchid house by spraying water over the paths and earth and on the staging between plants. Do this early in the morning; as the day progresses, the water will be drawn up as vapour. This daily damping down may be discontinued when natural conditions are cold and damp. Be careful, however, because in extremely cold weather the heating system may make the air very dry, and the greenhouse may need to be damped down more often.

Orchids grown in the home as windowsill plants must be chosen from those that do not demand very high humidity. Even these may benefit from additional local humidity by standing them on a layer of moist gravel or expanded clay aggregate in a tray or deep saucer.

Feeding

Since modern orchid composts contain little nourishment, orchids will need feeding during their growing period. Liquid fertilizers are the most convenient and these can be added during watering. Any proprietary, general-purpose brands sold for pot plants may be used. Orchids are not heavy feeders, so it will be necessary to dilute the fertilizer to half the strength recommended for other pot plants. Feed the orchids once every three weeks from spring to autumn, and only every six weeks (if at all) during the winter.

Ventilation

Most orchids, especially the popular cool-greenhouse kinds, require free-moving air conditions. They dislike cold draughts, however, which can cause flower buds to drop and slow down growth. Ventilators should be only partially opened in spring, when sunny days may be accompanied by chill winds, and closed well before the temperature starts to drop in the late afternoon. As days become warm, ventilators may be opened wider and for a longer time. Remember, however, that water vapour is quickly lost through open ventilators and humidity is reduced, so that extra damping down is needed. A small electric fan, inexpensive both to buy and run, will keep the air moving without letting out humidity or letting in draughts.

Shading

Although different orchids may have different light requirements, from the shade-loving *Paphiopedilum* orchids to the sun-loving *Laelia* species and hybrids, some form of shading is needed to protect new growth from being scorched by the sun and to prevent the greenhouse from overheating. The cheapest method is to use a greenhouse shading compound. White is more efficient than green in reflecting back the sun's rays, and it becomes almost transparent in rain, letting in more light on dull days. More effective, but more expensive, are manual or automatic roller blinds, made either of wood slats or plastic mesh.

Resting

An important and integral part of an orchid's lifecycle is the resting period, when growth is halted. During this time, which in the case of some orchids may last only a few weeks and in others several months, they need very little water, if any, in order to survive.

Although plants' requirements vary, the general rule is that those orchids that lose their leaves when resting should not be watered until new growth begins. Water sparingly at first, then normally (taking care not to overwater). Plants that keep their leaves will need to be given only a little water during the resting period to avoid dehydration.

Propagation

Vegetative propagation methods are the easiest for the amateur to learn. They also have the advantage of

---

HOW TO PROPAGATE BY ADVENTITIOUS GROWTHS

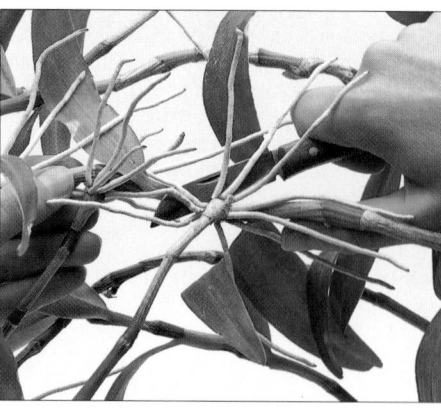

1 *When a new plantlet with aerial roots has formed from a leaf node, cut it away carefully from the parent plant with a sharp knife.*

2 *The selected cutting should have healthy leaves and an evenly developed root system.*

3 *Holding the plantlet by its stem at planting level, pot up the young plant in a 6cm (3in) pot with the roots just below the compost surface.*

HOW TO PROPAGATE BY STEM CUTTINGS

1 *Using a sharp knife, cut off a section of stem at least 25cm (10in) long, just above a leaf node or at the base of the plant.*

2 *Divide this into lengths of about 7cm (3in), cutting midway between leaf nodes. Each cutting should have at least 1 node.*

3 *Lay the cuttings in a tray on a layer of moist sphagnum moss and store in a humid place out of direct sunlight.*

4 *After several weeks, the dormant buds will have developed into plantlets, which will then be ready to pot up.*

producing offspring which are identical to the parent plant, so that the results are predictable.

Adventitious growths

The simplest cuttings, which are commonly known to orchid growers as "keikis", are small plantlets that appear adventitiously (that is, atypically) from the nodes on stems of monopodial orchids, such as *Dendrobium*. As soon as these plantlets have developed a few vigorous roots, they should be severed from the parent plant with a sharp knife, and then potted into a standard orchid compost. Water them sparingly at first, but remember to spray the leaves with a fine mist until the roots have become established and the plants have had a chance to become accustomed to their new environment.

Stem cuttings

Cuttings may also be made from the stems (often called canes) of many *Dendrobium* and *Epidendrum* orchids. With a sharp knife, cut off sections up to 30cm (12in) in length. Divide these into cuttings 7.5–10cm (3–4in) long, each with at least one dormant bud. Lay the cuttings on damp sphagnum moss or a similar moist material, and keep them in a humid place, shaded from the sun. When the buds have developed to produce plantlets, detach these and pot them up separately.

Division

The usual method of propagating sympodial orchids such as *Cattleya*, *Cymbidium*, and *Odontoglossum* is by division. Simply cut through the rhizome between pseudobulbs and pot up the pieces separately. Each piece should have at least three healthy pseudobulbs and a healthy dormant bud to produce new growth.

Back-bulbs offer another way of propagating sympodials such as *Cymbidium*. Remove a back-bulb, preferably one with roots, by pulling or cutting the rhizome just beyond it. Insert the back-bulb in grit, sharp sand, or standard orchid compost, place in a cool, shady place, and keep moist. Shoots should appear in two or three months. When the bulbs have developed roots, pot them on.

Commercial techniques

Growing orchids from seed is a difficult technique and requires specialized knowledge and skills. Orchids raised commercially from seed are germinated in flasks of nutrient jelly in a strictly controlled laboratory environment. They are sometimes also propagated by meristem culture, in which microscopic pieces of plant tissue are grown on under laboratory conditions in order to mass-produce replicas of the original plant. As a result, first-class cultivars may now be purchased at a reasonable price. Both are, however, highly specialized techniques seldom practised by the amateur gardener.

HOW TO PROPAGATE BY DIVISION

1 *When the orchid has grown too large for its pot and has several leafless bulbs, it may be divided. The plant shown here is a* Cymbidium.

2 *Remove the orchid from its pot, then divide the plant by separating or cutting it into 2 sections; each section should have at least 3 healthy pseudobulbs.*

3 *When dividing the orchid, any leafless back-bulbs may be pulled away. Discard shrivelled ones, and retain those that are firm for potting up separately.*

4 *Trim each section of the divided plant by removing surplus compost and cutting off any dead roots with secateurs.*

5 *To replant each section, hold the plant with the oldest pseudobulbs at the back of the pot and at planting level, and place the compost around it. New growth will develop in front of the plant.*

PROPAGATION BY BACK-BULBS

1 *Plant selected back-bulbs singly in 6cm (3in) pots. Plant at one side of the pot, leaving space for new growth.*

2 *Within 2 or 3 months the old back-bulb will produce a healthy new shoot.*

PROPAGATION IN FLASKS

Meristem culture takes place under sterile conditions. Microscopic pieces of plant tissue are placed in a flask on a special nutrient medium such as agar-agar jelly; they then develop into young orchid plants.

Routine care

UNLIKE plants grown outdoors, indoor plants are not subject to the extremes of the seasonal cycle so need relatively little attention. They require only watering and fertilizing, and an annual potting on, to perform at their best.

Watering and humidity

A common problem in the care of indoor plants is overwatering. In general, water when the compost is nearly dry. Take special care with coconut fibre composts because the surface is inclined to dry out while the rest stays moist.

Water plants frequently while they are in active growth, less in winter when they are dormant – twice a month or even less may be enough. Wet the compost thoroughly, but do not leave the pot standing in water. Some plants, such as cyclamen, are susceptible to root rot; to water them, stand the pots in a little water until the compost is dark and damp. If tap water is hard, use distilled water or rainwater for lime-hating plants.

Buildings are often poorly ventilated and the atmosphere dry and unsuitable for many indoor plants. Maintain humidity by grouping pot plants on wet gravel in trays or in containers (see "Grouping plants", p.438), or on capillary matting (see "Care of house plants before going away", p.448).

Electric and ceramic humidifiers are readily available; bowls containing water placed in a room so that the water evaporates are also effective. Plants that need high humidity benefit from being mist sprayed with soft water. Use sprays sparingly on plants with hairy leaves, and avoid sunlight since spots of water on the leaves can cause scorch.

Cleanliness

Always remove dead leaves and flowers promptly since they may harbour diseases or pests. Do not allow dust or grime to build up and block the leaf pores; dust the foliage with a soft brush. Thoroughly spray the plants occasionally to keep them clean and fresh, but do not spray cacti or plants with hairy leaves unless it is warm enough for any excess moisture to evaporate rapidly, or the leaves may rot. Only use leaf shine on glossy-leaved plants and check that it is compatible with individual species.

Fertilizing

Pot plants grow in relatively small volumes of compost and soon use up the available nutrients. Frequent watering also leaches out nutrients and the plants could starve without regular feeding throughout the growing season.

Balanced fertilizers are available in various forms: water-soluble or liquid (most convenient for indoor plants), granular, and solid. Always be careful to follow the manufacturers' instructions and never apply fertilizer to dry compost as it will not soak through evenly and may damage the roots.

Stopping

The appearance of many pot plants, especially trailing plants, may be improved by pinching out growing tips on young plants to encourage production of more sideshoots. This keeps the foliage bushy and increases the number of flower buds. Only stop plants that are in active growth.

CLEANING SMOOTH-LEAVED PLANTS
Gently wipe each leaf (here variegated Ficus elastica) *with a clean, moist, soft, and lint-free cloth.*

REMOVING DEAD LEAVES
Pinch out dead leaves and stems at the base of the plant (here Nephrolepis exaltata) *or cut them out.*

Neglected plants

With the exception of orchids and palms, most plants that have weak, leggy, or damaged growth, or sparsely spaced leaves, produce new, vigorous growth if cut hard back to a healthy bud or joint in early spring. Cut back a neglected fern to the crown; keep the root ball moist and in medium light to induce new growth.

Plants that root readily are best renewed from cuttings, while some plants are rejuvenated by air layering (see p.456). Revive exhausted plants by repotting or with a rest in a shaded greenhouse. To rescue an overwatered plant, remove all the sodden compost from the root ball, trim off rotting foliage and roots, and repot it in fresh compost. Refresh an underwatered plant by immersing the pot in water until the bubbles stop rising; then let the pot drain.

Potting on and top-dressing

Indoor plants also need periodic potting on to accommodate their growth and to replenish the compost. A pot-bound plant has retarded growth, fails to thrive, and water rinses clean through its pot. Pot on before this stage so that the plant's development is unimpeded. A few plants, such as *Hippeastrum*, enjoy confined roots, so do not pot them on.

The best time to pot on is at the start of the growing season, although fast-growing plants may need potting on several times in one season. The process may delay flowering because the plant initially concentrates its energy on new root growth. Never pot on a dormant plant.

Potting on

Ensure that the root ball is completely moist so that it comes easily out of its pot without damaging the roots. Turn the pot upside down and slide the plant out into your hand. If the pot is too big to lift easily, run a knife around the inside; then lay the pot on its side. Support the plant

HOW TO RENEW TOP-DRESSING

HIPPEASTRUM

1 *Use a widger to remove the top 2½–5cm (1–2in) of the old compost, taking care not to damage the plant's roots.*

2 *Replace it with fresh, moist compost to which a small amount of fertilizer has been added. Firm the compost well around the crown and water.*

PRESERVING HUMIDITY AROUND POT PLANTS

Create suitably humid conditions for indoor plants by providing them with their own microclimate. Loosely pack a shallow tray with clay pellets or gravel and fill it with water. Group several pot plants on the tray. Keep the water topped up so that the gravel or pellets remain wet.

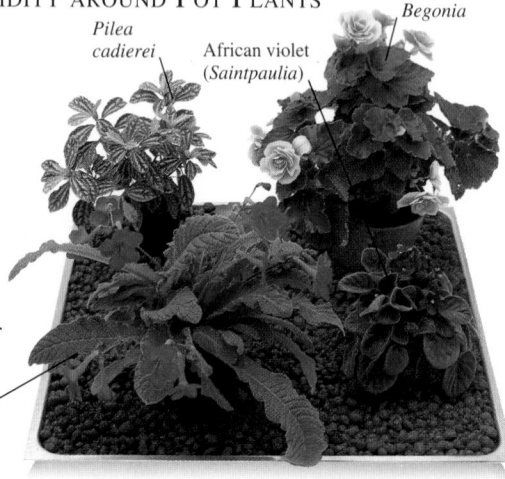

Pilea cadierei

African violet (Saintpaulia)

Begonia

Streptocarpus

with one hand and rotate the pot, gently tapping the sides with a wood block to loosen the compost fully before removing the plant.

Put fresh potting compost in the new pot until the plant is positioned at the same depth as before, with space allowed for watering. Check that the roots are spread out and the plant centred, fill in with more compost, and firm gently. Water, but do not feed the plant for four to six weeks so that it will send out new roots into the compost in search of food. Keep the plant out of direct sun for a few days to recover.

Repotting

If a plant is in the largest available container, has grown to its full size, or is very slow-growing, repot it into the same size pot to renew the compost. Take the plant out of its pot, removing as much of the old compost as possible. Prune out damaged or diseased roots before repotting the plant in fresh compost.

Top-dressing

With plants that react badly to root disturbance, or enjoy confined roots, do not repot, but at the start of each growing season replace the old, surface compost with fresh compost of the same type and enrich it with balanced fertilizer.

Hanging baskets

Hanging baskets need regular care. Never allow the compost in a basket to dry out. Water it thoroughly; in very warm weather, this will need to be done both morning and evening. If the plants wilt, soak the basket in a bowl filled with water.

Feed plants in a basket regularly with a balanced liquid feed, and control any pests. Dead-head flowering plants, clip back over-long trailing plants, and thin out any untidy or tangled growth. Remove and replace any dead plants.

Maintaining terrariums and bottle gardens

A closed container rarely needs water; but if required use a long-necked watering can to trickle water against the glass inside to avoid disturbing the compost. Use just enough water to clean the glass and moisten the surface. If the glass is continuously obscured by mist, the compost is too wet – remove the cover or cork until it clears. To get rid of condensation or algae inside the glass, use a small

HOW TO POT ON AN INDOOR PLANT

1 *Before potting on a plant (here* Dracaena sand- *eriana), make sure that its root ball is moist by watering it thoroughly an hour beforehand. Select a pot that is one or two sizes larger than the old one. Make sure the pot is clean (whether washed, disinfected, or new) to avoid spreading diseases. The fresh potting compost should be of the same type as that in the old pot.*

2 *Remove the plant by inverting the pot and sharply tapping the rim on a hard surface to loosen the root ball. Support the plant as it slides out of the pot.*

3 *Gently tease out the root ball with a hand fork or fingers. Put some moist potting compost in the base of the new pot.*

4 *Insert the plant so that its soil mark is level with the rim base. Fill in with compost to within 1.5cm (¹/₂in) of the rim, firm, water, and place in position (right).*

Keeping plants from year to year

When all danger of frost is past, plunge flowering plants grown for winter colour indoors, in their pots in outdoor beds to "rest" during the warmer months. Choose a cool place, with indirect light, and keep them watered with soft (lime-free) water. At the end of summer, repot or top-dress them, bring them indoors, and feed them regularly once flower buds appear. To keep a cyclamen after flowering, do not water it until new growth starts, then remove old roots, and repot in loam-based potting compost so that the corm is level with the surface. Put it in a cool, well-lit place, and water regularly.

WINTER-FLOWERING POT PLANTS
In late spring, transfer the plants, here azaleas (Rhododendron), to a plunge bed in semi-shade outdoors. Sink each pot up to its rim in weed-free soil or another suitable plunge material, allowing space for the plants to grow. Bring them in before frost threatens, and keep them cool until the buds open.

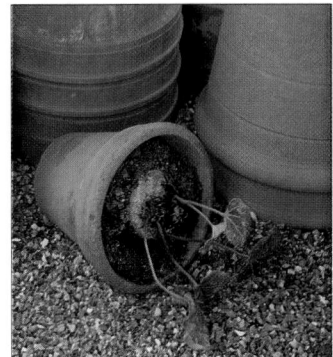

CYCLAMEN
Let the leaves die down naturally after flowering. Place the plant on its side, in its pot, under a green-house bench or in a cold frame.

REPLANTING A TERRARIUM

Asparagus densiflorus 'Sprengeri'

Ficus pumila 'Variegata'

Hypoestes phyllostachya 'Splash'

Dracaena reflexa cv

Selaginella kraussiana 'Aurea'

Fittonia verschaffeltii

Selaginella martensii

1 *When a terrarium becomes overgrown, carefully remove any plants that have grown too large. Divide them or select new, small plants. Try to leave the surrounding compost undisturbed.*

2 *If needed, trim the remaining plants with scissors. Thin out the surface moss where necessary by removing some with tweezers, keeping adjacent plants firmly in place with a cork and cane tamper.*

3 *Divide low-growing plants that have outgrown their allotted space. Use a widger to replant the divisions and the new plants (see inset). Firm with a little fresh compost, using the tamper.*

4 *Trickle water down the inside of the glass until the compost is just damp. Then replace the lid.*

---

sponge attached to a length of cane. Keep the container out of direct sunlight and move it occasionally, especially if it is in a shaded place in winter. Remove dead leaves and control pests and diseases.

Trim the plants from time to time so that each has enough light and space. A razor blade inserted into the end of a cane is useful for pruning plants in small-necked bottle gardens. If any plants encroach upon others, either replace them with smaller plants, or replant the entire container (see above).

Plants in greenhouses

These need regular, sometimes daily, attention, even if the greenhouse is equipped with automatic systems. Watering, ventilation, misting, and feeding are especially important in summer, as is heating in winter, and proper hygiene at all times. Routine care of pot plants, including feeding and potting (see pp.446–7), is similar to that of indoor plants.

Watering

In the enclosed greenhouse environment, correct watering is crucial. The amount needed varies with the season and the weather. In summer, water more on sunny than on cloudy days. Use a hose in a big greenhouse, with a low water pressure to avoid washing surface compost away from the roots. A watering can is best in a small or mixed greenhouse, where plants have differing water needs:

some pot plants may need watering several times on a hot day. Stand the can in the greenhouse until the water temperature is the same as that of the plants. Do not overwater, especially in winter, since wet soil leads to rotting. For full instructions on watering (e.g. by capillary matting, drip feeds, or trickle systems), see p.485. Self-watering pots are also useful; an outer pot holds water that is borne by capillary action along a wick to the compost in an inner pot.

Humidity

Plants need moist, but not stagnant, air. In hot, sunny weather, damp down by splashing the floor, particularly hard surfaces, with water each morning and evening, or more often in very hot weather. This keeps the greenhouse humid and temporarily cools the air. (Soil floors hold most moisture, while tiled or concrete floors dry most quickly.) If the air is too humid, plants cannot transpire water vapour from the

leaves to keep cool, and may overheat and wilt, so ventilate the greenhouse to dry out the air. In very hot climates, or for plants with particular needs, automated damping down systems and special humidifiers may be necessary (see GREENHOUSES AND FRAMES, "Humidity", p.484).

Dank, cold air encourages fungal diseases to attack plants. In winter, keep the air dry by ventilating when weather permits, or install a fan or a de-humidifier.

Care of indoor plants before going away

When going away, it is possible to ensure that indoor plants do not dry out. To keep water loss to a minimum, move plants into the shade and use one of the following watering methods. To use a capillary mat, group pot plants on an upturned tray, draining board, or shelf. Let the mat trail into another tray, the sink, or bath that is filled with water to supply the plants. Holes in plastic pots allow water through,

and clay pots are as good if saturated beforehand. Stand large or single pots on wick waterers, which draw water into the compost from a reservoir by means of a wick. Alternatively, water

the plant thoroughly, allow it to drain, and place it in a sealed, plastic bag to avoid moisture loss. Check for and control any pests or diseases before going away.

Guzmania lingulata

Syngonium podophyllum 'Albolineatum'

Calathea

CAPILLARY MATTING
Place pot plants on one end of a piece of wet matting. Leave the other end submerged in a water reservoir. The plants must be above the water so that they can draw it up as they need it.

Adiantum capillus-veneris

Ficus pumila 'Variegata'

PLASTIC BAG
Hold a clear, plastic bag away from the foliage with split canes. Seal with a plastic twist-tie or fold the neck of the bag under the pot.

Temperature regulation

Use ventilation to control temperatures in the greenhouse and avoid severe fluctuations that can harm plants. Too much ventilation slows growth; too little leads to high temperatures. On windy days, ventilate the greenhouse on the leeward side to avoid harmful draughts. For further information, see GREENHOUSES AND FRAMES, "Ventilation" (p.483) and "Shading" (p.484).

Hygiene

Keep the greenhouse clear of all debris that may harbour pests, and remove dead leaves and flowers before they rot. Wash or renew the aggregates on benches if they are infested with tiny snails or clogged with soil. Each autumn, take the plants outside and clean the greenhouse. Choose a still, warm day when the change in their environment is least likely to affect the plants. A thorough scrub-down is preferable, otherwise give the greenhouse a good sweeping and hosing down (see GREENHOUSE AND FRAMES, "Routine maintenance", p.491).

Frost protection

In unheated greenhouses, stop plant roots freezing in cold weather by keeping them nearly dry. Cover plants with a layer of plastic sheeting, fibre fleece, or newspaper, and beds with bracken or straw. Lag the base of shrubs and climbers with insulating material, secured with netting or twine. Plunge small pots in sand.

Pests and diseases

Regularly check buds, growing points, and the backs of leaves, and take early remedial action. Destroy badly infested plants, and isolate less affected specimens until they are clear of trouble. Isolate newly purchased plants for two weeks and control pests and diseases before placing them with other plants. Particular problems may be caused by vine weevil larvae (p.564) and red spider mites (p.550), especially in dry, centrally heated air in winter.

In warm, moist, greenhouse conditions, pests and diseases, such as grey mould/*Botrytis* (p.557) and powdery mildew (p.550), aphids (p.550) and hence viruses (p.553), and whiteflies (p.550), can spread rapidly. During the annual clean-up, (see "Routine maintenance", p.491) remove plants likely to be harmed by chemicals; fumigate the greenhouse and control any pests or diseases before replacing the plants. See also PLANT PROBLEMS (pp.545–77).

Hydroculture

This system has developed from hydroponics, which is a technique for growing plants in water to which all necessary nutrients are added. In hydroculture, "water roots" (which are slightly different from plant roots growing in soil) are supported in an open-mesh pot of inert growing medium and nutrients added to water in an outer, watertight container. A calibrated, floating marker in a clear, plastic indicator measures "maximum", "optimum/best", or "minimum" water levels.

Hydroculture has several advantages: it is easy to provide the plants with a precise and appropriate amount of air, water, and nutrients; the growing medium is clean, well drained, odourless, free from overacidity and clogging, which discourages weeds, pests, and diseases; and growth is often faster and stronger than in soil. Bulbs, cacti, orchids, and many plants that are commonly grown in offices flourish under hydroculture; see also the "Planter's guide to indoor plants", p.435.

Preparing plants

Plants are best obtained from specialist nurseries or raised from cuttings, although some will transfer from soil. Between early spring and early autumn, choose a young, healthy plant and remove it carefully from its pot. Soak the root ball in water at room temperature for half an hour until the soil comes away from the roots, and gently rinse the roots clean.

Planting

If using a fertilizer cartridge, clip it firmly into the culture pot base before planting. Wash and soak some clay pellets, then half-fill a culture pot with them. Place the plant in the pot, then spread out its

WASHING PLANT ROOTS

Wash off soil traces under slowly running, cool water while holding the plant (here a Dieffenbachia).

The inner culture pot holds the plant and the growing medium (here clay pellets), which may be placed in any suitable watertight container.

Water level indicator in moulded holder

Inner culture pot of flexible plastic

Open mesh to allow free flow of water and nutrients

Water

Recess for fertilizer cartridge

CLAY PELLETS

Clay pellets

Outer, watertight container

Plant developing "water roots"

A TABLE-TOP DISPLAY

Chamaedorea elegans

Aucuba japonica 'Variegata'

Syngonium podophyllum

Euphorbia milii

Pilea 'Norfolk'

Group several plants in inner culture pots in a larger bowl.

roots, and carefully fill the pot to its rim with pellets. Insert the water level indicator. Place planted culture pots either singly or in groups in watertight containers; clear glass is unsuitable because it lets light reach the roots. Water to the "optimum/best" level on the indicator. Keep the plants at 18–25°C (64–77°F). If they have previously been grown in soil, cover them with clear, plastic bags to prevent them drying out while water roots are developing.

Watering

The roots are kept moist by the capillary action of the porous growing medium and dislike being in water for long periods, so let the level drop to "minimum" before watering. Occasionally keeping to "minimum" level for 2–3 days encourages new root formation. Never keep to "optimum" for more than two weeks.

Before going away, top up the containers to "maximum" level or

stand the culture pots in a tray. Add water and nutrients until the level rises to about 3cm (1¼in).

Feeding

Various soluble fertilizers are available; follow the supplier's instructions. Minerals in the tap water react with the fertilizers to release nutrients, which are then absorbed as needed by the plant.

Propagation from cuttings

Prepare cuttings in the normal way (see p.453), then root them in a jar of water or plant directly in small culture pots. Insert the cuttings 3–4cm (1–1½in) deep in 2–4mm (1/16–1/8in) clay pellets. Cover them with a plastic bag or place in a propagator to reduce evaporation, and keep them in bright, indirect light for two weeks. As soon as new growth appears, remove the cover. Start normal watering and feeding two weeks after planting.

TYPES OF FERTILIZER

Slow-release cartridge, containing granular fertilizer, to clip into base of inner pot

Soluble, granular fertilizer

Soluble tablets

Fertilizers for use with hydroculture pots are formulated to suit tap water of various hardnesses.

Training and pruning plants grown under cover

T HE BASIC principles of training and pruning under cover are much the same as for outdoors, although it may be necessary to adapt these to accommodate extended flowering periods and limited space. Climbing plants that are too tender to be grown in the open may be readily cultivated under cover. If properly trained and pruned, they make efficient use of confined space and provide shade for other plants.

Plant supports

Plants that need support when grown under cover include ornamental climbers, some shrubs, annuals, fruiting vegetables, fruit trees, and vines (*Vitis*). True climbers find their own way up supports (see "Climbing methods and supports", p.94), while shrubs, grown as climbers against a wall for example, need tying in.

Some vines require a permanent, rigid support securely attached to the framework of a wooden greenhouse or to the glazing bars of an alloy-framed one. Wires, stretched horizontally along the walls of the greenhouse, are useful for training all climbers. In lean-to greenhouses,

CLIMBING PLANTS FOR GROWING UNDER COVER

Prune after flowering
Allemanda cathartica
  'Hendersonii' ❋ ◉
Bougainvillea ❋
Clerodendrum thomsoniae ❋ ◉
Distictis buccinatoria ❋
Jasminum, some ❋
Kennedia rubicunda ❋
Mandevilla splendens ❋ ◉

Mandevilla splendens

Pandorea
  jasminoides ❋
Passiflora ❋
Senecio, some ❋
Solanum wendlandii ❋ ◉
Stephanotis floribunda ❋ ◉
Thunbergia ❋

Prune as required
Agapetes macrantha ❋
Hoya ❋
Asarina erubescens ❋
Cissus ❋
Cobaea scandens ❋
Gynura aurantiaca ❋ ◉
Ipomoea horsfalliae ❋

KEY
❋ *Not hardy*
◉ *Requires high humidity*

ESTABLISHING THE SUPPORT FRAMEWORK

Stretch wires tightly between vine eyes (see inset). Tie in the stronger shoots and prune them to downward-growing buds to encourage horizontal growth.

stretch the wires between vine eyes attached to the rear wall to avoid cutting out light. Alternatively, attach the wire to drilled and bolted, vertical wall battens. Keep the wires taut by using a straining bolt at the end of each wire. Space the wires at equal intervals: vines require a 25cm (10in) spacing; fruit trees 38–45cm (15–18in). Tie in the stems of climbers with soft string to horizontal or vertical support wires.

Netting may be attached to the framework of the greenhouse and used to support plants. Plastic netting perishes and needs replacing after one or two seasons, so it is not suitable for perennials. Instead, use plastic-coated wire netting.

There are also some useful purpose-made, wire-mesh frameworks and various forms of wooden trellis available: fix them securely to battens attached to the greenhouse wall. Train the plants gently along netting or mesh as they grow, and tie them in with soft string.

Annual ornamental climbers, or fruiting vegetables such as tomatoes, may be tied with soft string to bamboo canes placed vertically at 15–30cm (6–12in) intervals. Alternatively, drop lengths of strong string from secure fixings in the roof to the base of the plants. Tie the string loosely below the plant's first true leaf, then wind it around the stems and run it back to the frame. Never let the string become too tight around the stem of the plant. For details of the treatment you should give to particular plants, see the pruning and training sections in the relevant chapters.

Pruning plants grown indoors

Like plants that are grown outdoors, many indoor plants require regular pruning to maintain their vigour and encourage flowering. Others simply become too big for the available

space, or need cutting back to maintain an attractive and balanced framework. With pruning, cutting back, or pinching out, most plants may be trained and shaped. Drastic pruning is required only to remove old, weakened sections or to renovate a neglected plant.

Always use tools with well-sharpened blades to avoid damaging the remaining stems, and make a downwards, sloping cut above a bud to stimulate the growth of new shoots. A sharp knife is ideal for working on soft stems; use a pair of secateurs for woody ones.

When and what to prune
The best time for pruning depends on the flowering season of the plant and on the age of wood on which plants bloom. Some plants flower only on the new season's growth, and on these the old growth may be safely cut back in the spring without harming production of the next season's flowers. Others flower on older wood, so should be cut back only after flowering. See guidelines given on pruning for ornamental shrubs (pp.75–82), climbers (pp.104–107), and on pruning to produce fruit on vines (pp.401–407) and tree fruits (see pp.375–400).

CUTTING BACK AFTER FLOWERING

Cut back the flowered shoots to leave two or three buds. This encourages the production of next season's flowering shoots, which should be tied horizontally into the wires.

Pruning to restrict growth
Under glass, space for shrubs and climbers is always limited. Although major problems may be avoided by choosing the most suitable plant for the size of the greenhouse, it may be necessary to restrict growth to stop plants blocking the light. Climbers growing in the ground have to be rigorously controlled when they have filled their allotted space since they may overwhelm other plants.

Few shrubs and ornamental climbers grown under glass flower on old wood (but do check first), so pruning back fairly hard after flowering is generally advisable and safe; the time of flowering varies not only from species to species but also according to temperature and location. Cut back over-long stems in autumn; remove stray shoots whenever they appear, regardless of whether it is time to prune or not.

Some plants flower for much of the year under glass, yet must be pruned to control them. In early spring, cut out the previous season's growth on mature *Abutilon* hybrids, and cut back *Coronilla* and *Hibiscus*. *Hoya* species and cultivars continue to flower on old stems, so do not remove them. *Agapetes* also flowers on old wood, but may need cutting back to induce bushiness.

Pinching out
To improve the shape and increase the number of flowering shoots that are produced on young, scandent, or trained shrubs, pinch out the tips of new shoots throughout the growing season.

Shrubs that respond well to this treatment include fuchsias, *Abutilon*, *Brunfelsia*, *Centradenia*, *Hibiscus*, *Reinwardtia*, and *Tibouchina*.

AUTUMN PRUNING TO RESTRICT GROWTH

In the autumn, cut out the weaker shoots and reduce dense growth; this allows plenty of light to penetrate the foliage and encourages the development of strong shoots to form a sturdy framework.

Propagation

PROPAGATING indoor plants is an economical way to increase your stock and to replace old plants with younger, more vigorous specimens. Successful propagation requires clean conditions, warmth, light, and sufficent humidity.

The easiest method of propagation is by division, which produces only a few plants at one time. The majority of new plants for growing indoors or under cover are grown from seed or cuttings, however, since these methods usually yield a greater number of new plants. Some plants may be increased by layering.

Propagation by division

Division is a quick way of propagating plants. Many plants produce plantlets, runners, offsets, or bulbils, which root themselves and may be severed from the parent and potted up.

Dividing the rootstock
Before dividing a pot plant, water the root ball thoroughly and allow it to drain. Herbaceous and clump-forming plants may be gently pulled apart or cut into separate pieces, each with its own root system, and repotted. Use a sharp knife to separate the fleshy roots of rhizomatous plants; retain vigorous sections with young growth and fibrous, feeding roots. Prune any long, thick roots, and any that are damaged. Dust the wounds with fungicide. Replant each division in a clean pot using a similar compost to that used for the parent plant. Water the plants and keep them in good light, but out of direct sun, until they are established. See also "Potting on and top-dressing", p.446.

Dividing plantlets
Plantlets are small versions of the parent plant that grow on its leaves, stolons, stems, or inflorescences. Once they are large enough to handle, detach them with about 3cm (1¼in) of the leaf stalk or stolon, where appropriate. Insert the plantlet stalk in a pot of peat-substitute- or peat-based potting compost so that the plantlet rests on the surface. Water the pot and cover it with a plastic bag to preserve the humidity. Roots should form in about three weeks. After this, the plantlet takes up to five weeks to resume growth, at which point it is ready to pot on.

Dividing rooting runners
Some plants, such as *Saxifraga stolonifera* (syn. *S. sarmentosa*) and *Episcia*, spread by runners. If these are rooted individually in pots of compost, they may then be severed from the parent to make new plants.

Dividing offsets and bulbils
Offsets are small plants that develop around the base of plants. Choose a well-developed one with some roots; cut or break it off cleanly from the main stem and insert it in a pot of

HOW TO PROPAGATE POT PLANTS BY DIVISION

1 *Thoroughly water the plant (here Calathea) an hour before dividing it. Support the plant, then invert the pot and tap its rim on a hard surface. Slide out the plant.*

2 *Remove surplus compost, either by gently shaking the plant or by teasing some of the compost away with your fingers, so that the roots are accessible.*

3 *Use hands or a hand fork to prise the root ball into sections, each with a portion of roots. Take care not to damage the stems or fibrous roots.*

4 *Using a clean, sharp knife, trim back any thick roots so that the divisions will fit into their new pots, but take care to leave the delicate, fibrous roots intact.*

5 *Select sections with healthy, young shoots (see inset) for replanting. Insert each section in a pot of moist, loam-based potting compost. Gently firm the compost and water well to encourage the roots to establish. Label the pot.*

PROPAGATION BY ROOTING RUNNERS

1 *Peg down runners (here Saxifraga stolonifera) in individual 6cm (3in) pots of moist, standard cutting compost. Keep them well watered.*

2 *After a few weeks, separate each rooted plantlet, in its pot, from the parent by cutting the runner close to the young plant. Label the pot.*

451

moist potting compost. Cover the pot with a plastic bag until new growth is produced.

Some plants produce bulbils on the fronds or in the leaf axils. Detach these and root them in moist, loam-based potting compost. For further information, see LILIES, *Propagating from Stem Bulbils*, p.243.

Growing indoor plants from seed

The seed of pure species breeds true but that of many hybrid indoor plants does not. Uniform results may be obtained, however, from selections, or first generation (F1) hybrids of biennials, annuals, and a few perennials, such as cyclamen and pelargoniums.

Seed composts and containers
Use a compost prepared specifically for seed (see SOILS AND FERTILIZERS, "Propagation composts", p.534). It should be a free-draining and open-textured mix, which holds moisture without becoming sodden or forming a hard crust on the top.

A variety of containers may be used, such as half-pots, pans, and half or quarter seed trays. Always use a size of container that is appropriate to the number of plants required. Special cellular trays that allow each seed to grow in its own individual plug of soil are also readily available.

When to sow
Most seeds are spring-sown, but seeds of early spring-flowering species are usually sown in autumn. Annuals may be sown in several batches from spring to early summer for a succession of blooms. Seeds of many exotic species are spring-sown but often germinate freely if sown as soon as they are ripe. It may be difficult, however, to keep the young seedlings alive in winter.

Preparing the seed
Some seeds need special treatment to help them germinate. Seeds with hard coats often need pre-sowing treatment, such as soaking in warm water; the time required varies from about 10 minutes for *Cordyline australis* to about 72 hours for banana seed. Other hard-coated seeds, such as *Caesalpinia pulcherrima*, will not germinate unless the seed coat is chipped with a knife or file. If the seed is too small to handle, gently abrade it between two sheets of fine sandpaper. Follow the supplier's instructions on the seed packet to ensure success.

Sowing the seed
Overfill the container with standard seed compost and tap it on the bench; scrape off the surplus so that the compost is level with the container rim. Firm the compost to within 1cm ($\frac{1}{2}$in) of the rim.

Water the compost before sowing the seed, and allow the container to drain well. Watering with a watering can after sowing may "bunch" the seed or wash it together, leading to problems with overcrowding and damping off later.

Sow all seed thinly and evenly. Tiny seed is easier to sow if it is first mixed with horticultural sand. Place large seeds far enough apart to allow the seedlings to grow without being thinned later on. Alternatively, sow the seeds singly into small pots, cellular trays, or soil blocks.

As a general rule, cover seeds with compost to the depth of their smallest diameter. Very tiny seeds, however, or seeds that require light to germinate, should be left uncovered on the surface of the compost. Cover the container with a sheet of glass, a plastic bag, or a propagator lid to maintain humidity and stop the compost drying out. Place the container in the correct temperature, in good light but out of direct sunlight, and leave the seed to germinate.

Germination temperatures
Seeds usually germinate at 5°C (10°F) higher than the minimum needed by the same plant in growth. As a general rule, a temperature of 15–18°C (59–64°F) is suitable. The correct temperature varies for different seed, so follow the instructions given on the seed packets. Plants that are raised under cover for growing outside germinate at 10°C (50°F) or less. Many tropical or subtropical plants need 24–6°C (75–9°F) to germinate. If it is hard to maintain such temperatures indoors, consider using a heated propagating case. Although there are many different types and sizes, most have thermostats that allow a specific temperature to be maintained.

Aftercare of sown seed
Wipe off any condensation on covers to discourage fungal diseases. After seven to ten days, check the containers daily for signs of germination and remove the covers as soon as the seedlings appear. Germination times vary greatly, however, so some larger seeds may take several months to germinate. Keep the compost moist; use either a watering can or, for very delicate seedlings, a mist-sprayer.

Feeding should not be necessary if seed was sown in compost containing a small amount of nutrient, although seedlings that are to stay in their container for some time may benefit from a liquid feed as they grow. If the seedlings start to bend towards light, turn them daily and shade with cardboard or shade netting if there is danger of sun scorch.

Pricking out the seedlings
When the seedlings are 1cm ($\frac{1}{2}$in) high, they may be pricked out into larger pots or packs. Water them first, allow them to drain for an hour, then loosen them by tapping the side of the container. Lift the seedlings out of the container using a small, flat implement. If the seedlings are clumped together, use a dibber or pencil to tease them apart. Handle the seedlings carefully by the leaves since the stems are easily damaged.

Use a dibber to make holes in some fresh compost in a container. Lower each seedling into place so that it is at the same depth as before. Place more compost around the roots and lightly firm in each seedling. Small seedlings should be set about 2.5cm (1in)

INDOOR FLOWERING PLANTS THAT MAY BE RAISED FROM SEED
Alonsoa ❁
Begonia (fibrous-rooted and tuberous kinds) ❁ ◎
Browallia ❁
Caesalpinia pulcherrima ❁
Campanula ❁ ◎
Clitoria ❁
Cobaea ❁
Cuphea ❁
Cyclamen, some ❁ ◎
Exacum affine ❁ ◎
Impatiens ❁ ◎
Jacaranda mimosifolia ❁
Pelargonium (modern multi-bloom hybrids) ❁
Primula x *kewensis* ❁ ◎,
   P. malacoides ❁ ◎,
   P. obconica ❁ ◎,
   P. sinensis ❁ ◎

Primula malacoides

Salpiglossis ❁
Schizanthus ❁
Senecio x *hybridus* ❁
Sinningia ❁ ◎
Thunbergia ❁
Torenia ❁

KEY
❁ *Not hardy*
◎ *Requires high humidity*

RAISING INDOOR PLANTS FROM SEED

1 *Mix very fine, dust-like seed (here* Campanula*) with dry, fine sand in a bag; this makes it possible to sow the seed more evenly. Sow larger seed by hand.*

2 *Sow the mixture thinly onto a pot of moist, seed compost, using a small funnel of paper held close to the compost surface. Label, and place in a propagator.*

3 *When the seedlings are large enough to handle by their leaves, use a dibber to prick them out into a container of moist potting compost.*

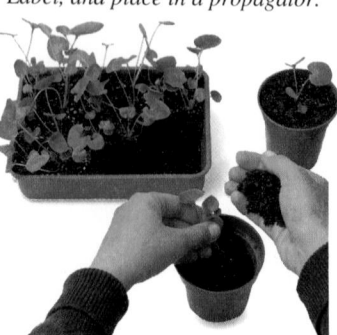

4 *Once the seedlings have become established, pot them on singly into individual pots or modules to grow on. Water, and label each pot.*

apart, and larger ones about 5cm (2in). Water the seedlings with a fine-rosed watering can. For seedlings sown individually in a cellular tray, lift the seedling with its plug of compost, and pot it up.

Potting on
Once the roots of plants have filled the containers, they need potting on (see p.446). The new pot should be large enough to allow for a 2.5cm (1in) gap all around the root ball. Insert the plant so that the base of its stem is level with the surface of the compost. Settle the compost by tapping the pot on a bench, firm it lightly, and water it using a fine rose.

Once potted on in normal compost, the new plants can be treated as mature specimens. Ensure that the correct conditions are maintained; different indoor plants have widely varying requirements.

Propagation from cuttings

Most tender, indoor plants may be readily propagated from softwood (tip) cuttings (rooted in compost or in water), leaf-bud or leaf cuttings. Semi-ripe or woody cuttings may be taken from indoor shrubs. The important factors for success with cuttings are timing, hygiene, warmth, and humidity.

Semi-ripe cuttings
Take cuttings of semi-ripe wood from the current season's growth, in summer after the main flush of fast, spring growth but before the wood is fully ripe; suitable material is firm, but flexible, and offers some resistance if bent. Plants grown under cover may reach maturity before mid-summer, so check new shoots carefully from early summer onwards. For details of the technique, see ORNAMENTAL SHRUBS, "Semi-ripe cuttings", p.84.

Leaf-bud cuttings
Genera such as *Ficus* and *Hoya* may be increased by leaf-bud cuttings, a type of semi-ripe cutting. Cut stems into 2.5–5cm (1–2in) lengths, each with a single leaf and leaf axil bud. Then insert them into pots of cutting compost and place the pots in a propagator at a temperature of 15–18°C (59–64°F). For further details, see ORNAMENTAL SHRUBS, "Leaf-bud cuttings", p.85.

Softwood cuttings
These are taken in early spring. Select new, short-noded sideshoots and remove them with a clean, sharp knife. When preparing cuttings, make clean, precise cuts so that no snags are left on the stems. Dip the base of each stem in hormone rooting powder, and, using a dibber or a pencil, insert several cuttings into a pot of standard cutting compost. The cuttings may be close together in a pot or placed around the edges as long as their leaves do not touch.

Place the pot in a propagator or cover it with a plastic bag to reduce water loss – make sure that the bag does not touch the cuttings, however. Leave the pot in a warm, light position but out of direct sunlight. Check the cuttings each day or two and, if necessary, clear any condensation by opening the propagator or bag for a while.

It should take about four to six weeks for new roots to form. At this stage, when young growth may be seen, transfer the cuttings to individual pots of peat-substitute- or loam-based compost to grow on. Keep the young plants in a warm, lightly shaded place until they are well established.

PROPAGATING FROM SOFTWOOD CUTTINGS

1 *Fill a 13cm (5in) pot with moist cutting compost and tamp it down until it is level.*

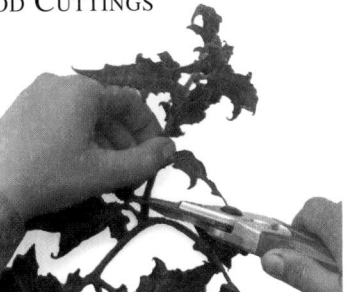

2 *Using secateurs or a clean, sharp knife, cut off, just above a node, some new, short-noded shoots 10–15cm (4–6in) long. The plant shown here is* Gynura aurantiaca.

3 *Trim each cutting just below a node, removing the lower leaves to create a length of clean stem at the base (see inset). Do not leave snags, which might rot.*

4 *Dust the cuttings with hormone rooting powder and insert them in the pot so that the leaves are just above the compost.*

5 *Water and label the cuttings. Place the pot in a propagator in a warm, light place and maintain a soil temperature of 18–21°C (64–70°F) until the cuttings are rooted and ready to pot on.*

INDOOR PLANTS THAT MAY BE PROPAGATED BY SOFTWOOD CUTTINGS

Abutilon, some ✿
Acalypha ✿ ◎
Aeschynanthus ✿ ◎
Alloplectus ✿ ◎
Bougainvillea ✿

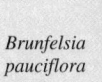

Brunfelsia pauciflora

Brunfelsia pauciflora ✿ ◎
Callisia ✿
Catharanthus ✿
Cissus ✿
Codiaeum ✿ ◎
Coleus blumei ✿ ◎
Columnea ✿ ◎
Crassula, some ✿ , ◎
Crossandra ✿ ◎
Epiphyllum ✿ ◎
Epipremnum ✿
Euphorbia pulcherrima ✿
Ficus benjamina ✿
Fittonia ✿ ◎
Gardenia ✿ ◎
Gynura ✿ ◎
Hibiscus, some ✿

Hibiscus rosa-sinensis 'The President'

Hoya ✿
Impatiens repens ✿ ◎
Iresine ✿ ◎
Ixora coccinea ✿ ◎
Jasminum mesnyi ✿
Justicia ✿
Kalanchoe ✿
Mandevilla splendens ✿ ◎
Pachystachys ✿
Passiflora ✿
Pelargonium ✿
Pellionia ✿
Pentas lanceolata ✿
Peperomia ✿ ◎
Pilea ✿ ◎
Plumbago auriculata ✿
Polyscias ✿ ◎
Rhipsalidopsis gaertneri ✿ , R. rosea ✿
Rhipsalis ✿ ◎
Rhoicissus capensis ✿
Ruellia ✿ ◎
Schlumbergera ✿ ◎
Sonerila ✿ ◎
Sparmannia ✿ ◎
Stephanotis ✿ ◎
Streptosolen ✿
Syngonium ✿ ◎
Tibouchina ✿ ◎
Tradescantia, some ✿ , ◎

KEY
✿ *Not hardy*
◎ *Requires high humidity*

Rooting softwood cuttings in water

The simplest method of rooting softwood cuttings is to place them in a glass or jar of water in a light, warm position. Prepare each cutting as for a normal softwood cutting, ensuring that the lower leaves are cleanly removed. Support the cutting on netting placed over the glass so that the stem is suspended in the water. When the roots develop and there is fresh growth, pot up the cuttings. Prepare pots with drainage material and 2.5cm (1in) of compost. Hold each cutting in a pot with its roots spread and fill in with compost until the roots are covered. Firm and water the cuttings thoroughly.

Propagating from leaves

Some plants may be propagated easily from whole leaves or leaf sections. In some cases, the leaves are inserted in compost (or water), while in others they are scored or cut up before being inserted or secured flat onto the compost. Each leaf should produce a number of small plantlets where the leaf veins have been cut.

Whole leaves

Certain plants, often those with fleshy leaves growing in rosettes such as African violets (*Saintpaulia*) and gloxinias (*Sinningia speciosa*), as well as Rex and rhizomatous begonias, and some succulents (see p.271) may be increased from leaf cuttings.

For the cuttings, choose healthy, undamaged, fully grown leaves and cut them off close to the base of the leaf stalks. Trim each stalk with a straight cut 3cm (1¼in) below the leaf blade; insert the cuttings individually into prepared pots of cut-ting compost (1 part sand and 1 part peat substitute or peat), label, and water. Place the pots in a propagator or cover each one with a clear plastic bag or improvised cloche (see below). As soon as each cutting produces plantlets, remove its cover. Grow on the cuttings until the plantlets are large enough to be teased apart and potted on individually. Alternatively, leaves with long stalks (especially African violets) may be rooted in water, although rooting tends to take longer than in compost.

Scored or cut leaves

The leaves of plants with prominent veins, such as Rex begonias and

PROPAGATING SOFTWOOD CUTTINGS IN WATER

1 *Using a sharp, clean knife, remove healthy, short-noded cuttings, 10–15cm (4–6in) long, from a healthy, vigorous plant (here Coleus). Cut each just above a node.*

2 *Trim each cutting below a node and remove the lower leaves to create a length of clean stem at the base (see inset).*

3 *Insert the stems through a piece of wire netting over the top of a jar of water. Ensure that the stems are in the water.*

4 *Keep the water topped up so that the lower end of each cutting is always below the surface. A network of roots should develop.*

5 *When the cuttings are well rooted carefully plant each one into a 6cm (3in) pot of sandy potting compost.*

HALF-LEAF SECTIONS

1 *Divide the leaf (here Strepto-carpus) by cutting out the midrib and exposing the veins.*

2 *Insert the sections, cut edges down, in shallow trenches. Gently firm them in.*

PROPAGATING INDOOR PLANTS FROM LEAF CUTTINGS

1 *Cut healthy leaves from the parent plant (here Saintpaulia). Insert each stalk in a small pot of cutting compost so that the leaf blade touches the compost.*

2 *Water, label, and cover the pots. Small cloches made from the bases of plastic drinks bottles are suitable. Leave them in a warm, light place out of direct sunlight.*

3 *Each leaf should produce several plantlets. When these develop, remove the covers, and grow them on until they are large enough to pot up individually.*

various members of the family Gesneriaceae, for example *Strepto-carpus*, will produce small plantlets if they are scored or cut up and the cut veins are then kept in contact with moist compost; the leaves may be either divided in half or into small sections, or they may be scored through.

Whichever method is used, keep the container in a propagator or in a clear plastic bag in a light place but out of direct sunlight; inflate the bag so that it does not touch the leaf sections, and seal it. The leaves being propagated should be kept at 18–24°C (64–75°F).

When clumps of plantlets develop from the cut veins, carefully lift and separate them, retaining a little compost around the roots of each one, and pot them up individually into 6cm (3in) pots of cutting compost.

Some succulent plants, including *Sansevieria* and those that have flattened, leaf-like stems such as *Epiphyllum*, may also be propagated from "leaf" sections although these are treated slightly differently. For details, see CACTI AND OTHER SUCCULENTS, "Propagation from stem sections", p.272.

PROPAGATION FROM CUT LEAVES

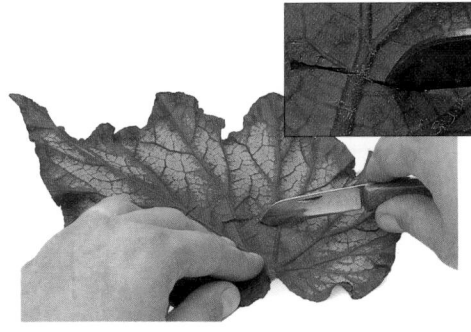

1 *Select a young, healthy leaf (here* Begonia rex) *and make a 1cm (¹⁄₂in) long incision with a sharp knife straight across each of the strongest veins on the underside of the leaf (see inset).*

2 *Place the leaf, cut side downwards, on a tray of cutting compost. Pin its veins to the compost. Label, and place the tray in a propagator or a plastic bag.*

3 *Leave the tray in a warm place out of direct sunlight. When the plantlets have developed, carefully separate them from the leaf (see inset) and pot them on singly.*

LEAF SQUARES

1 *Cut 4 or 5 square sections the size of a postage stamp from a healthy leaf. Each piece should include a strong vein.*

2 *Place the sections, veins downwards, on moist compost. Pin with wire hoops, then treat as other leaf sections.*

Propagation of tuberous begonias

When begonia tubers die back naturally in autumn, store them in their pots at 5–10°C (41–50°F) in a dry place over winter. Alternatively, lift and clean the tubers, dust their crowns with fungicide, and store them in boxes of dry sand, peat substitute, or peat.

At the beginning of the growing season, place the tubers in a tray of moist, sandy compost (1 part sharp sand, 1 part peat-substitute- or peat-based compost). Store them at a minimum temperature of 13–16°C (55–61°F). When new buds are clearly visible, cut the tubers into sections, making sure that each has at least one bud and some roots. Dust the sections with fungicide and leave them to dry for a few hours in a warm place. When the cut surfaces have formed calluses, pot up the sections in loam-based compost. Do not firm the compost heavily or water it, since this encourages fungal attack.

Alternatively, allow new shoots to develop on the tubers, and use these as basal cuttings. Take the cuttings so that each retains an eye. Dip the base of each cutting in hormone rooting powder and insert them, 2cm (³⁄₄in) deep, around the edge of a pot or pan of loam-based potting compost.

1 *In autumn, lift the dormant tubers and clean them. Dust the crowns with fungicide and overwinter them in a dry place.*

2 *In spring, place the tubers, concave side upwards, 5cm (2in) apart and 2.5cm (1in) deep, in a tray of moist, sandy compost.*

3 *When shoots appear, cut the tubers into sections, each with a bud and some roots. Dust cut surfaces with fungicide and allow to dry.*

4 *Pot up the sections singly in 13cm (5in) pots, with the top of each level with the compost surface. Water a little, and label.*

5 *Keep the pots in a propagator in a warm, frost-free place until the sections are established, then pot them on singly.*

BASAL CUTTINGS

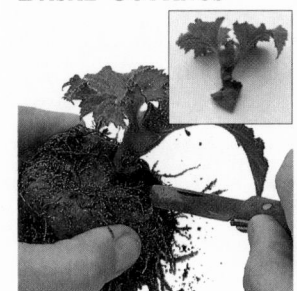

Remove 5cm (2in) shoots from the tuber, each with an eye of tuber at the base. Pot them up and treat as divided tubers.

Propagation by layering

Layering involves wounding the stem of a plant, inducing it to produce roots, and then separating the rooted stem. This method has a high success rate since the layered stem receives nutrients from the parent plant while it is developing.

Some indoor plants may be propagated by layering – either in air or in the soil. Air layering produces a fairly large, new plant from an older specimen but it may take some considerable time. Simple layering in soil provides new stock quite quickly.

Air layering

This is an excellent method for replacing old or damaged house plants, for example the rubber plant (*Ficus elastica*) and its relatives. The top of the plant, or tip of a branch, may be encouraged to form new roots, and is then severed from the parent.

Choose a section of stem of new growth that is straight, about 10cm (4in) long, and of at least pencil thickness. Cut the bottom off a clear, plastic bag to create a transparent sleeve and slip it over the stem or, if the leaves are too large to permit this, fold a clear, plastic sheet around the stem and tape up the seam. Secure the sleeve below the selected area of the stem.

Using a sharp knife, make a shallow, upward-slanting cut in the side of the stem, then wedge this tongue open with moist sphagnum moss. Alternatively, on woody plants, score two rings 1–2cm ($\frac{1}{2}$–$\frac{3}{4}$in) apart below a healthy leaf joint on the selected area of the stem; the scores should be just deep enough to penetrate the bark without harming the wood. Peel off the bark between the rings, leaving the cambium undisturbed.

In both cases, dust the cut area with rooting powder. Pack the sleeve with damp moss, and seal it so that the area is tightly enclosed to prevent it from drying out. If the stem is heavy, provide cane support.

It may be many months before the roots show. If the moss begins to dry out, open up the plastic, add a little water, and reseal. When roots appear, sever the layered stem from the parent and pot it up into a loam-based potting compost. Water the young plant sparingly until it is established.

Simple layering

Climbing or trailing shoots may be layered into soil while they are still attached to the parent plant.

Choose a long, vigorous shoot and peg it down into a small pot of moist cutting compost. After three to four weeks, roots should start to grow into the compost and new shoots begin to form; the rooted layer may then be detached from the parent plant. If required, several shoots may be layered at the same time, each in its own pot.

When severing the new plants, always take care not to spoil the shape of the parent plant. For further information, see CLIMBING PLANTS, p.115.

SIMPLE LAYERING

Select a long, healthy shoot and peg down the young growth into a small pot filled with moist cutting compost. Leave it until roots have formed before detaching it from the parent plant.

Parent plant

Long, vigorous stem

Leaf node

Wire staple

Moist cutting compost

PHILODENDRON SCANDENS

HOW TO PROPAGATE BY AIR LAYERING

1 *Trim the leaves (here* Ficus elastica) *from a straight length of stem (see inset). Slide a plastic sleeve over the stem and fix the lower end with adhesive tape.*

2 *Fold down the sleeve. Hold the stem firmly and cut a "tongue" in it, making a slanted, upwards incision 5mm ($\frac{1}{4}$in) deep and 2.5cm (1in) long.*

3 *Apply hormone rooting powder to the wound and push moist sphagnum moss into the incision, using a split stake or the back of a knife blade.*

4 *Roll the sleeve back into position around the packed incision. Fill the sleeve with more moist sphagnum moss.*

5 *When the sleeve is tightly packed with moss, secure the upper end to the stem with adhesive tape.*

6 *When the new roots are visible through the sleeve, cut through the stem just below the root ball with secateurs. Remove the plastic sleeve.*

7 *Gently loosen the moss ball and tease out the roots. Pot the rooted layer into a container that allows a 5cm (2in) space around the root ball. Fill this with loam-based potting compost and firm it very gently, making sure that the new roots are not damaged. Water, label, and place the pot in a shaded position until the young plant is established.*

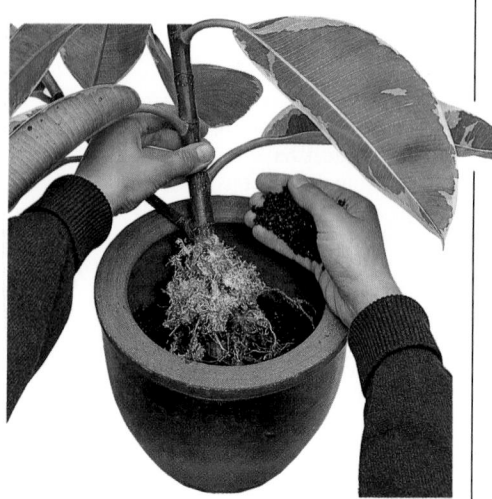

PART TWO

MAINTAINING THE GARDEN

*How to choose tools and greenhouse equipment,
style your garden with structures and surfaces, manage the effects
of climate and soil, and control pests, diseases, and weeds*

TOOLS AND EQUIPMENT

KEEPING A GARDEN *looking its best throughout the year involves a certain amount of maintenance, from routine tasks such as mowing the lawn and raking to occasional procedures such as hedgetrimming and rotavating. While it is unnecessary and expensive to invest in an entire catalogue's worth of garden equipment, having the correct tool for the job undoubtedly makes the work easier and faster, and produces a more professional result. Besides basic tools, for example a spade or a fork,* which will be in almost constant use, there will be other items of equipment that you cannot do without. Depending on individual requirements, these might include such things as a wheelbarrow for moving garden materials and refuse, a sprinkler for watering, or a supply of plastic seed trays. Assessing the type and amount of work you do in the garden makes it easier to decide exactly which tools you need; choosing them with care ensures that they will be durable and comfortable to use, as well as functional and effective.

Buying and using tools

Most modern gardening tools are based on traditional designs, although some may be improvements or variations on old concepts. A few completely new tools, however, have been successfully introduced. For example, until the 1980s, shredders and nylon-line trimmers were hardly known; yet they are now firmly established because they fulfil a demand not met by traditional tools.

Before buying a tool, the most important point to bear in mind is its function – it must perform correctly the task it is meant to do. Consider exactly what you need a particular tool for and how frequently you will use it. A simple, inexpensive pair of secateurs, for example, will be adequate if wanted only for pruning a few rose bushes once a year; if needed for intensive use, however, it is better to invest in a high-quality, more heavy-duty pair. Before purchasing a tool, wherever possible always try to check that it is:
• the best type of tool for the task;
• the right size and model to suit your needs;
• comfortable to use.
In large gardens, or for laborious or time-consuming tasks, consider using powered tools; since they are expensive and need careful handling and safety precautions, however, be sure that they are really needed.

To ensure that tools perform well and last a long time, it is important that they are properly maintained. Immediately after use, clean off any soil, grass clippings, or other plant material and wipe metal parts with an oily rag; all pruning and cutting tools will also need regular sharpening. Tools that are not needed over the winter months should be especially well oiled and then stored in a dry place.

In addition, factors such as expense and storage space must be taken into account: if a tool is needed only infrequently, hiring may be a more sensible option, especially for relatively expensive, bulky tools.

Hiring tools

If you decide to hire, book equipment in advance, especially tools likely to be in seasonal demand, such as powered lawnrakes and cultivators, and check whether the hire firm will deliver and collect the tools.

The condition of hired tools varies considerably. Some, especially powered tools, may even be potentially dangerous to operate. For this reason, you should always:
• Check for missing or loose parts. These may not be obvious, but if in doubt do not accept the tool.
• Look for loose bolts and fittings on tools such as powered cultivators that are subject to vibration.
• Ask for powered tools to be started, and check carefully for excessive vibration and noise.
• On electrical tools, check that the voltage is correct or that a suitable transformer is supplied if relevant. Look for frayed, cut, or exposed wires. Do not assume that the wiring is satisfactory just because the tool works adequately.
• On four-stroke engines, check the oil in the engine and transmission.
• Ask for a demonstration or instructions if you have never operated the tool before. This is particularly important with tools such as chainsaws, which can be dangerous to use.
• Buy or hire any recommended protective clothing (e.g. goggles, gloves, and ear protectors).
• Before signing the delivery note, comment on the contract or delivery note, if you have noticed any faults.

Safe use of tools

If you are not sure how to use a tool, ask for advice when buying or hiring, or contact the manufacturer. Correct use gives good results and helps prevent accidents. Make sure that the weight and length of the tool are suitable: a tool that is too heavy will be difficult to handle; one that is too short may cause back strain. Keep all powered tools in good repair and follow any safety recommendations. To minimize risks, make sure that a mains electric tool is fitted with a residual current device – sometimes called an earth leakage circuit breaker – which severs the supply in microseconds if the circuit leaks power (see also "Electrical safety", p.464).

DIGGING CORRECTLY
Keeping your back straight, not curved, when digging, hoeing, or raking helps to prevent backache.

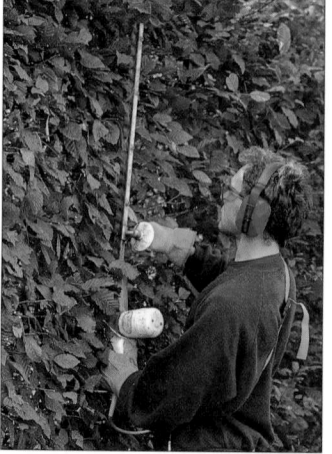
USING POWERED TOOLS
Take particular care when using powered tools, and always wear appropriate protective clothing.

Cultivation tools

The type of cultivation tools required depends on the nature of your garden. If you grow mainly vegetables or are cultivating a new garden, tools for digging will be a priority. If, however, the garden is well established, with lawns and perennial borders, surface cultivation tools such as hoes will be more important.

Spades

A spade is an essential tool, excellent for general cultivation, lifting soil, and digging holes for planting. There are two major types: standard digging spades, and the smaller and lighter border (also called ladies') spades. Some manufacturers also produce an intermediate-sized or medium spade that is suitable for general digging but lighter than a standard spade.

Some spades have a tread, which makes it easier to push the blade into the soil and less likely to damage footwear; these spades are, however, heavier and more expensive. For extensive digging, a larger spade (known as a "heavy"), which has a 30x20cm (12x8in) blade, may prove quicker to use.

If you find digging difficult or if the soil is very heavy, it may be worth buying an automatic spade to make the task less of a strain.

Forks

Garden forks are used for general cultivation, lifting rootcrops (which are more likely to be damaged with a spade), and shifting bulky material such as manure and garden compost. Most garden forks have four square metal prongs, and are generally available in two sizes: standard and border (or ladies'). Less common are medium, or youth, forks, an intermediate size between standard and border forks.

Other variations are also sometimes found. For example, a potato fork has broad, flat prongs and, generally, a larger head than a standard fork; it may be easier to use than a spade when digging heavy ground.

The head and neck of a fork should be forged in a single piece, with no welds or rough surfaces, the shaft fitting into a long socket in the neck. Some forks have shorter necks, the head held in place by two long metal plates riveted to the front and back of the wooden shaft. These are usually weaker and are now uncommon.

STANDARD
DIGGING SPADE
This is useful for shifting large amounts of soil, but it is heavy and therefore may be unsuitable or uncomfortable for some gardeners. It has a rectangular blade of about 28 x 19cm (11 x 7in).

"D"-type moulded hilt gives a good grip

Plastic hilt is comfortable even in cold weather

Tread makes digging easier

Coated blade may be easily cleaned

STAINLESS
STEEL BLADE
This is useful for a spade as it makes light work of digging and never rusts.

AUTOMATIC SPADE
Operating on a spring-and-lever system, the spade throws the soil forward without the need to bend. It is expensive, but may be worthwhile for the disabled or for those with back trouble.

BORDER SPADE
With a blade only 23 x 13cm (9 x 5in), this is designed for digging in confined spaces, for example a planting hole in a border, but it is also good for any general light work.

STANDARD FORK
This fork is useful for cultivating heavy soil, lifting vegetables, and shifting large loads, but some people may find it heavy to manoeuvre. Its head is about 30 x 20cm (12 x 8in).

Wooden shaft fitting into long socket in neck

Neck and head formed from one piece of metal for strength

Head

POTATO FORK
Primarily for lifting potatoes, this flat-tined fork may also be used for digging, and moving compost or garden refuse.

BORDER FORK
This is best for light work in borders and similar restricted areas. The size of the head – 23 x 14cm (9 x 5¹/₂in) – makes it suitable for anyone needing a small, lightweight fork.

Which metal?

Carbon steel is used for most garden tools. If cleaned and oiled after use, it should not rust, and it can be sharpened. Although stainless steel is more expensive and cannot be sharpened, it does make digging easier since the soil falls away from the blade more readily. Tools that have a "non-stick" coating may make working the soil and cleaning easier but the coating may wear off after long use.

Handles and hilts

A spade or fork shaft should be the correct length for the user's height to minimize back strain. The standard shaft length is 70–73cm (28–29in); a longer shaft, available up to 98cm (39in) long, will almost certainly be more comfortable for people over 1.7m (5ft 6in) tall.

Shafts are made from wood or metal, the latter sometimes covered with plastic or nylon. Both are generally strong, but even metal shafts may break if put under too much stress, and, unlike wooden ones, they cannot be replaced. Metal shafts, even plastic-coated, are colder than wood to hold in winter. Handle the tool, as if using it, to assess which type feels best.

"D"-TYPE HILTS
These are the most common type, but they may be uncomfortable for those with large hands, particularly when wearing gloves.

"Y"-TYPE HILTS
Similar to "D"-type hilts, but they may be weaker as they are formed by splitting the shaft wood.

"T"-TYPE HILTS
These have a cross-piece joined to the shaft end. Some gardeners find them comfortable, but they are not commonly available and may have to be ordered.

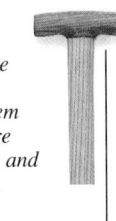

Hoes

Hoes are excellent for weeding and aerating soil; some types may be used to form seed drills. The Dutch hoe is probably the most versatile and is ideal for weeding between rows of plants and for creating drills. Apart from draw, digging, and onion hoes, there are proprietary hoes available for specific uses.

USING A DUTCH HOE
Hold the hoe so that the blade is parallel to the soil surface.

DUTCH HOE
This traditional hoe is excellent for weeding around plants. It cuts through surface weeds without damaging the plant roots.

COMBINATION HOE
This is suitable for chopping off weeds, drawing drills, and earthing up. Use the prongs to break up soil and draw seed drills.

TRIANGULAR HOE
Use the point for drawing a "V"-shaped drill; the flat side is for weeding narrow spaces in between plants.

DIGGING HOE
This has one or two chisel-like blades. It is used with a swinging motion to break up small areas of hard ground.

Moulded handle ensures a secure grip

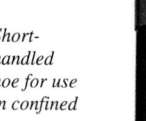

Short-handled hoe for use in confined areas

ONION HOE
This small hoe (above), also called a hand, or rock garden, hoe, is for weeding between onions and other closely grown plants where a normal hoe might cause damage. It is like a short-handled version of a draw hoe, and is used while squatting or kneeling.

DRAW HOE
This hoe (right) is good for chopping weeds, drawing up earth around plants, making flat-bottomed drills, and, with the blade corner, making "V"-shaped drills.

Curved neck makes the hoe easier to use in between plants without damaging them

Rakes

Rakes are excellent for levelling and breaking up the soil surface before planting and for gathering garden debris. There are two main types: general garden rakes and lawn rakes (see "Rakes and aerators", p.467).

A one-piece rake head is stronger than a bolstered (riveted) one, and the more teeth it has, the faster an area is covered; 12 teeth are adequate, 16 or more are preferable for large areas. A 1m (3ft) wide wooden rake is useful in a large garden.

Heads and shafts

Most rake and hoe heads are made from solid carbon steel; stainless steel ones are more expensive and do not work any better, although they are easier to clean and do not rust. Some rakes have a "non-stick" coating.

Shafts may be made from wood, aluminium, or plastic-covered metal. Shaft length is important: you should be able to stand upright while hoeing or raking to reduce strain on the back. Most people find a 1.5m (5ft) shaft comfortable, but a longer handle may be preferred.

GARDEN RAKE
This has short, wide, rounded teeth and is valuable for levelling soil, clearing the ground, and general garden tidying.

BOLSTERED RAKE
This cheaper garden rake has nail-like, riveted teeth.

Trowels and hand forks

A trowel is useful for digging holes for small plants and bulbs, and for working in containers and raised beds. A hand, or weed, fork may be used for weeding, lifting small plants, and for planting.

Most trowel blades and hand fork prongs are made from stainless steel, coated steel (e.g. chrome-plated), or ordinary carbon steel. Unlike carbon steel, stainless steel does not rust and is easy to keep clean but it is expensive. Coatings gradually tend to wear off in time. Some trowels have extra-long handles – up to 30cm (12in) – for more leverage. Hand forks with handles 1.2m (4ft) long reduce the need to bend when weeding the back of a border. Wooden, plastic, and plastic-coated handles are all generally comfortable to hold; metal ones tend to be cold.

HAND FORK
Often used for lifting small plants or loosening the soil when weeding. Unlike a trowel, it does not compact the soil, so it may be preferable to use when planting in heavy soil.

NARROW-BLADED TROWEL
Sometimes known as a rock garden or transplanting trowel, this is ideal for working in very confined areas such as rock gardens as well as for general transplanting tasks.

WIDE-BLADED TROWEL
This is useful for planting bulbs and bedding or other small plants, especially in confined areas such as containers and windowboxes.

Hand-weeding tools

For weeding between paving, bricks, or rocks, a patio weeder, which has a narrow, hooked blade, is ideal. A daisy grubber has a pronged blade suitable for levering up lawn weeds.

SPECIALIZED
WEEDERS
*A patio, or
paving stone,
weeder (right)
can be used
in narrow
crevices.
A daisy
grubber
(far right) may be
used to lift lawn weeds
without damaging the turf.*

Manual cultivators

A hand, or pronged, cultivator is used to break up the surface of compacted soil or to loosen weeds. It has a three- or five-pronged, metal head on a long shaft and is pulled through the soil, generally from a standing position. Some adjustable models have removable, central prongs.

Specialized hand cultivators may be useful for certain regular tasks. A star-wheeled cultivator, or miller, for example, forms a fine tilth when pushed to and fro through the soil, so is good when preparing a seedbed.

ADJUSTABLE MODELS
Cultivators with removable central prongs are suitable for tasks such as cultivating each side of a row of seedlings. Some models have a detachable handle which may be fitted to other types of compatible tool head, for example a rake or hoe.

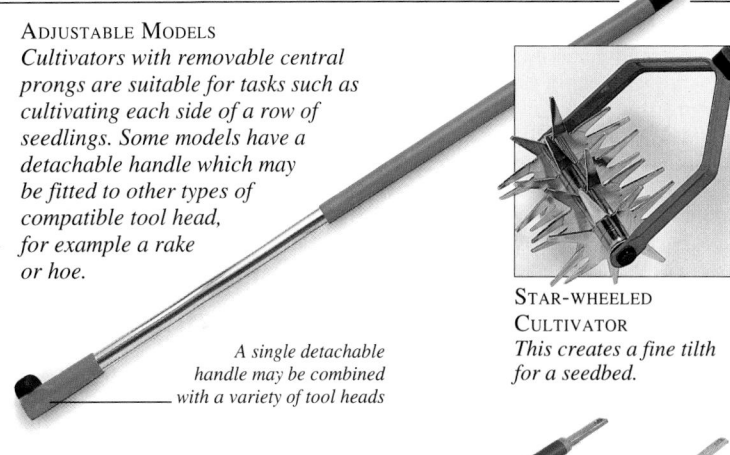

STAR-WHEELED
CULTIVATOR
This creates a fine tilth for a seedbed.

A single detachable handle may be combined with a variety of tool heads

REMOVABLE PRONGS
When working in very confined areas, it may be useful to remove some prongs to make the head smaller.

Powered cultivators

A powered cultivator is used for tackling laborious tasks like turning over the soil in neglected ground. It breaks up compacted soil and reduces it to a tilth fine enough for planting. It is impractical for use in heavily planted areas, however, and does not eliminate the need for hand digging. Petrol-powered cultivators are powerful and generally have a wide range of attachments but need more maintenance than electric ones. Electric cultivators are excellent for small jobs. They are easier to manoeuvre, less noisy, and cheaper than petrol-engined types but trailing cables may be a problem.

On most cultivators the handle height is adjustable. Some also have handles that pivot and lock sideways, allowing you to walk alongside the machine without trampling the ground already cultivated.

Cultivators come in three main types: front-, mid-, and rear-engined. **Front-engined cultivators** have rotors behind the driving wheels. They are easy to steer, but, because of the way the weight is distributed, are suitable only for shallow cultivation. **Mid-engined cultivators** are propelled by rotors rather than wheels. This may make control difficult, but the engine weight over the rotors makes deep cultivation easier than with a front-engined type. **Rear-engined cultivators** are best for manoeuvring in difficult places and for forming deep holes. The rotors, on a boom at the front, are swept from side to side as the cultivator is propelled along. The machines may be tiring to control.

POTATO LIFTER
This attachment lifts potatoes out onto the soil surface for easy collection.

FIVE-TINE
CULTIVATOR
ATTACHMENT
This is used to weed between rows and for general cultivation. The tines can be adjusted for depth and width.

POWERED CULTIVATOR
This front-engined petrol model is stable and easy to control. It is expensive, but makes an excellent job of straightforward cultivation over a large area.

Deadman's handle (cuts power if grip relaxed)

Blade engagement

Accelerator

Clutch

Horizontal handle adjuster

Vertical hand height adjuster

Choke

Lever adjusts depth of cultivation

Fold-away stand ensures stability when machine is not in use

Rotors should be well away from operator's feet

Rear rotors produce a fine finish for a seedbed

Transporter wheel aids steering

461

Pruning and cutting tools

When pruning, it is important to use the appropriate tool for the task and to make sure that it is sharp so that it cuts cleanly, easily, and safely. Using a blunt blade can leave a plant with a ragged wound that is prone to infection or that can cause dieback. Take particular care when working with powered tools, such as hedge-trimmers or brushwood cutters (see "Electrical safety", p.464).

Secateurs

Secateurs are used for pruning woody stems up to about 1cm ($^1/_2$in) thick and soft shoots of any thickness; they may also be used for taking cuttings for propagation. They can be used single-handed and are more controllable and easier to handle safely than a knife, particularly by inexperienced gardeners.

There are three main types of secateur: by-pass, curved, or side anvil; parrot-beak; and anvil. By-pass and parrot-beak secateurs have a scissor-like action, anvil secateurs have a sharp, straight-edged upper blade that cuts against a square-edged lower anvil. In some designs (swing anvils), the blade is pivoted in such a way that it remains parallel to the anvil as it cuts, preventing the stem from sliding out.

For cutting soft-stemmed plants, a light, comparatively cheap pair is adequate. For pruning fruit trees and shrubs with woody shoots up to 1cm ($^1/_2$in) thick, a pair of heavy-duty secateurs is preferable.

If possible, try out the secateurs to check that they are comfortable and easy to operate; the handle material and shape, how wide they open, and the pressure of the spring keeping them open all vary considerably.

BY-PASS SECATEURS
These use a scissor-like action. They have a sharp, convex, steel upper blade that cuts against a concave or square, steel lower blade to make a clean cut.

Brightly coloured handles are easy to spot

Moulded grip is comfortable in use

Sharp, steel blade makes a clean, precise cut

Safety catch may be moved with the thumb

ANVIL SECATEURS
These must be kept sharp, otherwise the blade crushes the stem against the anvil instead of cutting it.

FLOWER GATHERERS
These are designed to grip the flower stem after cutting.

SAFETY CATCH
This catch clips the handles together.

RATCHET SYSTEM
This makes cutting tough stems easier.

PARROT-BEAK SECATEURS
These give a clean cut, but may be damaged if used to cut wood more than 1cm ($^1/_2$in) thick.

Metal handles may be very cold to hold, but most handles are now plastic or plastic-covered metal. All secateurs are fitted with a safety catch that locks the blades in the shut position. Check that it is easy to operate with one hand and that it cannot be flicked off accidentally.

Secateur blades may be made from stainless steel, carbon steel, or coated steel. Coated blades are easy to wipe clean, but are unlikely to last as long as high-quality stainless or carbon steel blades, which keep their sharpness and cut cleanly and easily. When buying high-quality secateurs, ensure that they can be dismantled for sharpening without special tools and that new blades are available.

Some models have a ratchet system for cutting through a shoot in stages. These require less effort and so are suitable for those who find conventional models a strain, but they are slower to use.

Flower gatherers, or flower pickers, hold the flower stem after cutting. They are invaluable if cutting flowers often, otherwise secateurs or scissors will suffice.

Maintenance

Clean the blades of cutting tools after each use with an oily rag or wire wool to remove any sap that has dried on; then lightly oil them. Periodically tighten the blade tension of garden shears; this makes them cut more efficiently and produces a better finish.

Most pruning tools are easy to sharpen. Remove blades that are badly blunted or damaged, and regrind or replace them.

Long-handled pruners or loppers

A pair of long-handled pruners, or loppers, is useful for removing woody stems or branches 1–2.5cm ($^1/_2$–1in) thick, where secateurs might be damaged, and for thinner branches that are difficult to reach.

The long handles give additional leverage, making it easier to cut through thick stems. They are usually wood or plastic-covered tubular steel or aluminium. Blades are made of stainless steel, carbon steel, or coated steel, as for secateurs.

The weight and balance of long-handled pruners are important as you may have to hold them at full stretch or above your head. Make sure that you will be able to operate them easily and without strain.

Most long-handled pruners have a by-pass blade motion, others an anvil action. Both are satisfactory designs, and the choice is a matter of personal preference. Designs with a ratchet are sometimes available and are particularly useful for cutting through thick or tough branches and to reduce the strength needed for cutting.

All long-handled pruners require regular maintenance to keep them in peak working condition.

LONG-HANDLED BY-PASS PRUNERS
Using long-handled pruners makes it possible to prune stems that are high up or that are too tough or thick for secateurs.

Buffers prevent jarring when operating pruners

ANVIL PRUNERS
The blades open wide for cutting thick stems.

Tree pruners

A tree pruner is suitable for cutting branches up to 2.5cm (1in) thick that would otherwise be out of reach. The cutting device is positioned at the end of a pole that is usually 2–3m (6–10ft) long, although some extend to 5m (15ft). The carbon steel blade is operated by a lever system or a cord; both are efficient, although the lever system is more popular. Some cord models have telescopic poles so that the length may be adjusted; they are also more convenient to store. Tree pruners may have saw or fruit-picker attachments.

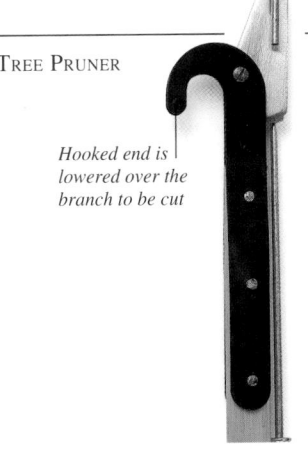

TREE PRUNER
Hooked end is lowered over the branch to be cut

Pruning saws

Use a pruning saw for severing branches more than about 2.5cm (1in) thick. As sawing in a confined space between other branches, and often at an awkward angle, may be difficult, various types of pruning saw have been developed. Those that are most commonly available are: general-purpose pruning, Grecian or rigid-handle curved, double-edged or two-edged, folding, and bow saws. If pruning is a major task in the garden, it may be necessary to have more than one saw for different types of work. A Grecian saw is one of the most useful pruning saws for an amateur gardener.

All pruning saws should have hardpoint, heat-treated teeth, which are harder and stay sharper for longer than ordinary saw teeth. They must be professionally sharpened. Saw handles are plastic or wood; choose whichever feels more comfortable and has a secure grip. Score a groove in the branch in which to insert the saw blade in order to reduce the risk of its slipping during use.

GENERAL-PURPOSE PRUNING SAW
Invaluable for most pruning jobs, this saw has a small blade, generally not more than 45cm (18in) long, so that it can be easily used in confined areas and at awkward angles.

FOLDING SAW
The saw blade folds into the handle, like a knife. It is suitable only for small branches, as it is designed to fit into a pocket and is not particularly strong.

GRECIAN SAW
This is excellent for confined spaces as it has a curved blade and cuts only on the pull stroke. In restricted areas, it is easier to use pressure on a pull, rather than a push, stroke.

DOUBLE-EDGED PRUNING SAW
This is very flexible as it has both coarse and fine teeth but may be difficult to operate in confined spaces without the top teeth damaging a nearby branch.

BOW SAW
This is used to cut through thick branches quickly, but is too large to operate in a confined area.

Garden knives

A garden knife may be used for light pruning tasks instead of secateurs, and is more versatile. It is also convenient for taking cuttings, preparing material for grafting, harvesting certain vegetables, and cutting string.

There are various types of garden knife available, including general-purpose, grafting, budding, and pruning or peach pruners. Most knives have a carbon steel blade which is either fixed or folds into the handle. If choosing the folding type, check that it is easy to open, and that the spring holding the blade in position is neither too strong nor too slack. Always dry knife blades after use, and wipe them over with an oily rag. Sharpen knives regularly, to the same angle as when new.

Most gardeners prefer a knife with a plastic or wooden handle, rather than a metal one, which may feel cold and uncomfortable.

GENERAL-PURPOSE GARDEN KNIFE
This is useful for all cutting tasks except heavy pruning.

MULTI-PURPOSE KNIFE
There are various models available. This one has a large blade for general use and pruning, a small one for grafting, and an attachment for budding.

GRAFTING
This straight-bladed knife is suitable for general tasks, and for making accurate cuts when grafting.

BUDDING
The blade projection is used for prising open the rootstock incision when propagating by bud-grafting.

PRUNING
The large blade curves downwards for a controlled cut when pruning.

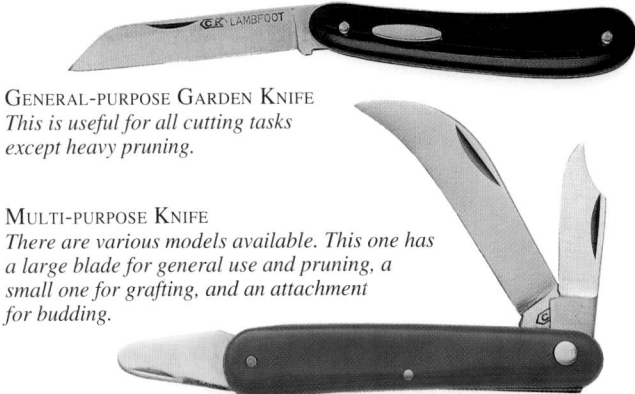

Garden shears

Shears are used mainly for trimming hedges, but are also invaluable for cutting small or awkward areas of long grass (see also "Lawncare tools", pp.466–7), clipping topiary, and cutting back herbaceous plants.

For soft-stemmed hedges, a light pair is adequate but for large hedges with tough, woody stems a heavy-duty pair will be needed.

Weight and balance are important; before buying, check that the shears are centrally balanced and the blades are not too heavy, or they will then be tiring to operate.

Most shears have straight blades although a few have wavy-edged blades: these cut through mature wood easily and help to trap the shoots so that they are not pushed out with the scissor-action of the blades. They are difficult to sharpen (see also "Maintenance", p.462).

STANDARD SHEARS
Shears usually have one notched blade to hold a thick shoot during cutting.

SINGLE-HANDED SHEARS
These have a spring mechanism similar to secateurs that allows them to be operated with one hand. Some types have blades that swivel – useful for cutting at an angle or vertically (as for edging a lawn). They are only suitable for cutting grass or very soft stems.

Hedgetrimmers

For gardeners with large hedges to cut, a powered hedgetrimmer may be worthwhile as it takes much less time and effort to use than ordinary manually operated shears.

The longer the blade, the faster the hedge can be cut and the easier it is to reach a tall hedge or across the top of a wide one. Hedgetrimmers with very long blades are heavy and often poorly balanced, however. A 40cm (16in) blade is adequate for normal garden use, but if cutting extensive hedges a 60cm (24in) blade saves considerable time. Blades may be either single- or double-sided; the latter speed up the cutting time but are not as easy to control as single-sided blades, so hedge-shaping may be more difficult.

The ease of handling is also affected by the blade action. Models with reciprocating- or double-action blades, which move against each other, are generally preferable for most gardeners. Single-action models, in which one moving blade cuts against a second, stationary blade, cause vibration and can therefore be tiring to operate.

The finish of the cut is largely controlled by the spacing of the teeth along the blade. Teeth that are narrowly spaced produce a smooth, even

PROTECTIVE CLOTHING
When operating powered tools, wear protective clothing such as goggles, ear protectors, and thick gardening gloves (see also p.471).

POWERED HEDGETRIMMER
This makes hedgetrimming faster and easier than it is when using garden shears. Electric models are light and easy to manoeuvre, while petrol versions are powerful and unhampered by trailing cables.

finish on a hedge that is regularly trimmed, while more widely spaced teeth usually cope better with thicker twigs but leave a rougher cut.

Petrol or electricity?

Hedgetrimmers may be powered by petrol or electricity, either from the mains or batteries. Petrol hedgetrimmers may be operated anywhere and are generally powerful and relatively free from vibration. They are, however, noisier, heavier, and more expensive than electric ones and usually require more maintenance.

Electric hedgetrimmers are more commonly used by amateurs and are better for small jobs. Being lighter, they are easier to handle than petrol trimmers; they are also cleaner to use and cheaper to buy.

Mains electric hedgetrimmers are the most convenient for hedges within 30m (100ft) of a power supply. As with other electric tools, the trailing cable can be inconvenient and even hazardous, and the machine must not be used in wet conditions. Safety features are very important when handling such a potentially

dangerous tool: for example, they should always be operated with a residual current device, or earth leakage circuit breaker (see also "Electrical safety", below).

Battery-powered hedgetrimmers are good for hedges in a distant part of a large garden or where there is no convenient power supply. They are usually run from a spare car battery. When fully charged, they are reasonably powerful but maintaining a charged battery and moving it around the garden can be time-consuming and laborious. They are more expensive than mains electric models.

Rechargeable hedgetrimmers

Hedgetrimmers powered by a rechargeable battery are cordless, easy to manoeuvre, and comparatively cheap. They are excellent for small, regularly trimmed hedges, but they lack the power to cut thick shoots and long hedges satisfactorily. As there are no trailing cables, rechargeable machines present fewer safety hazards than other types of electric trimmer. They can be recharged from a special mains unit.

Brushwood cutters

Second handle makes tool easier to balance and control

A brushwood cutter is excellent for slashing through tough weeds, undergrowth, and very long grass. The rotating head has a metal slasher or fine-toothed blade. This makes it suitable for far heavier tasks than those that can be tackled with a nylon-line trimmer (see "Lawncare tools", pp.466–7), but it is more tiring to operate. Some models take

plastic blades, but these are not as tough or durable. In addition to their cutting blade, some may be fitted with a nylon line for trimming grass.

As they need powerful engines to work effectively, most brushwood cutters are petrol-driven. Electric models are usually lighter, less noisy, and require less maintenance, but are less efficient for heavy work.

Electrical safety

• Keep leads only just as long as is necessary. Trailing cables are inconvenient and potentially hazardous, as they may be cut by moving blades.

• Have outside sockets installed by a qualified electrician at suitable points in the garden to keep leads short and safe.

• If extension leads are needed, ensure that they have the same number of wires as the tool: if the tool is earthed, the extension cable should be too.

• If the circuit is not already protected, attach a plug fitted with a residual current device (RCD) to the tool, or buy an adaptor RCD to insert between the plug and socket.

• Do not use an electric tool during or just after rain as this may cause electrical faults.

• Always disconnect the power supply before adjusting, inspecting, or cleaning a tool.

• Never touch a severed or damaged cable before disconnecting it from the mains.

Chainsaws

Chainsaws are suitable for sawing logs or large branches and for extensive tree surgery and felling. As they cut with a powered, toothed chain revolving at high speed, they can be dangerous and should be handled with great care; it is advisable to be trained in their safe use.

Electric chainsaws are useful for small jobs and are cheaper than petrol types, but strict safety precautions are essential (see right).

Petrol-driven chainsaws are more powerful and therefore suitable for very large gardens or woodlands but they are noisy, heavy, often difficult to start, and create fumes.

ELECTRIC CHAINSAW
An electric chainsaw is suitable for most sawing tasks; it is lighter and easier to handle than a petrol-powered version and generally requires less maintenance.

Revolving, toothed chain

Lawnmowers

When choosing a lawnmower, take into account the size of your lawn and the type of cut required. If only a small area needs mowing, a manual lawnmower should suffice, but for a larger lawn, buy a powered one. There are cylinder, rotary, and hover mowers available: cylinder models usually provide the finest cut, while rotary types are better for long, overgrown grass; hover mowers are the easiest to manoeuvre.

Grass should be mown more closely in summer than in winter, so check that the height of cut is easily adjustable (see also THE LAWN, "Frequency and height of cut", p.285). If you need a fine finish without loose grass, choose a model with a grass collector (see also "Grass clippings", p.285).

Manual lawnmowers

Manual mowers are relatively cheap, quiet, have no awkward cables, and require very little maintenance.

There are two types of manual lawnmower: those driven by wheels at the side and those operated by a chain drive from a heavy rear roller. A side-wheel mower is easy to push but may be difficult to use at the edge of a lawn: if its side wheels are not in contact with the grass, they do not turn the cylinder blades. As there is no rear roller, it does not produce a striped effect on the turf. Mowers with a rear roller make it easy to mow over an edge.

Powered lawnmowers

There are two basic types of powered lawnmower: cylinder, and rotary or hover (hover mowers work on the same principle as rotary ones). Most run on petrol or mains electricity. Powered mowers are potentially dangerous on steep slopes as they are designed for flat surfaces.

Cylinder mowers are either entirely self-propelled or with a powered blade; the latter type may be heavy and tiring to operate. Most have a rear roller, which is essential if you want a lawn with a striped pattern; the heavier the roller, the more pronounced the stripe.

Petrol-driven cylinder mowers often have broader cutting widths than electric ones. This reduces the cutting time but makes them more difficult to manoeuvre. Ride-on or tractor-hauled petrol models are convenient for very extensive lawns.

SELECTING A LAWNMOWER

MANUAL, REAR-ROLLER MOWER
With this kind of mower it is easy to mow up to and over a lawn edge, as the cylinder is supported by a back roller.

POWERED, CYLINDER MOWER
A mower of this type provides a fine, close-cut finish and is probably the best choice for a high-quality lawn. The blade cylinder is driven by a rear roller.

PLASTIC BLADE
Cheap to replace, the blade rotates horizontally to cut the grass.

CYLINDER BLADES
The blades are set along a cylinder that rotates forward and cuts against a fixed blade.

Deadman's handle (cuts power if grip relaxed)

ELECTRIC HOVER MOWER
A hover mower is ideal for cutting grass on small lawns and in awkward places such as beneath low, overhanging plants and next to paving. It is easy to manoeuvre on flat surfaces and shallow slopes but may overbalance and cut out on a steep slope. Most hover mowers do not have grass collectors.

PETROL-DRIVEN ROTARY MOWER
This is useful for extensive grassed areas, including rough and long grass, as it has a powerful engine. The replaceable metal blade cuts horizontally so is unlikely to scalp uneven turf.

Large grass collector needs emptying less frequently

Rotary and hover mowers have replaceable metal or plastic blades that cut the grass with a scythe-like motion as they rotate horizontally. Rotary mowers have wheels while hover mowers ride on a cushion of air. Only a few rotary mowers are fitted with rollers. Both types work better than cylinder mowers for sites that are slightly uneven or have long grass, but most models cannot cut the grass very low.

Which power source?

Electricity is more convenient and cleaner than petrol, but is not suitable for powerful engines. If used for tough jobs, such as very long grass or extensive areas, an electric mower may overheat. Convenience and safety should also be considered. Access to a power supply is essential, while the trailing flex may be a hazard. Electric mowers should not be used on wet grass.

Petrol lawnmowers are not hampered by cables but are more expensive to purchase and maintain. They may not start readily unless they are fitted with an electric ignition.

Safety

• Blades must be well protected so that they do not come into contact with the operator's feet. However safe the mower appears, the operator should always wear strong shoes.
• The blade brake must stop the blades rotating within five seconds of being turned off.
• The mower should have a lock-off switch, which requires two operations to turn on an engine. This reduces the risk of a child accidentally switching it on.
• A deadman's handle should be fitted. Held when mowing, this turns off the engine when released.

Maintenance

A few simple precautions keep a mower working efficiently.
• After use, disconnect power, then clean engine and blades.
• Check that the blades are sharp and replace blunt ones.
• Oil and lubricate regularly.
• Service the mower yearly.
• Periodically check that spark plugs are clean and adjusted.
• Clean filters and air intakes of petrol mowers regularly.
• Periodically check the oil level on four-stroke engines.
• Before you store a petrol-powered model, drain the tank.

Lawncare tools

As well as a lawnmower, a number of other tools are useful for maintaining a healthy and attractive lawn. Manual tools are usually adequate for most lawns but, for large areas, powered tools are faster and less tiring to use.

Edging tools

A neat, well-defined edge provides the perfect finishing touch to a well-mown lawn and emphasizes the lawn's shape and outline (see also *Cutting the Edge of the Lawn*, p.286). There are two main lawn edging tools: half-moon edgers and long-handled shears, although powered edging machines and certain nylon-line trimmers may be used.

Shafts for long-handled shears are wooden, steel, or plastic-coated steel; all are strong and the choice is really a matter of personal preference.

LONG-HANDLED
EDGING SHEARS
These are useful for trimming overhanging grass around the lawn edge. The handles should be sufficiently long so that there is no need to stoop. If either too short or too heavy, the shears may be tiring to operate.

HALF-MOON EDGER
Also known as an edging iron or lawn edger, this is used with a rocking motion to cut away worn or uneven lawn edges and to remove small areas of turf for repair. It has a sharp, curved, metal blade attached to a long, wooden or metal handle.

Tang of blade is well secured to shaft neck

Lawn edging materials

To prevent a lawn from gradually decreasing in size when turf is removed with tools such as a half-moon edger, outline the lawn with bricks, paving slabs, terracotta edging tiles, or metal or plastic edging strips. This helps to ensure an even edge to the lawn and inhibits grass from spreading onto paths and borders. A brick or paving-slab edge also enables hover and side-wheel mowers to be driven right to the lawn edge. Plastic strips, which are usually coloured green, are less likely than metal edging strips to damage mower blades, and are also cheaper.

Nylon-line trimmers

A nylon-line trimmer is useful for trimming grass in awkward areas that cannot easily be reached by a mower. It may also be used for slashing ground-cover plants or soft-stemmed weeds, although a more powerful brushwood cutter may be needed for tough undergrowth (see p.464). As the nylon cutting line is flexible and easily replaced, it is possible to work right up to a wall, tree, or paving without damaging

the tool. It is also safer than a fixed blade or cutter if there is an accident. Always wear goggles, however, as flying stones may be hazardous.

As for most other powered tools, nylon-line trimmers may be driven by electricity or petrol, and similar considerations of safety, convenience, and weight apply. Electric models are more common and are suitable for gardens where they are needed for small areas only.

They are light and easy to operate, but their area of use is restricted by the cable length. For safety, they should have a deadman's handle and be used with a residual current device. Under no circumstances must they be used on wet grass (see also "Electrical safety", p.464).

A petrol-driven nylon-line trimmer is ideal for larger gardens and for areas where there is no power supply. It is more expensive and needs more maintenance than an electric trimmer. It is also heavier and therefore may be more tiring to manoeuvre. For safety, it should have a quick, easy way to stop the engine.

Garden rollers

A garden roller, which may be made of metal or water-filled, hollow plastic, is used to level the surface during initial ground preparation before sowing grass seed or laying turf. It also settles the soil around young grass seedlings. Rolling established lawns regularly is no longer recommended, however; on heavy soils particularly, it tends to compact the turf and therefore impede drainage, which may cause problems such as moss and poor grass growth.

TRIMMER
This has a flexible, nylon, cutting line which rotates at high speed to cut through grass and other soft-stemmed plants or weeds. Some models have an adjustable head that may be tilted vertically for trimming lawn edges.

A shaft-handle makes the tool easy to manoeuvre

Shield protects user from whirling cutting line

CUTTING GUIDE
This keeps the nylon line just off the ground to stop it cutting too low and to produce an even trim.

Long-handled lawn shears

Long-handled lawn shears are helpful for trimming grass in awkward places, such as beneath overhanging plants or around trees, paving, or walls, and for tidying any stalks missed during mowing. The blades, set at right angles to the handles, are positioned parallel to the ground, not vertically as in edging shears.

While lawn shears are useful for very small areas, they have now largely been superseded by powered, nylon-line trimmers, which are faster and more versatile. Trimmers are heavier to hold and manoeuvre than shears, however, and more expensive as they are powered tools.

LONG-HANDLED LAWN SHEARS
These may be useful for cutting grass in small areas that would be difficult to cut with a mower.

Rakes and aerators

Tools for clearing up fallen leaves and garden debris and for reducing thatch (a layer of decaying organic matter) and soil compaction help to keep a lawn in good condition.

Lawn rakes are primarily used to gather up fallen leaves. Some types may be helpful in removing thatch and dead moss. There are three types of lawn rake: spring-tined, flat-tined, and scarifying, or aerator, rakes (see also "Rakes", p.460). In addition, powered lawn rakes are available, which are suitable for large lawns.

Aerators help to reduce thatch and let air into the soil, encouraging good root growth. On very small areas, aerating may be done with a garden fork, but for most lawns a purpose-built machine such as a hollow-tined aerator or a slitter is better.

SPRING-TINED LAWN RAKE
This is used for clearing out dead grass and moss, removing small stones and debris, and lightly aerating a lawn. Its light head has long, flexible, rounded wire tines.

FLAT-TINED LAWN RAKE
Excellent for gathering up leaves and loose material, this has long, flexible, flat tines of plastic or metal, and a light head to minimize damage to new growth.

SCARIFYING RAKE
This cuts deeply into thatch and even into the turf itself. Its rigid, metal tines are usually flat, with sharp points. As it may be heavy and tiring to use, a model with wheels either side of the rake head may be preferable.

POWERED LAWN RAKE
Easier to use than an ordinary rake, its plastic or metal tines effectively scarify turf, while its collecting box removes debris.

STAR-WHEELED SLITTER
This aerates the turf faster than a hollow-tined aerator but, if the ground is hard, it may not penetrate enough to be effective.

HOLLOW-TINED AERATOR
This powered, hollow-tined aerator penetrates deeply through the turf into the soil. The tines remove cores of soil, opening up compacted turf.

Sweepers and blowers

At its simplest, a leaf sweeper may be an ordinary besom brush or stiff broom used to sweep away small debris; this kind of basic sweeper is ideal for clearing pathways and small areas of the garden.

For large-sized lawns, however, using a purpose-designed leaf sweeper saves both labour and time. The leaves are lifted from the surface of the grass by rotating brushes and they are then thrown into a large collecting bag, from which they can be easily disposed of.

Powered vacuum leaf collectors and blowers may prove worthwhile in very large gardens, but they are expensive to buy and they may be noisy to operate.

Some powered models have flexible attachments designed for use among flower beds and other areas of the garden that are particularly hard to reach.

BESOM
This is an inexpensive brush suitable for sweeping up leaves and light debris.

LEAF SWEEPER
This gathers up garden leaves, using rotating brushes, and collects them in a large bag. It is light, easy to push, and quiet in operation.

POWERED LEAF BLOWER
This tidies up garden leaves by blowing, rather than sweeping, them into a pile for collection. It is best suited to a large garden as it is noisy, bulky to store, and unnecessary in gardens where tidying tasks are easily done by hand or other simpler tools.

Fertilizer spreaders

A fertilizer spreader is suitable for the accurate distribution of fertilizer, grass seed, and granular weedkillers. It comprises a hopper on wheels with a long handle. Check that the application rate is adjustable and that the flow may be switched off when turning at the lawn edge. After setting the application rate always check that it is correct by fertilizing a test area first (see "Applying fertilizers", p.531). A hose attachment for applying a fertilizer with water is useful for feeding a lawn (see *Hose-end Attachments*, p.468).

FERTILIZER SPREADER
A spreader applies fertilizer evenly, so avoiding scorching the grass.

Watering aids

Irrigation makes it possible to grow plants that require more water than is provided by rainfall, and to grow plants both indoors and in the greenhouse. Equipment such as hoses and sprinklers help make routine watering easier and faster.

Watering cans

A watering can is practical in the house, greenhouse, or for small areas outside. Choose a lightweight can that will not be too heavy to carry when full. The opening of the watering can should be wide enough to make filling easy, and the can itself should feel comfortable and well balanced. A can that has a strainer at the base of the spout helps to prevent the rose from becoming clogged by debris in the water.

Water butts

A water butt collects and stores rainwater from the house or greenhouse roof, invaluable during dry periods and for acid-loving plants. The butt should have a tap, and a lid to keep out insects and debris, which pollute the water and might block the tap. If necessary, raise the butt on blocks to allow room for a watering can to fit beneath the tap. Some water butts divert water back to the drain when the butt is full.

GARDEN WATERING CANS
These should have a generous capacity to reduce the need for repeated refilling. For general-purpose use, a 9 litre (2 gallon) can, which holds 8kg (18lb) of water, is a convenient size.

PLASTIC OR METAL?
Most watering cans are now made from plastic, but traditional galvanized metal ones, which are heavier and more expensive, are still available; both types are sturdy and durable.

GREENHOUSE
WATERING CAN
This has a long spout, so that it is easy to reach plants at the back of a bench, and a reversible rose for both fine and coarse sprays for watering seedlings and mature plants.

INDOOR WATERING CAN
This should have a long spout to reach into plant pots and windowboxes, and to help control the flow.

Caution with weedkiller

Do not use the same watering can for watering the garden and dispensing liquid weedkillers. Keep a special can with a dribble bar, clearly marked, for applying chemicals.

Which rose?

Coarse-spray rose

Fine-spray brass rose

Fine-spray, brass-faced, plastic rose

A fine rose is best for seeds and seedlings as the resulting spray does not damage them or wash the compost or soil away from them. For more established plants, a coarse-spray rose, which delivers the water faster, is preferable.

Roses are manufactured in a choice of materials: brass, brass-faced plastic, and all-plastic. Plastic is less durable and cheaper than brass but is still satisfactory for most uses. In general, metal roses give a finer spray.

Using a dribble bar, which is attached to a watering can, makes it more accurate than a rose for applying weedkiller. It also reduces spray drift which can be a problem with a rose.

Hosepipes

A hosepipe is invaluable for irrigating distant parts of the garden and for areas that require copious watering. Most hosepipes are made from PVC; they vary in the way they are finished or reinforced, which affects their flexibility and their resistance to kinking. Any kinks interrupt water flow and eventually weaken the hose wall. Double-walled and reinforced hoses are resistant to kinking but relatively expensive. Whichever type of hose you choose, make sure that it is long enough to reach all parts of the garden; some types may be lengthened with an extension.

A flat hosepipe is mounted on its own reel and cannot be used unless the entire hose is unreeled. Flat hoses are made in fixed lengths with connectors and nozzles pre-fitted. Some kink readily unless laid in a straight line and they may also be difficult to wind up because all the water must be drained out first.

HOSE REEL
A reel with a handle or wheels is easy to move around the garden. Some reels allow waterflow through the hose even when partially wound.

FLAT HOSE
A flat hose winds neatly onto its own reel and is easy to store.

Sprayers

Use sprayers, either portable devices or attachments fitted to the end of a hosepipe, to apply pesticides, weedkillers, and fertilizers, and to water or mist-spray plants. Compression types, pumped up before use, are most suitable for general use; small trigger-pump sprayers are for misting houseplants or applying pesticides to a few plants. For a large area, use a knapsack sprayer.

TRIGGER-ACTION
HOSE ATTACHMENT

Nozzle allows spray to be adjusted to jet or mist

Trigger

FERTILIZER
PULSE HOSE
ATTACHMENT

Central chamber for fertilizer

KNAPSACK SPRAYER
The sprayer is pumped up by the lever and is suitable for large areas.

HOSE-END ATTACHMENTS
These may be connected to a hose to spray large numbers of plants. Some have a trigger-action nozzle and most an adjustable spray. Special attachments (below left) are available for applying fertilizer and water together.

Garden sprinklers

A garden sprinkler automatically delivers a fine spray of water over a specific area. As it works while unattended, it saves time and effort. It also distributes the water economically since the spray, when applied over a long period, penetrates the soil better than water delivered from a watering can or hand-held hose. A sprinkler is generally attached to a garden hose or a static water-pipe.

There are various types of sprinkler to suit a range of needs: some are best for a lawn, for example, while others are preferable for irrigating a flower bed or vegetable patch. The simplest form is a static sprinkler, which usually produces a circular pattern of limited area. It is suitable for lawns, but is liable to form puddles, so must be moved around to achieve an even distribution. In a flower bed the spray is often obstructed by foliage, giving unsatisfactory results, although some models are sold with a long spike to raise the head above the surrounding plants.

Other forms of sprinkler in which water pressure is used to rotate the sprinkler heads give better, more even coverage. Rotating sprinklers and pulse-jet sprinklers swing round to deliver water in a wide circle; oscillating sprinklers deliver water over a rectangular area through a series of holes in a bar that rocks to and fro when the water is turned on.

A travelling sprinkler (also called a walking sprinkler) is useful for large, level areas such as a big lawn; it is convenient but expensive. The sprinkler delivers spray over a rectangular area while it is propelled along a straight track (usually a hosepipe) by the force of the water. The rate of travel and size of area covered either side of the track depends on the water pressure.

TYPES OF SPRINKLER

STATIC SPRINKLER
Static sprinklers are intended primarily for use on lawns, most being mounted on a spike to push into the ground. They usually deliver water in a circle, but a few water in a semi-circular, rectangular, or fan shape.

ROTATING SPRINKLER
Good for lawns, beds, and borders, this type of sprinkler covers a large circular area and applies the water evenly. The spray is delivered through nozzles on the arms, which are attached to a spinning pivot, driven by the force of the water. Those that are fitted with long stems are the best type for watering beds and borders.

PULSE-JET SPRINKLER
This type of sprinkler is invaluable for covering large, circular areas of lawn, beds, or borders. It has a single jet on a central pivot, which rotates in a series of pulses, ejecting spurts of water. Except on lawns, the delivery head is generally set on a tall stem for increased coverage.

OSCILLATING SPRINKLER
This is best used at ground level; it is not suitable for positions where surrounding foliage will interfere with the range of the spray. Water is sprayed through the brass jets in the oscillating arm. This sprinkler delivers water fairly evenly over a rectangular area, the size of which may be easily adjusted.

Underground sprinkler systems
These are permanent systems, ideal for irrigating lawns and rock gardens. They are unobtrusive and simple to operate, and are best installed when the area needing irrigation is first constructed, preferably by a professional. PVC pipes and connecting joints are laid in the form of a grid so that they supply various watering heads, to which hoses or sprinklers are attached. The sprinkler from each head delivers an even supply of water to a circular area.

Always continue watering until the ground is thoroughly wet, as this helps to even out the distribution to any overlapping areas. This type of watering system is usually the most expensive, and requires anti-siphon valves to meet water authority standards, and possibly a water meter and other special fittings.

Seep hoses

Seep hoses are useful for irrigating lawns or rows of plants. They are plastic or rubber hoses with small perforations along their entire length. With the holes facing upwards, a seep hose produces a fine spray over a rectangular area and can be used to water lawns. With the holes placed towards the ground, water is directed to the base of plants – an excellent way to irrigate vegetables and other plants grown in rows. Choose a seep hose carefully because some cannot be used as sprinklers, since their holes are so small that the water just trickles out even when the holes are facing upwards.

Porous hoses are a variation on seep hoses. A network of porous hoses enables water to seep slowly into the soil. They are particularly suitable for newly planted beds and borders. The connections may be varied and the system moved around as required on the soil surface, or the hoses may be buried at a depth of 10–15cm (4–6in) below the surface as a permanent irrigation system.

Hose timers

Hose timers may be used with ordinary garden sprinklers or more elaborate watering systems. They fit between a tap and the hose or irrigation pipe. Most hose timers turn off the water after a predetermined time. The more sophisticated ones also turn on the water. Some may be linked to a soil-moisture detector that overrides the programme if the ground is already sufficiently wet.

COMPUTERIZED TIMER
This allows you to programme watering times and duration in advance, to irrigate plants while you are busy or on holiday.

WATER TIMER
This can be set to turn off the water after a pre-set period, from about 5 minutes to 2 hours.

Trickle, or drip feed, systems

These are used for plants that benefit from individual watering; plants, for example, that need more water than others growing around them. The water drips gently beside the plant, minimizing disturbance to the soil around the roots. A trickle system works well in a shrub border, along a hedge, or for rows of vegetables. On a smaller scale, it is ideal for plants in containers, growing bags, and windowboxes. Unless fitted with a hose timer, trickle systems tend to waste water, and they need regular cleaning to prevent the tubes and drip heads from becoming blocked with algae and debris.

TRICKLE WATERING SYSTEM
The delivery hose is connected to a unit that filters the water and reduces the pressure. The water then flows along a network of tubes supported by spikes stuck into the ground. Systems of this kind can be extended by buying additional drip heads and lengths of tube.

Filter removable for cleaning

Connector for tube

Hose connection

Central unit reduces water pressure

Drip heads

Spike

Cleaning tool

General garden equipment

As well as tools for cultivating and maintaining the garden, a wide range of other accessories, such as carrying equipment and planting aids, may be useful, depending on your own individual requirements.

Wheelbarrows

Wheelbarrows are useful for transporting plants, soil, and materials such as compost and garden debris. They may be made of metal or plastic, the former being more durable. Painted metal soon rusts if the paint is chipped; even galvanized metal bins rust eventually. Plastic bins, although lighter, may split.

A ball-wheeled wheelbarrow is more stable than a standard model, making it easier to use over recently dug ground. Most suitable for very heavy work is a builder's barrow, which has an inflatable tyre to cushion the load. Barrows with two wheels and a pram-type handle (sometimes called garden carts) are stable and easy to load and unload, but are less manoeuvrable than standard barrows on uneven ground.

Sheets and bags

A carrying sheet or bag is suitable for transporting light but bulky garden waste such as hedge clippings; when not in use, it takes up very little space. It should be lightweight,

CARRYING BAG

CARRYING SHEET

TRUG

with strong handles, and made of a tough, tear-proof material, such as woven plastic. Carrying bags have a larger capacity than sheets. Trugs and baskets are good for light tasks such as carrying flowers or fruit.

TYPES OF WHEELBARROW

TRADITIONAL WHEELBARROW
Most barrows have a single, solid wheel and a shallow bin, although some models may be fitted with an extension to increase their capacity.

BALL-WHEELED WHEELBARROW
If you are transporting very heavy loads or using a barrow on rough ground, a model with a ball wheel or inflatable tyre is easier to push than a solid-wheeled one, but the wheel may become punctured.

Plastic bags

Clear plastic bags are excellent for a number of purposes: preventing cuttings material from drying out after collecting it, for example, and for covering cuttings in pots to raise humidity around them. Most food and freezer bags are suitable provided that they are not too thin, as they are then less effective at retaining moisture.

Kneelers and knee pads

A kneeler or knee pads, cushioned and covered with a water-proof material, make kneeling more comfortable, when weeding, for example. Knee pads are simply strapped to the knees; they are often sold in only one size, so check that they fit

before buying. Kneeling stools support the knees on a slightly raised platform and have hand rests to give support when kneeling down and standing up. They may also be turned upside-down for use as a small stool for working at raised beds or greenhouse benches.

KNEELERS
A kneeling stool (top) can be inverted for use as a stool and is light to carry. A cushioned pad (bottom) keeps knees clear of damp, hard ground.

Compost bins

A compost bin should have a lid to keep warmth in, easy access to the compost by slats or panels, and a capacity of at least 1cu m (1cu yd) to generate sufficient heat to accelerate the rotting process. Avoid wire mesh bins or those with large gaps between the slats, because they allow the heat generated to escape.

Traditional, wooden compost bins are available pre-cut for easy

self-assembly. Plastic compost bins are generally more effective than metal or wooden ones because they conserve moisture and reduce the need to water. There are plastic bins available that may be rotated to turn the compost, but this does not necessarily make good compost more quickly than a well-designed, traditional bin. See also SOILS AND FERTILIZERS, *Making a Compost Bin*, p.533.

Incinerators

Incinerators burn rubbish more quickly and cleanly than bonfires, but many gardeners now prefer to recycle garden waste by shredding and composting it. Open-mesh incinerators, some of which may be folded up after use, are good for burning dry material such as twigs and leaves, while galvanized steel, dustbin-type incinerators are suitable for slowly burning damp, woody material. Both types must be well ventilated.

Shredders

A compost shredder chops woody or tough garden waste, such as old Brussels sprout stems, hedge trimmings, and prunings, until it is fine enough to break down quickly on a compost heap. Shredders are usually electrically powered and should not be left outdoors when not in use. They are heavy to move around, so choose one with wheels, unless there is space to use and store it in one place.

For safety, make sure that the power is automatically disconnected when the hopper is removed (see "Electrical safety", p.464). The funnel should be easy to use, but you must not be able to touch the blades.

Power should cut out if inlet funnel is removed

Three sturdy legs ensure shredder is stable in use

USING A SHREDDER
The inlet funnel should not allow direct access to the blades. Wear goggles and gloves to protect against flying debris and thorny stems.

Planting and sowing aids

General garden tools or household items are often used for planting and sowing; for example a stick or pencil, instead of a dibber, will make a planting hole. Specialized tools, however, do make some tedious and repetitive jobs simpler and quicker.

Seed sowers and planters

These facilitate accurate and even sowing of seed. There are four main types: shakers, plungers, wheeled sowers, and seed-tray sowers.
Shakers are hand-held devices that may be used for sowing seed in prepared drills. Skill is required to ensure even seed distribution.
Plungers insert each seed individually to a predetermined depth.
Wheeled seed sowers are good for distributing seeds evenly in an outdoor drill. With a long handle, they can be worked from a standing position, making sowing less tiring.
Seed-tray sowers are thin, plastic or wooden boards with moulded protrusions on one side. When pressed onto the seed compost they firm the surface and make evenly spaced holes for sowing seed.

Bulb planters

A bulb planter is useful if planting a number of bulbs individually; for planting groups of small bulbs, a trowel or hand fork is better. A bulb planter removes a plug of soil or turf, which is then replaced on top of the bulb after planting; those with a claw-like action release the plug by pressure on the handle.

Gardening gloves

There is a range of gardening gloves for various purposes: some keep hands clean when working with soil or compost, while others also provide protection against thorns.

Leather and fabric gloves are useful for tasks such as pruning roses to guard against thorns. When buying leather ones, check that the leather extends far enough to protect all of the palm. All-leather or suede gloves give very good protection, but may be uncomfortably hot in warm weather. Gauntlet types cover the wrists and lower forearms.

Many gloves are made of fabric and vinyl. Some are impregnated with vinyl, others just have a vinyl grip on the palms. They are good for most jobs and keep hands cleaner than fabric alone. Vinyl-coated gloves are useful for messy jobs, such as mixing concrete, but are too thick for jobs needing a sensitive touch.

FABRIC WITH VINYL GRIP

SUEDE GAUNTLETS

SUEDE AND FABRIC

COTTON FABRIC

Dibbers and widgers

A dibber is a pencil-shaped tool used for making planting holes. Use a small dibber to transplant seedlings or insert cuttings, a large one for transplanting vegetables such as leeks that require a wide hole to allow space for growth, and for planting through a plastic mulch. A widger, which is like a narrow spatula, is good for lifting seedlings and rooted cuttings with the minimum of root disturbance.

Garden lines

A garden line is mainly used in vegetable plots as a guide for forming straight rows, but is also invaluable for other tasks, such as marking out areas when planning or designing, or forming a straight edge when planting up a hedge or constructing a wall or patio.

GARDEN LINE
Most garden lines have a pointed stake at either end for inserting into the ground. Grooves allow you to stretch a level line between the stakes.

Sieves

Garden sieves generally have a mesh of 3–12mm ($^1/8$–$^1/2$in) and are used to separate out coarse material from soil or potting compost. Choose a sieve with a large mesh to remove twigs and stones from soil before sowing or planting; use one with a smaller mesh when covering fine seeds after sowing. Those with a wire-mesh tend to be more effective and durable than plastic ones.

WIRE-MESH SIEVE

SIEVE WITH FINE, PLASTIC MESH

Thermometers

The best type of thermometer for garden and greenhouse use is a minimum-maximum thermometer, as this records both the lowest and highest temperatures reached. It also helps determine the warmest and coldest parts of the garden when deciding where to site particular plants. A soil thermometer registers soil temperature, and is helpful in deciding when to sow seed.

MINIMUM-MAXIMUM THERMOMETER

GREENHOUSE THERMOMETER

Rain gauges

A rain gauge is used for measuring amounts of rainfall or irrigation; it is helpful for identifying areas of the garden that are affected by rain shadow. It should have clear markings and a smooth inside surface for easy cleaning. Many gauges have a short spike for inserting into the ground.

Measurements are clear so that water level is easy to read

Spike for stability

PLASTIC RAIN GAUGE

PLANTING AND SOWING TOOLS

SMALL DIBBER

WOODEN GARDEN DIBBER FOR OUTDOOR USE

BULB PLANTER

WIDGER

WHEELED SEED SOWER

METAL GARDEN DIBBER

Ties and supports

Ties are used for various purposes in the garden but in particular to secure a climbing, scrambling, or fragile plant; supports are needed to protect some plants from wind or rain. Ties must be secure without constricting the stem; use a light material such as twine or raffia on soft-stemmed plants, which are readily damaged.

General ties

Garden string or twine in 3-ply is adequate for most tying jobs. Raffia, which is good for binding joins after grafting and as a lightweight tie, and soft strings, such as jute fillis, may disintegrate after a year or so. Clear plastic tape is excellent for use in grafting; special rubber ties are also available. Tar-impregnated string or polypropylene twine is a reliable, weather-resistant tie but, if used to secure plants to a support, may have to be loosened and retied annually.

Plastic-coated tying wire is strong and, as it lasts for several years, needs adjusting as the plant grows. It is good for fixing labels to training wires or trellis and joining canes. It may come on a reel with a built-in cutter, which is convenient to use.

Plant rings

These are split rings of wire; plastic-covered rings are also available. Plant rings are designed to be opened and closed easily around a plant

Labels and markers

Labels for garden use should be durable, weather-resistant, and large enough to contain all the information you want to note. Plastic labels are cheap and may be reused; if written on with pencil, they should remain legible for a season. Most plastic labels discolour gradually with age and become brittle, but they are ideal for labelling trays of seeds and cuttings. Looped labels and those with ties may be secured around the stem of a plant and are useful if labels at eye level are required.

For more permanent, water-resistant markers, use those coated with a black material; these are written on by scratching through to the white plastic beneath, but they cannot be marked with a new name. Aluminium labels, which are more expensive, will last almost indefinitely, but the lettering may have to be renewed every few years.

stem and its support. They are suitable for light jobs, such as attaching a houseplant to a cane.

Tree ties

Rubber tree ties are strong, durable, and good for securing a young tree to a stake. They should be easily adjustable so that an expanding stem is not constricted. Select one with a buffer so that the stake does not chafe the stem, or use a padded tie in a figure-of-eight form (see also "Tree ties", p.41). Nail ties to the stakes.

Wall fixings

Purpose-designed plant stickers may be used for tasks such as securing the stem of a climber direct to a wall

or other support. Lead-headed nails are stronger; they have a soft spur that may be bent over to fix stems and small branches to a wall.

Vine eyes hold stretched wires to which wall plants are then secured. On wall masonry, use flat vine eyes; for timber and wall plugs, screw in eyelet vine eyes.

Canes and stakes

Bamboo canes are excellent for supporting single-stemmed plants, but they eventually split and rot. More permanent and expensive are PVC stakes and plastic-covered steel rods. Support clumps of border plants with metal link or ring stakes (see PERENNIALS, "Staking", p.156). Trees and standard roses should be supported with sturdy, wooden stakes.

Netting

Netting is available in various materials and mesh sizes for a range of uses, such as supporting plants, protecting fruit from birds, and shading greenhouse plants (see "Shading", p.484). For plant support, choose a mesh of 5cm (2in) or more; it may be hard to disentangle plants from a smaller mesh. For plants such as sweet peas, thin, flexible plastic netting is adequate; heavier plants need semi-rigid plastic nets. For fruit protection, use purpose-designed, plastic netting with a mesh of 1–2cm ($\frac{1}{2}$–$\frac{3}{4}$in). Protect seedlings and winter vegetables from birds with 2.5cm (1in) mesh netting.

WALL FIXINGS

FLAT VINE EYE

EYELET VINE EYE

LEAD-HEADED NAIL WITH SPUR

Wire netting may be placed around plants to provide protection from animals such as rabbits. It is also useful for reinforcing concrete when constructing a pond or trough.

Use windbreak netting to protect vulnerable plants in exposed sites (see "Windbreaks", p.521). Knitted plastic netting may deteriorate in about four years, whereas moulded plastic should last at least twice as long. Windbreak webbing is even more long-lasting but very obtrusive. If a temporary windbreak is needed, durability is less important.

NETTING

PLASTIC NETTING
Shade netting

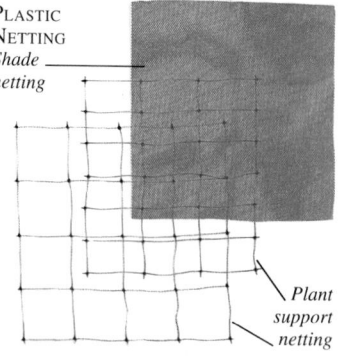

Plant support netting

WIRE NETTING

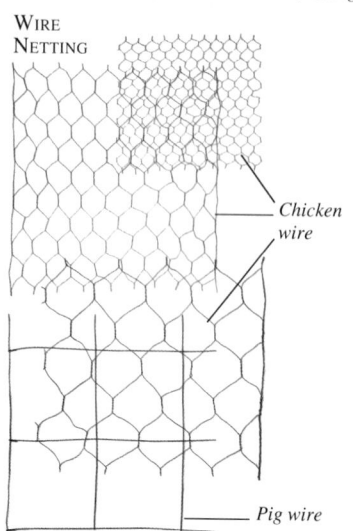

Chicken wire

Pig wire

PLANT SUPPORTS AND TIES

STAKES AND SUPPORTS

Tree stake

Bamboo cane

Rose stake

Green bamboo cane

Moss pillar

Split cane

TREE TIE

ROSE TIE

PLASTIC TIES

PLANT RINGS

RING STAKE

LINK STAKES

GARDEN TWINE

TWIST TIES

Pots and trays

Pots are available in a wide range of sizes but there are two basic shapes: round and square. Although round pots are traditional, square pots hold more compost for the same diameter; to save space use square pots, which pack neatly together. Round pots are classified by the inside diameter at the rim; square ones by the length of the rim along one side. Most pots have slightly sloping sides so that a plant and its root ball may be easily removed intact for repotting or planting out.

Pots are made of clay (terracotta) or plastic. Clay is traditional; plastic, however, is more common. Most plastic pots are manufactured from polypropylene, which deteriorates in cold weather. Pots made of a polypropylene and polythene mix do not become brittle in cold weather and are preferable for raising plants outdoors. Pots made of polythene only are cheapest and least durable; they fold flat for storage.

Standard pots are as deep as they are broad; they are the most common type of pot. Pans or seed pans are one third the depth of a standard pot of the same diameter. They are useful for germinating seeds. Half pots are half to two-thirds the depth of a standard pot of the same diameter. They are often used commercially for plants with relatively small root balls, such as evergreen azaleas. For very deep-rooted seedlings, sweet pea tubes or – for plants that

POTS AND PANS
Pots as well as other containers, such as troughs and urns, are used for cultivating and displaying plants both indoors and outside. The smaller pots, pans, and half pots are suitable for propagating and growing on young plants.

Standard pots

Ornamental terracotta pots

Large standard pot

Half pot

Seed pan

Pans

Seed, seedling, and cutting pots

will remain in the pot for some time – long Toms are used. Whalehide ring pots are designed to be used for the ring culture of tomatoes (see "Tomatoes: Growing under cover", p.338) in greenhouses.

Other pots designed for specific uses include lattice pots (which have mesh sides), hydroculture pots (forms of double pot), and specially designed forcing pots, which are placed over plants to exclude light.

Degradable pots and pellets
These are good for plants that resent root disturbance, as they can be planted out into the bed. The plants' roots grow through the sides and base of the pots into the surrounding ground. They are generally made

from compressed peat and various other fibres (often sphagnum moss and wood fibre, sometimes impregnated with plant food).

Peat pellets are good for seeds and rooting cuttings and must be expanded with water before being used. Many gardeners create their own degradable pots from cones made from double-thickness newspaper.

Pot saucers
These are particularly good for indoor use, when watering plants from beneath and to catch surplus water, which should then always be emptied to prevent waterlogging the growing medium. Saucers are available to match clay or plastic pots.

Seed trays
Traditional, wooden seed trays have largely been replaced by plastic ones, which are easier to clean but often more fragile. Very thin plastic trays are cheap and flexible but are unlikely to last more than a season. Strong plastics are more rigid and expensive; they may become brittle and split with age but, if stored out of sunlight when not in use, they should last for several years.

Which material?

Plastic pots are:
- light to handle and ideal where weight is important (e.g. on indoor shelves or on balconies);
- inexpensive;
- easy to clean;
- durable, although they may eventually split or crack;
- more or less impermeable, so compost dries out more slowly than in clay pots;
- good for use with capillary watering systems (see p.485);
- available in various colours.

Clay pots are:
- heavy and stable, so are good for large plants that might be top-heavy in a plastic pot;
- expensive but attractive, so they are often preferable for displaying plants;
- difficult to clean;
- breakable and, unless frost-proof, may crack or flake;
- porous so the compost is less likely to become waterlogged, although plants may need more frequent watering;
- excellent for alpines because they provide extra drainage;
- fair for capillary watering systems (see p.485).

Modular systems
With modules, or modular systems, plant roots are not damaged when separating each module, whereas seedlings grown in seed trays suffer some initial root damage when transplanted. Expanded polystyrene trays with individual planting cells insulate the compost, encouraging growth. They are useful for seeds or pricked-out seedlings, and are as expensive as good-quality polypropylene seed trays but do not last as long.

TRAYS AND MODULAR SYSTEMS
These are used for sowing seeds, inserting cuttings, or growing on young plants. Use a rigid, outer tray to hold flimsy, single-use modules containing plastic cells. Cells are useful for pricking out seedlings and sowing seeds singly.

LONG TOM
This pot suits deep-rooted plants that would be restricted by a standard pot.

WHALEHIDE RING POT
This bottomless pot for ring culture holds the compost over the growing aggregate.

SWEET PEA TUBES
These are excellent for seedlings that quickly develop long root systems.

HYDROCULTURE POT
The outer pot holds the water supply; the inner one contains the growing medium.

BIODEGRADABLE POTS
Use for propagating plants that resent root disturbance when transplanted.

LATTICE POT
This pot for aquatics lets in water, but should be lined with hessian to retain soil.

2
GREENHOUSES AND FRAMES

MANY PEOPLE RESIST *the idea of installing a greenhouse in the mistaken belief that it is expensive or requires much detailed gardening knowledge to maintain and use properly. This is not the case. As well as being the perfect all-weather space for tasks that crop up throughout the year, a greenhouse can be an extremely cost-effective investment, allowing you to propagate and grow on plants that may later be transferred outside to the garden itself at little cost. Cold frames, like greenhouses, are a boon to gardening, and can easily be integrated into the smallest of spaces. On a large site, greenhouses and frames can be screened from the garden proper by shrubs, climbing plants, or trees. In a smaller site, a greenhouse may need more careful integration to ensure that it does not visually jar or become too discordant a feature. The rewards of gardening under cover more than compensate for the initial cost and effort and open up a whole new world of gardening pleasures.*

Gardening under cover

Greenhouses, cold frames, and cloches are useful additions to any style of garden and are available in a range of sizes to fit whatever space is available. Each type of structure has a distinctive function but they are usually used in conjunction with each other. The most productive gardens use all three.

Unheated structures

Unheated greenhouses are used primarily to advance or extend the growing season of hardy and half-hardy plants. Cold frames fulfil a similar function, although they are also often used for hardening off plants that have been propagated in the greenhouse and for storing "resting plants". Cloches are used *in situ* over plants in the garden itself.

Heated structures

A heated greenhouse is far more versatile than either an unheated greenhouse or a cold frame, and allows a much greater range of plants to be grown. These include many frost-tender species that do not grow satisfactorily in temperate or cold climates without protection. In addition, a heated greenhouse provides a suitable environment in which to propagate plants.

GREENHOUSE STYLE
This traditional-style greenhouse is an integral part of the garden, which extends right up to the sides of the greenhouse. The hedges and trees provide shelter but are not close enough to reduce light penetration significantly. The timber framework will need to be treated every year or so with wood preservative to give weather resistance but otherwise only minimal maintenance is required.

ELEGANT DESIGN
Greenhouses with plastic-covered frames can be extremely attractive, as well as functional. This one is a decorative garden feature in its own right.

Siting the greenhouse

An amateur greenhouse is best positioned so that it blends in with the overall garden design. It should also be positioned in a sheltered site but where enough light is available for the plants to grow and thrive: too much shade will limit the range of plants that may be grown easily, whereas an exposed site will make the greenhouse expensive to heat or may mean that the plants are not adequately protected on cold nights.

Early planning
It is always worth spending the time to make sure that you have chosen the right spot before buying a greenhouse. If possible, make detailed notes in winter or spring of where shadows are cast in the garden by

POSITIONING THE GREENHOUSE

If the greenhouse is used mostly in the summer, its longer axis should run north to south. If good light in spring is a priority, however – when the sun is lower in the sky – orient the greenhouse east to west to make the best use of available light.

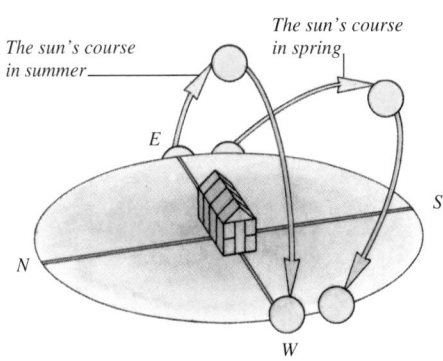

The sun's course in summer

The sun's course in spring

houses and any neighbouring garages, trees, or other large, nearby features, so that you do not site a greenhouse where it will be in shade for more than a few hours each day. Orienting the greenhouse north–south by its longer axis makes the best use of light in summer. For raising plants in spring, or overwintering tender specimens, an east–west orientation provides good light for much of the day.

If there is a possibility that you will want to extend the greenhouse later, or build a second, smaller one, allow enough space on the site.

Free-standing greenhouse
The best place to site a free-standing greenhouse is in a sheltered, light area away from buildings and large trees. If the site is high or exposed, choose a position that is sheltered by a hedge that acts as a windbreak, or build a fence or other screen. Windbreaks should not cast too much shade onto the greenhouse itself, however; they need not be tall – a 2.5m (8ft) hedge provides shelter for a distance of 12m (40ft) or more.

Do not position a free-standing greenhouse near or between buildings, since this could create a wind funnel effect that may damage the greenhouse and the plants inside. Positions at the bottom of a slope or near walls, hedges, or fences on the side of a slope should not be used to site a greenhouse because cold air may become trapped there (see CLIMATE AND THE GARDEN, "Frost pockets and frost damage", p.515).

Lean-to greenhouse
Place a lean-to greenhouse against a wall that receives a mixture of sun and shade. Do not site it where there is sun for most of the day, otherwise the greenhouse may overheat in summer, even with shading and a good ventilation system.

Access
Bear in mind the need for easy access. A site that is reasonably close to the house is preferable to one at a distance. Also make sure that there is a clear area in front of the greenhouse door for loading and unloading. Any paths leading to the greenhouse should be level. They should preferably have a hard, resilient surface and be wide enough to accommodate a wheelbarrow.

Mains services
Choose a site that will be convenient for mains water and electricity connection, if these services are needed. Although electricity is not essential for heating, it is useful for lighting as well as for some thermostatic controls and timing switches. A mains water connection makes watering plants more convenient, especially if an automatic system is used, and reduces the need to trail lengths of hose around the garden.

CHOOSING THE SITE

An open but sheltered site is best for a greenhouse – it should not be positioned in the path of a wind funnel. If there is no natural protection from the wind, construct a windbreak.

This greenhouse is in an open position, away from the shade cast by buildings and trees.

POOR POSITIONS

A line of trees provides shelter from the prevailing wind.

GOOD POSITION

This greenhouse lies in the shade cast by the nearby tree and will also be affected by falling leaves in autumn if the tree is deciduous.

This greenhouse lies directly in the path of a possible wind funnel. It is also too close to the hedge, which may make maintenance difficult.

A wind funnel may be created between 2 adjacent buildings.

Shade cast in summer

Shade cast in winter

Choosing a greenhouse

Before buying a greenhouse, consider carefully how it will be used in order to select the most suitable style, size, and materials – a greenhouse that is used as a garden room, for example, will differ significantly from one that is purely functional. If growing tropical and subtropical plants, an attractively shaped greenhouse, perhaps with room for central staging, might enhance the floral display.

Many different styles of greenhouse are available. Some make best use of space or provide optimum ventilation; others conserve heat well or allow better light penetration. When priorities have been decided, the final choice of style will depend on personal preference.

Conventional greenhouses

The more conventional types of greenhouse are suitable for a wide range of plants and include traditional span, Dutch light, three-quarter span, lean-to, and Mansard (or curvilinear) greenhouses. All of

TRADITIONAL SPAN

DUTCH LIGHT

these may have an aluminium or timber framework, and either all-glass or part-solid walls (except Dutch light greenhouses). Conventional greenhouses also have a wide range of compatible accessories, including staging and shelves.

Traditional span
The vertical sides and even span roof of a traditional span greenhouse are extremely practical in terms of

growing space and headroom. For raising seedlings and growing border crops, a traditional span greenhouse is likely to provide the best use of space for the least cost.

Dutch light
The sloping sides of Dutch light greenhouses are designed to allow in maximum light, so these greenhouses are suitable for border crops, especially low-growing ones such

as lettuces. The large sheets of glass are expensive to replace because of the size – the traditional dimensions are 145 x 77cm (59 x 30³/₄in). The glass panes slide into the frame and are secured using cleats fixed with galvanized nails.

The panes of glass on the roof overlap slightly to keep out rain and increase rigidity. This may cause loss of heat, however, if the panes overlap too loosely.

THREE-QUARTER SPAN LEAN-TO MANSARD

Three-quarter span
A three-quarter span greenhouse is positioned with one of its sides against a wall. Light is a little more restricted than in a free-standing model, so this type of greenhouse is best positioned beside a sunny wall, although this may mean that extra shading is required in summer. The wall provides extra warmth and insulation in the greenhouse, especially if it is a house wall (see also "Lean-to", right).

Lean-to
Where there is insufficient space for a free-standing structure, a lean-to greenhouse is an invaluable choice, particularly if a mainly decorative show-house is favoured.

Many are similar in appearance to conservatories, and may be used as garden rooms. Installing electricity, mains gas, or a water supply in a lean-to that is adjacent to a house wall is cheaper and generally involves less work than laying cables

or pipes to a greenhouse that is some distance from the house. In addition, the warmth of the house wall may reduce the level of heating required; brick walls store heat, from both the sun (especially if the wall is south-facing) and the domestic heating system, which is then released into the greenhouse.

The brick wall also provides good insulation, so that less heat escapes from a lean-to than from many other types of greenhouse.

Mansard
The Mansard (curvilinear) greenhouse has slanting sides and roof panels that are designed to allow maximum entry of available light. The full benefit is gained only in an open position with no shade from surrounding buildings or trees. A Mansard greenhouse is suitable for plants that need maximum light during the winter, when daylight hours are short and light levels are also frequently low.

DOME-SHAPED

POLYGONAL

ALPINE HOUSE

Specialist greenhouses

There are many specialist types of greenhouse, including dome-shaped, polygonal, alpine house, conservation, mini, and "polytunnel", all of which differ markedly in appearance from the more conventional types. Some are designed as highly decorative garden features in their own right, while others may offer particularly good value for money or be for specific types of plant.

Dome-shaped
This is an elegant design that is particularly useful in exposed positions as it is stable and offers less wind resistance than traditional greenhouses. Light transmission is excellent because the multi-angled glass panes and aluminium frame allow in maximum light. Dome-shaped structures may have limited headroom around the edge, and plants may also be difficult to reach. Extensions are not generally available and fittings may be limited to those produced by the manufacturer.

Polygonal
Octagonal and other polygonal greenhouses are frequently chosen where appearance is important, and may provide a focal point within the garden. They are generally more expensive than traditional greenhouses of similar size and, because they are not very common, there may be a limited choice of accessories. The irregular shape may also restrict growing space. Fitting replacement panes of glass in a polygonal greenhouse is more difficult than in a conventional structure.

Alpine house
This type of greenhouse is traditionally timber-framed with louvre vents extending all along the sides for the most effective ventilation. Usually, alpine houses are not heated and are closed only in the coldest winter weather, so insulation is not required. Unsuitable for tender plants, they are used for plants that thrive in bright, well-ventilated conditions, yet which require some overhead protection from dampness and rain. Their shape is similar to that of a traditional span greenhouse.

CONSERVATION

MINI

POLYTUNNEL

Conservation greenhouse
This type of greenhouse has many special features that are designed to save as much energy as possible. It is therefore usually more expensive than other types of greenhouse of similar size. The roof panels are angled to allow optimum light penetration, and mirrored surfaces are also used to reflect light within the greenhouse itself. Plastic double glazing and purpose-made insulation are fitted as standard.

Mini-greenhouse
This provides a useful, low-cost introduction to greenhouse gardening. Mini-greenhouses are usually aluminium and placed against a wall or fence. They should preferably face south–east or south–west so that maximum light penetrates. It is the best choice if only a small number of plants is to be grown, since space is limited. There is often useful space beneath the staging for overwintering plants or for storage.

Access may be a problem – all work has to be done from the outside. Ventilation may be inadequate, and rapid temperature changes often occur. Shading in summer is therefore essential if plants are not to become scorched.

Plastic "polytunnel" greenhouse
Where visual appearance is not important and low-cost protection is required – such as in the vegetable plot – a "polytunnel" greenhouse has many benefits. It comprises a large, tunnel-shaped frame covered with heavy-duty transparent plastic sheets and is widely used for crops that require some protection but not the warm conditions of a traditional greenhouse. Polytunnels keep out the worst of the winter cold and provide useful wind protection throughout the year. Since they are light and relatively easy to move, they are often used in plots where crop rotation is carried out.

For a large growing area, commercial "polytunnels" are a cost-effective investment, but for a small garden a more traditional shape may be a better choice. Some polytunnels include staging, although most are intended primarily for growing crops at ground level, planted either directly in the soil, in pots, or in growing bags.

Ventilation may be a problem: the door offers a reasonably efficient method of ventilation – especially in large tunnels with openings at each end – and some have sides that roll up. The plastic sheeting should be replaced every year or two – it gradually becomes opaque, restricting light penetration.

Choosing the size

The greenhouse will almost inevitably seem too small once it is filled with plants so, if possible, buy one that may be extended. Although a large greenhouse costs more to heat than a small one, it is possible to partition off a section in winter, and leave the remainder unheated (see "Thermal screens", p.482).

Space considerations

A greenhouse that is used primarily for ornamentals should have plenty of room inside for staging, which may be tiered, and possibly a central or end display. To provide space for propagation and growing on, it may be necessary to divide up the space with a partition. Alternatively, use a cold frame for propagation.

Length, width, and height

A length of 2.5m (8ft) and a width of 2m (6ft) are the minimum, practical dimensions for a general-purpose, traditional greenhouse. A smaller greenhouse than this limits the range of plants that may be grown, and may make it difficult to control the environment – draughts and rapid heat build-up in summer tend to be more of a problem in small greenhouses, and may lead to sudden fluctuations in temperature. In greenhouses that are more than 2m (6ft) wide, it may also be difficult to reach pots and ventilation towards the back of the staging. Staging to a width of 60cm (2ft) on either side allows a path of the same width down the middle.

If border crops are to be grown, choose a greenhouse that is 2.5m (8ft) wide with borders to a width of 1m (3ft). A width of 2.5m (8ft) is also suitable if a wider path is required for a wheelchair or to enable a wheelbarrow to be used easily.

Many small greenhouses have low eaves and comparatively low ridges, which make it tiring to work over the border or staging for long periods. To gain more height, build the greenhouse on a brick base or dig out a sunken path.

Choosing the materials

Greenhouses are made in a range of materials. The most important considerations when choosing both the framework and glazing for the greenhouse are practicality, expense, and the amount of maintenance required. The appearance of the materials may also be important.

BUYING A GREENHOUSE

Before buying a greenhouse, use the following as a checklist; it may save disappointment later.

Ridge height should be at least 1.7m (5ft 6in); remember to allow for roof ventilator openings protruding.

Roof ventilators are usually inadequate as supplied – the total ventilation area should equal one sixth of the floor area. Extra ventilators may be needed.

Glass should be easy to replace; use panes of a standard size – 60cm (24in) square or 60 x 45cm (24 x 18in). The large panes of Dutch light greenhouses are expensive to replace. Consider double-glazing if high temperatures are to be maintained, although this adds considerably to the cost.

Cross bracing on aluminium alloy greenhouses must be strong enough to make the structure rigid.

Eaves height affects the headroom – it should be at least 1.35m (4ft 6in) for ease of working.

Doors may be hinged or sliding. They must be wide enough: 60cm (24in) is the minimum practical width. For wheelchair or wheelbarrow access they should be wider and without a "lip". Sliding doors are easily adjusted for ventilation and are less likely to slam in wind than hinged doors. Check that doors are a good fit when closed, otherwise they may let in draughts.

Use ground anchors if the structure is not secured to a brick base.

Gutters and downpipes reduce the risk of water cascading from the roof and damaging the plants nearby.

A base may be an optional extra – bear this in mind when comparing prices since most timber-framed greenhouses need one. Some have a step that makes wheelchair access and use of a wheelbarrow difficult.

Use base cladding to reduce heat loss in the winter, unless border crops are to be grown.

Side ventilators allow free circulation of air. Louvre windows must close tightly to minimize heat loss in cold weather.

A kick panel at the foot of the door minimizes the risk of breaking the glass panel.

The framework

Timber frameworks have been the traditional choice and are generally considered to be the most attractive. They tend to be expensive, however, and are also heavy to construct. If possible, choose a durable hardwood. Cedar is an excellent choice.

It is rot-resistant, does not warp easily, and, if treated every year or two with special cedar preparation, retains its colour well.

Greenhouses constructed with redwood and deal are cheaper than those built with cedar but, before being assembled, they should be

pressure-treated with preservative; they also require regular painting to prevent rotting (see also "Timber framework", p.491).

Greenhouses with aluminium alloy frames are almost completely maintenance-free. They do not retain heat quite as well as timber

CONSTRUCTION MATERIALS

TIMBER
A timber frame is the traditional choice for garden greenhouses. Hardwoods are low maintenance.

ALUMINIUM
Aluminium alloy frames are light but extremely sturdy and need only minimum maintenance.

STEEL
Plastic-coated, steel frames are very strong but must be treated regularly to prevent rust.

frames but the difference is minimal and should not be considered a serious disadvantage.

Galvanized steel is also often used for greenhouse frames. Steel frames are light and easy to construct but extremely strong. They are cheaper than timber or aluminium frames but must be painted regularly (see "Metal framework", p.491).

Aluminium and steel frames are narrower than timber ones and allow larger panes of glass to be used, resulting in better light penetration.

Glass panes
Horticultural glass is the most satisfactory glazing material for a greenhouse: it allows excellent light penetration but is thinner and less expensive than ordinary glass. It is easy to clean, does not discolour,

and retains considerably more heat than plastic glazing materials. Glass is not as robust as plastic glazing, however, so breakages and cracks may be a problem, since the panes must be replaced quickly.

Plastic glazing
Plastics are generally more expensive and less durable than glass; they discolour more readily and also tend to become scratched over time, which is both unsightly and, more importantly, may cut down on the amount of light that is transmitted if the discoloring is severe.

Acrylic sheets are used to glaze the curved eaves of many greenhouses because the acrylic may be shaped easily to give an elegant outline to the structure. Condensation occurs more readily on its surface

than on a conventional glass pane. Rigid polycarbonate sheets are also often used to glaze greenhouses. They are easy to handle, lightweight, virtually unbreakable, and have good insulating properties. They are relatively easily scratched, however, and tend to discolour.

Twin-walled polycarbonate has particularly good insulating qualities, but its opacity may be a major problem in the greenhouse.

Sizing
Most local glass merchants will cut glass panes to size for little cost. It is important to make sure that any measurements you give are accurate; calculate them carefully, ensuring that there will be sufficient clearance for the glass to engage with the mounting system that is to be used.

GLAZING MATERIAL

Rigid plastic glazing material is light and easy to fit. This is twin-walled polycarbonate, which provides good insulation.

If plastic glazing material is used it will be supplied in sheets and is not usually difficult to cut to size at home using a sharp craft knife and straight edge.

Erecting the greenhouse

A greenhouse requires far less maintenance and lasts much longer if it is properly erected in the first place. The information listed below is necessarily of a general nature, because it applies to many different greenhouse types and designs: always follow the manufacturer's instructions for particular advice. If in doubt on any point, check the details with either the supplier or the greenhouse manufacturer.

Some manufacturers that supply by mail order also erect greenhouses, if required, but usually expect the ground to be levelled beforehand and any brick base (see below) to be prepared in advance.

Preparing the site

Always erect a greenhouse on firm, level ground, otherwise the frame may warp and become twisted and cause the glass to crack. The chosen site must first be cleared of weeds, since persistent weeds are very difficult to eradicate when the greenhouse is erected and in position. If the site selected for the greenhouse has been recently dug over, allow the soil to settle for a few weeks, and then consolidate it with a heavy roller.

Foundations
Aluminium greenhouses that are smaller than 2m wide and 2.5m long (6 x 8ft) do not usually require a thick concrete base. Simply dig a hole at each corner approximately 25–45cm (10–18in) deep, then wedge in the ground anchors (see

p.480) with rubble and pour in a concrete mix to fix them securely.

If a more substantial foundation is required, dig a trench approximately 25cm (10in) deep, filling it with 15cm (6in) of consolidated hardcore. Fix the anchoring bolts in place and finish off with poured concrete or paving slabs, making sure that the ground is level.

Brick bases
A brick base must be constructed to the precise measurements provided by the greenhouse manufacturer, on solid concrete footings approximately 13cm (5in) deep (see *How to Make a Concrete Footing*, p.504). The finished level of the footings should be at or below soil level.

Wooden greenhouses

The sections of a wooden greenhouse are usually supplied complete and only need to be bolted together and then fixed to the base.

Base
Interlocking concrete blocks may be used for the base, otherwise a solid concrete foundation or brick base should be built (see "Foundations" and "Brick bases", above).

Sides, gable ends, and roof
Before the greenhouse is delivered, check what kind of bolts or fixings are required and whether they will be supplied. First bolt the sides and gable ends together to form the main framework. Follow the manufacturer's advice for the exact method

of fixing this to the base or foundations, as designs vary. The foot of the frame may contain integral anchorage points for securely bolting it down. Bolt any internal partitions to the frame, then add the roof sections and bolt them in place.

Some wooden greenhouses are supplied as sections with unglazed frames, with the glass or plastic glazing supplied separately. Others have pre-glazed frames but these are heavy to move – two or more people may be required to support them.

If the timber has not been treated and is not rot-resistant, it is important to paint all the woodwork with a preservative at this stage, before the greenhouse is glazed.

BUILDING A BRICK BASE

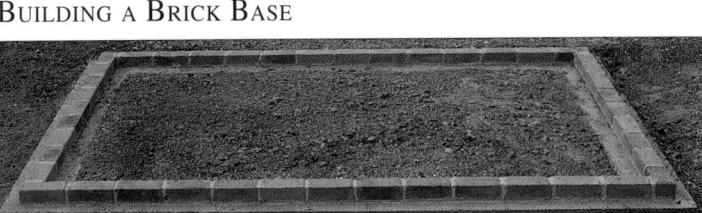

If using a brick base for the greenhouse, build it in advance, and lay proper foundations first. Check with the greenhouse manufacturer before building the base to make sure that the dimensions are correct.

Glazing
If putty is to be used for glazing it is usually supplied with the greenhouse. Apply it to the glazing bars, and bed-in the glass carefully. The glass panes are usually secured in place with galvanized steel or brass sprigs; if these are not supplied, they may be purchased from any hardware shop.

If a dry glazing system (that is, one that does not require putty) is to be used, simply follow the supplier's instructions.

Whichever method is used, glaze the sides and gable ends first, overlapping the panes by 1cm (1/2in). Use soft metal overlap clips to hold the glass panes firmly together.

CONCRETE FOUNDATIONS

For solid greenhouse foundations, dig a trench to match the dimensions of the greenhouse, filling it with hardcore and a layer of concrete.

Ground level

10cm (4in) layer of concrete

15cm (6in) layer of hardcore

GLAZING BARS AND CLIPS FOR METAL GREENHOUSES

GLAZING BARS
These form the framework of the greenhouse.

"W"-SHAPED WIRE CLIP
Use this type of clip to hold glass and plastic panes firmly in place.

SPRUNG BAND CLIPS
An alternative clip, these fix onto the frame.

Ventilators and door

Ventilators are supplied as an integral part of the pre-assembled sections, so the number you ordered should be in place. Screw on hinged doors and simply insert sliding doors into the runners.

Metal greenhouses

Greenhouses with metal frames are delivered in home-assembly kit form, and the frame is supplied in sections – the base, sides, gable ends, and roof. The sections are in turn divided into separate component pieces that need to be bolted together.

Base

Assemble the base first, ensuring that it is perfectly level and square to prevent any warping and twisting of the frame; measure from each corner to the one diagonally opposite – the measurements must be the same. The base must be securely anchored; this is particularly important in windy or exposed areas.

If fixing ground anchors to a concrete foundation, use the anchoring

A GROUND ANCHOR

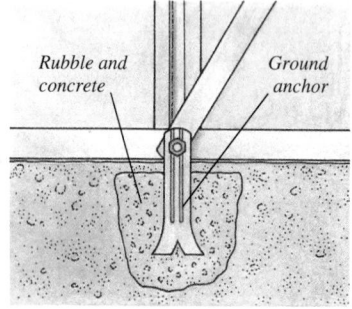

Rubble and concrete

Ground anchor

Small greenhouses may be secured using ground anchors. Wedge them in place with rubble first before pouring in a concrete mix.

bolts provided, otherwise simply set the ground anchors in rubble and concrete at each corner of the base.

Sides, gable ends, and roof

Assemble the sides, gable ends, and roof sections in the sequence recommended by the manufacturer in the instruction sheet. The sides are usually put together first.

First make sure that everything has been included, then before assembling lay out on the ground all the pieces for each section, in their correct relative positions. Bolt the pieces for each section (sides and gable ends) together. Decide at this point where the vents are to be positioned and leave suitable gaps for them, as necessary. Do not tighten the nuts until all the sections are fully assembled and have been loosely put together.

Bolt the sections together one to another, and then to the base, then bolt on the roof bars and ridge bar.

Ventilators

Ventilator frames are assembled separately, then bolted onto the roof and sides as required, before glazing. This gives greater flexibility than with wooden greenhouses when choosing both the number and position of ventilators. The hinges of roof ventilators usually slide in a groove in the moulding.

Glazing

Glazing strips are usually used for metal greenhouses. Cut the strips to the appropriate length and then press them into the grooves in the glazing bars – shaped pieces of metal that form the framework to hold the glass securely in position.

Glaze the sides of the greenhouse first, placing the glass squarely between the glazing bars, leaving about 3mm (1/8in) clearance on each side

of the glass panes for the glazing clips to be attached. The upper panes of glass should overlap the lower ones by about 1cm (1/2in). Secure them with overlap glazing clips – pieces of metal bent into "S" shapes that hook over the lower pane and hold the upper one firmly in position.

Once each pane is in position, use glazing clips, pressing them into place between the glazing bars and panes to hold the glass. A little pressure will be required to overcome the natural spring in the metal.

Glaze the gable ends of the greenhouse and then the roof, using the same technique.

Fitting the door

Metal greenhouses usually have sliding doors. These should be bolted together and slid into the runners provided in the end frame. A stop is supplied for bolting on afterwards to prevent the door from coming off the runners if it is opened too quickly. The door should be glazed when it has been fixed in position.

Installing electricity, gas, and water

Installing an outdoor power supply is not a job for the amateur. The installation of electricity in a greenhouse must be properly carried out by a qualified electrician, although considerable savings may be made by excavating the trench for the cable yourself and then refilling it later when the job is completed. Alternatively, the cable may be run overhead if your greenhouse is close to the house and it will not be unsightly; your electrician will be able to advise you on whether or not this is a practical option. Armoured cable and water-proof fittings should always be used for safety.

Electricity has many practical uses in the greenhouse: it provides power for heating, lighting, propagators, timers, soil-warming cables, and electrically powered garden tools of various types.

Mains gas is useful for heating the greenhouse, although mains gas heaters are less widely available than bottled gas heaters. Consult an approved fitter to discuss the feasibility and cost of laying on mains gas. Again, you can save money by offering to do the spadework yourself.

If you already have an outdoor water tap, you may be able to take a spur from this and run it to the greenhouse. The pipe must be buried below frost level – at least 30cm (12in) deep – and the above-ground parts should be very well lagged. In the UK, it is essential that an anti-siphoning device is incorporated in order to meet legal requirements.

Fitting the staging

The staging supplied by the manufacturer is designed to be bolted or screwed to the framework. This is best done at the same time as the greenhouse is erected, if possible, especially for octagonal and dome-shaped greenhouses, which have staging specially designed to fit. If solid staging is used, leave a gap several inches wide between the inside of the greenhouse and the staging, to allow free air circulation.

FITTING A PANE IN A METAL GREENHOUSE

Attach overlap glazing clips to the base of the pane. Wearing gloves, lift the pane into place, gently pressing the top edge into position before hooking the bottom edge onto the lower pane. Secure the pane with glazing clips (see inset), pressing them gently until they slot into position.

Creating the right environment

Creating the right balance of conditions in a greenhouse to suit the plants grown there is the essence of successful greenhouse gardening.

For tender plants, the temperature maintained is vital. In a heated greenhouse, choose an efficient, reliable, and economic heater. In any greenhouse, good insulation to retain heat and keep out draughts must be balanced with the need for thorough ventilation. Shading is essential in most greenhouses during the summer to help prevent the plants from overheating; see PRINCIPLES OF PROPAGATION, *Shading Greenhouses (Temperate climates)*, p.542.

Atmospheric humidity should be kept at a level that suits the plants being grown. Automatic methods of watering tend to increase humidity so, for most plants, special humidifiers may not be essential. Special lighting is often useful to increase the growth potential of plants.

Greenhouse temperature

The choice of plants to be grown in a greenhouse is determined largely by the temperature at which it is maintained (see "The greenhouse environment", p.433). There are four categories of greenhouse: cold, cool, temperate, and warm. The environment is controlled slightly differently in each type.

Cold

A cold greenhouse is not heated at all. Insulation (see p.482) is needed to keep out the worst of the winter cold and some form of shading (see p.484) is needed in summer. Thorough ventilation (see p.483) is important all year round.

A cold greenhouse may be used to grow summer crops, to overwinter slightly tender plants, or to propagate cuttings (although a propagator will increase the success rate, see p.488). An unheated greenhouse may also permit an early display of hardy plants and many types of spring bulb.

An unheated greenhouse is suitable for alpines – some are specifically designed to provide maximum ventilation for this type of plant (see "Alpine house", p.477), although any greenhouse with louvre ventilators along the sides is adequate.

Cool/frost-free

A cool greenhouse is one that is heated just enough to keep out frost. This means that a minimum daytime temperature range between 5°C (41°F) and 10°C (50°F), and a night-time temperature of no less than 2°C (35°F), is needed.

To ensure that these temperatures are maintained, a heater capable of a large temperature lift is a necessity in winter, in case the outside temperature falls many degrees below freezing. An electric heater with a thermostat (see p.482) is most likely to do this efficiently.

Insulation, thorough ventilation, and shading control are necessary, as with cold greenhouses.

A frost-free greenhouse may be used to grow all the types of plant mentioned for cold greenhouses. In addition, frost-tender plants may be overwintered, and summer crops or flowering pot plants grown. A propagator will be needed for germinating seeds. Young seedlings will benefit from the extra light provided by a growing lamp (see p.485).

Temperate

A slightly warmer greenhouse with a minimum daytime temperature range between 10°C (50°F) and 13°C (55°F), and with a minimum night-time temperature of 7°C (45°F), is suitable for growing a good selection of hardy, half-hardy, and tender pot plants, as well as vegetables.

Additional warmth is necessary in spring for propagation, supplied by a propagator or by boosting the ordinary heating for the required period. Supplementary lighting provided by a growing lamp is useful. Shading and good ventilation are required, especially in summer.

Warm

A warm greenhouse has a daytime temperature range between 13°C (55°C) and 18°C (64°F), with a minimum night-time temperature of 13°C (55°F). Such high temperatures enable the amateur gardener to grow a large range of plants, including tropical and subtropical ornamentals, fruits, and vegetables. A warm greenhouse may also be used for propagating plants and raising seedlings without the aid of propagation equipment, although a growing lamp will be useful.

Very good ventilation, preferably automatic, an efficient method of shading, and high humidity (see p.484) in hot weather are essential.

THE "GREENHOUSE EFFECT"

Light passes through glass as short-wave radiation, warming everything inside, including floor, staging, soil, and plants. Heat then reradiates from these as long waves, which cannot pass through the glass, leading to a build-up of heat inside the greenhouse.

HOW TO BALANCE THE ENVIRONMENT OF A GREENHOUSE

	HEATING (see p.482)	INSULATION (see p.482)	VENTILATION (see p.483)	SHADING (see p.484)	HUMIDITY (see p.484)	WATERING (see p.485)	LIGHTING (see p.485)
COLD No minimum temperature	None.	Insulate against severely cold draughts and damp, foggy weather in winter.	Thorough ventilation is essential to prevent damp, stagnant conditions in winter.	Shade vulnerable plants in summer with a shading wash, blinds, meshes or fabric, or rigid sheets.	Unlikely to be a problem in summer. Maintain a "dry" atmosphere in winter by ventilating.	Water by hand in winter. Use a capillary system, seep hose, or trickle system in summer.	Growing lamps are unlikely to be needed for the type of plants grown.
COOL Minimum temperature 2°C (35°F)	A thermostatically controlled electric heater is preferable but gas or paraffin heaters may also be used. A frost alarm is useful if tender plants are grown.	In winter, as for a cold greenhouse. In spring, good insulation is extremely important if frost-tender plants are grown.	Ventilate freely, especially if a gas or paraffin heater is used, to disperse water vapour and toxic fumes.	Shade to control the temperature in summer – shading washes or blinds do this most efficiently. Fit automatic blinds, if possible.	"Damping down" is beneficial to increase humidity in summer.	As for a cold greenhouse, except that an overhead system may also be used in summer.	Growing lamps may be useful, especially in spring when natural light is poor, for plants at an early stage of development.
TEMPERATE Minimum temperature 7°C (45°F)	A heater (preferably electric) fitted with a thermostat is required. A frost alarm is also essential.	As for cold and cool greenhouses. Thermal screens are useful in spring for propagation.	As for a cool greenhouse. Automatic vent openers are extremely useful in summer.	As for a cool greenhouse.	Maintain high humidity in spring and summer, especially around cuttings and seedlings.	An automatic watering system is useful throughout the year.	Growing lamps are useful in winter and spring for extending daylength.
WARM Minimum temperature 13°C (55°F)	As for a temperate greenhouse.	Good insulation is essential throughout the year to minimize heating costs.	Automatic vent openers fitted to several vents simplify temperature control enormously.	Automatic blinds are desirable in summer.	High humidity is required throughout the year.	As for a temperate greenhouse.	As for a temperate greenhouse.

Heating

It is important to maintain the correct temperature in the greenhouse for the range of plants you have chosen to grow. Select a heater that is powerful enough to maintain the required minimum temperature efficiently. Other factors to consider when choosing a greenhouse heater include convenience, the cost of installation, and running costs.

Electric heaters

These are the most reliable, efficient, and convenient to use in the greenhouse, although an electricity supply will be needed to run them (see "Installing electricity, gas, and water", p.480). They are usually thermostatically controlled, which means that no heat is wasted, and they do not require regular refuelling or maintenance. In addition, electric heaters do not produce fumes or water vapour.

A number of different types of electric heater is available. These include fan heaters and water-proof tubular heaters, both of which heat the greenhouse effectively. Convector heaters are also used but these do not distribute heat as efficiently. Tubular heaters need to be fitted to the sides of the greenhouse, just above floor level. Other heaters may be moved around as desired.

Electric fan heaters are particularly useful because they promote good air circulation, which helps to maintain an even temperature and minimizes the spread of disease. They may also be used to cool the greenhouse in warm weather if the heating element is switched off.

Gas heaters

Gas heating systems may be run off the mains supplies (see "Installing electricity, gas, and water", p.480) or from bottled gas. They are not as convenient to use as electric heaters: although they may have thermostats, these are not usually calibrated in degrees so you will need to experiment to find the correct setting.

If bottled gas is used, the cylinders need to be regularly replaced: always have two bottles connected by an automatic switch-over valve in case one runs out. Propane gas releases fumes and water vapour as it burns, so ventilation is important. Keep gas cylinders in a safe place and have them checked regularly by an authorized dealer.

Paraffin heaters

These are not as efficient as electric or gas heaters in their use of fuel because they are not controlled by a thermostat. Paraffin heaters may therefore be expensive to run if a high temperature needs to be maintained, since some energy may be wasted, although they are inexpensive to buy in the first place and there is no installation cost.

When using paraffin heaters, thorough ventilation is required because some plant-toxic fumes and water vapour are produced as a byproduct of combustion – a humid, stagnant atmosphere may encourage disease if ventilation is poor. Other drawbacks include the need to transport and store fuel, and to check the fuel level and wick every day (to ensure that it is burning cleanly).

Circulated hot water

Solid fuel hot water systems are now rarely used in greenhouses. Oil- and gas-fired circulated hot water systems are still sometimes used, but seldom on the small scale of the amateur greenhouse.

Although the distribution of heat through hot water pipes provides good heat transfer, often only about 50 per cent of the energy released is used – the rest is lost through the glass walls. The need for regular stoking and clearing out of the fire also makes solid fuel inconvenient.

Thermometer and frost alarm

If the heater in a greenhouse is not thermostatically controlled, use a maximum/minimum thermometer to check that the correct overnight temperatures are being maintained for the plants grown.

In regions that suffer extremely low temperatures, a frost alarm is a useful safeguard if the greenhouse contains tender plants. If the air temperature unexpectedly drops to near freezing, for example through a power failure or heater breakdown, an alarm bell will sound remotely (this will usually be somewhere in the home), allowing you time to protect the plants.

A FROST ALARM

Install a frost alarm if growing tender plants that may be damaged or killed if the temperature falls.

INSULATION MATERIAL

Bubble plastic is useful for insulating a greenhouse and reduces heat loss considerably. Cut it to size and attach it securely to the framework.

Insulation

Insulation in the greenhouse may reduce heating costs considerably; if a minimum temperature of 7°C (45°F) is required, for example, the cost of insulation may be recovered within just a few seasons – and even in a single winter period in particularly cold areas. The higher the temperature to be maintained, and the colder the region, the more cost-effective insulation is likely to be. Care in choosing the right material is required, however, since some insulation materials may reduce the amount of light reaching the plants.

Double-glazing

The most efficient method of insulating the entire greenhouse is to fit double-glazing. This is best done at the time of construction, if possible. Double-glazing is expensive, of course, but the benefits could be enormous.

Flexible plastic insulation

Bubble plastic, which consists of double or triple skins of transparent plastic with air cells in between, is a very efficient method of insulation. A single layer of plastic sheeting is not as efficient as bubble plastic at reducing heat loss but is less expensive and does not cut out so much light. Plastic sheets may be used in winter as a form of double-glazing. To attach the insulation material, use suction-pad fasteners or clips that fit into the greenhouse frame.

Thermal screens

These consist of sheets of clear plastic or translucent material, such as a cross-laminated fabric, that are attached to wires between the eaves and drawn horizontally across the width of the greenhouse in the evening. They are useful for conserving heat at night because they restrict the amount of heat that rises above the eaves, trapping the warmth lower down around the plants.

Vertical screens may also be used to partition off a heated section at one end of the greenhouse with plastic sheeting, leaving the remainder of the area unheated. Plants may be overwintered and early seedlings raised in the heated section.

Special kits for making thermal screens are available, or plastic sheeting and the necessary fixings may be obtained separately.

Base cladding

Base cladding on the floor of glass-to-ground greenhouses reduces heat loss significantly. In winter, place polystyrene panels along the foot of the glass panes to provide extra insulation, removing them before summer border crops are planted.

THERMAL SCREENS

Horizontal screen between the eaves

Vertical screen that acts as a partition

Thermal screens may be drawn horizontally between the eaves. They may also be drawn vertically to partition off a section of the greenhouse that needs to be heated to a high temperature.

Ventilation

Good ventilation is essential in a greenhouse, even in winter, to avoid a build-up of stuffy or damp, stale air, and to control temperature. It is important that the area covered by ventilators should be equal to at least one sixth of the floor area.

Extra ventilation

Few greenhouses are supplied with enough ventilators as standard, so order additional air vents, hinged and louvre windows, or extractor fans when buying a greenhouse. This is an especially important consideration with timber greenhouses, since it is usually difficult to add them later.

Extra ventilation is particularly important if paraffin or bottled gas heating systems are used, to prevent water vapour and fumes from building up to an unacceptable level.

Wind ventilation system

Air exchange in a greenhouse occurs when external movements of air, caused by gusts of wind, replace interior warm, humid air with fresh air. If ventilators are placed on the sides and roof of the greenhouse, and are also staggered, this will ensure that air circulates throughout the entire area – if vents are placed directly opposite one another, air will simply blow straight through the greenhouse.

Doors may also be kept open in summer to increase ventilation; it is worth fixing a sheet of netting across the doorway, however, to keep out birds and pets.

Chimney ventilation system

Chimney effect ventilation depends on warm, humid air rising out of roof vents and being replaced by fresh air that is drawn in as a result through lower ventilators, which are usually positioned along the sides of the greenhouse either above or below the staging.

Fan ventilation system

Fan ventilation is a mechanically driven system that works by extracting air from the greenhouse at head height, or slightly higher, and drawing in fresh air through vents lower down and usually at the opposite end of the greenhouse.

Hinged ventilators

These may be fitted to the sides or roof of the greenhouse and should open wide, to an angle of about 45°. This will allow maximum airflow while at the same time preventing direct gusts of wind from entering

THE PRINCIPLES OF GREENHOUSE VENTILATION

WIND EFFECT
Fresh air blows into the greenhouse, circulates, and then escapes through an open vent on the opposite side.

CHIMNEY EFFECT
Warm air rises and escapes through open vents in the roof, drawing fresh, cooler air in lower down.

FAN VENTILATION
Air is drawn out by a fan at the top of the greenhouse and drawn in through open vents lower down.

the greenhouse and possibly causing damage to the plants or even to the structure itself.

Louvre ventilators

Usually positioned below the height of the staging, louvre window ventilators are particularly useful for controlling the flow of air throughout the greenhouse in winter, when roof ventilators may allow too much heat to escape. The louvre vents must close tightly, however, so that they exclude all draughts.

Automatic vent openers

Autovent openers simplify temperature control significantly in the greenhouse, since they are designed to open automatically whenever the temperature inside rises above a predetermined level. These devices are essential if a heating system that has no thermostat has been installed in the greenhouse.

With any type of greenhouse, automatic vent openers should be fitted to at least some of the hinged or louvre ventilators; this is easily done by closely following the manufacturer's instructions.

They may be set to open at a range of temperatures, but make sure that you choose an automatic system that will function within the temperature range required in your greenhouse. It is best to set this to operate at a temperature that is just

below the optimum for the plants. In this way, the vents will open and the greenhouse will be well ventilated before the temperature inside rises to an unsuitable level for the plants.

Many different designs of autovent are available. Some models work by the expansion and contraction of a plug of wax that is contained in a metal or plastic cylinder; the movement of the wax works a piston that opens and closes the ventilator. Other models make use of metal rods that alter their shape as the temperature rises and falls, activating the ventilation mechanism.

Extractor fans

The type of extractor fan that is designed primarily for use in kitchens and bathrooms is also ideally suited for use in the greenhouse. An additional bonus with using these extractor fans is that most of them are fitted with a thermostatic control, which is an essential requirement for the greenhouse.

Choose a fan that is powerful enough for the particular size of your greenhouse – the extraction rate is usually quoted in cubic metres or cubic feet per hour. As a general guide, a 2 x 2.5m (6 x 8ft) greenhouse requires a fan with a capacity of 300cu m (10,000cu ft) per hour, but a smaller one may be perfectly adequate if other types of ventilation are also used.

A louvre window – positioned at the opposite end of the greenhouse to the extractor fan and set lower down – is essential to provide a flow of fresh air to replace the stale air that is drawn out by the fan.

Buy a fan that is fitted with louvre flaps that close when the fan is not actually working so that draughts are excluded. To extend the working life of the fan, the motor should not be set to run at maximum capacity; it is much better to choose a model that is slightly more powerful than is strictly necessary for the greenhouse.

LOUVRE VENTS

These are fitted on the side of the greenhouse above ground level to improve the flow of air through the interior. The opening mechanism has a lever and is simple to operate (see insets).

HINGED VENTS

Vents that open by a hinge mechanism are normally fitted to the roof of the greenhouse. Make sure that they open wide and that they are securely fixed when open.

AUTOVENT OPENER

This autovent works by the expansion and contraction of wax in a cylinder as the greenhouse temperature rises and falls.

Shading

This will help to control the temperature of the greenhouse if the ventilation system is insufficient. It also protects vulnerable plants from too much direct sunlight, reducing the risk of leaf scorch, and preventing flower colours from fading in strong sunlight. Shading applied primarily to control heat should be on the outside of the greenhouse; internal shading is unlikely to reduce the temperature significantly.

The amount of shade required in a greenhouse depends on the season and the plants being grown. In the months of strongest sunlight, shading that reduces the light by 40–50 per cent is suitable for a typical mixed greenhouse. Ferns generally prefer approximately 75 per cent filtered light, while most cacti and other succulents require very little or no shading at all.

Shading washes

These are often the most effective method of reducing heat from the sun, while still allowing enough light to penetrate for good plant growth. Paint or spray the wash onto the outside of the glass at the beginning of the sunny season and remove it in late summer by washing or rubbing it off, using a cleaning solution.

Shading washes are inexpensive to buy but they may be messy to apply and remove, and their appearance is sometimes unattractive in a small garden where the greenhouse is a major feature. Some washes become more transparent when wet, so that on rainy days or when the weather is dull they allow more light to penetrate.

Blinds

These are used mainly on the outside of the greenhouse and control temperature effectively. They are more versatile than shading washes, since they may be rolled up or down, depending on the intensity of light required. They may also be used where only a section of the greenhouse needs to be shaded. Manually operated blinds need constant attention, however. Automatic blinds, which come into operation as soon as the temperature rises to a predetermined level, are more convenient to use, but they are expensive.

Meshes and fabrics

Flexible mesh shading materials are suitable for either interior or exterior use. They are less adaptable than blinds because they are generally fixed in position for the entire season, and they are less satisfactory than shading washes in helping to control plant growth.

Woven and knitted fabrics are also suitable for both interior and exterior greenhouse use. The amount of light reduction varies considerably, depending on the type of fabric fitted, but the quality of light allowed through to the plants is usually perfectly adequate for good growth, although the temperature is not significantly reduced.

FLEXIBLE MESH

Plastic mesh netting may be cut to length and used either internally or externally for shading plants in a greenhouse.

SHADING THE GREENHOUSE

Shading washes are applied to the outside of a greenhouse to prevent the temperature inside from rising too high, without greatly reducing light. The washes may be left on throughout the season.

ROLLER BLINDS

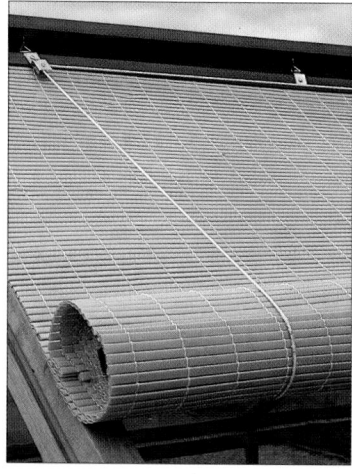

Blinds are a versatile method of shading the greenhouse. They should be hard wearing, since they will be in place for long periods.

Cross-laminated fabric, and some plastic meshes, are recommended for internal shading only.

Tinted bubble plastic may also be used for shading. It cuts down the light by almost 50 per cent, but it reduces temperature only slightly.

Rigid sheets

Rigid polycarbonate sheets (usually tinted) are sometimes used for shading in greenhouses. The sheets may be fixed either inside or outside, as recommended by the greenhouse manufacturer. They cut down the light effectively, but unless they are white in colour the quality of light transmitted may not be sufficient for good plant growth.

Humidity

Humidity is a measure of the quantity of water vapour in the air. The humidity of the air affects the rate at which plants transpire; this is their mechanism for drawing water (along with nutrients) from roots to leaves, where the water then evaporates from leaf pores into the air. As water evaporates, the plant is cooled down.

Establish the preferred humidity levels of the plants in your greenhouse, then control the amount of moisture in the atmosphere to suit them. Humidity may be increased using various techniques (see "Humidifiers", below) and reduced by ventilation (see p.483).

Plant requirements

A very humid atmosphere reduces the rate of transpiration and evaporation to a level that may be harmful to some plants and they may suffer damage from overheating unless cooler, drier air is brought in by ventilation. Many tropical plants from humid climates, however, require high levels of humidity for healthy growth, and will not survive in a dry atmosphere.

If the air is dry and the humidity level low, plants transpire more rapidly, often losing a great deal of moisture. Plants that are not adapted to cope with low humidity will wilt as a result, unless additional water is supplied at the roots. Dry-climate plants often have specific anatomical features that reduce the transpiration rate in drought conditions (see CLIMATE AND THE GARDEN, "Drought", p.517).

Measuring humidity

The level of humidity in a greenhouse depends to an extent on the temperature of the air – warm air is capable of holding more moisture than cold air before it becomes saturated. Relative humidity is a measure of the amount of water vapour in the air expressed as a percentage of saturation point at the same temperature. A "humid" atmosphere is defined as having a relative humidity of about 75 per cent; a "dry" atmosphere has a relative humidity of about 35 per cent.

Wet and dry bulb thermometers, used in conjunction with hygrometric tables, may be used to measure the relative humidity of the atmosphere. Hygrometers, which have a dial that gives readings for both the temperature and the humidity, are also available. As a general guide, a relative humidity below 75 per cent, but above 40 per cent, is beneficial for most greenhouse plants during the growing season – at levels above 80 per cent, diseases such as grey mould/*Botrytis* and mildew may become a problem.

In winter, humidity should be maintained at a lower level, but the exact level required will depend on the types of plant grown and the temperature of the greenhouse.

Humidifiers

Greenhouses may be "damped down" during the summer by splashing water – predominantly on the floor and on any staging – from a watering can or hose. This has the effect of increasing the level of atmospheric humidity. An automatic spray system simplifies humidity control, especially for plants that require very high humidity. In a small greenhouse, mist-spraying by hand or providing a tray filled with water that slowly evaporates into the air is usually adequate.

Watering

A traditional watering can is still the most efficient, if perhaps a time-consuming, method of watering a mixed collection of plants in a small greenhouse. Since you can easily monitor the flow, it ensures that all the plants are watered according to their individual requirements.

An automatic watering system is a useful addition to the greenhouse in summer, however; if the greenhouse is left unattended on a regular basis, an automatic system becomes essential, since some pot plants may need to be watered several times a day in very hot weather.

Capillary systems
Watering systems that rely on capillary action to draw up water are often used in a greenhouse.

Plant pots may be placed on a 2–5cm (³/4–2in) layer of clean sand (which retains moisture well) that is placed on the greenhouse staging and kept permanently wet. Moist sand adds considerable weight to the staging, however, so make sure that it is sturdy enough to take the extra load. In addition, protect wooden staging from the wet sand by lining it with sheets of plastic or kitchen foil, otherwise it will rot. Alternatively, the sand may be placed in aluminium trays.

Add a length of plastic gutter to the edge of the bench and keep it filled with water. This may be done by hand or automatically from an overhead tank connected to the mains, in which case the system should be controlled by a ballcock.

Capillary matting, which is widely available in rolls and is simply cut to the required size, is far lighter, easier to keep clean, and just as effective as sand. To keep the capillary matting continuously moist, trail the edge into a water trough or other reservoir of water. The water may be topped up by hand or supplied automatically from the mains, as above.

For a capillary system to be effective, there must be sufficient contact between the compost in the pots and the source of moisture so that water is continuously supplied to the plants' root systems. Plastic plant pots usually allow good contact between the compost and the moist sand or matting. Clay pots, however, may each require a wick. This is cut out of a piece of spare capillary matting and placed in the drainage hole of the pot to bridge any gaps between the compost and the mat.

During the winter months, do not use capillary watering systems in the greenhouse, since most plants are dormant, or growing only slowly, and therefore require a reduced intake of water. The perpetually damp mat or sand may also increase humidity in the greenhouse to unsatisfactory levels for the plants (see "Humidity", p.484).

Overhead systems
A system of overhead pipes, with nozzles from which water is sprayed onto the plants below, is widely used in commercial greenhouses. This is an ideal system for watering a large number of plants that are all at a similar stage of growth. It is not suitable for the small, amateur greenhouse, however, that contains a wide variety of plants. Overhead watering systems are also expensive to install and create too humid an atmosphere if used in the winter.

Seep hoses
These are widely used in the garden, and may also be used inside the greenhouse to water border crops or to keep capillary matting moist. In very hot weather, however, seep hoses may not supply a sufficient flow of water to the plants.

Trickle irrigation systems
This type of irrigation system consists of a series of small-bore tubes, each with an adjustable nozzle. The tubes are placed in the individual pots or growing bags, or near plants growing in the greenhouse border.

Most trickle irrigation systems are fed with water from a reservoir that is filled in turn from a hose connected to the mains water supply. It is possible, however, to use water supplied direct from the mains.

The rate of water delivery must always be monitored very carefully and adjusted according to the needs of the plants; these needs vary depending on time of year and the vagaries of the weather.

Lighting

If an electric power supply is already installed in the greenhouse (see "Installing electricity, gas, and water", p.480), lighting units are not expensive to add at any time, and running costs are also low. In addition, the lights produce a little extra heat for the plants. Ordinary fluorescent lamps provide enough illumination to work by comfortably.

Growing lamps
The special quality of lighting produced by growing lamps is required to increase daylength (see THE VEGETABLE GARDEN, "Daylength",

WATERING SYSTEMS

Overhead reservoir

Tubes supply each plant with water

Gutter filled with water

Capillary matting

CAPILLARY WATERING
An overhead reservoir feeds water to a gutter fixed to the staging. The matting soaks up water, which is absorbed by compost in the trays.

TRICKLE IRRIGATION
Trickle systems supply water directly to each pot by means of tubes, which are fed from an overhead reservoir.

p.307) for specific purposes during the spring and winter months when light levels are consistently low.

Fluorescent tubes that produce good light to improve plant growth may be obtained from specialist aquarium suppliers and garden centres. They do not produce much heat, and so may be placed close to the plants. The lights are fitted with reflectors that cast the light downwards, where it will do the most good. For greatest effectiveness, the tubes should be mounted 25–30cm (10–12in) above the foliage. Mercury fluorescent lamps and mercury vapour lamps also provide a suitable quality of light to encourage good plant growth.

Metal halide lamps are the best, if most expensive, form of growing lamp, emitting light that is close to the spectrum of natural light. They illuminate a large area but cast their light in a circular pattern, which may be inconvenient in a small greenhouse, since the corners may not be strongly lit.

Most growing lamps that are suitable for use in the greenhouse need special fittings because of the moist, humid atmosphere. If in any doubt, always ask the advice of a qualified electrician.

Light meters
Where lighting is a very important factor, special plant light meters may be useful in the greenhouse, because they measure light levels much more accurately than can be judged by eye.

Light meters are usually supplied with information about the light levels that are preferred by a wide range of commonly cultivated plants, so follow the instructions for the particular plants grown.

A GROWING LAMP

This provides additional light to improve plant growth. Secure it directly above the plants, if possible.

Using the space

To make best use of the limited space in a greenhouse, plan the layout carefully. Cultivation in raised beds, borders, growing bags, or containers placed on the ground, staging, or shelves are all suitable methods; often, a combination is best.

Raised beds

These are used mainly in alpine houses, where sharp drainage is required. Raised beds may be expensive to construct using new bricks, but old bricks are satisfactory. Leave a large gap between a raised bed and the wall of a greenhouse so that air

can circulate and moisture from the compost does not penetrate the wall. For details see STRUCTURES AND SURFACES, "Raised beds", p.507.

Beds that are raised to normal bench height are suitable only for lean-to greenhouses or for those with a tall brick base. For small plants that do not require a great depth of soil, a stone trough placed on brick pillars or "legs" may be used. Alternatively, construct a raised container by fixing rigid metal sheets or paving slabs on top of brick pillars, making the walls by laying several brick courses around the top, and lining with a sheet of butyl rubber. The butyl sheet should have several holes

pierced in it to ensure that the bed will be adequately drained.

Raised beds for taller plants need not be so high and so do not need to stand on brick pillars. They are usually built up from ground level with basal seep holes for drainage and simply filled with compost.

Borders and growing bags

A glass-to-ground greenhouse is required to grow plants directly in the border, to ensure that plants receive enough light. Borders with a width

of 1m (3ft) are acceptable in a greenhouse that is 2.5m (8ft) wide but make the beds wider if staging is placed over the borders, so that the staging does not prevent you from reaching the far side easily. Plants in containers may also be placed on top of the border rather than on staging, if required.

The soil in greenhouse borders may become infected with disease if the same plants are grown repeatedly over many years. If this is the case, or if the greenhouse floor is concreted over, growing bags may be used. Growing bags provide a convenient method of cultivation, since they retain moisture well and

INSIDE THE GREENHOUSE

Organize the elements within the greenhouse sensibly to make the best possible use of the limited space. Here is a well-planned layout for a lean-to greenhouse.

Vent

Automatic vent opener

Water reservoir irrigating the plants in the tray beneath

External shading blinds

Display shelf for plants

Thermometer

Shelf fixed to the wall

Electric sockets

Heated propagator

Water supply

Louvre vents

Seedlings and cuttings growing in trays

Slatted bench staging

Shade-loving plant beneath staging

Pots sunk into sand underneath the bench

Fan heater

Growing bag

Paved area

DISPLAYING THE PLANTS

Plants in the greenhouse should be arranged to make attractive displays. If the greenhouse is heated, a wide variety of plants may be grown throughout the year to maintain the display of flowers and foliage. Place dormant or "resting" plants beneath the staging to make more room for other plants in season.

remove the need to dig and fertilize the soil before planting. Most of the nutrients in the compost contained in the growing bags are used up during the season, so fresh growing bags should be used each year.

Staging

Staging is important for any ornamental or mixed greenhouse – by bringing plants closer to the light it encourages healthier growth. Even if removed for summer border crops, staging is necessary for propagating and growing on young plants.

Positioning the staging
The most satisfactory arrangement for a small or mixed greenhouse is to have a central path with staging along the sides, and possibly across one end, removing half of it for border crops when necessary and retaining the permanent staging to display ornamentals. The permanent staging should be positioned on the side where it will cast the least shade on the border crops.

Central staging
Larger ornamental greenhouses that are designed primarily as show houses may have staging placed in the centre, with a path around the edge. Two staging benches may be placed back-to-back, preferably with tiered staging in the centre to enhance the display of plants.

The right size and height
Most staging benches are 45–60cm (18–24in) wide. Wider benches are useful in a large greenhouse but they may be difficult to reach across. All staging needs to be of sturdy construction to support the considerable weight of plants, containers, and compost. Always leave a generous gap between the back of any staging and the sides of the greenhouse to allow air to circulate.

Most amateur greenhouses also have to serve as a potting shed. A convenient height for staging that is also used as a work surface is approximately 75–90cm (30–36in); it should be lower if a sitting working position is required.

Free-standing staging
It is sometimes useful to have staging that can be dismantled and stored away, bringing it into the greenhouse for short periods, for instance when raising seedlings in spring. Free-standing staging may not fit

FREE-STANDING STAGING

Movable benches allow great flexibility, since they may be moved around to accommodate the plants, or removed altogether.

FIXED STAGING

Most greenhouse manufacturers supply permanent, purpose-built staging that is made from the same materials as the greenhouse. It is best fitted at the same time as the greenhouse is constructed.

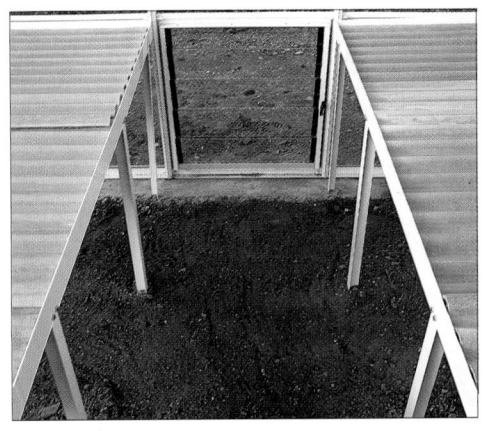

the greenhouse quite so well as staging that is built-in and may not look as attractive but is more flexible in use. It must be easy to assemble and sturdy since it will be in use for many years. If border crops are grown for most of the year, open-mesh staging which folds back neatly against the side of the greenhouse is convenient for short periods.

Free-standing modular staging systems can be built up into tiers and provide an attractive way of displaying plants. Slatted, mesh, or solid modular systems are available.

Permanent staging
Built-in staging and shelves may put a strain on the framework of a greenhouse, especially light, aluminium alloy structures. Gravel or sand, if used, adds extra weight to the staging, particularly when it is wet. Buy staging that is purpose-built, if possible; if in doubt, check with the greenhouse manufacturer before fitting any permanent staging.

Slatted and mesh staging
If you are growing alpines or cacti and succulents in pots, it is preferable to use slatted or mesh benches, which allow a freer flow of air than solid staging. However, slatted and mesh staging are not suitable for capillary watering systems.

SLATTED STAGING

Wooden-slatted staging is an attractive choice. The slats allow better air circulation around the plants than solid-surface staging does, but slats are not suitable for a capillary watering system, unless pots are placed in trays on the bench.

For a timber greenhouse, use wooden slatted benches; for an aluminium alloy or galvanized steel greenhouse, metal or plastic-mesh benches are more appropriate.

Solid surface staging
Solid staging allows more pots to be accommodated than slatted staging (it is difficult to keep pots upright between the slats), but may require more ventilation.

If using a capillary watering system, choose solid aluminium staging that has a level surface for the matting or sand. Some types of staging have reversible sections that produce raised flat surfaces for mats if placed one way, and dish-like sections for sand or gravel if reversed.

Shelves

Shelves in the greenhouse may be used for both storage and display. Permanent shelves often cast shade on the plants below so it is preferable to install fold-away shelves, which may be used in spring when space is short and then put away for the rest of the year.

In a small greenhouse, shelves can be used to display trailing plants where there is not enough headroom for hanging baskets.

Propagation aids

The propagation of many plants requires higher temperatures than may realistically be maintained in the greenhouse. To save on fuel bills, therefore, propagation aids are often used to provide the extra heat required. They may also increase the success rate when sowing seed or taking rooting cuttings. Choose a propagator for the greenhouse that is large enough to hold at least three standard seed trays.

An electric power supply in the greenhouse is essential if heated propagators, mist units, or soil-warming cables are to be used. Mist units require a mains water supply as well as a power supply.

Unheated propagators are of limited use in the greenhouse but usually provide sufficient humidity for rooting cuttings in summer.

Heated propagators

A heated propagator should have a heating element that is capable of providing a minimum compost temperature of 15°C (59°F) in winter and early spring, when temperatures outside may fall below freezing.

If tropical plants are to be propagated, the unit must have a more powerful heating element that can maintain a temperature of 24°C (75°F). The propagator should preferably be fitted with an adjustable thermostat, which allows greater flexibility of temperature.

Use rigid plastic lids, since these are more likely to retain the heat than thin plastic covers. Adjustable ventilators are useful because they allow moisture to escape and prevent the atmosphere inside the propagator from becoming too humid.

Domestic propagators
Some small heated propagators are designed for windowsill use. Usually holding just two seed trays, they are generally too small to be of practical use in the greenhouse and often do not have a thermostat. They may not generate enough heat in a cold or cool greenhouse, since the heating element is intended to operate in a room indoors.

Propagators designed for windowsills are best used in a greenhouse only during summer, when temperatures are high.

Heated bases
These are designed to be used with unheated propagators or ordinary seed trays, either of which may be placed on the heated base. A plastic hood must be placed over seed trays to maintain warmth and humidity. Heated bases do not raise the temperature as efficiently as heated tray propagators (see below) and are only suitable for one or two trays.

Heated tray propagators
These have a self-contained heating element in the base, and are more useful than heated bases (see above), especially if they are fitted with an adjustable thermostat.

Mist units

Cuttings may often be rooted more rapidly and in greater numbers in a mist unit than by using other more conventional means. Mist units are convenient, since they remove the need to water cuttings frequently.

The easiest and most convenient mist units to use are self-contained, enclosed units that include a heating element, thermostat, transparent cover, and a misting head. The constantly humid atmosphere created by the misting head provides a suitable environment in which to root cuttings quickly – by maintaining a constant film of water on the propagating material. Heat loss by evaporation is also reduced, and there is also less risk of the cuttings being affected by fungal diseases because, when the misting head is in operation, most disease spores are washed out of the air and from the leaves before they can infect plant tissues. On a small scale, a similar effect is created by enclosing a pot of cuttings in a clear plastic bag.

For large numbers of plants, a mist propagation unit is more practical. Some units are designed for use without a cover on an open greenhouse propagating bench; they are used in conjunction with soil-warming cables and also require a specially constructed greenhouse bench. If sited in a greenhouse where a mixed collection of plants is grown,

A soil thermostat controls the temperature of the compost, which is heated by cables. The misting head is controlled by a sensor (connected to a solenoid) located near the cuttings – when the atmosphere becomes too dry, the misting head is activated.

however, the high humidity created by an open mist unit may prove unsuitable for some types of plant. In this situation, it would be preferable to install a closed mist unit.

Soil-warming cables

Intended primarily for heating the compost in a conventional propagator or on a mist bench in the greenhouse, soil-warming cables may also be used to heat the air in an enclosed space, such as a cold frame or homemade propagator. The safest system to use is a cable with a wired-in thermostat that is connected to an insulated, fused socket.

In this propagating case, cables are used to heat both soil and air. Each set of cables has a thermostat, which ensures that the temperature never falls below a pre-set level.

however, the high humidity created by an open mist unit may prove unsuitable for some types of plant. In this situation, it would be preferable to install a closed mist unit.

Buy a screened cable, because it is much less dangerous if the cable is accidentally cut.

Soil-warming cables are sold in lengths that are designed to heat a given area. A 75-watt cable, for example, measures 6m (20ft) and provides enough heat for a bench area of 0.7sq m (7sq ft) in a greenhouse that has some form of heating. A cable with a higher wattage would of course be needed for use in a similar area in an unheated greenhouse or in a cold frame that is outside the greenhouse.

The cable should be laid at a depth of 5–8cm (2–3in) in a series of "S" bends (ensuring that the loops do not touch) in a bed of moist sand.

Cold frames and cloches

Cold frames and cloches relieve pressure on greenhouse space, but they are also extremely useful in their own right. They are likely to be used most intensively in spring to harden off plants raised in a greenhouse, but they may also be used throughout the year to grow a wide range of crops. In the colder months, they are useful for protecting winter flowers, overwintering the seeds of hardy annuals sown in autumn, and sheltering vulnerable alpines from the worst of the wet weather.

Cold frames

The most popular type of cold frame has glass (or clear plastic) sides as well as glass "lights" (frame tops which contain the panes of glass), although sometimes timber and brick are used for the construction. Glass-to-ground models usually have a metal framework.

Frame lights

Choose a frame that has removable or sliding "lights" for easy access; some also have sliding front panels, which may be useful for extra ventilation. Hinged "lights" that are wedged open still provide protection from heavy rain but sliding "lights"

are often removed entirely during the day, leaving the plants very vulnerable to heavy rain. Lightweight aluminium frames with their "lights" wedged open may be at risk in strong winds, however, so choose a model which has a hinged top and adjustable casement stays to secure the "lights" safely.

Wooden frames

Traditional timber frames are now difficult to obtain and are usually expensive, but may be made cheaply at home from second-hand timber. The wooden sides retain heat well. It is not very difficult to fix soil-warming cables (see p.488) to the inside of the frame to provide extra warmth. Paint or stain the wood to preserve it.

Aluminium alloy frames

These are widely available and relatively inexpensive. They vary considerably in design but are usually sold packed flat for easy transportation, and assembled on site. Aluminium alloy frames let in more light than either wooden or brick frames, but they do not have such good insulating qualities and may not be as strong or robust. It may be necessary to use ground anchors for lightweight frames.

HINGED LIGHTS
Hinged tops may be wedged open on warm days to prevent the plants from overheating.

SLIDING LIGHTS
Sliding tops are less vulnerable to gusts of wind but plants are not protected from heavy rain.

Brick frames

These are rarely used nowadays but they may still be built at home if a cheap supply of old bricks is available and if the "lights" can be made. Brick frames are generally warm and draught-proof.

Suitable sizes

The minimum practical size for a cold frame is 1.2m x 60cm (4 x 2ft). Often, however, the frame has to fit into whatever space is available (as near the greenhouse as possible), so choose the largest affordable frame that fits the space.

Height is important if the frame is to be used for plants in pots or for tall vegetable crops. In order to increase the height of a frame temporarily, raise it on loose bricks.

Insulation

The range of plants that may be successfully overwintered in a frame is increased if the frame is well insulated. The frame needs to be draught-proof; there should be no gaps around the glass or framework, and the top and any sliding front panels must fit well.

Glass-to-ground and plastic-sided frames may need insulating in cold weather with sheets of expanded polystyrene. Cut the sheets to size, and place them against the inside of the frame to reduce heat loss.

On cold nights, particularly when a sharp frost is predicted, frames may require additional outer protection: use layers of hessian or old carpet to cover the tops, tied down firmly or held in position with pieces of heavy timber. This protective covering should always be removed during the day, otherwise plants may suffer from lack of light. Alternatively, use several layers of thick,

clear plastic sheeting for extra protection – this may be left in place during the day since it does not reduce the light to the same degree.

Ventilation

Good ventilation is essential in warm weather. Most frames have "lights" that may be wedged open to allow fresh air inside; often, the "lights" also slide along to allow more ventilation, and are eventually removed completely when young plants need to be hardened off.

Light

Aluminium frames (but not brick or wooden frames) may be moved around the garden to take advantage of the best light at various times of the year. If a frame is permanently sited, it should be positioned where it will receive the maximum amount of light in winter and spring, provided that the site is not too exposed.

Frames need shading in summer but, for year-round use, one that lets in as much light as possible is best.

Glazing materials

Horticultural glass is the best glazing material for cold frames; it transmits light well, allows the frame to warm up quickly, and retains heat better than most plastic materials. Broken or cracked panes should be replaced as soon as possible, so a frame that allows the individual panes to be replaced easily should be chosen. Some are glazed using glazing clips or glass panels that slide into the framework, making glass replacement relatively simple.

Where glass may be a potential danger for children or animals, or where the cost of the frame is the main consideration, use plastic glazing material.

HOW TO USE COLD FRAMES

PLANTING IN THE FRAME
Plants may be grown directly in the cold frame, if required. Always prepare the base with a thick layer of drainage material, such as broken crocks or coarse gravel, before adding a 15cm (6in) layer of good garden soil or compost.

PROTECTING CROPS
Here, the cold frame has been placed directly onto the soil in the vegetable plot. Vegetables are growing through slits in a plastic mulch (see The "No-dig" System, *p.534) laid on the surface of the soil.*

Cloches

A range of cloche designs and materials is available – choose a cloche that suits the types of plant to be grown. Cloches tend to be used mainly in the vegetable garden but they are equally useful for protecting ornamental plants and seedlings that need a little extra warmth early in the season.

Materials

Glass is the best choice of material if cloches are to be used extensively for most of the year and moved from crop to crop. It has good light transmission and allows the frame to warm up quickly in sunlight. Clear plastic material (of various thicknesses) is an alternative; plastic cloches are generally less expensive than those made of glass but do not allow such good light penetration, nor do they retain as much heat.

Single thickness plastic is the least satisfactory material for retaining heat, but is cheap and useful where high temperatures are not necessary. Plastic cloches last longer if they have been treated with an ultraviolet inhibitor and are stored out of direct sunlight when not in use.

The minimum thickness that is suitable for cloches is 150 gauge, but 300, 600, or 800 gauge provides much greater protection. PVC is thicker and more rigid, and has similar qualities to polypropylene (see below). Moulded PVC and PVC sheeting should last for at least five years or more if treated with an ultraviolet inhibitor.

Cloches made from twin-walled polycarbonate offer good insulation and should last for ten years or more. Polypropylene is used in some injection-moulded cloches and in corrugated sheets; it retains heat better than plastic, but not as well as glass or twin-walled polycarbonate. It lasts for five years or more if treated with an ultraviolet inhibitor.

BARN CLOCHE

End pieces

These are an important part of most cloches – without them a cloche may become a wind tunnel, damaging the plants inside. The end pieces should fit well to preclude draughts but they should be easy to remove to provide additional ventilation when required.

Tent cloche

A tent cloche is inexpensive and simple to construct from two sheets of glass to form a tent shape. It is suitable for germinating seeds, for protecting young seedlings in spring, and for low-growing plants.

Tunnel cloche

A tunnel cloche may be made from either rigid or flexible plastic. Generally, flexible plastic, continuous tunnel cloches are used for crops such as strawberries and early carrots. The plastic must be supported by wire hoops (positioned over the row of vegetables) and tensioned with wires. Use heavy-duty plastic that has been treated with an ultraviolet inhibitor.

Rigid models are generally more attractive but more expensive than tunnel cloches that are made of flexible plastic. They are also easier to move around, since they do not need to be dismantled first.

Some tunnel cloches have self-watering features (see right).

Barn cloche

This has almost vertical sides supporting a sloping, tent-shaped top. Its extra height makes it useful for relatively tall plants but extra materials and complicated fittings make it more expensive than a tent cloche.

Some glass and rigid plastic barn cloches have lifting or removable tops to provide ventilation in warm weather, while still offering wind protection. This makes weeding, watering, and harvesting easier.

Flexible PVC is sometimes used for barn cloches, but these tend to be lower and therefore less versatile than those using other types of material, unless the top is removable or can be wedged open.

Dome-shaped cloche

Made from rigid plastic, dome-shaped cloches are easy to move around but are more expensive than tent or tunnel cloches. They have more space at the edges than tent and tunnel cloches, although the overall height may be no greater.

Self-watering cloche

Watering plants beneath cloches is difficult and time-consuming if the cloches have to be lifted or moved.

A self-watering cloche is designed to allow rainwater to trickle through gradually to the plants below. Alternatively, it may have a tubular system that is connected to a hosepipe.

SELF-WATERING CLOCHE

Floating cloche

A "floating" cloche (also known as a floating mulch) consists of a sheet of perforated plastic sheeting or polypropylene fibre fleece, which is placed over the ground where crops have been sown.

Floating cloches are permeable, allowing rainwater to penetrate to the soil below. This is a great advantage, since it reduces the need to water. The perforations in plastic floating cloches enable the sheet to stretch a little as the crop grows beneath it. Fibre fleece is sufficiently lightweight to rise with the growing crop. Both perforated plastic and fibre floating cloches allow air to

pass freely through the material and also have useful insulating properties; fibre fleece also protects plants from one or two degrees of frost. For further information, see THE VEGETABLE GARDEN, p.315.

The sheets or fleeces should be anchored firmly into the soil at the edges of the beds with soil, stones, or pegs. Whole beds may be covered with a floating cloche, if desired, or pieces may be cut to fit smaller areas or even individual plants.

Individual cloche

These are usually used to protect individual plants in the early stages of growth but they may also be placed over any vulnerable, small plants during severe winter weather, such as frost, deep snow, heavy rain, and high winds.

Home-made individual cloches, such as waxed-paper protectors and cut-off plastic bottles, are easy to make and are much less expensive than purpose-made models but may not be so attractive.

INDIVIDUAL CLOCHE

Wall-of-water cloche

This unusual design of cloche is useful for single plants and consists of a circle of hollow, clear plastic tubes, into which water may be poured. The tubes form the wall of the cloche, which alters in shape depending on the water level. If the tubes are half filled, they "cave in" at the top, protecting the plant from above as well as from the sides.

TENT CLOCHE

TUNNEL CLOCHE

WALL-OF-WATER CLOCHE

Routine maintenance

Regular maintenance is necessary to preserve greenhouses, and to keep frames and cloches clean. Autumn is usually a convenient time to attend to the maintenance work: cleaning and disinfecting the greenhouse structure and equipment at this time of year minimizes problems from overwintering pests and diseases.

It is important to do this work on a mild day before the very cold weather begins. Tender plants may then be put outside while the preparations for winter are carried out.

CLEANING BETWEEN PANES

To remove dirt from between overlapping panes in the greenhouse, use a thin, rigid strip of plastic to loosen any deposits before spraying or hosing down with water.

Exterior maintenance

Choose a dry, still day for routine work on the outside of the greenhouse. Before making a start, gather together all necessary materials for cleaning, repairing, and repainting.

Cleaning glass and plastic glazing

Glass may be cleaned with water only, using a hose and long-handled brush, but if it has become very dirty, better results are achieved by brushing with a solution of kettle descaler. Protect skin and eyes by wearing gloves and goggles, and rinse off the solution thoroughly with running water.

A proprietary window cleaning solution may also be used but it will not remove ingrained dirt. Dirt also tends to become trapped between overlapping panes. Push a thin, plastic label between panes to loosen dirt and algae, then remove using a water jet from a hose. Shading washes are best removed by rubbing them off with a cloth.

Repairing glass

Panes of glass and plastic panes that are slightly cracked may be temporarily repaired with transparent glazing tape. Broken and badly cracked panes, however, should be replaced completely, as soon as possible after the damage is noticed, to prevent harm to plants.

To replace a pane in an aluminium alloy greenhouse, remove the spring glazing clips and the adjoining pane, if necessary, and reglaze using the old clips (see p.480).

If the panes are bedded on linseed putty (as in many older wooden greenhouses), remove the glazing tacks and the panes of glass carefully. Chip away the putty with a chisel to leave a smooth surface. Clean the glazing bars with abrasive paper before reglazing.

Apply a priming paint to any unpainted or untreated wood on the glazing bars. Pay particular attention to knots in the wood which may be potential entry points for moisture. When the paint is fully dry, replace the panes by setting them on a bed of putty or glazing mastic, using glazing tacks to hold them.

Gutters and downpipes

Check that gutters and downpipes are in good repair. Use a hosepipe to clear any blockages. Small leaks in gutters may be sealed with mastic or other sealant, but badly leaking sections of gutter will need to be replaced completely.

Metal framework

Aluminium greenhouses require only minimal structural attention. Although they lose their bright colour, the greyish patina that forms protects the metal from the weather.

Steel frames and fittings should be checked for rust and, if necessary, treated with rust remover. Repaint every few years.

Timber framework

Cut out any rotting wood and replace it, applying woodworm killer, and renewing rusty hinges, as necessary. Softwood greenhouses need regular painting: strip off flaking paint, wash down, then apply primer and good-quality exterior paint. Hardwood greenhouses are more rot-resistant, only requiring a coat of wood preservative every year or two, which also restores the colour.

Ventilators

Windows and ventilator fans should be checked for ease of operation, working parts oiled if necessary, and glass or plastic cleaned.

Inside the greenhouse

Before cleaning and disinfecting the inside of a greenhouse or frame, turn off any electric power supply at the mains, cover electric sockets and fittings with plastic, and remove all plants to a safe place.

Cleaning and disinfecting

Glass and plastic glazing materials should be cleaned as described under "Exterior maintenance", above. Clean the glazing bars by scrubbing with a disinfectant solution – fine wire wool may be used (but not on anodized "coloured" aluminium).

Scrub brickwork and paths with a garden disinfectant and rinse with clean water. The disinfectant may be used, diluted according to the manufacturer's instructions, to sterilize the staging and other surfaces. Paint it on with a paintbrush or spray on as a coarse spray, wearing protective gloves and a face mask and goggles while spraying.

Fumigation

Return the plants to the greenhouse and, carefully following the instructions supplied, use a fungicidal and insecticidal smoke to fumigate inside. Make sure that all vents are closed before lighting the fumigant. Do not inhale the smoke, and lock the door until it is safe to re-enter.

MAINTAINING THE GREENHOUSE

An annual check in autumn will be enough to keep your greenhouse in good working order.

Check all ventilators, ensuring they are watertight.

Check for rusty hinges and treat with rust remover or replace.

Give panes a thorough clean, inside and out.

Replace cracked panes.

Repair broken ventilator fittings.

Clear leaves etc. from gutters.

Cover electric power points with plastic before cleaning inside the greenhouse.

Remove weeds from inside the greenhouse.

Check for dirt between overlapping panes. Clean, as necessary.

Strip areas of flaky paint and repaint or treat with preservative.

Remove rotten wood and replace it.

Clean and disinfect all inside surfaces.

3

STRUCTURES
AND SURFACES

THE STRUCTURES AND *hard surfaces of a garden act as the framework around which plants can grow and mature over the seasons. If thoughtfully designed, pergolas, fences, or trellis can add vital height to any planting scheme, as well as providing privacy and shelter. Paths can lead visitors along planned routes, revealing piecemeal the garden's splendours; a terrace adjoining the house makes a perfect setting for breakfast, while a patio, perhaps at the rear of the garden, might be an ideal place to relax in the warmth of the afternoon sun. As well as being practical elements, structures and surfaces are often attractive features in their own right, providing year-round architectural and textural interest. They may be designed so that they blend or contrast with the planting: the bold shape of a circular patio would make a striking contrast with the gentler lines of sprawling plants, for example, while a rustic arch would form a complementary support for rambling roses and other climbers.*

Designing with structures and surfaces

Hard landscape elements are vital in helping to form the framework of a garden design and may be as ornamental as they are functional. In a new garden, features such as a terrace or a pergola are valuable for providing interest while the plants are growing and becoming established. In a more mature garden, sympathetically designed structures complement softer elements such as a lawn or the planting in a border and give the garden solidity and substance all year round.

When planning and designing structures, consider them in the context of their setting and in relation to each other. Materials, style, size, and shape should all be congruous both with the house and the overall design of the garden. A terrace or wall adjacent to the house often looks most effective if built of the same materials, forming a cohesive link between house and garden. Local materials are often preferable because they tend to look appropriate in the setting. The degree of formality is another important consideration to be made; in a formal garden, for example, a mellow brick wall boundary would be ideal, while in an informal, cottage garden a picket fence or woven wattle hurdles would be more suitable.

Structures may be used to link, define, or separate different elements or parts of the garden. A gently curving path leads the eye along the garden, providing a unifying line, while a wide, straight path separates the features on either side. Steps create an interesting change of level and demarcate separate areas as well as joining them visually and providing access from one part to another. If the steps adjoin a patio, they may look best if constructed from the same materials and in a similar style – curved steps would look attractive linked to a circular patio, for example.

DESIGNING WITH HARD LANDSCAPE Here, hard materials have been used to form the main framework of the design, creating interest while the planting is becoming established and providing a foil for the softer shapes of the plants. The curving path adds a sense of movement, while the innovative use of mixed materials provides satisfying textural contrasts.

The order in which you undertake construction work largely depends on your individual priorities and the requirements of the site. It might be, for example, necessary to erect a flanking wall first because it will help to retain the soil of a raised bed; in another garden, laying a path might be the first priority to allow easy access with wheelbarrows to the rear of a site where work is in progress.

This chapter covers most straightforward structural projects that may be undertaken by an amateur, from hard surfaces such as patios, terraces, and paths, to boundaries and divisions, for example walls and fences, as well as other structures such as raised beds and pergolas. In addition, certain hard elements are covered in full in other chapters: see THE WATER GARDEN, pp.250–54, for details on constructing ponds and watercourses; see THE ROCK GARDEN, pp.196–206, for rock gardens, alpine troughs, and peat beds.

Patios and terraces

A patio is an ornamental feature as well as a functional one, providing an area for meals and relaxation, with plants in beds or containers, and perhaps a raised pool. An open paved area, with a balustrade or low wall, is more accurately described as a terrace. Patios and terraces are usually paved, although timber decking (see pp.499–500) is popular as an alternative in some countries.

Choosing a site

Patios and terraces are usually sited close to the house, often with French windows allowing direct access. This is convenient for providing power sources for lights and other equipment, but if the site is not warm and sheltered, it may be better to choose an alternative position. Designing the patio at an angle of 45° to the house, perhaps at a corner, may ensure that it receives sun for most of the day. A patio may also be built away from the house to make use of a fine view across the garden.

Two or more small patios may be more useful than one large one. One may be sited in an open, sunny spot, the other in a cooler position to provide a welcome, shady retreat on a summer's day.

Shelter and privacy

A warm, sheltered patio can be enjoyed both earlier and later in the season than one that is subject to strong winds. If the site is overlooked, or exposed to winds, provide both shelter and seclusion with screens, such as trellis, covered with climbing plants. A pergola (see pp.511–12) roofed with trellis will screen the patio from above and provide shade. Avoid siting a patio near large trees, however: these will cast too much shade and drip long after rain has stopped, their roots may dislodge the paving, insects could be troublesome, and falling leaves may be a nuisance.

DRAINAGE SLOPE

Mark a number of pegs at the same distance from the top of each, then knock them in, in rows 2m (6ft) apart – the first at the top of the slope. Put a 2.5cm (1in) offcut on a peg in the second row. Make the two rows of pegs level, remove the offcut, and repeat.

2.5cm (1in) offcut of wood

Levelling pegs

Slope of patio

A suitable size

Size is less important for a terrace that is simply a link between house and garden than for a patio that is to serve as an "outdoor room". It should be in proportion to the garden: if too small it may look trivial, if too large it may overpower a small garden. As a guide, allow about 3.3sq m (4sq yd) for each person likely to use it. For a family of four, a patio about 13sq m (16sq yd) is a practical size.

Choosing a surface

Simplicity is the key to good design. If the patio is to accommodate furniture, climbers, and container plants, paving should be unobtrusive. Bear in mind that coloured paving may look fussy and often weathers to dreary shades. Variety is best achieved by mixing textures: small areas of brick or gravel among paving slabs, railway sleepers intersecting bricks or clay pavers, or cobbles with stone slabs.

Also decide if, for example, a hard-wearing surface is needed, or one that is not slippery when wet: choose from such materials as concrete (p.494), paving slabs (p.495), natural stone (p.496), tiles (p.496), bricks and pavers (p.497), or granite setts and cobbles (p.499).

Foundations

Patios, paths, and drives (see p.501) need firm foundations to ensure that the paved surface remains stable once in use. The load-bearing requirements must also be taken into account: few patios will be required to support very heavy loads, but drives need more substantial foundations because they may be used by heavy vehicles as well as cars. Climate is another factor: in areas with prolonged dry periods, for example, concrete foundations may crack if not sufficiently deep; seek local advice if necessary.

Before undertaking any excavation work, check the location of all the service pipes and cables on your property with the local authority or supplier to avoid damaging them.

Water run-off

To drain off water, the surface of a patio should slope slightly; a fall of about 2.5cm/2m (1in/6ft) is usually sufficient. Calculate the combined depth of the sub-base and surface material and mark this as a line at the same distance from the top of each of a number of levelling pegs. Insert one row at the top of the slope so that the mark is at soil level, the top of the peg indicating the desired level of the finished paving. Insert a second row of pegs 2m (6ft) down the slope. On each peg in this row in turn, place a small, 2.5cm (1in) thick offcut of wood, a "shim", and lay a spirit level on a plank between this peg and one in the first row. Adjust the height of the lower peg until the top of the shim and the upper peg are level. Remove the shim and repeat the process down the slope. Then rake the soil so that it is level with the mark on each peg. The base and surface of the finished construction should be parallel.

Basic procedure

Remove any plant growth from the area, including tree roots, then dig out loose topsoil until firm subsoil is reached. Consolidate this using a plate compactor. For most patios and paths, but not those that might bear heavy loads (see p.494), firm subsoil or a 10cm (4in) layer of hardcore, covered with 5cm (2in) sand, is an adequate foundation. Use more hardcore if necessary to bring the surface of the sub-base up to the required level.

On unstable soils, such as peat or heavy clay (which may shrink in dry weather and cause damage to the paving), lay 15cm (6in) of compacted hardcore as a sub-base. Top this up with sand or ballast to produce a level surface for laying.

PREPARING THE SUB-BASE FOR PATIOS AND PATHS

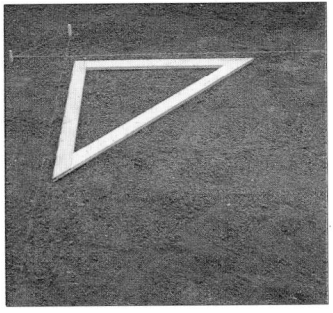

1 Mark out the area with pegs and string, setting the string at the ultimate level of the path or patio. Use a builder's square to check that the corners are set at right angles.

2 Dig down to firm subsoil and tamp down with a plate compactor. Allow for a 10cm (4in) depth of hardcore, a 5cm (2in) layer of sand, if required, plus the thickness of the surface layer.

3 Drive in a grid of levelling pegs every 2m (6ft). For a patio, incorporate a slight slope so surface water drains away. Use a spirit level and plank to ensure that pegs are level with strings.

4 Spread a 10cm (4in) layer of hardcore over the entire site, and then compact it so that it is level, using the pegs as a guide. Add sand, if necessary, and compact the area again.

HOW TO LAY CONCRETE

1 After marking out the site, dig it out to a depth of 20cm (8in). Drive levelling pegs into the ground 1m (3ft) apart along the string lines. Set them horizontal using a plank and a spirit level.

2 Remove the string lines and nail wooden planks to the inner faces of the pegs, butted end-to-face at the corners. This formwork holds the concrete in place until it sets hard.

3 Divide large sites into sections no more than 4m (12ft) long using formwork. Spread hardcore 10cm (4in) deep and tamp it down with a roller or stout timber.

4 Starting with the first section, tip in the concrete and spread it level so that it is just proud of the formwork. Work the concrete well into the edges.

5 Using a wooden beam that spans the width of the formwork, compact the concrete with a downward chopping motion. Then slide the beam from side to side to level the surface.

6 Fill any hollows that appear after levelling using fresh concrete, and level it again.

7 Lay a protective, water-proof covering such as plastic sheeting over the concrete until it dries. Remove the formwork when the concrete has set hard.

Load-bearing surfaces

For areas such as drives that need to support heavy weight (such as cars), lay a sub-base of at least 10cm (4in) of compacted hardcore or rubble, with a further 10cm (4in) of concrete on top. This concrete may be used as the top surface or as a base for another material such as asphalt or pavers bedded in mortar. On clay or unstable soils, or if the surface is to be used by heavy vehicles, lay 15cm (6in) of concrete on top of the hardcore. If mixing your own concrete for the foundations, see below. When laying large areas of concrete, it is essential to leave expansion gaps (see "Expansion joints", p.502).

Concrete

Concrete is relatively quick and easy to lay and makes a hardwearing and durable surface. It may be made more attractive by adding a textured finish (see p.502).

Ordering concrete

If you intend to lay a large area of concrete and there is access for large vehicles, having ready-mixed concrete delivered will make the job easier and quicker. Give the supplier the site measurements and information about the intended use of the surface to ensure that the correct amount and mix is delivered or use a supplier who will mix it for you on site. This saves time and effort, but requires advance preparation and usually some helpers, since you have to tackle the job straightaway.

Concrete and mortar mixes

The following proportions for concrete and mortar mixes are suitable for most projects. For an explanation of terms, see p.499.

Wall footings, drive foundations, and bases for pre-cast paving
1 part cement
2$\frac{1}{2}$ parts sharp sand
3$\frac{1}{2}$ parts 20mm ($\frac{3}{4}$in) aggregate
(or 5 parts combined aggregate to 1 part cement, omitting the sand)

***In situ* (poured) concrete paving**
1 part cement
1$\frac{1}{2}$ parts sharp sand
2$\frac{1}{2}$ parts 20mm ($\frac{3}{4}$in) aggregate
(or 3$\frac{1}{2}$ parts combined aggregate to 1 part cement, omitting the sand)

Bedding mortar (for bedding paving, and jointing paving bricks)
1 part cement
5 parts sharp sand

Masonry mortar (for garden brickwork)
1 part masonry cement
3 parts soft sand

All these proportions are measured by volume and not by weight. The consistency of the mix required for different jobs varies considerably. When mixing either concrete or mortar, start by adding only about half a part of water to one part of cement. This will provide a very stiff mix. Continue to add water gradually until you reach the consistency you need.

In hot climates, setting retardants may sometimes be necessary in mortar and concrete mixes, while in cold climates, antifreeze products may have to be incorporated. Seek local advice, if necessary. It is best to avoid laying concrete and mortar when the weather is close to freezing or above 32°C (90°F).

Laying concrete

First mark out the area to be concreted with string and dig down about 20cm (8in) until firm subsoil is reached. Drive a number of wooden levelling pegs into the ground at intervals of 1m (3ft) around the edge, using the string as a guide. Nail planks to the inside faces of the levelling pegs to make a formwork at least 20cm (8in) deep, which confines the concrete until it sets.

Divide large sites up into small sections no more than 4m (12ft) long using more planks. On top of the subsoil, spread a 10cm (4in) layer of compacted hardcore. Taking one section at a time, pour the freshly mixed concrete inside the formwork to a depth of 10cm (4in) and work it well into the edges. Use a wooden beam spanning the width of the formwork to compact the mix, then level the concrete by drawing the beam back and forth across the top of the formwork.

Inspection covers

Inspection covers that allow access to mains services must always be unobstructed, so should never be paved over. Proprietary metal trays are available in which to bed paving slabs, clay pavers, or other materials. These minimize the unsightly impact of an inspection cover sited in an area of paving and may simply be lifted out when necessary. When it is important to maintain the same pattern of laying as the surrounding area, it may be necessary to cut the slabs or pavers that fit within the tray. The trays may also be filled with turf, or used for planting.

Paving slabs

Concrete paving slabs are popular for patios, paths, and drives. They are available in a range of sizes, textures, and colours, and are easy to lay once the base has been prepared. Many garden centres and builders' merchants stock a range of pre-cast concrete slabs. Some designs may be available only in one area. Large suppliers usually produce catalogues and deliver direct.

Sizes and shapes

Most slabs are either 450 x 450mm (18 x 18in) or 450 x 600mm (18 x 24in), with smaller slabs designed to integrate with them. Not all slabs have a shaped edge designed to butt join; a half slab may be slightly less than half the size of a full one, to allow for mortar between the joints.

Circular slabs are suitable only for stepping stones and small areas of paving with an infill of a loose material, such as gravel. Hexagonal slabs are useful if you prefer a pattern without regular, parallel lines; half slabs are available for a straight edge. Some slabs are made with a "bite" out of one corner, so that four slabs together form a planting hole.

Quantities

If laying a pattern with slabs of different sizes or colours, draw a plan on graph paper to calculate the number of each required, and allow up to 5 per cent extra for breakages (especially if many have to be cut, see p.496). Try to work to dimensions that minimize the need to cut slabs.

Laying paving slabs

If laying a patio, establish a line that you can use as a straight edge and ensure that there is a slight slope for drainage; always slope the patio away from a building. A house wall is a practical base line to work from, but you may want to leave a small gap between the wall and paving for planting. The top of the paving must be a minimum of 15cm (6in) below the damp-proof course. Mark out the area to be paved with pegs and string. Make it a size that requires as few slabs as possible to be cut. If the slabs are not to be butted, allow about 0.5–1cm ($^1/_4$–$^1/_2$in) for mortar joints; metric slabs are usually designed to be laid with narrower joints than imperial slabs; if in doubt, seek advice from the supplier.

Preparing the site

Clear the site and prepare a sub-base or hardcore (see p.493). You will need wooden spacers about 1cm ($^1/_2$in) thick to place between the paving slabs to allow for mortar.

Positioning the slabs

Work from one corner, placing a row of slabs in each direction with spacers between to make sure that the dimensions are correct. Adjustments are easy to make at this stage. Using a bricklayer's trowel, lay a strip of bedding mortar along each edge where the slab is to be laid, to form an area slightly smaller than the slab. If the slab is 45cm (18in) across or more, lay a cross of mortar within the box. The mortar ridges should be about 3–5cm ($1^1/_4$–2in) high. This "box and cross" method combines strength with easy adjustment. Lay the slab in position and tamp it down with the handle of a club hammer or mallet. Use a spirit level to check that it is firm and straight. Repeat with successive slabs, using spacers between each one. Check the levels in each direction after every three or four slabs. Remove the spacers while you can

PAVING SLAB STYLES

TEXTURE
Surface textures range from smooth to stippled, scored, or roughly pebbled.

HEXAGONAL PAVERS
These are an attractive alternative to rectangles or squares. Half blocks are used for straight edges.

WEATHERED PAVERS
If a more natural look is desired, a range of "weathered" stone pavers is available.

POINTED SLABS
Some slabs are pointed to give special patterns or effects. Those with a "bite" taken out may be fitted together for a planting gap.

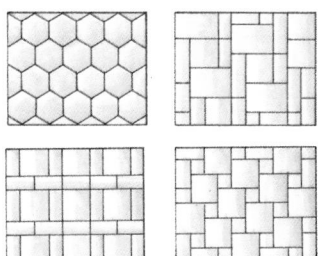

PAVING PATTERNS
A variety of pleasing patterns may be created with different shapes and sizes of paver.

CAST AND PRESSED SLABS
Cast slabs (sloping edges) are for light/medium use. Pressed slabs (straight) are lighter but stronger.

HOW TO LAY PAVING SLABS

1 *Mark out the area and prepare the sub-base (see p.493). Lay strips of mortar to form a square just smaller than the slab. Include a cross strip for large slabs.*

2 *Position the slab and tamp down. Use a spirit level to check it is level. Repeat, using spacers for 1cm ($^1/_2$in) mortar gaps between the slabs.*

3 *Remove the spacers before the mortar sets. After about 2 days, fill the joints with a stiff mortar. Tamp down so they are recessed 2mm ($^1/_{16}$in). Brush slabs clean.*

USING A JIGGER
This device has a central slit. After aligning the slit and joint, the gap can be filled without spilling mortar on the slabs.

still reach them without walking on the paving, and before the mortar sets. If you have to walk on the paving before the mortar has dried, stand on planks to spread your weight.

Finishing off
After a couple of days, fill the joints with a very stiff mortar mix (it should almost be "crumbly" to avoid staining the surface of the paving). Rub a

dowel or a rounded piece of wood over the pointing for a crisp finish, leaving it about 2mm (^{1}/₁₆in) below the paving surface. Alternatively, brush a dry mortar of 1 part cement to 3 parts sand into the joints. Brush any surplus off the surface. Spray the joints with a fine mist from a compression sprayer or a watering can fitted with a fine rose. Sponge excess mortar from the surface immediately, before it stains the slabs.

Cutting paving slabs

If you have many slabs to cut, it is best to hire a block splitter or angle grinder. For only a few, use a bolster (a broad-edged cold chisel) and club hammer. Always wear goggles when cutting paving blocks. Score the line where you need to cut with a corner of the bolster all around the slab, then chisel a groove about 3mm (^{1}/₈in) deep along this line; you may have to work around the slab several times, using the bolster to define and deepen the groove. If the slab has to fit into a tight space, cut it about 6mm (^{1}/₄in) smaller than needed to allow room for any rough edges that may be left when the slab splits.

Place the slab on a firm surface and raise the smaller part of the slab to be cut on a length of timber. Tap it sharply with the handle of a club hammer until a split forms along the line of the groove. Trim any rough pieces carefully with the bolster.

Crazy paving

Crazy paving has an informal appearance. It can be laid on sand, which will allow plants to be grown

between the joints, or on mortar for a firmer finish; if using the latter, fill in the joints with bedding mortar.

Defining the edges
Use string lines to mark out the area to be paved and prepare a sub-base for the paving (see p.493). Allow a slight slope for drainage (see "Water run-off", p.493) if necessary. Define the edges by laying a few metres (yards) of edging material first, working from one corner if laying a patio, the two edges if laying a path. This may simply be large pieces of crazy paving, with at least one straight edge, which can be laid to form the sides of the patio or path, or it could be wood, brick, or concrete. If using paving slabs, mortar these into position, even if bedding the remaining slabs on sand.

Laying the crazy paving
Loose lay an area about 1m (3ft) square without mortar, fitting the pieces together like a jigsaw. Keep the gaps small. It may be necessary to trim some pieces to size. Introduce a large piece occasionally, and infill with smaller ones.

Bed the pieces on sand or mortar, using a spirit level on a straight edge to ensure that they are level. Use a mallet or a block of wood and a hammer to bed each piece firmly in position. Lift pieces and add or remove sand or mortar as necessary until they are level.

Filling the joints
If bedding crazy paving on sand, finish off by brushing dry sand into the joints. If using mortar, mix a stiff, crumbly, almost dry mortar and use a pointing trowel to fill the joints (see "Finishing off", above). If using a dark-coloured stone, such

as slate, use a concrete dye (a powder you mix with the sand and cement) to make the joints less conspicuous. The colour will look different when dry, so test the dye on a small area and leave it to dry before deciding on the amount of colour to add.

Natural stone

Natural stone looks good, but is expensive and difficult to lay. Some types, such as sandstone, may be available cut into regular sizes and with an even edge. "Dressed" stone looks more natural; it is trimmed to a regular shape and has an attractive, uneven finish.

Lay sawn or dressed stone in the same way as paving slabs, adding or removing mortar to produce a level surface. Random stone is irregular in outline and thickness, and has no straight edges. This stone is suitable for laying as crazy paving, and it looks much more appealing than broken concrete paving slabs.

Tile surfaces

Quarry tiles, which are made of clay fired to a very high temperature, are useful for linking outdoor and indoor areas – perhaps where the paving inside a conservatory links with that outside. Glazed ceramic tiles may be more ornamental, giving an enclosed patio the impression of a Mediterranean courtyard for example, but many are not frost-proof. When selecting tiles, always check that they are suitable for using outdoors in your area before buying them. Tiles are difficult to cut,

---

How to Cut Slabs

1 Place the slab on a firm, flat surface and, using the corner of a bolster and a straight edge, score a groove on both faces and edges to mark the cutting line.

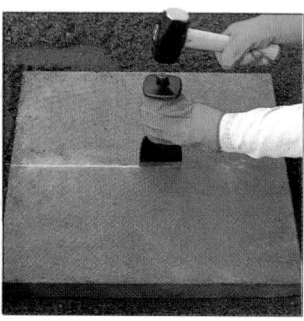

2 Using a bolster and club hammer, carefully work along the scored line to deepen the groove on the faces and edges of the paving slab.

3 Raise the slab onto a length of timber. Align the groove with the edge of the timber and tap the slab sharply with a hammer handle until it splits.

How to Lay Crazy Paving

1 Using string lines and pegs to mark the height of the edges, prepare a sub-base (see p.493). Lay the edging pieces first, placing their straight edges outermost.

2 Fill in the centre with large slabs, infilled with smaller ones. Check that central slabs are level with the edging pieces and bed them on sand or mortar. Use a block of timber and a club hammer.

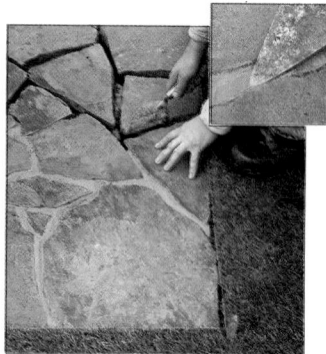

3 Fill the joints with almost dry mortar, or brush in sand. With a mortar finish, use a trowel to bevel the mortar so that any surface water drains away from the slabs.

especially if they are not rectangular, so where possible design the area to make use of full tiles.

Laying tiles

Since tiles are thin and sometimes brittle, they need to be laid on a concrete sub-base (see "Load-bearing surfaces", p.494). Quarry tiles may be laid on bedding mortar (see p.499). Soak the tiles for a couple of hours before use so that they do not absorb too much moisture from the mortar.

Glazed ceramic tiles are best glued to a level concrete base using outdoor tile adhesive (obtainable from a builders' merchant). Spread this on the back of the tiles, following the manufacturer's instructions, then press the tiles into position on the prepared concrete base.

Finish off an area of glazed tiles with a grout (available from builders' merchants) to fill the gaps, perhaps coloured to match or contrast with the tiles.

Bricks and pavers

Bricks and clay or concrete pavers are most effective when laid in small areas; a large expanse is best broken up with other materials, such as gravel or railway sleepers, otherwise the effect may well prove to be overwhelming.

For a patio situated next to a house built of brick, using bricks or pavers is an excellent way of linking the house and garden visually. Bricks and pavers also offer greater design flexibility than large, stone or

HOW TO LAY BRICK PAVING

1 First, prepare the sub-base (see p.493), allowing space for the edging bricks. Use string lines and pegs to set the edging bricks at the desired height.

2 Mortar in the edging bricks, and bed the others in the required pattern, tamping them level. At intervals, check levels in all directions.

3 Spread a thin layer of dry mortar over the surface and brush it between the joints. Sprinkle with water to set the mortar, and clean the surface.

concrete slabs, as they can be laid in a variety of patterns.

Choosing bricks

The range of bricks available is sufficiently extensive for it to be possible to find a type that suits a patio or terrace designed and constructed in any style.

For a large volume of bricks, contact a brick company to see if they will deliver. Builders' merchants supply bricks in any quantities. Be sure to choose bricks that are appropriate for outdoor paving and resistant to wetting and freezing.

Choosing pavers

Clay pavers are as attractive as bricks and are usually produced in shades of red. They have a thinner profile

than concrete pavers or bricks. Concrete pavers may lack the warm colours of bricks but they will make a practical surface. They are generally found in grey, blue-grey, or buff shades and are produced in a range of shapes.

Laying bricks

First make a suitable sub-base (see p.493). Bricks should ideally be bedded on mortar. First lay edging strips (or edging bricks), bedded on a concrete footing and then fixed with mortar between the joints. Prepare the bedding mortar (see p.494) and lay it to a depth of 2.5cm (1in). Bed the bricks onto this, spacing them evenly to leave joints for

mortar; use thin strips of hardboard or wood as spacers between bricks if desired. Once an area is complete, brush a dry mortar over the bricks. To remove air pockets, press this into the gaps with a narrow piece of wood. In damp weather, moisture from the ground and air will set the pointing; in dry weather, speed up setting by spraying with water.

Patterns in brick

Bricks may be laid in several different ways to create attractive patterns; three examples are shown below.

BASKET-WEAVE

INTERLOCKING BOXES

HERRINGBONE

Types of brick

Bricks are available in a wide range of styles, textures, and colours, providing an attractive and practical building material; take care to choose the most appropriate type so that they are suitable for the proposed purpose and that they co-ordinate well with the house, patio, or other hard landscape features.

ENGINEERING BRICKS
Engineering bricks are very hard-wearing. If used for paving, make sure they have good wet-weather grip. They may cost more than ordinary bricks.

CORED BRICKS
Cored bricks have holes. They may be used on edge for paving with a narrower profile, but are not economical for large areas.

FACING OR STOCK BRICKS
These are used to "face" buildings, providing an attractive finish. They are available in a variety of colours, and may be rough or smooth in texture. They may be unsuitable for paving as they may not be able to withstand severe weather conditions.

BRICKS WITH "FROGS"
A frog is an indentation in one side of a brick. Frogged bricks may be used for paving, if they are laid on edge or the frogs face downwards.

Cutting bricks and pavers

Bricks and thick pavers may be difficult to cut. If cutting is necessary, the easiest option is to use a hydraulic block splitter. These are often available from hire shops and are operated by applying pressure on a lever. Using this method, the bricks and pavers are cut quickly and neatly.

Alternatively, bricks and pavers may be cut to the desired shape with a bolster and club hammer (see "Cutting paving slabs", p.496).

Laying pavers

Pavers are bedded onto sand using a plate compactor; they nest together with small gaps between. Since the pavers can be lifted and relaid, this type of paving is sometimes called "flexible paving". Blocks 6–6.5cm (2½–2¾in) thick are adequate for garden projects.

Preparing the site and laying edge restraints

First, prepare a sub-base of 7.5cm (3in) compacted hardcore on firm soil (see p.493). Where there are no existing firm edges (such as walls), lay permanent edging strips. The simplest way to do this is to use specially made edge restraints or edging pieces, which are available from paving manufacturers. These must be concreted into position. Alternatively, use 100 x 38mm (4 x 1½in) treated or creosoted timber held in place with strong pegs at least 50mm (2in) square.

Large areas should be broken up into manageable sizes, such as 1m (3ft) squares, using temporary timber rails. Spread a layer of sharp

Pavers, tiles, setts, and cobbles

Pavers (also called paviors) vary greatly in size, colour, and thickness. They are also finished in many different ways, so that their texture and final shape, either formal and geometric or more informal and natural, contribute greatly to the style of the garden. More distinctive effects may be possible using terracotta tiles, granite setts, Belgian blocks, or rounded cobbles.

CLAY PAVERS
These red pavers may be laid either as "stretchers", that is longitudinally, or as "headers", placed end on.

WIRE-CUT CLAY PAVERS
Wire-cut clay pavers have a dragged finish and a roughened surface on all sides, which serves to provide extra grip in the finished paving.

INTERLOCKING PAVERS
These clay or concrete pavers can be used to create unusual patterns. Pressed pavers in blocks (far right) are produced in a range of colours.

TERRACOTTA TILES
Like bricks, terracotta tiles are made of clay but allowed to dry in the sun. They are porous and may crack if used in areas prone to frost.

GRANITE SETTS
Cut from hard granite, this form of paving is extremely durable. Like cobbles, the roughened surface of the setts creates a natural effect.

"BELGIAN" BLOCKS

IMITATION GRANITE SETTS
These reconstituted stone pavers are lighter and cheaper than granite. "Belgian" blocks have a more weathered look.

COBBLES
Cobbles (below) are large, rounded stones formed by the action of the sea or glaciers. They may be set in mortar to form an interestingly textured finish, but are uncomfortable to walk on and should be used only in small areas or in combination with other paving materials. When laying cobbles, form firm edges with bricks or lengths of concrete edging, set in concrete.

HOW TO LAY FLEXIBLE PAVING

1 *After preparing the sub-base (see p.493), set edging strips of concrete or timber in position around the edges of the site. Use a spirit level and a club hammer to tap the edges level.*

2 *Divide large areas into bays 1m (3ft) square with battens. Add 5cm (2in) of sand. Level the sand to the tops of the battens with a length of wood. Remove the battens and fill the vacated spaces with sand.*

3 *Lay the pavers to the required pattern, working from one corner of the site. Lay only whole blocks at this stage, leaving until last any cut ones required to fill the gaps in the design.*

4 *Vibrate the pavers into the sand or tamp down with a club hammer and length of timber. Brush dry sand over the surface and make 2 or 3 passes with a plate compactor.*

sand evenly to a depth of about 5cm (2in). The top surface of the sand should be about 4.5cm (1³/₄in) below the desired level of the finished paving when using 6cm (2³/₈in) pavers, or about 5cm (2in) below when using 6.5cm (2¹/₂in) blocks.

Positioning and bedding the pavers

Do not walk on the sand while laying the pavers, and keep it dry. Working from one corner of the site, lay the pavers. When some are laid, place a kneeling board over the pavers to continue working. Lay as many whole blocks as possible, then fill in with cut pavers around obstacles such as inspection covers as necessary (see p.494).

When about 5sq m (6sq yd) of paving has been laid, bed the pavers into the sand. The easiest way to do this is with a plate compactor, but do not go too near the incompleted edge. If only laying a small area of paving, the blocks may be tamped down with a heavy club hammer over a block of wood that is large enough to span several pavers at once. Continue to lay pavers and bed or tamp them down. When the whole area is finished, brush dry sand into the joints and settle in position with the plate compactor.

A mowing edge

Use bricks, pavers, or concrete slabs where it is difficult to mow to the edge of a lawn. Bed these on mortar, with the top just below the grass, so that the mower is not damaged.

A COMBINATION OF PAVING EFFECTS
A mixture of different paving materials, including square stone slabs, crazy paving, and brick edging, blends well with informal planting.

Setts and cobbles

Bed granite or imitation setts on 5cm (2in) of bedding mortar (see p.494) and brush stiff mortar into the joints (see "Finishing off", p.496). Spray the surface with water to clean it and set the mortar mix.

Cobbles may also be set in mortar. They are uncomfortable to walk on, so use them for small areas or with other materials. When laying, form firm edges with bricks or lengths of concrete edging. Lay 3.5cm (1¹/₂in) of bedding mortar over 7.5cm (3in) of compacted hardcore.

Terms explained

Aggregate is crushed stone or gravel used in making concrete. Graded 20mm (³/₄in) aggregate is suitable for most concreting jobs. Combined aggregate contains sand as well as stone.
Ballast is combined aggregate.
Bedding mortar is used for laying paving stones. It is made with sharp sand instead of soft (builders') sand.
Cement is a grey powder containing limestone, the setting agent of concrete and mortar.
Concrete is a hard-setting building material made of a mixture of cement, aggregate, sand, and water.
Dry mortar is a stiff mix often used to fill the joints in paving.
Hardcore is rubble such as broken bricks used as a sub-base under concrete foundations.
Masonry cement has additives that make it unsuitable for concrete. Use only for mortars.
Mortar is a mixture of cement, sand, and water used principally for bricklaying.
Portland cement is not a brand name, but a type of cement. Use ordinary Portland cement for most concreting jobs. It can also be used for mortars.
Sand is graded by particle size. Sharp or concreting sand is coarse; soft sand is more evenly graded for masonry mortar.

Decks

Timber decking is popular as a hard surface in warm, dry climates. Decks may be used anywhere, however, provided that timber pressure-treated with preservative is used.

It is best to build the deck on a level or gently sloping site. For a raised deck on a steep, sloping site, it is advisable to seek specialist assistance, since it will need to be well designed and constructed.

In some countries there are building regulations that state that all exterior areas of decking must be able to support a stipulated minimum weight. It may also be necessary to obtain a building permit in some areas and have the work inspected. If in any doubt concerning the regulations, check with your local authority building department. Simple parquet decking (see p.500), which is laid on gravel and sand, should not require permission.

TIMBER DECKING
A wooden patio or verandah overlooking the garden makes a very imposing feature, especially when crowned with a pergola to provide summer shade. Timber decking, however, needs to be very well constructed, and it is usually best to have the job done by experts. Features such as rails, steps, and timber supports require regular maintenance (see p.500).

Timber for decking

Western red cedar is a good choice because of its natural rot resistance, although regularly treating it with a preservative ensures a longer life. Other timbers are suitable but must be pressure-treated with a preservative. Timber merchants will advise on the most suitable timber and grade to use. Short lengths of timber can be made up into decking panels to produce a variety of attractive patterns.

CHEQUERBOARD   HERRINGBONE   PARALLEL SLATS   ANGLED CHEQUERBOARD   PARALLEL JOINTED

Slatted decking

This type of decking is suitable for level or gently sloping ground. It is simple to construct and requires few special fittings.

For an area beside a house, construct a concrete foundation (see *How to Lay Concrete*, p.494) with a gentle fall away from the house for water drainage. Onto the concrete base, mortar a row of bricks spaced about one brick apart at right angles to the intended direction of the decking. Add further rows of bricks at intervals of 40cm (16in). Check constantly that all the bricks are level, because they will support the joists.

Lay joists 75 x 50mm (3 x 2in) over the bricks, inserting a sheet of plastic or other damp-proof material between the bricks and the joists. If joining lengths of timber, make sure there is a brick beneath the point where the joists abut and screw a plain bracket across the join. Check levels between joists accurately with a spirit level and a straight edge.

DECKING STEPPING STONES
Decking can be used to create an unusual "stepping-stone" path across a pond. When positioned and angled for aesthetic effect, the squares add a stylish, geometric element to informal planting and the soft play of light on the pond surface. Here, parallel slats are laid in alternate directions to add a dynamic sense of movement to the overall design.

Lay 250 x 25mm (10 x 1in) planks at right angles to the joists. Allow 10mm ($^3/_8$in) gaps for free drainage and a little movement in the timber. Ensure that joints in the decking are staggered from row to row and that the planks are butt-joined over a supporting joist. Secure the planks with brass or other rust-proof screws, countersunk beneath the surface. Fill the holes with wood filler that matches the colour of the wood.

Finish the deck neatly with a low brick or block edging, cutting the decking so that it overlaps the edging by 5cm (2in). Alternatively, a length of facing timber can be screwed or nailed along the cut edges.

Parquet decking

It is possible to buy small, parquet-type, timber squares intended primarily for paths, which can also be used for decking. Alternatively they can be easily made. About 1m (3ft) square is a practical size. Buy

100 x 50mm (4 x 2in) treated timber, cut into 1m (3ft) lengths, and sand the ends smooth. Two lengths form the supports at opposite sides of the square, while the others are laid across them as slats. Use spacers to ensure that the slats fill the area evenly and fix the slats with two nails at either end. Prepare a base on firmed ground or subsoil with 7.5cm (3in) of compacted gravel topped with 7.5cm (3in) of sand. Level and tamp before laying the squares in alternate directions. Nail them together if necessary to stop them moving, driving the nails in at an angle.

Applying stains

Western red cedar turns a very obvious red colour when wet. It may, however, be stained any colour to suit the surroundings. It is best to use microporous stains, which allow any moisture in the wood to escape; if trapped beneath an impermeable layer, it would eventually cause the surface colour to lift. All wooden surfaces for staining should be dry and free from dirt. Follow instructions regarding stirring or thinning

and apply the stain with a good-quality paint brush, brushing in the direction of the grain. Do not overload the brush, since this will lead to uneven coverage, but work the stain well into the wood. Several applications will be needed, but wait until each coat is completely dry before applying more.

Maintenance

All wooden surfaces need regular maintenance. Once a year, check all surface areas for splits or cracks. Damaged timbers will need to be replaced. Check, too, that no bolts, screws, brackets, or nails have rusted. If galvanized fittings are abraded, their protective coating may be damaged and rust will appear. Brass fittings, which do not rust, are preferable in timber decking. If the stain wears thin in areas of heavy foot traffic, clean the surface and re-apply the stain (see above). Fungus growths are likely to appear at some stage. Fungicides are available, but it is better to remove growths by brushing with a stiff broom or use a scrubbing brush and a mild solution of bleach.

SUPPORT FOR TIMBER DECKING

Planks butt-joined over a joist

Joists butt-joined over a supporting brick

Damp-proof membrane

When joining two lengths of timber to form a joist, make sure that the join lies over one of the supporting bricks. Lay the planks at right angles to the joists, positioning all butt-joints directly over a supporting joist.

Paths and steps

Paths and steps play a valuable part in good garden design. They help form the framework of the garden, link its various elements, and may lead the eye to a focal point. Consider setting a path at an angle, off-centre, or following an indirect route. Steps provide interesting changes of level and create very different effects, depending on whether they are straight or curved, wide or narrow, and shallow or steep.

Practical considerations

Paths to the garden shed or the greenhouse need to be wide enough to take a wheelbarrow and should also provide a dry and solid surface. Those to the front door or for strolling through the garden should be sufficiently wide for two to walk abreast: about 1–1.2m (3–4ft).

Materials and design

The choice of materials and the laying pattern may be used to set or enhance the garden style. Combining materials, for example paving stones with cobbles, bricks with gravel, or concrete paving slabs with bricks or clay pavers, often makes a very effective design for a path.

"Stepping-stone" paths may be laid in many parts of the garden. They are a good choice, for example, when you do not want to spoil the line of a lawn, but they can become muddy in wet weather. Place the paving stones on the surface first to check the spacing; they should be spaced at a natural pace. On lawns, set them into the grass so that their surface is safely below mowing level.

Where winters are relatively dry, paths may be made of timber, either in the form of log sections used as stepping stones or to make a series of square, slatted units as described in "Parquet decking", opposite.

On sloping sites, steps may be an essential part of a path. They may also be valuable as a design feature even on a relatively flat site. Steps should harmonize with their setting: for example, in a woodland garden, shallow log risers and gravel treads would be suitable while, in a modern setting, brick risers and concrete slab treads would be more appropriate.

Drives

A drive can have a considerable impact on a design, especially in a small garden. There may be little choice in where to position a drive, unless a new garage is to be built at the same time; it is possible to make a drive look attractive, however, by choosing a suitable surface and positioning ornamental plants nearby.

Asphalt

Asphalt is best used for drives and paths that need not be attractive – the path to the shed, for example. It can also be used to cover a damaged concrete path. As well as black, asphalt is available in red and green. Stone chippings may be rolled into the surface to add texture. Asphalt is best laid in warm weather. Unless well laid, asphalt may break up after a few years; for heavily used areas such as a main drive it is worth having it laid by a qualified contractor.

Preparations

Asphalt can be laid on any firm surface, such as concrete or gravel. Never lay it on bare earth or hardcore

SUBTLETY WITH STONE
Here, the mottled texture of the embedded stones is complemented by Alchemilla mollis *and defined by seams of moss.*

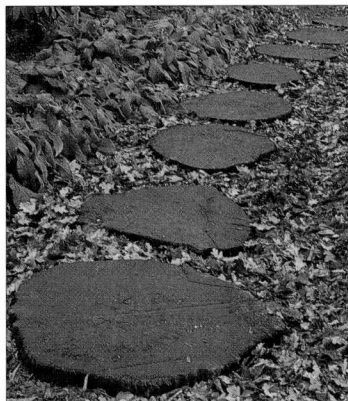

LOG SECTIONS
Logs sawn into sections make a harmonious series of stepping stones through an area of woodland, blending perfectly with the setting.

BRICK PATHWAYS
A brick path can become a design feature in its own right, adding texture and colour to a garden entrance. Here, the soft pink of the brick harmonizes with the surrounding plants and leads the eye to the rose-covered arch and the informal grass area beyond.

since it will be difficult to obtain a firm and level surface that will last. If necessary, make a stable base by spreading a mixture of gravel and sand 5–8cm (2–3in) thick over firm ground or compacted hardcore. If an old path or drive is the base, first paint inside any holes or cracks with bitumen emulsion (tar paint) and leave for about 20 minutes before filling them with macadam. To ensure good water drainage, lay a drive on a slight slope.

The edges of an asphalt path often weaken and crumble, so use concrete edging blocks (from builders' yards), bricks, or lengths of creosoted timber to provide a firm edging.

Application

Apply a layer of bitumen emulsion to bind the surface. Stir it first, then pour it from the container and spread it with a stiff brush. (Wash the brush in hot, soapy water afterwards.) When the emulsion has turned black, apply the macadam and rake it to an even depth of about 2cm (³/₄in).

Firm the surface by tamping it with the back of a rake to remove large air pockets, then make several passes with a heavy garden roller. Keep the surface of the roller damp to prevent the macadam sticking to it. Top up any visible depressions, and roll the surface again. If using stone chippings, sprinkle evenly and roll again to bed them in.

Bricks and pavers

The sympathetic colouring of bricks and clay pavers makes them excellent materials for paths within the garden. Because the individual units are small, it is relatively easy to adjust to changes of level and even to lay a path to a curve. A variety of effects can be created depending on the laying pattern used (see "Patterns in brick", p.497).

Construction

Mark out the proposed line of the path with pegs and string, calculating where cut bricks or pavers may be needed to create a sharp curve. If the path will be subjected to heavy wear, prepare a concrete foundation (see "Load-bearing surfaces", p.494). For one that will receive lighter use, an 8cm (3in) sub-base of firmed hardcore levelled with ballast should be sufficient.

First lay a suitable edging (see p.502) along one side of the path, then lay the path itself in sections about 1m (3ft) long. Pavers should be bedded in a 5cm (2in) layer of dry sand (see "Laying pavers", p.498), while bricks will require a 2.5cm (1in) bed of mortar (see "Laying bricks", p.497). As you complete each section, tamp the bricks or pavers into place, checking that they are level with a straight edge and spirit level. Then lay the edging on the other side of the path to complete this section. Repeat the process until the path has been laid.

To finish off a path made of pavers, brush dry sand into the joints. For a brick path, brush a dry mortar mix in between the joints (see "Finishing off", p.496), making sure that there are no large air pockets. If necessary, compact the mortar using a piece of wood slightly thinner than the joints. Finally, sprinkle with water from a watering can fitted with a fine rose, or use a compression sprayer to moisten the mortar and clean the bricks if necessary.

Concrete

Concrete cast *in situ* is a practical and hard-wearing surface material that is especially suitable for wide paths and drives. Its appearance can be made more attractive by adding texture (see below). Concrete can also be coloured using special dyes added to the mix. Since the colour often looks different once the concrete has dried, use dyes with caution. Colour a small test piece first and let it dry rather than judge the effect by the wet mix.

Break up a wide concrete path with rows of bricks or lengths of broad timber that will become part of the finished design. These will avoid the need for laying expansion joints during construction.

Preparing a base
Prepare a suitable foundation (see "Basic procedure", p.493). Next, make the formwork to hold the concrete in place until it sets. Use lengths of timber 2.5cm (1in) thick, and at least the depth of the concrete. Use 5 x 5cm (2 x 2in) pegs, not more than 1m (3ft) apart to hold the formwork in place. Lengths of timber may be satisfactorily joined by nailing a block of wood to the outside of the two pieces to bridge them together.

Making curves
To make gentle curves, mark out the shape that you want to create, and hammer pegs into the ground set closely together. Soak lengths of softwood in water to make them pliable and then bend and nail them to the pegs. Sharp curves can be made in a similar way, with the addition of a series of saw cuts on the inside of the curve. The saw cuts should reach about half-way through the timber to increase its flexibility. Alternatively, use several thicknesses of thin hardboard, which is easy to bend and shape.

Expansion joints
Concrete will crack if not laid with breaks to allow for expansion and a degree of movement. Divide the area into sections no more than 4m (12ft) long, using fixed pieces of timber as temporary divisions. If using ready-mixed concrete, where the load has to be used all at once, use hardboard cut into sections and leave these in position until the concrete has set.

Adding texture

An *in situ* concrete path can be made more attractive by adding texture. Use these techniques on a few sections only, or alternate patterns between sections, to create an interesting overall effect.

Exposed aggregate gives a pleasant, non-slip finish. Spread gravel or crushed stone evenly over the concrete before it sets, then tamp it gently into the surface. When the concrete is nearly hard, brush the surface to expose more of the aggregate, then spray it with water to wash away fine particles.

Brushed finishes are extremely easy to create. After tamping the concrete gently, push the bristles of a soft broom all over the surface to produce a fairly smooth finish; for a ridged effect, use a stiff broom once the concrete has begun to set. You can also brush in a series of swirls, or straight or wavy lines, as desired.

Stamped patterns can be made with special tools, but ordinary objects found in the home or garden may also be used imaginatively, for example pastry cutters and sea shells. This technique is best kept to very small areas. To create attractive leaf impressions, use large leaves, such as sycamore or horse chestnut. Press the leaves into the surface with a trowel and then brush them out once the concrete has hardened.

Coarse texture

Medium-coarse texture

Fine texture

HOW TO LAY A GRAVEL PATH

1 Dig out the base of the path to a depth of 18cm (7in) and set the edges. Compact the base. Drive in pegs at 1m (3ft) intervals to anchor the edge restraints.

2 If the path borders a lawn, excavate an extra 2.5cm (1in) so that the path is below turf level (inset). Put down successive layers of hardcore, sand and coarse gravel, and pea gravel. Rake level.

Laying concrete
Make up the concrete (see p.494) and pour it into the formwork. If mixing in small batches, fill alternate "bays", then remove the dividers once the concrete has set and pour concrete into the remaining bays. Use a length of wood to tamp the concrete level, working from the centre towards the joints. If the path or drive is wide, a tamping board used with a helper will make the job easier. Tamping leaves a slightly ridged surface. If you require a smooth finish, use a wood float in gentle, sweeping motions. A steel float will produce an even smoother surface.

Concrete paving slabs

Paving slabs are available in a wide range of colours, shapes, and finishes. They are easier to lay than *in situ* concrete, but are more difficult to lay to a curve than bricks or pavers. They combine well with other materials, for instance with cobbles set along the edge, or with small strips of gravel between each slab. This is a useful technique for creating curved paths since it makes the uneven joints less obtrusive. For details on laying paving slabs, see p.495.

Grass

Grass paths are useful for linking a series of lawns, or for broad walks between beds. They should be as wide as possible or they will not stand up to concentrated wear. Put down turf for a grass path in the same way as for a lawn – for full instructions, see LAWNS, "Laying turf", p.283.

Gravel

Gravel is easy to lay, presents no problems when creating curves, and is not expensive. There are drawbacks, however: unless well bedded and used with retaining edges, loose gravel can get onto adjoining surfaces, it can be uncomfortable and noisy to walk on, and it is not an easy surface on which to push a wheelbarrow or a pushchair.

Construct a firm base by excavating the ground to take about 10cm (4in) of compacted hardcore, 5cm (2in) of a sand and coarse gravel mix, and 2.5cm (1in) of gravel. For a fine finish choose pea gravel.

In a formal setting with mainly straight edges, concrete edging strips can be used; in other settings bricks or treated timber may be more appropriate. If using timber, anchor it with pegs about 1m (3ft) apart. Apply the gravel in several stages, raking and rolling it to produce a slight camber for drainage. To help compaction, water the gravel occasionally while rolling.

Edging paths

Plastic edge restraints are available, easily cut to size, that will hold a path of bricks or pavers in place invisibly. Turf over the top of the edge restraint to hide it. Lengths of treated timber may also be used, held in place with wooden pegs. It is also possible to use timbers temporarily while building the path, then remove them and fill in the gaps with concrete. For a brick edging, lay the bricks on edge or angled at 45° to the edge of the path and secure them with a little mortar.

Building steps

To calculate the number of steps you need to build, divide the height of the slope by the height of one riser (including the depth of the paving slab and mortar). It may be necessary to adjust the height of the steps to fit the slope. Mark the position of the risers with wooden pegs and then excavate the soil to form a series of earth steps.

Make a concrete footing (see p.504) for the base riser and leave it to set. Then construct the riser using bricks or blocks set in masonry mortar (see p.494). Check that they are level using a straight edge and spirit level, and backfill behind the riser with compacted hardcore or sand and gravel.

Prepare a bed of mortar on top of the riser and lay the first tread; it should slope forward slightly to shed water, and overlap the riser at the front by 2.5–5cm (1–2in). Mark the position of the next riser on the tread and mortar it into position.

Tread to riser ratio

For ease of use, it is important that the width of the tread and the height of the riser are in the correct proportion to each other. As a general rule, the width of the tread and double the height of the riser should total about 65cm (26in). First, choose the height of the riser, double it and deduct it from 65cm (26in) to give the width of the tread. You may wish to add 2.5–5cm (1–2in) for an overhang.

For the steps to be safe, the treads should measure at least 30cm (12in) from front to back. The height of the risers is normally between 10cm (4in) and 18cm (7in).

Paving stone treads

Brick risers

Gravel infill

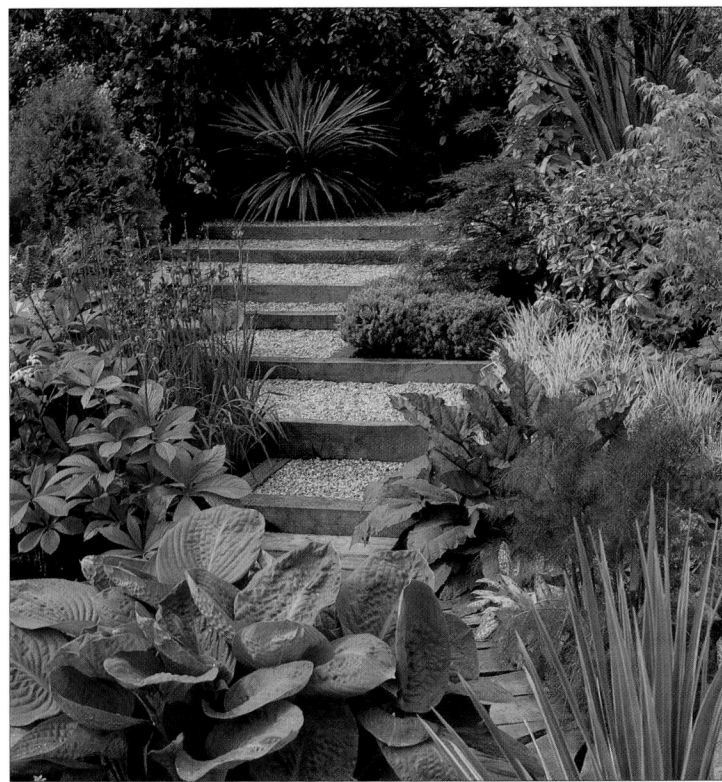

TIMBER AND GRAVEL STEPS
Here railway sleepers are infilled with gravel to create a curving flight of gently rising steps, with flanking plants softening the edges.

HOW TO BUILD STEPS INTO A BANK

1 *Measure the height of the bank to work out how many steps are needed (see left). To do this, drive a peg into the top of the slope and a post at the bottom. Tie string horizontally between the two, then measure the distance between ground level and the string.*

2 *Use string and pegs to mark the sides, then run strings to mark the fronts of the treads. Dig out the steps and compact the earth at each tread position.*

3 *Construct a footing for the riser, 15cm (6in) deep and twice the width of the bricks. Fill with concrete over a 7cm (3in) hardcore base.*

4 *When the concrete has set, lay the first riser on the footing. Use a string line stretched between pegs to ensure bricks are straight and level.*

5 *Backfill with hardcore to the height of the bricks and tamp down. Set the paving slabs on 1cm (½in) of mortar, with a small gap between them.*

6 *The slabs should have an overhang of 2.5–5cm (1–2in) at the front and a slight, forward slope for drainage. Mark the position of the second riser on the slabs and mortar the bricks in place. Fill in and set the treads as before. Continue for the remaining steps. Lastly, mortar the joints between the slabs.*

Walls

Boundary walls have been a feature of gardens since the early days of enclosures, and in the last century walled gardens were a common feature on large estates. Nowadays, however, large boundary walls are uncommon, having given way to cheaper fences or hedges.

Garden walls are often decorative as well as practical. If they have a planting cavity, low walls can be particularly effective and, because they require less substantial foundations and supporting piers, they are also easy and cheap to construct.

Materials

Boundary walls may be constructed from various materials including brick, and, for low walls, concrete walling blocks. Screen block walls (opposite) are a practical and decorative alternative to solid walls and are also suitable for dividing off parts of the garden. These blocks are purpose-made for outdoor use. When buying bricks, however, always check with the supplier that they are suitable for garden walls: they should be frost-proof and able to withstand moisture penetration from both sides.

Walls may also be constructed from a combination of materials, for example brick with facing panels of local stone such as flint. Large, plain walls may be painted with a masonry paint (usually white or a pale colour) on the garden side. This reflects the light and contrasts well with wall shrubs or other plants.

How high to build?

There may be restrictions placed on the height of walls in the deeds of the property, or in local authority or highway regulations. Check this before building. A low, screen block wall is a straightforward DIY job, but brick and concrete block walls higher than about 1m (3ft) require advice from a builder or structural engineer. Any wall higher than 1m (3ft) should have a strengthening pier every 2.5m (8ft).

COMBINED MATERIALS
Brick and flint are juxtaposed here to create a striking garden divider. The mixture of straight and curved lines reinforces the blend of styles. When combined in this way, diverse materials can effectively enhance each other.

Concrete footings for walls

The width of the footing for all walls should be two to three times the width of the wall. For walls lower than 1m (3ft), deep and substantial foundations are not necessary.

For a half-brick wall (i.e. the width of a single brick), dig a trench the length of the wall and 38cm (15in) deep. Place 13cm (5in) of hardcore in the bottom and tamp it down. Then pour in 10cm (4in) of concrete. Allow this to harden completely for a few days before laying the bricks or concrete blocks. For a

---

Walling materials

Bricks are the most popular choice of walling material, although concrete blocks manufactured to imitate natural clay bricks may also be used. If you want to build a wall to match the brickwork of existing buildings, used bricks are available in many colours and styles.

SMOOTH-TEXTURED BRICKS
These are most suitable for facing the front of a wall. They come in a range of colours.

MOTTLED ENGINEERING BRICKS
These contribute a rough-hewn appearance; they are also the hardest of all the bricks.

PRE-CAST CONCRETE BLOCKS
These contain medium-textured aggregate.

ROCK-FACED CONCRETE BLOCKS
The brick-red colour imitates the look of clay bricks. They are also available coloured to look like sandstone.

SMOOTH BLOCKS
These concrete blocks suit a modern design.

HOW TO MAKE A CONCRETE FOOTING

1 Mark out the site of the foundations with string lines stretched between wooden pegs.

2 Dig a trench of the required depth. Check that the base is level and the sides vertical. Drive in pegs to the level for the concrete. Align with a spirit level and a length of wood spanning the pegs.

3 Soak the trench with water and allow it to drain. Then add 13cm (5in) of hardcore and tamp it down. Pour in concrete, slicing into the mix with a spade to work it in and dispel air bubbles.

4 Compact the concrete by tamping it down firmly with a length of timber. Level it to the tops of the pegs. Leave the surface rough as a key for the mortar for the first course of bricks.

HOW TO BUILD A SCREEN WALL

1 *Place a course of blocks and pilasters alongside a prepared footing to position the supporting iron rods. Before the footing sets, knock in the rods, leaving enough exposed to reach the middle of the highest pilaster.*

2 *Lay a 1cm (¹/₂in) bed of mortar around the rod. Lower the pilaster onto the mortar and level it with a spirit level. Then fill the inside of the pilaster with concrete for reinforcement.*

3 *Mortar the footing and the first screen block. Repeat at the other end of the section.*

4 *Position one block at either end of the first section. To align the intervening blocks, push pegs into the ground and stretch a string between them, passing it over the pilasters and the blocks.*

5 *Position the next block, and knock it gently into place with the handle of a trowel. Repeat this procedure along the row of blocks, regularly checking the alignment with a spirit level. Remove the string.*

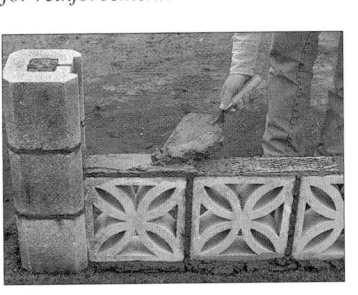

6 *Start the second row by placing the pilasters and filling them with concrete as before. Then lay the second row of blocks using chicken wire bedded in the mortar to strengthen the bonding.*

7 *Finish the second row. Mortar the pilaster caps and coping stones into position. Check levels, tidy up the pointing and square off the mortar at the base of the wall with a trowel.*

---

full-brick wall, which is two bricks wide, or for a double wall with a space for planting cavities, dig the trench 5cm (2in) deeper and add 5cm (2in) extra concrete. For a brick or concrete block wall, the top of the footing need only be 15cm (6in) below ground level. For concrete screens, the top of the footing may be just below ground level, provided reinforcing rods are used. On heavy clay or in cold areas, increase the depth of the footing so that it is below the frost line. For higher walls, specialist advice should be sought.

Block patterns

Many different geometric and free-form patterns of screen wall blocks are available for easy-construction garden walls.

LEAF

SQUARE

CURVED DIAMOND

Bricklaying

To ensure that the first course is straight, stretch two parallel strings along the footing, the space between them equal to the width of the wall. Lay a 10mm (³/₈in) bed of masonry mortar (p.494) along the footing. The first brick of a course is laid un-mortared, then the second is "buttered" on one end and laid up against it. As you lay, check frequently with a spirit level that the bricks are level and horizontal. If too high, tap them down gently with the trowel handle. Insert more mortar under any that are too low. Check also that the mortar joints are all 10mm (³/₈in) thick.

Repeat the process for subsequent courses. For walls with planting cavities, leave "weep" holes (un-mortared gaps between bricks) for drainage in the first course that is completely above ground level.

Before the mortar dries, use a pointing trowel to give the joints a neat, bevelled finish. Vertical joints should all be bevelled in the same direction, horizontal ones should slope slightly downwards to aid water run-off.

Brick bonding
There are many brick bonding patterns. If you are a beginner at bricklaying, keep to one that is easy to lay and does not require many cut bricks. The simplest of all is a running, or stretcher, bond, in which all the bricks are laid lengthways.

Screen walling

In parts of the garden where a brick wall would form too solid a barrier, a screen wall of purpose-made, pierced concrete blocks (see left and above) may be more appropriate. Walls of this kind are supported at each end and at 2.5–3m (8–10ft) intervals by piers built of hollow pilaster blocks. These are normally reinforced with iron rods set in the footing and filled with mortar or concrete. Even so, screen walls are not strong, so for walls higher than 2m (6ft) seek professional advice.

Some popular bonds

Running bond is used for walls one brick thick; Flemish and English bonds combine stretchers and headers (bricks laid respectively lengthwise and widthwise) in a full-brick wall.

RUNNING BOND

FLEMISH BOND

ENGLISH BOND

A DECORATIVE FINISH
Upright stones have been set in mortar as a coping for a dry limestone wall.

A FULL-BRICK WALL
This Flemish-bonded wall is topped by a course of "headers"– bricks laid across the full width of the wall.

STONE COPING
Large, stone slabs form a solid coping that complements a wall of flints mortared in courses.

SOFTENING THE WALL
The hard line of the wall's edge is softened by a colourful display of trailing flowering plants to create a curtain effect. The crevices between the dry stones provide ideal spaces for shallow-rooting rock garden plants.

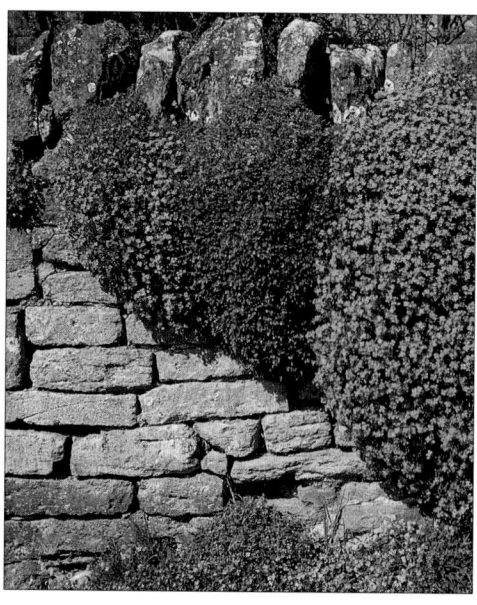

Coping

Coping, which forms the top course of a wall, prevents frost damage by shedding rainwater so that it does not seep into the joints. It also gives the wall a "finished" appearance.

Specially made, curved coping bricks are available, but these are often only the width of the wall and are strictly cappings, as they do not throw the drips clear of the wall. Wider concrete slabs are used for copings on brick as well as concrete block walls. If an ordinary brick finish is required, lay a double course of flat roof tiles before the final row. Coping is especially important for pierced concrete block walls, because it helps to bond the blocks.

Dry-stone walls

Dry-stone walls may be laid on a concrete footing (see p.504) or a foundation of rubble. They may be planted with alpines (see p.204), and look particularly attractive if a cavity is left in the top for trailing plants.

Dig a trench and make a firm base of compacted hardcore or rubble. The base of the wall should be one or two courses below ground level. Use a taut line to maintain a level construction, and build up the wall with broad tie-stones and smaller random stones to bond the wall together. The wall should be wider at the bottom than at the top. To achieve a consistent slope or "batter", make a batter board, a wooden frame in the shape of the desired cross-section of the wall. An inward slope of about 2.5cm in every 60cm (1in in every 24in) is usually sufficient. Use a spirit level to keep the batter board perpendicular. Finish off with large,

flat stones or a row of vertical stones laid on edge (and mortared if desired) as a decorative coping.

Retaining walls

Retaining walls may be used to terrace a garden or contain the soil in a raised bed (see p.507). Dry stones, concrete walling blocks, or bricks may be used. Seek professional advice for any retaining wall more than 75cm (2½ft) high or one on a steep slope, because it may be necessary to reinforce it to withstand the pressure of soil and water. Rather than building one large retaining wall,

terracing the garden in a series of shallow steps may be easier. In some countries, permission is required to build a high retaining wall, and regulations may demand that contractors be hired to construct it from poured concrete.

Insert a drain (see "Installing drains", p.529) running horizontally along the back of the wall, and backfill the lower half of the wall with gravel or rubble. If using bricks or concrete blocks, build the wall on a concrete footing (see p.504) set below the lower soil level, and leave "weep" holes for drainage between every second or third brick in the lower courses of the wall.

Dry-stone walling is a good choice for a low retaining wall, since alpines can be grown in the exposed face. Place large stones on a firm foundation of concrete or compacted hardcore, and lay subsequent courses of stone with an inward slope (a batter) of 2.5–5cm for every 30cm (1–2in for every 12in) of height. The wall should be perpendicular on the retaining side (see THE ROCK GARDEN, *How to Build a Dry-stone Retaining Wall*, p.204). If it is not to be planted with crevice plants, the wall may be mortared to make it stronger (see "Bricklaying", p.505); otherwise pack garden soil between the stones for additional stability.

Constructing retaining walls

Coping

Weep hole

Gravel infill

Mowing edge

Any retaining wall used to hold back soil on a slope must be extremely strong. Bear in mind that the higher the wall, the stronger it will need to be. Remember, too, that wet earth is heavier than dry earth, and water must be allowed to drain out through weep holes left at the base of the wall. If the units of construction are large, the retaining wall will be even stronger than if small bricks or blocks are used.

CONSTRUCTION
On the left is a section of a brick wall with a vertical, unmortared joint acting as a weep hole. On the right is a wall built of hollow concrete blocks (see below). Hollows may be filled with wet concrete, or with soil for plants.

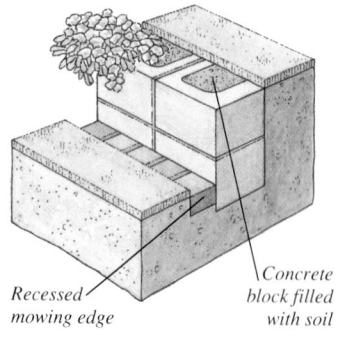

Recessed mowing edge

Concrete block filled with soil

REINFORCING RODS
The strength of a wall built with hollow concrete blocks will be greatly increased if hooked rods are set in the concrete foundation. Further reinforcing rods may be added passing up through the blocks.

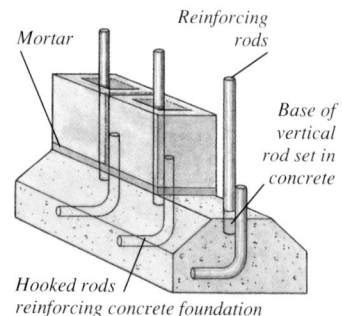

Mortar

Reinforcing rods

Base of vertical rod set in concrete

Hooked rods reinforcing concrete foundation

Raised beds

Raised beds provide a strong design element in a garden, perhaps surrounding a sunken garden or providing changes of level. Small groups of raised beds, or a series of linked beds, are ideal for an area that is mainly paved, while a single, distinctive raised bed makes a good foil for an attractive specimen plant.

Where the soil in a garden is poor, or unsuitable for growing certain plants, raised beds can be extremely useful: they enable acid conditions to be created in a garden with alkaline soil, for instance. Moreover, plants in raised beds have more room to develop and require less attention than those in tubs and other containers, in which the soil dries out fast.

Raised beds have the great advantage that they can be reached from a sitting position. A well-planned series of raised beds makes gardening a practicable possibility for elderly, disabled, or infirm gardeners. The height of the beds will need to be tailored to the requirements of the individual gardener and narrow enough for the whole bed to be within easy reach. The beds should be linked by easily negotiated, wide garden paths (see pp.501–2).

Materials

Raised beds may be built from a wide range of materials: mortared bricks (see "Types of brick", p.497), concrete walling blocks (see "Walling materials", p.504), unmortared natural stone (see "Dry-stone walls", p.506), railway sleepers, or sawn logs. If using bricks or concrete blocks, you may wish to finish off the bed with a coping (see p.506) wide enough to sit on.

Brick beds

A large, rectangular, brick bed is easy to construct, but may appear rather unimaginative. A number of smaller, linked beds at different heights will create a more visually stimulating feature, as will a circular raised bed. Always choose frost-proof bricks; ordinary house bricks may be unsuitable – check with the supplier. A half-brick wall is usually strong enough.

Rectangular beds

Prepare a footing (see *How to Make a Concrete Footing*, p.504) at a depth that allows the first course of bricks to lie below ground level. When the footing has set, use a masonry mortar mix (see p.494) to lay the courses

of bricks (see "Bricklaying", p.505). Lay whole bricks at right angles to form the corners.

Circular beds

For a circular bed, the bricks should ideally be cut to give a smooth curve but it is possible to use full bricks: first lay the bricks loosely to a circumference large enough to ensure that there are no wide gaps at the edge. Prepare the footing, and, when this has set, lay the bricks so that they almost touch on the inside edge of the wall. Use wedges of mortar to fill the gaps on the outer face. Stagger the courses as with a conventional bond and use half bricks for the final course to give a better curve.

Ericaceous plants

If plants that require acid soil are to be grown in the raised bed, line the inside of the walls, when completed, with a butyl rubber liner or several coats of a water-proof, bitumen-based paint. This stops lime in the mortar from leaching into the bed.

Concrete block beds

Concrete walling blocks are a good choice for raised beds if matching materials have been used for other garden structures and surfaces. The blocks may be too large for circular beds, but are ideal for rectangular ones. The beds are constructed in a similar way to brick beds.

Natural stone

Raised beds may be built using natural stone laid dry. Use the technique for dry-stone retaining walls (see "Dry-stone walls" and "Retaining walls", p.506), but keep the beds low and small.

For a bed higher than about 60cm (24in), it is best to mortar the stones securely in place. Even with a low bed, it may be necessary to use a certain amount of mortar at the corners for stability.

Sleepers

Railway sleepers, which blend unobtrusively with most plants and garden surfaces, are ideal for large, low, raised beds, but they are heavy and difficult to handle: do not make the walls more than three sleepers high. Use a chainsaw to cut the sleepers to length, but build the walls

Half-brick wall using a running bond

Soil level

Hardcore base

2.5cm (1in) concrete footing

BRICK BED
Ideally, brick beds should be built with frost-proof bricks. After preparing the concrete footing (see p.504), lay the first course of bricks below soil level. Stagger the courses to strengthen the walls.

Sleepers laid like bricks in a running bond

Rammed gravel base

SLEEPERS
Railway sleepers are particularly good for low raised beds. No footing is needed because the sleepers are themselves very stable. Ensure that they have not been treated with a preservative that is toxic to plants.

in multiples of full or half sleeper lengths. This will reduce the amount of sawing involved.

It is not necessary to provide a footing, since the length and weight of the sleepers make them extremely stable. Create a level surface to lay them on, using rammed gravel, then bond the sleepers like bricks, and, if more than two courses high, use metal rods driven into the ground to secure them in place: either drill holes for the rods in the sleepers, or position the rods on the outside of the raised bed as a brace.

Sleepers may already be impregnated with bitumen or a wood preservative that is toxic to plants, so ask the supplier for ones that have not been treated in this way.

Sawn logs

Logs make attractive edgings for woodland-style beds, and for very low, informal beds in a natural setting. For higher raised beds, logs of

a uniform size and thickness should be used. These may not be readily available, however, and the corner joints are difficult to construct. If this type of raised bed is to be built, it may be better to buy it in easily assembled kit form.

Watering

The growing medium in a raised bed will drain more rapidly than the soil in ordinary garden borders, so it is important to water plants more frequently. In particular, the soil in immediate contact with the retaining walls tends to dry out and shrink. In extreme conditions, this could expose the fibrous feeding roots of plants growing around the edges of the bed, making them vulnerable to frost, heat, or drought. Depending on the plants to be grown, it may also be necessary to add more humus to the soil to help retain moisture (see SOILS AND FERTILIZERS, "Using soil additives", p.527).

Fences

Fences are commonly used as property boundary markers, but they may also act as windbreaks or as a decorative feature within the garden. They may be erected more quickly and cheaply than brick- or block-built walls, and they have the additional advantage of affording almost instant privacy. In general they do, however, require more maintenance than a wall. To make a fence into a decorative element, it may be clothed with climbers or have trellis panelling fixed to the top.

The first step before erecting any fence is to mark out the line of fencing with a string line. If it is to be on a boundary between two properties, all the fencing and fence posts must be on your side of the boundary. For other legal requirements regarding fences, see "Laws on fences", p.510.

Panel fences

One of the simplest forms of fencing is a panel fence. It may be constructed using wooden or concrete posts. With concrete posts, the panels are simply slotted into grooves on either side of the post. For details, see *How to Erect a Panel Fence*, opposite. Another advantage of concrete is that it does not rot.

If you prefer timber posts, the panels have to be screwed or nailed into position. Protect the bases of timber fence posts by using either metal post supports or concrete spurs (see opposite). The latter are short posts that are embedded in a firm concrete foundation. They are bought ready made with two holes through which the timber posts are bolted to the spur just above ground level.

To build a fence with timber posts dig a hole for the first post, then stretch a string line along the run of the fence to ensure that it is straight. For a panel 2m (6ft) high, you will need 2.75m (8½ft) lengths of timber for the posts and the post holes should be 75cm (30in) deep. Fill the bottom with a 15cm (6in) base of hardcore, then stand the post in the hole and pack it round with more hardcore to

HOLE BORER

If a number of holes are needed for fence posts, hire a "corkscrew" hole borer. This device is reasonably easy to operate – simply turn the handle and apply a little pressure to make clean, deep holes. Powered versions are also available but they are heavy to support and can be difficult to use at first.

Fence types

Basket-weave fencing is usually sold as prefabricated panels, generally in a range of heights. Thin, interwoven slats of pine or larch are fixed in a light, softwood frame. It provides good privacy, but is not very strong.

Closeboard fencing consists of overlapping, vertical, feather-edged boards, usually of softwood, nailed to a pair of horizontal arris rails. The thick edges of the boards are nailed over the thin edges. It may be constructed *in situ*, but is also available (as shown here) in the form of panels. Closeboard is one of the strongest forms of fencing, offering good security and privacy.

Waney-edged fencing, made of overlapping, horizontal planks, is one of the most commonly used forms of panel fencing (see also p.513). It provides adequate levels of security.

Shingle fences consist of overlapping cedar shingles (wooden "tiles") that are nailed to a timber framework to produce a strong, solid fence. They offer good security and privacy, depending on their height.

Wattle hurdles are flimsy panels of interwoven woody stems. Two examples are shown here. They may be made *in situ* or bought as ready-made panels. They are held in place by stout stakes and are particularly useful when a new hedge is becoming established in a garden, offering interim privacy as well as good protection against both small and large animals. Within a relatively short period of time, however, they can begin to look ragged and unattractive, and they are also troublesome to maintain and repair.

Lattice fences are made from sawn timber or rustic wood. They resemble large partitions of diamond-shaped trellis. They are useful for an informal boundary marker, but offer little privacy.

Picket fences have vertical wooden "pales" spaced about 5cm (2in) apart, fixed to horizontal rails, and are more decorative than functional. Plastic picket fences are available that require far less maintenance than traditional wooden ones. Neither kind offers much security or privacy.

Ranch-style fencing uses thin, planed planks attached horizontally to stout posts. The timber is either painted or simply treated with preservative. There are plastic versions of this style of fencing available, which need less maintenance, but neither is secure.

Cleft chestnut paling consists of split vertical stakes about 7.5cm (3in) apart, linked by strands of galvanized wire. It is suitable only as a temporary fence.

Post-and-rail fences have two or more horizontal poles or rough sawn timber rails fixed between adjacent posts. They form an inexpensive boundary marker.

Interference fencing has horizontal boards fixed on both sides of the posts, the planks on one side facing the gaps on the other. It makes a better windbreak than a solid fence, and it provides acceptable if not total privacy.

Chain link consists of a wire mesh, which is usually attached to concrete, timber, or iron posts. Galvanized wire mesh lasts for ten years, plastic-coated wire mesh longer. It is a good choice where an animal-proof boundary is required.

Welded wire consists of an open, wire mesh stapled to wooden posts and rails. It is used primarily as a barrier to fence off larger animals where appearance is unimportant.

Post-and-chain fences may have chains made of metal or plastic which are attached to wooden, concrete, or plastic posts. They are used to mark boundaries where more substantial fences are not allowed.

Concrete fences are made of concrete panels, usually pierced, slotted into concrete posts. They offer the security and permanence of a masonry wall and require much less maintenance than a timber fence.

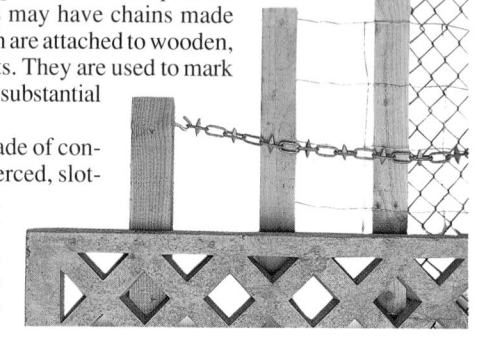

hold it in position. Check that it is upright with a spirit level. Using the panel as a width guide, dig a hole for the second post, making sure that it is aligned with the string line. Level the ground between the post and the hole and lay a gravel board – a length of wood (or concrete) fixed between

fence posts at ground level to prevent panels from coming into contact with the soil and rotting. A wooden gravel board should be secured to the first post with galvanized nails. Attach a fence panel to the post using 75mm (3in) galvanized nails driven through pre-drilled holes, or screw them

together with metal fixing brackets. Place the second post into its hole, ensuring that it is vertical and fits closely against the fence panel; fix the gravel board and panel as before. Repeat with the remaining posts, gravel boards, and panels.

Saw the tops of the posts to an equal height above the panels if necessary. Treat any sawn surfaces with wood preservative and finish each post with an overhanging wooden cap that deflects rainwater.

Lodge the posts firmly in position with wedges of scrap timber and hardcore, checking that they are vertical with a spirit level. Pack a stiff concrete mix (see p.494) around the base of each post, and use a trowel to create a slope away from each side as a run-off for water.

Metal post supports

Instead of digging holes for fence posts, metal post supports may be sunk into the ground instead, and

wooden posts inserted into them. This reduces the length of the timbers needed for fence posts and keeps them out of contact with the soil, thus prolonging the life of the wood. Use 60cm (24in) supports for fences that are up to 1.2m (4ft) high and 75cm (30in) supports for fences up to 2m (6ft).

Before driving the support into the ground, fit an offcut of wood from a post into the socket. This protects the support from damage. Most manufacturers also provide a special attachment that fits over the offcut of wood while the support is hammered into place.

Check continually that the spike is entering the ground vertically. Hold a spirit level against each of the four sides of the socket in turn. To secure the post, tighten the clamping bolts in the socket, or if these are not provided, fix it with screws or nails through the slatted holes. For added strength, metal post supports may also be set in a foundation of hardcore and concrete.

HOW TO ERECT A PANEL FENCE

1 Dig a hole 75cm (30in) deep and pack a 15cm (6in) layer of hardcore in the base. Insert the first concrete post and check the height of the post against the fence panel.

2 Pack hardcore round the post and pour in concrete. Tamp it down. Add more concrete and tamp again. Keep checking that the post is vertical.

3 Lay a fence panel on the ground to position the next hole accurately. Use a string line as a guide, then dig the next hole.

4 Fit a gravel board between the post holes. Level the ground until the board lies horizontally. Check with a spirit level.

CONCRETE SPURS

To avoid damage through contact with damp soil, bolt timber fence posts to a concrete spur set in a concrete foundation.

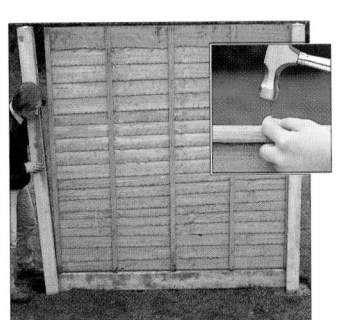

5 Slot the panel into the groove in the first post. Insert the next post and pack into position with hardcore. Secure moulded wooden coping to the top of the panel.

ERECTING A FENCE USING METAL POST SUPPORTS

1 Place an offcut of wood and the fixing accessory in the socket of the post support. Use a sledgehammer to drive the support directly into the ground.

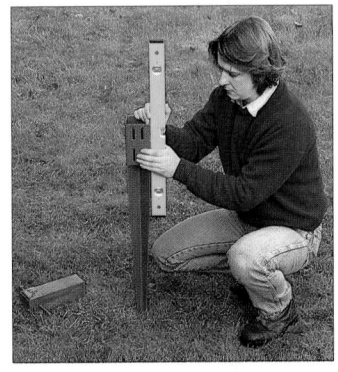

2 Keep checking that the support is being driven in vertically. Hold the spirit level against all four sides in turn.

3 Insert the fence post into the socket at the top of the support and secure it by nailing through the slatted holes. Some sockets are fitted with clamping bolts.

4 Using a string guide, hammer in further post supports. Nail fencing (here a panel of picket fence supported on bricks to keep the rails horizontal) to the posts.

USING ARRIS RAILS

The ends of the rails are chiselled to fit into mortise slots cut in the support posts. Vertical, feather-edged boards are nailed to the back of the rails.

Closeboard fencing

The overlapping vertical boards of a traditional closeboard fence are nailed to two horizontal rails, triangular in section, which are known as arris rails. Fence posts are available with mortise slots cut into the sides to hold the rails, but it is possible to chisel out the slots yourself. The usual heights for the rails are 30cm (12in) below the top of the fence and 30cm (12in) above the ground. Shape the ends of the arris rails so that they fit into the mortise slots and treat the cut ends with preservative.

Set up the fence posts as for panel fences (see p.508). Insert the arris rails into the mortise slots as you go. Wedge the first post firmly in place with hardcore, then prop the next post loosely in position. Insert the first pair of arris rails in the slots, pulling the second post into position. Attach the arris rails so that the flat backs face the correct side for the panels. Check with a spirit level that the second post is vertical and that the rails are horizontal. You may need to raise or lower the post a little. When satisfied, ram hardcore around the base to secure it.

Assemble the remaining posts and rails in the same way and nail them together for added strength. Cement round the bases of the posts to make permanent foundations. As a base support, lay gravel boards along the bottom of the fence (see "Panel fences", p.508). Nail small blocks of wood to the bottom of the fence posts as brackets for the boards, or nail the boards to pegs driven into the ground.

To fix the first feather-edged board, rest it on the gravel board and attach it to the back of the arris rails by nailing through the thicker edge. Then lay the thicker edge of the next board over the thin edge of the first, overlapping it by about 1.2cm (^{1}/2in) and hammer nails through the boards

into the rails. Cut a spacer from a piece of scrap wood to ensure that the overlap for all the boards is uniform.

Sloping ground

There are two ways to erect a fence on sloping ground: the fence may be constructed as a series of stepped horizontal sections or may slope with the ground. The method you should employ is largely dictated by the type of fencing you want to use.

A stepped fence
Panel fences, which cannot be satisfactorily cut, should be stepped. The upright posts need to be longer than they would be on level ground, the extra height depending on the width of the fence panels and the gradient. The triangular gap beneath each panel may be filled by building a low brick wall, stepped so that the panels sit on it. Alternatively, cut angled gravel boards and fix them in the gaps.

SLOPING GROUND

STEPPED FENCE
The panel fence is erected as it would be on level ground, except that the posts must be longer by the height of the supporting brick wall.

SLOPED FENCE
The line of the fence runs parallel to the slope, while the posts and the fencing boards are the same height they would be on level ground.

A sloped fence
To build a fence that slopes with the ground, set a temporary post at the top of the slope and stretch a string line between this and the bottom post. Use a fencing system that consists of individual planks nailed to rails (such as a closeboard or a picket fence). Instead of running horizontally between the posts, the rails run parallel to the slope. Cut the base of each plank at an angle to match the slope. Fix the planks to the rails vertically, resting them on a gravel board.

Wood preservatives

If possible, buy timber that has been factory-impregnated with preservative in a special vacuum press, since home treatments, usually applied only with a brush, are much less effective in penetrating below the surface of the wood.

Unless fences are made of a natural rot-resisting timber, such as oak or cedar, treat them regularly with a wood preservative. Re-apply creosote or water-based preservatives every four years, solvent-based products every two or three years.

Creosote is a widely used and effective treatment for preserving fencing. It has a very powerful smell, however, which many people find unpleasant. Wear protective clothing when applying this substance, since it is poisonous if swallowed, inhaled, or absorbed through the skin. Creosote is not recommended for fences used to support plants. Organic-based preservatives may also be effective. These and creosote both come in a range of colours.

Water-based preservatives are less unpleasant to use, and less toxic to plants. They improve the appearance of the timber and prevent the growth of surface moulds. They are, however, generally less effective at controlling rot.

Preservative should only be applied to dry timber. When erecting a fence, any cut ends should be soaked in preservative for 24 hours before

use. Keep all preservatives away from plants, and always wear gloves.

Various wood-pitch preservatives are also available. These create a barrier that prevents water penetration, making the wood too dry for bacterial action.

Maintenance

Broken timber support posts are one of the most common problems. If the damage is at soil level, the most effective method of repair is to use a concrete spur (see p.509). This is a short post sunk into the ground alongside the existing one and bolted to it to give support.

Dig a hole 45–60cm (18–24in) deep around the damaged post and saw off the rotten part. Paint the cut end of the timber post with a wood preservative. Place the concrete spur in the hole, resting it against the post, and pack hardcore around the base to support it. Push bolts through the holes in the spur and tap them with a hammer hard enough to leave an impression on the wooden post. Remove the bolts and spur, then drill holes through the post for the bolts. Bolt the concrete spur onto the post, tightening the nuts from the spur side so that the wooden post is not damaged.

Make sure that the post and spur are vertical, if necessary bracing them in position temporarily with stakes driven into the ground. Then fill the hole with a fairly stiff concrete mix (see "Concrete and mortar mixes", p.494), ramming it down firmly to remove any air pockets. After about a week, once the concrete has set, remove the supporting stakes and saw off any surplus length from the protruding bolts.

Broken arris rails are easily repaired with specially angled metal brackets. Some of these brackets are designed to brace a broken rail in the middle, others to support a rail that has rotted where the end fits into the post. Both types are simply screwed into place.

Laws on fences

It is always prudent to consult your neighbours before you construct any fencing. On certain sites, you may also need to consult your local authority's Building Control Department for permission according to the planning rules: these govern the size and appearance of constructions and their effect on, for example, neighbouring gardens and adjoining paths.

Structures that front a boundary on a road must conform to building regulations, especially with regard to safety. Planning permission may need to be granted. Bear in mind the following points about gates, walls, and fences: they should not be more than 2m (6ft) high, and should be no more than 1m (3ft) high if they adjoin a public thoroughfare.

Trellises

Trellises, which are usually made of wood, are both a practical and a decorative feature in a garden. They may be secured to the tops of fences or walls or fixed against them. Alternatively they may be used on their own as partitions or screens. Curved and more intricately designed trellis panels are available for creating garden arbours. Panels come in a range of shapes and patterns, most consisting of standard diamonds or squares; herringbone trellis is particularly effective for screening.

Trellises are most frequently used to support climbing plants. For a free-standing screen, heavy duty trellis is essential, particularly if it is to support vigorous climbers; the timber frame should be at least 2.5cm (1in) in section. If the trellis is to be used to extend the height of a wall or a fence, a lighter weight may be acceptable. When buying trellis, make sure it has been pressure-treated, and treat any sawn ends with a wood preservative (see p.510).

Trellis primarily intended for supporting climbers is also available in wire and plastic.

Erecting trellis

For a free-standing trellis, panels may be fixed to fence posts in the same way as ordinary fence panels (see "Panel fences", p.508). To attach panels to a fence with timber posts, use metal post extenders. Remove the post cap and slide the metal extender over the top of the post. Insert the required length of extension post and replace the original cap on top of the extension. To fix a lightweight trellis above a masonry wall, attach long battens of 5 x 2cm (2 x $^3/_4$in) timber to the sides of the trellis and screw them to the wall. If the trellis is to be fixed against a wall, allow at least 2.5cm (1in) between the wall and the trellis for good air circulation. Hinged fixings allow access for maintenance (see CLIMBING PLANTS, "Fixing a trellis panel to a wall", p.100).

Pergolas and rustic work

The term pergola originally meant a covered walkway formed by plants grown up trellis. Today the term describes any structure consisting of uprights supporting horizontal beams, over which plants are grown.

Traditionally pergolas were made of rustic poles, but sawn timber is often a better choice, especially where the pergola is combined with timber decking, or where the house forms one of the supports. Sawn timber may be used in combination with brick columns or with painted scaffold poles serving as uprights. Hardwoods such as oak are often used for sawn timber pergolas, but softwoods are perfectly adequate, provided they have been pressure-treated with a preservative.

Pergola construction

Draw your design on graph paper to work out the quantities of materials required, but buy a little more than you think you will need, as you may wish to modify the design slightly during construction. The height of the pergola should be at least 2.5m (8ft) if plants are to be grown over it so as to allow room to walk beneath. If the pergola spans a path, the uprights should be positioned far enough apart to allow for the growth of plants on either side.

Supports

Set wooden support posts in hardcore and concrete in holes at least 60cm (2ft) deep (see "Panel fences", p.508), or use metal post supports (see p.509). If you are building a pergola over a patio, special metal shoes designed to be fixed in a concrete base are available. To avoid breaking up an existing concrete or paved surface, build a brick shoe and fit the post into it (see *Joints and Supports*, p.512).

Sawn timber support posts should be 10 x 10cm (4 x 4in) in section. Scaffold poles may be used instead of timber uprights but must be set in concrete because of their greater weight. Alternatively, if the weight that is to be carried is substantial, build brick or concrete block columns on substantial footings (see "Bricklaying", p.505).

Cross-beams

For cross-beams (roof beams), use either the same timber as for the uprights or planks 5 x 15cm (2 x 6in) in section. These are sometimes sold ready-shaped and notched to fit

TIMBER PERGOLA ON A BRICK PATIO
The materials used to construct this pergola are few and simple, yet the design is most effective. A large square trellis has been fixed behind the square brick pillars that support the cross-beams.

JOINTS AND SUPPORTS

WOODEN PERGOLA
The basic unit of construction of most pergolas is a simple arch.

BRICK SHOE
A metal-lined shoe is used on top of a solid flat surface such as concrete.

BRICK AND WOOD PERGOLA
Brick columns support a wooden cross-beam.

DOWEL JOINT
To anchor a wooden beam on top of a brick column, use a wooden dowel mortared into the brick.

SINGLE-SIDED PERGOLA
The timber cross-beam is supported on one side by a scaffold pole and on the other by a joist shoe fitted into the wall.

NOTCHED JOINT
A wooden cross-beam fits neatly over an upright support.

HALF-LAP JOINT
Intersecting, horizontal beams may be joined almost invisibly.

BIRD'S MOUTH JOINT
This joint fixes a horizontal strut into an upright rustic pole.

CONCRETE CASING
If using metal uprights, sink them in a concrete casing.

JOIST SHOE
A joist shoe gives adequate support for a lightweight beam. Heavy beams may require a timber wallplate.

over the tops of the uprights. Lighter timber may be used for decorative rafters laid between the cross-beams.

Joints for beams and uprights

It is possible to assemble all the overhead timberwork by means of galvanized brackets and screws, but the structure will be stronger, and more attractive, if you use carpentry joints (see above). To fix an overhead beam to an upright, use a simple notched joint. This kind of joint is especially useful if the cross-beams are to project beyond the uprights – to serve as supports for hanging containers, for example.

Treat the cut surfaces of the joint with wood preservative (see p.510) before nailing them together. Avoid driving the nails in at right angles; skew-nailed joints hold together better when the structure flexes in the wind. If extra strength is needed, screw a "T"-bracket where the upright meets the horizontal.

If you are using scaffold poles to support timber cross-beams, effective joints may be created by drilling circular holes of the same diameter as the scaffold into the beams. The depth of the holes should be half the thickness of the timber.

Timber pergolas are often supported by a wall of the house. To attach a wooden cross-beam to the wall you will need to use a metal joist shoe mortared into the brickwork. When the supports are brick columns, the wooden horizontals are

fixed with dowels, which are mortared into the brick (see above).

You may wish to roof over the pergola with a network of intersecting rafters. Where two beams of equal thickness meet, a half-lap joint gives a strong, neat finish.

Many designs also incorporate corner braces between the uprights and the cross-beams to give the pergola greater rigidity. The timber for the braces should measure about 5 x 5cm (2 x 2in) and should fit as closely as possible into notches cut in the beams.

Cut the braces to the required length, then hold them up to the framework to mark the position and shape of the notches. Use a drill and chisel to cut the notches. When all the necessary adjustments have been made, treat all the cut surfaces with preservative before nailing the braces into the notches.

Rustic work

Rustic work comprises all kinds of garden structures made from poles (usually of larch or fir), rather than sawn timber. A popular material for arches and screens as well as pergolas, the poles may either be dressed, that is with the bark stripped off, or be left with the bark on as an attractive finish. If you use poles with bark, bear in mind that the bark is likely to become a refuge for garden pests.

The vertical poles that support the structure should be about 10cm (4in) in diameter. They may be bedded in concrete (see "Panel fences", p.508) or set in the open ground. In the latter case, sink them to 45–60cm (18–24in) of their length to ensure stability. If the bark is to be left on, strip it from the bases of the poles up to a point that extends 2.5cm (1in) above soil level when they are in position. Whether the bark is left on the poles or stripped off, soak the ends in wood preservative overnight. Set the uprights in their positions. The cross-beams and corner braces needed to complete the structure may be fixed later, once the concrete around the supports (if this is used) has set.

The poles used for the main cross-beams and corner braces should have a diameter of about 7cm (3in), but thinner poles may be used for the decorative latticework.

It is possible to pre-assemble some sections of the structure by laying them out on the ground according to the design, then cutting some of the poles to length and making the necessary joints. Saw all the cross-pieces only as you need them to ensure that they fit exactly.

There are many joints that may be used in the construction of a rustic pergola or arch. Half-lap joints (see above), similar to those used for sawn timber, are useful where the poles intersect. To attach a horizontal cross-beam to an upright, use a

bird's mouth joint (see above). All cut ends should be painted with a wood preservative before you assemble the structure.

As with sawn timber, it is always best to nail the joints together at an angle to give them extra rigidity.

Other plant supports

It is possible to provide permanent support for climbing plants without erecting a trellis or a pergola. Striking effects can be achieved with relatively simple structures.

Tripods

Rustic tripods are an excellent way of integrating climbers into a mixed or herbaceous border. Dressed rustic poles are better than those with bark for this purpose, as they are less likely to attract potential pests. For large plants, use poles with a diameter of about 15cm (6in). If the tripod is in a bed, sink the poles in holes filled with gravel.

Pillars

For a more formal effect along the back of a border or to flank a path, erect a row of single pillars made of brick or reconstituted stone. The bases of the pillars should be set firmly in concrete. To help climbers grow up the pillars, use plastic-covered large-mesh netting. Secure the net around the pillars by tying it together with plastic-covered wire.

Garden sheds

Sheds are valuable outbuildings for storing garden tools and equipment. They may house a miscellany of domestic items from bric-à-brac to bicycles, and sometimes double as a workshop, too. A simple tool store will keep hand tools dry and clean, but a larger shed with space to set up a workbench along one of the walls is a better investment.

Designs

Different designs of shed are available. Some have an apex roof (like an inverted "V"), while others have a pent roof (sloping in one direction only) or a flat roof.

An apex-roof shed has more headroom in the centre than a pent-roof shed, an advantage if a workbench is to be placed along one side.

A pent-roof shed usually has its door and window on the higher side.

A sensible arrangement is to place a workbench beneath the window and to store tools on the lower side.

As a rule, flat roofs are found only on sheds made of concrete.

Materials

Garden sheds may be constructed from a variety of materials – wood, concrete, steel, aluminium, or glass-fibre. The choice of material depends on the intended life and uses of the shed as well as on expense and maintenance requirements.

Wood

The most widely used material for a garden shed is wood; it blends in sympathetically with plants, especially after the new timber has weathered with age. Durable woods such as cedar are preferable, since they are naturally resistant to rot.

Most sheds, however, are made of softwood, which is much cheaper than cedar. Try to find a shed made of pressure-treated timber rather than of wood that has simply been dipped or painted. Treat with a preservative when new, and maintain regularly. Wooden sheds should be lined with water-proof building paper (from a builder's merchant) to reduce the risk of moisture penetration and to protect tools from rusting.

Concrete

Sheds made from concrete are robust and long-lasting but not particularly attractive, so are best sited alongside the house rather than in a conspicuous part of the garden. Generally constructed of pre-cast concrete sections, the roof is usually flat; many have plastic sections in the roof to admit light. A concrete shed must be erected on a firm, concrete base (see p.494).

The concrete walls may have a finish of exposed aggregate or imitation brick. When painted, these may make an excellent background for climbers and wall shrubs.

Metal

Steel sheds are very durable if they have been treated during manufacture to resist rust. They are usually green, but may be painted and usually do not include windows.

Sheds made of interlocking sheets of aluminium are also available. Most have a sliding door, and some an acrylic sheet window. Often small, these sheds are intended primarily as tool stores and are virtually maintenance-free.

Glass-fibre

Small glass-fibre sheds are available that are easy to assemble, and require no maintenance. They are just large enough to store tools.

ROOFING FELT
Choose a thick felt with a stone-chip finish. Poor felt will let in moisture that will damage the wood after three or four years.

ROOF
It must be strong, and should not sag or flex if you push the centre of one of the roof panels.

GUTTERS
They can help to extend the life of the shed by keeping the cladding dry. Although not a standard fitting, they are easy to fix yourself.

WINDOWS
These must fit well and should have rust-proof fittings. If hinged from the top, water is less likely to enter if they are left open in the rain. Check that there is a sloping sill and a drip groove underneath to prevent water from damaging the cladding.

EAVES
These should overhang the sides and ends by at least 5cm (2in).

HEADROOM
Make sure that you can stand comfortably; bear in mind that cross-braces are found in some designs.

DOOR
This should be solid with good cross-bracing. Check for strong hinges and a good lock. Metal fittings should be rust-resistant – galvanized metal or aluminium.

CLADDING
Inspect the shed from the inside to make sure that no daylight is visible through the boards. See right for different types of cladding.

FLOOR
It should be firm – test it by jumping up and down on it.

BEARERS
If the shed is not erected on a concrete base, pressure-impregnated bearers help to keep the shed timber dry. If not using bearers, lay the shed on a damp-proof material.

TYPES OF CLADDING

TONGUE-AND-GROOVE
This cladding usually offers good weather protection.

FEATHER-EDGED, OVERLAPPING WEATHERBOARD
This may warp or buckle unless it is thick.

REBATED WEATHERBOARD
This gives a closer fit than feather-edged weatherboard.

REBATE SHIP-LAP
As well as being durable, this has an attractive finish.

WANEY-EDGED WEATHERBOARD
This rough-edged board (also called rustic cladding) may be less weather-proof.

4

CLIMATE AND THE
GARDEN

CLIMATE HAS A *considerable influence on plant growth and, perhaps more importantly, on garden practice. Much of the satisfaction in gardening lies in meeting the challenges of the weather, often by exploiting its effects to the gardener's advantage. Choosing plants that thrive in the prevailing climate is fundamental to success, but although some plants will only perform well in their natural habitat, many are more adaptable and may be grown elsewhere, as long as suitable conditions are provided. The effects of climate on plants are complex, and made more so because the weather is constantly changing, often with interaction between two or more elements. A plant's responses to weather conditions are also shaped by its location within the garden, stage of maturity, and the length and intensity of the plant's exposure to inclement weather conditions. Through an understanding of the weather and an awareness of its effects, a gardener will be better able to grow healthy, productive, and attractive plants.*

Climate zones

World climate may be divided into four broad but clearly defined zones; these are tropical, desert, temperate, and polar.

Tropical climates are characterized by high temperatures and heavy, sometimes seasonal, rainfall, and support luxuriant, evergreen vegetation. Deserts have average daytime temperatures in excess of 38°C (100°F) but often very cold nights, with annual rainfall of less than 25cm (10in); only adapted plants, such as cacti, survive in these conditions. Temperate regions have changeable daily patterns but rainfall is generally evenly spread throughout the year and temperatures are less extreme than in the tropics or deserts; deciduous plants are more common than evergreens, as they are better adapted to these conditions. Polar regions experience extreme cold, strong winds, and low rainfall, so little plant growth is possible.

In addition to these four broad zones, intermediate zones, including subtropical and Mediterranean, are also recognized.

Regional climate

Conditions within climate zones are determined by geographical factors such as latitude, altitude, and proximity to the sea, which increases rainfall and moderates temperature.

The European continent
The great extremes of summer and winter temperature in north-eastern and central parts of Europe are influenced by latitude and the continental land mass. The Atlantic ocean and Mediterranean sea are too far away to have any moderating influence on temperatures in winter, when the cold land mass of Asia is more influential.

Further south, however, the combined influences of the sea and relative proximity to the equator mean that the Mediterranean climate consists of mild winters with limited rainfall and hot, dry summers.

The British Isles
The maritime climate of the British Isles is influenced by warm air currents and rain from the surrounding oceans. Westerly parts, in particular, benefit from the tempering influence of warm air currents from the Gulf Stream, so winters there are milder and prolonged frosts rare.

The North American continent
North America has much regional variation. For example, the average minimum temperature in the region from Saskatchewan to Labrador in the north of the continent is between -50°C (-58°F) and -35°C (-31°F), whereas that in the area between Arizona and Virginia in the south is between 5°C (41°F) and 10°C (50°F).

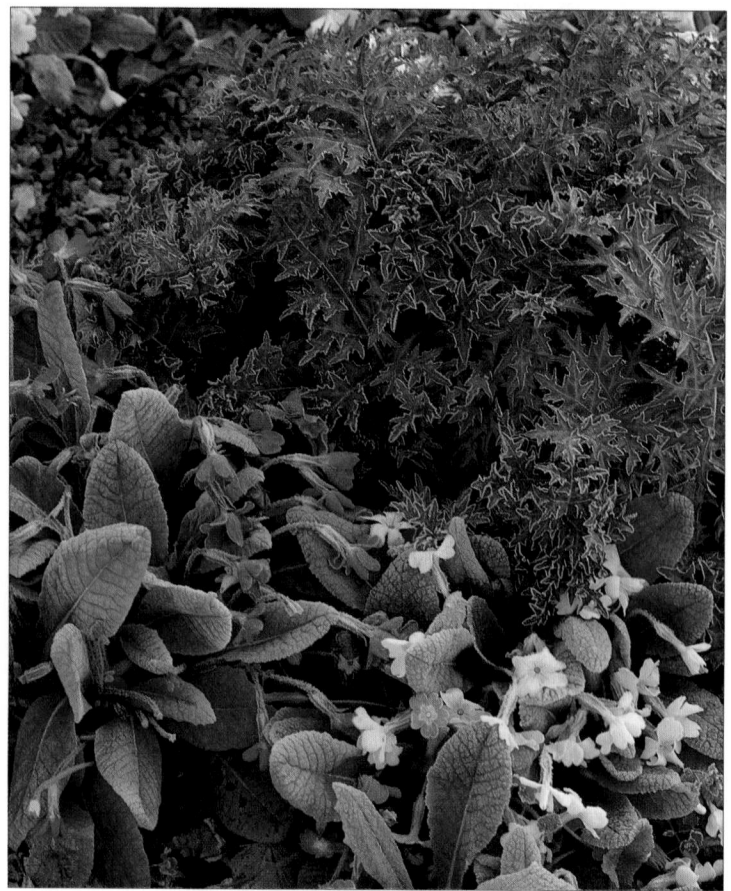

SPRING FROST
The play of light on the frost-tinged foliage and flowers of hardy plants brings an ethereal quality to the garden. Working with the weather rather than against it will ensure satisfying results throughout the year.

Elements of climate

The elements of climate that directly affect plants and the techniques used to grow them are temperature, frost, snow, rain, humidity, sun, and wind. Of these, temperature is usually regarded by gardeners as the most important: it determines the choice of plants to be grown as well as the length of the growing season.

Temperature

Vital plant processes such as photosynthesis, transpiration, respiration, and growth are significantly affected by temperature. Each plant species has a minimum and a maximum temperature beyond which these processes fail to take place. The maximum temperature is around 35°C (96°F) for most plants, while the minimum is highly variable. Where extremely low temperatures occur, plant tissue may be physically destroyed (see "Freezing and thawing", below).

Air and soil temperatures are the most important climatic factors influencing the onset and breaking of dormancy in plants, which, in turn, largely determine the length of the growing season.

Air temperature

Sunshine produces radiant energy that raises the ambient or air temperature significantly. In temperate and cooler climates, a sheltered site that benefits from the warming effect of full sun may be used to grow plants from warmer regions that might not otherwise thrive.

Altitude has an important effect on air temperature: given the same latitude, highland sites are cooler than lowland ones – for every 300m (1,000ft) increase in altitude, the temperature drops by 0.5°C (1°F). High-altitude sites thus have a shorter growing season, which together with the cooler temperatures affects the range of plants that may be grown.

Soil temperature

The temperature of the soil is important for good, healthy, root growth and affects the rate at which plants are able to absorb water and nutrients from the soil. The successful germination of seeds and development of shoots also depend on suitable soil temperatures (see PRINCIPLES OF PROPAGATION, "Requirements for germination", p.536).

The speed at which soil warms up and the temperature maintained during the year depend on soil type and the aspect of the site. Sandy soils warm up more quickly than clay, and well-drained, fertile soils stay warm longer than those that are compacted or infertile (see also "Soil types", p.522).

Sites with a natural, gentle incline towards the south warm up quickly in spring because they gain more benefit from the sun than level or north-facing ground. They are therefore ideal for early vegetable crops. North-facing slopes, on the other hand, stay relatively cool and may be used to grow plants that thrive in cooler conditions.

Dormancy

Plants become dormant to limit their exposure to winter weather, most having at least a short period of full dormancy. Many woody plants shed their leaves in autumn to avoid excessive transpiration, while most herbaceous and bulbous plants die down completely in winter and remain dormant below the ground.

The temperature of the soil and air are the most important factors involved in the onset and breaking of dormancy. It is possible to exploit this knowledge by, for example, keeping plants in a dormant state through cold storage – dormant scions for grafting may be stored until sap begins to rise in the rootstock, and shrubs may be stored in the same way, if necessary, until the soil is warm enough for planting.

On the other hand, bulbs grown in pots and winter-flowering azaleas, for example, may be awakened from dormancy and brought into early flowering if they are placed in a warm greenhouse.

Frost

Frost is a great hazard in gardening and considered to be more crucial than the average minimum temperature for the area. An unexpected severe frost has serious implications; even hardy plants may be vulnerable to unusually low temperatures, particularly after they have produced new growth in spring.

Frost occurs when the temperature is consistently below freezing, and takes several forms: in a hoar frost, crystals of ice are formed from water that has condensed from a humid atmosphere; black frost is more likely in a dry atmosphere, and blackens the leaves and stems of plants. Ground frost results whenever the temperature of the soil falls

FROST POCKETS

Since cold air sinks, frost will always collect at the lowest point it can reach, forming a "frost pocket" of air. Valleys and ground hollows are therefore most susceptible to frost pockets, and any plants in the vicinity will suffer as a result. Frost also collects behind closely planted hedges and other solid obstructions such as walls and fences, with the same effect.

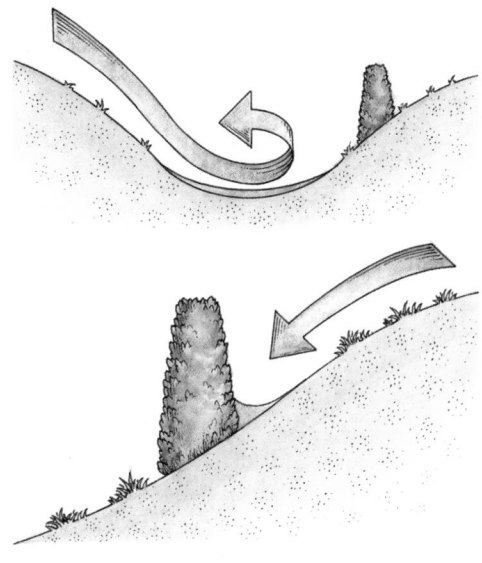

below freezing point; the depth of penetration of ground frost depends on its intensity and duration. Still, clear nights when the cold air collects at a level just above the ground are particularly dangerous. Most at risk are those trees, shrubs, and climbers whose woody tissue has not ripened (hardened) well, usually due to a lack of sun and warmth during autumn.

The risk of spring frost in any area determines the date after which it is safe to sow or plant out tender plants, such as chrysanthemums, runner beans, tomatoes, dahlias, and half-hardy bedding plants, and the onset of the autumn frost determines the end of their growing season. If to be kept from year to year, tender plants should be taken indoors or given adequate protection (see FROST AND WIND PROTECTION, pp.520–21).

Frost pockets and frost damage

Where dense, cold air flows downwards, pools of frost tend to collect and become trapped; any valley or hollow is therefore a potential frost pocket. Cold air accumulates in the depression, increasing the area of potential damage as it backs up the sloping sides of the valley.

Thick barriers formed by established trees or hedges along hillsides may obstruct the passage of cold air down a slope, but frost pockets will form in front of them. The problem may be avoided by thinning or removing the trees or hedge to allow cold air to flow through.

When the ground is frozen, water is no longer available to the roots of plants. Deep-rooted trees are not affected by heavy frosts, as their roots penetrate well below the frost-line,

but plants with shallower roots, such as small evergreen shrubs, may not be able to replace the moisture lost by continued transpiration. Severe ground frost also often causes newly planted, young, or shallowly rooted plants to rise or "lift" out of the soil; these should be carefully refirmed as soon as the thaw begins.

The risk of frost damage to plants kept permanently outside in the garden may be reduced by various means. For full details, see FROST AND WIND PROTECTION, pp.520–21.

Freezing and thawing

Frost itself does not always cause great damage to plants, but alternate freezing and thawing does. Frozen cell sap expands on thawing, which destroys plant cell walls, often killing tender plants. The flowers, shoots, buds, and leaves of hardier plants may also be damaged when the thaw begins, and sometimes even the roots are harmed as well. In cases of severe frost, the bark of some woody plants may split.

Repeated hard freezes followed by rapid thaws and subsequent waterlogging of the soil causes the greatest damage to roots. Late frosts in spring are particularly damaging to new top-growth, causing blackening of the leaves and injury to new buds and flowers.

Duration of frosts

The duration of the frost is also relevant to the amount of damage caused: for example, a temperature of -3°C (27°F) for a quarter of an hour would cause no damage, whereas the same temperature sustained over three hours could result in substantial losses.

THE CLIMATE OF EUROPE

N

0　　　　300　　Kilometres

0　　　　200　Miles

Temperature and rainfall

This map shows the average winter minimum temperature as well as the average annual rainfall of Europe. The areas of highest rainfall occur where moisture-laden winds meet mountain ranges; at high altitudes the winds cool and drop their moisture as rain. Altitude, as well as latitude, also has a clear effect on temperature; in mountainous regions, such as in the Pyrenees and Alps, precipitation often falls as snow. The continental interior endures extremely low winter temperatures, compared with more equable, maritime regions whose climate is influenced by the warming effects of the oceans. In these areas, the surrounding waters also ensure higher rainfall throughout the year.

AVERAGE WINTER MINIMUM TEMPERATURE		AVERAGE ANNUAL RAINFALL	
°C	°F	cm	in
4 to 6	39 to 43	0 to 25	0 to 10
2 to 4	36 to 39		
0 to 2	32 to 36	25 to 50	10 to 20
-2 to 0	28 to 32		
-5 to -2	23 to 28	50 to 75	20 to 30
-10 to -5	14 to 23		
-15 to -10	5 to 14	75 to 100	30 to 40
-20 to -15	-4 to 5		
-25 to -20	-13 to -4	100 to 150	40 to 60
-30 to -25	-22 to -13		
-35 to -30	-31 to -22	150 to 250	60 to 96

THE EFFECTS OF SNOW

SNOW DAMAGE
The considerable weight of thick snow may force apart hedges or evergreen shrubs and trees if it is allowed to settle for too long. Always clear snow from such plants as soon as possible.

ARCHED HEDGE
Shape a hedge to prevent snow collecting on it.

Frost as an aid to cultivation
Despite the danger to plants, frost may sometimes be helpful in cultivation. For example, soil water expands when it freezes, shattering clods into much smaller soil particles; this is particularly useful on clay soils, which may otherwise be unworkable. Low soil temperatures also reduce the numbers of some soil-inhabiting pests.

Snow

When atmospheric temperature falls close to (but not below) freezing, water droplets freeze in clouds or rain and may fall as snow.

Snowfall provides a useful supply of water on thawing and often provides valuable insulation for plants; a blanket of snow prevents the soil beneath from falling below 0°C (32°F) even though the temperature of the air may drop below this point. Heavy snow followed by severe frost, however, may damage shoots and boughs. Wherever possible, remove thick layers of snow from vulnerable plants.

Rainfall

Water is the main constituent of cell sap and is vital for photosynthesis, the complex means by which carbon dioxide and water are converted into living plant tissue. Photosynthesis is also fundamental to the process of transpiration, whereby a plant is kept turgid and nutrients are transported through it. Respiration, germination of seeds, and the subsequent development of roots, shoots, leaves, flowers, and fruit are also dependent upon good water supplies.

Rainfall is the principal source of water for plants grown in the open. Much rainfall is lost through evaporation and runoff but any moisture that soaks into the soil is absorbed by soil particles or held as a thin film around them. Water and essential nutrients, which are absorbed in solution, are then extracted from the soil by plant root hairs.

SNOW PROTECTION
A snow blanket protects high-altitude plants from freezing temperatures.

For optimum growth, plants need a steady supply of water. In practice, rainfall is variable, however, in both regularity and quantity.

Waterlogging
In badly drained soil, a build-up of water leads to waterlogging. Most plants are able to survive an occasional heavy downpour, but where waterlogging is prolonged, roots may die through asphyxiation, except in the case of specially adapted plants, such as marginal aquatics, swamp cypress (*Taxodium distichum*), and willows (*Salix*). On permanently waterlogged sites, most plants fail to establish unless drainage is improved (see SOILS AND FERTILIZERS, p.529).

Drought
Plant development is more often restricted by too little available water rather than by too much. Drought during the summer, when temperature and sunlight are at or near maximum levels, is a common problem. Wilting is the first outward sign of drought; plant functions are slowed down until more water is available, and water loss by transpiration is reduced by partial closure of the stomata on leaf surfaces.

Plants that originate in regions of low rainfall often have special adaptations, such as hairy, sticky, glossy, spiny, narrow, or fleshy leaves, that help to reduce water loss through transpiration. Cacti and other succulents, which have water-storing tissue in their leaves, stems, or roots, can survive long periods of drought.

The soil
In areas of low rainfall, various techniques may be used to increase the amount of water available to

RAIN SHADOW

Ground in the lee of a wall or solid fence (see shaded area above) receives less rainfall than ground on the windward side, since the wall or fence creates an area of rain shadow.

plants from the soil, such as removing weeds (see pp.573–7), mulching, and increasing humus content by digging in organic matter (see SOILS AND FERTILIZERS, "Mulches", p.532, and "Using soil additives", p.527). In addition, plants derive more benefit from rainfall if grown in an open position away from buildings, fences, and trees, which often produce areas of rain shadow.

Torrential rain may damage soil structure but the worst effects may be avoided by gardening on well-drained sites. Where this is not possible, drainage may be improved by deep digging or by installing artificial drainage aids (see SOILS AND FERTILIZERS, "Double digging", p.526, and "Installing drains", p.529).

Humidity

Humidity levels are determined by the quantity or proportion of water vapour in the atmosphere and the moisture content of the soil.

The point at which the air becomes saturated varies according to sunlight, temperature, and wind. Atmospheric humidity is usually referred to as "relative" humidity,

SUNSHINE AND SHADE

The shade cast on a garden by buildings and fences, as well as trees and large shrubs, changes according to the angles of sunlight, which differ according to season.

Shade cast in summer

Shade cast in winter

which is the amount of water vapour present in the air expressed as a percentage of saturation point.

The effects of humidity

In areas of heavy rainfall, atmospheric humidity is high. Certain plants thrive in conditions of exceptional humidity – ferns and mosses, for example. If necessary, humidity may be increased by damping down around plants (see GREENHOUSES AND FRAMES, "Humidifiers", p.484). This is also of great value when propagating plants to reduce loss of water by transpiration.

High relative humidity may have unfavourable effects, however: fungal diseases, for example grey mould, flourish in the moist conditions created by high humidity.

Sunlight

Sunlight provides radiant energy to raise the temperature and humidity of soil and air, and plays a major role in stimulating plant growth.

For most plants, sunlight and the consequent high temperatures encourage maximum new growth, flowering, and fruiting. A sunny summer also results in greatly enhanced food storage in plants and helps to firm protective tissue, which means that better propagating material is produced.

Daylength

The duration of daylight in a given 24-hour period (daylength) is determined by latitude and season, and affects flowering and fruiting in some plants, such as strawberries, *Kalanchoe*, and chrysanthemums. "Short" days have less than 12 hours of daylight, while "long" days have more than 12 hours. By using artificial lighting or blacking out the natural light, the flowering times of plants that are daylength-sensitive may, if required, be manipulated for

WIND TURBULENCE

Exposed areas on rising ground may suffer severe wind damage. Gusts of air meeting resistance from the land are diverted around the sides and over the top of hills, gathering in intensity at the same time.

WIND FUNNELLING

A wind funnel created between buildings and trees may cause a great deal of damage to plants in its path, since air is forced through the narrow channel at great speed. If gardening in such an area is unavoidable, construct a windbreak to protect your plants.

exhibitions or flower shows. Germination of seeds and seedling development are advanced by the same method (see GREENHOUSES AND FRAMES, "Growing lamps", p.485).

How plants respond to sunlight

Plants always grow towards the direction of sunlight: a shrub that is positioned close to a wall, for example, will develop more shoots and foliage on the side farthest from the wall. In the same way, plants that are subjected to a poor or localized light source become drawn or etiolated as they try to reach more light. The intensity of sunlight dictates flower opening in some plants: for example *Ornithogalum umbellatum* only opens its flowers in good light conditions.

Sun or shade

Most leafy plants require the maximum amount of light to achieve optimum growth. Some garden plants thrive in direct, strong sunshine, while others will not tolerate it. Half-hardy plants, most fruits and vegetables, roses, and plants of Mediterranean origin all thrive best in full sun. On the other hand, many rhododendrons prefer to have some shade, whereas ivies (*Hedera*) and periwinkles (*Vinca*) tend to do best in heavily shaded areas.

Excessive sunshine

Strong sunlight may scorch the flowers and leaves of plants, especially if they have been recently watered. It may also split fruits or

the bark of shrubs and trees. To prevent these problems from occurring, always choose an appropriate site when planting, and for vulnerable plants provide artificial shade in summer, most especially in greenhouses and frames (see GREENHOUSES AND FRAMES, "Shading", p.484).

Wind

Wind often damages plants and their environment but it also has some benefits: it plays an important part in pollen and seed dispersal and may also be useful in cooling plants down, provided that they have enough water to prevent desiccation. In addition, gentle winds prevent the development of a stagnant atmosphere, and deter plant diseases that might otherwise thrive.

On the other hand, wind may discourage beneficial insects and make it difficult to control pests, diseases, and weeds: spraying is dangerous in windy conditions because the spray drifts onto other plants. Many more serious problems are caused by the wind, however, although there are various ways of protecting plants.

Wind damage

If woody plants are exposed to strong winds continuously, their top-growth becomes unbalanced, giving the plants a one-sided appearance. The exposed shoot tips are also likely to be damaged or "scorched". Trees that grow on hill tops and on exposed, coastal sites are examples.

Strong winds and gales

The greater the velocity of wind, the more damage it causes. In high winds, shoots and stems of plants may be broken and, in gale force conditions, trees may be uprooted or their root systems seriously weakened. Strong winds may also cause damage to fences, greenhouses, and other structures in the garden. On sandy or peat soil, the wind may cause soil erosion.

Scorching and frost damage

Strong winds in high temperatures increase the rate at which water is lost from plants, leading to desiccation of leaves and shoots. Even moderate winds have a detrimental effect, and may prevent plants from reaching their full growth potential. Where temperatures are low and there is continuous wind, plants will suffer frost damage (see p.515).

Effects of topography

The severity of the wind depends to a large extent on topography. Coastal sites often have no natural protection from salt-laden wind coming in off the sea. Hill-top sites may be equally exposed, because the wind gusts around and over the hill, causing additional turbulence.

Wind funnels are created by the channelling of air between hillsides and along valleys, through corridors of established trees, or between adjacent buildings. This has the effect of considerably intensifying wind speed and strength, so avoid planting in these areas. Windbreaks are an effective means of providing shelter from wind. They may be either artificial, such as fences or screens, or natural, for example tree or shrub hedges.

How a windbreak works

Whichever type of windbreak is used, it should be approximately 50 per cent permeable. Solid barriers deflect the wind upwards, producing an area of low pressure directly behind them, which draws air downwards to fill the vacuum, causing further turbulence.

Fences or screens need to be up to 4m (12ft) high for maximum protection as a garden boundary, but may be as low as 0.5m (20in) for low-growing plants such as vegetables and strawberries. To achieve the greatest benefit across a large area, windbreaks should be placed at regular intervals roughly equal to ten times their height.

WINDBREAKS

Place windbreaks at a distance of 10 times their height.

A SERIES OF WINDBREAKS
Across a large area of flat ground, construct several, semi-permeable fences or screens to break the force of the wind.

REDUCING WIND SPEED
A windbreak should be semi-permeable. Gusts of air still pass through, but at reduced speed.

NON-PERMEABLE WINDBREAK
A solid windbreak is ineffective. Air is forced upwards, then pulled down to create a downdraught.

Microclimate

Differences in topography often mean that local climate varies considerably from that within a climate region. A site in a natural dip or hollow may be relatively warm if it is protected from the wind; on the other hand, if the hollow is shaded from sunshine it will be quite cool. Rainfall may be significantly less in gardens in the lee of high ground than in others in the same locality but on the windward side.

The garden and its plants further adapt local climate and introduce features that give rise to a microclimate specific to the garden; this may differ markedly from that of the surrounding area.

Exploiting a microclimate

To alter the microclimate of a garden, the gardener can easily adapt certain features to provide specific conditions. For example, the soil in raised or sloping beds that face the sun will warm up quickly in spring, producing ideal conditions for early crops or flowers. If the soil is free-draining, the same area may be used for plants that prefer dry conditions. South-facing fences and walls are excellent places to grow tender climbers, wall shrubs, and trained fruit trees, since they are in sun for much of the day; they also absorb a great deal of heat that is then released to the plants, which improves flowering and fruiting.

Wind shelter

A row of trees or a fence provides a sheltered area for plants that might otherwise suffer wind damage. The growing conditions on each side of such a windbreak will be different: the ground close to a hedge or fence on the leeward side will rarely receive rain and may also be sheltered from the warming effect of the sun.

Shaded areas

Areas of shade in the garden beneath tree canopies, hedges, or large shrubs receive the same sort of light as in natural woodland and may be suitable for plants that enjoy such an environment. If a greater degree of shade is required, plants may be grown against north-facing walls, although these sites may be colder.

A bog garden

The edges of a pond or stream, or a low-lying part of the garden, may be used to create the bog-like conditions that moisture-loving plants thrive in.

Greenhouses and frames

Using greenhouses, frames, and cloches gives complete control over the elements, enabling the gardener to create a variety of microclimates in a small space (see GREENHOUSES AND FRAMES, pp.474–91).

THE MICROCLIMATE OF A GARDEN

The potential for several different growing environments exists in even the smallest gardens. Naturally occurring features create their own areas of microclimate and garden features may be either exploited or manipulated, as necessary, to provide the conditions that plants from many different regions enjoy.

Avoid planting in areas of wind turbulence.

Raised beds provide well-drained conditions.

Trees provide a natural windbreak.

A sunny terrace is suitable for tender and sun-loving plants.

The edges of a pool may be planted with bog plants.

A greenhouse provides a suitable environment for tender plants.

Water plants thrive in a pool.

Frost and wind protection

SELECT plants that will thrive in a given climate zone rather than attempting to alter the growing conditions. Trying to grow very tender plants in a cold climate will almost certainly end in disappointment. For species that normally do well in a site but may suffer in harsh winters, providing protection against frost and wind is a sensible precaution. Efficient wind protection enables the gardener to grow a wide range of plants and is particularly useful for large plants, for those in open ground that cannot easily be brought under cover, and for early flowering plants and trees that are more susceptible to frost than later-flowering species. Protection is also needed from strong winds, which can break the stems of woody plants and damage fragile ones; winds may also carry salt spray from nearby roads or the sea, causing browning of the foliage.

Preventive measures

Gardeners can take precautions to avoid the worst effects of frost: do not plant in frost pockets and choose sheltered sites (such as in front of a warm wall or on a sunny bank) for susceptible plants. Tender climbers,

---

PROTECTING SMALL TREES AND SHRUBS

BRACKEN OR STRAW INSULATION
Tie in the branches, then surround the tree with wire netting secured to 3 canes in a partial circle 30cm (12in) from the tree. Pack bracken into the gap, then secure the netting to a fourth stake. Cover the top with more straw. Attach a sheet of plastic to the netting.

STRAW BARRIER
Pack a thick layer of straw between 2 layers of wire netting. Surround the plant, filling any gaps with extra straw, and tie in place.

HESSIAN STRIPS
Tie in the branches or leaves of the crown, then wrap the tree in strips of hessian, winding it round and tying it in place at intervals with string or twine. Protect the base of the trunk with straw or bracken.

HESSIAN AND STRAW COVER
Pack straw around the shrub's branches, working from the bottom up. Loosely wrap hessian around, and tie with string.

NETTING OVER A FRAMEWORK
When wall-trained fruit trees blossom, protect them from frost at night with woven nylon netting, rolled down to cover the tree but held away from the blossom by canes.

STRAW AND NETTING FOR WALL-TRAINED PLANTS
Protect a tree or shrub against a fence or wall by packing straw or bracken behind the branches. Fix netting at the top and bottom of the fence. Pack more straw between netting and plant, until it is covered.

TRENCHING ROSES

MOUNDING UP EARTH
Protect the graft union of bush roses from extreme cold by mounding up earth around the crown, to a depth of 12cm (5in).

1 *Loosen the root ball then dig a trench long enough to take the height of the bush when laid on its side and about 30cm (12in) deeper than the width of the bush.*

2 *Line the trench with a 10cm (4in) layer of straw and lay the bush down. Pack straw around and above the shoots.*

3 *Insert stakes and tie strings between them to hold the bush down. Infill with soil, mounding it up to cover the bush to a depth of 30cm (12in).*

for example, may be grown against a house wall (which will be warmer than a garden wall) or in containers that can easily be moved to a sheltered position. Seedlings, summer bulbs, and tubers should only be planted out when all danger of spring frost has passed, and roses and other shrubs should not be fed late in the season, since this encourages new soft growth that may then be damaged by autumn frost. Allowing herbaceous plants to die down naturally means that the foliage and stems will protect the crowns in winter, while a deep mulch of slowly decomposing organic matter provides useful protection for the roots of all plants. Check plants regularly in winter, firming any that have been lifted out of the ground by frost.

Frost protection

The aim of frost protection is to insulate the plants from the extremes of freeze and thaw conditions by maintaining a constant temperature.

Insulation

Wrapping plants in hessian, carpet, or double thicknesses of newspaper is effective in protecting the top-growth from damage. Any warm air escaping from the soil is trapped beneath the cover and acts as an insulating layer. Hessian helps to slow the warming process caused by a thaw and keeps the plant dormant through any mid-winter mild spells. Bracken or straw packed around the plant beneath the hessian provides additional insulation and is suitable for wall-trained trees and shrubs, climbers, potatoes, strawberries, and small fruit trees and bushes. Once

temperatures rise above freezing this cover can be removed. Wall-trained plants need to be detached from their support if possible and the stems gathered together before wrapping.

Small shrubs and trees growing in areas below their usual winter hardiness level can be protected by building a loose wire-netting cage around them and then packing this with dry leaves or straw. Plastic sheeting tied or stapled over the top of the cage will keep the insulating layer dry. Alternatively, pack the straw in between and behind the stems before covering over.

Mounding with mulches or soil

For perennial plants that die down to a resting crown, place a mulch or a few forkfuls of leaves over the crown and keep it in place with bracken or prunings from evergreens. Roses and other woody plants can be protected by mounding earth around the base or laying them in a trench. In very cold regions, the earth mound should be covered with a layer of straw. Root vegetables can be protected from frost damage in the same way and can then be harvested even during frosty spells.

Cloches

If only a few individual plants need protection, the best solution is to use a cloche, which acts like a miniature greenhouse, warming the soil and maintaining an even temperature. Emerging shoots of frost-sensitive plants, such as asparagus, can be protected with almost any household container: an old bucket, a large plant pot, or a tough cardboard box will all do the job quite adequately. Specially designed, clear plastic cloches are commercially available. More permanent cloche protection

can be provided by glass cloches, polythene panels, polytunnels, or cold frames (see GREENHOUSES AND FRAMES, pp.474–91).

Wind protection

Wind protection aims to reduce the wind speed before it reaches any plants, thereby reducing physical damage to branches and stems and preventing further water loss. Many tender plants have greatly improved chances of survival if they are planted in the lee of a good hedge. A 1.5m (5ft) hedge will reduce the wind speed by 50 per cent for plants within 7.5m (23ft) of the hedge (see HEDGES AND SCREENS, pp.60–62).

Tree and shrub species vary widely in their ability to withstand wind. The most tolerant are those with small, thick, spiny, or waxy leaves, such as x *Cupressocyparis leylandii*, *Escallonia*, and hollies (*Ilex*). Of deciduous trees, alders (*Alnus*), rowan (*Sorbus aucuparia*), willows (*Salix*), common elder (*Sambucus nigra*), and hawthorn (*Crataegus monogyna*) are particularly wind hardy. Windbreaks made from canes and netting, or proprietary windbreaks, can be used while the hedge grows.

WINDBREAKS

DOUBLE NETTING
Protect plants with fragile stems from wind by using flexible double netting supported by canes pushed into the soil.

PROPRIETARY WINDBREAKS
Protect plants with proprietary windbreaks fixed to stout stakes.

WOVEN HURDLES
Place woven hurdles at intervals between the plants, setting them at an angle into the prevailing wind, to deflect any strong gusts.

COVERS FOR FROST AND SNOW PROTECTION

CLOCHE
Use a cloche to protect seedlings, tender herbaceous plants, or young shrubs. Cover the open ends with glass or plastic to stop wind blowing straight through.

LOW POLYTUNNEL
Protect low-growing plants such as strawberries with a polytunnel stretched over wire hoops. The polythene may be raised at either side for ventilation during the day.

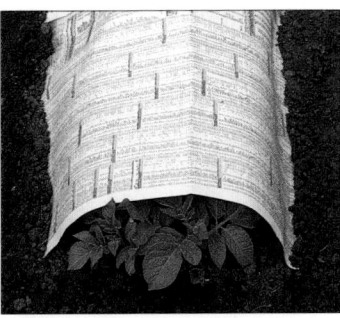

NEWSPAPER
Protect the new growth of potatoes and other tender crops against frost at night by covering them with sheets of newspaper, earthed in on either side to keep them in place.

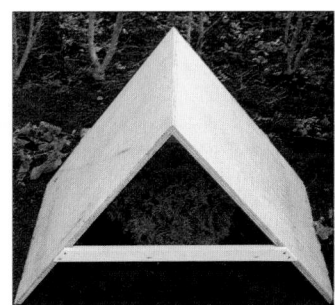

SNOW FRAME
Use plywood panels, cross-braced with a wooden strut, to protect shrubs such as some types of juniper (Juniperus) from heavy snow fall.

5

SOILS AND FERTILIZERS

SOILS ARE HIGHLY *complex and dynamic materials that are made up of minute particles of weathered rock of different types and accumulated organic matter, known as humus, as well as plant and animal life right down to the microscopic level. Healthy soil is essential to successful plant growth: it physically supports plants and supplies them with water, air, and a range of mineral nutrients. If the soil in your garden does not at first appear to be ideal, there is a range of possible solutions: virtually any soil may be improved with a little time and effort. It is possible, for example, to drain the soil if it is waterlogged and improve its structure and water-holding capacity by the addition of organic matter such as garden compost or well-rotted manure. Extra nutrients are easily added to the soil with fertilizers, and lime may be added to make acidic soils more alkaline. Mulches and top-dressings improve plant growth by preventing weed seeds from germinating and reducing water loss from the soil, and some also have an ornamental function. For container-grown plants, there is a wide range of potting composts available to suit every purpose.*

Soil and its structure

Most soil is classified according to its clay, silt, and sand content. The size and proportion of these mineral particles affect the chemical and physical behaviour of the soil. Particles of clay are less than 0.002mm ($^1/_{16,000}$in) in diameter; silt particles are up to 25 times larger than the largest clay particles; and sand particles may be 1,000 times larger – up to 2mm ($^1/_{16}$in) in diameter.

Soil types

Loam soils have the ideal balance of mineral particle sizes, with between 8 and 25 per cent clay, which results in good drainage and water retention, combined with high fertility.

Clay soils are heavy, slow draining, and slow to warm up in spring, but are often highly fertile. They are easily compacted, however, and may bake hard in summer.

Both sandy and silt soils have a low proportion of clay particles, making them much less water-retentive than clay. Sandy soils are particularly light and free-draining and need frequent irrigation and feeding; however, they warm up quickly in spring and are easily improved with organic matter. Silts are more retentive and fertile than sandy soils but tend to compact more easily.

Soil characteristics

Clay soils have more than 25 per cent clay particles and are characteristically wet and sticky. Soils containing less than 8 per cent clay are classified as either silt or sandy soil, depending on whether silt or sand particles predominate. Peat is formed where wet, acid conditions prevent full decomposition of organic matter, which therefore remains on or near the soil surface. Chalky soil, however, is alkaline and free-draining, and allows organic matter to decompose rapidly.

SANDY SOIL
A dry, light, free-draining soil, easy to work but relatively infertile.

PEAT
Rich in organic matter, peat is dark and moisture-retentive.

CLAY
A heavy, slow-draining soil, usually with a high nutrient value.

CHALK
Pale, shallow, and stony, chalk is free-draining and moderately fertile.

SILT
Silt is reasonably moisture-retentive and fertile but compacts easily.

Organic or peat soils are wet and acidic; they support excellent plant growth, however, if drained, fertilized, and limed.

Chalk or limestone soils are shallow, free-draining, and alkaline, and have moderate fertility.

The profile of the soil

Soils may be divided into three layers, or horizons: topsoil, subsoil, and a layer derived from the parent rock. Topsoil contains most soil organisms and many of the nutrients. It is generally dark, because it contains organic matter that is added artificially or naturally by leaf fall. Subsoil is usually lighter in colour; if it is white, the parent rock is probably chalk or limestone. If there is little or no colour change between topsoil and subsoil, the topsoil may be deficient in organic matter.

Weeds and wild plants help to indicate the type of soil in a garden and any characteristics it may have, although their presence is only a guide. Birch (*Betula*), heathers (*Calluna, Daboecia, Erica*), foxgloves (*Digitalis*), and gorse (*Ulex europaeus*) are all signs of acid soil, as are many garden plants such as rhododendrons. Beech (*Fagus*) and ash

SOIL PROFILES

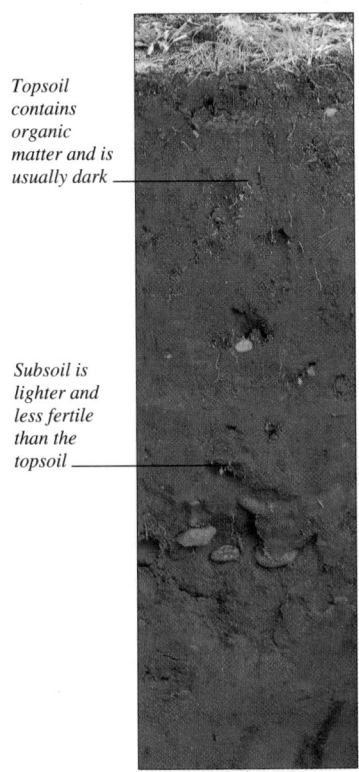

Topsoil contains organic matter and is usually dark

Subsoil is lighter and less fertile than the topsoil

Soil is usually made up of layers of topsoil and subsoil, and a lower layer derived from underlying rock. The depth of each layer can vary.

Identifying your soil

Rub a small amount of moist soil between your fingers. A sandy soil feels quite gritty and will not stick together or form a ball, although a sandy loam is slightly more cohesive. A silt soil feels silky or soapy to the touch. A silty loam may show imprints when pressed with a finger. A loamy clay soil holds together well and may be rolled into a cylindrical shape. Heavy clay soil may be rolled even more thinly, and develops a shiny streak when smoothed. All clay soils feel sticky and slightly heavy.

SANDY SOIL
Sandy soil feels gritty when rubbed between finger and thumb. The grains do not stick together.

CLAY SOIL
Clay soil feels sticky when wet and may be rolled into a ball that changes shape when pressed.

(*Fraxinus*) indicate that the soil is likely to be alkaline. Wild plants may also indicate the chemical profile of the soil: nettle and dock, for example, suggest a rich, fertile soil that is high in phosphorus, while clover indicates a soil that is low in nitrogen.

Acidity and alkalinity

Soil pH is a measurement of acidity or alkalinity – the scale ranges from 1–14. A pH below 7 indicates an acid soil, while a pH higher than 7 indicates an alkaline soil. Neutral soil has a pH of 7.

The pH of soil is usually controlled by its calcium level. Calcium is an alkaline element that almost all soils tend to lose through leaching (meaning that it is washed through the soil by water). Soils over chalk or limestone, which are rich in calcium, are more or less unaffected; other soils, especially sands, gradually turn more acidic.

Alkalinity may be increased, if necessary, by liming (see p.531), or introducing lime-rich material such as mushroom compost.

TESTING pH LEVEL

Soil test kits use a chemical solution that changes colour when mixed with soil in a small test tube. The colour is then matched against a chart that indicates the pH level of the soil sample.

A yellow or orange colour indicates acid soil

Bright green indicates neutral soil

Dark green indicates alkaline soil

Electronic pH meters and soil test kits may be used to measure soil pH. Make several tests across the garden, as the pH often varies; readings are particularly unreliable after liming.

The effect of pH
Above all, pH affects the solubility of soil minerals and hence their availability to plants. Acid soils tend to be deficient in phosphorus and sometimes contain excess manganese and aluminium. Alkaline soils tend to lack manganese, boron, and phosphorus.

Soil pH also affects the number and type of beneficial soil organisms, as well as pests and diseases. For example, worms dislike acid soils, but clubroot, leatherjackets, and wireworms are common in acid conditions. On alkaline soils, potato scab occurs more frequently.

Optimum pH
The pH range for good plant growth is between 5.5 and 7.5. A pH of 6.5 is usually optimum, depending on the plants to be grown. Peaty soils have an optimum pH of 5.8, however. The highest vegetable yields are

generally obtained from neutral soils but most ornamentals tolerate a wide pH range. Some are more sensitive; calcicoles (lime lovers) and calcifuges (lime haters) are adapted to extreme pH ranges and their growth suffers if they are planted in soil with the wrong pH level.

Soil organisms

Certain soil organisms are essential to maintain soil fertility. Beneficial bacteria and fungi prefer well-aerated soil and generally tolerate a wide pH, although most fungi prefer acidic conditions. One group of fungi (mycorrhizae) live in association with plant roots, and improve the take-up of nutrients from the soil.

Small soil animals, such as mites, play a vital part in the breakdown of organic matter. Microscopic worms and nematodes (eelworms) help to control pests – although some are themselves pests.

Larger soil animals, particularly earthworms, improve soil structure when feeding and burrowing; the passage of soil through an earthworm's body binds soil particles into crumbs, increasing aeration and improving drainage.

BENEFICIAL ORGANISMS

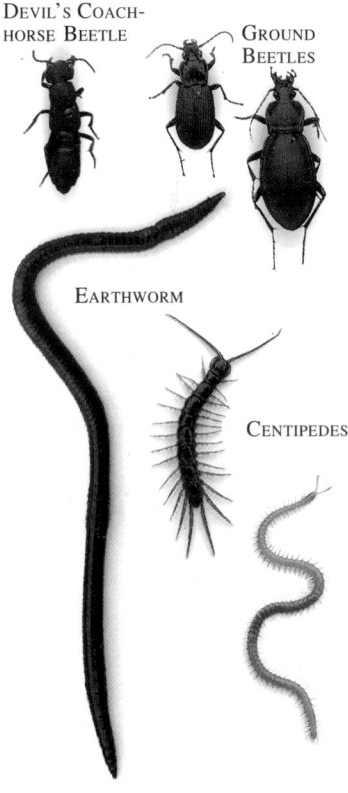

DEVIL'S COACH-HORSE BEETLE

GROUND BEETLES

EARTHWORM

CENTIPEDES

Healthy soil contains a teeming community of earthworms and other organisms, which help to aerate the soil and break down organic matter.

Soil cultivation

Correct methods of soil cultivation, including weeding, digging, and adding soil improvers, are vital to successful long-term plant growth.

Weeds compete with cultivated plants for space, light, nutrients, and water – in fact, all the essentials. They may also harbour diseases of many types, which makes their eradication or control vital.

Several digging techniques are used to cultivate the soil in different ways, depending on the condition of the soil and the plants that are to be grown. If the condition of the soil is poor, it may be improved by the addition of organic material, usually at the same time as digging.

Clearing an overgrown garden

Badly neglected, overgrown plots may be cleared using either tools or chemicals: use whichever method is convenient (see also PLANT PROBLEMS, "Controlling weeds", p.574).

Mechanical clearance
Slash as much top-growth as possible using a nylon-line trimmer, brushwood cutter, or scythe, and clear it away from the area. Then, with a rotary mower, cut any remaining growth as low as possible before digging out and removing all the vegetation that is left on the site.

Alternatively, use a rotavator to churn up the soil and chop up the weeds. Make several passes with the rotavator to break up the matted vegetation, then rake it up and remove it from the surface. The chopping action of the tines, however, will cut the roots or rhizomes of

perennial weeds into pieces that regenerate rapidly. After rotavating, therefore, it is essential to rake over the plot and remove by hand all remaining weeds.

Chemical clearance
Following the manufacturer's instructions carefully, spray with a translocated weedkiller, leave it to take effect, and then cut down the top-growth. If necessary, respray any vegetation that escaped the first application of weedkiller.

Remove the dead vegetation or incorporate it into the soil. Most gardeners prefer to prepare the whole site for planting, but trees, shrubs, and other vigorous ornamentals may be planted directly into holes prepared in the dead vegetation.

On sandy soil, many weedkillers are rapidly leached out, so use only contact weedkillers, which break down when in contact with soil. In organic gardens, where it is not desirable to use chemicals, or if the layout of a garden makes it difficult to apply weedkiller evenly, use mechanical or other methods of weed control, for example mulching (see p.532) and organic practices such as the deep-bed system (see p.534).

Weed control

In practically all gardens the soil is full of weed seeds and fragments of perennial weed roots. Weed seeds are brought into the garden from neighbouring land by the wind and in the soil or compost around bought plants. Cultivation, by its very nature, disturbs the soil, and often brings weed seeds to the surface, where they are able to germinate

CLEARING A SITE OF WEEDS

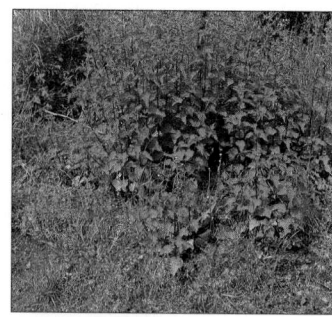

USING WEEDKILLER
A neglected or weed-infested site must be thoroughly cleared before planting takes place. Treat coarse weeds with a chemical weedkiller.

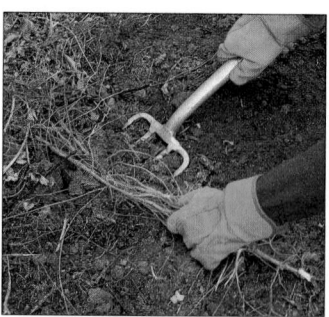

FORKING OUT WEEDS
Fork up the roots of large weeds and pull them out, holding the main stem close to the soil so that the whole root system is removed.

(see "The stale seedbed technique", p.526). Soil cultivation also allows small pieces of perennial weed roots to regenerate and start a new growth cycle over again.

It is virtually impossible to clean a soil completely of weeds, but regular weeding, rather than sporadic attempts that are then followed by periods of neglect, is the best method of control. Although tedious, hand-weeding, using a hand fork, is one of the most effective methods of controlling weeds, since you can ensure that the whole plant is removed from the bed. It also causes the least disturbance to existing plants.

Hoeing
Hoes are used to remove annual weeds and also help to aerate the soil (see also p.460). Unless used carefully, however, they may damage the surface roots and top-growth of

nearby cultivated plants. Hoeing mainly affects the surface soil and seldom goes deep enough to destroy the roots of perennial weeds; pull these out by hand or destroy them with a translocated weedkiller (see PLANT PROBLEMS, "Foliage-acting weedkillers", p.575).

Sterilizing the soil

Some soil pests and diseases, such as honey fungus (*Armillaria*) and nematodes, are so aggressive and persistent that soil sterilization may be the only effective treatment to eliminate them.

Soil sterilants should only be used as a last resort, since they are indiscriminate and kill all organisms, beneficial as well as harmful. This may lead to long-term problems in the garden, because harmful pests are likely to re-invade and thrive

SOIL STERILIZATION

Soil sterilization may be the only method of eradicating some pests or diseases. Cover the sterilized soil with plastic weighted down (any soil used for this should be discarded).

ROTAVATING THE SOIL

1 *For cultivating large areas of soil, it is worth hiring a motorized rotavator. Adjust the handlebars to a comfortable position and press down on the handlebars so that the tiller blades penetrate the soil to their full depth.*

2 *After rotavating, rake up and remove any pieces of perennial weeds from the surface of the soil, otherwise they will re-establish and grow again.*

unhindered, since there will be no natural predators to control them.

Chemical soil sterilants are highly poisonous and should be applied only by a trained operator. The sterilant is applied as a drench that percolates and vaporizes through the pores of the soil. The soil surface is then covered with plastic to prevent the gases from escaping. After a soil sterilant has been applied, it will be several weeks before it is safe to plant in the treated soil.

Digging and forking

Cultivating the soil by digging and forking helps to provide suitable conditions for good plant growth by aerating the soil and breaking up any surface crust (cap). Organic matter and fertilizers may be incorporated at the same time, if required. On heavily compacted ground, digging helps to improve both soil structure and drainage.

The most common method of cultivation is digging with a spade; single and double digging are in general the most effective and labour-efficient digging methods. Some garden beds, however, may not be suited to such a methodical approach to soil cultivation, especially where there are already many established plants. In these circumstances, forking and simple digging may be useful alternatives.

Disadvantages of digging

There are some disadvantages associated with digging. It increases the rate of breakdown of organic matter, particularly in sandy soils, which in the long term reduces soil fertility. In addition, while soil structure is temporarily improved by cultivation, after a while the soil settles down and may become compacted,

resulting in poor aeration and drainage unless the soil is dug again.

When to dig

It is preferable to dig in autumn, if possible. The soil is then exposed to winter frosts and snow, which help to break down large clods of soil and improve soil structure, especially on heavy ground.

From mid-winter until early spring, the ground is frequently wet or frozen and impossible to work. Heavy soil must never be dug when it is wet, since this may cause severe and permanent structural damage.

Using a fork

Much digging work involves lifting and turning the soil. Forks, which are shaped to penetrate the soil easily, are excellent for opening up and loosening soil – but not for lifting it. Forking is less harmful to the soil structure than using a spade, because it tends to break the clods along existing, natural, fracture lines rather than along artificially sliced ones.

Forking is suitable for rough digging and for turning the soil but not for creating fine tilths (see "Forming a tilth", p.526). It is also useful for clearing weeds from the soil, particularly perennial weeds such as couch grass (*Elymus repens*), without leaving behind small pieces that will regenerate.

Simple digging

When digging, some gardeners prefer simply to lift out a spadeful of soil, invert it, drop it back in its original position, and chop it up. This method is known as simple digging. It is a quick and relatively easy form of cultivation and is suitable for cleaning the soil surface of any debris and non-persistent weeds, incorporating small amounts of manure and fertilizers, or creating a surface tilth. Simple digging is often the best option when working in irregularly shaped beds or around existing plants.

Single digging

Single digging is the term applied to a methodical and labour-efficient approach to cultivation that ensures an area has been completely dug, to a uniform standard, and to the depth of a spade (known as a "spit").

Mark out with lines the area to be cultivated; then, beginning at one end of the plot, dig out trenches to a spade's depth and about 30cm (12in) wide. Place the soil from the first trench in a pile on the ground in front. Work backwards along the plot, turning the soil from each subsequent trench into the one in front.

FORKING

Fork over the soil when it is moist but not waterlogged. Work methodically, inserting the fork then turning it over (*see inset*) to break up the soil and aerate it.

SIMPLE DIGGING

Most spades have a blade 25cm (10in) long. This is the depth of trench required when digging 1 "spit" deep.

1 Drive the spade into the soil to its full depth, keeping the blade upright. Press down firmly on the blade with the ball of your foot.

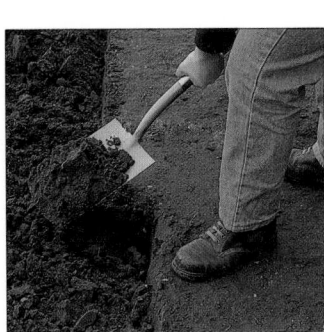

2 Pull back on the handle and lever soil onto the blade. Bend knees and elbows to lift the spade; do not try to lift too much, especially where the soil is heavy.

3 Twist the spade to turn the soil over. This introduces air into the soil and encourages the breakdown of organic matter.

SINGLE DIGGING

Mark out the bed, then dig a series of trenches, working backwards so that you do not compact the soil. Turn the soil from each trench into the one in front, using soil from the first trench to fill the last.

1 Dig out a trench 1 spit deep and about 30cm (12in) wide. Insert the spade vertically and lift the soil onto the ground in front.

2 Dig a second trench, turning the soil into the trench in front. Invert the soil to bury annual weeds and weed seeds.

Adopt this method on regularly shaped plots and in situations where soil uniformity is important – in vegetable gardens and allotments, for example. Single digging is also useful where large quantities of organic matter need to be dug in.

Take the opportunity to incorporate lime (if needed) and fertilizers, such as bonemeal, into the bottom of each trench before replacing the soil. Weeds, especially deep-rooting perennial ones, should be removed as a matter of course.

Double digging

Double or trench digging, in which the soil is worked to a depth of two spits rather than one, should be carried out if the ground has not been previously cultivated or if drainage needs to be improved.

In grassed areas, the turf may be stripped off the top, thrown into the trench bottom, and chopped up with a spade before backfilling the soil. Lime and fertilizers should also be incorporated, if required, and perennial weeds removed, as in single digging.

When double digging, it is essential that subsoil is not mixed with topsoil. On sites where the topsoil is less than two spits deep, standard double digging should be used, since this method ensures that the soil from the upper and lower spits are kept separate. The lower spit does not need to be brought to the surface – it may be forked or dug over *in situ*, although if more thorough cultivation is required it is also turned.

First mark out the area with lines, as for single digging, then remove the soil from the upper and lower spits of the first trench and from the upper spit of the second, laying it aside on the ground in three separate, clearly marked, piles. Soil may then

DOUBLE DIGGING

STANDARD DOUBLE DIGGING
Dig out trenches 2 spits deep and turn soil from each trench into the ones in front; do not mix soil from the upper and lower spits.

DOUBLE DIGGING FOR DEEP TOPSOILS
Where the topsoil is at least 2 spits deep, soil from the upper and lower spits may be mixed or transferred. Dig out 2 spits from the first trench, setting the soil aside to fill the final trench, then transfer soil from the upper spit of the second trench to the bottom of the first. Soil from the lower spit of the second trench should be transferred to the top of the first, and so on.

be transferred from the lower spit of the second trench to the base of the first trench, and from the upper spit of the third trench to the top of the first. In this way, topsoil and subsoil remain completely separate. Continue digging further trenches in the same way and, at the end of the bed, use soil saved from the first two trenches to fill the appropriate spits of the final two.

If the topsoil is more than two spits deep, there is no need to keep soil from the upper and lower spits

separate, and all the soil from one trench may simply be transferred to the trench in front (see above).

Forming a tilth

A "tilth" is a fine surface soil that is suitable for seed germination. It consists largely of small, even soil particles, and is moisture retentive and level. A surface tilth ensures good contact between seed and soil, so that moisture is absorbed easily.

To improve soil structure, dig in organic material such as well-rotted manure or compost, according to the needs of the soil.

Prepare seedbeds about one month before sowing by digging the soil and then leaving it to weather. Just before sowing, break up any remaining clods of soil with a rake, level the ground by treading gently, and then rake the surface to provide the fine tilth required for seeds.

Soil structure and water content

For plants to grow and flourish over a period of many years, the soil needs to have a good, inherent structure. On medium and heavy soils, in particular, plant growth depends on good soil structure.

In a well-structured soil, the particles form crumbs that exist as part of an interconnecting network of pores, through which water, nutrients, and air circulate. The structure of the soil therefore affects its ability to hold water, the rate at which it drains, and soil fertility. A poorly structured soil may become too freely drained or waterlogged, and nutrients will be lost by leaching.

SURFACE TILTH

A crumbly, even-textured soil with fine particles provides a good tilth for seed germination. It is water-retentive yet also provides free drainage.

The stale seedbed technique

This method of cultivation involves disturbing the soil by shallow digging to bring weed seeds to the surface. Any existing weeds are removed at the same time. The weed seeds are then allowed to germinate and grow, and the seedlings killed with a contact weedkiller or by shallow hoeing – this time disturbing the soil as little as possible. Seed may then be safely sown in the weed-free ground, as required. Further weed seeds inevitably germinate during the season, but since the main weed flush has been destroyed, subsequent weed control will be relatively simple.

1 *As an experiment, the soil on the right of this plot has been dug over, while the soil on the left has been left undisturbed.*

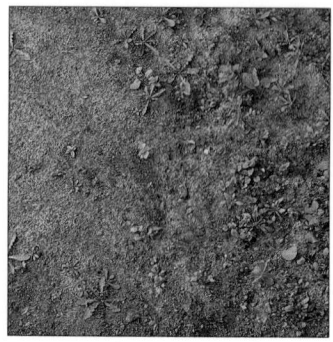

2 *After a few weeks, weed seeds have germinated on the cultivated ground. The undisturbed soil has relatively few weeds.*

Poorly structured soil

A poorly structured soil tends to be too wet in winter and too dry in summer. Water frequently runs off the surface rather than percolating deep down, yet once the soil is wet it drains slowly. A soil such as this is difficult to work, and in summer it may become hard and concrete-like. As a result, plant roots have great difficulty penetrating the soil and plant growth is adversely affected.

Cultivating heavy soil during wet weather may make it compacted. When soil particles are compressed, the amount of air in the soil is reduced and so drainage is hindered.

Walking on the soil in wet conditions damages the structure of the surface layer – the soil crumbs break down and fine particles at the surface form a crust, which then effectively prevents air and thus oxygen from reaching the plants' roots and also prevents seeds from germinating. This is known as "capping" and may occur on some soils, particularly silts, following heavy rain or if the soil is watered too heavily.

Improving soil structure

To improve poor structure, cultivate the soil to as great a depth as possible by double digging (without mixing subsoil with topsoil), incorporating organic or inorganic additives to help bind the soil particles into crumbs. This will do much to improve both aeration and water retention. On severely waterlogged sites, a suitable drainage system may need to be installed (see p.529).

Using soil additives

The choice of additives to use is dependent on the type of soil. Most may be either applied to the surface or incorporated into the soil. Organic material such as animal manure and garden compost improves the structure of any type of soil and also provides valuable nutrients. In addition, animal manure encourages earthworms, which will further benefit soil structure (see "Soil organisms", p.523).

A light, sandy soil may be improved with small amounts of clay (a process known as marling), but enormous quantities of grit or sand would be needed to lighten a very heavy soil.

On compacted soil and clay soil, add manure, compost, and/or lime (but not for acid-loving plants) to improve its structure by encouraging crumb formation.

On silt, add small amounts of clay to improve soil structure, and use manure and compost to encourage crumb formation.

The amount of additive required depends on the soil condition, but a good rule of thumb is to apply about a 5–10cm (2–4in) layer of bulky additives. Some materials, particularly inorganic compounds and water-retaining gels, should be added in much smaller quantities, so it is important to follow the manufacturer's instructions.

Subsidiary benefits of soil additives

Additives also maintain a good balance of air and water in soil. Sand, gravel, and coarse organic matter may be used to improve drainage in silty, compacted, and heavy clay soils. Sand or gravel should be used along channels in the soil, keeping a path open for water, rather than being worked in. Some additives, such as peat substitute, peat, well-rotted manure, and water-holding gels (which hold many times their weight in water) act as "sponges" and may be used to improve water retention in free-draining, sandy soil. On compacted soil, water-holding gels are useful for improving water retention without reducing aeration.

Additions of clay will improve the fertility of impoverished soil. Clay, peat substitutes (or peat), and, to some extent, bark help to retain nutrients that might otherwise be lost by leaching.

Problems with additives

Some additives should not be used in certain soil conditions. Fine sand, for example, added in small amounts to heavy soil may make poor drainage worse by blocking the soil pores. Use a more open material, such as gravel or coarse sand, instead.

Fresh manure gives off ammonia and sometimes other substances that may be toxic to plants. If it is not possible to compost the manure or mature it until it is well rotted, apply it to the soil surface in the autumn and leave the soil uncultivated over winter. The manure will gradually rot down and be incorporated into the soil by earthworms.

Fresh straw, leaves, and bark use up nitrogen during their decomposition process, contributing to a possible nitrogen deficiency in the soil unless additional nitrogen fertilizer is applied to the soil at the same time.

For garden compost (see p.533), never use plant remains that are infected with viruses or any material that contains perennial weeds – both are difficult to control or eradicate. This material should be burned.

SOIL ADDITIVES

Adding composts, well-rotted manure, or peat substitutes such as coconut fibre improves the soil structure and helps to hold moisture in the soil. Mushroom compost is alkaline in nature and therefore should not be used with plants requiring acid conditions. Lime (also alkaline) binds clay soil particles into crumbs by a process known as flocculation.

MUSHROOM COMPOST

MANURE

LIME

COCONUT FIBRE

COMPARING SOILS

GOOD SOIL
A well-structured soil has a crumbly, moist texture, with a network of pores that holds both air and water. The soil crumbs bind together but do not form a hard "cap".

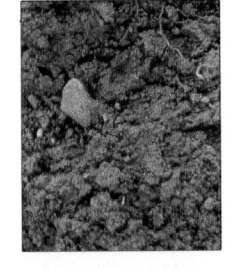

POOR SOIL
This topsoil is hard and compacted, making it almost impossible to cultivate. Drainage will be poor. Cracks appear where the soil has dried out.

SOIL PROBLEMS

COMPACTION
In compacted soil, the pores between the soil particles have been badly compressed. This results in slow drainage and poor aeration.

BLUE MOTTLING
Blue mottling on the soil surface indicates stagnant, waterlogged soil that needs to be drained. The soil may also have an unpleasant smell.

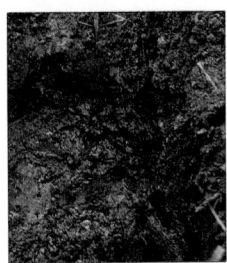

HARDPAN
This is an almost impermeable layer of severely compacted soil. Water will not drain through until the hardpan is broken up and drains are installed.

CAPPING
A crust or "cap" forms on the soil when soil crumbs on the surface are damaged by heavy rain or watering, or by walking on the soil when it is wet.

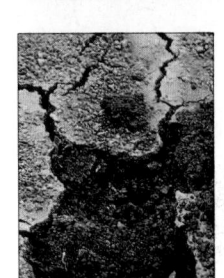

Water

Adequate water is crucial for good plant growth; the amount available depends to some extent on the plant itself but also on soil type and structure, and the method of watering. Water is often in short supply and should not be wasted, so it is important to use good watering and water-conserving techniques. It is also useful to know which (and when) plants are susceptible to drought and which are drought resistant.

An excess of water in the soil (waterlogging) can be as damaging to plants as a lack of soil water. Cultivating the soil and adding organic matter and grit will do much to improve drainage in saturated soil but on severely waterlogged sites an effective drainage system should be installed.

Soil water

In a well-structured soil, water is held in fine capillary pores (which are usually less than 0.1mm (^{1}/$_{160}$in) in diameter), with air in the larger pores; it is therefore possible for soil to be described as "both moist and well drained".

Water is most readily available to plants from pores of the largest diameter. As the pores become smaller, it becomes increasingly difficult for the plants to extract moisture, which means that some soil water always remains unavailable.

Clay soils

Clay soils hold the greatest amount of water but they have a high percentage of fine capillary pores, so plants are not always able to extract enough water for their needs.

HOW NOT TO WATER

Do not water plants at a rate that causes puddling on the soil surface, since this leads to run-off and erodes the soil.

METHODS OF WATERING

BASIN WATERING
Scoop out soil from around the base of the plant, and fill the resulting basin with water.

POT WATERING
Bury a large pot that has a drainage hole close to the plant and fill the pot slowly with water.

Sandy soils

Sandy soils contain coarse pores, and so the water held within them is more readily available than in clay. Sandy soils, however, have a high drainage rate, and there is relatively little capillary movement of water sideways and upwards.

Loams

Loams usually contain a balanced mix of coarse and relatively fine pores – the coarse pores allow rapid drainage while the finer ones retain water, much of which may be extracted by plants in dry conditions.

The water table

Moisture rises to the soil surface by capillary action from the water table below. Heavy clay soils may be saturated to 2m (6ft) above the water table, with some moisture available to plant roots as much as 3.5m (11ft) above it. Silt and most clay soils are saturated to 1.5m (5ft), with moisture available to roots 2.5m (8ft) above the water table. The figures for fine sand are 1.5m (5ft) and 2.4m (7^1/$_2$ft) respectively, and for coarser sand 30cm (1ft) and 1m (3ft). On gravel, there is no water rise at all.

Watering techniques

The aim of watering is to recharge the soil so that reserves will be sufficient to last until the next watering or rainfall.

Always water thoroughly so that water is available deep in the soil. Frequently applying a little water is of limited value, because much of it simply evaporates off the soil surface before it has a chance to penetrate down to the roots of plants.

Moisture take-up

The water supply to a plant is limited by the size of its root system. By improving drainage (see p.529) and rectifying compaction by double digging (see p.526), if necessary, plants are able to develop deeper root systems, with a comparative increase in growth.

The main limitation when watering, however, is the rate at which the soil takes up the moisture. On average, soil absorbs only about 8mm (^{3}/$_8$in) depth of water per hour. Water applied to the soil faster than it is absorbed (for example, by a hand-held hose or watering can with a rose) collects in a pool on the surface until the area covered is sufficient to take it all in. After watering in dry conditions, it is worth examining the soil with an auger – it may be surprising just how little the water has penetrated. If the soil around the roots of the plants is still dry, give the area several further applications once the water from the first application has soaked in.

To reduce water run-off, the ground may be modified by terracing or "dishing" to create a hollow trough around each plant (see above), which ensures that water reaches the roots. Pot watering (see above), garden sprinklers (see p.469), and trickle or drip feed systems (see p.469) are efficient methods of watering, since water is supplied to the roots over several hours.

Water-conserving techniques

Mulching the surface of the soil (see p.532) improves rain penetration and minimizes evaporation. By controlling weeds effectively (see p.524), you will ensure that no soil water is wasted on unwanted plants.

Water deficiency

Once a plant begins to wilt, its growth rate has already begun to slow down. In many areas, water use will exceed water supply during summer, so the soil suffers a net loss of moisture. Digging additives such as manure into the soil improves structure (see p.527) and water retention, which helps to prevent a water deficit from occurring, but unless an existing deficit is made up by irrigation, the soil becomes progressively drier. Regular watering is therefore essential.

The local meteorological office will have figures for the typical monthly water loss from the soil and through leaves by transpiration (known as potential evapotranspiration), and also for the average monthly rainfall. These figures are useful when calculating how often to water but, for greater accuracy, it is better to take your own rainfall measurements each month rather than using the average figures.

Seasonal needs

The point at which a water deficit begins to affect plant growth depends on the plants themselves. High-yield plants usually need plenty of water, so the soil should be kept moist. Some plants have critical periods of growth, during which time water supplies are vital: the first half of summer, for example, is much more important than the second for young ornamental trees. Fruit trees need ample water as the fruits swell, as do potato tubers, and standard trees are likely to require watering throughout their first season since their top-growth is frequently out of proportion to their roots.

Watering is especially important for newly planted or transplanted plants, and those in shallow soils and in containers. Seedlings, too, have low drought resistance, and a reliable water supply is essential.

Drought conditions

Even well-established garden plants suffer during prolonged drought, although no perceptible damage may be seen for some time. Moderate drought may, however, improve the flavour of some fruits and vegetables, especially tomatoes.

In areas of low rainfall, there is increasing interest in using plants that are adapted to droughts (xerophytes): *Cistus*, lavenders (*Lavandula*), and *Phlomis*, as well as many grey- and silver-leaved plants, are good examples. Grass tolerates prolonged, dry weather well; although lawns may become brown, they quickly recover once rain falls. Regular watering in summer is not essential, therefore, unless you want to keep your lawn looking green.

Waterlogged soil

Waterlogging occurs when the amount of water entering the soil exceeds the amount that drains out of it. Particularly vulnerable are those areas where the water table is high (see p.528) or where the soil is compacted and thus poorly structured.

Roots (except those of bog plants) are unable to function effectively in waterlogged soil and may eventually die if drainage is not improved. Wet soil is often low in certain nutrients (notably nitrogen) and, as a result, mineral deficiencies may prove a problem. Since wet soil tends to be cold, plant growth may be slow in spring. Diseases such as clubroot also flourish in waterlogged soil.

Rushes, sedges, and mosses growing on the ground suggest that the soil may be waterlogged. A sharp dividing line between peaty topsoil and subsoil also indicates poor drainage. On waterlogged clay, the soil may have a stagnant smell and a yellow or blue-grey colour, which is known as gleying.

Poor drainage may be confirmed by pouring water into a hole that is 30–60cm (12–24in) deep. If the water remains for hours or even days, then the soil needs draining. If digging deeper or trying to push a sturdy metal rod into the soil meets with resistance, this indicates that there is a layer of hardpan (see *Soil Problems*, p.527).

Improving drainage

Where waterlogging is not severe and there is excess surface water only, this may be diverted from the site by shaping garden surfaces so that the water flows into drainage ditches. To improve drainage on sites where there is a high water table, install an underground drainage system, preferably using a specialist contractor to carry out the work. If drains already exist on the site, check for blockages in the drainage ditches, or for damaged drainage pipes.

Drainage ditches and French drains

A system of open ditches is the best method of carrying away any excess water. These should be 1–1.2m (3–4ft) deep, with sloping sides. Just as effective but less obtrusive are French drains, which are gravel-filled drainage ditches topped with upturned turf and topsoil.

Drainage systems and soakaways

A soakaway is a gravel-filled pit into which excess water runs via underground drains or drainage ditches (see below). This method of drainage is effective on sites where there is surface compaction, since it breaks through any layer of hardpan. To construct a soakaway, dig a trench approximately 1.5m (5ft) wide and up to 2m (6ft) deep. Fill it with crushed stone, topped with a layer of coarse sand or gravel, and lay turf or a grate over the top. Install drains about 60cm (24in) below ground (see below) to lead from the surrounding land to the soakaway.

Water storage areas

Alternatively, create a water storage area where water collects in a pond or large container, or gradually soaks away. A pond is beneficial to wildlife, but its success depends on the degree of sediment in the drainage water – too much will make the pond rich in nutrients, therefore becoming prone to silting up and excessive algal growth.

Water that is collected in containers may be recycled for use in the garden. Collecting water that is allowed gradually to soak away helps to replenish groundwater reserves and reduces silt pollution of rivers.

HOW TO LAY DRAINAGE PIPES ON A FLAT SITE

Topsoil

Inverted turves

Coarse sand or gravel

Large gravel or crushed stone

Tile drain

This cross-section of a drainage trench shows a tile drain in place on a layer of gravel or crushed stone, with another layer on top, followed by coarse sand and inverted turves.

Drainage ditch

Pipe slopes down into the ditch

On a flat site, the plastic pipes or tile drains should be sloping. This will allow the water collecting in them to flow into a connecting ditch or a soakaway in another part of the site.

Installing drains

A system of perforated plastic pipes or tile drains laid in a herringbone pattern underground provides an effective method of drainage. Lay the pipes or tile drains in trenches on a bed of gravel, then cover them with further layers of gravel and sand, before refilling the trench with topsoil. Water from the surrounding site can seep through the gravel and into the pipes, which then carry it to a drainage ditch or soakaway. On level ground, slope the pipes, to encourage water to drain away quickly. Where the ground slopes, simply lay pipes parallel to the ground. Install drains before plants are in place, if possible, since the work causes considerable upheaval.

A DRAINAGE SYSTEM ON A SLOPING SITE

High ground

On sloping ground, lay the pipes or tile drains to run parallel to the ground. Simply butt them together in a gravel-filled trench.

Arrows show the direction of water flow

Trenches for pipes or tile drains, about 60cm (24in) deep

Gravel in trench surrounding pipes or tile drains

Gravel-filled drainage ditch or soakaway

Lowest level

Soil nutrients and fertilizers

The nutrients needed by plants are composed of mineral ions, which are absorbed in solution from the soil through the roots and used with carbon dioxide and water to make food. Macronutrients include nitrogen (N), phosphorus (P), potassium (K), magnesium (Mg), calcium (Ca), and sulphur (S); these are required in relatively large amounts by plants.

Micronutrients, or trace elements, are equally important but required only in small amounts; they include iron (Fe), manganese (Mn), copper (Cu), zinc (Zn), boron (Bo), molybdenum (Mb), and chlorine (Cl).

To ensure healthy plant growth, fertilizers containing nutrients may be added to the soil but this is only necessary when the soil is unable to provide adequate amounts of the nutrients required. On the majority of soils, only nitrogen, which promotes vigorous growth, phosphorus (phosphates), for assisting strong root growth, and potassium (potash), which improves flowering and fruiting, need to be added regularly. This is because the commonest nutrient deficiency problems for plants are caused by a lack of either nitrogen or potassium. Nitrogen deficiency (see p.554) causes reduced growth, and potassium deficiency (see p.554) causes leaf discoloration. Phosphate deficiency (see p.554) is less common. Manganese/iron deficiency (see p.555) causes browning of leaves, and may be a problem if acid-loving plants are grown in alkaline soil or watered with hard water.

Types of fertilizer

Deciding the amount and which type of fertilizer to apply can be complex. Understanding how each type works will make gardening more productive and even perhaps more environmentally friendly.

Bulky organic fertilizers
Weight for weight, bulky organic fertilizers supply fewer nutrients than inorganic fertilizers. For example, one tonne (0.98 tons) of manure typically contains 6kg (13.2lb) of nitrogen, 1kg (2.2lb) of phosphorus and 4kg (8.8lb) of potassium; the equivalent amount of nutrients in a chemical form is provided by only 30kg (66lb) of inorganic fertilizer.

Manures are, however, integral to organic growing because the organic "waste" matter that makes them so bulky provides greater benefits than a simple nutrient analysis would suggest. Manures normally contain high levels of micronutrients, and are a long-term source of nitrogen, although they may vary in quality, some batches having a poor nutrient content. Manures also provide the conditions in which worms thrive. Additions of manure improve the structure and water content of most soils (see p.526); and since this encourages root growth, it increases the uptake of nutrients by plants.

Concentrated fertilizers
Proprietary mixtures of blood, fish, and bone are good examples of concentrated organic fertilizers; they are easy to handle and contain fairly consistent proportions of nutrients but are relatively expensive for each unit of nutrient. Their characteristic slow release of nutrients is partly dependent on breakdown by soil organisms, so they may not be effective when these organisms are inactive, as in cold weather.

Soluble fertilizers
Soluble inorganic fertilizers contain high percentages of a given nutrient, weight for weight, and most are easy to transport, handle, and apply, although a few are unpleasant to handle. They are usually the cheapest source per unit of nutrient. They give a quick-acting boost to plants deficient in nutrients, and permit precise control over the timing of nutrient release. However, a large proportion of soluble fertilizer may be wasted on sandy soils because of leaching.

When using soluble inorganic fertilizers, be selective about which mineral ions are applied to the soil, since some may be damaging to particular plants. Redcurrants, for example, are sensitive to chloride salts, such as potassium chloride, so sulphates should be used instead. Large applications of some inorganic salts make the soil more saline and may harm beneficial soil organisms. Apply soluble inorganic fertilizers in split applications, sparingly but fairly frequently, rather than in a single, large dose.

Slow-release fertilizers
These are complex fertilizer formulations that are designed to release nutrients gradually. Some slowly degrade in the soil, while others absorb water until they swell and burst open. Many have membranes that gradually release nutrients from an internal store. By varying the thicknesses of these membranes, a mix is produced that will supply nutrients to plants over many months or even years in some cases.

Slow-release inorganic fertilizers are expensive but they overcome many of the drawbacks of soluble fertilizers, such as the need for split applications and loss of nutrients from the fertilizer by leaching. They make feeding container-grown plants much less time-consuming,

NUTRIENT CONTENT OF FERTILIZERS			
	% Nitrogen (N)	% Phosphate (P_2O_5)	% Potash (K_2O)
ORGANIC			
Animal manure	0.6	0.1	0.5
Garden compost	0.5	0.3	0.8
Bone meal	3.5	20	–
Fish, blood, and bone	3.5	8	–
Hoof and horn	13	–	–
Seaweed meal	2.8	0.2	2.5
Mushroom compost	0.7	0.3	0.3
Rock potash	5	8	10
Rock phosphate	–	26	12
Wood ash	0.1	0.3	1
Cocoa shells	3	1	3.2
INORGANIC			
Growmore	7	7	7
Ammonium nitrate	35	–	–
Triple superphosphate	–	44	–
Potassium chloride	–	–	60
Potassium sulphate	–	–	49

COMPARING FERTILIZERS

GARDEN COMPOST

MUSHROOM COMPOST

COCOA SHELLS

FISH, BLOOD, AND BONE

SOLUBLE INORGANIC FERTILIZER

These comparisons show the relative amounts of different types of fertilizer required to supply roughly the same quantity of nutrients.

SLOW-RELEASE FERTILIZERS

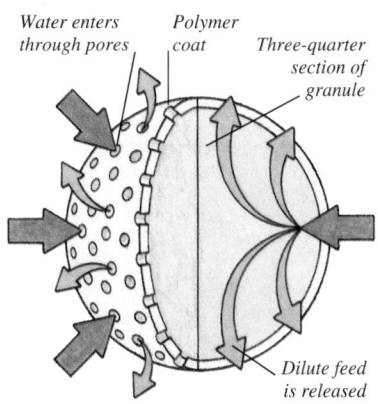

Water enters through pores *Polymer coat* *Three-quarter section of granule*

Dilute feed is released

Water enters the fertilizer granules through pores in the polymer coat, which builds up pressure inside, splitting the granules open.

since they remove the need to add fertilizer each time the plants are watered during the growing season. The nutrient release pattern of slow-release fertilizers may be difficult to predict, however, especially with long-term formulas, since the breakdown depends on the pH level of soil, as well as on the moisture content and temperature of the soil.

Green manures

These are plants that are grown purely to be dug back into the soil to improve fertility and add to the organic content. They are used on land that would otherwise be left fallow and can help to prevent nutrients from being washed away, since fallow land is more prone to leaching. Do not use invasive plants as green manures, however.

Borage (*Borago officinalis*), ryegrass (*Lolium perenne*), and comfrey (*Symphytum officinale*) are excellent perennial green manures. Mixtures of fast-germinating annuals are also used. Plants such as peas and annual lupins (*Lupinus*) have nitrogen-fixing bacteria in root nodules which

enable them to obtain nitrogen from air in the soil. The organic matter these plants provide may contribute as much nitrogen as would be added in a standard fertilizing regime; it has a low carbon:nitrogen ratio and so breaks down rapidly, providing easily available nitrogen.

Applying fertilizers

Fertilizers may be scattered over the surface of the soil or placed around individual plants. Some fertilizers are also available in liquid form for application to the soil surface or as foliar feeds directly onto leaves.

When applying fertilizers, always use gloves and do not breathe in any of the dust or vapour arising from them. Use only the recommended quantities, since too much fertilizer could damage the plants.

Broadcast fertilization

Scattering fertilizer over the whole soil surface benefits the greatest area of soil and minimizes the risk of plant injury from overfeeding. In dry weather, however, the uptake of some nutrients may be poor, particularly of immobile nutrients such as phosphates so, whenever possible, dig phosphates into the soil.

When broadcast fertilizing, do not allow any of the material to touch the leaves or stems of plants, since scorching may result.

Fertilizer placement

Fertilizing around the base of a plant (but not so that it touches the stem) is an economical and efficient feeding method, as plant roots quickly spread through the fertilized area.

Liquid fertilizers

Dissolving fertilizer in water before application is a particularly efficient method of applying nutrients, especially if the soil is dry. Do not use

liquid feeds when rain is forecast, since the liquid may be washed away, and apply the feeds early in the day to avoid possible sun scorch.

Foliar fertilizers

Liquid fertilizers sprayed onto leaf surfaces are known as foliar feeds; they may be used to correct mineral deficiencies that are caused by certain soil conditions, such as high pH. For deep-rooted plants, such as fruit trees, foliar feeds may also be used to correct deficiencies in nutrients that are relatively insoluble.

Liming

Liming or adding lime-rich material such as mushroom compost increases the alkaline balance of the soil. This is sometimes desirable to improve yields on the vegetable plot but is seldom worthwhile for ornamental plants – it is preferable to choose plants that are adapted to the existing conditions.

Types of lime

Ordinary lime (calcium carbonate) is usually the best choice because, although bulky, it is easy to handle and relatively safe to use. Quicklime (calcium oxide) is more efficient at raising pH but as it is caustic it may scorch plant material; there is also a risk of over-liming with quicklime. Slaked, or hydrated, lime (calcium hydroxide) is made by treating quicklime with water; it is slightly less efficient than quicklime but it is less caustic and easier to handle.

Applying lime

Lime may be spread on the soil at any time of year, but it should be applied as far in advance of planting as possible and preferably be well dug in. Choose a windless day and always wear protective goggles. Do not lime the soil every year, because

LIMING

Using a spade, spread the lime over the surface of the soil, then distribute it evenly with a rake (see inset). Do not plant or sow for about a month.

overliming may contribute to nutrient deficiencies, and always take pH readings in several different parts of the plot first, since any uneven rates of breakdown may cause temporary, localized problems. The following table indicates the average amount of lime required (in g/sq m) for a particular type of soil of a given pH to achieve a level of 6.5pH (see also "Optimum pH", p.523):

STARTING pH	SAND (g/sq m)	LOAM (g/sq m)	CLAY (g/sq m)
4.5	190g	285g	400g
5.0	155g	235g	330g
5.5	130g	190g	260g
6.0	118g	155g	215g

To raise soil pH quickly, add lime during digging or other cultivation methods. If required for established plantings, lime may be applied as a top-dressing and watered in.

Do not apply lime at the same time as manure because lime reacts with the nitrogen-rich manure, releasing nitrogen in the form of ammonia. This may damage plants and wastes nitrogen. If required, apply lime and manure in alternate years.

GREEN MANURING

Sow seed for green manures on fallow ground. Cut the plants to the ground when about 20cm (8in) tall, digging them in after a day or two.

HOW TO APPLY FERTILIZER

BROADCASTING
To apply fertilizer in accurate amounts over large areas, mark out the plot into square metres or yards, using string or canes. Fill a pot or bowl with the recommended quantity of fertilizer and sprinkle it evenly over each section of the plot.

PLACEMENT
Sprinkle the fertilizer around the base of the plant, making sure that none touches the leaves or stem.

Top-dressings and mulches

Top-dressings and mulches are materials that are applied to the surface of the soil. They are used to improve plant growth in some way, either by adding nutrients to the soil, by increasing the organic content, or by reducing water loss from the soil. Alternatively they may be used in a decorative manner.

Top-dressings

The term "top-dressing" is used in two ways. First, it describes surface applications of soluble fertilizers around plants. Second, it refers to additives that are applied to the soil surface or to lawns. For example, a lawn may be top-dressed with sand or fine organic material, which will eventually be washed in by rain.

Gravel or grit is sometimes used as a top-dressing for plants in beds and containers to provide quick drainage away from the "collars" of plants that are sensitive to excess moisture. They also act as a mulch and discourage growth of mosses or lichens on the soil surface.

Plants may also be top-dressed with gravel or stone chippings simply to achieve a decorative effect.

Mulches

Mulches are available in organic and inorganic forms and improve plant growth in several ways: they regulate soil temperature, keeping

MATERIALS USED AS TOP-DRESSINGS

TOP-DRESSINGS AS ADDITIVES
Some top-dressings, such as peat and well-rotted compost, are added to the soil around plants to provide humus and a steady supply of nutrients. Sand, mixed with loam and peat, is used as a top-dressing on lawns to improve aeration.

SAND

DECORATIVE TOP-DRESSINGS
Materials such as gravel and grit are added to the compost surface in containers or to the soil surface in a border or bed, particularly around low-growing plants such as alpines. These materials improve surface drainage as well as setting off the plants.

GRAVEL

PEAT   COMPOST   COARSE GRIT   CORNISH GRIT

plant roots warm in winter and cool in summer; they reduce water loss from the soil surface; and they help to stop weed seeds germinating by preventing light from reaching them.

Always remove all perennial weeds before mulching, otherwise they benefit from the effects of the mulch, to the detriment of your plants. A mulch should not be applied when the soil is cold or frozen, since the insulation effect will be counter-productive, and the soil remain cold – instead, wait until the soil has warmed up in spring.

Organic mulches

To be effective, an organic mulch should be long-lasting and not easily dislodged by rain. It should also have a loose structure that allows water to pass through it quickly.

Coarse bark is one of the most useful organic mulches because it prevents weed seeds in the soil beneath from germinating, and weeds that do appear are easily removed.

Garden compost and peat substitutes (or peat) are not quite as effective because they provide an ideal medium for the germination of weed seeds and are quickly mixed into the soil, although they do improve the texture of the soil as a result.

Inorganic mulches

Inorganic mulches made of horticultural paper or thin sheets of plastic or fibre fleece are widely available and easy to use. Lay them in place over the soil surface and secure them with metal pegs to stop them blowing away.

Plastic sheet mulches raise the soil temperature slightly and are particularly useful when growing crops. A disadvantage of sheet mulches is that, once they are in place, organic matter cannot be incorporated into the soil; it also decays more slowly underneath a sheet mulch. If required, extra nutrients may be added through holes punched with a dibber in the plastic sheeting, and then watered in. Unless sheet mulches are perforated, almost no water evaporates from the soil, and rain cannot penetrate it; do not, therefore, place a sheet mulch on dry soil or on soil that is waterlogged.

Floating mulches are sheets of light plastic or fibre fleece that are used like cloches – as the crop grows, the floating mulch is raised by the plants. Floating mulches are often perforated or permeable to allow rain and air through to the soil. Their main purpose is to increase soil temperature; they may also act as a barrier against pests.

LOOSE MULCHES

APPLYING THE MULCH
A loose mulch regulates soil temperature, retains moisture, and discourages weeds. It should preferably be about 10–15cm (4–6in) deep.

AREA TO MULCH
For small to medium-sized plants, spread a mulch to the full extent of the foliage canopy.

SHEET MULCH

A plastic sheet mulch controls weeds effectively over a large area and raises soil temperature slightly. Using a spade, anchor the sheet by sinking the edges into 5cm (2in) slits dug into the soil.

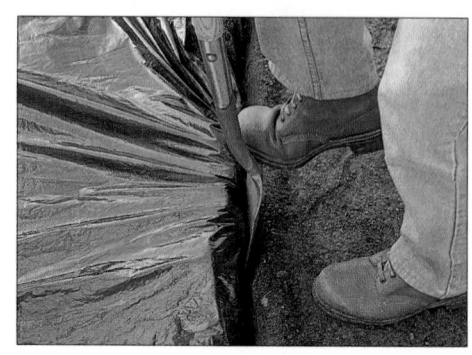

Composts

There are two distinct forms of compost: garden compost is decayed organic matter and is a soil additive; potting and propagation composts are made from precise combinations of (mainly) organic materials, and are used for growing plants in containers and for propagation.

Garden compost

The contribution of garden compost to the productivity of the garden can be enormous. It should be added to the soil when the rate of breakdown of the organic matter has levelled off; by this stage, it should be dark, crumbly, and sweet-smelling.

Making garden compost

To make a compost heap, build up a mixture of nitrogen-rich material (such as grass clippings) and carbon-rich material (such as bark and shredded paper), preferably in a ratio of 1:2. Almost any vegetable waste may be composted, but meat and cooked foods should not be used, as these attract vermin. Do not use thick layers of grass clippings, as they inhibit air movement. Pruning clippings may be used, although any woody stems must be shredded first. Use only young weeds; those with seed, or about to set seed, should be burned, as should all pernicious, perennial weeds.

Compost additives

Many materials compost satisfactorily, but additional nitrogen will speed up the process. The nitrogen may be provided as artificial fertilizer, proprietary starter compost, or, preferably, as manure, which has the advantage of containing high levels of soil organisms. Add this, as necessary, to the compost heap so that there are alternate layers of organic material and manure.

If the material in the compost heap is acidic, micro-organisms will not work efficiently – adding lime will make it more alkaline.

The composting process

The process of making compost generates a high temperature, which encourages the natural breakdown of organic matter and also helps to kill weed seeds and some pests and diseases. To heat up sufficiently, a compost heap should be at least 1 cubic metre (1 cubic yard) in size but 2 cubic metres is preferable. Compost reaches its maximum temperature in two or three weeks and

matures in about three months. Turning the heap speeds up the process and ensures complete breakdown. An ammonia odour indicates that the compost is too rich in nitrogen; a smell of rotten eggs means that the heap lacks air.

Slow composting

Composting may be undertaken in a non-intensive way. Heaps of moist leaves, for example, eventually rot down, even if they are not in a bin. No starter material is added, and the heap is not turned. There will, however, be some material that does not break down fully – this will need to be composted again.

Potting composts

Pot plants need a growing medium that is both well aerated and water-retentive, with a resilient structure that can withstand heavy watering. For best results, always use the most suitable type for the purpose. Standardized potting composts were first formulated by the John Innes Horticultural Institute of Great Britain in the 1930s. These are loam-based and also contain peat and coarse sand. Loamless (or soil-less) potting composts (mainly peat-based) were not promoted until the 1960s.

Loam-based potting composts

These should contain high-quality loam that is rich in organic matter. The loam is usually obtained by stacking turf for six months or more, and should be sterilized, either chemically or by heating the soil to a high temperature, to kill pests and weed seeds and eliminate diseases.

Loam-based composts provide better conditions than loamless ones for long-term growth. They contain a steady supply of nutrients, and are free-draining, with good aeration and structure. They do not dry out as rapidly as peat-based composts and are less prone to waterlogging. Plants also grow on more readily when transplanted to garden soil.

Loamless potting composts

These are lightweight and clean to use. Many are based on peat, which combines moisture retentiveness with good aeration, and is relatively stable and long-lasting. Peat is low in nutrients and does not hold these well compared with loams, however, so plants must be fed more often than with loam-based compost. Plants grown in loamless potting compost

MAKING A COMPOST BIN

1 *To make the first side, lay 2 timber battens (to act as the uprights) on the ground at least 1m (3ft) apart. Nail planks across them, butting the joints together. Leave an 8cm (3in) gap at top and bottom.*

2 *Make the second side; nail scraps of wood across the top to hold the sides in place temporarily. Nail on the back planks.*

3 *Nail 2 battens inside each upright (inset) for the front planks to slide between. Fix a piece of wood at the base as a "stop".*

4 *Nail planks across the top and bottom of the front panel, to stabilize the bin when the front planks are removed.*

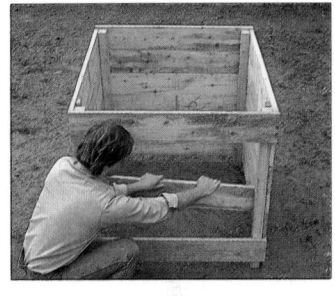

5 *Check that the front planks slide easily between the battens. If necessary, saw a little off the ends.*

USING THE BIN
Place a thick layer of twiggy material at the base; build up the heap in 15cm (6in) layers, sprinkling each layer with a little manure.

Manure

Garden and kitchen waste

may also find it difficult to adapt when transplanted to garden soil. Most loamless potting composts break down rapidly, so that the volume of compost shrinks and the remaining material loses much of its

structure. For long-term containerized plants, the more fibrous the compost the better. Loamless composts dry out rapidly and are hard to re-wet. They also become waterlogged if plants are overwatered.

Peat substitutes

The use of peat-based potting composts poses environmental problems in countries where peatlands are an endangered habitat. Alternative composts, such as those based on coconut fibre and bark, are available but trials on their effectiveness are not yet complete.

Standard potting compost

Potting compost may be either loam- or peat-based. John Innes formulas are loam-based and are made using 7 parts (by volume) good quality, sterilized loam, 3 parts peat substitute (or peat), and 1 part sand. To each cubic metre is added 594g ground limestone, or1.2kg hoof and horn, 1.2kg superphosphate of lime, and 594g potassium sulphate.

The figures for a cubic yard of compost are 1lb each of ground limestone and potassium sulphate, and 2lb each of hoof and horn and superphosphate of lime.

The amount of fertilizer contained in proprietary potting compost may vary, to suit the varying needs of plants. JI No.1 potting compost has relatively little fertilizer; it is suitable for short-term use, as when growing on seedlings and sowing large seed. JI No.2 and No.3 potting composts have twice and three times as much fertilizer respectively as JI No.1 compost and are therefore suitable for larger, established plants.

Loamless potting composts are now used extensively. They are made using 3 parts (by volume) coarse, well-structured peat substitute (or peat) and 1 part sand, and may have varying nutrient levels.

Universal composts

These have physical properties and nutrient supplies somewhere between those of seed and potting composts, and have a wide range of purposes, from growing on seedlings to potting many types of plant.

Special composts

These are used for plants that have specialized growing requirements. Orchid composts are free-draining and often contain charcoal and fine bark. Alpine and cactus composts are very free-draining and sometimes poor in nutrients, to suit the needs of the plants. Ericaceous composts have a low pH and are suitable for growing lime-haters, such as rhododendrons.

Blocking composts

These are peat formulations that are compressed when wet and then moulded to make planting containers and seed modules. These may be planted direct into the soil so there is little disturbance to plant roots.

Bulb fibre compost

This is made from undecomposed sphagnum moss, which has an open structure, and is used to grow bulbs in containers that do not have drainage holes, when poor aeration may be a problem. It gives physical support and retains moisture reasonably well. Its lack of nutrients is unimportant, since bulbs have food reserves.

Propagation composts

When sowing seed (particularly fine seed) and rooting cuttings, a higher success rate is achieved if propagation composts are used.

Standard seed compost

Fine seed needs good contact with the compost to germinate and should be sown in purpose-made seed compost, which is fine-textured, moisture-retentive, and low in nutrients, as salts may damage seedlings.

Standard seed compost (based on the John Innes formula) is made using 2 parts (by volume) sterilized loam, 1 part peat substitute (or peat), and 1 part sand. To each cubic metre is added 1.2kg superphosphate of lime and 594g ground limestone (2lb and 1lb respectively for a cubic yard).

Standard cutting compost

Compost mixes for rooting cuttings are free-draining and intended for use in high-humidity environments. They may be based on bark, perlite, or mixes containing a high percentage of coarse sand. Cutting composts are low in nutrients, so cuttings need feeding once rooted.

A standard cutting compost typically contains 50:50 sand and peat substitute (or peat). To each cubic metre (yard) is added 4.4kg (7$\frac{1}{2}$lb) dolomitic lime; 1.5kg (2$\frac{1}{2}$lb) each of hoof and horn or dried blood, superphosphate of lime, and calcium carbonate; and 148g (4oz) each of potassium nitrate and potassium sulphate. An absence of loam may mean that specialist micro-nutrient fertilizer should be added.

Organic practices

Organic growing methods often aim to minimize the need for cultivation of the soil to preserve natural fertility and reduce weeds. Materials such as manure and other organic fertilizers (see p.530) are integral to organic growing practices, since they help to maintain a good soil structure.

The "no-dig" system

Cultivating the soil paradoxically creates the conditions in which weeds flourish and sometimes causes the natural soil structure to deteriorate. The "no-dig" system is a method of soil cultivation which, in order to preserve the soil structure and prevent loss of nutrients, uses minimal digging, favouring the use of a trowel whenever possible. The "no-dig" system also makes use of mulches for suppressing weeds and conserving moisture. At its extreme, potatoes, for example, need not be buried in the soil but may, instead, be "planted" on the soil surface below a thick covering of mulch.

The deep-bed system

Using the deep-bed system, the soil structure is improved to the required depth with one thorough cultivation (see "Double digging", p.526). Large amounts of organic matter are incorporated at the same time, after which further digging is avoided. If compaction is prevented, by not walking on the beds, further cultivation becomes unnecessary. A natural soil structure develops, encouraged by the organic matter and the high worm population. Further organic matter is added only as mulches and top-dressings.

Because the only disturbance to the surface occurs when planting, any weed seeds below germination level remain dormant and only weed seedlings from wind-blown seeds need to be removed.

THE DEEP-BED METHOD

1 Cultivate the ground deeply and dig in organic matter. To make the bed, mound the surface, using topsoil from the surrounding area, so that the bed is raised slightly.

2 The bed should be no more than 1.5m (5ft) wide, to allow easy access. Because the soil condition is so much improved, it is possible to plant over 4 times as densely as in a conventional bed.

THE "NO-DIG" SYSTEM

1 To grow potatoes, lay the tubers on the soil surface, then cover with a 15–20cm (6–8in) layer of mulch.

2 Cover the potatoes with black plastic, fixing it down securely. Make slits for the seedlings to grow through.

6

PRINCIPLES
OF PROPAGATION

PROPAGATING PLANTS IS *often instinctively undertaken by a gardener, for example when he or she divides up an overcrowded clump of perennials or bulbs, and is a natural extension of plantsmanship. Plant propagation is not difficult once the underlying principles are understood, and it is the best, most satisfactory, and cheapest way to extend the number of plants in the garden. In addition, it provides many opportunities for exchanging plant material with other gardeners, and thereby further increases the range of plants available in cultivation. More advanced techniques include hybridizing in order to create plants with new characteristics such as a different growth habit or flower colour, for example. To many people, the transition from a seed into a healthy plant, the development of a seemingly lifeless hardwood cutting into a vigorous, new tree or shrub, or the formation of a young plant on a piece of leaf is a fascinating process. An understanding of the techniques outlined in this chapter should bring the many rewards to be gained from successful plant propagation within the reach of every gardener.*

Seeds

Seed is much the commonest way by which flowering plants reproduce in nature. It is a sexual method and, as such, always presents the possibility of a variety of genetic combinations, so that the resulting seedlings are variable. Such variation provides the basis by which plants adapt to their environment, and enables the breeding and selection of cultivars with new combinations of desirable characteristics. Seeds may more or less breed true but frequently vary considerably within a species. In horticulture, variation is disadvantageous if the plants raised are to retain particular characteristics, but advantageous when new, improved characteristics are being sought.

REPRODUCTIVE PARTS OF A ROSE FLOWER

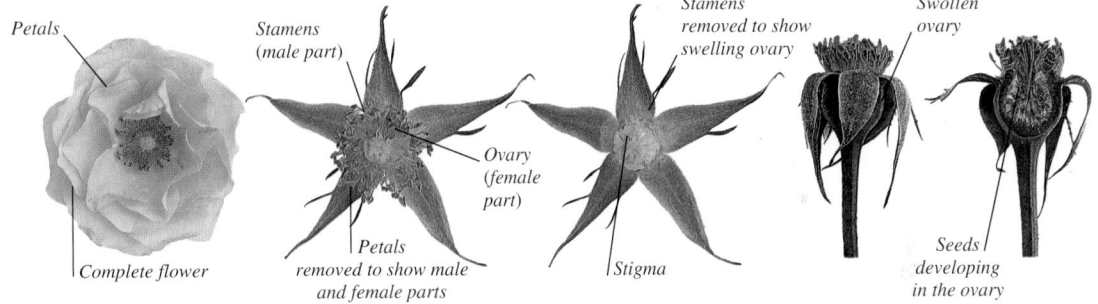

Petals · *Stamens (male part)* · *Stamens removed to show swelling ovary* · *Swollen ovary* · *Ovary (female part)* · *Complete flower* · *Petals removed to show male and female parts* · *Stigma* · *Seeds developing in the ovary*

The parts of a flower needed for reproduction are the stamens – the male part, which bears the pollen – and the pistils – the female part, which comprises one or more stigmas, style, and ovary. The petals attract pollinators.

How the seed develops

Most plants are hermaphrodite – that is, each flower bears male and female parts. As the flower matures, pollen is transferred onto one or more stigmas of the same flower (self-pollination) or of a flower on another plant of the same species (cross-pollination) by insects, birds, water, or wind. The pollen grains then produce pollen tubes, which grow down the style towards the eggs in the ovary, and fertilization occurs when the male and female nuclei fuse. From these develop the embryos, which, nourished by adjacent storage tissue within a seed, are capable of forming complete new plants.

Collecting and storing seed

In general, seed should be collected from a plant as soon as it is ripe and then stored in a dry, dark, airy place at 1–5°C (34–41°F) until it is used. Certain seeds, however, have special requirements. Some are viable for only short periods and should be sown as soon as possible. Others may be stored for very long periods at low temperatures without losing viability. Fleshy fruits should be soaked and softened in water, the seeds removed from the flesh, and then air-dried at 10–20°C (50–68°F). Before they are dry, however, seeds of most stone fruits (e.g. cherry) and that of some berried shrubs (e.g. *Berberis* and cotoneaster) need stratifying (see p.536).

Keep a close watch on fruits that split to release their seeds. As soon as a seed capsule splits, harvest it together with other capsules that are nearing maturity, even though they have not yet opened. Dry them in clean paper bags before separating out the seeds. When a few wind-distributed seeds blow away, collect the mature seed by covering the seed-bearing branches with fine muslin or paper bags; or cut one or two seed-bearing branches and place them in water indoors to mature.

How to overcome dormancy

The seeds of some plants have in-built mechanisms to assist in controlling the time of germination; for example, many seeds do not germinate in late autumn, when conditions are unfavourable for seedling growth, but remain dormant until the temperature and other factors are more suitable. This dormancy is achieved by a variety of means including the presence of chemical inhibitors in the seed, by hardened seed coats that must rot or be breached before the seed can germinate, or by the need for the seed to experience alternating cold and warm periods. Several methods have been developed horticulturally to overcome this natural dormancy so the seeds will germinate more quickly and are therefore less likely to fail.

Scarification
The aim is to break down the hardened seed coat and allow water to enter, thereby speeding up germination.

SCARIFICATION

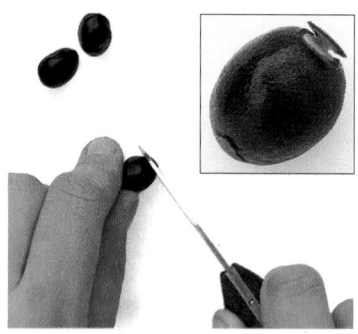

Before planting, carefully nick the hard coat on seeds such as Paeonia lutea *with a clean, sharp knife so that the seed can absorb moisture.*

Large, hard-coated seeds, such as those of the legume family, may be nicked with a knife. Smaller seeds may be shaken in a jar lined with abrasive paper or one containing sharp gravel.

Warm stratification
This is used for hard-coated seeds of many woody species (see *Tree Seed Requiring Stratification*, p.57, and *Shrub Seed that Requires Special Treatment*, p.87). Place the seeds in a plastic bag in an equal volume of sand and leaf mould, or an equal volume of peat substitute (or peat) and sand, and store for 4–12 weeks at 20–25°C (68–77°F). This is usually followed by a period of cold stratification prior to the seeds being sown.

Cold stratification
Soak the seeds for a period of up to 24 hours, then add them to a mix of moist peat:sand in a plastic bag or place them in an open dish with moist filter paper. Refrigerate the seeds at 1–5°C (34–41°F) for 4–12 weeks until germination starts. Alternatively, place the seeds in a perforated tin containing 1 part seed to 3 parts moist sand and bury the tin outdoors, at a depth of 60cm (2ft), for one or two winters. Periodically, dig up the tin and check for germination. Once this occurs, sow the seeds immediately.

COLD STRATIFICATION

Before / *After*

Lupin seeds, after soaking in water for 24 hours during cold stratification, will have swelled slightly.

Requirements for germination
In order to germinate, a seed needs water, air, warmth, and, for some species, light. The growing medium needs to be a fine compost capable of drawing water up to seeds placed near its surface. To aid this capillary rise, the compost is firmed lightly using a presser board. Without this firming, air pockets occur, and the water columns essential for capillary rise are broken. The compost, however, must not be compacted or so damp that air cannot penetrate; seeds will almost certainly fail in such anaerobic compost as they cannot obtain the oxygen vital for growth. Seed composts have only about a quarter of the fertilizer content of potting composts and often contain a fungicide to prevent "damping off" diseases (p.568). For most successful results, the temperature for germination of most seeds should be 20–30°C (68–86°F); heated propagators are useful for maintaining a steady temperature (see "Heated propagator units", p.543).

Light requirements vary during germination: some seeds need light (e.g. *Alyssum*, begonia, *Calceolaria*, and *Genista*), but others are inhibited by it (e.g. *Allium*, delphinium, *Nigella*, and phlox). There is no way of distinguishing seeds requiring dark conditions from those needing light by physical examination; if the dark/light requirement is unknown, initially sow the seed in the dark; if it fails to germinate after a period of some weeks, place it in the light.

Sowing and aftercare

After sowing the seed in containers or in open ground, do not allow the compost to dry out or become too waterlogged; cover the containers with glass or plastic and set in an appropriate environment (see "The propagation environment", p.542). The first sign of germination is the emergence of the radicle, or primary root, followed, in epigeal germination, by the cotyledons, or seed leaves, which

HOW A SEED GERMINATES

In hypogeal germination (right), the cotyledons, or seed leaves, stay below soil level, whereas in epigeal germination (far right), they appear above ground.

Radicle

True leaves

Soil level

Cotyledon

True leaves

Cotyledon

Radicle

SEEDLING GROWTH

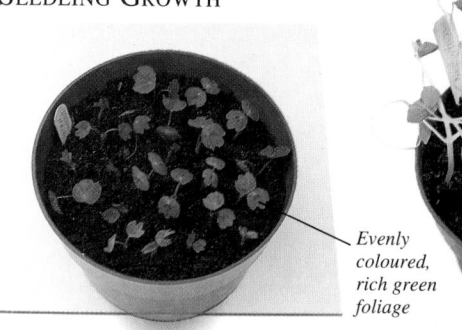

Evenly coloured, rich green foliage

Long, thin stems

HEALTHY SEEDLINGS
Sturdy, well-spaced nasturtium (Tropaeolum) *seedlings flourishing under glass and ready to be pricked out.*

UNHEALTHY SEEDLINGS
If not pricked out early enough, the seedlings will become pale, crowded, and etiolated – and may die.

provide the initial food reserves. The true foliage leaves appear later and generally differ from the cotyledons.

When the seedlings are large enough to handle, they should be "pricked out" (see ANNUALS AND BIENNIALS, "Pricking out", p.183). Failure to do so results in weak growth, because the crowded seedlings compete for light and nutrients and readily succumb to fungal infection. Once transplanted, return the seedlings to the warm germination environment to re-establish; then gradually harden them off by placing the containers in cooler conditions (see "Hardening off", p.543). A

TRUE LEAVES

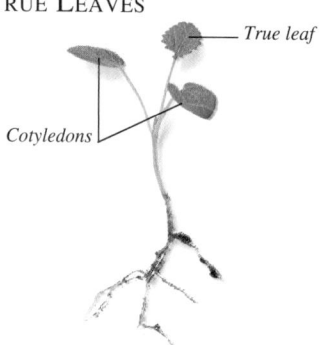

True leaf

Cotyledons

As the cotyledons, or seed leaves, wither, the true leaves gradually take over the process of photosynthesis.

cold frame, closed at first, then opened in stages, provides a suitable environment for hardening off seedlings.

Producing hybrid plants

When hybridizing plants, it is important to prevent self-pollination. For controlled cross-pollination, petals, sepals, and stamens are removed from the flowers on the proposed female parent and the denuded flowers protected from insects by paper or plastic bags until the stigmas on the female plant are sticky and receptive. Pollen, previously collected from air-dried stamens, is then transferred to the stigmas and the flowers are protected from insects once again until fertilization has occurred. Hybrid seed will develop in the ovaries and should be collected when ripe and according to its requirements (see also THE ROSE GARDEN, "Hybridizing", p.134).

F1 and F2 hybrids
For the gardener seeking uniformity and near-perfection, F1 and F2 hybrid seed is available for a limited range of plants, mostly annuals. Such seed needs a complex plant breeding technique and is therefore more expensive.

The first generation derived from crossing two carefully maintained, genetically inbred plants of the same species is termed "first filial generation", or F1, hybrid. This process combines the benefits of greater uniformity that can result from inbreeding with the vigour that can flow from cross-breeding. F1 hybrids are usually more vigorous than their parents and give uniformity in flower characteristics such as colour and form that seldom occurs with open-pollinated seed. Sometimes two controlled crosses from four selected lines are used to produce a "second filial generation", or F2, hybrid – retaining some of the vigour and uniformity of the F1 parents but often with other favoured characteristics less evident in the F1s.

Layering

Layering is a natural form of propagation: roots are induced to develop by covering a stem with soil while it is still attached to the parent plant. The rooted portion of stem is then separated from the parent plant and grown on.

The stem to be layered is often cut, ring-barked, or twisted. This partially interrupts the flow of hormones and carbohydrates, which, as they accumulate there, help to promote root growth. The tissues beyond the constriction are slightly water-stressed, and this, too, favours root formation. Another important root stimulus is the exclusion of light from the stem: light-starved cells then become thin-walled and roots form more readily. In order to stimulate rooting further, use a rooting hormone at the point of layering.

Methods of layering

Layering methods are classified in three groups: those in which a stem is brought down to the soil (simple, serpentine, natural, and tip layering); those in which soil is mounded over a stem (stooling, trench layering, and French layering); and air layering, where the "soil" is brought up to the plant stem. The word "soil" is used loosely here to mean any growing medium such as peat, sand, sawdust, or sphagnum moss.

Simple layering

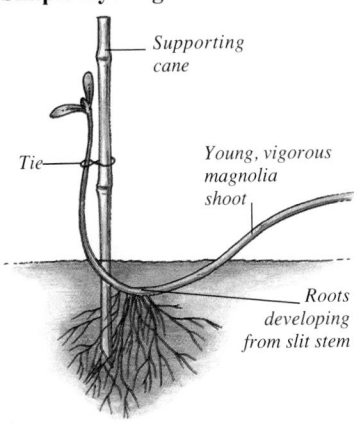

Supporting cane

Tie

Young, vigorous magnolia shoot

Roots developing from slit stem

This method is best carried out between autumn and spring. The parent plant should be young and pruned the previous season to produce vigorous, flexible stems, which can be brought down to soil level and will root readily. A slanting cut is made on the underside of the stem to be layered, which is firmly pegged or secured at this point into the soil. The shoot tip is tied to a vertical cane, inserted in the soil. The following autumn, if the layer is well rooted, it can be cut from the parent plant (see also ORNAMENTAL SHRUBS, "Simple layering", p.88, and CLIMBING PLANTS, "Simple layering", p.115).

SERPENTINE LAYERING

Parent plant

Soil level

Peg holding clematis stem under mounded soil

Roots appearing between nodes

Serpentine layering

This modified form of simple layering is used for plants with pliable stems, such as clematis. Long, young stems are mounded with soil, leaving buds exposed to produce aerial shoots (see also CLIMBING PLANTS, "Propagation by serpentine layering", p.115).

Natural layering

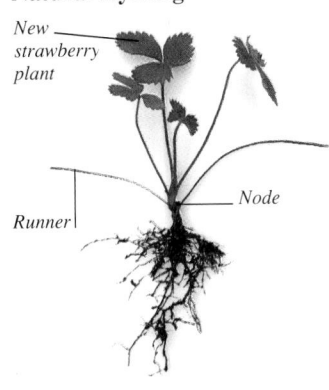

New strawberry plant

Runner

Node

Some plants, such as strawberries, reproduce naturally by sending out a series of runners. These then root at a node, forming a new plant. Once the new plant is fully established, sever it from the parent and grow on (see also "Strawberries: Propagation", p.410).

Tip layering

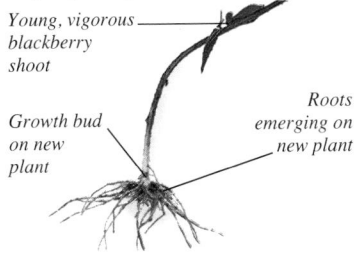

Young, vigorous blackberry shoot

Growth bud on new plant

Roots emerging on new plant

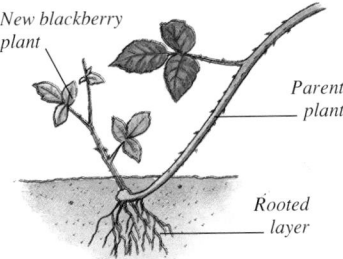

New blackberry plant

Parent plant

Rooted layer

This method is for shrubs and climbers that produce roots from their shoot tips; one of the commonest examples in nature is the blackberry. In summer, a young, vigorous shoot tip is buried in soil in a hole 7–10cm (3–4in) deep. A new shoot, which has developed from

the tip, appears a few weeks later; the young plant may then be separated from its parent. Grow on the rooted layer *in situ*; transplant it the following spring, if required (see also "Blackberries: Tip layering", p.411).

Stooling

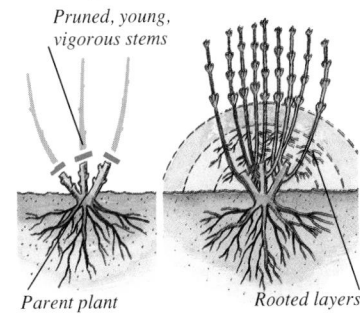

Pruned, young, vigorous stems

Parent plant

Rooted layers

Although important for the commercial production of rootstocks, stooling, or mound-layering, is used by amateurs only for a few woody plants. The stems of a young parent plant are cut back in late winter or early spring to within 8cm (3in) of the ground. When the new shoots are about 15–20cm (6–8in) long, mound soil up over their bases, and again twice more until summer. With plants that root easily, such as thyme and sage, there is no need to cut the stems back before mounding. By autumn, the stems will have rooted; they are then separated from the parent plant and transplanted (see also THE HERB GARDEN, "Mound layering", p.301).

Trench layering

Trench, or etiolation, layering is primarily for fruit rootstocks, especially those that are hard to root. The parent plant is planted at an angle, so that its shoots can readily be pegged down in shallow trenches and covered with soil. The rooted shoots can be detached from the parent to form new plants.

TRENCH LAYERING

Parent planted at 30–40° angle

Soil level

5cm (2in) deep trench

Young, vigorous shoots pinned in position

French layering

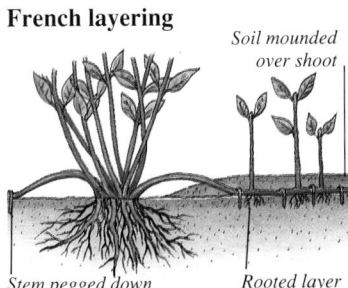

Soil mounded over shoot

Stem pegged down

Rooted layer

French, or continuous, layering is a modified form of stooling. In late winter, peg young shoots from the parent stem to the ground. Any new growths are gradually earthed up to a depth of 15cm (6in). These new shoots should have rooted by autumn and after leaf fall may be separated and grown on (see also ORNAMENTAL SHRUBS, "French layering", p.89).

Air layering

Sealed, plastic sleeve packed with moist sphagnum moss

Diagonal slit in stem to form a tongue

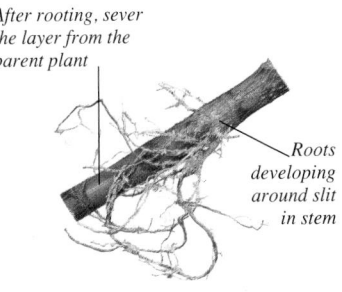

After rooting, sever the layer from the parent plant

Roots developing around slit in stem

Use air, or Chinese, layering – also known as marcottage – on some trees, shrubs, and house plants. In spring or summer, slit an aerial shoot and pack the tongue with sphagnum moss; cover with plastic until roots develop (see *Air Layering a Shrub*, p.89, and THE INDOOR GARDEN, "Air layering", p.456). Rooting may take up to two years.

Cuttings

Propagation from cuttings is the commonest vegetative method. There are three main types: stem, leaf, and root. Stem cuttings produce roots directly from the stem itself or from the mass of thin-walled, wound-healing tissue (callus) that develops at its base. These roots are called adventitious, which means added, or artificial. Some large leaves can be used as cutting material and will develop adventitious roots from near their veins. Vigorous, young roots may also be used for cuttings – propagation by root cuttings is a simple and economical method neglected by most gardeners. Suitable species will produce both adventitious stem buds and roots on the root cutting.

How roots form

Adventitious roots most often develop from young cells produced by the cambium – a layer of cells that generates tissues involved in the thickening of stems. They are usually located close to food- and water-conducting tissues, which provide nourishment as they develop.

Adventitious root growth is also helped by natural hormones called auxins, which accumulate in the base of a cutting. Natural auxins can be supplemented by synthetic auxins, which are available as talc-based powders or as solutions. These aid rooting when applied to the bases of cuttings and are recommended for all plants except those that root very easily. Use only a little hormone, however, as too much could harm immature tissue.

Rooting hormones can be bought with low concentrations of active ingredient for soft cuttings and higher concentrations for hardwood material; some contain a fungicide, which helps to prevent infections entering the cuttings through the wounded tissues.

CALLUS PADS

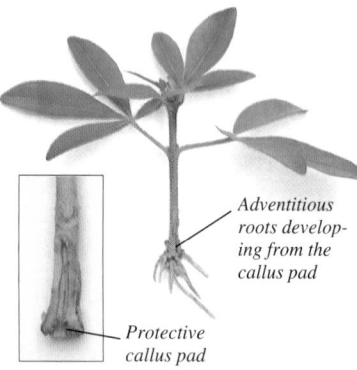

Plants that are difficult to root (here Choisya ternata) form a callus pad of wound-healing tissue at the base of a stem cutting, where they have been severed from the parent plant.

Adventitious roots developing from the callus pad

Protective callus pad

SOFTWOOD CUTTINGS

Prepared cutting trimmed below the node

Rooted cutting

The soft, green stem on a softwood cutting (here Hydrangea macrophylla) usually turns brown as it matures and develops its root system.

Stem cuttings

Stem cuttings are often classified by the maturity of the stem tissue into softwood, greenwood, semi-ripe, and hardwood (or ripewood). The distinction is useful, though imprecise, because tissues develop continuously throughout the growing season.

Softwood cuttings
These are taken in spring, when the new shoots of the parent plant are almost fully developed and just beginning to harden. Such cuttings are generally made from the tips of shoots (tip cuttings), but the new, young basal shoots (basal cuttings) of herbaceous perennials are also used (see PERENNIALS, "Basal stem cuttings", p.166). Since young material roots most readily, softwood cuttings often provide the best chance of rooting species that are difficult to propagate. However, they need a supportive environment, as they lose water and wilt quickly (see "The propagation environment", p.542).

Greenwood cuttings
These are taken from early to midsummer, from slightly more mature wood, when growth begins to slow. They root slightly less readily but survive better than softwood cuttings, although they still require a supportive environment in which to develop into new plants before being hardened off.

Semi-ripe cuttings
Taken in late summer, semi-ripe cuttings are less prone to wilting since the stem tissues are firmer and woody (see ORNAMENTAL SHRUBS, "Semi-ripe cuttings", p.84). Some species with large leaves, for example Ficus and

camellia, may be propagated more economically by taking a short section from a semi-ripe stem just above and below a leaf bud, retaining a single leaf (see ORNAMENTAL SHRUBS, "Leaf-bud cuttings", p.85).

Hardwood cuttings
Fully mature, hardwood (or ripewood) cuttings are taken at the end of the growing season from autumn through to spring, when the tissues are fully ripened. They are the easiest to maintain in a healthy condition but are often slow to root. Hardwood cuttings fall into two categories: leafless deciduous cuttings and broad-leaved evergreen cuttings. Growth of many glossy-leaved evergreens, such as holly (*Ilex*) and rhododendron, wilts readily when young early in the season since their protective leaf waxes develop slowly; they are therefore best propagated by semi-ripe or hardwood cuttings (see also ORNAMENTAL TREES, "Hardwood cuttings", p.54; CLIMBING PLANTS, "Propagation by hardwood cuttings", p.113; and THE ROSE GARDEN, "Hardwood cuttings", p.131).

SEMI-RIPE CUTTINGS

Stem with opposite buds cut below a node

New growth has developed from each node

The green stem (here Weigela) has a darker and woodier base.

LEAF-BUD CUTTINGS

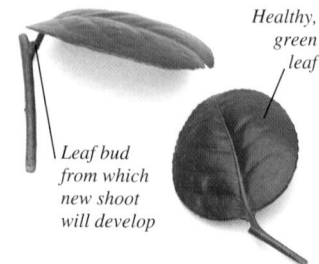

Healthy, green leaf

Leaf bud from which new shoot will develop

A short piece of semi-ripe stem (here camellia) provides sufficient food reserves for a leaf-bud cutting, since it produces some food through its leaf.

HARDWOOD CUTTINGS

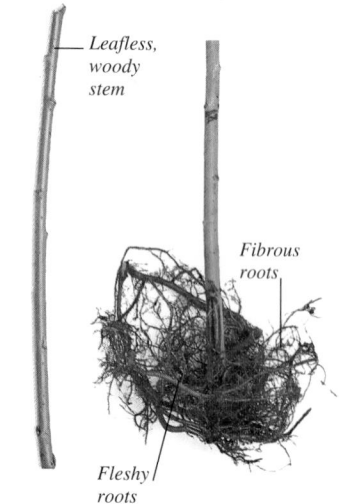

Leafless, woody stem

Fibrous roots

Fleshy roots

Hardwood cuttings (here Salix alba) are the longest type of stem cutting since they need large food reserves while their roots slowly develop.

When to take stem cuttings

There are no hard and fast rules about when to take stem cuttings of a particular species, so if cuttings taken in spring fail to root, further cuttings can be taken later in the season and treated according to the relative maturity of the shoots.

Plants that are difficult to root are best propagated early so that the new plants have time to mature before winter. As the action of root-producing hormones is suppressed by flower-initiating ones, use cuttings without flower buds wherever possible; if cuttings with flower buds have to be used, remove the flower buds.

Preparing stem cuttings
Stem cuttings are normally prepared by trimming just beneath a node, or leaf joint, where the cambium (the layer of cells involved in stem thickening) is most active. A few easy-rooting

NODAL CUTTING

Sharp, clean blade reduces the chances of infecting the cutting

Node

Most cuttings (here Hydrangea paniculata) root most satisfactorily at their nodes and so should be trimmed just below a node.

INTERNODAL CUTTINGS

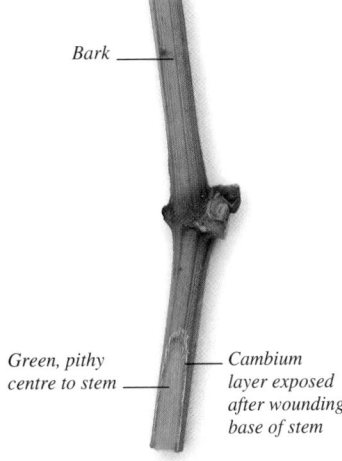

Internodal cuttings (here Clematis montana) *utilize scarce propagating material in an economical way.*

cuttings, for example willows (*Salix*), have pre-formed roots at the nodes, and these start to develop when the stem is cut from the parent plant. For these and for cuttings with densely crowded leaves on each stem, cut between nodes (internodal cutting).

The length of the cutting will depend on the species but is commonly 5–12cm (2–5in) or about five or six nodes in length. The lower leaves are stripped to give a clean stem for insertion. To assist the cuttings in rooting, semi-ripe and hardwood cuttings are often "wounded" by removing a sliver of bark from the lowest 2.5cm (1in) of the cutting. This exposes a greater area of cambium and thereby stimulates roots to form. Some cuttings, especially semi-ripe ones, may be taken by pulling a sideshoot away from the main shoot with a small "heel" of bark still attached (see ORNAMENTAL SHRUBS, "Heel cuttings", p.85). A heel may provide a cutting with added protection until it has produced roots, although there is no satisfactory scientific explanation for this response.

With the exception of leafless, hardwood stem cuttings, which contain food reserves from the previous

WOUNDING

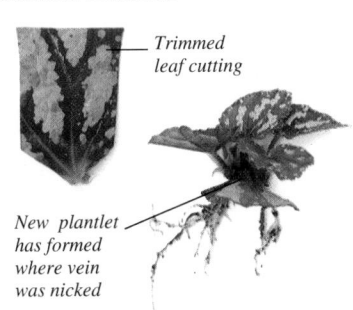

Bark

Green, pithy
centre to stem

Cambium
layer exposed
after wounding
base of stem

*Use a very sharp, clean knife to make a shallow, angled, downward cut at the base of semi-ripe and hardwood cuttings such as vine (*Vitis*).*

PREPARING CUTTINGS

Unprepared
cutting

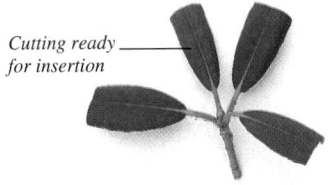

Cutting ready
for insertion

To reduce stress from water loss on leafy cuttings (here rhododendron), remove some leaves, halve others.

growing season, few cuttings are able to produce roots and shoots without supplementing their food reserves through photosynthesis. However, active leaves lose water through their pores, which is not easily replaced, and excessive water loss will cause failure. To achieve a balance between retaining photosynthetic tissue and reducing water loss, trim away all but three full-sized leaves, leaving any immature leaves. If the remaining leaves are large, as on many broadleaved trees and large shrubs, reduce each by half to minimize water loss.

Leaf cuttings

For some plants, whole leaves (with or without leaf stalks) or sections of leaves may be taken as cuttings and inserted or secured onto the compost. With whole leaves laid flat, the veins should be nicked at intervals since new plantlets form at the cut surfaces of large leaf veins. Propagate plants such as *Sinningia* and *Streptocarpus* from cut sections of fully expanded, undamaged leaves. African violets

LARGE LEAVES

Trimmed
leaf cutting

New plantlet
has formed
where vein
was nicked

Large leaves of plants such as begonia may be divided into small pieces, each of which will form callus at a nicked vein and then adventitious roots.

(*Saintpaulia*) and *Peperomia* may also be propagated from entire leaves with their stalks (see also THE INDOOR GARDEN, "Leaf cuttings", p.454).

Root cuttings

Root cuttings are taken in the dormant season from young, vigorous roots of about pencil thickness for most trees and shrubs but the roots may be somewhat thinner for some herbaceous plants such as phlox.

The length of the cutting

This is dependent on the environment in which the root cutting is to develop: the warmer the environment, the faster new shoots will appear and, therefore, shorter cuttings with smaller food reserves may be used successfully although these should not be less than 2.5cm (1in) in length. Root cuttings that are 2.5–5cm (1–2in) long are best grown on in a greenhouse, and those over 5cm (2in) long in a cold frame. For *Ailanthus* and lilac (*Syringa*), which can be propagated in open ground, 10–15cm (4–6in) long root cuttings should be used.

Inserting root cuttings

It is important to insert root cuttings the correct way up since the new roots always form at the distal end (that is, the end that was farthest from the crown of the parent plant). Cuttings should be inserted vertically so that their other (proximal) ends are flush with the soil surface; herbaceous root cuttings, however, are frequently inserted horizontally (see also PERENNIALS, "Root cuttings", p.167).

The rooting medium

Cuttings need air (to obtain oxygen) and water in their rooting medium, but if the medium is too wet, the cuttings rot. Standard cutting compost must, therefore, have a more open structure than loam-based potting compost. The rooting medium should also be warm in order to speed up

SMALL LEAVES

Leaf
cutting

Leaves
of new
plantlet

Adventitious
roots

To encourage callus to form, and rooting to occur, small leaves such as Peperomia may be trimmed at the edges.

ROOT CUTTINGS

Straight cut
at proximal
end, nearest
the crown of
the parent
plant

Shoots
appearing
just above
roots

Roots
appearing
from the
distal end

Slanted cut
at distal end

To help distinguish the two ends when taking root cuttings (here Acanthus mollis), *make differently angled cuts.*

PROTECTIVE ENVIRONMENT

Leafy cuttings grow best in a humid environment, such as within a plastic bag secured over a container; keep the plastic away from the leaf surfaces.

development of the roots: 18–25°C (64–77°F) is ideal for cool temperate species, and up to 32°C (90°F) for those from warm climates. If necessary, use bottom heat (see p.542).

Caring for the cuttings

After insertion, keep leafy cuttings turgid in the humid atmosphere of a closed case, mist unit, propagator, or other similar environment. Leafless cuttings that have been planted outdoors, either direct in the soil or in a container, as appropriate, should be protected by either a clear plastic tunnel or a cold frame.

Every ten days or so, water the rooting medium lightly if required, and spray with a fungicide to help prevent disease; at the same time, lift the lights or remove the plastic over enclosed cuttings, to enable air to circulate, for a 5–10 minute period.

Once rooted, cuttings should be potted up individually and those growing under cover gradually hardened off (see p.543).

Storage organs

Storage organs have diverse structures, and include bulbs, corms, rhizomes, root and stem tubers, and turions. Most plants with storage organs will increase naturally by producing offsets, which should be lifted and divided to prevent overcrowding. Offsets will flower more quickly than seed-raised plants and will be identical with the parent, whereas seed-raised plants may be variable in character.

The main propagation methods apart from division are to cut the storage organs into sections and to stimulate them to produce offsets by wounding; these sections or offsets will soon form complete plants if provided with a warm, dark place in which to develop. The cut surfaces should always be dusted with a fungicide as they easily succumb to fungal attack.

Bulbs

NON-SCALY, OR TUNICATE, BULB

Wide, fleshy, inner scale leaves

New shoot arising from leaf axil

Membranous, dry, outer scale leaves on Narcissus bulb

Root

SCALY BULB

New shoot

Narrower, fleshy scale leaves of lily bulb

Root

Bulbs may be propagated by chipping; division of offsets, bulbils, or bulblets; scaling or twin-scaling; and scooping or scoring. The gardener can tell only from experience which is best for which bulb, but for lists of plants appropriate to each method, see BULBOUS PLANTS, "Propagation", pp.237–42.

Chipping

Non-scaly, or tunicate, bulbs such as snowdrops (*Galanthus*) that do not naturally increase quickly may be multiplied rapidly by chipping. This method involves cutting each bulb into up to 20 pieces, depending on its size. Each piece, which generally comprises three or more scale leaves and a

CHIPPING

Bulblets develop between the scale leaves on a chipped bulb such as snowdrop (Galanthus) in air temperatures that do not exceed 25°C (77°F).

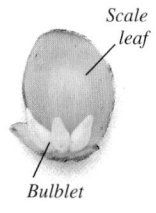

Scale leaf

Bulblet

section of basal plate, is then soaked in or dusted with a fungicide. The chips may be incubated (see "Chipping", p.241) or placed in a 1:1 mix of peat substitute (or peat) and perlite in a container in a frost-free greenhouse and left undisturbed for up to two years. Then separate the bulblets and repot or replant as required.

Division of offsets

Bulbs have wide, fleshy scale leaves, which act as food storage organs. At their base are axillary buds, which may enlarge naturally to form offsets. When the bulbs are lifted at the end of the growing season, these may be separated and planted out individually (see "Division of large bulbs", p.237).

DIVISION OF OFFSETS

Carefully remove each offset from a bulb (here Narcissus) by cutting or pulling.

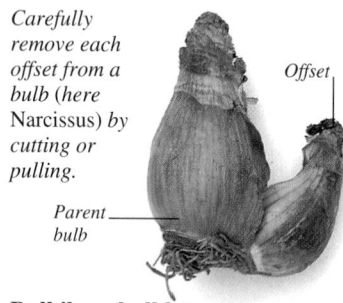

Offset

Parent bulb

Bulbils or bulblets

Bulbils are produced on flowerheads or stems; bulblets develop on the bulb itself or on stem roots. Both may be detached and planted up to develop into new bulbs (see also LILIES, "Bulbils and bulblets", p.243).

Scaling

Scaling involves the removal of bulb scales, which are then induced to form bulblets. It is used for bulbs such as fritillaries (*Fritillaria*) and lilies

BULBLETS AND BULBILS

Some lilies (Lilium), for example L. lancifolium, produce small, bulb-like structures known as "bulbils" on their stems above the ground. Others, for example L. longiflorum, may develop similar bulblets on bulbs or stem roots in the soil.

Lily bulbils

Lily bulblets

Old stem, which has developed roots

SCALING

Bulblets appear at the base of individual scale leaves of loose-scaled bulbs, here lily (Lilium).

Scale leaf

New top growth

Rooted bulblet

TWIN-SCALING

Two bud scales and a section of basal plate are used for non-scaly bulbs (here Narcissus).

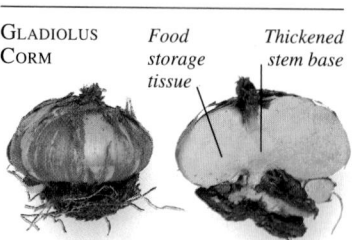

Fleshy scale leaves

Bulblet

Basal plate

(*Lilium*) that are made up of fairly loose scales. Individual scale leaves are pulled away from the basal plate of a mature bulb and then left in a plastic bag containing moist vermiculite or a peat:grit mix, in a warm, dark place. Bulblets appear at the scale bases, usually after two months. Grow on the scales in a container until the bulblets are large enough to be separated (see also "Scaling", p.240).

Twin-scaling

Non-scaly, or tunicate, bulbs such as daffodils and snowdrops may be twin-scaled. In this, the bulb is cut vertically into eight to ten sections and each of these is divided into pairs of bud scales with a small section of basal plate. These are then incubated and grown on in the same way as in scaling above. (See also "Twin-scaling", p.241.)

Scooping and scoring

Some bulbs, such as hyacinths, can be propagated by either scooping or scoring the bulb. This causes callus tissue to develop, which encourages bulblets to form. For scooping, the basal plate of a mature bulb is scooped out at the centre, leaving just the outer

SCORING

Callus tissue

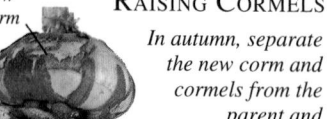

Bulblets developing inside cut

Basal plate

Shallowly cutting the basal plate of some bulbs (here hyacinth) stimulates the growth of bulblets.

edge of the basal plate intact; for scoring, two shallow cuts at right angles are made into the basal plate. The bulb is then stored in a warm, dark place until bulblets have formed; these are then detached and grown on separately (see also "Simple cutting", p.242; "Scooping hyacinths", p.242; and "Scooping and scoring *Trillium*", p.242).

Corms

GLADIOLUS CORM

Food storage tissue

Thickened stem base

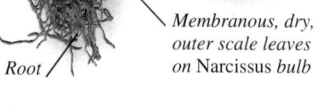

Corms are reduced, compact, underground stems with a solid internal structure. Most corms produce several buds near the apex; each bud naturally forms a new corm. Miniature corms, or cormels, are produced as offsets

RAISING CORMELS

New corm

In autumn, separate the new corm and cormels from the parent and grow on.

Cormels

Old corm

DEVELOPMENT OF A CORMEL

Cormels may take up to three years to reach flowering size. The sequence below shows their development in the first year.

between the old and new corms in the growing season (see also BULBOUS PLANTS, "Gladiolus cormels", p.237).

Larger corms may be increased artificially by cutting them into pieces, each with a growing bud, just before the growing season. When planted in a pot or the open ground and lightly covered with soil, these cut sections will develop into new corms.

Rhizomes

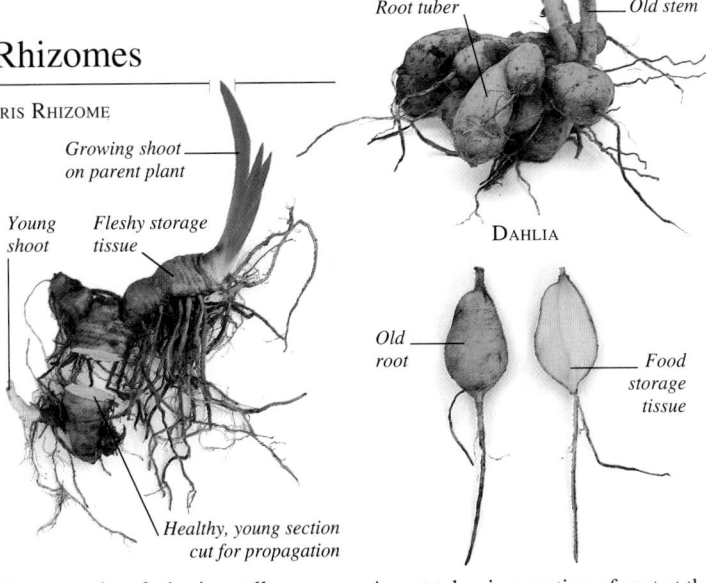

IRIS RHIZOME

Growing shoot on parent plant

Young shoot

Fleshy storage tissue

Healthy, young section cut for propagation

These consist of a horizontally growing shoot, usually beneath but sometimes on the soil surface. They are propagated by cutting the rhizome into young, healthy sections, each with one or more growth buds, which are planted up individually (see also PERENNIALS, "Division of rhizomatous plants", p.165; BULBOUS PLANTS, "Scooping and scoring Trillium", p.242; and ORCHIDS, "Division", p.445).

Root tubers

Root tuber

Old stem

DAHLIA

Old root

Food storage tissue

A root tuber is a portion of root at the stem base that swells during summer and is modified into a storage organ, or tuber, as in dahlias. Such plants may be propagated in spring by dividing a cluster of tubers into healthy pieces, each with a developing shoot (see also *Cutting up Bulbs for Propagation*, p.241). Root tubers may also be propagated by basal cuttings of the young, emerging shoots in spring (see DAHLIAS, *How to Propagate by Basal Cuttings*, p.227).

Stem tubers

The stems of some plants (e.g. potatoes and Jerusalem artichokes) are modified to produce tubers, which act as storage organs. Tuberous begonias, for example, form perennial tubers at the bases of their stems, which enlarge each year. In spring, these can be cut into pieces, each with a growth bud. Each piece will produce basal shoots, which can be used as basal cuttings (see DAHLIAS, *How to Propagate by Basal Cuttings*, p.227) or grown on to form a new tuber (see "Propagation of tuberous begonias", p.455).

JERUSALEM ARTICHOKE

Old stem

Stem tuber

Food storage tissue

Other types of storage organ

Plants such as *Saxifraga granulata* and some *Kalanchoe* and asparagus species develop round, bulb-like buds at their shoot axils. These buds can be separated and grown on individually in the same way as bulblets or cormels (see p.540).

In some water plants, such as *Hydrocharis* and *Myriophyllum*, these relatively large bud structures are known as "turions". When mature, they drop off the parent plant naturally, sink to the bottom of the water, and develop into new plants.

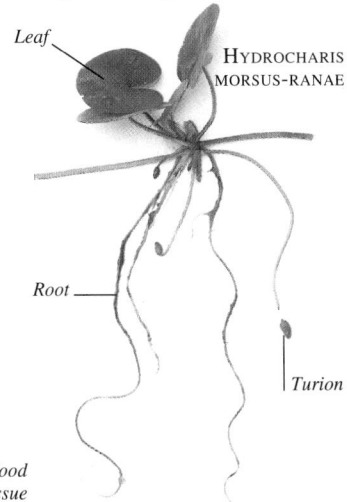

Leaf

HYDROCHARIS MORSUS-RANAE

Root

Turion

Grafting and budding

In a wide range of woody plants and a few herbaceous ones, a budded stem, or scion, is grafted onto a rootstock, or stock, of another species or cultivar, to achieve a composite plant with more desirable characteristics. Most apple, pear, and stone fruit trees are propagated in this way. The stock may be more resistant than the scion to root disease or more suited to a particular environment. Often (especially with fruit trees), the stock is selected because it controls the growth of the scion to produce a dwarfed or a particularly vigorous plant. Sometimes, a scion cultivar that is difficult to increase from cuttings is grafted onto easily rooted stock. The rootstock also influences the age at which the tree bears fruit and its size and skin quality – dwarfing rootstocks generally conferring earlier fruit-bearing. Conversely, the rootstock's growing cycle may be affected by the scion cultivar, which in its turn influences cold hardiness. Reactions to soil acidity can also be affected by interactions between rootstock and scion cultivars.

The scion may take the form of a single bud on a short portion of stem (usually known as budding) or it may be a multi-budded length of stem.

When to graft

Most grafting is normally undertaken in late winter to early spring, when the cambium is particularly active; these warm conditions also favour the growth of callus cells. Hot weather later in the season may dry out the thin-walled, cambial cells.

T-budding, on the other hand, is most often done in mid- to late summer, when well-developed scion buds are available and young stock material is of suitable diameter. For success, the stock plant needs to be growing actively, so that the bark can be lifted from the wood to allow the bud to be inserted – an action known as bark slipping. Chip-budding, however, may be undertaken over an extended season because the chip is positioned beside the stock rather than slipped under its bark.

How to graft

Because grafting cuts inevitably damage plant cells, and the thin-walled cells at the graft union are vulnerable to fungi and bacteria, it is essential that knives are sterile and sharp, so that a single cut is sufficient. The propagation environment, prepared plant material, and ties must also be scrupulously clean.

Once stock and scion material have been selected and cut to shape, according to the type of graft, position the two pieces carefully so that there is maximum cambial contact. If the grafting materials are of different widths, ensure the cambium on at least one side of the graft is in contact. Central

CAMBIUM LAYER

Node

Bark

Cambium

Pithy centre

For successful grafting, the scion cambium must be matched as closely as possible to that of the stock.

to the grafting process is the activity of the cambium – a continuous, narrow band of thin-walled cells between the bark and the wood – which produces new cells that are responsible for stem thickening. Within days of grafting, the region between the stock and scion should fill with thin-walled callus cells. The cambial cells on the stock and scion next to the young callus then influence neighbouring cells, so that a complete cambial bridge forms between the two parts. Further divisions of this new cambium produce water- and food-conducting tissue, which functionally joins the scion and stock.

Traditionally, grafts were bound with raffia, and then coated with wax to prevent drying. However, waxing is used less often now that raffia has mainly been superseded by clear plastic tape, which seals the join better. Pot-grown stocks once grafted should be kept in a suitable protective environment (see "Greenhouses", p.542, and "Cold frames", p.543).

Regularly examine the graft, and remove the tape once the graft appears to have taken. The following growing season, cut back the stock plant just above the new shoot that has developed from the grafted scion.

Chip-budding

A "chip" of ripe wood is removed from the rootstock and replaced with a matching "chip" of similar size from the scion, or budstick, containing a bud (see THE FRUIT GARDEN, "Chip-budding", p.372).

T-budding

In this technique, just the scion bud is grafted onto the rootstock by cutting a "T" in the stock bark and inserting the bud beneath (see THE ROSE GARDEN, "Bud-grafting", p.132).

Side-veneer grafting

A short, downward cut through the cambium layer of the stock is followed by a sloping cut down towards the base of the first cut. The chip is removed and replaced by the scion, which is shaped to match the stock (see ORNAMENTAL TREES, "Side-veneer grafting", p.58, and ORNAMENTAL SHRUBS, "Side-veneer grafting", p.90).

Side-wedge grafting

A downward, slightly inward cut is made into the side of the stock. The scion is then prepared by making two oblique cuts at the base. The scion's wedge-shaped base is inserted into the rootstock cut so that the cambium aligns and is bound in position.

Apical-wedge grafting

The stock is cut flat and a wedge-shaped chip is removed from the centre, into which the scion is then inserted (see ORNAMENTAL SHRUBS, "Apical-wedge grafting", p.91).

Saddle grafting

The top of the stock is saddle-shaped, with upward-sloping sides. The scion is then shaped so that it fits closely over the top of the rootstock (see ORNAMENTAL SHRUBS, "Saddle grafting", p.90).

Basal-whip grafting

Cut back the stock at an oblique angle to 5–8cm (2–3in). Then prepare the scion to match. If the scion is thinner than the stock, first cut the stock horizontally, then obliquely to match.

Flat grafting

Both the stock top and scion base are cut horizontally (see CACTI AND OTHER SUCCULENTS, "Flat grafting", p.275).

Whip-and-tongue grafting

Make matching sloping cuts on the rootstock and scion, then cut shallow tongues along the sloping cuts, so that the scion interlocks securely with the stock (see THE FRUIT GARDEN, "Whip-and-tongue grafting", p.373).

WHIP-AND-TONGUE GRAFT
The rootstock and scion gradually unite to function as one plant.

The propagation environment

During propagation, plants are at their most vulnerable and their environment is, therefore, vitally important. The choice of environment depends on which propagation method is chosen and on the relative maturity of the plant material itself. Propagation from leafy cuttings, for example, requires a more closely regulated environment than for leafless cuttings.

Greenhouses

It is essential that the greenhouse has adequate ventilation and, in the growing season, appropriate shading (see "Creating the right environment", p.481). For two months on either side of mid-summer, apply a shading wash to the outside of the glass so that propagated plants are not stressed unnecessarily by extreme weather conditions (see "Shading washes", p.484). Additional protective shading can be provided by mounting some shade cloth on wire runners across or along the length of the bench or greenhouse. The curtain can be withdrawn during dull weather.

Protecting leafy cuttings

Because leafy cuttings, initially, have no roots and cannot easily take up water to replace that lost from the leaves, they must have further protection within the greenhouse.

Clear plastic sheeting or a plastic bag placed over a tray of cuttings and tucked under is perfectly satisfactory if appropriate shading is provided. Water vapour condensing on the inside of the plastic helps to protect the cuttings against desiccation. Soft cuttings may succumb to disease if the plastic touches them; insert a framework of split canes or wire in the compost to keep the plastic off the cuttings. In such closed systems, however, excessive air temperatures may build up in

RIGID-TOPPED PROPAGATOR

Because most of the moisture in a rigid-topped propagator is retained within the unit, cuttings remain turgid and so are more likely to root quickly and healthily.

very hot conditions and the containers of cuttings should be kept in a shaded but light place out of the sun.

Rigid plastic propagators need similar shading to plastic sheeting, and generally provide a drier environment, because water vapour may leak through their ventilation openings: these should be kept closed until the cuttings have rooted and are ready to be hardened off.

A mist unit provides the best system for summer propagation, but for winter and early- and late-season propagation it should be combined with bottom heat. Ideally, the mist unit should maintain a constant water film on the leaf surfaces; some water will still be lost from the leaves by transpiration but this is amply replaced by "applied" water from the misting process. Since the mist is applied in bursts, however, the greenhouse humidity fluctuates and so, inevitably, each leaf's water film is imperfect, and some water loss occurs. Complete

mist systems comprise supply pipes, water filter, nozzles, and a solenoid and sensor to regulate the misting frequency (see "Mist units", p.488).

For softwood cuttings, which wilt readily, the best system is to arrange a low, clear plastic tent just above the misting nozzles. This ensures a higher ambient humidity between mist bursts than does open mist. It is important to shade such a closed mist system in bright weather.

Bottom heat

Most biological processes are speeded up when temperatures are higher, and therefore raising the temperature of the compost usually increases the rapidity with which seeds germinate and cuttings root.

Cables or heating mats are most convenient for small greenhouses (see "Propagation aids", p.488). The temperature is controlled by a rod thermostat or electronic controller. If they are used in closed mist systems, excessive

---

SHADING GREENHOUSES (Temperate climates)

To prevent the greenhouse from overheating when propagating, add one or more layers of shading, depending on the weather conditions and season. Greenhouses in open, sunny sites are particularly vulnerable to overheating.

		Spring	Summer	Autumn	Winter
DULL DAYS	Whitewash		▬▬▬▬		
BRIGHT DAYS	Layer of shade cloth	▬▬▬▬▬▬▬▬▬▬			
	Additional shade cloth	▬▬▬▬▬▬			
	Whitewash		▬▬▬▬▬		

EFFECTS OF BOTTOM HEAT

CUTTING
GROWN
WITH
HEAT

CUTTING
GROWN
WITHOUT
HEAT

*Poor,
short roots*

*Long, strong,
healthy roots*

air temperatures may build up in bright conditions, during which the heating must be switched off.

Heated propagator units

These self-contained units are very useful for extending the propagation season in otherwise unheated greenhouses (see "Heated propagators", p.488). Since the units have heat loadings well in excess of the 160 watts/sq m (15 watts/sq ft) recommended for mist systems, they must be fitted with effective thermostats, otherwise damagingly high temperatures may occur in sunny weather.

Cold frames

Cold frames provide a valuable gain in soil and air temperatures while maintaining high humidity and providing adequate light for young plants to grow successfully. They can be used to raise

CIRCULATING AIR IN A COLD FRAME

*Since cold air expands
and rises as it heats up,
the lid of a cold frame
must be propped
open in warm
weather to allow
some air to escape
and the temperature to
remain reasonably cool.*

seedlings early in the season, protect grafts, and propagate leafless and leafy cuttings. They may also, if required, be fitted with bottom heat (see p.542).

Because such low structures have no great volume, they easily overheat in sunny conditions unless ventilated and shaded well (see "Cold frames", p.489). Conversely, when temperatures fall below -5°C (23°F), frames must be insulated with thick layers of hessian or coconut matting to avoid frost damage to the plant material.

Cloches and polytunnels outdoors

Glass and clear plastic cloches and tunnels are most often used to give seedlings an early start in the season in the vegetable garden. A wide range of easily rooted cuttings also do well in such an environment (see "Cloches", p.490). Additional shading, such as shade netting, is required in bright, sunny weather.

Growing the propagated plant

To propagate plants well, the gardener needs not only to prepare the material properly but also to care for and grow on the young plants in a suitable environment until they have developed sufficiently to survive in the garden. At key stages during propagation, practical inexperience or carelessness may kill well-rooted plants.

Caring for plants being propagated

Since most forms of propagation involve cutting various parts of the plants being increased, plant tissues are exposed to possible disease infection; it is therefore important to maintain hygienic conditions in the propagating area. Tools and benches should be regularly and thoroughly cleaned (using a mild disinfectant if necessary), and dead and damaged plant material removed. Potting composts must always be fresh and sterile. Fungicidal solutions may also be applied to protect seedlings (e.g. Cheshunt compound) and leafy cuttings (e.g. captan or benlate), following the manufacturer's instructions.

When preparing pots or trays of compost for sowing seed, lightly firm the compost using a presser board, especially around the edges of the container. Water is drawn up through the compost by capillary action and, without this firming, air pockets occur and the water columns essential for capillary rise are broken. However,

FIRMING THE COMPOST

*Ensure that seeds
are germinated in
evenly pressed,
level compost so
that capillary
action and
therefore seedling
growth are not
hindered by air
pockets in the
compost.*

Air
holes

*Continuous
capillary action*

*Broken
capillary action*

do not firm loam-based composts: a medium filled with roots must be well aerated and have an open structure for optimum plant growth.

The composts in which propagated plants are growing should be moist, but not wet, at all times. Too wet a medium will reduce the oxygen available and the roots may die or succumb to disease. It is also important to maintain the correct environment until the young plants are sturdy enough to be hardened off (see "The propagation environment", p.542). Prick out seedlings to avoid them becoming overcrowded, as unless air is allowed to circulate freely around the young plants stagnant conditions may arise and cause damping off (p.564). Remove fallen leaves and dead matter immediately.

Most organic potting mixes are acid, that is, with a pH value of less than 7, and the ideal range for an organic mix is pH 5–5.5. Simple test kits are available to measure the pH. A very alkaline soil or compost reduces the amount of phosphorus, iron,

manganese, and boron available to the plant, whereas too acidic a soil means that calcium and magnesium may be in short supply. For feeding the plants, apply a proprietary liquid fertilizer strictly in accordance with the manufacturer's instructions.

DAMPING OFF

*Seedlings are more likely to damp off
if they are overcrowded, especially if
grown in damp, poorly ventilated
conditions, or if they are allowed to
suffer frost damage.*

Hardening off

Hardening off the propagated plants, by which process the young plants are acclimatized to the outside air temperature, must not be rushed, because, over a period of days, the natural waxes coating the leaves need to undergo changes in form and thickness to reduce water loss. The stomatal pores on the leaf also need to adapt to less supportive conditions.

First, turn off the heat, if appropriate, in the propagator or mist unit. Then, during the daytime, raise the covers for increasingly long periods. Finally, the covers may be removed for both day and night. If the plant has been in the protective environment of a greenhouse and eventually needs to be planted outdoors, move it next into a cold frame. This, too, should be closed at first, then opened in stages. The hardening off process may take two to three weeks.

Outdoor nursery beds

If propagating plants in any quantity, an outdoor nursery bed can provide the best conditions in which to grow on recently propagated plants and young seedlings in pots and other containers, once they have been hardened off. The nursery bed may be of any suitable size. First prepare a level site and then enclose it with 8cm (3in) high, wooden edging boards. There are two types of outdoor bed: water-permeable fabric beds and sand beds.

WATER-PERMEABLE FABRIC BED

Use edging boards to enclose the nursery bed and line with water-permeable fabric placed directly onto the soil.

Edging board 8cm (3in) above soil level

Water-permeable fabric

Two-way flow of water through the soil

Soil level

SAND BED

With this type of nursery bed, the containers are set directly onto the coarse sand topping.

Edging board 8cm (3in) above soil level

Sand

Two-way flow of water through the sand

Plastic sheeting cut 2.5cm (1in) below the top of the edging boards

Soil level

Prepared seedbed

Water-permeable fabric beds
In this, the simpler option, black polypropylene, woven fabric, or weed matting is laid over the prepared soil surface within the wooden edge boards. The fabric suppresses weeds, and helps to isolate plants set on its surface from soil-borne diseases. Such a water-permeable fabric bed also enables containers to drain freely, yet gives the plants access to soil water through capillary action. If the soil is not well-drained and sandy, or if the prepared surface remains uneven, cover it with some sand before laying the fabric.

Sand beds
A sand bed has the advantage over a water-permeable fabric bed of reducing the amount of watering necessary.

Lay an oversize plastic sheet that is folded double over the prepared soil and up over the edging boards. Cover the plastic with coarse, lime-free sand to within 2.5cm (1in) of the top of the edge boards. Then trim the plastic sheeting to the sand level. Infill to the top of the edging boards with more sand and level off by drawing a plank across the top of the boards.

Place containers directly on the sand. The sand enclosed within the plastic liner provides a water reservoir, which reduces the frequency of watering needed and prevents potting composts from drying out. Excess water drains away between the boards and the plastic sheeting. More complex sand-bed designs incorporate drainage pipes and automatic watering systems.

Advanced techniques

Since the mid-20th century, many new propagation methods have been introduced commercially. These are, as yet, generally confined to "laboratory nurseries" using advanced technologies, but the results of their developments are affecting several branches of horticulture.

Micropropagation

Micropropagation uses explants, or tiny pieces of young plant material. Each explant is grown on in a glass or plastic container in a medium containing organic nutrients, mineral salts, hormones, and other elements needed for growth, and is placed in a closely controlled, sterile environment. The explant multiplies to form numerous shoots or complete plantlets, which are then rooted as "microcuttings" or, if they have already rooted, weaned to greenhouse conditions. Sterile conditions are vital throughout, and transfer of the plant material from the culture to a greenhouse is especially difficult.

Micropropagation is used mainly for high-value plants, for example for the rapid introduction of new cultivars, for plants difficult to propagate by other means, and to produce disease-free stock. Technical improvements and automation should eventually reduce costs substantially.

Genetic engineering

It is now possible to identify and even extract particular genes from a plant's cells and to introduce these into another cell, not necessarily of the same species. Using such methods, resistance to certain fungi, viruses, and pests has been introduced into otherwise susceptible species. For example, some lettuce, tomato, and pepper cultivars that are susceptible to cucumber mosaic virus can be given a gene that minimizes its effect. Petunias and tobacco plants can now also be made resistant to certain herbicides.

The potential for genetic engineering is vast, especially for the development of agricultural crops such as rice and other vegetables. Examples include special potatoes that do not suffer from low-temperature sweetening for crisp manufacture; rape seed that has been altered so that it yields more oil for margarine manufacture; and tomatoes into which a gene has been inserted to allow them to be harvested commercially while red and ripe (rather than while green and unripe), so that they are tastier but firmer and less prone to damage during transportation to market.

Advances in seed propagation

New methods have been developed to improve the speed and uniformity of seed germination for the gardener. Seeds are soaked in solutions of salts, such as sodium chloride or potassium nitrate, or in polyethylene glycol solutions. They are thus primed for germination but are dried before the radicle emerges and are then packaged ready for sale. The seeds can be sown conventionally as required.

Fluid drilling and pelleted seed have been developed to make uniform seed sowing easier. In fluid drilling, seed primed for germination is contained within a gel base, for example in a fungicide-free wallpaper paste, which can then be squeezed along the seed drill. In pelleted seed, primed seed is coated in an inert material that may contain fungicides, nutrients, and/or a fluorescent dye. The seeds can then be handled individually and sown more evenly. Pelleted seed is made for small-seeded bedding plants and some vegetable crops.

Artificially produced seeds

Some flower tissues, when introduced into a special liquid culture medium, develop numerous embryos – each similar to the embryo within a seed. If these are separated from the medium and given a synthetic coating, artificial seed may be produced. This process is known as somatic embryogenesis and may eventually lead to the manufacture of vast numbers of genetically uniform, so-called "seeds".

Hydroculture

Instead of compost, seeds and cuttings are propagated in a culture solution or an inert supporting medium, such as sand, gravel, clay granules, or rockwool, bathed in nutrient solution (see THE INDOOR GARDEN, "Hydroculture", p.449). This technique is used in regions where a suitable compost is not easily obtainable.

MICROPROPAGATION

A microscopic portion of plant tissue is extracted from a plant under sterile conditions. This portion, or explant, is then divided (right) and grown on in test-tube conditions (far right). Once sufficiently large, these embryo plants may be further divided or grown on to form plantlets.

Embryo plant

Sterile, test-tube conditions

7

PLANT PROBLEMS

*E*VEN THE MOST *experienced gardener may suffer problems caused by plant diseases and disorders, the ravages of pests, and the choking of plants by weeds. By following all the principles of good cultivation outlined in this book, it should be possible to keep these problems to a minimum. Occasionally, however, in severe cases it will prove necessary to diagnose a problem, and then to decide upon the appropriate course of action required in order to remedy the situation. The choice of treatments now includes a variety of organic and biological methods, as well as the use of chemicals. Good garden management depends upon learning how to prevent plant problems from occurring, and, if this fails, to recognize them at an early stage when they can be treated more easily.*

Pests, diseases, and physiological disorders

Most plant problem symptoms are easy to see. A tree, shrub, or plant may wilt or become discoloured, or it may fail to come into leaf or to bloom at all. Insects, which may be the cause of the plant's poor health, may be seen on part or all of the plant. Sometimes an infestation or disease in the roots may be noticed first through symptoms in the leaves. This chapter gives detailed information on how to prevent and control the pests, diseases, and physiological disorders that can cause such problems.

What is a pest?

Pests are animals that cause damage to cultivated plants. Some, such as slugs, snails, and rabbits, are well known; most, however, are small invertebrates such as mites, eelworms, woodlice, and millipedes, which are less evidently plant pests. The largest group by far in this category are the insects. Pests may damage or destroy any part of a plant or, in some cases, even the whole plant. They feed in various ways – by sap sucking, leaf mining, defoliating, or tunnelling through stems, roots, or fruits. Sometimes they cause abnormal growths known as galls. Some pests also indirectly damage plants by spreading viral or fungal diseases, while others coat plants with a sugary excrement that encourages the growth of sooty moulds.

What is a disease?

A plant disease is any pathological condition caused by other organisms, such as bacteria, fungi, or viruses. Fungal diseases are commonest; bacterial diseases relatively rare. The symptoms that these organisms produce vary considerably in appearance and severity, but the growth or health of the plant is almost always affected and, in severe attacks, the plant may even be killed. The rate of infection is affected by factors such as weather and growing conditions. In some cases, the disease-causing organism (pathogen) is spread by a carrier, such as an aphid. The pathogen is sometimes visible as a discoloration on the plant, as with rusts. Symptoms such as discoloration, distortion, or wilting are typical signs of disease infection.

HOW TO DIAGNOSE PLANT SYMPTOMS

In a case where it is obvious that the leaves have been eaten away by some kind of pest, turn to the section on "Eaten leaves" to identify the cause.

When a plant shows several symptoms, look either in the section on the whole plant or in the part that deals with the worst aspect, here discoloured leaves.

What is a disorder?

Plant disorders usually result from nutritional deficiencies or from unsuitable growing or storage conditions. An inappropriate temperature range, inadequate or erratic water or food supply, poor light, or unsatisfactory atmospheric conditions may all lead to physiological disorders. Problems may also be caused by deficiencies of the mineral salts that are essential for healthy plant growth.

Weather, cultural, or soil conditions may lead to a range of plants being affected. The problems become apparent through symptoms such as discoloured leaves or stem wilt. A plant that lacks water, food, or the appropriate environmental conditions will not only appear unhealthy but will also be far less able to resist attack from either insect pests or diseases caused by fungi, viruses, or bacteria. Unless problems are correctly diagnosed and treated, affected plants may die.

How to use this chapter

This part of the book enables the gardener to diagnose and treat plant problems. It is organized according to the site of the symptoms (such as distorted flowers or discoloured leaves) in sections covering leaves, stems, flowers, fruit, roots and tubers, bulbs, whole plant, and lawns. Within the main sections the problems are grouped by the type of symptom; for example, all yellow leaf spots will be found together.

To identify a problem, look in the appropriate section. If you cannot find it there, turn to the cross-references at the end of that section. Each entry lists the plants affected, the symptoms, the cause of the problem, and how to control it. On p.572 is a list of the controls mentioned, together with the names of treatments currently available (these are subject to change).

Prevention of problems

Always buy strong, vigorous plants that look healthy. Do not purchase plants that are showing dieback or discoloured stems, that have leaves that are an abnormal colour for the time of year, or that are wilted or distorted. Do not buy plants showing significant pest infestations or disease. Check the root ball of container-grown trees and shrubs: do not buy them if they are either pot-bound or showing poor root development.

Check that the plant is suitable for its intended position, taking into account the type, texture, and pH of the soil, the aspect of the site, and whether the plant is prone to frost damage. Plant carefully, making sure that the ground is well prepared and that the roots are properly spread out. Each type of plant has different requirements for watering, feeding, and, where appropriate, pruning. If a plant is badly diseased or infested by pests, it may be impossible to revive it; such plants should be removed, especially if there is a risk that the trouble might spread to healthy plants nearby. If the plant does not thrive, try to discover the underlying cause and treat as necessary to overcome the problem.

Organic control

Organic control uses natural methods to help plants both resist and recover from attack by pests and diseases. Such methods have long played their part in gardening, but in recent years they have attracted an increasing level of interest.

Organic treatments and traps
A few chemical preparations originate from natural sources; pyrethrum, for example, is derived from the pyrethrum daisy. Other organic treatments are derris dust, soft soap, and sulphur dust. These may be obtained as ready-made powders or liquid sprays; they are safe to use and spray damage is not a problem. They have short persistence, however, and act only on contact with the pest or disease, which necessitates regular and thorough applications. Organic traps may easily be constructed. Earwigs may be trapped in inverted flower pots, and wireworms in old potatoes or carrots spitted on a stick and buried. In greenhouses, whiteflies (which are attracted to the colour yellow) may be caught on a piece of yellow card smeared with grease. Inspect these traps regularly and dispose of the pests.

COMPANION PLANTING
French marigolds (Tagetes patula) *attract hoverflies, which feed on aphids that may attack nearby plants.*

An inverted flower pot filled with dried grass and placed over a cane attracts earwigs (see p.548). Remove the pot and burn the grass every other day.

Companion planting
Certain companion plants grown in association with a crop can help to reduce pest and disease attack. For example, some strong-smelling herbs such as mint and garlic may repel pests that are attracted to plants by smell, thereby keeping them away from nearby plants. Deliberate planting of host plants may deflect pests away from other plants or attract predators to feed on the pests: as nasturtiums (*Tropaeolum*) are susceptible to aphids plant French marigolds (*Tagetes patula*) nearby as these attract hoverflies, which feed on the aphids.

Resistant plants
Some plants are resistant to attack by pests or diseases. Plant breeders have been able to profit from this, and have produced cultivars with a higher-than-average resistance to some pests or diseases. Cultivated plants resistant to pests include some butterhead lettuces, which are seldom affected by the lettuce root aphid. Plants resistant to disease include some tomato cultivars, which resist tomato leaf mould, and the climbing rose 'Maigold', which shows some resistance to diseases such as powdery mildew, rust, and black spot.

In some cases, the resistance appears to be total, but even a resistant plant may succumb to a given disease if its growing conditions are poor, for example, or if other factors, such as the weather, weaken the plant. Before buying plants, check if there are disease- or pest-resistant cultivars readily available. The availability of resistant plants varies from year to year, so check catalogues annually for this type of information.

Garden hygiene
Maintaining a tidy and well-managed garden is one of the most important ways to keep pests and diseases under control. Select vigorous plants and ensure that they have the optimum growing conditions for successful growth. Examine plants to identify any new problem as soon as possible, since a well-established infection or infestation is always far more difficult to deal with than one that is identified and treated early.

The regular removal and disposal of diseased parts of plants, and some pests such as cabbage white caterpillars, will certainly help to control infections. Any debris from infested or diseased plants (or any material suspected of being infested or diseased) should be burned; otherwise the pest or

pathogen may survive, overwinter, and re-infect the plant in spring. Garden rubbish should be destroyed or, where appropriate, composted.

Crop rotation
Rotating vegetable crops, usually on a three- or four-year basis, helps prevent soil-borne pests and diseases from building up to a damaging level. For further details on planning a crop rotation system, see THE VEGETABLE GARDEN, "Rotation", p.307. Although a strict rotation plan is generally used for vegetables, it is also worth rotating annuals and bulbs where feasible, as this reduces the build-up of diseases like pansy sickness and tulip fire.

Growing a particular kind of plant in the same ground for a number of years may also lead to problems (for example "Rose-sick soil", p.122). If a disease such as pansy sickness becomes evident, remove all the plants and grow other, botanically unrelated plants that are not susceptible on the site.

Biological control

This term describes the limiting of pest damage by the deliberate introduction of natural enemies, such as predators, parasites, and diseases. In the greenhouse, where pests may have developed immunity to chemicals, it is often the only effective way of controlling them.

Use of biological controls is less practicable in the relatively uncontrolled conditions of the open garden, especially where pesticides are used, since they may kill the controls as well as the pests. Not all pests and diseases can be countered by appropriate biological controls; other controls may be introduced as more work is done on insect and disease ecology.

Greenhouse controls
Biological controls for use in the greenhouse may be obtained from specialist suppliers. Some examples are listed below.

PEST	BIOLOGICAL CONTROL
Red spider mites	Predatory mites (*Phytoseiulus persimilis*)
Whiteflies	The parasitic wasp *Encarsia formosa*
Mealybugs	Ladybirds (*Cryptolaemus montrouzieri*)
Soft scale insects	The parasitic wasp *Metaphycus helvolus*
Aphids	Fly larva predators (*Aphidoletes aphidimyza*)
Thrips	Predatory mites (*Amblyseius* spp.)
Vine weevil larvae	Nematode predators (*Heterorhabditis* spp.)
Caterpillars	Bacterial disease (*Bacillus thuringiensis*)

Introduce the control before plants are heavily infested, as it may be a number of weeks before it becomes effective.

Most predators and parasites require daytime temperatures of at least 21°C (70°F) and good light intensity in order to breed faster than the pests. Restrict the use of pesticides, since most are harmful to biological controls; the exceptions are pirimicarb against aphids, and insecticidal soaps,

FRIENDS AND FOES

FOE:
MILLIPEDE

FRIENDS:
CENTIPEDES

FRIEND:
HEDGEHOG

FRIEND:
GARDEN
SPIDER

*Flat
centipede*

*Snake
centipede*

which control a wide range of small insects and mites. Some of the most troublesome pests, especially red spider mites, whiteflies, and vine weevil larvae, have now developed such a high degree of immunity to the pesticides that were employed against them that biological control is usually the only effective treatment now available.

Beneficial garden animals

Insects and other creatures found in gardens are by no means all destructive. Many are not only useful to the plant but actually essential for its survival; for example, a large number of fruits, vegetables, and flowers rely on pollinating insects, such as honey bees, to carry pollen from one flower to another to enable fertilization to take place. In other cases, some species of natural predator can help to control certain types of pest and should therefore be encouraged to visit the garden.

Hedgehogs, shrews, frogs, and toads feed on many ground-dwelling plant pests. Birds may be the cause of some damage in the garden, but this disadvantage is usually far outweighed by the enormous quantities of insect pests that they devour. Some invertebrates, for example centipedes, prey on soil-dwelling pests. It is possible to distinguish centipedes from the somewhat similar millipedes (which are often harmful) by the number of legs that are carried on each segment of their bodies: centipedes have only one pair per body segment, whereas millipedes have two pairs.

Spiders are also useful allies as their webs trap countless insects. Certain insects, however, may be invaluable in the garden. Ladybird beetles are a familiar example in many countries, and both the larvae and the adult beetles feed on destructive pests such as aphids. Ants and wasps, whose activities might damage some plants, may still help the gardener by preying on other insect pests.

BIOLOGICAL CONTROL
Encarsia formosa *wasps parasitize whitefly larvae, causing them to blacken and eventually die.*

Chemical control

Chemical control is the term used to describe the action of destroying plant pests and diseases by applying synthetic compounds to plants or soil. Although the emphasis on organic control is presently becoming stronger, the responsible and sparing use of chemicals still has a valuable role to play in pest and disease control. A sensible combination of the most suitable aspects of both methods may often provide the best solution to these difficult and often recurrent problems.

Pesticides and fungicides

Most pesticides (which are used to kill insects, mites, and other pests) and fungicides (which are used to control diseases caused by fungi) either work by being brought into contact with the pest or disease organisms, or they are systemic.

Contact pesticides kill pests when they crawl over a treated surface or when they are directly hit by the chemical (when sprayed, for example). Contact fungicides may kill germinating fungal spores and prevent further infection, but they have little effect on established fungal growths.

Systemic chemicals are absorbed into the plant tissues and are then transported by the sap stream throughout the entire plant. Fungicides of this type, for example benomyl, thiophanate-methyl, and carbendazim, kill fungi in the plant tissues. Systemic pesticides, such as dimethoate and heptenophos, are predominantly used against sap-sucking pests and are less useful (unless they are mixed with a contact compound) against pests that have chewing mouthparts, such as caterpillars, beetles, and earwigs.

Thorough spraying of affected plants, especially on the undersides of leaves, is essential with all pesticides. Pesticide-resistant strains may sometimes occur, particularly with persistent greenhouse pests such as whiteflies and red spider mites.

Fungi that are frequently treated with systemic fungicides may also develop resistant strains. This problem can sometimes be overcome by using a different type of compound, but with greenhouse pests the use of biological control (where possible) is often a better alternative (see p.546).

Formulation of chemical preparations

The active ingredient of a chemical preparation kills the organism, and the way in which a preparation has been formulated determines its efficacy and use. Pesticides and fungicides are available as concentrated liquids, dusts, powders (with which a wetter may be incorporated to ensure thorough penetration of the active ingredient), smokes, baits, and ready-to-use diluted liquids. These are now formulated for maximum effectiveness and safety, for gardeners and for the environment, although in the past many environmentally harmful chemicals were available.

(see p.546)

Using chemicals safely

If the instructions are followed precisely – that is, only in the way and for the purpose that the manufacturer describes – chemicals should prove effective with little risk to the user or to the environment. It is now illegal in some countries for gardeners to use chemicals other than in accordance with the instructions provided. Always take the following precautions:

• think before you spray: is it really necessary?
• choose the chemical carefully – make sure it is the right one for the job;
• apply the preparation at the rate and frequency stated on the label;
• never mix chemicals unless the manufacturer recommends this;
• always observe any suggested precautions;
• do not spray in the wind, to avoid damaging adjacent plants;
• do not spray during the middle part of the day (or at any time of the day on hot days) as hot, sunny weather increases the risk of scorching plants;
• avoid contact with the skin and eyes;
• do not inhale dusts, smokes, or sprays;
• make sure that the chemical does not drift into other people's gardens;
• keep pets and children away during treatment;
• never eat, drink, or smoke when applying a chemical;
• dispose of any excess carefully and wash out any apparatus thoroughly;
• do not use apparatus for anything other than chemicals;
• store chemicals out of reach of children and animals;
• store chemicals in their original containers, with their original labels, and keep any explanatory leaflets with them.

Phytotoxicity

Some plants are liable to suffer adverse reactions to fungicides and insecticides. This is known as phytotoxicity. The manufacturer's instructions often list those species that should not be treated. Such lists cannot, however, be complete, since the reaction of many ornamental plants to certain chemicals is as yet unknown. If in doubt as to whether a certain chemical may be suitable, first test the fungicide or pesticide on a small area of the plant, to gauge the likely reaction, before undertaking treatment of the whole plant. Alternatively, where several plants of the same type are grown together, test the chemical on only one of them.

Various other factors, including the stage of growth and the environmental conditions surrounding the plant, can also increase the likelihood of a plant being damaged by chemical treatments. For example, young seedlings, cuttings, and flower petals are much more sensitive than is mature foliage to variations in the growing conditions, and may therefore be adversely affected by the application of some chemical treatments. Similarly, plants that are suffering any stress should never be treated with chemicals.

In order to avoid problems with side-effects on mature plants, never spray them when they are in bright sunlight, or when they are either dry around the roots or have been exposed to unusually high or low temperatures.

Leaf problems

Eaten leaves

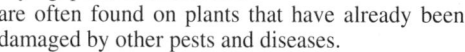

Slugs and snails

Plants affected All seedlings, climbing plants, herbaceous perennials, small annuals, bulbous plants, vegetables, including potatoes (see also "Slugs", p.566), and strawberries.

Symptoms Holes appear in the foliage and stems may be stripped; silvery slime trails may be left on the leaves or the soil surface. Small holes are visible on the outside of bulbs and the underground part of

Slugs under leaves

Holes in leaves

Silvery slime trails

Stems stripped

their stems, leading to large cavities inside.
Cause Slugs (e.g. *Milax*, *Arion*, and *Deroceras* spp.) and snails (e.g. *Helix aspersa*), slimy-bodied molluscs that feed mainly at night or after rain.
Control Cultivate regularly to expose eggs, and avoid the use of organic fertilizers and mulches. Scatter methiocarb or metaldehyde slug pellets among plants, or spray with liquid metaldehyde or one of the aluminium sulphate-based products.

Earwigs

Plants affected Shrubs, perennials, and annuals, commonly dahlias, chrysanthemums, and clematis. Also apricots and peaches.
Symptoms Young leaves are eaten in summer. See p.561 for other symptoms.
Cause The earwig (*Forficula auricularia*), which is a yellowish-brown insect 15mm (³/4in) long with a pair of curved pincers. Earwigs hide during the day and feed at night.
Control Place inverted pots, that have been loosely stuffed with hay or straw, on canes among susceptible plants; earwigs use

Adult earwigs

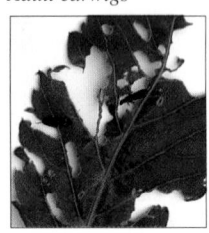
Leaves eaten away

these as daytime shelters from which they can be removed and destroyed. Alternatively, spray at dusk with permethrin, pirimiphos-methyl, or HCH.

Woodlice

Plants affected Seedlings and other soft growth, including strawberry fruits.
Symptoms Holes may appear in seedlings and in leaves near shoot tips but woodlice are not generally pests; they mainly eat decaying plant material and are often found on plants that have already been damaged by other pests and diseases.
Cause Woodlice (e.g. *Oniscus*, *Porcellio*, and *Armadillidium* spp.), also known as slaters or pill bugs. They are grey or brownish-grey, sometimes with white or yellow markings, and up to 1cm (¹/2in) long with hard, segmented bodies. They feed at night and hide away out of sight in dark shelters during the day.
Control Always clear away plant debris and keep greenhouses tidy to reduce shelter. Protect seedlings with HCH dust or scatter methiocarb slug pellets.

Millipedes

Plants affected Seedlings and other soft growth, strawberry fruits, and potato tubers.
Symptoms Seedlings and soft growth are eaten; slug damage on bulbs and potato tubers is enlarged. Damage is rarely serious.
Cause Millipedes (e.g. *Blaniulus*, *Brachydesmus*, and *Cylindroiulus* spp.), black,

Common millipedes

grey, brown, or creamy-white animals that feed below or at soil level. They have hard, segmented bodies with two pairs of legs per segment (centipedes, which are beneficial predators, have only one pair per segment). The spotted snake millipede (*Blaniulus guttulatus*) is the most damaging species. Its slender, creamy-white body is up to 2cm (³/4in) long with a row of red dots along each side. Millipedes are encouraged by soils that have a high organic content.
Control Cultivate the soil thoroughly and maintain good hygiene. Use inorganic rather than organic fertilizers in areas where millipedes are a problem, especially where potatoes are being grown. Millipedes, once present, are difficult to control, but HCH dust or methiocarb slug pellets may occasionally have some effect.

Flea beetles

Plants affected The seedlings of brassicas, leafy vegetables, radishes, wallflowers (*Cheiranthus*), and stocks (*Matthiola*).
Symptoms Small holes and pits are scalloped from the upper surface of the leaves; plants may die.

Cause Small, black or metallic-blue beetles (e.g. *Phyllotreta* spp.), sometimes with a yellow stripe running down each wing case. They are usually 2mm (¹/16in) long, with enlarged hind legs that enable them to leap off from plant surfaces when disturbed. They overwinter in plant debris.
Control Clear away plant debris, particularly in autumn. Sow seed in warm soil and water seedlings regularly to help rapid growth through the vulnerable stages. Apply an HCH seed dressing before sowing, or dust emerged seedlings with HCH, derris, pirimiphos-methyl, pyrethrum, or carbaryl.

Asparagus beetles

Plants affected Asparagus.
Symptoms Leaves are eaten; the epidermis is removed from stems, causing the upper growth to dry and turn brown. Damage occurs between late spring and early autumn.
Cause Both the adult and larval asparagus beetle (*Crioceris asparagi*). The adult beetles are 7mm

Adults   *Larvae*

(¹/4in) long, with yellow and black wing cases and a reddish thorax. The larvae are greyish-yellow.
Control Pick off light infestations by hand. If serious, spray with pyrethrum, derris, or permethrin; if plants are in flower, spray at dusk to protect bees.

Viburnum beetles

Plants affected *Viburnum*.
Symptoms Holes are eaten in the leaves; this occurs first in early summer, when the foliage may be reduced to just veins, and then again in late summer.
Cause The viburnum beetle (*Pyrrhalta viburni*). The initial period of damage in early summer is caused by the creamy-white larvae, which are up to 7mm (¹/4in) in length and have black markings. The second phase of damage, occurring in late summer, is caused by the adult beetles, which are greyish-brown in colour.

Control Spray with permethrin, pyrethrum, malathion, pirimiphos-methyl, or fenitrothion when the larvae first appear.

Red lily beetles

Plants affected Bulbous plants, especially lilies (*Lilium*) and fritillaries (*Fritillaria*), and occasionally *Polygonatum*.
Symptoms Leaves and flowers are eaten from early spring to mid-autumn.
Cause The adult and

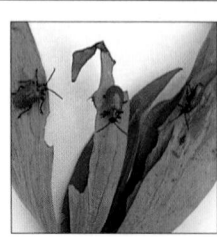

larval red lily beetle (*Lilioceris lilii*). Adults are 8mm (³/sin) long and bright red. Larvae are reddish-brown with black heads, and covered in black excrement.
Control A long egg-laying and emergence period (mid-spring to mid-summer) makes control difficult. Pick off by hand; otherwise spray with permethrin, pirimiphos-methyl, or fenitrothion.

Vine weevils

Adult vine weevil

Irregular holes in leaf margins

Plants affected Shrubs, mainly rhododendrons, hydrangeas, *Euonymus*, and camellias; also grape vines (*Vitis vinifera*), strawberries, and other herbaceous plants.
Symptoms Notches appear in leaf margins, often near the ground, from mid-spring to mid-autumn.
Cause The adult vine weevil (*Otiorhynchus sulcatus*), a greyish-black beetle 9mm (³/sin) long, with a short snout and a pair of elbowed antennae that feeds at night and hides by day.
Control Damage occurs over a long period, and control is difficult, although good hygiene and the removal of plant debris reduce the number of hiding places. Established plants can tolerate damage, but if the problem is serious spray at dusk with permethrin, HCH, or pirimiphos-methyl.
See also "Vine weevil larvae", p.570.

Capsid bugs

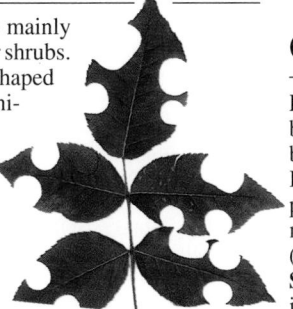

Plants affected Shrubs and perennials (especially chrysanthemums, fuchsias, hydrangeas, *Caryopteris*, and dahlias), annuals, vegetables (rarely), and fruits.
Symptoms The leaves at shoot tips are distorted with numerous small holes. Damage occurs throughout the summer. See p.561 for other symptoms.
Cause Capsid bugs (e.g. *Lygus rugulipennis* and *Lygocoris pabulinus*), green or brown insects 6mm (¹/4in) long that suck sap from shoot tips. Their toxic saliva kills plant tissues, causing leaves to tear.
Control In winter, clear up plant debris. Spray at first sign of damage, with dimethoate, fenitrothion, pirimiphos-methyl, HCH, pyrethrum, or permethrin.

Leaf-cutting bees

Plants affected Roses mainly but also trees and other shrubs.
Symptoms Lozenge-shaped or circular pieces of uniform size are removed from the margins of the leaf.
Cause Leaf-cutting bees (*Megachile* spp.), which use the leaf pieces to build their nests. They are up to 1cm (¹/2in) long, and have ginger hairs on the underside of their abdomen.
Control Leaf-cutting bees are of some benefit as pollinating insects and, unless plants are heavily damaged, control is not necessary. If they are a persistent nuisance, swat them as they return to the leaf.

Sawfly larvae

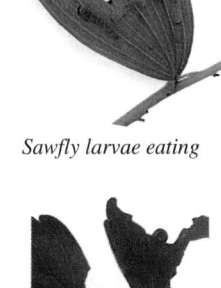

Sawfly larvae eating

Leaves eaten away

Plants affected Trees, shrubs, perennials, bulbous plants, and fruits. Particularly affected are conifers, willows (*Salix*), *Aruncus dioicus*, *Geum*, *Aquilegia*, Solomon's seal (*Polygonatum*), roses, gooseberries, and currants.
Symptoms Plants are defoliated.
Cause The larvae of various sawfly species (e.g. *Nematus*, *Pristiphora*, and *Diprion* spp.); caterpillar-like larvae that are up to 3cm (1¹/4in) long and generally green, sometimes with black spots. The larvae of the Solomon's seal sawfly (*Phymatocera aterrima*) are usually greyish-white in colour. Most larvae grip the leaf edge and wave their bodies in an "S" shape when they are disturbed, but this does not occur with those on *Geum* or Solomon's seal.
Control Where possible, remove by hand. Spray serious infestations with pyrethrum, permethrin, fenitrothion, pirimiphos-methyl, or malathion.

Winter moth caterpillars

Plants affected Many deciduous trees, fruit trees, and roses.
Symptoms Leaves are eaten between bud burst and late spring. Blossom and fruitlets may also be severely damaged.
Cause Pale green caterpillars, 2.5cm (1in) long, of the winter moth (*Operophtera brumata*).
Control Place sticky grease bands at least 15cm (6in) wide around tree trunks in mid-autumn, in order to prevent the wingless female moths from climbing up to lay eggs on the branches. Spray after bud burst with derris, pyrethrum, permethrin, pirimiphos-methyl; alternatively, use the bacterial control *Bacillus thuringiensis*.

Cabbage caterpillars

Plants affected Mainly brassicas, including cabbages, cauliflowers, and Brussels sprouts. Some perennial and annual ornamentals, e.g. nasturtiums (*Tropaeolum*).
Symptoms Holes appear in the foliage between late spring and early autumn, and caterpillars may be found in the hearts of brassicas and on leaves.
Cause Caterpillars of the large cabbage white butterfly (*Pieris brassicae*), which are yellow and black with distinct hairs; those of the small cabbage white (*P. rapae*), pale green with velvety hairs; and those of the cabbage moth (*Mamestra brassicae*), yellowish-green or brown, with few hairs.
Control Pick off the young caterpillars by hand. For serious infestations, apply derris, pyrethrum, permethrin, pirimiphos-methyl, carbaryl, or use the bacterial control *Bacillus thuringiensis*.

Wood pigeons

Plants affected Brassicas and bush fruits, especially blackcurrants, and the seeds of peas, beans, and other vegetable crops.
Symptoms Leaves of brassicas are eaten, especially in cold weather, and young plants are uprooted; blackcurrants are stripped of buds, leaves, and fruits; seeds are eaten.
Cause Wood pigeons.
Control Netting is the only effective means of preventing damage to crops. Scaring devices, such as humming tapes, scarecrows, or aluminium foil strips, work only initially; they soon lose their deterrent effect as birds become used to the devices. Repellent sprays, based on quassia or aluminium ammonium sulphate, must be used very frequently if their effectiveness is to be maintained.

Caterpillars

Plants affected Many garden plants.
Symptoms Leaves, and occasionally also flowers, are eaten away.
Cause Caterpillars of various species of butterfly and moth, which feed on plant material. The most common in gardens are winter moth and cabbage caterpillars (see left), webber moth caterpillars (see p.551), and tortrix moth caterpillars (see p.552).
Control Pick off caterpillars by hand, if practicable. For serious infestations, spray with pirimiphos-methyl or fenitrothion.

Rabbits and hares

Plants affected Low-growing plants, young trees.
Symptoms Low-growing leaves are eaten, and the bark of young trees is gnawed away, especially during spells of cold weather.
Cause and control See p.570 for details.

Deer

Plants affected Most garden plants, especially trees, shrubs (including roses), and herbaceous plants.
Symptoms Shoots and leaves are eaten; tree bark is rubbed and frayed, and stripped in winter.
Cause and control See p.570 for details.

See also "Webber moth caterpillars", p.551; "Tortrix moth caterpillars", p.552; "Bacterial leaf spots and blotches", p.552; "Shothole", p.552; "Cutworms", p.559; and "Birds", p.561.

Discoloured and wilted leaves

Aphids

Plants affected Trees, shrubs, climbing plants, perennials, annuals, bulbous plants, vegetables, and fruits.

Symptoms Leaves are often sticky with honeydew (aphid excrement), blistered, or blackened by sooty moulds; stems and buds may also be covered. See also p.555.

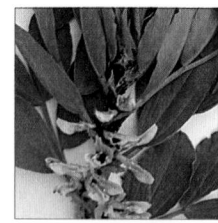

Blackfly on stem

Cause Aphids (including those known as greenfly, blackfly, or plant lice) that cluster on stems and the undersides of leaves, sucking the sap; some attack roots. They are up to 5mm (^{1}/4in) long, either wingless or winged, and green,

Blistered leaf

yellow, brown, pink, grey, or black; some, e.g. the woolly beech aphid, are covered in a fluffy, white wax. Aphids may transmit viruses (see p.553).

Control Apply a tar oil wash in winter against aphid eggs on deciduous fruit trees and bushes. Spray other plants, before heavy infestations develop, with malathion, fenitrothion, pirimiphos-methyl, insecticidal soaps, pyrethrum, or derris, or use a systemic insecticide, such as dimethoate, heptenophos, or pirimicarb. Pirimicarb is selective, leaving most other pests and beneficial insects unharmed.

Whiteflies

Plants affected Both indoor and greenhouse plants, also some vegetables and fruits.

Symptoms Leaves are covered with sticky honeydew (whitefly excrement) and a form of sooty mould. Small, white insects fly off the plants when they are disturbed.

Adult whiteflies

Cause Whiteflies, active, white-winged insects 2mm (^{1}/16in) long that rest beneath young leaves; the immature, scale-like nymphs, which are immobile, whitish-green (or black if dead), flat, and oval are also found here. Several species occur, the most widespread of which

Whitefly nymphs

is the glasshouse whitefly (*Trialeurodes vaporariorum*). In the open, brassicas are attacked by the cabbage whitefly (*Aleyrodes proletella*).

Control The parasitic wasp *Encarsia formosa* provides effective biological control in greenhouses from mid-spring to mid-autumn, if introduced early. Both greenhouse and garden whiteflies may be sprayed with permethrin, pyrethrum, pirimiphos-methyl, or insecticidal soaps on three or four occasions at five-day intervals; pesticide-resistant strains of greenhouse whitefly do, however, occur.

Mealybugs

Plants affected Indoor and greenhouse plants, cacti and other succulents, vines (*Vitis*), some tender fruits, *Citrus*.

Symptoms A fluffy, white substance appears in leaf and stem axils. Plants may be sticky with honeydew (excrement) and black-

ened with sooty moulds. Roots may also be affected.

Cause Various mealybugs (e.g. *Pseudococcus* and *Planococcus*); soft-bodied, greyish-white, wingless insects up to 5mm (^{1}/4in) long, often with white, waxy filaments trailing from their bodies. Root damage is caused by root mealybugs.

Control During the warmer months the introduction of the ladybird *Cryptolaemus montrouzieri* provides biological control. If this fails, spray with malathion, pirimiphos-methyl, or an insecticidal soap on several occasions at intervals of two weeks.

White blister

Plants affected The Cruciferae family, commonly brassicas, honesty (*Lunaria*), *Arabis*, and *Alyssum*.

Symptoms White, glistening, fungal spore clusters, often grouped in concentric circles, develop on lower leaf surfaces. Severely affected foliage, and the heads

of brassicas, may also be distorted by this condition.

Cause The fungus *Albugo candida*, which is most troublesome on closely spaced plants.

Control Remove and burn affected leaves. Rotate plantings where feasible, and increase spacing.

Powdery mildew

Plants affected Trees, shrubs, roses, perennials, annuals, bulbous plants, vegetables, fruits, and many indoor plants.

Symptoms A fungal growth, usually white and powdery, appears on the leaves; on rhododendrons it is buff-coloured and felty. Usually found on the

upper surface, it may appear on the lower side only or on both sides. A purple discoloration may develop. Leaves yellow and fall early. Flowers and fruits (see p.562) are also affected.

Cause Various fungi, including species of *Sphaerotheca*, *Oidium*, and *Uncinula*, which thrive on plants growing in dry soil. Some have restricted host ranges; others attack widely. Spores are spread by wind and rain splash, and the fungus may overwinter on host-plant surfaces.

Control Avoid growing susceptible plants on dry sites, and water and mulch as necessary. Remove affected areas immediately. If the problem persists, spray with a suitable fungicide, e.g. benomyl, sulphur, or bupirimate with triforine.

Downy mildew

Plants affected Perennials, annuals, bulbous plants, vegetables, including brassicas, some fruits, stocks (*Matthiola*), lettuces, and seedlings.

Symptoms A fluffy or mealy, white, fungal growth develops on the lower surface of the foli-

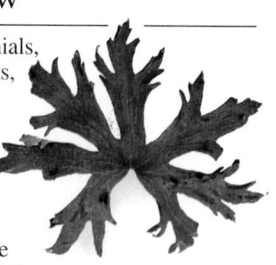

age, while the upper surface is blotched either yellow or brown; the older leaves are usually the most seriously affected. Growth is stunted and the plant is prone to secondary infections such as grey mould/*Botrytis* (see below).

Cause Species of *Peronospora* and *Bremia* fungi, which are encouraged by humid conditions.

Control Sow seeds thinly and do not overcrowd plants. Improve ventilation, air circulation, and drainage; avoid overhead watering. Remove affected leaves and spray plants with mancozeb.

Grey mould/*Botrytis*

Plants affected Trees, shrubs, perennials, annuals, bulbous plants, vegetables, fruits, and most indoor plants. Soft-leaved plants are particularly vulnerable to this condition.

Symptoms A fuzzy, grey, fungal growth appears on the foliage, causing it to discolour and rapidly deteriorate; the infection may then spread into the main body of the plant. See pp.557, 560, and 562 for other symptoms.

Cause and control See p.557 for details.

Red spider mites

Plants affected Trees, shrubs, perennials, annuals, bulbous plants, cacti and other succulents, vegetables, and fruits. Beans, cucumbers, melons, apples, and plums are particularly susceptible.

Symptoms The leaves become dull and increasingly yellowed as a fine, pale mottling develops on their upper surface. They fall prematurely, and a fine silk webbing may cover the plant.

Cause Red spider mites, eight-legged animals less than 1mm (^{1}/16in) long. They are yellowish-green with black markings, but may be orange-red in autumn. There are several species, the most common of which is the two-spotted, or glasshouse, red spider mite (*Tetranychus urticae*); this affects both garden and indoor plants in summer.

Control The rapid reproduction of the mites and the existence of pesticide-resistant strains make control difficult. Discourage those in greenhouses by spraying water underneath leaves and maintaining high humidity; the predatory mite *Phytoseiulus persimilis* provides an effective biological control of *T. urticae* if introduced before heavy infestations develop. Non-resistant red spider mites may be controlled with sprays of malathion, pirimiphos-methyl, dimethoate, or insecticidal soaps on three or four occasions at five-day intervals.

Thrips

Plants affected Shrubs, perennials, annuals, bulbous plants, vegetables, fruits, and indoor and greenhouse plants. Gladioli, privets (*Ligustrum*), lilacs (*Syringa*), honeysuckles (*Lonicera*), peas, and onions are often attacked.
Symptoms A silver-white discoloration with tiny black dots appears on the upper leaf surface. See p.560 for other symptoms.
Cause Various species of thrips or thunderfly (e.g. *Thrips simplex*, *T. tabaci*, *Frankliniella occidentalis*, and *Kakothrips pisivorus*), which are brownish-black insects with narrow bodies up to 2mm (^{1}/16in) long, sometimes crossed with pale bands. The immature nymphs are a pale yellow-orange but otherwise resemble the adults. Both adults and nymphs feed on the upper surface of the leaf. They thrive in hot, dry conditions.
Control Water plants regularly and reduce the temperature in greenhouses with shading and ventilation. Spray with permethrin, pyrethrum, malathion, pirimiphos-methyl, HCH, or dimethoate as soon as damage is seen.

Silver leaf

Plants affected Broad-leaved trees and shrubs, especially those in the Rosaceae family; plums and cherries are most commonly attacked.
Symptoms A silver-grey discoloration appears on the foliage, often starting on a single branch and then gradually spreading throughout the crown. The branches subsequently die back and infected limbs have a central dark stain.
Cause The fungus *Chondrostereum purpureum*, which is also commonly found on felled logs and dead branches. The spores are produced from small, leathery brackets attached to the bark. The upper surface of the bracket is pale grey and slightly hairy, the lower surface purple and smooth. Spores may infect fresh wounds (less than a month old). There is no risk of infection from the silvered foliage.
Control Avoid injury to plants. Prune susceptible trees in summer, when infection is less likely to occur, and apply a wound paint. Remove affected limbs to 15cm (6in) past the stained wood.

Leafhoppers

Plants affected Trees, shrubs, perennials, annuals, vegetables, and fruits. Rhododendrons, roses, pelargoniums, primulas, and tomatoes are usually the most vulnerable.
Symptoms A coarse, pale spotting appears on the upper leaf surface, except on rhododendrons where damage is restricted to the spreading of rhododendron bud blast (see p.560).
Cause Leafhoppers, such as the rose leafhopper (*Edwardsiana rosae*) and the glasshouse leafhopper

Spots on leaves

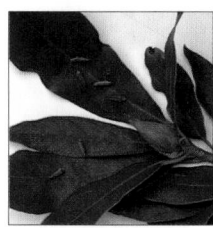
Adult leafhoppers

(*Hauptidia maroccana*), green or yellow insects 2–3mm (^{1}/16–^{1}/8in) long that leap from the plant when disturbed. Their bodies are widest just behind the head and taper back. The rhododendron leafhopper (*Graphocephala fennahi*) is turquoise-green and orange, and 6mm (^{1}/4in) in length. The creamy-white, immature nymphs are less active.
Control Spray beneath the leaves with malathion, pirimiphos-methyl, dimethoate, permethrin, or pyrethrum when leafhopper activity is seen.

Pear and cherry slugworms

Plants affected Pear and plum trees; also fruiting and ornamental cherries (*Prunus*), *Chaenomeles*, hawthorns (*Crataegus*).
Symptoms The leaves develop whitish-brown patches where the larvae graze away the surface.
Cause The pear and cherry slugworm (*Caliroa cerasi*), which is the larval stage of a small black-bodied sawfly. The larvae are up to 10mm (^{1}/2in) long and are broadest at the head end. They are covered by a black slimy substance and consequently resemble slugs. They feed mainly on the upper leaf surface. Two or three generations occur between early summer and early autumn.
Control Spray thoroughly with pyrethrum, derris, permethrin or pirimiphos-methyl as soon as the larvae are first seen.

Suckers (psyllids)

Plants affected Bay (*Laurus nobilis*), box (*Buxus*), and pears.
Symptoms The leaf margins of bay are yellowed, thickened, and curled; box leaves are stunted; pear leaves are sticky with honeydew (excrement) and blackened with sooty mould. Damage occurs throughout the summer. See p.555 for other symptoms.
Cause Suckers (e.g. the bay sucker, *Trioza alacris*, the box sucker, *Psylla buxi*, and the pear sucker, *Psylla pyricola*), the flattened and immature nymphs of small, aphid-like, winged insects. The nymphs are 2mm (^{1}/16in) long and usually grey or green.
Control Prune out and burn affected shoots immediately. Spray the plant thoroughly with dimethoate or pirimiphos-methyl, either in spring or when the damage is first seen.

Leaf and bud eelworms

Plants affected Annuals and most herbaceous perennials. Most commonly attacked are begonias, chrysanthemums, and *Anemone* x *hybrida*.
Symptoms Brownish-black patches appear on leaves as islands or wedges between the larger veins.

Dark patches

Cause Microscopic nematodes (*Aphelenchoides*) that feed in large numbers inside infested leaves.
Control Burn all affected leaves or destroy the whole plant as soon as the infestation is noticed. For chrysanthemums, dip the dormant stools in clean water held at 46°C (115°F) for at least five minutes to obtain clean cuttings. There is no chemical control available to the amateur gardener.

Wedges between veins

Leaf miners

Plants affected Trees, shrubs, perennials, and vegetables, especially lilacs (*Syringa*), hollies (*Ilex*), apples, cherries, chrysanthemums, and celery.
Symptoms White or brown areas appear within the leaf, often of characteristic shape for the particular leaf miner, e.g. linear, circular, or irregular.
Cause Larvae of various flies, e.g. the celery leaf miner (*Euleia heracleii*) and the chrysanthemum leaf miner (*Phytomyza syngenesiae*); moths, for example the apple leaf mining moth (*Lyonetia clerkella*); beetles, such as the beech leaf mining weevil (*Rhynchaenus fagi*); and sawflies, such as the birch leaf mining sawfly (*Fenusa pusilla*).
Control Remove and destroy affected leaves if the plant is lightly infested. Spray seriously infested plants with pirimiphos-methyl, dimethoate, or HCH when damage is first noticed.

Linear blotching

Irregular discoloration

Webber moth caterpillars

Plants affected Many trees, shrubs, perennials, and annuals, but most particularly fruit trees, willows (*Salix*), *Euonymus*, junipers (*Juniperus*), hawthorns (*Crataegus*), and cotoneasters.
Symptoms Shoots of the affected plant are defoliated, and the feeding area is completely covered with a dense, greyish-white, silk webbing.
Cause The caterpillars of various moths, such as the brown tail moth (*Euproctis chrysorrhoea*), the lackey moth (*Malacosoma neustria*), small ermine moths (*Yponomeuta* spp.), the hawthorn webber moth (*Scythropia crataegella*), and the juniper webber moth (*Dichomeris marginella*). The caterpillars of the last two species are no more than 2cm (^{3}/4in) long; the other caterpillars are up to 5cm (2in) long and often have hairy bodies.
Control Remove small infestations by careful pruning. If the problem is very serious, spray the plants with permethrin, pirimiphos-methyl, pyrethrum, or *Bacillus thuringiensis*.

Tortrix moth caterpillars

Plants affected Trees (ornamental and fruit), shrubs, perennials, annuals, and bulbous plants.
Symptoms Two leaves may be bound together with fine, silk threads, or one leaf may be either similarly attached to a fruit or folded over on itself.

Brown, dry, skeletal patches appear on the leaves.
Cause The caterpillars of tortrix moths, such as *Cacoecimorpha pronubana*, which graze away the inner surfaces of leaves. They are up to 2cm (³/₄in) long, and are generally dark green with brown heads. The caterpillars wriggle backwards rapidly when they are disturbed.
Control Squeeze bound-up leaves to crush the caterpillars or pupae. Pheromone traps are available for use against *C. pronubana*; these trap the males and reduce the likelihood of the females mating successfully. If the problem is serious, spray the affected plants very thoroughly with permethrin or pirimiphos-methyl.

Scale insects

Plants affected Trees, shrubs, cacti and other succulents, fruits, and indoor and greenhouse plants.
Symptoms The foliage is sticky with honeydew (excrement) and blackened with sooty moulds. Plant growth may be slow. White, egg-containing deposits may also appear. See also p.557.
Cause Scale insects, such as soft scale (*Coccus hesperidum*), mussel scale (*Lepidosaphes ulmi*), and horse chestnut scale (*Pulvinaria regalis*). They are yellow, brown, dark grey, or white, up to 6mm (¹/₄in) long, flat or raised, and circular, pear-shaped, or

Soft scale

Egg deposits

oval. They are found on lower leaf surfaces and stems.
Control Spray deciduous fruit trees with a tar oil wash in winter. Other plants may be sprayed with malathion or pirimiphos-methyl. This is most effective when the newly hatched scale nymphs are present – throughout the year on greenhouse plants, early to mid-summer outside.

Bacterial leaf spots and blotches

Plants affected Trees, shrubs, roses, perennials, annuals, bulbous plants, vegetables, fruits, and indoor plants.
Symptoms Various spots or patches develop. They may appear water-soaked, and are often angular with a yellow edge or halo ("halo

Spots   *Yellowing*

blight"). As they coalesce, the leaf is killed. Black spots appear on rose and delphinium leaves.
Cause *Pseudomonas* bacteria, spread by insects, rain splash, or wind-borne seeds.
Control Avoid wetting the foliage. Remove all affected leaves; spray with Bordeaux mixture. Spray roses with benomyl, thiophanate-methyl, carbendazim, or triforine.

Black spot on rose

Rusts

Plants affected Trees, shrubs, perennials, annuals, bulbous plants, vegetables, fruits, and indoor plants.
Symptoms Small, bright orange or brown patches of spores develop on the lower leaf surface, each corresponding to a yellow discoloration on the upper surface. Spores may appear in concentric rings or pustules, sometimes pale beige, e.g. those of chrysanthemum white rust. Winter spores, dark brown or black, are sometimes also produced. The leaves may also fall early. See p.557 for other symptoms.
Cause Fungi, most often species of *Puccinia* and *Melampsora*, which are encouraged by high humidity. The spores are spread by rain splash and air currents. A few rusts are systemic.
Control Remove all affected areas. Improve air circulation by increasing ventilation and plant spacing wherever possible, and try to discourage the development of lush growth.

Small, brown spores

Pale discoloration

Rust on bluebell leaf

Affected plants should be thoroughly sprayed with a fungicide containing propiconazole or mancozeb.

Corky scab

Plants affected Cacti and other succulents, especially *Opuntia* and *Epiphyllum*.
Symptoms Corky or brown, irregularly shaped spots appear. These areas later become sunken.
Cause Either extremely high humidity or excessively high light levels.

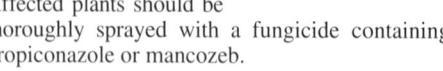

Control Take measures to improve the growing conditions of the plant. In extreme cases, however, the plant must be discarded, after having been used for propagation purposes, if desired.

Shothole

Plants affected Edible and ornamental cherries (*Prunus*), peaches, nectarines, plums, gages, and *Prunus laurocerasus*; also other trees, shrubs, and woody perennials.
Symptoms Discoloured (usually brown) spots develop on the foliage; the

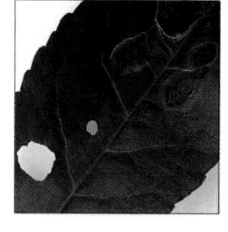

dead leaf tissue then falls away, leaving holes and giving the plant an untidy, ragged appearance. In severe cases large areas of leaf are lost.
Cause The fungus *Clasterosporium carpophilum* is usually responsible for this condition, but occasionally other fungi or bacteria are involved. Plants that are lacking in vigour are most likely to show symptoms of shothole.
Control Try to improve the general growing conditions and the overall health of the affected plant. If the problem persists, spraying the plant thoroughly with a copper-based fungicide may help.

Fungal leaf spots

Plants affected Trees, shrubs, perennials, annuals, bulbous plants, vegetables, fruits, and many indoor plants.
Symptoms Discrete, concentrically zoned spots appear on the leaves; close

inspection may reveal pinprick-sized, fungal, fruiting bodies. Spots may be a range of colours but are frequently brown or slate grey. In severe cases they coalesce, sometimes obscuring most of the leaf surface. Early leaf fall may occur, but in some instances there is little damage or effect on the overall vigour of the plant. The condition known as anthracnose also causes cankers on stems.
Cause A wide range of fungi.
Control Remove all affected parts, and rake up and burn any leaves that have already fallen. Spray with benomyl or a copper-based fungicide.

Tomato leaf mould

Plants affected Almost exclusively greenhouse tomatoes.
Symptoms Purplish-grey, fuzzy, fungal patches develop on the lower leaf surface, each corresponding to a yellow discoloration on the upper surface. Leaves wither and die but

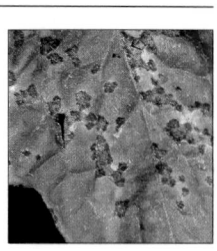

do not fall. The lower leaves are affected first.
Cause The fungus *Fulvia fulva* (syn. *Cladosporium fulvum*), which thrives in warm, humid environments. The spores are spread by insects, tools, and handling, or on air currents. They overwinter on plant debris and on greenhouse structures.
Control Remove affected leaves, and improve ventilation and air circulation. Consider growing cultivars bred for resistance to the disease, e.g. 'Shirley', 'Grenadier', and 'M. M. Super'. Spray with a suitable fungicide, e.g. benomyl, mancozeb, or carbendazim; it is not worth spraying if the disease occurs towards the end of the season.

Chocolate spot

Plants affected Broad beans.

Symptoms Chocolate-coloured spots or streaks appear on both the leaves and the stems, sometimes coalescing to cover a whole leaf. In extreme cases the plant is killed.

Cause *Botrytis fabae*, a fungus that thrives in wet spring weather. Plants growing in very acid soils are susceptible, as are those with soft, lush growth. Winter-sown crops are most severely affected by this condition.

Control Sow seed thinly, first dressing the soil with sulphate of potash, and avoid excessive use of nitrogen fertilizers. Remove and burn affected plants at the end of the harvest. Spray with benomyl.

Scab

Plants affected Pears, *Citrus*, loquats, pyracanthas, and *Malus*, including both ornamental and fruiting species.

Brown patches

Symptoms Dark and greenish-brown patches, scabby and sometimes blistered, develop on the foliage; any affected leaves may fall early. See p.562 for other symptoms.

Cause The fungi *Venturia inaequalis*, *V. pirina*, *Spilocaea pyracanthae*, and *S. eriobotryae*, which thrive in damp weather. They may overwinter on infected leaves or shoots.

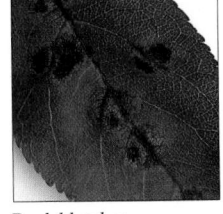
Dark blotches

Control Keep the plant open-centred by pruning, remove any scabby shoots and fruits, and rake up and burn all the fallen leaves. Spray plants with a suitable fungicide, such as thiram, triforine + bupirimate, benomyl, or carbendazim. Do not store any affected fruits.

Lily disease

Plants affected Lilies (*Lilium*), especially *L. candidum* and *L. x testaceum*.

Symptoms Dark green, water-soaked blotches develop on the leaves, later turning a pale brown; the foliage then withers but remains on the stem. Where the pathogen enters a leaf axil the stem may rot. Black sclerotia (fungal resting bodies) may form on dead tissues.

Cause The fungus *Botrytis elliptica*, which is encouraged by wet weather. Spores produced on the leaf lesions (or, in spring, from the sclerotia) are spread by rain splash and wind.

Control Grow on a well-drained site; clear away affected debris. Spray with Bordeaux mixture or benomyl at the start of the season.

Viruses

Plants affected All plants.

Symptoms Leaves are undersized, distorted, or grouped in rosettes. Patterns of yellow discoloration (mosaics, ringspots, mottles) are common. See pp.560 and 563 for other symptoms.

Yellowish streaks

Cause A large number of viruses, some with very wide host ranges. Submicroscopic virus particles in the sap of infected plants may be transmitted to healthy tissues by sap-feeding pests such as aphids (p.550), by nematodes or other soil-borne pests, through handling, or on pruning or propagating tools; some are seed-borne.

Ringspots

Control Buy certified (virus-free) plants where possible. Keep potential carriers, e.g. aphids (see p.550), under control, and make sure that the site is free of weeds as these may harbour viruses. Remove and burn affected plants as soon as possible; always handle suspect plants after those which appear healthy, and do not propagate from them. Always use a new site for any replacement plants.

Tulip fire

Plants affected Tulips.

Symptoms The leaves are covered with pale brown, spore-producing blotches. Both leaves and shoots are deformed and stunted, and later become covered in dense, grey, spore-bearing, fungal growths, and black sclerotia (fun-

gal resting bodies). The bulbs develop sunken, brown lesions and small, black sclerotia. See p.560 for other symptoms.

Cause The fungus *Botrytis tulipae*, which flourishes particularly in wet seasons; the spores are spread by wind and rain. The sclerotia persist in the soil, later germinating when tulips are planted again in the same area.

Control Remove and burn affected leaves and shoots (or preferably the whole plant) immediately. Plant from early winter onwards. Lift and dry bulbs at the end of the season, discarding any with sclerotia, and dip the remaining bulbs in a suitable fungicide solution, e.g. carbendazim. Wait at least two years before replanting the site with tulips; alternatively, change the soil.

Clubroot

Plants affected The family Cruciferae, especially brassicas (e.g. cabbages, Brussels sprouts, swedes), and radishes. Also some ornamentals, such as stocks (*Matthiola*), candytufts (*Iberis*), and wallflowers (*Cheiranthus*).

Symptoms Plants are stunted and discoloured; foliage wilts in hot weather. See also p.564.

Cause The slime mould *Plasmodiophora brassicae*, which thrives in poorly drained, acid soils, and is also found on manure and plant debris. It is easily spread on boots and tools, and the spores are very resilient, remaining viable for 20 years or more, even in the absence of a host plant. Weeds that are susceptible to the disease (e.g. shepherd's purse and charlock) may be a source of infection.

Control Remove and burn affected plants. Keep the area free of weeds, where feasible improve drainage, and lime the soil. Raise new plants in pots of soil-based compost so that their roots are well developed when planted out. Proprietary chemical dips may be used at the planting stage.

Tomato/potato blight

Plants affected Tomatoes (in the open and occasionally under cover), potatoes.

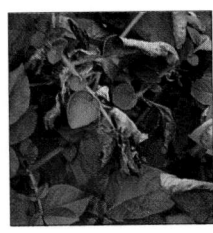

Symptoms Patches of brown discoloration develop on the leaf tips and edges; in damp conditions these may often be ringed with a white, fungal growth. The leaf tissue is killed, and where the patches coalesce the whole of the affected leaflet may eventually die. See pp.562 and 566 for other symptoms.

Cause The fungus *Phytophthora infestans*, which thrives in warm, moist conditions. Spores produced on the foliage of tomato and potato plants, and on potato haulms, are carried from plant to plant by wind and rain, and these may be washed down into the soil to infect potato tubers.

Control Avoid overhead watering. Earth up potatoes deeply to provide a barrier for the tubers against falling spores, and choose resistant cultivars, for example 'Kondor', 'Romano', 'Cara', and 'Wilja'. Protect both tomatoes and potatoes by spraying thoroughly with mancozeb or a copper-based fungicide. In wet seasons spray plants before the blight appears; spray tomatoes as soon as they have been stopped.

Fireblight

Plants affected Members of the family Rosaceae that bear pome fruits, mainly pears, apples, some *Sorbus*, cotoneasters, and hawthorns (*Crataegus*).

Symptoms The leaves generally turn blackish-brown, shrivel and die, and they remain clinging to the stem; those of some *Sorbus* and hawthorns may turn yellow and fall. Oozing cankers appear on the branches, and the whole tree may eventually die. See p.569 for other symptoms.

Cause The bacterium *Erwinia amylovora*, which is produced from the cankers, attacks via the blossom. It is carried from plant to plant by wind, rain splash, insects, and pollen.

Control Remove the affected plants or prune out affected areas to at least 60cm (24in) past the damaged area; remember to dip the saw in disinfectant before using it on another tree. Fireblight is no longer a notifiable disease.

Pansy sickness

Plants affected Violets (*Viola*) and pansies (*Viola* x *wittrockiana*).

Symptoms The petals and leaves discolour and wilt as the stem rots at ground level. Roots are also susceptible to attack, and may eventually become quite loose in the ground.

Cause Microscopic fungi (primarily *Pythium violae* and *Aphanomyces euteiches*), which are soil-borne and build up in soils where pansies and violets have been grown for several years. Sclerotia (fungal resting bodies) are produced and the soil may remain infected for several years.

Control Dig up and burn any affected plants as soon as the problem is noticed. Grow susceptible plants on a new site each year.

Primula brown core

Plants affected Primulas.

Symptoms Leaves yellow, wilt, and die, and the plant becomes loose in the ground as the roots rot back from the tips.

Cause and control See p.565.

Insecticide/fungicide damage

Plants affected Some indoor and garden plants.

Symptoms Discrete spots or patches, often bleached or scorched, appear on leaves, which may fall; the plant usually survives.

Cause Commonly chemicals used at the wrong rate or interval, or applied during hot, sunny weather. Some plants are damaged by fungicides or insecticides applied correctly and susceptible species should be noted on the packaging; check carefully before using.

Control Only use proprietary chemicals and always follow the manufacturers' instructions.

Contact weedkiller damage

Plants affected All plants.

Symptoms Pale, bleached spots appear on the contaminated foliage, sometimes turning brown, and small bumps may appear on stems. Bulbs exposed to contact weedkillers before their foliage has died down show a very pale, almost white, leaf colour the following season. In severe cases, vigour may be reduced and the plant may even die.

Usually plants grow out of the symptoms.

Cause Spray drift due to windy conditions, or to careless application. Poorly cleaned sprayers and watering cans may also lead to contamination.

Control Follow the manufacturers' instructions. Use a dribble bar applicator or watering can in preference to a sprayer, and keep all equipment for use with weedkillers only.

Drought

Plants affected All plants, especially those that are young and container-grown, or in light, sandy soils.

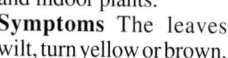

Symptoms Autumn colour develops early and defoliation may occur, sometimes followed by dieback. Plants wilt and growth is stunted. See pp.561 and 568 for other symptoms.

Cause Prolonged or repeated water shortage due to dry soil, excessive water loss from leaves of plants on exposed sites, injured or restricted roots, or soil compaction. Plants in small containers are vulnerable in hot weather, since peat-based composts allowed to dehydrate are hard to re-wet.

Control Water plants regularly; check those growing in hot or sunny positions. Mulch, where appropriate, to improve moisture retention. It is easier to prevent drought than to treat it; plants exposed to prolonged water shortage are less likely to recover once adequate water is supplied or temperatures lowered than those suffering a sudden shortage.

High temperatures and scorch

Plants affected In particular plants with fleshy leaves or flowers, those near glass, and seedlings; also trees, shrubs, perennials, annuals, bulbous plants, vegetables, fruits, and indoor plants.

Symptoms The leaves wilt, turn yellow or brown, become dry and crisp, and may die; the tips and margins are often affected first. In extreme cases the stems die back. Scorching produces brown patches on the upper or exposed parts of the plant; foliage close to glass is very susceptible. Affected leaves may shrivel completely. Scorched petals turn brown and become dry and crisp. Roses may show "balling" (as the outer petals dry up they enclose the bud). Fruits are also affected (see p.562).

Cause Very high or fluctuating temperatures in a closed environment (e.g. a greenhouse); scorching is caused by bright, but not necessarily hot, sunlight. Scorch problems are increased by moisture on the leaves and fruit, and by faults in the glass near plants, both of which magnify the sun's rays. Apple fruits may discolour if picked too early or stored with insufficient ventilation.

Control Where possible shade greenhouses, provide adequate ventilation to keep temperatures down, and move plants away from any faults there may be in the glass. Avoid overhead watering and spraying in sunny weather. Harvest only ripe apples and store them under suitable conditions.

Low temperatures

Plants affected Trees, shrubs, perennials, annuals, bulbous plants, vegetables, fruits, indoor plants; seedlings and young plants are most vulnerable.

Symptoms Leaves, especially those of seedlings, are sometimes bleached, and brown, dry patches develop; evergreen foliage may turn completely brown. Frost injury results in puckered, withered, or discoloured (often blackened) leaves, and a lifting of the lower leaf surface, which gives the foliage a silvered appearance. Rotten patches, brown and dry or dark and soft, develop on the petals, especially on exposed flowerheads. Frost injury may leave petals withered or discoloured and the whole flower may be killed. See p.557 for other symptoms.

Cause Low temperatures or occasionally great fluctuations in temperature. Plants in exposed positions or frost pockets are likely to be affected.

Control Provide winter protection for young or tender plants, and those grown in exposed positions.

Nitrogen deficiency

Plants affected Trees, shrubs, perennials, annuals, bulbous plants, vegetables, fruits, and indoor plants.

Symptoms Pale green leaves are produced, and these sometimes develop either yellow or pink tints. Overall growth is reduced and the whole plant may eventually become slightly spindly.

Cause Growing plants either in poor, light soils or in restricted surroundings such as hanging baskets, windowboxes, or other types of container.

Control Use green manures on affected areas, or apply a high-nitrogen fertilizer, e.g. sulphate of ammonia, nitrochalk, or dried blood.

Potassium deficiency

Plants affected Edible and ornamental fruiting plants, mainly currants, apples, and pears.

Symptoms The foliage turns blue, yellow, or purple, with a brown discoloration either in blotches or on the leaf tips or margins. Some leaves may roll inwards; they are fairly soft and therefore prone to attack by pathogens. Flowering, fruiting, and general growth of the whole plant may be reduced.

Cause Growing plants in soils either with a light texture or with a high chalk or peat content.

Control Improve the soil texture. Dress with sulphate of potash or a high-potash fertilizer.

Phosphate deficiency

Plants affected Potentially all plants may suffer; but this particular deficiency is unlikely to occur in most gardens.

Symptoms Plant growth is slow and the young foliage may appear dull or yellowed.

Cause The leaching out of phosphates in acid soils and areas of high rainfall. Plants growing in either heavy clay soils or deep peat soils, as well as those overlying iron pans, are the most likely to be at risk from this condition.

Control Apply bone meal or superphosphate.

Manganese/iron deficiency

Plants affected Trees, shrubs, perennials, annuals, bulbous plants, vegetables, fruits, and indoor plants. Acid-loving plants growing in alkaline soils are often affected.
Symptoms A yellowing or browning starts at the leaf margins and extends between the veins. The overall leaf colour may also be rather yellow.
Cause The cultivation of plants in unsuitable soils or composts; acid-loving plants, in particular, are unable to absorb adequate trace elements from alkaline soils. Regular watering with very hard water, buried debris (e.g builders' rubble), and rain run-off from mortar in walls are all possible causes of a locally raised soil pH.
Control Choose plants that are compatible with the soil type and clear the area of any builders' debris. Use rain water, not tap water, for susceptible plants. Acidify the soil before or after planting, and apply acid mulches. Apply a chelated or fritted form of trace elements and sequestered iron.

Magnesium deficiency

Plants affected Trees, shrubs, perennials, annuals, bulbous plants, vegetables, and fruits; also many indoor plants. Tomatoes, roses, and chrysanthemums are most often affected.
Symptoms Distinct areas of discoloration, usually yellow but occasionally red or brown, develop between the leaf veins (interveinal chlorosis), and the affected leaves may fall early.
Cause Acid soils; heavy watering or rainfall, both of which leach out magnesium; or high potash levels, which make it unavailable. Plants fed on high-potash fertilizers to encourage flowering or fruiting (e.g. tomatoes) are susceptible.
Control Treat plants and/or soil with Epsom salts in autumn; either add them neat to the soil at a rate of 25g/sq m (1oz/10sq ft), or apply a foliar spray of 210g Epsom salts in 10 litres of water (7½oz in 2¼ gallons), adding a wetting agent such as soft soap.

Waterlogging

Plants affected Potentially all plants.
Symptoms Leaves turn yellow and the plants wilt.
Cause Too much water in the growing medium, owing to poor structure or drainage, or overwatering.
Control Improve soil structure and drainage.
See also pp.564 and 568.

> **See also** "Irregular water supply", "Oedema", "Peach leaf curl", "Hormone weedkiller damage", "Mycoplasmas", all below; "Azalea gall", p.556; "Smuts", p.556; *Verticillium* wilt", p.557; "*Fusarium* wilt", p.558; "*Phytophthora* root rots", p.558; "Foot and root rots", p.558; "Etiolation", p.559; "Blossom wilt", p.560; "Carrot flies", p.564; "Narcissus eelworms", p.567; "Iris rhizome rot", p.567; "Onion flies", p.567; "Blackleg on potatoes", p.568; "*Coryneum* canker", p.568; "Clematis wilt", p.569; and "Willow anthracnose", p.570.

Distorted leaves

Irregular water supply

Plants affected Potentially all garden plants, especially those grown in containers.
Symptoms Leaves and flowers become puckered and distorted, or are undersized. See pp.557 and 563 for other symptoms.
Cause An irregular supply of water, leading to irregular patterns of growth and consequent distortion in the upper parts of the plant.
Control Provide a regular and adequate supply of water for plants, especially in hot or windy weather, and pay particular attention to any plants that are growing in containers. Apply a regular mulch around the plants, where appropriate, since this will do most to conserve the moisture in the soil and prevent problems from occurring.

Oedema

Plants affected Potentially all plants, but particularly pelargoniums, camellias, *Eucalyptus*, and succulents.
Symptoms Raised, warty patches appear on the foliage. These are initially of a similar colour to that of the rest of the leaf but later turn brown.
Cause Excessively high moisture levels in either the air or the growing medium, which give the plant cells an unusually high water content. As a result of this, small groups of cells swell, forming the outgrowths, and later burst, leaving brown patches on the leaves.
Control Improve air circulation around the plants by increasing ventilation, and by attending carefully to plant spacing. Decrease the amount of watering and wherever possible try to improve drainage. Leaves affected with this condition should not be picked off at any time.

Peach leaf curl

Plants affected Peaches, nectarines, almonds, and related ornamental species (*Prunus*) in the open.
Symptoms Leaves become distorted, blistered, and sometimes swollen, later turning a deep red; a white, fungal growth then develops on the leaf surfaces. The foliage falls, but a second flush of healthy leaves will be produced afterwards.
Cause The fungus *Taphrina deformans*, which is encouraged by cool, wet conditions. Spores are carried by wind or rain to shoots, bud scales, and cracks in the bark, where they overwinter.
Control Pick off affected leaves before they turn white. Shelter plants so that spores cannot land; an open-sided, wooden frame covered with heavy-duty plastic is ideal. To prevent infection, spray leaves with a copper-based fungicide in mid- to late winter, repeating the application 14 days later.

Hormone weedkiller damage

Plants affected Broad-leaved plants, mainly roses, tomatoes, grapes, and conifers.
Symptoms Leaves are small, narrow, often thickened, and with prominent veins. They may be cup-shaped and extremely distorted. The petioles become twisted. Small bumps may appear on stems. See p.563 for other symptoms.
Cause Contamination by a growth regulator or hormone-type weedkiller, often from a considerable distance; minute quantities may cause extensive damage. Common sources of trouble are spray drift, the use of contaminated sprayers or watering cans, and water from polluted butts.

Distorted leaves

Stunted leaf buds

Control Always apply weedkillers according to manufacturers' instructions, placing protective barriers around adjacent garden plants to prevent spray drift. Keep one sprayer or watering can for use with weedkillers only. Store weedkillers in their original containers, away from compost, fertilizers, and plants. Affected plants usually grow out of the symptoms.

Aphids

Plants affected Trees, shrubs, climbing plants, perennials, annuals, bulbous plants, vegetables, and fruits.
Symptoms Leaves are stunted and distorted.
Cause and control See p.550 for details.

Suckers (psyllids)

Plants affected Bay (*Laurus nobilis*), box (*Buxus*), and pears.
Symptoms The leaf margins of bay are yellowed, thickened, and curled; box has stunted stems and cupped, slightly distorted leaves. Damage occurs to box in spring, and to bay throughout the summer. See p.551 for symptoms on pears.
Cause and control See p.551 for details.

Mycoplasmas

Plants affected Trees, shrubs, perennials, annuals, bulbous plants, vegetables, fruits (especially strawberries), and indoor plants.
Symptoms Leaves may be undersized, distorted, and covered with patterns of discoloration. This condition on strawberry plants, which is known as green petal, produces young leaves that are small, irregularly shaped, and yellowed; in addition, the older foliage turns a distinctly red colour when flowering has ceased. See p.560 for other symptoms.
Cause Mycoplasmas, which are believed to be

related to bacteria. Many mycoplasmas are spread from plant to plant by aphids (see p.550), but strawberry green petal is more frequently carried by leafhoppers (see p.551), which commonly pick up the infection from clover plants that are suffering from a condition known as phyllody disease.
Control Discard all affected plants, buy only certified fruit stock, and control both pests that are potential carriers (aphids and leafhoppers), and weeds, which may harbour the disease.

Gall mites

Plants affected Trees and shrubs, including plums, pears, walnuts, vines (*Vitis*), maples (*Acer*), limes (*Tilia*), elms (*Ulmus*), hawthorns (*Crataegus*), rowan (*Sorbus aucuparia*), broom (*Cytisus/Genista*), beeches (*Fagus*), and blackcurrants.

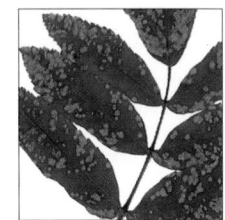
Pale leaf blotches

Symptoms These vary according to the species of mite, and include: whitish-green or red pimples or spikes on foliage (maples, elms, limes, and plums); creamy-white or pink hairs on lower leaf surfaces (maples, limes, and beeches); raised, blistered areas on upper leaf surfaces, with pale hairs underneath (walnuts and vines); thick, curling leaf margins (beeches and hawthorns); pale leaf blotches, later turning brownish-black (rowans and pears); and stunted

Stunted leaves

leaves (broom). Plant vigour is not affected.
Cause Microscopic gall mites, or eriophyid mites, secreting chemicals that induce abnormal growth.
Control Remove affected leaves and shoots if desired. There is no effective chemical control.

Gall midges

Plants affected Many garden plants, especially violets (*Viola*), *Gleditsia*, and blackcurrants.
Symptoms Violet leaves thicken and fail to unfurl. *Gleditsia* leaflets swell and fold over to form pod-like galls. Blackcurrant shoot-tip leaves fail to expand normally and the shoot tips may eventually be killed.
Cause Whitish-orange maggots up to 2mm (¹/₁₆in) long that feed within the galled tissues; three or four generations may occur in a summer. These are the larvae of three types of midge: the violet gall midge (*Dasineura affinis*), the gleditsia gall midge (*D. gleditchiae*), and the blackcurrant gall midge (*D. tetensi*). The adults are tiny, greyish-brown flies.
Control Remove and destroy affected leaves. The larvae are well protected inside the galls, but spraying with dimethoate or pirimiphos-methyl in late spring, when the galling first occurs, may provide some control.

Gall wasps/cynipid wasps

Plants affected Oaks (*Quercus*) and roses.
Symptoms Symptoms on oaks include: flat discs on the lower surface of leaves in autumn; benign, spherical, woody growths (marble galls) or pithy oak apples on shoots in spring; yellowish-green or red bunches of

currant galls on the catkins; and yellowish-green, sticky "knopper" galls on acorns. Species rose stems and hybrid rose suckers develop swellings covered in yellowish-pink, moss-like leaves ("bedeguar" galls or "Robin's pincushions") in late summer. Damage to the plant is minimal.
Cause The larvae of gall wasps, or cynipid wasps; they secrete chemicals as they feed.
Control No treatment is necessary.

Azalea gall

Plants affected Rhododendrons and azaleas, especially Indian azalea (*Rhododendron simsii*) grown as an indoor plant.
Symptoms Fleshy, pale green swellings (galls) develop on the foliage or flowers, later turning white.

Cause The fungus *Exobasidium japonicum*, which is encouraged by high humidity. The spores are insect- or air-borne.
Control Remove and destroy the galls before they turn white. If the disease persists, spray the plants with Bordeaux mixture.

Whiptail (molybdenum deficiency)

Plants affected All brassicas, most particularly cauliflowers and sprouting broccoli.
Symptoms The leaves develop abnormally and appear narrow and ribbon-like; the heads of cauliflowers and sprouting broccoli are extremely small or, more commonly, do not develop at all.
Cause A deficiency of the trace element molybdenum, most often occurring in acid soils.
Control Increase the alkalinity of the soil by liming. Treat the soil with molybdenum before sowing or planting out susceptible crops.

Bulb scale mites

Plants affected *Hippeastrum*, especially those grown indoors, and daffodils.
Symptoms Growth is stunted, the leaves become curved, and saw-toothed scarring starts to appear along the leaf margins and flower stems.

Cause The microscopic, white bulb scale mite (*Steneotarsonemus laticeps*), which feeds in the neck region of the bulb.
Control Discard infested bulbs. Buy only those of good quality from reputable suppliers. There is no chemical control available to amateur gardeners.

Rose leaf-rolling sawflies

Plants affected Roses.
Symptoms Rose leaflets roll downwards at the edges to form tight tubes during late spring and early summer.
Cause Rose leaf-rolling sawfly (*Blennocampa pusilla*). The females lay their eggs in the leaflets, secreting chemicals that cause the rolling. Pale

green, caterpillar-like larvae then feed inside the rolled leaflets. The adults are black-bodied insects 3–4mm (¹/₈in) long with transparent wings.
Control Pick off and burn rolled leaves. Alternatively, spray thoroughly with pirimiphos-methyl.

Smuts

Plants affected *Anemone*, *Trollius*, violets (*Viola*), and also winter aconites (*Eranthis hyemalis*).
Symptoms Round or elliptical swellings, often pale green or dirty white, develop on the leaves. They rupture, releasing powdery, black masses of

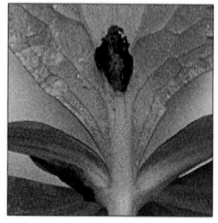

spores; severely affected leaves then wither and die. Leaf stalks may show similar symptoms.
Cause Various fungi, e.g. *Urocystis* and *Ustilago*; the spores are spread by rain splash and air currents.
Control Burn affected plants; infection may recur even if the problem appears to have been controlled.

Eelworms

Plants affected Phlox and *Allium*, including onions.
Symptoms Leaves may be spotted with small, rough, yellow patches known as spickels. Phlox are stunted, with narrow shoot-tip leaves and swollen stems; onion leaves and stems are swollen and

soft. Plants may be killed by a heavy attack.
Cause Microscopic eelworms or nematodes (*Ditylenchus dipsaci*) feeding in the plant tissues.
Control Burn affected plants. Where infested onions have been growing, plant non-susceptible vegetables for the next two years. Eelworm-free phlox can be obtained from root cuttings. There is no chemical control available for garden use.

See also "Powdery mildew", p.550; "Leaf and bud eelworms", p.551; "Scab", p.553; "Viruses", p.553; "Leafy galls", p.559; "Ink spot", p.567; and "Willow anthracnose", p.570.

Stem, branch, and leaf-bud problems

Stems discoloured or with pests visible

Low temperatures

Plants affected Trees, shrubs, perennials, annuals, bulbous plants, vegetables, fruits, and indoor plants. Soft-stemmed and young plants are most vulnerable.
Symptoms Brown, dry patches develop on the stems – especially those of *Acer*. Stems may blacken, wither, and crack or split, giving access to various organisms that cause dieback. The cracks become enlarged if moisture accumulates within them and then freezes, and this may lead to the death of the whole plant. See p.554 for other symptoms.
Cause Low temperatures or occasionally great fluctuations in temperature. Plants that are growing in exposed positions are the most likely to be affected by this problem.
Control Provide winter protection from frost and wind for young or tender plants, as well as for those growing in exposed positions.

Verticillium wilt

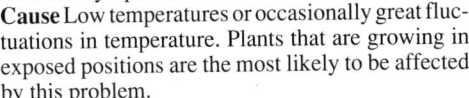

Plants affected Many garden and greenhouse plants.
Symptoms Staining of the vascular system of stems and roots, creating longitudinal brown stripes (revealed by removal of bark or outer stem). Woody plants deteriorate over several years, and may die.
Cause Several species of the fungus *Verticillium*, which may be present in the soil or in plant remains, or are introduced in new stock.
Control Remove any affected plants and soil in the immediate vicinity of the roots. Clean pruning tools thoroughly after use on diseased or suspect plants. Keep weeds under strict control and do not grow susceptible plants on the affected area.

Slime flux/wet wood

Plants affected Trees, shrubs, and woody perennials; clematis is particularly affected.
Symptoms The stem dies back and a pink, yellow, or off-white slime oozes from its base. This is often thick and may have an unpleasant smell.
Cause Injury to the stem (often through frost or wounding) when sap pressure is high, just before the leaves break. The sap released from the wound has a high sugar content and is colonized by various micro-organisms (in particular yeasts, bacteria, and fungi), which cause the thickening and discoloration.
Control Avoid injury to stems, particularly those of susceptible plants. Remove the affected stems immediately, cutting well back into healthy growth, below ground level if necessary. Given adequate food and moisture, the plant should subsequently produce more shoots.

Spur blight/cane blight

Plants affected Raspberries. Spur blight may also attack loganberries.
Symptoms With spur blight (shown here), purple areas develop around the nodes in late summer; these increase in size and turn a silvery-grey. Numerous tiny, black sclerotia (fungal resting bodies) develop in the centre of each blotch. Buds may die, or may produce shoots that die. With cane blight, deterioration starts just above soil level as the fungus enters through points of injury and causes the base of the cane to develop dark discoloration and to become brittle. The foliage withers. Weakened plants are much more likely to be affected by this problem than well-maintained, strong specimens.
Cause The fungi *Didymella applanata* (spur blight) and *Leptosphaeria coniothyrium* (cane blight).
Control Maintain plants well. At the first sign of disease, cut out affected canes, going to below soil level for cane blight.

Scale insects

Hemispherical scale (above) and mussel scale (right)

Plants affected Indoor and greenhouse plants, trees, shrubs, fruits, and cacti and other succulents.
Symptoms The stems are sticky with honeydew (excrement), and they appear blackened with sooty moulds. Heavily infested plants may also show slow growth. White, waxy deposits containing eggs also occasionally appear on the stems.
Cause and control See p.552 for details.

Rusts

Plants affected Trees, shrubs, perennials, annuals, bulbous plants, vegetables, fruits, and indoor plants; mints (*Mentha*), roses, raspberries, and blackberries are commonly affected.
Symptoms Pustules containing bright orange or dark brown spores develop either on, or apparently bursting from within, the stem. Some plants, e.g. junipers, develop gelatinous growths. In severe cases stems become extensively distorted and ruptured. Dieback may follow. See also p.552.
Cause A range of fungi encouraged by high humidity. Spores are spread by rain splash and air currents, and may overwinter on plant debris.
Control Remove affected areas and improve air circulation, increasing ventilation and plant spacing. Spray with a suitable fungicide, e.g. propiconazole or mancozeb.

Grey mould/*Botrytis*

Plants affected Trees, shrubs, perennials, annuals, bulbous plants, vegetables, fruits, and indoor plants. Soft-leaved plants are vulnerable.
Symptoms Dead and discoloured patches develop on the stems and leaves. Rapid deterioration may occur, causing the upper parts of the stem to die. Fungal spores develop on decaying plant material. See pp.560 and 562 for other symptoms.
Cause The fungi *Botrytis cinerea* and, on snowdrops (*Galanthus*), *B. galanthina*, which thrive in damp conditions and where air circulation is poor. Fungal spores are spread on air currents or by rain splash; infection is most likely where plants are damaged. Fruits may also become infected by contact with those already diseased. Hard, black, resilient sclerotia (fungal resting bodies), produced on plant remains, fall to the ground and may cause later infections.
Control Avoid injury to plants, clear up dead and dying plant material, and provide good air circulation, ensuring at all times that plants are adequately spaced and those under cover are well ventilated. Remove and burn any affected areas (and in the case of snowdrops the entire clump) immediately. Spray with a fungicide that contains benomyl, thiophanate-methyl, or carbendazim.

Irregular water supply

Plants affected Potentially all plants, especially those in containers.
Symptoms The outer stem layer or bark of the stem or trunk may split or crack. See pp.555 and 563 for other symptoms.
Cause An irregular supply of water, leading to irregular growth. Sudden availability of water after a drought caused by climatic conditions or a prolonged dry period due to erratic watering brings rapid swelling, which causes the stem to rupture and crack.
Control Provide a regular and adequate supply of water, especially during hot or windy weather. Do not suddenly overwater plants after drought conditions in an attempt to make up for a severe lack of moisture. Mulch, where appropriate, to conserve as much moisture in the soil as possible.

Dutch elm disease

Plants affected Elms (*Ulmus*) and *Zelkova*.
Symptoms Notching appears in twig crotches, and young twigs may be crook-shaped. Longitudinal, dark brown streaks develop under the bark. Leaves in the crown wilt, yellow, and die. The tree

Crook-shaped twigs

may die within two years.
Cause *Ceratocystis ulmi*, a fungus often spread by elm bark beetles as they tunnel under the bark. Infected trees may pass the disease to healthy ones via common root systems.
Control Fell and remove affected trees.

Longitudinal streaks

Woolly aphids

Plants affected Apples, cotoneasters, pyracanthas.
Symptoms A fluffy, white, mould-like substance appears on the bark in spring. Starting on the larger branches around old pruning cuts and in bark cracks, it later spreads to the new shoots where soft swellings may develop. Aphids may be visible.

Cause The woolly aphid (*Eriosoma lanigerum*), which is a small, greyish-black insect that sucks sap from the bark and secretes white, waxy threads.
Control Spray plants with dimethoate, heptenophos, or pirimicarb when the pest is seen.

Froghoppers (cuckoo spit)

Plants affected Trees, shrubs, perennials, annuals.
Symptoms Globules of white froth containing a small insect appear on stems and leaves in early summer. Where the pest feeds on shoot tips growth may be distorted but damage is minimal.

Cause Froghopper nymphs, or spittlebugs (e.g. *Philaenus spumarius*), cream-coloured sap-suckers that secrete a protective froth over themselves. The adults are darker in colour, up to 4mm (^{1}/sin) long, and live openly on the plant.
Control If treatment is necessary, remove nymphs by hand or spray with dimethoate or permethrin.

Adelgids

Plants affected Conifers, particularly *Abies*, pines (*Pinus*), spruces (*Picea*), *Pseudotsuga menziesii*, and larches (*Larix*).
Symptoms A fluffy, white, mould-like substance appears on the leaves and stems. Knobbly swellings develop on *Abies*, and

swollen stem tips (known as pineapple galls) appear on the young shoots of spruce.
Cause Adelgids, or conifer woolly aphids (for example *Adelges* spp.), which are small, greyish-black, aphid-like insects that suck sap from the bark or the leaves. The bark- and leaf-feeders secrete white, waxy threads.
Control Established trees can tolerate the damage, but spray small trees with HCH on a mild, dry day in mid- to late winter or early summer.

Fusarium wilt

Plants affected Perennials, annuals, vegetables, and fruits; most commonly affected are China asters (*Callistephus*), carnations (*Dianthus*), sweet peas (*Lathyrus odoratus*), beans, and peas.
Symptoms Black patches develop on the stems and the foliage; these patches are sometimes covered with a white or pale pink fungal growth. Roots turn black and die.
Cause Various species of the microscopic fungus *Fusarium*, which are present in the soil or on plant debris, or are sometimes seed-borne; they may also be introduced on new stock. They will build up in the soil when the same type of plant is grown in the same site year after year.
Control There is no cure for affected plants. Remove them and the soil in their vicinity, and destroy the plants. Avoid growing susceptible plants in the area. Propagate only from healthy stock; if possible, grow resistant cultivars.

Phytophthora root rots

Plants affected Trees, shrubs, and woody perennials; maples (*Acer*), Lawson cypress (*Chamaecyparis lawsoniana*), apples, yew (*Taxus baccata*), rhododendrons, raspberries, and heathers are most commonly attacked.

Symptoms Patches of dead tissue may appear on the stem or the trunk with bluish-black stains in the tissue beneath; the foliage is sparse and chlorotic. Dieback may follow, and plants may even be killed. See p.565 for other symptoms.
Cause Various species of the fungus *Phytophthora*, which is frequently found in wet or waterlogged soil. Roots are attacked by swimming spores that build up in the soil and in infected plant remains.
Control Always avoid heavy watering, and wherever possible improve soil drainage in the area. Dig up and burn all affected plants. Buy only good-quality plants from reputable sources, and choose those that are tolerant or resistant to *Phytophthora*, such as *Tsuga heterophylla* and x *Cupressocyparis leylandii*. There is no effective chemical control available to amateur gardeners.

Foot and root rots

Plants affected A wide range, especially petunias and other bedding plants, tomatoes, cucumbers, peas, beans, and young, container-grown plants.
Symptoms The stem bases discolour and shrink inwards. This causes the upper parts of the plant to wilt and die off; the lower leaves will usually show the symptoms first. The roots turn black and break or rot (see p.565).

Cause A range of soil- and water-borne fungi that flourish where growing conditions are not adequately hygienic. They are often introduced through the use of unsterilized compost and non-mains water, and build up in the soil, especially if susceptible plants are repeatedly grown on the same site.
Control Rotate susceptible plants. Maintain strict hygiene and only use fresh, sterilized compost, and mains water. Remove affected plants and the soil in the vicinity of their roots.

Seedling blight

Plants affected Many vegetable crops grown in warm climates, including beans, peas, peanuts, cabbages, sweet potatoes, and tomatoes.
Symptoms Seedlings show symptoms of damping off (see p.564). The collar or stem of older plants rots at soil level, and shoots yellow, wilt, and die.
Cause Invasion via the base of the plant by the fungus *Sclerotium rolfsii* (syn. *Corticium rolfsii*); nematode and insect wounds promote infection. Plants in light, sandy soils, well supplied with moisture, are most at risk.
Control Maintain crops well, remove diseased plants and debris, and avoid growing plants in contaminated areas; burn infected residues or bury them deeply. Seed may be treated with thiram.

Boron deficiency

Plants affected Carnations (*Dianthus*), lettuces, celery, and tomatoes; also all fruits (most commonly pears, plums, and strawberries). The condition is fairly rare.
Symptoms The growing tips die, causing the plants to become stunted and bushy. Celery stems

start to develop transverse cracks and the exposed tissues turn brown; lettuces fail to heart up. Pears become distorted and dimpled with brown, flecked flesh (very similar symptoms to those of the virus disease called stoney pit). Plums are misshapen and may show gumming (see "Pests and diseases", p.388). Strawberries are small and poorly coloured. See p.566 for other symptoms.
Cause and control See p.566 for details.

Clematis wilt

Plants affected Clematis, especially large-flowered hybrids, e.g. 'Jackmanii', and *C. montana*.
Symptoms The terminal shoots wilt, starting with the youngest stems, and the petioles darken where they join the leaf blade. Whole sections of the plant may be affected and start to die back. See also p.569.
Cause The fungus *Ascochyta clematidina*, which produces spore-releasing, fruiting bodies on the older stems. Other, non-pathogenic causes of wilt (e.g. drought, poor drainage, and graft failure) may be mistaken for this disease.
Control Cut back any affected stems to healthy tissue, below ground level if necessary. Spray all the new foliage produced later in the year, and that appearing the following spring, with Bordeaux mixture or benomyl.

See also "Mealybugs", p.550; "Powdery mildew", p.550; "Chocolate spot", p.553; "Lily disease", p.553; "Contact weedkiller damage", p.554; "Smuts", p.556; "Etiolation", p.559; "Fungal brackets", p.559; "Lightning", p.559; "Chafer larvae", p.564; "Leatherjackets", p.564; "Damping off", p.568; "Blackleg on cuttings", p.568; "Blackleg on potatoes", p.568; "Coral spot", p.569; "Honey fungus", p.569; "Crown rot", p.569; "Replant disease/soil sickness", p.569; "Rose dieback", p.569; "Fireblight", p.569; "Peony wilt", p.569; and "Vine weevil larvae", p.570.

Stem distortion and abnormal growth

Etiolation

Plants affected Seedlings of all garden plants, and soft-stemmed plants.
Symptoms Stems are elongated and often pale, and the plant may grow towards the available light source, developing a lop-sided habit. The leaves are chlorotic and flowering is often reduced.
Cause Insufficient light, often due to poor siting of the plant or shading from adjacent plants, buildings, and similar structures. Overcrowded plants are susceptible to the condition.
Control Choose and site plants carefully. Ensure that adequate light is provided for seedlings as soon as germination has occurred. Plants only slightly affected should recover if conditions are improved.

Cutworms

Plants affected Low-growing perennials, annuals, root vegetables, and lettuces.
Symptoms Stem bases and leaves of low-growing plants are visibly gnawed and roots may also be affected. Plants grow slowly, wilt, and may ultimately die.
Cause Caterpillars of various moths (e.g. *Noctua* and *Agrotis* spp.), usually creamy-brown in colour and 4.5cm (1³/₄in) long. At night they feed above soil level.
Control Where damage is seen, search for and destroy the cutworms. Spray any vulnerable plants with pirimiphos-methyl; alternatively, the soil may be treated with chlorpyrifos + diazinon.

Hormone weedkiller damage

Plants affected Broad-leaved plants (mainly roses, tomatoes, and grapes), and conifers.
Symptoms Small bumps may appear on stems. Leaves are distorted and petioles twisted or spiralled. See also pp.555 and 563.
Cause Contamination by a growth regulator or hormone-type weedkiller, often from a considerable distance; even minute quantities may cause extensive damage. Sources of trouble are spray drift and the use of contaminated sprayers or watering cans. Plants that have been affected usually grow out of the symptoms.
Control Apply weedkillers according to the manufacturers' instructions, placing protective barriers around adjacent plants. Keep one sprayer or watering can for use with weedkillers only, or preferably use dribble bars. Store weedkillers away from compost, fertilizers, and plants.

Leafy gall

Plants affected Shrubs, perennials, and annuals, especially dahlias, chrysanthemums, and pelargoniums.
Symptoms Tiny, distorted shoots and leaves develop on the stem at or near ground level.

Cause *Corynebacterium fascians*, a soil-borne bacterium that enters host plants through small wounds. It is easily spread on tools or through propagating from infected plants.

Control Destroy affected plants and remove the soil in their immediate vicinity, and wash after handling them. Do not propagate from infected plants. Maintain strict hygiene, sterilizing tools, containers, and the greenhouse regularly.

Crown gall

Plants affected Trees, shrubs (most commonly cane fruits and roses), and woody perennials.
Symptoms Irregular, rounded, often woody, swellings occur on or burst from the stem, but plant vigour is not seriously affected. See p.565 for other symptoms.
Cause *Agrobacterium tumefaciens* bacteria, prevalent in wet soils, which enter through surface wounds.
Control Avoid plant damage and improve soil drainage. Cut out and destroy all the affected stems.

Forsythia gall

Plants affected Forsythias.
Symptoms Rough, woody rounded galls form on the stems. They persist from year to year but rarely have adverse effects.
Cause Unknown; possibly bacterial infection.
Control No action is strictly necessary but the unsightly galled stems may be removed and the plant sprayed with a copper-based fungicide.

Fungal brackets

Plants affected Trees, shrubs, woody perennials.
Symptoms Fungal fruiting bodies, often bracket-shaped, appear commonly on the lower trunk, but also on the upper section or on the crown, sometimes near branch stubs or
other wounds. Either short-lived or perennial, they vary in appearance, often according to weather conditions. General growth is slow, and the tree may develop an excess of dead wood and a thin crown.
Cause and control See p.565 for details.

Witches' brooms

Plants affected Trees, mainly birches (*Betula*) and hornbeams (*Carpinus*); shrubs; woody perennials.
Symptoms Dense clusters of small shoots appear on otherwise normal branches. Leaves discolour early and remain small but vigour is unaffected.

Cause Fungi (especially *Taphrina*) and mites (for example *Eriophyes*), which cause the mutations.
Control Cut branches back below the affected area.

Big bud mites

Plants affected Commonly hazels (*Corylus*), yew (*Taxus baccata*), brooms (*Cytisus/Genista*), and blackcurrants.
Symptoms The buds are abnormally enlarged and fail to break.
Cause Microscopic gall mites feeding inside the buds. Hazels are attacked by *Phytoptus avellanae*, brooms by *Eriophyes genistae*, yew by *Cecidophyopsis psilaspis*, and blackcurrants by *C. ribis*. Blackcurrant big bud mites can spread the virus-like disease known as reversion.
Control Remove and burn affected buds in winter. Yew and hazels are fairly tolerant but heavily infested blackcurrants and brooms should be destroyed. The fungicide carbendazim gives blackcurrants some protection if applied three times at 14-day intervals, starting when the first buds open, but there is no effective control for established infestations.

Lightning

Plants affected Tall trees, especially those in isolation.
Symptoms Bark may be stripped, and a deep furrow may appear down one side, often following the spiral grain. The heartwood may be shattered, weakening the tree and leaving it susceptible to disease. Dead wood increases

in the crown and the upper crown may be killed.
Cause Lightning.
Control Lightning conductors may be fitted to valuable tall trees but this is unlikely to be feasible.

Mechanical wounding

Plants affected Potentially all plants.
Symptoms A neat-edged wound is visible on the stem or bark. Sap from the injured area may ferment into a slime flux (see "Slime flux/wet wood", p.557), and pathogens entering the wound cause dieback or even death. A healed wound may leave a raised area.
Cause Careless use of garden machinery and tools.
Control Remove severely damaged shoots or stems. Wounds on woody plants should be left alone.

Voles

Plants affected Shrubs and young trees.
Symptoms Bark is gnawed from stems and roots.
Cause Voles.
Control Traps are the most effective solution. See also "Mice, rats, and voles", p.566.

See also "Asparagus beetles", p.548; "Vine weevils", p.549; "Eelworms", p.556; "Rusts", p.557; "Irregular water supply", p.557; "Fasciation", p.561; "Grey squirrels", p.563; "Nectria canker", p.568; "Coryneum canker", p.568; "Honey fungus", p.569; "Replant disease/soil sickness", p.569; "Willow anthracnose", p.570; "Rabbits and hares", p.570; and "Deer", p.570.

Flower problems

Discoloured flowers

Grey mould/*Botrytis*

Plants affected Trees, shrubs, perennials, annuals, bulbous plants, vegetables, fruits, and indoor plants.
Symptoms A fuzzy, grey, fungal growth appears on the flowers in patches, leading to total deterioration. This may later spread to the stems and body of the plant. See also pp.557 and 562.
Cause The fungi *Botrytis cinerea* or *B. galanthina*.
Control Avoid injury to plants, clear up dead material, and provide good ventilation. Remove affected areas. Spray with a fungicide containing benomyl, thiophanate-methyl, or carbendazim.

Fungal patches

Total deterioration

Viruses

Plants affected Most flowering plants, mainly bulbous plants and sweet peas (*Lathyrus odoratus*).
Symptoms Flowers are small and distorted, patterned with streaking or colour-breaking. See also pp.553 and 563.
Cause A large number of viruses. Submicroscopic virus particles in the sap of infected plants may be transmitted to healthy tissues by aphids, nematodes, and certain other pests, through handling, or on garden tools; some are seed-borne.
Control Buy certified (virus-free) plants. Control potential carriers, for example aphids, and keep down weeds. Remove and burn affected plants; handle suspect plants after healthy ones, and do not propagate from them. Use a new site for any replacement plants. There is no chemical control.

Thrips

Plants affected Perennials, often *Achimenes*, *Primula obconica*, *Sinningia*, *Streptocarpus*, African violets (*Saintpaulia*), chrysanthemums, cyclamens, roses, gladioli, pelargoniums.
Symptoms White flecks appear on the petals, and loss of pigmentation can be severe. Heavy attacks prevent the buds opening. Leaves develop a silver-white discoloration.
Cause Various species of thrips, e.g. gladiolus thrips (*Thrips simplex*) and rose thrips (*T. fuscipennis*) in gardens, and western flower thrips (*Frankliniella occidentalis*) in greenhouses. They are sap-suckers that may enter and damage unopened flower buds. The adults are narrow-bodied, up to 2mm (¹/₁₆in) long, and brown or black; the immature nymphs are creamy yellow. They thrive in hot, dry conditions.

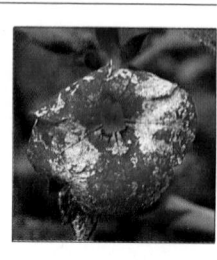

Control Water plants regularly and, in greenhouses, maintain a cool, humid atmosphere. Spray with malathion, pirimiphos-methyl, permethrin, or dimethoate as soon as symptoms appear.

Blossom wilt

Plants affected Apples, pears, cherries (*Prunus*), and quinces.
Symptoms The flowers turn brown and wither, but remain tightly clinging to the stem. The adjacent leaves then turn brown and die, and in severe cases the spur may be extensively damaged. Many tiny, buff-coloured spore masses appear on the affected areas, and in winter pustules form on the bark.
Cause *Sclerotinia* spp., which flourish in damp conditions. The spores are carried on air currents and infect the plant via the flowers.
Control Remove and burn all infected areas in summer, and spray plants with either benomyl or a copper-based fungicide.

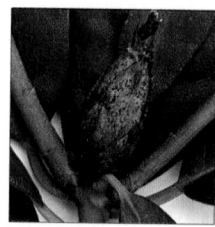

Tulip fire

Plants affected Tulips.
Symptoms Bleached, and often elongated, spots appear on the petals; severely affected flowers may wither. Some of the buds remain tightly closed and become covered in a dense, grey, fungal growth.
See p.553 for symptoms affecting the leaves.
Cause The fungus *Botrytis tulipae*, which flourishes in wet seasons, because the spores are spread by wind and rain. The sclerotia (fungal resting bodies) persist in the soil, and will later germinate when tulips are planted in the area again.
Control Remove and burn affected leaves and shoots immediately. Lift and dry off bulbs at the end of the season, discarding any with sclerotia, and dip them in a suitable fungicide solution, e.g. carbendazim. Wait two years before replanting the site with tulips, or change the soil. Plant from early winter on.

Mycoplasmas

Plants affected Trees, shrubs, perennials, annuals, bulbous plants, vegetables, fruits (especially strawberries), and indoor plants.
Symptoms Flowers are green, undersized, and sometimes distorted. They do not revert to their usual colour and subsequent flushes are also green. Symptoms on clematis are similar to those caused by frost injury, but "frost-damaged" flowers will be replaced by normal-coloured blooms later in the season. On strawberries,

the condition is called green petal. See also p.555.
Cause Mycoplasmas, which are believed to be related to bacteria. Many are spread by aphids, (see p.550), but strawberry green petal is more frequently carried by leafhoppers (see p.551), which commonly pick up the infection from clover plants suffering from phyllody disease.
Control Discard affected plants, buy certified fruit stock, and control both pests (potential vectors) and weeds (which may harbour the disease).

Rhododendron bud blast

Plants affected Rhododendrons and azaleas.
Symptoms The buds form but do not open. They turn brown and dry, sometimes developing a silver-grey sheen, and during spring become covered in black, fungal bristles. The affected buds are not shed.
Cause The fungus *Pycnostysanus azaleae*, which is passed from plant to plant by the rhododendron leafhopper (*Graphocephala fennahi*).
Control If practicable, remove and destroy all the affected buds before mid-summer, when the leafhoppers become prevalent; also spray against the leafhoppers (see p.551).

Potassium deficiency

Plants affected Both edible and ornamental fruiting plants, but mainly currants, apples, and pears.
Symptoms Flowering, subsequent fruiting, and general growth may be reduced. See p.554 for details of other symptoms.
Cause Growing plants in soils with either a light texture or with a high chalk or peat content.
Control Improve the soil texture. Dress with sulphate of potash or a high potash fertilizer.

Apple suckers

Plants affected Apples.
Symptoms The blossom browns as though it is frost-damaged; small, green insects appear on the flower stalks.
Cause Apple sucker (*Psylla mali*) nymphs, which are flattened, pale green insects up to 2mm (¹/₁₂in) in length that suck sap. Heavy attacks will both kill the blossom and prevent fruit set.
Control Apply a tar oil wash in winter. Alternatively, spray with dimethoate, pirimiphos-methyl, fenitrothion or permethrin at the green cluster stage of bud development, before the petals show colour.

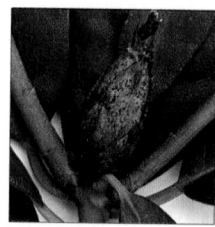

> **See also** "Powdery mildew", p.550; "High temperatures and scorch", p.554; "Low temperatures", p.554; "Azalea gall", p.556; "Chrysanthemum petal blight", p.561; "Michaelmas daisy mites", p.561; and "Fireblight", p.569.

Distorted and eaten flowers

Drought

Plants affected All plants, especially those in light, sandy soils or containers.
Symptoms The buds fail to develop fully, and the flowers are small and sparse. See also pp.554 and 568.
Cause Chronic (prolonged) or repeated drought. Plants in small containers are particularly vulnerable during hot weather, and peat-based composts that are allowed to dry out too much are extremely difficult to re-wet. Dry, brown buds on certain plants, e.g. camellias and rhododendrons, are the result of a water shortage the previous year during the period of bud initiation.
Control Water plants regularly, and frequently check those in hot or sunny positions. Mulch, where appropriate, to improve moisture retention. Try to prevent drought rather than treat it: plants exposed to a chronic water shortage are far less likely to recover than those suffering a sudden shortage.

Capsid bugs

Plants affected Shrubs, perennials, and annuals, mainly dahlias, fuchsias, hydrangeas, chrysanthemums, and *Caryopteris*.
Symptoms Flowers develop unevenly with undersized ray petals. Fuchsia flowers abort completely.
Cause and control See p.549 for details.

Earwigs

Plants affected Shrubs, perennials, and annuals, commonly chrysanthemums, dahlias, and clematis. Also apricot and peach trees.
Symptoms Petals are eaten in summer. See p.548 for other symptoms.
Cause The earwig (*Forficula auricularia*), which is a yellowish-brown insect 15mm (³/₄in) long.
Control Place inverted pots, stuffed with hay or straw, on canes among plants; earwigs hide in these, and can be destroyed. Alternatively, spray at dusk with permethrin, pirimiphos-methyl, or HCH.

Fasciation

Plants affected All plants, most commonly delphiniums, forsythias, *Daphne*, and *Prunus subhirtella* 'Autumnalis'.
Symptoms Peculiar, broad, flattened flower stems develop. The main stems are also broad and flattened.
Cause In many cases, early damage to the growing point caused by insect, slug or frost attack, or handling; it may also be due to bacterial infection or genetic malfunction.
Control Fasciation does no harm; affected areas may either be left on the plant or pruned out.

Proliferation

Plants affected Mainly roses, especially the older varieties, but occasionally other ornamentals and fruiting plants.
Symptoms The flower stem grows through the centre of the existing flower, and a new flower may form above the first. In some cases several flower buds form together, surrounded by one set of petals.
Cause Early damage to the growing point of the bud, often through frost or insect attack. Where the problem recurs, a virus (see p.560) may be the cause.
Control Severely and repeatedly affected plants, which may be virus-infected, should be destroyed. In all other cases treatment is unnecessary.

Chrysanthemum petal blight

Plants affected Chrysanthemums and other members of the Compositae family and *Anemone*. The disease is rare.
Symptoms The outer florets develop brown or water-soaked oval spots; if the whole flowerhead becomes affected, it withers and dies. *Botrytis cinerea* may colonize the affected bloom (see "Grey mould/ *Botrytis*", p.560), masking the original symptoms.
Cause The fungus *Itersonilia perplexans*, which attacks susceptible plants, usually those under glass.
Control Remove and destroy affected blooms.

Michaelmas daisy mites

Plants affected Michaelmas daisies (*Aster*), especially *A. novi-belgii*.
Symptoms Plants flower poorly; some flowers may be converted into rosettes of small leaves. Greyish-brown scars appear on stunted stems.
Cause The Michaelmas daisy mite (*Tarsonemus pallidus*), a microscopic mite that feeds in flower buds and shoot tips.

Distorted and healthy (inset) flowers

Control Discard infested plants, replacing them with less susceptible perennial asters, e.g. *Aster novae-angliae* or *A. amellus*. There is no effective chemical control available to amateur gardeners.

Hemerocallis gall midges

Plants affected *Hemerocallis*.
Symptoms Flower buds become abnormally swollen and fail to open. The problem occurs between late spring and mid-summer.
Cause The *Hemerocallis* gall midge (*Contarinia quinquenotata*), a tiny fly that lays its

eggs in the developing buds. Affected buds will be found to contain white maggots, up to 2mm (¹/₁₆in) long, feeding between the petals.
Control Pick off and burn galled buds. The late-flowering cultivars escape damage.

Pollen beetles

Plants affected Roses, sweet peas (*Lathyrus odoratus*), daffodils, marrows, runner beans, and other garden plants.
Symptoms Small, black beetles are found in the flowers in spring and mid- to late summer.
Cause Pollen beetles (*Meligethes* spp.), which are 2mm (¹/₁₆in) long and black. They eat some pollen but otherwise cause little direct damage to the blooms.
Control Pollen beetles cannot be controlled, because vast numbers fly into gardens from oil seed rape fields, where they breed. It is not advisable to use insecticides – they can cause damage to the petals and harm useful pollinators, e.g. bees. Cut flowers can be freed of the beetles by placing them in a shed or garage with one source of light (e.g. a window or a lamp) towards which the beetles fly.

Birds

Plants affected Trees (ornamental and fruit), most fruits, and shrubs, especially forsythias, cherries (*Prunus*), strawberries, almonds, and *Amelanchier*, crocuses, primrose (*Primula vulgaris*), and polyanthus (*Primula*).
Symptoms Flower buds are pecked from trees and shrubs; outer bud scales are left scattered on the ground. Crocus and primrose flowers are shredded. Vegetables, especially peas and beans, fruits, seeds, and seedlings are pecked or eaten.

Bullfinch damage

House sparrow damage

Cause Birds, including bullfinches (trees, shrubs, and fruits) and house sparrows (crocuses and primroses). Vegetables, fruits, and seedlings may be pecked or eaten by many birds including wood pigeons (p.549), blackbirds and starlings (p.563), and jays (p.563).
Control Netting is the only effective means of preventing damage. Scaring devices, e.g. humming tapes, scarecrows, or aluminium foil strips, are effective only initially; birds soon lose their fear. Repellent sprays, usually based on quassia or aluminium ammonium sulphate, must be used frequently to maintain their effectiveness.

> **See also** "Caterpillars", p.549; "Low temperatures", p.554; "Irregular water supply", p.555; "Azalea gall", p.556; "Etiolation", p.559; "Viruses", p.560; "Thrips", p.560; and "Mycoplasmas", p.560.

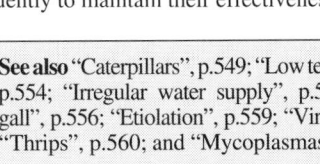

Fruit, berry, and seed problems

High temperatures and scorch

Plants affected Soft fruits, tree fruits, tomatoes, and apples, especially green-skinned cultivars.
Symptoms Discoloured patches develop on the skin, particularly on the upper-most surfaces of fruits, or on the ones that are more highly exposed.
Cause and control See p.554 for details.

Grey mould/*Botrytis*

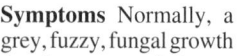

Plants affected Fruiting trees, shrubs, perennials, annuals, and indoor plants. Soft, thin-skinned fruits, e.g. strawberries, raspber-ries, grapes, and tomatoes, are vulnerable.
Symptoms Normally, a grey, fuzzy, fungal growth develops on a soft, brown rot. The damage spreads rapidly and the whole fruit may collapse. Unripe tomatoes may develop "ghost spot", where a pale green ring appears on the skin but the rest of the fruit colours normally and does not rot (the unaffected parts may be eaten). See also pp.557 and 560.
Cause and control See p.557 for details.

Powdery mildew

Plants affected Most fruits, commonly grapes, peaches, and gooseberries.
Symptoms Whitish-grey, fungal patches appear on the skin, often turning brown as they mature. The berries of grapes become hard and extensively cracked, and may fail to swell fully; secondary fungi may then invade. Cracking of gooseberries is uncommon and fungal growth can be rubbed off.
Cause and control See p.550. Grow gooseberries showing some resistance, for example 'Invicta' and 'Lancashire Lad'.

Brown rot

Plants affected Culti-vated fruits, especially apples, plums, peaches, nectarines, and pears.
Symptoms Soft, brown areas develop on the skin, and penetrate throughout the flesh. Concentric rings of creamy-white pustules then start to appear on the surface. Affected fruits either fall or may become dry and wizened and remain on the tree.
Cause The fungus *Sclerotinia* (*S. fructigena* and *S. laxa*). The pustules produce spores, and these are then carried by wind or insects to other fruits;

---

infection occurs through wounds or blemishes on the surface of the fruit.
Control Prevent injury to fruits (e.g. that caused by pests), and pick off and burn those affected.

Tomato blight

Plants affected Tomatoes, mainly in the open but also in greenhouses.
Symptoms The fruits first develop a brown discoloration and then start to shrink and rot. Even fruits that may have appeared to be healthy when picked may begin to deteriorate rapidly within a few days.
Cause and control See p.553 for details.

Raspberry beetles

Plants affected Mainly rasp-berries, but also blackberries and hybrid cane fruits.
Symptoms Ripe fruits are dried up and brown at the stalk end; an insect larva may be found inside the fruit.
Cause The raspberry beetle (*Byturus tomentosus*). The females lay eggs on the flowers in early to mid-summer. Brownish-white larvae up to 6mm (1/4in) long hatch two weeks later. They feed initially at the stalk end of the fruit but then move to the inner plug.
Control Only chemical sprays provide an effective control. Apply malathion, fenitrothion, permethrin, or derris to raspberries when the first pink fruit appears; to loganberries when 80 per cent of the petals have fallen; to blackberries when the first flower opens. A second application may be required for raspberries and loganberries two weeks after the first. Spray at dusk to avoid harming bees.

Scab

Plants affected Pears, pyracanthas, *Citrus*, *Malus*, and loquats.
Symptoms Blackish-brown, scabby patches develop on the skin, and a severe attack will leave fruits small and distorted. In some cases cracks may develop, which will make the fruit vulnerable to secondary infections.
Cause and control See p.553 for details.

Calcium deficiency

Plants affected Apple (the condition is known as bitter pit), container-grown tomatoes, and sweet pep-pers (blossom end rot).
Symptoms The flesh of apples is brown-flecked and tastes bitter; the skin is

Bitter pit

---

sometimes pitted. Bitter pit may affect fruits on the tree or in store. Tomato and pepper fruits develop a sunken, blackish-brown discoloration at the flower end.

Blossom end rot

Cause A lack of cal-cium, possibly combined with other nutritional im-balances, resulting from an irregular or poor supply of moisture to the roots, preventing adequate cal-cium uptake. Groups of cells deprived of calcium collapse and discolour.
Control Avoid very acid growing media. Water regularly and, where feasible, mulch plants. Apples may be sprayed with calcium nitrate every ten days from early summer until harvesting.

Pear midges

Plants affected Pears.
Symptoms The fruitlets turn black, starting at the eye end, and fall from the tree. Small maggots are found inside fruitlets.
Cause The pear midge (*Con-tarinia pyrivora*). The adults lay eggs on the unopened flower buds; these hatch into orange-white maggots 2mm (1/16in) long that feed in the fruitlets, leaving them black and rotten.
Control Collect and burn damaged fruitlets before the maggots fall into the soil to pupate. Spray with fenitrothion, pirimiphos-methyl, or HCH when the blossom is at the white bud stage. Pear midge is difficult to control on large trees.

Shanking of vines

Plants affected Grape vines (*Vitis vinifera*).
Symptoms Berry stalks wither. Berries have a watery or sour taste; black varieties turn red, and white ones remain translucent. They may remain on the bunch but shrivel up and are vulnerable to disease, e.g. grey mould/*Botrytis* (see above).
Cause Heavy cropping, either over- or under-watering, or stagnant soil conditions.
Control Cut out withered berries and regularly apply a foliar feed. Decrease the crop for a few years and try to improve general soil conditions.

Blue mould on citrus

Plants affected All *Citrus*, especially oranges.
Symptoms Circular patches of mould, usually with a central depression, appear on the rind. They extend rapidly and develop a distinct, blue coloration.
Cause The fungus *Penicillium italicum*, which en-ters fruits through bruised, wounded, or insect-damaged areas. It typically occurs on stored fruits.
Control Wash fruits immediately after harvest with a suitable fungicide, e.g. benomyl at 1 part/1,000.

Irregular water supply

Plants affected Potentially all fruiting plants.
Symptoms Fruits are mis-shapen and undersized, and a sudden availability of water may cause their skin and flesh to crack, leaving them vulnerable to the diseases that cause rotting. See pp.555 and 557 for other symptoms.
Cause and control See p.555 for details.

Viruses

Plants affected Pears, cucumbers, melons, pumpkins, tomatoes, strawberries, and raspberries.
Symptoms Fruits may be undersized, distorted, dis-coloured, and grouped in rosettes. Cucumber mosaic virus produces warty, distort-ed cucumber, melon, and pumpkin fruits, blotched dark green and yellow; pear stony pit virus produces distorted and pitted pear fruits with patches of dead, stony cells. See also pp.553 and 560.
Cause and control See p.553 for details.

Hormone weedkiller damage

Plants affected All fruits, but commonly only tomatoes.
Symptoms Plum-shaped toma-toes form. Although they ripen normally and are safe to eat, they may taste unpleasant and be hollow. Fruits that have formed be-fore contamination occurs are not usually affected. See p.555 for other symptoms.
Cause and control See p.555 for details.

Fruit flies

Plants affected Tropical and subtropical fruits.
Symptoms Holes are bored in fruits. Secondary fungal and bacterial infection may occur.
Cause Larvae of fruit flies (*Dacus* and *Ceratitis* spp.), including the Mediterranean fruit fly (*C. capitata*).
Control Lay a bait of malathion and sugar solution.

Wasps

Plants affected Grapes, plums, pears, apples, and figs.
Symptoms Large cavities are eaten in ripe fruits in late summer; wasps may be seen feeding.
Cause Wasps, which are attracted to fruits initially damaged by birds.
Control Protect fruits by placing bags made of muslin or nylon tights over the trusses before damage begins. Locate and destroy wasp nests, placing permethrin or bendiocarb dust in the entrance.

Blackbirds and starlings

Plants affected Tree and soft fruits.
Symptoms Peck marks ap-pear on ripe tree fruits, leav-ing them susceptible to brown rot (see p.562); soft fruits are eaten whole.
Cause Blackbirds, starlings, and other birds (see p.561).
Control Either net the plants at fruiting time or grow them in a permanent bird-proof cage.

Codling moths

Plants affected Apples and pears.
Symptoms Holes are tun-nelled in ripe fruits.
Cause The caterpillars of the codling moth (*Cydia pomonella*), which feed in the core of the fruit; when they are mature, each cat-erpillar makes a frass-filled tunnel to the outside of the fruit.
Control Hang pheromone traps in the trees from late spring to mid-summer to catch the male moths, thus reducing egg fertilization. Use of traps will also indicate when the males are flying, enabling sprays to be timed more accurately to control the caterpil-lars as they hatch. If necessary, spray with permethrin, pirimiphos-methyl, or fenitrothion in early summer and again three weeks later.

Plum moths

Plants affected Plums.
Symptoms The fruits ripen prematurely and then drop. A pink cater-pillar and its excrement may be found inside the fruit.
Cause The plum moth (*Cydia funebrana*), which lays its eggs on the fruitlets during early summer. These hatch into caterpillars known as red plum maggots, which grow up to 12mm (1/2in) long.
Control Spray with permethrin, fenitrothion, or pirimiphos-methyl once in early summer and then again three weeks later. Pheromone traps hung in the tree in late spring catch the male plum moths, thus enabling the use of sprays to be timed more accurately. Traps, if used on their own, can reduce the mating success of the females and consequently result in fewer maggoty fruits.

Apple sawflies

Plants affected Apples.
Symptoms Fruitlets are tunnelled and drop off during early to mid-summer. The damaged fruits sometimes remain on the tree and become mature, but they are mis-shapen and have a long, ribbon-like scar on the skin.
Cause The larvae of the apple sawfly (*Hoplocampa testudinea*), white caterpillar-like insects up to 1cm

(1/2in) long with brown heads. They are less wide-spread than codling moths (see above).
Control Spray with pirimiphos-methyl, permethrin, fenitrothion, or HCH within seven days of petal fall; spray at dusk to avoid harming bees.

Pea thrips

Plants affected Peas.
Symptoms The pods turn silver-brown and they may remain flat apart from a few seeds at the stalk end.
Cause The pea thrips (*Kakothrips pisi-vorus*), which is a narrow-bodied, blackish-brown, sap-feeding insect up to 2mm (1/16in) long. The immature nymphs are orange-yellow. Both the adults and the nymphs feed on the plants; they thrive in hot, dry conditions.
Control Water plants regularly where the damage occurs and spray the plants with dimethoate, pyrethrum, permethrin, pirimiphos-methyl, mala-thion, or fenitrothion.

Pea moths

Plants affected Peas.
Symptoms Peas in pods are eaten by caterpillars.
Cause The pea moth (*Cydia nigricana*), which lays eggs on pea plants in flower in early to mid-summer. The caterpillars are creamy-white with brown heads, and are up to 1cm (1/2in) long.
Control Use pheromone traps to catch the males, reducing the chances of the females mating success-fully; or spray plants with fenitrothion, pirimiphos-methyl, or permethrin, 7–10 days after flowering begins. Early- or late-sown peas should not need spraying.

Jays

Plants affected Peas and broad beans.
Symptoms Developing pods are pecked and the seeds are eaten.
Cause Jays.
Control Netting is the only effective protection. Scaring devices are only effective initially as birds soon lose their fear. Repellent sprays must be used frequently if their effectiveness is to be maintained.

Grey squirrels

Plants affected Young trees, flower buds, fruits, and nuts.
Symptoms Bark is gnawed away. Flower buds, ripening fruits, and nuts are eaten.
Cause Grey squirrels.
Control Traps work only if used over a wide area.

> **See also** "Woodlice", p.548; "Millipedes", p.548; "Winter moth caterpillars", p.549; "Wood pigeons", p.549; "Potassium deficiency", p.560; "Birds", p.561; "Boron deficiency", p.566; and "Drought", p.568.

Root and tuber problems

Waterlogging

Plants affected Potentially all plants.
Symptoms Some roots may rot off completely. Those remaining are frequently blackened with a peeling outer surface. The first visible symptom is usually wilting leaves.
Cause Excessive water

levels in the growing medium, owing to factors such as poor soil structure, compaction, impeded drainage, or overwatering.
Control Where feasible, improve the structure and drainage of the soil and, if necessary, choose plants that are likely to survive in wet conditions. Check that drainage holes for container-grown plants are adequate, and that flow through them is not impeded. Regular application of a foliar feed during the growing season may help to stimulate growth, allowing waterlogged roots to be replaced.

Damping off

Plants affected The seedlings of all plants.
Symptoms Affected roots darken and rot off, causing the seedling to collapse and die. The disease often starts at one end of the seed tray, spreading rapidly to the other. A fluffy, fungal growth may

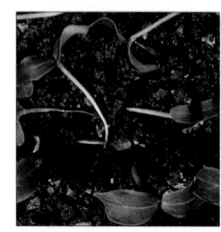

appear on the compost as well as on dead seedlings.
Cause Various fungi – in particular *Pythium ultimum* and some *Phytophthora* – which are soil- or water-borne and attack seedlings via either the roots or the base of the stem. They flourish in moist and unhygienic conditions.
Control There is no effective control once the disease is established, so it must be prevented. Sow seed thinly, improve ventilation, maintain strict hygiene, and avoid overwatering. Use only sterilized compost, mains water, and clean trays and pots. Water occasionally with a copper-based fungicide.

Root-knot nematodes

Plants affected Many garden plants, including fruit trees, vegetables, and ornamentals. Plants growing in greenhouses are also susceptible.
Symptoms Galls or swellings appear on the roots or tubers. Overall growth is stunted, and the plant may wilt, yellow, and sometimes even be killed.
Cause Root-knot nematodes (*Meloidogyne* spp.), which are thin, transparent, and only 0.5mm ($^1/_{32}$in) long. The larvae penetrate the roots.
Control Burn all affected plants. Rotate vegetable crops; choose resistant plants. There is no chemical control available to amateur gardeners.

Vine weevil larvae

Plants affected Many shrubs, perennials, annuals, bulbous plants, and indoor plants; most commonly affected are begonias, cyclamens, fuchsias,

Impatiens, primulas (including the Polyanthus Group), *Sedum*, and strawberries. Container-grown plants are particularly vulnerable.
Symptoms The outer tissues of woody seedlings and cuttings are gnawed from the stem bases and roots below ground level. Plants grow slowly, have a tendency to wilt, and finally collapse and die.
Cause and control See p.570 for details.
See also p.570; and p. 549 for information on damage caused to leaves by adult vine weevils.

Chafer larvae

Plants affected Young annuals, bulbous plants, and vegetables.
Symptoms Large cavities appear in root vegetables. Stem bases are eaten, and small plants wilt and may eventually die.
Cause The root-feeding, creamy-white larvae of beetles such as cock chafers (*Melolontha melolontha*) and garden chafers (*Phyllopertha horticola*). They are plump, "C"-shaped, and up to 2cm ($^3/_4$in) long, with brown heads and three pairs of legs.
Control Search for and destroy the larvae. Water vulnerable plants with pirimiphos-methyl, or treat the soil with chlorpyrifos + diazinon.
See also p.571 for problems caused on lawns.

Cutworms

Plants affected Low-growing perennials, annuals, root vegetables, and lettuces.
Symptoms Cavities appear in root crops, and tap roots may be severed, causing plants to wilt and die. See p.559 for other symptoms.
Cause The caterpillars of various moths (e.g. *Noctua* and *Agrotis*), usually creamy-brown in colour and up to 4.5cm ($1^3/_4$in) in length. They eat roots and the outer tissues of stem bases.
Control Search for and destroy the cutworms. Water vulnerable plants with pirimiphos-methyl, or treat the soil with chlorpyrifos + diazinon.

Leatherjackets

Plants affected Young annuals, bulbous plants, and vegetables.
Symptoms The roots are eaten, the stems are severed at ground level, and plants turn yellow, wilt, and may eventually die.
Cause The larvae of crane flies, also known as daddy-long-legs (e.g. *Tipula*), which feed on roots and stems. Leatherjackets are up to 3.5cm ($1^1/_2$in) long; they have tubular, greyish-brown bodies with no legs.
Control Where damage is seen on the plants, search for and destroy the leatherjackets. Water any vulnerable plants with pirimiphos-methyl; alternatively, treat the affected soil with chlorpyrifos + diazinon. Leatherjacket damage most commonly occurs on land that has recently been brought into cultivation, and as a consequence the problems should diminish within a few years.
See also p.571 for problems caused on lawns.

Carrot flies

Plants affected Mainly carrots, parsnips, parsley (*Petroselinum crispum*), and celery.
Symptoms Rusty brown tunnels are bored under the outer skin of mature roots. Small plants develop discoloured foliage and may eventually die.
Cause Creamy-yellow maggots, larvae of the carrot fly (*Psila rosae*), which feed in the surface tissues of the larger roots; in autumn they may bore deeper. They are slender, legless, and up to 1cm ($^1/_2$in) long.
Control Enclose susceptible plants within a clear polythene fence at least 60cm (24in) high, to exclude the low-flying female flies. Treat seed rows with chlorpyrifos + diazinon or pirimiphos-methyl dust; growing plants may be protected against the second generation of larvae by watering with pirimiphos-methyl in mid-summer. Lift carrots for storage in autumn to limit damage.

Cabbage root flies

Plants affected Brassicas (including cabbages, cauliflowers, Brussels sprouts, turnips, swedes), radishes.
Symptoms Plants grow slowly and wilt; seedlings and transplants die; tunnels appear in root crops.
Cause Root-feeding larvae of the fly *Delia radicum*, white, legless maggots up to 9mm ($^3/_8$in) long. Several generations occur between mid-spring and mid-autumn, causing damage mainly to young plants.
Control Place collars of carpet underlay, roofing felt, or cardboard, about 12cm (5in) in diameter, around the base of transplanted brassicas to prevent the female flies from laying eggs in the soil. Alternatively, both transplanted brassicas and seed rows can be protected with chlorpyrifos + diazinon or pirimiphos-methyl dust.

Clubroot

Plants affected The family Cruciferae, especially certain brassicas (for example cabbages, Brussels sprouts, and swedes) and radishes, and some ornamentals, including candytufts (*Iberis*), wallflowers (*Cheiranthus*), and stocks (*Matthiola*).
Symptoms Swollen and distorted roots; stunted and often discoloured plants; wilting in hot weather. See p.553 for other symptoms.
Cause The slime mould *Plasmodiophora brassicae*, which thrives in poorly drained, acid soils, and may also be found on manure and plant debris. It is easily spread on boots and tools, and the spores remain viable for 20 years or more, even in the absence of a host plant. Weeds susceptible to this disease (e.g. shepherd's purse and charlock) may be a source of infection.
Control Remove and burn affected plants. Keep the area free of weeds, improve drainage, and lime the soil. Raise new plants in soil-based compost to encourage root development. Proprietary chemical dips containing benomyl may be used when planting.

Violet root rot

Plants affected Vegetables, mainly carrots, parsnips, asparagus, swedes, turnips, potatoes, celery.
Symptoms Roots, tubers, and any other parts below ground level are covered in a dense, matted, purple, fungal growth to which soil particles become attached. The upper parts of the plant become stunted and discoloured. There may be secondary rotting.
Cause The fungus *Helicobasidium purpureum*, which is spread as the mycelium grows from plant to plant, and harboured by some weeds. It thrives in both acid and waterlogged soils.
Control Remove and burn infected or suspect plants immediately. Avoid growing susceptible plants on the affected site for at least four years, and keep the area entirely free of weeds.

Phytophthora root rots

Plants affected Trees, shrubs, and woody perennials; commonly maples (*Acer*), yew (*Taxus baccata*), Lawson cypress (*Chamaecyparis lawsoniana*), apples, rhododendrons, raspberries, and heathers.
Symptoms The larger roots die back from the stem or trunk, although the fine roots may appear perfectly healthy; affected roots usually turn black. See p.558 for other symptoms.
Cause Various species of the fungus *Phytophthora*, often found in wet or waterlogged soil. The roots of plants are attacked by swimming spores that build up both in the soil and within infected plant remains.
Control Avoid heavy watering and where possible improve soil drainage. Dig up and burn affected plants. Buy plants from reputable sources and choose those that are tolerant or resistant, e.g. *Tsuga heterophylla* and x *Cupressocyparis leylandii*. There is no chemical control available to amateurs.

Foot and root rots

Plants affected A wide range, especially petunias and other bedding plants, tomatoes, cucumbers, peas, beans, and young, container-grown plants.
Symptoms The roots turn black and break or rot. See p.558 for details of other symptoms.
Cause A range of soil- and waterborne fungi that flourish where growing conditions are unhygienic. The fungi are often introduced in unsterilized compost and non-mains water, and will build up in the soil over several years if susceptible plants are repeatedly grown on the same site.
Control Rotate susceptible plants. Maintain strict hygiene, and use only fresh, sterilized compost and mains water. Remove affected plants and the soil in the vicinity of their roots.

Tropical root rots

Plants affected Annual and perennial crops, temperate and tropical, including broad beans, French beans, cucumbers, melons, pumpkins, peanuts.
Symptoms Annual plants show a mid-season wilting, with rotting of the base of the stem and upper portion of the root; the infected tissues develop lesions and often turn red before decaying. The leaves become chlorotic as their water supply is restricted, and young seedlings may show signs of damping off (see p.564). Groundnut shells become blackened and rapidly decay. The infected tissues of perennial crops turn purple and the plants wilt.
Cause Various forms of the soil-borne fungus *Fusarium solani*, which often occur as secondary infections. The disease is carried in the soil and infected debris; crops grown in poorly drained, acid soils are particularly at risk. High soil temperatures will encourage the development of pea root rot (*F. solani* f. *pisi*).
Control Rotate crops on a long cycle. Treat seeds with hot water at 55°C (162°F) for 15 minutes. Where possible, improve soil drainage.

Crown gall

Plants affected Trees, shrubs (most commonly cane fruits and roses), and woody perennials.
Symptoms Irregular, rounded swellings develop on the roots, and occasionally the whole root system is distorted into a single, large swelling. See p.559 for symptoms.
Cause The bacterium *Agrobacterium tumefaciens*, prevalent in wet soils. The bacteria enter the plant through wounds made on the surface and cause cells to proliferate.
Control Avoid damaging plants and improve soil drainage. Cut out and destroy any affected stems in order to prevent secondary infection.

Honey fungus

Plants affected Trees, shrubs, climbers, and some woody perennials; most commonly affected are privets (*Ligustrum*), rhododendrons, and *Wisteria*.
Symptoms In autumn, fruiting bodies sometimes develop in clusters on underground roots, at the base of the trunk, and occasionally at some height from the ground; they die back after the first frost. The plant deteriorates and eventually dies. See p.569 for other symptoms.
Cause The fungus *Armillaria* (principally *A. mellea*) spread either by rhizomorph movement from an infected plant or stump, or through root contact.
Control Dig out and burn affected plants, stumps, and as much of the root system as possible; if necessary, have the stump chipped or ground out by a contractor. Avoid the more susceptible plants, choosing those showing some resistance, e.g. yew (*Taxus baccata*), *Cornus*, beech (*Fagus*), and *Hebe*.

Fungal brackets

Plants affected Mainly trees, and especially mature or overmature specimens, but also shrubs and woody perennials.
Symptoms Fungal fruiting bodies, often bracket-shaped, may appear above ground, following the line of the roots; they are attached to the roots by tiny fungal threads. They vary in appearance, often according to weather conditions. The roots may become hollow and eventually die, making the tree extremely unstable in the ground. Stems are also affected (see p.559).
Cause Various fungi, e.g. *Meripilus* or *Ganoderma*.
Control Seek professional advice, particularly if the tree poses a potential hazard. Removal of fruiting bodies will not prevent further internal decay, but does reduce the chances of spread to other trees.

Parsnip canker

Plants affected Parsnips.
Symptoms The shoulders of affected parsnips discolour and rot; the crown, shank, and roots of the plant may also rot, and the foliage may show some spotting. This condition occurs mainly in autumn and winter.
Cause Various species of fungus, primarily *Itersonilia pastinaceae*. Some are soil-inhabiting and others produce spores that are washed into the soil from leaf lesions.
Control Rotate crops. Prevent injury to parsnip roots, particularly the type of injury caused by carrot fly larvae (see p.564). Sow late and closely in order to produce parsnips with small roots, which are less prone to disease, and earth up the rows to provide a barrier against spores washed down from the leaf lesions. Remove all affected plants immediately. Grow parsnips in a deep loam soil with a high pH, and choose a resistant cultivar, e.g. 'Avonresister'.

Verticillium wilt

Plants affected A large number of garden and greenhouse plants.
Symptoms The roots deteriorate and die, and if cut longitudinally in the early stages of degeneration they may show a central, vascular column of brown discoloration.
Cause and control See p.557 for details.

Fusarium wilt

Plants affected Perennials, annuals, vegetables, and fruits; most commonly affected are China asters (*Callistephus*), carnations (*Dianthus*), sweet peas (*Lathyrus odoratus*), beans, and peas.
Symptoms The roots of affected plants turn black and eventually die.
Cause and control See p.558 for details.

Primula brown core

Plants affected Primulas.
Symptoms The roots rot and, if split longitudinally, show a distinct brown core; many are killed and plants become loose in the ground. Leaves yellow, wilt, and die. Flowers wilt.
Cause The fungus species *Phytophthora primulae*, which can remain viable in the soil for many years.
Control Dig up and burn all the affected plants. Grow any new primulas on an entirely fresh site.

Mice, rats, and voles

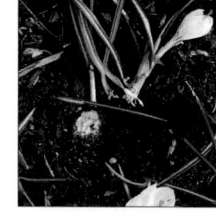

Plants affected Shrubs, young trees, crocus corms, seedlings of peas and beans, seeds, vegetables, and fruits kept in storage.
Symptoms The outer layer of stems and roots is gnawed. Seeds, seedlings, corms, vegetables, and fruits are eaten.
Cause Mice, rats, and voles.
Control Traps provide the best solution; poisoned baits containing alphachloralose or coumatetralyl may also be used.

Boron deficiency

Plants affected Roots of carrots, parsnips, swedes, turnips, and beetroots. The condition is fairly rare.
Symptoms The roots are of a poor shape and texture, and are rather grey. They may split longitudinally and sometimes contain cavities. A brown discoloration – known as brown heart – may occur in the lowermost sections, often in concentric rings; it is found mainly in turnips and swedes, and leaves them poor tasting and fibrous. Beetroot shows internal discoloration and may develop cankers. See p.558 for other symptoms.
Cause A lack of boron in the soil, or an inability of the plant to take up the trace element owing to unsuitable growing conditions. Most common on very chalky or heavily limed soils, those that have been very dry, and those where the boron has been leached out. It rarely affects greenhouse plants.
Control Maintain correct soil moisture levels and avoid excessive liming. Before introducing a susceptible plant to a problem site, apply borax at 35g/20sq m (1oz/20sq yd), mixing with horticultural sand for easy and accurate application. Use fritted trace elements.

> **See also** "Aphids", p.550; "Mealybugs", p.550; "Pansy sickness", p.554; "Slugs", "Wireworms", below; "Onion flies", p.567; "Fungus gnat or sciarid flies", p.570; and "Bean seed flies", p.570.

Potato tuber problems

Slugs

Plants affected Potatoes.
Symptoms Circular holes are bored in the outside of potato tubers, and extensive cavities appear in the interior, during late summer.
Cause Slugs.
Control Scatter methiocarb or metaldehyde pellets, or spray plants with liquid metaldehyde. Grow less susceptible cultivars; harvest tubers as soon as mature.
See also "Slugs and snails", p.548, for leaf problems.

Wireworms

Plants affected Potatoes and other root crops, seedlings, perennials, annuals, and bulbous plants.
Symptoms Tunnels up to 3mm (¹/₈in) in diameter, superficially similar to those made by slugs, are bored through root crops. Underground parts of other plants are damaged. Small plants wilt and die.
Cause The slender, stiff-bodied, yellowish-orange larvae of click beetles (e.g. *Agriotes* spp.), which feed on roots and stem bases. They are up to 2.5cm (1in) long, with three pairs of short legs at the head end and a peg-like protuberance beneath the rear end. The problem mainly occurs when grassland is brought into cultivation.
Control Where damage is seen, search for and destroy the wireworms. Lift root crops as soon as they are mature. Water vulnerable plants with pirimiphos-methyl, or treat the soil with chlorpyrifos + diazinon. The pest usually disappears once the ground has been cultivated for about five years.

Potato blight

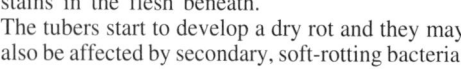

Plants affected Potatoes.
Symptoms Dark and sunken patches begin to develop on the skin, and there are reddish-brown stains in the flesh beneath. The tubers start to develop a dry rot and they may also be affected by secondary, soft-rotting bacteria.
See p.553 for symptoms that affect the foliage.
Cause The fungus *Phytophthora infestans*, which thrives in warm, moist conditions. Spores produced on the foliage and on potato haulms are carried from plant to plant by wind and rain, and may be washed down into the soil to infect potato tubers. The same fungus may also attack tomatoes.
Control Avoid overhead watering. Earth up potatoes deeply to provide a barrier against falling spores, and choose resistant cultivars, e.g. 'Kondor', 'Romano', 'Cara', or 'Wilja'. Spray with mancozeb or a copper-based fungicide; in wet seasons spray before the blight appears.

Common potato scab

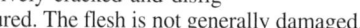

Plants affected Potatoes.
Symptoms Raised, scabby patches develop on the skin, and these sometimes rupture. Damage may be superficial, but in some cases the tuber becomes extensively cracked and disfigured. The flesh is not generally damaged.
Cause *Streptomyces scabies*, a bacterium-like but mycelium-producing organism, common in soils that are sandy and light with a high lime content, and those only recently cultivated. Disease development is most common during hot, dry summers, and when soil moisture levels are low.
Control Improve soil texture and avoid liming; water regularly. Do not plant potatoes on soil that has recently been used for brassicas. Grow resistant cultivars, for example 'King Edward'; very susceptible cultivars include 'Maris Piper' and 'Desiree'.

Bacterial rotting

Plants affected Potatoes.
Symptoms. The tuber is rapidly reduced to a slimy mass that has a strong smell, while growing or in storage.
Cause Bacteria enter the tuber either through wounds or through damage caused by infections.
Control Maintain good growing conditions, and harvest potatoes carefully in order to avoid injury. Remove all affected tubers immediately.

Internal rust spot

Plants affected Potatoes.
Symptoms Rust-brown flecks develop throughout the flesh of the tubers.
Cause Cultivation either in sandy, acid soils that are low in organic matter, or in soils that are generally low in nutrients – in particular potash and phosphorus.
Control Incorporate humus into the soil before planting and apply a general fertilizer in spring. Water regularly. Grow only potatoes showing some resistance to this condition, for example 'King Edward'.

Potato spraing

Plants affected Potatoes.
Symptoms A brown, arc-shaped discoloration, sometimes with a corky texture, develops inside the often misshapen tuber. Potatoes alone show these symptoms, but the viruses (p.553) can infect *Nicotiana*, China asters (*Callistephus*), gladioli, tulips, hyacinths, and *Capsicum*.
Cause A number of viruses, including tobacco rattle virus, and, less often, potato mop-top virus; these are transmitted by free-living nematodes in the soil.
Control Avoid growing other host plants on the affected site, and grow all potatoes on a fresh site.

Ring rot

Plants affected Potatoes in store.
Symptoms The vascular tissues of tubers become soft and decay. The disease may eventually reach the tuber surface, producing cracks near the eyes, and secondary rots may develop. Symptoms usually develop late in the growing season.
Cause *Corynebacterium sependonicum*, a bacterium transmitted by infected tubers used as seed potatoes.
Control Inspect tubers on lifting, do not store any that are suspect, and ensure that all storage containers are clean. Plant only disease-free tubers.

> **See also** "Millipedes", p.548; "Blackleg on potatoes", p.568; and "Potato cyst eelworms", p.570.

Bulb, corm, and rhizome problems

Storage rots

Plants affected Bulbs and corms, especially if damaged or poorly stored.
Symptoms Discoloured, sometimes sunken patches develop on the surface of the bulb, or beneath the outer scales or skin. A fungal growth may appear on the patches, spreading

through bulb tissues, which become light and dry.
Cause A range of fungi. Infection is often restricted to a very few, closely related bulbs or corms, and may affect both those in the ground and those in store. Temperatures that are too low or too high and over-damp conditions encourage the disease.
Control Store and plant only healthy bulbs, and avoid injury to them. Store in suitable conditions, and immediately remove any that show signs of deterioration. Dipping them in a fungicide solution, e.g. carbendazim, or in sulphur may prevent attack.

Bulb flies

Plants affected Daffodils, *Hippeastrum*, snowdrops (*Galanthus*), bluebells (*Hyacinthoides non-scriptus*), *Cyrtanthus purpureus*, and *Sprekelia*.
Symptoms Bulbs fail to grow or produce only a few grass-like leaves. Maggots may be found in the bulbs.
Cause The large narcissus bulb fly (*Merodon equestris*), which attacks sound bulbs, and the small narcissus bulb fly (*Eumerus* spp.), which attacks damaged bulbs. Large bulb flies lay eggs singly on bulbs in early summer. Adults resemble small bumblebees; larvae are brownish-white, up to 2cm (³/₄in) long, and fill the centre of the bulb with muddy excrement. Small bulb fly larvae are similar but never more than 8mm (³/₈in) long; there are usually several in a bulb.
Control Avoid planting in warm, sheltered places, which attract adult flies. Discourage egg-laying by firming the soil around the necks of bulbs as they die down, or cover with fine-meshed screens in early summer. There is no effective chemical control.

Ink spot

Plants affected Bulbous irises, *Crocosmia*, *Lachenalia*.
Symptoms Inky stains appear on bulbs, and yellow dots or black craters on fleshy scales. Bulbs may rot away. Black patches or blotches appear on leaves.
Cause The fungus *Myriosporium adustum*, which spreads through the soil to nearby bulbs.
Control Destroy diseased bulbs. Lift bulbs every year, and plant in a new area. Spray with Bordeaux mixture.

Narcissus basal rot

Plants affected Daffodils.
Symptoms After about one month in store, the basal plate of the bulb becomes soft and brown, and rots. The deterioration spreads to the inner scales, which turn dark brown, and a pale pink, fluffy, fungal growth may then appear

between the scales and on the basal plate. The bulb gradually dries out and becomes mummified. Bulbs which become infected in the ground may, if not lifted, rot away in the soil. In some cases, foliage symptoms of yellowing and wilting occur first.
Cause The soil-borne fungus *Fusarium oxysporium* f. *narcissi*, which infects bulbs through the basal plate; the fungus is encouraged by high soil temperatures. If the infected bulb is not lifted, it may infect adjacent bulbs. Stored bulbs that are infected but do not show symptoms also act as a source of infection when planted.
Control Lift bulbs early in the season, before soil temperatures rise, and dip them in a solution of carbendazim or thiophanate-methyl. Check bulbs thoroughly for signs of disease before storing.

Narcissus eelworms

Plants affected Daffodils, bluebells (*Hyacinthoides non-scriptus*), and snowdrops (*Galanthus*).
Symptoms Bulbs cut transversely reveal brown concentric rings. Plant growth is stunted and distorted, and infested bulbs invariably rot.
Cause The narcissus eelworm (*Ditylenchus dipsaci*), which is a microscopic nematode that feeds within bulbs and foliage. Where bulbs have been naturalized, the area of infestation will increase each year as the pest spreads through the soil. Weeds may also harbour narcissus eelworms.
Control Dig up and burn both the infested plants and any others within 1m (1yd) of them. Immersing dormant daffodil bulbs in water at 44°C (112°F) for three hours kills the eelworms without causing bulb damage, but the constant temperature is difficult to maintain without special equipment. Avoid replanting affected areas with susceptible plants for at least two years, and keep weeds under control. No chemical treatment is available.

Iris rhizome rot

Plants affected Irises.
Symptoms The base of outer leaves decays and the rot then spreads into the rhizome, attacking the youngest parts first. The infected area is reduced to a foul-smelling mass.
Cause The bacterium *Erwinia carotovora* var. *carotovora*, which thrives in waterlogged soil. The bacteria enter the rhizomes through wounds or other damaged areas.
Control Check all rhizomes for any kind of damage before planting, and be extra careful to avoid injuring them. Plant the rhizomes shallowly, and always in good, well-drained soil. Take steps to ensure that slugs (see p.566), which may be the cause of injury to rhizomes, are kept under control. The prompt removal of any rotting tissue may help to check the problem temporarily, but in the long term the whole rhizome is best discarded.

Onion white rot

Plants affected Onions, shallots, leeks, garlic.
Symptoms The base of the bulb and the roots are covered in a fluffy, white, fungal growth in which hard, black sclerotia (fungal resting bodies) become embedded.

Cause The fungus *Sclerotium cepivorum*. Sclerotia in the soil will remain viable for at least seven years and, when stimulated by the presence of new host plant roots, they will germinate, causing infection again.
Control Dig up and burn affected plants as soon as possible. Do not grow susceptible crops on the affected site for at least eight years.

Onion neck rot

Plants affected Onions and shallots.
Symptoms The scales at the neck become soft and discoloured; a dense, fuzzy, grey, fungal growth develops on the affected area; and hard, black sclerotia (fungal resting bodies) may form. In some

severe cases the bulb eventually becomes mummified. The symptoms frequently do not appear until the bulbs are being kept in storage.
Cause The fungus *Botrytis allii*, spread mainly by seed-borne fungal spores and the sclerotia present on plant debris.
Control Obtain sets and seed from a reputable source. Encourage the growth of hard, well-ripened onions; do not feed after mid-summer, avoid high nitrogen fertilizers, and water regularly. After harvesting, allow the tops of onions to dry off as rapidly as possible. Store under cool, dry conditions with good air circulation, discarding damaged bulbs. Avoid the more susceptible white-bulbed onions.

Onion flies

Plants affected Mainly onions, sometimes shallots, less often garlic and leeks.
Symptoms Growth is poor, the outer leaves turn yellow, and maggots may be found in the bulb.
Cause The root- and bulb-feeding larvae of the onion fly (*Delia antiqua*),

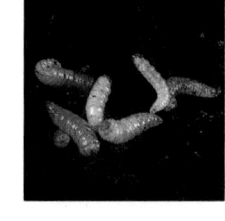

white maggots up to 9mm (³/₈in) long.
Control Carefully lift and burn infested plants. Treat the soil with chlorpyrifos + diazinon or pirimiphos-methyl dust when sowing or planting sets. Seedlings are less tolerant of damage than sets.

See also "Slugs and snails", p.548; "Millipedes", p.548; "Red lily beetles", p.548; "Tulip fire", p.553; "Bulb scale mites", p.556; "Grey squirrels", p.563; and "Mice, rats, and voles", p.566.

Whole-plant problems

Drought

Plants affected All plants, especially those that are young, container-grown, or in light, sandy soils.

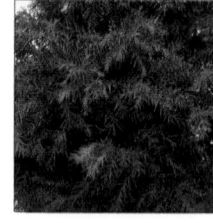

Symptoms Autumn coloration develops early and defoliation, followed by dieback, may occur. Plants wilt and growth is stunted. Flowering and fruit set may decrease markedly. Fruits may be small, sometimes distorted, and of a poor texture. See pp.554 and 561 for other symptoms.

Cause Chronic (prolonged) or repeated drought due to inadequate or unavailable soil moisture; excessive water loss from the leaves of plants on exposed sites; injured or restricted roots; or soil compaction. Plants in small containers are vulnerable during hot weather, and peat-based composts that dry out too much are extremely difficult to re-wet. Dry, brown buds on certain plants, such as camellias and rhododendrons, are the result of a water shortage the previous year during the period of bud initiation.

Control Water plants regularly, and frequently check those in hot or sunny positions. Mulch, where appropriate, to improve moisture retention. Drought is more easily prevented than treated; plants exposed to chronic water shortage are less likely to recover once adequate water is supplied or temperatures fall than those suffering acute (sudden) shortage.

Low temperatures

Plants affected Trees, shrubs, perennials, annuals, bulbous plants, vegetables, fruits, indoor plants; seedlings and young plants are especially vulnerable.

Symptoms The leaves are sometimes bleached, and brown, dry patches develop; evergreen foliage may turn brown. Rotted patches develop on petals, especially on exposed flowerheads. Frost injury causes leaves to pucker and petals to wither or discolour. In some cases, whole flowers may be killed. See also pp.554 and 557.

Cause and control See p.554 for details.

Waterlogging

Plants affected Potentially all plants.

Symptoms Leaves may turn yellow, and plants tend to wilt. Bark peels off branches. Roots may rot off completely. Those remaining often begin to blacken and their outer surface peels away very easily.

Cause Excessive water levels in the growing medium, owing to poor soil structure, compaction, impeded drainage, or overwatering.

Control Where feasible, improve the structure and drainage of the soil and, if necessary, choose plants that are most likely to survive in wet conditions. Check that drainage holes for container-grown plants are adequate, and that flow through them is not impeded. The regular application of a foliar feed during the growing season may help to stimulate growth, allowing waterlogged roots to be replaced.

Damping off

Plants affected The seedlings of all plants.

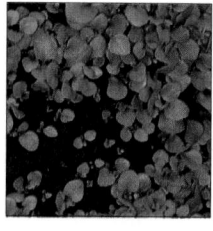

Symptoms The seedlings collapse and die as their roots darken and rot off; the disease often attacks seedlings at one end of a seed tray, rapidly spreading to the other. A fluffy, fungal growth may appear both on the compost and on any dead seedlings.

Cause Various fungi (most particularly *Pythium ultimum* and some *Phytophthora*), which are soil- or water-borne and attack the seedlings via the roots or stem bases. These fungi flourish in moist and unhygienic conditions.

Control There is no control once the disease is established, so it must be prevented. Sow seed thinly, improve ventilation around seedlings, maintain strict hygiene, and avoid overwatering. Always use sterilized compost, mains water, and clean trays and pots. Water seedlings occasionally with a copper-based fungicide.

Blackleg on cuttings

Plants affected Cuttings, most particularly those of pelargoniums.

Symptoms The stems become blackened, shrunken, soft, and rotten, usually at the base; the plant discolours and eventually dies.

Cause A variety of micro-organisms, e.g. *Pythium* and *Rhizoctonia*, which are often spread by propagating in unhygienic conditions. Unsterilized compost, dirty pots, trays, and tools, and the use of non-mains water are commonly to blame. The disease is also transmitted by soil moisture.

Control Use clean equipment, sterilized compost, and mains water. Dip cuttings in rooting powder containing a fungicide before potting up. Remove affected cuttings immediately.

Blackleg on potatoes

Plants affected Potatoes.

Symptoms The stems collapse, blacken and rot at the base, and the foliage discolours. The disease usually occurs at the start of the season, but any tubers that have formed may also rot. Most of the crop remains healthy; only a few plants show symptoms.

Cause The bacterium *Erwinia caratovora* var. *atroseptica*, which is usually introduced on slightly infected seed tubers that do not show any symptoms at all when they are being planted.

Control Remove affected plants immediately. Inspect tubers on lifting and do not store any that are suspect. The bacteria are unlikely to build up to dangerous levels in the soil, and potatoes can be planted on the site again under a rotation scheme.

Bad pruning

Plants affected Woody perennials, shrubs, and trees.

Symptoms The plant has a poor, unnatural, or uneven shape. Vigour may be reduced and flowering is limited. Snags or whole limbs may die back.

Cause The removal of limbs too close to, or far from, the main limb or trunk. A flush cut, where no snag is left, leaves a large wound and, more importantly, no branch collar – the area that most rapidly produces callusing wood to heal the wound. Conversely, too long a snag encourages dieback. Carelessly removed branches may damage adjacent bark.

Control When pruning a tree or shrub always be careful to follow the correct method at the appropriate time of year, checking the extent of pruning necessary. Use sharp pruning tools and do not leave any snags or flush cuts. If necessary, employ a reputable tree surgeon.

Nectria canker

Plants affected Woody perennials, shrubs, trees, especially apples, flowering crab apples (*Malus*), beeches (*Fagus*), poplars (*Populus*), *Sorbus*, mulberries (*Morus*), and hawthorns (*Crataegus*).

Symptoms Small areas of bark, often close to a bud or wound, darken and sink inwards; the bark cracks, forming loose, flaky, concentric rings. Enlarged cankers restrict nutrient and water flow, and lead to stem and leaf deterioration. In extreme cases the whole shoot becomes ringed and dies back. White pustules appear in summer, red pustules in winter.

Cause Spores of the fungus *Nectria galligena* infect wounds caused by pruning, leaf fall, irregular growth, frost, and woolly aphids (see p.558).

Control Prune affected branches or, on larger limbs, remove the cankered area; treat with a canker paint containing cresylic acid. Spray the affected tree with an appropriate fungicide. Avoid susceptible cultivars, e.g. the apples 'Cox's Orange Pippin', 'Worcester Pearmain', and 'James Grieve'.

Coryneum canker

Plants affected Conifers, mainly cypresses (*Cupressus*) especially *C. macrocarpa* and *C. sempervirens*, and x *Cupressocyparis leylandii*.

Symptoms Some scattered branches develop dull foliage, which later yellows, dies, turns brown, and is eventually shed. Affected branches develop cankers, which produce copious amounts of resin and are covered with pinhead-sized, black, blister-like, fruiting bodies. When cankers girdle a branch or main stem it dies.

Cause Air-borne spores released from the fruiting bodies of the fungus *Coryneum cardinale* invade trees through the ends of cut branches, fine cracks in the bark, leaf scales, and twig crotches. Infection occurs most readily during the dormant season.
Control Cut out all affected branches or, if severely damaged, remove the whole tree. There is no available chemical control.

Bacterial canker

Plants affected Mainly apples and *Prunus*, in particular cherries and plums.
Symptoms Flat or sunken, elongated cankers develop on the stems; droplets of golden or amber-coloured gum ooze from the affected area. The stem starts to deteriorate, and the foliage and flowers may wither and die, or the buds do not break. Foliage may show symptoms of shothole (see p.552).
Cause The bacteria *Pseudomonas syringae* and *P. mors-prunarus*.
Control Remove cankered branches and treat the wounds with a wound paint. Spray the foliage with Bordeaux mixture or other copper fungicide in late summer and early autumn.

Coral spot

Plants affected Broad-leaved trees and shrubs, especially *Elaeagnus*, elms (*Ulmus*), beeches (*Fagus*), maples (*Acer*), magnolias, and currants.
Symptoms Affected shoots die back, and the dead bark becomes covered in orange-pink pustules about 1mm ($^1/_{16}$in) in diameter. Until recent years, the

disease was most commonly found on dead branches and woody debris, but it has become more aggressive and now affects living shoots as well as dead.
Cause The fungus *Nectria cinnabarina*. Spores that have been released from the orange pustules are spread by rain splash and on pruning tools. They enter the wood through damaged or dying areas and wounds and infect the plant.
Control Clear away all woody debris. Cut back affected branches to a point well below the obviously infected area.

Honey fungus

Plants affected Trees, shrubs, climbers, and some woody perennials; mainly rhododendrons, privets (*Ligustrum*), and *Wisteria*.
Symptoms A creamy-white mycelium develops under the bark at the base of the trunk or the stem, sometimes it also extends upwards; tough, black rhizomorphs (i.e. fungal strands) appear. In autumn fruiting bodies grow in clusters and die back after the first frost. Gum or resin exudes from cracks in the bark of conifers. Plants deteriorate and finally die; prolific flowering or

Mycelium under bark

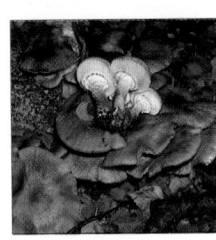

Fruiting bodies

fruiting may occur shortly before death. Roots are also affected (see p.565).
Cause The fungus *Armillaria* (principally *A. mellea*) spread either by rhizomorph movement from an infected plant or stump, or through root contact.
Control Dig out and burn affected plants, stumps, and root systems; if necessary, have stumps chipped or ground out by a contractor. Avoid susceptible plants; choose those with some resistance, e.g. yew (*Taxus baccata*), *Cornus*, beech (*Fagus*), and *Hebe*.

Crown rot

Plants affected Mainly perennials and indoor plants; also trees, shrubs, annuals, bulbous plants, vegetables, and fruits.
Symptoms The base of the plant rots and may smell unpleasant. Plants may wilt, wither, and die.
Cause Bacterial and fungal organisms entering the stem through surface wounds; over-deep planting also leads to infection.
Control Avoid injury to the stem base and keep the crown free of debris; do not mulch right up to the plant. Ensure that planting depths are correct. Complete removal of the affected area may prevent disease spread, but frequently the whole plant is killed and should be dug up and destroyed.

Replant disease/soil sickness

Plants affected Mainly roses, commonly those on *R. canina* rootstocks, and fruit trees.
Symptoms Vigour is reduced and growth stunted. Roots are small and dark.
Cause Several factors may be involved, including soil-dwelling nematodes and the viruses they transmit, soil-borne fungi, and nutrient depletion.
Control Do not grow replacement plants in a site previously occupied by the same or a closely related species. Change the soil to a depth of 45cm (18in) and a width several centimetres greater than the spread of the roots. There is no suitable chemical sterilizer available to amateurs, but the ground can be treated by a contractor.

Rose dieback

Plants affected Roses.
Symptoms The plants die back, and may discolour. A fungal growth may develop. Deterioration is extensive in some cases.
Cause Poor planting, poor maintenance, or a poor environment. Severe or repeated attacks of frost, leaf disease, or fungi may also be responsible.
Control Plant roses correctly. Feed and water them regularly. Prune them, and keep diseases and pests under control. Remove dead tissue, then spray or dust cankered roses with a copper-based fungicide.

Fireblight

Plants affected Members of the family Rosaceae that bear pome fruits, mainly pears, apples, cotoneasters, hawthorns (*Crataegus*), and some *Sorbus*.
Symptoms Blossoms wilt and adjacent stem areas discolour. The foliage turns blackish-brown, shrivels, and dies, but remains on the stem. Dark greenish-brown cankers then form on the branches, producing a bacterial ooze varying in colour between yellowish-brown and white, depending on the host. The inner surface of the bark and the wood beneath it may be stained brown. Affected limbs die and the tree is killed. See p.553 for other symptoms.
Cause The bacterium *Erwinia amylovora*, which is produced from the cankers and attacks via the blossom. It is carried by wind, rain splash, insects, and pollen grains.
Control Remove affected plants or prune out affected areas 60cm (24in) past the damage; dip the saw in disinfectant before using it on another tree. Fireblight is no longer a notifiable disease.

Clematis wilt

Plants affected Clematis, mainly large-flowered hybrids, e.g. 'Jackmanii', and *C. montana*.
Symptoms The terminal shoots wilt, starting with the youngest foliage, and the petioles begin to darken where they join the leaf blade. Whole sections of the plant may eventually die back.
Cause The fungus *Ascochyta clematidina*, which produces spore-releasing, fruiting bodies on the older stems. Other, non-pathogenic causes of wilt (e.g. drought, poor drainage, and graft failure) may be mistaken for this disease.
Control Cut back any affected stems to healthy tissue, below ground level if necessary. Spray all the new foliage produced later in the year, and that appearing in the following spring, with Bordeaux mixture or benomyl.

Peony wilt

Plants affected Peonies (*Paeonia*).
Symptoms Affected shoots wilt, wither, and turn brown. The infection generally starts at the stem base, which may become covered in a grey, fuzzy, fungal growth resembling grey mould. Small, hard, black, sclerotia (fungal resting bodies) form both on and within the affected stems.
Cause The fungus *Botrytis paeoniae*. The sclerotia drop into the soil and remain until conditions are favourable (wet years in particular); they then cause new infections.
Control Cut out the affected shoots of herbaceous peonies to below ground level and dust with Bordeaux mixture; thin out dense plants. Spray the foliage with benomyl or thiophanate-methyl.

Willow anthracnose

Plants affected Willows (*Salix*); *S.* x *sepulcralis* 'Chrysocoma' mainly.
Symptoms Dark, elliptical, roughened cankers about 6mm (¹/₄in) long form on the stems; they may coalesce, and badly affected shoots die back. Leaves develop small, dark brown spots, then turn yellow, curl, and fall early. The disease is rarely fatal.

Cause The fungus *Marssonina salicicola*, which is usually encouraged by mild, damp weather conditions. Spores produced from the cankers and foliage lesions are spread by rain splash.
Control Rake up and burn all the affected leaves, and where possible cut out the cankered shoots. Spray with Bordeaux mixture, starting in spring as soon as the leaves break.

Potato cyst eelworms

Plants affected Potatoes and tomatoes.
Symptoms Plants yellow and die, starting with the lower leaves, and potato tubers remain small. Roots of lifted plants show numerous white, yellow, or brown cysts up to 1mm (¹/₁₆in) in diameter.

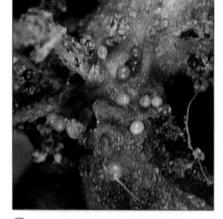

Cysts on roots

Cause Root-dwelling eelworms, or nematodes, that disrupt water and nutrient uptake. Mature females swell and their bodies (known as cysts) burst through the root walls. Cysts contain up to 600 eggs; these remain viable for many years. Cysts of the golden cyst eelworm (*Globodera rostochiensis*)

Yellowed leaves

change from white through yellow to brown as they mature; those of the white cyst eelworm (*G. pallida*) change directly from white to brown.
Control Crop rotation discourages the build-up of infestation. Some potatoes are resistant to the golden cyst eelworm, e.g. 'Pentland Javelin', 'Pentland Lustre', 'Ukama', and 'Revelino' (earlies), and 'Maris Piper', 'Montana', 'Kingston', and 'Minsand' (maincrop); others, e.g. 'Cara', 'Morag', and 'Sante', are also tolerant of the white cyst eelworm. There is no chemical control available for amateur use.

Vine weevil larvae

Plants affected Shrubs, perennials, annuals, bulbous plants, and indoor plants; fuchsias, begonias, cyclamen, *Impatiens*, *Sedum*, primulas (including the Polyanthus Group), and

strawberries are commonly affected. Container-grown plants are also particularly vulnerable.
Symptoms Plants grow slowly, wilt, collapse, and die. The outer tissues of seedlings of woody plants and cuttings are gnawed from the stems below ground.
Cause The plump, white larvae of the beetle *Otiorhynchus sulcatus*, which are up to 1cm (¹/₂in) long and slightly curved, with brown heads and no legs. The adults lay eggs in spring and summer, and damage occurs from autumn to spring.
Control Maintain good hygiene to avoid providing shelters for the adults. Treatments using nematodes (*Steinernema* and *Heterorhabditis* spp.) are now available; watered onto the potting compost in late summer, these treatments kill the larvae; a moist, well-drained compost with a temperature of 10–21°C (50–70°F) is required. Alternatively, treat susceptible plants with a drench of HCH or pirimiphos-methyl in mid-summer, and again one month later, to kill small larvae. The older larvae are tolerant of pesticides; none available to amateur gardeners has enough persistence to give good protection.
See also "Vine weevils", p.549.

Fungus gnats or sciarid flies

Plants affected Plants grown under cover. Seedlings and cuttings are more susceptible than established plants.
Symptoms Both seedlings and cuttings fail to grow; greyish-brown flies run over the compost surface or fly among the plants. Larvae may be visible.

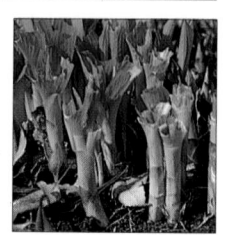

Cause The larvae of fungus gnats or sciarid flies (for example *Bradysia* spp.), which feed mainly on dead roots and leaves but may also attack young roots. They are slender, white-bodied maggots up to 6mm (¹/₄in) long with black heads. The adult flies are of a similar length. They do not cause any problems on healthy, established plants.
Control Keep greenhouses tidy, and remove dead leaves and flowers from the soil surface to avoid providing shelters. Use sticky yellow traps suspended above plants to trap the adult flies. If necessary, water the compost with pirimiphos-methyl or permethrin to control the larvae.

Bean seed flies

Plants affected French and runner beans.
Symptoms Seeds either fail to germinate or emerge blind. Seedlings are eaten.
Cause The larvae of the fly *Delia platura*, which are white, legless maggots up to 9mm (³/₈in) long that eat the germinating seeds and seedlings.
Control Avoid sowing when the soil is cold and wet (to encourage rapid germination), or pre-germinate seeds before sowing. If the problem is recurrent, sow seeds in pots or trays in a greenhouse and transplant once the seedlings have emerged. Alternatively, treat the soil with pirimiphos-methyl dust when sowing seed.

Ants

Plants affected Most annuals and low-growing perennials.
Symptoms Plants grow slowly and have a tendency to wilt. Heaps of soil may also appear, sometimes even burying some low-growing plants.

Cause Various species of black, yellow, or reddish-brown ants (e.g. *Lasius* and *Formica* spp.), which disturb the roots as they construct their nests. They do not usually feed on the plants, however, and cause relatively little damage.
Control Ants are often abundant and impossible to eliminate; as far as possible their presence should be tolerated. If the problem is severe, water plants with HCH or pirimiphos-methyl.
See also p.572 for problems caused on lawns.

Rabbits and hares

Plants affected Young trees; low-growing plants.
Symptoms Tree bark is gnawed away, especially during cold weather. Low-growing plants are eaten, sometimes grazed down to ground level.
Cause Rabbits and hares.
Control Exclude the ani-

mals from gardens with wire netting at least 1m (3ft) high and sunk another 30cm (12in) below ground level. Alternatively, place less elaborate fencing around individual susceptible plants. Protect the base of trees with wire netting or spiral tree-guard collars. Repellent substances, based on quassia, aluminium ammonium sulphate, or pepper dust, give only limited protection and need frequent application, especially during wet weather or periods of rapid plant growth.

Deer

Plants affected Most plants, especially trees, shrubs (including roses), and herbaceous plants.
Symptoms Shoots and leaves are eaten; tree bark is rubbed and frayed. In winter, bark may be eaten.
Cause Mainly roe and fallow deer, which feed on shoots, leaves, and bark. Bark is frayed when males mark trees with their scent glands or rub the velvet from new antlers.

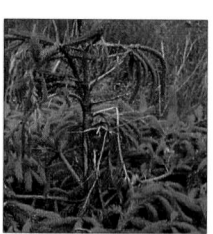

Eaten rose shoots

Control Protect gardens with wire mesh fences at least 2m (6ft) high, or place wire netting around stems and trunks. Repellent sprays or scaring devices, such as hanging tin cans, provide only short-term protection from deer.

Branch damage

See also "Clubroot", p.553; "Pansy sickness", p.554; "Irregular water supply", p.555; "*Verticillium* wilt", p.557; "Slime flux/wet wood", p.557; "Spur blight/cane blight", p.557; "Grey mould/*Botrytis*", p.557; "Dutch elm disease", p.557; "*Fusarium* wilt", p.558; "*Phytophthora* root rots", p.558; "Foot and root rots", p.558; "Cutworms", p.559; "Crown gall", p.559; "Fungal brackets", p.559; "Lightning", p.559; "Mechanical wounding", p.559; "Blossom wilt", p.560; "Root-knot nematodes", p.564; "Chafer larvae", p.564; "Leatherjackets", p.564; "Carrot flies", p.564; "Cabbage root flies", p.564; and "Wireworms", p.566.

Lawn problems

Drought

Plants affected Lawns and other grassed areas.
Symptoms Yellowish-brown, straw-like patches of variable size develop on the lawn; in extreme cases the whole area may become discoloured. Damage usually occurs in late spring or summer.
Cause Dry weather and inadequate watering. Free-draining, sandy soils are most at risk.
Control Water regularly in the early evening, providing enough water for deep penetration. To improve drought resistance, feed regularly, leave cut grass on the lawn if drought conditions are forecast, and spike and top-dress in the autumn. Allow the grass to grow fairly long before cutting, and avoid mowing too closely.
See also pp.554, 561, and 568 for problems caused to other plants.

Cats and dogs

Plants affected Lawns, seedlings, garden plants.
Symptoms Gardens, especially lawns and other grassed areas, are fouled with droppings; grass and foliage are scorched with urine; and newly planted areas are scratched up.
Cause Cats and dogs. Cats prefer dry soil and newly cultivated areas.
Control Where other people's dogs are a problem, site plants away from the most public, accessible parts of the garden; alternatively, protect them with netting. Areas visited consistently by cats should be regularly watered. Repellent substances based on pepper dust, naphthalene, or aluminium ammonium sulphate are available, but these often fail to give more than temporary protection.

Dollar spot

Plants affected Lawns and other grassed areas, particularly those containing fine-leaved bents and creeping fescues.
Symptoms Small, pale, straw-coloured patches develop in early autumn. At first they are 2.5–7.5cm (1–3in) in diameter, but coalesce to form larger areas. They darken with age.
Cause The fungus *Sclerotinia homeocarpa*, encouraged by heavy or compacted soils and by a high pH; alkaline soils or those treated with lime are likely to produce symptoms. The disease appears mainly in mild, damp weather.
Control Improve soil aeration and remove thatch. Treat the area with a suitable fungicide, e.g. benomyl, carbendazim, or thiophanate-methyl.

Starvation

Plants affected Lawns and other grassed areas.
Symptoms The grass is thin, patchy, and often rather pale; it may be invaded by moss and weeds or attacked by pathogens. Growth is likely to be slow.

Cause Inadequate feeding or unsuitable fertilizers.
Control Feed the lawn in spring and preferably also in summer and autumn, choosing feeds appropriate to the time of year.

Snow mould/*Fusarium* patch

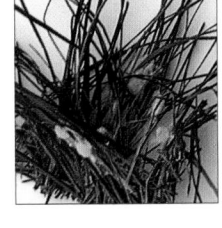

Plants affected Lawns, particularly those that contain a high proportion of annual meadow grass (*Poa annua*).
Symptoms Patches of grass become yellow and die, often coalescing to form large areas. In damp weather a white, fungal growth appears, causing the grass blades to stick together. It is most prevalent in late autumn and winter, especially on areas of grass that have been walked on while snow-covered.
Cause Principally the fungus *Fusarium nivale*, which is encouraged by poor aeration and the overuse of nitrogen fertilizers.
Control Improve maintenance, regularly aerating and scarifying the turf. Avoid using high-nitrogen fertilizers in late summer to early autumn. Treat affected turf with benomyl, carbendazim, or thiophanate-methyl.

Slime moulds

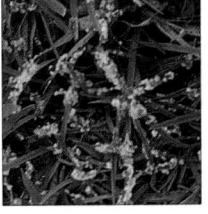

Plants affected Common grasses, and occasionally some other plants.
Symptoms Clusters of beige, orange, or white fruiting bodies smother individual blades of grass, and spores are then released, giving the slime mould a grey appearance; the grass looks unsightly but is not harmed. The condition is particularly common in late spring and again in early autumn.
Cause Slime moulds. They tend to thrive during periods of heavy rain.
Control Hose down the affected area.

Red thread

Plants affected Lawns, especially of finer grasses.
Symptoms Tiny, pale pink to red, gelatinous, branching threads of a fungus develop on small patches of grass, which later become bleached. The lawn is very rarely killed completely.
Cause The fungus *Corticium fuciforme*, which is common after heavy rain. It is also troublesome when the soil is nitrogen deficient or poorly aerated.
Control Improve turf maintenance, aerating, scarifying, and feeding as necessary. Fungicides should not be necessary on a well-kept lawn, but where the problem is severe benomyl, thiophanate-methyl, or carbendazim may be used to control the problem.

Dog lichens

Plants affected Lawns and other grassed areas, particularly those that are in poor condition.
Symptoms Groups of greenish-black, curled, or leafy growths with a pale creamy-white lower surface appear in the lawn.
Cause *Peltigera canina*, which is most troublesome on grassed areas that are badly drained, poorly aerated, compacted, or shaded.
Control Rake out the lichens and treat with a suitable chemical. Improve aeration of the lawn and, if possible, the drainage. Remember to feed and top-dress the grass regularly.

Algae and gelatinous lichens

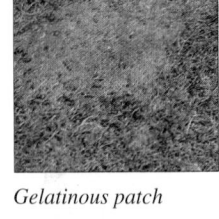

Gelatinous patch

Plants affected Lawns and other grassed areas.
Symptoms Slippery patches of green or greenish-black form on the surface.
Cause Gelatinous lichens and algae, which are particularly commonly found on any poorly drained, poorly aerated, or compacted sites.
Control Try to improve the drainage, and also aerate the lawn. Prune back any trees or shrubs that noticeably overhang the area, creating densely shaded, damp sections. Apply any proprietary lawncare products that contain dichlorophen.

Green, algal slime

Leatherjackets

Plants affected Lawns and other grassed areas.
Symptoms Brown patches appear in the lawn in mid-summer, and maggots are sometimes visible.
Cause Leatherjackets, the larvae of crane flies, or daddy-long-legs (e.g. *Tipula* spp.), which feed on the roots. They are greyish-brown, tubular, legless maggots up to 3.5cm (1¹/₂in) long.
Control Soak affected areas of the lawn with water, and cover with sacking or black plastic sheeting for a day to bring the leatherjackets to the surface; they can then be removed and killed. Use carbaryl against newly hatched larvae in early to mid-autumn. Problems are worse following wet autumns. On plants, search for and destroy the leatherjackets.
See also p.564 for problems caused to other plants.

Chafer larvae

Plants affected Lawns and other grassed areas.
Symptoms Patches of the lawn are ripped up by birds, foxes, or badgers as they feed on chafer larvae. Damage occurs in autumn, sometimes continuing through a mild winter, and is found mainly on sandy soils where grass growth is already poor.

Cause The root feeding larvae of certain beetles, in particular the cock chafer (*Melolontha melolontha*), the garden chafer (*Phyllopertha horticola*), and the welsh chafer (*Hoplia philanthus*). The larvae are plump, "C"-shaped, and can be up to 2cm (³/₄in) long. They have white bodies, brown heads, and three pairs of legs.
Control Feed and water the lawn as necessary, to encourage good growth. If damage is severe, spray lawns with carbaryl in late spring to early summer, as this is when the adult beetles emerge and lay their eggs, and treatment is therefore most effective.
See also p.564 for problems caused to other plants.

Toadstools

Plants affected Lawns and other grassed areas.
Symptoms Fungal, fruiting bodies develop, sometimes in distinct circles ("fairy rings"), and often on buried, woody material. Most cause little damage, but fairy rings are both harmful and disfiguring. Two circles of very lush, green grass form, one within the other, sometimes several metres in diameter, and the grass in between them dies off;

toadstools then emerge on the outer part of this middle zone. A white, fungal growth permeates the soil in the area of the ring.
Cause Various fungi, including *Coprinus*, *Mycena*, and the fairy-ring-producing *Marasmius oreades*. They all have underground mycelia and are spread to new sites by wind-borne spores.
Control Brush off *Coprinus* and *Mycena* when they first appear, before their spores are produced. If the fungi are on buried wood, remove them. There is no chemical control available to control fairy rings.

Ants

Plants affected Lawns and other grassed areas.
Symptoms Small heaps of fine soil are deposited on the surface of the lawn, mainly in summer.
Cause Ants (e.g. *Lasius flavus*), usually yellow-brown, which carry soil particles up to the surface as they remove it to extend their underground nests.
Control When the soil dries, brush it away. Water the nest site with pirimiphos-methyl, carbaryl, HCH, permethrin powder or dust, or pyrethrum.
See also p.570 for problems caused to other plants.

Earthworms

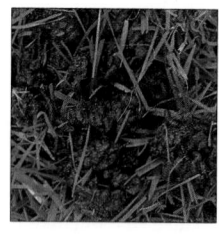

Plants affected Lawns.
Symptoms Small, muddy deposits or worm casts are left on the lawn surface in spring and autumn.
Cause Earthworms, mainly surface-casting types, especially *Allolobophora* spp.
Control Disperse dry casts by brushing. If numerous, apply carbaryl when the soil is warm and damp.

Moles

Plants affected Lawns, seedlings, young plants.
Symptoms Heaps of soil (molehills) appear on the lawn and cultivated areas. Roots of young plants and seedlings are disturbed.
Cause Burrowing moles.
Control Moles are most efficiently controlled by trapping, although they may sometimes be driven away by mole smokes; these are less effective in dry, sandy soils, however.

Controls currently available (with proprietary names, where applicable)

Aluminium ammonium sulphate Vitax Stay Off

Aluminium sulphate-based slug killers Fertosan Slug Killer; Fieldspray Nobble

Bendiocarb Doff Portland Ant Control Powder; Secto Ant & Crawling Insect Powder; Secto Wasp Powder

Benomyl ICI Benlate + 'Activex' 2

Bone meal Bio Bone Meal; Vitax Bone Meal

Borax Nippon Ant Control System; Nippon Ant Killer Liquid

Bordeaux mixture Vitax Bordeaux Mixture

Brodifacoum ICI 'Mouser'

Bupirimate + triforine ICI 'Nimrod'-T; ICI 'Roseclear'

Calcium ammonium nitrate ICI Nitrochalk

Carbaryl PBI Autumn & Winter Toplawn; May and Baker Total Weedkiller Granules; May & Baker Wasp Nest Destroyer; Murphy Lawn Pest Killer

Carbendazim Bio Supercarb Systemic Fungicide; Fisons Turfclear; Murphy Systemic Action Fungicide

Chelated/fritted forms of trace elements Doff Portland Sequestered Iron Plant Tonic (with chelated iron); ICI Miracid Soil Acidifier Plant Food; ICI Miracle-Gro Plant Food

Chlorpyrifos + Diazinon Bio Chlorophos

Copper-based fungicide Bio Cheshunt Compound; Murphy Traditional Copper Fungicide; Spraydex General Purpose Fungicide

Coumatetralyl Bio Racumin Mouse Bait; Bio Racumin Rat Bait

Cresylic acid Vitax Medo

Derris Bio Friendly Insect Spray; Bio Friendly Pest & Disease Duster; Bio Hexyl; Bio Liquid Derris; ICI Derris Dust; Murphy Derris Dust

Dichlorophen Baby Bio Roota; Bio Moss Killer; ICI 'Moss Gun!' for Lawns & Paths; Murphy Super Mosskiller RTU

Difenacoum ICI 'Ratak'

Dimethoate Bio Long-Last; Doff Portland Systemic Insecticide; Secto Rose & Flower Spray

Epsom salts

Fenitrothion Bio Fenitrothion

Grease banding Bio Boltac Greasebands; Vitax Corry's Fruit Tree Grease

Gypsum Vitax Claybreaker

HCH Bio Hexyl (gamma HCH)

Heptenophos Murphy Systemic Action Insecticide; Murphy Tumblebug

High potash fertilizer Bio Flower Maker

Insecticidal fatty acids (soaps) Bio Friendly Pest Pistol; Phostrogen Safer's Houseplant Insecticide; Phostrogen Safer's Insecticide; Phostrogen Safer's Ready-to-use

Fruit & Vegetable Insecticide; Phostrogen Safer's Ready-to-use Rose & Flower Insecticide; Ad Chem Savona Ready-to-use Rose Spray

Lime Vitax Garden Lime

Malathion Bio Crop Saver; Bio Malathion Greenfly Killer; Murphy Liquid Malathion; Murphy Malathion Dust

Mancozeb Bio Dithane 945

Metaldehyde Bio Slug Mini-Pellets; Doff Portland Quality Slug Killer (Economy); Doff Portland 'Slugoids' Blue Mini-Pellets; Murphy Slugit Liquid

Methiocarb Bio Slug Gard

Molybdenum

Naphthalene Vitax Scent-Off Buds; Vitax Scent-Off Pellets

Permethrin Baby Bio Flydown; Bio Crop Saver; Bio Kybosh; Bio Long-Last; Bio Multirose; Bio Sprayday; Fisons Insect Spray for Houseplants; ICI Fumite Whitefly Smokes; ICI 'Picket'; Murphy Permethrin Whitefly Smokes; Murphy Systemic Action Insecticide; Murphy Tumblebug; Nippon Ant Killer Powder; Nippon Ant & Crawling Insect Killer; Nippon Fly Killer Spray; Nippon Ready-to-use Ant & Crawling Insect Killer Spray; Secto Extra Strength Insect Killer Powder; Spraydex Greenfly Killer; Spraydex Houseplant Spray; Spraydex Insect Killer

Phoxim Fisons Soil Pest Killer; Murphy Kil-Ant

Pirimicarb ICI 'Rapid'; ICI 'Roseclear'

Pirimiphos-methyl ICI Fumite General Purpose Insecticide Smokes; ICI Antkiller Dust; ICI Kerispray; ICI 'Sybol'; ICI 'Waspend'

Propiconazole Murphy Tumbleblite

Pyrethrum Bio Anti-Ant Duster; Bio Friendly Anti-Ant Duster; ICI 'Bug Gun!' for Fruit & Vegetables; ICI 'Bug Gun!' for Roses & Flowers; Fisons Nature's Answer to Insect Pests; Doff Portland Fruit and Vegetable Spray; Py Garden Insecticide; Py Spray Insect Killer; Doff Portland Rose and Flower Insect Spray; Vitax House Plant Pest Killer

Quassia Bio Friendly Insect Spray

Sequestered iron (iron chelate)

Sulphate of ammonia

Sulphate of potash

Sulphur Bio Friendly Pest & Disease Duster; Bio Multirose; Phostrogen Safer's Ready-to-use Garden Fungicide; Vitax Sulphur

Superphosphate

Thiophanate-methyl May & Baker Liquid Club Root Control; May & Baker Systemic Fungicide Liquid

Thiram Bio Hexyl; Secto Hormone Rooting Powder; Secto Rose & Flower Spray

Triforine Bio Multirose

Triple phosphate

Weeds

WEEDS are, quite simply, plants that grow where they are not wanted. They have important features in common: they are usually fast-growing and invasive, competing with cultivated plants for food and water; they are able to grow in almost any soil or site; and they often show a marked resistance to control. Weeds may occur in almost any part of the garden.

Cultivated plants may be placed in the weed category in certain circumstances, depending on their habit. If they prove too invasive for their site and overwhelm their neighbours, or if they self-seed freely throughout the garden, they may properly be classified as "weeds".

Categorizing weeds

Annual weeds complete their entire lifecycle within one year. They set seed which germinates freely; occasionally, as in the case of groundsel (*Senecio vulgaris*), they may even produce several generations in one season. It is important, therefore, to remove annuals at the seedling stage, before they are able to produce seed.

Perennial weeds, by contrast, survive from year to year. Some grow readily from seed, like annuals, but more usually persist by means of various storage organs, such as rhizomes, bulbs, bulbils, tubers, and thick tap roots. Many perennials are able to proliferate because of poor cultivation techniques that leave small pieces of rhizome or root in the soil when digging over or rotavating.

Controlling weeds

Weeds may be controlled in two main ways: they may either be discouraged from growing by the use of good, basic gardening techniques; or they may be removed by manual, mechanical, or chemical means.

The choice of how to remove different weeds depends on various factors: the habit of the plants themselves, the preference of the gardener, and the location of the weeds – whether in borders, lawns, paths, or neglected sites.

CULTIVATED PLANTS AS WEEDS

SNOW-IN-SUMMER
Any plant may become a weed if it dominates other garden plants. The dense growth and rapid spread of Cerastium tomentosum *may cause problems in a rock garden.*

RUSSIAN VINE
Although often planted to cover unsightly features rapidly, the Russian vine (Fallopia baldschuanica) *is an invasive climber that can soon swamp more delicate plants in the vicinity.*

Annual weeds

In common with other annual plants, annual weeds grow, flower, set seed, and die within one year. They occur most frequently in regularly cultivated areas, such as vegetable plots or annual borders, where frequent digging deters perennial kinds. Their rapid growth makes them troublesome among crops raised from seed *in situ* as they smother slower-growing plants and reduce yields of others by competing for moisture, nutrients, and light.

The need for control

It is most important to destroy annual weeds before they produce seeds, since many seeds are small, light, readily wind-borne, and quick to germinate. Quick-maturing species such as shepherd's purse (*Capsella bursa-pastoris*) may produce several generations in a single season. Common chickweed (*Stellaria media*) smothers nearby plants and is another weed that should be controlled at the seedling stage. Its seeds start to germinate in the autumn and continue growing in a mild winter to form dense mats.

Many seeds may be buried once they are shed, and lie dormant for many years until they are brought to the surface during site or crop cultivation. The weeds then germinate and grow rapidly. If a site is heavily infested, it should be cultivated regularly when it is crop-free in order to kill germinating seedlings.

Annual weeds may be controlled by hand, mechanical, or chemical means (see "Preventing weeds", p.574).

COMMON ANNUAL WEEDS

Shepherd's purse
(*Capsella bursa-pastoris*)

Hairy bittercress
(*Cardamine hirsuta*)

Annual meadow grass
(*Poa annua*)

Common chickweed (*Stellaria media*)

Groundsel
(*Senecio vulgaris*)

Annual nettle (*Urtica urens*)

Perennial weeds

Perennial weeds persist from year to year, surviving and resting through winter cold and summer heat by storing food reserves in fleshy roots, bulbs, rhizomes, or tubers.

They may be divided into two groups: herbaceous kinds and woody-stemmed kinds. Herbaceous perennials die back to ground level in the autumn. They survive the winter by storing food in their roots and then reappear in spring. Examples are the perennial stinging nettle (*Urtica dioica*), broad-leaved dock (*Rumex obtusifolius*), and field bindweed (*Convolvulus arvensis*). Also included in this group are the stemless herbaceous perennials that have leaves arising directly from their roots or rhizomes, for example, dandelion (*Taraxacum officinale*) and ground elder (*Aegopodium podagraria*).

Woody-stemmed perennials, such as common elder (*Sambucus nigra*) and bramble (*Rubus fruticosus*), survive the winter by storing food in stems and branches. The woody-stemmed, evergreen, common ivy (*Hedera helix*) can also be an invasive weed.

The need for control
Perennial weeds have underground fleshy roots, rhizomes, and other storage organs that are not easily controlled. Hoeing and digging, along with machine cultivation, tend to break the roots and rhizomes into sections without killing them; many survive to grow and increase the infestation. With most perennial weeds, use of weedkillers is the most practical and effective approach.

Preventing weeds

Both annual and perennial weeds may be prevented from establishing in various ways. These will do much to avoid the need for tedious weeding later on.

Working the soil
Before planting, clear the site of all weeds, either manually or with chemicals. Weeds are often difficult to eradicate from among established plants, which may need to be lifted and the weeds extracted from the washed root system.

Conditioning very acid soils with lime will deter some lawn weeds, such as field woodrush (*Luzula campestris*), that thrive where the soil is acid.

Cultivating healthy plants
Vigorous, healthy plants are able to compete more effectively with weeds than are poor, weak specimens. Plants with spreading foliage provide a dark cover over the soil that discourages weed germination under the canopy.

Some vegetable crops, for example potatoes, compete well with annual weeds and may be grown to help maintain clean ground for a subsequent crop (see THE VEGETABLE GARDEN, "Rotation", p.307).

Ground-cover plants
Some plants grow in dense carpets that suppress the germination of weed seeds. They are particularly useful for parts of the garden where, because of shade, or very wet or dry soil, weeds thrive. Choose ground-cover plants carefully as some are invasive (see GROUND COVER, pp.150–51).

Mulching
In early spring, apply a mulch 1–2in (2.5–5cm) thick of weed-free, organic material such as leaf mould, peat substitute, or processed bark to help prevent weed seeds germinating and smother weed seedlings. Do not use garden compost or insufficiently rotted manure as they often contain weed seeds.

Established perennial weeds may grow through the mulch but, as they tend to root into the loose material, they are easy to remove.

Black plastic sheeting
Laid directly over the soil, black plastic sheeting prevents annual weeds from establishing. It can also be effective with perennial weeds: horsetail (*Equisetum arvense*) and field bindweed are both less likely to grow if the area is covered for at least two seasons. Cover the sheeting with a bark mulch to improve its appearance. Black plastic sheeting is particularly useful in fruit and vegetable gardens; make slits in it through which the crops can grow.

Grassing down borders
Some persistent perennial weeds, such as horsetail and oxalis (*Oxalis corymbosa* and *O. latifolia*), may resist repeated attempts to eradicate them with weedkiller or to dig them out. An alternative approach is to grass down heavily infested borders and maintain them as close-mown turf for several years. Given time, this treatment will clear the soil and usually eliminate most of the infestation.

Controlling weeds

Once weeds are present, they may be eradicated in one of three ways: hand-weeding, mechanical control, and chemical control. There are three

PERENNIAL WEEDS
WEEDS WITH RHIZOMES AND STOLONS

Hedge bindweed
(*Calystegia sepium*)

Creeping thistle
(*Cirsium arvense*)

Ground elder
(*Aegopodium podagraria*)

Field bindweed (*Convolvulus arvensis*)

Couch grass
(*Elymus repens*)

Coltsfoot
(*Tussilago farfara*)

Willow herb
(*Epilobium* sp.)

Horsetail
(*Equisetum arvense*)

Creeping yellow cress
(*Rorippa sylvestris*)

different types of weedkiller: those that act on the leaves, those that act on the soil, and those that act on specific types of plant.

Hand-weeding and hoeing

Hand-weeding, hoeing, and forking are often the only practical ways of removing weeds in flower beds, the vegetable garden, and small patches of ground, where weedkillers cannot be used safely without risk of harming nearby garden or crop plants.

Small patches of perennial weeds, such as ground elder or couch grass, may be forked out, but great care must be taken not to leave in the soil sections of rhizomes, roots, or bulbils that will grow again. Check a month or so later and remove any regrowth.

Hand-weed or hoe in dry weather, if possible, so that the weeds are easily loosened from the soil. In wet weather, remove uprooted weeds from the site to prevent them from rooting back into the soil. Hoe only lightly around cultivated plants to prevent their surface roots from being damaged.

Removing weeds mechanically

Market gardeners often use rotary cultivators (rotavators) with hoeing or cultivating attachments for annual weed control between rows of vegetables, but they may be unsuitable for perennials. They simply cut the rhizomes of weeds such as couch grass

and ground elder into many pieces that will continue to grow as new plants. Wherever possible, use weedkillers to kill perennial weeds before digging or cultivating.

Foliage-acting weedkillers

Leaf-acting products enter the weeds through leaves or green stems and are applied with a sprayer or watering can and fine rose or dribble-bar. There are two different types. The first acts by translocation, moving from the leaves to the roots, and so destroys both annual and perennial weeds. For maximum effect the weeds should be in vigorous growth. The second type works by contact, killing only by direct touch. They destroy annual weeds and the green leaves and stems of perennial weeds, although not the roots of perennials, which will usually regrow strongly. Some weedkillers act through both leaves and roots.

Soil-acting weedkillers

These are applied to the soil and are absorbed into the roots of growing weeds. From there they move to the parts above ground, killing the weeds by interfering with their metabolism. They remain active in the soil, sometimes for months, killing weeds as the seeds germinate. They kill established annual weeds and may also kill or suppress many established perennial weeds. When planning to use areas

that have been treated with soil-acting weedkillers, check the manufacturer's literature for details of residual activity and do not sow or plant until the recommended period has elapsed.

Selective weedkillers

Most selective weedkillers kill broad-leaved weeds and leave narrow-leaved grasses unharmed. Conversely, however, alloxydim-sodium kills the majority of grasses but is harmless to non-grassy ornamental plants.

The range of chemicals

Gluphosinate ammonium (contact action) and **paraquat with diquat** (contact action) are both quick-acting and will kill annual weeds but only check broad-leaved weeds. They are useful for killing overwintering annual weeds before spring sowing or planting and are inactivated in soil.

Glyphosate (translocated, foliage-acting) is one of the most useful weedkillers for controlling perennial weeds. It is a foliage-acting weedkiller that moves down to the roots, killing or strongly checking even the most difficult weeds. It is not selective and should be kept well away from all garden plants. With the majority of weeds, it is most effective when weed growth is well advanced, usually from about mid-summer onwards, but check the manufacturer's recommendations. As it does not persist in the soil it is safe

to cultivate as soon as weeds are dead.
Alloxydim-sodium (absorbed through foliage) is a selective weedkiller that kills most perennial weed grasses without affecting non-grassy ornamentals. It is particularly useful for eradicating couch grass in borders and rock gardens.

Ammonium sulphamate (foliage- and soil-acting) controls woody-stemmed perennial weeds such as bramble and various tree seedlings. Where they cannot be dug out easily, cut them back with secateurs or a pruning saw to leave a short stump. Then wet the newly cut surface and the whole stump down to ground level with a solution of ammonium sulphamate. Avoid run-off into the soil where there may be underlying roots of nearby garden plants.

Dichlobenil (soil-acting, granular) is a weedkiller that may be applied, before growth begins, to the soil around well-established fruit trees and bushes and some ornamental shrubs, including roses, to control or suppress some perennial weeds, such as ground elder, and to control germinating weed seeds. It is residual and continues to act for several months.

Amitrole (foliage-acting, translocated) is usually combined with contact and soil-acting herbicides to control weeds that have become established in cracks and crevices in paved areas, paths, and drives.

WEEDS WITH TUBERS AND FLESHY ROOTS

Bryony
(*Bryonia dioica*)

Oxalis (*Oxalis corymbosa* and *O. latifolia*)

Lesser celandine
(*Ranunculus ficaria*)

WEEDS WITH DEEP ROOTS

Japanese knotweed (*Polygonum japonicum*, syn. *P. cuspidatum* and *Fallopia japonica*)

Dock (*Rumex* sp.)

Perennial stinging nettle (*Urtica dioica*)

Bramble
(*Rubus fruticosus*)

Using weedkillers safely

Care must always be taken when applying weedkillers:
• wear protective clothing, for example rubber gloves and old clothes, when mixing and applying weedkillers;
• do not apply weedkillers in windy conditions when there is a risk of spray being blown across to nearby plants, which may suffer serious damage;
• use only for appropriate purposes as recommended on the product label, for example do not use a path weedkiller to keep down weeds in a rosebed;
• always dilute soluble weedkillers according to the manufacturer's instructions;
• always apply weedkillers at the recommended rates on the labels;
• always keep in original containers and make sure that the labels are well secured to the containers so that contents are known and no errors in usage occur;
• never store diluted weedkillers for future use;
• store away out of reach of children and animals, preferably in a securely locked cupboard in a workshop or shed.

Lawn weeds

Various perennial weeds can be troublesome in lawns. Their common survival factor is their ability to grow and thrive in the adverse conditions of short, regularly mown grass. They usually originate from seeds carried by the wind or by birds. Once lawn weeds have germinated, most are then rapidly spread by the action of mowing and early treatment is necessary if they are to be eradicated.

Among the most troublesome lawn weeds are: slender speedwell (*Veronica filiformis*), field woodrush (*Luzula campestris*), annual meadow grass (*Poa annua*), and mind-your-own-business (*Soleirolia soleirolii*, syn. *Helxine soleirolii*). These persistent weeds do not respond to treatment by lawn weedkillers, and need other forms of treatment.

In lawns where the grass is too sparse to offer adequate competition, moss may also become a problem.

Preventing weeds and moss

Good lawn care is an effective preventive measure. The presence of numerous weeds in a lawn usually indicates that the grass is not growing sufficiently vigorously to prevent weeds from establishing. Lack of regular feeding and drought are among the most common reasons for poor growth. Soil compaction and mowing the grass too closely and too regularly may also lead to the spread of moss. For further details on lawn care, see THE LAWN, "Routine care", pp.285–90.

Coarser weed grasses (for example, *Holcus lanatus*) may remain a problem, and clumps, or affected areas of turf, may need to be removed, and the cleared patch returfed or re-seeded.

Raking before mowing and lifting creeping stems may help to check the spread of creeping weeds, such as trefoils (*Trifolium* spp.), slender speedwell, and sorrels (*Rumex* spp.) if the grass is mown straight afterwards.

Removing weeds

If weeds are already present in the lawn, there are two main ways of treating them, depending on the severity of the problem. They may either be removed by hand if they are not too widespread, or they may be treated with an appropriate weedkiller.

Weeding by hand

Hand-weeding is an effective method of removing a few, scattered rosetted weeds such as daisy (*Bellis perennis*), dandelion (*Taraxacum officinale*), and plantains (*Plantago* spp.). Use a daisy grubber or hand fork to lift the weeds, then firm back displaced turf.

Dealing with moss

Moss may be killed with moss preparations or lawn sand. This is only a short-term solution, however: unless the original conditions that encouraged moss are identified and corrected, the problem usually recurs.

Removing weeds with chemicals

Weedkillers intended specifically for use on lawns work by translocation – moving within the plant from the leaves to the roots – and the weeds begin to distort and shrivel within a few days of application. The chemicals are selective and do not harm lawn grasses at normal dilution rates, but do not use them on seedling grasses within six months of germination.

You should also avoid using lawn weedkillers on newly laid turf, sprigs, or plugs within a six-month period of laying or planting.

LAWN WEEDS

Yarrow (*Achillea millefolium*)

Common mouse-ear chickweed (*Cerastium fontanum*, syn. *C. vulgatum*)

Mouse-ear hawkweed (*Hieracium pilosella*)

Field woodrush (*Luzula campestris*)

Broad-leaved plantain (*Plantago major*)

Self-heal (*Prunella vulgaris*)

Creeping buttercup (*Ranunculus repens*)

Sheep's sorrel (*Rumex acetosella*)

Pearlwort (*Sagina procumbens*)

Lesser yellow trefoil (*Trifolium dubium*)

Common white clover (*Trifolium repens*)

Slender speedwell (*Veronica filiformis*)

The range of chemicals

Proprietary lawn weedkillers normally combine two or more active ingredients in order to control a wider range of weeds.

2,4–D is a selective weedkiller that is particularly effective against broad-leaved, rosetted weeds, such as plantains and daisies. This chemical is usually combined with mecoprop.

Mecoprop kills various difficult, small-leaved, and creeping weeds, such as trefoils (*Trifolium* spp.) and yarrow (*Achillea millefolium*). It is usually combined with 2,4–D.

Dichlorophen kills moss in lawns. It is quick-acting.

Ferrous sulphate is the active ingredient in lawn sands; it is used to eradicate moss.

MCPA is a selective herbicide used in both problem-weed mixtures and lawn weedkillers to control weeds that have resistance to other chemicals.

Dicamba is usually combined with 2,4–D or MCPA to control a wider range of weeds.

Lime may be applied on very acid soils as a light winter dressing in the form of ground chalk or limestone at 50g/sq m (2oz/sq yd) to deter sorrels and field woodrush. Sorrels can also be controlled by repeat treatment with 2,4–D preparations but field woodrush is resistant to all lawn weedkillers.

Buying weedkillers

Lawn weedkillers are usually sold as a concentrated liquid and therefore need to be suitably diluted. They may also be obtained in the form of soluble powder, ready-to-use spray, aerosol, wax bar, or in combination with liquid or granular lawn fertilizers.

Applying weedkillers

Feed the lawn at the start of the growing season, applying weedkiller two to three weeks later when grass and weeds are growing strongly. In the spring, creeping lawn grasses soon colonize any bare patches left as weeds shrivel and die. Great care should be taken when applying weedkillers (see the recommendations on p.575).

Wheeled sprayers can be used for large areas; a watering can with a fine rose or dribble-bar attachment is better for small lawns. Divide the lawn into strips using two garden lines to ensure that the grass has been given complete and uniform coverage.

If possible, wait for two or three days after mowing before applying the weedkiller so that the weeds have time to develop new leaf surfaces to absorb the chemicals. Do not mow the grass for two or three days after spraying to allow time for the weedkiller to work its way down towards the roots.

How often to apply

Some lawn weeds, such as daisies and plantains, are killed by one or two applications of weedkiller; others, for example the trefoils, may need two or three applications, at four-to six-week intervals. Occasionally a species such as slender speedwell (*Veronica filiformis*) may survive several applications.

Where a weed shows no response to repeated applications of various weedkillers, the only solution is to remove it by hand. This will either mean removing and replacing infested areas of turf or, alternatively, feeding, scarifying, and aerating the turf to strengthen it and weaken the weed.

Neglected sites

Different treatments need to be adopted according to how long the area has been neglected and how great a hold the weeds have obtained. Sites that have been neglected for some time may take a season, or even longer, to clear for vegetable growing.

Short-term neglect

On sites that have been neglected for up to a year, most of the weeds are likely to be annuals. Kill these with one or two applications of the contact weedkillers paraquat with diquat or gluphosinate ammonium in the spring or summer. This has the added advantage of defoliating and weakening any young perennials that may have appeared; it does not kill them, however. Dig these up two or three weeks after the treatment, when they have resprouted and can be identified.

If any weed seedlings appear in the meantime, either dig them in or destroy them with a further application of contact weedkiller.

Winter clearance

If the site is being cleared during the winter, remove any overwintering top-growth of annual weeds with a rotary mower. Then dig out any perennial weeds by hand, if possible, before cultivating the area. Clear neglected vegetable plots and allotments progressively, beginning at the warmer, sunnier end, where the earliest sowings of crops are to be made and the seedbeds are to be sited.

Longer-term neglect

After a second year of neglect, perennial weeds will become well established, competing vigorously with annual weeds. If the site remains neglected for a further year, by the end of the third growing season the weed population will usually be largely, or entirely, strong-growing perennial weeds. Badly infested sites are difficult to clear by hand or by use of a rotavator (the latter may do no more than turn the weeds back into the soil again). It is more practical to use translocated and soil-acting weedkillers, allowing a full growing season for treatment to take effect.

Cutting down weeds

If beginning clearance in spring, cut down weeds with woody stems, for example brambles or elder, to within 30–45cm (12–18in) from the ground, then spray the whole weed-infested area with ammonium sulphamate.

Using this weedkiller has a dual purpose: it not only kills woody weeds but is also effective against coarse grasses and broad-leaved perennial weeds. It persists in the soil for about three months, which is a disadvantage; being highly soluble, it spreads easily through the soil and, for this reason, should not be used where there are underlying tree or shrub roots, or where it may leach into cultivated areas and affect plant growth there.

Any weeds that survive treatment with ammonium sulphamate and produce regrowth in late summer can then be treated with glyphosate.

Summer spraying

Another method is to cut the weeds back in spring and then allow them to grow unchecked until mid-summer; then spray the site with glyphosate, which acts more effectively on the vigorous young growth stimulated by the spring cut. It is a translocated weedkiller and it usually takes three to four weeks to show any effect; it leaves no harmful residues in the soil and as soon as weeds are dead the site can be cultivated and planted. Very persistent weeds, such as horsetail and bindweed, may need subsequent spot-treatment, again with glyphosate, possibly for a further two or three growing seasons, to control them fully.

HAND CLEARANCE

To remove perennial weeds from a recently neglected site, dig them out by hand. Be sure to extract all the roots to prevent new growth the following spring. If you are clearing the site in spring or summer, defoliate with weedkiller, then wait a few weeks before digging the weeds out by hand. In winter, dig up the perennials that remain after rotavating.

Uncultivated ground

Where previously cultivated land is to be left uncultivated, and is free from perennial weeds, it can be kept clear by regular light cultivations, at intervals throughout the year, with a hoe or with a mechanical tool, such as a rotary cultivator. Alternatively, at intervals, developing weed seedlings can be killed by application of the contact weedkillers, paraquat with diquat, or gluphosinate ammonium.

If there are perennial weeds infesting the site, let them grow until mid-summer, then spray with glyphosate.

Weeds in cracks and crevices

Weeds in the cracks in paths and brickwork are hard to remove by hand, so chemical control is usually required.

Path weedkillers

In early spring, apply a proprietary path weedkiller. Such weedkillers are mixtures of contact and soil-acting chemicals, the latter usually remaining active in the soil for several months. They may also include a foliage-acting, translocated herbicide, such as MCPA or amitrole, to deal with any established perennial weeds, not usually controlled by the low-strength, soil-acting chemicals in these mixtures.

Spot treatment

Perennial weeds in paths may be spot-treated or sprayed with glyphosate when regrowth is vigorous. Dichlobenil granules carefully sprinkled or brushed into the spaces between paving stones will control weeds but should not be applied if crevice plants are being cultivated.

8

BASIC BOTANY

BOTANY – THE SCIENTIFIC *study of plants – covers a number of disciplines. Familiarity with the basics of botany helps the gardener to understand the principles underlying many horticultural techniques, to maintain plants in good health so that they provide fine ornamental displays and high-quality fruit and vegetables, and to obtain appropriate plant material for propagation. The study of the internal arrangement of plant structures (anatomy) and their external construction (morphology)* *can, for example, provide an explanation of how to graft successfully, create new hybrids, or make pruning cuts that heal quickly. Physiology is the study of a plant's metabolism. It aids understanding of a plant's need for water and light, the role of nutrients in plant growth, and the processes of photosynthesis, transpiration, and respiration. Taxonomy – the identification and classification of plants – can indicate close relationships between genera or species that frequently have similar cultivation needs.*

Plant diversity

There are more than 250,000 species of seed-bearing plant. They include annuals, which flower, seed, and die in a year or less; biennials, which grow from seed in their first year and then flower, seed, and die in the second season; and perennials, which live for several to many years, and include woody plants. Commonly, the term perennials is applied to herbaceous or border plants, while trees and shrubs are referred to as woody plants. All plants have roots, stems, leaves, and flowers; these may be modified for particular purposes and environments.

Roots

These anchor the plant in the soil and absorb water and mineral salts from which the plant manufactures its food. Fleshy tap roots penetrate vertically downwards, forming sparse lateral roots that are, in turn, finely branched. Fibrous roots comprise a network of fine, thread-like roots that emerge from the base of the stem or from tap roots in some plants. The root tips bear fragile root hairs, which are in intimate contact with soil particles from which water and mineral salts are absorbed. Roots are sometimes modified to form storage organs, as is the case in many terrestrial orchids or swollen tap roots such as carrots.

Stems

Plant stems provide the above-ground framework of the plant, supporting the leaves, flowers, and fruits. Some stem cells are specialized to provide a strong framework; some conduct water and mineral salts (the xylem), or manufactured food (the phloem) from

BASIC PARTS OF A PLANT

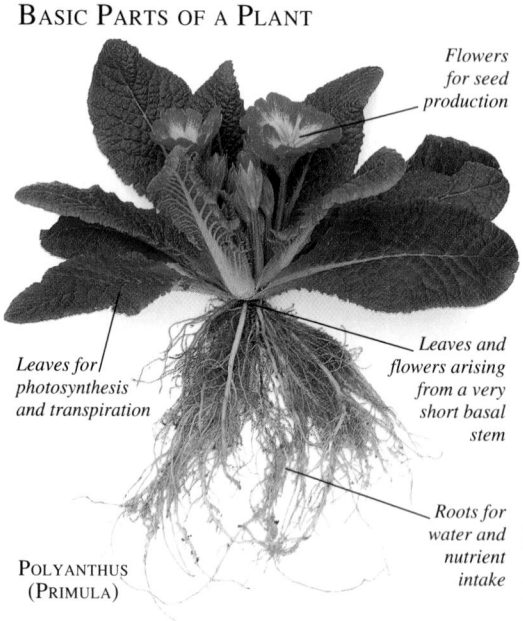

Flowers for seed production

Leaves for photosynthesis and transpiration

Leaves and flowers arising from a very short basal stem

Roots for water and nutrient intake

POLYANTHUS (PRIMULA)

ROOT SYSTEMS

All roots draw up water and minerals and anchor the plant in the soil; some also store food.

FIBROUS ROOTS
These fibrous roots are adventitious as they arise directly from a rhizome (here of a bearded iris) – a specialized, often swollen stem

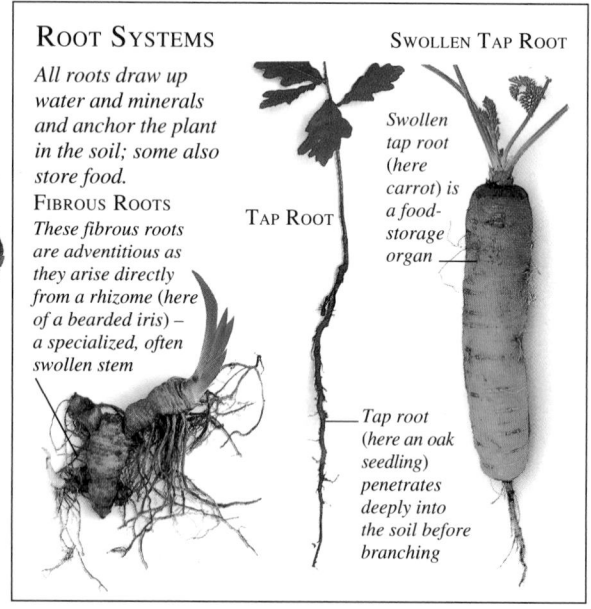

SWOLLEN TAP ROOT

TAP ROOT

Swollen tap root (here carrot) is a food-storage organ

Tap root (here an oak seedling) penetrates deeply into the soil before branching

TYPES OF STEM

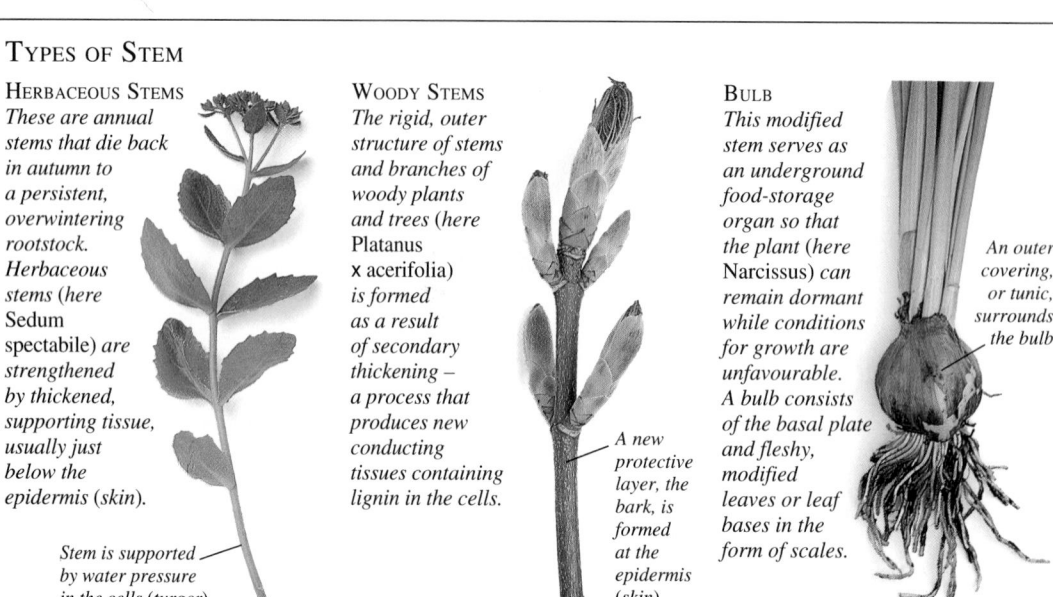

HERBACEOUS STEMS
These are annual stems that die back in autumn to a persistent, overwintering rootstock. Herbaceous stems (here Sedum spectabile) are strengthened by thickened, supporting tissue, usually just below the epidermis (skin).

Stem is supported by water pressure in the cells (turgor)

WOODY STEMS
The rigid, outer structure of stems and branches of woody plants and trees (here Platanus x acerifolia) is formed as a result of secondary thickening – a process that produces new conducting tissues containing lignin in the cells.

A new protective layer, the bark, is formed at the epidermis (skin)

BULB
This modified stem serves as an underground food-storage organ so that the plant (here Narcissus) can remain dormant while conditions for growth are unfavourable. A bulb consists of the basal plate and fleshy, modified leaves or leaf bases in the form of scales.

An outer covering, or tunic, surrounds the bulb

LEAF FORMS

SCALE-LIKE LEAF (*Chamaecyparis obtusa* 'Nana Aurea')

PINNATE LEAF (*Robinia pseudoacacia*)

BROADLY OVATE LEAF (*Camellia japonica*)

PINNATIFID LEAF (Swiss-cheese plant, *Monstera deliciosa*)

COMPOUND PINNATE FROND (*Dryopteris filix-mas*)

DIGITATE LEAF (Horse chestnut, *Aesculus hippocastanum*)

LINEAR LEAVES (Annual meadow grass, *Poa annua*)

the leaves to all parts of the plant. Stems are often modified for other functions. Tubers, corms, and rhizomes, for example, are swollen, underground stems that are modified for food storage; in cacti, the often swollen stems contain water-storage tissue.

Leaves

Leaf form is extremely diverse and may be modified as spines, as in some cacti, or as tendrils, as in the garden pea. Whatever their form, leaves are the manufacturing centres of a plant.

They contain the green pigment chlorophyll, which absorbs the energy of sunlight in order to convert carbon dioxide from the air and water from the soil into carbohydrates by the process known as photosynthesis. The by-product, oxygen, is essential to all life. The energy required to drive the plant's metabolism is produced through respiration, which breaks down carbohydrates to release energy, carbon dioxide, and water.

Leaves present a relatively large surface so that they maximize absorption of light; they are thin enough for light to penetrate to the cells that

PHOTOSYNTHESIS

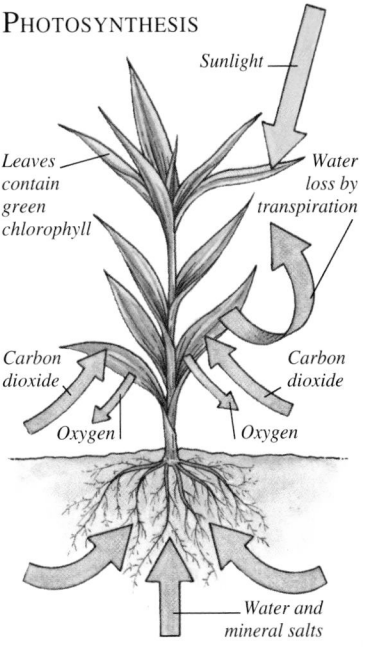

Sunlight

Leaves contain green chlorophyll

Water loss by transpiration

Carbon dioxide

Carbon dioxide

Oxygen

Oxygen

Water and mineral salts

Water and carbon dioxide are converted into carbohydrates and oxygen using the energy of sunlight, which is trapped by the chlorophyll in a plant's leaves.

contain chlorophyll, and to allow rapid movement of gases to all cells. Their surfaces contain numerous pores (stomata) through which oxygen and carbon dioxide pass in and out of the leaf. The stomata also control water losses through transpiration. A high evaporation of water vapour from the leaves and a lack of water entering through the plant roots is the cause of plants wilting in dry conditions.

Although only 1 per cent of the fresh weight of a plant consists of minerals, they are essential. In solution they are directly concerned with the water

balance of the cells, and help regulate the passage of substances between cells. They maintain the correct pH for biochemical reactions and are essential components of chlorophyll and enzymes, the biological catalysts of the plant's internal chemistry.

Fruits and seeds

Seeds are a flowering plant's means of reproduction. Each seed develops from a single, fertilized egg and one or more seeds is contained in a fruit. There are many types of fruit that disperse their seeds in various ways. In some fruits, the seeds germinate rapidly with no special treatment; in others, it may be necessary for the seeds to undergo specific treatment in cultivation for them to germinate fairly rapidly. For further information, see PRINCIPLES OF PROPAGATION, "How to overcome dormancy", p.535.

Pods and capsules are dehiscent fruits, splitting along a regular line or lines to release the seed, as in *Aquilegia* and violets (*Viola*). Indehiscent fruits do not split. Good examples are the fruits of hazel (*Corylus*) and sweet chestnut (*Castanea sativa*), in which a single seed (kernel) is enclosed in a tough shell. These large seeds have a high moisture and fat content, and deteriorate quickly unless sown fresh or stored in cool, moist conditions. In roses, many small, indehiscent fruits, each containing one seed, are enclosed in a hollow receptacle – the hip. The individual seeds (strictly fruits) need to be extracted before sowing.

Succulent fruits, where the seed is enclosed in flesh, include berries (e.g. bananas, tomatoes, grapes), which have many seeds; drupes (e.g. plums, cherries, peaches), which typically have

TRANSPIRATION

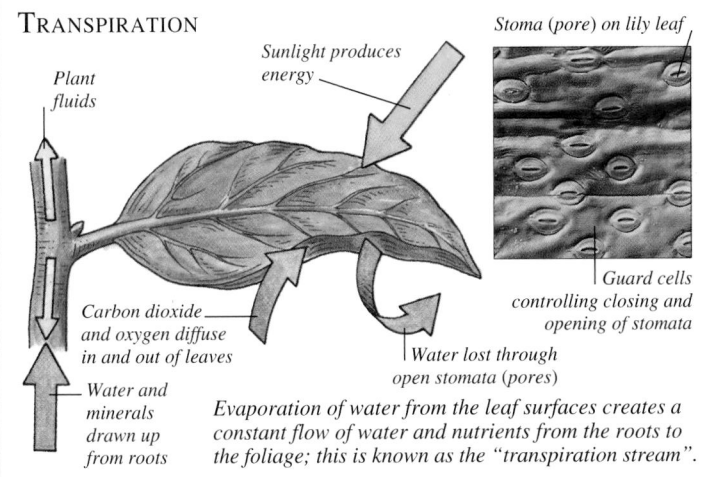

Sunlight produces energy

Plant fluids

Stoma (pore) on lily leaf

Carbon dioxide and oxygen diffuse in and out of leaves

Guard cells controlling closing and opening of stomata

Water lost through open stomata (pores)

Water and minerals drawn up from roots

Evaporation of water from the leaf surfaces creates a constant flow of water and nutrients from the roots to the foliage; this is known as the "transpiration stream".

FRUIT TYPES

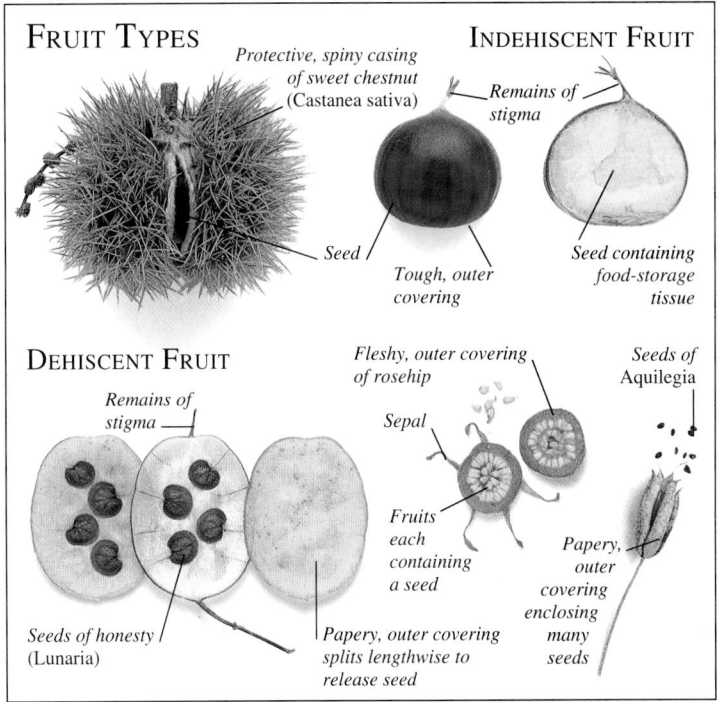

Protective, spiny casing of sweet chestnut (Castanea sativa)

INDEHISCENT FRUIT

Remains of stigma

Seed

Tough, outer covering

Seed containing food-storage tissue

DEHISCENT FRUIT

Remains of stigma

Seeds of honesty (Lunaria)

Papery, outer covering splits lengthwise to release seed

Fleshy, outer covering of rosehip

Sepal

Fruits each containing a seed

Seeds of Aquilegia

Papery, outer covering enclosing many seeds

one seed in the form of a stone or pip; and pomes (e.g. apples, pears), which develop from parts of the flower as well as the ovaries. In all these types of fruit, the seed should be removed from the pulped flesh and cleaned before being sown.

Flowers

Flowers are the fourth basic part of a plant and they show extraordinary diversity in colour, scent, and form, with a wide range of adaptations to ensure that they fulfil their reproductive function. They may be borne as showy, individual flowers (*Hibiscus*, tulips) or in many-flowered spikes (*Kniphofia*), racemes (hyacinth), panicles (*Gypsophila*), umbels (*Agapanthus*), or in heads consisting of numerous small florets such as dahlias in the family Compositae.

A flower has four main parts: petals or tepals, sepals, stamens, and one or more carpels, which are collectively known as the pistil. Most conspicuous are the petals, carried above a whorl of (usually) green sepals. The male reproductive nuclei are carried in pollen grains, enclosed in an anther attached to a stem, the filament – the whole male part being a stamen; these vary greatly

PARTS OF A FLOWER

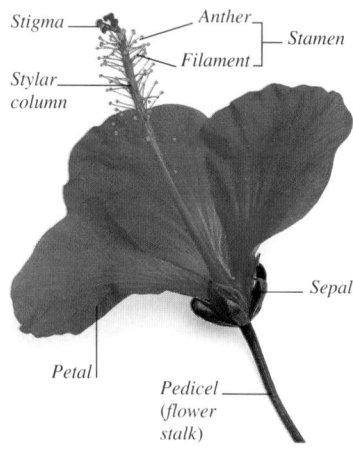

Stigma
Anther
Filament — Stamen
Stylar column
Sepal
Petal
Pedicel (*flower stalk*)

SEXUALITY IN FLOWERS

Dioecious plants – being either male or female – need a plant of each sex growing close to one another to set seed. Monoecious plants bear separate male and female flowers on the same plant. Bisexual (hermaphrodite) flowers contain both male (stamens) and female (carpels) parts in the same flower.

FEMALE PLANT   MALE PLANT

DIOECIOUS (*Skimmia japonica*)

MONOECIOUS (*Begonia*)

BISEXUAL (*Schlumbergera*)

Female flower (*without stamens*)

Male flowers (*with stamens*)

Stigma (*female part*)

Stamens (*male part*)

in number from three in crocuses to 30 or more in buttercups. The carpels enclose the female egg nuclei and have a projecting style, or stylar column, with a stigma at its tip to receive pollen grains. Pollen grains germinate on the stigma and a pollen tube containing the male nuclei grows through the tissue of the style to fuse with the female nuclei (the process of fertilization) eventually forming seeds.

Many plants bear separate female and male (unisexual) flowers on the same plant, for example birch (*Betula*) and hazel (*Corylus*). They are known as monoecious plants. Bisexual, or hermaphrodite, plants have the male and female parts in each flower. A few species bear unisexual and bisexual flowers and are known as polygamous plants. In dioecious plants all the

flowers produced are of one sex only; examples are many holly species (*Ilex*), *Garrya*, and some *Skimmia* variants. Male and female plants must be grown together if they are to set seed; this is especially important in cases where plants are grown for their ornamental berries, as with many hollies and *Pernettya* species and cultivars.

Different but related species do not normally interbreed because they often occur in dissimilar habitats, flower at varying times, or possess minor variations in flower characters that prevent successful interbreeding. In cultivation, such barriers can sometimes be overcome, and hybrids are often created by design (see "Producing hybrid plants", p.536).

Flowering plants of the division Angiospermae produce seeds that are enclosed in an ovary. They differ from the Gymnospermae, which comprise non-flowering plants that bear naked seeds. Angiosperms are divided into monocotyledons and dicotyledons, based on whether there are one or two seed leaves (cotyledons) within the seed itself. Monocotyledons also have leaves with (usually) parallel veins, flower parts in threes or multiples thereof, and often relatively slender, insignificant, non-woody stems. Dicotyledons have leaves with a broad network of veins; the petals and sepals are in multiples of two, four, or five; and the stems are thickened (and, in trees and shrubs, woody), originating from a special layer of cells within the stem called the cambium. Monocotyledon stems do not possess a cambium layer and so are generally smaller.

CLASSES OF FLOWER

Flowering plants are grouped into two classes: monocotyledons and dicotyledons

Petals in multiples of two, four, or five

DICOTYLEDON (*Ranunculus repens*)

Stamens in threes or multiples of three

Tepals in threes or multiples of three

Three-lobed stigma

MONOCOTYLEDON (*Lilium*)

LEAF VEINS

Monocotyledon

Dicotyledon

Leaf vein patterns in monocotyledons (here Curculigo recurvata*) are usually parallel; those in dicotyledons (here primula) generally form a network.*

Classification and nomenclature

Plants are referred to scientifically by two names, generally written in italics. The first name, which always has its initial letter capitalized, is of the genus, the second is the species name, or specific epithet: for example, *Rosa canina*. In nature, species often show minor variations in character; they are given a third name, prefixed by "subsp." (subspecies), "var." (varietas), or "f." (forma): thus *Rhododendron rex* subsp. *fictolacteum*. A cultivar (cultivated variety) is one that has been selected either from the wild or from gardens and grown in cultivation, and whose characteristics are preserved by some means of controlled propagation. The name of such a plant is written in Roman script with an initial capital letter and in single quotation marks: thus *Choisya ternata* 'Sundance'.

Mutation

A mutation, also known as a sport, is a genetic change in a plant, either natural or induced, that may be exploited horticulturally by propagating the mutated material in order to introduce a new cultivar. Mutations may occur in all parts of the plant but those of horticultural interest are mainly colour mutants or doubled flowers and variegated shoots that occur on a normally green-leaved plant.

Chrysanthemum cultivars often produce mutations, for example one flowerhead in a spray having a different colour from the parent plant.

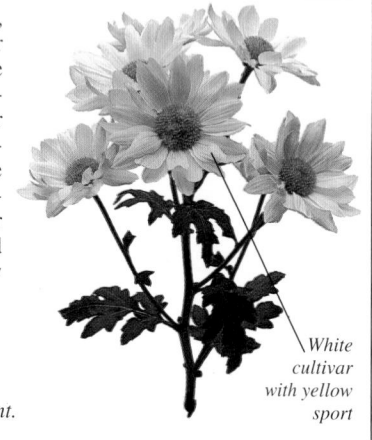

White cultivar with yellow sport

Seasonal reminders

KEY

♂ *Soil preparation and planting*
✤ *Routine care*
✿ *Pruning and training*
✾ *Propagation*

THESE NOTES, distilled from Part One of this book, serve as reminders of important tasks to be done during the gardening year, and of the best times to do them. They should be taken only as a guide, not as rules to be followed rigidly. If you live in a cold region, you may have to delay some tasks; if in a warm region, you may be able to start them earlier and finish later. Every garden is unique: its position (sheltered or exposed) and soil type (wet or dry, heavy or light) affect the rate at which the plants grow and therefore the time when various activities are best undertaken. Certain year-round operations are not covered here (e.g. controlling pests, diseases, and weeds, or potting up cuttings). For full details of how to carry out the tasks mentioned, refer to the appropriate specific chapters.

Spring

ORNAMENTAL TREES	♂ When conditions permit, plant trees in prepared ground or in containers. ✤ Apply artificial fertilizer. Water newly planted trees or those in containers. Mulch. Check stakes and ties in early spring. Remove suckers. Top-dress or repot trees in containers.	✿ In early spring, cut out dead, diseased, and damaged wood; root prune established trees if necessary. Carry out formative pruning, coppicing, and pollarding in early to mid-spring. Prune deciduous trees that flower in late summer (except those that	"bleed" heavily), if needed. Start regular clipping of topiary. Renovate evergreen hedges in mid-spring. ✾ Take softwood cuttings. Sow seed. Carry out air layering and, in early spring, simple layering.
ORNAMENTAL SHRUBS	♂ Plant all shrubs in prepared ground or in containers when conditions permit. ✤ Feed and mulch established shrubs in early spring. In late spring, carefully dead-head flowering shrubs, unless seed is required. Remove suckers and reverted shoots. Transplant deciduous shrubs.	Repot or top-dress any shrubs in containers. ✿ Prune shrubs that flower on new wood and all hydrangeas. Root prune vigorous shrubs or those in containers. In early spring, renovate deciduous shrubs. Coppice or pollard plants grown for summer foliage or winter stems. In mid-spring, carry out	formative training and pruning; prune and renovate evergreens. Prune shrubs that flower in winter or early spring in late spring. ✾ Take softwood and, later, greenwood cuttings. Sow seed of tender shrubs under cover. Carry out simple and tip layering and stooling. Divide suckering shrubs in early spring.
CLIMBING PLANTS	♂ In mid-spring when conditions permit, plant climbers in prepared ground or in containers. ✤ In early spring, feed and mulch established plants. Water young plants, if necessary. Dead-head repeat-flowering species,	unless seed is needed. Repot or top-dress climbing plants in containers (except spring-flowering plants). ✿ In early spring, carry out formative and renovation pruning; prune deciduous climbers that flower on new wood, and evergreens.	In late spring after flowering, prune spring-flowering species that flower on old wood. ✾ Sow seed of half-hardy and annual climbers. In early spring, carry out layering. In late spring, take softwood cuttings.
THE ROSE GARDEN	♂ When conditions permit, plant container-grown roses in prepared ground. In early spring in cold areas, plant bare-root roses. ✤ Water newly planted roses if necessary. After pruning, remove weeds, and feed and	mulch established roses. In late spring, begin spraying against pests and diseases. Repot or top-dress roses in containers. ✿ Prune large- and cluster-flowered bush roses, miniature and standard roses, Bour-	bons, Hybrid Perpetuals, and newly planted roses. Carry out formative pruning of species roses. Cut back roses on pillars. ✾ In early spring, divide rooted suckers from roses growing on their own roots.
PERENNIALS	♂ In early spring if conditions permit, start planting hardy perennials in prepared ground or in containers. ✤ Feed and mulch established plants. Water new plants, if necessary. In early to mid-	spring, remove dead growth of half-hardy plants and cut back shrubby perennials. In mid- to late spring, thin dense shoots; stake plants that will need support later on. In late spring, "stop" young shoots, if required.	Transplant half-hardy plants. Repot or top-dress plants in containers. ✾ Sow seed collected the previous autumn. Divide fleshy-rooted plants. Take basal cuttings and start taking stem tip cuttings.
ANNUALS AND BIENNIALS	♂ **and sowing** Start planting all biennials, hardy annuals, and plants grown as annuals in prepared ground or in containers, when	conditions permit. Sow half-hardy and hardy annual seed, and in late spring, hardy biennial seed outdoors.	✤ Water regularly. Stake climbers and tall plants. In late spring, begin to "stop" plants as necessary.
THE ROCK GARDEN	♂ In early spring, plant out rock garden plants in prepared ground or in troughs. ✤ Remove winter protection from alpines outdoors. Feed established plants. Replenish top-dressings on plants outdoors if necessary.	Cut back over-vigorous and straggly plants, and any dieback, in early spring; prune rock-garden shrubs and woody perennials. Cut out dead rosettes. In mid-spring, repot herbaceous and shrubby plants. Plunge	alpines and dwarf bulbs after flowering. ✾ Take leaf and basal cuttings. In early spring, divide mat- and clump-forming plants. In late spring, take softwood cuttings.
BULBOUS PLANTS	♂ In early to mid-spring, plant snowdrops "in the green" and summer-flowering bulbs in prepared ground, under cover, or in containers. ✤ Feed and water established plants. Dead-	head regularly unless seed is needed. Stake tall plants. Repot or top-dress bulbs in pots. In late spring, cut grass as bulbs die down; recover bulb frames after flowering.	✾ Collect ripe seed of early-flowering plants. Take basal stem cuttings of dahlias and begonias in early spring. Divide dahlia tubers.
THE WATER GARDEN	♂ In late spring, prepare the planting sites and start planting aquatics and marginals. Plant bog and moisture-loving plants and deep-water plants.	✤ In mid-spring, clear blanketweed. Thin out oxygenating plants. Divide and replant or repot overcrowded aquatic and bog plants. In late spring, overhaul neglected ponds.	✾ Sow seed of tropical water lilies. Take softwood cuttings of oxygenating plants. In late spring, divide marginal plants and collect turions for replanting.
CACTI AND OTHER SUCCULENTS	♂ In mid- to late spring, plant succulents in prepared raised beds or desert gardens. ✤ In early spring, feed and start watering.	Keep soil moist for epiphytes still in bloom. Start repotting as necessary. ✾ Sow seed under cover until late spring. In	early to mid-spring, take leaf and stem cuttings or sections. Start to carry out flat and side grafting.
THE LAWN	♂ **and sowing** Thoroughly prepare the site for a new lawn at least a month before sowing seed or laying turf in mid- to late spring.	✤ Roll lawns before mowing if turf has been lifted by frost. In mid-spring, repair damaged areas. In mid- to late spring, lightly scarify,	and apply fertilizer, or lawn sand if moss is present. Treat fine lawns with a wormicide, if needed. Begin appropriate mowing routine.

THE HERB GARDEN	♂Plant container-grown plants in prepared ground or in pots, when conditions permit. ❧ **and harvesting** Water and feed newly planted herbs. In cold areas, before growth starts, cut back herbaceous plants. In early	spring, repot or top-dress plants in containers; start watering and feeding them in late spring. Harvest leaves as appropriate. ✒Hard prune shrubby herbs. ♨Sow seed of perennial herbs. Make	successive sowings of seed of regularly used annuals and biennials. Take softwood cuttings in late spring. Mound-layer shrubby herbs.
THE VEGETABLE GARDEN	♂In early spring, plant perennial vegetables in prepared ground, and start planting container-grown, annual vegetables, under cloches if necessary.	❧Water newly planted vegetables. Erect supports for peas and climbing beans. Force rhubarb and chicory. In late spring, mulch planted vegetables.	♨Sow tender vegetables indoors and hardy vegetables outdoors (under cover in cold areas). Sow tender vegetables outdoors from late spring.
THE FRUIT GARDEN	♂When conditions permit, plant strawberry runners in prepared ground. ❧Begin feeding and mulching. Water as necessary. Protect flowers from frost. Thin fruitlets on peach and nectarine fans under cover. Check nets, stakes, and ties. Pollinate	peach and nectarine flowers and strawberries under cover; aid pollination on vines. ✒Pinch out and disbud new vine shoots. Disbud/deshoot fans of stone fruits under cover. Prune young stone fruit trees, acid cherries, blueberries, cobnuts, filberts, figs,	and branch leaders on trained trees and plum pyramids. Carry out bark-ringing on over-vigorous apple and pear trees. ♨Sow alpine strawberries. Graft fruit trees.
THE INDOOR GARDEN	♂Prepare greenhouse beds and soil benches, and plant all ornamentals. Plant up terrariums, bottle gardens, and hanging baskets. ❧In early spring, "stop" young trailing plants. Pot on, repot, or renew top-dressing of established plants as necessary. Start feeding	and increase watering once growth is under way; mist-spray plants that need high humidity. Start removing dead leaves and flowers, unless seed is needed. Plunge winter-flowering plants outdoors. ✒Cut back weak or damaged growth. Prune	shrubs and climbers that flower on new wood. In early spring, cut back shrubs and climbers that are in growth all year round. ♨Start sowing seed of annuals. In early spring, take leaf and softwood cuttings and leaf sections. Carry out division and layering.

Summer

ORNAMENTAL TREES	♂In early summer, plant container-grown trees, if necessary. ❧Water as necessary. Remove suckers. ✒In early summer, prune spring-flowering	trees. In mid-summer, prune deciduous trees that "bleed" heavily and mature, pleached trees. Prune young, pleached trees in late summer; remove diseased or dead branches	from evergreens. Clip topiary as necessary. In late summer, prune deciduous hedges. ♨In mid-summer, carry out chip-budding. In late summer, start taking semi-ripe cuttings.
ORNAMENTAL SHRUBS	♂Plant container-grown shrubs, if necessary. Plant up ornamental containers in late summer. Prepare soil for autumn planting. ❧Water as needed. Dead-head unless seed is needed; remove suckers. Feed shrubs in pots.	✒Regularly pinch out sideshoots to produce standards. After flowering, prune shrubs that flower on old wood, mature standards, and informal hedges. Prune deciduous shrubs that "bleed" heavily in mid-summer.	♨In mid- to late summer, take semi-ripe and mallet cuttings; start taking leaf-bud cuttings. In late summer, carry out chip-budding and side-graft deciduous shrubs.
CLIMBING PLANTS	♂Plant container-grown climbers, if needed. ❧Water, if necessary. Dead-head unless seed is required.	✒Tie in new shoots to supports. After flowering, prune climbers that flower in summer on old wood. In late summer, carry	out the first stage of pruning *Wisteria*. ♨Take softwood cuttings. In mid- to late summer, take semi-ripe cuttings.
THE ROSE GARDEN	♂Plant container-grown roses, if necessary. ❧Water, if needed. Start dead-heading unless seed is needed. Remove suckers and blind shoots. After mid-summer, apply fertilizer.	✒Thin Gallica roses and train new shoots of climbing roses and ramblers. In late summer, prune ramblers and most old garden roses after flowering. Renewal prune non-remontant	shrub, species, and ground-cover roses. Peg down Bourbons and Hybrid Perpetuals. ♨In late summer, take semi-ripe cuttings; also bud-graft, layer, or hybridize roses.
PERENNIALS	♂Plant container-grown perennials. ❧Water, if necessary. Dead-head unless seed	is required. "Stop" shoots, and tie in supports. ♨In early to mid-summer, collect and	sow seed of early-flowering perennials. Take stem tip cuttings.
ANNUALS AND BIENNIALS	♂ **and sowing** Plant annuals, biennials, and plants grown as annuals. Until mid-summer, sow seed of all annuals and biennials. In late	summer, sow hardy annuals and biennials in pots for planting in autumn. ❧Water as necessary. Dead-head unless seed	is required. Stake and tie tall plants and climbers. Collect ripe seed.
THE ROCK GARDEN	♂Plant alpines and rock-garden plants. ❧Water as necessary. Dead-head unless seed is required. Cut out dead rosettes. After flowering, cut back spring-flowering plants	as appropriate. Ventilate and shade alpine houses as necessary. ♨Sow fresh seed. Take basal, "Irishman's", and leaf cuttings. In early summer, take	greenwood cuttings; from mid-summer, take semi-ripe cuttings, and, from late summer, ripewood cuttings.
BULBOUS PLANTS	♂In mid-summer, prepare soil, and plant all autumn-flowering bulbs by late summer. Plant out pot-grown bulbs when foliage has died down. ❧Dead-head unless seed is needed. Tie in	tall plants to supports. Lift early-flowering bulbs and heel in. Divide and replant over-crowded clumps. Water summer-flowering bulbs in containers and under cover; feed and spray them, if needed. Stop mowing when	autumn-flowering bulbs appear in grass. ♨Collect bulbils and remove bulblets from dormant bulbs; pot them up. Collect ripe seed. In late summer, start scaling and twin-scaling lilies and other bulbs.
THE WATER GARDEN	♂Plant aquatics and marginals until mid-summer; deep-water plants until late summer. ❧Clear any blanketweed from ponds. In	mid-summer, feed water lilies. ♨In mid-summer, sow seed and take softwood cuttings. Collect ripe seed and sow in	containers under cover. Take softwood cuttings of marginals and oxygenating plants. In early summer, divide water lilies.
CACTI AND OTHER SUCCULENTS	❧Repot as necessary. Feed and water regularly; mist-spray indoor plants lightly and hose down succulents in the garden or in	the greenhouse. In mid-summer, use shading as necessary. ♨Carry out grafting. In early summer, divide	offsets of clump-forming and some tuberous-rooted plants.
THE LAWN	♂ **and sowing** Lay turf. If sowing seed, keep the ground well-watered.	❧Mow lawns as appropriate. Feed in early or mid-summer. Water thoroughly, if necessary.	Apply weedkiller. Aerate areas subject to heavy wear.

THE HERB GARDEN	♂ Plant container-grown herbs, if necessary. ✿ and harvesting Feed and water newly planted herbs and those in containers. Mulch moisture-loving herbs. Dead-head unless seed is needed. Harvest leaves, flowers, and seeds. ✄ Cut back herbaceous plants after flowering, earlier if flowers are not required. In late summer, start cutting back shrubby herbs. ✿ In early summer, sow regularly used annuals and biennials. From mid-summer, take semi-ripe, softwood, and stem cuttings. In late summer, sow winter and spring crops.
THE VEGETABLE GARDEN	♂ Plant winter brassicas, salad vegetables, container-grown annuals, and tender vegetables in prepared ground. ✿ and harvesting Water, if needed. Mulch planted crops. In early summer, earth up potatoes; stake and tie cordon tomatoes. Train climbing vegetables in mid-summer. "Stop" tomatoes and lift and dry onions in late summer. Harvest and store crops. ✿ Make successive sowings of summer crops. Start sowing oriental brassicas and winter vegetables.
THE FRUIT GARDEN	♂ Plant new strawberry runners. ✿ and harvesting Top up mulch and apply liquid feed where required. Irrigate fruit trees and mow grass. Thin fruitlets on plums, apples, etc., if needed. Burn rotten fruit. Cut back summer-fruiting strawberries after picking. Shade greenhouses. Pick fruits as appropriate. ✄ Pinch out and train shoots on fan-trained, stone fruit trees. Pinch out new fig shoots. Remove water shoots on trained trees. Break new sideshoots on cobnuts and filberts. Prune summer-fruiting raspberries and train in new canes. Prune acid cherries. Start summer-pruning trained pears and, in late summer, trained apples, pears, and pyramid plums. ✿ Transplant rooted strawberry runners. Bud-graft fruit trees. Tip layer and take leaf-bud cuttings of blackberries and hybrid berries.
THE INDOOR GARDEN	✿ Feed and water regularly. Pot on, repot, or renew top-dressing of plants, if necessary. Mist to maintain humidity and damp down the greenhouse as necessary. Remove dead leaves and flowers unless seed is required. ✄ Regularly pinch out growing tips, if necessary. Prune climbers that flower on old wood. ✿ Sow annual seed in early summer, and biennial seed. Take semi-ripe and stem cuttings.

Autumn

ORNAMENTAL TREES	♂ Plant container-grown trees. In mid-autumn, plant bare-root and root-balled trees in prepared ground. ✿ Apply mulch of organic fertilizer. Check stakes and ties. Transplant established trees. In late autumn, protect tender plants. ✄ Carry out annual, formative, and renovation pruning of deciduous trees (except those that "bleed" readily) and hedges. Prune mature pleached trees for shape. ✿ Take semi-ripe cuttings in early to mid-autumn and hardwood cuttings later on.
ORNAMENTAL SHRUBS	♂ Plant shrubs in prepared ground. ✿ Mulch. In mid-autumn, transplant established shrubs. Protect tender plants in late autumn; in cold areas, move shrubs in containers under cover. ✄ Prune and renovate deciduous shrubs (except those that "bleed" heavily). In windy sites, shorten shoots that flowered in late summer. In early autumn, prune evergreen hedges. In late autumn, cut out all dead, diseased, and damaged wood. ✿ Take leaf-bud cuttings in early autumn and hardwood cuttings in mid-autumn. Collect and sow ripe seed of hardy shrubs outdoors. Carry out simple layering. Divide shrubs.
CLIMBING PLANTS	♂ Plant climbers in prepared ground. ✿ Mulch. Renew ties and supports if necessary. Repot or top-dress plants in containers. In late autumn, protect tender climbers. ✿ Sow seed of hardy climbers. Take semi-ripe and hardwood cuttings. Carry out layering.
THE ROSE GARDEN	♂ In early autumn, prepare soil. In late autumn, plant roses and rootstocks for budding. ✿ Remove all plant debris. In mid-autumn, cut back taller large- and cluster-flowered roses. Check stakes and ties. In late autumn in cold areas, provide winter protection. ✄ Prune large- and cluster-flowered bush roses, miniature, standard, and newly planted roses. Formative prune species roses. Prune climbing roses and train in new shoots. ✿ Take hardwood cuttings. In late autumn, collect and sow ripe seed.
PERENNIALS	♂ Plant hardy, bare-root and container-grown perennials in prepared ground. ✿ Mulch. Dead-head (except plants with decorative seedheads) unless seed is needed. After flowering, start to remove stakes and plant debris; cut back hardy plants to the base (except in cold areas). Begin transplanting established plants. Lift plants for storing over winter. In cold areas, move tender plants in containers under cover. ✿ Collect and sow ripe seed. Divide fibrous-rooted plants. Take stem tip cuttings.
ANNUALS AND BIENNIALS	♂ and sowing Plant out biennials. Sow hardy annuals that overwinter outdoors. ✿ Dead-head unless seed is required. In late autumn, remove dead annual plants. Cut down to base perennials grown as biennials. Lift perennials grown as annuals and pot up.
THE ROCK GARDEN	♂ In early autumn, plant small bulbs in pots or in the rock garden. Plant shrubs and conifers in mid-autumn, if conditions permit. ✿ If necessary, renew top-dressing on rock gardens, screes, and troughs. Cut out dead rosettes. Prune rock-garden shrubs and woody perennials. Protect plants outdoors from winter weather as appropriate. Raise heat in alpine houses to prevent plants freezing. ✿ Sow seed in mid-autumn. Take basal, root, and ripewood cuttings. Divide mat- and clump-forming plants.
BULBOUS PLANTS	♂ Plant spring-flowering bulbs in prepared ground or in containers, and prepared bulbs in pots for forcing. ✿ Water, and spray if necessary. Start watering resting bulbs, bulbs under cover, and forced bulbs. Lift and store dahlias after first frosts. Move indoors or lift and store summer-flowering bulbs in containers. ✿ Sow seed. "Chip" bulbs.
THE WATER GARDEN	✿ Remove all dead and dying growth, and seedpods of invasive plants. Cover ponds with net to keep out fallen leaves. In mid- to late autumn, protect frost-tender crowns. Move tender floating plants to a frost-free place. Service and clean the water pump. In early autumn, thin oxygenating plants. In mid- to late autumn, cut back leaves of waterside plants and excess growth of submerged plants. ✿ In early autumn, divide established clumps of marginal and bog plants.
CACTI AND OTHER SUCCULENTS	✿ Water plants regularly until mid-autumn, then begin to restrict watering. Allow desert plants to dry out, but keep epiphytes in moist soil. Feed plants that are in active growth from mid-autumn.
THE LAWN	♂ and sowing Lay turf when conditions permit. Sow seed in prepared ground. ✿ Mow lawns as appropriate. In early autumn, feed, and water if needed. Control moss, if necessary. Aerate, then top-dress. Start clearing fallen leaves in mid-autumn.
THE HERB GARDEN	♂ Plant all herbs while conditions permit. In early autumn, lift, divide, and pot up mature plants for winter use indoors. ✿ and harvesting Cut back dead foliage of herbaceous perennials (except in cold areas). In late autumn, remove fallen leaves from low-growing, evergreen herbs. Protect tender herbs and those in containers. Harvest roots and seedheads as appropriate. ✄ In early autumn, cut back shrubby herbs. ✿ In early autumn, sow annual and biennial seed. Take hardwood and semi-ripe cuttings. Divide clump-forming and rhizomatous herbs. Mound-layer shrubby herbs.

THE VEGETABLE GARDEN	♂ Plant overwintering "bulb" vegetables in prepared ground. In early autumn, plant winter salad vegetables and oriental brassicas under cover. In mid-autumn, start digging and manuring empty beds.	❧ **and harvesting** In early autumn, stake and earth up winter brassicas, if necessary. Harvest and store crops as appropriate. From mid-autumn, lift plants for forcing. Protect tender crops and perennials and root	vegetables in the ground. ♨ In early autumn, sow salad crops under cover. In mid-autumn, sow hardy, over-wintering vegetables.
THE FRUIT GARDEN	♂ In early autumn, plant strawberry runners for the greenhouse. In late autumn, in prepared ground, plant tree, bush, and cane fruits, and grapes. Transplant tree fruits. ❧ **and harvesting** Water newly planted strawberries. Mow grass. Harvest fruits and	burn debris. Prepare storage for tree fruits. Check stakes and ties. ⚘ Shorten pinched shoots on plum, apricot, and sweet cherry fans. Remove old canes from hybrid berries and blackberries; tie in young canes. Prune fan-trained peaches and	nectarines after fruiting. In late autumn, start to winter-prune apples, pears, and bush fruits. ♨ Sow alpine strawberries. Plant hardwood cuttings of currants and gooseberries in open ground. Divide rooted suckers of raspberries, cobnuts, and filberts.
THE INDOOR GARDEN	♨ In early autumn, bring in winter-flowering plants and repot or top-dress. Reduce feeding and watering of other plants as growth slows.	Scrub down and fumigate the greenhouse. In late autumn, protect plants in an unheated greenhouse from frost.	⚘ Prune long shoots on shrubs and climbers. ♨ Sow seed of early-flowering plants. Store begonia tubers over winter.

Winter

ORNAMENTAL TREES	♂ Plant container-grown, deciduous bare-root, and root-balled trees, when conditions permit. Prepare seedbeds. ♨ Mulch, when conditions permit. Transplant deciduous trees. In early winter, protect tender	trees. In late winter, repot or top-dress trees in containers. ⚘ Cut out dead, diseased, and damaged wood. In early winter, carry out formative pruning and renovation of deciduous trees and hedges.	Start coppicing and pollarding in late winter. ♨ Take hardwood cuttings. Carry out apical-wedge, saddle, and side-veneer grafting. In late winter, prepare trees for simple layering in spring.
ORNAMENTAL SHRUBS	♂ Plant shrubs, when conditions permit. ♨ Mulch, when conditions permit. Transplant young shrubs, if necessary. In early winter, protect non-hardy shrubs.	⚘ Cut out all dead and damaged wood. Carry out formative pruning and renovation of deciduous shrubs. ♨ Take hardwood cuttings. In mid-winter,	take root cuttings. Collect and sow seed. Carry out simple layering, and apical-wedge, saddle, and side-veneer grafting. From late winter, "drop" heathers. Divide shrubs.
CLIMBING PLANTS	♂ When conditions permit, plant container-grown stock in prepared ground. ♨ Mulch. Protect non-hardy climbers. ⚘ In early winter, prune ornamental vines.	Carry out the second stage of pruning *Wisteria* in mid-winter; prune deciduous climbers for shape. In late winter, carry out formative pruning and training; prune hardy, deciduous	plants that flower on new wood. Check ties and supports. ♨ In early winter, take hardwood and root cuttings. Carry out layering.
THE ROSE GARDEN	♂ Plant all roses, when conditions permit. ♨ In late winter, tie in shoots of climbers and ramblers loosened by winds. Transplant	established plants if required. ⚘ Renewal prune remontant shrub roses. In warmer climates, prune roses to induce an	artificial rest period. ♨ In late winter, cut back any budded rootstocks. Sow seed from hybridizing.
PERENNIALS	♂ In late winter, plant hardy perennials when conditions permit. ♨ Remove supports and plant debris. Protect	non-hardy plants. When conditions permit, transplant established plants. ♨ Sow seed in containers. Take root cuttings.	Graft *Gypsophila* cultivars that do not root from cuttings.
THE ROCK GARDEN	♂ **and construction** Build raised and scree beds and rock gardens, when conditions permit.	♨ Protect alpine houses. Fill gaps in top-dressing. In mid-winter, look for early signs of aphids in alpine houses, and spray accordingly.	♨ Complete seed sowing, except for tender or half-hardy plants. Take root cuttings and "scoop" rosette-forming plants.
BULBOUS PLANTS	♂ In mid-winter, prepare soil for summer-flowering bulbs to be planted in spring.	♨ Water forced bulbs and bulbs under cover, if necessary.	♨ Start dahlia tubers into growth under cover, for cuttings or division.
THE WATER GARDEN	♨ Protect raised ponds with planks or plastic covers; cover them completely during severe	frosts. Ensure that at least a small area of the pool remains ice-free throughout winter by	using a pool heater or floating a ball on the surface.
CACTI AND OTHER SUCCULENTS	♨ Keep soil moist as epiphytes come into bud. Keep other plants dry.	♨ In late winter, sow seed under cover.	
THE LAWN	♂ Prepare the site for a new lawn. Lay turf when conditions permit.	♨ Mow established lawns only if necessary, when conditions permit. Clear fallen leaves.	Service lawn mowers and other equipment, if necessary.
THE HERB GARDEN	♂ Prepare ground for spring planting.		
THE VEGETABLE GARDEN	♂ Finish digging and manuring empty beds. Plant outdoors with protection, if conditions permit. Prepare seedbeds for spring sowing.	❧ **and harvesting** Force chicory and rhubarb. Stake and protect windswept vegetables. Harvest and store crops as appropriate.	♨ In mid-winter, sow seed indoors. In late winter, set potatoes to sprout indoors.
THE FRUIT GARDEN	♂ Plant tree, bush, and cane fruits, and grape vines in prepared ground. ♨ Apply fertilizer in late winter. Top-dress vine borders; scrape old bark from vines. Check stakes and ties. Protect tender fruits	outdoors. Repot or top-dress plants in containers. Pollinate peaches under cover. ⚘ Winter-prune. Prune autumn-fruiting raspberries and young tree roots. Tip prune summer-fruiting raspberries, blackberries,	and hybrid berries. ♨ Divide rooted suckers of raspberries, cobnuts, and filberts. In late winter, plant hardwood cuttings of grape vines in well-drained, open ground.
THE INDOOR GARDEN	♨ Reduce the frequency of watering. Keep the air around plants fairly dry by using ventilation or a de-humidifier. In an unheated	greenhouse, keep plants nearly dry to prevent roots from freezing; if necessary, cover plants with plastic sheeting or similar	material, or plunge small pots in sand.

GLOSSARY

The glossary explains horticultural terms that are used in this book. Words in italic in a definition have a separate entry. Fuller explanations and illustrations may be found elsewhere by looking up the term in the index.

Acaricide. A *pesticide* used to control mites. (Cf *Insecticide*.)

Acid (of soil). With a *pH* value of less than 7. (Cf *Alkaline* and *Neutral*.)

Adventitious. Arising from places where growths do not normally occur; for example, adventitious roots may arise from stems.

Adventitious bud. See *Bud*.

Aerate (of soil). Loosen by mechanical means in order to allow air (oxygen and carbon dioxide) to enter; for example, using a spiked roller to aerate a lawn.

Aerial root. A plant root growing above ground to provide anchorage and, on an *epiphyte*, to absorb atmospheric moisture.

Air layering. See *Layering*.

Alkaline (of soil). With a *pH* value of more than 7. (Cf *Acid* and *Neutral*.)

Alpine. A plant that grows above the tree line in mountainous regions; loosely applied to rock garden plants that may be grown at relatively low altitudes.

Alpine house. An unheated, well-ventilated greenhouse used for cultivating *alpine* and bulbous plants.

Alternate (of leaves). Occurring successively at different levels on opposite sides of a stem. (Cf *Opposite*.)

Anemone-centred (of flowers). Flowers or flowerheads in which the central petals or flowers (modified *stamens*) form a cushion-like mound and the outer rim of petals or ray florets are flat and spreading, as in some chrysanthemums.

Annual. A plant that completes its lifecycle (*germination*–flowering–seeding–dying) in one growing season.

Anther. The part of a *stamen* that produces *pollen*; usually borne on a *filament*.

Apical. See *Terminal*. Apical bud: see *Bud*.

Apical-wedge grafting. See *Grafting*.

Aquatic. Any plant that grows in water; it may be free-floating, totally submerged, or rooted on the pond bottom with leaves and flowers above the water surface.

Asclepiad. A member of the *family* Asclepiadaceae.

Asexual reproduction. A form of reproduction not involving *fertilization* and in propagation often involving mechanical methods (see *Vegetative propagation*).

Auxins. Naturally occurring or artificially synthesized plant growth substances controlling shoot growth, root formation, and other physiological processes in plants.

Awn. A sharp point or bristle, commonly found on a *glume* of a grass *inflorescence*.

Axil. The upper angle between a leaf and a stem, between a main stem and a lateral branch, or between a stem and a bract. (See also *Bud*: *Axillary bud*.)

Axillary bud. See *Bud*.

Back-bulb (of orchids). A dormant, old *pseudobulb* without leaves.

Backfill. To fill in a planting hole around a plant's roots with a soil mix.

Ball. See *Root ball*.

Balled. 1) Of trees and shrubs that have been lifted and had their *root ball* wrapped in hessian or other material to keep it intact during *transplanting*. 2) Of a flower that does not open properly and rots when still in bud.

Bare-root. Of plants sold with their roots bare of soil.

Bark-ringing. The removal of a ring of bark from the trunk or branches of certain fruit trees, to reduce vigorous growth and to encourage fruit cropping. Also known as "girdling".

Basal plate. A compressed *stem*, part of a *bulb*.

Basal stem cutting. See *Cutting*.

Basal-whip grafting. See *Grafting*.

Base dressing. An application of fertilizer or humus (manure, compost, etc.) applied to or dug into the soil prior to sowing or planting.

Basin irrigation. A form of irrigation whereby soil is scooped out from around the plant or made to form a ridge around it, creating a basin into which water is introduced.

Bastard trenching. See *Double digging*.

Bed system. A method of planting vegetable crops in closely spaced rows, often in blocks or narrow beds for easy access.

Bedding plants. Annuals and biennials (or plants grown as such) raised almost to maturity and then planted out, "bedded out", often in large blocks for temporary display.

Biennial. A plant that flowers and dies in the second growing season after *germination*.

Biennial bearing. The production of a heavy fruit crop in alternate years, with little or no blossom or fruit in the intervening years.

Blanch. To exclude light from developing leaves or stems in order to keep the plant tissue soft and palatable.

Bleed. To lose *sap* through a cut or wound.

Blind. Of a plant that fails to produce flowers, or a stem in which the growing point has been damaged.

Bloom. 1) A flower or blossom. 2) A waxy, white or bluish-white coating on a stem, leaf, or fruit.

Blown. Of flowers or hearted vegetables that are past full maturity and fading.

Bog plant. A plant whose natural habitat is soil that is permanently damp, or one that thrives in such conditions.

Bole. The *trunk* of a tree from ground level to the first major branch.

Bolt. To produce flowers and seed prematurely.

Bract. A modified, often protective, leaf at the base of a flower or flower cluster. Bracts may resemble normal leaves, or be small and scale-like, or large and brightly coloured.

Branch. A shoot arising from the main stem or trunk of a woody plant.

Brassica. A member of the cabbage *family*.

Break. A *shoot* growing from an *axillary bud*.

Broadcasting. Scattering seed or fertilizer evenly over the ground, rather than in furrows or *drills*.

Broad-leaved. Of trees or shrubs that bear broad, flat leaves rather than needle-like foliage.

Bromeliad. A member of the *family* Bromeliaceae.

Bud. A rudimentary or condensed shoot containing an embryonic leaf, leaf cluster, or flower. **Adventitious bud**: one produced abnormally, for example from the stem instead of from a leaf *axil*. **Apical** (or terminal) **bud**: the topmost bud on a stem. **Axillary bud**: one that occurs in an *axil*. **Crown bud**: a flower bud at the shoot tip, surrounded by other, usually smaller, flower buds. **Fruit bud**: one from which leaves and flowers (followed by fruits) develop. **Growth bud**: one from which only leaves or a shoot develop.

Bud union. The point at which the *scion* bud unites with the *rootstock*.

Budding. Bud-grafting, a form of *grafting*.

Budding tape. See *Grafting tape*.

Bud-grafting. See *Grafting*.

Budwood. A shoot cut from a tree to provide a *scion* for *bud-grafting*.

Bulb. A modified *stem* acting as a storage organ and consisting mainly of fleshy, more or less separate or tightly packed, scale leaves (a modified *bud*) on a much reduced stem (basal plate).

Bulb fibre. A mixture of *peat*, oystershell, and charcoal, in which *bulbs* are grown in containers, often without drainage holes.

Bulbil. A small *bulb*-like organ, often borne in a leaf *axil*, occasionally on a stem or in a *flowerhead*. (Cf *Bulblet*.)

Bulblet. A small developing *bulb* produced from the basal plate of a mature bulb outside the *tunic*. (Cf *Bulbil* and *Offset*.)

Bush. 1) A small shrub. 2) An open-centre fruit tree with a *trunk* of 90cm (3ft) or less. **Bush fruit**: used of soft fruit bushes such as blackcurrants and gooseberries.

Cactus. A member of the *family* Cactaceae, characterized by fleshy, water-storing tissue in the stems and areoles (specialized groups of cells) from which spines, flowers, and shoots develop.

Calcicole. *Lime*-loving; a plant that thrives in *alkaline* soil.

Calcifuge. *Lime*-hating; a plant that will not grow in *alkaline* soil.

Callus. Protective tissue formed by plants over a wounded surface, particularly in *woody* plants but also at the base of cuttings.

Calyx (pl. **calyces**). The collective name for the *sepals*, the outer *whorl* of, usually green, segments that enclose the flower in bud.

Cambium. A layer of meristematic tissue capable of producing new cells to increase the girth of stems and roots. (See also *Meristem*.)

Capillary matting. Matting made of synthetic fibre that is used to draw water upwards by capillary action to irrigate pot plants on capillary beds or benches.

Capping. A crust that forms on the surface of soil damaged by compaction, heavy rain, or watering. (Cf *Pan*.)

Capsule. A dry seed case that dehisces (splits open) when ripe to release its seeds.

Carpel. The female part of the flower of flowering plants that contains the *ovules*; several carpels in a flower are collectively known as the *pistil*.

Carpet bedding. The use of groups of closely planted, low-growing, colourful *bedding plants* in various patterns or designs.

Catkin. A racemose (see *Raceme*) flower spike, or a spike-like *inflorescence*, with conspicuous *bracts* and small, often unisexual flowers lacking petals.

Central leader. The central, usually upright stem of a *tree*.

Certified stock. Plants certified by the Ministry of Agriculture, Fisheries and Food (U.S.D.A. in the USA) as free from certain pests and diseases.

Chilling requirement. The requirement of plants for a specific period of dormancy below a particular temperature in order for them to initiate flowering.

Chinese layering. An alternative name for air layering; see *Layering*.

Chip-budding. See *Grafting*.

Chlorophyll. The green plant pigment that is mainly responsible for light absorption and hence *photosynthesis* in plants.

Clamp. A method for storing *root crops* outdoors. The crops are heaped up and protected against frost by layers of straw and soil; a "chimney" hole filled with straw provides ventilation.

Climber. A plant that climbs using other plants or objects as support: **self-clinging climbers** by means of supporting, *adventitious*, *aerial roots* or adhesive tendril tips; **tendril climbers** by coiling their leaf stalks, leaf *tendrils*, or modified *terminal* shoots; **twining climbers** by coiling their *stems*. **Scandent**, **scrambling**, and **trailing climbers** produce long, usually flexuous, stems that grow over or through plants or other supports; they attach themselves only loosely, if at all, to the support.

585

Cloche. A small, usually portable, structure made of clear plastic or glass, normally in a metal framework; used to protect early crops on open ground and to warm the soil before planting. (See also *Floating cloche*.)

Clone. 1) A group of genetically identical plants produced by *vegetative propagation* or *asexual reproduction*. 2) An individual plant in such a group.

Cold frame. A glazed, box-like, unheated structure, made from brick, wood, or glass, with a hinged or removable glass or clear plastic *light*, used to protect plants from excessive cold.

Collar. 1) The part of a plant where the roots meet the stem; also known as the "neck". 2) The part of a tree where a main branch meets the *trunk* (or a side branch meets a main branch).

Companion planting. Positioning plants together that are reputed to have a beneficial effect on neighbouring plants by discouraging pests and diseases or improving growth.

Compositae. The daisy *family*.

Compost. 1) A potting medium comprising a mixture of *loam*, sand, *peat*, *leaf mould*, or other ingredients. 2) An organic material, rich in *humus*, formed by decomposed plant remains, and other *organic* matter, used as a soil improver or *mulch*.

Compound. Divided into two or more subsidiary parts, for example a leaf divided into two or more *leaflets*. (Cf *Simple*.)

Cone. The densely clustered *bracts* and flowers of *conifers* and some flowering plants, often developing into a woody, seed-bearing structure as in the familiar pine cone.

Conifer. Gymnosperms, usually evergreen trees and shrubs that are distinguished from flowering plants (Angiosperms) by the naked *ovules* that are not enclosed in an *ovary* but are often borne in *cones*.

Contact action. The action of a *pesticide* or weedkiller that kills or damages the pest or weed by direct contact.

Coppicing. The annual pruning back of trees or shrubs close to ground level to produce vigorous, usually decorative, *shoots*.

Cordon. A trained plant (usually a fruit tree) generally restricted to one main stem by rigorous pruning. A **single cordon** has one main stem, a **double**, or **"U"**, **cordon** has two, and a **multiple cordon**, three or more stems.

Corm. A *bulb*-like, underground, swollen *stem* or stem base, often surrounded by a papery *tunic*. A corm is replaced annually by a new corm that develops from a *terminal*, or *lateral*, *bud*.

Cormel. A small *corm* developing around a mature corm, usually outside the main corm *tunic*, as in *Gladiolus*.

Cormlet. A small *corm* arising at the base (and usually within the old *tunic*) of a mature one. (See also *Offset*.)

Corolla. The interior *whorl* of the *perianth* of a flower, comprising several free or fused *petals*.

Cotyledon. A seed leaf; the first leaf or leaves to emerge from the seed after *germination*, often markedly different from mature leaves. Flowering plants (Angiosperms) are classified into *monocotyledons* (one) and *dicotyledons* (two) depending on how many cotyledons are contained in the mature seed. In Gymnosperms (*conifers*) they are often produced in *whorls*.

Crest. A ridged outgrowth, often on *perianth segments*, as in orchids and some irises.

Cristate. An exaggerated *crest*, commonly seen in fern fronds and the *inflorescences* of *Celosia* or the stems of cacti.

Crocks. Broken pieces of clay pot, used to cover the drainage holes of pots in order to provide free drainage and air circulation to the root system and to prevent the growing medium from escaping from or blocking the drainage holes.

Crop rotation. A system in which vegetable crops are grown on different sections of a plot on a three- or four-year cycle to minimize the build-up of soil-borne pests and diseases in one section.

Cross-fertilization. The *fertilization* of the *ovules* of a flower as a result of *cross-pollination*.

Cross-pollination. The transfer of pollen from the *anther* of a flower on one plant to the *stigma* of a flower on another plant; the term is often loosely applied to *cross-fertilization*. (Cf *Self-pollination*.)

Crown. 1) The basal part at soil level of a *herbaceous* plant where roots and stems join and from where new shoots are produced. 2) The upper, branched part of a tree above the *bole*.

Crown bud. See *Bud*.

Culm. The usually hollow stem of a grass or bamboo.

Cultivar. A contraction of "cultivated variety" (abbreviated to "cv"); a group (or one among such a group) of cultivated plants clearly distinguished by one or more characteristics and which retains these characteristics when propagated either asexually or sexually. (Cf *Variety*.)

Cupped. Usually of leaves or flowers, shaped like a cup.

Cutting. A portion of a plant (a leaf, shoot, root, or bud) that is cut off to be used for *propagation*. **Basal stem cutting**: one taken from the base of a (usually *herbaceous*) plant as it begins to produce growth in spring. **Greenwood cutting**: one taken from the soft tips of young growth after the spring growth flush has slowed down; slightly harder and woodier stems than are used for softwood cuttings. **Hardwood cutting**: one taken from mature wood of both deciduous and evergreen plants at the end of the growing season. **Heel cutting**: one taken with a portion of the bark or mature wood at the base. **Internodal cutting**: one in which the basal cut is made between two *nodes* or growth buds. **Leaf cutting**: one taken from a detached leaf or part of a leaf. **Leaf-bud cutting**: one consisting of a short section of stem and a single or double pair of buds or leaves. **Nodal cutting**: one trimmed at the base just below a growth bud or *node*. **Ripewood cutting**: one taken from ripened wood, usually of evergreens, during the growing season. **Root cutting**: one taken from part of a semi-mature or mature root. **Semi-ripe cutting**: one taken from half-ripened wood during the growing season. **Softwood cutting**: one taken from young, immature growth during the growing season. **Stem cutting**: one taken from any portion of a plant stem. **Stem tip cutting**: any cutting taken from the tip of a shoot; sometimes applied to softwood and greenwood cuttings.

Cyme. A usually flat-topped, *determinate inflorescence* in which the central or *terminal* flower opens first.

Damping down. Wetting greenhouse floors and staging with water to increase humidity, particularly in very hot weather.

Dead-heading. The removal of *spent* flowers or *flowerheads*.

Deciduous. Of plants that shed leaves at the end of the growing season and renew them at the beginning of the next; **semi-deciduous** plants lose only some of their leaves at the end of the growing season.

Degradable pot. A pot made from degradable material such as compressed peat or paper.

Dehiscence. Term used of *fruits* (usually *capsules*) and *anthers* to describe the process of opening at maturity to release their contents.

Dehiscent. Of a *fruit*, usually a *capsule*, or an *anther* that splits along definite lines to release seeds or pollen.

Determinate. 1) Used of *inflorescences* where the central or terminal flower opens first so that the main axis cannot extend further. (Cf *Cyme*.) 2) Used of bushy or dwarf tomatoes. (Cf *Indeterminate*; *Semi-determinate*.)

Dibber. A tool used for making holes in soil or potting compost into which seedlings or cuttings are inserted.

Dicotyledon. A flowering plant that usually has two *cotyledons* or seed leaves in the seed; it is also characterized by the (usually) net-veined leaves, the *petals* and *sepals* in multiples of two, four, or five, and by the presence of a *cambium*. (Cf *Monocotyledon*.)

Dieback. The death of tips of shoots as a result of damage or disease.

Dioecious. Bearing male and female reproductive organs on separate plants.

Diploid. Having two basic sets of chromosomes. (Cf *Triploid*.)

Disbudding. The removal of surplus *buds* to promote the production of high-quality flowers or fruits.

Distal end (of *cuttings*). The end that was originally farthest from the *crown* of the parent plant. (Cf *Proximal end*.)

Division. A method of increasing plants by dividing them into pieces, each with a root system and one or more shoots (or dormant buds).

Dormancy. The state of temporary cessation of growth and slowing down of other activities in whole plants, usually during the winter; **seed dormancy**: non-*germination* of seed when placed in conditions suitable for germination due to physical, chemical, or other factors inherent in the seed; **double (seed) dormancy**: non-germination of seeds due to two dormancy factors in the seed.

Double (of a flower). See *Flower*.

Double cordon. See *Cordon*.

Double digging. A cultivation technique in which the soil is worked to a depth of two *spits*. Also known as "trench digging" or "bastard trenching".

Drainage. The passage of excess water through soil; the term is also applied to systems of drainage used to remove excess water.

Drill. A narrow, straight furrow in the soil in which seeds are sown or seedlings planted.

Drupes. See *Stone fruits*.

Earthing up. Drawing up soil around the base of a plant to help prevent *wind-rock*, to *blanch* the *stems*, or to encourage stem rooting.

Emasculation. The removal of the *anthers* before the pollen is shed to prevent *self-pollination* and hence *self-fertilization*.

Epicormic shoots. Shoots that develop from latent or *adventitious* buds on or from the *trunk* of a tree or shrub. (See also *Water shoots*.)

Epigeal. Type of seed *germination* in which the seed is pushed above soil level by elongation of the *hypocotyl*. (Cf *Hypogeal*.)

Epiphyte. A plant that grows on another plant without being parasitic, and obtains moisture and nutrients from the atmosphere without rooting into the soil.

Ericaceous. 1) Term describing plants of the *family* Ericaceae, usually *lime*-hating and requiring soils of pH6.5 or less (see also *Calcifuge*). 2) Of compost, with an appropriate *pH* or acidity for growing ericaceous plants.

Espalier. A plant trained with the main stem vertical and (usually) three or more tiers of branches horizontally placed on either side in a single plane; often applied to fruit trees.

Evergreen. Of plants that retain their foliage for more than one growing season; **semi-evergreen** plants retain only a small proportion of their leaves for more than one season.

Explant. A tiny portion of a plant prepared and inserted in an aseptic growing medium for *micropropagation* purposes.

Eye. 1) A dormant or latent growth *bud*, such as the eye of a potato or dahlia tuber. 2) The centre of a flower, especially if different in colour from the petals.

F1 hybrids. First-generation plants obtained from crossing two selected pure-breeding parents to produce uniform, vigorous, and high-yielding offspring. Seed from F1 hybrids does not come *true*. **F2 hybrids**: plants that result from *self-* or *cross-fertilization* of F1 hybrids; they are less uniform than their parents.

Falls. The pendent or horizontally placed *tepals* or *petals* of irises and some related plants.

Family. A category in plant classification, a grouping together of related *genera*, for example the family Rosaceae includes the genera *Rosa*, *Sorbus*, *Rubus*, *Prunus*, and *Pyracantha*; the family Iridaceae includes the genera *Iris*, *Crocus*, *Dierama*, and *Crocosmia*.

Fastigiate. With the branches (usually of trees and shrubs) growing vertically and almost parallel with the main stem.

Feathered. Of *maiden* trees that have several *lateral* branches ("feathers").

Fertile (of plants). Producing viable seed; shoots bearing flowers are also said to be fertile shoots as opposed to non-flowering (sterile) shoots.

Fertilization. The fusion of a *pollen* grain nucleus (male) with an *ovule* (female) to form a fertile seed.

Fibrous. 1) Of roots, fine and often branching and dense. 2) Of loam, containing fibre derived from (dead) grass roots.

Filament. The *stalk* of the *stamen* which bears the *anther*.

Fimbriate. Of part of a plant that has a fringed margin. Plant organs with a fringe of hairs are said to be ciliate.

Flat. An American term for a shallow seed-box or container.

Flat grafting. See *Grafting*.

Floating cloche. Lightweight sheet, usually of woven polypropylene (fibre fleece), placed over a crop, which is lifted up by the plants as they grow. It provides some frost protection while allowing water and light penetration. Also known as floating mulch. (See also *Cloche*.)

Floret. A (generally) small flower in a *flowerhead* consisting of many flowers.

Flower. The part of the plant containing the reproductive organs usually surrounded by *sepals* and *petals*. The basic flower forms are: **single**, with one row of usually four to six petals; **semi-double**, with two or three times the normal number of petals usually in two or three rows; **double**, with more than the normal number of petals in several rows with few or no *stamens* produced; **fully double**, flowers usually rounded in shape, with densely packed petals and with the stamens obscured or absent. (Cf *Flowerhead*.)

Flowerhead. A mass of small *flowers* or *florets* that together appear to form a single flower as in members of the family Compositae.

Force. To induce plant growth, usually of flowers or fruit by control of the environment, normally by increasing the temperature.

Forma (f.). A variant within a *species* usually distinguished only by minor characteristics. *Clematis montana* f. *grandiflora* is a larger-flowered, more vigorous form of *C. montana*; also loosely used for any variant of a species.

Formative pruning. A method of pruning that is carried out on young trees and shrubs to develop the basic branch structure of the desired form or shape.

Foundation planting. The basic, and usually permanent, structural and shelter planting of trees and shrubs in a garden.

Frame. See *Cold frame*.

Framework. The permanent branch structure of a tree or shrub; the main branches that determine its ultimate shape. **Framework plants**: the plants in a garden that form the basis or structure of the design (cf *Foundation planting*).

Frame-working (of fruit trees). Pruning back all side growths to the main framework and grafting *scions* of a different *cultivar* onto each main framework branch.

French layering. See *Layering*.

Friable (of soil). Of a good, crumbly texture; capable of forming a *tilth* that can be worked easily.

Frond. 1) The *leaf*-like organ of a fern. Some ferns produce both barren and *fertile* fronds, the latter bearing *spores*. 2) Loosely applied to large, usually *compound* leaves such as those of palms.

Frost hardy. See *Hardy*.

Frost pocket. A site, often a hollow, where cold air gathers, that is subject to severe and often prolonged frosts.

Frost tender. See *Tender*.

Fruit. The fertilized, ripe *ovary* of a plant containing one to many seeds, for example, berries, hips, *capsules*, and nuts; the term is also used of edible fruits.

Fruit bud. See *Bud*.

Fruit set. The successful development of fruits after *pollination* and *fertilization*.

Fully double. See *Flower*.

Fully reflexed. See *Reflexed*.

Fungicide. A chemical that kills fungi, especially those responsible for various plant diseases.

Genus (pl. **genera**). A category in plant classification ranked between *family* and *species*. A group of related species linked by a range of common characters, for example, all species of horse chestnut are grouped under the genus *Aesculus*. (See also *Cultivar*, *Family*, *Forma*, *Hybrid*, *Subspecies*, and *Variety*.)

Germination. The physical and chemical changes that take place as a seed starts to grow and develop into a plant.

Girdling. 1) The removal of bark all round a stem or branch caused by animal or physical damage or by a constricting tie that prevents the flow of water and *nutrients* to the upper part of the plant, eventually causing the death of all the tissue above the girdled trunk or branch. 2) See *Bark-ringing*.

Glaucous. With a blue-green, blue-grey, grey, or white bloom.

Glume. A chaff-like, dry *bract* in the *inflorescences* of grasses and sedges.

Graft. To join artificially one or more plant parts to another.

Graft union. The point at which *scion* and *rootstock* are joined.

Grafting. A method of *propagation* by which an artificial union is made between the *scion* of one plant and the *rootstock* of another so that they eventually function as one plant. Methods include apical-wedge grafting; basal-whip (or splice) grafting; bud-grafting (including chip-budding and T-budding); flat grafting; saddle grafting; side grafting (see CACTI AND OTHER SUCCULENTS, "Side grafting", p.275); side-veneer grafting; side-wedge grafting; and whip-and-tongue grafting. (For details see PRINCIPLES OF PROPAGATION, "Grafting and budding", pp.541–2.)

Grafting tape. Tape used to protect a *graft union* during healing.

Green manure. A quick-maturing, leafy crop such as mustard that is grown specifically to be dug back into, and thereby enrich, the soil.

Greenwood cutting. See *Cutting*.

Ground colour. Main (background) colour of petals. (See also *Laced*.)

Ground cover. Usually low-growing plants that quickly cover the soil surface and suppress weeds.

Growth bud. See *Bud*.

Half hardy. Used of a plant not tolerating frost in a given climatic zone. The term generally implies an ability to withstand lower temperatures than *tender*.

Half standard. A tree or shrub that has a clear stem of 1–1.5m (3–5ft) between ground level and the lowest branches.

Hardening off. Gradually acclimatizing plants that have been raised under cover to cooler, outdoor conditions.

Hardpan. See *Pan*.

Hardwood cutting. See *Cutting*.

Hardy. Able to withstand year-round climatic conditions, including frost, without protection.

Haulm. The top-growth of plants such as potatoes and legumes.

Head. 1) The part of a tree above a clear *trunk*. 2) A dense *inflorescence*.

Head back. To prune back the main branches of trees or shrubs by half or more.

Heading. See *Heart up*.

Heart up. The stage at which vegetables such as lettuces or cabbages begin to produce tight "hearts" or "heads" of inner leaves.

Heavy (of soil). Having a high proportion of clay.

Heel. A small piece or strip of bark or wood that is retained at the base of a *cutting* when it is pulled away from a main stem.

Heel cutting. See *Cutting*.

Heeling in. Temporary planting until a plant can be placed in its permanent position.

Herb. 1) A plant grown for its medicinal or flavouring properties or for its scented foliage. 2) Botanically, a *herbaceous* plant.

Herbaceous. A *non-woody* plant in which the upper parts die down to a rootstock at the end of the growing season. It is chiefly applied to *perennials*, although botanically it also applies to *annuals* and *biennials*.

Herbicide. A chemical used to control or kill weeds.

Hull (of nuts). To remove the outer casings.

Humus. The chemically complex, organic residue of decayed vegetable matter in soil. Also often used to describe partly decayed matter such as *leaf mould* or *compost*.

Hybrid. The offspring of genetically different parents usually of distinct taxa (see *Taxon*). Hybrids between *species* of the same *genus* are known as interspecific hybrids. Those between different but usually closely related *genera* are known as intergeneric hybrids. (See also *F1 hybrids* and *F2 hybrids*.)

Hybrid vigour. An improvement in growth and yield shown by some hybrids.

Hybridization. The process by which *hybrids* are formed.

Hydroculture. The cultivation of plants in nutrient-rich water, sometimes with sterile aggregates. (See also *Hydroponics*.)

Hydroponics. Growing plants in dilute solutions of nutrients. Applied loosely to any form of soil-less culture.

Hypocotyl. The portion of a *seed* or *seedling* just below the *cotyledons*.

Hypogeal. Type of seed *germination* in which the *seed* and *cotyledons* remain below the soil surface while the young shoot (plumule) emerges above soil level.

Incurved. Applied to petals of flowers and *florets* that curve inwards to form a compact, rounded shape. **Incurving** flowerheads are less compact with more loosely arranged but still incurved florets.

Indehiscent. Of a *fruit* that does not split open to release its seeds. (Cf *Dehiscent*.)

Indeterminate. 1) Used of an *inflorescence* not terminated by a single flower, in which the primary axis (stem) continues to develop as the lower flowers open (e.g. a *raceme* as in delphiniums). 2) Used of tall or *cordon* tomatoes, which, in a suitable climate, can grow to an indefinite length. (Cf *Determinate*; *Semi-determinate*.)

Inflorescence. A group of flowers borne on a single axis (stem). *Racemes*, *panicles*, and *cymes* are all types of inflorescence.

Informal. Applied to some cultivars of chrysanthemums, dahlias, and other flowers with irregular flower formation.

Inorganic. Of a chemical compound, one that does not contain carbon. Inorganic fertilizers are refined from naturally occurring chemicals or produced artificially. (Cf *Organic*.)

Insecticide. A *pesticide* used to control or kill insects.

Insert. To place cuttings in a growing medium.

Intercropping. The growing of quick-maturing vegetable crops between slower-growing crops to make maximum use of the available space.

Intergeneric hybrid. See *Hybrid*.

Intermediate. 1) A term applied to chrysanthemums with flowerheads intermediate in shape between *reflexed* and *incurved*. 2) A hybrid with characters intermediate between its two parents.

Internodal cutting. See *Cutting*.

Internode. The portion of stem between two *nodes*.

Interplanting. 1) The planting of fast-maturing plants between slower-growing plants to provide a display while they mature. 2) The planting of two or more types of plants together to provide a display of different colours or textures (e.g. tulips among wallflowers). Often used in relation to bedding.

Interspecific hybrid. See *Hybrid*.

Irrigation. 1) General term for watering. 2) The use of a system of basins, channels, or sprinkler systems to provide a controlled supply of water to plants.

John Innes compost. *Loam*-based *composts* devised by the John Innes Horticultural Institute in Norwich, UK, and made to a standard formula.

Knot garden. Beds laid out in a formal, often complex, pattern, formed from dwarf hedges or clipped herbs.

Laced. A term applied to *Dianthus* cultivars in which the petals have a narrow band of colour contrasting with the ground (main) colour.

Lamina. The blade of a leaf, usually flattened, not including the petiole (leaf stalk).

Lateral. A side growth that arises from a shoot or root.

Layer planting. A form of *interplanting* in which groups of plants flower in succession having been planted closely together.

Layering. A method of *propagation* by which a *shoot* is induced to *root* while still attached to the parent plant. The basic form is self layering, which occurs naturally in some plants. Methods include: air layering (also known as Chinese layering or marcottage), French layering, mound layering (see THE HERB GARDEN, "Mound layering", p.301), serpentine layering, simple layering, stooling, tip layering, and trench layering. (For details, see PRINCIPLES OF PROPAGATION, "Layering", p.537.)

Leaching. The loss from the top soil of soluble *nutrients* by downward drainage.

Leader. 1) The main, usually central, stem of a plant. 2) The *terminal* shoot of a main branch.

Leaf. A plant organ, variable in shape and colour but often flattened and green, borne on the stem, that performs the functions of *photosynthesis*, *respiration*, and *transpiration*.

Leaf cutting. See *Cutting*.

Leaf mould. Fibrous, flaky material derived from decomposed leaves, used as an ingredient in potting media and as a soil improver.

Leaf-bud cutting. See *Cutting*.

Leaflet. One of the subdivisions of a *compound* leaf.

Legume. A one-celled, *dehiscent fruit* splitting at maturity into two, belonging to the *family* Leguminosae.

Light. 1) The movable cover of a *cold frame*. 2) Of soil, with a high proportion of sand and little clay.

Lime. Loosely, a number of compounds of calcium; the amount of lime in soil determines whether it is *alkaline*, *acid*, or *neutral*.

Line out. To plant out young plants or insert cuttings in lines in a nursery bed or frame.

Lithophyte. A plant naturally growing on rocks (or in very stony soil) and

usually obtaining most of its nutrients and water from the atmosphere.

Loam. A term used for soil of medium texture, often easily worked, that contains more or less equal parts of sand, silt, and clay, and is usually rich in humus. If the proportion of one ingredient is high, the term may be qualified as silt-loam, clay-loam, or sandy loam.

Lute. A piece of equipment used for working (luting) top-dressings into lawns.

Maiden. A *grafted* tree in its first year. (See also *Whip*.)

Maincrop (of vegetables). Those cultivars that produce crops throughout the main growing season, doing so over a longer period than either early or late cultivars.

Marcottage. An alternative name for air layering; see *Layering*.

Marginal water plant. A plant that grows partially submerged in shallow water or in constantly moist soil at the edge of a pond or stream.

Medium. 1) A *compost*, growing mixture, or other material in which plants may be propagated or grown. 2) Applied to those soils that are intermediate in character between *heavy* and *light*. (See also *Loam*.)

Mericlone. Genetically identical offspring produced by *meristem* culture.

Meristem. Plant tissue that is able to divide to produce new cells. Shoot or root tips contain meristematic tissue and may be used for *micropropagation*.

Micronutrients. Chemical elements essential to plants but needed only in very small quantities, also known as trace elements. (See also *Nutrients*.)

Micropropagation. Propagation of plants by *tissue culture*.

Midrib. The primary, usually central, vein of a leaf or leaflet.

Module. Applied to various types of container, particularly those used in multiples for sowing seed and pricking out seedlings.

Monocarpic. Flowering and fruiting only once before dying; such plants may take several years to reach flowering size.

Monocotyledon. A flowering plant that has only one *cotyledon* or seed leaf in the seed; it is also characterized by narrow, parallel-veined *leaves*, and parts of the flower in threes or multiples of three.

Monoecious. Bearing separate male and female reproductive organs on the same plant.

Monopodial. Growing indefinitely from an apical or *terminal bud* on a stem. (Cf *Sympodial*.)

Moss peat. See *Peat*.

Mound layering. See *Layering*.

Mulch. A material applied in a layer to the soil surface to suppress weeds, conserve moisture, and maintain a preferably cool, even root temperature. In addition to organic materials such as manure, bark, and garden compost, polythene, foil, and gravel may also be used. (See also *Floating cloche*.)

Multiple cordon. See *Cordon*.

Mutation. An induced or spontaneous genetic change, often resulting in shoots

with variegated foliage or flowers of a different colour from the parent plant. A mutation is also known as a sport.

Mycorrhizae. Soil fungi that live in beneficial association with plant roots.

Naturalize. To establish and grow as if in the wild.

Neck. See *Collar*.

Nectar. Sugary liquid secreted from a *nectary*; often attractive to pollinating insects.

Nectary. Glandular tissue usually found in the flower, but sometimes found on the leaves or stems, that secretes *nectar*.

Nematicide. A *pesticide* used to control nematodes (eelworms).

Neutral (of soil). With a *pH* value of 7, i.e. neither *acid* nor *alkaline*.

Nodal cutting. See *Cutting*.

Node. The point on a stem from which one or more leaves, shoots, branches, or flowers arise.

Non-remontant. Flowering or fruiting only once in a single flush. (Cf *Remontant*.)

Nursery bed. An area used for germinating seeds or growing on young plants before planting them out in their permanent positions.

Nut. A one-seeded, *indehiscent* fruit with a tough or woody coat, for example an acorn. Less specifically, all fruits and seeds with woody or leathery coats.

Nutrients. Minerals (mineral ions) used to develop proteins and other compounds required for plant growth.

Offset. A young plant that arises by natural, *vegetative* reproduction, usually at the base of the parent plant; in bulbs, offsets are initially formed within the bulb *tunic* but later separate out. Also known as offshoots.

Offshoot. See *Offset*.

Open-pollination. Natural pollination. (See also *Pollination*.)

Opposite. Term describing two leaves or other plant organs, at the same level on opposite sides of a stem or other axis. (Cf *Alternate*.)

Organic. 1) Chemically, referring to compounds containing carbon derived from decomposed plant or animal organisms. 2) Loosely, applied to mulches, composts, or similar materials derived from plant materials. 3) Also applied to crop production and gardening without the use of synthetic or non-organic materials.

Ovary. The basal part of the pistil of a flower, containing one or more *ovules*; it may develop into a *fruit* after *fertilization*. (See also *Carpel*.)

Ovule. The part of the *ovary* that develops into the *seed* after *pollination* and *fertilization*.

Oxygenator. Submerged aquatic plant that releases oxygen into the water.

Packs. Compartmented trays in which individual seeds or seedlings are grown.

Pan. 1) A shallow, earthenware or plastic pot that is much wider than it is deep. 2) A layer of soil that is impermeable to water and oxygen and impedes root growth and drainage. Some pans (hardpans) occur naturally on clay or iron-rich soils. Soils capped (see *Capping*) by heavy rain or excess

watering, or by continuous use of cultivation machinery are also known as pans or hardpans.

Panicle. An *indeterminate*, branched *inflorescence* often consisting of several racemose branches (see *Raceme*). The term is also loosely used to describe any type of branching inflorescence.

Parterre. A level area containing ornamental beds, often with low-growing plants and enclosed in dwarf hedges. (Cf *Knot garden*.)

Parthenocarpic. The production of fruit without *fertilization* having taken place.

Pathogens. Micro-organisms that cause disease.

Peat. Partially decayed, humus-rich vegetation formed on the surface of waterlogged soils. **Moss** or **sphagnum peat** is largely derived from partially decayed *sphagnum* moss and is used in potting composts. **Sedge peat** is derived from sedges, mosses, and heathers; it is coarser than moss peat and less suitable for potting composts.

Peat bed. Beds usually constructed from *peat* blocks and filled with very peaty soil; used to grow acid-loving plants, particularly in soils with a high *pH*.

Peat blocks. Blocks of peat cut from natural peat deposits.

Peat substitute. A term applied to a number of different organic materials – such as coconut fibre – used in place of peat for potting composts and soil improvers.

Peduncle. The *stalk* of a *flower*.

Peltate (of leaves). A leaf with the stalk usually attached centrally beneath the leaf blade; sometimes the stalk may be off-centre within the leaf margin.

Perennial. Strictly, any plant living for at least three seasons; commonly applied to *herbaceous* plants and *woody* perennials (i.e. trees and shrubs).

Perianth. The collective term for the *calyx* and the *corolla*, particularly when they are very similar in form, as in many bulb flowers.

Perianth segment. One portion of a *perianth*, usually resembling a *petal* and sometimes known as a *tepal*.

Perlite. Small granules of expanded, volcanic minerals added to growing media to improve aeration.

Perpetual. Of plants that bloom more or less continuously throughout the growing season or over long periods of time.

Pesticide. A chemical substance, usually manufactured, that is used to kill pests including insects (insecticide), mites (acaricide), and nematodes (nematicide).

Petal. A modified leaf, often brightly coloured; one part of the *corolla* usually of a *dicotyledonous* flower. (Cf *Tepal*.)

Petiole. The *stalk* of a *leaf*.

pH. A measure of alkalinity or acidity, used horticulturally to refer to soils. The scale measures from 1 to 14; pH7 is neutral, above 7 is alkaline, and below 7 acid. (See also *Acid*, *Alkaline*, and *Neutral*.)

Photosynthesis. The production of organic compounds required for growth in plants by a complex process involving *chlorophyll*, light energy, carbon dioxide, and water.

Picotee. A term describing *petals* with a narrow margin of a contrasting colour.

Pinching out. The removal of the growing tip of a plant (by finger and thumb) to induce the production of *sideshoots* or the formation of flower buds. Also known as "stopping".

Pistil. See *Carpel*.

Pith (of stems). The soft plant tissue in the central part of a stem.

Pleaching. A technique whereby branches from a row of trees are woven together and trained to form a wall or canopy of foliage.

Plumule. See *Hypogeal*.

Plunge. To sink a pot up to its rim in a bed of ashes, peat, sand, or soil to protect the roots of the plant or plants in the pot from extremes of temperature.

Pod. An ill-defined term generally applied to any dry, *dehiscent fruit*; it is particularly used for peas and beans.

Pollarding. The regular pruning back of the main branches of a tree to the main stem or trunk, or to a short branch framework, usually to a height of about 2m (6ft). (Cf *Coppicing*.)

Pollen. The male cells of a plant, formed in the *anther*.

Pollination. The transfer of *pollen* from *anthers* to *stigmas*. (See also *Cross-pollination*, *Open-pollination*, and *Self-pollination*.)

Pollinator. 1) The agent or means by which *pollination* is carried out (e.g. insects, wind). 2) Used in fruit growing to describe a *cultivar* required to ensure fruit set on another self- or partially *self-sterile* cultivar.

Polyembryonic. Containing more than one embryo in an *ovule* or *seed*.

Pome fruit. A firm, fleshy *fruit* formed by the fusion of the *ovary* and the hypanthium (the fused base of *calyx* and *corolla*); for example an apple or pear.

Pompon. Usually small, almost globular *flowerheads* made up of numerous *florets*.

Potting compost (also potting mix or potting medium). A mixture of *loam*, *peat substitute* (or *peat*), sand, and *nutrients* in varying proportions. Soil-less *composts* contain no loam and mainly comprise peat with nutrients added.

Potting on. Transferring a plant from one pot to a larger one.

Potting up. Transferring seedlings into individual pots of compost.

Pricking out. The transferring of young seedlings from where they have germinated in beds or pots to positions where they have room to grow on.

Propagation. The increase of plants by *seed* (usually sexual) or *vegetative* (asexual) means.

Propagator. A structure that provides a humid atmosphere for raising seedlings, rooting cuttings, or other plants being propagated.

Proximal end (of *cuttings*). The end that was originally nearest to the *crown* of the parent plant. (Cf *Distal end*.)

Pseudobulb. The thickened, *bulb*-like *stem* of a *sympodial* orchid arising from a (sometimes very short) *rhizome*.

Quartered rosette. A rosetted flower with the petals arranged in four, more or less equal, sections.

Raceme. An *indeterminate*, unbranched *inflorescence* with usually many stalked flowers borne on an elongated axis (stem).

Radicle. A young root.

Rain shadow. An area of ground next to a wall or fence that is sheltered from prevailing winds and therefore receives less rain than open ground.

Rambler. A trailing *climber*.

Ray flower (or floret). Small flower with a tubular *corolla*, as borne in the outermost ring of a *Compositae* flowerhead.

Recurved. Applied to petals of flowers and florets that curve backwards.

Reflexed. Applied to petals of flowers and florets that bend sharply backwards at an angle of more than 90°. They are sometimes called fully reflexed. Also loosely applied to any flower in which the petals or *perianth segments* are *recurved*.

Remontant. Of a plant that flowers more than once during the growing season (often applied to roses and strawberries). (Cf *Non-remontant*.)

Renewal pruning. A system in which the *laterals* are constantly cut back to be replaced by young laterals stimulated by pruning.

Respiration. The release of energy from complex *organic* molecules as a result of chemical changes.

Revert. To return to an original state, for example when a variegated plant produces a plain green leaf.

Rhizome. A specialized, usually horizontally creeping, swollen or slender, underground *stem* that acts as a storage organ and produces aerial shoots at its apex and along its length.

Rind. The outer bark of a shrub or tree outside the *cambium* layer.

Ripewood cutting. See *Cutting*.

Root. The part of a plant, normally underground, that anchors it and through which water and *nutrients* are absorbed. (See also *Aerial root*.)

Root ball. The roots and accompanying soil or *compost* visible when a plant is removed from a container or lifted from the open ground.

Root crops. Vegetables such as carrots and potatoes grown for their edible roots.

Root cutting. See *Cutting*.

Root run. The area of soil into which a plant's roots may extend.

Rooting. The production of roots, usually from cuttings.

Rooting hormone. A chemical compound synthesized in powder or liquid form and used at low concentrations to encourage root production.

Rootstock. A plant used to provide the root system for a *grafted* plant.

Rose (of a watering can). A perforated nozzle that diffuses and regulates the flow of water.

Rosette. 1) A cluster of leaves radiating from approximately the same point,

often borne at ground level at the base of a very short stem. 2) A more or less circular arrangement of petals.

Rotation. See *Crop rotation*.

Rounded. Regularly curved, as in a circle.

Runner. A horizontally spreading, usually slender, stem that runs above ground and roots at the *nodes* to form new plants. Often confused with *stolon*.

Saddle grafting. See *Grafting*.

Sap. The juice of a plant contained in the cells and vascular tissue.

Sapling. A young tree; a seedling or any young tree before the wood hardens.

Scandent. Ascending or loosely climbing. (See also *Climber*.)

Scarification. 1) Abrasion or chemical treatment of a seed coat in order to speed up water intake and induce *germination*. 2) Removing moss and thatch from a lawn using a scarifier or rake.

Scion. A *shoot* or *bud* cut from one plant to *graft* onto a *rootstock* (stock) of another.

Scrambling climber. See *Climber*.

Scree. A slope comprising rock fragments formed by the weathering of rock faces: simulated in gardens as scree beds, in which high-altitude *alpines* that need excellent *drainage* may be grown.

Sedge peat. See *Peat*.

Seed. The ripened, fertilized *ovule* containing a dormant embryo capable of developing into an adult plant.

Seed dormancy. See *Dormancy*.

Seed leaf. See *Cotyledon*.

Seedhead. Any *fruit* that contains ripe seeds.

Seedling. A young plant that has developed from a seed.

Selection. A plant selected for particular characteristics and usually propagated to retain the same characteristics.

Self layering. See *Layering*.

Self seed. To shed fertile seeds that produce *seedlings* around the parent plant.

Self-clinging climber. See *Climber*.

Self-fertile. Of a plant that produces viable *seed* when fertilized with its own *pollen*. (See also *Fertilization*, *Pollination*, *Self-pollination*, and *Self-sterile*.)

Self-incompatible. See *Self-sterile*.

Self-pollination. The transfer of *pollen* from the *anthers* to the *stigma* of the same *flower*, or alternatively to another flower on the same plant. (Cf *Cross-pollination*.)

Self-sterile. A plant unable to produce viable *seed* after self-fertilization, and requiring a different *pollinator* in order for fertilization to occur. Also known as "self-incompatible" – incapable of self-fertilization.

Semi-deciduous. See *Deciduous*.

Semi-determinate. Used of tall or *cordon* tomatoes that will only grow to 1–1.2m (3–4ft) long. (Cf *Determinate*; *Indeterminate*.)

Semi-double. See *Flower*.

Semi-evergreen. See *Evergreen*.

Semi-ripe cutting. See *Cutting*.

Sepal. The outer *whorl* of the *perianth* of a flower, usually small and green, but sometimes coloured and *petal*-like.

Serpentine layering. See *Layering*.

Set. 1) A small onion, shallot bulb, or potato *tuber*, selected for planting. 2) A term describing flowers that have been successfully fertilized and have produced small *fruits*.

Sexual reproduction. A form of reproduction involving *fertilization*, giving rise to *seed* or *spores*.

Sheet mulch. A *mulch* using an artificially produced material (e.g. plastic).

Shoot. A branch, stem, or twig.

Shrub. A woody-stemmed plant, usually branched from or near the base, lacking a single *trunk*.

Side grafting. See *Grafting*.

Sideshoot. A stem that arises from the side of a main *shoot*.

Side-veneer grafting. See *Grafting*.

Side-wedge grafting. See *Grafting*.

Simple (mainly of leaves). Undivided. (Cf *Compound*.)

Simple layering. See *Layering*.

Single. See *Flower*.

Single cordon. See *Cordon*.

Single digging. A method of digging in which only the topsoil is turned over to a depth of one *spit*.

Snag. A short stub or frayed end left after incorrect pruning.

Softwood cutting. See *Cutting*.

Soil mark. The usually noticeable point on a plant's stem that shows the original soil level before the plant was lifted.

Species. A category in plant classification, the lowest principal rank below *genus* containing closely related, very similar individuals.

Specimen plant. A striking plant, usually a tree or shrub in prime condition, grown where it can be seen clearly.

Spent (of flowers). Dying or dead.

Sphagnum mosses. Mosses common to bogs; their moisture-retentive nature is valued when used as a component of growing media, for example in orchid cultivation.

Spike. A racemose (see *Raceme*) and hence *indeterminate inflorescence* that bears unstalked flowers along a common axis (stem).

Spikelet. A small spike, forming part of a compound *inflorescence*; often applied to grasses where the flowerhead consists of several flowers with basal *bracts*.

Spit. The depth of a spade's blade, usually 25–30cm (10–12in).

Splice grafting. An alternative name for basal-whip grafting, see *Grafting*.

Spoon-type. Applied to the *florets* of chrysanthemums (and some other flowers) in which the quill-like florets expand to form a spoon shape at the tips.

Sporangium. A body that produces *spores* on a fern.

Spore. The minute, reproductive structure of flowerless plants, such as ferns, fungi, and mosses.

Sport. See *Mutation*.

Spray. A group of *flowers* or *flowerheads* on a single, branching stem, such as occurs on many chrysanthemums and carnations.

Spur. 1) A hollow projection from a petal, often producing *nectar*. 2) A short branch or branchlet bearing flower buds, as on fruit trees.

Stalk. A general term describing the stem of a leaf or flower (e.g. petiole, peduncle).

Stamen. The male reproductive organ in a plant, comprising the pollen-producing *anther* and usually its supporting *filament* or *stalk*.

Standard. 1) A tree with at least 2m (6ft) of stem below the first branches (see also *Half-standard*). 2) A shrub trained so that it has a clear length of stem below the branches (1–1.2m/3–4ft for roses). 3) One of the three inner and often erect *perianth segments* of the iris flower. 4) The largest, usually uppermost petal of a flower in the *subfamily* Papilionoideae (peas and beans) of the *family* Leguminosae.

Station sow. To sow seed individually or in small groups at fixed intervals along a row or *drill*.

Stem. The main axis of a plant, usually above ground and supporting leaves, flowers, and fruits.

Stem cutting. See *Cutting*.

Stem tip cutting. See *Cutting*.

Sterile. 1) Not producing flowers or viable seed. (Cf *Fertile*.) 2) Of flowers without functional *anthers* and pistils (see *Carpel*).

Stigma. The apical portion of a *carpel*, usually borne at the tip of a *style*, which receives *pollen* prior to *fertilization*.

Stock. See *Rootstock*.

Stock plant. A plant used to obtain propagating material, whether seed or vegetative material.

Stolon. A horizontally spreading or arching stem, usually above ground, which roots at its tip to produce a new plant. Often confused with *runner*.

Stone fruits. Fruits, also known as "drupes", with one or more seeds ("stones") surrounded by fleshy, usually edible tissue. They are common in the genus *Prunus* (e.g. apricots, plums, cherries) and some other plants, such as mangos, that produce *indehiscent*, woody fruits.

Stool. A number of shoots arising, more or less uniformly, from the base of an individual plant, for example some shrubs cut back regularly to produce propagating material and also chrysanthemums.

Stooling. 1) See *Layering*. 2) The routine pruning back of woody plants by *coppicing*.

Stopping. See *Pinching out*.

Strain. A loose, undefined term sometimes applied to races of seed-raised plants; not a term accepted under the International Code for the Nomenclature of Cultivated Plants

because of its imprecise definition.

Stratification. Storage of seed in warm or cold conditions to overcome *dormancy* and aid *germination*.

Stylar column. A column of joined *styles*.

Style. The usually elongated part of a *carpel* between the *ovary* and *stigma*, not always present.

Subfamily. A category in plant classification, a division within the *family*.

Sub-lateral. A sideshoot originating from a *lateral* shoot or branch.

Subshrub. 1) A low-growing plant that is entirely *woody*. 2) A plant that is woody at the base but has soft, usually *herbaceous*, growth above.

Subsoil. The layers of soil beneath the *topsoil*; these are usually less fertile and of poorer texture and structure than the topsoil.

Subspecies. A subdivision of a *species*, higher in rank than varietas (see *Variety*) or *forma*.

Succulent (of plants). A plant with thick, fleshy leaves and/or stems adapted to store water. All cacti are succulents.

Sucker. 1) A shoot that arises below ground from a plant's roots or underground stem. 2) On *grafted* plants, a sucker is any shoot that arises below the *graft union*.

Sympodial. Definite growth of a *shoot* terminating in an *inflorescence* or dying; growth is continued by *lateral* buds. (Cf *Monopodial*.)

Systemic. Term describing a *pesticide* or *fungicide* that is absorbed and distributed through a plant when applied to the soil or foliage.

T-budding. See *Grafting*.

Tap root. The primary, downward-growing *root* of a plant (especially a tree); also applied loosely to any strong, downward-growing root.

Taxon (pl. **taxa**). A group of living organisms at any rank; applied to groups of plants or entities that share distinct, defined characters.

Tender. Of a plant that is vulnerable to frost damage.

Tendril. A modified leaf, branch, or stem, usually filiform (long and slender) and capable of attaching itself to a support. (See also *Climber*.)

Tepal. A single segment of a perianth that cannot be distinguished either as a sepal or petal, as in *Crocus* or *Lilium*. (See also *Perianth segment*.)

Terminal. At the tip of a stem or branch; usually refers to a bud or flower.

Terminal bud. See *Bud*.

Terrarium. An enclosed container made of glass or plastic in which plants are grown.

Terrestrial. Growing in the soil; a land plant. (Cf *Epiphyte* and *Aquatic*.)

Thatch. A layer of dead, *organic* matter intermingled with living stems that accumulates on the soil surface in lawns.

Thin (of soil). Used loosely of poor soil, prone to *capping* and drought.

Thinning. The removal of seedlings, shoots, flowers, or fruit buds to improve the growth and quality of the remainder.

Tilth. A fine, crumbly, surface layer of soil produced by cultivation.

Tip layering. See *Layering*.

Tip prune. To cut back the growing tip of a shoot to encourage sideshoots or to remove damaged growth.

Tissue culture (of plants). The growing of plants under sterile conditions in artificial media.

Top-dressing. 1) An application of soluble fertilizers, fresh soil, or *compost* to the soil surface around a plant or to lawns to replenish nutrients. 2) A decorative dressing applied to the soil surface around a plant.

Topiary. The art of clipping and training trees and shrubs into various, usually intricate, geometric or free shapes.

Topsoil. The uppermost, normally fertile, layer of soil.

Trace element. See *Micronutrients*.

Trailing climber. See *Climber*.

Translocated (of dissolved nutrients or weedkillers). Moving within the vascular system (conducting tissues) of a plant.

Transpiration. The loss of water by evaporation from the leaves and stems of plants.

Transplanting. Moving a plant from one position to another.

Tree. A *woody*, perennial plant usually with a well-defined *trunk* or stem with a *head* or *crown* of branches above.

Trench digging. See *Double digging*.

Trench layering. See *Layering*.

Triploid. Having three basic sets of chromosomes. Such plants are normally *sterile*. (Cf *Diploid*.)

True (True-breeding). Of plants that when self-pollinated (see *Self-pollination*) give rise to offspring similar to their parents.

Trunk. The thickened, woody, main stem of a tree.

Truss. A compact cluster of flowers or fruits.

Tuber. A swollen, usually underground, organ derived from a stem or root, used for food storage.

Tufa. Porous limestone rock that absorbs and retains moisture; used for cultivating alpine plants difficult to grow in garden soil.

Tunic. The fibrous membranes or papery outer skin of *bulbs* or *corms*.

Tunicate. Enclosed in a *tunic*.

Turion. 1) A detached, overwintering, usually fleshy, *bud* produced by certain

water plants. 2) A term sometimes applied to an *adventitious* shoot or *sucker*.

Twining climber. See *Climber*.

"U" cordon. A double *cordon*.

Underplanting. Low-growing plants planted beneath larger plants.

Union. See *Graft union*.

Upright. Term describing the habit of a plant with vertical or semi-vertical, main branches. (Cf *Fastigiate*.)

Urn-shaped (of flowers). Globose to cylindrical in shape with a somewhat constricted mouth; "U"-shaped.

Variable. Varying in character from the type; particularly of seed-raised plants that vary in character from the parent.

Variegated. Marked with various colours in an irregular pattern; particularly used for leaves patterned with white and yellow markings but not confined to these colours.

Variety. 1) Botanically, a naturally occurring variant (varietas - var.) of a wild *species*, between the rank of *subspecies* and *forma*. 2) Also commonly but imprecisely used to describe any variant of a plant. (Cf *Cultivar*.)

Vegetative growth. Non-flowering, usually leafy growth.

Vegetative propagation. The increase of plants by asexual methods normally resulting in genetically identical individuals.

Vermiculite. A lightweight, mica-like mineral allowing good water retention and aeration when used in cutting compost and other potting media.

Water shoots. Applied usually to *epicormic* shoots that frequently arise close to pruning wounds on tree trunks or branches.

Whip. A young seedling or grafted tree without *lateral* branches.

Whip-and-tongue grafting. See *Grafting*.

Whorl. The arrangement of three or more organs arising from the same point.

Widger. A spatula-shaped tool used for transplanting or *pricking out* seedlings.

Wind-break. Any structure but often a hedge, fence, or wall that shelters plants and filters strong winds.

Wind-rock. The destabilizing of a plant's roots by strong wind.

Winter wet. Excessive amounts of water that accumulate in the soil during the winter months.

Woody. Ligneous, a term describing stems or trunks that are hard and thickened rather than soft and pliable. (Cf *Herbaceous*.)

Wound. A cut or broken area in a plant.

Wound paint. A specialized paint applied to a cut surface of a plant after pruning.

INDEX

(*entry cont.*)

(*entry cont.*)

E

N

O

P

W

(*entry cont.*)

XYZ

ACKNOWLEDGMENTS

Photography credits

The position on the page is given from top to bottom and across the page from left to right. The photographs in plant portrait boxes are numbered sequentially from left to right across the rows and from the top row to the bottom row. Where the picture is in a step-by-step sequence it is given the number of its caption.

ADAS Crown ©: 527 bottom 1–6, 564 centre left
Ted Andrews: 178 centre left
Heather Angel: 547 bottom left
Jane Aspden: 65 bottom, 262, 263 top left
A-Z Collection: 424 centre left, 428 centre left
Harry Baker: 360 bottom, 428 bottom left and right
B & B Photographs: 556 bottom centre above, 564 bottom right, 566 bottom left
Gillian Beckett: 224 portrait box 1 and 8
Birmingham Botanical Gardens: 422 left
Boys Syndication: 95 top left, 307 bottom left
Christopher Brickell: 53 top right, 206 top sequence 4
Prof. Chin: 332 bottom right 333 top left, 340 centre left, bottom right, and inset, 419 centre right, inset, and bottom left, 426 bottom, 427 top left, centre, and bottom left
Trevor Cole: 197 top
Eric Crichton: 7 top right, 11, 22, 24 bottom left, 25 top left, 30 bottom right, 31 top, 38 top, 61 top, 66 bottom left and right, 67 bottom right, 96 bottom right, 119 bottom right, 120 top and bottom left, 121 bottom, 138, 139 top right, 140 top left, 142 top, 150 bottom right, 159 bottom left, 174 bottom, 189, 194 top, 217, 218 box 3, 220 bottom left, 224 top left and right, 225 top left and 226 portrait box 2, 246 top, 277 top right, 278 bottom, 279 top and bottom, 291, 307 top, 308, 506 top right
Geoff Dann: 194 bottom
Jack Elliott: 190 top, 221 bottom left
Raymond Evison: 97 top, 108 portrait box 7, 109 bottom left
Forestry Commission: 557 bottom left, 559 centre right
John Galbally: 161 bottom left above and bottom far right
Garden Picture Library: 120 bottom left, 172, 174 top left and top right, 175 top, 193 top, 218 box 4, 245 top right and bottom, 264 bottom left, 433 top right
John Glover: 67 bottom left, 95 bottom right, 244, 474, 475 top
Jerry Harpur: 2 courtesy of Chris Grey-Wilson, 14 top, 15 top, 16 top left, 21 bottom right, 24 top and bottom right, 28 top, 29 top, 30 top and bottom left, 31 bottom, 33 top left, 36 top and bottom left, 94, 96 top, 119 bottom left, 139 bottom, 142 bottom, 146 bottom, 191 bottom, 276, 303, 305 top, 359, 360 top, 362 bottom, 363 bottom, 430, 501 top
Holt Studios International: 552 bottom right, 554 centre, centre left, centre right above, centre right below and bottom right, 560 bottom right, 562 top left, 566 bottom centre, 568 top centre and bottom centre, 569 top right, 570 centre left above, 571 bottom centre right and bottom left, 575 bottom left, 576 top centre left

Horticultural Research International, Kirton: 242 top sequence 3, 554 bottom centre, 558 right, 565 bottom left
ICI Agrochemicals: 553 top right
Clive Innes: 264 top
Andrew Lawson: 13 top left, 21 bottom left, 23 top, 25 top right to bottom right, 26 top right, 29 bottom, 33 top right, 119 top, 121 top left, 137, 139 top left, 218 bottom, 221 top left and bottom right, 246 bottom right, 305 bottom, 434 top
Elvin McDonald: 264 bottom right, 341 centre left and inset, 348 centre right, 398 bottom
MAFF Crown ©: 561 centre, 568 centre left
S. E. Marshall: 180 bottom right
Silvia Martin: 499 bottom
Tania Midgley: 361 top
Graeme Moore: 277 top left
J. Nicholas: 544 bottom right
Oxford Scientific Films: 96 bottom left, 569 bottom left, 572 left
Park Seeds: 342 bottom left and right
Photos Horticultural: 363 top, 564 top left, 569 top centre and centre right
Royal Botanic Gardens, Kew: 423 centre
Royal Horticultural Society, Wisley: 306 bottom, 549 top right, 553 bottom left and right, 556 bottom and centre, 557 top right and bottom centre, 558 centre and centre left below, 559 bottom left, 560 centre and bottom centre, 563 top right, centre left above, centre right, and bottom right, 565 top right, 566 top left and centre right above, 567 centre, centre right and bottom right, 570 top left, top right, centre left bottom, bottom centre, and bottom right
Harry Smith Horticultural Photographic Collection: 60 bottom left, 173 top left, 265, 333 centre left, 420 bottom, 423 top left, 424 centre right, 429 centre, 434 bottom, 571 centre left
Sports Turf Research Institute: 571 centre right above
Lauren Springer: 33 portrait box 1
Prof. H.D. Tindall: 325 centre left and bottom right, 353 bottom, 355 centre, 407 bottom, 420 top, 421 top, 423 top right and bottom, 426 top left and right
Elizabeth Whiting Associates: 28 bottom, 32, 35 bottom, 36 bottom right, 64 top, 190 bottom, 245 top left, 252 top, 293 bottom left
Steve Wooster: 12, 15 bottom, 16 bottom left and right, 17 bottom, 25 bottom left, 52 bottom left, 63, 98 bottom left, 116, 121 top right, 140 top right, 158 top, 492, 501 bottom, 503 bottom left, 514
Tom Wright: 97 bottom, 175 bottom
Additional photography by:
Jane Burton, Peter Chadwick, Eric Crichton, Geoff Dann, John Glover, Jerry Harpur, Neil Holmes, Jacqui Hurst, Dave King, Andrew McRobb, Andrew Lawson, Andrew de Lory, Tim Ridley, Karl Shone, and Gerry Young

Dorling Kindersley would like to thank the following for:

Specialist advice
Mr Ted Andrews (sweet peas); Peter and Fiona Bainbridge (landscape design and construction); Harry Baker (fruit); Dr Bob Ellis (vegetable cultivar lists); Dennis Gobbee (rose hybridizing); Patrick Goldsworthy, British Agrochemical Association (chemical controls); Ken Grapes, Royal National Rose Society; Peter Orme (rock garden design and construction); Terence and Judy Read (grape cultivar lists); Prof. S. Sansavini (fruit cultivar lists); Pham van Tha (fruit cultivar lists); and in particular the many staff at the RHS Garden, Wisley, who so patiently and freely gave of their time to advise on horticultural techniques throughout the duration of the project.

Providing plants or locations for photographs
Mrs Joy Bishop; Brickwall House School, Northiam; Brinkman Brothers Ltd, Walton Farm Nurseries, Bosham; Denbies Wine Estate, Dorking; Mrs Donnithorne; Martin Double; J.W. Elliott & Sons (West End) Limited, Fenns Lane Nursery, Woking; Elsoms Seeds Ltd, Spalding; Mrs Randi Evans; Adrian Hall Ltd, Putney Garden Centre, London; Mr & Mrs R.D. Hendriksen, Hill Park Nurseries, Surbiton; The Herb and Heather Centre, West Haddlesey; Hilliers Nurseries (Winchester) Ltd, Romsey; Holly Gate International Ltd, Ashington; John Humphries, Sutton Place Foundation, Guildford; Iden Croft Herbs, Staplehurst; Mr de Jager; Nicolette John; David Knuckey, Burncoose Nursery; Mr & Mrs John Land; Sarah Martin; Frank P. Matthews Ltd, Tenbury Wells; Mr & Mrs Mead; Anthony Noel, Fulham Park Gardens, London; Andrew Norfield; Notcutts Garden Centre, Bagshot; Bridget Quest-Ritson; Royal Botanic Gardens, Kew; Royal Horticultural Society Enterprises; Lynn and Danny Reynolds, Mrs Rudd, Surrey Water Gardens, West Clandon; Rolawn, Elvington; Miss Skilton; Carole Starr; Mr & Mrs Wagstaff; Mrs Wye.

Tools for demonstration photographs
Spear and Jackson Products Ltd, Wednesbury, West Midlands; Felco secateurs supplied by Burton McCall Group, Leicester.

Supplying equipment
Agralan, Ashton Keynes; Bob Andrews Ltd, Bracknell; Black and Decker Europe, Slough; Blagdon Water Garden Products PLC, Highbridge; Bloomingdales Garden Centre, Laleham; Bulldog Tools Ltd, Wigan; Butterley Brick Ltd, London; CEKA Works Ltd, Pwllheli; Challenge Fencing, Cobham; J. B. Corrie & Co Ltd, Petersfield; Dalfords (London) Ltd, Staines; Diplex Ltd, Watford; Direct Wire Ties Ltd, Hull; Robert Dyas (Ltd), Guildford; Fishtique, Sunbury-on-Thames; Fluid Drilling Ltd, Stratford-upon-Avon; Gardena UK Ltd, Letchworth Garden City; Gloucesters Wholesales Ltd, Woking; Harcros, Walton-on-Thames; Haws Elliott Ltd, Warley; Honda UK Ltd, London; Hozelock Ltd, Birmingham; ICI Garden Products, Haslemere; LBS Polythene, Colne; Merck Ltd, Poole; Neal Street East, London; Parkers, Worcester Park; Pinks Hill Landscape Merchants Ltd, Guildford; Qualcast Garden Products, Stowmarket; Rapitest, Corwen; Seymours, Ewell; Shoosmith & Lee Ltd, Cobham; SISIS Equipment Ltd, Macclesfield; Thermoforce Ltd, Maldon.

Additional assistance
Sarah Ashun, Jennifer Bagg, Kathryn Bradley-Hole, Lynn Bresler, Diana Brinton, Susan Conder, Jeannette Cossar, Diana Craig, Penny David, Paul Docherty, Howard Farrell, Roseanne Hooper, David Joyce, Steve Knowlden, Mary Lambert, Claire Lebas, Margaret Little, Louise McConnell, Caroline Macy, Eunice Martins, Ruth Midgley, Peter Moloney, Sarah Moule, Fergus Muir, Chez Picthall, Sandra Schneider, Janet Smy, Mary Staples, Tina Tiffin, Roger Tritton, Anne de Verteuil, John Walker.

Abbreviations

C	centigrade	ml	millilitre(s)
cf	compare	mm	millimetre(s)
cm	centimetre(s)	oz	ounce(s)
cv(s)	cultivar(s)	p(p).	page(s)
F	fahrenheit	pl.	plural
f.	forma	sp.	species
fl oz	fluid ounce(s)	spp.	species (pl.)
ft	foot, feet	sq	square
g	gram(s)	subsp.	subspecies
in	inch(es)	St	Saint
kg	kilogram(s)	syn.	synonyms
lb	pound(s)	var.	varietas
m	metre(s)	yd	yard(s)

Note: The generic and species names of plants are abbreviated to their initial letters after their first full mention in a sentence or a list.